# SCALE, SPACE AND CANON IN ANCIENT LITERARY CULTURE

Greek culture matters because its unique pluralistic debate shaped modern discourses. This groundbreaking book explains this feature by retelling the history of ancient literary culture through the lenses of canon, space and scale. It proceeds from the invention of the performative "author" in the archaic symposium through the "polis of letters" enabled by Athenian democracy and into the Hellenistic era, in which one's space mattered and culture became bifurcated between Athens and Alexandria. This duality was reconfigured into an eclectic variety consumed by Roman patrons and predicated on scale, with about a thousand authors active at any given moment. As patronage dried up in the third century CE, scale collapsed and literary culture was reduced to the teaching of a narrower field of authors, paving the way for the Middle Ages. The result is a new history of ancient culture which is sociological, quantitative and all-encompassing, cutting through eras and genres.

REVIEL NETZ is the Patrick Suppes Professor of Greek Mathematics and Astronomy at Stanford University. He is a prolific author in many fields, from verse through literary theory to modern environmental history, and his core field is the history of the ancient exact sciences. He has pursued a more cultural, cognitive and literary approach to the history of science and has published a series of studies, beginning with *The Shaping of Deduction in Greek Mathematics* (Cambridge, 1999). He is also the translator and editor of the Cambridge editions of the works of Archimedes, two volumes of which have been published to date, and one of the main contributors to the study of the Archimedes Palimpsest, on which he co-authored (with William Noel) *The Archimedes Codex*, which has been translated into 18 languages.

# SCALE, SPACE AND CANON IN ANCIENT LITERARY CULTURE

REVIEL NETZ

*Stanford University, California*

# CAMBRIDGE
## UNIVERSITY PRESS

University Printing House, Cambridge CB2 8BS, United Kingdom

One Liberty Plaza, 20th Floor, New York, NY 10006, USA

477 Williamstown Road, Port Melbourne, VIC 3207, Australia

314–321, 3rd Floor, Plot 3, Splendor Forum, Jasola District Centre, New Delhi – 110025, India

79 Anson Road, #06–04/06, Singapore 079906

Cambridge University Press is part of the University of Cambridge.

It furthers the University's mission by disseminating knowledge in the pursuit of education, learning and research at the highest international levels of excellence.

www.cambridge.org
Information on this title: www.cambridge.org/9781108481472
DOI: 10.1017/9781108686945

First published 2020

Printed in the United Kingdom by TJ International Ltd, Padstow Cornwall

*A catalogue record for this publication is available from the British Library.*

*Library of Congress Cataloging-in-Publication Data*
NAMES: Netz, Reviel author.
TITLE: Scale, space, and canon in ancient literary culture / Reviel Netz.
DESCRIPTION: Cambridge, UK ; New York : Cambridge University Press 2019. | Includes bibliographical references and index.
IDENTIFIERS: LCCN 2019019510
SUBJECTS: LCSH: Greek literature – History and criticism. | Greek literature, Hellenistic – History and criticism. | Greece – Intellectual life – To 146 B.C. | Civilization, Western – Greek influences.
CLASSIFICATION: LCC PA3009 .N48 2019 | DDC 880.9–dc23
LC record available at https://lccn.loc.gov/2019019510

ISBN 978-1-108-48147-2 Hardback

*To Maya, Darya and Tamara*

# Contents

# Maps

# *Abbreviations*

BNP      *Brill's New Pauly: Encyclopaedia of the Ancient World,* 22 vols., eds. H. Cancik, H. Schneider and M. Landfester. 2002–10. Leiden.

CEDOPAL      Centre du documentation de papyrology littéraire. University of Liège.

CLA      *Codices Latini Antiquiores: A Palaeographical Guide to Latin Manuscripts Prior to the Ninth Century,* 12 vols., ed. E. A. Lowe. 1934–71. Oxford.

DPA      *Dictionnaire des philosophes antiques,* 7 vols., ed. R. Goulet. 1989–2018. Paris.

EANS      *Encyclopedia of Ancient Natural Scientists: The Greek Tradition and Its Many Heirs,* eds. P. T. Keyser and G. L. Irby-Massie. 2008. London.

LDAB      Leuven Database of Ancient Books. Catholic University of Leuven.

PGRSRE      *Prosopography of Greek Rhetors and Sophists of the Roman Empire,* P. Janiszewski, K. Stebnicka and E. Szabat. 2014. Oxford.

RE      *Realencyclopädie der classischen Altertumswissenschaft,* 84 vols., eds. A. Pauly, G. Wissowa and W. Kroll. 1893–1980. Stuttgart.

TLG      *Thesaurus Linguae Graecae.*

# *Acknowledgements*

In the next pages, as the book proper unfolds with the Preface, I begin with a note of gratitude to my teacher, Geoffrey Lloyd. Gratitude and reverence to my teachers are my starting point.

Those who shaped me the most, early on, were (in Tel Aviv) Benjamin Cohen, Gideon Freudenthal, John Glucker and Sabetai Unguru and (in Cambridge, U.K.) Myles Burnyeat, Geoffrey Lloyd and David Sedley.

My PhD is now 25 years old, and I have had most of my education since. The names, then, of some of my teacher-colleagues: mentioning just those who taught me directly on the topics that went into this book. Among these are Markus Asper, Avi Avidov, Alessandro Barchiesi, Mary Beard, Karine Chemla, Serafina Cuomo, Richard Duncan-Jones, Rivka Feldhay, Margalit Finkelberg, Maud Gleason, Ian Hacking, Brooke Holmes, Keith Hopkins, Paul Keyser, Christopher Krebs, Bruno Latour, John Ma, Irad Malkin, Richard Martin, Stephen Menn, Julius Moravcsik, Franco Moretti, Grant Parker, Anasatasia-Erasmia Peponi, Eleanor Robson, Malcolm Schofield, Robert Sharples, Susan Stephens, Patrick Suppes, Liba Taub, Dorothy Thompson and Tim Whitmarsh. I want to mention in particular three ancient historians at the Department of Classics at Stanford who have influenced me almost as much as did my very first teachers, back in Tel Aviv: Ian Morris, Josh Ober and Walter Scheidel. I would not have written this book without them.

Many of my colleagues went further and helped me reach audiences from whom I have learned even more. Portions and versions of the argument put forward here were discussed at workshops in Kyoto University; Tel Aviv University; Humboldt University, Berlin; ETH, Zurich; Cambridge University; CNRS – SPHERE Paris; Yale University; Columbia University; New York University; Princeton University; Cornell University; McGill University; University of Pennsylvania; University of Chicago; University of Arkansas; and University of Texas – Austin. Particularly helpful were the audiences at the Stanford Humanities

Center, where I completed the draft of the manuscript in the academic year 2015/2016, and at Stanford's Center for Advanced Studies in Behavioral Sciences, where I am now putting the finishing touches to it, in the academic year 2018/2019. I have been very lucky in the generosity of my department and my deans.

Many of the students who studied with me at the Department of Classics at Stanford have become, effectively, my student-teachers. Many have read portions or all of my manuscript (a few, indeed, have been kind enough to check my English tenses). With all of them I experienced the magic of graduate teaching: how an argument – theirs, and mine, together – is built up by being questioned. And also that other miracle, inherent to classical studies: how the distinct branches of the classical world come together, as if all those rivers were connected, mysteriously, by subterranean canals. Among those teacher-students I can mention: Scott Arcenas, Melissa Bailey, Nicholas Boterf, Amy Carlow, Leonardo Cazzadori, David Driscoll, Simeon Ehrlich, Nicholas Gardner, Jacqueline Montagne, Jack Mitchell, Mark Pyzyk, Courtney Roby, Veronica Shi, Verity Walsh and Johannes Wietzke.

I wrote this book as a labor of love, without contract at hand, and it was with some dread that I sent it to Cambridge. Michael Sharp, editor of classics at Cambridge University Press, was, as always, the perfect editor. Emma Collison led the project of the making of this book with rigor and kindness; Mike Richardson was a precise and tactful copy-editor. I am especially grateful to two outside readers, who made many, many comments that have greatly improved this book.

I remain responsible for all errors and mistakes. Indeed, even with all the many friends along the way, the writing of this book, as of any other, remained, at its core, a lonely enterprise. Yet I did not feel lonely, writing this book. Instead – as will be apparent to my readers – this book was written with great excitement and joy. I owe this joy to the people to whom this book is dedicated: my wife, Maya Arad, and our two daughters, Darya and Tamara. Thank you, all.

# General Introduction

An introduction is a good moment in which to express gratitude. It was a little more than 20 years ago that I submitted the last file of my dissertation to my supervisor, Geoffrey Lloyd. At this stage of the dissertation work, I already knew what to expect. A couple of days later the manuscript chapter, littered with Geoffrey's scrawls, was in my mailbox, and I settled down to decipher that handwriting.

This last chapter concerned the historical context of the Greek mathematical genre. Why did Greek mathematicians write the way they did? I explained this in terms of the historical context in which the genre was formed, which I identified as the early fourth century BCE. So: a product, like so many other facets of Greek culture, of the polis and of Athenian democracy. I then went on to note, almost in passing, that the form then survived "because some aspects of the relevant background remained in force throughout antiquity", by which I meant to say that, in many ways, the culture of the democratic polis remained dominant throughout antiquity. Next to those words I found scribbled "I am not so sure" – in which, of course, Geoffrey Lloyd was right. I knew that I needed to find another account. More than 20 years late, I offer this book: my second try.

For, you see, Lloyd's question really puts in doubt much of the scholarship concerning the rise of Greek civilization – including that of Geoffrey Lloyd himself! Let me explain. Perhaps the central insight of twentieth-century scholarship on Greek culture was the emphasis on the role of public, face-to-face debate, in turn related to the culture of the classical polis and, in particular, its democratic experiment. This cultural feature was taken to explain most aspects of Greek culture: agonistic, performative, radically innovative. Lloyd himself, especially in his 1979 and 1990 books (following upon earlier suggestions, in particular Vernant, 1962), has argued for a thesis that traces the rise of Greek science to the culture of the democratic experiment. Such a thesis serves to historicize the rise of science and to make "rationality" a feature not of some nebulous "mentality" but, rather, of a concrete historical practice.

Contemporary scholarship into ancient culture often follows this template: (1) explain a Greek cultural form through a moment of origin in the classical era – and then (2) ignore the question of the long-term survival of that moment.

But this is clearly in some sense wrong. The democratic experiment was the affair of a subset of the classical poleis: no more. It was to a large extent over already by the end of the fourth century.[1] Now, of the roughly 49 million words of Greek currently on the Thesaurus Linguae Graecae (TLG), dated to not later than the end of the fifth century CE, just a little more than 5 million are dated to not later than the end of the fourth century BCE. The legacy of Greece, in such crude terms, is about 90 percent post-classical and only 10 percent (archaic and) classical. But there is in fact a much stronger argument to be made: the 10 percent "classical" segment of the Greek legacy no doubt had a major influence on later civilizations. But it did so only through the efforts of post-classical Greek civilization to keep this segment alive, not only to preserve a group of texts but also to maintain a body of knowledge surrounding them that infused such texts with meaning.

As Ian Morris puts it (2010: 260), "Democracy disappeared from the West almost completely in the two thousand years separating classical Greece from the American and French revolutions." And so, Morris argues, it is absurd to find the explanation for the special achievement of the West in the Greek democratic experiment. But should we therefore throw out our accounts of the specific achievements of Greek culture, anchored in the classical polis? We need a different kind of account: one that explains Greek civilization as a phenomenon larger than the democratic polis – and yet accounts for the centrality of the Athenian experiment within this civilization. We need to understand how the Athenian experiment was canonized – and the kind of influence this canonicity had.

This book, then, is an attempt to answer Lloyd's question, and along the way to explain the shape of the Greek legacy, and its significance for

---

[1] This has to be qualified: the end of Athens as a major political agent (which can be precisely dated to 338 BCE, or to 322 BCE at the latest) did not translate into a total collapse of democratic practices around the Greek world. There has recently been more interest in the extent to which democracy survived into the Hellenistic era (for which a good starting point is Mann and Scholz, 2012), a point to which we shall return in Part III. Even so, there is no doubt that, after the fourth century, democracy gradually became less central – and that most cultural activity was around the major cities governed by, or subservient to, monarchic courts.

the West. Ultimately, I argue that the survival of a classical canon was important in two ways: (1) in that it left behind a tradition that, in literary form, preserved the ideals of the face-to-face city (what I refer to as "the polis of letters"); and (2) in that it created a gap between culture and state: what was canonized was not a state ideology but in some sense defined a social space away from the state – providing, as it were, the conditions for the emergence of civic society. These are the two main upshots of the book, providing together an outline of how a modestly scaled event in the classical Greek-speaking world carved out a unique historical path for the Mediterranean. All civilizations were mostly monarchical but those of the West ended up being committed to those two ideals: public debate, and a culture distinct from that of the state. Another claim I develop is that, thanks to the failure of Greek civilization to develop a monolithic state ideology, a space was opened for more or less autonomous cultural practices, of which the most significant, in the long term, was the rise of a distinctive scientific practice in the Hellenistic era. This combination – public debate, civic society and scientific practice – arguably accounts for the distinctive achievements of western Europe in the early modern era.

Strong claims, and I am required to produce a detailed historical account: how the classical canon was formed, and why it was never replaced. Which means that this is mostly an account not of the classical canon itself but of post-classical reception: a history of literary practices in Hellenistic, Imperial and late ancient times.

The duration is long, and the scale is big. The relevant level of analysis is that of culture as a whole: technical as well as strictly literary. Part of the difficulty I had in constructing the argument towards the end of my dissertation was that I was trying to determine the causes for the stability of a particular cultural form – mathematics – in isolation from its larger cultural setting. But culture is a system. This is not merely a structuralist declaration of faith but, rather, a straightforward point about how one may study a canon. The very meaning of such terms as "canon" and "genre" is positional: they entail a certain relation to the literary field taken as a whole. And so one has to reach beyond one's training and address something such as "Greek civilization as a whole": the many genres, the many places, the many periods.

I come to this book, as it were, as a historian of mathematics, but – in a process familiar to mathematicians – the problem has meanwhile been *generalized* and need no longer refer to its original terms. This is a book not about Greek mathematics but about Greek literary culture as a whole.

The key methodological commitment of this book, then, is to the study of literary culture as a whole. From this follow certain other methodological consequences. Studying literary culture as a whole implies an attention to overall patterns more than to individual details. I thus regularly offer statistics and maps. While I do make many qualitative pronouncements, these are, with a few exceptions, generalizing and impressionistic, and not based on close readings. Studying the regularities of literary culture as a whole also implies adopting a perspective which need not have been available to the ancient actors themselves (they had pursued their own practices, without necessarily pausing to consider their literary culture as a whole). For this reason, I make no effort to identify the authors' concepts and am content to deploy my own observer's concepts throughout. The result is a book very different from traditional classical philology. The complex footnote with its plethora of primary and secondary sources is almost entirely avoided (my footnotes, instead, merely point to the key, recent studies with which the reader, wishing to pursue a point of detail, may begin her research).[2] Only rarely do I offer close readings of individual passages or reconstructions of the meanings of original terms. Fortunately for me, traditional philology now has few champions, and I will not spend time arguing against the straw man of the philological critic. Instead, I will apologize to him.[3] I have no interest, as such, in debunking close reading or in debunking the recovery of actors' concepts: I find such research exciting and rewarding (as well I should, spending most of my working life as Archimedes' philologist). I am not even interested in promoting in general this or that methodology: one should simply use the tools that are useful for a task. I write a book on a broad-brush question and so I use a broad brush; for other projects, other, finer brushes are more appropriate.

The Greek classical legacy is the subject of the first part: "Canon". In this first part I offer an account of the position of the Athenian democratic experiment for ancient culture as a whole. The second part, "Space", concentrates on the Hellenistic era: how the system of oppositions between

---

[2] One reason we, classical scholars, often write very long footnotes is to display our mastery of a field: about the topic of the footnote, we know less, perhaps, than von Wilamowitz-Moellendorff, but, anyway, more than practically anyone alive. Not me, not here. This book ranges widely – you will see – and, on most pages, I write on topics on which there are at least a hundred classicists better informed than myself. (This book aims to be, simultaneously, a work of scholarship *and* a work of synthesis: is this combination at all possible? I am not sure, but, at any rate, this is the gamble underlying this work.)

[3] I was about to write "to her" and then realized that straw men are male by definition – as were the great bulk of ancient authors and readers. In this book, the generic lyrical poet will be "he or she"; otherwise, generic ancient authors and readers will be referred to as "he".

Athens and Alexandria was constructed, and how it gave way to another system dominated by Roman networks. In particular, in the third century BCE the opposition between Athens and Alexandria made possible a nearly autonomous practice of science. In general, my emphasis would be on a Hellenistic duality, on a Roman plurality. The crucial point is that somehow, in the post-classical era, the Mediterranean became monarchical – and yet failed to develop a unifying ideology. Ultimately, I would argue, this was because of the specific ways in which space and canon interacted to prevent the rise of a replacement to the Athenian canon. The third part, "Scale", attempts a reconstruction of the absolute numbers of authors, books and their audiences in antiquity. This is found to be especially important for the account of culture through the Imperial era and into late antiquity. I follow the contexts and consequences of a rise in scale, through the Imperial era, followed by a major decline through the third century CE. This final transition into late antiquity achieved, finally, something of a stable, revered corpus of writing, across all fields: the pluralism of the democratic experiment, finally curtailed. It was shot through with the contradictions and legacies of more than seven centuries of debate, however: a treasure house of heterogeneity that will shape future Mediterranean civilizations.

In the first part I show the homogeneity of the central canon. In the second part I show how this homogeneity of the canon led, paradoxically, to the heterogeneity of the specialized genres. In the third part I show how the specialized genres, finally, became homogeneous – only in late antiquity.

I draw maps, make counts. The key technique is statistical. Would that I could say that this book thus shows, in such a way, my background in mathematics! But in fact I am no mathematician, still less a statistician. I am better prepared to offer close readings of Greek lyric poetry than I am to measure statistical significance. This book displays no statistical sophistication; it offers no more than simple tables and a few correlations. I could have hired a statistician and deployed t-values and chi-squares; I chose not to, for a reason. With the kind of evidence available to the ancient historian, the potential biases in our evidence are so huge so as to swamp any statistical artifacts of randomness. We need to look not for mathematical but "archaeological" significance: a sense of how the evidence was formed and what its biases of selection were. This qualitative grasp of the evidence is, in general, the one most important in the application of statistics to historical questions. And so the appropriate response is to consider bias explicitly – and to concentrate on clear, qualitatively meaningful results. Percentages are always discussed in rough approximations: where I find 17 percent, I discuss them as "roughly 20 percent". And, while raw figures are provided precisely, I expect such numbers to be wrong in detail and am not concerned about this. Even if I count 29 philosophers at a given place, and a better scholar will count 33, the types of conclusions I draw will never depend on such detail: I leave room for error, for error there will be.

I rely throughout on simple tools: mostly, counts of citations, papyrus fragments and authors based on reference works and indices. The tools are simple but they are solid, for the study of the ancient world is now based on remarkable databases and reference works, in turn based on the collection, edition and preservation of an enormous corpus. So it is for a reason that I feel gratitude to traditional philological scholarship. But the point is deeper than just my gratitude to past scholars, who created information and then aggregated it in ways that make possible an impressionistic synthesis such as the one offered here.

Rather, the truly remarkable thing is the presence of a tradition that preserves a robust image of a civilization as a whole. The statistical approach is not favored by classical scholars, I suspect, because of a widely shared assumption that our knowledge of antiquity is too fragmentary. Part of the argument of this book will be that this is not true. The ancient literary practice is very well attested, *for a reason*. It was a self-aware, widely dispersed activity which kept recording itself in rich, pluralistic detail – and which continued to be treasured by a chain of civilizations that defined, through the centuries, an ever-expanding Mediterranean. Let us begin to explore this, starting right at the top of the chain: the Greek canon.

# PART I

# *Canon*

The response to Lloyd's note is, I think, rather simple. Appropriately – for a question raised by Geoffrey Lloyd – I begin with a comparison with China.

Mark Lewis' book *Writing and Authority in Early China* (1999) studies the formation of the Chinese canon during the Han period. This canon was a particular Confucian interpretation as well as a reconstruction of the "classics". A single group of texts triumphed, arranged hierarchically according to degrees of authorial remove: anonymous classics at the top, a constructed author "Confucius" (quoted but not authoring himself) interpreting them, trailed by the various authored texts that interpret Confucius. And that was indeed a single group of texts, promoting the ideals of a single group, the servants of the state: ritual-literate masters (*ru*). Thus, this group of texts both represented an ideal polity (*Zhou Li*: this polity was imagined to exist in mythical, early dynasties) as well as *con-stituting*, in itself (Lewis' key observation), such a polity. Lewis insists throughout on this duality: hierarchy and unity were ideals promoted by the texts – as well as a material/textual reality, embedded in the works themselves. Here is Lewis' summary of the significance of this canon formation (1999: 362):

> The imaginary state of *Zhou Li* came to define the imperial order, and the textual realm fashioned in the coded judgements of the [texts of the canon] endured, while the substantial realities of actual administration all turned to dust. In this way the Chinese empire became a realm built of texts.

My point will be obvious. The Greek case was exactly complementary: the political conditions of the democratic experiment in Athens became established not so much in the political realm but, rather, as the Greek literary canon – forming an alternative, *cultural* realm. It represented a realm of face-to-face agonistic encounters between free individuals anchored in the polis. It also constituted, in its very formation as a group of texts, a principle of multiplicity (many genres, many authors and many works), tied to clearly defined locations in city states, commemorating a Greek world of multiple city states, above all commemorating Athens; the multiple authors being fundamentally on an equal footing as far as their authorial status is concerned; and the system as a whole based on the tension of synchronic individuals. The canon spoke of the realities of the early polis and constituted, in itself, a kind of textual polis: what I would call the "polis of letters".

The Mediterranean saw little democracy in the actual political sphere. It saw Hellenistic kingdoms, a Roman empire and its Christian and Muslim heirs (in those later civilizations, an ideal of political unity sat side by side with an ideal of religious orthodoxy). Through all that, though, the canon survived as an alternative frame of reference, sometimes more active, sometimes less, but always a guide for a cultural conduct at variance with the realities of monarchy; it also served to qualify and even obstruct the formation of a more direct, "Confucian" state ideology. The individual in face-to-face debate always remained as a central model of intellectual and literary practice. In particular, through many centuries, the specialized genres could be inspired by a canon enshrining the democratic polis, without being canonized themselves. Within the specialized genres, one continued to struggle for a leading position, creating a varying range of intellectual alliances throughout a shifting Mediterranean.

My argument is in a sense simpler than Lewis'. I do not need to argue that the cultural canon was a historical force that shaped later politics; rather, I just need to argue that the cultural canon was a historical force that shaped later culture. This should hardly be controversial. The key observation is simply that the cultural canon was a more significant force than the contemporary political culture. What mattered most for cultural practice was not the presiding role of a Ptolemy or an Augustus but that of Euripides, Plato and Demosthenes. Culture was shaped not by its contemporary politics but by its foundations on a canon.

Throughout much of antiquity, the spirit of debate in the canon was enacted in the specialized genres, against the background of spaces in contest: Athens against Alexandria, and then a Roman synthesis that was deliberately distinct from either preceding model. It was also enacted within a cultural space that was big enough to contain debate: a large audience, many cultural contestants and many books. Late antiquity saw a collapse in scale. Under the pressure of this collapse, the specialized genres changed their character, and they assimilated to the structure of canonicity of the literary field. Canon, at this point, became all-pervasive, and this pervasive canon of Greek antiquity was bequeathed to the Middle Ages. But, at this point, it was shot through and through with a variety and tensions, marked by a bizarre cultural hybrid of the pagan and the Christian. At some point the conditions would be finally ripe for the polis of letters to reassert itself. This would happen, most significantly, in early modern Europe and would define, finally, the place of the Greek legacy in world history.

Such is the outline of my claim. The roles of space and scale in the growth of the specialized genres of antiquity are discussed in Parts II and III of this book. For this part, my task is to discuss in detail the structure of the ancient canon and to offer a historical account for its stability.

Chapter 1, "Canon: The Evidence", discusses the sources of evidence for the canon – above all, the papyri – and along the way maps the canon itself. Its main claim is simply that the canon was real: the same authors were both more prestigious as well as more popular, and this seems to be true, equally, across times and places: from as soon as our evidence for the canon emerges, and everywhere across the Mediterranean. Chapter 2, "Canon in Practice", has two distinct tasks. It first describes the canon structurally, arguing in detail for the validity of my central metaphor, the canon as a "polis" of letters: this is crucial for the argument of the lasting impact of the canon. It then accounts for the canon historically, arguing for its early formation and providing a part of the account of its stability (an account picked up by later parts of the book) – the stability which ultimately, I argue, answers Lloyd's query.

This part of the book, in short, argues that the Greek canon was real. A brief caveat, then. Whether or not the canon is "real" is often taken, in contemporary discourse, as a question of value: do certain works of art (and perhaps also the ideology they convey) stand for timeless realities? It should be obvious that I have no interest in this question. When I claim that the Greek canon was real, I make a purely sociological observation: certain Greek authors were more frequently read, and more widely valued, and that, throughout all antiquity, the overall ranking of such authors remaining nearly unchanged. Even this purely sociological claim is controversial, and so I shall need to bring in the evidence.

CHAPTER I

# *Canon: The Evidence*

Near the beginning of his commentary to Plato's *Parmenides*, Proclus tries to account for the very purpose of the dialogue.[1] He mentions that some consider it to be primarily an agonistic response to Zeno of Elea, and he notes the variety of ways in which Plato engages in such agonistic responses. Sometimes, Plato simply tries – so Proclus – to outdo his opponent, for instance in the way in which, in the *Menexenus*, he tries to write a funeral oration even better than that of Thucydides.[2] There are many ways in which this is a suggestive passage: to begin with, it reminds us that authors of Proclus' time found it natural to write commentaries on works roughly 800 years old; that, even while engaged in an emulation and almost a religious celebration of that distant past,[3] they understood the past authors themselves to have been engaged in an agonistic practice (the authors they emulate, Proclus understood, did not emulate each other); and, finally, that Proclus and his audience had a very clear idea of some of the figures they referred to. The name "Thucydides" occurs twice – no more – in all of Proclus' extant, prodigious output, and, on both occasions, it is brought in with no explanation: the audience would know perfectly well who Thucydides was, and also, indeed, how the *Menexenus* could be seen as being in implicit competition with it.

---

[1] Proclus, a fifth-century CE author, had a huge output: more than 50 works may be ascribed to him with confidence, of which the bulk take the form of philosophical commentary (SEP, s.v. Proclus, *Supplement*: 52, non-dubiously attested works, of which 27 are explicitly commentary; but many of the non-commentary works are in fact introductory to the reading of Plato, while the explicit commentaries tend to be more bulky than the more systematic works). This is in line with the overall project of commentary in late antiquity: a teacher, brokering a text to his audience; such brokerage requires, perhaps primarily, an account of the purpose of writing (Mansfeld, 1994: 10). See pp. 775–7 in Part III.

[2] Proclus, *in Parm.* 631.27–8.

[3] A two-day festival of celebration of the birthdays of Socrates and Plato is attested in Marinus, *Life of Proclus* 23 (Penella, 1984).

Most remarkably, Proclus was quite likely right.[4] In other words, the historical writings of Thucydides were so clearly present to a late ancient philosopher such as Proclus that he not only took them for granted but also could have interpreted correctly their meaning for an early reader such as Plato. Proclus was at home in the literary practice of fourth-century BCE Athens.

At this point it is customary to cite Borges. I will use him to bring out a contrast. In "Averroes' Search" ("La Busca de Averroes"),[5] Borges imagines how – in the Andalus of the twelfth century – Ibn Rushd (or Averroes, in Borges' Eurocentric spelling) sets himself the task of writing a commentary on Aristotle's *Poetics*, and how Ibn Rushd concludes that "[Aristotle] gives the name 'tragedy' to panegyrics and the name 'comedy' to satires and anathemas".[6] Ibn Rushd gets it wrong, you see, because *he has no idea what Greek theater was like*. How could he have one?

Borges' story is a wonderful literary evocation and a rendering of a Corduba which is as distant from Borges as Plato was from Proclus. Borges' point was how difficult it was, in general, to evoke a different culture (and so the story ends on a self-reflective, ironic note, undermining Borges' own effort). And indeed, while Borges is a bit unfair to Ibn Rushd (who did get it half right, and whose original purpose was explicitly to map Aristotle's terms onto Arabic literary forms),[7] he does get something essential right. Not perhaps a universal point, but a particular historical one: Borges accurately reveals the contrast between the reception of the Greek canon within the continuous transmission of the Greek tradition itself, and outside that transmission. The Greeks have always transmitted simultaneously Plato – and Thucydides; Aristotle – as well as tragedy and comedy. It was a canon that traveled together, its parts in mutual support. This is distinctive, and non-obvious: other cultures did not take on board, similarly, the entire system; hence Proclus' success, and Ibn Rushd's failure.

This was a self-evident system of genres, visible from any vantage point offered by the many forms of cultural life. Galen, an Imperial-era medical author, famously thought that the best doctor should know how to reason properly, hence should know philosophy; he also thought that he should know the meaning of words. And so Galen also wrote 12 books with

---

[4] At least as early as Berndt (1881) modern scholars have pointed out the allusions Plato seems to direct at Thucydides; see Coventry (1989: 3 n.8).

[5] Borges (1962 [1947]: 148).

[6] The quotation is from Borges, not Ibn Rushd; I understand that Borges relies on reliable translations.

[7] Mallette (2009).

commentary on fifth-century BCE Athenian comedies.[8] This is Galen: frantically piling up his cultural capital (on this tendency in the Roman era, see in Chapter 6, section 6.3). Archimedes, the Hellenistic mathematician – a much more subtle author – wrote *The Sand-Reckoner*, a treatise setting out to show that the number of the grains of sand can be expressed. Among other things, this surely is a subtle allusion to Pindar: a scientific-literary move typical of Hellenistic Alexandrian culture (more on this in Chapter 4, pages 670–7).[9] Proclus on Thucydides, Galen on Aristophanes, Archimedes on Pindar. We have covered the three post-classical eras (Hellenistic, Imperial and late), the three main branches of non-belletristic writing (philosophy, medicine and the exact sciences) – and we find an important continuity. In all cases we see a non-literary author referring to a literary author, and *nothing in this appears to be remarkable*. That the authors and their audience share the knowledge of the literary authors is taken for granted. Ibn Rushd's difficulty was, after all, that Aristotle took for granted his audience's familiarity with a particular canon of fifth-century plays, and so he did not even bother to explain what they were. The same familiarity could still be taken for granted nearly a millennium later.

This continuity was maintained, materially speaking, in the form of books. And so we should look for the ancient book. Concentrating just on the Nile Valley (that is, excluding the spectacular find of the library at Herculaneum), even considering only "pagan" works, we now have at least a rough description of some 7,000 literary papyri (the terms "literary" and "papyri" both being understood in an expansive sense: more on this below). Those are 7,000 *fragments*, containing on average less than 4 percent of their original text.[10] Let's start from there.

## 1.1  Data from the Papyri

Our notion of "canon" has two distinct components: first, what we may refer to as *prestige* – the familiarity and positive attitudes regarding (for instance) given authors; second, *popularity*, for instance as measured in the circulation of books. In the modern context – under the pressure of mass

---

[8] Nutton (2009: 30).

[9] *Ol.* 2.98: "Since sand escapes number. . ." While the use by Pindar may well be the most canonical (and is Sicilian in theme, suitably for Archimedes' purpose), this is in fact a widespread trope (Nisbet and Hubbard, 1970: 321).

[10] As I note below, I calculate an average 4 percent fragment size from the data of Johnson (2004, tab. 3.7). Johnson selects for study *identified* texts, however, which creates a bias for larger fragments. Note also that there are many papyri fragments as yet unpublished even in rudimentary form, most of them being on the small side.

literacy – a (qualified) divide has formed between the two, in a process classically described by Bourdieu 1993 [1983]. In some cases, authors directly base their cultural capital – that is, their prestige – on their low circulation. This has got to the point that "non-canonical literature" is understood to refer primarily to such genres in which high circulation coincides with low brand reputations for the genre as a whole (such as the detective novel). All this is a modern phenomenon, and, to the (restricted) extent that this now holds, the modern canon is, historically speaking, an anomaly. In the case studied here, the two – prestige and popularity – coincide (with qualifications that will be discussed below), and I will use the term "canonical" to mean both. But I start with the evidence regarding circulation.

The following table lists, in descending order, all the Greek authors for whom two or more papyri fragments (found other than in Herculaneum) are identified.[11] The author name is followed by the number of fragments. I divide the list into sub-tables according to tiers (which are of course my own construction). For each author, I note genre and date.[12] I note immediately the most obvious shortcoming of this table: it does not include the currently unidentified papyri. Their potential impact (which I argue to be minor) is discussed in section 1.4.1.

---

[11]  This does not mean "all authors for whom two or more fragments were found": about a third of the fragments of literary papyri are adespota and could hide a few more authors frequently surviving (as well, of course, as changing the numbers for the identified frequently surviving authors; I return to discuss this on pp. 79–88 below). It is obvious that Herculaneum would badly corrupt the sample; I return to this point below. The source is CEDOPAL, an online database that represents the current state of Mertens–Pack, originally a database tracking all non-Herculaneum, "pagan" papyri (with a few exceptions). I will have a few more notes to add below concerning Christian papyri, as well as returning to the overall nature of the databases. It should be said immediately that CEDOPAL allows a minor amount of overcount, in that deleted or dubious entries are still counted. For most purposes I ignore this, though in a few cases I will note that an individual author is especially inflated. I use CEDOPAL and not LDAB (a more comprehensive, and better-thought-out system) because CEDOPAL is good enough for the purpose of gaining general statistics, and had a much easier interface when the data were compiled. Put simply, I would never have been able to compile all the statistics of papyrus count generated in this book from the LDAB database. I avoid in this book the convention of providing the date in which an internet resource has been accessed, as I have accessed the sites multiple times. In general, the data on papyri used in this book were compiled in 2011, but, prompted by readers for the press, I then went and recounted this first table, in the first week of July 2018, so as to ensure that no significant changes had occurred (only one interesting development was noted: a significant rise in the number of papyri by Plutarch; see p. 93 below). As a consequence, I allowed myself in most cases, in the following tables in this book, to reuse the data from 2011 without recalculating them.

[12]  My genres are constructed here in a coarse-grained sense. Dates are given for the multiple of 50 which occupies the largest segment of the author's productive life (a date such as –400 means that most of the author's work was produced during the period –425 to –375). Even when in doubt, I give a speculative precise date; specific numbers, with recognition of error, are better than fuzzy numbers.

## Tier 1: The central canon (over 30 fragments) – 17 authors[13]

| | | | |
|---|---|---|---|
| Homer | 1,680 | Poetry: ep. | Archaic |
| Demosthenes | 204 | Prose: rhet. | −350 |
| Euripides | 169 | Poetry: trag. | −400 |
| Hesiodus | 137 | Poetry: ep. | Archaic |
| Isocrates | 132 | Prose: rhet. | −350 |
| Menander | 105 | Poetry: com. | −300 |
| Plato | 103 | Prose: phil. | −350 |
| Thucydides | 98 | Prose: hist. | −400 |
| Callimachus | 77 | Poetry: ep.[14] | −250 |
| Aristophanes | 59 | Poetry: com. | −400 |
| Apollonius | 55 | Poetry: ep. | −250 |
| Pindar | 55 | Poetry: lyr. | −450 |
| Aeschines | 50 | Prose: rhet. | −350 |
| Xenophon | 50 | Prose: hist. | −350 |
| Herodotus | 48 | Prose: hist. | −450 |
| Sophocles | 37 | Poetry: trag. | −450 |
| Aeschylus | 33 | Poetry: trag. | −450 |

## Tier 2: Less dominant canonical authors (9–29 fragments)[15] – 17 authors

| | | | |
|---|---|---|---|
| Hippocrates | 29 | Prose: med. | −400 |
| Alcaeus | 28 | Poetry: lyr. | −600 |
| Theocritus | 28 | Poetry: ep. | −250 |
| Sappho | 25 | Poetry: lyr. | −600 |
| Archilochus | 19 | Poetry: lyr. | −650 |
| Plutarch | 16 | Prose: phil. | +100[16] |

[13] The cutoff point is in a sense arbitrary. The bottom of the list has very significant non-papyrological support, however: it is historically plausible that Xenophon, Sophocles and Aeschylus should be considered as forming part of the central canon. I shall return to discuss below the relationship between papyrus frequency and other sources of evidence for ancient reputation.

[14] The coarse-grained division into genres is problematic here, for the first time in this table. I return to the example of Callimachus and his genres, and the general question of pigeonholing ancient authors, on pp. 127–35 below.

[15] The bottom cutoff point is in this case truly arbitrary, but I believe it is better to make some distinction than none; it comes in handy that there happened to be, in both 2011 and 2018, no eight-papyrus authors.

[16] Plutarch is the first author in this list whose numbers should be adjusted for date. Since he wrote in the first century CE (and, as we shall see below, wide circulation usually took some time to achieve in antiquity), he had a smaller chronological range in which to circulate, and so the 16 fragments are the equivalent of, say, 20 to 25 fragments from a classical author (the adjustment is not much greater than that, since most of our literary papyri are from the Imperial era, indeed beginning with the second century). This type of adjustment is especially important for the genre of the novel as a whole. Note finally that Plutarch is the author whose fortunes improved the most from 2011 to 2018 (from nine to 16 – almost doubling his count). It now becomes clear that Plutarch was a massively successful author *already in antiquity*. His

*(cont.)*

| | | | |
|---|---|---|---|
| Aesopus | 15 | Prose: varia | −450 |
| Alcman | 15 | Poetry: lyr. | −600 |
| Aristoteles | 14 | Prose: phil. | −350 |
| *Anthologia Graeca* | 12 | Poetry: lyr | −100[17] |
| Aratus | 12 | Poetry: ep. | −250 |
| Bacchylides | 11 | Poetry: lyr. | −450 |
| Galen | 11 | Prose: med. | +200 |
| Astrampsychus | 10 | Prose: varia | +300 |
| Lysias | 10 | Prose: rhet. | −400 |
| Euphorion | 10 | Poetry: ep. | −250 |
| Stesichorus | 9 | Poetry: lyr. | −550 |

### Tier 3: Sporadic but perhaps significant survival (5–7 fragments) – 18 authors

| | | | |
|---|---|---|---|
| Achilles Tatius | 7 | Prose: novel | +150 |
| Aelius Aristides | 7 | Prose: rhet. | +150 |
| Epicharmus | 7 | Poetry: com. | −450 |
| Euclides | 7 | Prose: math. | −300 |
| Eupolis | 7 | Poetry: com. | −450 |
| Hyperides | 7 | Prose: rhet. | −350 |
| Ptolemaeus math. | 7 | Prose: math | +150 |
| Simonides | 7 | Poetry: lyr. | −500 |
| Alcidamas | 6 | Prose: rhet. | −400 |
| Anubion | 6 | Poetry: ep. | −50 |
| Dioscorides | 6 | Prose: med. | +50 |
| Lycophron | 6 | Poetry: trag. | −250 |
| Anacreon | 5 | Poetry: lyr. | −550 |
| Antimachus of Colophon | 5 | Poetry: ep. | −400 |
| Hipponax | 5 | Poetry: lyr. | −500 |
| Oppian | 5 | Poetry: ep. | +150 |
| Philo | 5 | Prose: phil | +0 |
| Strabo | 5 | Prose: geog. | +0 |

massive corpus was preserved *for a reason*. This is typical of the way in which the later choice to preserve authors into the main manuscript transmission can be predicted directly from the papyrus selection. The ranking – stable. More on this below!

[17] "Anthologia Graeca" is an author field in CEDOPAL's filing system, and so for consistency's sake I include it here; this is of course, in the ancient context, a composite category, so what we find here is a lump of truly minor poets, not a fairly widespread, single anthology. In other words, this is not a "tier 2" author.

## Tier 4: Sporadic survival (2–4 fragments)[18] – 41 authors

**4 fragments:** Astydamas (poetry: trag., –350); Babrius (poetry: lyr., +200); Chariton (prose: novel, +50); Dionysius Thrax (prose: tech., –150); Rhianus (poetry: ep., –250); Theophrastus (prose: phil., –300); Theognis (poetry: lyr., –500)

**3 fragments:** Aeschines Socraticus (prose: phil., –400); Antiphon (prose: rhet., –400); Antonius Diogenes (prose: novel, +150); Callisthenes (prose: hist., –350); Cercidas (poetry: lyr., –250); Corinna (poetry: lyr., –500); Cratinus (poetry: com., –400); Dinarchus (prose: rhet., –300); Dionysius Scytobrachion (prose: tech., –250); Libanius (prose: rhet., +350); Lollianus (prose: novel, –100); Lycurgus (prose: rhet., –350); Nicander (poetry: ep., –150); Nicarchus II (poetry: lyr., +50); Posidippus of Pella (poetry: lyr., –250); Tyrtaeus (poetry: lyr., –650)

**2 fragments:** Apollodorus of Athens (prose: tech., –150); Arrian (prose: hist., +150); Choerilus (poetry: ep., –400); Chrysippus (prose: phil., –200); Critias (poetry: trag., –400); Dionysius (bassarika) (poetry: ep., –250); Ephorus (prose: hist., –350); Herodianus (prose: tech., +200); Herondas (poetry: lyr., –250); Isaeus (prose: rhet., –350); Pancrates (poetry: ep., +150); Parthenius (poetry: lyr., +0); Philemon (poetry: com., –300); Satyrus (prose: hist., –300); Sophron (poetry: com.; –400); Timotheus of Miletus (poetry: lyr., –400); Triphiodorus (poetry: ep., +300); Tryphon (prose: tech., +0)

## Tier 5: Currently hapax papyrus authors – 76 authors

Here I prefer not to quote the list at all, as, taken individually, the names are misleading: there is not much of a difference between surviving in one papyrus fragment and zero. As a group, however, those authors acquire meaning. Of the 76 authors, 61 are prose authors and 15 are poets;[19] this appears meaningful. Indeed, we should compare now all five tiers, as wholes.

---

[18] It is misleading to think of this part of the list as in any sense "canonical": the evidence is compatible with the author being rare in antiquity. To signal the different meaning of the list, I no longer present it in table form but in a paragraph format.

[19] The names, without elaboration, are: Africanus (Julius), Anatolius, Anaximenes rhet., Andocides, Antiochus of Syracusae, Antipater of Tarsus, Antiphanes, Appianus, Areius, Aristodemus, Aristophanes of Byzantium, Aristoxenus, Artemidorus, Ausonius, Carcinus, Chares, Charisius, Conon, Cornutus (L. Annaeus), Ctesias, Didymus, Dio Chrysostomus, Diodorus Siculus, Empedocles, Eratosthenes, Erinna, Eudoxus, Favorinus, Gregorius of Corinth, Gregorius of Nyssena, Harpocration, Hecataeus, Heliodorus med., Heliodorus novel, Hellanicus, Heraclides gramm., Heraclides Lembus, Hermarchus, Hermesianax, Herodotus med., Hierocles, Himerius, Hippolytus, Ibycus, Josephus, Leo gramm., Lucianus, Manetho, Meleager, Menelaus, Mnasalces, Moschus, Musonius Rufus, Nechepso, Nonnus, Olympius med., Pamprepius, Pherecydes, Philaenis, Philicus, Philostratus, Phlegon, Phoenix, Polybius,

|           | Poetry % (authors) | Prose % (authors) | Average date |
|-----------|--------------------|-------------------|--------------|
| Tier 1    | 59                 | 41                | −410         |
| Tier 2    | 59                 | 41                | −350         |
| Tier 3    | 56                 | 44                | −220         |
| Tier 4    | 49                 | 51                | −180         |
| Tier 5    | 20                 | 80                | −90          |

The central observation out of this table is straightforward: canonicity, in antiquity, was associated with more performative genres, such as poetry and rhetoric. In a way, this book is a series of observations on this correlation.

Higher up, the papyrus evidence is more poetic, more anchored in the classical era. Lower down, it is constituted more by prose, and by later works. It seems reasonable to extrapolate the table further, with a surprising result: it seems very likely that the bulk of the authors circulating in antiquity in small numbers – those who currently are not among the identified papyri – would be prose authors of the Roman era. More on this below, especially in Part III.

In some other ways the top names in the tables themselves offer few surprises. It is well known that the papyri are heavily dominated by Homer, and that in general the "canonical" authors are indeed very frequent; it is also widely recognized that, among the authors not transmitted via the manuscript tradition, Menander is extremely frequent in the papyri. So this first table is not inherently surprising. What is perhaps worth noting is its most obvious feature: it is a *descending* list of *authors*. Take the "authors" first. Whereas the typical medieval codex is often an anthology in char-acter – a collection organized typically by subject matter[20] – the elementary unit of ancient literary culture was a roll containing a work by a single

---

Posidippus com., Posidonius, Pythagoras, Sextus Pythag., Simias of Rhodus, Soranus, Sosylus, Strattis, Themistius, Theon gramm., Theon rhet., Theopompus. To clarify: this is the list of one-fragment authors from 2011 (in my recounting of numbers of fragments, I went through all the authors of tiers 1 to 4 and recounted them; it should be noted that already in tier 4 the changes found were minimal, so continuing this work seemed otiose, though doubtless it would have come up with a few minor changes).

[20] To make a suggestive comparison: I have made a survey of (1) a random selection of Paris codices in the ancient exact sciences in Greek, Latin and Arabic (random: selecting all the manuscripts whose inventory number divided by five) and (2) all the Laurentian and Vatican Greek codices in the ancient exact sciences. A total of 98 codices include works on a single topic by various authors, while 19 include multiple works by the same author; 71, with a single treatise each, cannot be classified in the same way. We find that, when codices in the exact sciences join together several works, relatively little effort is made to keep together works by the same author, but there is a common practice of bringing together works on a single topic. That my example involves a technical field is of course significant: the codex, unlike the roll, did often collect technical (or, in the most frequent case, liturgical) works.

author. Often the roll would contain a part of a work (hence the division into "books" we are familiar with from modern editions), and sometimes it would contain more than a single work by the same author. But a multi-authored volume, with multiple works by *different* authors, is extremely rare.[21] Of the 413 papyri in the sample studied in Johnson (2004), only one contains works by more than one author (P.Lond. Lit. 134+130, Demosthenes and Hyperides). Obviously, our finds are fragments, and so it is possible that we merely hit upon one work contained in a roll and that elsewhere on the same roll a different author is represented; the numbers appear robust, however, even with this taken into consideration.[22]

We find that the ancients collected authors. This is made even more evident when we bring in the other obvious feature of this table: its rapid descent. Imagine, for instance, that ancient readers were interested in having the various genres represented in their book baskets, so that they made sure they had tragedy and comedy, elegy and prose, philosophy and medicine; but they couldn't care less which authors they happened to own

---

[21] Anthologies in the strict sense, with brief extracts from many individuals, are also quite rare (fewer than 100 fragments are identified: but this must be an undercount, as fragments with a single work could derive from anthologies). More importantly, they derive mostly from the context of education and were not collected as "books"; I return to discuss this on pp. 42–3 below. The evidence of the titles is relevant; based on Caroli (2007) I have surveyed 61 extant book titles: all of them specify a single author, unsurprisingly, as they almost always specify a single work (an interesting exception is Caroli, 203–4, P.16, P.Ant. I 21 – an external etiquette: "Pindar, whole" [the name, exceptionally, is in the nominative and not the genitive: perhaps kept on a box with multiple rolls]). None specifies multiple authors. The evidence is suggestive but not dispositive, because multiple-author works might theoretically have had, instead, multiple individual titles scattered through them. I return to discuss this evidence on pp. 80–1 below.

[22] I estimate the average survival of columns out of original rolls, based on Johnson (2004, tab. 3.7), as about 3 to 5 percent. (I say "estimate" because I did not sum up the entire table – I do not have the original spreadsheet – and so, to make the calculation practical, I took a sample of every sixth entry and derived the result: 3.86 percent. The error introduced by this sampling is smaller than the range of 3 to 5 percent – which I adopt because there are other sources of error in Johnson's original sample). In other words, each papyrus fragment has about 4 percent probability of hitting upon the transition from one author to the other (assuming there is just one; the probability is higher if there are multiple such points). Also, many papyrus fragments cover non-contiguous text and so "stretch out" across more than 4 percent of the original papyrus; further, they tend to come away from the end/beginning – see p. 80, n.137, below – raising further the probability that they might detect transitions between authors). At face value, then, we would have expected to find 20 or so transitions within 413, while we find one. Likely, then, most ancient rolls did not contain more than a single author. Finally, it should be said that P.Lond. Lit. 134+130 is a very atypical roll of more than a single scribe and huge dimensions. As for the report based on Tzetzes, according to which the "palace library" in Alexandria had 400,000 "mixed" rolls and 90,000 "unmixed" rolls (Kaibel CGF 19; discussed in Fraser, 1972: II.485 nn.170–7; see the more critical discussion in Bagnall, 2002: 351–2, however), all I can say is that the evidence of the papyri suggests something is seriously wrong with this passage – whose numbers, anyway, are clearly stylized. Did Tzetzes have in mind the conditions of the codices of his own time and place?

in the various genres. The resulting curve would have been much less steep in that case: we learn, therefore, that ancient readers did not collect *genres* but, instead, collected *names*, showing a marked preference for just a few.

The next set of tables is perhaps somewhat less familiar. In what follows, I consider the numbers not for authors but for works, picking out only those works for which six or more fragments survive (with a few extrapolations thrown in).[23] Instead of providing raw fragment counts, though, I divide the number of fragments by the word count (which I estimate in some cases). I also adjust for the different format of prose and poetry. Thus, the following table provides a basic outline of the relative numbers of copies for given works. The rationale is obvious: when two works of the same length are represented, one by 20 fragments but the other by ten fragments, the simplest assumption is that the work with the more fragments had twice as many copies. Conversely, when two works are represented by the same number of fragments, but the length of one was 10,000 words while the length of the other was 100,000 words, the simplest assumption is that the shorter work had ten times more copies. I divide the list into tiers, in an obvious way.

| | | Pap. count | Word count | Pap./word × 1,000 (including prose adjustment)[24] |
|---|---|---|---|---|
| **Tier 1: The *Iliad* (24 rolls)** | | | | |
| Homer | *Iliad* | 1,557 | 115,477 | 13.5 |
| **Tier 2: *Odyssey*/Hesiod level; roughly 20 to 30 percent of the *Iliad* (32 rolls)** | | | | |
| Isocrates | *Nicocl.* | 30 | 3,119 | 12[25] |
| Isocrates | *Demon.* | 23 | 3,000 | 9.5 |

[23] A set of six, in and of itself, has no statistical value. The set of all works with six or more surviving fragments, however, is already a useful object to consider, and it is valuable to consider the broad patterns of the order of frequency within the set. In this case I reproduce the numbers based on the count from 2011. Since then CEDOPAL has changed its interface, so searches by individual works are no longer practical. Since, in this table, what interests us are the relative frequencies, and I have established in my comparison of papyrus numbers per author in the previous table that those were overall very stable, this should not come as a problem (the author who changed most from 2011 to 2018 – Plutarch – did so through many different works and so would not be visible in this table).

[24] I calculate, based on Johnson (2004: tab. 3.7), that poetry would have on average something like 25 percent more papyrus footprint per word. I thus adjust the prose numbers up by 25 percent (the sheer count by words tends to overestimate the frequency of poetry, as it occupies more papyrus for the same amount of words and therefore is more likely to be present on the papyrus evidence).

[25] It appears that the survival of Isocrates' exhortations on papyrus is almost entirely a phenomenon of the classroom; hence those numbers are the most misleading. I return to discuss this on p. 42 below.

*(cont.)*

| Hesiod | *Theogony* | 40 | 6,969 | 5.75 |
|---|---|---|---|---|
| Hesiod | *Works and Days* | 32 | 5,900 | 5.5 |
| Demosthenes | *Olynth.* | 28 | 6,350 | 1.5 |
| Homer | *Odyssey* | 283 | 87,765 | 3.25[26] |
| Demosthenes | *Chers.* | 10 | 4,291 | 3 |
| Hesiod | *Shield* | 9 | 3,336 | 2.75 |
| Euripides | *Phoe.* | 28 | 10,477 | 2.75 |

**Tier 3: The Menander/Hellenistic range; roughly 10 to 20 percent of the *Iliad* (17 rolls)**

| Isocrates | *Peace* | 17 | 8,278 | 2.5 |
|---|---|---|---|---|
| Callimachus | *Hymni* | 17 | 7,443 | 2.25 |
| Hesiod | *Catalogue* | 58 | 27,800?[27] | 2? |
| Menander | *Epitrepontes* | 14 | 7,000?[28] | 2? |
| Menander | *Misumenus* | 14 | 7,000? | 2? |
| Demosthenes | *Philip.* | 21 | 14,300 | 2 |
| Aeschines | *Ctesiph.* | 27 | 19,171 | 2 |
| Aratus | *Phaen.* | 14 | 7,867 | 1.75 |
| Euripides | *Orestes* | 19 | 10,753 | 1.75 |
| Isocrates | *Paneg.* | 16 | 11,249 | 1.5 |
| Callimachus | *Hecale* | 13 | 9,000?[29] | 1.5? |
| Euripides | *Androm.* | 12 | 7,763 | 1.5 |
| Euripides | *Medea* | 12 | 8,394 | 1.5 |

**Tier 4: The normal Demosthenes/Aristophanes range; roughly 5 to 10 percent of the *Iliad* (42 rolls)**

| Euripides | *Hecuba* | 9 | 7,676 | 1.25 |
|---|---|---|---|---|
| Apollonius | *Argon.* | 52 | 39,090 | 1.25[30] |
| Theocritus | *Idyl.* | 24 | 20,501 | 1.25 |

[26] It will be noticed that the sum of the *Iliad* and the *Odyssey*, in this table (based on 2011 numbers), is higher than the figure for Homer as a whole from the previous table (based on 2018 numbers). This paradoxical result is the outcome of CEDOPAL's choice, between 2011 and 2018, to remove "homerica" (grammatical and purely educational material) from the category of Homer. (See below, also, a similar effect with Aratus: there are now only 12 Aratus counted, but 14 were counted in 2011, because CEDOPAL has improved its filtering for false attributions and double-counting.)

[27] 4,000 lines is a standard guess (Osborne, 2005: 6). I extrapolate based on word and line counts from extant Hesiodic works.

[28] I simply resort to the desperate measure of considering the *Dyskolos* "typical".

[29] Hollis (1990): from *c.* 900 to *c.* 1,800 lines? Extrapolating from the *Argonautica*, we get 6,000 to 12,000 words, from which I take the mid-point.

[30] Here is a good example of how stable the results are. I found 52 Apollonius fragments in 2011; now there are 55. But at the level of granularity which matters to us here – rounding the fraction pap./ 1,000 × words to the nearest 0.25 – this difference simply does not register at all.

*(cont.)*

| | | | | |
|---|---|---|---|---|
| Demosthenes | *False Leg.* | 25 | 23,576 | 1.25 |
| Demosthenes | *Crown* | 24 | 22,893 | 1.25 |
| Aeschines | *Timarch.* | 14 | 13,961 | 1.25 |
| Demosthenes | *Lept.* | 10 | 11,543 | 1.25 |
| Demosthenes | *Midias* | 14 | 16,013 | 1.25 |
| Hippocrates | *Aphor.* | 6 | 7,374 | 1.25 |
| Euripides | *Bacchae* | 8 | 8,207 | 1 |
| Aristophanes | *Nubes* | 8 | 10,463 | 1 |
| Menander | *Dysc.* | 7 | 6,693[31] | 1 |
| Demosthenes | *Timocr.* | 11 | 14,896 | 1 |
| Callimachus | *Aetia* | 33 | 30,000?[32] | 1? |
| Menander | *Pericir.* | 6 | 7,000? | 1? |
| Archilochus | | 18 | 21,000? (4 r.?) | 1?[33] |
| Pindar | | 57 | 90,000?[34] (17 r.) | 0.75? |
| Aristophanes | *Achar.* | 6 | 7,818 | 0.75 |
| Euripides | *Hippo.* | 6 | 8,647 | 0.75 |
| Aristophanes | *Equites* | 7 | 9,764 | 0.75 |
| Aristophanes | *Plutus* | 7 | 8,864 | 0.75 |
| Aristophanes | *Pax* | 7 | 8,796 | 0.75 |
| Aeschines | *False Leg.* | 8 | 12,758 | 0.75 |
| Thucydides | | 96 | 153,260 | 0.75 |
| Lycophron | *Alex.* | 6 | 7,527 | 0.75 |
| Anubion | | 6 | ? | 0.75?[35] |

[31] This text has some small lacunae; but this is probably true of many other texts with "normal" survival.

[32] I make the desperate assumption that the work would have been somewhat shorter than the *Argonautica*.

[33] Did Archilochus' work circulate in four rolls, one for each of his main genres (see, e.g., Tarditi, 1968: 15)? Were the rolls as small as they seem to be for some other lyric poets? If so, we should project a rather significant penetration, higher even than Pindar's. Archilochus was indeed a decisive influence in the canonization of lyric poetry, as we will note below, and so the result is not impossible. (My hunch is that Archilochus' rolls were longer than the lyric average: if his poems really were squeezed into four rolls, this was done so as to fit a generic definition.) Was he "actually" more important than Pindar? Or perhaps better put: the ranking of the lyric poets was not as rigid as that of authors in other genres (see more on this on pp. 67–8 below).

[34] Assume that the Theognid collection represents the equivalent of two ancient bookrolls (the text itself was extremely unstable; see the summary in Lane Fox, 2000: 46–7, but apparently circulated in roughly the same scale as that transmitted through the manuscript tradition); then the Theognid poems and the extant Pindar cover roughly 32,000 words for six books, or roughly 5,300 words per book, which I use for my calculations.

[35] The fragments comprise 3,060 words while the much-abbreviated prose paraphrase has 3,222 words. A ratio of 0.75, implying roughly 8,000 words in the original, seems reasonable.

**Tier 5: Lyric, philosophy and history; less than 5 percent of the *Iliad* (more than 100 rolls)**

| | | | | |
|---|---|---|---|---|
| Plato | *Phaedo* | 11 | 22,633 | 0.5[36] |
| Plato | *Phaedrus* | 8 | 17,221 | 0.5 |
| Isocrates | *Antid.* | 7 | 18,731 | 0.5 |
| Alcaeus | | 28 | 53,000? (10 r.) | 0.5? |
| Sappho | | 23 | 47,500? (9 r.) | 0.5?[37] |
| Alcman | | 15 | 26,500? (6 r.) | 0.5? |
| Ptolemy | *Handy Tables* | 6 | (n/a)[38] | 0.5? |
| Astrampsychus | | 10 | ? | ? |
| Aesop | | 14 | 46,077 | 0.25[39] |
| Herodotus | *Hist.* | 47 | 189,489 | 0.25 |
| Achilles Tatius | *Leuc.* | 6 | 43,440 | 0.2[40] |
| Plato | *Republic* | 12 | 89,358 | 0.15[41] |
| Xenophon | *Mem.* | 6 | 36,426 | 0.15 |
| Xenophon | *Cyr.* | 13 | 80,684 | 0.15 |

[36] This level of 0.5 is probably also that of the somewhat less central plays by Euripides (for instance, Cresphontes, Heracles, Iphigenia T., Telephus, Alcestis, Cretenses, Hypsipyla, Iphigenia Aul. and Trojan W. all have three to four fragments: identifications not always secure and numbers not significant, but the sense that there were plenty of quite widely circulating plays by Euripides is clear) as well as by Menander (Samia, Georgus, Aspis, Colax and Sicyonioe all have three to five fragments). One would probably also have encountered Sophocles or even Aeschylus at this stage: Sophocles' Ajax and Oedipus Rex have three to four fragments. For the incredible result, that Aeschylus' rare fragments are mostly of the lost drama and that there are not more fragments of the Oresteia, see Morgan (2003); the point is that collection of Aeschylus was an especially erudite project: more on this on pp. 49–50 below.

[37] For reasons explained on p. 81, n.139, below, I wonder if her rolls were not especially short, so that her works in fact had higher circulation, perhaps comparable to Pindar?

[38] TLG's word count is 5,239, which misses the mark of the actual extent on papyrus, however, since this work is composed of tables. I just multiply by three to get the sense of three rolls (30 meters is Jones' count, in Swerdlow, 1999: 315, from which, based on Johnson, one derives three rolls).

[39] Even this number is an overcount, however: the bulk of the "Aesopian" fragments are brief citations from the classroom context. Kurke (2011) suggests that Aesop provides an example of popular literature, appropriated by elite rhetorical education, which is of course possible, but I am not sure the evidence is inconsistent with Aesop's text being, right from the beginning, primarily an anthology for schoolroom use.

[40] This number needs to be adjusted for the chronological reasons explained above for Plutarch: the ancient novel had a smaller chronological range in which to circulate. Indeed, as Cavallo (1996) points out, the circulation of the ancient novel was above all a phenomenon of the Imperial era, adding somewhat to the chronological adjustment: instead of 0.2 the number should be 0.4 or 0.5. Indeed, it appears that a number of novels circulated at this level or just beneath it. The question of the circulation of the novel has been discussed by Stephens (1994), who argues for its relative infrequency; the argument is bolstered by considering the sheer length of ancient novels. Even so, we find that during their heyday the most popular novels circulated about as widely as Plato did, perhaps more than Herodotus: an elite genre no doubt – that is Stephens' argument – and certainly not on a par with the central performative canon, but, for all that, a fairly popular genre.

[41] As I will point out below, it is likely that the entire works of Plato circulated roughly at this frequency.

(*cont.*)

| | | | | |
|---|---|---|---|---|
| Bacchylides | | 14 | 90,000?[42] | 0.15? |
| Euclid | | 6 | (n/a) | 0.1?[43] |
| Stesichorus | | 9 | 100,000?[44] | 0.1 |
| Xenophon | *Hell.* | 7 | 67,924 | 0.1 |
| Plato | *Laws* | 9 | 106,297 | 0.1 |

The first set of tables, counting total fragments per author, measures the sheer papyrus footprint of an author. This second set of tables looks at the rate of penetration of a given work. Using the simplified assumption of no more than one copy of a work per household (I will return below to qualify this assumption), this may be considered a measure of the relative number of households in which the work could be found.

This set of tables is more surprising, because we do not normally pause to consider the sheer bulk of some of the works circulating in antiquity. Two types of works are especially bulky, at the two ends of the circulation pattern. At the top: Homer wrote *long* epics. Thus Homer's enormous papyrus footprint implies a less sharp break at the rate of penetration: the *Iliad*, indeed, was more widely circulated than any other work, but not so much more as implied by sheer fragment counts. At the bottom: Greek non-performative prose, we notice, tends to be much bulkier than other Greek forms (where the single-roll size, or at most a few rolls, is often appropriate: a speech, a drama, a dialogue; also, a small epic, a collection of lyric poems).[45] Thus, for non-performative prose, large papyrus footprints are compatible with fairly modest rates of penetration.

All this should be used to supplement, not replace, the evidence of sheer papyrus footprint. Was Plato not canonical? Of course he was: it is very remarkable that a significant number of households may have collected the entire works of Plato, so that we need to say that his canonicity took the

---

[42] In date and range of work – though of course not in his impact – he is comparable to Pindar. For this reason, and also in view of the substantial number of fragments, I use arbitrarily the number (arbitrarily calculated) for Pindar.

[43] TLG's word count for the Elements is 155,536; but it appears clear that several of the Euclid fragments are from a schoolroom epitome. The entire exercise is at its most fictional in this case: we learn not only that Euclid was extremely rare in book collections but also (more surprisingly) that he was not that rare in the classroom.

[44] Stesichorus could well have been an especially ample lyric poet, with near-epic proportions (West, 1971). "A little more than Pindar" seems justified.

[45] The two observations may well be related: the pattern for very long works in non-performative prose was set by Herodotus, certainly among other things as a claim for Homeric status (for the innovation of Herodotus' bulk, see Flory, 1980).

form of *an extensive collection by relatively few collectors*. Indeed, the division into tiers of penetration, and especially the contrast between the top four tiers and tier 5, suggests a division into two ideal-type libraries: (1) libraries which collect just the canon in the narrow, performative sense (Homer, and then – not that far behind – early poetry and performative prose, by a few major authors); and (2) more specialized libraries with much larger holdings, where one also finds philosophy, history and lyric poetry as well as the minor authors from the more central genres. Some authors were canonical in that they could be found in the ideal-type small library; others were canonical in that they could not be omitted in the ideal-type big library.

We end our observation of the basic papyrological data with two oppositions: between the performative and the non-performative (it is the performative which tends to get canonized), and between the small library and the big library. The relationship between these oppositions will engage us for the remainder of the book.

## 1.2 The Significance of the Data from the Papyri

### 1.2.1 General Remarks

Conclusions, already! But can the evidence support them? The rest of the chapter will have to be, among other things, methodological, defending the use of literary papyri for statistical purposes.

It is rare to see the question explicitly addressed. One often finds casual notices of papyrus counts – mostly by non-papyrologists – used as evidence for an author's popularity.[46] Papyrologists, on the other hand, regularly advise caution, insisting on the danger of statistical extrapolation from the papyri.[47] Sustained efforts at the interpretation of the papyri as statistical sources are less frequent and do not engage in arguments for the validity of such a use.[48] Thus we are left with a blanket admonition of caution, which,

[46] Two examples taken at random: Csapo (2010: 143): "Statistics from papyrus-finds make Menander the third most purchased or copied poet after Homer and Euripides"; Pelliccia (2009: 248): "This proportion [the Epinicians, about a quarter of Pindar's poetry] corresponds to…the papyri surviving from before the mid-third century CE" (exaggerated, in my view; see p. 122, n.52, below).
[47] I will return to cite more on this below. This is not just a tendency of the past: a recent work such as McNamee (2007) dedicates most of its introduction to the discussion of "the evidence and its limitations", going through the central points of papyrological caution: provenance in the periphery of Greek culture; haphazard finds; large chronological span.
[48] I note a few: Stephens (1994) (the ancient novel was an elite genre); many works by Cavallo, in particular 1997 (late antiquity) and 1996 (once again, primarily the novel). Morgan (2003) is the study most directly focused on the statistics of papyri, but her subject matter is, cautiously, the

salutary as it is, offers but a poor substitute for proper methodological discussion.

How come the scholars of literary papyri give this question so little space? This is a question about the history of the discipline. And so I have followed this through a survey of *Proceedings of the International Congress of Papyrology*, starting in 1928.[49]

Until the mid-1960s we see mostly technical descriptions of collections (e.g. Collart, 1935: "Les papyrus inédites de la Faculté des lettres de Paris") alongside generalist papers on Greco-Roman Egypt (e.g. Kerényi, 1935: "Die Papyri und das Wesen der alexandrinischen Kultur"). By the mid-1960s, however, the gentlemanly talks dedicated to broad characterization had largely disappeared. Their place was taken by studies in social history, using documentary sources; or the editions of individual literary papyri. On the one hand, papers such as Lewis, 1965, "Exemption from Liturgy in Roman Egypt", on the other hand papers such as Gigante, 1965, "Nuovi resti dell'ode Pindarica *nomos pantōn basileus* (P.Oxy. 2450)".

The 1960s were a period of professionalization in the humanities as a whole. In papyrology, the study of documents *professionalized outwards*, while the study of literary texts *professionalized inwards*. (This, indeed, may be true of the discipline of classics as a whole, history and literature bifurcating with the coming of academic professionalization.) Documentary papyri gained a world of meaning when viewed from the perspective of a more sociological history of the quotidian, and so documentary papyrologists were quick to join post-war developments in the discipline of history. The study of literary papyri, on the other hand, seemed to have little to gain from structuralism or from "new criticism", and the scholars of the papyri of, say, Greek lyric, stood back from an alien world of literary theory. Things have changed since: but it should be emphasized that, when papyrologists sum up, even now, the potential contribution of the evidence of papyri for the study of ancient literature, they most often limit themselves to the discovery of new texts and to the study of the textual history of known works. This is

---

spread of tragedy *in Egypt*. She thus avoids the much more difficult problem of extrapolation from Egypt to ancient culture as a whole.

[49] I have chosen this as a relatively small corpus, which is, however, a venue where scholars discuss issues of fundamental importance, as they see it, to the discipline. Other venues, such as the *Zeitschrift für Papyrologie und Epigraphik*, tend to be much more dominated by isolated, technical works.

a supremely philological enterprise.[50] This perhaps should not come as criticism: the 7,000 published literary papyri are 7,000 monuments to heroic scholarship.[51]

I suspect part of the resistance to statistical mining of the papyri emerges from some elemental resistance to probability as such. We may start by quoting Turner (1968). Here is his remark, following upon a description of the fortuitous nature of the Oxyrhynchus discovery (1968: 30):

> [I]n view of the present-day trend to statistical treatment of data from papyrus finds,[52] it is important to show the extent to which caprice governs the survival and discovery of papyri of any given epoch.

Or we may consider a footnote from one of the more quantity-friendly of ancient historians, Hopkins (1991: 133 n.2):

> The survival ratio, the ratio of texts surviving to those ever produced, is clearly a critical dimension... Consider the following: the Romans conducted 17 censuses...and we have less than 1,000 surviving census returns [so] the survival ratio is c. 1:12,000. ...3 surviving copies of the Oracle of the Potter could mean anywhere between 3 and 35,000+ originals.[53]

Both Turner and Hopkins make valid points. Turner is right that, in treating samples, we should consider their bias, and when the specific nature of the bias is hard to establish we must bring more caution into the sample's interpretation. Hopkins is right about the numbers – indeed,

---

[50] So the various contributions by Haslam, Luppe, Manfredi and Parsons (1992), summing up the field in the 20th congress (dedicated to celebrating 100 years of papyrology); and Renner (2009), in the recent *Oxford Handbook of Papyrology* (Bagnall, 2009a).

[51] Criticism or not, the above of course was a generalization, most valid for just one generation and allowing for major exceptions. In Italy and France, especially, a tradition was developed of studying the papyri for the light they throw on reading practices or "the history of the book" (benefiting, then, from contemporary trends in French and Italian historiography, inspired by the seminal Febvre and Martin, 1958). Cavallo has been leading this type of research since the 1960s, and his book (with Capasso) from 1983, *Libri, scritture, scribi a Ercolano*, is the first major landmark in this tradition. It is joined by others, of which some are very important to this study: McNamee (1995) and elsewhere for the practices of commentary; Cribiore (1996 and later publications) and Morgan (1998; 2003) for the practices of education; and Blanchard (1989) for ancient book collection practices. Most recently, Johnson has produced both a study of the bookroll and its scribes (2004) and a study of the bookroll and its readers (2010); Dorandi (2007) is fundamental to the study of authorial practices based on the evidence of the papyri. Structuralism, post-structuralism and historicism have all gone by, and literary papyri finally re-emerge to join a contemporary trend in literary studies.

[52] What did Turner have in mind? Perhaps he was reacting to the first tentative steps towards the digitization of the study of papyri, proposed as soon as computing resources began to be available around university campuses (see, e.g., Tomsin et al., 1973).

[53] Compare also Bagnall (1996: 103): "It is doubtful that the audience for [the literary] authors exceeded a few thousands in all of Egypt in any period, after all, and the survival of their manuscripts out of many millions of papyri of all kinds is a very chancy affair." Evidently, the fact that there were originally *many millions of papyri* is seen as materially weakening the significance of the sample.

this quotation from him is the best entry point I am aware of into the problem of the absolute scale of writing in antiquity. We shall consider it in much greater detail in Part III. But both Turner and Hopkins also appear to me to be not far removed from relying on layperson's misperceptions of the use of statistics. The layperson's belief is that, in order to find out about large groups, we need to have as large a selection as possible; and that we should intentionally select as "representative" a selection as possible, and not let it be formed by sheer chance. It appears as something of a black art, for example, that one can call strictly at random no more than a thousand or so households in the entire United States, and be able to tell within a few percent the fraction that will vote for each of the candidates for the presidency. But such miracles happen regularly, for a good reason: samples should be governed, as far as possible, to use Turner's terms, by sheer caprice; they need not be very large, and it certainly hardly matters in what ratio they stand to the original set. The significance of a sample derives almost entirely from the combinatorics, hence the probabilities, of the set itself. The absolute sample size matters a lot: a few hundred are good to have, and a thousand or so are perfect for most purposes. The same numbers would do almost equally well to find out about political affiliation in a polity as big as the United States or as small as Switzerland. And the more random the selection, the better.

We should therefore note immediately that the papyri dug in Egypt form by now a very large sample. They are not a perfectly random set (indeed, true randomness is rare anywhere, and, in some metaphysical sense, impossible: this is the main challenge in the application of statistics to *any* field). But, as we shall see below, they come close.

The size of the sample is big. Indeed, it has been big for a long time now. I study papyri based on two online databases, LDAB and CEDOPAL; the latter is the digitized version of a system of cataloguing pagan literary papyri first developed by Roger Pack in 1952 and then expanded in 1965. Before Pack, papyrologists relied on C. H. Oldfather (1923).[54] It is instructive to consider this early publication. Oldfather has 1,167 literary papyri to catalogue.[55] Not that many, perhaps, and Oldfather's was not even meant

---

[54] Oldfather never got established as a unique standard reference, however, in the way in which Pack did. The field of papyrology was dynamically evolving, visibly so; an annual publication – *Bibliographie Papyrologique*, instituted by Marcel Hombert in 1932 (similar in conception to the more familiar *Année Philologique*) – was the preferred resource.

[55] The – troubled – three decades between Oldfather and Pack saw the publication of a little over 1,000 literary papyri, or 41.5 per annum (Pack, 1952, had 2,369 entries). Thirteen years later Pack's second edition already had 3,026 – a growth of 50.5 per annum. About 50 years later we have 4,000 papyri more, so the rate has been going up steadily (thus, the seven years between the first and second

strictly as a catalogue (unlike Pack, as well as Mertens following him, who set out to produce a comprehensive, accessible list). Oldfather's motives were different. This, his PhD, followed a project suggested by W. L. Westermann but, I suspect, motivated by Michael Rostovtzeff.[56] Oldfather conceived of his project as, primarily, an opportunity to use the accumulated evidence of papyri as a window into Hellenistic and Roman civilization.

Oldfather was patently naïve, in papyrology and statistics as well as in Hellenistic history. The PhD was his only genuine scholarly contribution.[57] And yet the point is that many of Oldfather's observations hold surprisingly well. The most important are these: the close correlation between texts used in the classroom, and elsewhere; and the overall continuity of literary taste across the centuries. We will soon return to consider those two observations in more detail. Oldfather further listed as the most frequent authors, in order (Oldfather, 1923: 74): Homer (1), Demosthenes (2), Euripides (3), Menander (6), Plato (7), Thucydides (8),[58] Aristophanes (10), Isocrates (5), Xenophon (14). Within brackets I provide the current standing, with our sevenfold larger pool of papyri. The difference is exaggerated by a simple clerical error in Oldfather's calculations: he did not notice that Hesiod, then with 20 fragments and now with 158 fragments, number 4 on the list, was then as frequent as Isocrates and more frequent than Xenophon (the last had 16 fragments only). We find that

counting I made of papyri – 2011 and 2018 – saw the totals rise by several hundred or a few percent of the total). Yet more papyri await to be published, though the consensus appears to be that, within our collections, we are nearing the bottom of the barrel and that the – rather many – unpublished papyri are usually smaller fragments (Johnson 2004: 3 n.1). But how many still survive underneath Egyptian villages, unexcavated?

[56] Oldfather (1923: vi): "To Professor M. Rostovtzeff of the University of Wisconsin I am especially indebted for his interest in [the study's] completion and for his helpful suggestions."

[57] For more on the person – a fine, old school classicist, devoted above all to translation – see http://unlhistory.unl.edu/exhibits/show/oldfather.

[58] In 2011, when I first wrote this passage, Thucydides was slightly above Plato. The fragments published between 2011 and 2018 actually made our statistics fit Oldfather's *better*. This in itself is a sheer anecdote, but its implication is real and should be emphasized: as new fragments came in through the last century, the overall statistics did not gradually diverge away from their original shape but, instead, largely oscillated around a fixed point. I note here further a major consequence. In conversations with colleagues, one reason frequently cited for doubting the statistical accuracy of the papyri is the nature of editorial bias. Many papyri are still unpublished, and so the statistics we have show not only the selection of archaeological fortune but also that of active editorial taste. This is a serious concern, but it is largely dissipated by the evidence of the stability, through the last century, of the major contours of the statistics. The discipline of classics went through a major transformation through the twentieth century; for a generation now (a generation highly fecund in its publication of papyri!) we have come to appreciate the unexpected and non-canonical. And yet the statistics barely budge. The aggregate of editorial choices, probably, did not matter so greatly: for, after all, few papyrologists ever resisted the desire to publish *minor* ancient literature!

nine of our current top ten authors were top ten authors already in 1923. Further, consider Oldfather (1923: 83–4): "[Demosthenes'] absence until the first century BC can very likely best be explained by the lack of organized city life. . .where there was little opportunity for the advocate." I doubt the interpretation, but the observation is surprisingly robust. Oldfather counted 43 Demosthenic fragments in his table IV. This had a total of 786 papyri. It also had no more than 93 pre-first-century papyri, in total! Now, the simple assumption (assuming no random variation) would have predicted four to five Demosthenes pre-first-century fragments. Oldfather, instead, found zero. The subsets are tiny, however, and a statistician would have recoiled from any conclusion. And yet Oldfather has noted a reality. We now have 204 Demosthenes fragments, and also about 500 pre-first-century fragments out of a total of about 7,000. We would expect by now to have roughly 15 pre-first-century Demosthenes papyri. That we still find *zero* begins to appear meaningful, and I will return to discuss this phenomenon as the most important exception to the rule of Ptolemaic-to-Roman continuity. But what I want to emphasize now is more general: here, again, is a case in which the overall pattern of the evidence was stable, throughout the twentieth century and beyond.

The statistical observations made by Oldfather in 1923 remain valid, almost a century and 6,000 papyri later. The point is that this is essentially unsurprising. A statistician would consider it rather meaningless to expand his random sample size from 1,000 to 7,000. This is perhaps obvious for a statistician but it ought to be spelled out as a specifically papyrological prediction. A word of caution often heard is "Who knows what the future may bring, what the next findings of papyri are going to reveal?". Now, the expansion of the universe of papyri from 1,000 to 7,000 did not change materially the pattern of frequency among authors. And so, it may be predicted, with considerable confidence, that the same will be true as the universe is expanded further – to 15,000 or 20,000 or even more. A century ago Oldfather has already our statistics; and I think it much likelier than not that, a century hence, the same statistics will still be found. It is of course useful that we now have many more papyri, but this is mostly not for the purposes of the wide observations on papyri as a whole but for the sake of smaller subsets: now, even a set with some 5 to 10 percent of the total papyri can have some statistical significance. This is especially important for our interpretation of Ptolemaic papyri; and, a century hence, we will be able to make even more precise fine-grained observations. But, for now, the coarse-grained observations stand.[59]

## 1.2.2   Spatial Homogeneity inside Egypt

Size by itself settles nothing. Big samples may be corrupt. And yet one worry we may dispel immediately. Our sample is not flawed with the presence of some big idiosyncratic caches that skew the evidence. This can be seen through a comparison of the Oxyrhynchus evidence with the rest.[60] As a very elementary statistical exercise, I compare the 15 most popular authors, comparing their numbers from Oxyrhynchus and from the rest of Egypt.[61]

| Author | Oxyrhynchus | Non-Oxyrhynchus |
| --- | --- | --- |
| Homer | 846 | 822 |
| Hesiod | 91 | 67 |
| Demosthenes | 89 | 97 |
| Euripides | 79 | 91 |
| Thucydides | 66 | 30 |
| Menander | 61 | 56 |
| Plato | 50 | 40 |
| Isocrates | 46 | 72 |
| Callimachus | 45 | 38 |
| Aristophanes | 27 | 30 |
| Apollonius of Rhodes | 36 | 20 |
| Aeschines | 37 | 13 |
| Herodotus | 26 | 21 |
| Pindar | 40 | 6 |
| Xenophon | 16 | 26 |

I promised to avoid statistical jargon, but the correlation coefficient between the two columns is well above 0.99, meaning that, by and large,

[59] Having established this point, I will from now on allow myself to use, without recalculation, figures derived from the 2011 counting of papyri. In many cases such a recalculation would be otiose.
[60] Roughly a half of all literary papyri are *known* to have been found at Oxyrhynchus. Our papyri come from the Nile Valley; within it, Oxyrhynchus was among the bigger cities (not as easy to establish as one would think: Bagnall, 1996: 52–3. Only Arsinoe appears to have been larger, and it is indeed very well represented by documentary papyri). It was also a fairly northern one (if we imagine that sheer proximity to Alexandria made a city closer to metropolitan literary culture – and this seems to be the conclusion of Morgan, 2003 – then this should matter).
[61] "Non-Oxyrhynchus" means not *known* to be from Oxyrhynchus. Many papyri emerge from shady transactions in which provenance is impossible to ascertain. In short, many "non-Oxyrhynchus" papyri may well in fact be Oxyrhynchian. Even so, had Oxyrhynchus (or any other site) been truly distinctive, the contamination of the non-Oxyrhynchian by unprovenanced Oxyrhynchian papyri would not have been enough to mask any genuine discrepancies.

one can use the papyri from Oxyrhynchus to predict how many will be found outside it. A scatter-plot is more useful perhaps (ignoring Homer so as to gain better resolution).

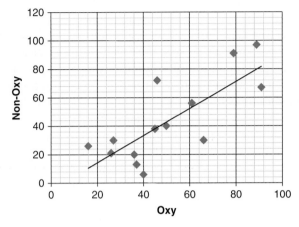

Figure 1.1

Thucydides, Aeschines and especially Pindar are rather better represented in Oxyrhynchus; Isocrates and Xenophon are rather better represented outside it. We do note perhaps a tendency for more sophisticated material to be represented by the more metropolitan center of Oxyrhynchus (Morgan, 2003, documents this in a more fine-grained manner for Aeschylus and Sophocles as well).

And so we note: Oxyrhynchus displayed essentially the same taste as that of the composite of many other independent finds from across Egypt. Whatever biases governed the selection of Oxyrhynchus papyri, then, they would have to be essentially the same as those governing the selection of papyri in the most general terms.

Why is this significant? Suppose one had found Herculaneum's Villa dei Papiri in the Nile Valley rather than in Italy. This would make our sample bigger by about 15 percent (about 1,100 rolls added to our about 7,000), and also much worse. In case you haven't heard of Herculaneum: in the eighteenth century a fantastic site was excavated near Pompeii; buried by the Vesuvian eruption was an entire library (or section of a library). This villa of papyri held a dedicated collection with a single, highly distinctive cache: almost entirely Epicurean and most frequently by a single author,

Philodemus.[62] Suppose, then, we were to add this to our papyri. Would we have to say then that Philodemus was the second most popular author in antiquity after Homer? This would clearly be wrong: the villa would have skewed our data. But, conversely, we also can see, from the table above, that no such distinctive, large find skews our *Egyptian* data, because, had there been one, it would have to be either in Oxyrhynchus or elsewhere – which would have been visible in our data, because, had there been such a preserved Egyptian villa, it would turn out in our evidence as a case of particular authors (popular in that particular villa) being substantially more frequent at either Oxyrhynchus or outside it, depending on where that villa happened to be.

Undoubtedly there are some small caches in our finds, and a few can be identified.[63] And yet we do not find in Egypt big literary caches, for a reason. The Villa Dei Papiri is a freak case of papyrus conserved in situ through disaster. But, for literary papyri, what we have are mostly rubbish dumps, or – for Ptolemaic papyri – the secondary use of papyrus in mummy cartonnage. Our finds were formed not by the wholesale removal of entire libraries but, rather, by the piecemeal culling of isolated rolls that were no longer required (I shall return below to discuss the conditions for such decisions).[64]

We could perhaps expect mini-caches: that is, even if rolls were discarded in small, separate acts, there is no reason to expect them to be discarded strictly individually. One way to look for the traces of such mini-caches is through the small groups of papyri. Tier 4 in the table on page 17 above lists the authors with two to four papyri each. Do they represent two

---

[62] Zarmakoupi (2010) is a survey of the archaeology and reception of the villa as a whole, with an in-depth article by Sider on the papyri; the literature on the papyri is now enormous, with a journal (*Cronache Ercolanesi*) dedicated to their publication and interpretation, published since 1971. As noted in p. 27, n.51, above, Italian papyrologists, trained in the study of this unique library, have been at the forefront of the study of the ancient book.

[63] Houston (2009: 249–50) lists all known literary caches. The largest non-Herculaneum one has 52 manuscripts (PSI 11–12). It is not deeply distinctive in its choice of authors. Aristotle's *Constitution of Athens* was found in an impressive small cache (see details and reference to past literature in Privitera, 2012: 119); it surprising, however, not in its very authors but simply in having a somewhat distinctive variation on the common authors (so, the Athenian constitution itself; also, for instance, not just Demosthenes and Isocrates but also Hyperides...): this is typical of the continuity we do find between big and small libraries. The most distinctive cache is P.Oxy. XVI, Group A (Jones, 1999), 45 astronomical texts. Since, as explained by Jones, astronomical texts are most likely the working materials of practicing astrologers, such a cache is perhaps better understood on the model of a documentary survival (where, indeed, caches are commonplace).

[64] Rolls were typically "shredded" to be more easily carried in a basket, suggesting the simultaneous discarding of several papyri, but not more than a handful. In general, for the discarding of papyri, see Cuvigny (2009).

to four ancient libraries, or are some of these simply two to four papyri being discarded from the *same* library? If the latter, we should expect to see quite a few cases in which the two to four papyri are all from the same provenance and period.

Now, we are not looking strictly for the same century (why not discard simultaneously, say, a mid-second-century book and an early third-century one?); and many papyri are unprovenanced. Thus, we look for a very low threshold. The condition is this: for the given tier 4 author, no more than one provenance should be identified, and the centuries must be at least adjacent.

How low is this threshold? About half the papyri are from the second or third centuries CE and are either known to be of Oxyrhynchus or are non-provenanced. Thus, the null result is pretty unlikely. And yet, our attested numbers appear to support this null result.

| | Total number of authors | Could be mini-cached[65] | Null result[66] |
|---|---|---|---|
| 4 fragments | 7 | 1[67] | ~1 |
| 3 fragments | 16 | 5[68] | ~4 |
| 2 fragments | 18 | 7[69] | ~9 |

In short, the result is likely to be almost entirely random. None of the potential mini-caches are from anywhere other than Oxyrhynchus. Only two are outside the second and third centuries CE. These are interesting: Sophron, with two fragments from the first and second centuries CE (and Sophron represents the precarious transmission of non-Attic drama); Nicarchus II, with three fragments from the first century. Two of Nicarchus' fragments could simply come out of the same papyrus roll. In general, before us is a very rare case: a Roman-era poet, preserved on papyrus almost immediately upon his activity. I can well believe that his three – or two – fragments represent no more than a single Oxyrhynchus collection. But, if so, his case would be nearly unique. Even when we find no more than two to four fragments of a single author, we are likely to witness more than a single act of discard, from more than a single

[65] In the sense that they are all from a single location, and from the same or adjacent centuries.
[66] In the sense that this is the number likely as a random result.    [67] Cratinus.
[68] Aeschines Socraticus, Antiphon, Lollianus, Lycurgus, Nicarchus II.
[69] Arrian, Choerilus, Critias, Pancrates, Satyrus, Sophron, Triphiodorus.

collection.[70] But, if so, it is likely that the bulk of our literary papyri come from a very large number of independent acts of discard.

In all this, literary papyri differ from documentary ones. There were certain types of documents one held on to for a long time, forming gradually personal (family) or more official archives. Such archives could then be deposited en masse, perhaps to be recovered later by their owners or perhaps because there was no longer any need for the archive. Such documentary caches are relatively frequent,[71] and they form an important contrast to the fate of literary papyri. Documents were of use for a generation or two and, when no longer in use, could often be archaeologically cached; books were forever, and so they entered the archaeological record only piecemeal. Literary books: a stable, permanent possession.

We end up with a surprising result: it turns out that literary papyri are statistically more useful than are *documentary* papyri. Indeed, when studying documentary papyri one always has to be wary in isolating the impact of a few caches on one's overall statistics (most obviously, in the impact of the Zenon papyri on our understanding of Ptolemaic documentary papyri; but also in the impact of the Apion estate on our understanding of Byzantine Egypt).[72] Documentary papyri represent a very coarse structure: perhaps about a half derive from isolated acts of discard comparable to those of literary papyri, while something like the other half derive from a mere 150 or so acts of discard that vary enormously in size and content.[73] That documentary papyri are more often treated in sheer quantitative terms, while literary papyri are not, is a consequence of the history of the disciplines that goes against the grain of the data themselves.

---

[70] This does not mean that there would not be mini-caches; rather, that they involved more frequent – that is, less distinctive – authors (as we see, indeed, from the caches documented in Houston, 2009).

[71] Montevecchi (1988: 248–61, 575–8) lists 135 Greek archives (a scholar of brilliance and caution, Montevecchi never claims that her lists are exhaustive, yet one doubts much more can be added; of course, there are also non-Greek archives, as well as many archives that have not yet been identified). They range in size from a handful of private documents bundled together – for instance, the 14 letters by Apollonius of Bakchias (Smolders, 2004: 233–7) – to the 3,000 documents of the Ptolemaic estate of Zenon.

[72] The best introduction to the Zenon archive is online: www.lib.umich.edu/reading/Zenon/index .html. This cache contains the majority of all papyri from the third century (Habermann, 1998: 147). The significance of the single Apion estate for the history of early medieval economy as a whole is enormous (see Hickey, 2012, for the debate), though this may be based not on a statistical argument but, rather, on a wider historical interpretation by which this estate was, indeed, representative of important trends (with a little over 250 papyri, this cache is large but not unique).

[73] Verhoogt (2012: 508): "Many archives are very small…but there are about a dozen archives with more than one hundred texts."

### 1.2.3   *Chronology and Continuity*

We do not find caches and our evidence is not skewed in *space*. But is it skewed in *time*? The preponderance of our evidence is (not surprisingly) from the Imperial era, peaking (more surprisingly) not only in the second but also in the (troubled) third century (more on this in Part III). Perhaps Oxyrhynchus, as well as other similar cities, really did collect Demosthenes more than Xenophon; perhaps really about four to five times as much. But is this true for any period other than the second and third centuries CE?

Let us consider, then, the chronological evidence, this time comparing the dates −300 to +100 with +200 to +500 (I leave a century's buffer, so as to reduce the overlap: bear in mind that many papyri are dated to a wide range that can easily take up a century or so; also, my unorthodox choice of eras was meant simply to have the sums as close to each other as possible).

| Author | −300 to +100 | +200 to +500 |
|---|---|---|
| Homer | 585 | 714 |
| Hesiod | 48 | 65 |
| Demosthenes | 29 | 94 |
| Euripides | 134 | 58 |
| Thucydides | 17 | 45 |
| Menander | 43 | 52 |
| Plato | 16 | 34 |
| Isocrates | 24 | 65 |
| Callimachus | 27 | 27 |
| Aristophanes | 3 | 43 |
| Apollonius of Rhodes | 7 | 29 |
| Aeschines | 6 | 29 |
| Herodotus | 8 | 25 |
| Pindar | 11 | 30 |
| Xenophon | 7 | 20 |

The correlation coefficient is still a very respectable 0.979 – that is, one can fairly confidently predict how many papyri a given canonical author might have in the late Imperial era/late antiquity, based on how many he had in the Hellenistic/early Imperial era. But some differences do spring up, and the scatter-plot (excluding Homer once again) is rather more interesting.

Clearly, there were some changes of taste: Aristophanes emerged to rival Menander as the chief comic author (eventually, of course, Aristophanes alone would remain to survive through the manuscript transmission). On the whole, rhetoric became somewhat more prominent, supplanting to some extent tragedy (more on this below).

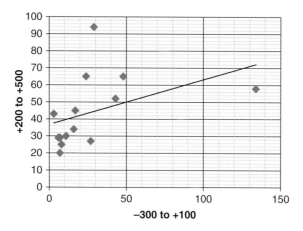

Figure 1.2

There are some real differences, then, and it is always necessary to qualify statements about Egyptian literary papyri by reference to their eras. Indeed, the effect becomes much more obvious once we isolate papyri dated to −300 to −100. We noted above Oldfather's observation concerning the absence of Demosthenes from this group. Oldfather was rash, in my opinion, in using such numbers to make fine-grained claims concerning individuals; but our overall figures are now considerably higher, making subsets meaningful, and it has now certainly become valid to compare entire genres. In the following table (produced in 2011) I took the two top tiers in the table on pages 15–16 above and clustered the authors according to the coarse-grained generic definitions used there, ignoring "varia" and "med.". I provide the percentage within the original group, so that, for instance, by dividing the 2,160 non-Ptolemaic epic papyri by the 6,628 non-Ptolemaic papyri total, I derive 33 percent.

|  | (Total minus Ptolemaic) | Ptolemaic |
|---|---|---|
| Epic | 33% | 13% |
| Rhetoric | 5% | 1% |
| Tragedy | 3% | 8% |
| Comedy | 3% | 1% |
| History | 3% | 1% |
| Philosophy | 2% | 1% |
| Lyric | 2% | 1% |

Viewed like this, the contrast is quite sharp. This is seen first at the level of total domination by the canon. Top authors in the top six genres account for 51 percent of all post-Ptolemaic literary papyri (these also include many paraliterary papyri, so the fraction among strictly literary papyri is in fact larger). They account for just 26 percent of the Ptolemaic literary papyri – half the fraction. Homer leads the difference but does not account for it entirely. One genre alone forms an exception: tragedy, for which the canon is considerably more frequent among the Ptolemaic papyri. There are 30 Ptolemaic papyri of Euripides alone. The numbers suggest that the rate of penetration by some plays by Euripides could have been, in the Ptolemaic era, not far behind that of the *Iliad* itself.[74]

We need a close-up picture. I have constructed a random sample of 48 papyri dated to between −300 and −100, and another one of 48 papyri dated to between +100 and +200.[75] Here are the results.

| −300 to −100 | | +100 to +200 | |
|---|---|---|---|
| Homer | | Homer | |
|     *Iliad* | 3 |     *Iliad* | 11 |
|     *Odyssey* | 2 |     *Odyssey* | 1 |
|     Homerica | 2 |     Homerica | 2 |
| Drama | | Drama | |
|     Euripides | 3 |     Euripides | 1 |
|     Other known | 1 |     Other known | 1 |
|     Adespota | 5 |     Adespota | 1 |
| Literary | | Literary | |
| prose | | prose | |
|     Known authors | 1 |     Known authors | 10 |
|     Adespota | 5 |     Adespota | 1 |
| Other poetry | | Other poetry | |
|     Known authors | 6 |     Known authors | 5 |
|     Adespota | 6 |     Adespota | 5 |
| Other | | Other | |
|     Technical | 7 |     Technical | 5 |
|     Schooltexts | 3 |     Schooltexts | 4 |
|     Unidentified | 4 |     Unidentified | 1 |

[74] A rough estimate: for a typical tragedy by Euripides (a little over 10,000 words) to have the same level of saturation as the *Iliad* (115,000 words), it will have to have 1/11 as many fragments as the *Iliad*: so the 55 Ptolemaic fragments of the *Iliad* correspond to five fragments of a Euripidean tragedy with the same incidence. Among the Ptolemaic papyri of Euripides, Orestes actually surpasses that number and has six fragments. Clearly, this, standing alone, signifies nothing, but it is worth noting that seven more plays have two to three fragments. This might well be considered the "normal" level for Ptolemaic Euripides – that is, many of his more popular plays had about half the incidence of the *Iliad*.

[75] CEDOPAL (in its 2011 interface) opened 48 screens of papyri from −300 to −100, one per each ten papyri, and I took the first from each; for the second century CE I skipped to each seventh screen and then added two more by picking the fifth fragment from each of the 16th and the 32nd screens.

The broad picture is clear enough: Ptolemaic papyri have fewer *Iliad* and known prose authors; they compensate by having more, obviously, of everything else, notably drama but also prose adespota.

First of all, we should qualify the contrast. There are important continuities: in particular, the broad order *within* genres seems to be stable. Homer dominates epic, Euripides dominates tragedy, Menander dominates comedy (he has seven Ptolemaic fragments), Plato dominates philosophy (six fragments). Beyond that, the Ptolemaic numbers are too small to make such claims, but it is significant that the famous authors are often represented on the Ptolemaic papyri: Hesiod (5), Sophocles (4), Isocrates, Callimachus, Aeschylus, Archilochus (3 each), Thucydides, Sappho (2 each), Herodotus, Xenophon, Hippocrates, Aratus, Lysias, Euphorion and Stesichorus (1 each). Missing from the top tier are Demosthenes, Aristophanes, Apollonius, Aeschines and Pindar.[76] Of these, only the absence of Demosthenes is genuinely surprising (the absolute numbers for the other missing authors are quite small) – and has been remarked upon already by Oldfather. Thus, the evidence does not suggest a reworking of the levels of canonicity within genres between the Ptolemaic and Roman eras.

What does the evidence suggest?

Once again, it is indeed reasonable to suppose that drama as a whole was more popular in the Ptolemaic era, oratory as a whole less so. It is worth mentioning that we have six to eight Ptolemaic papyrus fragments containing musical notation for classical tragedy, and no more than six Roman-era papyri containing drama with musical notation, of which at least some may contain post-classical drama: since Ptolemaic papyri are less frequent by about an order of magnitude, this implies a very significant drop in the frequency of musically annotated drama.[77] The more general point is that not a single Roman-era papyrus with musical notation is identified as containing classical compositions – this, even though literary papyri of the Roman era as a whole are dominated by classical works. The natural interpretation is that there was some continuous tradition of full-fledged

[76] Of the second tier, missing are Alcaeus, Theocritus, Alcman, Aesop, Bacchylides, Aristotle and of course Astrampsychus and Plutarch: so there are five missing out of 13 that could have been represented. Since authors in this tier have on average fewer than 16 fragments, and the Ptolemaic papyri are about 1/15th of the total, Ptolemaic representation of five out of 13 is, essentially, chance level.

[77] Ptolemaic music papyri with drama are: DAGM 3, 4, 5–6, 8, 9–14 (perhaps three fragments: 9–10, 11, 12–14), 15–16; Roman era: DAGM 38, 39–40, 42–43, 45, 49, 53–54 (I ignore DAGM 56, which clearly is not a notated music text but, rather, a study in composition, perhaps a rare document of music education).

performance of ancient drama, music and all, through the Hellenistic period, but that it did not last into the Roman era.[78] Thus, the relative decline of drama may be related to the relative decline of its performative presence – a presence which was replaced, to some extent, by the rise of oratory. We note that the power of genres is related to their perceived performativity. This would serve as a first approximation; we will return to this issue many times in this book.

But this is not the entire story: independently of the ranking of genres, there is also the less "elite" status of Roman-era papyri, visible above all in the sheer presence for the *Iliad*. Was there a dumbing down? Did people stop reading more sophisticated and rare works? I doubt that. An alternative account might perhaps have been that Roman-era papyri were more heavily dominated by the educational context. This is tempting but probably wrong: as I will note below, I do not think that the sheer size of the educational context is enough to make such an impact, and, as a simple empirical matter, the obvious schooltexts are not at all rare in the Ptolemaic context.[79] The next option is to bring in our ideal-type division into big and small libraries. Then the hypothesis would be that the Roman-era material is more heavily populated by the ideal-type small library. This is plausible: Greek acculturation of Egypt, together with the general competition for the status of paideia in the Roman era (more on this in Chapter 6, section 6.3), would mean that more people owned books. The more libraries there are, the less the entire landscape of books is dominated by the few big libraries. All those Roman-era *Iliad*s, then, represent not *dumbing down* but *trickle-down*.

Speculative as it is, this argument is in some sense forced on us because of the obvious saturation of the population by *Iliad*s. If we assume that the relative frequencies of big and small libraries were the same in the Ptolemaic and in the Roman eras, then we would either

---

[78] See T. J. Fleming (1999) for the (minority) position that ancient music was transmitted by notation. He seems to ignore the very likely possibility that musical notation was an internal technical device shared by professional musicians that did not have the status appropriate to bookrolls (I return to this on pp. 676–7 below). That musical traditions survive mostly without the use of writing is obvious (and is the key claim of the monumental Taruskin, 2010); we should envisage long generations during which musical traditions survived orally: even though it was written down on occasion, writing itself would not be the main medium of continuity. But this oral tradition, then, could be subject to gradual erosion. Through whatever mechanism, it is clear that dramatic traditions were carried over to the Imperial era mostly through mime rather than full-fledged productions of ancient drama (see pp. 498–9 below).

[79] Cribiore (1996: 175–284) has 412 school exercises, 33 of which, by my count, are from the third and second centuries BCE: so the Ptolemaic-era material has an (insignificantly) *higher* ratio of school exercises.

have to believe that many big libraries did not possess the *Iliad* in the Ptolemaic era or, conversely, that in the Roman era it became customary for big libraries to possess the *Iliad* many times over (the default Bar Mitzvah gift, as it were). I am sure there was some over-saturation of libraries with the *Iliad*,[80] but this cannot be the pervasive account distinguishing the Ptolemaic era from the Roman. So, if we assume that essentially all big libraries already had the *Iliad* in the Ptolemaic era, and that hypersaturation by the *Iliad* was not much more common in the Roman era, the only option left is that big libraries became less frequent. And so, as book owning becomes more widespread, it changes its overall character.[81]

The fundamental point is that we can accommodate the evidence we have for Ptolemaic literary papyri without the assumption of a rupture in the canon taking place at around –100 BCE. We do note a change (less drama, more rhetoric), representing, I would argue, a different ranking of the genres in terms of their perceived performativity; and we do note another change (fewer adespota, more *Iliad*), representing, I would argue, a rise in the relative number of small libraries. But the main lesson is that of stability.

I looked in detail at the contrast between the Ptolemaic- and Roman-era papyri, which is indeed the most significant case of papyri displaying any heterogeneity. And yet: in the year 250 BCE, as in 350 CE, one could pick books at random in any Egyptian city and find, to a large extent, the same authors. What is surprising is not that some details change but that, through all those centuries, so little does. There is little surprise in the spatial homogeneity of the papyri; why should we expect, after all, Oxyrhynchus to possess a very distinctive literary culture? The temporal homogeneity is startling, however. Such is the stability of the canon. We set out to look for discrepancies in our evidence, simply so as to test its reliability. But we have come up with an unexpected, positive result: it appears as if the canon was subject to no more than minor variations through the centuries.

---

[80] There are in fact parallels to this in the collection of Epicurus in Herculaneum, where in particular Epicurus' central work, *On Nature*, was present in multiple copies (some books are attested two or three times: for a brief summary, see Gigante, 1995 [1990]: 18; given the fragmentary nature of the survival of the villa, this suggests perhaps ten to 20 copies held originally at the same library, at least of some of the books! But this is of course the central canonical work of Epicureanism, in a professional Epicurean library. This is the equivalent of grammarians – who certainly would have multiple copies of their Homer.).

[81] For a similar argument – with better evidence to support it, in Victorian British circulating libraries – see Moretti (1999: 147).

*1.2.4   Education and Scholarship, Curation and Discard*

One of the most striking features of the papyrological evidence is the role of papyri from the educational context. Cribiore (1996), the most systematic study in the field, catalogues 412 papyri related to the study of basic literacy alone (a simple extrapolation suggests that a similar study today would have closer to 500 documents). As I note below, many other documents no doubt belong to the context of education – e.g. mathematical exercises, anthologies, etc. How far does that skew our evidence? In some sense, not substantially. The following table provides the number of writing exercises taken from tier 1 authors (and counted in all the tables above!).

| | |
|---|---|
| Homer | 129 |
| Menander | 29 |
| Euripides | 25 |
| Isocrates | 14 |
| Demosthenes | 7 |
| Hesiod | 4 |
| Herodotus | 2 |
| Callimachus | 2 |
| Aristophanes | 1 |
| Apollonius | 1 |
| Aeschines | 1 |
| Pindar | 1 |
| Xenophon | 1 |

The Isocratean writing exercises derive entirely from his exhortations, and this is the only case in the top tier where writing exercises represent a very significant fraction of a work's survival (in this case, about half: Aesop's ratio is even higher, though his selections for the classroom are of a different kind). About a quarter of the *identified* Menander fragments (an important qualification), as well as a sixth of the identified Euripides fragments, are writing exercises (both authors had easily extractable gnomic passages) – as are less than 10 percent of the Homer fragments.

And yet, the overall correlation is striking. The overall evidence of papyri largely predicts the use of papyri for writing exercises, but *more so*. The writing exercises are hyper-canonical. But, then again, is this not perhaps suggestive for other literary papyri? Maybe a professional-looking copy of the *Iliad* could have served as a tool for the teaching of basic literacy – just as a professional-looking copy of Demosthenes could have served as a tool for the teaching of rhetoric. Cribiore (2001: chap. 8, 201–4) returns to this problem and keeps noting the same difficulty: at the level of education in which mature reading of the canon was to be expected (with the possible exception of mere anthologies, or of the *Iliad* and of Isocrates' exhortations), would not "normal" texts be used instead of the obvious schooltexts of the level surveyed in Cribiore (1996)? Thus Cribiore ends up using the frequency of literary-looking papyri as evidence for the papyri used in the classroom. Undoubtedly this is sound; but what does that mean for the overall origins of papyri as a whole, in literary collections as against the use in schools? So many papyri were "merely" educational; perhaps this is where they generally came from?

And yet this impression is, I would argue, deceptive. It arises from the extremely high frequency of writing exercises within the literary papyri, which, at first glance, seems to suggest that the consumption of literature was dominated by the classroom. You graduated, and then put away childish things such as reading and writing – lifelong readers being the exception rather than the rule.

But this is obviously an illusion. The frequency of educational papyri in our evidence is clearly exaggerated because of their discard-to-curation ratio.[82] It would not be at all extraordinary for a literary roll to have remained in circulation for a century or two.[83] Would a writing

[82] For the general questions of discard and curation, studied by archaeologists under the heading "formation processes of the archaeological record", see, e.g., Schiffer (1996). As Lamotta and Schiffer (1999: 19) put it: "[E]arly studies tended to assume that variability in house floor assemblages—i.e. differences and similarities in the kinds and quantities of artefacts—could be attributed to differences in the activities carried out in those structures. Since the mid-1970s, however, there has been a concerted effort to identify additional sources of variability contributing to house floor assemblages, principally the formation processes of the archaeological record—both cultural and noncultural."

[83] Houston (2009: 250–1). Perhaps rolls could be kept for up to five centuries (!) – a fantastic number, but well within the experience of the medieval curation of manuscripts. In fact, the loss rate for medieval manuscripts is estimated by Buringh (2011: 227) at about 25 percent per century, implying a half-life closer to two centuries. (Parchment manuscripts are arguably made of a more durable material than papyrus, but the same cannot be said for paper. And yet – paper manuscripts from the high Middle Ages are commonplace: see Bozzolo and Ornato, 1980. The Ravenna papyri – for which, see Tjäder, 1955 and 1982 – have been kept in continuous curation for up to 1,500 years!). Lewis (1974: 60–1) sums up the evidence simply as "hundreds of years" for the longevity of a papyrus book, though our sources mostly relate to especially valued documents. I have used the LDAB data to produce a very crude average age for the papyri in Herculaneum, simply taking each century as its middle point (thus, assigning all "first-century BC" rolls to the year 50 BC). The average roll turns out to have been produced at 59 BC, so it was 128 years old when it became carbonated by the volcano (the equivalent of a contemporary library whose books were printed, on *average*, when Bismarck retired from office). But for how long would the rolls be curated even further, absent the eruption? To clarify: that this was an elite, well-curated library should not necessarily mean a longer curation; maybe rich collections are those that can more easily commission replacements for deteriorating rolls? I will return to such considerations below. The one major difficulty with such exercises – making them produce more of an upper bound – is that we do not know how many rolls the library *had already lost*. At any rate, the Herculaneum evidence definitely shows that, when the will is there, rolls could very definitely be preserved in substantial numbers for one to two centuries or more.

exercise remain "in circulation" for even ten to 20 years? While many dozens of Cribiore's exercises on papyrus are written on the back of documents – or on the back of other exercises – only one or two of these exercises have a document written on their *own* back, the exceptions being number 185, and perhaps 250 (but, even then, it is quite possible that the fragmentary account on 185 was made by the schoolmaster himself: so, not a secondary use of a piece of paper left lying around but, rather, two documentary engagements by the same individual). The impression, then, is that school exercises simply did not lie around so as to be reused. A piece of papyrus was valuable to the classroom in that it contained space on which exercises could still be entered, but once it was covered by exercises it lost its value. It is not at all outlandish to suggest, then, that the typical curation period of a school exercise would be no more than ten to 20 years, or an order of magnitude less than that of a literary roll; quite likely, less. If so, Cribiore's 412 writing exercises would represent not 7 percent of the total literary papyri in circulation at any given moment but 0.7 percent, or quite likely less.[84] All in all, perhaps a low percentage of the total written documents in circulation at any given moment could be concentrated in the school, probably rather less.

Stephens, 1994: 411, points out the relative frequency of the first books of the *Iliad* as evidence that "large numbers of copies of books 1 and 2 owe their existence to their use as school texts". This in fact is an important observation, which ought to be generalized and qualified for its wider significance. The following table measures the incidence of "first books" among the relatively frequent, multi-roll works.

---

[84] The evidence is even more skewed towards educational papyri, in that many of them are not papyri, strictly speaking, at all, but ostraka. The survival rate of ostraka must be significantly higher than that of papyrus, so that, if a low percentage of our extant "papyri" are educational ostraka, we must assume that such artifacts constituted a vanishingly small fraction of the pieces of writing in circulation at a given moment (surely less than one-tenth of a percent). On the other hand, a substantial amount of writing for educational purposes would have to be produced on wax tablets, a type of artifact that barely survives at all; there were thousands of these in the Egyptian chora, inscribed and reinscribed daily: the bulk of all ancient ephemeral writing – which remained, indeed, ephemeral and lost from sight. (For a famous case, outside Egypt, of a wax tablet retrieved with all its multiplicity of writing, see Zalizniak on the Novgorod Codex: www.csad.ox.ac.uk/CSAD/news letters/newsletter10/Newsletter10d.html.)

|  | Total | First book | Survival factor for first book[85] |
|---|---|---|---|
| Homer's *Iliad* | 1,421 | 201 | 3.8 |
| Homer's *Iliad* | Second book: | 150 | 2.8 |
| Homer's *Iliad* | Third book: | 92 | 1.6 |
| Homer's *Odyssey* | 252 | 18 | 1.8 |
| Thucydides | 97 | 23 | 2.2 |
| Apollonius | 56 | 25 | 2.4 |
| Herodotus | 47 | 20 | 5.2 |
| Callimachus' *Aetia* | 33 | 13 | 2.0 |

The effect is real and consistent. Still, it is not necessarily *just* a schooltext effect (though to some degree, of course, it is, as can be verified for Homer: many of the exercises are indeed from the first books: Cribiore, 1996: 194). Another part of the effect must involve the influence of the small library. We may note that the top tiers of the table on pages 20–4 above are dominated by short works: a single play, a single speech, a brief epic work – Homer himself forming the main exception. If so, it is tempting to believe that some smaller libraries could have opted to hold a single roll from larger works; perhaps this was, indeed, most frequent with Herodotus: too famous to ignore, too bulky to collect.

Yet a third account should be mentioned as well. I introduce it with a completely separate piece of evidence: the frequency of Ptolemy's *Handy Tables*. As noted in the table on page 23 above, the six fragments found in 2011 (for a work occupying probably three rolls) are fairly impressive for a second-century CE work. If we take them as the equivalent of, say, 12 fragments for 30,000 words of prose, we find a frequency comparable to that of, say, Sappho or Plato. Yet another fragment (of the introduction to the *Handy Tables*) was published in 2014 (Acerbi and Del Corso, 2014): so, seven fragments, of a single second-century CE work! The *Handy Tables* present no interest to any reader other than the sophisticated astrologer, and it does seem likely that antiquity had fewer sophisticated astrologers than it had readers of the *Republic*.[86] This merely illustrates the wider

---

[85] In this column, I calculate the average number of fragments predicted, by the total (column 1), for an arbitrary book; and divide it by the actual number (column 2) found for a given book. I treat all books as of equal length, a simplification which cannot be verified for Callimachus and which is slightly, but not significantly, wrong for all the rest. Generally speaking, first books tend to be somewhat longer, hence my numbers are slightly exaggerated, perhaps by 10 percent or so. In my calculation, I compare the number of first-book fragments to the average number of non-first-book fragments.

[86] The point seems to me fairly evident but I return to discuss the number of copies of Plato on pp. 118–21 below. Roughly put, sophisticated astrologers – those who owned Ptolemy's tables – served the elite – who owned Plato. And there were surely, on average, more craftsmen than clients in the sophisticated astrology business!

problem of the astrological (or, very rarely, astronomical) papyri, of which we have 245 fragments. This is to some extent because we are especially lucky in the editor of those papyri – Alexander Jones, who scoured the Oxyrhynchus collection for its astrological contents (Jones, 1999). Even so, Jones is responsible for only 168 out of the 245 fragments. The basic fact, then, is that astrological papyri, taken as a whole, are more frequent than those of any author other than Homer himself. This surely is not an artifact of the schoolroom, neither is it entirely (as was the case with writing exercises) a consequence of there being little incentive to curate the artifacts in question for a long period. Certainly, some astrological papyri are literally "ephemerids", and so to some extent ephemeral – tabulating predicted observations for a certain chronological range and thus losing much of their value as their window of accuracy expires. Others are individual horoscopes and are perhaps comparable to documents, certainly not to collectible literary papyri. But many astrological papyri have lasting content, of which the *Handy Tables* form one example. Procedure texts are always valid; epoch tables can be valid for very long periods. We have at least 60 such long-lasting papyri in Jones' collection alone. These are not merely long-term documents; they are extremely useful long-term documents, always of value to any practicing astrologer. Such documents, we should expect, could be curated indefinitely. And yet the sheer numbers among surviving documents are extremely high.

In short, the seven fragments of the *Handy Tables* are not a fluke: it appears that long-lasting astrological tables are surprisingly over-represented in the papyrus evidence, even though there would be clear incentives to curate them for as long as one curated any literary text, so that the explanation through quick discard cannot apply in an obvious way.

But perhaps quick discard needs to be assumed, for a contrasting reason: useful astrological tables would have to be discarded frequently just *because* they were so useful. The use of astrological tables entails the continuous rolling, unrolling and thumbing of the papyrus, and it stands to reason that such repeated use would have to shorten the document's life and so inflate the frequency of the document in the papyrus evidence.[87] The *Handy*

---

[87] I briefly entertained the idea of considering this question in terms of the material properties of the extant fragments – are the manuscripts that I predict to be the more thumbed in fact the more tattered? – but I quickly despaired of this route. Astrampsychus' P.Oxy. 47.3330 is indeed, to my untrained eye, fairly decrepit. But not more so than, say, P.Oxy. 76.5107, from Plato's *Statesman* – a work of the big library lovingly to be curated. The papyri in our possession all share the trauma of discard, all were deliberately shredded and cast out: it is perhaps impossible to tell now how they might have appeared, just prior to discard, in their full form. I simply have to assume, then, that books subject to more wear and tear would have deteriorated more rapidly.

*Tables* were *handy*. And, once a copy of Ptolemy's *Handy Tables* had deteriorated through heavy use, its owner would have commissioned *a new copy*.

This effect must be seen in other parts of the papyrological evidence as well. The case of Astrampsychus is directly comparable. Having ten fragments for a work of perhaps 300 CE[88] – equivalent to roughly 40 fragments of a classical work – and of the size of roughly a single roll implies a penetration rate comparable to that of Hesiod. Surely those ten fragments were well thumbed by late ancient readers anxious to discover their fate, in the process ruining their rolls. Another example: we have 26 to 28 fragments of musical notation from antiquity. Historians of music routinely lament this small number but historians of the book should be struck to find it so large. Music notation was a rare professional skill, apparently the outcome of ad hoc compilation by isolated individuals rather than the recopying of standard notated texts.[89] If so, 26 to 28 fragments would suggest a fantastic frequency. But, once again, notated papyri would be more heavily used and for this reason more frequently replaced.

This must also be part of the explanation for the first book effect. After all, there were not *that* many teachers in antiquity, certainly not enough to produce three times more copies of Book I of the *Iliad* than one would find in all other libraries put together. No: schoolmasters stood out not in that they had more copies of *Iliad* I but in that they constantly opened and reopened them. So, perhaps the entry into the canon is over-represented, in the evidence of the papyri, through sheer attrition? The most often read, and so the most quickly damaged?

The wider point of the discard effect is its converse: works which suffered less attrition would have been kept longer and so would have been more visible in the actual circulation of papyrus. It is clear that the best-curated and longest-maintained papyrus would have been that of the literary roll. Documents could sometimes be kept for long periods, for legal reasons, but many were ephemera and are not known to have been preserved for more than several decades.[90] It would not be too far off to

---

[88] So, Browne (1976).    [89] West (1992: 270 ff.).

[90] The Dioscorus archive was maintained for some 70 years and may be among the longest-lasting (on this archive, see p. 190 below); that of the strategos Apollonius, another major collection (see Kortus, 1999), lasted for a similar period. The largest archive of all – that of Zenon (see p. 35, n.72, above), was maintained for only about 30 years. (The assumption is that the latest deposit into an archive is not far removed from the end of the active maintenance of the archive.)

suggest that the average curation of a document would be not much more than a third the length of that of a literary roll. If so, we find that, in the Roman era at least, the amount of papyrus in circulation used for documents was not much more than that used for literary rolls.[91] When we first think of papyri, we tend to think of the ancient bookroll; a closer acquaintance with papyrology soon convinces us that this impression is wrong and that papyrus in antiquity was essentially a bureaucratic and economic tool. But this, too, is a false impression, created by the more frequent discard of documents. The ancients themselves were familiar not with the papyrus which we now know – the one which was cast out or hidden away. They knew the papyrus above ground. And so, writing must have presented itself, to them, as it still does today: as the vehicle, above all, of literature – or, more precisely, of the canon.

Be that as it may: we have noted that the papyri of elementary education did not differ substantially from those of the canon. They were, indeed, hyper-canonical, emphasizing, in a non-linear relation, the very top of the canon, with a special emphasis on poetry.

An exactly complementary result can be found for sophisticated scholarship. The evidence, in this case, derives from annotations. These are genuinely very hard to classify, deriving as they do from all manner of literary culture: some, basic glosses used for the intermediate level of teaching of literacy; others, scholarly texts. McNamee (2007) cautiously avoids any strict classification, and notes how the more obviously elementary glosses correlate well with the evidence for basic literate education (56–8). Yet it is clear that the evidence of annotated papyri as a whole belongs most typically to a scholarly, elite context. The sheer numbers based on the table in McNamee (2007: 514–29) (ignoring Latin and adespota, which are not numerous, however) are listed below. I note the percentages of the total papyri that are annotated (which is the relevant measure of the tendency of an author to become annotated: absolute fragment counts are very misleading in this regard). I avoid this measure for authors of unique annotated fragments, which, as usual, are nearly meaningless from a statistical point of view.

---

[91] I suggest the hypothetical ratio 1:3 because it is the one adopted in Habermann (1998: 157, tab. 11), where documentary and literary papyri are presented side by side, the vertical axis for literary papyri scaled at one-third that of documentary papyri. The two graphs are then made roughly to coincide. This surely is a substantial undercount of documents, however (whose rate of publication is considerably lower than that of literary rolls).

*Annotated percentage of total papyri per author*

| | | |
|---|---|---|
| Homer | 26 | 1% |
| Aristophanes | 17 | 30% |
| Alcaeus | 14 | 50% |
| Pindar | 14 | 25% |
| Menander | 13 | 11% |
| Euripides | 12 | 7% |
| Callimachus | 11 | 13% |
| Plato | 10 | 11% |
| Aeschylus | 8 | 25% |
| Sophocles | 8 | 22% |
| Thucydides | 7 | 7% |
| Demosthenes | 6 | 3% |
| Theocritus | 6 | 25% |
| Aratus | 5 | 36% |
| Bacchylides | 5 | 44% |
| Alcman | 4 | 27% |
| Apollonius | 4 | 8% |
| Euphorion | 4 | 40% |
| Hesiod | 4 | 3% |
| Simonides | 4 | 67% |
| Stesichorus | 4 | 44% |
| Anacreon | 3 | 60% |
| Archilochus | 3 | 17% |
| Epicharmus | 3 | 43% |
| Sappho | 3 | 13% |
| Xenophon | 3 | 7% |
| Herodotus | 2 | 4% |
| Hippocrates | 2 | 8% |
| Hipponax | 2 | 40% |
| Isocrates | 2 | 2% |
| Lycophron | 2 | 33% |
| Parthenius | 2 | 100% |
| Antiochus | 1 | |
| Aristoxenus | 1 | |
| Cercidas | 1 | |
| Corinna | 1 | |
| Cratinus | 1 | |
| Critias | 1 | |
| Eratosthenes | 1 | |
| Herodas | 1 | |
| Hierocles | 1 | |
| Ibycus | 1 | |
| Nicander | 1 | |
| Theognis | 1 | |

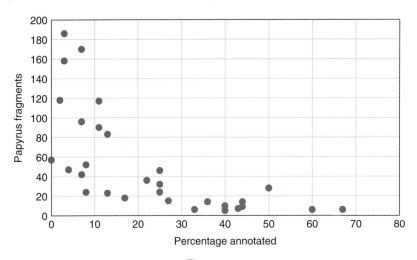

Figure 1.3

Once again the practice involves primarily poetry, and in this it super-ficially resembles elementary education. Just which poetry, however? The following table takes the results for poetry alone (ignoring, for better resolution, the two extreme cases of Homer and Parthenius),[92] showing a striking correlation: the less widely a poet was circulated, the more likely that he or she would be annotated.

As explained in note 92, this is not a mere effect of size as such. Rather, it shows that annotation was not attached to a fixed fraction of works, instead attaching to particular *types* of work. And, indeed, our result generalizes a point made more narrowly by Perrone (2009), regarding commentary to comic fragments: annotation peaks with regard to minor authors.

Does this mean, however, that scholarly readers would disdain the central canon, picking instead an alternative canon of minor poets? But this is wrong as well: as McNamee points out (2007: 127), not only are there many annotated copies of the most central canonical poets, but those copies also sometimes contain the most sophisticated annotation found anywhere. It is not as if Homer contained trivial glosses and Alcaeus sophisticated scholarship; to the contrary. Thus, what we see is that,

[92] There is an obvious difficulty with this comparison, in that an author who survives in very small numbers, and is annotated at all, would have to have a fairly high percentage of annotated fragments. To circumvent this problem, I ignore the single-annotated-fragment authors. The remaining authors all have at least five fragments overall (typically, rather more) and the typical rate of annotation is in the range of about 10 percent; hence this threshold effect is largely avoided.

whereas, in the circulation of papyri as a whole, there were many more copies of the central canon than of the rest, in the sphere of annotated texts the curve was much gentler.

This is predictable, as the leveling effect is a feature of big libraries. There were, say, ten times more libraries containing Hesiod than those containing Sappho. But, within those libraries that did contain Sappho, the sheer number of Hesiod rolls was not any larger than the sheer number of Sappho rolls: hence we find four annotated Hesiods and three annotated Sapphos. The *Iliad* was much more widespread than the *Odyssey*. But annotated texts were typical to the kind of library that had both, and so it is not surprising to find 15 annotated texts of the *Iliad*, and 11 of the *Odyssey*. And so the evidence is suggestive, once again: the big library contained the small library as a subset (this, indeed, is the fundamental sense in which prestige and popularity, in antiquity, went hand in hand). The cutoff point was different, with important consequences for how the literary field would have been conceived from the perspective of the small, or of the big, library. But both dealt with the same literary field, similarly ranked.

Driscoll (2016) is a study of the use of Homer, especially, within the culture of what I call here "the big library". He goes through many close readings as well as statistical observations concerning the sympotic authors of the Imperial era, namely Plutarch, Aulus Gellius and Athenaeus, who, thanks to Johnson (2010), we have come to interpret as representations of the ideology of elite book culture in the Imperial era. To me, the most significant result comes in Driscoll's appendix I, "Is the Use of Homer Distinctive?". Driscoll puts side by side the uses Plutarch makes of Homer, lyric poets and Euripides. He goes through the manner in which citations are introduced and their function, concluding that (246), "in general, quotations of Homer fall into the same broad continuum of quotation as with Euripides and lyric". The only significant difference found is not between Homer and the lyric poets (which is indeed a contrast between the small and the big libraries) but between Homer and *Euripides* (citations from the latter, more than those of other authors, tend to be taken out of context and "flattened" into a mere background, a kind of verbal wallpaper ornamenting the conversation).[93] So this, once again, is continuous with

---

[93] It seems that this is indeed a contrast between Euripides and the lyric poets: since he is so well known, he can be cited out of context. Homer, of course, could have been cited in the same way, as well, but this is less frequent in his case because he is, most often, the direct *theme* of conversations – as shown abundantly by Driscoll.

the evidence from the papyri as a whole and from the annotated papyri in
particular: the big library and the small library, on a *continuum*.

We return to the homogeneity of the ancient canon, this time not in
space or time but across the axis of literate education. This is, after all, the
fundamental point observed by the historians of education: the very same
works would have been repeatedly encountered throughout a pupil's career.
And those works would have been chosen to some extent on the basis of
their perceived value in moral education (hence Isocrates) but above all as
a reflection of canonic status. The canon of education was formed on the
basis of the general canon, concentrating on the most canonical poets (so:
Homer, Hesiod, Menander, Euripides and some Pindar). Prose was more
difficult, in being less memorable; but, even then, one took the most
memorable piece of canonical prose – Isocrates' exhortations – and made
it the basis of education in prose. A single text was taken from the margins
of the canon (or perhaps was specific to the educational context), namely
Aesop. With this single exception, ancient education relied on the set of
authors it had available already: it had its very starting point in the canon.
Ultimately, as one reached the big library, the entirety of the literary field
would have been perceived, all the way down to tiers 3 or even 4. But it was
the same field, throughout: the same, monolithic canon.

## 1.3   Out of Egypt

### 1.3.1   *The Internal Evidence of the Papyri*

But are the papyri representative of anything other than the Nile Valley?
I believe we have already come across an important piece of evidence for
this question – in the very stability of the papyri. It is hard to imagine
Oxyrhynchus maintaining its fixed literary culture while everything else
changed about it – a calm in the eye of a Mediterranean literary storm. No:
stability must have been forced on the Egyptian chora from the outside.

What is the empirical evidence for this a priori consideration? First, our
evidence does not appear to be biased by local patriotism – or even by
temporal patriotism. There is no preference for local or recent authors. To
the contrary; one finds throughout a preference for a set of authors distant
in space as well as time. This would make it inherently unlikely that the
favorite authors were peculiar to Egypt.

The following table lists the pagan Greek authors who are usually
assumed to have been at least related to Egypt, identified on Egyptian
papyri. Within each locality, the authors are arranged chronologically.

**Alexandria**

| | | |
|---|---|---|
| Euclid | 6 | −300? |
| Rhianus | 4 | −250 |
| Herondas | 2 | −250 |
| Callimachus | 83 | −250 |
| Apollonius | 52 | −250 |
| Theocritus | 24 | −250 |
| Lycophron | 6 | −250 |
| Posidippus | 3 | −250 |
| Philicus | 1 | −250 |
| Aristophanes | 1 | −200 |
| Eratosthenes | 1 | −200 |
| Heraclides | 1 | −150 [Lembus] |
| Philo Judaeus | 4 | +0 |
| Tryphon | 2 | +0 |
| Areius | 1 | +0 |
| Theon rhet. | 1 | +50 |
| Heliodorus | 1 | +100 [Medicus] |
| Menelaus | 1 | +100 |
| Soranus | 1 | +100 |
| Achilles Tatius | 6 | +150 |
| Ptolemy | 6 | +150 |
| Pancrates | 2 | +150 |
| Appianus | 1 | +150 |
| Harpocration | 1 | +200 |

**Diospolis**

| | | |
|---|---|---|
| Anubion | 6 | −50 |

**"Egypt"**

| | | |
|---|---|---|
| "Nechepso" | 1 | −100? |
| Ps. Manetho | 2 | +150 |

**Panopolis**

| | | |
|---|---|---|
| Triphiodorus | 2 | +300 |
| Nonnus | 1 | +450 |
| Pamprepius | 1 | +450 |

This list, with its 228 fragments, is entirely dominated by the Alexandrian literary culture of the early Ptolemaic period, some of whose members certainly became major figures of ancient culture as a whole. Callimachus, Apollonius and Theocritus are responsible for 159 of the fragments (Theocritus, of course, had only tenuous Alexandrian connections). Other than them, what we find are technical works – grammatical, medical and mathematical – for which Alexandria was certainly objectively central.

The prominence of Alexandrian poetry in the Egyptian papyri should not strike us as a local phenomenon. Perhaps the strongest evidence for this comes from the finding, among the papyri, of non-Alexandrian Hellenistic poetry. Aratus is an obvious example (the Hellenistic courts with which he is associated in our – untrustworthy – evidence are at Pella and Antioch, not Alexandria).[94] Otherwise, the most significant example is that of Euphorion. Here is a fairly important Hellenistic poet, though not at the level of the major poets – if importance is judged (as it must be) by influence on Roman poetry.[95] He was not active in Alexandria, however (hailing from Chalcis, with ties to Athens and to Antioch).[96] Would Egypt still collect him? It does, with a very respectable ten fragments: a fair measure of the importance of this author. A non-Alexandrian origin was not penalized by the papyri; as a correlate, I do not think we should assume there was a bias in favor of collecting Alexandrian poetry just because it was Alexandrian.

And, finally, even if we can prove conclusively the cross-Mediterranean canonicity of the Hellenistic poets only for the Roman era, then it is surely significant that their papyri are *not* specifically Ptolemaic: of the 159 fragments of the Alexandrian Hellenistic poets, no more than four are Ptolemaic-era. Indeed, the relative frequency of those poets is *smaller* in the Ptolemaic period. This result is expected and follows from the overall tendency of the lesser domination of the Ptolemaic papyri by the canon. And so, as a consequence, there are, relatively speaking, more Ptolemaic papyri of lesser Hellenistic poets (just as there are more Ptolemaic papyri, relatively speaking, of lesser authors as a whole) – Posidippus being just the most famous example.[97] This brings up a wider phenomenon: the papyri as a whole do *not* testify to any contemporary trends. Geographical proximity does not matter, but neither does chronological proximity. Here is another table, setting out all the papyrus fragments whose century of production as papyrus roll (as estimated by papyrologists) is the same as their century of composition as literary work (as judged by literary scholars).

---

[94] Aratus' itinerary is recounted in lively fashion by Green (1986: 148). It is known through the prism of literary biographical legend; the connection to Pella and the absence of any significant Alexandrian ties seem safe.

[95] Was Euphorion an influence on Gallus? Was this taken by the Romans themselves to be an emblematic example of Greek influence? See Hunter (2006: 24–6) (Hunter, as most scholars do, tends to see in Euphorion essentially an imitator of Callimachus).

[96] Dickie (1998: 52).

[97] I refer of course to the Milan Papyrus (see Gutzwiller, 2005), a nearly intact book produced in a matter of decades following the poet's death.

**Third–second centuries BCE, ten identified same-century literary papyri out of 482 total (21 per thousand)**

Callimachus ×2, Aratus, Cercidas, Chares, Dionysius Scytobrachion, Philicus, Phoenix, Posidippus, Sosylus, Meleager

**First century BCE to first century CE, five identified same-century literary papyri out of 1,717 total (three per thousand)**

Meleager, Dioscorides, Nicarchus II ×3

**Second–third centuries CE, 32 identified same-century literary papyri out of 3,940 total (eight per thousand)**

Achilles Tatius ×2, Antonius Diogenes ×2, Aelius Aristides ×2, Arrian, Chariton ×3, Dictys Cretensis ×3, Dionysius (Gigantias), Harpocration, Heraclides, Herodotus med., Hierocles, Lollian ×2, Menelaus, Pancrates ×2, Phlegon, Plutarch ×5, Ptolemy, Triphiodorus ×2

**Later antiquity, one identified same-century literary papyrus out of 1,538 total (below one per thousand)**

Themistius

I will take up in detail in the next section the question of adjustment for unidentified authors: to anticipate, these do not materially change the picture (so, for instance, papyri with unidentified Attic drama are certainly not contemporary!).[98] Further, the average author's productive period would be a fraction of a century, which more than cancels out the effect of unidentified papyri. Papyri distributed during the

[98] The major exception was pointed out in Cavallo (1996): quite a few papyri with ancient novels are extant from the first to second centuries CE, and most of these are likely to have been written at about the same time. To be more precise, however, there are 44 anonymous novels, likely to have been written in the first or second century CE, distributed as follows in terms of their century of papyrus production: six first century, 14.5 second century, 16.5 third century, six fourth century, 0.5 fifth century, 0.5 sixth century (we get "half" papyri when a papyrus is attributed to a range of two centuries). This should be measured against the total number of papyrus fragments from the century, however, so the actual incidence of anonymous novels is (numbers per thousand papyrus fragments): 6.7 first century, 5.3 second century, eight third century, eight fourth century, 0.8 fifth century, one sixth century. It is therefore not quite correct to say that the novel had its greatest distribution in the era of its composition, that of the high Empire. Rather, it is correct to note that it established its position fairly rapidly (though as a distinctly minor genre: about 1 percent of literary papyri, including papyri by known authors; one should note once again at this point that novels are fairly long). Then, at the end of the fourth century, it rapidly fell out of fashion.

author's own lifetime would have had, we find, a minuscule presence in the Nile Valley.[99]

There are hardly any exceptions to this emphasis on a single, dead, foreign canon.[100] One is formed by the group of Triphiodorus, Nonnus and Pamprepius, with four fragments between them. As Cameron (1965: 470) puts it, "In the later Roman Empire Egypt, not for the first time in its history, became the home of Greek poetry."[101] As MacCoull (1988: 59–60) notes, it is striking that so much of the attested literary activity seems to come from just this region of Panopolis (situated well to the south of Oxyrhynchus): to the four fragments above one should definitely add *The Vision of Dorotheus*, an adespota Christian hexameter from the early fourth century CE,[102] and probably also the Blemyomachia, certainly yet another upper Egyptian and late ancient hexameter, found on an upper Egyptian papyrus.[103] It would not be shocking to discover that this poetry was more popular in Egypt than outside it. At the very least, it is noticeable that no late ancient non-Egyptian poets are represented in CEDOPAL. And the six fragments considered above are not all that trivial, if we consider that we are looking at very late authors – fourth and fifth centuries CE – who had a much more limited scope for being preserved. The six fragments of late ancient Egyptian poets are perhaps a meaningless fluke, but they could also be the equivalent of several dozen papyri from an earlier period.

We need bigger numbers to form a clearer picture of papyri in late antiquity. And so we should extend our vision to encompass Christian authors. Van Haelst (1976) had 52 well-located patrological texts (I ignore apocryphal writings). Of these, 28 are by fathers of the Church associated with Egypt (typically, of course, with Alexandria). Origen dominates this corpus, with 12 fragments, but there are ten authors in this group of Egyptian fathers of the Church preserved in papyrus and published by 1976.[104]

---

[99] That the numbers are somewhat higher in the Ptolemaic era is, once again, simply a function of the overall higher incidence of rare authors in that era. We find that small libraries are safe libraries, keeping just the established canon; and that big libraries are more open to experiment. (Stephens, 1994, raises the question as to which library the ancient novel belonged to. Her conclusion – in my terms, that it was a big library phenomenon – is the one more in line with the evidence we accumulate throughout this chapter.)

[100] I put aside discussion of one other exception – the Acta Alexandrinorum, surely a text circulating primarily in Egypt – until the discussion of adespota below. As will be noted, this appears to have been in some sense a sub-literary group of texts.

[101] Cameron (1965)     [102] Kessels and van der Horst (1987).

[103] Livrea (1978) ascribes it to Olympiodorus from Thebes.

[104] I have to rely on Van Haelst here, because LDAB does not allow an easy interface with which to survey the detail of large groups of papyri. It is reassuring to note, for instance, that LDAB now has 27 fragments by Origen (the numbers are much bigger because LDAB also counts late ancient manuscripts with translations into Latin that survive through the manuscript tradition).

| Athanasius | Alexandria | CE4 | 1 |
|---|---|---|---|
| Clement | Alexandria | CE2 | 1 |
| Cyril | Alexandria | CE5 | 3 |
| Didymus the Blind | Alexandria | CE4 | 6 |
| Isaiah | Scetis | CE5 | 1 |
| Julius Africanus | Libya?/Jerusalem | CE3 | 1 |
| Origen | Alexandria | CE3 | 12 |
| Theonas | Alexandria | CE3 | 1 |
| Theophilus | Alexandria | CE4 | 1 |

Once again, this may simply reflect Egypt's, and Alexandria's, role in the scholarly life of early Christianity (on which there is more in Chapter 6, pages 777–8). Egyptian Christians did possess papyri of the works of such non-Egyptian authors as Irenaeus, Melito of Sardis and the Cappadocian fathers of the Church – though none, other than Melito, survived in huge numbers.

What to make of this? It is certainly true that, while Ptolemaic and Roman Egypt possessed authors from across the Greek-speaking Mediterranean, Egyptian authors formed no more than a fraction among them. But, then, Christian and Byzantine Egypt possessed a considerably larger fraction of Egyptian authors. Partly this could reflect a certain Byzantine fragmentation of Mediterranean culture.[105] We shall revisit this claim in Part III. But, if so, the evidence becomes even clearer, by contrast, for the central centuries of the Hellenistic and Imperial eras. We begin to see evidence that the canon was not merely frozen in time but also homogeneous across the Mediterranean.

### 1.3.2 The TLG Evidence

From Ptolemaic times, until the Byzantine fragmentation, the selection of books found in the Egyptian countryside appears to have been Mediterranean rather than Egyptian. Spatial proximity to a given author did not matter. Indeed, it is even possible that this was *especially* true of places such as the Egyptian countryside. It would be rather incredible had the typical Athenian library in the Hellenistic era not included a rather larger fraction of Athenian philosophy; if the cities of the Islands and of Asia Minor did not display some preference, at least, for their native sons.[106] There ought to have been some

[105] While this is no more than an anecdote, it is worth mentioning that Van Haelst has one papyrus by Tatian of Mesopotamia (in Greek), and it is also the only papyrus he has from Dura Europos, a rare papyrus find from the Fertile Crescent – i.e. Tatian's own cultural area.

[106] We have some evidence for the local commemoration of cultural figures through monuments (Zanker, 1995: 161–6): Clazomenae minting a coin with Anaxagoras on it, Sicilian Himera doing

geographical variability there, because there were significant local literary
traditions. The Nile was rich with tradition, just not a Greek one. That its
Greek-speaking elites showed, in their collections of Greek works, so little
interest in their own *Egyptian* heritage is shocking. You would think
Herodotus Book *II* would be the most frequent. But in fact Herodotus, as
we just saw, is the most heavily skewed towards Book I. He was cast aside just
as his treatment was about to reach the Nile. No: the Egyptian countryside
did not possess its own native *Greek* literary tradition (and, until the
Byzantine era, it does not appear to have over-represented even
Alexandria), and so it carried a bland, unmarked literary culture, one we
may therefore use as our guide or baseline for other geographies, in locations
with a more storied literary past.

In what follows, I compare the number of fragments of papyrus
(counted in 2011) to the number of citations in ancient literature as
a whole. The following table presents the number of TLG citations of
a given author's name up to the fifth century CE, followed by the
number of papyrus fragments, and then by the ratio of the first to
the second; and then the same not with the numbers of citations but
with the numbers of authors who make such citations. The TLG
searches were run in 2011 on all authors with 12 fragments or more.
They are ordered by TLG counts.

I hasten to explain: as classical scholars know all too well, references
in antiquity were often implicit (through allusion or through citations
of varying accuracy, unaccompanied by an explicit mention of their
author's name).[107] This impression is correct though exaggerated. With
some exceptions, it was generically inappropriate to cite historical
names explicitly in verse (indeed, would the names even scan?), and
also, with some exceptions, authors in theoretical-technical fields such

the same for Stesichorus; monuments were erected for Homer in the cities with which he was
associated (and then in others as well), but, suggesting a clearer local tradition, there was one for
Bias, in Priene, and another for Archilochus, in Paros. The last one is especially significant for the
extensive inscriptions found there, dating from the Hellenistic era, containing detailed biographical
anecdotes (Kontoleon, 1963): these suggest a continued dedication to Archilochus the imagined
author. It is hard to believe that the city erecting such monuments to its dead poet would not also
collect his papyri with greater zeal. Notice that this evidence relates primarily to archaic figures,
"heroic" semi-founders of their cities; it should not be assumed that the same attitude would
necessarily have extended to more recent, and more mundane, local authors. In general, for the
question of local identities in a globalized Roman world, see the collection of essays Whitmarsh
(2010) and references therein.
[107] See Stanley (1990) for citation practices in the Imperial era (when, indeed, they become somewhat
more stable and modern-looking). It is telling that this study is produced from within the tradition
of Christian *biblical* scholarship: classical scholars tend to be less interested in the nature of their
texts, as canons, within antiquity itself.

as philosophy, medicine or mathematics often referred only sparingly to individual names (unless, that is, they were commentators, in which case they frequently cited names: the commentary verges on the "scholarly"). In those two cases, then, references by one author to another were often mediated and allusive. This leaves out a large body of literature, however, especially historical and scholarly, in which names were cited very frequently. As a consequence, the census of explicit mentions of names involves big numbers which appear meaningful enough. Indeed, concentrating on explicit mentions (and not indirect allusion) is precisely the relevant measure for our purposes. What we try to find is the extent to which certain names gained cultural currency. The hypothesis, then, is that this census can serve as a proxy for ancient reputations.

| Author | TLG cites | Papyri | Cites/ papyri | TLG authors | Authors/ papyri |
|---|---|---|---|---|---|
| Aristotle | [4,180] 3,950 | 12 | 330 | 270 | 22.5 |
| Hippocrates | [3,516] 3,400 | 24 | 140 | 118 | 4.9 |
| Plato | [9,771] 9,350 | 90 | 105 | 311 | 3.5 |
| Sophocles | [1,505] 1,400 | 36 | 40 | 158 | 4.4 |
| Aratus | [988] 500 | 14 | 35 | 91 | 6.5 |
| Aristophanes | [1,952] 1,600 | 57 | 30 | 140 | 2.5 |
| Xenophon | [1,100] 1,050 | 42 | 25 | 132 | 3.1 |
| Aeschylus | [791] 750 | 32 | 25 | 133 | 4.2 |
| Demosthenes | [3,399] 3,300 | 186 | 20 | 162 | 0.9 |
| Herodotus | [1,145] 1,000 | 47 | 20 | 174 | 3.7 |
| Archilochus | [430] 400 | 18 | 20 | 100 | 5.6 |
| Sappho | [402] 400 | 23 | 20 | 85 | 3.7 |
| Euripides | [2,211] 2,200 | 170 | 15 | 226 | 1.3 |
| Aeschines | [932] 800 | 50 | 15 | 96 | 1.8 |
| Alcman | [280] 250 | 15 | 15 | 62 | 4.1 |
| Hesiod | [1,369] 1,250 | 158 | 10 | 217 | 1.4 |
| Thucydides | [1,158] 1,150 | 96 | 10 | 132 | 1.5 |
| Menander | [1,058] 1,030 | 117 | 10 | 114 | 1 |
| Pindar | [738] 650 | 57 | 10 | 146 | 2.6 |
| Alcaeus | [296] 300 | 28 | 10 | 72 | 2.6 |
| Homer | [5,733] 5,500 | 1815 | 5 | 332 | 0.2 |
| Isocrates | [641] 600 | 118 | 5 | 103 | 0.9 |
| Callimachus | [602] 500 | 83 | 5 | 127 | 1.5 |
| Theocritus | [171] 150 | 24 | 5 | 50 | 2.1 |
| Bacchylides | [99] 100 | 14 | 5 | 37 | 2.6 |
| Apollonius | [1,369] 100 | 52 | 0 | 161[108] | 3.1 |

[108] The problem of multiple Apolloniuses is very significant in this case; this part of the table is nearly meaningless.

There's some work put into this table: it is not an unmediated count.[109] You will notice that the first column includes a number in square brackets; these are the raw numbers of a lemma search of the name up to the end of the fifth century CE. This is followed by another, estimated, "real" number, obtained as follows. First, quite obviously, we removed references that preceded the author as well as references from within the corpus of the author himself. Following that, we sampled the citation lists to estimate how many of the references are merely of homonyms, adjusting accordingly.[110] Finally, TLG counts give rise to some double-counting of fragments (so, if the name "Plato" is mentioned in a context in which, say, Athenaeus provides a fragment from Alexis, this will be counted by TLG twice as two separate cites of "Plato": by Alexis as well as by Athenaeus). This was estimated by counting the number of references from fragments where the author's name is cited and reducing a little under its half ("a little under", since occasionally the double-counting involves a later source which is not included in our survey). Such estimates are not precise, and so I round the result to the nearest multiple of 50; I then further simplify by rounding the ratio of cites to papyri to the nearest multiple of five.[111]

And as we do so we find quite significant results. First of all, many authors fall squarely into a fairly narrow range, between roughly 40 and 15 cites per papyrus fragment. These are the following: Sophocles, Aristophanes, Xenophon, Aeschylus, Demosthenes, Herodotus, Euripides and Aeschines (among the core Athenian canon), Aratus (among the Hellenistic authors) and Archilochus, Sappho and Alcman (among the archaic authors).

Why is Euripides, for instance, on the low side of this range? Because the simple division of cites by papyri is clearly misleading and a non-linear regression would do a better job. There is a certain ceiling, and, as citations approach it, their rate of growth slows down. Ancient literature just did not have room for, say, 5,000 explicit citations of Euripides. This accounts also, to some extent, for the Homer and Hesiod anomalies, and

---

[109] Much of the work has been done by my research assistant, Amy Carlow.

[110] The sample was typically "every 30th occurrence" but when the results were more difficult we went to "every 15th occurrence". This result is much more statistically robust than it appears, since the results are arranged by authors, and since references are to the author, or homonymous, in a manner highly correlated within the citation pattern of a single author: so if, for instance, Galen has 60 cites of the name, and all are homonymous, we will indeed pick it exactly twice.

[111] The same adjustments were not made on the number of authors citing, which is therefore generally an overcount.

is an important background to take into account when considering the Menander anomaly.[112]

The remaining anomalies are divided into two: authors who have surprisingly many citations, given their papyri; and those who have surprisingly few. Let us go through these in turn. Those authors with surprisingly many citations are Aristotle, Hippocrates and Plato. The reason for this is self-evident: citation by name is common in the particular genre of the commentary, which survives extensively for philosophy and science.[113] It should be pointed out, though, that the presence of philosophers is in fact much more impressive than that, when we consider the number of *citing authors* (which is much less sensitive to hyper-citation within commentaries): with 311 and 270 citing authors, respectively, Plato and Aristotle are outliers. They are unlike almost anyone else – but they are like Homer. (Hippocrates is not of the same order; indeed, his huge citation number is driven almost entirely by a single author, Galen.) Now, to be like Homer is a very rare accomplishment indeed, and we may begin to note that the reception of philosophy follows a separate route – in the very elite levels represented by the citation counts – from that of the papyri. At some elite level, philosophy could become not a genre within literature but the equivalent, or the alternative, to literature.

Another "scientific" author is Aratus, and this should serve to deflate his apparently robust cites-to-papyri ratio: it is in fact largely a function of mentions by Hipparchus' so-called commentary. Without such scientific references, Aratus should in fact be included with the other Hellenistic authors, in the group of surprisingly low ratio of cites to papyri.

This group includes, then, the following authors: several archaic authors (Pindar, Alcaeus, Bacchylides); all the Hellenistic authors; Menander (perhaps best considered alongside the Hellenistic authors); and Thucydides and Isocrates.

There are several hypotheses for such low ratios of cites to papyri. The first one is that such authors were in fact specifically popular in the Nile Valley, and for this reason we find many more papyrus fragments of such authors than their overall reputation would lead us to expect. The second

---

[112] But the case of Menander is more difficult, as the number of papyri may be an undercount; see p. 86 below. Further, it also seems relevant that with dramatists, in particular, it is natural to attribute a citation to the speaker rather than to the author (this seems to be the implication of Driscoll, 2016: 237).

[113] For all three authors, there was an impressive publication burst between 2011 and 2018, raising their papyrus counts by 10 to 20 percent; this also slightly removes their anomaly.

one is that such authors have a lower disposition to have their name cited by later authors, relative to their circulation on papyrus.[114]

The case of Isocrates is the simplest in this regard: his papyrus count is inflated by the school use of the Cyprian orations. Thucydides is something of a surprise: on closer look, his case may reflect a version of the non-linear "ceiling" effect. All three historians have, in fact, very similar cite counts – just over 1,000 – which is apparently as much as a historian could get, regardless of his papyrus count.

The remaining anomalies are driven by eras. In general, archaic authors are not cited as often as classical authors (indeed, even those within the 40-to-15 range are on the lower side); Hellenistic authors are cited *much* less. The archaic effect cannot be due to the influence of the Nile: we certainly do not think that Bacchylides, Pindar and Alcaeus were, among all the regions of the Mediterranean, especially popular in the Egyptian chora. (Admittedly, they were more popular among the editors of Greek papyri – but not more popular than, say, Aeschylus.) On the other hand, it is clear why they would be cited less often than their Athenian counterparts. After all, a considerable fraction of our citations – by my estimate, about half – comes from the context of Atticism, in the form of lexica and anthologies focused on Athenian history and literature as well as on Attic usage. This must account in part for the low number of cites of the Hellenistic authors – though, in this case, the doubt returns: are these, after all, not over-represented on the Nile? Surely both forces operate: the cites-to-papyri ratio of Hellenistic authors is low due both to their low citability (because of their non-Athenian origin) and to their high incidence as Egyptian papyri (because of their at least quasi-Egyptian origin). But which force is the more important?

I set aside this question, and set aside the Hellenistic authors as a group. Otherwise, the result is powerful: the discrepancies that do arise between papyrus fragment and TLG counts are mild and explicable. This is quite significant. TLG citations were not made in the Egyptian countryside. The authors in the TLG corpus lived in the major centers of Greek Mediterranean culture, hailing from across the Mediterranean and active in such places as Athens, Asia Minor, Rome and Alexandria. In short, this is the culture of the richest, greatest metropolitan centers: and yet it is not very easy to tell it apart from Oxyrhynchus.

[114] It is also possible that the sheer numbers of papyri finds, or of cites, are for some reason an outlier (we have accidentally lost many authors who did cite the particular author; or we happen to have dug up, or simply published, a disproportionate amount of papyri for just this particular author).

This could be put somewhat differently. What the comparison between TLG citations and papyrus fragments brings out is just how *plausible* the distribution of papyrus fragments is. The papyrus fragments do not shock us by bringing in many authors in the wrong proportions; rather, they seem to capture quite well what we would have expected, based on the pattern of attestation in ancient literature (so that even Menander, the most spectacular case of wealth hidden in the papyri, was after all very well attested in advance: the surprise of his many fragments was in a sense predictable).

The results are plausible. What is implausible is that we get them. There is no obvious way in which TLG citations influence papyrus fragments, or vice versa. And, indeed, the correlation is not any direct cause and effect. Rather, TLG cites are a good enough proxy for ancient reputations, and, as I noted early on, it is a likely hypothesis that, in antiquity, reputation and circulation went hand in hand: the main reason to collect an author was if his or her reputation was high. This was not Bourdieu's modernism.

### 1.3.3 The Evidence of the Portraits

We need to find more ways to assess reputations: to study the pictures that the ancients formed of their own culture. So let us consider their pictures. These are harder to quantify, but I did compile a count based on Richter's (1965) survey of Greek portraits (somewhat expanded in Richter and Smith, 1984), considering just the portraits of "cultural icons".[115] I count only the reasonably safe reconstructions of portraits in marble.[116] (Other formats are less common and show more eccentric patterns of preservation; and it is better to compare like with like.)

[115] So that I ignore portraits of political and military figures. Richter's approach is positivistic and often bordering on the naïve. We may doubt the very meaning of a "portrait of. . ." – could a Roman copy of a Greek portrait (whatever that meant originally) not have been commissioned just as a generic Greek or a generic cultured person, or just as a nice piece of marble (see, for instance, Dillon, 2006)? Richter, in fact, in the detail of her argument, does pay attention to such nuance, and the pattern of distribution forces one to believe, after all, in the reality of the phenomenon, for, if these were just nice pieces of marble to look at, why should their distribution have responded to the cultural function of the subjects? For a sophisticated discussion, ultimately sympathetic to Richter's project (and engaging with the role of such portraits in canon formation!), see Wallis (2016). My study is based on an Oldfather-type resource: a somewhat antiquated survey. In this case, the rate of new discoveries is more muted (though not negligible: see, e.g., Fittschen, 1991), but, at any rate, this is the most recent *comprehensive* resource, and so the one I use.
[116] I count as "portrait" any compelling evidence that a piece of marble hailing from an ancient statue (in any format) survived till modern times. Reliable reports of lost statues, and of course mere bases, count as well. Ancient reports are not counted.

I arrange the portraits by tiers of extant number of portraits, in two separate columns: literary, and philosophical.

### Tier 1: The literary leaders[117]

| Literary | | |
|---|---|---|
| Sophocles | 54 | Trag. |
| Menander | 54 | Com. |
| Demosthenes | 47 | Rhet. |
| Homer | 43 | Ep. |
| Hesiod | 38 | Ep. |

### Tier 2: The philosophical leaders (with Euripides)

| Literary | | | Philosophical | | |
|---|---|---|---|---|---|
| | | | Socrates | 37 | (Above the schools) |
| Euripides | 30 | Trag. | Epicurus | 29 | Garden |
| | | | Plato | 23 | Academy |
| | | | Hermarchus | 23 | Garden |
| | | | Metrodorus | 19 | Garden |
| | | | Aristotle | 18 | Lyceum |
| | | | Chrysippus | 18 | Stoa |

### Tier 3: Less dominant figures (5 to 11)

| Literary | | | Philosophical | | |
|---|---|---|---|---|---|
| Anacreon | 11 | Lyr. | | | |
| Aeschines | 10 | Rhet. | Zeno | 10 | Stoa |
| Aeschylus | 9 | Trag. | Carneades | 9 | Academy |
| Herodotus | 8 | Hist. | Antisthenes | 8 | Cynic |
| | | | Colotes | 8 | Garden |
| Hyperides | 6 | Rhet. | Cleanthes | 5 | Stoa |
| Thucydides | 5 | Hist. | Diogenes | 5 | Cynic |
| | | Also: | Hippocrates | 5 | Med. |

[117] It is useful to have a sense of the scale of the phenomenon. Højte (2005: 591–606) is a survey of the known bases for statues of emperors from the Imperial era, with about 2,300 entries (an undercount, relative to Richter's measure, since she counts extant statues as well as bases, though this difference is not all that dramatic: bases are more common). This compares with about 550 statues in the list provided here. Put differently, portraits of Homer were at about the same scale as portraits of Augustus.

**Tier 4: More sporadic survival**

| Literary | | | Philosophical | | |
|---|---|---|---|---|---|
| Moschion | 4 | Trag. | Theophrastus | 4 | Lyceum |
| Pindar | 3 | Lyr. | | | |
| Alcaeus | 3 | Lyr. | | | |
| Panyassis | 3 | Ep. | | | |
| Isocrates | 3 | Rhet. | | | |
| Aristophanes | 3 | Com. | | | |
| Philemon | 2 | Com. | Heraclitus | 2 | Presocratic |
| Xenophon | 2 | Hist. | | | |
| Thespis | 2 | Trag. | | | |
| Lysias | 2 | Rhet. | | | |
| Corinna | 1 | Lyr. | Aristippus | 1 | Cyrenaic |
| Posidippus | 1 | Lyr. | Archytas | 1 | Pythagorean |
| Timotheus | 1 | Lyr. | Posidonius | 1 | Stoa |
| Bacchylides | 1 | Lyr. | Thales | 1 | Presocratic |
| Ibycus | 1 | Lyr. Also: | Eudoxus | 1 | Math. |
| Aratus | 1 | Ep. | | | |
| Stesichorus | 1 | Lyr. | | | |
| Protagoras | 1 | Rhet. | | | |

The evidence represents primarily the reception of the Greek canon by the highest stratum of the Roman elite. Some of it is from the Greek east, however, and may represent the public spaces of the Greek city. Provenance, at any rate, is rarely certain: the statues had usually reached modern collections already by the Renaissance – and would have been moved about, a lot, in antiquity itself. The division into tiers is not quite arbitrary: the contrast between the first, literary, tier and the second, philosophical, one is manifest, and it is heartening to have the gap between tiers 2 and 3 (none in tier 2 has fewer than 18 portraits, none in tier 3 has more than 11). Thus, even with such small numbers, and with the many difficulties concerning identification, the evidence appears coherent, and indeed, once again, plausible in its own way.

The one major surprise in this evidence is the place of philosophy. As usual, with regard to ancient philosophy, we should make an effort to remember that this is not some academic pursuit. Philosophy was the search for a solution to a lived problem: that of the happy life.[118] Perhaps portraits represented past solutions to this problem and displayed the patron's own moral nature? Or perhaps, regardless of one's "real"

---

[118] Classical statement by Burnyeat (1982). (For instance, page 30: "[The Skeptic] is still, like any other Hellenistic philosopher, a man in search of happiness.")

philosophical affiliation, a group of Epicurean philosophers, say, tele-graphed pleasure and otium: just what was needed at that corner? The point, in general, is that philosophical identities constituted a semiotic system, independent of the semiotics of literature itself.

Even so, the sheer numbers of philosophical portraits do add to the impression gained from the TLG cite counts and begin to suggest that, perhaps, the Egyptian papyri could underplay the significance of philoso-phy, especially of the Hellenistic schools, relative to the metropolitan centers.[119] While the Villa dei Papiri is essentially an anecdotal find – a single event, however massive – the fact that its excavated collections were so heavily centered around Epicurean philosophy does become some-what less surprising given the evidence of the portraits (the villa, after all, furnishes quite a few portraits, as well!).[120]

Otherwise, what is most significant is not the relative numbers as such (we would not expect, with this very different medium of recording prestige, any quantitative correlation) but the ordinal structure. This, then, seems to be the overall ranking of the genres, as implied by the portraits:

Tragedy > epic > rhetoric > comedy > lyric > history

The only surprise is in the relative positions of tragedy and epic. We are reminded of the Ptolemaic papyri, and, indeed, the models for the icono-graphic tradition were formed in the fourth and third centuries BC; but why should the Roman *relative frequency* reflect any Hellenistic pattern? Instead, it is tempting to imagine some kind of context in the sites of performance, real or imagined. Why have a portrait of Thespis, for instance? One is a Roman copy, the other an inscribed base (Roman era) from the theater in Athens (Richter, 1965: 73). Sophocles, Menander and Demosthenes evoked the culture of Athenian performance, whether in Athens itself or elsewhere. A portrait emphasizes the sense of a lived presence in space: the more performative authors suited the medium best. Thus even Homer himself, as well as Hesiod (who must frequently have accompanied him in the iconographic programs), was not more

---

[119] It is interesting to compare the program of the Ptolemaic portraits in the Serapeum in Memphis (Lauer, 1955): identified are Homer, Pindar and Hesiod; Thales, Heraclitus, Protagoras and Plato. The rough parity between literature and philosophy is suggestive of the future Roman villa (is this parity, then, perhaps yet another Roman imitation of a Hellenistic model?); the choice – which philosophers to represent – is distinctive.
[120] For a survey of this magnificent sculptural set, and its place within modern scholarship, see Mattusch and Lie (2005).

dominant than the representatives of the most obvious forms of performance.

Let us now look inside the genres themselves. The case of epic is clear:

Homer > Hesiod    > Panyassis, Aratus

Why Panyassis? I shall return in Chapter 2, page 215, to the explicit, scholarly lists of canonical authors, in which he is indeed included. We do not need to imagine any undetected popularity in antiquity (his TLG cite up to the end of the fifth century CE is a mere 43). Probably there were sufficiently many cases when the iconographic program called for *more than two* epic poets. There was no obvious way to choose which, and Panyassis suited just as well.

Comedy is more interesting:

Menander    > Aristophanes, Philemon

The two less common portraits of comic authors were *much* less common than Menander's. Typically one needed just one comic author, and when one needed more – two – the second could be either the second-ranked author of "new comedy", or the first-ranked author of "old comedy".

History presents a slight difference from the evidence of the papyri, but not a very surprising one:

Herodotus > Thucydides > Xenophon

The numbers are small, and yet this is in line with the impression we had already from the TLG cites (as well as from a closer consideration of the papyri fragments themselves), that Thucydides may have been less absolutely popular than the sheer number of his fragments suggests.

Consider next the case of rhetoric:

Demosthenes > Aeschines > Hyperides > Isocrates, Lysias, Protagoras

Once again, the numbers are not large. And yet we have one more reason to wonder whether the large number of Isocrates' papyri could not be to some extent a function of his educational role.

Lyric, with very small numbers distributed between many authors, mostly fails to replicate the evidence of the papyri (or, for that matter, of TLG cites):

Anacreon > Pindar, Alcaeus > Corinna, Posidippus, Timotheus, Bacchylides, Ibycus, Stesichorus

Probably Anacreon fitted well the iconographic program of sympotic sites. Otherwise, the relative frequency of Pindar and Alcaeus is based on tiny numbers – and yet is as we would have predicted (the absence of Sappho, though, is surprising; a statistical accident?). As for the rest, it is obvious that these lyric poets, to the mind of the Roman patrons commissioning their portraits, just did not break out of the pack. Perhaps they were typically framed in groups of several – maybe even many – poets; the emphasis would be on the variety of one's acquaintance with the lyric. We shall return to this point below, concerning the manner in which lyric poetry presented itself to its ancient audience.

The portraits represent 15 out of 17 authors in the first tier of the table on page 15 above, 11 out of 15 authors in the second tier. It is true that in some cases portraits are identified based on general assumptions concerning ancient popularity, so that the exercise is somewhat circular; but, while circular, it is also solid. Here, then, are the top missing author portraits (listed by 2011 papyrus counts):

| | |
|---|---|
| Callimachus | 83 |
| Apollonius | 52 |
| Sappho | 23 |
| Alcman | 15 |
| Aesop | 14[121] |
| Euphorion | 10 |

We recall the observation concerning TLG cites: the active elite commemoration of the canon tended to focus on its Athenian component. It does remain intriguing that Roman poets wrote their poetry "in the shadow of Callimachus" (to quote the title of Hunter, 2006) – yet only in a metaphorical sense. Once again, this may represent a certain over-representation of the Alexandrian poets among the papyri – or perhaps it may already direct us towards a more nuanced sense of the mental map that accompanied the canon. The Alexandrians have joined the canon – and yet, somehow, in a qualified sense; because, you see, they joined it when it was already formed.

The evidence of the TLG and of the portraits, taken together, tends to confirm the evidence of the papyri. It does suggest, however, that the position of the Alexandrian poets in the canon could have been qualified. More important, it underlines how poorly the papyri serve us in capturing the place of philosophy in the very top levels of metropolitan culture. An

---

[121] The absence of Aesop portraits (in the sense of marble statues) is somewhat surprising, as the visual possibilities are obvious; there might be a small trace of an iconographic tradition in other media (but even this is uncertain: Lissarrague, 2000). But, once again, here is a case in which sheer papyrus counts are misleading, as most of the Aesop fragments derive from the classroom.

important conclusion: the specialized genres (of which philosophy may have been supreme) did pursue a distinct trajectory from that of canonical literature.

### *1.3.4 The Codices and the Big Library*[122]

We have compared the papyri with the TLG – so, moving from Egypt into the Greek-speaking metropolitan centers of antiquity. We have compared them with the portraits – so, moving especially into the very elite, Imperial Roman reception of the Greek canon. Now we move to compare the papyri with the practices of narrow circles of elite Christian scholars and patrons, especially in Constantinople, mostly in the fifth to sixth centuries, and then in the ninth to tenth centuries (when the major process of codification took place, first in the transition to parchment and then in the transition to minuscule).[123] We consider the slaves of Roman Oxyrhynchus, carrying their baskets full of shredded papyri into the rubbish dump; and it turns out that their activity predicts very precisely that of the scholars of Byzantine palaces, half a millennium and more later. More precisely, it is dictated by two parameters: previous circulation, and genre. The more papyrus fragments an author has, the likelier he or she is to survive through the manuscript tradition; the more an author writes in prose (or, failing that, in hexameter), the likelier he is to survive. This suffices to account for the Byzantine selection of ancient works.

Of tier 1 (page 15), only one author is missing from the manuscript tradition:[124] this is the famous case of Menander. It is often said that Menander's reputation fell in Byzantine times relative to that of Aristophanes (e.g. Cribiore, 1996: 201). This contains only part of the truth, as the more significant story is that of the rise of Aristophanes rather than that of the decline of Menander. The latter was still very well stocked by late ancient libraries (I return to discuss this in Chapter 6, pages 770–1). In truth, the Byzantines did not do a fantastic job of transmitting Aristophanes, either: five early manuscripts, of which only one contains all the 11 plays we now possess.[125] Perhaps Menander just had worse luck with Byzantine fires. I would not be surprised were a minuscule palimpsest

---

[122] For the sake of this discussion, I use "codices" to mean "manuscript transmission".

[123] In what follows, I take the liberty of using "Byzantium" as a synecdoche of Greek-speaking medieval culture as a whole.

[124] I rely on the TLG canon of Greek authors, compiling a list of all authors marked by the field "[cod.]".

[125] Sommerstein (2010).

to surface – as it did recently for Hyperides, bringing this author, only in 2002, from the "papyrus, but not codex" column to the column of "papyrus, as well as codex".[126]

This brings us to tier 2. It is best considered together with tier 3, as the two show similar survival into codex: about 60 percent. The losses are:

| | |
|---|---|
| Alcaeus | Lyr. |
| Sappho | Lyr. |
| Archilochus | Lyr. |
| Alcman | Lyr. |
| Bacchylides | Lyr. |
| Euphorion | Ep. |
| Stesichorus | Lyr. |
| Epicharmus | Com. |
| Eupolis | Com. |
| Simonides | Lyr. |
| Anacreon | Lyr. |
| Antimachus (< Colophon) | Ep. |
| Hipponax | Lyr. |

The pattern is clear: a papyrus top-tier author who wrote in prose would always be preserved. Epic poetry would be preserved but, other than the case of Homer, this survival would be qualified (indeed, even Hesiod did not have all his works transmitted). Drama was even more precarious and lyric was entirely lost. Several poets do survive from the Hellenistic era, but in the case of Callimachus, in particular, this is through a restricted and disappointing selection (only the hymns). Apollonius and Aratus are better preserved – but this is because they were known, already in antiquity, almost entirely on the basis of a single work each. So we find, once again, that the preservation of the Hellenistic poets is qualified. But I pause to note immediately that the survival of Hellenistic poetry into the manuscript tradition, while qualified, is in fact very remarkable given the evidence of the TLG citations and the Roman statues. We see a clash: papyrus counts, traditional interpretations of Latin poetry and, now, survival into manuscript all suggest that the major Hellenistic poets enjoyed a canonical status; TLG citations as well as (the absence of) portraits suggest they didn't. Perhaps we need to distrust some of our evidence, but the likeliest account is that canonicity, in this case, actually carried a different meaning. In this case, the key works became canonical, but not so

---

[126] See Tchernetska (2002). Menander does have two parchment palimpsests, both, however, early majuscule: LDAB 2713, 10072. Their upper text is from the eighth to ninth centuries, so we know that his texts survived until that date at least.

much their authors, because they reached their canonicity on the strength of their allusion to past, canonical masters. Hence the *Phaenomena* and the *Argonautica* were collected, alluded to, preserved; but their authors did not become powerful cultural currencies, on par with the Athenian masters.

Moving below tier 3, the rate of survival at first glance appears to be surprisingly stable. Tier 4 has preserved 23 out of 43 authors; tier 5 has preserved 32 out of 76 authors. The overall pattern is (percentages rounded to the nearest five):

| | Byzantine survival |
|---|---|
| Tier 1 | 95% |
| Tier 2 | 60% |
| Tier 3 | 60% |
| Tier 4 | 60% |
| Tier 5 | 40% |

There is a sharp drop between tier 1 and 2, but tiers 2, 3 and 4 are (statistically speaking) identical and even tier 5 does not yet get into free fall. This masks a compositional effect, however. The top tiers are more poetry-heavy, so that we would have predicted higher losses; the lower circulation of tier 4 is cancelled out by its prose contents, so that it ends up surviving equally as well as tier 3. And so it continues: tier 4 loses 13 out of 22 poets, tier 5 loses 13 of its 15 poets – keeping, that is, only the late ancient poets Pamprepius and Nonnus.

Perhaps the most remarkable point in all this is that, in fact, *all* prose authors of tiers 1 to 3 ended up on Byzantine manuscripts. A prose author? No problem, then: to put this in slogan form – collect five papyrus fragments and you're guaranteed a Teubner edition. (We are grateful for the Hyperides find, then, which allows us to see the power of this generalization.) Tiers 4 and 5 do differ from tiers 1 to 3 in that they lose *some* prose authors. Once again, the drop is not dramatic: in tier 4, 14 prose authors are preserved out of 21 (65 percent survival); in tier 5, 30 out of 61 (50 percent survival). The precise percentages are misleading as they are to a large extent a reflection of our ignorance regarding adespota, but the relative frequency is significant: the greater the number of papyrus fragments, the smaller the chances of Byzantine survival, the correlation holding all the way down.

In short, it is clear that the Byzantine pagan canon was a subset of the ancient canon. It is also clear that this subset was informed by Byzantine

preferences in terms of genre. But it appears to have been a subset of
precisely the same ancient canon we have seen so far – *preserving the same
papyrus ranking.*

It is worth pursuing this comparison further. We consider the fraction of
the papyri authors who survive on codex, and note the strong correlation
between papyrus fragments and survival. But what about ancient authors
found on codex who are *not* represented among the papyri? What do they
correlate with? Do they represent, in some sense, a literary culture which
the evidence of the papyrus ignores?

I count 173 authors extant on codex but not on papyrus: the size of this
database is promising. The chronological breakdown is as follows.

| | |
|---|---|
| Classical | 10 |
| Hellenistic (3rd–2nd centuries BCE) | 21 |
| 1st century BCE[127] | 11 |
| Roman era[128] | 81 |
| Late ancient | 45 |

This, once again, is promising: had the list been dominated by late
antiquity, the interpretation would be that codex-but-not-papyrus authors
are those who came *too late for papyrus.* But most of the authors preserved on
codex but not on papyrus are from the Roman era, and the papyri have only
themselves to blame for not keeping such authors. Indeed, it is helpful to
ignore the late ancient authors and consider the generic breakdown of the
remaining authors: just which *kind* of authors did the papyri not represent?
I break the list of codex-but-not-papyrus down into two categories of genres:
those atypical among the papyrus canon, and those typical among it.

| Genres atypical to papyrus | | Genres typical to papyrus | |
|---|---|---|---|
| Grammar | 25 | Rhetoric | 21 |
| Technical | 23 | History | 9 |
| Mathematics | 20 | Novel | 1 |
| Philosophy | 18 | | |
| Medicine[129] | 9 | | |

---

[127] I see this century as belonging more to the Roman era (it includes, for instance, Dionysius of
Halicarnassus), but in deference to the standard periodization I count it separately.
[128] I include the TLG category "3rd century", exclude "3rd–4th century" and beyond. Since our
papyrus evidence drops at about the end of the third century, and since there was a certain delay in
entry into the papyrus evidence (see p. 55 above), authors straddling the centuries are to be excluded.
[129] The number of medical codex-only authors is very small; they are crowded out as a consequence of
the decision made to preserve a monumental amount of the works of Galen.

The only belletristic author extant on codex but *not* on papyrus is the novelist Longus. This is extraordinary, as the numbers involved in such attestations are so small – often no more than one or two papyrus fragments. In all likelihood, then, Longus, too, "should" have had papyrus fragments by now and, instead of, say, three, he has zero because of sheer randomness. The likely conclusion of this tight correlation is that the only way a belletristic author could survive into manuscript form is if he were extremely popular in antiquity itself.

Within the codex-but-not-papyrus subset, Greek literature was essentially written in prose alone. Of the "typical" papyrus genres, history and rhetoric are perhaps "normally" represented: these are such authors as Dionysius of Halicarnassus, Cassius Dio, Diogenes Laertius, Herodes Atticus, Philostratus. . . This is the "Second Sophistic" in its widest sense: was it perhaps less frequent on papyrus? Mostly, too late. (But also: such authors did not get ranked as uniquely canonical, for their ancient audiences, as did those of an earlier age. Even those who were no doubt a sensation in their own lifetime may not have been enduring – as noted already, on page 55, n.98, above, for the novel.) But beyond that is a system of genres very foreign to the world of papyrus, entirely dominated by theoretical or, indeed, technical works. So was this perhaps the "metropolitan" taste, different from that of provincial Egypt?

This conclusion is perhaps not entirely wrong: the theoretical genres must have been better represented in big libraries, which must have been more common in the real centers. But, methodologically, we are still making the wrong comparison. We set side by side the codex-only authors, and the papyrus authors. But by "the papyrus authors" we do not really mean "the authors who circulated as Egyptian papyri". We mean "the authors identified so far among the excavated papyri", which actually means something like "the top 168 authors among all those who circulated as Egyptian papyri" (this is a simplification, but it is not far off the mark and it brings the point home). But we should not compare the codex-only authors with the top 168 authors. We should compare them with the papyrus authors *further down*. We are looking at 129 codex-only authors of the relevant eras, and so our comparison should be, as a first approximation, with the authors ranked numbers 169 to 297 among all those who circulated as Egyptian papyri. But wait: we found that the Byzantine selection removed essentially all poetry at that level (and there would have been *some* poetry among the papyri, at this level). Thus we are looking at something rather like the prose authors ranked 169 to 320 among all those who circulated as Egyptian papyri. But wait again: we noticed that the tendency to preserve a prose author declined somewhat as one went down the papyrus count, from 71 percent at tier 4 to 49 percent at tier 5; here, at tiers 6 and 7, it would be lower still. Maybe a third of the prose authors should be represented, likely fewer. We find, then, that we are looking at the prose authors ranked roughly 169 to 600 or beyond, among all those who circulated as Egyptian papyri. Could those authors have been in some ways comparable with the codex-only authors?

We need to compare the codex-only authors with tiers "6, 7 and below" of the list of authors extant on papyri – the list that we would have had *had all papyri survived*. And so, in the following table, I consider the same numbers as above, now as percentages, considering only prose works. The codex-only authors are compared with the prose authors before late antiquity from tiers 4 and 5. And, if we assume that "codex-only" authors are similar to "tiers 6, 7 and below" authors, we should expect to see a continuity, in the transition from tier 4 to 5, to 6 and beyond.

In the table below, I look at the generic composition of the following three categories.

**Tier 4 (excluding late antiquity), tier 5 (excluding late antiquity), codex-but-not-papyrus authors (excluding late antiquity)**

| Tier 4   N = 22 | | Tier 5   N = 54 | | Codex-only   N = 127 | |
|---|---|---|---|---|---|
| Gram. 23% | Rhet. 23% | Gram. 19% | Rhet. 13% | Gram. 20% | Rhet. 16% |
| Tech. 5% | Hist. 18% | Tech. 9% | Hist. 20% | Tech. 18% | Hist. 7% |
| Math. 0% | Novel 14% | Math. 4% | Novel 2% | Math. 16% | Novel 1% |
| Phil. 14% | | Phil. 28% | | Phil. 14% | |
| Med. 5% | | Med. 6% | | Med. 7% | |
| Total 45% | Total 55% | Total 65% | Total 35% | Total 76% | Total 24% |

The continuity is remarkable. If we were to try to extrapolate the codex authors as "tiers 6 and 7", working mechanically from tiers 4 and 5, we would not be too far off the mark: we would have predicted correctly the genre clusters – that is, we would have expected the lower tiers to be dominated by theoretical and even technical works. We would be surprised to see that the "literary" genre best represented was not history (as tiers 4 and 5 would have us expect) but, rather, rhetoric; we would be delighted to discover that, among the "theoretical/technical" genres, mathematics was heavily represented (disappointed, however, that philosophy was less so).

These surprises are not meaningless. It is clear that the ancient literary universe was populated by many obscure historians, providing rich regional and anecdotal variety: the stuff that fills Jacoby (more on this in Chapter 5, pages 598–604). Such literature had mere local interest. It probably did circulate in Egypt in small numbers, and so Jacoby must have been heavily represented among the papyrus authors ranked 169 to 600. It is not so surprising that this literature disappeared from Byzantium. As for the comparison between mathematics and philosophy, this may once again be a real feature of the evidence: it could be that the Nile Valley simply did not possess mathematical works, which circulated almost entirely in a few metropolitan centers. Even more: it is possible that the large-scale collection of mathematical authors was much more common in Byzantium than it was in earlier metropolitan centers, as a reflex of Neoplatonist habits in late antiquity.

But the key observation is that, in its overall generic composition, we see traces that suggest that the big library of the Nile Valley was not entirely unlike those big libraries of Constantinople, out of which emerged our manuscript tradition. The precise *choice of authors within genres* may have changed, and the emphasis shifted as well from genre to genre, but overall, it appears, the basic nature of a big library was, once again, fairly stable.

We do, in fact, get a glimpse of the Egyptian big library via the (few) extant catalogues: 19 papyri fragments of library catalogues or requests for books, collected in Otranto (2000).[130] The catalogue or request for a book is a bibliophile, scholarly act and it suggests an exceptionally well-stocked library (one does not bother with producing a book catalogue only so as to write "Homer's *Iliad*, Homer's *Odyssey*"). Indeed, Homer is mentioned directly in only two of the catalogues. One (Otranto 2000: 90–1; 16 in Otranto's list) is a fairly complete survey of the collected works of Plato and of Xenophon, followed by a mention by name only of four authors – Homer, Menander, Euripides and Aristophanes – at which point the roll becomes illegible (but would it present any major surprises?). The other (Otranto 2000: 10; 3 in Otranto's list) is a more detailed catalogue of rolls by the authors: Homer, Callimachus, Pindar, Hesiod, Aeschines and Demosthenes, with a few other names illegible, impossible to identify ("Dionysius" – of whom there are so many) and tantalizing ("Aelian" – is this the correct reading? Who is the reference, in the date of the papyrus, the middle of the first century CE?). Homer also appears in the more scholarly context of commentary: Otranto, 2000: 108 (18 in Otranto's list),

---

[130] For a recent discussion of this body of evidence, see Houston (2009). Papyri may be compared, in this case, with epigraphic finds: pinakes in Taurmina, detailing works by relatively rare historians and perhaps a philosopher (Philistus, Callisthenes, Fabius Pictor, and then Anaximander [!]; see Battistoni, 2006).

lists commentaries by Callimachus; to Aeschines, Demosthenes and Homer's *Iliad*; by Callinicus; and then historical works by Herodotus, Xenophon, Aristotle (Ath. Pol.), Thucydides and – once again – Callinicus (which one?). A list of more grammatical works, perhaps, used for the reading of the *Iliad* and of Plato, as well as Priscus and Rufus (?) – perhaps commentators rather than poets? – is in Otranto (2000: 73–4) (14 in Otranto's list).

We mostly see tier 1 authors so far, though perhaps glanced from its more erudite grammarians. Other book catalogues are richer. Seven, in particular, detail erudition related to drama.[131] The remaining four catalogues, remarkably, are more "theoretical/technical", and primarily philosophical. Let us consider them in more detail.

Four is a private letter (Otranto, 2000: 18) that originally accompanied a package with works by Metrodorus, Epicurus and perhaps others. Five is a very well preserved letter sent by Theon, in Alexandria, to Heraclides "the philosopher" (from Oxyrhynchus, probably, where the papyrus was dug up). The letter accompanied works by well-known Stoic authors: Boethus, Diogenes, Chrysippus, Antipater and Posidonius. This is all tier 5 or, let us say, tier 6. None is extant through the manuscript tradition; all belong to a genre which is reasonably represented in the manuscript tradition.

Otranto's number 17 (2000: 98–9), from third-century CE Arsinoe, is a fragment from a larger catalogue that apparently made various counts of the numbers of rolls in the collection: the biggest number, 296, is legible in line 28 and appears to be some interim summation. The entire library could well include thousands of rolls. The few names that survive fall into two sections, the first appearing to be philosophical, the second medical: (1) Geminus, Diogenes of Babylon, some "Socratic", then authors from Tarsus and Citium followed by Hierocles, Glaucon (?), Xenophon and Chrysippus; (2) Thessalus, Erasistratus, Themison, Harpocration. This appears to be, then, a large library including, inter alia, philosophy of a Stoic flavor[132] alongside medical works. Perhaps we see here an example of the library of an elite medical practitioner? Once again, excluding the canonical Xenophon, all these authors are no longer extant, though their genres are.

---

[131] These are Otranto (2000) 2, 6, 7, 8, 9, 10 and 11.

[132] There is some debate in the literature concerning Geminus' intellectual profile: more of a scientist or a philosopher? If the latter, how much of a Stoic? This papyrus has not, to my knowledge, been brought to bear on this question; it adds some probability to the traditional view that he was, indeed, a Stoic philosopher (this question will interest us again on page 467 below).

Otranto's number 15 (2000: 80–1) is perhaps the most remarkable catalogue of all. Excavated in Memphis and dated once again to the third century CE, this catalogue refers to (quoting only identifiable works):

- Socratic letters
- Aristotle, "On *Aretē*"
- Posidonius, from "On Anger"
- Elements of Medicine by Theodas (an empiricist)
- Theophrastus, "On Sophrosyne"
- Dio of Prusa, "On Distrust"
- Aristotle, Ath. Pol.
- Socratic works (dialogues?) by Crito, Simon and Cebes
- Nigrinus, *Apology*[133]
- Diogenes (of Babylon? If so, a Stoic), "On Freedom from Pain"
- Chrysippus, a logical work
- Aristotle, *Constitution of the Athenians*

At this point the relatively well reconstructed section of the papyrus ends and we are left with mere names and fragments, such as "Apion" "Theophr-" (this would have to be Theophrastus – right?), "Hippias", "Diogen-", "Aeli-", "Eukri-", "Archim-", "Chrysip-" (so Chrysippus, again) and "Aristo-" (Tle?).

The confirmed impression is of a very well stocked – indeed, ecumenical – philosophical library (though perhaps avoiding Epicurean works?). We even see a little bit of science showing through: a medical work and also, stunningly, an "Archim-" that one is sorely tempted to reconstruct as "Archimedes" – the only mention of Archimedes in the evidence of the papyri. For a moment, we reach the point, at the circulation of papyri, where even advanced mathematics is represented. Indeed, we also see here a few more extant authors! Swamped, however, by those we have lost.

Byzantium was like this but much more. That is: the fundamental fact of the codex survival is that it contains *so many authors*. Classicists do not normally feel this way but what must be realized is that Byzantium, taken as a whole, must have collected many more authors than almost any single library did in antiquity. And it achieved this with far fewer total books, dedicated to pagan literature, than circulated in antiquity itself. In other words, Byzantium was a *leveler*. We saw throughout this chapter the

---

[133] Probably two works, both by Lucian? We consider them "belletristic", but would this library take Lucian as a philosopher/sophist?

dramatic gap between the top authors and the more minor ones, the top authors (even putting Homer aside) being more frequent (by two orders of magnitude?)[134] than even the relatively frequent, yet not quite canonical, authors. In Byzantium, a pagan author could have more manuscripts, or fewer, but the range was always the same: a few. It acted, in other words, rather like an ideal-type big library. Which is precisely the way we need to conceive of the transmission of classical literature via the manuscript transmission: it was the distillation of the ancient literary sphere, originally divided into many libraries of varying size, via a smaller set of (mostly) big libraries. It thus reflected Alexandria more closely than it did Oxyrhynchus. But the two, we find, would not be unrelated. To be precise: among the canonical authors, Byzantium chose precisely the same authors as did earlier antiquity. Below the canon, Byzantium preserved the same genres (with some shifts of emphasis) but was not committed to the same ranking of authors; naturally enough as, indeed, outside the canon, by definition, such rankings would have been less rigid.

This bears repeating, as the point is not widely recognized. When we note that "Byzantium did not differ from the world of papyrus" we mean two different things. We mean that it collected *the same authors*, at the top tiers (i.e. in the literary canon); and that it collected *the same genres*, at roughly the same propositions, in lower tiers (i.e. in specialized genres). The ranking of the authors was established within the literary canon but less so within the specialized genres. This carries a very weighty conse-quence: there was room left for post-classical authors to emerge and dominate the later tradition – a Euclid, a Ptolemy, a Galen, a Proclus. The literary canon was homogeneous; the specialized genres were not. Everywhere, throughout the history of Greek antiquity, at all levels of its reception, the same literary authors were read according to the same ranking of their reputations. But the specialized genres were – well, specialized: this or that genre being more or less popular at different times and places; the reputations of the authors in genuine contest. Which underlines the stability of the literary canon itself: it is not as if the Greeks adopted the notion that a literary system, as such, has to be stably ranked. They stably ranked one system – the performative one – and this alone, but not others; until, that is, late antiquity, a point to which we shall return in Part III.

---

[134] In the table on pp. 20–4 above, Hesiod's *Theogony* circulates at 5.75 when Plato and Xenophon are at 0.15: 40 times more! So would the *Theogony* have been more frequent by two orders of magnitudes than, say, tier 3?

## 1.4  Adjusting the Sample

Our sample is, in many ways, reliable. Even so, it should certainly not be taken as a *direct* measure of the distribution of papyri in antiquity. To consider this distribution, we need to bring in four adjustments, each bringing in its own uncertainty.

First, we need to bring in the papyrus adespota – mentioned only in passing so far – so as to get a more realistic sense of the sample itself.

Second, we need to consider the selection bias of the sample relative to papyri in the Egyptian chora. Papyri, as noted on several occasions already, were not all equally discarded, and we should consider the effect this could have had on the relative frequency of papyri in circulation.

Third, we need to consider the variation between the Egyptian chora and the Mediterranean as a whole. We have emphasized throughout the continuities between Egyptian papyri and other sources of evidence; but we did note some potential discrepancies, and these should be brought in as well.

Fourth, we need to address explicitly the limitations of extrapolation from a sample. Even with a perfect sample, statistical error must be present.

The next section deals with the adespota; adjustments two and four are then taken by the following section. (I leave aside adjustment three, for which I have, so to speak, already exhausted the arsenal of evidence; I return to it, in a qualified sense, in Chapter 5. While we cannot add much more on the direct evidence for the Mediterranean distribution of *books*, there is certainly much more evidence on the Mediterranean distribution of *authors*.)

### 1.4.1  Bringing in the Adespota

The methodology of section 1.3.4 above hides a difficulty. I compared the authors extant through the manuscript tradition, but not identified on papyrus, to the authors rarely identified on papyrus. Throughout, I used "identified on papyrus" as no different from "extant on papyrus", but this is wrong in a significant way: authors are often identified on papyrus *because* they are extant through both papyrus and the manuscript tradition (the tradition providing the basis for the identification).

This criticism has some truth in it, but it has to be qualified. First of all, many of our identifications are based on ancient fragments and testimonies rather than full, direct manuscript transmission.[135] Second, the fact remains that a very substantial fraction of the excavated literary papyri are indeed identified: the group of actual adespota is, in some sense, not that large.

We may consider the case of the fragments that would have been identified with or without being attested through the manuscript transmission. These are the fragments that contain a title. Caroli (2007) lists all the external and initial titles extant on papyri, and surveys less systematically the extant final subscriptions or "colophons".[136] With a few additions, the list has 61 titles.[137] It is not without interest, then, to consider the division of those titles by tiers, as follows.[138]

[135] The following example involves a parchment manuscript being identified, but it is structurally similar to many papyrus identifications and is worth retelling as a spectacular piece of recent scholarship – to which I was eyewitness! In 2002 Natalie Tchernetska recognized several leaves in the Archimedes Palimpsest as coming from speeches by Hyperides, thanks to the fact that a very small legible sequence was nearly identical with the small Hyperides fragment 164, preserved in the *Suda* (Tchernetska, 2005: 1).

[136] Caroli's survey is motivated by an interest in ancient library practices, hence the emphasis put on initial and external titles (which would be more visible to the user) and the mere passing note of subscriptions, surveyed in Caroli (2007: 59–60).

[137] Caroli's list has 16 legible external notes (written directly on the outside of the roll, or attached as an etiquette), and 16 legible internal, initial titles. One should add Cribiore (1996: 246, entry 301); this is a papyrus with a school exercise copying Euripidean material, expressly so titled, and so, by our methodology, this indeed is a case when we would have identified the text even without a transmitted parallel (which in fact is not extant). Caroli also surveys 26 subscriptions; I have also noted through my leafing through the papyrological records two titles not noted by Caroli: P. Monac. 2.23 (inv. 339), Heliodorus; and P.Ant. 1.28, Hippocrates. Doubtless there are more, though not many more. The 61 extant titles represent about 1 percent, a reasonable survival rate when we consider an overall survival rate on average of 4 percent of the bulk of the roll, and that the external parts of rolls would have been the first to deteriorate; but, even more likely, not all rolls carried external titles (the use of such titles reserved to the somewhat bigger collections: if your entire library is constituted by a single roll of the *Iliad*, you will not attach to it an identifying mark).

[138] A word on methodology. Statistics manuals will tell you that the margin of error on a sample as small as 61 is very large, 12 percent or more, which means that a number such as 12 tier 5 papyri, or 20 percent, means, in this sense, a range of 8 to 32 percent. But margins of error are relative to confidence levels, and the default calculation is for a confidence level of 95 percent (it is 95 percent likely that the result falls within this range). This confidence level should be taken as a normative tool within science: it acts to define the minimal size of scientific experiments when population size is constrained by the scientists' resources. It thus tells scientists how to allocate their resources. We do not have such freedom to choose our sample size, and for this reason we are constrained to use lower confidence levels. A sample size of 61 generates quite precise results at the confidence level of 75 percent, which can be translated to mean "suggestive, but not demonstrative".

|  | Extant titles | Total pap. fragments, from table on pages 15–18 above (2011 numbers) |
|---|---|---|
| Tier 1 | 29 | 3,241 |
| Tier 2 | 11[139] | 234 |
| Tier 3 | 4 | 96 |
| Tier 4 | 5 | 126 |
| Tier 5[140] | 12 | 76 |

The column of extant titles seems to have somewhat surprisingly few found in tier 1, and significantly surprisingly many in tier 5. This is for several reasons. First, the extant titles display a certain bias to rare authors.[141] Second, the fraction of tier 1 authors in the papyrus evidence as a whole is definitely somewhat exaggerated by school use, especially in the case of Homer. Third, consideration of the adespota would indeed bring in more minor authors.

To the statistician of papyri, the adespota are a scary notion. At first glance, they are a large mass of some 3,000 fragments (almost as many as the identified fragments we have studied so far!), the lot being rather chaotically catalogued by Mertens–Pack and, subsequently, by CEDOPAL and LDAB. Who knows what we may find there?

Here, then, is what I set myself to do: to go through the list, genre by genre, and consider the probable distributions of the fragments in each, even absent a clear identification of each individual fragment. The exercise is extremely conjectural, but it is better, I believe, to have explicit numerical guesstimates than some vague qualitative statements. The following tables, then, attempt an impressionistic classification of the adespota according to the following categories. Let me explain my methodology, such as it is. Through my repeated searches through

---

[139] It is probably sheer accident that we have three titles by Sappho. Note, however, that very short rolls make it more likely that a survival might include a title, and that the division of her work into nine rolls (obviously a forced number, to stand for the nine muses) could well have meant fewer words per roll. If so, the 5,000 words of her fragments could well represent something like a quarter of her output known to antiquity.

[140] Tier 5 in this case really means "tier 5 and below", since a roll with a named title (and all titles are named) is automatically an identified author roll.

[141] Sixteen of the extant titles are external marks, written on the roll itself or attached as an etiquette; this practice seems to be associated with libraries with more advanced cataloguing (and thus more comparable to the book catalogues considered in the preceding section). From this category, we have: (Tier 1) Demosthenes, Aristophanes, Menander, Pindar; (2) Alcaeus, Stesichorus, Bacchylides; (3) Eupolis, Simonides; (4) Tryphon, Sophron; (5) Sosylus, Theopompus, Hermarchus, Olympius, Posidippus the Comic author. Note the frequency of tiers 4 to 5, as well as the absence of Homer.

CEDOPAL I got some working familiarity with the distribution of the papyrus evidence as a whole. Over several days I went through the listing more systematically, reading all the entries on the adespota and forming a rough guess concerning their nature. It would obviously take a few years' work (a dissertation, anyone?) to produce this kind of study in a scientific way, reading all the adespota together with their secondary literature and classifying them according to precise criteria; and it is likely that such a scientific study will obtain different results from mine. But note that the purpose of my guesses was not to establish, for each papyrus, to which category it belonged but, rather, to develop a sense of the range of likelihoods that a given papyrus of a certain type would belong to a certain category. At this level, I believe, the guesstimates are not *that* hard to establish. And so, to the guesses.

My main object was to classify adespota into the following categories.

1. <u>School texts</u>: texts produced by pupils, or for use by pupils, at various educational levels.
2. <u>Ad hoc private compilations</u>: this includes such objects as musical scores used by musicians, tables used by astrologers, etc. The fundamental feature of this group is that the piece of papyrus in question is not seen to be due to an "author" at all (those are, as it were, the private *documents* – of such individuals whose professional life engaged with literate culture).
3. <u>Unidentified canonical works</u>: some adespota are not yet assigned to a canonical author (this term is no more than shorthand for the "authors in tiers 1 to 3 from the table on pages 15–18 above", and does not involve any assumptions about relative frequency). This would most typically come about because such fragments derive from an unknown work by a known author (many of the adespota are tiny, difficult fragments, however, and it is possible that they have simply not been properly deciphered yet). By far the most significant case here is that of Menander (more below).
4. <u>Occasional literature</u>: sometimes literary works get written down, but are not understood to become part of circulated literature. They are, instead, locally used. It seems that a small but meaningful number of papyri fragments, especially poetic, are of this category.
5–6. <u>Minor prose and poetry</u>: these are the remaining true literary adespota. These are works by authors other than those of the first through third tiers of the table on pages 15–18 above.

For the following set of tables, I slightly rearranged CEDOPAL's categories.[142] Each row is a CEDOPAL category or cluster of categories. For each such row, I produce a guesstimate as to the division of this row in terms of my six categories above.

I arrange the rows or CEDOPAL categories into several groups, based on their similar character. This is strictly my own grouping. Finally, note that my numbers are stylized and rounded throughout.

*Mostly school*

| | School | Ad hoc | Canon | Occasional literature | Minor prose | Minor poetry | Total |
|---|---|---|---|---|---|---|---|
| Beginners poetry[143] | 90 | | | 9 | | 10 | 109 |
| School exercise | 406 | | | | | | 406 |
| Math/metrology | 120 | 14 | | | 3 | | 137 |
| Grammar/ scholarship[144] | 120 | 15 | 5 | | 47 | | 187 |
| Oratory | 40 | 15 | 18 | 10 | 15 | | 98 |
| Tachygraphy | 70 | 10 | | | 1 | | 81 |
| Total | 846 | 54 | 23 | 19 | 66 | 10 | |

*Mostly ad hoc, private compilation*

| | School | Ad hoc | Canon | Occasional literature | Minor prose | Minor poetry | Total |
|---|---|---|---|---|---|---|---|
| Magic[145] | | 25 | | | 4 | | 29 |
| Artists' tools[146] | | 50 | 3 | | | | 53 |
| Astronomy | 20 | 200 | | | 27 | | 247 |
| Law | 10 | 30 | | | 8 | | 48 |
| Myth/religion[147] | | 80 | | | 23 | | 103 |
| Medicine | 30 | 130 | | | 98 | | 258 |
| Total | 60 | 515 | 3 | | 160 | | |

[142] Among CEDOPAL's categories, I suppressed: the category "parody", one item entering "grammar/ scholarship", the other "school exercises"; and also the category "catalogues" (very interesting, but documents). I also lumped together several closely related categories, each case explained individually.

[143] Anthology, fable/gnomic poetry; minus the "Anthologia Graeca" author field.

[144] Glossary/grammar, metric, criticism/rhetoric.

[145] Alchemy, divination. There are many more strict magical papyri in the sense of actual spells (Betz, 1992, is a translation). These are rightly not included among literary papyri.

[146] Music, illustrations (effectively, all unidentified illustrated papyrus are in fact illustrations not accompanied by text: not illustrated works, then, but artists' notebooks).

[147] These are mostly religious documents, rather than literary texts of a religious content.

*Prose*

| | School | Ad hoc | Canon | Occasional literature | Minor prose | Minor poetry | Total |
|---|---|---|---|---|---|---|---|
| Philosophy | 20 | 5 | 2 | | 87 | | 104 |
| History[148] | 5 | 5 | 5 | 10 | 146 | | 171 |
| Various prose[149] | 10 | 5 | | 2 | 20 | | 37 |
| Practical arts[150] | | 5 | | 2 | 5 | | 12 |
| Novel | | | | 4 | 45 | | |
| Unidentified prose[151] | 30 | 30 | 100 | 10 | 180 | 10 | 360 |
| Total | 65 | 50 | 107 | 28 | 483[152] | 10 | |

*Poetry*

| | School | Ad hoc | Canon | Occasional literature | Minor prose | Minor poetry | Total |
|---|---|---|---|---|---|---|---|
| Comedy and mime | 30 | 5 | 70 | 5 | | 38 | 148 |
| Tragedy and satyr[153] | 10 | 1 | 40 | | | 20 | 71 |
| Lyric[154] | 10 | | 40 | 20 | | 38 | 108 |
| Unidentified verse | 20 | 5 | 40 | 20 | | 36 | 121 |
| Elegy/epigram | 7 | | 5 | 10 | | 15 | 37 |
| Hexameter | 20 | 3 | 20 | 40 | | 75 | 158 |
| Total | 97 | 14 | 215[155] | 95 | | 222 | |

[148] Including geography and biography.     [149] Anthology, dialogue, epistolography.

[150] Combining agriculture, botany/zoology, hunt and cuisine.

[151] The most difficult category, these are mostly fragments that are too small or too hard to identify; some are certain to be misidentified and to be in fact poetry; quite a few might be documents after all.

[152] This column is significant. It is relatively large, because Byzantium was so zealous in maintaining the ancient prose canon that there are few slots for the admission of hitherto unidentified prose fragments.

[153] Satyr is rare to non-existent.

[154] Quite a few of the lyric fragments could be choral, hence perhaps dramatic; perhaps my count is overgenerous for "minor poetry", in this sense.

[155] Adespota poetry, unlike prose, has plenty of slots to fit in the canon. My impression is that editors, impressed by the adespotic character of a work and the sense that "there was so much lost!", often tend to err on the side of exoticism. I wonder if the probabilities are taken into considerations strongly enough. If we have identified over 100 fragments of Menander, and only a handful of all other new comedy authors taken together, the probability must be overwhelming that a given unidentified new comedy fragment was in fact by Menander. A somewhat weaker case can then be made for the other poetic genres, with the important caveat that unidentified epic cannot be by Homer!

The grand totals are as follows.

School: 1,068
Ad hoc: 633
Otherwise unidentified fragments by authors from tiers 1 to 3: 345
Occasional literature: 145
Minor prose: 709
Minor poetry: 242

Truly, the main thrust of this exercise is the observation (which is in fact fairly obvious) that Mertens–Pack tends to err on the side of generosity, counting as "literary" papyri many semi-literary or simply documentary artifacts. It is especially this observation that limits the statistical impact of adespota papyri.

   Following this exercise, then, we find that we have (2011 numbers) 3,926 fragments belonging to tiers 1 to 3, and 1,153 belonging to tiers 4 to 5 "and below". This comes to much better agreement with the evidence of the titles, where we have 44 titles to works from tiers 1 to 3, and 17 to works from tiers 4 to 5. If we think of tiers 1 to 3 as canonical, we have:

| | | | |
|---|---|---|---|
| Fragments (with adespota) | Canonical 77% | Other 23% |
| Titles | Canonical 72% | Other 28% |

Or, put conversely: it is helpful to find that the set of guesstimates provided in the tables above adds up to a number of fragments by minor authors that largely coincides with the evidence from the titles. Small as this sample is, it serves as heuristic corroboration.

   If we erred, it was perhaps on the side of assuming too *many* adespota, particularly in poetry. The argument derives from the consideration of annotated adespota. From McNamee (2007: 525–9) I count the number of annotated adespota, which I put side by side with my guesstimate above:[156]

| Genre | Annotated adespota | Guesstimate of minor authors in the adespota |
|---|---|---|
| Comedy | 7 | 38 |
| Tragedy | 2 | 20 |
| Hexameter | 10 | 75 |
| Lyric | 8 | 91 |

---

[156] I count only poetry, excluding Latin, writing exercises, magical texts and anthologies. The Pack numbers are: comedy (including mime): 1625, 1628, 1629, 1631, 1638.2, 1645, 1745; tragedy (including satyr): 1739.1, 2463.3; hexameter: 1800.2, 1837.3, 1840, 1846, 1857.3, 1874, 1957.1, 1957.5, 1962, one uncatalogued; lyric: 1846, 1890, 1892, 1903, 1949.3, 2861.21, 2867, one uncatalogued.

The guesstimate above is tantamount, we find, to the assumption that, among our adespota, about 10 percent of the papyri of minor poets are annotated. But, extrapolating from the discussion on pages 49–50 above, we should expect some 20 to 40 percent of the papyri of minor poets to be annotated. To some extent, this may be due to the presence of post-Callimachean poetry (a class of literature which we see very little, which will tend to remain adespota and which probably indeed did not attract annotation). But, at the very least, the evidence of annotated adespota suggests that our guesstimates for minor poetry among the adespota are on the high side.

At most, then, roughly 950 minor authors – perhaps even fewer – among the adespota: a very meaningful category, but not the scary mass of little-understood 3,000 fragments we started with. Let us pause to consider, then, how precisely the addition of the adespota fits in within the interpretation of the fragments offered so far in this chapter. I consider the consequences as we go down the canon.

First, Menander. It is clear that the number presented for him in the table on page 15 above – 105 fragments – is a serious underestimate. His real number must come much closer to the numbers for the two top authors below Homer, Demosthenes (204) and Euripides (169); I would not find it shocking if we were to find that Menander's fragments are, in fact, the most numerous immediately following Homer. This result makes the incidence of his Roman portraits easier to understand, that of his TLG cites more difficult.

Was Menander the second most frequent author? Only if we do not assign more papyri to Euripides. There are far fewer tragic adespota, but a few must be by Euripides. These will not change the overall impression of his significance but will underline its extreme width: we need to consider the tragic adespota, to estimate how many of Euripides' fragments derive from his non-transmitted plays.

No more than a handful of fragments appear to derive from the cyclic epic poems (that there are no annotated adespota epic papyri is decisive). Perhaps there are a few more of Hesiod's catalogue; but the bulk of the poetry that remains to be assigned to the canonical authors would be divided between the Hellenistic and archaic poets. The papyri probably transmit a more varied picture of the major Hellenistic poets than comes through their identified fragments (indeed, there could even be fragments of their scholarly prose); likely, more of Callimachus' epic is yet unidentified. As for archaic poetry, there surely is some more hidden in the adespota. But there is no special reason to believe this should be mostly from such lyric poets as correspond to the frequencies established at the moment. The numbers, in this case, are too small, the ratios too equal, to support such assumptions. All we can say is that we need to treat the ranking of lyric poets with added caution.

It is intriguing to speculate on the identity of dark horses, waiting in the adespotic wings, ready to storm into the top tiers. There is in fact one very striking case, that of the Acta Alexandrinorum. This prose work had, in 2011, 39 counts by CEDOPAL; Harker (2008: 179–211) has a more expansive category of "Acta Alexandrinorum and related literature", under which he files 73 (!) fragments. As the numbers suggest, this is not so much a single work but an entire genre. Harker (2008: 78) suggests that we should refer to them as "the Alexandrian Stories". This is a special Egyptian take on the genre of the novel as a whole. It is Alexandria in the years 38 to 41 CE, and upright Greek citizens try to stand up against the wickedness of their Jewish neighbors. An embassy is sent to Rome, in vain; the emperor is on the side of the Jews, and the Greek ambassadors are martyred. The Acta Alexandrinorum remove the theme of "love" from the novel, and put in anti-Semitism instead. ("The Protocols of the Elders of Alexandria", perhaps.) Indeed, there is something very strange about the distribution of this work. It is hard to think of a parallel, in the evidence for literary papyri, for a literary work where so many of the copies are made by untrained hands on the verso of documents (so, at least 29 out of Harker's 73 fragments). It was once customary to imagine that the novel, as a whole, was a more "popular" literature, and, when Stephens debunked this, she relied in part on the professional look of the papyri of the novels (Stephens, 1994: 413). But here we come across a work truly popular in its place and time. For once, this was a specifically Egyptian phenomenon. Circulation stopped in the third century CE (as was to a lesser extent true of the novel as a whole); mercifully, the work did not survive through to codex, and it left no traces on ancient literature as a whole. Such is not the canon. It is true that we have obtained here, for once, a Bourdieu-like case: a textual category for which fairly large circulation coincides with little prestige. But the point is not just that this is a rare case but that the genre of the Acta Alexandrinorum stands out in that it did not possess a well-recognized figure of an *author*.[157] This seems to clarify the sense in which

---

[157] See the discussion in Luiselli (2016), who takes the Acta Alexandrinorum as a case study for adespota – and comes to similar conclusions concerning their relatively marginal role in antiquity. They are something of a "literature of consumption", however (!) (which does not negate the fact that so was, for instance, Menander).

a certain type of canonicity operated in antiquity: attaching itself primarily not to works, but to authors. More on this in the following chapter.

What the Acta Alexandrinorum suggest, however, is that *we would have noticed* such dark horses. Had there been other substantial groups of papyrus texts all relating to a single textual core, then – fragmentary as the evidence is – it would have been picked up by papyrologists. Instead, the adespota seem to present a very scattered distribution; which is as one would expect. The adespota appear to be minor: the result of aggregating many works, each with very low distribution.

What we do notice is the sheer number of anonymous minor prose authors. We find history; medicine; philosophy; grammar and literary criticism; novels; even a little astronomy and astrology – and a few technical works. Why is it anonymous? After all, there are 127 Roman-era and earlier prose authors surviving through the manuscript tradition. We said above that they should be comparable with the authors ranked 169 to 600 among all the papyri in circulation in Egypt. As for history, our inability to identify the fragments is unsurprising: as noted above, Byzantium did not attempt to collect the enormous variety of ancient historiography. Medicine is also easy to understand: once Galen was established as the medical canon (which happened, possibly, only with Oribasus in the fourth century CE; see pages 765–6 below), little else would be collected. The medical papyri, accumulated in a pre-Galenic world, display a variety we can no longer tease apart into its various authors. (There might be significant authors hidden there: Herophilus and Erasistratus, perhaps?) Byzantium has been more generous in its preservation of philosophy, and yet it transmitted practically no philosophical works from the Hellenistic era and very few from the Roman era. At the same time, it is striking how few philosophical papyri appear to derive from the major Athenian schools of the Hellenistic era. CEDOPAL counts seven fragments as Stoic, Epicurean or Skeptic (there are no fragments, other than those of Aristotle and Theophrastus themselves, that we connect to the Lyceum). Once again, the specialized genres did not produce a ranking as stable, or as homogeneous, as that of the literary canon. Little wonder, then, that we may no longer identify the authors of so many of the specialized prose fragments: unlike their literary counterparts, the papyri of the specialized genres do a bad job of predicting ultimate Byzantine choices.

We consider here the selection bias within Egypt (which papyri get into the rubbish dump?);[158] and, finally, consider the consequences of the inevitable error in the sample.

We may perhaps think that the act of discard represents a certain disdain towards the work in question, so that the rubbish dumps should be filled with the less valued works. It is very obvious that what we do find is not pulp literature – with the unique exception, perhaps, of the Acta Alexandrinorum – and a moment's reflection reminds us that our expectations are anachronistic: graphocentric and print-based. The point concerning graphocentrism is more subtle, and I will return to explain my point in greater detail in the next chapter, but the fundamental point is that what the ancients valued in their literature was the actual or imagined performance, rather than the materiality of a written surface. We therefore predict less book fetishism. The ancient scribe is anonymous and indistinguishable,[159] the books plain and unillustrated.[160] Athenaeus, indeed, sings the praises of Larensis' library for its sheer size and variety, but not for the quality of the books owned as material artifacts.[161] Obviously it would be bad form to put one's fetishism on display, but even Lucian's *Adversus Indoctum* – a diatribe against a book fetishist, a great book collector who is not cultured enough, however, for the speaker's taste – represents the fetishism primarily as a matter of producing a large collection of books; not so much a matter of "first editions".[162] There was, admittedly, a certain fetishism concerned with owning books that belonged to famous individuals: when Galen lost his library to fire in 192, he lamented, among other examples, "Panaetius' Plato" (that is, presumably, a text of Plato that belonged to Panaetius). But even this seems to reflect the intellectual value attached to the notes, or corrections,

---

[158] I assume here that, once in the rubbish dump – or inside the mummy cartonnage – the survival rate of a papyrus fragment of a given size is not correlated in any way with its contents. (This assumption may be called into question, and it would be useful to consider the rates of survival according to different grades of papyrus make, for instance. This level of information is not available for statistical treatment, and so I leave this question to one side.)

[159] I do not say "undistinguished"; ancient scribal practices are professional, and often to high quality, but this is judged by Johnson (2004) precisely on the basis of the homogeneity of the artifacts. A medieval manuscript was marked for its high quality by its distinctiveness; an ancient manuscript was marked for its high quality by its conformity with a single standard of scribal polish.

[160] This is a contentious claim, though it is less controversial among the scholars who have looked at it recently; I return to discuss this on pages 146–7 below.

[161] For a discussion of Athenaeus and his patron, see Braund (2000); the key evidence, it should be admitted, is from the epitomized Book I.

[162] See the discussion in Johnson (2010: chap. 8).

inserted by a great reader (the grief over the lost Panaetius' Plato is paralleled, in Galen's text, by a grief concerning the loss of a Homer in a genuinely Aristarchean edition).[163]

Why no fetishism about "first editions"? Obviously, because there were no "first editions" of papyrus. Copies were interchangeable, and, if your copy became eaten by worms, you got a new one. Thus, discard was in fact an act of maintenance. When we see a papyrus fragment in the rubbish dump, we should not imagine some country bumpkin getting rid of his unwanted Euripides; rather, we should imagine a wealthy member of the elite who replaced his old Euripides with a brand new one.

Of course, rolls could sometimes have been discarded even without replacement, but we definitely cannot assume that discard implies little esteem. It implies, instead, heavy and careless use. As mentioned above, this would most strongly correlate with educational use. Many adolescents must have been warned, to no avail, to treat books more carefully. It seems reasonable to suppose that works that circulated only in big libraries, and were read only sporadically by sophisticated, and so perhaps careful, readers, would survive better. On the other hand, heavily studied books would be quicker to deteriorate, even if their scholars were mature and sophisticated. Johnson (2010: 185–99) studies in detail a group of 16 Oxyrhynchus papyri with variant readings attributed by name: a small subset of the evidence of McNamee (2007) considered above. In 13 of the 16 cases the notes are inserted by multiple hands, and Johnson's conclusion – that this is an example of a reading community in action, in this case scholars reading and annotating a text – is very compelling. He notes that the annotations are typically "contemporary with the text", which is taken by him to be a reflection of this reading community in action (that is, they actually spend time together with the book; it is not just a matter of the roll passing from hand to hand through the generations). I am convinced that Johnson is right, but the question remains as to why later readers did not feel the urge to reuse the book in the same fashion. But surely the intensive study of a book in consultation with other books, including the insertion of new writing by several hands, would all be very rough on the papyrus? It is true that such books also gained special value, and could perhaps have been curated by their owner in memory of those days spent reading with friends; but such are not the rolls that survive for a century or two. This is

---

[163] "On Freedom from Grief" 13 (Boudon-Millot, 2007). A book could also become a personal memento: Libanius, having become attached to the copy of Thucydides from which he always read, grieved greatly when it was lost, and was elated when it was found again (Oration 1.148–50).

significant, because our evidence shows a remarkable number of more "scholarly" books (commentaries and annotated rolls).[164] Was book collecting associated with active scholarship? To some extent it was, but it appears to me that our evidence would inevitably exaggerate the significance of this association. The papyri, taken at face value, suggest a world of literary papyri in which elementary education is dominant and sophisticated scholarship is quite significant. In the actual circulation, elementary education must have been of very modest significance and active scholarship of small proportions – each, perhaps, responsible for not more than 1 to 2 percent of actual texts in circulation. The bulk of ancient bookrolls were simply the collections of elite members who needed to display their mastery over the canon.

The two adjustments for heavy use – of elementary education, and of sophisticated study – have opposite consequences. Elementary education involved, above all, Homer, Isocrates and, to some extent, the top tier of the table on pages 15–18 above - that is, Euripides, Menander, Hesiod and Demosthenes. Adjusting for that would be to move Isocrates down a notch, and somewhat reduce the gap between the very top and those who come just underneath it. So the *Iliad*'s rate of penetration was not ten times that of Apollonius' *Argonautica*; it would have been, say, between five and eight times. Hesiod's *Theogony*'s rate of penetration was not ten times that of Plato's *Phaedrus*; it would have been, perhaps, between six and nine times. The ranking of the top canon would remain the same, but it would be more "compressed".

The typical subjects for active scholarly study, as we noted, would be the rare authors among the highly valued, ancient canonical poetic works, especially archaic lyric poetry and minor drama (in a sense of "minor" which includes Aristophanes, Sophocles and Aeschylus). We find, then, that such authors would tend to be somewhat over-represented in our sample. We should bear in mind, however, that the numbers of those authors would be somewhat expanded by bringing in the adespota. In the end, however, the single most important selection bias in the editing of papyri involves just those rare authors and poetic genres. For many editors, rare poetry was what papyri were *for*. (Yet another case when attitudes towards the canon rarely budged through the centuries: the scholars studied by McNamee simply anticipate the attitudes of McNamee's colleagues!) Above all, we achieve, once again, more uncertainty in our

---

[164] McNamee (2007: 2) counts 293, or about 5 percent of strictly literary pagan papyri, that carry annotations.

knowledge of the relative ranking of such minor authors. But, if anything, the balance of probability, I believe, is that archaic poetry and minor drama are over-represented in our sheer count of papyri.[165]

Finally, there remains the hand of error. One's first impression is surprise with the sheer plausibility of the results: would our statistics be as good as that? In fact, the margin of error with such a large sample is not very high. We have about 5,000 tokens (about 7,000 CEDOPAL papyri, minus the paraliterary), distributed between about 150 types; a confidence level of 99 percent will get us ranges that fit practically all authors.[166] Let us translate the key points of the tiers into 99 percent confidence margin of error terms.

| | |
|---|---|
| ~200 (top authors) | 165–235 |
| ~40 (Xenophon) | 28–60 |
| ~25 (Theocritus) | 12–40 |
| ~10 (low-ish tier 2) | 4–17 |
| ~6 (typical tier 3) | 1–15 |
| ~3 (typical tier 4) | 0–12 |
| ~1 (tier 5) | 0–8 |

This is a very high confidence level, so that it is rare for individual results to get even near the borders of the range (and it is extremely rare, though likely attested at least once in our data, for them to get beyond it).

For the very top authors, we probably can form a very precise guess concerning their absolute numbers. With Homer, the very serious problem is that of adjusting for the impacts of education and overall heavy use; but, if we could only adjust for that, his numbers should be within a percentage point or two of the "real" number. The ranking of tier 1 is probably mostly correct within a few places in the ladder (with the

---

[165] This all concerns the distribution within Egypt. The implications of such distributions for the distributions elsewhere were clarified above, with one major caveat: we have not discussed yet the relative frequencies of big, and small, libraries inside and outside Egypt. I shall return to discuss this in Part III, pp. 539–41.

[166] A "99 percent level of confidence" means the following. Suppose you find, in a random sample whose size is 5,000, that category X has 200 members. This is likely to be somewhat wrong: the true frequency in the original population the frequency of X is likely not precisely 200/5,000 (or 4 percent). Perhaps the true frequency is 211/5,000; perhaps it is 188/5,000. *If indeed the only source of error is the one introduced by random sampling as such*, we may calculate with mathematical precision how big the error is likely to be. Statisticians often do so by saying that, with X confidence – say, 99 percent – you can say that the true frequency falls within a certain range. In this case, it is 99 percent likely that the true frequency is roughly around 165–235/5,000 (that is, there is no more than a 1 percent chance that the true frequency is below 165/5,000, or above 235/5,000).

exception of the over-represented Isocrates, who has to remain higher, however, than his closest rhetorical competitor, Aeschines).

Lower down, the results are at least suggestive: we cannot be sure in each individual case, but, if we find seven fragments of Achilles Tatius, this does tell us something real. But at this stage results are mostly meaningful in the aggregate: there are 76 fragments in tier 5, and so the authors of tier 5 are more than 75 percent likely to have had between 66 and 86 fragments *between them*: an important, precise result.

Recall that there was, in fact, one significant move from 2011 to 2018: Plutarch jumped from nine to 16 fragments – just barely within the confidence level of 99 percent. Of course, it is predicted that one or two of our authors should contain an error even higher than that. But the interesting point is that Plutarch's move was in "the correct direction": an author who we always assumed to have been highly successful was indeed shown to have been so. This is an anecdote, but it is also a predicted outcome. Random variation goes in all directions, but normal, predicted results are – generally speaking – more frequent in the original sample than strange, surprising results. Thus, random variation is more likely to go from the mean to the outlier than vice versa. As more data are collected and we correct for random variation, we tend to "revert to the mean". Likely enough, a generation from now – when this book is no longer read – I will be vindicated: overall, the distribution of papyri is likely to end up *even more plausible* than it is right now.

So, stop worrying, and learn to love the evidence of the papyri. Hard to believe – but the gods of archaeology have heard our prayers and have granted us, for once, a true window into the past.

## 1.5  The Ancient Greek Canon: Conclusions

No need to be coy. The evidence of the papyri is statistically useful *for the literary canon.*[167] In this chapter, I used it to recover the overall contours of the ancient literary system. In the next, I will concentrate on the top tier so as to understand, finally, the nature, and origins, of the canon.

Here, then, is the ancient canon.

[167] As explained above, however, our confidence in the papyri should not be extended from the literary canon to other parts of the literary field. The papyri do not tell us which Hellenistic philosophers were more popular, or how popular Hellenistic philosophy was as a whole; or who the leading scientists were and what their overall impact was. This was not stable.

**The small-library permanent must-haves**
1. Homer; but also
2. Menander, 3. Euripides, 4. Hesiod; and also, in a different sense
5. Callimachus, 6. Apollonius, 7. Theocritus, 8. Aratus

So far, the permanent canon of the small library. Three authors joined this canon in Roman times (having been, before that, big-library canonical authors).

**Roman-era additions to the small-library must-haves**
9. Demosthenes, 10. Isocrates, 11. Aeschines

All small libraries were similar to each other, but each big library was big in a different way. It could not be imagined without the following, big-library canonical authors, however.

**The permanent big-library canon (arranged by genre)**
12. Thucydides, 13. Herodotus, 14. Xenophon
15. Sophocles, 16. Aeschylus
17. Plato
18. Aristophanes
19. Pindar

Eight small-library authors; eight big-library authors; three transitional. Nice. We have isolated a significant, but manageable, group of authors. The most important outcome of this chapter is the precise isolation of the list of names: we know now (but we always did, did we not?) whom we need to study. The question concerning the rise of the Greek canon involves, precisely, these. The next chapter will study the structure formed by these authors (give or take a few) and the historical process that made them canonical.

But we have also discovered, already, rather more. I started out by claiming the absence of any ancient opposition between prestige and popularity, and the discussion has amply demonstrated this, with no more than a few wrinkles of detail: yes, philosophy existed on its own plane; yes, there was the Acta Alexandrinorum. But the key point, throughout, was the *lack* of oppositions within the canon. Wherever we went, we found variations on the same system of ranking for the literary canon. Elementary education was based on the small library, because this represented the very top of the canon; and, also, this is probably what schoolmasters owned. But, then, those humble school-masters of Oxyrhynchus did not know a literary culture any different from that known to a Roman senator, to an Asia Minor author, to an Alexandrian grammarian, to Athenaeus, to Proclus, to Galen or to Archimedes. They all shared the same literary system of ranking of both prestige *as well as* popularity.

This first result must be emphasized. It has become an established procedure in the humanities to display the heterogeneity underlying apparent units. We have learned to argue that the naïve assumption of homogeneity prevails just because of the power of words to draw an essentialist spell. Thus, we have learned to decry the error of assuming that there was something such as "the Greeks". "Nonsense," the sober contemporary humanist comments. Surely there were many varieties of being Greek? There must have been "cultures within ancient Greek culture" – to quote the title of an influential recent collection (Dougherty and Kurke, 2003). I do not question the particular claims made in such a volume, and by the research tradition it represents. Surely, we can point to the tension between the use of a lyre or an aulos, between the implicit ideology of an Aesop and that of a Delphi. Greeks had their tensions. And yet we should not be blinded to the facts of homogeneity. Through the centuries studied in this book, across an expanding Greek Mediterranean, the top literary field was unique and stable. In fact, the paradox was deeper: a world made of local identities, of the sense of attachment to one's own city – shaped by a universal and homogeneous canon. It was always like that: epichoric but, above all, Panhellenic.[168]

The opposition we do see, historically, was not between different senses of popularity – between the canonical and the non-canonical. Rather, it was the opposition of the canonical and the specialized. This is what we have returned to, again and again, in our observation: the parallel structure of literature – and philosophy; the duality of the small and big libraries. Above all: the opposition between performative and non-performative literature. Stability reigned supreme – in the literary, small-library, performative canon. Elsewhere, diversity and change – and the continued life of Greek civilization.

Here, then, is my plan for the remainder of the book. As promised already, I now move on to investigate the structure and stability of the central literary canon. Following that, in Parts II and III, we will study how the more specialized Greek cultural forms played out against this background of the stable canon – and how the structure of a canon was finally made supreme in the literary field in its entirety, in late antiquity.

---

[168] For this tension, of the local within a universal Greek world, see especially the collection of essays in Whitmarsh (2010).

CHAPTER 2

# Canon in Practice
## The Polis of Letters

## 2.1 Introduction

### 2.1.1 Setting the Questions...

In the preceding chapter we established that the canon was real. In this chapter I try to understand what this meant in practice. What was it that an ancient audience possessed when it was in possession of its canon? And how and when was this canon formed? Two questions: one structural, the other historical. I study these two questions in order, in sections 2.2 and 2.3, respectively.

This chapter is in places more "theoretical" than most parts of this book (I get to cite Foucault!), and, as it touches on the earlier phases of Greek cultural history, it is also in places more "speculative". I bring in a variety of tools and approaches. But the key observation is simple: we should not cease to marvel at the fact that the Greeks had *authors*. This contingent historical development is so natural to us that we have become immune to its precise historical specificity. One of the goals of this chapter, then – and why I find its variety of approaches helpful – is that of estrangement.

But I aim to achieve more than just estrangement. It is not enough to point out that the author had to be invented historically. This would still be to assume an ahistorical category of the "author". It was a specific type of author that the Greeks invented and canonized: the performative author, who may also be seen as the author-within-a-genre.

Through this chapter, I will gradually develop an account of what the author-within-a-genre was: a vivid presence, understood relative to a concretely imagined site of performance. From this, several important consequences follow. We see precisely how the canon could have functioned as a kind of cultural correlate to the political reality of the city. And we can see how it had to be anchored, historically, in certain realities of performance: why it emerged, quite naturally, at a certain place and time,

96

and not afterwards. The canon was not made in Byzantium, as we have demonstrated in the previous chapter. Nor, I shall argue now, was it made in Alexandria: how could the librarians have achieved such a task? The reception of the ancient literature that ended up in the canon was tied to its concrete social setting in performance – which makes it the less surprising that its canonicity emerged early on, from the very act of performance. It was a canon made by audiences, not by erudites; because, to begin with, it was a literature intimately bound with its audience.

The canon, then, was made by the performativity of the classical city, above all Athens; and its survival meant the cultural survival of the polis.

And so, we begin with that obvious observation: the various comparisons made in Chapter 1 – for instance, between papyri fragment counts and TLG citations – were all made between authors' *names*. This, of course, is more than a point of methodology: it is already a result. What the ancients collected was not just "literature"; they collected named authors – so much so that even essentially anonymous works were attributed to real or fictional persons. We do not find anything such as the Chinese *Book of Odes* – a literary tradition in which genre is marked but authors are essentially unattributed[1] – or, say, "the Gospels of Socrates according to Xenophon, Plato, Aeschines and Antisthenes" – a literary tradition in which the subject matter overrides the figure of the author. Works were primarily collected on the basis neither of genre nor of contents but on the basis of named authors.

We may consider the fate of the epic cycle. The *Iliad* and the *Odyssey* managed to obtain a clear authorial status, being ascribed, without serious challenge, to Homer; for other epics, controversy surrounding authorship was the rule.[2] Such loosely authorial epic poetry had little classical impact[3] and, at most, a tiny papyrus footprint.[4] In short, from the fifth century BCE onwards

---

[1] Beecroft (2010) is, among other things, a rich study of attempts by considerably later Chinese readers to read authorship out of the *Book of Odes*, the point being that the songs themselves were not originally assigned to named authors and were not collected on the basis of authorial reputations. (China, too, went through its revolution of inventing the named author, but it did so much later relative to canonization; thus, clearly defined named authorship subsisted mainly beneath the central canon.)

[2] West (1999) attributes the invention of Homer as the author of the two epics to the late sixth century; see West (1999: 380) for some of the controversies concerning the authorship of the other epics.

[3] For what it's worth, I count the following (optimistically defined) ten fragments and testimonies to the epic cycle from the classical period: Plato (*Euthyphro* 12a, *Phaedrus* 269a); Herodotus (II.116.6–7, IV.32); Aeschines, *In Tim.* 128; Hippocrates, *Articul.* 8; Aristotle (*Poetics* 1451a19, EN 1116b26, Pol. 1338a22; and then *Poetics* 1459a37: a famous passage on the epic cycle whose fame makes our imagination increase, by association, the fame of the epic cycle itself).

[4] P.Rain. 3.5 (P.Vindob. inv. G 26762) is perhaps from a cyclical epic, perhaps (I would say, probabilistically preferable) from Hesiod's catalogue (Traversa, 1951: 131–2); P.Oxy. 30.2510 is

the epic cycle was essentially a scholarly showpiece.[5] If we believe with West (1999) that the firm attribution of the *Iliad* and the *Odyssey* is a product of the late sixth century BCE, then this means that, almost as soon as the naming was made, the epic cycle effectively disappeared. It could not have been absolutely rare before that – how would it survive otherwise? The likeliest account is that the naming took the two best-known epic works and endowed them with the Homeric brand, the consequence being that the two *more* famous works become the two *much, much more* famous works.

Or was the epic cycle not collected simply because it was not good enough?[6] (And, for the same reason, it could not find an author to claim it?) We reach a deep question: the relationship between quality and canonicity. But we may set aside discussion of this question (it deserves a big monograph of its own; I will limit myself to a brief footnote, at the end of this chapter: page 237, note 290). For, clearly, the operating mechanism in this case has something to do with the presence or absence of an author's name, not with the differences of quality as such. The evidence is from the *Shield of Heracles*, which managed to attach itself unshakably to the name of Hesiod. It is hard to believe the quality of the epic cycle was much worse; and yet those poems disappeared while the *Shield of Heracles* was widely copied.[7] And so the impression begins to build: works were collected in antiquity *because of their authors*. This has to be qualified. Homer was also identified as the author of the *Hymns*,[8] perhaps also of the *Margites* and other works.[9] Of

---

assigned by its editor, Bravo (2001), to either the *Aethiopis* or the *Iliad Parva*. But these are optimistic attributions (West, 2013: 47; in general, editors are overzealous in ascribing hard-to-identify fragments to minor sources; sober considerations of base probabilities imply otherwise). At most, one or two fragments for a literature that, in its totality, must have occupied not much less papyrus than Homer himself is very little indeed. Strictly speaking, the implication is that of three orders of magnitude difference between the penetration of Homer and that of the epic cycle; or, in absolute numbers, if we imagine a few dozen thousand households with Homer, we should imagine a few dozen households with the epic cycle: but perhaps this is a case when we should not directly extrapolate from the Nile Valley.

[5] To scholars, it was definitely known, and our evidence derives from a variety of such Roman-era (perhaps late ancient) scholars, so that we have multiple fragments and testimonies from the likes of Pausanias, Athenaeus, Plutarch, the scholiasts to Pindar and to Homer and of course the *Chrestomatheia* itself.

[6] So, implicitly, Griffin (1977).

[7] Fourteen fragments for a work of 480 lines, suggesting a typical Hesiodic frequency. The reading most sympathetic to the aesthetic of the *Shield* is Martin (2005), considering it as "pulp epic".

[8] The survival of the *Homeric Hymns* into medieval manuscripts is remarkable and a sign of some genuine ancient familiarity; but it is clear that close knowledge of the hymns – unlike the Homeric epics – was a matter of specialized erudition (and so cause for boast by grammarians: Driscoll, 2016: 124).

[9] See Graziosi (2002) for the early reception of Homer – dominated, obviously, by the reception of the epics in performance.

the first, not a single papyrus fragment has been identified; of the latter, the three fragments may perhaps derive from later developments of the genre. The case of Homer is therefore more complicated: he was identified with a specific genre (hexameter heroic narrative). He was collected as an author, but filtered through the genre constraint – in the manner in which Tolstoy, say, is globally a household name as the author of two massive novels, while his plays are only very rarely produced outside Russia. This formula – "author, within genre" – is one we will see again and again in this chapter.

In general, the Greek "anonymous" was a failure. The TLG Canon of Greek Authors and Works lists its anonymi through 14.5 columns of text (1986: 21–8) out of roughly 652 total columns, so less than 3 percent; but this overstates the fraction. A considerable number of our so-called anonymi are papyri adespota (so the bulk of the anonymi grammatici).[10] Many others are now identified as anonymi because the contents of their work happen to be cited without a mention of the author's name (most anonymi historici are created in this way).[11] Many others are very short technical treatises, copied into codices without the author's name. It is difficult to argue that this is how they circulated in antiquity itself (some even appear to be Byzantine creations – so, for instance, Euclid's *Elements* XV[12] – as well as several philosophical commentaries; these are essentially late scholiastic accretions rather than ancient works). It is noteworthy that very many of the short technical works are medical in content – 26 anonymi medici, mostly a few hundred words long. Some, but not all, must be Byzantine, yet it is just possible that a few medical works always did circulate without an author (this would be continuous with that other strange phenomenon, the Hippocratic corpus). Other than this there is just one group of real anonymi, the epigrams in the anthologies (we shall return to discuss this, in

---

[10] To some extent this category was created through the zeal of Wouters (1979), who edited and published a large selection of grammatical papyri (and implied that they emerged from book-like, authored publications: perhaps some of his papyri are mere ad-hoc compilations). Partly, this category is large simply because so few ancient theoretical treatises in grammar are now extant, making it harder for us to assign authorship.

[11] And so, effectively, these anonymi were created by Jacoby. Thus Kaldellis (2007), on Jacoby 479, "De Lesbo": "These 'fragments' do not correspond to any particular author, much less a 'historian'. Under the misleading category of Anonymoi, Jacoby placed two passages, one of which is from a poem (the Ktisis Lesbou) while the other was probably a piece of Lesbian religious lore."

[12] See Keyser and Irby-Massie (2008), EANS, s.v. Isidorus of Miletus' Student (the name derives from a reference made inside the work to "Isidore of Miletus, our teacher"). This kind of scholastic work was made in a context in which the distinction between writing and teaching was blurred, allowing for a qualified re-emergence of a non-authorial attitude to one's writing. They could be made as side notes to Euclid – and could survive that way.

Chapter 5, in considering the post-classical fate of poetic authorship: many authors of epigrams in the post-classical era did not consider themselves primarily as "poets", so their poetry would be effectively non-authorial). Beyond the category identified by the TLG as "anonymi", there is also a group of works that modern scholarship chose to identify by the work's name, some of which became quite popular, especially in late antiquity; chief among these are the *Life of Aesop* and especially the *Alexander Romance*. The point about this small group is not merely that it is, indeed, small but, more significantly, that it seems to be playfully aware of its position relative to a "normal" literary space. Following Arthur-Montagne (2016), we can see such works as parodies of *paideia*. It seems that some students (or teachers?) of rhetoric took up the standard rhetorical exercises around such figures as Aesop and Alexander, and turned them into literature that was lively by virtue of its upending of classroom expectations. (In a different register, the same account of course holds for the *Batrachomyomachia*'s anonymous parody of Homer). We can see why this was popular, and also how the lack of authorial status correlates with a derivative position relative to the literary field. The literary was authored, and so the metaliterary or nearly counter-literary, in this case, became unauthorial.

The late anonymous novel, the epigram, perhaps also medicine, are no more than qualified exceptions to the rule, then: named authorship was a nearly non-negotiable condition for the very circulation of literature in antiquity, from the naming of "Homer" onwards. The importance of being named: readers collected names, and so the unnamed would also have to be uncollected.

What are those names? Several of them are effectively mere labels: Homer, Hippocrates and Aesop. A significant set of authors: the most important; the only widely circulated technical author; the most enduring prose fiction (albeit enduring because of its place in the elementary curriculum?). They are significant because they were all positioned right at the *cusp* of the invention of the authorial persona: in literature as a whole (Homer, who survives from a pre-authorial stage of literature), in science (Hippocrates, who is the earliest extant technical author) and in prose fiction (Aesop, emerging out of unauthorial, folk fiction). We recall something important: the author happened *during* Greek literature. They did not have authors by way of imitation of a previous literary culture; they had to invent them, and, along the way, transform them, and so they always went on carrying the remains of the author's absence.

All this is, of course, in some sense familiar. All modern vernacular literatures are constructed with the same building block of the named author. And so it has to be emphasized that this is not a cultural universal.

In all early cultures we find a much more complicated relationship between authors and works. The classics are unattributed (or are understood to be later compilations of materials due to various past authors, some entirely anonymous, some amorphous). Later works (among classical Chinese literature) are often imbued with the aura of a single master, most famously Confucius himself – but even these are expressly not presented as the works of the master himself but, rather, as later collections made by followers who are sometimes anonymous, and who – even when not so – then at least carry a much less powerful aura than that of the original master.[13] As Harbsmeier (1999) explains, "Traditionally...the function of the editor/compiler was separate both from that of the originator of the linguistic content of the text and from that of the person responsible for the production of a given inscribed material object." This fundamentally editorial mode of authorship is reminiscent of the Talmudic literature, in which names are frequent enough but are arranged as a chain of quotations made by anonymous editors. Indeed – stepping earlier – Near Eastern literature is essentially all anonymous, of which Israelite literature is the most familiar. To quote Smith (1972: 194): "In the Israelite literary tradition...authors' names are rarely reported and when they are reported the reports are almost always false... (The books of the prophets usually contain some prophecies by the men whose names they bear, but were not composed by them.)" To this we may add, from our perspective, that the prophets insist on the divine source of their prophecy, with a quite unironic stridency (whereas already Hesiod's invocation of the Muses – to say nothing of the lyric tradition as a whole – implies at the very least a complex attitude to the notion of divine inspiration).[14] And this seems to be the point: early literature derives its aura of authority not from the figure of an author but, rather, from its numinous origins and themes, and for this reason the aura of the author is superfluous if not

---

[13] For an account of the Confucian Five Classics, where this mode of authorship is most influentially enshrined, see Nylan (2001).

[14] And so, what does it mean that the Muses "know how to tell lies similar to truth"? Perhaps not all that much: this line, Hesiod's *Theogony* 27, is the subject of massive debate (for a recent discussion with references, see Nagy, 2010), but, likely enough, we see here some recognition of the nature of fiction – ascribed to the very divine authority of poetry!

problematic. (Why have the author, when you can have the divine? Would the author not *stand in the way* of the divine?)[15]

Now, to be clear, China would eventually invent the "author" – independently from Greece – but this invention did not displace a canon whose numinous, unauthored or semi-authored identity was perpetuated through the centuries. It is not as if the only route to the invention of the author has to pass through Homer. And yet, we should not make the opposite mistake implicit in most studies of the figure of the author in non-Western traditions. There, the standard move is to take Western literature as the norm and to reflect upon the non-standard, weak status of the author in the relevant tradition. But this is clearly wrong, for the Greeks, too, as we noted, started out un-Greek. The author is not normal; it had to be invented, historically, and – with it – the entire structure of a literary field. This is the topic of this chapter, then: the study of a specific, contingent historical form.

Two complementary observations emerge. First, as we insist, the author has to be *invented*. Structuring a literary field around authors' names has to be historically constructed and is not the cross-cultural norm for early literature (which is, instead, that of ascribing the source for literature in the transcendent – the divine, or the heroic author-figure whose sayings are "collected"). Second, the author *remains*. Once invented, this practice does not get undone: literatures do not move *away* from the authorial practice and, within authorial literatures, anonymous and pseudepigraphic authorship tends to be marginal. (Greco-Roman literature would eventually absorb the Israelite authorial practice, through the Bible; but the tendency would be to normalize this practice with authors such as "Moses", "David" and "Solomon" – and, once this Israelite canon was absorbed, later Christian authors tended to follow the rules of the Greek authorial game).[16] We seem to see something like a "natural progression" from the transcendent to the author – a claim that might strike my readers as outrageous: one of those Comtean teleologies that lead from the theological to the positivist, or, closer to our field, a claim perhaps reminiscent of Bruno Snell's (1953 [1946]) account of the Greek "discovery of the mind" – as if it took Greek literature and philosophy to discover the existence of an authorial "I"...

---

[15] Thus, the Vedas – the foundational canonical text of all Sanskrit traditions – are explicitly assumed to be authorless because they arise with *cyclical creation itself* (Lutsyshyna, 2012: 453–4).

[16] Previous to that, early Jewish/Christian literature in Greek is often ambiguous between traditional Israelite and Greek authorial practices, giving rise to another minor group of Greek texts with weak to no authorship.

But the empirical observation is real, and perhaps what we ought to say is that, underlying the big metaphysical account of a dawning of the identity of the individual in the classical world, what we see, in practice, is the rise of a new, effective, literary technique – which, because of its sheer efficacy, ended up winning the day. The Greeks may not have discovered the secular "I"; what they did create, however, was the practice of the author, and, with it, a very compelling way of going about literature.

The metaphysical dimension is surely relevant in some other ways, however. The absence of a religiously sanctioned canon, within Greek literature, reflects a broader point. The Greeks – perhaps here alone among early civilizations – did not have priest-kings. The social groups with access to the divine did not acquire any powerful political role. Morris (2005: 11) and Ober (2015: 136) stress this point, as a major background to the emerging egalitarianism of the early Greek polis, one which would ultimately translate into a more open political field of debate and, eventually, democracy. We should note that this idiosyncrasy made possible the rise not only of a political field but also that of a literary field, dominated by free agents. Authors, writing in their own name: made possible, because the gods don't.

The Greeks invented the structure of a literary field defined by named authors. When? Clearly, this had already been achieved by the sixth century – a very poorly documented period. How? We need all the explanatory tools we can find, and in this chapter we look at this through two perspectives. First, we study the structure of the literary field, in its mature form: the "polis of letters", made of genres, authors and works. Following that, we look at the chronological question, first establishing the dates when the canon become entrenched, and then considering its process of formation. But, first of all, we discuss the "author"; we can't avoid literary theory altogether.

### 2.1.2    . . .And Theory

"Sans doute en a-t-il toujours été ainsi" ("No doubt this is how it always has been"); so writes Barthes (1977: 61) – a text would always be primarily a text and therefore not in the control of an "author", who therefore, finally, must be seen as a fiction. Barthes immediately qualifies this by saying that the "sentiment" of this phenomenon is variable (simple societies have shaman mediators, not "authors", for instance), but the argument of Barthes' essay – expressed in its title, "Death of the Author" – transcends historical and cultural boundaries. "This is how it always has been"; there

never was an author but there always was the illusion as if it were real. . .
Foucault 1977 [1969], too, raises the same question – "What is an author?" –
and then swirls in fantastic circles around the question of the historicity of
the category. At the end, it appears that Foucault believes the following: the
figure of the author arises from the modern state, from capitalism; it is
a bad thing. Foucault makes some remarkable statements in this regard:

> [T]he author is not an indefinite source of significations that fill a work. . .
> [H]e is a certain functional principle by which, in our culture, one limits,
> excludes, and chooses; in short, by which one impedes the free circulation,
> the free manipulation, the free composition, decomposition, and recompo-
> sition of fiction. [. . .] The author is therefore the ideological figure by which
> one marks the manner in which we fear the proliferation of meaning. [. . .]
> Although, since the eighteenth century, the author has played the role of the
> regulator of the fictive; a role quite characteristic of our era of industrial and
> bourgeois society, of individualism and private property, still, given the
> historical modifications that are taking place, it does not seem necessary that
> the author function remain constant in form, complexity, and even in
> existence.

The author – in some sense, invented in the eighteenth century! Foucault
was fond of the idea of recent historical ruptures, such that would tend to
make the present appear radically contingent and therefore eminently
replaceable. Such was the sentiment of the 1960s. But even this nod
towards historicity was, in this essay by Foucault, no more than an
aside – rounding up the usual suspects – while making a point which
was not so much about historicity (with its emphasis upon precise historical trajectories) as upon constructedness as such.

For indeed, to Barthes and Foucault – and to the half-century of literary
theory following – it was profoundly important that "the author" was
*constructed*. As often happened with late twentieth-century theory in the
humanities, the recognition that a category was constructed was somehow
transformed, in theoretical discourse, to the impression that it was *merely*
a construct. Worse: the construct was understood (certainly by Foucault
himself) as in some sense a "false consciousness", a tool of hegemony. To
criticize that which is constructed, then, was a "critique": an act of libera-
tion. Thus, the recognition of the author as a constructed category was read
not as an invitation to a further historicization of authorial practices
(which, as we note, Barthes and Foucault hardly acknowledged); it was
the goal itself. If it served anything, it was as an invitation to a new kind of
literary theory, perhaps structuralist (whereby text is liberated from its
presumed biographical author), perhaps post-structuralist (whereby text is

immersed within an open-ended network of intertextualities). The claim that the author was a construct was taken not as a historical question but as a theoretical answer.

Of course, we have now a plethora of historical studies showing the historical settings of various figures of the "author". But what seems not to have been noted yet is that, by "the author", we essentially mean a particular form of constructing the author, and that this particular form is not "constructed" in some vague, ahistorical sense. It was, in fact, initially an invention of a particular historical moment, within Greek literature. Entrenched in the Greek literary canon, mirrored later by the Roman literary canon, this particular historical form was then the model for European vernacular literatures, which now dominate the model of the "author" globally. It was indeed transformed in the romantic and modern traditions, as I will return to note below. But its invention was Greek.

Nor do we gain much by understanding this reality as "false consciousness", imposed by hegemony. Of course, Foucault is right that a construct that succeeds in surviving must be good for something; he then took it for granted that, obviously, it will be good for *capitalism*. But the author is more than a successful construct: it is universally so, easily exported, enduring through profound social and economic transformations. Capitalism alone is not a good explanation, then.

Let us start from Foucault's central insight:

> [A]n author's name is not simply an element in a discourse. . .it performs a certain role with regard to narrative discourse, assuring a classificatory function. Such a name permits one to group together a certain number of texts, define them, differentiate them from and contrast them to others. In addition, it establishes a relationship among the texts. . . The author's name serves to characterize a certain mode of being of discourse: the fact that the discourse has an author's name, that one can say "this was written by so-and-so" or "so-and-so is its author," shows that this discourse is not ordinary everyday speech that merely comes and goes, not something that is immediately consumable. On the contrary, it is a speech that must be received in a certain mode and that, in a given culture, must receive a certain status.

Naming is a tool of classification: it delimits the literary (named!) from the non-literary; it classifies the literary field into its constituents. So far we go with Foucault – and immediately notice that he seems to miss a key question. For why would the classification based on the author be so powerful – and not one based on, say, genre, subject matter, number of words, any other category we might think of? This seems to be our best clue so far: names – an especially *compelling* category!

Now, if I read Google Scholar correctly this afternoon (January 19, 2016), Foucault's (1977 [1969]) "What Is an Author?" has 5,544 citations, while Bar-Hillel et al. (2012), "A Rose by Any Other Name", has five. This is wrong, since, I believe, Bar-Hillel offers the most promising response, yet, to Foucault's question. Let me begin to redress the balance.

Bar-Hillel et al. (2012), "A Rose by Any Other Name", is a study in the power of *names*. It is also a study in cognitive psychology (the subtitle is "A Social-Cognitive Perspective on Poets and Poetry"). Here is how it works. We start with four genuine poems by four canonical poets (of the modern Israeli Hebrew canon). Four fake poems are invented as terrible pastiche of the originals.[17] Four bland names are invented alongside the original names of the authors. We now have eight poems (four real, four fake), eight names (four real, four fake). We zoom in on 16 combinations. Each of the eight poems is titled, once with its "real" author name, once with a fake name. Several hundred students in Jerusalem's Hebrew University were then asked to rate the various poems, randomly assigned, on a scale from 0 to 100. And then the results (Bar-Hillel et al., 2012: 9):

> Poet reputation was the only statistically significant effect. Poems attributed to famous poets were rated higher (M=76, SD=12) than poems attributed to bogus poets (M=70, SD=15; $F(1,273=14.65, p<.001$). Authenticity of the poems made no difference – both real and fake were rated 73 on average.

Empirically, we see, there is such a thing as an author function, which we can even quantify. The author function adds to our experience in consuming an

---

[17] Here is the example – Emily Dickenson, and an awful pastiche – provided by Bar-Hillel et al. to illustrate the *kind* of effect produced in the original study, which was conducted in Israel with modern Hebrew poetry (texts by Goldberg, Amichai, Zach and Rabikovich):

| Authentic poem | Fake counterpart |
|---|---|
| Wild Nights – Wild Nights! | Blue Dawns – Blue Dawns! |
| Were I with thee | For my babie |
| Wild Nights should be | Blue Dawns decree |
| Our luxury! | A fantasy! |
| Futile – the winds – | Empty – the crib – |
| To a heart in port – | No nursery – |
| Done with the compass – | No bibs, no nappies |
| Done with the chart! | No luxury! |
| Rowing in Eden – | Roaming the gardens – |
| Ah, the sea! | Oh, the grass! |
| Might I moor – | Tonight – Seeking a laddie |
| In thee! | Seeking a lass! |

object from an established set. The result is an asymmetry: the consumption of objects from the established set is favored, and so they are consumed more, creating a feedback loop through which the established set dominates its type of consumption.

There's something going on in your head which the name causes, hence you end up liking that name... We recently find this to be the case, everywhere – and this is how Bar-Hillel et al. might provide a starting point for answering Foucault's question. The direct inspiration for Bar-Hillel et al.'s study was from wine tasting. There, wines – expensive and cheap – were presented with price tags, false and true; tasters were asked to rank their experience.[18] One can go further than that, scanning brains to detect the response brain scientists believe is associated with pleasure.[19] Pepsi and Cola;[20] beer with and without vinegar (!)[21] – long is the list of beverages drunk, in recent years, by the subjects of marketing experiments. The results are always the same: the real pleasure – not just the reported one – seems to be correlated *entirely* with one's conceptual knowledge of the consumed object, not at all with the physical properties of the object itself.[22] Ariely and Norton (2009) refer to this as "conceptual consumption", and, clearly, this is the relevant category for our understanding of audience preferences.

So far, then, a straightforward idea: we can understand the domination of a literary field by its named authors, on analogy with the domination of a market by its favorite brands. Straightforward enough, and I suppose readers trained in any kind of literary theory have forsaken me by now. Is that all I offer – the sheer simple-mindedness of business school vapidity, offered, seriously, as a response to Foucault? Have we descended that low?

I hear you. No, this kind of business school think is certainly constrained and ahistorical, and indeed it is time to turn the model of the brand on its head: we should definitely not try to understand ancient literature on the

[18] Goldstein et al. (2008).
[19] Plassman et al. (2008). Or consider Berns et al. (2010): teenagers really *do* enjoy more the music they perceive to be preferred by their peers. (The authors suggest that the regions of the brain affected imply that the mechanism for preference formation is driven by the anxiety over committing a social faux pas through the wrong valuation: we were all teenagers and can appreciate the plausibility of the suggestion.)
[20] McClure et al. (2004). [21] Lee, Frederick and Ariely (2006).
[22] Bar-Hillel et al. did not scan the brains of the readers of poetry. They did, however, produce another experiment in the same study, in which respondents were told that one poem in each pair was real, one fake, and were asked to identify the real one. The results were at chance level, suggesting that the valuation based on a provided author's name was the "genuine" appreciation (and that there was no other, more basic valuation based on direct cues from the poems themselves, somehow suppressed by the author's name).

model of modern marketing. Instead, both should be seen as deriving from more basic structures – or, indeed, if anything, it is modern marketing that stands to learn from the study of literature. For a good enough reason: the author came *first*.

Marks used by guilds and, more generally, reputations conveyed by areas or towns of origins, are attested early on in medieval Europe[23] and China,[24] and in some ways (especially in the "area of origin" form) go back to antiquity: I shall return to this in Chapter 3. As Richardson (2008) points out, these are authenticating devices, conveying the assurance of quality in a market plagued by low information: how would you know the merchant is not cheating you?[25] So much is ancient. The modern brand – a name designating a particular line of product owned by a particular firm – arose only in the English-speaking world, in the late nineteenth century, as the state became more powerful, markets more informed. Consumers worried less about being cheated; producers worried less about being copied. And so consumers could begin to trust brands, and producers gained the incentive to develop them; at this point, the structural logic of domination by marked names made the development of brands irresistible.[26]

To make the modern brand, one first had to bridge the gap of trust between producer and consumer. In the economic domain, then, the brand had to wait for the emergence of developed capitalism and, in particular, the emergence of strong enforcement of property rights, even for commercial intellectual property. Not so in the cultural sphere, where incentives work differently. Before the modern market of print, literary cultural production sought status, not income: fame, not sales. If so, passing under another author's name was less attractive.[27] Thus, the expectation was set early on

---

[23] Richardson (2008).    [24] Eckhardt and Bengtsson (2010).

[25] Bang (2008) argues for an extremely low-information Roman Mediterranean market, so much so that it was effectively not an integrated economy at all. The argument here does not rely on this strong and controversial claim, but it is worth consulting Bang to get a sense of how precarious information – hence, trust – could be in pre-modern markets, rendering impossible the formation of commercial brands. It is striking, then, that the "market" in culture was so thoroughly homogenized! Was it so, then, in culture *alone*?

[26] There is no good general history of the emergence of the brand as a social phenomenon, though there are many asides in semi-professional historical studies produced by scholars of marketing. The rise of the brand is best studied historically in the context of legal history, in which the growth of trademark law is understood as a central example of the expansion of property rights beyond the rights in physical property, through the nineteenth century but, in fact, fully achieved only in the twentieth (see, e.g., Bone, 2006).

[27] I have mentioned above the failure of the ancient author "anonymus". Pseudo did even worse. Pseudepigrapha are a very minor Greek tradition, sometimes reflecting the absorption of Near Eastern non-authorial tradition into Greek (pseudepigraphy is in fact central in Second Temple Judaism and Christianity), sometimes showing the enduring attraction of a literature ascribed to

that literary activity was pursued for the sake of personal fame, and for this reason was prima facie genuine. The bridge of trust was constructed automatically and did not require the legal power of the state to sustain it. This happened in the archaic Greek world, because a numinous, priestly canon was absent there, and for specific reasons having to with the historical context of the archaic world – to which we will return in the conclusion to this chapter. But, then, once the model of the author had become established, the logic of the brand was irresistible; of course, poems by Sappho, or by Archilochus, were recited, memorized, preserved, perhaps even written down, more than those by others, *and those that had no names behind them.* The Sapphic corpus had a brand name to sustain it: those few extra percentage points calculated by Bar-Hillel et al.

And so the brand first emerges: as the author. It would take the economic sphere some 25 centuries to catch up. Foucault had it exactly upside down: imagining that the figure of the author arose with capitalism, responding to the economic sphere. A tempting mistake – to base the cultural superstructure on the economic base! Culture and economy are related, in this case, not through cause and effect but through a parallel logic, a logic whose operation came more naturally in the cultural sphere.

And so, in a way, I say that Foucault's problem is hardly a mystery: of course literature would be defined by named authors, because named authors are a kind of brand, and there is indeed an effective power to the brand name, so that – whenever conditions allow the rise of brands – brands do emerge.

But this observation is merely the starting point. We still have not brought in yet any historical sense of the phenomenon of the brand, other than commenting on the economic logic that makes such brands possible. However much brands are grounded in human cognition as such,

---

numinous origins (so, in the pseudo-Pythagorean literature). But most authors now listed as "pseudo-" are pseudo-pseudo authors, so to speak. In fact, they are an offshoot of the anonymus phenomenon. Thus pseudo-Scymnus: a geographical text circulating in the manuscript tradition without an authorial mention; identified in 1635 as by the ancient author Scymnus, of whom only fragments remain; the identification has since been retracted and the treatise finally stuck with the author "pseudo-Scymnus". It is along such lines that most so-called pseudo-author ascriptions now circulate. What we do not see in such episodes is the desire to pass off as Scymnus. Finally, three of the pseudo-authors cited by TLG are medical (which is typical of the distribution of anonymi): Hippocrates, Dioscorides and Galen. This puts into context Galen's famous introduction to "On My Own Books", in which he watches with satisfaction a customer unmasking a pseudo-Galenic text. (Galen brags, as usual: *he has become a brand.*) There could not have been that many such scenes in actual life. Another form in which anonymity abounds, and so ultimately leads to the accretion of pseudo-authorship, is the epigram, or in general the short lyric: thus Anacreon's or Theognis' many spuria.

it seems obvious that their expression will depend on cultural and historical conditions. And, to understand this, we need to go back to an even more basic question: even within the reductive terms of the business school theorization, we have not yet brought out the main question about the power of brands.

Just why are brands so effective? How do they contribute to our consumption? Here we need to be more speculative with regard to the literary field: the experimental research has not yet been conducted. But it is available already in the economic field, and I believe this may be relevant for our purposes. For we seem to have learned, over the last couple of decades, how to make sense of the mechanism through which brands make themselves effective. This is through their *personality*. See Aaker (1997: 347), for example: "Absolut Vodka personified tends to be described as a cool, hip, contemporary 25-year-old." And 348: "The personality traits associated with Coca-Cola are cool, all-American and real." Aaker ends up developing a measurement that manages to capture the actual responses to actual brands based on five dimensions of personality (351): "sincerity, excitement, competence, sophistication, ruggedness". This is all absurd, I know; but it is based on empirical research, and it then becomes an effective tool in the hands of marketers. There is a *theory* behind the two guys staring at you and saying "Hi, I'm a Mac" and "I'm a PC".[28] It works. We should call this effect, perhaps, *the pathetic fallacy of the brand*. Through this pathetic fallacy the identity of a product ends up influencing the experience of its consumption. It possesses a certain human warmth; it may be identified as in some sense "like us"; we may more easily develop an emotional attitude towards it. One way or another, we relate much more effectively to products when they strike us as persons.

My point is by now obvious: once again, the author comes first. Certain product lines, if you will, come *naturally* packaged as persons. This, then, would automatically serve to make their brands stick. A key example of that would be, then, the bundle of works associated with a named author. A brand name strives to gain a personality; but we naturally ascribe a personality to the works of an author. This is, of course, an illusion, which is precisely why Barthes wanted the author dead. He wanted us to stop falling prey to the pathetic fallacy of the brand of the author, stop believing that there is a little person in there, inside the text, who tries to communicate with us. When we contemplate a volume of Balzac and

---

[28] For a discussion of this classic example of a campaign built around a brand (officially titled "Get a Mac"), see Livingstone (2011).

imagine a person, Balzac, in there, this is in a sense just like contemplating an Apple machine and imagining a hip and casual kid. But, then, we do, both, which is how Apples, and Balzacs, sell.

And the beauty of it is that it all comes naturally. Since speech is highly indicative of personality, there is no need for an extra marketing campaign. The writing does all the marketing required. Encounter the works and the sense of a personality will engulf you all by itself: Homer, heroically performing; Plato, hiding within his ironies; Callimachus, forever erudite. The authors come to be defined as a personality, conveyed via their works; and the works, in turn, come alive with the sense of the personality of a brand. This is the fundamental contribution of Bar-Hillel et al. They put the category of the "author" within the context of the "brand". And then – following Aaker – we may solve Foucault's implicit puzzle: why is it the "author" that serves as the key classificatory principle in all literatures that came by its invention? Simple enough: because the category of the "author" is the most effective in projecting a personality and thus the most effective in building a brand.

Exasperating ahistoricism, all that! And of course we should immediately stop and qualify – as even the scholars of brands do, after all. Even Aaker does not claim that "sincerity, excitement, competence, sophistication, ruggedness" are cultural universals (the "ruggedness" sort of gives the game away: these are contemporary American concepts).[29] And so this is how we may historicize the concepts of the brand and of the author: we need to find the culturally specific mechanism through which the pathetic fallacy of the author is conveyed. The argument, then, is that the way in which a group of texts proclaim a "personality" is historically constructed. And, in this sense, the modern author is indeed very different from the ancient one.

The form in which the "author" presented him- or herself did change, around 1800, in ways which we will be better able to explain at the end of section 2.2. But we may begin, once again, from Barthes and Foucault. What motivated the French structuralists, when they had denied the "author"? They started out from formalism, from "new criticism". "Down with the author" meant "Down with authorial intent/authorial biography". One, instead, was instructed to explore the textual strategies through which a purely written artifact (apart from the intentions of its author and the circumstances of its writing) might broadcast – or not – its

---

[29] Aaker (1997: 355) concludes that seminal article with the expectation that cross-cultural comparisons will give rise to significant differences; Aaker and Schmidt (2001) follow on with the comparison, though limited within the polarity of "individualistic" versus "collectivistic" societies. It is alien to this research tradition – relying on the experiment, geared towards practical applications in marketing – to raise the possibility of historical, and not just cultural, specificity.

implied maker.³⁰ Such was "new criticism", trained in the careful parsing of conceptual structures, writerly strategies, points of view, ironies. The question posed by Barthes and Foucault was whether or not, following "new criticism", the category of the "author" was even meaningful. They went beyond "new criticism", but stayed on its path, and the category they had questioned was that of that "new criticism" persona: the writerly strategist, the crafter of texts.

Clearly, this would not be the way in which the question of the author presented itself to the ancient reader. The key term, scholars have come to recognize in recent decades, must be that of *performance*. In the pre-modern context, literature did not imply an author and its literary craft; it implied voice, body, stage. An author, no doubt: but not the authorial presence of, say, a *Nabokov*; rather, a bit more like the authorial presence of a *Nijinsky*. We went beyond the mere observation, that early epic poetry was oral improvisation. We now recognize that, when a literature primarily assumes the context of a performance, this will demand a poetics different from our own book-centered one. Thus, in early poetry, whether in epic (a locus classicus? The field is still dominated by the shadow of Lord: but try Nagy, 1996), or lyric (locus classicus: Gentili, 2006 [1984]). Then again, we also went beyond recovering just the performances that underlay the earliest and primarily oral stage of Greek literature. The point is that the Greeks never did shed this poetics of performance (how could they, indeed, not having shed the canon to which it gave rise?). As this becomes recognized, classicists begin to pay attention, for instance, to the performative character of Athenian civilization as a whole (Goldhill and Osborne, 1999), debate again the actual role of performance in Hellenistic poetry (Alan Cameron, 1995), recover the performance of the Second Sophistic (Gleason, 1995) and recognize that even the literate, unsung poetry of the Romans can be understood only in relation to an implied, performed, model of poetry (Barchiesi, 2007). I quote a few *loci classici*, but in truth one could open any recent publication in ancient literature at random: literary scholarship in the classics, through the last quarter-century, was largely dedicated to the discovery of ancient performance.³¹

---

³⁰ The concept made famous by Booth (1961). Is it even possible to extract a single "implied author"? Is it desirable? It was around this question that the post-structuralist debate concerning the author was framed.
³¹ And so, the one essay engaged directly with the question of the author function in classical Greece ends up with a conclusion which is perhaps the same as mine (Calame, 2004: 39, my translation): "The classical Greek author-function arises in a way from an authorial prototype, at the same time emblematic and a guarantee of a discursive practice of a po(i)etic order." What Calame means,

And so, the sense in which a text approaches us and, "personified", says "Hi, I'm a Mac" – or, let's say, "Hi, I'm a Pindar" – is quite direct and material. We actually do imagine a person as we read the text. We imagine his or her voice, his or her body in performance, or the space where his or her works are to be staged. Indeed, we may well engage in performance as we read: many reading events involved the reading together, aloud – with an emphasis on correct elocution and performance – of the canonical works.[32]

This may be turned into a prediction. I suggest that, in the ancient context, the brand potential of the name of an author was correlated with one's ability to imagine the author's works in performance. This prediction is borne out.

Technical works are less performative; correspondingly, we see a much weaker organization according to authors in the technical sphere.

The following table puts side by side the papyrus fragments by the "top author" in a given genre, and the total number of fragments by adespota in that genre (which may serve as proxy for "less famous authors" in that field. The strict number of adespota is useful as an objective number; I add in brackets the – impressionistic – estimated number of minor authors, produced in the table on pages 83–4 above.) This yields a top/periphery (T/P) ratio which measures the dominance of the core authors in their field, or the degree to which a field was dominated by its more canonical authors (2011 numbers).

| | | |
|---|---|---|
| Homer 1,861 | Epic 157 (75) | T/P ratio 11.9 (24.8) |
| Demosthenes 186 | Oratory 96 (15) | T/P ratio 1.9 (12.4) |
| Euripides 170 | Tragedy 65 (20) | T/P ratio 2.6 (8.5[33]) |
| Menander 117 | Comedy 131 (38) | T/P ratio 0.9 (3.1[34]) |
| Pindar 57 | Lyric 108 (38) | T/P ratio 0.5 (1.5[35]) |
| Plato 90 | Philosophy 102 (87) | T/P ratio 0.9 (1) |
| Thucydides 96 | History 154 (146) | T/P ratio 0.6 (0.7) |
| Hippocrates 24 | Medicine 286 (98) | T/P ratio 0.1 (0.2) |

I think, is that the author function is a sign referring to an imagined author-in-performance, which in turn is a sign of the performative genre as a whole.

[32] Johnson (2000; 2010); this is distinct from the once popular claim that the ancients only read aloud, now thoroughly debunked (Knox, 1968; Gavrilov, 1997).

[33] This number should be slightly adjusted upwards: several tragic adespota are in fact by Euripides.

[34] This number should be significantly adjusted upwards: many comic adespota are in fact by Menander.

[35] This number should be slightly adjusted upwards: several lyric adespota are in fact by Pindar.

Arrangement according to tiers would once again be useful. The first tier to itself is epic; the second tier is (in this order, apparently) oratory, tragedy and comedy; the third tier, in order, is lyric, philosophy and history; medicine (and, so, technical literature as a whole) follows at some distance.

Now, the ordering of tier 2 is a matter of historical period: among the Ptolemaic papyri, Euripides reigns almost as supreme, in his genre, as does Homer. In the Roman era we see a retreat of tragedy, a rise in rhetoric; which accords with a pattern of *vividly present performativity*. Epic performances were always a given, at least in one's early education if not beyond. One always learned how to pronounce Homer properly.[36] Not only that: the performance was not understood to require access to any original, lost music. Tragedy and lyric did rely on their musical performance (new comedy less so). The music of lyric was lost before the Hellenistic era; that of tragedy was lost later. We thus understand the ordering of tragedy, comedy, lyric and oratory and its historical transformation. We have come to take this for granted, but it is a distinctive feature of ancient literature: that philosophy, as a real literary presence, was dominated by the genre of dialogue – specifically, by Plato, a master of the vivid, present voice. Equally, it is probably not an accident that history was dominated by works that contained powerful speeches. Still, the genres of history and philosophy were already primarily written and so did not develop as powerful an authorial presence, as powerful a structuring, based on the named author.

The claim that the presence of the author was mediated through performance implies, we notice, a relation between author and genre. This is the evidence we look for: the overall position of the authors, within the literary field as a whole. Let us look at this structure.

## 2.2 The Polis of Letters: Structure

The larger system within which we need to put the author was a three-layered graph made of genres, authors, works. In what follows, we will study this topology in detail. I first look (section 2.2.1) at the connection between the layers of author and works. I then look (section 2.2.2) at the connection between the layers of author and genre. Once both have been considered, I bring in more evidence to consider the graph as a whole (section 2.2.3). I emphasize, above all, that the presence of the ancient author emerged from genre, not from works. With this, we can understand the function of the canon, as a whole, for its ancient readers. It was the

---

[36] Mitchell (2006).

authors pitted as avatars of embodied performance: preserving, through many centuries, a cultural model of the political realities of the small city state. Hence, the polis of letters (section 2.2.4).

### 2.2.1 *Genre/Author/Work: The Works beneath the Author*

The Greek canon was big. But it was also structured. Instead of remembering a set of 50 to 100 independent entries, the ancient reader knew a work as occupying a niche in a structured order of three major layers: "genre", "author" and "work".

Let us first take a rather expansive category – works that now (2011) have at least six papyrus fragments – a group which I then adjust.[37] With this definition in mind, we can find a little over 100 works,[38] spread between 27 authors.[39]

| Author | Works | Number of heavily circulated works / their total word count |
|---|---|---|
| Homer | *Iliad*; *Odyssey* | (2/203 K) |
| Menander | *Epitrepontes*; *Misumenus*; *Dysc.*; *Pericir.*; *Samia*; *Georgus*; *Aspis* | (*c.* 7/47 K) |
| Euripides | *Phoe.*; *Orestes*; *Androm.*; *Medea*; *Hecuba*; *Bacchae*; *Hippo.* | (7/62 K) |
| Hesiod | *Theogony*; *Works and Days*; *Catalogue*; *Shield* | (*c.* 4/44 K) |
| Callimachus | *Hymns*; *Hecale*; *Aetia* | (*c.* 3/46 K) |
| Apollonius | *Argo.* | (1/39 K) |
| Theocritus | *Idyl.* | (1/20 K) |
| Aratus | *Phaen.* | (1/8 K) |
| Demosthenes | *Olynth.*; *Chers.*; *Philip.*; *False Leg.*; *Crown*; *Lept.*; *Midias*; *Timocr.* | (*c.* 8/115 K) |

---

[37] I extrapolate from Plato's works with many fragments (*Phaedo, Phaedrus, Republic, Laws*) to Plato's collected works: I explain this below. I remove technical works whose fragments probably represent rapid discard: Hippocrates' *Aphorisms*, *Astrampsychus*, Ptolemy's *Handy Tables*, Euclid's *Elements*. I also bring in plays by Menander with four fragments or more, to compensate for (I suspect) his many adespota fragments; I also put in the play with the most fragments by both Sophocles and Aeschylus. In all such cases, the identification of the "real" ranking of the plays is, of course, especially difficult.

[38] In what follows I count "the collected works" of a lyric poet as a single work.

[39] These are the 19 canonical authors identified at the end of Chapter 1, together with several more lyric poets (Alcaeus, Sappho, Archilochus, Alcman, Bacchylides) as well as Aesop (as usual, a question mark); and then a few exceptional cases: Achilles Tatius (allowing us to consider the reception of the novel), and Lycophron's *Alexandra* (surprising, but perhaps we should believe the evidence of the fragments – and of the manuscript tradition).

*(cont.)*

| Author | Works | Number of heavily circulated works / their total word count |
|---|---|---|
| Isocrates | *Ad Nicocl.*; *Ad Demon.*; *Peace*; *Paneg.*; *Antid.* | (*c.* 5/45 K) |
| Aeschines | *Ctesiph.*; *Timarch.*; *False Leg.* | (*c.* 3/46 K) |
| Thucydides | | (1/153 K) |
| Herodotus | | (1/189 K) |
| Xenophon | *Mem.*; *Cyr.*; *Hell.* | (3/185 K) |
| Sophocles | *Ajax* | (1/8 K) |
| Aeschylus | *Septem contra Thebam* | (1/6 K) |
| Plato | | (*c.* 36/587 K) |
| Aristophanes | *Nubes*; *Achar.*; *Equites*; *Plutus*; *Pax* | (5/46 K) |
| Pindar | | (1/90 K?) |
| Alcaeus | | (1/53 K?) |
| Sappho | | (1/47 K?) |
| Archilochus | | (1/21 K?) |
| Alcman | | (1/36 K?) |
| Aesop | | (1/46 K) |
| Bacchylids | | (1/90 K?) |
| Achilles Tatius | *Leuc.* | (1/43 K) |
| Lycophron | *Alex.* | (1/8 K) |

A genuinely surprising result is the stability of the number of curated words per author. This has a very powerful center of gravity at around 45,000 words: the extremely narrow range of 43,000 to 47,000 words was reached, by the methodology above, for eight authors – almost a third of the authors represented: Menander, Hesiod, Callimachus, Isocrates, Aristophanes, Sappho, Aesop and Achilles Tatius. Slightly below and above are three more: Apollonius, Alcaeus and Euripides. The word count is sensitive to my particular choice of the threshold of canonicity and of course to random noise; it is reconstructed for most authors and is most probably wrong for Sappho if not for others.[40] And yet: I did not expect any such result and did not cook my books to get it! Some 43,000 to 47,000 words; this stands for a reality: it is not just word count but is, instead, a measure of a particular scale, comparable to the ultimate choice of seven plays for Aeschylus (43,000) and Sophocles (61,000). This is the

---

[40] I suspect that if we had the real word counts for lyrical poets, however, we would find that they are clustered near the low end of the range; that is, I suspect we undercount Archilochus (his rolls were big) and overcount Pindar as well as, surely, Bacchylides (some at least of their rolls were small).

scale studied by Blanchard in his work on the ancient antecedents to the eventual selection of canonical works. It is the scale of the *basket* with two or so clusters of three to four rolls.[41] Eventually, this would become the scale of the codex. Not too much emphasis should be put on the material constraint, of course. They could have afforded bigger baskets. Rather, we see a material counterpart to cognitive and social thresholds: 30,000 to 60,000 words – or works counted according to the magic number seven plus or minus two – or the same number of rolls in a single work – was as much of their mental space as the Greeks normally set off for an author for whom they deeply cared.

The exceptions? Of course, Homer; Demosthenes is exceptional in a different way, as is Plato. Then the three historians, who break the 30,000 to 60,000 threshold mainly through their very large size of roll.[42] The remaining exceptions are of small author corpora. The case of Sophocles and Aeschylus is probably misleading, and it is perhaps better to dismiss the papyri count for individual plays and just consider them each as a normal, 40,000 to 60,000 author, whose overall circulation was too small to register (that is, too much confined to the big library). The remaining cases form a genuine exception. These are three Hellenistic poets whose collected output was on the small side, with a single work each: Theocritus (24,000: perhaps not significantly below the normal), Aratus and Lycophron.

And so, we recall the qualified presence of the Hellenistic poets in the canon. Callimachus was the last author to be collected as such; later additions to the canon (including Apollonius himself) would do so on the power of a single *work*. It is thus misleading to think of such poets as brand names: their name was not powerful enough to carry the interest in them as an author, beyond the single work. In their case, it was not the author who was made canonical, then, but the work itself: hence the absence of portraits, TLG mentions and biographies. Something in the power of brand making eroded, at just this moment, early in the third century.

And, conversely: up to Callimachus himself, canonization was of an author as such, not just of an individual work. It thus entailed the collection of 30,000 to 60,000 words, in a few cases more. There was an active brand making, which made names, such that those names carried with them a larger authorial corpus.

---

[41] Blanchard (1989).
[42] Herodotus: nine rolls; Thucydides: eight rolls; Xenophon: three major works of eight, seven and four rolls, respectively.

The precise structure of works' frequency within an author's corpus would vary. The three options at work seem to be: the collected works; fixed selection according to tiers; and a curve of works by the author, suggesting a freer selection based on the aggregate of random preferences.

It appears possible that some canonical authors had a single-level corpus of the "collected works"; and, indeed, it seems natural that the lyric poets would often circulate in the manner suggested by the extant library mark to Pindar's works: "Pindar, whole" (Caroli, 2007).[43] So much is speculative; we can be more precise in one case: that of Plato. The following table sets out, for each of Plato's works, the number of words followed by the number of fragments (Plato's numbers were augmented somewhat from 2011, and such a table could be sensitive to this; I therefore calculated the numbers again on July 6, 2018).

| | | |
|---|---|---|
| *Euthyphro* | 5,463 | 1 |
| *Apology* | 8,854 | 1 |
| *Crito* | 4,329 | 1 |
| *Phaedo* | 22,633 | 12 |
| *Theages* | 3,650 | 1 |
| *Rival Lovers* | 2,424 | 1 |
| *Theaetetus* | 23,803 | 6 |
| *Sophist* | 17,404 | 1 |
| *Euthydemus* | 13,030 | 2 |
| *Protagoras* | 18,079 | 1 |
| *Hippias Minor* | 4,505 | 0 |
| *Cratylus* | 19,201 | 2 |
| *Gorgias* | 27,824 | 6 |
| *Ion* | 4,091 | 0 |
| *Philebus* | 19,055 | 2 |
| *Meno* | 10,396 | 2 |
| *Alcibiades I* | 11,317 | 4 |
| *Alcibiades II* | 4,422 | 2 |
| *Charmides* | 8,410 | 2 |
| *Laches* | 8,021 | 5 |
| *Lysis* | 7,319 | 1 |
| *Hipparchus* | 2,426 | 0 |
| *Menexenus* | 4,908 | 0 |
| *Statesman* | 18,592 | 8 |
| *Minos* | 3,078 | 1 |
| *Republic* | 89,358 | 14 |
| *Laws* | 106,297 | 9 |

---

[43] The view of Pelliccia (2009: 248) is that the ultimate selection of the epinician poems, to survive from among Pindar's oeuvre, was a late (Byzantine?) choice: more on this below.

| *Epinomis* | 6,389 | 0 |
| *Timaeus* | 24,104 | 1 |
| *Critias* | 5,040 | 1 |
| *Parmenides* | 16,434 | 2 |
| *Symposium* | 17,530 | 1 |
| *Phaedrus* | 17,221 | 8 |
| *Hippias Major* | 8,911 | 1 |
| *Epistles* | 17,213 | 2 |
| *Spuria* | 14,839 | 3 |

On average, each 6,000 words of Plato now transforms into one papyrus fragment. The great majority of the works are represented in the papyrus fragments almost precisely according to this average value. The more notable exceptions are these, in ascending order of significance.

- *Laches*: five fragments, about 8,000 words. Almost certainly, this result is random noise (which is to be predicted among 36 small-number entries).
- *Laws*: nine fragments, about 106,000 words. Plato's longest (and most boring) work,[44] it could have discouraged some prospective collectors. It could also have been unlucky.
- *Phaedrus*: eight fragments, about 17,000 words. This is a reasonably marked deviation, and it seems likely that the work – understood perhaps primarily as Plato's statement on rhetoric – would have had a special appeal for anyone pursuing a rhetorical education.[45] (The implication, then, is that Plato, at least in Egypt, was not collected primarily by "philosophers"; which is obvious, given his wide reception. He belonged to the literary canon). Nevertheless:
- *Statesman*: eight fragments, about 19,000 words. There is no very compelling argument for this deviation; perhaps this is, once again, random noise.
- *Phaedo*: 12 fragments, about 23,000 words. This is the most striking result, in quantitative terms, and it is easy to see why the *Phaedo* would attract special attention:[46] it is biographically interesting as a depiction of Socrates' death, it discusses a doctrine of supreme importance

---

[44] Subjective judgement! For, whatever it's worth, there are no known ancient commentaries to the *Laws* and the dialogue is not among the core sources of doctrine for later Platonists (Plotinus relies most on the *Phaedo*, *Phaedrus*, the *Symposium* and the *Timaeus*: see Armstrong, 1967: 214 – a Neoplatonist set of emphases which moderns may still appreciate, and which is somewhat suggested, as noted below, even by the Egyptian papyri).

[45] For the reception of the *Phaedrus* in the Second Sophistic, see Trapp (1990).

[46] For the ancient reception of the *Phaedo*, see Delcomminette, d'Hoine and Gavray (2015).

regarding immortality and indeed, for this reason, could well have been read as a kind of summa of Platonic philosophy (for whatever it's worth, the earliest extant philosophical commentary other than the Derveni papyrus itself is a commentary on the *Phaedo*: a third-century BCE papyrus).

What we see is that, with the exception of two works, the numbers of papyrus fragments of Plato are best understood on the hypothesis of a flat distribution between all the works (with a few deviations due to random noise). Several non-exceptional works are very striking. That the *Republic* should be so exactly predicted by a simple "flat" distribution is uncanny.[47] That the *Timaeus* is not more popular is very surprising, given what we usually think about Plato's ancient reception. (The work has by far the most attested commentaries – see note 47 above – and it remains possible that among philosophers it was appreciated the most. In the papyri, however – representing, perhaps, a more general reception? – it is, if anything, under-represented, albeit not in a significant way.) The *Alcibiades* – a set of two dialogues, one of which was occasionally taken to be isagogic to Plato's works,[48] and therefore likely to leave more traces of Plato as a figure in the educational process – is not greatly common. The sophisticated, mature works of epistemology and metaphysics – *Theaetetus*, *Sophist*, *Statesman* and *Parmenides* – are very well represented, even though it is hard to see how anyone, other than a professional philosopher, could have made much sense of them. In short, the distribution, with two exceptions, is very hard to associate with particular preferences or avoidances. The two exceptions – the *Phaedo* and the *Phaedrus* – comprise 20 fragments, of which 6.5 would be predicted "anyway", so that only 13 to 44 of the 103 Platonic papyri fragments are due to the "overcount" of the *Phaedrus* and the *Phaedo*. The great bulk of the Platonic papyri fragments, then, seem to emerge from a random, "flat" distribution, whereby all dialogues are equally likely to survive.

---

[47] The *Republic* may not have had in antiquity the pre-eminent position it gained in modern times. The database of ancient commentaries (www.ancientphilosophers.net/commentaries/</u) lists only two attested commentaries to the *Republic* (*Timaeus* has nine, *Parmenides* six, *Alcibiades I* and *Phaedo* five, *Cratylus* and *Philebus* three; alongside the *Republic*, *Phaedrus* and *Sophist* also have two). Even so, the *Republic* did become a major emblem of Platonic writing: its beginning was chosen by Dionysius of Halicarnassus as an example of Plato's diligence as a stylist (*De Comp. Verb.* 25). Most important, criticism and emulation of Plato sometimes took the form of imitations of the *Republic* – from Zeno of Citium, through Cicero and beyond.

[48] Mansfeld (1994: 94–5).

We find, in short, that Plato was most typically collected (at least, away from the philosophical schools) not through one's education in philosophy, nor through one's developed preference for this or that work, but through the desire to have his collected works present in one's library (which was the case in roughly 5 to 10 percent of all libraries – if we take the *Iliad*'s penetration to represent "all libraries").[49]

The circulation pattern in Plato's case is easier to discern, because he was a major author with a well-articulated corpus that survives intact. How far can this be extended for other authors? Aristophanes clearly did not circulate as "collected works"; the methodology taken above suggests the selection of just five plays: *Clouds, Acharnians, Knights, Peace, Wealth.* Delving beneath the six-fragment threshold, however, we find the *Wasps* with four fragments, and the *Birds, Lysistrata, Frogs* and *Women in the Thesmophoria* with three fragments each.[50] The impression is that the papyri represent a selection of Aristophanes comparable to the ultimate selection made by the codex, perhaps arranged in two tiers.[51] This may be bolstered by the clearer case of Homer and Hesiod, who were certainly collected in two tiers each: the *Iliad* as against the *Odyssey*, in Homer's case (other "Homeric" works being discarded altogether); *Theogony* and *Works and Days* in the top Hesiodic tier, the *Shield* and the *Catalogue* in the lower one.

So, alongside the "collected works" model, we may envisage the "two-tier" model. Is this perhaps the more central rule? Plato himself, after all, did have, we suggested, two dialogues more frequent than the rest: so maybe the *Phaedo* and the *Phaedrus*, taken together, should be envisaged

---

[49] This is based on the table on pp. 15–18 above, with the assumption (see pp. 89–92 above) that the extant papyri over-represent Homer and slightly under-represent the big library, with its better curatorial practices. Note that Xenophon is perhaps comparable to Plato, though the numbers are too small to make a clear judgement. We have (title followed by number of words, rounded to nearest thousand, and by number of fragments; from this point on in this section I rely on 2011 numbers): *Symposium* 10,000, 3 frr.; *Memorabilia* 36,000, 6 frr.; *Cyropaedeia* 81,000, 13 frr.; *Hellenica* 68,000, 7 frr.; *Anabasis* 58,000, 5 frr.; *Apologia* 2,000, *De Vectigalibus* 4,000, *Res Publica Laecedaemoniorum* 5,000, *Agesilaus* 8,000, *Cynegeticus* 9,000, *Oeconomicus* 18,000, 1 fr. each. By the standards developed for studying Plato's distribution, we find that *Symposium* is slightly over-represented, *Hellenica* and *Anabasis* slightly under-represented. This may perhaps best be interpreted as a two-tier scheme, the "philosophical"/"novelistic" works constituting a top tier which is roughly at Plato's level.

[50] *Women in the Assembly* has one fragment only; probably sheer bad luck.

[51] Indeed, this is an author surviving mostly from late antiquity: the choice of the papyri is nearly *contemporary* with the choice of the codex. (Note that the number of potential Aristophanic adespota is small and unlikely to change this result.) It is customary to refer to a "Byzantine triad" – *Wealth, Clouds, Frogs* – perhaps joined also by *Birds*, as the plays most central to the later, Byzantine reception (Sommerstein, 2010). This roughly agrees with the evidence of the papyri (and, with such a small sample, we should expect no better than very rough agreement).

as the top-tier Plato – and all the rest second-tier Plato? Indeed, we recall the first-book effect, which is also a tier effect, the first tier constituted by a work's first book, the second tier by all the rest (the *Iliad*, as usual, presenting the exception of a *gradual* layering). Is the first book of Herodotus, or of Thucydides, then, their first tier, their "portable" version?

Then again, is the distribution of Pindar truly just an artifact of our ability to attribute his fragments? Of the 57 fragments, 25, or 44 percent, are from the four transmitted books of victory odes; but, if we assume that the rolls were all roughly of equal length, we should have expected victory odes to constitute 24 percent of the total.[52] Could it be the case – here, too? – that antiquity itself gave the cue to the medieval transmission, and that the victory odes constituted a slightly more elevated tier in antiquity itself? But the evidence is insufficient.

In the case of Aeschylus and Sophocles, we have Morgan's (2003) analysis: their fragments are never found away from the more urban and northern sites, and the implication is that they are indeed strictly confined to the big library.[53] This would help account for the relatively undifferentiated survival of their works. They have each a little over 30 fragments (36 for Sophocles, 32 for Aeschylus; but the result is actually a bit more impressive for Aeschylus, with his much shorter plays). This is about 40 percent of the number of fragments by Plato that we associate with the big library. Plato's collected works take up the equivalent of 500,000 words of poetry, or about 60 Sophoclean plays (or perhaps 80 Aeschylean plays). We end up with the following hypothesis: that the type of library that contained Plato's collected work could also contain a very large selection of plays by Sophocles and Aeschylus; not the complete works, but nevertheless much more than late antiquity ended up choosing.[54] But we cannot rule out the existence of an ancient tier

---

[52] Pelliccia (2009: 248) points out that this is to some extent an effect of the late ancient survival of Pindar (all papyri from the fourth century onwards are epinician; likely, circulation was now limited to that). There are only seven such papyri, however: among papyri of the Hellenistic and the Roman era, 18 out of 50, or 36 percent, are epinician. Then again, some of the lyric adespota must be non-epinician Pindar; bringing this in, the fraction of the epinician among the extant pre-300 CE Pindar papyri becomes, essentially, the predicted 23 percent. To add to the uncertainty, we do not know if the epinician rolls were longer or shorter than the average Pindar roll.

[53] Which indeed is paralleled to some extent in the case of Pindar, 40 of whose 57 fragments are, as noted above, *known* to be from Oxyrhynchus.

[54] It is true, as Finglass (2012: 13–14) points out, that the selection of the seven plays seems to have been made already in late antiquity, but, while the transmitted plays are more prominent in the papyri from the Imperial era as well, the numbers are too small to draw conclusions and, more important, are so few as to be sensitive to even a handful of unidentified adespota (which by necessity will not be among the transmitted plays). As Finglass adds, the pattern of quotations by ancient authors does not reveal a clear picture of an emphasis, in the Imperial era, on a small selection of plays.

system for them, too, which simply escapes our current papyrological evidence.

Still, the "selected works" of Sophocles and of Aeschylus had certainly emerged by late antiquity, if not before; it is then, once again, that we find the selection for Aristophanes. This might even have continued a tier of sorts, the "portable" version, with something like five plays, collected in smaller libraries. Finally, there may also have been perhaps a set of collected poetic narrative by Callimachus; the *Hymns*, perhaps, were the portable version. This principle of "collected works"/"portable" seems to cover, then, most of the canonical authors of whom enough survives to justify such claims. It operates with the major epic poets (among whom we should count Homer, Hesiod and Callimachus), who obtained the kind of status that justified wide collection in a complete set; and also with the more sophisticated authors, who were therefore collected primarily by big libraries.

A more complex case was that of the major, small-library, performative authors. They produced somewhat shorter works, which fit the size of a single performance – i.e. typically a single roll. They also produced plenty of them. (The same was also true for Aristophanes, of course, but his collection was more a matter for the big libraries.) The smaller libraries that made the choices to collect speeches and drama had to make choices from a wide variety. The result is selection and curved slopes that mimic, in miniature, the structure of the canon as a whole. Rhetoric had three major authors in clear descending order (Demosthenes, Isocrates, Aeschines). The same was repeated within each of those authors' corpora. If we ignore Isocrates' exhortations, we find that the *Peace* is much more frequent than the *Panegyricus*, in turn much more frequent than the *Antidosis*, nothing else being very frequent at all.[55] Aeschines, too, has three speeches: in descending order, *Against Ctesiphon*, *Against Timarchus* and *False Embassy*. Demosthenes has a very similar sloping pattern of three: the *Olynthiacs*, then *Chersonese*, then the *Philippics* (so, some of the major political speeches involving the war against Macedon). In his case, however, this is just a first tier, followed by a second tier of five

---

[55] It appears that Callimachus' hymns were more frequent than the *Hecale*, or the *Aetia*, which in turn were more frequent than any of his other works; on the other hand, it seems possible that a few epic fragments still should be assigned to either the *Hecale* or the *Aetia*, in which case we should simply say that Callimachus was collected as an author of hexameter (broadly defined).

speeches from a more varied group of occasions (*False Leg.*; *Crown*; *Lept.*; *Midias*; *Timocr.*), all roughly of equal frequency.

Menander's pattern is the most difficult to reconstruct. Two or more fragments are:

| | |
|---|---|
| *Epitrepontes* | 14 |
| *Misumenus* | 14 |
| *Dyskolos* | 7 |
| *Periciromene* | 6 |
| *Samia* | 5 |
| *Georgus* | 4 |
| *Aspis* | 4 |
| *Colax* | 3 |
| *Sicyonioe* | 3 |
| *Citharista* | 2–3? |
| *Theophoroumene* | 2 |

This surely over-represents the better-preserved plays, however: unassigned fragments (which are many, in Menander's case) would surely make the distribution even flatter. Perhaps Menander's distribution took, once again, a two-tier form, of a few plays with many more copies. (The top two? A few more, assuming that, perhaps, a play such as the *Dyskolos* could have been unlucky in its survival into papyri?) And then, many more plays that were less frequently collected though still popular enough. The latter is unambiguously the case with Euripides:

| | | |
|---|---|---|
| *Phoenician W.* | 28 | Extant |
| *Orestes* | 19 | Extant |
| *Andromache* | 12 | Extant |
| *Medea* | 12 | Extant |
| *Hecuba* | 9 | Extant |
| *Bacchae* | 8 | Extant |
| *Hippolytus* | 6 | Extant |
| *Cresphontes* | 4 | |
| *Heracles* | 4 | Extant |
| *Iphigenia T.* | 4 | Extant |
| *Telephus* | 4 | |
| *Alcestis* | 3 | Extant |
| *Cretenses* | 3 | |
| *Hypsipyla* | 3 | |
| *Iphigenia Aul.* | 3 | Extant |
| *Trojan W.* | 3 | Extant |
| *Alcmaeon* | 2 | |
| *Antiope* | 2 | |
| *Electra* | 2 | Extant |

(*cont.*)

| | | |
|---|---|---|
| *Helen* | 2 | Extant |
| *Rhesus* | 2 | Extant |
| *Theseus* | 2 | |

This is followed by no fewer than 17 plays for which just one fragment is identified, of which only one is extant: an eccentric exception, the satyr play *Cyclops* (indeed, as a satyr play is roughly half the size of a tragedy, this should count as the equivalent of two fragments!). Once again, it is striking to see how effectively the papyrus frequency predicts survival in the manuscript tradition (or else we have to assume – less likely in my view – that a great many of the papyri currently unassigned by Euripides are not only by him but also fit into no more than a handful of unknown plays; more likely, bringing in unidentified fragments and adespota would lift and extend the tail of the curve but would not change its shape). But the fundamental point for our purposes is that, since so many of these plays are extant, the ranking by number of fragments is fairly robust – and it is clearly a *continuously* sloping curve. In the case of Euripides, at least, the intensity of critical reception – a field of competing preferences – produced the kind of differentiation seen in the structure of the canon as a whole.

So: Euripides and, perhaps, Menander. But they are exceptional: selection overall involves less well-articulated differentiation, based instead on a coarse-grained division into two tiers or a sequence of just three works. What the gradation within the truly popular authors, Menander and, above all, Euripides, shows is the nature of the small library. There was not a single size for the small library; there were larger and smaller libraries, and they differed from each other. How? Primarily, in how many Euripides and Menander pieces they contained. Hence, many more of the more popular plays by these authors, fewer of the less popular. For most authors, however, collection was restricted to the big library, and there the main principle was that of the collected works or of a well-defined selection thereof.

The big library is where critical reception took place: and what we find, then, is that the intensity of *distinction* did not extend much from the level of the author to the level of the work. The ancients ended up distinguishing their authors and ranking them individually, but, once such distinction had been established, the works within the individual corpora were largely packaged together as entire sets or as large subsets. Canonization, we recall, operated, primarily, at the level of *authors*: this means that it operated much less at the level of *works*.

### 2.2.2    Genre/Author/Work: The Genre above the Author

Let us look again at the list of more-frequent works from the preceding section. My structuring simplifies it into a list structured according to 28 categories, each an author, typically with no more than a handful of entries in each.

But of course the 28 authors are structured as well. I have repeatedly referred to the authors as falling into generic categories. This is perhaps once again best understood in terms of a tree, as follows.

| Poetry | | | | | Prose | | | | |
|---|---|---|---|---|---|---|---|---|---|
| Epic | Drama | Lyric | Oratory | History | Philosophy | | | Other | |
| | Tragedy Comedy | | | | | | Fable | Nov. | Sci.[56] |
| 3 (5) | 3 (4)[57]    2 | | 1 (7) | 3 | 3 | 1 | (1) | (1) | (1) |

The numbers here are the numbers of canonical authors in the genre; in brackets are the numbers when single-work authors are added in (or, in the case of lyric poetry, when authors other than Pindar are added in).

This tree controls seven to ten base categories, arranged from left to right in a progression that, I suggest, is roughly from center to periphery. Comedy is the "other" of drama; lyric is the "other" of poetry, the least canonical and canon-forming of the genres. For this reason, it has more canonical authors in multitude, each rather weak in magnitude (it cannot establish a powerful canonical center). Prose is the "other" of poetry (for this reason, it generates more genres, less clearly defined); the "Other" category in "Prose" is "other" several times over and obtains only qualified status.

In short, everything operates by hierarchically defined pairs and triads, down to the level of the individual author: poetry/prose; epic/drama/lyric; tragedy/comedy; canonical prose/other; oratory/history/philosophy; and then:    Homer/Hesiod/Callimachus;    Euripides/Sophocles/Aeschylus; Menander/Aristophanes; Demosthenes/Isocrates/Aeschines; Thucydides/ Herodotus/Xenophon. Indeed, this may even be extended, in a weaker form, further down into the authorial corpora themselves, which, as we saw, so often involve a pair (core or "portable edition"/other or "collected

---

[56] I count Anubion as the sole (surprising!) representative of "science" in the canon, under this (greatly expanded) definition.

[57] I do count again Sophocles and Aeschylus: obviously, they were present as central canonical authors in the bibliosphere, even if none of their individual works were.

works") or, in the case of the orators, a triad. Usually the first term is considerably more powerful than the rest, and, the more "central" a category is, the more powerful is this asymmetry. It is more powerful within poetry than within prose: most between epic poets, least between historians. There is less layering of lyric poetry, less layering within the Platonic corpus. We are tempted to say: this all fits structuralism like a glove; it is the manner in which society structures its cultural map via comparative rankings. Hierarchical pairs and triads. The mind just works this way.

Which mind, though? We have learned to become wary of the ease of this kind of structuralism. Whose pairs and triads, whose tabulation? Is it not that of the modern categorizer? Are those genres even historically real?

Consider Xenophon, my number three historian. Or was he perhaps the number two philosopher? Indeed, the *Hellenica* (which most obviously makes him join the group headed by Herodotus and Thucydides) does not appear to have been in his "portable edition", which, instead, was more philosophical – indeed, Socratic (*Symposium, Memorabilia* and the *Cyropaedia*). And yet – I would argue that there is no doubt that the genre of "history" is a real, ancient category. It is not merely our project, to cluster authors by genres; ancient audiences and even the ancient authors themselves must have conceived of literature as governed by genre.

Xenophon's case is an example of what happens when historians are prolific: genres tend to get blurred (more on this below). Another atypical case – but a telling one – was that of Callimachus. In a sense here is an author who truly straddles all genres: poetry and prose, epic and lyric. In practice he is present in the evidence of the papyrus strictly as a poet, and above all as an author of hexameter (in a sense which includes elegy).[58] This is reminiscent of the way in which the ancient tradition, which understood Homer to have been the author of four works – *Iliad, Odyssey, Hymns* and *Margites* – collected the first more than the second, and the third and fourth, essentially, not at all. Authors were collected within the boundaries of what was understood to be their defining genre. In the case of Callimachus, this presents a relatively minor complication (we need to decide on how to define "hexameter").[59] Even in the case of Xenophon the genre is complicated

---

[58] It is possible that certain scholastic adespota could derive from Callimachus; there are no positive indications of that, however. This is one further example of how the specialized genres did not construct, before late antiquity, a canonical ranking.

[59] It is a central question in the study of Callimachus: was he a bold innovator in his choice, for various occasions, between hexameter and elegy? As Cameron (1992) has pointed out, it may well be that the choice appeared less urgent for Callimachus, and for his readers, than it does for us. These were close variations on the same epic theme.

and original: historical writing of a reflexive, philosophical variety. But he was primarily the author in this single genre, and was collected as such.

Let us take a single, yet comprehensive example of the way in which ancients could classify authors: the surveys of homonymous persons (those who have the same name as the subject of the biography) in Diogenes Laertius. While the work of a single individual, it is edited from various sources (occasionally it borrows explicitly from Demetrius of Magnesia's study of homonymous authors, but it is clear that Diogenes has other sources as well).[60] It is useful to note that there is no single formula of classifying an individual. The dyad "genre/place", in either order, as in "Archytas, a musician from Mytilene" (VIII.82), appears to be the most common, but this is not more than 27 out of the 183 entries, or 15 percent. As in all levels of Diogenes' work, variety is prized and the multiplicity of heterogeneous sources is embraced. In short, we do not need to see in the classifications the expressions of Diogenes' idiosyncratic fancy. They appear to be the composite product of scholars from Demetrius down to Diogenes – that is, from the first century BCE to the second century CE. This is how antiquity classified authors.

Above all, through genre. If we include "philosophical school" as a category analogous to genre (and also count the handful of non-author endeavors, as well as the fairly frequent painters and sculptors), we find that 126 out of the 183 individuals are classified according to their genre of activity. Place – which looms so large in Diogenes, and, as we shall note, in Greek representations of culture in general – comes only second to genre. Eighty-five of the individuals, fewer than half, are provided with a spatial classification, which in practice is almost always the name of a city. Still, this 85 is a large number: it is important to contrast space with time. To us, chronology may be the starting point in classifying an individual (we think of ancient authors primarily in terms of eras, perhaps centuries). It seems clear that Diogenes Laertius typically had the information with which he could determine eras, and that he just did not consider this important as such. I count no more than nine individuals – about 5 percent – for whom rough dates are mentioned. The range of those dates is significant. Almost all are marked for being very early.[61] Diogenes does not mention dates to

[60] See Mejer (1981) for an attempt to extract the Demetrian layer, and for the argument as to why Diogenes must have been eclectic in his sources.
[61] A Thales (I.38, *archaios panu*), a Xenocrates (IV.15, *archaios sphodra*), a Bion (contemporary with Pherecydes of Syrus, IV.58), a Strato (V.61, *archaios*), a Demetrius (V.83: an orator "older than Thrasymachus" – so not archaic while being very early for his genre) and all three extra Pythagorases (Diogenes does not assert that they were old, merely that all four Pythagorases were near contemporaries: VIII.46).

help us locate an individual in our mental maps. He does so in order to tell us something noteworthy about the individual. They are akin to the brief biographic comments (a critical assessment in two or three words, name of a famous individual an author was related to, etc.) which make the lists of homonyms into microbiographies.[62] One's date (specifically, being very ancient) was a particular anecdote. But one's *essence* was given by the composite of genre and city.

Works are named for 34 of the 183 individuals, or a little below 20 percent. What is even more significant is the generic category of such works. Twenty-eight of the 34 individuals for whom individual works are named are scholars or (most typically) historians. So, for instance, one of the Demetrii was from Kallatis and wrote 20 books on Asia and Europe. His genre is not "history" or "geography"; he is simply an author of books, *gegraphōs. . .biblous* (V.83). This is the typical way to classify historians, and, indeed, the adjective "historian", *historikos*, is rather infrequent (six times).[63] Historical (and scholarly) authors were primarily classified via their works while all other authors were primarily classified generically.

We find that it was essentially taken for granted that an individual would readily be pigeonholed into a generic category: one just was a poet of the old comedy, an orator, a peripatetic, a physician, a sculptor or a painter. This is how lives were supposed to be lived. There is no impression left at all that Diogenes *struggles* to contain his individuals within such generic categories. Indeed, he is happy to report the rare crossings of such divisions, as no doubt interesting anecdotes. The final of the Heracliti (IX.17) was a citharode who then became a clown (!) – a rare specimen (should we rule out the possibility of a joke concerning Heraclitus' philosophy, misunderstood by Diogenes or one of his sources?). Two of the

---

[62] Fifty-two of the individuals are microbiographically/critically treated, often very briefly (Carneades was a poet of *frigid* elegies: IV.66).

[63] In general, *suggrapheus*, which roughly means perhaps "the one compiling pieces of writing", is a word meaning "prose author" in general (so that Greek, unlike English, had a special word for this purpose, analogous to the word for "poet", *poiētēs* – literally "maker", but the metaphor might be largely dead in the post-classical era). There were specialized words, however, such as *rhetōr* (orator), *philosophos* (philosopher) or *iatros* (physician), used much more naturally for authors in the various prose genres other than history. In that case, *historikos* seems to have preserved its etymological sense of "related to empirical enquiry". (The close association of the term *historia* with the genre of history is a Roman phenomenon – see Krebs (2015: 506) – i.e., in a context in which the word lost something of its etymological resonance. Contrast with "lover of wisdom", which did become a dead metaphor in Greek itself, *philosophos* referring simply to a certain generic endeavor.) Hence the Greek word for "prose author", *suggrapheus*, came to mean also what we call a "historian" (in a wider sense which also includes scholarship and geography of a certain kind).

Demetrii explicitly crossed generic boundaries: the one nicknamed *graphikos* was a lucid prose writer (of which genre?) who was also a painter (V.83).[64] The other, finally, was truly an author of many genres (V.85): a *poikilographos*, or many-spangled-author; a poet who also wrote historical and oratorical works. Writing in many genres is, we find, extremely rare, and calls for special comment.[65]

I argue that genre, in antiquity, was a reality, and not just a construct that we throw back upon our evidence. This is somewhat akin to my claim, in the preceding chapter, that the canon was a reality, and in both cases the tendency of scholarship over the last generation – if not longer than that – is to resist such traditional categories. Our resistance to genre, in particular, is imbued with value judgement, and in fact genre is often discussed, in contemporary scholarship, through the praise of its subversion.[66] There is nothing wrong with our own value judgements, nor should we be afraid to bring them to our own judgement of ancient works. But we should also be careful not to let them bias our historical interpretation: the fact that we feel that genre should be resisted should not lead us to think that the ancients did, and, indeed, the bulk of the evidence suggests they did not. Which brings us to another important methodological point. The way scholars in the humanities often go about answering a question, such as "Was genre a reality in antiquity?", is to scan their memory for examples. If one wishes to show that genre was not a reality then one would simply have to scan one's memory for examples of authors whose work straddled many genres. But, obviously, such authors can be found: the question is one of statistical preponderance, and for this statistical question we require the tools of statistics. Scanning one's memory as a methodology is simply the equivalent of "cherry-picking" – the practice of avoiding randomness and, instead, willfully constructing arguments based on a small, hand-picked, unrepresentative sample.

---

[64] The absence of a more specific generic marker suggests, as noted above, that he wrote historical or scholarly works; did he write perhaps on painting? If so, his generic oddity would be eliminated.

[65] Note also the parallel case of philosophical schools, in which identity was supposed to be lifelong: for the few exceptional cases when school boundaries were crossed (sometimes noted as scandals), see Dorandi (1999b: 60).

[66] In July 2018 I found on Google Scholar 1,060 works of scholarship, published since 2014, using the words "genre-bending". These words are apparently always applied positively – "a groundbreakingly genre bending memoir..."; "genre-bending writers like...are getting increasing (and deserved) attention"; "some of the most innovative, genre-bending, and generally mind-bending fiction in contemporary literature" – and so on: value is placed on being *new*, being *other*. This is all fine, but it is also distinctly unlike the ancient Greek reception of literature.

And so, to have a genuine empirical test, I produced a random sample of 100 authors (taking up the TLG canon of authors and choosing the first author whose entry starts on every *second* page, then filling up with an extra 18 authors picked by leafing at random).[67] I then tried to identify the genres within which those authors were active. As far as we could tell, 79 were clearly active in a single genre. So, for instance, my survey includes Alexander of Aphrodisias: an extremely prolific author – about a million extant words, but we have lost many more. Prolific – but not promiscuous. All those words are either commentary on Aristotle, or more self-contained philosophical studies arising directly out of Aristotelian scholarship. Another author in my survey is Plato, whose 650,000 words are all preserved, and then some (the corpus contains a few obvious spuria). A handful of the letters might be genuine (were they strictly speaking "works" in the sense of the dialogues?), but everything else is...well...Platonic dialogue, relentlessly pursuing exactly the same form, year after year, book after book, perhaps for the duration of 50 years. This is amazing, when we consider how polymorph an author Plato was, hiding behind his many personas, shifting (perhaps) his views and his interests – indeed, writing dialogues which are extremely diverse in their make-up. And yet the one constant core was genre.[68] So, in general: the bulk of the authors appear to have had only a single genre. This may be because we know relatively little. Very often what we have is a citation mentioning that so and so, a historian, notes a particular fact – and that's enough for Jacoby to form an entry and later for TLG to count an author.[69] It is clear that the loss of information makes it more likely for us to undercount cross-generic authors than to overcount them from among the authors extant on TLG[70] – but it should be borne in mind

---

[67] Note that it is important, when constructing such samples, to pick not (1) the author whose entry is the first in a page, but (2) the author whose entry is the first to *start* on a given page. Option (1) creates a powerful bias for authors with long entries.

[68] The idea that Plato wrote poetry in his youth is one of the most often repeated in the literature of Platonic anecdotes (anecdote 14 in Riginos (1976: 43–8); he was also said to be a wrestler, and a painter). This is almost certainly apocryphal, and Riginos hypothesizes that this was extrapolated from Plato's own comments concerning education.

[69] The single largest group is that of historians – 20 in my random sample. This may be partly the thoroughness of Jacoby's work, but it seems to be also a real feature of ancient literature. There was always room for new, regional histories: they seem to form one of the major groups of adespota in our papyri. (I shall return to discuss this in Part III.) It will be noted that this is not more than a very small plurality.

[70] Note, however, that authors of whom only a single work is reported are relatively rare: only 26 among my 100. For the rest, we typically know that they produced more than one work, and produced all their work in the same genre. I also should explain how overcounts can come about. We may overcount cross-generic authors by relying on false testimonies that confuse separate

that the authors extant on TLG would also, for another reason, tend to include more cross-generic authors. I explain: the TLG is a list of the extant authors (in an expansive sense of "extant" that includes "in fragments only"). Now, one important way towards ending up extant was to have been prolific. Those who wrote more survived more. Thus, the TLG has a bias towards the more prolific authors. It is clear that many of our lost authors would have written little, and so would probably have fewer opportunities to cross generic boundaries. In short, then, I suspect my sample over-represents, if anything, the frequency of generic crossing in antiquity: all those scholarly authors with a massive output, crossing several genres, are relatively well attested now but would have been comparatively rare in antiquity.

For, indeed, what is truly significant is not the frequency of generic crossing as such but its character. Let us look at the minority of authors – 21 – whose classification into genres is more problematic.[71] I arrange them according to chronological categories.

*Early polymaths: 2*

| Name | TLG number | Era | Genre |
| --- | --- | --- | --- |
| Democritus | 1304 | CL | Philosophical/scientific |
| Aristotle | 0086 | CL | Philosophical/scientific |

*Hellenistic and early Roman polymathy: 3*

| Eratosthenes | 0222 | Hel. | Mostly "scholar" but much more |
| --- | --- | --- | --- |
| Semus | 1663 | Hel. | History (Delos) but also "on Paeans" |
| Juba | 1452 | Rom. | History, "scholarship" |

authors (it was Demetrius' project, after all, to prevent such confusions). It is clear that the *Suda*, in particular, is guilty of such confusions (so Jason – TLG author 1921 – was probably a historian, and the *Suda*'s mention of him being a "grammarian" is most likely a confusion). All in all I count three errors of this kind in my random sample of 100 authors: Perigenes, TLG 1021 (a medical author, not a mechanical author); Hypsicrates, TLG 1983 (a historian, not a grammarian); and the Jason mentioned above.

[71] I do not list here three authors who had a clear generic identity but also, added on to it, produced epigrams (apparently epigrams form a small exception to the genre rule: they were something one was supposed to do "on the side"; the epigram was lyric par excellence, so here is yet another indication for the weak generic force of lyric poetry). Those are: Archelaus, TLG 0570, paradoxographer; Marcus Argentarius, TLG 0132, Latin orator; and Philodemus, 1595, philosopher. I also leave out a case of "sequential identities": Androtion, TLG 1125, was first an Attic orator and then, being exiled, assumed another identity, that of the historian. Radical changes in one's life could entail one's taking up of new generic identities: but this reinforces rather than undermines the decisive nature of a generic choice as a choice of *life*.

*Second Sophistic authors: 5*

| | | | |
|---|---|---|---|
| Aelius Aristid. | 0284 | Rom. | Speeches; prose hymns; autobiography |
| Favorinus | 1377 | Rom. | Philosophy with a Second Sophistic |
| Galen | 0057 | Rom. | Medicine, philosophy, scholarship |
| Plutarch | 0007 | Rom. | Philosophy, history (biography), "scholarship" |
| Polyaenus | 0616 | Rom. | History, tactics, "rhetor" |

*Late ancient/Church context: 8*

| | | | |
|---|---|---|---|
| Athanasius | 2035 | LA | Theology, hagiography |
| Basilius | 2040 | LA | Theology, quasi-scholarship |
| Callinicus | 2189 | LA | Rhetoric, history |
| Gregorius Naz. | 2022 | LA | Theology, rhetoric, etc. |
| Gregorius Thau. | 2063 | LA | Theology, rhetoric, etc. |
| Hippolytus | 2115 | LA | Theology, history, law, etc. |
| Methodius | 2959 | LA | Dialogue, theology |
| Themistius | 2001 | LA | "Speeches" and philosophy |

The numbers are not entirely driven by the presence of a large *extant* corpus; it is clear that both Democritus and Eratosthenes showed a great generic variety, even though no more than a tiny fraction survives of either's work (furthermore, we deduce Aristotle's generic variety not just from the extant corpus but from its combination with the works known through the fragments). True, we certainly see here some of the largest corpora to survive from antiquity. Authors such as Galen and Plutarch aimed to do amazingly much, and part of the amazement had to do with variety.

Everything in this set has to do with scholarship. "Scholarly" authors are those reflective upon the canon. And so we find the following result: authors who took up the genres that constituted the canon – poetry as well as non-scholastic prose – had to make a commitment. It was, literally, a choice of life. We all remember how, at the end of the *Symposium*, Socrates buttonholes the somnolent Aristophanes and Agathon and proves a typical, paradoxical Socratic position: the same person should write both tragedies and comedies.[72] The two barely follow and fall asleep, defeated,

---

[72] *Symposium* 223d; see Patterson (1982).

and yet, in their very person, refute Socrates... In antiquity, Socrates' advice was not heeded. The occasional citharode could become a clown, just as the occasional philosopher could switch schools. On the whole, one made one's choice and stayed with it.

There was of course much generic experimentation among the Hellenistic poets. But it was the reflective attitude towards the canon that allowed the spirit of Alexandrian experimentation (see Chapter 4, on the "surveying" character of Alexandrian literature). The generic experiment was taken up again, in a different way, when the Romans picked up the Alexandrian project: so Ovid, Cicero, Seneca... But this once again involved the project of constructing a new literary project, reflectively picking up the various elements from a tradition.

Perhaps most remarkable is the strength of generic identities where they would seem to matter least – in science. It is a received idea among modern historians of science that scientific disciplines follow scientific institutions.[73] If so, absent our institutions, pre-modern authors should not have our disciplines. And yet ancient scientists had an extremely strict disciplinary regime. Not a single author contributed to both medical and mathematical literature.[74] A few mathematicians were also philosophers (a work in logic is ascribed to Ptolemy, who certainly displayed considerable philosophical interests;[75] and philosophers in the Platonic tradition, especially in late antiquity, often engaged with mathematics, sometimes in

---

[73] This seems to be inspired primarily by the rich variety of scientific life in early modern Europe, which was indeed gradually eroded through the rise of the university as a setting for scientific research, constraining the scientific life through the regimented terms of institutionalized disciplines: a social reality, accepted yet constantly lamented by the scientists themselves (see, e.g., Daston, 1998). And, indeed, in many other civilizations (such as those of ancient Mesopotamia) scientific genres do follow the institutional realities, primarily of education. It is a specific feature of Greek science: to have genre fill the role that, elsewhere, is filled by institutions (Asper, 2007: 147–56).

[74] The most serious contender for a counter-example is the report in Diogenes Laertius (VIII.86) that Eudoxus was a physician. The only reason this carries any weight is that Diogenes says that he has it on the authority of Callimachus' Pinakes that Philistion of Locri was Eudoxus' teacher. But most probably Diogenes misunderstood his source (the most likely source of the entire confusion is another report preserved by Diogenes VIII.89, that a certain Chrysippus was the pupil of both Eudoxus, in astronomy, and Philistion, in medicine – a report that itself could have got mixed up with the many Chrysippi from the fourth and third centuries; see discussion in Berrey, 2014a). The certain observation is that there is no individual for whom we have testimonies of both medical authorial activity (in the sense of any positive doxography) and mathematical activity (in the sense of composing an original piece of mathematics). This is remarkable, in that this combination is ubiquitous in the most faithful heir to the Greek scientific tradition, medieval Islam, from Al-Kindi to Ibn-Sina and beyond. It is not as if the two, the ancient exact sciences and the ancient medical tradition, cannot be pursued by the same mind!

[75] For Ptolemy the philosopher, see Taub (1993).

a sustained, professional way).[76] Galen certainly was both a medical author and a philosopher. We will see in Chapter 4, section 4.5.5, how this was especially natural in the Imperial era. But even then – and even though Galen repeatedly asserted the value of a mathematical education – he himself did not engage at all significantly with mathematics anywhere in his writing, and, at any rate, however prolific and generically varied, always remained first and foremost a doctor.[77] The same, a fortiori, was true of all scientists in antiquity: they were first and foremost that thing which they were. Archimedes, Hero, Ptolemy: very different authors but certainly "mathematicians" contributing to a particular genre, namely the exact sciences. The mix could have been different – the combination of geometry, various ludic works, and the study of the physical world in Archimedes; the combination of mechanics and elementary school geometry in Hero; the survey of the mixed sciences, with a touch of philosophical curiosity, in Ptolemy. *Within* a generic boundary, there would have been considerable freedom. But the freedom stopped at the generic border.[78]

An author's career would be defined by a genre. Indeed, it would be defined: authors would be aware of their choices of writing as falling into the pattern of their overall output. Perhaps this was done most self-reflectively in the Roman case (Roman authors were actively setting out a new canon and so actively considered their position within it) – so Farrell (2002) and the collection of essays edited by Hardie and Moore (2010). The key example is Vergil: first you write *Eclogues*; then *Georgics*; then *Aeneid*. Pastoral, didactic, epic – the ladder of the hexameter. The fundamental point is that, the more serious your ambitions, the more you would concentrate on a single genre and consider your career within it (Cicero and Pliny were forced into their multiform activity, or cast themselves as amateurs so as to justify it: so Gibson and Steel, 2010).

Now, this should be put against modern literary careers. Our own value judgement is different – and is related to the ideal, very modern poetic persona of the "genius". The best case to consider is Russian culture, where

---

[76] So, most obviously, Proclus' commentary to Euclid's *Elements*, as well the passage in Simplicius concerning Hippocrates' quadratures (in *Phys.* Diels 60–8); in a sense, this may also be the context for Eutocius' commentaries as a whole.

[77] I argue for the extremely narrow engagement of Galen with mathematics, in Netz (2017a).

[78] I began this book with the question, scrawled by Geoffrey Lloyd on the margins of my PhD: did the mathematical genre indeed remain stable, throughout antiquity, "because some aspects of the relevant background remained in force throughout antiquity"? Come on! Of course not! The cultural and political background changed a lot but what remained the same is the power of genre. To become a mathematician, then, was to pick up a particular authorial life, with all its literary accompaniments. Little wonder the style did not change much. Ancient genre was *like that*.

the figure of the author looms most powerfully. There, an author's career is made by the *crossing* of generic boundaries. The pattern, as ever, was set by Pushkin, who actively expanded his output from short lyrical forms (the launching pad to him as to so many others) to narrative poems, then a play and then short prose (he died before writing his novels). And so for all of later Russian literature: a substantial fraction of canonical prose, from Lermontov down to Pasternak, was written by noted poets. The dramatic canon includes major works by Turgenev, Tolstoy and Gorky (famous in the West strictly as prose authors; Chekhov, uniquely, had become globally canonical for both prose and drama). Even Dostoyevsky – his career choices severely limited by financial needs – was noted as a journalist and an essayist no less than as a novelist.

Genre breaking is typical to post-Romantic literature for reasons which are obvious enough: the more an author can flout generic constraints, the more he puts on display his *idiosyncratic* power. He breaks from the pack. The figure of the author, in the post-Romantic era, is made like that; the more powerful it is, the more so, hence the Russian extreme (because, there, for well-known political reasons, literary authorship carried special significance). It is therefore remarkable that the – very powerful – figure of the author emerged in an ancient context which frowned upon such breaking of generic boundaries, in which authors were imagined *inside* their packs.

But we are pushing ahead, and we should sum up the interim result. In antiquity, genre reigned supreme: because an author was imagined as taking up a *life*. Authors were marked more by their genre, and so, conversely, authors were defined less by their works. Let us proceed to see this final observation in more detail.

### 2.2.3   *The Topology of Ancient Literature*

We find that the canon ranged primarily over authors, selecting a certain group of individuals. This group was defined primarily through genres, however. This suggests a paradox: the canon worked through the logic of brand names through which certain individuals stand out from their peers. It primarily identified those individuals, however, according to what they *shared* with others – their genre – and not with what set them apart – their works. The literary tree was structured according to authors, but it looked up from authors, to genre, and now down, to works.

This is correlated with the following strong claim, for which I will gradually build the evidence through the remainder of this section: in antiquity, works, quite simply, did not identify authors. The contents of one's work were not the key to one's distinctive mark as an author. This is striking for a modern reader, who takes it for granted that authors are, above all, the artificers of imaginative worlds and that they become canonical by carving out a piece of virtual reality as their own – so that this becomes, in a sense, author-restricted. The name (and the age) *Lolita* and "Nabokov"; *madeleine cakes* and "Proust"; *whales* and "Melville"; even the whole of *Dublin* – indeed, even the whole of *June 16th* – and "Joyce". Modern authors are primarily marked by the contents of their work, and vice versa; the author–content nexus defines the literary field. But, then again, it is quite obvious that the idiosyncratic fictional domain – the one used in one work and then never used again – is marginal in the ancient literary system. It is only in very narrow cases that one can find, in antiquity, anything like Austen's Highbury, Flaubert's Yonville, Mann's Berghof.[79] One may think, in more general terms, of the cast of characters as the more abstract "domain" of a work. This, too, is typically idiosyncratic and fictional in the modern novel, but, as I note in more detail below, it is shared across many works and authors in antiquity in the form of *myth* or *history*. More precisely: ancient fictional domains are associated with a non-performative genre (the novel), which for this reason is the genre that creates the weakest authorial presence. (Comedy, as usual, is an errant case; see below.) Achilles Tatius was indeed "the author of *Leucippe and Clitophon*", characters who belong just to him. But who was Achilles Tatius himself? We have no clue, and the same, apparently, was true even back then, there being no biography, no grammarian scholarship, no critical reception focused on the identity of this, undoubtedly popular, author.

And indeed, most generally, ancient authors' works take place in the shared domains of myth (in poetry) and history (in prose). The question is this: when the ancients thought about particular mythical events, did they think of them primarily as particular representations in poetry? It would be

---

[79] This is all related to a central question in the history of literature, having to do with the invention of fiction. It is widely recognized that the understanding of literary "fiction" changed simultaneously with the rise of the novel, mostly through the eighteenth century, creating our standard practice of the suspension of disbelief (for a compelling statement, see Gallagher, 2006). Finkelberg's (1998) argument that, in some ways, "fiction" was an ancient invention is also valid: her point is that the ancients came to think of literary craft as due not to divine inspiration but – as I keep insisting in this chapter – to the author. This author, however, at least in the central genres of Greek literature, did not control a separate, suspended-in-a-vial universe all for himself (which is the sense in which "fiction" is indeed a modern invention). For that, one would need the modern author and her novels. I return to this large-scale opposition between "the ancients and the moderns" on p. 155 below.

bizarre indeed if they did so while myth was primarily oral: as Herington (1985: 63) has pointed out, archaic myth had to form a "shared world". To some extent, all we will note below is that the habit of the shared world of myth never died. And so let us look very far ahead of the archaic era. My starting point is the ekphrastic authors of the third century CE and beyond. Theirs was the highly literate, reflective culture of the canon of the late Imperial era and late antiquity. And yet these works make surprisingly few explicit allusions to literary works. Philostratus the elder does refer regularly to Homer (seven times out of 64 described paintings), and does mention Pindar explicitly, once, for the figure of Theiodamas (II.24), as well as Euripides (for Heracles the Mad, II.23) and, very remarkably, Xenophon, for the figure of Pantheia (II.9). And yet, stories we would think of as primarily literary are not explicitly referred to a literary source (*Bacchae*, I.18, *Hippolytus*, II.4, no mention of Euripides; *Argo*, II.15, no mention of Apollonius; *Polyphemus*, II.19, no mention of Theocritus; *Antigone*, II.29, no mention of Sophocles). Philostratus the younger has one explicit mention of Sophocles, for *Philoctetes* (17); Callistratus has two explicit mentions of Euripides, once for *Dionysus* (8) and once for *Medea* (13). Otherwise, they just describe scenes without a reference to their literary depiction. It is indeed intriguing that the tale of deserted Ariadne – one of the central episodes in Vesuvian iconography and certainly, among other things, a Euripidean one – is assumed by Philostratus to be known as a *nursery tale* (I.15: nurses, we are told, like to recount and weep over this story). Indeed, the imagined addressee is truly young, and these works could emerge from the classroom context.[80] All the more remarkable: the authors that Philostratus could have named but did not are among those that the highly educated youngsters were supposed to know. The overall impression is that the iconography of myth, even for the late ekphrastic authors, was not defined primarily via canonical literary descriptions and that myth, instead, existed primarily as cultural material separate from the literary sphere, accessible to literature but not owned by it, so that when art accessed the same space it did so on its own, unmediated by literature.

The question of the visual depiction of literature is of course contested. Taplin (2007: 22–6) addresses the debate concerning the presumed depiction of drama on vases, dividing the field into "philodramatists" (who see

---

[80] See Arthur-Montagne (forthcoming), who sees such references to the classroom as somewhat ironic, however: her reading is that the ekphrastic authors pretend to speak from the perspective of the classroom while engaging with the sophisticated concerns of the elite audience.

vases as illustrations of plays) and "iconocentrics" (who see vases as autonomous artistic creations). Scholars today naturally gravitate towards the iconocentric position. It combines structuralist attention to form with the historicist acknowledgement of the agency of artists. It elevates the visual to be the equal of words, turning upside down age-old academic traditions in an act of thrilling subversion. The fully iconocentric position is made by Small (2003), whose book is even titled *The Parallel Worlds of Classical Art and Text* – the point, for her, being that art, as such, was independent. Indeed, even Csapo (who is keen on the argument that vases do provide important information on theater, thus revealing theater's ubiquitous presence) has this to say on the display of tragic myth on vases (Csapo, 2010: 3):

> There are at best five Attic pots or fragments that can be said to depict tragedy in performance. Tragic performance is even harder to find in West Greek pottery. Of some twenty thousand known vase paintings, as many as 450 can be reasonably argued to show influence of tragedy – but of these no more than two could be said unambiguously to "show tragedy".

How does Csapo recover the use of art as the depiction of drama? Through an insistence that the relation between art and its dramatic contents never left the realm of the visual. So, Csapo (2014: 96): "Dramatic performance is a visual (even if not just a visual) art and the visual arts in Greece shared in a commonwealth of motifs." This idea of sharing in a commonwealth is suggestive for the type of shared universe of content that we approach.

On the other hand, take Taplin, as his example is in fact suggestive of a certain opposition between antiquity and modernity (2007: 25):

> Suppose that we have a series of paintings that all evidently share the same basic iconography: they show a young man in black, with a white blouse, staring at a skull. [Taplin points out that it is possible – and, indeed important – to read all those images iconocentrically, inspired by iconographic traditions and differing in their artistic execution.] [T]hey do not need the Hamlet story, let alone Shakespeare's text. But even a rudimentary recollection of the Shakespeare…will surely inform and enrich the picture [in this sense, then, Taplin suggests that the drama enriched the vases].

But perhaps the very point is that there was no obvious ancient parallel to Shakespeare's Hamlet, no figure that, by virtue of a powerful treatment by a canonical author, comes to be defined as essentially *of that author*. Consider what might appear to be a leading contender: Euripides' *Medea*. It could have been Euripides' invention to have her kill her children, and it is indeed as a child killer that she is remembered from Euripides onwards. But even if this is Euripides' own invention, it does not take place in the enclosed domain of Euripides' fiction. Instead, it takes place in the shared domain of myth. That is: Euripides has, perhaps, changed the manner in which others will recall myth from that point onwards, and they were free to do so, writing their own Medea plays. There may or may not have been a previous infanticide version in a tragedy by Neophron; there were perhaps seven or eight tragic authors, as well as five comic authors (myth is a typical theme of "middle comedy"), writing versions of "Medea" in the century *following* Euripides' *Medea*.[81] Since our knowledge of drama in this century is extremely fragmentary, it is prudent to assume there were several dozen "Medeas" on the stage at Athens: a new one, perhaps, every other year. A major treatment of a particular mythical theme, then, could actually inspire a copycat phenomenon; or, more technically, a major work created an axis of intertextuality that defined, effectively, a *subgenre*. (Of course, the most powerful example of that is Homer himself, who sat at the top of the most powerful axis of intertextuality of them all, that of the Trojan Wars – which, for that reason, were never *just* Homeric.) For whatever it's worth, *none* of the six "Medea" vases cited by Taplin depicts a scene on the stage of Euripides' play (four – Taplin nos. 33 to 36 – depict, perhaps, offstage events; two seem to derive from alternative myths, perhaps alternative plays: Taplin nos. 94 and 102).[82] As for the Pompeian depictions of Medea – most significantly derived from the panel painter Timomachus[83] – we may now follow Gutzwiller (2004). She is keen to find a direct reflection of the text in the depiction, and her summary of the case is prudent (2004: 349–50):

> What vase painters almost always represented in their depictions of tragic scenes was not the realia of the staged event, such as masks and scenery, but the mental image created by the performance, what is called today the dramatic illusion. [...] So Timomachus conveyed, as it seems, what the viewer may remember as the power and meaning of Medea's monologue, not the scene as presented on stage. [...] Timomachus thus found it necessary to conflate several scenes from Euripides and to change the staged relationship of characters and props in order to convey the internal dynamic of Medea's monologue by a single visual image.

Undoubtedly Timomachus and his audience had the text of Euripides internalized. But did it supplant, as it were, myth – did "Euripides' *Medea*" replace, in their mental representation, "Medea" itself? We have direct

---

[81] Euripides' possible originality: Mastronarde (2002: 49–64); Medea's influence: (2002: 64–5).
[82] Todisco (2006: 246) counts altogether eight Medea vases: not a big number.
[83] For the Roman reception of Timomachus' Medea, see Vout (2012).

evidence for this question in the epigrams studied by Gutzwiller: AP 16.135 to 143 are all ekphrastic epigrams referring to the experience of viewing an image of Medea. They sometimes refer explicitly to Timomachus but – and here is the observation over which I differ from Gutzwiller – they *never* refer to Euripides or even unambiguously allude to him.[84] The point of the epigrams is to praise Timomachus, for his depiction precisely of "Medea" itself and not of "Euripides' *Medea*". Once again: I do not deny that, when thinking about Medea, viewers also thought of Euripides; I do not deny that, when they thought of Medea, they thought of her (at least to the extent they thought of her Corinthian phase) primarily as represented by Euripides. But what they did think about was her: Medea. She remained a creature of myth, not of tragedy.

The point is deeply counter-intuitive for readers steeped in the tradition of fiction. Two analogues might help. First, our fairy tales do not have the same cultural status as did ancient myth (precisely because fiction has supplanted myth as the major vehicle of narrative). But they are structurally not unlike myth, and, indeed, it is quite clear to us that a new telling of Sleeping Beauty is not a reference to the Tchaikovsky ballet, or even to the Disney movie, but is instead a reference to the tale itself, which has not been taken over by any of its particular tellings. Second, myth was not alone, in antiquity, as a field of narrative which authors could not take over for themselves. So was history, even at its most canonical (Plutarch could go back and write a biography of Pericles, which was not a retelling of Thucydides). This autonomy of narrative reference is still with us: it is quite obvious to us that even Tolstoy cannot make Napoleon "his", that a new retelling of the 1812 campaign would obviously, among other things, play intertextually with *War and Peace* but would deal with a realm that is understood to exist independently of any author.

In this sense, then, I would argue that Medea was not "Euripides'". Timomachus is not like the illustrator of Hamlet; rather, he is like the post-

---

[84] Gutzwiller analyzes in greater detail Antiphilus' epigram (AP 16.136) and convincingly argues for allusions to philosophical discussions of the character of Medea (she also points out the many, rather obvious allusions that the epigrams are making to each other: so we find that these are highly allusive texts). As for allusions to Euripides, she points out (2004: 367–8) the words μέλλησις (line 7), and χείρ (lines 1, 8): the first could very well be a philosophical allusion, but for it to work as an allusion to Euripides we need to emend the text – and then to read allusion into distinct forms of a single, very common word (Euripides has, perhaps, μέλλω, as well as μέλλομεν); then again, references to "hands" in such a context hardly count as allusion. At this point, it becomes significant that there is an explicit reference to Timomachus in some of the epigrams – as it shows that those very epigrams do *not* avoid referring to named historical persons as such. The absence of allusion or reference to Euripides begins to appear as a significantly non-barking dog.

Euripidean playwrights, returning to the same theme and offering their own version. And, indeed, Small (2003) is right: the worlds of art and literature were parallel, in antiquity, but not exactly (or not just) as an observation concerning the relationship between the different media, but also, more basically, as an observation concerning the relationship between creative reflections on the same shared mythical world: none could become the anchor to supplant myth itself.

Now, as Gutzwiller points out, this is a problem primarily for tragedy, with its emphasis upon myth. The vase painting of comedy, on the other hand, does depict the performance itself (for which see Taplin, 1993: also Csapo, 2010: 65–7). Why do vase paintings of comedies depict the actual performance of comedy, and not the "dramatic illusion" of a space in which the events of comedy unfold? Surely this has to do with the fictional status of comic scenes, which in turn is related to the fictional, ad hoc characters. Pisthetaerus and Euelpides are not designed to subsist in an openly narratable realm, such as that of *Medea*; there is no expectation that other dramatists would come along, to produce the sequel to cloud cuckoo land.[85] Such comic characters are enclosed within the ad hoc realm constructed by Aristophanes for the purposes of his own play. And where is this located? In one place only: on the stage. For this reason, then, depictions of comedy quite naturally are depictions of comic performance.[86] There is no other place for comedy to take place, whereas tragedy takes place in the mythical domain and is merely depicted on stage. Comedy – marked for its generic otherness.

Another, related way of looking at the marking of the individual work is through its literal marking – the title. One is reminded of Moretti (2009), a study of the transformation of the title of the English novel from the middle of the eighteenth century to the middle of the nineteenth. Titles become much shorter: from summaries of the narrative[87] they become catchy phrases or even words.[88] This corresponds with the radical

---

[85] While ancient literature did not possess Flaubert's Yonville, it did have the analogues of Swift's Lilliput: within parodic, metaliterary settings, locations that scream their non-existence.

[86] Green (1991: 26–7) emphasizes the complementarity phenomenon: the flouting of "dramatic illusion" or the meta-generic awareness, through the performance, that old comedy was just that, enhancing attention to the actual performed event (rather than its intended referentiality). The phenomena are complementary, because fictionality was, in the ancient context, a mark of artificiality.

[87] E.g. Moretti (2009: 139): *A letter from H—g—g, Esq; One of the Gentlemen of the Bedchamber to the Young Chevalier, And the Only Person of his Retinue that attended him from Avignon, in his late Journey through Germany, and elsewhere; Containing Many remarkable and Affecting Occurrences which happened to the P— during the course of his mysterious Progress. To a Particular Friend.*

[88] E.g. (Moretti, 2009: 145): *Persuasion.*

transformation of the literary field: the novel, originally rather marginal, becomes central to a large literary market, and as a consequence it becomes what we now still associate with the very idea of a "title": a competitor for the market's attention. A brief title, to catch the ear and the eye.

Now, notice an important presupposition: that a book's success should depend on the identity of the book itself (and not just on that of the author, let alone the genre). Thus the attention-grabbing title is a marker of the centrality, in the literary field, of the individual work. Its ancient absence comes, then, as no surprise. The ancient book did have a title, in the sense of a bibliographic marker at its outside, beginning or end.[89] Titles were sometimes variable – hence the many disjunctive transmitted titles; typically, they did not carry authorial sanction. A good summary of the entire practice is in Thrasyllus' arrangement of the Platonic dialogues, in which each dialogue was provided by Thrasyllus himself with two titles, one based on the main interlocutor, the other on the theme – e.g. "Euthyphro or On Holiness" (DL III. 57–61). As we see from this example, ancient titles are very often minimal and neutral descriptions of the work's content.[90] Titling by characters was the simplest: so tragedy as well as old comedy (main character or chorus), and rhetoric (often "for" or "against" an individual).[91] Note that the main tragic character would be known from the common character set and, to the extent that one knew one's Athenian history, the same would be true of the speeches. The alternative formula, as we have seen already from Thrasyllus, was that of the main theme or generic classification. It is by no means limited to the specialized technical fields and is instead the most basic literary norm from archaic epic onwards. (In lyric poetry, however, titles are avoided altogether: the sphragis or seal was an internal naming of the author and not an external titling of the work;[92] titles such as those of Pindar's victory odes are the – successful – effort of Hellenistic scholars to find as neutral titles to lyric

---

[89] The papyrological, as well as some of the iconographic evidence, is collected in Caroli (2007) (already mentioned on page 80 above). For a discussion of the origins of the practice (certainly well entrenched already in the fifth century), see Caroli (2007: 1–13). The central study in the field remains Nachmanson (1941) (the nature of the ancient title – with its very obvious significance for the nature of ancient authorship – remains, largely speaking, a curious omission by more theoretical scholarship; but see, e.g., Pinto, 2012).

[90] Thus, these are often belated (Schmalzriedt, 1970, for instance, plausibly suggested that the entire "On Nature" series is a title bestowed by later readers; one needed a named author, not so much a named work).

[91] If two works by the same author involve the same main character, later readers could choose to refer to them simply as, e.g., "the big Hippias" and "the small Hippias"! On this practice, see Leszl (2006: 43).

[92] See, e.g., Edmunds (1997).

poetry as possible: not so much titling as *classifying*.) Hellenistic poets, ambitious to insert themselves into the literary field, achieved canonicity with works whose titles offer neutral descriptions of contents (*Aetia*, *Phaenomena*), generic classification (*Hymns*) and main characters (*Hecale*, *Alexandra*). There could have been some originality in the choice of contents, genres and characters; but the consequent titling procedure was, to say the least, subdued.[93]

Still, attention-grabbing titles are attested from antiquity. Here are some examples I have come across.[94]

| Title | Author | Contents | Era |
|---|---|---|---|
| *Tritogeneia* (*Three-origined*) | Democritus (ps.?) | Ethics | Class.? |
| *Horn of Amaltheia* | Democritus (ps.?) | Ethics[95] | Class.? |
| *Triagmos* (*Triad*) | Ion of Chios | Philosophy | Class. |
| *Aletheia* (*Truth*) | Protagoras | Dialectic? | Class. |
| *Skutikoi Logoi* (*Cobbler's Discourses*) | Simon | Socratic dialogues | Class. |
| *Canon* (*Rule*) | Polyclitus[96] | Description and rules of sculpture | Class. |
| *Katoptron*[97] (*Mirror*) | Eudoxus | Descriptive astronomy | Class. |
| *Peplos* (*Robe*) | Aristotle | Biographic compilation | Class. |
| *Deilinion* (*Afternoons*)[98] | Theophrastus | ? | Class. |
| *Tripod* | Nausiphanes | Epistemology | Class. |
| *Canon* | Epicurus | Epistemology | Class. |
| *Grapheion* (*Pencil*) | Callimachus | ? | Hel. |
| *Silloi* (*Squint-eyed*) | Timon | Philosophical parody | Hel. |
| *Indalmoi* (*Hallucinations*) | Timon | Philosophical satire | Hel. |

[93] There is one major counter-example, namely the *eidullia* or "little types", the title of Theocritus' collection of poems (while scholarship is cautious on this important question, I believe the striking title most likely suggests an authorial design). The self-referential awareness of the textual presence of the collection is typical of such marked titles, and is perhaps to be understood alongside the origins of this poetry in what was, after all, a genre of comedy: the Sicilian mime. (See, however, Clayman, 2009: 167–9, who seeks a philosophical influence in the title. For Theocritus and mime, see, e.g., Burton, 1995.)

[94] These are my anecdota, aided by Zilliacus (1938). The list cannot claim to be complete, and it ignores dramatic works (including dialogues), to which I turn briefly in the discussion below.

[95] These two titles are from DL IX.46. It should be noted that they are two of a very long list, with about 70 entries, the rest titled in a more formulaic manner.

[96] Some of these titles, while definitely "attention-grabbing", were repeated (Epicurus, too, had a work titled *Canon*); this does not necessarily mean such titles would lose their striking nature. I do not try to cover, systematically, all such repetitions of the same title.

[97] Or *Enoptron*: both versions given in the fragments (frr. 6, 3, 68).

[98] The metaphor appears to be that one does one's important work in the morning, and lighter stuff is left to the afternoon (Aulus Gellius XX.5). The marked treatise-title – reserved for one's lighter moments!

*(cont.)*

| Title | Author | Contents | Era |
|---|---|---|---|
| *Lembeuticus (Of the Little Boat)* | Heraclides | Scholarly/philosophical?[99] | Hel. |
| *Batrachomyomachia (Battle of Frogs and Mice)* | Anonymous (ps. Homer) | Homeric parody | Hel. |
| *Epikichlides (Thrusherizing)* | Anonymous (ps. Homer) | Homeric parody | Hel. |
| *Soros (Heap)* | Posidippus? | Anthology of epigrams? | Hel. |
| *Anthologia (Flower-gathering)* | Meleager (and others) | Anthology of epigrams | Hel. |
| *Tripod* | Glaucias | Medical methodology | Hel. |
| *Psammites (Sander)* | Archimedes | Cosmological calculation | Hel. |
| *Ephodos (Approach)* | Archimedes | Geometrical methodology | Hel. |
| *Stomachion* | Archimedes | Combinatorics on a puzzle? | Hel. |
| *Ocytocion (Of Fast Delivery)* | Apollonius | Geometrical calculation | Hel. |
| *Musarum (Muses)* | Opillus | Varied scholarship? (phil.?) | Hel. |
| *Leschai (Grapevine [the term refers to a public space where gossip is exchanged])* | Heraclides the Younger | Scholarship | Hel. |
| *Pinax (Table)* | Ps. Cebes | Philosophical treatise | Rom. |
| *Leimon (Meadow)* | Pamphilus | Grammatical anthology | Rom. |
| *Narthex (Casket)* | Soranus (etc.?) | Pharmacological collection | Rom. |
| *Cesti (Embroideries)* | Julius Africanus | Encyclopedic technical work | Rom. |
| *Keria (Honeycombs)* | Sporus | Scientific/philosophical survey? | Rom. |
| *Silvae (Woods)* | Lucan | Anthology | Rom. |
| *Pratum (Meadow)* | Suetonius | Anthology | Rom. |
| *Florida* | Apuleius | Anthology | Rom. |
| *Stromateis (Blankets)* | Clemens | Anthology | Rom. |
| *Kleis (Key)* | Melito | Christian interpretation | Rom. |
| *Noctium Atticarum* | Aulus Gellius | Varied scholarship | Rom. |
| *Dyktiaka (Hunting-nets?)* | Dionysius of Aegai | Anthology of medical theory | Rom. |
| *Panarion (Medicine-box)* | Epiphanius | Heresiology | LA |

[99] DL V.94 claims that Heraclides Lembus got his nickname from the work; could this be in error? He was a Hellenistic scholar, a biographical compiler, and so an antecedent to Diogenes himself. The title could well refer to a boatload of anecdotes.

What jumps out immediately is the centrality of the technical genres – indeed, at their most abstruse. Archimedes is one of the most original contributors to this list!

An entire set parallel to that of the list above is that of comic titles. Often formulaic, they still sometimes evoke characters or choruses that are so marked as to make the title itself stand out. *Women in the Assembly* is certainly among other things an arresting title, as is *The War-Ender* or *Lysistrata*.[100] The last title suggests already the practice of new comedy: the chorus recedes and one concentrates on the main character, employing not its (anyway, generic) proper name, however, but instead its grotesque type: Menander's rogue's gallery contains, for instance, a "grouch" (*Dyskolos*), as well as "she whose hair was cut short" (*Perikeiromene*); that of Philemon, "he who slips in besides" (*Pareision*), "she who is made young again" (*Ananeoumene*). (But note that even such titles did not become author-restricted, and that we have, for instance, several comic authors writing about the "child who was brought in" [*Hypobolimaios*].)[101] Some comic titles are certainly *intended* as attention grabbers. The upstart Aristophanes was laughing at Cratinus (a drunkard, no longer his old self) and so Cratinus fought back with the *Pytine*, or *Wine Flask*, where Comedy asks for a divorce from her husband Cratinus, the drunkard.[102] This last title already recalls the typical realm of the marked name outside comedy: a suggestive artifact; it is a reflection upon the papyrus roll itself, signaling its physical, artifactual nature by metaphorically likening it to another artifact: a tripod, a gathering of flowers, a stomachion, honeycombs.

The attention-grabbing title was a rare exception associated primarily with the *funny*. So how come it is so closely associated with sophisticated technical works? Menander – and Archimedes. How to account for this pattern? Let us note, then, that this pattern is not unique: we can find the very same combination, again, in the illustrated bookroll. Now, it is in fact very rare to find any illustrations on literary papyri. Two classes of literature did carry illustrations in antiquity, however: science, in particular the

---

[100]  Unique, in referring to a protagonist and not to a chorus (Kanavou, 2011: 129).

[101]  Satire can take the complexion of comedy, and it can also take its attention-grabbing title. This is common in philosophy of an especially pugnacious character (we note Timon's titles above): Oenomaus of Gadara authored a *Charlatans Unmasked* (Branham and Goulet-Cazé, 1996: 15); perhaps we should add his contemporary Lucian with his *Sales of Lives*, often rendered into English as *Philosophers for Sale*.

[102]  See Bakola (2010: 59–65).

exact sciences; and comedy and parody.[103] There is a rather obvious connection between the attention-grabbing title and the illustration: both are textual strategies, located on the papyrus, amplifying its meaning beyond that which is written on the text itself. In other words, what the two share – the attention-grabbing title, and the illustration – is the marking of *textual artificiality*. To frame a work with a marked title is to foreground the conscious choice involved in making it, to foreground, perhaps, its being made as a writerly artifact. It becomes the *author's* wine flask; or it is a "robe", a "flower-gathering", a "meadow", a "casket" – all various metaphors for the artificiality of a *collection* (in fact, anthologies are the type of work that is most prone to possess an arresting title).

Further: the use of a marked title is related, we recall, to the use of the restricted character-set (one which derives not from myth as such, but from the author's own imagination: not so much in the novel, as in comedy). Now, even though the exact sciences, by their very nature, do not have access to a fictional realm, it is typical of a certain kind of exact science to invent new figures, sometimes labeled extravagantly (a hyperbola, a conchoid, an arbelos).[104] Active naming was, in antiquity, a feature of the sciences, more than of mainstream literature – with the exception, once again, of comedy. This is the marking of artificiality, now not through the semiotic marking of the papyrus as a vehicle of meaning but through the universe of referents itself: the marking of the artificiality not of the sign but of the signified. Rare in antiquity – aside from science, and comedy.

In general, then, the marking of artificiality was avoided in ancient mainstream literature. Works referred to a "given", neutral world of myth or of history; they did so without relying on the properties of the written text and instead were understood to emerge, organically, from socially sanctioned forms of performance.

To mark the textuality of the individual work, and to mark the fact that its referents were invented, was to mark its artificiality. And so, in the most

---

[103] I have discussed this in Netz (2013), arguing in detail for the absence of illustrations from main-stream illustrated rolls (contra Weitzmann, 1947, a masterpiece which is still worth reading – and is yet entirely false in its main argument. For a clear statement of the case by an art historian, see Squire, 2011: 129–39; this follows on Small's, 2003, argument: here, indeed, we definitely see art and text as parallels that do not meet.). It goes now almost without saying that the diagram was a generic marker of the ancient exact sciences (Netz, 1999a: chaps. 1–2); for its more nuanced role in medicine, see Netz (2013). Illustrated pagan literary papyri, excluding science (and magic), are: P.Oxy. 2652–3, P.Soc. It. 847 – both Menander; and P.Oxy. 2331, P.Colon. 179, P.Oxy. 3001 – aberrant poetic pieces all likely to be intended as parody.

[104] For the Hellenistic scientific name, see Netz (2009: 149–60). This has important parallels in medicine, as I emphasize in Chapter 4, pp. 360–1.

general terms: the marking of the individual work would have to be the
ironic, distancing marking of a work's textuality – and so, all the way down
to *Don Quixote*, or indeed to *Tristram Shandy* and *Eugene Onegin*. To set
up one's work as unique would be to lower its claim to seriousness.

Moretti's (2009) study of the rise of the marked title from the middle of
the eighteenth century to the middle of the nineteenth is, as Moretti explains,
a study in the rise of a market of books – a market that forced authors to
compete with rival titles. But more: when we position this study within the
longue durée of the book title, or more generally the longue durée of the
markedness of the individual work, we also see in it a study of *the naturaliza-
tion of artificiality*. As the artificiality of the novel loses its markedness,
attention to the individual work as a framed, devised artifact is no longer
ironic. It's no longer a joke to create your own world, your own cloud cuckoo
land: it becomes, simply, what literature is about. Hence, serious literature
can begin to force attention to the individual work: the arms race begins, to
make the individual work as marked as possible – to culminate, within a few
generations, with Proust and Joyce.

So, Proust and Joyce are not how ancient literature was. The individual
work was not marked.

We may compare Homer with Proust: or, even more to the point, we
may compare Aristarchus with the MLA. To consider how ancient literature was read, we should turn to ancient literary criticism itself. I insist on
excluding one central witness. Namely: I would contend that, while the
ancient tradition of literary criticism is well known, it is well known in a
misleading fashion. We have canonized a certain ancient work and in so
doing transformed the ancient practice. To us, Aristotle's *Poetics* looms
largest.[105] Indeed, the *Poetics* is a work of rare genius. Seen against the
background of ancient literary criticism, it is also an idiosyncratic exception. I explain: there is a tendency to think of Aristotle (alongside Plato) as
"the canonical Greek thinker", hence to take his *Poetics* as representative of
ancient thinking on, well, poetics. This is wrong, twice. First, to repeat the
point made in Chapter 1, canonization, in antiquity itself, tracked

---

[105] Examples can easily be multiplied. I quote from an online interview with a major literary scholar:
"What is your all-time favorite narratological study?" – *Phelan:* "Candidates...include the usual
suspects...from Aristotle's *Poetics* to Shklovsky's *Theory of Prose*, from Bakhtin's "Discourse in the
Novel" to Booth's *The Rhetoric of Fiction*, from Barthes' "Introduction to the Structuralist Analysis
of Narrative" to Genette's *Narrative Discourse*." [One of these, I note, is not like the others. Source:
www.diegesis.uni-wuppertal.de/index.php/diegesis/article/view/200/273]. Or Brooks, in his introduction to Todorov's *Introduction to Poetics* (it is in the introductions that the *Poetics* is most often
invoked) (Brooks, 1981: viii): "Why poetics? [...] In the Western tradition, the point of first
reference is ever and still Aristotle."

performativity. There was no unique canonization of philosophy or of any of the specialized, non-performative genres, prior to late antiquity (I return to this point in Chapters 4 and 6, in particular; this should be distinguished from the canonization of Plato – and of Xenophon – as literary, quasi-performative authors). Aristotle, in particular, was much less of a central figure during the Hellenistic era, when ancient literary criticism truly began.[106] Then again, even though Aristotle did become a canonical figure in late antiquity, his poetics still did not replace the rhetorical tradition, in the interpretation of literature itself – a transition which started to take place only in the Renaissance. While Aristotle's *philosophy* was canonized in late antiquity and the Middle Ages, his *Poetics* was almost entirely neglected: copied only in fragmentary form and very rarely commented upon.[107] We started our discussion in Chapter 1 with Borges' image of Ibn Rushd, failing in his commentary of the *Poetics*: but it should be emphasized that, through late antiquity and the Middle Ages, hardly anyone other than Ibn Rushd even bothered. When it came to the appreciation of literature, Aristotle's *Poetics* quite simply did not matter.

Why is the *Poetics* so modern-looking? Because it is concerned with the way in which literary works, taken as entire wholes, are structured through their use of literary device – above all, in his case (at least, in the sections of the work which call the attention of modern readers), through the use of mimesis and plot.

Even so, the *Poetics* never engages with the study of individual works on their own account, and, even while it does occasionally bring in examples from individual tragedies, it is organized through and through according to the principle of genre, beginning with a general classification of genres and devoting most of its extant text to a survey of the principles of the genre of tragedy: it is never "an interpretation of Oedipus Rex", always a classification of genre and a study in the genre of tragedy. Modern readers do not see this as jarring, because they read Aristotle's *Poetics* along the model of modern studies in poetics, in which general observations serve as a general theory or template from which individual interpretations of individual works may be produced. And it is, finally, *this* practice – the interpretation of the literary devices and conceptual structures informing the reading of a given individual work – that constitutes the great bulk of modern literary studies. Such is the natural practice of the reading of literature, when the literary tree is

---

[106] I return to this well-known observation in Chapter 4, pp. 486–7.
[107] Tigerstedt (1968: 7–10). The *Poetics* did not even form part of the Aldine edition: Deitz (1995).

marked by the author, who in turn is identified primarily through
individual works (and so: the modern interpretation of literature is
about making sense of how a particular author makes certain works her
own, through *her* devices, *her* conceptual structures). Finally, this practice – the interpretation of the literary devices and conceptual structures
informing an individual work – is entirely missing from ancient literary
criticism (missing, indeed, even from Aristotle!).

The first tendency of ancient literary criticism was to set an author
within very broad categories of style. The first question was: what was
an author like? And the answer would be a single adjective, taken from
a small, restricted repertoire. Demetrius has four types (36): spare,
elevated, elegant and powerful; Dionysius has three kinds (De Comp.
Verb. 21): austere, elegant, blended; Longinus' extant treatise is dedicated to a single variety, that of the "sublime". Hermogenes in "On
Ideas" looks, instead, for the abstract nouns that form the *elements* of
style (clarity, grandeur, beauty, rapidity, character and sincerity). This
variety is discussed in the terms of authors-within-genres. Hermogenes
chooses one author, Demosthenes, explicitly because he is said to be
paradigmatic of all types of style ("On Ideas" 215). Dionysius introduces each kind by stating who the paradigmatic authors are according
to genre of each; for instance, the paradigmatic blended authors are
(24): in epic, Homer; in lyric, Stesichorus and Alcaeus; in tragedy,
Sophocles; in history, Herodotus; in rhetoric, Demosthenes; in philosophy, Democritus, Plato and Aristotle. Modernity and antiquity are
near opposites in all of that. Modern critics end up praising the genius
of idiosyncrasy. Their ancient counterparts praised the master craftsmanship of paradigmaticity.

Most significantly, the discussion is never concerned with the level of the
work taken as a whole. Rarely, entire poems are analyzed, but even then
the analysis is focused on individual selections, ranging in size between the
clause and (rarely) the paragraph. This is because the project of detecting
paradigmaticity is based on the identification of features of verbal texture,
which are not taken to be unique to a given author but are, rather,
displayed in any given work, with many individual passages.

So, for example, *repetition* – so Demetrius – contributes to an elevated
effect, quoting Herodotus I.203 (Demetrius 66): "There were huge ser-
pents in the Caucasus, both huge and many." As do dactyls, notes
Longinus, quoting Demosthenes, *On The Crown* 188 (Longinus xxxix.4):
"A decree – that made the peril that covered our city disperse like a cloud."
Horace, in his *Ars Poetica*, spends many wonderful lines on the evocation of

the idea of propriety in its various forms, to conclude with an image of critical friendly advice in action (445–8): "[The friendly critic] condemns lifeless lines, blames harsh lines, draws a black mark with his pen across the inelegant, cuts out pretentious ornamental details..." This essentially follows the procedure of the critics of style, looking out for failed pieces of verbal texture. This is how criticism was supposed to aid the author. (The friendly critic becomes in line 450 an "Aristarchus": literary criticism personified.)

So what does an Aristarchus do, according to this model? Aristarchus is lost but we may consider, for instance, Dionysius of Halicarnassus' "On Composition", following the lead of de Jonge (2008). This is a contribution to literary studies that expressly combines what we may think of as "linguistics" with traditional philology (a type of combination which I see as typical to the first century BCE; see Chapter 4, pages 473–5). The two go easily together, because both are engaged with the level of individual expressions as verbal texture. A study of composition (*sunthesis*), it heavily relies on the analytic tool of *trans*position (*metathesis*). Thus, one takes a very brief passage from a canonical author, tries out a minor change in its verbal texture and derives an appreciation of the effectiveness of the original arrangement. From de Jonge (2008: 381):

> Thucydides 3.57.4: "And we fear, men of Sparta, lest you, our only hope, may fail in resolution."
> Dionysius de Comp. Verb. 7.18–21: "And we fear, men of Sparta, lest you may fail in resolution, that are our only hope."

Dionysius correctly notes that this transposition would destroy the "charm" and "feeling" (*pathos*) of the original. And so, time and again: one picks one of the works of the canon and, within it, identifies a tiny piece of verbal structure, and then one shows how this embodies certain generalized properties of style. Metathesis is one technique among several, but the overall strategy – atomize, then generalize for "style" – is practically the only one in evidence in the literary criticism extant from antiquity.

To be fair, such works as those by Demetrius and Dionysius represent a particular strand of ancient thought about literature: these are teachers of rhetoric of the Imperial era, and so it is perhaps less surprising that we do not find in them the same kind of disinterested contemplation of literature of Aristotle's *Poetics*. Their job is to mine the canon for its usefulness to the rhetor. But, then again, they could do so because literature was always made useful in precisely this way. The validity of metathesis as a critical tool seems to have been at least one of the key concerns of Philodemus' *On Poems*[108] – writing in the first century BCE and in polemic primarily with Hellenistic "critics" (Philodemus' own term)[109] – but, in more general terms, it is clear that the focus of critical attention we see through this work is fixed at a level very close to the smallest verbal unit (one critic discussed by Philodemus, Pausimachus, argued that composition mattered less; what mattered was the choice of *individual sounds*).[110] The original works of literary criticism (as distinct from their reflection in rhetorical theory) are now lost, but, as Nünlist (2009) reveals, they may be recovered to a certain extant from the many scholia extant now as part of the medieval transmission of the canon. What do we find, then, when we look – to use Nünlist's title – at "the ancient critic at work"? Unsurprisingly, perhaps, we find *scholia*. That is, we find comments that attach very clearly to a particular word, phrase or clause, and explain them. Of course, a central place is given to judgements of style (Nünlist, 2009: chap. 9; note that Nünlist confines himself to observations that go beyond single words or very short phrases, so that this very substantial chapter does not do justice to the sheer proliferation of such comments): so, for instance (220):

> He [sc. Homer] makes a transition [Il. 21.257–62] from the grand style to the plain and florid.

Nünlist's chapter on "characters" remains at the same level (249):

> By means of a single word ["unwillingly", Il. I.348] he [sc. Homer] has shown us the entire character of the person [sc. Briseis].

Even "Plot" – Nünlist's first chapter, highlighted by him precisely because it is the one most promising for "literary theory" – is always restricted to this microscopic level. The most that we find is that a particular puzzle about a small-scale unit of text is accounted for, by reference to another (29):

---

[108] This is the argument of Greenberg (1958), supported by Armstrong (1995).
[109] For their identity, see Janko (2000: chap. 5).
[110] This is known as "euphonicism"; see the brief discussion in Gutzwiller (2010: 350–3). In technical terms, the critics who favor metathesis emphasize the syntagmatic (the ordering of elements), those who favor euphonics emphasize the paradigmatic (the choice of elements), but, either way, we consider the smallest micro-elements possible; in the case of Pausimachus, indeed, we consider individual letters. (This, argues Armstrong, 1995, is part of the fascination of such theories for an atomist such as Philodemus.)

Why does only Peleus' spear not fit him [sc. Patroclus] whereas all the other arms do? Megaclides[111] says in book 2 of "On Homer" that Homer prepares for the "Production of the Armour".

Nünlist points out (2) that "the scholia provide a very good insight into how critics made use of the various scholarly tools in the daily business of explaining the Greek 'classics'", and the point is precisely that this daily practice was their *main* business. The critics made their name through commentary on the canon. It is not as if the scholiasts had to make their selections from general treatises on literary theory, where this or that passage from Homer was given as an example for some general, theoretical observation. The scholia were selected from larger works, in the forms of commentaries, whose structure was more or less homologous to that of scholia. Indeed, to the contrary: it was the rhetorical authors on style, whom we discussed above, that recomposed a tradition of commentary into somewhat more general statements.

Thus, the argument from silence is very significant. What we do not find among the scholia are general, theoretical statements of Aristotle's *Poetics* type, which got shoehorned somehow to fit a particular passage. Because, you see, the ancient literary critics were not like Aristotle. Literature was not approached, primarily, at the analytic unit of the individual work. It was studied, instead, at the analytic unit of a piece of verbal texture – which was taken as representative of particular effects of the literary voice.

Some attention is given in the scholia to considerations of genre (noting that a certain passage in comedy, for instance, is more "tragic": Nünlist, 2009: 218–19), and this of course is an important reference point for the rhetorical handbooks, but generally speaking genre is simply taken for granted – elided, as it were, just like the author. We know who the authors are, what the genres are: this is the basic presupposition of the canon. But, above all, literature, in this tradition, is approached as individual moments of verbal expression. That it is so useful for rhetorical education is perhaps key: this is rhetoric as master literature because all of literature is, quite simply, understood as a form of performance. What is the literary canon? The place in which you encounter the verbal performance that can have the effect of "the grand", "the florid", "the plain". This kind of verbal performance had several masters, arranged across several performative genres. One interiorized the canon, and in so doing one sensed the effect of style,

[111] Late fourth century BCE; the origins of such traditions considerably precede Imperial-era rhetoric.

of superb verbal performance as such. And, in so doing, one perfected one's
own rhetoric.

   This section has ranged widely, but the point is that the various strands
do come together. I started by pointing out the rather straightforward
observation that canonical ancient literature typically engaged with the
(shared) realm of myth. Thus, the contents of one's works were not very
individuated to oneself. This I brought together with the growing awareness, in contemporary scholarship, concerning the gap between verbal
and visual representations. My argument is that, even while the popularity of certain themes in art may be due to their popularity in literature, it
is still the case that, when an artist invokes a work of literature, he ends up
referring primarily to the shared mythical contents of the work, rather
than to their individual representation in the individual work. This, in
turn, is related to the very unmarked character of the ancient title. Not
only do the various Medea plays return to the same Medea theme; they do
so with the very same title! Finally, a separate but related observation
derives from the ancient critical reception of ancient literature: this
involved the appreciation not of the totality of a single work but, rather,
of the stylistic (that is, performative, voice-related) character of an
author. Ancient criticism appreciated authors *as such*, at the level of an
author's voice revealed, across his entire oeuvre, in various moments of
verbal texture; but it did not dwell on the artifice of a particular work,
taken as a whole. This, finally, is related to the observation made above,
on pages 118–25: ancient works were collected according to their named
authors – but more in the context of "collected works" or smaller
"portable editions", less in the context of a few, selected works with
which an author was primarily associated; while, on the other hand,
authors were understood by others – and also understood themselves –
primarily in terms of their chosen genre.

   We have returned several times to the idea of the topology of the Greek
literary field – its structure as a tree – and there is a clear observation
emerging concerning this topology. Indeed, the Greeks invented the
author (as the Chinese would do, independently, later on). Thus the
Greek literary field had three layers – genre, author, work – and not (as
was the case in other, comparable early literatures) the two layers only, of
genre and work. In its invention of the author, Greek literature already
leads the way to the modern literary system: I keep insisting upon that.
Nevertheless – and here is the main observation, from which so much else
follows – modernity does differ from antiquity in the *clustering* of its layers.
In the modern system, performance loses its significance. In modernity, the

author is not the expression of generalized principles of verbal style, expressed through genres, and is instead a master of a specific set of works with their idiosyncratic universe. The vividness of fiction comes to replace the vividness of performance. *The layer of the author is thus proximate not to genre but to that of the works.* The author marks her works and is marked by them; generic boundaries matter much less. The opposite was true in the Greek case, in which an author subsisted much more as an exponent of performance – and was much less marked by the contents of his works. The three literary systems can therefore be seen at a glance as follows.

### *The brief topology of world literature*

| Early | Greek[112] | Modern |
|---|---|---|
| Genre (performative) | **Genre (performative)** | Genre (non-performative) |
| | **Author** | **Author** |
| Work | Work | **Work** |

The Greek[113] and the modern literary system share the centrality of the author brand name. In the modern system, however, this brand name flows up, from the works; in the ancient system, it flows down, from the performative presence of the genres.

The modern figure of the author – whose identity springs from that of the works under his name – implies a much more powerful authorial control over the work itself. The author as such, the brand name that convinces you to collect *this* and not *that*, was invented in Greek antiquity; and yet the author, the romantic master of her own universe, was a new invention. In this modern system, authors are envisaged solipsistically, anchored in private and restricted fictional domains, living a non-performative practice of writing and consumed in the privacy of reading. A modern notion; perhaps, in fact, invented circa 1800. On which, then,

---

[112] It should be clear that when I talk about "Greek literature" here I mean precisely Greek *canonical* literature. This is important not just because most literature in circulation was canonical but also because, of course, the Greek understanding of literature was formed entirely on the basis of this canon.

[113] I follow Feeney (2016): it is a remarkable, contingent fact that the Romans chose to create a literature on the Greek model, in their own language. What this means, I believe, is that they adopted the Greek topology of literature: the principle of a brand-name author, primarily attached to his genre; from this it followed, also, that the Roman adoption of the Greek author went hand in hand, naturally, with the Roman adoption of the Greek system of genres as a whole.

Foucault was simply right. Indeed, the nature of the ancient author, as the exponent of performative practices that ultimately transcend him, is much more in keeping with a structuralist or even a post-structuralist account of literature. The ancient author really should be understood – because this is how he was understood by his own audience – as the channel for intertextual structures stronger than himself. The scholia, isolating textual segments and reading them as expressions of generalized "style": more or less as Kristeva would have it. The post-structuralists should be given their due, then, but, as we therefore notice, let us also pause to note that, when they rebelled against the social construct of the author, they did so in a narrow, ahistorical manner: the very rebellion of Kristeva, Barthes and Foucault was conceived in the terms of the romantic author. What they argued, effectively, was that the figure of the author was a misleading fiction, misleading precisely because it had assumed that authors were solipsistic masters of their own universes. This helps us, scholars of antiquity, in case we might be inclined (as few are now) to read the ancient author through the perspective of a post-Romantic image. But we need to make a different start altogether, if our goal is to understand the ancient understanding – the (seminal) ancient construction – of their own fiction of the author, anchored not in solipsistic fictions but, to the contrary, in public, shared performances.

And this seems to be the main starting point: in the ancient system, authors are tied to the space of shared myth and history, and are envisaged and consumed primarily through the practices of public performance (actual or imagined). What I would argue is that, as a consequence, ancient authors are naturally imagined as personas constituting, together, a public entity, one that could be imagined only in relation to some concrete social practices. Hence the polis of letters, imagined primarily through the practices of democratic Athens. Let us now proceed to see this argument in detail.

### 2.2.4    The Polis of Letters

For the critics of Foucault's generation, to deconstruct *the post-Romantic author* was the same as deconstructing *the author*, as such. And so for us: for anyone immersed in modern literature, it is hard even to envisage a strong authorial identity, mediated through any vehicle other than the craftsmanship of one's individual set of works. Hence, when I argue that, in the ancient world, genre and performance reigned supreme, that one's individual set of works mattered less, it sounds almost as if I am arguing that the *author* mattered less. But, after all, this was clearly not the case: the author was the central node in the literary system. His was the brand-name: primarily, literature was valued for the personas of certain authors.

How, then, was the author made present, how was the persona projected, if not through the craftsmanship of one's individual set of works? To answer, let us look at the manner in which authors were made present. I will construct my argument through a few qualitative examples, and I start with that typical ancient genre dedicated to the figure of the author – the literary biography. So, to begin with, a couple of vignettes.

The first is from the most elaborate biography of the most emblematic author. I pick as my example the beginning of Homer's career, according to the *Vita Herodotea* 9:[114] having reached Cyme – now fully blind – Homer stands in front of a shop and recites an epigram asking for hospitality ("Respect a man who needs hospitality and a home..."). Thanks to these words, he is favorably received. Enjoying this hospitality, he then produces poetry. During his stay, he repeatedly utters gnomic poetic phrases, which are repeated by his audience. Here, then, is the author made vivid: expressing brief, memorable words in public.

The second is a compressed example, taking the near-totality of an individual, or, indeed, of a field. The field with the least authorial presence is that of the exact sciences (it is, as it were, the opposite end of the spectrum from Homer). There is effectively only one fully imagined author: Archimedes; he is famous, essentially, for four episodes. To them we may add one for Euclid. In what follows, then, I nearly sum up the biographical image of the ancient exact sciences as a whole.

(1) Archimedes once pondered a case involving a forger trying to hoodwink the king. He found his clever solution while in the bath. In his excitement, he ran out naked, crying "I have found it! I have found it!"[115]

(2) The king once asked Archimedes to help launch the biggest ship in the world, in competition with those of Alexandria. Archimedes devised a mechanism to obtain this and, as he was pulling on it and

---

[114] The manuscript tradition ascribes this biographical essay (Vasiloudi, 2013) to Herodotus, hence its title – even though it is at the very earliest a Hellenistic work, most likely Roman era. (This is typical of the way in which the readers of the canon came to conceive of it as an ensemble: and here is how *Herodotus* approached *Homer*...)

[115] For the tradition of this story, see Jaeger (2008: 17–31). The story clearly telegraphs, in some sense, Archimedes' achievement in *On Floating Bodies* (with whose law of buoyancy one can indeed solve the Crown's problem). In general, for the ancient tradition of Archimedes – and whatever history underlay it – the best treatment remains Dijksterhuis (1987 [1938]: chap. 1).

launching the ship, he remarked "Give me a place to stand and I shall move the earth."[116]

(3)    As the Romans were besieging his city, Archimedes devised machines to protect the city walls, so effective that the very sight of a rope would drive the Romans away. The Roman general remarked: "Let us stop fighting this geometrical Briareus. . .who plays with our sambuca. . ." [a pun on an ancient war machine whose name suggested also a musical instrument].[117]

(4)    As the city fell, Archimedes told the Roman soldier who had come to take him "Move away from my diagrams", whereupon the soldier killed him in rage.[118]

(5)    The king once asked Euclid for an easier way to study mathematics, whereupon Euclid said: "There is no royal road to geometry."[119]

Archimedes running naked, shouting his brief words that hint at his science, is akin to Homer the blind man, reciting his epigram that hints at his epic. At both ends of the spectrum, authors are similarly made vivid: brief fictional words, uttered in public, stand in for the real words preserved by the author's reception on papyrus. This captures the main observation by Lefkowitz (1981): that the biographical tradition concerning poets was essentially manufactured from the poems themselves.[120] What I wish to note is that, as the biographers constructed their lives, based on their sources, they formed those lives as series of succinct, verbal encounters. Life was made: by turning source texts into a series of brief embodied texts.

But then, how significant are the two vignettes considered so far – the one example from Homer's biographical tradition, and the case of the biographical tradition for the field of the exact sciences? My approach in this section is qualitative, but it should not be cherry-

---

[116] Jaeger (2008: 101–22). This telegraphs *On Balancing Planes* (which derives, effectively, the law of the balance, hence the principle underlying the lever).

[117] Plutarsch, *Vita Marcelli* 17.     [118] Jaeger (2008: 77–100).

[119] Proclus, in *Eucl.* I 68 Friedlein. This clearly hints at the *Elements* and their massive size (and it is easy to see how this particular anecdote was invented by schoolmasters, frustrated at their students' attitude towards their textbook).

[120] This is often qualified in more recent scholarship (see, e.g., Graziosi, 2002; Kivilo, 2010; and Hendrickson, 2013) but never abandoned: it is clear that, whatever other sources were used, the biographical tradition was produced by authors immersed in the textual hints of the poems, and ready to extract them for their worth. Of course, all of this was in part because poetry was considered to contain a good measure of historical truth, in all sorts of ways which were readily seen, by the ancients themselves, as problematic and yet worthy of pursuit (Kim, 2010).

picked: it is easy to be misled by a few examples that one knows well. And so we need to have some kind of *sample* of the ancient figure of the cultural icon. What I look for is some indication of how cultural figures were made vivid in passing. My following set of vignettes is a preliminary effort towards a sample. I consider the 13 major authors of the classical era (the 19 canonical authors found at the end of Chapter 1, minus Homer, Hesiod and the Alexandrians). For each, I look for quotations taken from authors from whom significant writings remain – and in whose writing one finds only once or twice the mention of the author I am looking for. In this way, I try to catch the ancient authors unaware, when they cite a canonical name without intending to, without this being a major practice of theirs – they cite, just because citing that canonical name comes in naturally.[121] Hence, then, the following set of 13 vignettes,[122] arranged by the name of the mentioned canonical author (not by name of citing authority, given, instead, in parentheses).

### Pindar (Isocrates, *Antidosis* 166, tr. Norlin, 1980)

It would be even more absurd if, whereas **Pindar**, the poet, was so highly honored by our forefathers because of a single line of his in which he praises Athens as "the bulwark of Hellas" that he was made "proxenos" and given a present of ten thousand drachmas, I, on the other hand, who have glorified Athens and our ancestors with much ampler and nobler encomiums, should not even be privileged to end my days in peace.

### Aeschylus (Marcellinus, *Vita Thucydidis* 4–5, tr. Allen [online])

When [the Thracians and the Dolonians] were distressed by war and suffered not a little evil from the continuous hostilities, they took refuge in the oracle of a god. For they saw that a god alone discovers to them a passage out of their impractical situation because the strength of a god is above all, according to **Aeschylus**.

---

[121] I have a spreadsheet with the number of times each of the major 30 authors (in terms of papyrus frequency) has his name cited by any later author up to the end of the fifth century. I use this spreadsheet to look up references that satisfy "mentioned no more than once or twice", avoiding fragmentary contexts. I further restrict myself to contexts in which the figure of the author is in some sense relevant: I thus avoid grammatical quotations and the mere cataloguing of the names of authors. Within those constraints, I picked up the examples haphazardly, although, the choice being made by a person, my choice must have involved all sorts of unconscious biases. The number obviously is small and the set of vignettes is a suggestive reading, not a "representative" sample (the concept has no meaning with such a tiny sample size). I do believe this methodology is preferable to the one whereby we systematically seek out a group of passages that support a particular thesis.

[122] Where available, translations are Loeb, revised only when the English style is impossibly antiquated.

**Sophocles (Aelius Theon, *Progymnasmata* 65–6, tr. Kennedy, 2003)**
The teacher should collect good examples of each exercise from ancient
prose works and assign them to the young to be learned by heart; for
example, the kind of *chreia* [memorable anecdote used in rhetorical exer-
cises] found in Plato's *Republic*: "Someone once went up to the poet
Sophocles and said: 'How are you managing, **Sophocles**, in matters
Aphrodisial? Are you still able to have intercourse with women?' And he
replied: 'Hush, man. I have escaped these things most gladly, like a slave
running away from a mad and savage master.'"

**Herodotus (Sextus Empiricus, *Outlines of Pyrrhonism* 231–2, tr. Bury,
1990)**
[Context: various views on death.] We know, too, the things which
**Herodotus** says about Cleobis and Biton in the story about the Argive
priestess. [She asked the goddess for the best that mortals can get, for her
children; and so they died in their sleep.]

**Euripides (Theophrastus, *Metaphysics* 8a25–7)**
[Context: a discussion of the balance of good and bad in the cosmos.] Hence
it appears that **Euripides**, too, says in a general sense [i.e. one that goes
beyond the context of his play to a general metaphysical claim] that "good
things cannot fall apart".

**Aristophanes (Achilles Tatius, *Leucippe and Cleitophon* VIII.9, tr.
Gaselee, 1917)**
The bishop then came forward. He was no poor hand at speaking, and as
good at quip and gibe as the plays of Aristophanes, and he began his speech
with much humour, touching in a jesting vein on Thersander's own
lecherous depravity.

**Thucydides (Diogenes Laertius, *Life of Xenophon* II.57, tr. Hicks, 1925)**
It is said that even though he [Xenophon] could have removed **Thucydides'**
books – which were unknown – he made them famous. [Apparently this
tradition envisages Xenophon as, effectively, Thucydides' posthumous pub-
lisher – an act of extreme generosity, as it makes Xenophon's competition so
much harder.]

**Isocrates (Galen, *De Praenotatione ad Posthumum* K. XIV 672)**
[Context: the admiring audience asks Galen by which (single) sign he
was able to make a brilliant deduction.] I responded to them as I've
heard that **Isocrates** once responded [when asked if his, Isocrates',
entire art could be taught in the three years of prescribed study]:
"You, boy, let's pray that you can learn what you are taught in
one day; as for me, through the weakness of my mind, I have had to
teach myself for many years."

**Xenophon (Artemidorus, *Oneirocriticon* I.66)**

[Context: the significance of drinking wine in a dream.] It seems to me that **Xenophon's** Socrates' [expression] is in place[= "is fitting"?]: "Wine, like mandragora, puts to sleep human cares, even as it lights up friendliness, as oil does flame."

**Plato (*Cassius Dio* 43.11, tr. Cary, 1916)**

When evening was come, [Cato] secretly slipped a dagger under his pillow, and asked for **Plato's** book on the Soul. This was either in the endeavour to divert those present from the suspicion that he had any such purpose in mind, in order to be observed as little as possible, or else in the desire to obtain some consolation in respect to death from the reading of it. When he had read the work through and it was now near midnight, he drew forth the dagger, and smote himself upon the belly.

**Demosthenes (Callistratus, *Descriptions* 2.5, tr. Fairbanks, 1931)**

[The sculptor] Scopas, even when fashioning creatures without life, was a maker of truth and imprinted wonders on bodies made of inanimate matter; while **Demosthenes**, fashioning icons in words, almost made visible a form of words by mixing the drugs of the technē with the products of mind and intelligence.

**Aeschines (Clemens of Alexandria, *Stroma* VI.2.20.4–6, tr. Wilson, 1869)**

[Context: pagan wisdom was plagiarized from the Jews. As part of the argument, Clement argues for the pervasive presence of plagiarism within Greek literature: they keep repeating each other.] Andocides the orator says, "The preparation, gentlemen of the jury, and the eagerness of our enemies, almost all of you know." Similarly also Nicias, in the speech on the deposit, against Lysias, says, "The preparation and the eagerness of the adversaries, you see, O gentlemen of the jury." After him **Aeschines** says, "You see the preparation, O men of Athens, and the line of battle."

**Menander (Philostratus, *Epistle* 47, tr. Benner, 1949)**

[Context: a love letter to a lady; the conceit is the lover ponders the addressee's ethnicity, deducing from her coldness that she cannot hail from various localities, all of which were famed for mythical loves.] If, pretty one, you were Spartan, I would have mentioned Helen and the ship... [Eight further locality/myths follow.] [N]or from Attica, for in that case you would never have failed to know the night festivals and the holidays and Menander's plays.

There is some variety within this set. In some cases authors are evoked in more general terms, in others for precise quotations. It so happens that the two comic authors are recalled in the most general fashion, their work as a whole being suggestive (in both cases, of the erotic – in two quite distinct flavors). Demosthenes is recalled as a general emblem of the power of words. Plato is more specific, but is still represented through a single emblematic dialogue – the *Phaedo* (which was, as we have noticed, together with the *Phaedrus*, in his "portable edition"). This is the less common way of evoking an author, however. More typical is the small piece, or, literally, the fragment.[123] Herodotus is made of story lines, and so one recalls a particular story. From Pindar, Aeschylus, Euripides, Xenophon and Aeschines we have a brief quotation, a *fragment* (on which, more below). Sophocles, Thucydides and Isocrates are brought up in the context of a biographical anecdote, which, in the case of Sophocles, is explicitly (in the case of Isocrates, implicitly) that of a *chreia* – a brief, famous anecdote.

And yet, the variety is in fact quite restricted. One could bring up the author as a whole or as a fragment. But, in all cases, the ancient author was made present through the figure of *words-in-action*. Comedy could be an aphrodisiac; Plato's *Phaedo* could be the functional equivalent of a dagger; the words of Thucydides are physically hidden and salvaged, imagined in a potential contest with Xenophon; Demosthenes' words are in action in the most plastic manner, being made to do things as marble does.

We recall a central fact: reading a text, ancient readers wished to be able to conjure the presence of the author. Biographies are *extant*, at least in fragmentary form, for about two-thirds of the authors in tiers 1 to 3 (in the terms of the table on pages 15–18 above), with the exceptions of (removing late and technical authors):[124]

> Callimachus, Herodotus, Alcaeus, Theocritus, Archilochus, Alcman, Bacchylides, Euphorion, Stesichorus, Eupolis, Antimachus

It is very likely that a few of those authors did have an ancient vita, however.[125] The remaining authors are Hellenistic (Callimachus, Theocritus, Euphorion),[126] minor (the minor comic author Eupolis; the minor epic author Antimachus; this should be seen to cover at least some of

---

[123] My sample is biased against the fragment, since for this particular exercise I avoided grammatical sources and, more generally, frequent citers (the two categories often overlap); more below.

[124] In what follows, I am non-committal as to the dates at which such biographies were written. As pointed out by Kivilo (2010), the conventional assumption that such biographies were produced in late, perhaps Roman, times is at least subject to doubt, and it may well be that well-known authors had biographical tales told about them *from the beginning*.

[125] In all likelihood there was an ancient life of Archilochus (see, e.g., Compton, 1990: 333–6, and references therein; indeed, as noted on p. 57, n.106, above, there is something close to a biography, extant *epigraphically*); the same could well be true of Alcaeus (scholarly literature dedicated to him was enormously rich, for which see Porro, 1994; did it not generate a vita?).

[126] There were vitae of Aratus and of Apollonius of Rhodes, however, making the absence of Callimachus' vita puzzling.

the lyric poets). The one real puzzle is that of Herodotus, and the loss of any vita for him is probably mere accident. This is significant: to read, one needed to know who the author was, and so the canonical authors – even going beyond tier 1 – accumulated a biographical tradition.[127] Eventually, the rule that reading requires familiarity with the setting of the work would be generalized, and Mansfeld (1994) studies this phenomenon – a study we should now put in the context of Johnson (2010). As Johnson observes, at least from the Roman era onwards, certain types of serious reading would often be pursued in groups, in some contexts led by a master,[128] and, as Mansfeld shows, this reading was preceded – immersed? – by an "isagogic" discussion which put the text into its context. In some cases, the context became detailed and formulaic, involving such questions as "the goal of the treatise", etc.[129] Generally speaking, however, the isagogic involved the genre, the life of the author and then the character of the individual work read: "de arte, de opifice, de opere" (Quintilian II.14.5).[130] It seems that at least some of the vita tradition – not all[131] – emerges from this kind of context (and, indeed, it often survives physically as introductory material in the manuscript tradition).

We are reminded of the portraits, a closely related genre. In both cases, the tradition emerged in the fourth century BCE, but is attested primarily from the Roman era.[132] Portrait and biography bring up the canonical author in vivid detail. This quality of vividness must have been the most crucial one for the ancient biography. Momigliano seems to be disappointed, again and again, by the domination of the biographic material by the anecdote (1971: 68–9):

---

[127] This is why the vitae are made out of the contents of the works: they are designed with the works in mind, cutting and splicing the elements of the author's work much like a trailer to the movie. See Beecroft (2010) for a similar point, though one more sympathetic to the vita as the site for serious literary reflection.

[128] Snyder (2002).

[129] Mansfeld concentrates on the developed formula, which emerged, however, in the late ancient communities that dedicated themselves to the reading of Plato and Aristotle. For them, the authors themselves were a given, and so the isagogic emphasis was entirely on the individual treatise.

[130] See, e.g., Mansfeld (1994: 39, 52). The two cases cited by Mansfeld are Euclid and Hermogenes – i.e. less familiar authors.

[131] Aesop's lives were an early form of the novel (or should we imagine group-reading, with exegesis, of Aesop's fables?), as was the *Certamen Homeri et Hesiodi*. But these are the exceptions, involving non-historical figures.

[132] Textbook discussions: Richter (1965: 1–6); Momigliano (1971: 9–10, chaps. 2–3). Momigliano is on the whole fairly sanguine on early antecedents, while being very restrictive in his definition of "biography".

My favorite example of the irrelevant anecdote in Aristotle is his characterization of Hippodamus of Miletus at the beginning of a lengthy discussion
of Hippodamus' theories (*Politics* 2.1267b22). According to Aristotle,
Hippodamus son of Euryphon was a Milesian "who invented town planning and laid out Piraeus and had odd theories about other aspects of life
which he liked to make himself known for: accounts of his foibles mention
his long hair and expensive personal possessions and also the cheap but
warm clothes he wore in summer as well as in winter, and his desire to be an
expert in all the sciences". The cheap yet warm clothes that Hippodamus
paraded not only in winter, but also in summer, can hardly have struck
Aristotle as an argument against Hippodamus' political philosophy.

Of course not: but the function of the anecdote is not to tell us anything
profound about the author but to entertain us while *conjuring up the author
as a vivid presence*. In this case the effect is mostly visual, but very often
what is at stake is a vivid encounter, beginning already with the *Certamen
Homeri et Hesiodi*: two authors, acting out an agon. Plato, too, gets into
trouble: he tells Dionysius, the ruler of Syracuse, that virtue is more
important than "what is useful to the powerful". The tyrant becomes
upset: "Your speech is geriatric!" "Yours," so Plato, "is tyrannical."
Dionysius, now furious, arranges for Plato to be sold into slavery, and an
entire novelistic vignette ensues. All this is from Diogenes Laertius
III.18–21, which we can now understand is not idiotic. It is a kind of verbal
portraiture of a piece of literature, in this case turning a passage in the
*Republic* – the Thrasymachus conversation in the first book – into a vivid
historical event. Of course, it is not as if the original passage in the *Republic*
lacked in vividness. What Diogenes Laertius and his readers needed was an
opportunity to bring in not just Socrates but also Plato himself: to have the
author imagined in vivid detail. This is related to another ancient genre,
the fictional correspondence. Extant are letters attributed to at least the
following canonical authors: Euripides, Hippocrates, Plato, Xenophon,
Demosthenes, Aeschines, Aristotle, Aratus. Almost entirely fictional (a few
by Plato might be genuine), these are an extension of the vita tradition, one
more way of making the author speak in his own voice or in a more
personal way. One should of course add the letters of Socrates – in this
case, inventing a direct voice for a powerful presence which is otherwise
only mediated. Indeed, once again we see that philosophy occupies a role
roughly parallel to that of all other literature as a whole, its authors forming
a parallel canon. There is an extant pseudo-epistolary literature attributed
to several of the Seven Sages (but not by the lyric poets!), and then also by

Speusippus, Demetrius of Phaleron, Arcesilaus, Diogenes the Cynic and other philosophers (those by Epicurus, of course, are genuine).

Above all, these are words in action in the sense of the author being imagined, a vivid bodily presence, in the action of utterance. The voice of the author could be made even more living by embedding it in a narrative context, and for this reason we have the invented biographical anecdote, or – to use the ancient term – the *chreia*. This genre, in fact, adds another layer to our qualitative survey.

Our evidence for the ancient chreia is concentrated within the rhetorical handbooks (and it is surveyed by Hock and O'Neil, 1985; 2002). Throughout antiquity students of rhetoric were advised how they could memorize and employ chreiai in their speeches. For this reason, the few modern scholars who study this genre tend to consider it within the limited contexts of education and of rhetoric. This is a narrow focus, however: rhetors cited chreiai, and students were taught to imitate them, because they worked; the image of utterance-in-action was compelling.

As a rule, the chreia was based on the figure of the author engaged in a hostile encounter in public and winning it through a powerful phrase (as we have seen in the example above, involving Plato). The questions addressed to Sophocles and Isocrates, in the sample of passages considered above, were meant to embarrass them; they won the day through the power of words. Even in the absence of a hostile context, the utterance itself is shaped as an attack. Hock and O'Neil (2002: 10) quote what appears to be a beginning-stage reader composed of a series of five chreiai, all around Diogenes the Cynic:[133]

> Seeing a fly on his table, he said: "Even Diogenes keeps parasites." Seeing a woman being educated, he said: "Wow! A sword is being sharpened!" Seeing a woman giving advice to a woman, he said: "An asp is being supplied venom from a viper." Seeing an Ethiopian eating white bread, he said: "Look! Night is swallowing day!" Seeing an Ethiopian defecating, he said: "Look! A kettle with a hole in it."

This is extremely offensive to modern ears (as Hock and O'Neil are quick to point out), but the point is that, while the sentiment was more acceptable to an ancient ear, its contents would still be premised on *giving offense*. This is what makes the ubiquity of such chreiai in the educational context so striking. A few chreiai repeated in our sources are more anodyne and self-evidently schoolmasterish ("Aesop the fable-writer, on being asked

---

[133] The papyrus fragment as a whole is discussed in Hock and O'Neil (2002: 5–12).

what the most potent thing among men is, said: 'Speech'"; "Isocrates said that education's root is bitter, its fruits – sweet").[134] The bulk are of a sharper variety: "Socrates the philosopher, when a certain student named Apollodorus said to him, 'The Athenians have unjustly condemned you to death', said with a laugh: 'But did you want them to do it justly?'"[135] Words were more powerful, more memorable (surely the point for educational context), when they suggested the violent encounter. Chreiai are often binary – "upon seeing/hearing – he said" – an event followed by a statement (a statement standing on its own, as the progymnasmata explain, would be merely a gnome and thus more akin to the fragment, which I discuss below). The event very often involves a second person, creating a brief social interaction: the anonymous interlocutors doubting Sophocles' virility, Diogenes and the Ethiopian... In a formula: words, embodied in a social setting, become vivid.

Several of the chreiai preserved in the educational context make vivid, in such violent encounters, the main figures of the canon. So, for instance, the following, preserved on papyrus: "Demosthenes the orator, on hearing that Aeschines had died, said: 'The stylus of my speeches has perished.'"[136] Historians doubt that Aeschines did, in fact, predecease Demosthenes, but for this genre this is immaterial: what is being juxtaposed here are the creatures of the contemporary canon, present to the educated reader's mind. But it should be emphasized that the chreia was most prolific not with the major authors of the canon, but with those who were a literary presence without leaving behind a written text. This is a group comprised of the Seven Sages, of Socrates, and of the Cynics, above all, indeed, Diogenes, who dominated ancient collections of chreiai and is indeed attested *only* through this vehicle.[137] All this invites the question of the historicity of Diogenes. For any given chreia attributed to Diogenes, the overwhelming probability is that it was constructed by a later tradition; and yet it is likely enough that here there was an individual engaged primarily

---

[134] Nicolaus, Progymnasmata 22–3; Hock and O'Neil (1985: 259): the last chreia on Isocrates is among the most often recycled in this pedagogic genre.

[135] Aelius Theon, Progymnasmata 207–8; Hock and O'Neil (1985: 91).

[136] Hock and O'Neil (2002: 35). The concretization of words-in-action (person = stylus = speeches) is typical, but here it probably takes a polemical meaning: Aeschines as *merely* a scribbler, not a genuine speaker.

[137] Hock and O'Neil (2002: 8). Diogenes Laertius' *Life of Diogenes the Cynic* is of course no more than a chain of chreiai; the same is largely true for another performer-philosopher, Arcesilaus, and, in general, the chreia is Diogenes Laertius' central biographical technique; see Kindstrand (1986). It was a technique especially suited to philosophers, because they had a vivid presence, but typically wrote (less memorable) prose, and not poetry; their vividness therefore had to be constructed through an invented chreia.

in outré performances with intended philosophical consequences.[138] It is not as if the chreia co-opted Diogenes against his will, and perhaps the way in which the genericity of the chreia should be brought to bear on the question of the historical Diogenes is quite the opposite. We should say that Diogenes co-opted to himself the chreia. Recognizing the cultural power of the resonant gesture, he made a name for himself as an author of violent gestures, eschewing text.

So this was one way to present oneself as an author: the embodied verbal gesture. But above all, of course, one's presence as an author would be conveyed through words. And this is why brief citations pepper extant Greek literature. It is not a mere accident of survival that allows us to form our collections of ancient fragments. Rather, it was the ancients, already, who perceived their cultural heritage in the form of the fragment: brief verbal moments, worthy of being re-enacted on the space of one's own text, so as to endow it, locally, with the vividness of past authors being made present to the mind. Let us, see, then, how this was done. Once again, I will provide a close reading of sorts, of a tiny sample. I have carried out a search in the TLG for the string of Latin characters "fr.", which brings up more than 10,000 pre-Byzantine results. Some of these are from papyri, and the bulk are from the massively citing authors (which I avoid once again, so as not to bias our sample to one important, yet exaggerated type). I went through my results, looking for authors who appear less frequently (so as to avoid making this a study of particular authors' reputation), and picked ten. Here are my passages (arranged by the same principle as the preceding set of vignettes).

### Diagoras (Philodemus, *On Piety* 518–27, tr. Obbink, 1996)

Those who eliminate the divine from existing things Epicurus reproached for their complete madness, as in Book XII he reproaches Prodicus, **Diagoras** and Critias among others. (Context: followed by other targets of criticism such as Antisthenes, and by other authorities who cite the same passage in Epicurus such as Hermarchus.)

### Callinus (Strabo, *Geography* XIV 4.3, tr. Jones, 1932)

Herodotus says that the Pamphylians are the descendants of the peoples led by Amphilochus and Calchas, a miscellaneous throng who accompanied them from Troy; and that most of them remained here, but that some of them were scattered to numerous places on earth. **Callinus** says that Calchas died in Clarus, but that the peoples led by Mopsus passed over the Taurus,

---

[138] So, e.g., Bosman (2006), who emphasizes the comic resonance of such performances. A similar historiographical problem is that of the historical Jesus, whose biographical tradition – often compared in the scholarship to that of the Cynics – is once again dominated by the chreia (Gowler, 2006).

and that, though some remained in Pamphylia, the others were dispersed in Cilicia, and also in Syria as far even as Phoenicia.

### Solon (Philo, *The Creation of the World* 104, tr. Younge)

And **Solon**, the Athenian lawgiver, described these different ages in the following elegiac verses:

> In seven years from th' earliest breath,
> The child puts forth his hedge of teeth;
> When strengthened by a similar span,
> He first displays some signs of man.

(etc., the entire poem quoted. Context: discussion of seven-based periods; followed immediately by the views of Hippocrates.)

### Ion (Cleonides, *Harmonic Introduction* 12, tr. Strunk, 1978)

Those speaking of a seven-toned phorminx use the word in the sense of "note", just as do Terpander and **Ion**. The former says:

> We will no longer love the four-voiced ode

> But will sing to thee new hymns with the seven-toned phorminx.

The latter:

> Eleven-stringed lyre, having a ten-step order, three consonant roads of harmonia,
> Formerly all the Greeks raised a meager muse, strumming thee seven-toned by fours.

### Heraclitus (Sextus Empiricus, *Adv. Math* vii.126, tr. Bury, 1973)

And [as for] **Heraclitus**. . . Sensation he convicts by saying expressly "Ill witnesses for men are eyes and ears when they have barbarous souls." (Context: a long doxography of skeptical views concerning sense perception, preceded by a series of philosophers such as Plato, Democritus, Empedocles, immediately followed by Homer and Archilochus.)

### Empedocles (Achilles Tatius, *Introduction* 16, tr. Inwood, 2001: 111)

Some say that the sun is first, the moon second, and Saturn third. But the commoner opinion is that the moon is first, since they say it is a fragment of the sun, as **Empedocles** too says:

> A round and borrowed light, it whirls around the earth.

(Context: followed by mentioning the view that those planets move according to harmony, which is stated to be found in Aratus, Eratosthenes, Hypsicles, Thrasyllus and Adrastus, originally a Pythagorean view.)

### Heraclitus (Porphyry, *Cave of Nymphs* 4, tr. Taylor, 1917)

For the ancients thought that these souls are incumbent on water which is inspired by divinity, as Numenius says, who adds, that on this account, a prophet asserts, that the Spirit of God moved on the waters. The Egyptians likewise, on this account, represent all daemons and also the sun, and, in short, all the planets, not standing on anything solid, but on a sailing vessel; for souls descending into generation fly to moisture. Hence also, **Heraclitus** says, that moisture appears delightful and not deadly to souls; but the lapse into generation is delightful to them.

**Euripides (Iamblichus, *Theologoumenae Arithmeticae*, "On the Monad" 6, tr. Waterfield, 1988)**
And **Euripides** too, who was a disciple of Anaxagoras, mentions the earth as follows: "Those among mortals who are wise consider you to be the hearth."

(Context: following on a doxography in which Homer, Empedocles, Parmenides and "Pythagoreans" are mentioned.)

**Pherecydes (Damascius, *Problems and Solutions Concerning First Principles* 124, tr. Ahbel-Rappe, 2010)**
**Pherecydes** the Syrian makes Zas and Time and Chthonia exist eternally as the first three principles. (Context: list of views on beginnings expressed in Greek myths, following citations from Acusilaus and Epimenides, on the authority of Eudemus, citing also Orphic sources.)

**Xenophanes (Simplicius, *A Commentary on Aristotle's Physics* I.22)**
Theophrastus says of **Xenophanes** the Colophonian, who was the teacher of Parmenides, that the arche was one or that what is, i.e. the all, was one and neither limited nor unlimited nor in motion nor at rest. (Context: a doxography on views on the arche, preceded by the views of Melissus and Parmenides.)

In this case, my sample is shaped by the unsystematic metadata practices baked into the TLG. First, modern editors consider a citation to be a fragment, typically, when its source text has been otherwise lost. This distinction is immaterial for our purposes, and so we lose many citation moments, above all of Homer. Second, some editions insert a note, inside the text itself, that a certain passage is a "fragment", but others do not. The TLG simply follows on previous editorial choices. (Typically, fragments are noted in such texts that contain many: one reads Athenaeus for the fragments, hence editors note them explicitly inside the text itself; Plato's citations of lyric poetry are remarked upon, if at all, only in the critical apparatus.) Thus, the roughly 10,000 pre-Byzantine "fragments" should be seen as a significant undercount of actual ancient citations – heavily biased towards the recherché. By avoiding the massive citations – which are our main source for minor poetry – I have skewed the balance further in favor of recherché *prose*, hence the many Presocratic citations in my sample; but it should be borne in mind that this sample is not entirely absurd, either, in this way. Fragments of the Presocratics are indeed relatively frequent in ancient literature, especially compared to the truly tiny presence of Presocratic literature in the papyri.[139] Already, in antiquity itself, this group of writers was appreciated primarily through memorable quotations. It is not absurd to suggest that, just as Diogenes actively anticipated, in his philosophical practice, his eventual absorption into the collections of chreiai, so too many ancient philosophers actively anticipated, in their philosophical practice, their eventual absorption into the collections of gnomic statements. The very notion of the fragment is in this sense misleading, implying that all philosophers produced complex edifices out of which we now have only a few, unrepresentative, tiny chips. Many of them produced fragments – memorable phrases – from the beginning (evidently so, indeed, in the case of Heraclitus, twice cited in my tiny sample).

Even so: the sample seems plausible enough. Here are some of the key observations. First, the quoted element is usually atomic – the smallest possible. With one exception – Philo's quotation of an entire elegy of Solon – we find here no more than one or two lines of poetry, no more than a single statement in prose (paraphrased for the gist of its content). This certainly seems likely as a general observation for the ancient citation. Second, while the element of citation is "atomic" – the smallest possible – it is part of a "molecule" – a cluster of citations. In this sample, all the citations emerge from a context of an entire cluster of citations, sometimes two (in Cleonides, Ion – together with Terpander; in Philo, Solon – together with Hippocrates), but often rather more, usually about four to five authors named either for their citations or as mediating authorities for the authors cited. This number seems to be significant: what it stands for is *more than three*. That is, the cited authors are not easily parsed into a simple group and, instead, suggest a large, less structured heap.[140] Now, this should once again be considered in the light of the bias of the sample. The quotations here are biased for less frequent authors, which might

---

[139] Other than Epicharmus – seven fragments, typical for minor drama – and a single fragment of Antiphon (perhaps preserved as a piece of rhetoric rather than of philosophy? See Luginbill, 1997), the only unequivocal papyrus of Presocratic philosophy is the Strasbourg Papyrus of Empedocles – a work of poetry. Note further that my avoidance of heavy citations does not exclude only poetry: I also avoid Diogenes Laertius and Stobaeus, among others, so some of our main sources for the philosophical fragment are, in fact, avoided.

[140] Wietzke (2017) has studied the specific phenomenon of authors that are mentioned *only rarely*. His conclusion is that, in some cases (authors in a scholarly context), the sheer plurality of mentioned names is a manifestation of poikilia. Name dropping – not exactly to enhance one's social capital as to enhance the sense of vividness and variety.

mean our sources are more invested in the display of erudition; on the other hand, I avoid the authors of massive citation whose work is composed entirely of heaps of quotation. As a very raw check on this question, I looked at the citations of *mēnin aeide* (the first two words of the *Iliad*: so, the tritest of citations, at the opposite end from the erudite) in post-archaic, pre-Byzantine literature. There are 35 occurrences. Seven are from two authors who cite the words in a scientific/logical context: Sextus Empiricus, who quotes the line as an example of a logical statement; and Pappus, who produces a variation on it as part of a complicated alphabetic-numerical exercise.[141] In those cases the line is indeed cited alone. In all other cases the line is cited embedded within a larger structure of authors and citations (most typically – as part of an entire heap of citations from Homer). It was simply not the done thing, among the Greeks, to cite *one* thing. So, once again, it is not quite an accident that so much is preserved of the views of the Presocratic philosophers. It was not individual views that were preserved but, rather, entire doxographies.

This, then, is the rule: small, atomic citations, embedded within larger molecules of multiple citations. This rule governs much of ancient literature, and indeed defines entire subgenres, such as those of anthologies, doxographies and, above all, sympotic literature. At the extreme, such texts as those by Athenaeus, Plutarch and Aulus Gellius can read, to us, as postmodernist deconstructions of the figure of the author; they can read, to us, as literature reduced to its constituent intertexts, one tiny citation followed by another. They are, as it were, straight out of Kristeva. But, as I keep emphasizing: such, in fact, is how the figure of the author was sustained.

And it is clear, perhaps, from a modern perspective, how this could be so. We are reminded of Kristeva. For a reason: surely our ultimate insight should come from Bakhtin. The rule we find in ancient citations is that of *maximal polyphony*, and the juxtaposition of clashing, individual voices serves to highlight, then, individual voice. The fragment thus functions much like the chreia. It is the individual voice, distilled to a minimal atom, maximized for effect by its clashing proximity to other voices. A doxography – of opposing views.

Nightingale (1995) identifies this phenomenon within the context of Plato's use of certain canonical works from various genres that become embedded, and criticized, in his own dialogue (sometimes very extensively, as in the evocation of prose in the speeches of the *Symposium*, the *Phaedrus*

---

[141] Sextus Empiricus, *Adv. Math.* I.133.3, 163.3, 10, VIII.80.8, IX.350.3; Pappus II.26.2, 28.26.

and the *Menexenus*; very often the much briefer quotations of poetry). These are the "genres in dialogues" of Nightingale's title – which make Plato's works dialogic in the Bakhtinian sense. Semonides is being quoted in the *Protagoras*, first by Protagoras, then by Socrates; the brief quotations create a sharp contrast to their prose context and are offered as contrasting interpretations (self-contradicting? So Protagoras, contradicted by Socrates).[142] The sharp presence of the cited author's voice serves to present more directly Socrates and Protagoras themselves, and, through it all, create the magnificent vividness of voice which made Plato such a compelling author for his ancient readers. What we now need to note, then, is that dialogism – in the Bakhtinian sense – was not a specific Platonic phenomenon. Dialogism is typical of Greek literature as a whole, for a fundamental reason.

This should be put side by side with Bréchet's (2007) observation: how ancient citations are brought in not so much as textual artifacts but as spoken voices ("as Homer *says*..."). To quote, in antiquity, was to bring a voice into conversation: quotation, as dialogism. This is indeed often the context of ancient citation: the dialogue of sympotic literature.

What would be the opposite of dialogic literature? Literature in which the author-figure of the given text aims to erase the many-voiced presence of his characters and sources, leaving dominant just a single authorial presence. But already in the fourth century, and throughout its history, Greek literature never aimed at this kind of erasure. The goal was, throughout, to invoke the shared literary tradition. A fundamental tool for achieving this effect was the brief cited passage – cutting against its immediate context as well as against other brief cited passages. The goal was to maximize polyphony so as to maximize, as it were, phonia as such – the sense of the voice of past authors becoming present.[143]

Let us go back to the set of 13 vignettes in which a canonical name is evoked. Sophocles is recalled not directly but indirectly, via Plato.

---

[142] The famous passage is 339a–347a; see Beresford (2009) for a recent discussion that sums up the current scholarly opinion (Socrates' interpretation is absurd and ironic). Note that, for Nightingale's project, which I follow here, what matters is not the *content* of the engagement with the fragment but its *structural* effect of dialogism.

[143] And so we note that chreiai, and fragment collection, are not primarily driven by the educational process. This indeed mirrors the position of canon formation as such. In both canon formation, and fragment/chreiai collection, we find the same patterns in the educational as well as in the "elite" context. Which caused which? The question is wrong: it was just a cultural practice maintaining itself, among other things, through the process of education. There is no doubt that the memorability of apophthegms and gnomai made them useful specifically for the educational process of instilling literacy. But, in this, education did not differ from other cultural contexts in which memorability was valued, because it went hand in hand with vividness of presentation.

Xenophon is evoked through his own evocation of Socrates (which is implicitly contrastive: "Xenophon's Socrates" means, for Artemidorus' readers, "the non-Plato's Socrates"). Xenophon, once again, is imagined to be salvaging Thucydides. Demosthenes is set side by side with an artist, Scopas. Isocrates evokes Pindar, Galen evokes Isocrates – so as to compare oneself, hence to insert oneself into the literary tradition. Several of the remaining vignettes, finally, come from the context of the citation and form, naturally, part of a larger molecule of citations. The rule is preserved: the authors are recalled *together*.

The romantic image of the author is based on the author's craftsmanship of his own body of works, which are fictional, hence idiosyncratic to him. To be fully appreciated as an author, you must stand apart, solipsistically, in your realm. Ancient literary works were not like that: they concerned the shared world of myth and history, and they were much less central to the identity of the author. The author did not stand apart but was appreciated socially, as a member of a group of authors. He was vividly present, through the power of words to evoke the vividness of imagined encounter. Which was natural enough, as literature was understood, above all, as performative, so that its words were imagined as embodied, as uttered in a public space.

It is for a reason, after all, that the canonical author comes within small groups attached to genres. Each genre implies a form of performance and some kind of external reality, and then that reality is occupied by a small group of clashing individuals. Three tragedians, of which one, Euripides, is supreme: an echo of the dramatic festival in which a single victor emerges from three contestants. Homer, and Hesiod: but this was imagined very early on as a contest between two performers, in the *Certamen of Homer and Hesiod*. This was paralleled, of course, by the agon of Euripides and Aeschylus in Aristophanes' *Frogs*, the point surely being that, while the dramatic festivals brought together the two pairs Aeschylus/Sophocles and then Sophocles/Euripides, direct competition between Aeschylus and Euripides never took place, and for this reason was appropriate comic material. Indeed, even distant styles of performance were perceived together in a system of oppositions, such as "new" and "old" comedies. Only one author was canonized from each, and the two were separated by nearly a century, and yet they formed a pair – old and new, Aristophanes and Menander – and Roman-era authors, at least, could not fail to consider Menander and Aristophanes in competition with each other.[144] When

---

[144] Plutarch's *Moralia* 853–4, an epitome of a *Comparison of Menander and Aristophanes*.

poets were contemporary, strife had to be imagined: so Callimachus
rebuking Apollonius of Rhodes and causing his exile.[145] Politics involved
a direct confrontation between two viewpoints, and so the most dramatic,
and final, contest of Athenian democracy was canonized through its two
rival exponents: Demosthenes and Aeschines. Why have Isocrates as well?
Among other things, because he was in explicit competition with Plato.[146]
The ancient vita could not avoid imagining Thucydides envying and
implicitly competing with Herodotus[147] (though Xenophon, we noted,
was kind to Thucydides' memory). In general, the historians are best
understood not in terms of explicit contest but in terms of implicit division
of labor. Xenophon belongs to the genre of sequels to Thucydides (we shall
return to discuss this in the next chapter). What this suggests is
a recognition of Thucydides as a canonical author and the effort to become
equal to that canon. In poetry, we often see a return to the (unrestricted)
character set of myth in a manner which suggests the implicit competition
of intertextuality. Aratus surely positioned himself in such a manner
relative to Hesiod,[148] Apollonius to both Homer (a different return) and
Euripides (a different Medea).[149] Homeric competition defined both
Callimachus and Theocritus. Three authors competed in their accounts
of Socrates: Aristophanes, Plato and Xenophon. Plato, as Proclus keenly
noted, competed with Thucydides as well (indeed – Nightingale's point –
he competed with literature as a whole in order to create philosophy: I take
this to mean above all that he took on Homer, in the *Republic*). Finally,
Aristophanes directly confronted Euripides again and again (as, indeed, he
did with most of his contemporaries). All this may be expressed as a graph
in which the canon is visualized not chronologically but in terms of
patterns of contest.[150]

In the introduction to Chapter 1 I expressed my amazement at
Proclus' ability to identify Plato's *Menexenus* as an agonistic exercise

---

[145] Lefkowitz (1980): that the strife was likely invented out of whole cloth is precisely what makes it
useful for my argument.
[146] Nightingale (1995: chap. 1).
[147] Marcellinus, *Vita Thucydidis* 54. Plutarch's *On the Malice of Herodotus* repeatedly contrasts
Herodotus' failings with Thucydides' superior achievement, as did Dionysius of Halicarnassus
before him (Pritchett, 1975); in fact, it appears as if critical reception of either Herodotus or
Thucydides, at least from the Roman era on, was primarily about their competitive comparison.
[148] Obvious enough: Fakas (2001).
[149] For the (paramount) epic dimension, see Fantuzzi and Hunter (2004: chap. 3). For Apollonius and
Euripides, see Knight (1991).
[150] Excluded from this graph is Pindar – and lyric poetry as a whole. Lyric poetry was a canon that
preceded the established polis of letters and that was largely superseded by it; this development calls
for a different, chronological account, to which I turn next.

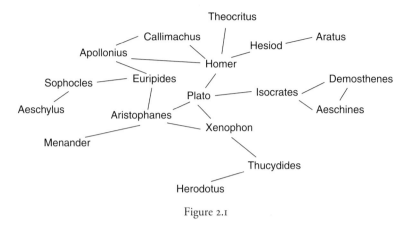

Figure 2.1

directed against Thucydides. I contrasted this with the fictional account, in Borges, of Ibn Rushd's failure to understand the meaning of Aristotle's references to tragedy and comedy. There was a certain web of knowledge that traveled throughout antiquity and was still available for Proclus to use in his reading of Plato. However fictional, Borges' story reminds us of the contingency, and frailty, of such webs. A culture can inherit certain of its monuments with or without context. Throughout antiquity a certain set of monuments – the canon – was transmitted in a rich contextual form, its authors fully made vivid. This tight, fully imagined web of individuals formed what I call the polis of letters. Authors were recalled through words in (violent) action, words taken in hostile encounter; in this abstract sense, the words of the polis were political words. Indeed, other than the epic/archaic component, the canon was mainly formed with authors who could be associated together in the events of a single polis – Athens – with its own set of ritual performances. Together, these Athenian authors formed a network of oppositions that in and of itself created the sense of a social group in active, fruitful tension, literature as city-in-miniature. Their heirs – the Hellenistic poets – fastened upon the loose valency of the big molecule: the availability of imitative competition with the epic/archaic compo-nent of the canon. They succeeded in doing so, and their works survived, but, since they could not carry the same aura of co-presence in a city, they survived in a qualified way and with relatively weak authorial presences. Somehow, after Athens, Athens remained essential – which will be the topic of the following part of this book.

This, then, is the account I provide of the shape of the Greek canon. The invention of the author was triumphant – once established – because of the inherent power of the author to organize a literary field through the attractive power of the brand. In the Greek context, authors were formed via their generic association: they were authors-within-genre. This also meant that they were perceived in terms of their style and performance, in terms of their words-in-action. Thus, the canon would be formed as the accumulation of many names associated together, each becoming a site for the cultural imagination of words-in-action. We understand the role of the occasion of performance; we understand the value of the sharp contest of the polis, which forms a powerful background to the power of words-in-action.

Many questions remain unanswered. How did the Greeks stumble upon the invention of the brand-name author in the first place? Once they did, why did Athens become such a major site for the construction of such brand names – and, following the achievement of Athens, why did canon formation become, later on, so constrained that, following the Alexandrian completion of the big molecule of contest, no further changes to the canon remained possible, thus enshrining the Athenian legacy?

We reach beyond structural description, towards an account of the historical growth, and ultimate immutability, of the canon. Why did archaic Greek readers begin to collect names? Why did Hellenistic Greek readers stop doing so? To answer these questions, we need a few more detours, a few more pieces of evidence, concerning the ancient formation of authorship.

## 2.3   The Polis of Letters: History

How was the canon made? More generally, how were authors made? I assume many of my readers come with the assumption – built into the late twentieth-century debate concerning the Western canon – that canons are deliberately (or functionally) constructed as forms of hegemony.[151] Putting aside the question of political critique, this assumes, effectively, that canon formation is at a remove from the site of creation. Canons, it is assumed, are a matter not of authors and their audiences but of

---

[151] A standard statement (Bennet and Royle, 2016: 47): "In recent years, much attention has been given to the construction of the literary canon. In particular, critics have explored the ways in which the canon is bound up with questions of education, class, economics, race, ethnicity, colonization, sexual and gender difference, and so on. [...] More than ever we are made aware of how far the canon is a fabrication."

gatekeepers, literary critics and the makers of cultural judgement.[152] This remove in social space then makes possible a remove in time as well. Under this model, then, of the *constructed canon* it is natural to assume that the Greek canon was made, say, with the Byzantine selection.[153] We have already seen in Chapter 1 the stability of the canon from the Ptolemaic era onwards, the passivity of Byzantium. There is no doubt that the canon substantially pre-dates the Byzantine transmission and must go back at least to the Hellenistic era. This does not yet rule out the possibility that the canon was made in Alexandria, however. In this chapter I argue that it was not and that the canon, quite simply, was not made at a remove. It was a judgement made by authors and audiences, merely reaffirmed by later critics. This, then, is simultaneously a question of chronology and of history, because the date of the making of the canon is entangled with the mechanism of its making.

The structure of the argument is as follows. First – still at a structural level of analysis – I set out in section 2.3.1 some evidence concerning the social prerequisites for the making of the ancient author. Following that, in section 2.3.2, I provide some of the dates that may be established for the canonical status of the central ancient authors. section 2.3.3, finally, offers a tentative model for the historical formation of the ancient canon.

### 2.3.1 Becoming an Author: What Did It Take?

The argument of this section is that one became a notable author through one's own accumulation of social capital. One had to be, oneself, socially eminent. This observation is the starting point for the claim that critics, at a temporal remove, simply could not have constructed the canonicity of past authors: social capital cannot be posthumously constructed. So, we need to turn to the sociology of ancient literary fame.

---

[152] From Guillory (1993) onwards study of the canon was often understood in terms of choices made by institutions of education. This is natural, given that the debate concerning the canon surrounded, primarily, school curricula.

[153] Often stated unreflectively by non-specialists, as an automatic application of contemporary assumptions concerning canon formation: Gorak (1991: 51–2): "[R]ecent scholarship also emphasizes the even more basic function of the Byzantine canon…the classroom elections of Byzantium guaranteed the survival of many texts." But sophisticated versions of the same claims are made even by classicists, who do know, of course, that the canon was there all along (see, e.g., Kaldellis, 2015, on the historiographical canon in Byzantium. In such readings, a particular form of reception of the canonical authors is described as the making of the canon. Expert scholars know the qualified sense of the "making" in place, but most readers come out assuming that Byzantium made authors such as Herodotus and Thucydides.).

To make a start on this sociology, I suggest we take two indirect approaches. The two pieces of evidence marshaled in this section are (1) the longevity of the ancient author and (2) the scarcity of ancient graphomania. I consider authorship, so to speak, from the top and from the bottom of the literary ladder.

We start at the top, and, to begin with, then, I take Tim Parkin's very useful compilation of older individuals from Greco-Roman antiquity (http://personalpages.manchester.ac.uk/staff/tim.parkin/oldancients.html), an online database complementing Parkin (2003). From the fifth century BCE on (I ignore early and truly dubious reports) the list comprises 97 philosophers and 74 non-philosophical authors.[154] Let us consider this in detail. There is no doubt that ages at death were misreported, generally stylized and often exaggerated in ancient sources.[155] Still, the authors surveyed by Parkin were all considered by their immediate circle to have died at an old age of 60 or more. More to the point, many ages can be historically corroborated, and some are remarkable indeed. Sophocles did participate in dramatic contests from the 460s to the 400s; he must have died more than 80 years old. There are good reasons to believe Galen lived to an age nearer 90.[156] (It is telling that the sources, in this case, actually under-report Galen's age at death as 70: stylized ages need not always be inflated ages.) Of the very top canonical authors (excluding of course Homer and Hesiod), the ages at death quoted by Parkin (but transformed into plausible figures) are:[157]

---

[154] That philosophers are so heavily represented is perhaps a mark of the density of the ancient biographical tradition concerning philosophy, and its survival. Partly, of course, it may have to do with the ancient perception of old age, wisdom and philosophy: a philosopher *ought* to have been old (he was bearded, was he not? See Zanker, 1995), his old age *ought* to have been reported.

[155] Parkin (2003: 36–46) himself discusses this in detail. In general, numerical values are typically stylized and rounded in ancient sources (Scheidel, 1996); in the case of age, there is also in some cases a tendency to exaggerate. Our response should be to round, ourselves (a rational response to uncertainty); and never to rely on a report of an age of death as such but, rather, on the evidence for the person's activity. Since the accumulated evidence suggests many notable persons did die at old age, however, we may begin to give credence to the bare statement of longevity (without paying much attention to the precise figure given by the ancient source). The reported age at death of Epimenides (157!) was certainly inflated, but this should not lead us to assume automatically that so was, say, that of Sophocles. As Parkin (2003: 273) concludes, "In spite of low expectation of life at birth, a not insignificant percentage of the population was in its 60s or 70s." We sometimes tend to assume a pre-modern Monty-Pythonesque regime of mortality, people dropping dead right and left. The reality of medical history is that life expectancy at birth did indeed rise dramatically, in the industrial world, through the twentieth century, mostly stemming from the eradication of infant mortality, changes in adult mortality being more incremental.

[156] This depends on the authenticity of *De Theriaca ad Pisonem*; if genuine, its historical references make it the product of Galen's 88th year (Nutton, 1997).

[157] I refer the reader for the sources in Parkin's list; I add a brief comment in brackets.

| Pindar | 80? | (Merely late reports; but long active life)[158] |
| Aeschylus | 69 | |
| Sophocles | 90? | (Dubious reports; but dramatic contests support this) |
| Herodotus | Mid to late sixties? Less? | (Problematic evidence)[159] |
| Euripides | 74 or 79 | (Same as Sophocles) |
| Aristophanes | 65 | (Same as above) |
| Thucydides | 65 or a bit less? | (Especially problematic; weak evidence)[160] |
| Isocrates | 90? | (Given as 98/100; clearly inflated, but very long active life) |
| Xenophon | 70? Much more? | (Reported as over 90, but this is likely inflated)[161] |
| Plato | 80 or 84 | (Very safe dating) |
| Aeschines | 75 | (A stylized report in a vita; but no reason to doubt) |
| Demosthenes | 62 | (Quite confident dates) |
| Menander | 51 | (Many sources, leaving little room for doubt)[162] |
| Callimachus | 70? | (Weak evidence; but long active life) |
| Apollonius | 60? More? | (Almost no real data)[163] |

The life expectancy at birth of a central canonical Greek author was, we find, about 67. This clearly is rather old. Is this perhaps a phenomenon of the hyper-canonical only? If we lower the threshold we repeat the same effect. I extend the list down to authors with at least three papyri fragments (so by no means highly central authors), to obtain 18 more authors for my sample, as well as adding the top 17 authors mentioned in the OCD ("top" measured by the size of the OCD entry) who have *fewer* than three papyri fragments – reaching down to authors who are fairly obscure to modern readers,

---

[158] Datable poems range from 498 to 446 BC.

[159] Most now follow Fornara (1971), who is the source of Parkin's older age at death.

[160] Not from Parkin. Thucydides was a general in 424, so certainly 30 years old or more then. He might be taking into consideration, in his history, an event that took place in 397; see Pouilloux and Salviat (1983), as well as the synthesis (Hornblower, 2002). Hornblower may be summed up as affirming the dates as "around 460" till "maybe later than 397" (but certainly not earlier than 399). The evidence can be squeezed to 454 to 399 and age at death of 55, but this is at the extreme of both probability distributions; 65, or a bit less, does appear to be the most likely. It is interesting that the biographical tradition did not choose to think of him as "old" at his death. His life was known to involve the violence of war as well as of plague. His memory did not suggest the tranquility of an old age.

[161] We know of his activities from 401 (the anabasis itself) to 355 (to which the *poroi* is dated). He was certainly more than a mere youth in 401, hence at least 70 years old at death and perhaps rather more.

[162] Obviously, not from Parkin; see De Marcellus (1996).

[163] The evidence is summed up in Hunter (1989: introd. [1–12]). Just about the one clear thing is that he was chief librarian for the Ptolemaic court around 270 to 245 BC. Scholars traditionally interpreted this to mean he was more than a mere youth in 270 and died not long after 245, so perhaps, then, "c. 305–245" is how we may sum this up.

although at their time they were still very significant (lowest in this set is the historian Theopompus of Chios). Altogether I add 35 authors, to reach a sample of 52 "top" authors, limited to such authors whose longevity can be plausibly reconstructed.[164] The average longevity of the top 17 authors was about 67; the average longevity of the next 35 was about 70.5.[165] Going down the scale actually *raised* the average longevity a little, albeit insignificantly.

Now, of course, to have become a well-known author, one would have to survive childhood, for sure: so we are looking not for e(0), the life expectancy at birth, but at e(X), the life expectancy at the age X, with X being a certain non-zero value. Let me explain with the aid of Scheidel (1999), whose discussion offers an interesting parallel: the age of emperors at death. They died, on average, at age 60. This would be very high for e(0), but obviously not because the emperors came from a supremely robust stock (indeed, Scheidel's main result is that many emperors must have come to a violent end!). Rather, the emperors were pre-selected as a group, by having acceded to the throne, on average, at age 41. For their longevity, then, one has to calculate the appropriate value for e(41), in their time and place (for which 60, it turns out, is somewhat low).

But, compared with the major cultural figures, emperors died young! True, some died violently – but so did Demosthenes, for instance, in the central canon of 17 authors (as well as Eupolis and Callisthenes, the only truly young deaths in the extended set of 52 figures). The conclusion is that cultural "accession to the throne" happened later in life for authors than it did for emperors. That is: there was an age when "authors were made", after which they could die and still end up famous. But they would, on average, have as many years to live, after that point, as an actuary would have expected. And so we can use the actuary tables to *reconstruct backwards* the age when "authors were made", based on the data of their actual longevities.

---

[164] The top 52 authors whose age at death can be estimated are a subset of, perhaps, the top 70 to 80 authors from antiquity. I do not think failure to estimate represents a younger age at death (the problem is most acute with archaic authors, who, if anything, are typically reported to have died very old – likely in a cultural context in which the social persona mattered even more, since there was no writing to compensate for the absence of one's person).

[165] The names and ages are as follows (note that throughout I provide not reported ages but estimates based on historical constraints; if none can be provided the author is excluded): Aristotle 62, Epicurus 71, Plutarch 74, Socrates 71, Himerius 71, Plotinus 66, Posidonius 84, Polybius 82, Democritus 80, Aristoxenus 65, Archimedes 70, Cassius Dio 70, Diogenes of Sinope 80, Eratosthenes 80, Erasistratus 75, Origen 69, Timaeus 80, Eusebius 76, Theopompus 60, Lysias 65, Galen 88, Hyperides 68, Aelius Aristides 64, Eupolis 40, Theophrastus 84, Cratinus 80, Dionysius Thrax 70, Philo 65, Aeschines Socraticus 60, Callisthenes 40, Cercidas 70, Chrysippus 73, Dinarchus 70, Lycurgus 65, Strabo 75.

An average life expectancy near 70, under the models one often uses for pre-modern societies, would suggest a life expectancy calculated at a little above 50.[166] This is intriguing: after all, it is very rare that we hear of any reasonably well-known ancient author who died before the age of 50.[167] And this might be significant in and of itself, because for a well-known author to have died young would have been a notable event, one perhaps to be marked by the sources.

Or take the following comparison. The following (small) list has all the scholarchs of the philosophical schools in Athens for whom we can determine the age at which scholarchate was attained.[168]

| | |
|---|---|
| Speusippus | 61 |
| Xenocrates | 57 |
| Theophrastus | 50 |
| Hermarchus | 55 |
| Cleanthes | 69 |
| Strato | 49 |
| Arcesilaus | 50 |
| Lyco | 30[169] |
| Chrysippus | 48 |
| Carneades I | 47 |
| Panaetius | 54 |
| Clitomachus | 58 |
| Phaedrus | 63 |

---

[166] Frier (1982) extrapolates from Ulpian's schedule of the paying out of annuities, which slide according to the age of the recipient. For youths, one calculated 30 years of disbursement; for a 50-year-old, one calculated nine. Frier's observation is that this must represent prevailing assumptions concerning the (median?) longevity at a given age, from which he recovered a model of mortality distributions in accordance with the standard used by demographers, the Coale–Demeny model life tables (Frier, 1982: 237; the bedrock of all such analysis is Coale and Demeny, 1966). Scholarship since then, especially Scheidel (2001), has pointed out the many uncertainties in this use of models: the not very surprising upshot of more recent discussions, however, is that the severe environment of endemic and epidemic disease in ancient urban centers would tend to make mortality at older ages worse. An ancient, metropolitan 50-year-old would have had to expect considerably fewer than 20 years.

[167] The exceptions emerge mostly from a single context: the Roman poets who have made their mark during the late Republic. I will return to discuss this below. I have also mentioned Eupolis and Callisthenes. The latter's fame rests on the fame of his subject, Alexander of Macedon. The case of Eupolis is more intriguing. Menander, too, died young; both – as well as Aristophanes (and Sophocles) – are reported to have had an early start in the dramatic contest. Drama, and especially comedy, was one arena in which fame could be obtained relatively rapidly. (Did the subversion of comedy invite, specifically, the carnivalesque reversal whereby the young mock the old?)

[168] The term may overstate Speusippus' actual position, as I note on p. 324 below; at any rate, he became the "first" within a certain group, in the year 347.

[169] A very marked choice, which Strato tried to defend: Lyco was appointed because "some are too old, some too preoccupied" (Diogenes Laertius V.62).

The average age is 53, remarkably similar to the "a little above 50" we find for intellectual achievement in general. To have been considered suitable to make this transition, to be considered a first in your group, you had to reach this age.

Now, all this of course is a very difficult argument to make: my sample is small; it is hard to adjust for the bias of survival of evidence concerning longevity; and even the application of the statistical models – the ones which supply the argument for its deceptive air of mathematical certainty – may not be safe, for the reasons spelled out (as noted in n.166 above) by Scheidel (2001). But in fact precision is unnecessary (and, to be clear, I avoid any pretense at precise calculation!). The broad contours are clear, and sufficient: it appears that a very great proportion of ancient eminent authors died at age 60 or above. Since we do not believe that becoming an eminent author was in and of itself conducive to health,[170] the conclusion must be that one's chances of becoming an eminent author would have been much reduced if one happened to die at the age of 50 or so. No country for young men, there.[171] And this is all that our argument requires.

Now, this can be seen in two ways. First, there ought to have been some kind of correlation between the sheer amount of one's productivity and one's future fame. After all, one publishes, or perishes. Dying at an older age grants one more time in which to produce more. And, indeed, the one

[170] There is a familiar hoax, as if winning the Oscar lengthens one's life (presumably, the boost to one's ego). It is a statistical artifact produced from the kind of effect discussed here. (For an elementary discussion, see www.causeweb.org/wiki/chance/index.php/Oscar_winners_do_not_live_longer). Greenspan, Heinz and Hargrove (2008) compare old master painters and sculptors. They note (2008: 1): "Analysis of the database revealed that Old Master painters lived 3 years less than their peer sculptors (63.6 ± 0.9 versus 67.4 ± 1.1)." Their conclusion – alarming to me as well as, I suppose, to most of my readers – is that sculptors lived longer because their occupation involved more strenuous exercise. (Maybe we should conduct a similar study on novelists versus poets: if, as I suspect, we find that poets tend to die younger, we could perhaps account for the longevity of novelists by the longer periods they spend sitting and writing – surely as healthy a lifestyle as any.) This was published in *Age and Ageing*, the journal of the British Geriatric Society, and fellow doctors were quick to point out that the results might point instead to the professional risk painters take through their exposure to hazardous materials. Exercise and toxicity: such are contemporary obsessions. A more sociological approach would note, first of all, the extremely high longevity as such (which also matches very well the evidence for antiquity, fragmentary and dubious as it is). What the evidence seems to suggest is the greater significance of patronage in the career of sculptors, where fame rests entirely on access to rare, monumental commissions.

[171] Philostratus, *Lives of the Sophists* 543, on Polemo: "When he died he was about fifty-six years old, but this age-limit, though for the other professions it is the beginning of senility, for a sophist still counts as youthfulness." I suggest that Philostratus was right about the profession he knew best – that of the sophist – but wrong about the rest. Fifty-something, in antiquity, was the real *beginning*. (Chrestus of Byzantium – so Philostratus tells us: *Lives* 592 – was neglected by posterity; this is because he never reached full mastery, having died, as he did, at the age of 50.) In Hanoch Levin's immortal words: "Life begins only at age sixty-two" (Levin, 2003: 33).

relatively young death in the core canon – Menander – coincides with
a very prolific author, and with a very young beginning of the productive
span (it appears that Menander produced his first comedy while still an
ephebe, so that, dead when aged 51 or 52, he had by then more than 30 years
of activity behind him – with perhaps as many as 100 plays?). This, then,
suggests that there is a certain tipping point, not so much in terms of
absolute age but in terms of sheer output.

This output effect is very likely. But there could also be another, more
subtle effect, of "just sticking around": that the very fact that one's name
was familiar to a group of contemporaries for long enough would somehow
lift one's reputation. It certainly mattered a lot that one survived long
enough to become the leading figure of one's day. Let us look more closely
at drama, where the didascalia allow a firmer grasp than usual of the
evolution of the career. This is the most obvious example of prominence
achieved through social performance, though patronage and network are
no less important than elsewhere: we note the phenomenon of the poetic
families (Csapo, 2010: 88). The most prolific family was that of Aeschylus,
beginning already with his father Euphorion; the clan would have 11
members (tragic Bachs, as it were). It helped some – perhaps even in
gaining one's first commissions – to have the family connection.

So let us look at the seminal career at the heart of this family – and at the
beginning of the Athenian canon. Aeschylus' debut took place in 499 (just
in time for the beginning of continuous didascalic record),[172] but it took
him 15 years to get his first victory. The dominant tragedian of that age, it
appears, was Phrynichus, whose career ended at some point after 476 (his
last recorded production of *Phoenician Women*). This left an opening: the
major competition was dead. It was just in time for the *Persians* to shine, in
472. During the remaining 14 years of his life Aeschylus won three more
documented victories. The entire sequence of years with recorded victories is:

> 484, 472, 467, "sometime between 465 and 459", 458.

And so the inter-victory gaps look roughly: 12, 5, 5 (?), 4(?).

The statistics are problematic (and surely we are missing several of his
victories,[173] so that the gaps must have been shorter, surely especially so
near the end of the career). The implication is of a career divided into three

---

[172] So, West (1989); Scullion (2002).
[173] The *Suda* claims a total of 13: but this appears to have been a stock number (Phrynichus, too, is
assigned the same number).

periods of 12 to 15 years each: 499 to 484, a minor presence (no victories); 484 to 472, a significant author (occasional victories); 472 to 458, the leading author (the default victor: though he did lose once to Sophocles!). The breakthrough moment – from merely successful to lead-ing – arrived at about age 55.

It helped to have been, at some point, number one: number two could serve as well, as it did for Euripides (always trailing, in his life, the established Sophocles) and for Menander (always trailing, in his life, the established Philemon). Rhetoric did have *three* major contemporaries – Demosthenes, Isocrates and Aeschines. But ancient Athenian attention would have been even more powerfully riveted on the stage of the assembly than on that of the theater.

Let us consider more closely the comparison with politics. Parkin's list of Greek political figures who are reported to have died old has 43 entries, including 15 royal heirs. This means he counts only 28 Greek figures who *achieved* greatness (not royal heirs – i.e. they did not have to wait for their predecessors to die so as to reach the throne, which would create a bias for longevity), and then died over 60 years old. This is a very low number. The conclusion seems to be that one could have achieved greatness, in the political sphere, at an earlier age than one could in the cultural sphere. There was no need, Menander-like, to grind out comedies, more than three per year, for over three decades... A few shining deeds, and you've *made it*. Cultural fame beckoned the would-be Nestor; the would-be Achilles aimed for political and, above all, military glory: Alexander died aged 33.

For another comparison, let me bring in another Alexander: I mean Sergeyevich Pushkin. (As usual, the purest specimen of the Romantic author is found in Russia.) During his twenties – at the same age as Alexander the Great crossing Asia – he published a series of lyrical, and long, narrative poems, in particular a major novel in verse. This, *Eugene Onegin*, was enough to establish him as Russia's favorite son. He died, at age 37, in a duel that contemporaries perceived to have been the outcome of state persecution. Anger at the government following Pushkin's death was picked up by Lermontov's poem "Death of a Poet", an underground sensation that, in turn, had catapulted its own author into a level nearly as elevated as that of Pushkin himself: a position Lermontov maintains in the Russian literary pantheon to this day, even though he himself was dead – through his own duel – at the even younger age of 27. The phenomenon is indeed familiar: from Pushkin onwards, Russian authors – in particular, poets – have been habitually crowned with the heroic garlands of a youthful death. In general, romanticism and (to a lesser extent) modernism has a remarkable number of hyper-canonical authors who die very young. Going outside Russian culture (there, it would be tedious to list all the major authors who have died young), we may note haphazardly a few super-famous names: Byron, Shelley and Keats; Kleist and Novalis; Leopardi; but also: Rimbaud and Apollinaire (to cross into France, and into modernism); Galois and Abel (to cross into mathematics);[174] and then Schubert, Chopin, Mozart (of course!); or Van Gogh, Egon Schiele and Modigliani (but also Raphael, Giorgione, Masaccio and Caravaggio)... – and the point is that the likes of all of these are not found in Greek antiquity.

Not that there are that many like them in the nineteenth and twentieth centuries, either. The great bulk of modern successful authors died old.[175] The advantages of old age remain as obvious as ever: so, for instance, *sticking around for a very long time* is an absolute prerequisite for the Nobel Prize for Literature. But, particularly in certain transformational cultural settings of the modern world, great fame would often be achieved by those who die young.[176] Now, we must separate two components of this phenomenon. First, there is certainly a cult of romantic agony. Byron and Keats, Pushkin and Lermontov, became even more famous just *because* they died young. But they would undoubtedly have reached fame even without the young death (as Wordsworth and Coleridge managed to do well enough). The 60 percent of hyper-canonical English Romantic poets who died young represent not just the cult of romantic agony but also something else, more mundane: people died younger, sometimes, back then. The one remarkable thing is that some of them had *already made their mark*. In the Romantic world, in the modern world, it sometimes becomes

---

[174] See Alexander (2010) – this time a surname – for a study of the romantic image of mathematics; the phenomenon is mostly about mathematics as against other sciences (in which a longer apprenticeship, apparently, is still crucial).

[175] I compared average longevities in the *Oxford Book of Verse* for the seventeenth and nineteenth centuries. The seventeenth century had average longevity of 59; the nineteenth century – the age of Romanticism! – had average longevity of 65. It appears that authors who died very young constitute 60 percent of the set of hyper-canonical English Romantic poets but only a small fraction of moderately successful English Romantic poets.

[176] Is death at a young age especially typical of Romanticism and high modernism? Perhaps: but notice in general that life expectancy at age 30 went up considerably from the early nineteenth century to the twentieth, so that e(30) and e(50) came to be less distinguishable. Camus and Sylvia Plath are two relatively recent examples of authors who made their mark at a young age. A mortality regime such as that of the early nineteenth century would surely have added more twentieth-century authors to their ranks.

possible to make one's mark at an early age.[177] Obviously, to do so, you would have to have a small body of work which in and of itself was sufficient to have established you. For this reason we find that death at a young age is especially prevalent among those who were truly great. That is: if you have made your name on the basis of a narrower body of works, then this body of works must have been especially compelling. The case of painting is very suggestive: Van Gogh, Egon Schiele and Modigliani, Giorgione, Masaccio and Caravaggio... (but not Raphael, a unique phenomenon of sheer craftsmanship). Such names conjure in our mind powerful, even disturbing images that seem to leap out of the panel. It is important to be truly great, and it is also important to be truly great in a way that commands attention. Finally, it is important to live at a time when intense attention is focused on one's form of creativity. The Russian case is probably best understood in such terms: because of the intensity of the engagement by Russians with their own literature (resulting, of course, from the position of literary culture as the unique outlet of civic society), there was always an intense interest in emerging literary talent, so that poets very often could become famous on the basis of a single, early work. Russian patterns of mortality took care of the rest but they were almost immaterial. Pasternak died aged 70 and Akhmatova aged 77, but they would both have been just as famous had they died at the more traditional age of 37. The point is not that Mayakovsky and his like died young; the point is that Russian poetic fortunes were made before one's 30th birthday.

The key to the entire phenomenon is the place of the body of works as commanding attention – often, indeed, the attention of peers whose critical judgement plays a key role in the process of reception (it takes a Verlaine to make a Rimbaud). This is internal reception, whereby poets make poets through their own networks, in which the capital of recognition is exchanged and accumulated. And we have proof, I believe, in the longevities of ancient cultural figures, that such processes were extremely rare in antiquity.

What was the ancient exception? Roman authors of the late Republic and (somewhat less) the early Empire, overwhelmingly the lyric poets. I select a few key names, followed by age at death:

---

[177]  Indeed, in certain contexts such as popular music, it is almost impossible to make one's mark unless it is made by a very young age. This – together with lifestyle – accounts for the age 27 phenomenon, from Janis Joplin down to Amy Winehouse.

Varro Atacinus (47), Catullus (30), Cornellius Galus (44), Cornificia (45), Licinius Macer (35), Lucan (26), Lucretius (44), Petronius (39), Priscus (41), Propertius (35), Tibullus (36)

These authors died on average aged 39, nearly the Russian age; this of course selects the young deaths, but there are, essentially, no old poets: 60 or so is roughly the maximum. It appears that the average age at death for a late Republican Roman poet was not much higher than 40, suggesting a fantastically low value for the age at which expectancy is to be calculated. Of course, it was also a bad time and place: crowded, marshy and violent.[178] But surely the main observation here is more specific than just that concerning Roman demography, for which we ought to consider Parkin's list of old deaths among Roman authors of the period – for, indeed, many Romans did die old. Parkin has 85 old deaths among Romans of the three centuries 2 BCE to 1 CE. His data may be summed up also as follows.

*Number of famous Romans recorded to have reached old age*

|          | 2nd century BCE | 1st century BCE | 1st century CE |
|----------|-----------------|-----------------|----------------|
| Politics | 10              | 18              | 31             |
| Poetry   | 6               | 2               | 0              |
| Prose    | 1               | 6               | 11             |

This is a phenomenon of genre. Prose writers died old, poets died young. Late Republican poetry was an exceptional context – which the poets themselves, as is well known, were keen to assert:

> Give way, Roman authors, Give way, Greeks:
> Something greater than the *Iliad* is being born.

So Propertius (Elegies II.34.65–6) on the *Aeneid*. Vergil himself died at the age of 51, old for a Roman poet of his time; but he became a super-canonical author, in his lifetime, based on a relatively small corpus that was effective through its sheer power to command attention.

---

[178] Scheidel (2009a), as ever emphasizing uncertainty but leaving no doubt that Rome was, quite simply, a deathtrap.

You see: here, for once, was intense attention fixed on a literary genre. Romans, after all, were setting up a monument, appropriating the canon into their own language. Not only was attention intensely focused; it was internally focused. It was an era of poets and authors in deep and direct dialogue, cataloguing and advertising each other's achievements. The major modern study of the distribution of works within an ancient author's lifetime is Starr (1987), concentrating on the one case when evidence is plentiful: the Roman authors of the late Republic and the early Empire. In Starr's formula, the Romans circulated texts (1987: 213) "in a series of widening concentric circles determined primarily by friendship". To be an ancient Roman author meant to belong to a tiny, elite network of friendship, within which one's work could subsist. One sent one's work to one's friends, who might or might not send it onwards, and one became an author by building a position within a network.[179] This is a significant observation concerning the way in which literary reception, in antiquity, depended on social reception. But note that the Roman case was exceptional – which is precisely why it is so well documented. Roman literary patronage, as explained by White (1993) (expanding White, 1978) was simply the practice of amicitia, with literary authors as its beneficiaries. It was not a matter of philanthropists seeking the advancement of culture, nor even that of statesmen in search of propaganda. It was Romans, doing what they always did: worrying about one's circle of friends. Now, as I will return to explain in more detail in Chapter 4, the central theme of the first century BCE was the absorption of literary practices into the Roman networks of amicitia. This happened as – and because – the political battle over such networks escalated. The intensity with which the Roman elite scrutinized its members spilled over, through networks of literary amicitia, to generate an intense scrutiny of the literary elite. And so, fame could be made fast. An exceptional case, coming from a rare moment, of literary attention being intense – but relatively narrow-based.

The intensity of the attention riveted upon literary amicitia made early success possible, but the general rule remains, even then, and can be stated clearly: in antiquity, to become accepted as a significant literary figure, one

---

[179] See more recently, e.g., Iddeng (2006) and Parker (2009). In recent scholarship there is a tendency to conflate Starr's central claim – that Roman literature was provided its status within tiny networks of amicitia – with a different debate, concerning the relative roles of orality and literacy in Latin literature (the question then becomes whether literature was consumed by small group of listeners or by large, widespread groups of readers). Thus, the recent emphasis on the literate nature of ancient literature is offered as a qualification to Starr (1987). In fact, as Starr already recognized, what made literature, above all, was the circulation, within the amicitia networks, of *written* texts.

first had to have become *socially* significant. The authors whom the Greeks knew – and who we hear of – needed not merely to have written plays; they needed somehow to get their plays, time and again, performed. Nor could one make one's poetry out of Alexandria's Latin quarter. You needed to gain entry into Alexandria's Versailles. Rimbaud could be made by Verlaine; but Callimachus had to be made by the Ptolemies. In short, ancient authors would be remembered to the extent that they managed to become *socially prominent*.[180] The significance of patronage was obvious for the Alexandrians (as well as for Pindar) and the significance of prominence in the democratic citizen body was obvious in the case of the orators and the playwrights. Of the canonical historians, two were established political players (Thucydides and Xenophon), while the remaining one, Herodotus, made his name through a work calculated to appeal to the Athenian citizen body. The one remaining centrally canonical author (later than Homer and Hesiod) was Plato: an exception to the Athenian democracy. He was also an aristocrat, one who used his social capital so as to create a cultural network of friends around the Museion in his villa in the Academos – the roots of the Hellenistic philosophical schools, found in a particular author's social prominence. We shall return to all this when considering the date at which authors entered the canon. But the rule can be stated already. There was one course towards literary achievement: via genre – that is, via an externally defined social occasion. It was a place at which the author contributed but society laid the rules: a Panhellenic festival, a symposium, the assembly, the theater, the court. One needed to fit in; get accepted; settle in for many years. By age 55 or so, you could have made it.

So much, then, for the view from the top. I now turn to the view from the bottom: looking down, once again, at the papyri dug from the sands of Egypt. In what follows, I look for the opposite of the established author, for those who strove – against the odds – to make their name. The fundamental point is not that such wannabes failed: the point, rather, is that they never tried. My quest for graphomania is nearly reduced to a single cache –

[180] A somewhat testable hypothesis is that works will remain in cultural memory to the extent that they managed to attach themselves to more socially prominent names. Wietzke (forthcoming) argues precisely this: a fairly high fraction of the attested dedications of works from antiquity is to royalty – clearly, significantly above the actual fraction of works actually dedicated to kings. The conclusion has to be that such dedications remain more in cultural memory (ultimately, not a very surprising result! Incidentally, Glenn Most has suggested – in a personal communication – that this might lie behind the survival of Vitruvius' *Architecture*. The dedication to the emperor may not have landed Vitruvius his desired public commissions; but it landed him everlasting fame.).

which is, in fact, only quasi-literary. This is the cache of poems by Dioscorus of Aphrodito.

I have briefly mentioned above, on page 56, a certain regionalism which is perhaps apparent among our very late papyri, suggesting that Byzantine Egypt may have developed something of a local literary culture. Upper Egypt, with its strong traditions of monasticism, may have formed the center of this cultural phenomenon.[181] Byzantine-era Aphrodito, at the very least a considerable village of Upper Egypt,[182] was therefore not an entirely marginal place and Dioscorus, its boss,[183] not a marginal person. The cache of papyri associated with his name, accumulated through most of the sixth century (Dioscorus' own lifespan was roughly 520 to 573), has 650 fragments, almost all documentary. The archive also conserved a small literary section: codices of the *Iliad* and of Menander, of course; but also a codex with commentary to the *Iliad* as well as a codex with minor comedies. It also had a vita of Isocrates with a rhetorical treatise, as well as a fragment from the *Greek Anthology*. This is more than a small library, with some elite aspirations, especially by early Byzantine standards (the commentary, the rare comedies: I return to discuss the shrinking scale of literary culture in later centuries in Chapter 6).[184] A member of the elite, at home in his classical education; but not a bibliomaniac and certainly not a senatorial-level member of the elite. The cache further contains 51 fragments of poetry by Dioscorus himself. I read a few random lines (P. Cair. Masp. II.67131 A, adapting MacCoull's translation):[185]

> Arise, the Thebaid, and dance and welcome peace
> For you shall now behold no evil any longer;
> The fear has come, the fear of spotless justice
> Meted by Victor the wise...

[181] Panopolis – from which hail both Nonnus and Pamprepius – is in Upper Egypt. It appears that Nonnus, in particular, might have influenced Dioscorus' style: a local tradition, here. For the specific phenomenon of Byzantine Greek poetry – "wandering poets", who ranged mostly through Upper Egypt, however – see Cameron (1965) and Miguélez-Cavero (2008).

[182] Bell (1944) is a charming narrative account of Aphrodito, Byzantine and British. The fundamental point about Aphrodito was its freedom to collect its own taxes, suggesting a level of significance, and a cause for friction, that define Dioscorus' career.

[183] Keenan (1985: 253); Wickham (2005: 411–19) provides a realistic portrait of the sociopolitics of this village.

[184] There are also a few paraliterary papyri involving literacy and metrology. (The list is taken from Fournet, 2008: 309.)

[185] I modify the text to provide a sense of a meter. Just what Dioscorus' own meter consisted of is unclear.

On this MacCoull (1988: 77) remarks: "In this poem Dioscorus is antici-
pating the beginning of his career as *nomikos* at Antinoe."[186] You see: the
Victor in question was the local prefect. As Fournet puts it: "One could
actually speak of a 'documentarisation' of literature. [Poetry] became a sort
of document itself." In the modern workplace we may have the colleague
who knows how to raise a toast, who knows how to compose a farewell
note. This is roughly what Dioscorus was. As part of his career, he would
put his relatively good culture to use in composing poems to celebrate his
superiors for various occasions such as a promotion. Did he daydream of
future glory? Perhaps, but we can be sure of one thing: his poetic production had a more immediate goal, functioning at local occasions, in a low-
level game of patronage. So: no graphomania here.[187]

Such was Dioscorus', occasional, poetry. Let us consider an analogue –
from the other chronological end of the papyrological evidence. Once
again, we witness an enormous documentary collection – this time, the
famous Zenon archive, collected during the years 261 to 229 BCE (so about
800 years older than Dioscorus). There is also one poem in this collection,
or, more precisely, two alternative versions of a single poem (suggesting we
are close, once again, to an authorial origin).[188] It may start: "This tomb
tells that Tauron the Indian lies dead," or "A young dog, Tauron, who lies
buried honorably beneath this tomb." So, either way, an epitaph for a dog.
Which dog? Both versions make it clear: the dog is commemorated for
having helped *Zenon* (Tauron died fighting a boar, so during a hunt: the
poem commemorates the leisures of the elite). The theme of the noble dog
is not necessarily frivolous, though probably at least in part ironic (nothing
extraordinary about irony in a Hellenistic epigram).[189] That the dedicatee
is no more than an estate overseer – granted, of a very significant estate –
suggests a very local type of production. This is, as it were, the other side of

---

[186] Local encomia are a typical form of Dioscorian poetry; many are written for the occasions of
weddings and birthdays of various local notables.

[187] Kundera (1980 [1979]): "Let us define our terms. A woman who writes her lover four letters a day is
not a graphomaniac, she is simply a woman in love. But my friend who xeroxes his love letters so he
can publish them someday – my friend is a graphomaniac. Graphomania is not a desire to write
letters, diaries, or family chronicles (to write for oneself or one's immediate family); it is a desire to
write books (to have a public of unknown readers)."

[188] P.Cair. Zen. IV 59532. I use the translation from Pepper (2010) – which is an extremely sophisticated study of this strange production.

[189] Though the nobility of dogs was much more in doubt in antiquity. Dogs are subaltern and inferior;
their courage in front of other animals is senseless (Franco, 2003, esp. 168–70). All of this suggests
even more powerfully the ironic context of the dog epitaph. Pepper (2010) suggests that praise of
a subaltern is modulated to fit the subaltern status of the dedicatee. In general, the two dog epitaphs
differ from Dioscorus' poetry in their careful execution. Perhaps a genuine poet, there; or a more
talented amateur.

Dioscorus' archive: here we have the official preserving the occasional poetry addressed to him. Either way, was the author of the epitaph on the dog Tauron seeking the status of a *poet*, any more than was Dioscorus himself? Is the poem addressed to Zenon in the hope that it will be circulated further and eventually heap glory on its author? Or is it addressed to achieve a local commission (perhaps, in fact, to set up a local monument),[190] to gain a local favor?

Or perhaps we have looked in the wrong place. Maybe the would-be authors are hidden elsewhere, among the mass of adespota. If so, the one relevant indication we have is that of the autograph in the scribal sense – literary papyri that appear to have been inscribed by the composer of their contents. Scribal autography would indicate only a subset of autography in the larger sense of papyri produced for their author: for instance, some professional-looking papyri (so, not autographs in the inscriptional sense) could be the cleaned-up version commissioned from a scribe by a private author – who, indeed, could also work by dictation to begin with. Still, scribal autography is the evidence we have got.[191] This field was opened up for papyrological study especially following Manetti's remarkable hypothesis (now widely accepted) that the medical treatise preserved in papyrus only, the *Anonymus Londinensis*, was in fact a draft, and so a scribal autograph.[192] Following on from that discovery, Dorandi has catalogued the apparent inscriptional autographs among papyri. Some of them are from the Herculaneum trove, and appear to be facsimiles of original drafts by Philodemus (not genuine autographs, then, but indications of an autographic practice). Dioscorus' poems form the other significant group of such autographs. Other than this I count 21 fragments in Dorandi's list, or 23 if we add in the *Anonymus Londinensis* itself as well as the Zenon dog epitaph,[193] which I then divide as follows.[194]

(1) Four fragments. Ambitious prose: medical doxography (*Anonymus Londinensis*), a history of the siege of Rhodes by Demetrius

---

[190] Indeed, the epigram – in its original sense of a one-off poetic event carved on stone – seems to remain as a main vehicle of this strictly local poetry; see Merkelbach and Stauber (1998–2004).

[191] It is also possible that some documents whose appearance suggests inscriptional autography (interlinear corrections, marks of intended corrections, etc.) could have been produced by professional scribes as a kind of "facsimile" of an original autograph. While not autographs in the strict sense, these are still indications of the character of ancient autographs and therefore serve us in our purpose.

[192] Manetti (1986).

[193] Pepper (2010) believes this is an autograph, and refers to the literature debating this question.

[194] Based on Dorandi (1991a: 19–20), expanded in Dorandi (2007: 48–50).

Poliorcetes (P.Berol. inv. 11632); a mythological compendium (P.Oxy 3702); vita of Socrates (P.Hibeh 182).

(2)   Two fragments. Ambitious poetry: erotic elegy (P.Oxy 3723); a cosmogony in hexameter (P.Oxy 2816).

(3)   15 fragments. Works (mostly poetry) with obvious local functions: speech notes (PSI 1399: the contents are local); three performance notes: an iambic trimeter – drama – on Odysseus (P.Köln VI 245)[195] as well as two pieces of poetry with musical notation (P.Oxy 3539, P. Berol. inv. 6870 + inv. 14097 verso); two drafts for epitaphs (PSI I 17, P.Cair. Zen. IV 59532); four encomia (P.Giss. 3, P.Oxy 1015, P.Oxy 3537; P.Lit. Lond. 62). One should probably add two hymns (PSI Carlini, P.Ross. Georg. I 11)[196] and perhaps also an epigram (P.Köln III 128).

(4)   Two fragments. Private exercises? A rhetorical exercise (P.Yale II 105); poetic notes (P.Wash. Univ. II 70).[197]

The last could well be an educational document in some sense – a person trying his hand in the application of his poetic or rhetorical studies, with or without being directed by his teacher, but at any rate without necessarily possessing the ambition of becoming recognized in any sense. The third category belongs to the ephemeral world of Dioscorus, though perhaps the self-identity of the author could have been that of a "poet". The Egyptian chora did need to produce hymns; there would always be occasions calling for encomia, local speeches, epitaphs, epigrams. We are left with a mere handful of apparently "ambitious" works. The number is tiny and its internal distribution is perhaps less significant; what matters is the absolute scarcity of the fragments. This is not about lower levels of ancient literacy. The point is precisely in the contrast between the many *owned* papyri and the few *authored* ones – and in the ephemeral character of the very few authored ones we can identify. Literary production was

---

[195]   This may be the production notes of a show, with the text freely altered by the troupe (i.e. a papyrus directly comparable with the musical papyri); see Gianotti (2005).

[196]   Related to such autographs are the hymns to Isis by Isidore (see, e.g., Fowden, 1986: 49–50). Surviving as stone inscription and not as papyrus, this occasional literature bears closest relation to epigraphy (in some cases, indeed, as with the epitaphs, it may be that the papyrus was made in preparation for inscription: once again, see Merkelbach and Stauber, 1998–2004). The hymn, made for a definite ritual event, remained *essentially* occasional even as poetry as a whole became only symbolically related to its roots in occasions. The only successful effort in the hymn as literary form was the ironic, self-conscious set by Callimachus himself.

[197]   This document, dated to the sixth to seventh centuries AD, uses the verso of a papyrus document that has a list of clothing. It comes from Dioscorus' world (this time, from Oxyrhynchus). It is not quite a poetic production; rather, a poetic doodle.

rare among *the most literate elite.* You see: there was not much point even *trying.*

Modern literature is arranged in a descending, sloping curve. The very top best-sellers, then somewhat less stellar but still highly respected authors, then all the way down through the many gradations of literary failure to reach, finally, those who did not succeed even in getting their work published but nevertheless persist trying: the extremely long tail of a sharply sloping curve. The ancient curve sloped as rapidly but it carried a short tail – or, more precisely, its tail carried a different meaning.

What I offer can be called a demand-side theory of graphomania: modernity knows many graphomaniacs, because it is not entirely absurd for would-be authors to believe in the existence of potential demand for their work. Just get a little more exposure – and you might get in there. In the ancient Egyptian chora, however, it would have been simply lunatic for a person to dream himself a Homer, a Demosthenes, a Euripides. Literature depended on becoming eminent in a socially defined role, which was not defined for the Egyptian chora but for the metropolitan centers. In short, you really must move to Alexandria or you'll be forever stuck writing epitaphs for dogs.

The absence of the long tail speaks to a fundamental feature of ancient literature – the one we have seen throughout this section and through the discussion in the previous sections – of the role of *genre* in constituting the author's brand. To be recognized as an author – even by oneself – one first of all required an appropriate position. Literature could subsist only in the medium of a thick understanding of its performance, genre and occasion.

I attack the material of this section from both flanks – the top elite and the lowest adespota – aiming for the advantage of the indirect approach. Perhaps the direct statement would have been enough: the conclusion of this section is not really very controversial. All I am saying is that, to become an eminent author in antiquity, one had to become, to begin with, eminent – in the social meaning for which "literary eminence" was defined. Hence, one could not have graphomania and, as a correlate, one could not have Rimbaud. You could not storm the walls of high literature from the outside because there was no space, outside literature, in which to marshal your literary prowess. Literature had to be done from the inside.

It is not clear how often reputations can be remade posthumously, even today: I shall return to this below (on pages 216–18). But the ideology of posthumous literary success is fundamentally that of *genius*: of an author making it against the odds. This, once again, is the Romantic author: and, once again, we need to remember that the ancient author was not like that.

So much from first principles; let me now move to the chronological evidence: is there, in fact, reason to believe that the reputations of the authors of the ancient canon were posthumously made?

### 2.3.2 *The Making of the Athenian Canon: Chronological Data*

To repeat: we have already established, in Chapter 1, that the canon was mostly stable from the Ptolemaic era onwards. As we seek the origins of the canon as a system, we do not need to look later than, say, the middle of the third century BCE. This simplifies our task to a considerable extent. To begin with, we may put aside the (difficult) question of the reception of the Hellenistic component of the canon. Clearly, the position of the Hellenistic poets was qualified; clearly, they came late, largely speaking, for our purposes. What they represent is an embellishment on a canon that preceded them.

We may also ignore, for the most part, the reception of archaic literature. As for lyric poetry, this was a marginal, erudite component of the big library, from the Hellenistic era onwards. It thus represents a past canon, replaced by the Athenian one. There is also no need, for the moment, to study the origins of the dominance of archaic epic in the canon: this clearly goes right back to the earliest written evidence, and holds steady since. I shall not ignore this archaic canon and shall return to discuss it in the following section, looking for the rise of the brand-name author. But, for the shape of the canon as it was transmitted throughout antiquity, what matters most is clearly the Athenian component.

The question, then, is very simple: at what point did the three tragedians, the two comic authors, the three orators, the three historians and the one philosopher – Plato – become pre-eminent?

Before we move on to consider the evidence, let us recall the two extreme options. One is that "critics make canons". If so, the canon should have been made in Alexandria of the first half of the third century. The other is that "audiences make canons". If so, the canon should have been made in Athens, through the fifth to the fourth centuries. We have a meaningful chronological spectrum: between about 400 and 250 BCE. Where does our evidence lead along this spectrum?

We should start with the dramatists, as these were – to judge from the papyri – the most important element of the Athenian canon in the Hellenistic era. Indeed, they set the stage for Athenian canonicity. The rise of the fifth-century dramatists coincides with a period for which we have relatively ample evidence; and it is abundantly clear that their fame was early.

As noted, we have a significant number of papyri: dated to the third and second centuries are 30 fragments by Euripides, seven by Menander, four by Sophocles and three by Aeschylus. We also find three fragments by Astydamas (the Younger: a fourth-century tragedian to whom we shall return below). Likely a few more fragments by the major tragedians lie hidden among the adespota.[198] But the impression is clear. Just to add one small, but telling example: Chrysippus, in the second half of the third century, would often quote brief literary passages to make philosophical points (as we will return to note in Chapter 4). The list of the extant citations is as follows.[199]

| | | |
|---|---|---|
| Homer | 60 | (*Iliad* 40, *Odyssey* 20) |
| Euripides | 21 | (12 adespota, 2 *Alc.*, *Phoen.*, 1 *Or.*, *Supp.*, *El.*, *Herc.*, and a mere mention) |
| Hesiod | 13 | (7 *O. et D.*, 5 *Theog.*, 1 adespota) |
| Tragic adespota | 8 | |
| Menander | 2 | |
| Comic adespota | 1 | |
| Lyric | 6 | (Tyrtaeus 2, Pindar 1, Theognis 1, Orpheus 1, Stesichorus 1) |
| Empedocles | 1 | |

As we have noted already: in the third century Euripides was second, in canonicity, only to Homer.

Let us then try and move back in time, closer to the authors themselves. Our evidence, indeed, is partly archaeological. The case of comedy is easy, and there we have no difficulty of principle in identifying the visual references (of course, there is always the usual scholarly debate concerning individual identifications). Tragedy is harder. As explained in section 2.2.3, the depiction of mythological themes treated by tragedies does not amount, in general, to an *illustration* of those tragedies. And yet, when we find a correlation between the mythological themes depicted on vases

---

[198] But not more than a few, as is seen by the near-total lack of annotated tragic adespota. I counted two on p.85 above: of these, P.Berol. 16984 is a late parchment codex (fourth to fifth century CE) for which only the annotation survives. That this is tragedy is supposition; that this is by a minor tragedian defies all probability. The other is P.Bodm. inv. 28 – an annotated satyr play.

[199] This is going through SVF and culling out examples which are obviously not by Chrysippus but by the sources quoting him; I try to preserve whatever could be by him, so I probably overstate the numbers. I do avoid P.Par. 2, however, now considered not by Chrysippus (Cavini, 1985), though it does reflect a cultural setting very similar to his (see pp. 412–13 below).

and those treated by successful plays, it becomes natural to assume that the theme was made prominent by the prominence of the drama. The correct model, then, is that a successful tragedy could create a referent for intertextuality: thus, we can rely, with caution, on the evidence of the vases, so as to reconstruct a possible trajectory for the popularity of tragedies.

There is a clear tendency, in south Italian vases, to represent themes that Euripides could have made prominent;[200] it is even clearer (incredibly so, given the peculiarly Athenian subject matter) that fourth-century south Italian vases repeatedly illustrated Aristophanes.[201] Indeed, in general terms, dramatic subject matters – most often, apparently, Attic drama – are one of the dominant themes of south Italian fourth-century art: one of the fundamental starting points for Csapo's claim – directly relevant to us – that Athenian drama quickly became prominent across the Mediterranean.[202] As pointed out by Taplin, early Panhellenic reception seems to be implied by the evidence for Aeschylus' *Oresteia*, which could have pushed its themes onto vases by the 440s.[203] Now, while this comes from a much later context, it should be mentioned that the prolific iconographic tradition related to Menander may plausibly be reconstructed to have originated in the early third century – i.e., once again, immediately on the heels of the author's own career.[204] So, of the five canonical Attic dramatists, four seem to have inspired, whether directly or indirectly, the kind of iconographic response that suggests a nearly immediate Panhellenic fame (Sophocles was perhaps an exception).

The archaeological evidence is useful, in that it is earlier than that of the papyri – and mostly from outside Athens. It is this, above all, which supports Csapo's argument for an early, fourth-century spread of the Athenian dramatic practice across the entire Greek-speaking world.[205] As we bring in the literary sources, our perspective become necessarily more

---

[200] Todisco (2006: 246, 249) counts 217 "Euripidean" south Italian vases; this is a very maximalist number.

[201] Csapo (2010: 55–61).

[202] Csapo estimates some 750 vases with dramatic themes; Taplin (2007: 15) estimates "more than 2000" elaborately painted vases (out of more than 25,000 currently catalogued). This agrees well with the position of drama we find in Ptolemaic papyri: it is almost as important as all other poetry taken together.

[203] Taplin (2007: 50). This is an isolated find; but Taplin emphasizes the overall impact of *Oresteia*-related themes in the iconographic evidence as a whole, with 11 vases (2007: 48–67). Todisco (2006: 246–7) finds 172 Aeschylean-themed south Italian vases, so trailing Euripides only by a small difference (in the case of Aeschylus, however, the vases come about a century later than the plays, whereas for Euripides the time gap is much smaller). Sophocles has a mere 76 south Italian vases. All these numbers, I repeat, are very optimistic.

[204] Csapo (2010: chap. 5).

[205] There is, of course, the sheer fact of the patronage of Athenian dramatists, late in their careers, outside Athens: Aeschylus in Sicily, Euripides in Macedon. I return to discuss this in Chapter 3, pp. 280–3.

Athenocentric.[206] Its contours are worth pursuing, however, and they have been meticulously studied in a major study of the Athenian reception of the dramatic canon, that of Hanink (2014). Now, Hanink's title, *Lycurgan Athens and the Making of Classical Tragedy*, is somewhat misleading, as it would seem to imply that, by her telling, the three tragedians were made canonical in the years following the Athenian defeat in Chaeronea in 338, when Lycurgus was the leading statesman. I am not sure how far Hanink herself would wish to pursue such an argument, but her evidence clearly shows that, for the authors of the third quarter of the fourth century, the three tragedians were a major reference point: repeatedly quoted by the orators (Chapter 4), invoked in comedy (Chapter 5)[207] and of course repeatedly used by Aristotle, most famously in his *Poetics* (Chapter 6). Indeed, as Lamari (2017) shows in great detail, the reperformances of the major tragedians had become, by Lycurgus' time, a constant, Panhellenic phenomenon *for over a century*. We may support this qualitative account with some numbers: a TLG count of mentions of the major dramatists, up to and including the fourth century BCE (but

---

[206] It would have been best had we possessed non-Athenian sources, from this era, alluding to the canonical tragedians. While in fact there was a massive explosion in writing outside Athens at just this period, this is also among the bodies of text least likely to survive from antiquity, even in fragmentary form (see Chapter 6, pp. 634–5). The one major exception is the Hippocratic corpus, which seems, however, for generic reasons, to avoid literary allusions (the absence of any unequivocal uses of Homer is revealing). There is a rich literature concerning the parallelism between tragedy and early medicine, often framed in the terms of the tragedians' potential knowledge of medicine (most of this concerns Euripides – see Kosak, 2004, a book-length treatment – but the evidence is significant for other dramatic authors: for Sophocles, in particular, see Allan, 2014). Recent scholarship at its best sees the two – medical and dramatic – as coexisting fields of literary practice, aware, dialectically, of each other (Holmes, 2010). Studies in the lexicon of the Hippocratic corpus have found there the reflection of poetic language, even, specifically, that of Euripides (Lanata, 1968), but Jouanna and Demont (1981) qualify this (by their interpretation, such poetic words in Hippocratic corpus merely reflect the Ionian dialect. We are at the mercy, then, of the accident of survival, which has preserved Ionian prose almost uniquely in the Hippocratic corpus.). Longer, genuine allusions are rare and difficult to prove. To take one example: *Breaths*, 3 (a late fifth-century text, more literarily ambitious than most others in the Hippocratic corpus). Air is that on which "the earth rides", *gēs ochēma*. A striking poetic phrase and paradox, which, sure enough, is *identical* to one used in Euripides in the year 415 (*Troad.* 884: there, said by Hecuba, on Zeus). Diels (1887: 14) plausibly suggested that both authors, Euripides as well as the Hippocratic author, might have been influenced by Diogenes of Apollonia, but the precise phrase is not attested for that – admittedly fragmentary – author, whose style, if vivid, is also quite literal and free of paradox. In fact, it is hard for me to imagine that Euripides would simply pick up, as is, a phrase in Diogenes, without poeticizing it; and, if the precise phrase *gēs ochēma* and its surrounding paradox are indeed due to Euripides, we must conclude, then, that the Hippocratic author was echoing a very recent dramatic production.

[207] The evidence brought in for comedy's interest in the tragic canon tends to be later – from new comedy more than middle comedy (Hanink, 2014: 167) – but this is typical for the bias of survival as a whole, whereby new comedy is better represented than middle comedy by more than an order of magnitude.

removing citations earlier than the author and from the corpus of the author himself), yields:

Aeschylus 118; Sophocles 121; Aristophanes 119; Euripides 258[208]

The similarity between Aeschylus, Sophocles and Aristophanes is uncanny and suggests that – at some distance from Euripides' unique place as, quite simply, the most popular author – the other major dramatists had become, already, the "classical" representatives of the genres as such. The classicizing tendency of the era is clear. Famously, Lycurgus was the author of laws that, among other things, erected a group statue of the three tragedians next to the Theater of Dionysius[209] and, even more remarkably, established the "official text" of the plays of the dramatists (discussed in Hanink, 2014: chaps. 2–3). There is no doubt that Lycurgus used the tragedians to a particular end – as a building block in a renewed city ideology of citizenship, based on reverence for fifth-century glories (Hanink, 2014: chap. 1, lays out this ideology). What we find here is an ideological use of the three tragedians that assumed, rather than constructed, their fame. To mention just one example: Diogenes Laertius tells us that some of the works attributed to Heraclides of Pontus were "on the <plays? passages?> of Euripides and Sophocles" as well as "on the three tragedians".[210] It seems likelier than not that, during the Lyurgean era, Heraclides of Pontus had already gone back from Athens to his native city.[211] He was an old man at the time, and Heraclides' studies of tragedy could well have been earlier still. Indeed, the most significant evidence we have for fourth-century drama clearly implies that the tragedians were seen as canonical already by the year 386:[212] an inscription notes that, in that year, "old drama" started to be reperformed in the city's dramatic festival, which – judging by

---

[208] It is true, as pointed out by Hanink (2014: 5), that these numbers crest at the third quarter of the century, but this is mostly a compositional effect due to the distribution of our evidence (it is then that we have extant the most oratory, as well as the works of Aristotle).

[209] The practice of setting up honorific statues is typically Hellenistic (and forms the basis of our statistics from Chapter 1 pp. 64–5, for the evidence of the portraits). Lycurgus' set of the statues of the tragedians belongs to an early generation of this practice and may well have been fairly rare in its time: a rare, therefore a more powerful, statement (Ma, 2013: 76; and, in general, see Ma, 2013, for the structure of the practice).

[210] Diogenes Laertius V.87–8. We should not over-interpret the reference to "the three" in "the three tragedians" (as scholars seem prone to do: e.g. Hägg, 2010: 115), and argue that one already did not need to specify *which* three; the title need not be authorial. But, clearly, the work assumed the canonicity of the three tragedians.

[211] This comes from the relatively reliable account by Philodemus (P.Herc 1021 col. VI.41–VII.10).

[212] Lamari (2017: 77–81) offers the likely guess that in 386, already, reperformances of the major tragedians could have served a political purpose, prefiguring Lycurgus: recalling, in Athens' more troubled time, her canonical authors.

the evidence from the didascalia – seems to mean that the three tragedians came to be reperformed (perhaps Euripides and Sophocles more than Aeschylus).[213] The year 386 is already not too far from the year 405, when Aristophanes' *Frogs* already assumes the triad of great tragedians, and the most economic assumption is that, starting near the end of the careers of Sophocles and Euripides, the perception was formed that these three tragedians tower over everyone else – a perception never shaken through the fourth century and beyond. Indeed, Hanink concedes this point in her discussion of Astydamas II, who did enjoy enormous contemporary success and even survived, to some extent (as noted above) in Hellenistic papyri – but with only four TLG citations from the fourth century, and no presence in the archaeological evidence. He was popular – and yet not canonical. Anecdotes from antiquity imply that he set up a bronze statue for himself, that he wrote angry epigrams denouncing his bad fate of a late birth robbing him of his just recognition.[214] The implication seems to be that canon was *already* formed, by the fourth century.

So, let us go back to the careers of the playwrights themselves. We recall that of Aeschylus: an apprenticeship, 499 to 484; a central place, 484 to 472; a dominant position, 472 to 458. It was indeed his final play – the *Oresteia* – that appears, based on the evidence of the vases, to have become emblematic. (Not so among the papyri, where Aeschylus is collected mostly by specialized bibliophiles who aim at comprehensiveness.) The case of Sophocles is more complicated. His debut was a victory at 468 – over Aeschylus, no less. This did not settle him as a leading author, however (he was too young, and, what is more important, Aeschylus was still alive). The next reported victory is from 447. Five more are reported, three of which are some year in the Olympiad 447–4, 442 and 438, a rate which compares in density with Aeschylus' major achievement. Aeschylus has vacated the position of "leading dramatist" in 458, and it appears that by 447, at the latest, Sophocles has captured it. (He was probably under 50 years old at the time.)

Sophocles' victories are usually not dated, but it is clear that he participated in, and often won, many competitions from 447 till his death in 406. The *Suda* assigns him 123 plays and 24 victories; the vita mentions 18 victories. The number of plays is not absurd for the length of his career – roughly 30 productions, or one every other year – and is in fact not even

---

[213] IG ii2 2318.1565–6.
[214] Hanink (2014: 183–8); see Ma (2013: 110) for a measured statement on the question of the historicity of Astydamas' statue.

much doubted by modern scholars.[215] If the number of competitions is roughly correct, then so perhaps is also the number of victories, at roughly 60 to 80 percent of his competitions. It may be assumed that he had roughly 20 productions in the years 447 to 406 and perhaps about 15 victories. This puts into perspective the evidence for Euripides' career. The point is that Euripides never had the stage to himself. He put on a production for the first time in 455, and was a victor for the first time in 441 (a 14-year gap, comparing very closely with Aeschylus); he had a total of four or five victories. Euripides came too late to exploit the post-Aeschylus gap, and, because of Sophocles' longevity, never had a post-Sophocles gap to exploit. But, then again, Athenian attention was primarily riveted upon contest: Euripides never became the top tragedian but the two, Sophocles and Euripides, formed the top with contest.

As noted above, Euripides was a unique case individual works forming the focus for selection. In the Hellenistic and Roman eras Aeschylus and Sophocles were collected only in large sets, by bibliophiles; Euripides was everywhere (and more discriminately so than Menander). We may do as follows: plot the popularity of his plays, as measured by papyri counts, against the dates of their first production (which may often be estimated with some precision). The following graph plots the survival of papyrus fragments of plays by Euripides as a function of original year of production, from 448 at the left to the posthumous plays at the right.[216]

The center of gravity of this graph – the date of original production of a "typical" Euripidean papyrus fragment (among the successful plays, with two or more fragments) – was 415.[217] The popularity of Euripides was the popularity of an elderly playwright: of about the age of the Aeschylus who produced the *Oresteia*. We note indeed several inflection points. 438 is the year of the first durable success, the tetralogy that included *Telephus*, *Alcestis* and *Cretan Women*. (Remarkably, this early success also has two of the successful plays which did *not* survive through the manuscript tradition: being early could be penalized as late as the date of the choice of the

---

[215] Endorsed, for example, by Beer (2004: 24–5); see there for more references.

[216] I use plays with two or more fragments only; dates are sometimes provided by editors by decades ("420s") and are sometimes known by Olympiad. In such cases I divide the fragment counts by ten or four and distribute them over the ten or four years, as appropriate.

[217] Morgan (1998: 116) notes this for the dramatic schooltexts: "There seems to be a slight bias in favour of later plays (*Troades, Helen, Orestes, Phoenissae, Electra, Bacchae* are all datable to *c.* 415 or later) although *Medea, Hippolytus* and *Alcestis* are considerably earlier." I do not understand how this bias comes to be characterized as "slight".

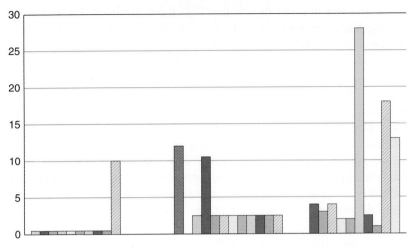

Figure 2.2

manuscript transmission?)[218] *Telephus* became a widely quoted, and parodied, play.[219] *Medea* came in 431, and several significant plays followed in the
420s, in particular *Andromache*, *Hecuba* and *Hippolytus*. At this point
Euripides was in his 50s and had probably already "arrived". But the real
success came very late: from 416 to 408 we find a successful play each year
(except for 409), among which are the perennial favorites, *Phoenician
Women* and *Orestes*. The posthumous works, too, left an important mark,
especially the *Bacchae*.

This is all a very surprising result. Why would book owners in
Oxyrhynchus, six centuries or so after Euripides' death, care about the
relative date of his plays, aiming to preserve his later works more often than
his earlier ones? Perhaps he became progressively better. The sheer
productivity through his final years is stunning. But the point is that this
judgement would have had to be formed at some point, and the likeliest
account is that it became formed *as the plays were performed*. This is all
consistent with the theory presented above concerning the author's rise to
eminence. The impression is that Euripides grew in stature – in a process

---

[218] If by "successful" we mean "with two fragments or more", we find that only seven are not extant:
*Cresphontes, Hypsipyla, Alcmaeon, Antiope* and *Theseus*, as well as *Telephus* and *Cretan Women*.
[219] I count 31 fragments in the TGrF; for parodies, see Csapo's account of the iconographic representation of Aristophanes' parodies (Csapo, 2010: 55–8).

slower than usual, because of the presence of Sophocles – and, so, each of his new productions became more of a big deal. This is not to say that his earlier work did not have a major impact; but it seems that, at around 416, Euripides achieved such a position to ensure that any of his works would become canonical.

Which means, of course, that we have evidence for Euripides' canonization in his (late) lifetime. So we should actually discount, in this case, the evidence of the victories. Let us assume that a "top tragedian" (as were, in succession, Phrynichus, Aeschylus and Sophocles) would become the default winner and would tend to keep that role out of sheer inertia and deference. This suggests that Euripides did not really have much of a chance each time he competed against Sophocles. Sophocles, at this established stage of his career, probably produced a show a little over half the years; this means that we should roughly double Euripides' victory count to get a measure of how many times he would have won had there been no Sophocles. His five victories are the equivalent of ten victories in a no-Sophocles world. But we focus on the wrong statistic: as if victories directly represent an author's contemporary impact. A much more significant number, I would argue, is the sheer number of plays. Let us note the following. A tragic production involved four plays, and so the 90 traditionally given for Aeschylus, the 123 for Sophocles and the 77 for Euripides are the equivalent of roughly 23, 31 and 20 productions, respectively, across careers whose documented length (based on the didascalia) was 41, 62 and 47 years, respectively.[220] The ratios are 0.56, 0.5 and 0.43, a sequence which might reflect a more difficult and competitive field through the fifth century. Most remarkable is the consistency of the figures: apparently, a very successful Athenian tragedian could have presented a show every two years on average. One imagines that this comes close to the human limit on the part of the author (to write 200 Sophoclean plays... Now, *that* would be too much),[221] so the impression is that, with these three authors, we see that they had a show *every time they wanted to*. This, as any performer would tell you, is no mean thing.[222] So, it is above all at this level that the didascalia are meaningful. We should not over-interpret the ranking of the three performing players in each given year.

---

[220] The numbers appear preposterous but are not beyond the range of performance cultures. Certainly, many, many Euripidean plays are attested with actual fragments – remarkably, no fewer than 77!

[221] Compare Müller (1984: 60–77) for the argument that tragic staging generally involved an interval of two years at least.

[222] So, Stevens (1956: 92): "[Euripides] could practically count upon production...should we regard this as a failure?"

The preceding step of selecting the three competitors for the year is much less clearly understood. It mattered less for the Athenian culture of *public* contest but it must have dominated the life of would-be playwrights.[223] What is clear is that the sheer presence gained by sustained, repeated performance was essentially limited to the three leading dramatists. Similarly long careers in the competitions are reported for Choerilus and Phrynichus, as well as for Pratinas;[224] and later in the fifth century, for Euphorion the Younger (25), Ion (23) and Philocles (19). Perhaps we do not know the full extent of their careers; it may be that they were, in their time, more popular than we can now imagine. Yet Euphorion's career was clearly an offshoot of his father's, Aeschylus, to the extent that he was at least on some occasions merely the posthumous producer of Aeschylean works. He does not appear to have become at all prominent (or frequently performing) in his own name. Philocles is another member of the Aeschylus clan, who may have built something of a separate career; the *Suda* report of 100 plays is probably garbled, and, without it, little remains to suggest a major presence on the fifth-century stage. Ion's 11 attested plays suggest a less consistent career,[225] albeit one that did gain some attention from future scholarly readers, hence a significant number of fragments and testimonies (though no known papyrus fragments).

Let us sum up. We have a wide range of evidence showing that by the middle of the fourth century BCE the three tragedians were recognized as canonical. There is significant archaeological evidence that Euripides and Aristophanes were Panhellenic canonical authors already in the early fourth century and (much less powerful) evidence that Aeschylus reached the same kind of success in the middle of the fifth century – i.e., in all three cases, the evidence points to the direct aftermath of the author's career. The evidence of the dates of production, victories and the overall pattern of

---

[223] For the role of the archon, see Csapo and Slater (1994: 105, 108–9). Snell (1971) counts 49 attested fifth-century tragedians (other than the three canonical playwrights), and the total was perhaps nearer 100; there were 300 slots for performance in the Great Dionysia, and the three canonical authors consumed, between them, perhaps a quarter of that. Competition for choruses must have been stiff; it is a wonder that we hear so little about it. But note the implication: the average non-canonical playwright would perform *twice*. (Probably, many did just once; failure could have been brutal.) More on all of this in Chapter 5, pp. 554–5, where I try to estimate the number of ancient tragedians.

[224] Those numbers are late inventions, however, representing later scholars' assumptions on how a successful dramatic career should look; see West (1989) for the claim that genuine *didaskaliai* – perhaps genuine drama? – began only in 502.

[225] For Ion's overall career, see Jennings and Katsaros (2007). He was noted for his crossing of generic boundaries – poet and prose writer, dramatist and philosopher. Unanchored in space, he was also unanchored in genre: the two, especially in the fifth century, go together.

survival suggests a process of canonization through the author's own career, reaching a point of inflection at about age 50 or later. In this case, then, canonization apparently took place in the fifth century itself.

It was important to discuss the case of tragedy in detail, because it is the one best attested: we have the didascalia, significant papyrus remains and many references through the fourth century. The evidence shows that: (1) by the middle of the fourth century, at the latest, the three tragedians were already canonical in a sense probably comparable to that of their ultimate reception; (2) the evidence of the vases, together with the reperformances studied by Lamari (2017), suggest that this status was Panhellenic and not just Athenian; but (3) at any rate it is clear that all three achieved dominating status, at least in Athens itself, late in their own lifetime. The simplest account of all this, I would suggest, is that the full canonicity of the three tragedians was in place already early in the fourth century.

We may sum up the case of comedy more briefly, along similar lines. The arrangement of tragedy – a major early author, followed by two near-contemporaries – was repeated in old comedy with Cratinus (active from the early days of the comic competition, before 450, and clearly the elder statesman of comedy), followed by Aristophanes and Eupolis, who both debuted in the 420s. Cratinus died in the 420s, Eupolis in 411. Aristophanes had a quarter-century of dramatic production left in him – in which he eclipsed everyone else in the profession. This condition, then, can be assigned to Aristophanes, as well: overpowering dominance in Athens itself, during his own lifetime. Perhaps Euripides would have been as pre-eminent, had Sophocles died two decades earlier; perhaps tragedy simply had a larger social role, hence could accommodate more pre-eminent figures. The evidence of the papyri as well as of TLG citations suggests that Cratinus and Eupolis survived only as erudite references; Aristophanes alone, as noted above, remained as nearly the equal of Sophocles and Aeschylus. As mentioned already, this dominant position, once again, is shown by the evidence of the vases to have been, likely enough, Panhellenic, in spite – or because? – of Aristophanes' Athenian themes.

It appears that the comic equivalents of Astydamas – those comic authors who enjoyed great contemporary popularity – were less hindered by the weight of the past. Reperformance of old comedies begins only in 339.[226] Prolific output of new plays is typical of the genre. The 100 or so plays attributed to the three major playwrights of the new comedy –

---

[226] Wilson (2000: 23).

Philemon, Menander, Diphilus – are a plausible number supported by the very large number of attested plays and, in the case of Menander, that of comic fragments. Something of the dynamics of the Sophocles–Euripides pairing was repeated, late in the fourth century, with Philemon and Menander. Once again, the older and more established poet survived throughout the career of his younger peer, who nonetheless, through manic labor (a play every four months?), quickly established himself as a worthy rival. Rarely a winner in the competitions (in which the shadow of the established author prevailed), Menander nevertheless had a remarkable contemporary success. In his case, the papyri are early enough. Four of the extant third-century BCE fragments are identified as by Menander – but there are also 17 new comedy adespota. As noted above, it would fit the pattern of Ptolemaic papyri if a larger fraction of these are not by Menander, compared to later papyri. Surely at least several, however, would be by Menander, who therefore had something like five to 15 third-century fragments. This is among 297 fragments altogether in the century: short of Homer and Euripides but probably above all the rest. As noted above, there is also some indication that the iconographic tradition relating to Menander's plays had formed already by the early third century BCE. Following about 275 BCE, comic production in Athens went into something of a decline (I shall discuss this in Chapter 5), and, so, Menander – and, less so, Aristophanes – it would remain.

The evidence is highly suggestive, though (naturally, given our sources) not decisive. This is why the general considerations of the preceding sections are so important. I have argued above that literary eminence would have to be predicated upon social eminence: one had to become an elder statesman, in a well-defined social niche. We now see this in action. It is only to be expected that canonization should be contemporary – or, more precisely: that it should amount to massive contemporary success which is not lost following the author's death. The contemporary success is built upon many performances which gradually build an author's status until an inflection point is reached. It is built in Athens itself – which, for the case of drama, provided the required social niche – but was broadcast to the entire Hellenic world. Canonization was achieved when Aeschylus was about 55 years old, Sophocles perhaps a bit younger than that, Euripides perhaps a bit older, Aristophanes and Menander rather younger.

There is no evidence for posthumous fame but there is posthumous oblivion a-plenty: not all contemporary, eminent authors survive to be considered canonical. The dynamics of canon formation are not the positive process of the "construction of the canon", imagined by so much of contemporary scholarship in the humanities. Canons are formed through a negative process of loss.

So much – from drama, the most significant and the best-documented case. As we move beyond tragedy and comedy, our evidence is generally weaker, but Plato's case, at least, is fairly clear. We now take for granted Western philosophy, as footnotes to Plato. There is considerable evidence that it was so, even very early on. Obviously, we are now without archaeological finds. But we do have papyri: Plato figures substantially among those of the third century – five fragments, including an anonymous commentary to the *Phaedo* (so, already a major factor of intellectual life: but do we need papyri to know this about the philosophy of the third century?). To recall, my fourth-century count for the TLG was: Aeschylus 118; Sophocles 121; Aristophanes 119; Euripides 258. Plato, by the same measure, has 577. This is not driven primarily by the Aristotelian corpus (which has – in itself massive – 124 explicit mentions of the name "Plato"). There are a large number of fragments from many diverse authors deriving from or referring to the Platonic corpus. Of course, even this can be qualified: it might be said that this shows merely that later Greek scholarship tended to recall the fourth century from around Plato's perspective.[227] Especially with regard to the philosophical reception, however, the evidence is real enough (and so Aristotle is unique merely in being extant). Typically, when we know anything of substance of a fourth-century philosopher, it appears he had something to do with Plato, whether in criticizing him or in being his direct or indirect disciple.[228] Plato became a major topic of philosophical study in his own right, and we know of at least nine authors in the late fourth century (or, perhaps, the early third century) writing directly about him: Dicaearchus,[229] Speusippus,[230] Praxiphanes,[231] Theophrastus,[232] Zeno of

---

[227] So, for instance, Diocles of Carystus: he has a TLG count of 14 citations of Plato. But this is an illusion: Diocles survives only as fragments collected from the medical doxographic tradition, and the TLG merely counts 14 passages (mostly from Galen) where Diocles' and Plato's views are recounted in close proximity.

[228] Twenty-two of the fourth-century philosophical authors whose TLG entries include a Plato citation have a genuine relation to him: Antisthenes, Dicaearchus, Hermodorus, Archytas, Xenocrates, Aristotle, Eudemus, Heraclides of Pontus, Speusippus, Simus, Praxiphanes, Theophrastus, Epicurus, Demetrius of Phaleron, Zenon of Citium, Chamaeleon, Clearchus, Crantor, Hermarchus, Persaeus, Timon, Nausiphanes.

[229] A biography/doxography of Plato; see the discussion in White (2001: 218–28).

[230] *Encomium*: DL IV.5.    [231] A dialogue with Plato as participant: DL III.8.

[232] An epitome of the *Republic*: DL V.43.

Citium,[233] Clearchus,[234] Crantor,[235] Hermarchus,[236] Persaeus.[237] This list is confined to philosophical authors whose titles are known to refer directly to Plato.[238] As we can see from Aristotle's work, however, works could be shot through with Platonic references without being explicitly about him.[239]

Already, in the first half of the fourth century, Plato is a stock comic figure (not an obvious achievement in this phase of comic writing, which no longer lingered so much in contemporary Athens). Once again, we can build a list of nine authors (Theopompus, Amphis, Anaxandrides, Cratinus Junior, Ephippus, Epicrates, Ophelio, Philippides and Alexis) all referring explicitly to Plato in their comedies. Doubtless there was a bias for later readers to cite such fragments. And yet, our knowledge of middle comedy is extremely fragmentary,[240] so there surely were many more references. Probably, over the last 30 years of Plato's life – when he had become prominent enough to be laughed at – Plato's name was uttered on the stage, mockingly, at least several times each year.

It is not clear that Plato had a comedy dedicated to him alone (it would be less in the style of middle comedy, anyway). This distinction was already reserved for Socrates in 423; the figure of Socrates preceded Plato into Panhellenic stature. I do not count Socrates in the Greek canon, since he was not a writing author, but there is no doubt that he won a commanding place in Greek memory and that this place was essential to Plato's position. It is therefore important to find out how, and when, this Socratic fame was achieved. Indeed, later doxographic tradition envisaged fourth-century philosophy – a rich and varied field – as proceeding directly from Socrates via his pupils (thus Diogenes Laertius I.14, II.47). The instinctive

---

[233] A "Republic", surely a response to Plato's *Republic*. For an overview, see Schofield (1999b: 756–60).

[234] A commentary on the mathematics in the *Republic* (Athenaeus IX 393a, where this is quoted for a method of catching quails: place a mirror and a noose in front of it, and the quails will fly into the mirror to meet their own reflection and get caught).

[235] The first commentary to the *Timaeus*: Proclus in *Tim.* 1, 76.1.      [236] "Against Plato": DL X.25.

[237] "Against Plato's Laws": DL VII.36.

[238] And then there are historians: Theopompus writes "Against the School of Plato" (from an Isocratean perspective?): Athenaeus 508c.

[239] This is all a more "professional" and anyway elite reception. This would always be true of Plato, however, whose canonical status was that of the most typical author of the *big*, specialized libraries.

[240] We have roughly 1,000 lines from both Alexis and Antiphanes, and a few scattered references from minor authors; 245 plays are ascribed to Alexis alone; surely there were many hundreds of middle comedies. The survival fraction of middle comedy is counted in hundredths of a percentage point (that of new comedy by tenths of a percentage point, that of old comedy by whole percentage points – already a respectable survival rate).

response of a modern scholar would be to doubt such reconstructions,[241] and yet Socrates' influence is evident.[242] I have made a list of philosophers known to be active around the middle of the fourth century, with 43 persons spread across the entire Greek world. Nearly all are related to figures who are indeed known to have been close to Socrates; if not to Plato, then to Aristippus of Cyrene or to Euclid of Megara. I find – incredibly – only one clear exception, Anaxarchus of Abdera, a minor follower of Democritus.[243]

Philosophy, then, was not so different from drama: in both cases, a specific Athenian form of performance (the Dionysia; Socratic inquiry) was canonized and made Panhellenic in the early years of the fourth century. Plato and Xenophon rode this wave of canonization of performance and achieved canonicity for their own writing. At first there were many Socratics, but cultural perception would eventually have to settle on a select few. Clay (1994: 26) notes that, early on, Plato was but "a minor Socratic". Of course he was: a 30-year-old author would have to be. By 375 or so he must have become canonical. He must have sensed it. Early Plato wrote from the subversive perspective of a minor author; late Plato wrote from the commanding perspective of the elder statesman.

Xenophon was the other widely successful Socratic. With him, we move into the genre of history, as well – and into the least well documented piece of (the early formation of) the Athenian canon. Now we are truly reduced to the vague study of "influence", which I shall therefore merely sum up in passing. The raw numbers for TLG counts (later than the author, until the end of the fourth century) are respectable: Herodotus, 148; Thucydides, 126; Xenophon, 88. But in this case only the numbers for Herodotus carry genuine meaning: "Thucydides" often refers to other Athenian namesakes. The many references to Herodotus are real and widespread, and Murray's (1972: 204–5) judgement, that "already in the fourth century B.C. the influence of Herodotus on the writing of history is strong", is certainly valid. Murray was engaged in arguing against the impression that later readers thought poorly of Herodotus as historian. Thus, Murray needed to explain the many polemic responses to Herodotus, the liar: a polemic

[241] So, e.g., Long (1999: 618): "From a historical point of view this procedure is much too contrived and uniform."
[242] For whatever it is worth, the iconographic tradition of Socrates – which ends up becoming one of the most prolific among ancient cultural portraits – seems to begin no later than the early fourth century (Zanker, 1995: 12).
[243] A lot depends on our understanding of the "minor Socratics" (such as the "Cyrenaics" – that is, Aristippus' followers). Were they "Socratic" in any important sense? The ancients thought they were; for a modern assessment sympathetic to the ancient point of view, see McKirahan (1994).

response which in and of itself confirms Herodotus' status. Flory (1980) doubts that Herodotus had a genuine wide reception, arguing primarily from a priori considerations regarding the sheer bulk of his work, and from the limited literacy of his audience. But this is irrelevant, as Herodotus' ultimate canonicity – not just that of the late fifth century BCE – was among the top literate elite. More recently, Priestley (2014) has gone through the evidence for Herodotus' reception during the Hellenistic era, from the late fourth century onwards. This is a difficult, qualitative kind of research. We need to show that (mostly) fragmentary texts were written in response to Herodotus (but this is when we have lost the other potential sources to which such texts could refer). But the qualitative point seems plausible enough. From Alexander's conquests onwards, the Greeks engaged intensively with a world described by Herodotus – and engaged with it, it seems, through Herodotean eyes. The implication is that by the late fourth century, at the latest, the Herodotean text was, for Greek intellectuals, a present cognitive resource. Indeed, when Aristotle points out that history and poetry do not differ in their use of meter, so that Herodotus would still be "history" even if cast in verse (*Poetics* 1451a38–b4), there is no doubt that he chooses an emblematic figure of "the historian" as such. Herodotus was canonical: we cannot prove this for the year 400, but we can prove this – which is what matters to us – *before Alexandria*.

Herodotus' influence, in this qualitative sense, is the easiest to prove. We have less evidence for the two other historians. A century ago Münscher judged that Xenophon was immediately received as a major historian, with recognition as a philosopher emerging only in the Hellenistic world (Münscher, 1920: 35). The evidence is limited, however (as we can see from the fairly small number of TLG citations). Hornblower (1995: 50) argues at length for Thucydides' significant reception already in the fourth century, for which the best evidence remains the tendency of later historians – including Xenophon – to take the (arbitrary) end point of Thucydides' history as the starting point for their own history. References to Thucydides are more oblique, though Hornblower's major difficulty – the lack of references by Polybius – is perhaps exaggerated: Polybius in general does not cite earlier authors unless to criticize them. It does seem reasonable enough to suppose that Thucydides did not yet enjoy, in the fourth century, the very same *kind* of position we see in the Roman-era papyri. With the rise of oratory as a genre in the post-Hellenistic era, the historian most closely associated with Attic oratory would benefit the most.

It goes without saying that the major orators were famous, as political figures, in their own time. The ultimate choice of antiquity was to elevate, above all else, some of the *later* Attic orators. This has the paradoxical consequence that we hardly have any evidence for the reception immediately following the death of the canonical authors. Demosthenes and Aeschines die – and then we enter into the third century, from which so little literature is extant (and when, to repeat, rhetoric as such was canonical mostly as a big-library, erudite pursuit). Still, it is useful to set the TLG citations down to the fourth century BCE against papyrus fragments from all of antiquity:

| | Fragments | TLG citations[244] |
|---|---|---|
| Demosthenes | 186 | 461 |
| Isocrates | 118 | 106 |
| Aeschines | 50 | 199 |
| Lysias | 10 | 93 |
| Hyperides | 7 | 54 |
| Dinarchus | 3 | 28 |

To repeat, the TLG citations measure, effectively, the orator's success *as a political actor*. (Isocrates, less so, hence his weaker TLG numbers; but his fragment count is bolstered, as mentioned above, by his role in education.) What this table reveals is the rather obvious observation that the ultimate reception of the orators was related to their original political prominence. This is suggestive of a continuity of reception (for, otherwise, if it were just later critics choosing their favorite stylists, why would they pick the more successful politicians?). It is typical, however, that, when we look for evidence for the reception of rhetoric in the Hellenistic era, we are driven to rely on late sources such as Dionysius of Halicarnassus and Cicero: otherwise, there is very little to rely upon. Plutarch's *Life of Demosthenes* 10 is our best guide (tr. Perrin 1919):

> Ariston the Chian records an opinion which Theophrastus also passed upon the two orators. When he was asked, namely, what sort of an orator he thought Demosthenes was, he replied: "Worthy of the city"; and what Demades, "Too good for the city." And the same philosopher tells us that Polyeuctus the Sphettian, one of the political leaders of that time at Athens,

---

[244] These, obviously, exclude citations from the authors' writings themselves, as well as spurious homonyms.

declared that Demosthenes was the greatest orator, but Phocion the most influential speaker; since he expressed most sense in fewest words.

The statements ascribed to Theophrastus and to Polyeuctus have the ring of chreiai, and, sure enough, a collection of chreiai is mentioned by Diogenes Laertius (VII.163) in the catalogue of works ascribed to the Stoic philosopher Ariston of Chios; almost certainly, these works were written by the peripatetic philosopher Ariston of Ceus, of the late third century BCE.[245] Since the point of the chreiai is to belittle Demosthenes in comparison with potential rivals, and since chreiai trade on surprise, the overwhelming likelihood is that, by the late third century BCE at the latest, it was already taken for granted that Demosthenes was canonical.[246] Wooten (1974) argues that the speeches in Polybius show a Demosthenic influence – which is later still, however: in the second century. More relevant to us is Kremmydas' (2007) discussion of P.Berl. 9781, a papyrus (likely) from the middle of the third century containing a rhetorical exercise (so, likely, an educational document), purporting to be a speech by Leptines – the adversary to Demosthenes' *Against Leptines* – responding to Demosthenes. We are here no more than decades later than Demosthenes' death – and his works are already the stuff of the curriculum. This provides some context for the wider evidence brought in by Kremmydas (2013), who brings together the remains of rhetorical education in the Hellenistic era. The basic observation is that there was a continuous tradition of rhetorical education stretching back in time to the fourth – or, indeed, the fifth – century BCE (as we will note in Chapter 5, page 592, rhetorical technai were regularly written throughout the centuries, regardless of the fortune of rhetoric, itself, as a literary form). At any rate, recent scholarship emphasizes that the major moment of critical reception of rhetoric happened not in Alexandria but in late Republican and early Imperial Rome.[247] This one thing can be certain, then: the canonization of the rhetors preceded their critical reception. The likeliest account,

---

[245] DPA, s.v. Archédèmos de Tarse, 403.

[246] Kremmydas (2007: 22) is wrong, however, in ascribing to Chrysippus a commentary on Demosthenes' speech *Against Leptines*. The entry in question in Diogenes Laertius' catalogue of Chrysippus' works (VII. 201) should be translated as "On *logos*, [addressed] to Leptines" – a logical treatise addressed (as was Chrysippus' wont) to a pupil. It does remain clear, from evidence preserved by Philodemus and Quintilian (Cooper, 2002: 226), that second-century philosophers discussing rhetoric did routinely assume the central position of Demosthenes (once again, we learn this in the context of the criticism of Demosthenes); that we do not have similar evidence from the third century is because we know so little of the views of third-century philosophers on rhetoric – related, perhaps, to a general retreat of third-century philosophy from literary questions (see Chapter 4).

[247] I return to discuss this on pp. 497–8 below, relying on Wisse (1995) and O'Sullivan (1997) for the critical tradition in the first century BCE. It is clear that third-century Hellenistic grammarians

then, is the simplest: there had to be some interplay between political fame, during the author's lifetime, and the author's survival as a reference in the rhetorical handbook. There had to be some churn as new rhetors came upon the political scene through the fifth and fourth centuries, but this largely came to a stop in the end of the fourth century: for many years thereafter no one could rival the fame of Demosthenes and Aeschines, and so the textbooks got frozen. (As for Isocrates, his survival is even more straightforward: he alone was both a famous protagonist in his own right – as well as a master teacher.) If so, the dynamic may parallel, to some extent, that of comedy: in a more fluid field, new names can replace old ones and the last standing would be the best preserved.

The hypothesis developed in this discussion is that the massively famous authors of antiquity acquired their fame through their own lifetime. Let us walk quickly through the evidence. In this section, we have seen the empirical confirmation: the eminence of the major authors can be established, in general, not much later than their death and, in a few better-documented cases, even within their lifetimes. Nothing points to the era of the third century and to the library of Alexandria as an era in which literary reputations were drastically remade; all the relevant reputations seem to be firm enough through the fourth century itself. (In the case of rhetoric, the same relationship holds, with later dates.) Further, this matches with our understanding of the structure of eminence in antiquity: if indeed literary eminence was a product of social eminence (as argued in the preceding section), then, of course, literary eminence would have to be produced within the author's own lifetime: you cannot be socially eminent as a corpse. And this also matches with our understanding of the structure of literary presence. I have emphasized, in the preceding section, that authors were present to their audiences as proponents of genres, located within embodied social practice. Thus, literary eminence was predicated on social eminence for a reason. Sociology – rooted in poetics. A poetics of performance demands a sociology of the writer as a highly visible social actor, which requires that the major author start out as a major contemporary presence.

The authors themselves had major social presence, through their poetics of performance. Conversely, it is simply not clear what kind of social power later agents could have, in transforming literary reputations. What was the mechanism through which the library of Alexandria could reshape the

focused almost entirely on poetry, with perhaps some attention to the canonical historians; but they produced no studies of the rhetors (Broggiato, 2014: 47–8).

literary perception of classical authors? It is not as if they acted as the Board of Education, issuing a new syllabus. How could Lycurgus, in the 330s (leader of a defeated Athens!), shape perceptions of the tragedians, away from his own city and across an expanding Greek-speaking world? Later mediators of the canon could not reshape it: because, you see, the canon was *already* powerful.

Let us look at a single, empirical test of this hypothesis. I have avoided in this section the question of the formation of the archaic canon and have simply taken it for granted, as, indeed, the canonicity of Homer and Hesiod is assumed in all extant Greek literature. But we can look at the question of the post-classical reception of the lyric poets. Here, for once, is a truly erudite field, one on which the critics could have a decisive effect. Were the relative reputations of the lyric poets, then, made by the grammarians?

In the following table I put side by side the numbers of papyrus fragments and the TLG quotes down to the fourth century (the survey includes all archaic lyric poets extant on papyrus, excluding Simonides, whose TLG search brings up, apparently, mostly namesakes).

| Poet | Papyrus fragments | TLG quotes down to fourth century (self and pre-self excl.) |
|------|-------------------|------------------------------------------------------------|
| Pindar | 46 | 102 |
| Alcaeus | 28 | 43 |
| Sappho | 23 | 65 |
| Archilochus | 18 | 53 |
| Alcman | 15 | 33 |
| Bacchylides | 14 | 7 |
| Stesichorus | 9 | 35 |
| Anacreon | 5 | 33 |
| Ibycus | 1 | 8 |

The outlier – we knew this already – is Bacchylides; maybe he was more popular in Egypt; maybe he was unlucky in his quoters; I consider it most likely that his sheer number of fragments is a fluke.[248] Pindar, with 102 TLG citations, is well above the other lyric poets – up there together with Aeschylus and Sophocles (which, remarkably, is where he also is in the evidence of the papyri!). But, clearly, the correlation is real enough (for

---

[248] And a case of a 2011 Mertens–Pack overcount: three of the 14 fragments are shadows of past attributions now revoked.

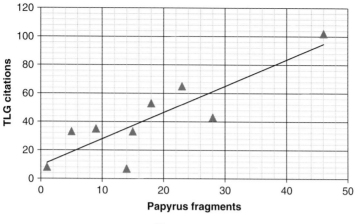

Figure 2.3

once, we may roll in statistics: coefficient 0.86). It actually makes for a nice picture.

What this figure means in English is that authors such as Plato cite Pindar or Sappho at about the same relative frequency in which such authors' fragments are retrieved from the sands of Egypt. Now, we may debate the order of causation (perhaps authors became central in later reception to the extent that they were enshrined in such canonical works as those by Plato), but this underlines the fundamental observation: the relative reputations, even of the lyric poets, were not transformed through the third century and, instead, had already been cast into their ultimate mold by the fourth.

So what did Alexandria do? Indeed, there is some evidence for ranking, among the Hellenistic scholars as well as their Roman-era counterparts. Hellenistic authors counted the Seven Wonders of the World,[249] but also the three authors of old comedy, the nine lyric poets, perhaps the four epic poets; later on, they would count the ten Attic orators. When and how each list was set up is contested by scholars.[250] Accordingly, let us consider this in more detail. One clear observation is that such lists are inflated. Take epic. Homer and Hesiod, Antimachus and Panyassis? This list of four is surely dead wrong (though it helps explain why we end up finding

---

[249] Hoepfner (2003).
[250] Especially for the orators, though the lists are probably late in this case. For the debate, and a (less than compelling) argument for an early list of ten orators, see Smith (1995).

a portrait of Panyasis). Or old comedy: Eupolis and Cratinus are indeed represented in the papyrus evidence (six and four fragments, respectively). If you want to choose *three*, this is the best choice. But there was only *one* enduring canonical author of the old comedy, and Alexandrian list makers were powerless to change this fact. The list of ten Attic orators similarly inflates the reality of a reception dominated by the three major orators Demosthenes, Isocrates and Aeschines.[251]

The impact of Alexandrian canon formation, then, was to *expand* (for a tiny minority of bibliophiles), not to *contract* (from the literary field as a whole). It took the (cognitively restricted) smaller set of truly central authors and added to them a certain ballast so as to reach larger, more interesting lists. Preserving the minor: is this, perhaps, the true vocation of the critic?

Moretti, as always, is incisive (2000: 209):

> The slaughter of literature [i.e. the process whereby 99.5 percent of novels disappear]. And the butchers – readers who read novel A (but not B, C, D, E, F, G, H, . . .) and so keep A "alive" into the next generation, when other readers may keep it alive into the following one, and so on until eventually A becomes canonized. Readers, not professors, make canons: academic decisions are mere echoes of a process that unfolds fundamentally outside the school: reluctant rubber-stamping, not much more.

(227):

> As for the exceptions to this model, they are neither as common nor as striking as the critical legend would have it. *The Red and the Black*, supposedly ignored by nineteenth-century readers, went through at least seventeen French editions between 1830 and 1900; *Moby-Dick*, another favorite counterexample, went through at least thirteen English and American editions between 1851 and 1900. Not bad.

What we do not see so much is the rise from anonymity.[252] Shklovsky's famous dictum (1990 [1925]: 190) – "The legacy that is passed on from one literary generation to the next moves not from father to son but from uncle to nephew" – points to a reality which is different nonetheless from that of posthumous fame. Successful authors very often find inspiration not from their most successful predecessors but, rather, from less canonical preceding forms (so, in Shklovsky's example, Alexander Blok being inspired by

---

[251] Minor orators survive on papyrus in numbers which are comparable with those of Cratinus and Eupolis: Lysias ten, Hyperides seven, Antiphon and Lycurgus three.

[252] Collins (1998: 59): "Canons do change, but only among those figures which have entered the long-term chain of reputation in the first place."

gypsy love songs). This is a kind of posthumous fame which offers little of the comfort of the rags-to-riches storyline. Shklovsky's dictum is sometimes understood in a different manner, referring to the way in which relatively minor figures are chosen as objects of canonization by a later generation – one that marks its new tastes through its new canon: so Gerard Manley Hopkins for twentieth-century modernist English poetry, or Kafka, of course, for modernist prose as a whole. Such cases are rare and defined by sharp sociological and chronological constraints. Posthumous canonization of this kind demands an early, zealous social focus led by a crusader to one's cause; and, for this reason, it can happen only relatively close to the author's death. Kafka was never as obscure as often imagined, already printed and appreciated by an important circle by his death in 1924.[253] The crusade is very famous in this case, led by Brod and joined by a motley group of Jews, Czechs and modernists; by the 1930s Kafka's future was assured, though he had to wait for the late 1940s to become iconic.[254] Hopkins' crusade, led by Robert Bridges and sustained by a circle of Catholic admirers, took even longer: 41 years after Hopkins' death, the second edition of his *Poems* published in 1930, as Hopkins was instantly sprung onto the canon of modernist poetry.[255] The immediate group, carrying on the living memory, is crucial: it preserves the making of the brand, allowing it to come to life once enough attention has been achieved.

These are rare events[256] – and such that are impossible to imagine in antiquity. Blok, inspired by gypsy song; Kafka and Hopkins, waiting in the wings; what such events demand is a typically modernist structure – the *heterogeneous literary field*. In the late nineteenth century the kind of

---

[253] Kittler, Koch and Neumann (1994) collect Kafka's publications during his lifetime with some notes on their reception.
[254] Durrani (2002).    [255] Mellown (1965).
[256] But myth making engages with such moments, magnifies them and imagines them everywhere. I will take a single example, so often repeated by music lovers. Schubert is often represented, especially in popular reception but also in some scholarly works, as an isolated genius, recognized only posthumously (his rediscovery ascribed, in this case, to Schumann, who did indeed champion Schubert in the decades following the composer's death). So, for instance, Daverio (2000: 604): "The publication of several large-scale instrumental works by Franz Schubert in the late 1820s and 1830s elicited little reaction from contemporary critics. One of the few voices to break the near silence was that of Robert Schumann." In fact it is well recognized, at least since the work of Biba (1979), that Schubert was extremely successful in his own lifetime (Euripides-like, though, he never had Vienna to himself: he died very shortly after Beethoven did – and when Rossini was still alive. The myth of his posthumous rediscovery also rests on the fact that, inhumanly prolific as he was, there most definitely remained a massive, never-yet-performed *Nachlass* at his very young death.). Such myths emerge naturally around a romantic figure such as that of Schubert. The full irony is that such naïve, nineteenth-century myths of genius end up being reinforced by the sophisticated, post-structuralist myth of criticism as hegemony. For both imagine the author's name – posthumously made.

literature consumed at St. Petersburg's cabarets was entirely distinct from the literature discussed at its salons; local, idiosyncratic literary circles could be developed at such semi-marginal places as Prague or Dublin; literary tastes were in competition, busily distinguishing themselves from each other, all the while engaging and disengaging from mass literature so as to construct their own cultural capital.

All this is well known to readers of Bourdieu and was absent in antiquity. I return to the fundamental observation of Chapter 1. The papyri display remarkable diachronic continuity, and at the same time the various pictures we may form of the canon – uncovering it at its various social levels – are all consistent. From the humble schoolroom at the Egyptian chora to the senatorial villa, there was but a single synchronic literary field. There were no major reappraisals – discoveries of minor authors who were suddenly pushed to the fore – because there were no social niches that could have maintained such minor authors as their own, private, heroes.[257] And so classical canonization had to be achieved within one's lifetime – or not at all.

### 2.3.3    The Invention of the Brand in Early Greek Philosophy and Literature[258]

So far through this chapter I have brought in some empirical evidence (not without a few generalizations!). The remaining two sections are more synthetic, and more speculative still. To some extent, what I say will be grounded in the evidence and theoretical framework provided in this chapter; but in some ways I anticipate arguments for which I will require more evidence, later on,

[257] This – in the literary canon, and prior to late antiquity. Reappraisals could take place in the specialized fields (the most striking case is the relative neglect, and then rise, of Aristotle). We may consider also the wide field of non-performative prose that did not have an Athenian component: narrative local histories; biographies; the novel; the Acta Alexandrinorum; the Gospels. All are closely related generically, with obvious differences that present different niches of reception: the educated elite for the history and the novel; a wider, but specifically Egyptian, literate public for the various Acta Alexandrinorum; wider, but specifically Jewish (in their fashion) reading communities, for the various Gospels. The ultimate historical transformation of the canon, in late antiquity, would indeed arise out of this minor family of synchronic difference.

[258] In general in this book I no more than glance at archaic Greece – the methods I usually apply become effective only once the habits of massive citation of historical names (related to the rise of prose genres) become established. This section is thus more speculative; and I note immediately a major limitation of my approach: in this book – which starts from the Greek canon! – I have rather little to say about *Homer*.

concerning space (especially from Chapter 3), and concerning scale (especially from Chapter 6).

The key outcome derived from the chapter so far is the following claim: ancient canonization is typically contemporary, and in fact can be dated fairly precisely to an author's mature age.

This means that we can replot the canon, transforming the series of names obtained through our various means of studying the canon into a series of dates. To the extent that we can date the activities of ancient authors (and, for the major authors who interest us, we usually can), we can also tentatively suggest the historical moment at which they began to attract wide acclaim. We can therefore study the pattern of such waves of acclaim – and, therefore, begin to suggest a historical narrative.

Here, then, is how our story may begin. Once upon a time the Greeks had a literary field dominated by epic poems circulating (in more or less fluctuating form) without named authors. The point is nearly uncontroversial – see, for example, West (1999) – and we need only note that, back then, the Greeks were normal: this is how, in early civilizations, literature circulates. And then, at some point, names and the persona of the author intervene. "Homer" is clearly a late invention; "Sappho", say, is demonstrably not so.[259] The names add up, and, eventually, the prominent Greek lyric authors and philosophers would number about a dozen each.[260]

As noted, I rely on the assumption above that, to become an established name, one needed to have reached a certain social prominence. This would be even more powerful in the context of oral transmission, in which, obviously, posthumous fame would be tricky to achieve. I therefore look not for the beginning of an author's career, or even for the ancient

---

[259] That is, at some point we see authors who refer to themselves by name in their poems, perhaps striving to make sure that future reperformances would acknowledge their authorship. On this "seal" motive, *sphragis*, see especially Calame (2004: 13–19). The case of Hesiod – on which see more below – is complicated. The name is used by the poet himself, but could it be, itself, a conventional bardic mask? (So Nagy, 1979: 296–7, etymologizing the name as "emitter of song". This has not won universal agreement; see Most, 2006: xv.)

[260] For the lyric poets, the list could include Pindar, Alcaeus, Sappho, Archilochus, Alcman, Bacchylides, Simonides, Stesichorus, Hipponax, Anacreon, Theognis, Tyrtaeus and Ibycus – all represented on papyri. For archaic figures of wisdom, the list could include the Seven Sages (the less apocryphal among them are: Thales, Solon, Chilon, Pittacus), together with at least Anaximander, Anaximenes, Pythagoras, Heraclitus, Parmenides and Xenophanes (the last might equally be counted among the lyric poets – as is of course true of Solon as well). The scale may well be constrained by the limits of a mostly oral form of transmission: I return to this question of scale in Chapter 5, pp. 566–8.

biographical device of an "acme" at age 40, but, rather, for what we may call the "post-acme" – not necessarily the period of maximal activity but the period when people begin to repeat your words, because they are the words of an established great author: say, age 60. To clarify: I do not mean that one would start singing at age 60. Rather: I mean that those whose songs would be heard with reverence, imitated and resung with the name of the original author would be the elder statesmen – and stateswomen – of song. Indeed, lyric poetry often engages with love, and with subversion, in manners which, to modern readers, are sometimes evocative of youth. Can we imagine a Sappho, aged 60? But these authors, I suggest, are champion horses that have raced many times already. When they sing of old age – as they do so often – it is from experience.[261] Now, the ranges within which "age 60" may fluctuate are very wide. We know little. And yet, events do not take place in vague "centuries". I therefore prefer to offer approximate dates, however speculative and arbitrary (which I find are best rounded, in this case, to the nearest decade). This would allow us to produce a speculative *timeline* of archaic canonization – by which, once again, I mean the dates at which the authors of the archaic canon turned 60.[262] Poets' names are given in varying font sizes according to their survival on papyrus, which I take to be the first-approximation measure of early success (as shown on pages 214–15 above, survival on papyrus is probably a good proxy for the fame of authors in the fourth century, which is already suggestive, perhaps, of the early reception).

---

[261] Mace (1993: 338): "Anyone who can say *dēute* ["again"] of an encounter with Eros is, de facto, giving an account of a fresh experience with desire from a veteran's point of view." (This, from Mace's analysis of a key formulation in archaic lyric poetry, is repeatedly found in many poets and poems, which she sums up as "Eros… Me, again!".) Another major theme is that of impending mortality (Hardie, 2005). Poetic authorship is born intertwined with the idea of how future audiences would reflect on one's poetry, after one's passing: musings of old age.

[262] I do not provide individual sources for the dates. The biographical data are almost always meager and are always well known (a historical reference here, a late notice of the Olympiad of the acme there). It has to be admitted that some of the dates are particularly problematic: especially so – naturally – the earliest date, that of Hesiod (Kõiv, 2011. Note that, *pace* Nagy, 1979, I consider him here as a historical poet, if only for the sake of the exercise). It should be emphasized that, while there is typically much room for debate, there is usually not much chronological wriggle room: for instance, a somewhat radical, revisionist proposal for Archilochus' date (Lavelle, 2002) merely pushes it back by about 20 years. I do not claim that we know the precise decade in which ancient poets became prominent – this would be preposterous – but I do claim that we may form some probabilities, and that the emerging clusters make us gain confidence in the process. (For more on my view on the role of probability in my dating, locating and counting of ancient authors, see pp. 619–21 below.) I try to report minor archaic poets as well (such that do not survive in the papyrus tradition), but I exclude those whose historicity is in doubt (this excludes, to my mind, Terpander, Arion, Aristoxenus of Selinus and Susarion), as well as those for whom the evidence for any dating is indeed too precarious (this excludes Callinus, Asius, Demodocus, Pythermus, Eumelus and Ananius). I take Pindar as my cutoff point.

## The Archaic Canon Timeline

| Year | Song | | | | Wisdom | |
|---|---|---|---|---|---|---|
| 680 | Hesiod | | | | | |
| 670 | | | | | | |
| 660 | | | | | | |
| 650 | | | | | | |
| 640 | Archilochus | | | | | |
| 630 | | | | | | |
| 620 | Tyrtaeus | | | | | |
| 610 | Mimnermus | | | | | |
| 600 | | | | | | |
| 590 | Sappho | Alcman | | | | |
| 580 | Alcaeus | | | Solon | Thales | |
| 570 | Stesichorus | | | | | |
| 560 | | | | | | |
| 550 | | | | | Chilon | Anaximander |
| 540 | Ibycus | | | | | |
| 530 | | | | | Anaximenes | |
| 520 | Hipponax | Anacreon | Phocylides | **HOMER**[263] | | |
| 510 | Semonides[264] | | | | Pythagoras | |
| 500 | Simonides | | | | Xenophanes | |
| 490 | Lasus | | | | Heraclitus | |
| 480 | Theognis | | | | Parmenides | |
| 470 | Timocreon | | | | | |
| 460 | Pindar | | Bacchylides | | | |

As we peer through the fog of the "seventh and sixth centuries" and look at dates – however dodgy – a certain landscape begins to emerge.

First, we might detect a tipping point near the end of the seventh century: names of poets are very scarce before that; from then on they are regularly accumulated; the same generation also constructs the figure of the named sage.

This tipping point can be accounted for in one of two ways: either there were as many names in circulation, in cultural memory, even before 620, but then these names were later lost (before the major commemoration of archaic poetry by written now extant sources, from the late fifth century onwards); or authorial names were actually more often accumulated from

---

[263] I follow West (1999) and take this as the date in which the name "Homer" becomes entrenched as a way of referring to the author of the *Iliad* and the *Odyssey*.

[264] A rather more controversial dating: Hubbard (1994).

that date onwards. The point is that there are in fact several names that do emerge from those mists of time – and they seem to be mostly fictional! Had there been a Terpander, how come nothing remained from his poetry?[265] Antiquity, if anything, would have served as motivation for memorization. Better, then, to assume that there was *nothing* to remember – surely some poetry, some wisdom, but very little of it *named*. Other than Hesiod and Archilochus, the early and middle part of the seventh century did not canonize its performers. All the more so for the eighth. I see no reason, then, not to believe that Hesiod was the start of named authorship in Greek literature.[266] This, in turn, provides some faith in the traditional date: it makes sense for Hesiod to precede, somewhat, the eventual *standardization* of authorship.

Indeed, Hesiod's was, we note now also, a false start. Whether or not there was an actual individual named Hesiod, the key point is that for the next 400 years no other Greek poet ever managed to make a major name for himself as the author of epic hexameter.[267] Archilochus provides the second and more assured beginning (perhaps, if Hesiod is a mere mask, Archilochus actually came first). And it is not very long after him – perhaps a couple of decades? – that the tipping point occurs and an entire group of named authors emerges.

This, then, is the suggested outline: Hesiod – but then Archilochus – and then a more or less "established" model of the named author. (Perhaps the sequence could indeed be understood in terms of generations, especially if the chronology above is taken quite literally. The gap of 30 to 50 years is as one would expect based on the assumption that authors need to reach old age before they become widely imitated. Under my reconstruction, then, Archilochus grows up as Hesiod's poems begin to be regularly reperformed; Sappho and her peers grow up as Archilochus' poems begin

---

[265] "A virtual poet" is how Beecroft (2010: 107) refers to Terpander, putting him in the category of Orpheus: the central point is that even the ancients had nothing to go by in constructing his persona.

[266] In itself not a very controversial idea; see, e.g., Griffith (1983). But, of course, to suggest that Hesiod was a real actor and not just a bardic mask is already to take a position in a scholarly debate (see p. 219, n.259 above). The key point, in my view, is not that Hesiod uses his own name but that, if we take on board the reality of a non-authorial literary field, why should such a mask take the form of a name? Is Nagy, suggesting the bards take up a particular persona, not anachronistically imposing back on an archaic era the assumptions of authorial literature?

[267] Antimachus of Colophon comes closest (five papyri fragments, 181 TLG citations through all of antiquity, 27 till the end of the fourth century – though the bulk of all those citations are homonyms). He was a classical author, experimenting with new ways of entering the canon following the closure of the archaic canon (more on this below): his experiment was a failure that was kept alive, in a qualified way, through Alexandrian efforts at canonization. That lyric, rather than epic, formed the main vehicle to the early brand-name author is understandable, as, indeed, is the fact that the social institution most significant for this authorship was the symposium.

to be regularly reperformed. An author born circa 700 would know that canonization is an option; an author born circa 650 would know that song is the most successful route leading there. I find this reconstruction plausible, but it does depend on a certainty that our dates cannot provide.) At any rate, it is clear that the character of the named author is well established, at the latest, by the generation of Sappho; once again, not a very controversial suggestion.[268] This will also explain how, as the canon of established names became established, the following generations – growing up on the expectation that any poetry would have a named author – would seek to assign an author even to the *Iliad*. I follow in my table above the (very debatable) suggestion by West (1999) that, near the end of the sixth century, the old epic itself became assimilated into the culture of the named author with the invention of "Homer".[269]

I have constructed Pindar to be the end point of my survey, but it is true that later lyric poets – with the qualified exception of Timotheus – never gained any significant prominence. A certain tradition does culminate with Pindar, and so the last major lyric poet, his memory undimmed by anyone following him, remained pre-eminent.[270] This, of course, is consonant with the dynamics of cultural memory we saw in the previous section. The

---

[268] One of the achievements of contemporary scholarship was the realization of the somewhat contrived nature of Sappho's "first person" stance; in fact, it is now believed that much of this poetry could have been originally sung by choruses, and not by the poet herself (see Lardinois, 1996, and references therein). The old image rests on a more basic reality, never lost sight of: the poetry is so attractive precisely because of its highly personal, indeed suggestive, voice; she was, indeed, the prototypical author for Snell (1953 [1946]).

[269] One also notes, in my table, a quasi-hiatus: over the period from 570 to 520 only a single poet is canonized, perhaps in a more minor way – Ibycus (even this is merely an addition to a relatively belated entry of the west, with Stesichorus: canonization in the core Aegean area between Alcaeus and Hipponax). If this is not merely a construct of my methodology, or of the bias of the sources, it may be of deep significance. Perhaps, at some stage, strictly oral transmission becomes saturated, and there is no more cognitive space left for the memorization beyond the established repertoire of the group of poets from Archilochus to Alcaeus. The further expansion of the repertoire may owe something to writing, in this case. This, then, would be the first, tentative closure of the canon.

[270] It generally helps to be the last in the series of the canonization in a genre: there are no later challengers to diminish your stature. Thus Pindar is the top lyric author; Euripides is the top tragedian; Aristophanes is the top author in old comedy but is overshadowed by Menander, the top author in new comedy. Demosthenes, finally, is the top orator. Obviously, this is true for canonical systems as a whole: the classical dominates over the archaic (but is not displaced by the Hellenistic). The late mover advantage applies in the more performative genres but not in history, in which Xenophon's position is secondary to that of his two predecessors, of whom Herodotus may retain the first position: the entire question of first movers versus late entrants merits further research. This question is intensively studied in economics, in which, generally, the first mover is considered to be at an advantage (locus classicus: Lieberman and Montgomery, 1988). The major difference seems to be that authors die while business brands are immortal. Thus, business brands maintain the kind of authority that Sophocles, say, kept through his lifetime. Real-life authors die and are then at a disadvantage.

closure following upon Pindar is of course significant; we shall return to it below, on page 233.

So far, the chronological landscape. What does it suggest in terms of potential causal accounts? Let us consider the possible routes for the maintenance of early Greek poetry.[271] Choral songs were very probably reperformed locally in their seasonally recurring ritual context (Herington [1985], though it is intriguing that the major piece of evidence is from hyper-conservative, highly visible Sparta). Surely, written transmission could have served to preserve at least Pindar's verse (the epinician, in particular, is obviously dependent on a particular occasion, and so scholars wonder sometimes whether reperformance could really serve as its main vehicle of survival);[272] clearly, such an account may serve for the latter generations of lyric poetry but not for the formation of the literary form. It is as uncontroversial a claim as one can make in such a field, that lyric poetry was maintained, in its early stages, primarily through the filter of the symposium. Perhaps in the competitive context of the skolion,[273] perhaps in more relaxed forms of entertainment, songs were reperformed in convivial gatherings of members of the elite (who, as such, were trained in musical performance), through the seventh and sixth centuries. Now, the gathering of the symposium is an event of multiplicity, in that it has several participants who address each other as equals. What we need to assume is that in symposia from around 640 BCE onwards it became quite common to summon an extra guest, as it were, in the person of Archilochus. Or, as it is better put, by Nagy (2004): the culture of the symposium involved the taking on of roles for the sake of performance (this, Nagy explains, is archaic mimesis). Archilochus took up the role of "Archilochus" in his songs performed among his circle of friends;[274] it was but an easy step for others, in other symposia, to take up that role for themselves, for the sake of

---

[271] That this was produced in the context of performance was repeatedly stressed over the last few decades; only a handful of studies concern themselves directly with the question – more pertinent for our purposes – of reperformance (I quote a few of the important exceptions to this). This is not because of scholarly neglect but, rather, because of the limitations of our evidence. We interpret lyric poetry primarily based on the poems themselves, and they are obviously informative above all for the context of their original performance.

[272] This is related to a wider question regarding the survival of choral lyric: how did this pass through the filter of the symposium in the first place? One option, emphasized by recent scholarship, is to make all poetry at least compatible with monody performance (say, as symphonies became familiar through solo piano transcriptions reperformed in nineteenth-century European salons); see, e.g., Heath and Lefkowitz (1991) for the case of Pindar's victory odes, Davies (1988) for the general claim. Just as first-person poetry was sometimes sung by choruses (see n.268 above), so choruses were often sung by a single person, taking up the voice of the implied author.

[273] See Griffith (1990, esp. 193) and Martin (2017).

[274] For this, the argument relies on Rösler (1980).

a song. The construction of "Archilochus" did not make a single, unique center of power and prestige. To the contrary: it added a further dimension of diversity – the other, borrowed voice – to an institution that prided itself on such variety.

Recall: we need a name, and we need a personality – the name *Archilochus* and the marked persona of "Archilochus". So, we need a cultural context where name-dropping was natural (you do not just stand up and say "Here is a new song I heard the other day"; you say instead "Here is a song which I think is really great; it is by Archilochus – you must have heard of him"); and we need a cultural artifact that marks the particularity of the singing persona.

Now, the symposium brings together members of the elite who present themselves to each other as equals – the social norm for interaction among members of the elite in the "horizontal" context bringing together the Greek aristocracy. (To borrow the model of Herman, 1986: on the one hand, the vertical context of the individual polis; on the other hand, the horizontal context of the aristocratic network.) As members of the elite meet to celebrate their status they see themselves as a set of individuals a cut above from their individual poleis, belonging essentially to a cross-polis network. And so it is only natural to bring in a foreign elite member, and have him clearly marked as a named individual on par with those actually present.

We can now offer a model for the rise of the archaic canon. In the seventh century members of the Greek elite would meet in symposia, where they sang (and perhaps repeated words of wisdom), occasionally ascribing their words to other individuals, perhaps from other poleis, not present in the symposium itself.

This practice created an opening: songs that markedly broadcast a particular persona of their maker would be more readily transportable and ascribed to a foreign member. Hesiod, of course, was very effective in broadcasting his particular persona (hence an epic *didactic*: the didactic creates an addressee, and as a consequence the persona of the singer, so, in this structural sense, there is no doubt that Hesiod was indeed a didactic poet; see Schiesaro, Mitsis and Clay, 1994). For reasons explained above, his model was not easily repeated (indeed: would the symposium be a natural vehicle for the transmission of epic? For the kind of persona projected by Hesiod?). An even more successful master of broadcasting a particular persona, however, was Archilochus. Aggressively contrarian, marked for his style, Archilochus could very naturally be reperformed as "Archilochus". The model is thus formed, and in the following generation we hear, again and again, the distinct voices of singers marking themselves as elite individuals ready to be invited – through their song – to the many symposia spanning the poleis of the Greek world. By the year 580 an entire set of individual names has been naturalized into the practice of sympotic reperformance; later in the century the origin of song in its individual maker is such an established idea that, in their efforts to sustain their status as authentic performers, the guild(s) of epic performance begin to ascribe their own songs to their own original performer, and Homer is made to join the canon – at which point the literary field dominated by the named author has been created.

This, then, is the theory. In poetic terms, it is straightforward: poetics are made by preceding poetics, genres by preceding genres. We have learned this point well enough since the work of Todorov, and, in this case, the moral is clear: the Greeks had a culture of performance; the genres of the named author had to construct him or her, then, as a projected performer. The named author would be the one whose performances could be imitated by others, while maintaining their identity.

Historically, the theory is no less straightforward: the Greek literary field was originally created as the projection of the cross-polis network of the elite. For this reason, it is important for me to argue that the field was always Hellenic rather than strictly epichoric. That is, I do not deny that many individual performances were originally tied to a particular space, and reperformance in some cases could have been primarily local as well (it is quite likely that this is how Spartan song, in particular, survived into the classical era). And yet, the model which needs to be avoided, I think, is that of Lesbian symposia, reperforming Sappho and Alcaeus; Thasian symposia, reperforming Archilochus – and so on for generations until, finally, a single canon is formed of the many epichoric traditions. Had this been the case, we would have seen the tradition dominated by the powerful spaces of the era of canonization (much more Solon, then, and many more Athenian, Theban and Corinthian poets). We would also expect to see even more names (there would be many canons, not one: and so the cognitive threshold on the repertoire would still allow the proliferation of many individual singers maintained, however tenuously).[275] Nor is such a model consistent with the plausible examples of mutual influence that

---

[275] Such may well be the case for the Chinese *Book of Odes*, which is indeed the belated conflation of several epichoric traditions into a unique canon – one in which the named author is not evoked, however (see Beecroft, 2010; I am not sure, however, that he would agree with my characterization of the Greek case).

poets exercise upon each other[276] – and of the reality of a highly mobile culture in which travel is the biographic information most typically provided for any member of the cultural elite.[277] And for a good reason: the very status of the Greek elite relied on its ability to transcend its individual polis. One sang – and made a mention of place ("epichoric") so as to make a statement, on a broader, Panhellenic arena.[278] Or, conversely: why would a Greek aristocrat wish to invite, to his symposium, just the members of his home town? Better to bring famous guests from elsewhere, whether in the flesh – or through their song. Quite simply, the demographic realities of the archaic Greek elite simply would not allow the formation of many local canons (see page 642 below). To maintain even this small community of poets one had to reach for the Greek world, as a whole.

And so a single canon was made, and it was made as a network of illustrious names, each with its own place; because it was as such a network – illustrious names, representing their cities – that Greek aristocrats liked to think of themselves.

The theory proposed here is that in the sixth century BCE Greeks already possessed a literary field similar in some of its broad structural features to that of the later canon. It anticipated the later canon in that it was widely shared among a wide Greek audience and in that it was formed of many named individuals anchored within their performance genres. It differed from the later canon in its more limited set of genres. Put simply, it did not include drama or prose. Its system was articulated not so much by genre as by variety, which spelled, to its audience, *spatial* difference, especially in dialect and musical form. Its variety thus represented the multiplicity of the many cities of the Greek world. What we need to understand in the following section, then, is the addition of new genres – which also pushed almost the entirety of the early canon into the margins of the new one – correlated with a sharp spatial concentration on the single city of Athens.

---

[276] This is typically discussed in terms of authors' *dialects* becoming reflected in that of others. Scholarship has tended to avoid the study of allusion in archaic poetry, since, on the model of oral composition, shared elements are understood to reflect not intentional reference from one author to another but the mere deployment of a common stock of tools. This may well blind us to some real practices of allusion (for a recent attempt to revive allusion in archaic poetry, see, e.g., Irwin, 2005, on Solon's use of his predecessors).

[277] So, the meetings of the Seven Sages (for their overall performance of wisdom, see Martin, 1993). As for the poets: travel, exile or settlement are reported, whether or not correctly, for every archaic poet for whom any biographic details of substance are available, with the single exception, I believe, of Tyrtaeus. (Sparta the exception – though it had to import its Alcman.)

[278] This is the interpretation provided by Boterf (2017) for the significant phenomenon of the emphasis on the local, in lyric poetry. A local emphasis – but one intended to resonate widely.

Before we proceed, a couple of observations.

In the book parodied in the title to this section ("The Discovery of the Mind in Greek Philosophy and Literature"), Bruno Snell argues that the early Greeks, through a long process of intensive introspection, discovered that they had the rich attributes of a personality. This thesis is still widely cited, though classicists, I believe, now refer to it only so as to debunk it in passing. It is not a silly theory to offer, coming from the background of a German scholarship dominated by Neo-Kantianism, with its emphasis on concepts and their historical growth. And so my point is not yet again to debunk Snell but, rather, to notice that *he had a point*. The persona of the author in Greek literature is strikingly different from that of other early literatures. The individual does come through in rich detail and specificity, which we have since come to associate with literature as such but which is absent from, say, the *Analects*, from the Old Testament – or, for that matter, from Homer. We should not lose sight of the radical innovation of archaic literature. The thing is to account for this innovation in historical terms. I trace it to the poetics of a literary practice – named authorship – which in turn is traced to social institutions.

A parallel case can be made for early Greek philosophy. Here I concentrate on an aspect different from that emphasized by Snell. For him, the innovation of early Greek philosophy was its emphasis on the knowing subject; important for Snell's philosophical tradition but of limited relevance for actual Presocratic thought. I would emphasize the turn to naturalism – that is, the proposal of explanations that do not evoke the divine. This is typical of Presocratic thought from its very beginning, and is, in comparative context, perhaps its most striking feature: so much is quite uncontroversial.[279] At some level, this is directly related to the weakness of Greek religious-political institutions – the absence of priest-kings (as noted above on page 103, following the work of Morris and Ober). The numinous did not possess, in the Greek world, quite the same social power it had in virtually all other civilizations. This does not directly determine the naturalism of the Presocratics, but it creates the conditions for it, through the shaping of the authorial practices of Greek wisdom.

---

[279] This is often made to be the starting point for discussion of the Presocratics – e.g. KRS 72–6, Algra (1999: 48) and Morgan (2000: chap. 2) – though scholars of ancient philosophy typically shy away from providing a direct account of this original development. (An account of the naturalism of Presocratic thought tends to celebrate the "enlightenment" of Greek civilization – embarrassingly anachronistic, hence the subject is typically left moot.)

Let us step back for a moment and consider why, in other early civilizations, words of wisdom are spoken from an anonymous or mediated perspective. Apart from the power of priest-kings, the fact is that to speak from a personal perspective is also to invoke contingency: why should a particular person have any special access to wisdom? Better to speak, then, from the point of view of impersonal, transcendent truth. There is therefore an inbuilt bias for anchoring claims of truth in distant authorities, the mythical and the divine, or the reported sage who is portrayed as possessing mythical wisdom: Confucius; or the physicians of the Yellow Emperor.[280] Indeed, this bias might be the most pronounced in medicine, wherein truth, freed of all contingency, is of most consequence; hence, even among the Greeks, medicine has its Hippocrates and, even later on, many anonymous and pseudonymous works, as noted on page 99 above. And, indeed, non-poetic wisdom was not the arena in which the figure of the author was invented and the named poet had to become entrenched before the first named sage appeared. For this reason, I do not see the absence of Greek priest-kings as the proximate cause for Greek naturalism. It is not as if they had no pharaohs, hence they had Thales; because, in the first instance, the absence of a pharaoh gave rise not to a Thales but to an Archilochus.

Archilochus did lead to Thales, though. By the early sixth century the author was a dominant mode of cultural transmission. It became natural for individuals to seek fame through their wisdom, and, for those who performed words of wisdom, to authenticate their sayings with the figures of the authors who had supposedly uttered them before them. As the authorial model was thrust upon the field of wise sayings, contingency was thrust upon the field of wise thought. And so it was embraced. One had to discover a new kind of wisdom, one which suggested not the immobile store of communal knowledge but the new claims of individuals – making radical, original claims. Wisdom was cut from its mooring in tradition. It became, instead, a critique – projecting persona in the Greek manner of words in violent action, arguing – the more forcibly, the better – against all traditional views. Hence nature, against myth.

---

[280] See Unschuld (2003): the foundational canon of Chinese medicine, this Han-era compilation is presented as a series of statement made by physicians at the court of the mythical Yellow Emperor of yore.

### 2.3.4    The Tyranny of Athens over Greece

To us, Athens in the fifth century was marked, above all, by its leading position within the democratic experiment. Indeed, I argue that its ultimate canonization in the polis of letters had the consequence of enshrining cultural practices of a perhaps "democratic" nature, in the heart of the Western tradition. But it should be emphasized that, if the Greeks ended up worshipping the city of democracy, they did so for reasons other than its politics. Look at whom they canonized: Aristophanes, Euripides, Socrates, Thucydides, Plato, Isocrates, Xenophon and Aeschines all were in some ways critical of or distant from the democratic avant-garde, or even from democracy as such; three went into forced or voluntary exile, one was executed.[281] (Aeschylus, a good citizen, belongs to an early generation when democracy was still in its first stages of evolution; Menander was active in a city whose democratic ethos was already somewhat compromised.) So, it is not that Greeks turned to Athens as their model because of political affinity with its distinctive politics. To the contrary: Greek elite members took comfort from the anti-democratic views expressed by major Athenian figures. I started my discussion with the observation that the Athenian canon was maintained by a society which no longer engaged in the democratic experiment. We can say more: at the very time of its formation, the canon was formed of authors who were mostly skeptical of this experiment and for an elite audience which must have to a large extent detested it.

So, it is all the more perplexing: why an *Athenian* canon? Why did the polis of letters need to be formed on the model of Athens?

Let us begin with some dates – which can now, indeed, be offered much more precisely (if, as usual, with a strong element of conjecture). The following is a timeline of the canonization of the Athenian component of the canon (plus Socrates), providing the date of canonization as implied from the history of reception; or, when all that fails, the date when the author reached age 50 or a little above (for Socrates, an oral author, the age of 60 is used again). Dates are rounded to the nearest multiple of five (in this case, the evidence has been covered in the chapter above).

---

[281] A familiar observation; usually put not in the terms of the nature of canonization but, rather, in terms of the attitudes of Athenian elites towards the institutions of the city (McClelland, 1989: chap. 1; Ober, 1989).

## The Athenian canon timeline

> [470   Aeschylus (canonization still within the archaic system)]
> [445   Sophocles (but this is Athenian: Panhellenic
>             canonization is post-Euripidean?)]

Canonization of the Athenian system

|         |     |               |               |
|---------|-----|---------------|---------------|
|         | 415 | Euripides     | Herodotus[282] |
| Stage A | 410 | Socrates      |               |
|         | 405 | Aristophanes[283] |           |
|         |     |               |               |
|         | 390 | Thucydides    |               |
|         | 380 | Isocrates     |               |
| Stage B | 375 | Xenophon      |               |
|         | 375 | Plato         |               |

Later developments

|         |     |             |
|---------|-----|-------------|
|         | 340 | Demosthenes |
|         | 340 | Aeschines   |
|         | 295 | Menander    |

The list has a clear core (stages A to B). Aeschylus entered the canon, perhaps indeed in a genuine Panhellenic sense, at about the same time Pindar did. He could have been, then, yet another addition to the repertoire of Panhellenic song, providing more representation to that suddenly hugely important place, Athens (that his choral productions were much more elaborate than their predecessors, however, must have presented a difficulty for reperformance: he died in Sicily, directing one).[284] Sophocles was canonized in the middle of the fifth century – primarily in

---

[282] The date of Herodotus' publication is contested (see Meister, 1990: 210 n.14, for sources; the debate appears to have quietened since). Are we to envisage publication around 445 or around 415? Was the author of the *Histories* aged 40, or 70? I choose the later date, with Fornara (1971), but not *all* that much rides on this, as Panhellenic reception could, once again, have waited a few years upon publication of the work – similarly to the fate of Sophocles, first an Athenian phenomenon and only somewhat later a Panhellenic one.

[283] The date is a compromise between that of the major plays (mostly earlier) and the absolute age of the author (still quite young in 405: as mentioned above, a phenomenon of comedy).

[284] This is not to say that his poetry did not mark a new departure; Herington's model (1985, esp. 138–44) has Aeschylus as the author of performances centered on song which also – crucially – exploit the full narrative potential of Homeric themes. Arguably, then, his originality lies in the way in which he brings together the various forms available to him: a culmination of the archaic which, dialectically, points in a new direction. Is the new form "democratic"? Not necessarily: the simultaneous invention of theater in Epicharmus' Syracuse shows that theater can be begotten of tyranny no less than of democracy. What the two historical moments share – Athens and Syracuse, at the beginning of the fifth century – is a sudden asymmetry between previously roughly equivalent cities. Athens in the Aegean; Syracuse in Sicily; suddenly prominent, to the point that a particular form of poetry, one which no longer is designed for export beyond its original city, gains enough confidence to become a central cultural form of that city.

the sense that he was an *Athenian* phenomenon.[285] (Finally, even if we prefer an earlier date for Herodotus, he represents such a radical generic departure that, in this case, it is harder to argue for the precise date of the major reception.) And so the first author whose entry into the canon clearly marks the beginning of a new form of canonicity, based upon Athens, was Euripides. (See pages 201–3 for the main fact: that Euripides was an extremely significant author indeed in his own lifetime.) Later on, Demosthenes and Aeschines, as well as Menander, in their respective genres, were certainly pre-eminent in their own generation. The key point, in both cases, is that it was already a given that the contemporary leading Athenian orators, or the leading comic authors in Athens, were figures of major Panhellenic valence: Athens, for them, was already canonical. (This is especially well documented for Menander, for which see page 206 above. The case of the orators is much more difficult to study, for the reasons explained pages 211–13: we do not have much by way of Hellenistic reception of rhetoric.) And so: the canonization of Athens was concentrated in stages A to B above. It was within the context of this canonization that Aeschylus changed his meaning – the last archaic poet became the first Athenian dramatist – and that Sophocles' reception expanded geographically. Herodotus may well have belonged in this context as well; and then the argument is that Demosthenes, Aeschines and Menander would each, in different ways, gain from the charisma of the place, accumulating in the years from 415 to 375.

Those dates are meaningful. We find that the canonization of Athens took place between the catastrophe of the Sicilian expedition and the Battle of Leuctra – coinciding with the generation of Spartan dominance.[286] The Athenian canon was formed neither because of Athens' democracy nor because of its empire. It was not politics which forced the Greeks to take Athens as their canon, and so, it appears, we must look for the *poetics* of the Athenian canon in its formation.

To understand the poetics of Athens in the years 415 to 375 we need to look back to the background against which this poetics was formed. Another set of dates that springs up from the table above is 470 to 415.

---

[285] See once again the evidence from Todisco (2006), quoted in n. 203. Taplin (2007: 88): "Sophocles did not 'travel' as well as the other two."

[286] Eras VIII–IX in Ober (2008: 64–6). Era VIII: "By the end of this era, Athens was at its lowest point..." Era IX: "Athenians hoped to regain control of parts of the old empire, but this proved a futile hope."

That is, we also note that – if indeed Sophocles' Panhellenic canonization is to be understood as a later development – there is a hiatus in the process of canonization. The canonization of Pindar, Aeschylus and Parmenides seems to mark a certain closure. Song is never canonized again; philosophy is dominated by responses to Parmenides; for more than 50 years, perhaps (the years of Athens' empire!), no new Panhellenic figures are made. A certain form of performance can no longer generate canonicity; an alternative is not yet ready. Perhaps for this reason: that poetics are made by past poetics; yet they are also constrained by social conditions. The Greeks in the middle of the fifth century were heirs to a poetics whose authorship was provided by the sympotic mimesis of singers. Socially, this was based on the central cultural position of the institution of the symposium, and what it reflected, ultimately, was the cross-polis network of the Greek elite. The rise of the democratic polis put an end to this centrality, and the symposium could no longer serve as guarantor of authorship. Imperial Athens could not, perhaps, yet create a new poetics; but it was powerful enough to close the old one.[287]

And then: stage A brings in the dramatic authors as well as that other Athenian performer, Socrates (Herodotus remains a unique exception, perched between performance and writing). One chronological step later, with stage B, we see the real admission of prose into the canon. Two transitions in the canon, then, cascaded: (A) the foregrounding of Athens; (B) the introduction of prose.

Now, the rise of prose is of course often discussed in the literature. Even as meta-historical accounts such as Snell's were going out of fashion, it was still possible to argue for the power of *literacy* to transform a culture's

---

[287] But note carefully: lyric depended, perhaps, on the symposium, with its aristocratic assumptions; epic did not. The consequences were that there were very few canonized epic authors (one invented, one perhaps historical), but also that *epic survived democracy*. Let me briefly spell out an important consequence of this. Homer would end up as the cornerstone of the Greek canon, and, while his epic poems did not project a polis of letters in the sense of the Athenian canon, they projected a set of *poleis* of letters. The world of Odysseus was a multi-city world, lacking major asymmetries between the many poleis. This historical reality was captured throughout the Homeric epics, in which, for instance, the mnemonics of the *Catalogue of Ships* was based on a shallow taxonomy of no more than one layer of hierarchy and a rough parity between the many places covered, the entire point being the great plurality of more or less equal places (see, e.g., Evans and Jasnow, 2014). Enshrined, Homer would certainly continue to provide at least one of the templates available for the Greek mental geography of their central landscapes: to give just one well-known example, references to Homer still structure Strabo's geography of Greece, Books VIII to X – produced in the Roman era! (For Strabo's reliance on Homer, see Biraschi, 2005, and Kim, 2007, for discussion.) The cultural memory of a Greek world, a pluralistic composite of many roughly comparable cities, would also serve to preserve, in monarchic empires, the attitudes and practices of the city state.

mentality so that one could display a new, literate mind at the turn of the fifth century: the starting point for grand theories of grand dichotomies, from Havelock (1963) to Svenbro (1988). Thomas (1992) marked a turn away from such grand theories, emphasizing instead the complicated nuance of the interaction of the written and the oral. More recent scholarship tends to follow Thomas' sobriety. The old theories of a grand dichotomy were indeed wrong about almost everything: the oral would always remain critical for Greek culture as a whole (as we have emphasized time and again), the written did not spring out of nowhere towards the end of the fifth century, the oral and the written always interact, in different ways, in different contexts; above all, the human mind is not so plastic that a single technology would radically alter it. There are no new minds; just new practices. The grand dichotomy theories were right about one thing, though: that there was a grand dichotomy. The structure of the literary field did change completely at a well-defined point near the end of the fifth century, and this had to do, ultimately, with the rise of prose and some kind of transformation in the dynamics of text and performance. Why is that?

My basic assumption remains simple: poetics are made by previous poetics. And so, even as the sympotic was downgraded as a vehicle of literary broadcast, the model of the performative author remained. A vividly imagined presence of the author, with his body, place, contests, would always remain the key regulating principle for ancient literature (hence the observations in section 2.2.4 above). And so, one needed another way of bringing in the sense of performance – not through direct imitation, and presence, but through indirect suggestion. One needed to be able to imagine a performance *from a distance*.

This could work only on the expectation that the audience could evoke the original sense of performance. And, for this purpose, one requires a familiarity with a particular set of performances. It is not surprising that, of all the sets of performances available in the Greek world in the fifth century BCE, that of Athens would stand the best chance of becoming widely familiar. And this for two reasons: not just the obvious one, that Athens now was the most famous city, but for a deeper reason, that Athens, with its democratic experiment, was also a place of endless public performance. Democracy made Athenian public events ever more central to the life of the city, and so it was not merely the most famous city but also the most intensely performative and thus, quite naturally, the focus around which performance could be imagined. And it was this, finally, which made Athens the school of Hellas. Elites could detest democracy but what they could not resist was a good show, and it was in this, above all, that Athens excelled.[288]

The system would quickly become self-sufficient. The principle is simple: in the Greek context, canonicity demands performativity. In the absence of actual mimetic performances as the site of literary reproduction, to obtain canonical status, works require their audiences to be in possession of a code of performativity: a code that translates a mere text into an imaginary performance. Such a code was found in the familiarity with the public culture of democratic Athens. And what provided this code? At some level, and perhaps most of all for the first generation that canonized Athens, this was direct familiarity with the fame of Athens. But, above all, this code could have been provided by the canonical Athenian texts themselves. As soon as a sufficient segment of the Athenian canon was assembled, familiarity with the canon would in and of itself constitute the code of performativity which allowed the reading of this very same canon as performative, hence as canonical. Such is the beauty of the Athenian canon and the reason why it always had *to travel together*– so that, almost a millennium later, Proclus could still remember Plato's precise relation to Thucydides. It all worked as a system – as the polis of letters.

The Athenian canon suggested that works depended on a code of performativity which came to depend on a site of performance – a city whose public life was keenly imagined.[289] Now, the earlier, archaic canon could not be sustained apart from the symposium, but the new, Athenian canon relied on texts alone, and on the information that they themselves provided. Once this principle had been achieved, texts meant for Panhellenic circulation began to circulate much more widely. One key feature of the late fifth and early fourth centuries, across the Greek-speaking world, was the explosion of writing in many cities, writings that no longer assumed, directly, a culture of reperformance and, instead, relied directly on written circulation and on the medium of prose. It was the way in which literature was reimagined, away from the symposium: emulating Athens' Panhellenic success as a cultural export, but without the benefit of Athens' fame. And it was only *after* this had been achieved – when prose

---

[288] The role of performance culture to Athens' democracy is by now familiar – though it was a shocking innovation to scholarship as it was introduced, late in the twentieth century. For a basic statement, see Goldhill and Osborne (1999).

[289] The argument of the following paragraph depends on claims concerning space and scale: when and where did prose authorship expand? I present here my conclusions; the evidence is summed up in section 6.1.1 below.

was established, across the Greek-speaking world as a whole – that Athens reached stage B of its canonization. Now it reached to prose, as well, and added in a new set of authors, who could trade on the charisma of the place, even apart from its staged performances.

The Athenian canon could now survive even though imperial Athens was gone, now becoming the ghost of a polis, a polis of letters. And this was because knowledge of the city as a site of performance now depended not on any contemporary realities but, instead, on the realities mediated through the canon itself. And, since this canon remained, and since it set the rules of any possible poetics, one could replace it, from now on, only through another, alternative site of public performance. And, since democracy, with its performance culture, was so sharply downgraded (see discussion, and qualifications, on pages 645–6 below), no other site of public life could begin to approach, in its level of intensity, that of Athens. The ghost of Athens, together with the memory of its culture of performance, was enough to block off the rise of a new, alternative canon and so to keep, in perpetuity, this system of the texts that carried their own code. No other texts could.

The rise of the Athenian empire gave rise to one first closure, that of the archaic poetics and the model of canonization based on the elite symposium. Its final collapse gave rise to the second closure, of the classical poetics and the model of canonization based on familiarity with the performativity of Athenian culture. The collapse of a poetics opens a period of experimentation, and we may notice the wide literary experimentation of the first generation or two of Hellenism. Little survived: how could works be canonized away from the central model of Athens? Of all the experiments, just one was successful, if in a qualified way. The performance of hexameter was always available as a central cultural model, and indeed, now that the literary field was conceived as an arena of explicit or implicit contest, works in hexameter that presented themselves as in contest with the two canonical hexameter poets filled a genuine gap in the literary system. The Hellenistic poets succeeded to the extent that they presented themselves as the belated contemporaries, and rivals, of the archaic poets. This served to complete the polis of letters, and so to cement its logic. Now that the molecule of literary competition was completed, there was truly no more room for expansion of the canon, and, once again, crucially, because there was no new Panhellenic site around which public performance could be imagined, no new works could be introduced so as to *replace* the old canon. It remained. Soon enough the memory of Athens would become, to the Greek-speaking elite, an invisible city more vivid than any one present. And such it would remain, to the heirs of Greek civilization.

This, then, is a sketch, accounting for the shape of the Greek canon. It is pursued here purely at a sociological level,[290] and, as I keep insisting, it is incomplete: we need to bring in, yet, space and scale. This is all, after all, a story about *imagining Athens*. And so this has to be recognized: that when the Greeks related to a literary work, they first of all located it, and it was for that reason that the more powerful location would have the more powerful hold on the canon. To understand the formation of the Athenian canon, then, we need to understand culture, as a spatial phenomenon: the subject of the following two chapters. In Chapter 3, we will look at space as a determining factor of Greek civilization; following that, in Chapter 4, we can begin to understand how, in the early third century, Athens was canonized – and how the culture of the Mediterranean was structured by an opposition between Athens and Alexandria.

As we move from the first to the second part of the book, we also move from the central canon of the performative genres to the wider literary field of specialized genres. And here it becomes important that canonization follows on performativity: the specialized genres, being non-performative, did not achieve any clear canonization prior to late antiquity. More than this: their authors wrote, with the model of the polis of letters, available from the canon – and hence aimed to make their name by inserting themselves within networks of contest against past masters. To become a notable author in a specialized genre, one made one's name against other names – and so, inspired by the canon, the great accumulation of greek specialized authors in competition – all the way down to late antiquity.

---

[290] I avoid in the main text the question of the quality of the canon, and it is clear that I believe that what makes texts canonical is that they were produced in a highly canon-making cultural context. This is not to say that I deny the quality of the canon. In fact, I believe canonical works, in general, are far superior in their quality to non-canonical works, and I suspect that this should be explained in social terms: the cultural context which is highly canon making is one in which the audience is riveted upon a particular cultural form. Likely enough, this kind of communication from the audience – all of Russia, waiting for its next poet; all of Attica, attending the Dionysia – contributes, in many different levels, to the quality of the work of art. As noted at the beginning of this chapter: this question calls for its own monograph!

# PART II

# *Space*

The discussion of canon was mostly about chronological stability: the main point was that one could find the same canon from the fourth century BCE down to the Byzantine transmission.

In the remaining parts of the book I look, first, at space, and then at scale. And, as I do so – *time*, too, becomes more significant: the discussion, from now on, often involves the changes in the distribution over space, or the rise and fall of scale. And so, the next two parts are arranged chronologically. In this part, concerning space, I discuss the rise, towards the beginning of the third century BCE, of a set of associations putting Athens and Alexandria in opposition. I finally discuss the dissolution of this opposition, in the first century BCE, with the Mediterranean renetworked around Roman patronage. In this part, then, I provide a background to the cultural history of the Hellenistic era. In the following part, concerning scale, I start once again from an observation concerning stability – the scale of authorship in the Hellenistic and Imperial eras, taken together, being fairly constant – and then produce a series of variations on the theme of stability, arranged in chronological order. One is the rapid rise in the scale of authorship during the fifth century BCE, preceding this era of stability. (This complements the account made just now in the previous chapter, concerning the formation of the Athenian canon: the missing piece in our argument so far is the rapid rise in prose in the late fifth century, which is best understood through the prism of scale.) Another is the possible dip in scale through the later Hellenistic era. The final moment of instability – and by far the most significant – is the collapse of the scale of authorship in the third century CE and beyond. In Part III, then, I revisit some of the ground covered in Parts I and II, but mostly I provide a background to the cultural history of the Imperial era and of late antiquity.

The next two parts, then, are mostly a study in the cultural history of post-classical antiquity. This is the era of monarchy, and it is in this era that our initial question arises: why did the ancient Mediterranean, throughout this period, preserve cultural attitudes that we typically explain by reference to democratic institutions? We have accounted for this, so far, in terms of the perseverance of a canon shaped by the city of Athens, though not in the sense that the contents of this canon reflected democratic ideals (not even the literate elites of the fifth and fourth century BCE would have had much interest in ideals of this kind: they preferred, even back then, Plato and Xenophon). Rather, the canon was, in and of itself, a polis of letters: strongly characterized individuals setting themselves in mutual contest. In this part, we note another feature of the legacy of Greek culture, only indirectly related to the democratic experiment: its diversity – as soon as one steps away from the performative canon. Alongside the central, performative canon, the Greeks produced, for many centuries following the end of Athenian domination, a variety of specialized works that never were canonized, and that never had a single order. The most important era for the specialized genres – the third century BCE – was marked by a major duality between a more "philosophical", Athenian culture and a more "scientific", Alexandrian culture. Perhaps the most significant legacy of Greek antiquity was its creation, in this period, of a relatively autonomous scientific culture. Later on, the Roman era was marked by a variety of eclectic responses to this rich variety. The Mediterranean could have produced, at around the year 300 BCE, an all-encompassing ideological structure, covering not just literature but also philosophical and technical knowledge. It failed to do so. The conditions which formed the homogeneous literary canon also prevented the unified canonization of anything other than literature. In this part, I try to explain how this happened.

CHAPTER 3

# Space, the Setting
## The Making of an Athens-against-Alexandria Mediterranean

Greek culture of the Hellenistic era had a simple and stable geographical pattern: Athens against Alexandria. This should call for an explanation. Following a methodological statement in section 1, I discuss in section 2 the ancient forces countervailing against any enduring centers, so that I end up emphasizing just how unlikely the duality of the Hellenistic Mediterranean was. Sections 3 and 4, then, try to account for the rise of these two centers, section 3 surveying the nature of Alexandria's centrality, and its historical route, section 4 following the geographical patterns of ancient philosophy and their culmination in the Hellenistic schools of Athens.

## 3.1 A Note on Measuring Cities

The preceding part of the book looked at authors and *counted* them: how many papyri by an author? How many mentions of an author in the TLG? This part looks at authors and *maps* them: where are they in the Mediterranean? This technique is open to doubt: just how well do we know the cultural geography of the ancient Mediterranean? Once again, I would argue – along the line of the claims above for the canon – *more than you might think*. To set some parameters, I use my sample of 100 ancient authors (based on the TLG canon, up to the end of the fifth century CE; see page 131 above). This may be divided into four categories.[1]

(1)     Authors for whom the overall contours of a biography/itinerary can be reconstructed with some confidence. Sometimes – more so for later authors – we possess a "real" biography (so Galen); as often, we can really understand an author's main trajectory with great confidence even when the data are very fragmentary (Eratosthenes: surely

---

[1] I try to avoid counting brief stays: each location stands for either a place of birth or a place that could have been reasonably considered, for at least some significant part of the author's active career, as his or her primary residence.

241

the overall trajectory was from Cyrene to Alexandria, with perhaps a little of Athens thrown in; or Androtion: from Athens to Megara). I found 43 such authors, the largest group.

(2)   Authors for whom there is no more than a tradition – albeit a fairly reliable one – attaching them to a particular place. Democritus was from Abdera? Probably this is true, though we do not know the precise significance of this connection (was he merely born there?). Was Geminus really from Rhodes? There was a classical comic author named Lysippus, who had a performance at the Dionysia; meager information, but he very likely was an Athenian, or at the very least worked there for a meaningful part of his career. In short, while there is a measure of uncertainty with this group, its locations are sufficiently informative and we should use them in our maps. I find 32 authors in this group.

(3)   Authors for whom spatial information is available but is vague to the point of being useless. This case is quite rare and arises especially from conflicting reports, when we cannot tell which of the several places associated with an individual was their "real" place. I find only eight authors in this group.

(4)   Finally, we have authors mentioned without any spatial references: 17 in my sample.

So, we find that 75 percent of (a not very large sample of) TLG authors are what we may call "localizable".

This represents above all the powerful sway of the *city*. (No individual in the 100-author sample used here is localizable by reference to an entire region but *not* to a city: so, Dionysius Thrax was in some unspecifiable sense "from Thrace"; but he was also quite certainly active in Alexandria.) We noted above, on page 128, that Diogenes Laertius spatially locates the individuals in his lists of homonyms about half the time, space coming as a close runner-up to genre as the key marker of identity. Indeed, we find that there would have to be special reasons for us to have an author attested – and yet remain unlocalized.[2] Sometimes these are medical authors (six in my list: the names are Cratippus, Lycomedes, Nymphodotus, Perigenes, Severus and Socrates). Such persons are mostly quoted in passing, with the name serving as a mere placeholder to better identify (and authenticate) a piece of pharmacological or clinical lore. We find a similar effect with the

---

[2]  This does not imply that authors in antiquity could not be active away from a city, in a state of exile. Indeed, the very markedness of "one's city" made this option the more significant: to be exiled was marked and powerful. Hence Selden's (1998) "alibis" and Whitmarsh's (2001a) exiles.

truly minor historians (seven in my list: Agathocles, Anaxicrates, Antiphanes, Comarchus, Diodorus, Heraclitus – a paradoxographer – and Heropythus). The few remaining exceptions are the truly obscure authors, especially post-classical poets. (Who was the Dionysius, the author of the *Bassarika*? The Hellenistic comic author Hipparchus? Where did Anyte come from? Or the epigrammatist Isidore?) We find the same principles we have noted all along: the Greek concept of author-ship is primarily performative, and for this reason it suggests an individual in space. Non-performative authors can sometimes escape spatiality but the presuppositions of performance linger, and it is for this reason that the spatial pattern of authors matters.

In the plurality of cases, the biography is mostly clear. But, almost as often, all we have is the mere attachment to a particular place. About half the time, when a biography is clear, it turns out that it is useful to think of the author as possessing more than a single location. And yet authors in the second category are almost always noted for just one city. And so, we probably miss a significant number of locations even for the authors we do list. This has an important implication. Suppose I find that, in a given genre and time, N percent of the authors are associated with place Y. In reality, more were: perhaps half as many again? "40 percent", then, means (even apart from the errors introduced by other biases of survival) "some-where between 50 percent and 70 percent", and so on. We shall return to this observation later on.

In this part of the book we look at the various geographical patterns of the distribution of authors across genres and periods.[3] But it is worthwhile to begin with a "baseline TLG" pattern – the one emerging from our random sample. Seventy-five individuals are localizable with reasonable confidence, and, of these, several are firmly associated with more than a single location. I have a total of 103 location markers, shown in Map 1.

---

[3] In Chapter 1 I pointed out that, while the extant papyrus fragments are but a small fraction of those circulating in antiquity, the size of the sample is big enough, and its composition random enough, to justify treating them as a fairly representative sample of all papyri in circulation (with the normal caveats of such samples). In this chapter, my evidence is the set of attested authors, which I use to draw conclusions for all authors in antiquity. Here my underlying argument is different. If we consider only the authors who already had a significant impact in antiquity, I suspect that most, or at the very least a great many of them, are still attested (though typically no longer extant, not even in fragmentary form). One always has to be aware of potential geographical biases in our evidence, but the prima facie implication of the pattern of geographical distribution among attested authors is that such, indeed, was the qualitative character of the distribution among significant authors in antiquity itself. (It is always reasonable to assume that the truly obscure authors, no longer attested, had a much more equal geographical distribution.) This argument relies on considerations of absolute scale and will therefore be developed – in some detail! – only in Chapter 5.

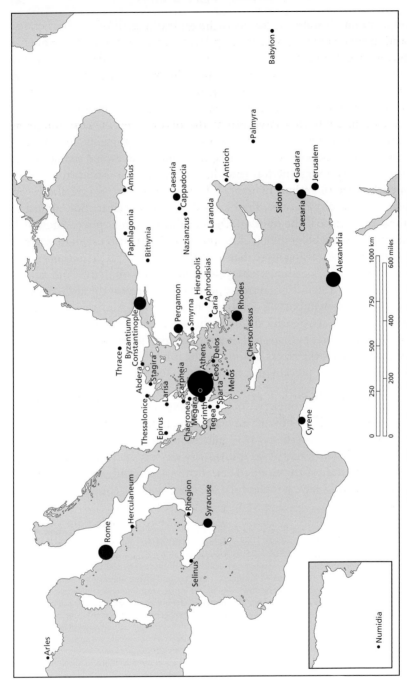

Map 1   The locations of authors randomly selected from the TLG

The fundamental observation is the great diffusion of places. The 103 location markers are spread over 47 locations; 33 of these appear exactly once and eight appear two to three times. The few more frequent places are Rhodes (four times), and then: Constantinople, Rome, Alexandria (six, eight and eight, respectively) and Athens, in a category of its own, with 25 located individuals – a third of the total.

This represents to a large extent the bias of the TLG. It counts as "author" an individual for whom we have at least a meaningful testimony – the definition of "meaningful" being quite elastic, however, it was extended much further for the central performative genres and much less for the scientific genres. In the terms introduced above, on page 216, the TLG surveys very extensively the *minor* authors, but it is much less effective for the *specialized* authors.[4] Thus, the gap between Athens, on the one hand, and Alexandria and Rome, on the other hand, is exaggerated in my sample. What the map does tell us is that, in the period of more than six centuries between the foundation of Alexandria and the foundation of Constantinople, the geography of the ancient Mediterranean was truly a tale of three cities: Athens, Alexandria and, later on, Rome. And, as we shall see, no other city in particular: other centers are always specific to a particular genre, and transient. Let us begin to see this in detail.

## 3.2   The Unlikelihood of an Enduring Center: Cities in Transit

It is surprisingly easy to locate most ancient authors – and, when we do so, the results are predictable. Generally speaking, authors tend to cluster according to their genres. This is surprising: even when Greeks did develop a clearly defined spatial system, this was in a social setting in which cultural practices hardly ever developed enduring institutional support and, instead, were conducted primarily as isolated generational events. The pull of space, generally speaking, was not the pull of a fixed institution.

General surveys still sometimes tell the linear narrative with individuals picking up, in sequence, impersonal continuities: "The History of

---

[4] The TLG category "medical author" has 56 entries; the category "comic author" has 171. I shall return to discuss the absolute numbers of practitioners in the various genres in the following part, but we can note already that this ratio is wrong by perhaps an order of magnitude. One consequence of this sampling bias in the TLG is that the number of localizable individuals is exaggerated (thus, not 75 percent but perhaps 50 percent of all ancient attested authors were localizable). Another consequence is to make my baseline map tilt to the old Greek core and even more to the mainland. (This, as we will note below, reflects a "literary" bias.)

Philosophy", "The History of Science"...[5] For Greek culture, this
Hegelian relay race is uniquely inept. Impersonal continuity makes sense,
to a point, in the description of social institutions – those that stay when
people don't. But Greek cultural life was typically structured not so much
around institutions as around genres. Thus there was no question of
individuals looking, actively, to become, say, the next "Regius Professor
of Mathematics". Instead, different individuals could choose to pick, or
not, one of the genres available on the cultural menu. Instead of lingering
institutions, we have the flickers of fascination: an individual pursuing a
field and perhaps acquiring a following – which dissipates soon after his
death.[6]

And so we recall: prior to Athens, literature does not develop spatial
foci – with two very qualified exceptions. There was, first, the Lesbian
moment, with Sappho and Alcaeus active in the same island, at the same
time. They establish Aeolian as a viable literary form, and yet there is no
school of poetry associated with Lesbos; by the next generation poetry is
already unmoored from Lesbos (Aeolian, but not Lesbos: genre, not institution).[7] And then: Simonides and his nephew Bacchylides, both active in
Ceus near the end of the sixth century and the beginning of the fifth: two
generations of poets. (In this case, this is possibly a *family* tradition.)[8] In both
cases the poets do not develop a distinctive local tradition – and there is no
real reason to suppose that behind the two extant authors lie many more,
now lost. We find, then, a small, brief clustering.

Philosophy does have many centers; even so, we notice several two-
generation effects – a figure, his immediate echo – and then, no more. I

[5] Consider Heath (1921), *A History of Greek Mathematics*. Volume I is titled, simply, *From Thales to Euclid*. Volume II is titled *From Aristarchus to Diophantus*. Take, for instance, volume II, chapter 15. This is titled "The Successors of the Great Geometers" and is arranged by the following sections: "Nicomedes"; "Diocles"; "Perseus"; "Isoperimetric Figures"; "Zenodorus"; "Hypsicles"; "Dionysodorus"; "Posidonoius"; "Geminus" – and so, almost two centuries pass by, and the relay race proceeds (incredibly misleading, for this transitional era; see p. 467 below). Antiquated? But Lindberg (1992) – still probably the best survey book in early science – follows a similar, if much more abbreviated, trajectory.

[6] The phenomenon I refer to as cities in transit is noted by Collins (1998: 89–97). His approach is perhaps marred, however – if I understand him correctly – by a tendency to ascribe an institutional reality to the many "schools of philosophy". The underlying reality of cultural life, in antiquity, was genre and not institution (I consider this the one blind spot in Collins' excellent study, which forms an obvious inspiration for my own).

[7] It is typical that scholarship into archaic lyric hardly ever attempted to extract any meaning out of the spatio-temporal coincidence of the two poets; for a rare exception (which focuses, however, on the ritual setting, not on any "school of poetry"), see Nagy (2007).

[8] Pelliccia (2009: 241) is skeptical (see references in Hutchinson, 2001: 321), but the base probability for such a family relation – in a fairly small island! – is considerable (compare the contemporary case of Aeschylus' family of poet-tragedians: p. 197 above).

emphasize such cases when the original voice, and his immediate echo, are close in space. Here is a list of some of the clearer earlier cases.

| Original voice | Immediate echo |
| --- | --- |
| Thales | Anaximander, Anaximenes |
| Pythagoras | Hippasus[9] |
| Parmenides | Zeno |
| Leucippus[10] | Democritus |
| Philoaus | Archytas |
| Pyrrho | Timon[11] |

In the following cases it appears clear that the philosopher served as an original voice, but his immediate echo is constituted by figures that are so minor and doubtful (or so individually rich) that this is best described as "X and his followers". Among such powerful, original voices are:

Socrates
Euclid of Megara
Phaedo of Elis[12]
Diogenes the Cynic
Diodorus Cronus[13]

---

[9] The biographical tradition on "Pythagoreans" is of course weak and contradictory; see Zhmud (2012: chap. 3). I take Hippasus to stand in for the generation of Pythagoras' followers, on the assumption that the basic notion that there was *some* following is indeed correct; the key point is precisely that ancient Pythagoreanism as a historical phenomenon falls into place the moment we recognize it not as an institutional-like continuity but, instead, as two separate generational events, around Pythagoras himself and then around Philoaus.

[10] Knowledge of Leucippus' origins – indeed, of anything distinctive about his philosophy – was lost early in antiquity; Stenzel 1925 (s.v. RE) preferred, rightly, not to choose between the very weak ancient testimonies that positioned him in either Elea, Miletus or Abdera. It was a case when the immediate echo drowned out the original voice. And yet the parallels provided here make it somewhat more likely that he was, after all, from Abdera – one of the options reported by Diogenes Laertius.

[11] Here is a case of a two-generation phenomenon reinterpreted in antiquity itself as the first two links in a much longer chain: ancient authors imagined an entire set of skeptic philosophers between Timon and Aenesidemus (see Decleva Caizzi, 1992, summed up 188–9: Aenesidemus in fact revived a dead tradition, extant purely in the form of ancient writing; see more in Chapter 4, p. 478). "Timon...was never the head of a skeptic school... Diogenes lists other students of Pyrrho, but they were never organized" (Clayman, 2009: 10).

[12] I return on pp. 313–14 below to discuss the evidence for the Socratic schools.

[13] Sedley (1977: 75–6): "The school itself [Diodorus Cronus' dialecticians] was perhaps somewhat makeshift in character. It barely outlasted two generations." Notice that, later on, philosophy is swallowed by the Athenian schools and so develops continuities; but that, as soon as it emerges away from them, we find similar local two-generation events, starting with Posidonius and his followers (Edelstein and Kidd, 1972–99: I.13–14). Much of the activity in this case appears to be epitomizing

During the fourth century three cities try for longer continuities.

(1) In Cyrene, a tradition is maintained by a family. Aristippus was a Socratic, pivoting away and returning to his home town, Cyrene; his daughter Arete, as well as his grandson Aristippus the Younger, both were his "followers", and then it appears that the voice of Aristippus the Younger could have had an immediate echo in Cyrene at around the turn of the third century.[14]

(2) Anything between zero and two philosophical schools, but at any rate considerable philosophical activity, is associated with fourth-century Megara, otherwise not a major center[15] – so, presumably a specifically *philosophical* center. Euclid of Megara pivoted away from Socrates – to have followers at all?[16] To inspire, directly or indirectly, Stilpo and Diodorus Cronus (was he at all associated with Megara?) – both of whom then inspired others?[17]

None of the evidence is clear but what we dimly sense in such episodes is the overlying pattern of several short-lived traditions: the Aristippus family

and editing, a pattern repeated much later with the pairs Epictetus/Arrian and then Plotinus/ Porphyry (followed by a pivoting away to Iamblichus).

[14] The evidence is collected in Giannantoni (1990–1: II.1–133), but the brief account in Dorandi (1999a: 47) is decisive.

[15] It is number 15 in Ober's set of 20 successful classical poleis (Ober, 2008: 47), number 24 in coin counts (50). EANS has three entries for Megara, one later and dubious, but the earlier ones are intriguing: the engineer Eupalinus, whom we will meet in p. 279 below at the court of the tyrant Polycrates of Samos; and Herodicus, a major gymnastic trainer of the fifth century, who settled, however, in the Megarian colony Selumbria. So, the two Megarians who rose to cultural prominence prior to Megara's philosophical century did so away from their native city.

[16] Those who are said to be among his followers, and who could fit the chronological frame of immediate echoes, are dubious and obscure: Euboulides, Ichthyas, Cleinomachus, Diocleides, Bryson of Heraclia. "Sur les disciples immédiats d'Euclide, peu de choses sont assurées" (Muller, DPA, s.v. Euclide de Mégare, 276, who indeed also remarks, correctly: "Les mégariques n'avaient d'institutions comparable à l'Académie ou au Lycée." Of course; no one did.).

[17] Sedley (1977: 75–7) cuts through the fog. The "eristikoi" (petty debaters – certainly a pejorative term) may be seen as Euboulides – perhaps a follower of Euclid himself, so pivoting away from him? – and then the immediate response to him; those who are strictly called "Megarians" are a later group, that of Stilpo and the response to him. Diodorus Cronus was certainly the original voice of the third of those groups – the "Dialecticians" – then echoed by Philo; a few other obscure names are mentioned. On both their localities it is known only that Diodorus originated from Iasus. Diodorus was active in Alexandria early in the third century BCE, and the latest that we hear of anyone called a "Dialectician" is near the middle of the third century. Sedley (1977: 77): "The dialektikoi. . .are those who took up the constructive study of logic. . .brought together by a common interest in propositional logic. . . [T]his. . .explains the brevity of their separate existence: within a few decades propositional logic found itself a home in the Stoa, thus depriving the Dialectical school of its raison d'être." At this point it should be clear that I think such formulations should be flipped around. The brevity of a given cultural tradition such as the "Dialecticians" is no puzzle – it is in the nature of ancient cultural practices to survive for roughly two generations; the longer inertia of the Stoa, instead, is what calls for explanation.

and then the response to Aristippus the Younger; the followers of Euclid, of Diodorus, of Stilpo.

(3) Finally, the rise of the philosophical schools in Athens should be seen against this background, with an especially rich pattern of layers. It is perfectly normal for Plato to pivot away from Socrates to create his own, very distinct, philosophical identity.[18] Plato's own voice developed its own echo – and, then, it was natural for Aristotle to pivot away again and indeed to try out other cities. Aristotle's return to Athens, as well as the decision of some other followers of Plato *not to pivot away*, eventually copied by Aristotle's pupils, both mark a turning point (to which I return at the end of this chapter). We begin to sense that Athens, around the end of the fourth century, was an exceptional place. (I return to discuss Athenian school formation in full, critical detail in section 3.4.2 below).

In fields other than philosophy, too, we may note the pattern of small, local or short-lived clusters. In the exact sciences we have, first, Hippocrates and Oenopides, both of Chios – a coincidence? (The first had an obscure follower, a certain Aeschylus.)[19] The concentration at Cyzicus at around the middle of the fourth century is hardly a coincidence: we have four names – Athenaeus, Callippus, Helicon and Polemarchus – to whom we may add the somewhat later Protagoras, as well as the undated Adrastus and Apollodorus. Epicurus attacks – in *On Nature* XI – a group engaged, above all, with astronomy, active in Cyzicus (Sedley, 1976); it is intriguing in this context that Diogenes Laertius reports that Eudoxus, late in his brief career, taught in Cyzicus. Do we see here Eudoxus, as an original voice – and then his echo, not in his native town but in a town in which he was, literally, in transit? It is interesting to reflect on this episode, Epicurus against Eudoxus. Epicurus was probably writing around 310, from nearby Lampsacus – where he was briefly located following a failed attempt to set up a school in Mytilene. Soon enough he would relocate to Athens, and become part of the great gelling of Greek philosophy. But at that moment, about 310, he provides us with a picture of cities in transit; the

---

[18] But since he was stuck in the same city as Socrates – not just any city, but Athens! – Plato had to build greater distance. He could be his own person only by becoming the opposite of Socrates the pure speaker – so he became Plato, the pure writer. Phaedo, Euclid or Aristippus switched cities; Plato switched genres.

[19] For Oenopides, see Bodnár (2007); of his biography, nothing is known save (inferred) date and location (stated by our city-minded sources). Aeschylus emerges out of a single note by Aristotle, *Meteorology* I.6, in which he is explicitly and confidently (342b36) said to have been Hippocrates' pupil (see discussion in Wilson, 2008).

ship of philosophy passing, briefly, next to that of astronomy. But they soon embark elsewhere and the entire meeting comes to nothing.

The bulk of creative work in advanced mathematics seems to have been pursued primarily by no more than two brief networks: the one described in Proclus' summary of the history of early Greek mathematics (Proclus, in *Eucl.* I 66–8, standardly understood to derive from Eudemus' history of Greek geometry),[20] and the one constituted by Archimedes, his correspondents and the authors in the following generation, reacting to Archimedes' achievement. Since we can see here the entirety of an intellectual pursuit – in the terms of generations – this is worth pursuing in more detail.

Proclus' list includes three names from the archaic era: Thales, Mamercus and Pythagoras; Hippias of Elis, Anaxagoras and Oenopides are mentioned based on their appearances in Platonic dialogues (the *Hippias* and the *Amatores*, respectively; those are the more likely to be Proclus' own Platonist additions to the original list). Following are:

> Hippocrates of Chios, Theodorus of Cyrene, Plato himself.[21]

And then:

> Leodamas of Thasos, Archytas of Tarentum, Theaetetus of Athens, Neoclides, his pupil Leon, Eudoxus of Cnidus (said to be a little later than Leon), Amyclas of Heracleia, Menaechmus (said to be a student of Eudoxus), Dinostratus, his brother, Theudius of Magnesia, Athenaeus of Cyzicus, Hermotimus of Colophon, Philippus of Mende.

Several of these individuals are mere names known only from Proclus' summary (these are Amyclas, Athenaeus, Hermotimus, Leon, Neoclides and Theudius), but the traditions that Theaetetus, Archytas, Eudoxus and Philippus knew Plato personally are quite solid, and there is no special reason to doubt Proclus' claim that so did the much less well known Leodamas. We are told that Theatetus was Theodorus' student, that Menaechmus was Eudoxus' student, that Dinostratus was Menaechmus' brother. We end up with a tight network whose core is Plato. This impression may well be because later tradition knew most and cared most about Plato, and Proclus himself produces his survey for the express purpose of emphasizing Plato's role in early mathematics. We do not need to subscribe to this particular philosophical interpretation to judge that a significant part of the early creative contributions to pure Greek mathematics was made by a single network, active mostly from the early fourth

---

[20] See Zhmud (2002: 179–90).     [21] Plato was most likely added to the list by Proclus.

century to about its middle, sufficiently close in time to constitute a near-generational event.

Then again, starting with Archimedes' correspondence with Conon, Dositheus and Eratosthenes, we may follow a similar concentration of contributions to pure mathematics; several authors are evidently responding to Archimedes' challenge, for instance in completing apparent lacunae in his works (Dionysodorus, Diocles), or in general in producing work which evidently aims at a similar type of brilliance, for instance in Apollonius' calculations.[22] Apollonius himself corresponds with Attalus, Eudemus and Philonides, and we may add the names of several other authors whose work clearly resonates with the interests of Archimedes and Apollonius: Knorr (1986: chap. 6) singles out for discussion, besides such names mentioned above, those of Nicomedes, Perseus and Zenodorus. Once again, the details might be debatable, but it seems clear that another significant part of the creative contribution to pure mathematics was made by a single network, active mostly from the middle of the third century to the early second century, connected via Alexandria.

Indeed, it is arguable that very little creative work in pure mathematics was ever done in the Greek world outside these two networks. In between the two networks we find Euclid's efforts of compilation, as well as a group of astronomers (Aristarchus was of course an astronomer; as were Aristyllus and Timocharis, charting the Alexandrian sky; and Pheidias, Archimedes' father; it is perhaps significant that Archimedes' primary correspondents, Conon and Dositheus, could well have been primarily astronomers, so that Archimedes could well have initiated the new turn towards pure mathematics); I will return below to characterize and qualify the character of this moment in the foundation of Alexandria. Later than Archimedes' network, we find sporadic responses as well as mostly efforts of collection and commentary – and, of course, a more creative work in the mixed sciences and in particular in astronomy (Hipparchus, already in the second century BCE, leads in this new direction; following him, there seems to be a genuine hiatus in the exact sciences: I return to this in Chapter 4).

This historical background is useful, once again, for the question often raised in the general histories: why did creative work in Greek mathematics

---

[22] I argue in Netz (2017b) that Apollonius might be dated to the generation immediately following Archimedes and so was in direct competition with him (such was the traditional dating, but since the work of Toomer, Gallo and Frazer in the 1970s a new orthodoxy has set in, according to which Apollonius was separated from Archimedes by at least 50 years). If so, it becomes possible to compress nearly the entirety of the creative work in advanced mathematics in the Hellenistic era within a generation and a half.

decline following its Hellenistic heyday?[23] Such a question is meaningful only in the context of the Hegelian relay race. In reality, Greek mathematics never declined; it always progressed brilliantly – in the two episodes in which it was pursued.

Or back to astronomy. Here is the historical observation: Greek astronomers (primarily Eudoxus) first developed an astronomy in which the motions of the planets are produced by a combination of homocentric spheres. Later on they developed a new astronomy, in which the motions of the planets are produced by a combination of epicycles and eccentrics.[24] Why is that? The only ancient evidence on this question comes from the context of the Roman era's renewed synthesis of science and philosophy. Sosigenes, a second-century CE Aristotelian, in his commentary upon *Metaphysics* Λ, had to confront the gap between the astronomy assumed by Aristotle and that used by contemporary astronomers. To account for this, he looked for objections raised to the astronomy assumed by Aristotle – that is, Eudoxus' model of homocentric spheres:[25] the strongest he could find was Autolycus' observation that some planets' brightness varies, suggesting that their distance from the earth is not a constant (impossible within the model of homocentric spheres). The implicit historical account, then, is that a certain observation by Autolycus was enough to kill an entire research program with the authority of Eudoxus behind it. While modern scholars sometimes advocate alternative accounts for this intellectual transition,[26] and some indeed go as far as to doubt the very existence of an early mathematical astronomy,[27] this – really, no more than a late commentator's speculation – has become the standard modern interpretation.[28] A crucial

[23] Heath's position (1921: II.197) is that there was simply no more room for progress, on the type of questions raised within Greek mathematics, by the techniques available; I offer (in Netz, 1999a: 237–8) no more than a variation on this observation, when I argue that Greek mathematics was confined to the "third floor" – the results based on the tools based on the *Elements* – but it is obvious, from the examples of both Islamic mathematics and the sixteenth century and early seventeenth, that, even within the confines of this third floor, there was so much to be achieved. The tools did not stop Greek mathematicians from achieving more; they stopped, on their own.
[24] Any history of Greek astronomy would cover the two models, though the question of the transition between them is usually avoided. Evans (1998: 305–12, 337–42) is precise and accessible.
[25] See Mendell (n.d.: 16) and Bowen (2013a: 165).
[26] Yavetz (2010) – whose reconstruction of the homocentric spheres model achieves high empirical success at the cost of analytic complexity – points out the computational advantages of an epicycles/eccenters model. Evans and Carman (2014) point out the (related) advantages of an epicycles/eccenters model for the sake of mechanical constructions (which may well have emerged only in the third century; see pp. 358–60 below on display mechanics in the Hellenistic world).
[27] So Goldstein and Bowen (1983) and in many publications since.
[28] "All homocentric systems have one severe drawback which in antiquity led to their early demise...the distance between a planet and the earth cannot vary" (Kuhn, 1957: 59).

point seems to have been overlooked: *all* the ancient authors who are known to have contributed to the homocentric spheres model were associated with fourth-century Cyzicus. In this case, we are especially misled by the picture of the Hegelian relay race – which makes us think of a single astronomical research program, whose transitions therefore require an account in terms of empirical refutations. In fact, there was no "single astronomy", going first through a homocentric spheres model stage and then moving on to epicycles. There were at least *two* – each taking its own approach. There was a particular generational event in Cyzicus, in the second half of the fourth century, and another (Apollonius to Hipparchus?), at the beginning of the second century. The first, but not the second, engaged with homocentric spheres; the second, but not the first, engaged with epicycles and eccentrics: an astronomical replay, with some of the same figures, and with a generation's delay, of the two episodes of pure mathematics.[29]

A similar observation can be made concerning the Hellenistic anatomical tradition. A deeply original departure in the early third century BCE – specific to Alexandria?[30] – was made by the generation of Herophilus and Erasistratus. Moving beyond the standard traditions of clinical practice aided by speculative accounts of the human body, such doctors engaged with a careful project of dissection, perhaps to some extent vivisection, of animals and likely also humans, resulting in a massive renaming of the human body as well as extended physiological theorizing. And then, following these two authors, Greek medicine reverts to form; for many generations there appears to be little evidence for any dissection or vivisection; by the middle of the third century BCE Hippocratic commentary seems to have become, instead, the central form of medical authorship. Once again, this is easy to tell as a story of decline, or perhaps of cultural taboos emerging to block the practice of dissection.[31] And this rupture, too, becomes much less enigmatic as soon as we recognize that Greek cultural traditions are local and bound to individuals and their immediate followers. Indeed, Herophilus'

---

[29] It seems that the original voice of homocentric spheres was Eudoxus, a late member of the first network of Greek mathematics, and that the original voice of epicycles and eccenters could have been Apollonius, a later member of the second network of Greek mathematics – once again, a case of a *pivot*: traditions of practice extend beyond the second generation by changing, a member of the second generation acting once as a response for the first generation and again, differently, as an original voice answered in the third generation.

[30] See p. 291, n.78, below for Erasistratus and Alexandria; Herophilus' Alexandrian connection is certain.

[31] From the abstract to von Staden (1992): "The paper explores possible reasons for the mysteriously abrupt disappearance of systematic human dissection from Greek science after the death of Erasistratus and Herophilus." But why should we consider disappearances to be mysterious?

immediate *Herophilean* followers are few[32] and his most prominent
disciple – Philinus – pivots away, in the typical manner we now know
from Greek philosophy, to form his rival empiricist approach (and to be
echoed by Serapion and a small cluster of "empiricists" around the end of
the third century; then, another cluster appears, near the beginning of the
first, theoretically distinct from the first cluster).[33] Later than Herophilus'
immediate followers we have, over the next two centuries, six names of
Alexandrian physicians, none prominent, who chose to attach themselves
to the fame of Herophilus; and then – a new school in the temple of Men
Karou in Phrygia, where three generations of physicians, identifying
themselves as Herophileans, were active from the later first century
BCE to the early first century CE – more than a two-generation episode
and clearly something approaching the foundation of a local institution,
but one which did not survive long, however, beyond the normal bounds
of an ancient cultural practice.[34] And yet, in none of those later echoes
was there a repetition of what, to us, is the most distinctive feature of the
original generation.

    Alexandria dominated grammar even more than it did medicine. The
one serious rival it had in the Hellenistic period itself was a school in
Pergamon in the middle of the second century BCE – yet another example
of a single individual with a powerful original voice, once again finding
only short-lived echoes. Crates (born, perhaps, in Mallos, and active in
Pergamon; not too much should be made of a single visit to Rome) was
indeed    the    most    important    ancient    grammarian    among    non-
Alexandrians.[35] Thanks to the influence of his work, a group of names
associated with him is further attested: at this zenith moment of around 150
BCE, then, Pergamon has six names to Alexandria's ten (in the very rough
enumeration that underlies the map on page 274 below). But this does not
mean that, at this moment, the Mediterranean became dual. Rather, it
means that grammar, at this point, became so important that it could
spawn local imitations of Alexandria. And this is all: there is no later
tradition of grammar in Pergamon – yet another city in transit.

---

[32] Von Staden (1989) counts four likely Herophileans, likely from the third century: Andreas,
   Callianax, Callimachus and Bacchius.
[33] In the first cluster we may note, beyond Philinus and Serapion themselves, Apollonius the Elder,
   Apollonius "Biblas" and Glaucias of Tarentum; in the second cluster we note Ptolemy of Cyrene,
   Zophyrus of Alexandria, Lycus of Naples, Diodorus, Archibius, Heraclides of Tarentum – credited
   with the theoretical reorientation of the tradition of empiricism at his time (Frede, 1987) – and
   Apollonius of Citium.
[34] Von Staden (1989: 529).     [35] For Crates' immediate influence, see Broggiato (2001, esp. 7–8).

Scholars are amazed by the short life of Alexandrian anatomy: so brilliant, and yet cut so short! But it should be seen as no more surprising than the short life of Alexandrian hexameter and elegy – and it ought to be emphasized how short that life was. "Hellenistic poetry" is, above all, the poetry of a particular generation, with authors such as Apollonius, Aratus and Theocritus responding to the original voice of Callimachus.[36] Alexandrian poetry is an episode – reflected, centuries later, in yet another local episode, that of Augustan poetry, a sudden burst of poetic activity in a particular place, in a particular language. Needless to say, the burst dies out, and scholars ever since have had to account for the decline of Latin poetry: following the Augustan generation, Latin literature entered its "silver age". This was a nineteenth-century verdict but one essentially repeated by our own, present-day, less judgemental scholars: "Augustus died at about the same time as Livy and Ovid, whose deaths set a term to the great achievements of Augustan prose and verse. The immediately subsequent years were comparatively fallow" (Mayer, 2008: 58). Indeed, this seems to be the rule everywhere in antiquity: the years of achievement are followed by the fallow years. This is because fields are never in continuous cultivation. Cultural life followed more the logic of slash-and-burn agriculture: quickly setting up a new tradition, exhausting it, moving elsewhere.

We have noted on page 233, note 287, how, with the enduring canonicity of Homer, the Greeks always preserved a polycentric image of their own world, one without any single city as clearly ascendant. Indeed, in a rather basic sense, this is simply what archaic space was like.[37] All of the above

---

[36] This is, of course, already an interpretation: there were more poets active in Alexandria, later than the generation of the followers of Callimachus (though it does appear that, quantitatively, poetry does peak early on; see p. 570 below). Nevertheless, we have reached a point at which we may be justified in deriving, from the later reception, reasonable guesses for the immediate impact, and the conclusion is that, within Hellenistic poetry, it was only this generational event that had a major presence as a wider cultural event.

[37] Ober (2008: 43–53) measures the success/prominence of archaic and classical cities. His main interest is Athens' success, which is mostly driven by the classical divergence, however. As he points out (47), "The other 19 top poleis of the top 20 are grouped quite tightly around the mean." In general it is hard to find stable regional systems in archaic culture. There are plenty of regional-looking labels, such as the dialect forms in poetry – which are markers of genre, however, not of ethnicity, let alone region (Mickey, 1981); the case is even clearer for the markers such as "Doric" in architecture or music, when it is clear that ethnics are no more than good to think with, while, in practice, a greater variety of capitals and of keys could everywhere be found (for architecture, see Barletta, 2001; for music, Woerther, 2008). Indeed, the very ethnic terms could have been applied later, certainly in the case of architecture (for which our evidence really begins only with Vitruvius!), and the very notion of Doric and Ionic ethnicity could have been less clearly defined in the archaic era itself (Hall, 1997), coming into sharper relief only with the antagonism between Athens and Sparta of the fifth century (Alty, 1982) – a consequence, once again, of the breaking of symmetry with the rise of Athens. The

does have one glaring exception, however – in the Athens of the fifth and fourth centuries. What emerges from this account, then, is, once again, the sheer exceptional character of classical Athens. I think we do not pause sufficiently to consider how exceptional this was, because we think of Athens on the model of a Paris, a London, and then take it for granted that national literatures possess national centers. But Greek culture was not national and it started out, in the archaic era, without possession of a center. Within the Greek context, the phenomenon of classical Athens was unprecedented and, in some ways, never repeated. It should loom large in our explanations of other, later concentrations.

On the other hand – now putting the Greeks in a wider, comparative context – it is, indeed, the Greek *weakness* of enduring centers that is inherently surprising. There is a very good reason why systems, in general, would tend to develop centers: because of network effects. It makes sense to be where others are already, hence agglomeration naturally takes off (I return to discuss this on pages 258–63 below).[38] This simple logic seems often *not* to have operated in Greek culture – likely because, against the centripetal force of the network effect, there were often set the centrifugal forces of the epichoric: culture, attached to particular places. The strong spatial dimension of each individual's life, marked in terms of one's city, militated against the rise of, as it were, *impersonal* centers. And so, even the rise of Athens as a center for the performative genres took place not so much through the logic of the network effect but through the logic of the local, the epichoric: Athens, for a while, became *the* local.

The end of the centrality of classical Athens gave rise, in some sense, to a renewed epichoric Greek world, with its emphasis on the plurality of local experiences. At any rate, what this section underlines is that, through many centuries, the Greeks never developed a model of culture, produced by a stable, institutional center. Continuities, such as we find, have to be accounted for otherwise.

And yet: in the Hellenistic era, in some cultural areas, there was a renewed emphasis on Athens as a center; in others, Alexandria is the central

---

world of Odysseus, with its many dispersed cities, simply did not develop any neat structuring geographies – and its centers, such as they were, were all ex-territorial – the main cultic centers such as Delphi and Olympia (a familiar observation: see, e.g., Snodgrass, 1986: 54).

[38] There is now a lively tradition of economic studies of agglomeration, its origins and its advantages: for a survey, see Fujita and Thisse (2002). Such ideas go back at least to Marshall (1890), who evidently reflected on the experience of industrial concentration in England – specifically in terms of the geographical advantages presented by the communities of technical knowledge. It is, once again, a field in which marketable commodities follow a logic that was first evidenced in non-monetary, cultural transactions.

city. The argument of the remainder of this chapter is that, in both cases, indeed, institution making, in and of itself, does not explain the centrality. I will be skeptical concerning the role of enduring institutions in Alexandria; I argue that, in the case of Athens, institutions follow centralization, and not vice versa. This, then, is the key outcome of the preceding section. If not institutions, what? My argument would be that the duopoly of Alexandria and Athens should be understood in two distinct ways: there were different modes of centrality at work. Both, however, reacted to the same reality: a Mediterranean, facing the closure of the Athenian performative canon. We shall follow this, first for Alexandria, then for Athens. In each case, we will need to see the detail of the centrality of each city, in the Hellenistic era; followed by an account of the rise of that centrality.

## 3.3 The Road to Alexandria

In what follows, I first discuss in section 3.3.1 the nature of Alexandria's centrality, considering the cultural history of the Mediterranean in the longue durée. The fundamental observation, there, is that, seen against this large background, Hellenistic Alexandria stands out as a model of centrality that does, after all, seem to be based on the advantages of the central node in a network. On a cross-cultural comparison, Alexandria was *normal*. In the following section 3.3.2 I discuss the nature of patronage before and after the rise of Macedon – and its potential meaning in the generations of Alexandria's foundation. Patronage mattered: but what mattered even more was the rise of a set of cultural pursuits that were more easily exportable. As the canon closed, with its performative-epichoric character, other, perhaps less epichoric practices, came to matter more. Finally, in section 3.3.3, I look at the granular history of Alexandrian culture in the early third century: it was above all a moment of a rise in local scale, and of the crystallization of intellectual practices, that created Alexandria's unique centrality.

### 3.3.1 *Alexandria and the Scientific Mediterranean*

The goal of this section is to collect the geographical evidence for the pull of Alexandria as a center for science in the Hellenistic era. This, then, is the most map-intensive segment of our discussion. By comparing maps – by noticing how distributions are analogous, or else contrast with each other – we may begin to form hypotheses concerning the historical formation of these distributions.

And so to my first analogy. The following pair of maps, Maps 2 and 3, display the known geographical distribution of mathematical authors in two periods: before and after the foundation of Alexandria.[39]

The analogy is clear enough. In both maps, just one center is discernible: Athens in Map 2, Alexandria in Map 3. In both, the center is dominant but not absolutely so: there are many authors that can be connected to other places as well. Indeed, roughly the same fraction of the localizable authors are *known* to be associated with the central place in both maps. These are about 50 percent with Athens, about 40 percent with Alexandria; the lower centrality of Alexandria might well be a fluke; it may simply reflect our even greater ignorance of later biographies in the exact sciences. As noted above, on page 243, both numbers provide a low estimate (because, when we are ignorant, even more contact with the center should be assumed). In short, it is clear that the majority of authors in the exact sciences had some kind of contact with either Athens, in the classical era, or with Alexandria, in the post-classical era. And yet many of them at the very least hailed from elsewhere, or even remained active elsewhere: so Eudoxus, returning to his native Cnidus (or setting up a transient center in Cyzicus?), or Archimedes, corresponding with his Alexandrian colleagues while staying in Syracuse. Athens and Alexandria never developed a *monopoly* on the exact sciences. But, given all we have seen so far, the remarkable thing is not the absence of a monopoly but the rise of the center: why, after all, Athens? Why Alexandria? In the case of the exact sciences, at least, these are perhaps best understood, indeed, as hubs of a network. Consider these two maps, Maps 4 and 5, with networks of mathematics in classical, and the Hellenistic worlds.

In Map 4, we see the origins of mathematical authors of the first network of Greek mathematics, as discussed on page 250 above. Seven are localizable outside Athens, and only one, Theaetetus, is a native-born Athenian. (Two – Menaechmus and Dinostratus – are only localizable to Athens to the extent that we trust Proclus' report of their connection to Plato; it would be surprising if their origins were Athenian.) In Map 5, we see the patterns of mathematical communication attested in the works of Archimedes (addressing, from his native Syracuse, Conon, Dositheus and Eratosthenes, all residing in Alexandria but hailing, respectively, from Samos, Pelusion and Cyrene), Apollonius (addressing, from Alexandria, Eudemus in Pergamon, mentioning their meeting in

---

[39] An early version of those maps was produced in Netz (1997); the data of EANS allow one to construct much better maps, though with similar results.

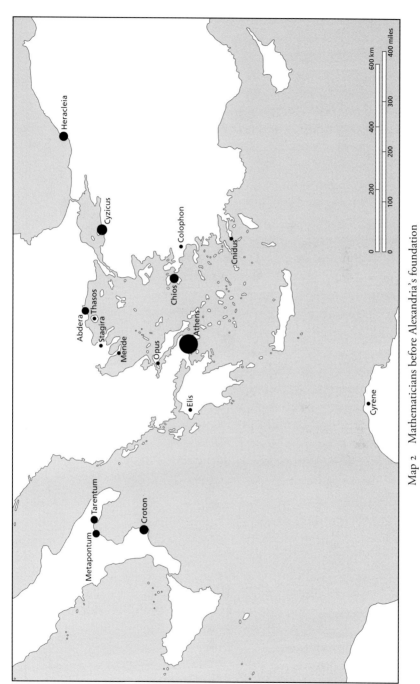

Map 2   Mathematicians before Alexandria's foundation

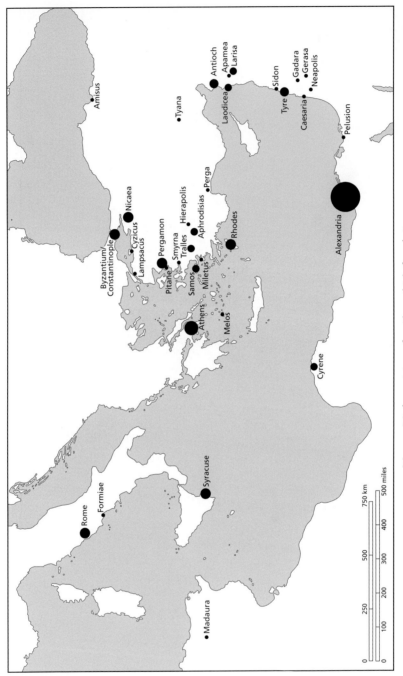

Map 3   Mathematicians after Alexandria's foundation

Amisus
Tyana
Antioch
Apamea
Larisa
Laodicea
Sidon
Gadara
Gerasa
Neapolis
Tyre
Caesaria
Pelusion
Byzantium/
Constantinople
Nicaea
Cyzicus
Lampsacus
Pergamon
Pitane
Smyrna
Tralles
Hierapolis
Aphrodisias
Perga
Rhodes
Samos
Miletus
Athens
Melos
Alexandria
Cyrene
Syracuse
Rome
Formiae
Madaura

0      250      500      750 km
0   100  200  300  400  500 miles

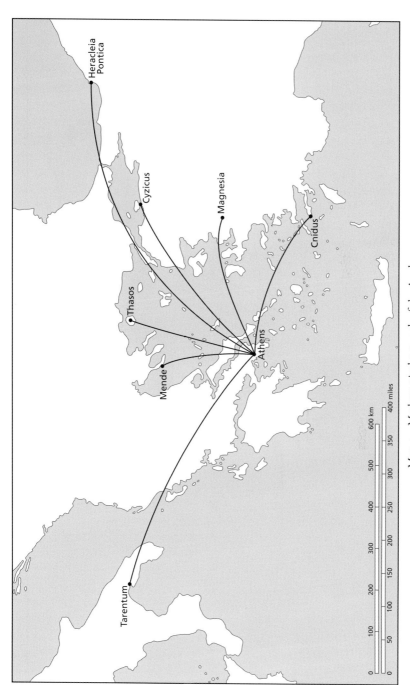

Map 4 Mathematical network of the Academy

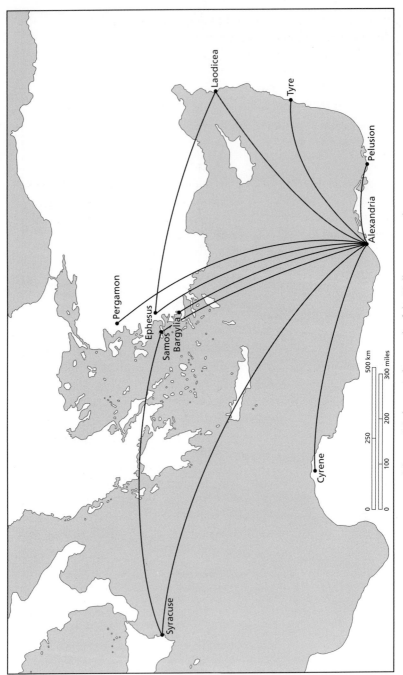

Map 5   Mathematical network of the Hellenistic period

Ephesus with their mutual friend Philonides from Laodicea; himself hailing from Perga) and Hypsicles (his father met, in Alexandria, Basilides of Tyre; he himself addresses Protarchus of – just possibly – Bargylia).[40] The center, in such a model, serves a *communicative* function. It is not necessarily (though of course it can be) a center of patronage.

The case of mathematics can be simply summed up:

Athens:Aegean::Alexandria:Mediterranean

In the two ratios constituting this proportion, we see the power of the network and the overall asymmetry of intellectual clustering. We recall not just the general principle of spatial agglomeration but, specifically, de Solla Price's (1976) principle of cumulative advantage in intellectual networks (in his specific case study: that the highly cited tend to get cited more, because they are more visible). Here we see de Solla Price's networks made spatial. One seeks to communicate with the spatially central individuals, because, being more spatially central, they are easier to communicate with. And so it is natural for intellectual endeavors in an environment of free agents to display a marked asymmetry whereby just one place becomes dominant. Modern academics are not free agents: they seek salaries, and these are distributed more evenly in space so that the asymmetry is curtailed. Ancient mathematicians, we find, must have been less influenced by such considerations; after all, there were no salaried positions in the exact sciences.

Now, there *were* some in medicine. Map 6 shows the distribution of medical authors around the Aegean in the four temporal nodes −450 to −300. Consider it now together as against Map 5, for the distribution of mathematicians, at the same period.

The mathematical map has the structure of a center (Athens) surrounded by periphery (mostly Aegean shores). The medical map has a different structure – a duopoly. There are two major centers: Athens again – but now also, and even eclipsing it, the island of Cos. Each carries a small planetary orbit: Athens carries a handful of near-Athenian islands

---

[40] The "visit" is a recurrent theme in Hellenistic mathematics. Archimedes mentions a Heraclides who serves as a go-between to Dositheus; Apollonius mentions his own son traveling to Pergamon in the same capacity, and also mentions, besides the meeting at Ephesus between Eudemus, Philonides and himself, the visit made to Alexandria by Naucrates (otherwise unlocalizable); Hypsicles mentions Basilides' visit to Alexandria; and Diocles, finally, mentions the visit paid him at Arcadia by Zenodorus (otherwise, unfortunately, unlocalizable: Jones (s.v. EANS) mentions that the name is common in Attica and in the Near East, which, for a Hellenistic mathematician, makes the Near East more likely). Notice that, while I consider Hypsicles for this exercise, his dating to the Hellenistic era is not secure: see Netz (2016).

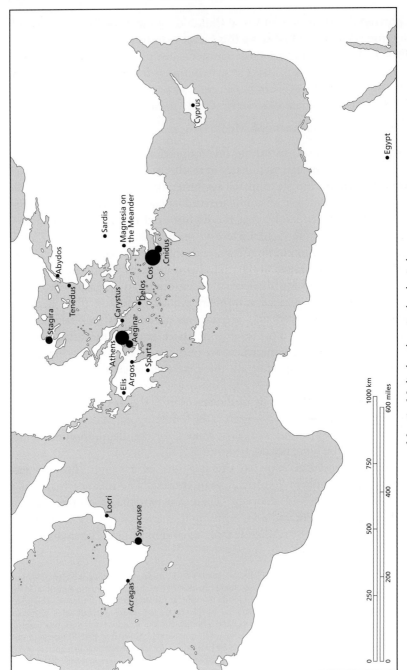

Map 6   Medical authors in the classical era

(Aegina, Carystus, Ceus, Siphnus; maybe Delos, not too far geographically and very close culturally); Cos carries its planet rival in Cnidus. Other than these two planetary systems, medical authorship seems to be rare and isolated. (Only one other place has more than one medical author: this is Syracuse, far from both Athens and Cos, and with its own patronage.) We should note that the Coan center is probably under-represented in our survey. We do not list the anonymous authors of the Hippocratic corpus independently. We do not know how many of them were indeed from Cos (or Cnidus; or how many were distinct from other, known Coan authors).[41]

The difference between medicine and mathematics in the classical era is twofold, seen once in the case of Cos, once in the case of Athens.

We cannot be sure what form the "school" in Cos took, and the flourishing of Cos seems to follow the usual rule of a generation-and-a-half event.[42] There was a certain power to the very association with Cos: a place – and its dialect – identified with medical education. With Athens, I offer a more speculative remark. We saw that, with the bipolar structure of the medical Aegean, Athens did not possess the same role as "center of exchange" which it possessed for the mathematical Aegean. Why, then, have the cluster at or near Athens? My speculation is that this has to do with the sheer concentration of population and wealth. For, after all, medicine, unlike mathematics, was a profession: it could be lucrative.[43] There would thus be an incentive for one to become a doctor in a place where this lucrative potential could be achieved. It makes more sense to be a doctor in Athens than in Cyzicus. (Syracuse is populated, and rich; it also had doctors.)

---

[41] The Ionic dialect of the corpus may or may not suggest origins in Cos: this is yet another case of an ancient identification between genre and dialect (Tribulato, 2010: 392).

[42] For the historicity of the school, see Joly (1983) and Mansfeld (1983a). For the Hippocratic "clan", see von Staden (1976).

[43] The evidence on the economics of the medical profession is very limited. There are sensationalist reports of astronomical incomes in Pliny, no more than a handful of indications in the papyri (where we sometimes see lower-status individuals engaged with healing – but always for a fee: see, e.g., Lang, 2012: 218). What's somewhat more visible in our evidence is the involvement of the state in ensuring the very presence of the medical profession, and its remuneration (so, something such as public physicians? – The best survey remains Cohn-Haft, 1956; Nutton, 1977, extends the evidence for the Imperial era. There is a medical tax mentioned in the Ptolemaic papyri, perhaps of related significance: Lang, 2004: 119–24.). This evidence is better known simply because state interventions are better documented. In general, it is hard to recover the economies of individual professions, but even the evidence for public physicians in the Greek city states as well as tax-supported Ptolemaic physicians seems to suggest some kind of support for practitioners who made most of their income from fees. The one clear feature of the evidence is that the medical profession was never composed of gentleman practitioners, engaged in their craft for philanthropic or theoretical reasons. It was a service industry. (Which was ideologically problematic, in antiquity: for the culturally difficult position of medicine, then, as a "liberal art", see Kudlien, 1976.)

In short, two centers. One center carries its centrality by virtue of its achievement in creating an institutional power over the profession; the other center carries its centrality by virtue of the various forms of centrality (political, economic or perhaps more widely intellectual) that Athens did after all develop in the classical period. Other locations are an unstructured, random set.

This is best compared with the map of medical authorship in the Roman era – the six temporal nodes from –50 to +200 (skipping, for the moment, medical authorship in the Hellenistic era). Let us put this new map, Map 7, side by side with that of medical authorship in the classical era.

The medical Roman-era system is long – two more nodes than I had for my Aegean map and longer than any of the other eras. There were no obvious ruptures in the intellectual history of the Mediterranean through this period. This is also an extraordinarily active Mediterranean, and my survey of medical authors for this period is bigger than the entire survey of mathematicians I had for all of antiquity. The most salient contrast to mathematics, then, is that of sheer numbers: more on this in Chapters 5 and 6.

The mathematicians in this era were dominated by Alexandria. Not so the doctors. Alexandria is a major center, but it does not have any monopoly: indeed, it is slightly beaten by Rome (with 23 individuals, as against the 20 at Alexandria). It is interesting to note that Alexandria does not seem to have a significant medical planetary system. In the mathematical map, we could see the persistence of mathematical authorship there and its vicinity, from Pelusion to Sidon. There are nine authors in my mathematical survey – almost a tenth of the Mediterranean production as a whole. And yet no one is recorded to have pursued medical writing along the pleasant shores of the Mediterranean, extending east of Alexandria and south of Sidon. (I shall return to mention medical Sidon below: in medicine, it is "Syrian", not "Alexandrian".) On the other hand, Rome is not only a major center but also, clearly, a center of gravity: around it we see Naples, Massalia, and a handful of authors in Sicily and Africa; perhaps Dyrrachium should be understood within the same system. Compared to this, the scarcity of mathematics in the western Mediterranean, in this period, is striking.

In the mathematical system of Alexandria we see (1) the paramount centrality of Alexandria, together with (2) the continuity of mathematical presence along the shores of the Mediterranean from Asia Minor to Egypt itself (such continuity, however, that (3) nowhere becomes locally established). None of the three features holds in the case of medicine in the

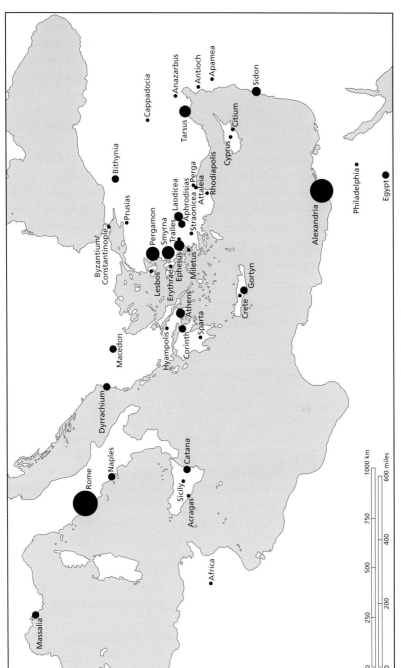

Map 7  Medical authors in the Roman era

Roman era. (1) Alexandria, as we have seen, is not paramount in its centrality. (2) Medical activity is not continuous along the Mediterranean, but is "punctuated" at least by the gap of Palestine. To this gap, one can add that southern Turkey – between Tarsus to the east and Aphrodisias to the west – is "less medical" than either the heartland of Asia Minor, from Aphrodisias to the north, or the Syrian area that includes Tarsus, Laodicea and Sidon. (3) Finally, one notes the presence of several local centers, minor, for sure, but no less real.

Let us try to characterize this polycentric system more carefully. In a sense, it is reminiscent of the system we have seen in the medical Aegean: the two major centers of Cos and Athens are now projected, upon a larger canvas, onto Alexandria and Rome (is Alexandria, once again, the more "intellectual", professional center, Rome the more "political" one?). So, perhaps:

Cos:Athens::Alexandria:Rome

This surely holds part of the truth. But one senses, rather, that a two-center model no longer will do: Asia Minor is too important, and, if so, the Syrian coast should be considered as yet another center, if lesser in importance. The remaining handful of medical authors from mainland Greece, Crete and Cyprus, on the other hand, appear as mere "scatter", or as planetary to the four-center model of Rome, Alexandria, Asia Minor and Syria.

Two conclusions seem to emerge. First of all, with more doctors to go around, the medical Mediterranean could spare more centers. Scale matters – and so, the medical Mediterranean had *centers*. Mathematics did not: it was scattered, composed by a string of autodidacts appearing here and there in random locations across the Mediterranean, dependent upon the single continuity of Alexandria. Medicine could develop schools – even *rival* schools. Thus, a Galen could travel across the Mediterranean in search of the best medical education on offer. (His mathematical education, on the other hand, depended entirely on the random event of being born to a mathematically minded father.)[44]

Second, a Galen would ultimately be led by ambition. The route from Pergamon to Rome is easy to understand – and does not pose the same ambiguities of interpretation as that from Cos to Athens, before it. One

---

[44] Galen's biography is nicely summarized in Mattern (2013): see, for the architectural/mathematical parentage, pp. 29–34; for the peripatetic education, chap. 2. The identities of Galen's teachers are in doubt but it seems that he studied in at least four cities: Pergamon, Smyrna, Corinth and Alexandria (Nutton, 1987).

went to Rome so as to enjoy Imperial patronage and the opportunity to shine upon the most majestic stage. Seen in this light, the four centers acquire a clearer meaning. Rome, Asia Minor, Alexandria and the Syrian coast could very well be, simply, the most significant concentrations of *wealth* in the Roman era, perhaps in this order.

I have skipped the Hellenistic system: let us now bring it back into consideration. I set the map for the medical Mediterranean for the temporal nodes –250 to –100, Map 8, side by side with Map 3, of the mathematical Mediterranean "after Alexandria".

It is striking to see that the mathematical model – a scatter surrounding a center – is, finally, answered by the medical one. In the Hellenistic period – and in the Hellenistic period alone – the two sciences shared the same topology – indeed, the very same geography, as the center is the same city of Alexandria. Does this imply that, especially in the couple of generations immediately following the foundation of Alexandria, medicine as a cultural practice approximated more closely the exact sciences? This would support an intuition that, in Alexandria's heyday, medicine came closest to becoming a *science*. I put this possibility aside and consider a few more sources of evidence.

Hellenistic medicine was exceptional, compared to medicine in other eras of antiquity, in that it came close to "science". I suggested above that we should normally think of it as a service industry. What would be the parallels to that? Perhaps astrology: this calls for another map, Map 9. The numbers are now much smaller. With 44 names altogether, we risk losing any meaningful information, by carving the data into contrasting maps. And yet the following seems meaningful: the distribution of astrologers in the central Imperial era (–50 to +250) as against the rest (+300 to +500 – lumped together, however, with the very first node of –100, when astrology first emerges: Map 10).

Other than in the Roman era, astrology does not show any geographical centers. Alexandria is nearly absent and all other places present a random scatter. This perhaps is just a function of the small numbers in our sample. And yet, with similarly small numbers, the distribution of astrologers in the *Roman* era is very clear. Roman-era astrologers did to some extent match Roman-era doctors. There were two centers: Rome and Egypt. The other, very minor locations match, to some extent, the medical distribution: a bit of Asia Minor, and then Vettius Valens from Antioch. But, all in all, the dominance of the two poles – of the "science" itself, in Egypt, and of its patronage, in Rome – is much more decisive.

But note: the non-Roman pole of the science of astrology is located, in this case, not in Alexandria but in a more nebulously defined Egypt. Sometimes we do not know of a specific location in Egypt; sometimes

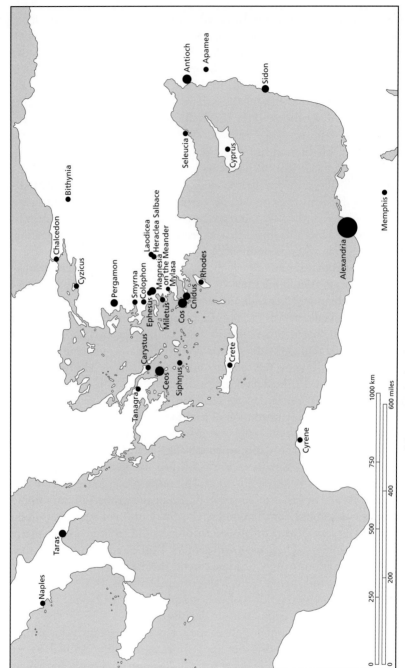

Map 8  Medical authors in the Hellenistic era

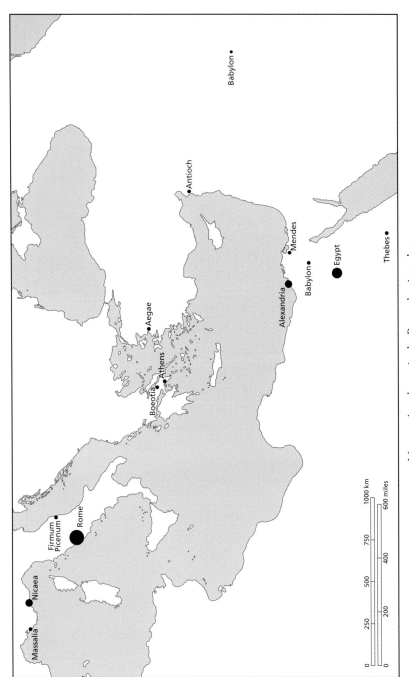

Map 9   Astrologers in the Rome-dominated era

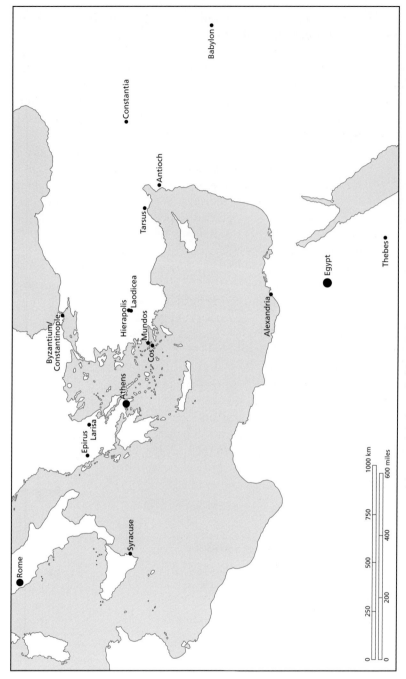

Map 10    Astrologers before and after the Rome-dominated era

we know of a specific non-Alexandrian origin. Of the two clearly Alexandrian astrologers of the Roman era, one is Ptolemy himself, primarily marked not as an astrologer but as a theoretical author in the exact sciences. (Did Ptolemy even cast horoscopes for pay?[45] The other Alexandrian astrologer is very obscure: Serapion of Alexandria.)[46] Our textbooks, of course, remind us that the same words could mean both "astronomy" as well as "astrology" in antiquity and that there was no hard-and-fast distinction between the two, up to and including Newton.[47] This appears to be simply wrong as far as the sociology of ancient science is concerned, and in fact Ptolemy – regularly cited to prove the case – is the only ancient author who can reliably be described as an author in both "astronomy" and "astrology" (if indeed – n. 45 – he was a practicing astrologer). This fact need not necessarily spell any epistemological concerns, and is, indeed, primarily sociological: astronomy was aligned, from the very foundation of Alexandria, with that city's tradition of the exact sciences; astrology was constructed, in the Roman era, as an "Egyptian" practice (I return to discuss the rise of astrology in the Roman era in Chapter 4). Perhaps the most important lesson we learn is that Alexandria was *not* Egyptian in the same sense: that is, in the eyes of potential Roman patrons an Alexandrian origin would not carry the esoteric cachet of Egypt. To them, at least, Alexandria was Greek: one of the two poles of the culture of the *Greek* Mediterranean. Your doctor should be Greek and therefore could well be Alexandrian. But horoscopes are better cast at the Egyptian chora, where old, exotic traditions keep their hold.

So, the light that astrology throws on Alexandria is, perhaps surprisingly, oblique. A more direct illumination is to be found in *grammar*. This automatic association is amply verified through the following two maps, Maps 11 and 12, of grammar in the Hellenistic era (here –300 to –100) and the Roman era (–50 to +200).[48]

---

[45] Riley (1987) emphasizes the paucity of tools directly relevant for individual horoscopes, in Ptolemy's astrological work: it is more focused on general influences of the stars and is consistent, therefore, with a more theoretical interest.

[46] This author is reported only by late Byzantine citations (s.v. EANS). I do not mean to imply that he need be fictional (of course, he might be) but, rather, that, at this late stage, the cultural meaning of "Alexandria" as distinct from Egypt may have been eroded.

[47] For some references, see Sela (2001 61 n.3).

[48] For medicine and the exact sciences, I have the resource of EANS: it is possible to quibble with some of its claims, but it is a very thorough survey. For grammar, I do not have a comparably exhaustive survey and so my numbers are an undercount (derived from search of a few relevant words, such as "grammar" and "grammarian", in the online Brill's New Pauly); see the discussion in Chapter 5, pp. 596–8.

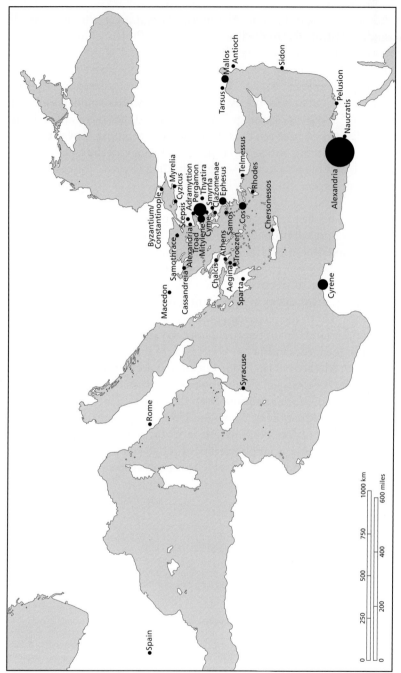

Map II    Grammarians in the Hellenistic era

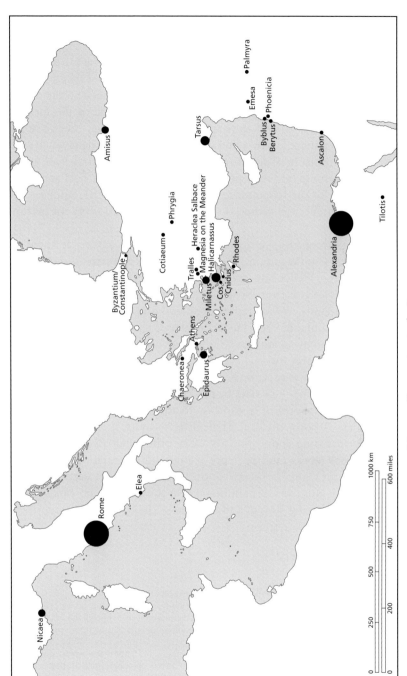

Map 12   Grammarians in the Roman era

Nicaea

Rome

Elea

Chaeronea
Athens
Epidaurus

Byzantium/
Constantinople

Amisus

Cotiaeum

Phrygia

Tralles
Magnesia on the Meander
Miletus
Cos
Cnidus
Rhodes

Heraclea Salbace
Halicarnassus

Tarsus

Emesa
Byblus
Berytus
Phoenicia

Palmyra

Ascalon

Alexandria

Tilotis

0      250     500     750    1000 km

0      200     400     600 miles

Of 138 localizable grammarians in my list, 59 have an Alexandrian connection: this is not surprising (though it bears recalling that grammar's connection to Alexandria was not determined by Ptolemaic patronage). Once again, the grammatical maps recall the medical ones. Once again, we see a two-center model in the Roman era: this has 22 names associated with Alexandria, and 24 with Rome (indeed, uncannily close to the medical numbers, which are 20 and 23, respectively). Once again, there is some evidence for patronage bestowed on grammarians (this is a field which even allowed some measure of social mobility: a remarkable number of grammarians have servile origins – perhaps not unnatural in a field somehow cognate to that of the schoolmaster).[49] And so we can once again see the duality of an intellectual center, on the one hand, and a center of patronage, on the other.

Other than these two – a scatter (with a transient center – as noted on page 254 above – in Pergamon). The geography of this scatter is significant, however. In the Hellenistic era this comes from the core areas of the classical Greek world: from Syracuse to Asia Minor, from Byzantion to Cyrene. The islands are well represented, and one even finds a smattering of the Greek mainland: Clazomenae, Athens, Sparta. All in all, I count 38 Hellenistic grammatical authors who have a very likely connection to that Greek core, and only two who have not (the two are Comanus, from Naucratis, and Dionysius, from Sidon, both active in Alexandria at around the age of Aristarchus – i.e. late in the Hellenistic era). The numbers are small but they do present a contrast to the cases of medicine and of mathematics. Among medical Hellenistic authors, I count ten "non-core" (with a strong connection to a city other than Alexandria or the classical Greek core) and 25 "core"; among mathematical Hellenistic authors, I count eight "non-core" and 17 "core". Another useful comparison is with the numbers of grammarians in the Roman era, which are 12 "non-core" (excluding Rome) and 21 "core". The bare percentages, then, are as follows.

---

[49] The place of freedmen among Greek-speaking intellectuals in Rome is not to be exaggerated: it was mostly the socially eminent who were worthy of elite patronage (see McNelis, 2002), but it is also clear that the most powerful among the Romans could create eminence through the sheer power of their patronage, so that their freedmen could be sufficiently eminent as intellectuals; for the phenomenon of the freedman-grammarian, see Christes (1979). In general, the truly opulent ancient household had an in-house grammarian, as family member – and tutor to one's sons; see, e.g., the entertaining summary of the evidence, mostly from Cicero's correspondence, in Bonner (1977: 28–32).

|           | Mathematics | Medicine | Rom. grammar | Hel. grammar |
|-----------|-------------|----------|--------------|--------------|
| Core      | 68          | 71       | 64           | 95           |
| Non-core  | 32          | 29       | 36           | 5            |

The absolute numbers are small but their stability is significant, and it suggests that about a quarter to a third of Greek intellectual life in the post-classical eras was recruited in the "post-classical regions" (excluding Alexandria). It is against this background that the mere 5 percent of Comanus of Naucratis and of Dionysius of Sidon – both, once again, also fairly late – seems to be suggestive. More to the point, this seems to make historical sense: for over a century Alexandria was engaged in the project of assembling its Greek identity through a bricolage of the classical Greek Mediterranean, executed verbally by Callimachus or by Apollonius[50] and played with actual individuals recruited into Alexandria through the power of Ptolemaic patronage from places such as Ephesus (Zenodotus), Rhodes (Simias), Cyrene (Callimachus and Eratosthenes) and Byzantion (Aristophanes). The newer shores of the eastern Mediterranean would make little contribution to this effort and so those shores figured neither in the *Aetia* or the *Argonautica* nor in the prosopography of the *Museion*. No surprise there, perhaps: but we are reminded of just how successful this project was in that Alexandria did, in fact, become master of the Greek language. We may now put this side by side with the negative observation concerning Alexandria's minimal role as an astrological center, as opposed to that of a loosely defined "Egypt". Alexandria, to reiterate, was perceived not as Egyptian but as Greek: so, negatively, for astrology – and positively, for grammar.

We have now followed the spatial distributions of mathematics and of medicine, of astrology and of grammar, comparing, in each case, the Hellenistic period with at least one other period. We have learned something about Alexandria – but, even at a more basic level, we have learned something about the spatial distribution of science. This seems to be driven by two major attractive forces: network effects and patronage. The pull of network effects attracts authors to the company of their famous peers; the pull of patronage attracts authors to the major centers of wealth and power. The two are not independent of one another, as prestige

---

[50] Thalmann (2011) is a survey of the spatial imaginary in the *Argonautica* (it ends up emphasizing how much the center and periphery, in this work, are still defined relative to the old Greek core); for Callimachus' *Aetia*, see Acosta-Hughes and Stephens (2012: maps 3–4).

would primarily be conferred via patronage itself. But they are not identical, and so there would be moments when one pole would be marked more by its intellectual pedigree and communicative power, the other by its patronage.[51] In the Hippocratic system, Cos and Athens may have hinted at such a system; it becomes clear in the Roman-era pattern of Alexandria and Rome.

The relative pull of the two forces may change historically and according to the discipline. Patronage is most powerful in astrology, which (at its high end of astrological authorship) becomes *primarily* an endeavor to be pursued in Rome; it is powerful enough in Roman-era medicine and grammar. But, in mathematics, network effects are clearly more powerful than patronage, and so a single-center model is more natural.

As we consider more contexts, we begin to develop a sharper sense of the plausible counter-factuals, and, in this way, we gain a sense of what needs to be explained. The main counter-factual, we find, is this: during the Hellenistic era there was no field in which Alexandria was the center of patronage, and some other city the center of education. This carries two meanings. First, there was no Athens-to-Alexandria transmission, with culturally prominent individuals routinely trained in the first, and then practicing in Alexandria.[52] This absence speaks, in practice, to the absence of Hellenistic philosophy in Alexandria. Second, there were no minor, local centers of cultural activity, serving as training grounds in the fields typical to Alexandria, away from that city. This speaks to the nature of such activities, in the precise era in which they emerge.

In the remainder of this section, I will point out that Alexandria's influence emerged at the moment when the relative roles of the genres were transformed. The performative genres, in which local tradition mattered more, lost their valence for creative meaning, as the canon froze into place. And so the non-performative – hence, non-canonized genres – assumed a more central role. But, there, network effects and patronage overwhelmed entrenched attachments to culturally defined spaces: hence, Alexandria. To follow this argument, then, let us take a step back and consider the emergence of cultural patronage.

[51] It is an attractive hypothesis, that there is a functional reason why the two poles ought to be distinct: by having prestige conferred away from patronage, there is a neutral, and so more reliable signaling mechanism, for merit, according to which patronage may be conferred. Wall Street – relying on Harvard's selection.
[52] There are a handful of exceptions, such as Eratosthenes and Sphaerus, both very qualified counter-examples; see pp. 409–10 below.

### 3.3.2    Courts and Canons – before and after Chaeronea

Cultural patronage – which must include the dependent attachment of one remarkable individual to another[53] – would be inherently problematic for an ideology of egalitarianism, whether democratic or aristocratic. It serves to mark the special status of the patron, through his unique ability to dispense patronage; it highlights a relation of subordination between two members of the elite. In a word, it is tyrannical. As indeed it generally was in early Greek history, for which the evidence can be summed up rapidly. There are six main episodes of cultural patronage, for the entire era preceding Macedon's dominance:

> (1) We may start with the tyrant of Samos, Polycrates, praised by the poets Ibycus and Anacreon[54] (it was under the same dynasty that a major piece of engineering – a tunnel dug to provide water to the city – had not only been successfully achieved but also inscribed, in cultural memory, as the work of a brilliant architect, Eupalinus of Megara: a foreigner in the court, once again?).[55] Polycrates was in power in the 530s and 520s – the generation when the named author is finally established as the unique form of cultural presence. Brand-name authors mattered, then.
>
> (2) Indeed, at nearly the same time, the Peisistratids in Athens may have had as guests the same Anacreon, as well as Simonides;[56] perhaps we may add Lasus of Hermione;[57] certainly, there is the evidence for the Peisistratids' cultivation of the text of Homer,[58] and it is at least possible that the earliest form of Athenian dramatic competitions evolved under the tyrants (even though the evidence becomes firm only with the foundation of

[53] There are many competing definitions of patronage (which I do not worry with here: we know well enough what we're talking about, and I prefer facts to semantics), but all insist on asymmetry; a foundational reference point is Kaufman (1974: 285): "[S]pecial type of dyadic exchange. . .between actors of unequal power and status."

[54] The historical evidence is late and weak (the most significant source for Ibycus, for instance, is the *Suda* s.v.): we mostly have to judge based on the fragments of the poems (and it was probably the poems themselves, and no more, that informed our historical sources). The best discussion is in Bowie (2009), to whose judgement I will return below.

[55] The tunnel is well known archaeologically (and is recognized as a technical marvel): Kienast (1990). Herodotus III.60 is our sole authority for the name of the architect.

[56] See, once again, Bowie (2009).

[57] All we have is Herodotus VII.6.3: the Athenian diviner Onomacritus was exiled by the tyrant Hipparchus, following the exposure of the former as a forger by the poet Lasus (see Dillery, 2005, for this episode). Our dependence on Herodotus is on the whole typical for the period, but it should be noted that the theme of court life in Herodotus is driven by his Eastern exoticism: thus, the Lasus episode is told as a flashback, from the perspective of Onomacritus, later on, in the *Persian* court.

[58] See, e.g., Kivilo (2010: 3); this will add Orpheus of Croton and Zophyrus of Heraclea, as well as Onomacritus himself, to the Peisistratid cultural establishment.

democracy).[59] The view that the Peisistratids had something of a "cultural program" is a cliché, but may hold some truth to it.

(3) Early in the fifth century the Deinomenids in Syracuse engage once again some very well-known poets: Aeschylus was likely commissioned for a play celebrating Syracusan ideology;[60] even better known are the songs of praise commissioned (and extant) from Pindar – as well as from Bacchylides.[61] (Epicharmus' comedy is produced in Syracuse in the same era – and so is perhaps parallel to the possible rise of drama in Athens under the Peisistratids?)[62]

(4) Right towards the end of that century King Archelaus of Macedon invites an entire host of cultural figures to his court, foremost among whom is said to be Euripides; also present were the tragedian Agathon and the poets Timotheus and Choerilus, as well as the painter Zeuxis; there is even a report suggesting that Socrates himself was invited to the court. The evidence for this episode is by far the shakiest.[63]

(5) Not long afterwards – from the very beginning of the fourth century onwards – Dionysius I cultivated many cultural figures in his court in Syracuse. In a fairly expansive form, the list could have included: the tragedians Antiphon and Carcinus, the poet Philoxenus, philosophers such as Aristippus of Cyrene, Aeschines the Socratic, and of course Plato, orators such as Lysias, Andocides, Isocrates and his pupil Eunomus, historians such as Xenophon, Philistus and Hermias of Methymna – and local Sicilian talent such as Xenarchus, the mime-

---

[59] Osborne (1993) notes the tension between the "ambition" inherent in dramatic competition and the ethos of democracy, and so tends to take seriously the suggestion that drama had roots older than democracy.

[60] The "Aetnae"; see Poli-Palladini (2001).

[61] See, e.g., Gold (1987: 21–30); as noted since, by Kurke (1991), the rise of the specific genre of praise poetry suggests, if anything, the greater tensions associated with outstanding achievement, rather than the entrenched positions of established elites.

[62] So Bosher (2014), who sees Syracusan theater as deliberately advanced by the tyrants (it was certainly they who built the actual theater!).

[63] The evidence is weak, because at this point we no longer have praise poetry (Hammond and Griffith, 1979: 149 n.1.) The least controversial is Agathon's invitation to the Macedonian court, implied by Aristophanes *Frogs* 83–5 (and confirmed by the ancient scholia to the line); Euripides' Macedonian sojourn became entrenched in ancient memory but its very reality has been doubted; see Scullion (2003). Later, the comic poet Anaxandrides is reported to have some kind of connection to Philip II, but this is especially weak – a confused notice in the *Suda* (A 1982 – "came to be in the competitions of Philip of Macedon") that seems to suggest, at most, being performed in festivals; scholars often suggest this has to be the festival at Dion in 348 (Webster, 1952: 18). The evidence, if anything, is marked for its silence: later Macedonian kings did not produce a court of poets, on the model of Archelaus. Aristotle might have been hired to serve as Alexander's tutor, however (the evidence is enormous – Düring, 1957: 288–94 – but entirely Roman-era or later. Quintilian is the earliest direct source, *Institutiones* I.1.23, and the story is the most detailed in Plutarch, *Alex.* 7.2 ff.; this entire tradition emerges out of a specific Roman-era ideology of paideia, whereby the governing elite's patronage of Greek scholarship is just taken for granted).

composer, and the orator Aristoteles.[64] While the overall fact of Dionysian patronage is secure, the details for each individual figure are doubtful in the extreme.

(6) Aristotle – whom we have noted already in a Macedonian connection – spent a few years in the 340s in the court of Hermias, tyrant of a small cluster of cities in the Troas. Aristotle's poem of praise for Hermias was well known in antiquity and survives through three separate sources (!).[65] In this case the evidence for any other intellectual at the court is exceptionally weak, even if in all likelihood Aristotle was not alone.[66] Later tradition amplified the episode – which involved a philosopher destined to become, in the Roman era, second only to Plato in his fame – but, in the 340s, all Hermias could manage to fetch was the most provincial (if most brilliant) of Plato's followers, merely in his thirties: small fish for a small pond.

The evidence is often unreliable. The encounter of the author and the ruler is among the more common and sensational tropes of ancient biography, and, so, we must always wonder if it may not be fictional; worse – as already mentioned in note 63 – many of our sources are Roman-era – that is, from a time when patronage was indeed decisive (I return to this in Chapter 6, section 6.3). The one reliable evidence is that of commissioned poetry, which survives most substantially for an early episode – Syracuse in the early fifth century. This, then, is our one clear case, and it is not a case of court patronage at all. The poet does not become the tyrants' client and, instead, performs a well-defined job for them. In the case of Pindar, we can see – following Kurke (1991) – how patronage is constrained by the ideologies of egalitarianism, the poet presenting himself as a superb craftsman and his patron as a figure within the continuum of wealth and power of the city. The tyrant appears not as patron of poetry but as its supreme consumer.

We know very little about the mechanics of earlier tyrannical courts: it could be that at Samos and at Athens poets were hired; or that they simply

---

[64] Sanders (1987: 1–2, with references). While the evidence is open to question on many details, it is much more extensive than that for the Archelaus episode.
[65] This poem is the subject of Ford (2011, text in chap. 1), which is also, overall, the best treatment of the entire Aristotle-and-Hermias episode. (Chroust, 1972, makes too much of the meager evidence we have for Aristotle as a political actor in the service of Macedon; Leroi, 2014, is hopelessly romantic in his image of Hermias as a patron of *biology*, of all things. It has been widely assumed, however, ever since Thompson, 1913, that Aristotle did spend much of his sojourn in Asia Minor, wading near the shore and observing sea life.)
[66] Ford (2011: 20).

stayed over, even if for extended visits, such friends as one would invite to one's banquet. It was only polite to sing, while there (so, Bowie, 2009). At any rate, throughout the evidence, we see no suggestion of a career made for patronage. An invitation to a court is sometimes welcome, but it comes as an episode within one's larger career.

And yet – if the tradition concerning his personal patronage is to be trusted – Archelaus *could* have had a considerable, and very weighty, group of individuals invited, all at about the same time: so, a real court? The evidence is thin but the possibility persists; the case of Dionysius I is so much clearer. If so, we find that, while court patronage was not a sustained form of Greek cultural life as a whole, still, for a very brief window of time – a couple of decades at the turn of the fifth century – this form suddenly emerges, with at least one and perhaps two major episodes. The timing must be significant: the moment of Athens' historical crisis – and its cultural triumph. I have argued on page 232 above that the canon was formed at exactly this moment, as a more mediated consumption of performance becomes possible. In a world in which everyone appreciates Euripides and imagines his vivid presence, it would have been much more impressive to bring over the man himself.

Neither Archelaus nor Dionysius set out to recruit Athenians specifically: they both had non-Athenians in their retinues as well, and it just so happened that Athenian figures were dominant. It is quite possible (especially in the case of Archelaus) that their programs of patronage benefited directly from Athens' crisis; it was a good time to move away. What is most evident is the change in the character of courtly patronage, in response to changing models of cultural life. Praise was the traffic of the archaic court. Archelaus' use of poetry is more subtle: perhaps, a play, carrying his name, by Euripides (already the Deinomenids had commissioned a play from Aeschylus, as we recall). Dionysius' is the first clear case of a cultural court – and it is also the first prose court. Indeed, beyond such names as those of philosophers, historians and orators, we should also mention Dionysius' direct patronage of engineering (perhaps prefigured by Eupalinus in Polycrates' Samos?). Architects and craftsmen are hired from across the Mediterranean, to help in the speedy construction of walls, ships and war engines – efforts that became associated, in later tradition, with the very invention of the catapult. Cuomo (2007: 43–4) recounts and deconstructs this episode very well (should we trust such stories of *invention*? A trope, after all: just like the figure of the poet-at-the-court).[67] It is hard to tell if "patronage" is the appropriate term; engineers are not mentioned by name (so this is perhaps not a matter of attracting celebrated authors),[68] and the gathering of talent is here for a purpose. And yet this remains clear: both Archelaus and Dionysius gathered together, from across the Greek world, individuals of highly prized skills. Archelaus looked only for the leading authors, especially the poets; Dionysius looked for prose authors and engineers as well.

What the discussion so far suggests is the thinness of patronage in the Greek world. The form simply did not carry that much cultural valence: after all, the main vehicle of canonicity had been *public* performance. The trend of Greek culture, from Pindar's time, was in an even more egalitarian direction; little wonder that the traffic in praise declined. Arrian explicitly contrasts Alexander with the early Sicilian tyrants: unlike Hieron, Gelon and Theron, he says that no praise poetry was written for Alexander.[69] He could have been wrong: there were poets, too, in Alexander's retinue,[70] but their memory did not survive. Alexander did not dismiss poetry as such; it was, rather, that the historical trajectory, outlined by the court of Dionysius, has now reached its zenith. Talent for hire was primarily concentrated in prose, and primarily of a more "useful" type. The role of the intellectual, now, becomes not so much that of a validator of the court but, rather, its servant: something, indeed, along the lines of a "government sector" of cultural production. Let us look at some evidence for this.

For the sake of the following exercise, I take the EANS Time-Line with the two periods 360 to 325 and 325 to 295. I reassign figures from the first period whose main activity post-dates Chaeronea to the second period, and

---

[67] As usual for Dionysius, the evidence is almost entirely from Diodorus Siculus, who asserts directly at 14.42: "Indeed, even the catapult was invented at the moment in Syracuse, what with the best craftsmen being brought together from everywhere into a single place." Diodorus goes on to ascribe the invention of quadriremes and quinqueremes (less plausibly, perhaps) to the same episode.

[68] On the other hand, the focus of Diodorus' stories of Dionysius' war preparations is on the tyrant's terrifying, Napoleonic energy; it is a narrative that would not lend itself to the mention of great inventors.

[69] *Anabasis* 1.12: among other things, of course, Arrian engages in the display of one's erudite mastery of lyric poetry.

[70] Weber (1993: 49) lists: Agis of Argos, Aeschrion (of Lesbos?), Choerilus of Iasus, and Pranichus (or Pierion? Even Plutarch – *Alex.* 50.8 – was not sure of the right name for this very obscure singer, known for a single episode: once, he happened to sing songs of invective against some generals, to Alexander's delight). Sextus asserts that Pyrrho wrote encomiastic poetry for Alexander, for sale (*Adv. Gramm.* 282). The extreme obscurity of all such poetry is remarkable (none survives), as is the ancient reputation of Choerilus, the most significant among them – and the very epitome of a bad poet for Horace (*Ars Poetica* 357–8).

assign figures who straddle both periods to the period with which their bulk of activity seems to be associated. The resulting absolute numbers of "scientists" covered by EANS are 63 just before Chaeronea, and 81 afterwards. Since my time frame for "before Chaeronea" is narrower, the numbers are in fact closely comparable on an annual basis (if anything, we may have a higher concentration in the years immediately preceding Chaeronea; this reflects EANS' bias, and perhaps that of the ancient sources themselves, towards "Plato's Academy" as a center of scientific research). In both cases, the numbers reflect EANS' definition of scientific activity, especially to the exclusion of many philosophers whose activity may not have overlapped with "science" in our own modern sense. While this emphasis on "science" is somewhat forced, it is, for that very reason, also somewhat useful as a sample: certain types of intellectual practices changed their relative weight, at precisely this moment. Let us see the evidence, then.

I provide a simplified scheme, in which I contrast what I call "the government sector" with the "non-government sector". The "government sector" is, of course, a loaded term. It refers to two main types of activity: on the one hand, architecture, mechanics, tactics and related, evidently practical activities; on the other hand, geography, which, in this era, as I will argue, is clearly tied to the state. The "non-government sector" is the more common forms of ancient science: philosophy (such as was judged by EANS to be scientific in character), medicine, mathematics and a few scattered "others". The numbers are given in percentages.

| | Government sector | | Non-government sector | | | |
|---|---|---|---|---|---|---|
| | Geography | Architecture etc. | Philosophy | Mathematics | Medicine | Other |
| Before Chaeronea | 8 | 3 | 38 | 21 | 17 | 11 |
| | 11 | | 89 | | | |
| After Chaeronea | 41 | 23 | 17 | 7 | 9 | 0 |
| | 64 | | 36 | | | |

The upshot is clear: before Chaeronea the "government sector" is marginal. Following it the bulk of non-literary intellectual life is dedicated to geography, mechanics and architecture (other than those fields, indeed, what remains is more and more concentrated in a handful of Athenian schools: more below).

It may be that our sources are especially rich with regard to the mathematics of the middle of the fourth century: many of our names are mentioned in Proclus' summary of Eudemus' history of geometry, which has its terminus with Eudemus himself and its focus of interest in Plato's Academy, discussed on page 250 above. Without this passage, we would have six names fewer in the non-governmental, pre-Chaeronea rubric (no Amyclas, Athenaeus, Hermotimus, Leon, Neoclides or Theudius), and the percentage of mathematics there would drop from 21 to 11 – i.e. not appreciably more than that after Chaeronea. But this type of argument is misleading: the argument from section 3.2 makes it inherently likely that the first major generation of Greek mathematics would indeed be a generational event. It is at the very least a genuine possibility that the decline in the relative position of mathematics was real. If we turn to the "philosophy" rubric in the pre-Chaeronea generation, we find many authors who are especially interested in the exact sciences: Platonists who are not mathematicians themselves and yet share Plato's fascination with mathematics, Pythagoreans, authors whose work reflects directly on music (Aristoxenus) or on astronomy (Heraclides Ponticus). Of my 24 philosophers, nearly all are of this character, with the possible exceptions of Metrodorus of Chios and, perhaps, Theophrastus. Of course, this is in some sense no more than EANS' bias of selection: philosophers who show no interest in science would not be mentioned in EANS. The telling point is that an interest in science, in this particular generation, seems to go hand in hand with an interest in mathematics. The simplest, and traditional, explanation would be that, in this generation, mathematics was indeed especially influential in intellectual terms, perhaps under the influence of Plato himself, perhaps a reflection of the intellectual achievement of the mathematics of that generation. If so, the striking comparison would be to what follows: in the generation after Chaeronea EANS mostly cites philosophers whose interests are more cosmological or logical in character, and sometimes explicitly anti-mathematical: Zeno, Diodorus Cronus, Epicurus... Eudemus of Rhodes himself, the peripatetic historian of science, is exceptional in this generation for his very interest in the exact science: in other words, we see that even the Platonic-Aristotelian tradition – to which the exact sciences once mattered so much – now turns to them as subjects of historical inquiry.[71]

---

[71] See Zhmud (2006) for the origins of the history of science in the Peripatos of this generation: another transient, generational practice! Looking further, there is no doubt that Hellenistic philosophy had comparatively little interest in mathematics; see section 4.4.4 below.

So, less mathematics. And, at the same time, more geography, architecture, mechanics. People have been building new war engines and monumental buildings throughout the fourth century. From its middle onwards, and, apparently, especially in the generation following Chaeronea, it becomes much more common for such craftsmen to be widely celebrated by name; could this be because such craftsmen more often took care to celebrate their own achievement in writing? At any rate, the grand monument, or the grand machine, becomes a celebrity object in and of itself. The mere *plans* of the new temple of Artemis at Ephesus, as well as of those of Apollo at Didyma, would be enough to bring fame to their architects, Daphnis and Paeonius.[72] Vitruvius (X.13) and Athenaeus Mechanicus (10–15) explicitly quote a book, or books, by Diades, on war engines; they also report that Diades accompanied Alexander in his campaign. Or consider this: how common is it for buildings to be called after their architects? The Leonidaion, a huge hostel set up for the accommodation of guests to Olympia around 320 BC,[73] was so-called after its benefactor and architect, Leonidas of Naxos. In all, EANS lists 44 authors under "Architecture"; eight are from the 330–295 generation (we would otherwise expect two architects among the roughly 100 authors of this generation, as EANS as a whole has about 2,000 entries). EANS lists 72 in total under "Mechanics"; nine are from the 330–295 generation (we would expect three). Perhaps this has something to do with the kind of visibility offered in this period. More monumental buildings, more war engines constructed. The visibility of the architect and of the mechanic, we note, is a function of his patronage. Not surprising, then, and yet noteworthy: a spurt of patronage in the post-Chaeronea era.

The (relative) numbers are even more robust for geography. Overall, in this field, EANS counts 246 authors (a significant category: it is mostly EANS' way of accommodating the contribution of the ancient genre of "history" to what we now call "science"). We would expect, then, 12 to 13 authors in the 330–295 generation – and we find 31 instead. This most certainly is not due to some random fluctuation, and indeed it is mostly due to Alexander's own patronage. Some intellectuals were invited to his court specifically so as to add to its luster and perhaps to its future, written, fame. Not only their histories, but also the memoirs of generals and other participants in the campaign tended to dwell primarily on the geography of

[72] Both temples took many more years to complete (for the temple of Apollo at Didyma: see Parke, 1986), so the fame of the architects must have been based on an anticipation, during their lifetime, of future monuments.
[73] Lavish enough for the Romans, who made it their headquarters in the city (Pausanias V.15.2).

new, exotic spaces. No fewer than 12 geographical authors from this campaign are still known by name. One imagines those tents at night, the candles burning late, quills running on papyrus.[74] Nor would the self-commemorating voice of geographical patronage be lost with the passage of Alexander. The first Ptolemy had Hecataeus in his service; the first Seleucus had Megasthenes as well as Patrocles; Pyrrhus had Cineas; Antigonus the First had Hieronymus.[75] Most of these should be seen as political actors who perhaps turned to writing only late in life, after the dust of their many battles had settled. And yet: they would follow a precedent set by the generation of Alexander. Ophellas of Cyrene is an intriguing case: a ruler himself, from 322 to 308, he was also a geographical author. It might be significant that he was a ruler of Cyrene, and that his geography covered the Atlantic – that is, moving in the opposite direction to Alexander. Indeed, the purview of geography was not confined to the Alexandrian spaces. Geographers were covering the entire Mediterranean (starting from the relatively early Pseudo-Scylax), and the west was the focus of the work of Timaeus of Taormina, and, of course, of Pytheas of Massalia himself – both among the most influential historical and geographical authors of their time. We may also mention Andron, author of a *Pontica*: was it commissioned by a ruler with Pontic interests? Aristides wrote on the Aegean, Mursilus on Lesbos; but Dicaearchus' geographical interests were dictated by the curiosity of the Lyceum and not by royal patronage.

In the generation following Chaeronea we see – whether explicitly commissioned by patronage or, more simply, bringing forth the wonders of a new age – a sudden profusion of cultural fame associated with the physical setting of the world. The city built – its architect; the city injured – the maker of war-engines; cities, and their world – described and measured. This is very far indeed from the intellectual world of Plato's Academy.

The physical setting of the world and its cities: what physical setting, which cities, furnish the authors of this new cultural pursuit? Map 13 is the map of the "government sector" authors of the post-Chaeronea generation.

---

[74] For Alexander's conquest as geographical expedition, see Bodson (1991). The identity of Alexander's contemporary historians is typically studied as a problem of historical sources: what are the early historians, underlying our several (Roman-era: see p. 660 below) histories of Alexander? For this question, see Zambrini (2007).

[75] Some of the names mentioned in this paragraph are very familiar (there are many publications, for instance, on Pytheas of Massalia: Cunliffe, 2002, is a fairly recent popular book). Others are barely known, and, for all, one should best refer to EANS.

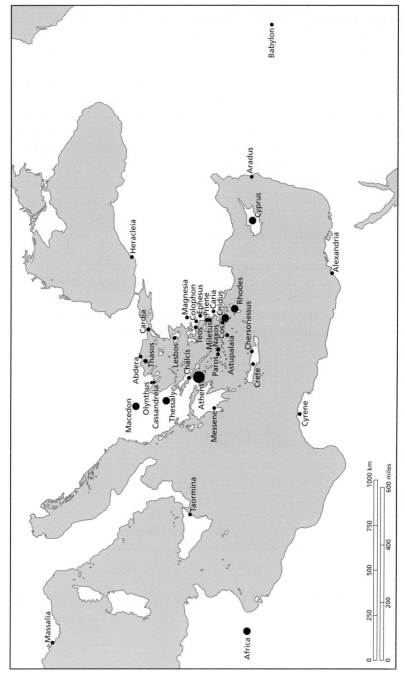

Map 13    "Government sector" authors of the post-Chaeronea generation

The presence of Alexandria, such as it is (Parmenion the architect, as well as Amyntas the geographer), arises perhaps from a somewhat later generation. There are also a couple of Near Eastern imports: Berossus, from Babylon, and Callias, from Aradus, both bringing in their own expertise in Babylonian astrology or Phoenician engineering. Otherwise, the map is resolutely old Greek – indeed, nearly archaic in its complexion: it surveys the Aegean core with perhaps somewhat more focus on northern Greece as well as Asia Minor and the islands facing it: perhaps Alexander's coalition; or just the usual locations of Greek civilization, once Athens' domination is thrown off. The key fact – once again, archaic in character – is the absence of a center: the couple of authors from Cnidus or Rhodes are perhaps no more than an accident, and even the five authors from Athens are a very small concentration by the standards of the late fourth century. For this cultural pursuit, it does not matter where you come from. The authors of geography are professionally itinerant, accumulating their autopsies of India, Aethiopia or Thule; engineers and architects travel from one location to the next, seeking new commissions. The main theme of the era, after all, was a huge expedition away from Greece.

And yet, most cultural figures of the fourth century were not geographers, let alone mechanicians; the main development was the growth of philosophy, and, as we saw, this growth took the form of the rise of local traditions. Cyrene or Cyzicus; Megara or Lampasacus; above all, Athens. And, indeed, what EANS identifies as science, in the years immediately *preceding* Chaeronea, still fits this overall trend. Athens dominates completely the "non-government sector", with 32 out of 56 entries plausibly associated with Athens (this already approaches the Athenian domination of philosophy in the third century). Medicine is an exception, with only one Athenian (Mnesitheus), but this is because Cos and Cnidus remain dominant in this particular field (so Dexippus, Dracon, Chrysippus, Philistion).[76] Nor, of course, do philosophers quit Athens after Chaeronea. EANS, simply, pays somewhat less attention to them – and for a good reason. Science, in a modern sense, does seem to occupy the Athenians less – which will be a major theme of the following chapter.

Such are the exact sciences, then, in the generation following Chaeronea. By EANS, one counts Aristyllus and Euclid (both, perhaps, in Alexandria), Autolycus (in Pitane), Lasus (in Magnesia) and Pheidias (in

---

[76] Only one Coan is clearly attested as active in the post-Chaeronea generation, though one is wary to read much into this, as this is the extremely influential Praxagoras. Clearly, Cos was a major center of medicine all the way through the end of the fourth century, and in some ways even beyond.

Syracuse). Perhaps one should have counted Hipponicus in Athens in this period;[77] Aristyllus and Euclid belong to a late-ish date, as does Pheidias (the father of Archimedes, he was probably prominent when Archimedes was young: closer to mid-century, and, at any rate, he never should have been counted by EANS in the 330–295 generation). Just as the second third of the fourth century witnessed an enormous concentration of mathematical activity, so the last third witnessed a near-disappearance of the field.

In all this, there are several distinct causal forces at play. We may see perhaps the coincidence of several generational events (mathematics, declining from its first heyday; the Platonic circle, giving way). Surely, the rise of even more powerful autocrats meant that patronage could be more significant. But we find that patrons look for whatever supply they can find. The Deinomenids paid for poetry of praise, Archelaus commissioned a tragedy, Dionysius invited historians and philosophers. Throughout, the very nature of the career was somehow resistant to the practice of patronage: epichoric poets and patriotic philosophers – what did they have to do, in the end, in a tyrant's court? But now, finally, there was a supply of careers, plausibly made for patronage. There was now a vitality in the most specialized of skills: machine making, building, geographical compilation based on personal autopsy. Thus, cultural life simply has less to do with the public and so with any concrete, local space. The late fourth century sees therefore a new style of culture, in which space – the place from which you came, at which you work – simply matters less. This is the context in which the network effects – the more powerful center, becoming powerful simply by virtue of its centrality – may take hold. Patronage, strategically allocated, could start a snowballing effect, creating new centers. And it is as such that Alexandria, indeed, triumphs.

### 3.3.3  *Alexandrian Generations*

Our ability to date third-century authors from Alexandria is surprisingly robust. A handful are astronomers, always useful for chronology; many more are reported in the context of specific events in the court, which are, typically, datable; others are merely correlated with particular kings. Most

---

[77] He is mentioned by our sources once (DL 4.32): Arcesilaus arrives in Athens and studies geometry with Hipponicus before turning to philosophy. Arcesilaus was born in 316 (hence EANS' date, "C. 285–250"), but the impression of a young man seeking his destiny suggests a Hipponicus active at around the turn of the century. Whoever he was, he failed to leave any other mark on the history of his profession.

of the authors are mutually correlated, in clusters of coeval or succession relations.

This makes possible the following list – likely not exhaustive, but still extensive – of 67 at least roughly datable figures of "cultural production" associated with early Alexandria. I date an author to the period in which he rose to some prominence. My set includes Eratosthenes but excludes Archimedes: effectively, the cutoff point is around the middle of the century. The sense of association with Alexandria includes any relation to the Ptolemaic court. Thus, authors who were summoned to the court even briefly, or who composed court poetry dedicated to the Ptolemies, are included, even if there is no compelling evidence that they would be identified by their contemporaries as residents of Alexandria. Sometimes the Alexandrian connection is very conjectural and based on the circular argument that authors in certain fields would likely be engaged with the Ptolemaic court or with Alexandria.[78] The list is arranged by a division into three generations and, within each, by endeavor. To repeat: as usual, the rough dating refers to the (conjectured) moment of cultural prominence.

### Generation one:[79] 27

**History/geography:**[80] 7 Hecataeus of Abdera, Manetho (Egyptian),[81] Ptolemy Soter, Cleitarchus of Colophon, Amometus (Cyrene?), Philon, Euhemerus[82]

---

[78] The clearest example for such an argument for an Alexandrian connection is that of Erasistratus (following Lloyd, 1975; *pace* Fraser, 1969). I argue in Netz (2015) that such seemingly circular arguments reflect sound, Bayesian probabilism.

[79] By "generation one" are meant such authors whose activity in Alexandria was primarily under Ptolemy I Soter. Forty years, from 322 to 282: it is likely that cultural activity in Alexandria was much more pronounced towards the latter half of this period. (The foundation of the library and the Mouseion is often assumed to have taken place at around the end of the fourth century – Blum, 1991, opts for 295 BCE – but there is no evidence for the date. A weak argument is that Soter was, for many years, engaged in campaigns of war and so perhaps less inclined to support culture; more important is the fact that the sheer size of Alexandria must have been growing rapidly through these years, and with it its likely patronage – a point to which I shall return below.)

[80] Hecataeus, Cleitarchus, Euhemerus and of course Ptolemy Soter himself are clearly defined historical figures and their early dates are not in doubt: FGrH 264, 137, 63 and 138, respectively. Amometus and Philon are much less well known and are dated primarily by association (FGrH 645, 670, respectively).

[81] Advised Soter together with Timotheus (Gmirkin, 2008: 242).

[82] A difficult case. Certainly primarily active in Cassander's court, Callimachus' *Iamb* I.9–11 seems to imply a prolonged stay in Alexandria as well (Fraser, 1972: I.292–3 and notes; Acosta-Hughes and Stephens, 2012: 166–7).

**Medicine:**[83] 6 Eudemus (the anatomist), Herophilus of Chalcedon (Cos), Erasistratus of Ceus, Xenophon of Cos, Chrysippus,[84] Cleophantus of Ceus

**Philosophy:**[85] 6 Strato of Lampsacus[86] (Athens), Demetrius of Phaleron, Theodorus of Cyrene, Hegesias of Cyrene, Diodorus Cronus[87] (Iasus, Megara), Stilpo of Megara

**Poetry:** 1 Rhinthon of Tarentum[88]

**Scholarship:** 1 Philitas of Cos[89]

**Astronomy:**[90] 2 Timocharis, Aristyllus

---

[83] A famous novelistic episode (several ancient sources: see discussion in Breebaart, 1967) finds Erasistratus at the court of Seleucus I in the year 293. A fiction, no doubt – so that the story should not even be used to argue that Erasistratus ever served the Seleucids (so, rightly, Lloyd, 1975) – it would still have to be chronologically likely. The implication is that Erasistratus was well established – sufficiently to have been trusted as the court physician – very early in the third century. The rest follows from the impression from the tendency of our sources to mention Herophilus and Erasistratus as peers; then, Eudemus may have been even older than Herophilus; Xenophon studied together with Herophilus; Cleophantus was Erasistratus' brother. For all, see EANS s.vv.

[84] "The chronology and the identity of the several physicians called Chrysippus remains chaotic" (von Staden, 1989: 46–7). But it is clear that a certain doctor Chrysippus got entangled in a court intrigue and was executed in around 280 (Fraser, 1972: II.502 n.46); see now Berrey (2014a).

[85] For the subject of philosophical sojourns in Alexandria, see Chapter 4, p. 410. I discuss Strato, Diodorus and Stilpo in separate notes. Demetrius of Phaleron became an exile in Alexandria in some year not much later than 307, till his death in 283. Theodorus is said by Diogenes Laertius (II.101–2) to have been protected in Athens by Demetrius of Phaleron and later sent by Ptolemy on a mission to Lysimachus, both statements presented as the premise for rather unconvincing anecdotes; an Alexandrian stay comparable to Demetrius' own is not unlikely. The evidence for Hegesias is worse: Cicero, *Tusc.* I.83–4 reports that the king Ptolemy forbade him to lecture as his (hedonistic) advocacy of suicide was acted upon by too many of his students. He is dated purely by considerations of the generations of the Cyrenaic school, which will make a king later than Soter unlikely; but can such a story carry any substance?

[86] Strato is said to have served as Ptolemy Philadelphus' tutor (DL V.58); he is known to have become the scholarch of the Lyceum in 286 (Sharples, 2011: 28–39). For some reason this is standardly interpreted to mean that Strato was in Alexandria until 286, but it appears, if anything, that Strato was in residence when Theophrastus' will was composed (DL V.53, 56: Strato is simply mentioned alongside the other leaders of the school). Alexander got his own tutor at the difficult age of 13, which Philadelphus reached in 295. So, a stay of five or more years?

[87] DL II.11–112 refers to a disputation in front of Ptolemy Soter between Diodorus Cronus and Stilpo; Stilpo wins, Cronus dies in despair. Callimachus in an epigram (fr. 393) has the crows inspired by the (logically minded) Diodorus, in paraphrase crowing: "Cronus! Consequence! Conditional!" So, Diodorus Cronus was likely present at the court, even if briefly, in the 280s (in time for a Callimachean ironic comment). The evidence for Stilpo depends on the anecdote in Diogenes Laertius.

[88] A weak entry. The *Suda* refers to him as "came to be under Ptolemy the first", which could be strictly chronological rather than stating any relation to Alexandria.

[89] *Suda*: born (or acme??) under Philip and Alexander; then, a tutor to Philadelphus (so, a colleague of Strato; like him, he seems later to have returned to Cos, based on references in Theocritus: Fraser, 1972: I.309).

[90] Timocharis' extant, datable observations – likely a subset of his entire range – are from the years 294 to 271 (for a discussion, see Goldstein and Bowen, 1989). The implication is that he was likely to have been active in Alexandria from the early years of Ptolemy Soter. Aristyllus' extant observations are of fixed stars without any interaction with the planets, and so are not datable; Maeyama (1984)

**Mathematics** 1 Euclid[91]
**Building** 2 Parmenion[92], Sostratus of Cnidus[93]
**Religion** 1 Timotheus of Eleusis[94]

**Generation two:**[95] 25

**Poetry:** 10 Asclepiades of Samos,[96] Apollodorus (author of

argues that they accord best with a generation later than Timocharis. Aristyllus is mentioned by Ptolemy only as a kind of alternate for Timocharis (in general terms – Aristyllus, in fact, precedes Timocharis – *Almagest* VII.1 Heiberg 3.3; particular observations in a single sequence, with observations by Timocharis and by Aristyllus mixed together: VII.3 Heiberg 20.4–22.12). We are informed of Aristyllus in the context of Hipparchus' discovery of the precession of the equinox, based on a comparison of his own fixed star observations with those of Timocharis and Aristyllus. Now, it is unlikely that fixed star observations as such would have been dated by their authors, so Hipparchus must have worked on the basis of an assumption concerning the general date of Timocharid–Aristyllan observations. Had they been known to have been separated by any considerable number of years, this in and of itself would have required some kind of mention (even if merely to note that a gap of a single generation is immaterial for such calculations), and so the absence of any reference to this problem affords some kind of an argument that Ptolemy – and so, perhaps, also Hipparchus – considered Timocharis and Aristyllus as contemporaries. (Note especially the observation by Goldstein and Bowen, 1991: 106–7: are Timocharis' observations systematically south of the Alexandrian zenith, Aristyllus' observations systematically to its north? Would this not suggest a deliberate division of labor between workers on a single enterprise?) If so, the two astronomers fit well a pattern of "clusters" in early Alexandria: the Pleiad, of course (Fraser, 1972: II.871–2 n.6); Zenodotus, Alexander and Lycophron dividing between them the literary field (unfortunately, we have to rely on Tzetzes for that: the evidence is compiled together in Fraser, 1972: II.649 n.14: but the parallel with the putative division of the celestial globe between Timocharis and Aristyllus is irresistible); Manetho and Timotheus acting together as religious authorities (one Greek, the other Egyptian) in the Greek–Egyptian identification of a cult statue; Asclepiades, Posidippus and Hedylus brought together in the introduction to Meleager's *Anthology*; should one also mention Herophilus and Erasistratus, as well as Callimachus and Apollonius themselves – so closely intertwined in our evidence? It was an age of *pairs*.

[91] Famously, there's very little to go by. Proclus in *Eucl.* I 68 is our only substantial source, asserting that Euclid lived at the time of Ptolemy the first (so far, so good), albeit then muddying his own claim with some very weak evidence: that Euclid preceded Archimedes (based on what? On the one – or two – probably late scholia in Archimedes' text? See Netz et al., 2011: I.276–7), but followed Plato (based on the fact Euclid was not mentioned in Proclus' reliable historical sources, stopping a little after Plato! See p. 251 above). Little wonder that scholars have suggested this evidence carries no value and wondered if Euclid could not have been substantially later (Schneider, 1979: 104 n.105).

[92] Architect of the Serapeion; apparently a Soterian but possibly even an Alexandrian foundation: Welles (1962: 285–7).

[93] An architect of the Pharos? Perhaps not; but it is useful to have this reminder of the major architectural program of Soter's Alexandria. That the Pharos was a Soterian initiative is inherently plausible, and accords even with the later date of completion in Eusebius; see Clayton and Price (1988: 143).

[94] The evidence is paired with that for Manetho; see above, n.90.

[95] This refers to the earlier part of Philadelphus' reign, into the 260s, though our dates now tend to be less precise.

[96] A question. Sens (2011: xxv–xxxii) suggests a birth date of *c.* 340–330 and a tenuous connection with Alexandria. The key fact is that he was a major presence for Theocritus at around the mid-270s to the mid-260s (Sens, 2011: xxv–vi); his prominence as a poet could have been achieved either late in the reign of Soter or early in the reign of Philadelphus.

Theriaca),⁹⁷ Glauce of Chios,⁹⁸ Posidippus of Pella,⁹⁹ Hedylus of Samos,¹⁰⁰ Theaetetus of Cyrene,¹⁰¹ Theocritus of Syracuse,¹⁰² Sositheus of Alexandria Troas,¹⁰³ Philicus of Corcyra,¹⁰⁴ Sopater of Paphos¹⁰⁵

**Scholarship:** 5 Zenodotus of Ephesus,¹⁰⁶ Alexander of Pleuron,¹⁰⁷ Lycophron of Chalcis,¹⁰⁸ Callimachus of Cyrene¹⁰⁹, Apollonius of Rhodes¹¹⁰

**Building:** 1 Purgoteles (of Paphos?)¹¹¹

**Philosophy:** 3 Sphaerus of Borysthenes (Athens),¹¹² Posidonius of Alexandria (Athens),¹¹³ Colotes of Lampsacus¹¹⁴

**Mechanics:** 1 Ctesibius¹¹⁵

⁹⁷ Little evidence; see EANS s.v.; and Overduin (2014: 7).
⁹⁸ Citharode; mistress of Philadelphus (Fraser, 1972: II.818 n.165).
⁹⁹ Court references make a distinguished activity in the 270s all but certain; that he was active, and honored, well beyond that is clear from both the evidence of inscriptions as well as from his own work (Thompson, 2005).
¹⁰⁰ Refers to both Glauce (Fraser, 1972: I.573) and Ctesibius (Fraser, 1972: I.571), the latter reference framed in a temple context – a dedication to Arsinoe – that allows a dating to the 260s.
¹⁰¹ Referred to by Callimachus (Fraser, 1972: II.843 n.318).
¹⁰² Griffiths (1979); Fraser (1972: I.666–7). Court poetry is established for the 270s.
¹⁰³ Dead by mid-century (Fraser, 1972: II.851–2 nn.356–7).
¹⁰⁴ Priest of Dionysius in Philadelphus' Pompe (Fraser, 1972: II.870 n.1, and also discussion in 872 n.7 and 859 n.407): so, likely (Foertmeyer, 1988) during 275/4.
¹⁰⁵ Athenaeus 71a–b: Born under Alexander, died under Philadelphus; as we recall from section 2.3.1, our tendency is to see an author as "distinguished" not at the presumed acme of 40 but at the more mature age of 50, which would fit best with the early years of Philadelphus.
¹⁰⁶ Vit. Zenod. 369 West: a pupil of Philitas; tutor to the "children" of Ptolemy (i.e. not a tutor to Philadelphus himself; Euergetes would have required a tutor at some point beginning between the mid-270s and the mid-260s).
¹⁰⁷ He is found at the court of Antigonus at around 270 (Vita Arat. V 147 Maass); Tzetzes, as noted above, saw Zenodotus, Alexander and Lycophron as contemporaries.
¹⁰⁸ Fraser (1972: II.649–50 n.17). He seems to lose at this point his passion for detailed footnotes ("the familiar links with Philadelphus, Arsinoe, etc."). In short, the 270s.
¹⁰⁹ Famously dated through court poetry of two distinct eras: the 270s and the 240s: as explained by Acosta-Hughes and Stephens (2012: 2), this is because Ptolemaic court poetry was primarily inspired by first ladies, of whom there was none in the 260s and 250s.
¹¹⁰ Second librarian, so in this respect might be considered "later than" Zenodotus; but very clearly also "a contemporary of Callimachus" (the vita evidence for the quarrel is now considered worthless – Lefkowitz, 1980 – but it does make clear that the two were always considered contemporary). The conclusion is that Apollonius assumed the librarianship at an older age than Zenodotus did.
¹¹¹ See EANS s.v.; the evidence is literary (implying genuine elite fame) as well as epigraphic.
¹¹² Subject of a short biography by Diogenes Laertius (VII. 177–8); I return to discuss the anecdote of this philosopher in the Ptolemaic court in Chapter 4, p. 410.
¹¹³ Diogenes Laertius VII.38: said to be among the pupils of Zeno.
¹¹⁴ A critique of rival philosophies, known through Plutarch's Against Colotes, was addressed to Philadelphus and singled out Arcesilaus for special criticism: so, likely, the 260s.
¹¹⁵ EANS s.v.; the dating depends on that of the poet Hedylos.

**Medicine:** 2 Callianax,[116] Strato the Erasistratean[117]
**Astronomy:** 1 Aristarchus of Samos[118]
**Geography:** 2 Dionysius,[119] Timosthenes of Rhodes[120]

### Generation three:[121] 15

**Medicine:**[122] 4 Bacchius of Tanagra, Callimachus, Philinus of Cos, Andreas of Carystus
**Scholarship:** 5 Eratosthenes of Cyrene, Aristophanes of Byzantium,[123] Hermippus of Smyrna,[124] Philostephanus of Cyrene,[125] Istrus[126]
**Astronomy:** 3 Conon of Samos,[127] Dositheus of Pelusion,[128] Dionysius[129]
**Mechanics:** 1 Philon of Byzantium[130]
**Poetry:** 2 Machon of Corinth (Sicyon?),[131] Dioscorides of Nicopolis (?)[132]

---

[116] Von Staden (1989: 478–9). [117] Sharples (2011: 14–17).

[118] Huxley (1964) provides the poor argument for Aristarchus' Alexandrian association (essentially, that he made observations even while Aristyllus and Timocharis did as well); poor as it is, it is inherently likely that he was connected with developments in Alexandria. An observation dated to 280 BCE is reported in Ptolemy's *Almagest* 3.1 on the good authority of Hipparchus.

[119] Jacoby 717; sent to India by Ptolemy Philadelphus.

[120] EANS s.v.; fleet commander under Ptolemy Philadelphus.

[121] These are the last years of Philadelphus, reaching into the early years of Euergetes: from the late 260s and into the 240s.

[122] For Andreas, Bacchius and Callimachus, see von Staden (1989: 472–7, 484–500, 480–3, respectively). Philinus was a major figure (founder of empiricism): Deichgräber (1930: 254–5). All the dates are produced by reference to Herophilus (the generation of his students).

[123] Eratosthenes and Aristophanes are among the most famous philologers of Alexandria, also apparently successive librarians, and so are tightly dated (Pfeiffer, 1968: 172).

[124] Fraser (1972: II.656 n.52). "Callimachean" (Athenaeus 58f., 213f.): this is taken by the literature to mean "Callimachus' student".

[125] Date, once again, produced by reference to Callimachus, perhaps his teacher; see Capel Badino (2010: 29–35).

[126] Jacoby 334: another "Callimachean". (As his inclusion in Jacoby implies, his scholarship touched more on history.)

[127] Dated through the Lock of Berenice (Gutzwiller, 1992: 359): so, prominent in the 240s.

[128] Addressee of several works by Archimedes (Netz, 1998a): so, active in the third quarter of the third century.

[129] What evidence there is is discussed in Jones (2003: 71–2). We have a certain Dionysius, said to be of Alexandria, whose calendar had the epochal year 285 BCE; observations according to that calendar are recorded for the years 272 to 241. The more economical assumption in my view would be to make Dionysius not only the maker of the calendar but also the observer (Jones, in EANS s.v., seems to date the author to 285, in which case we have one more astronomer in the generation of Aristyllus and Timocharis, while "our" astronomer, observing in the years 272 to 241, should be considered anonymous).

[130] A very important – and extant! – author, only weakly dated (he is aware of Ctesibius: EANS s.v.)

[131] Gow (1965: 1–11) has the floruit at around mid-century; perhaps he belongs better with the previous generation.

[132] Clark (2001: 2–5). A reference to Machon suggests that Dioscorides could have been somewhat younger.

Generation one, we may now see, is essentially the post-Chaeronea
government sector, only more so. Geography – and history of a contemporary, courtly bent – predominates, its seven authors giving the age
its tone. Several others are clear creatures of the court: two scholars acting
as tutors, a philosopher who's a political protégé in exile, a religious
authority invited to give the king advice on a cult statue. A notable
continuity with the post-Chaeronea patterns of patronage is the absence
of poetry (Philitas is a scholar and likely hired as such; Rhinthon is the
only author in this group who was primarily a poet – and his association
with Alexandria is the most tenuous). A new departure is the sheer
number of medical authors, once again probably a court phenomenon.
We are told, however fancifully, of Erasistratus as a court physician to
Selucus I; Diphilus of Siphnus was, at the same time, a court physician at
Lysimachus' court;[133] would Herophilus have been granted his famous
access to dead – or living – bodies without such a court position? The
obscure Chrysippus, for sure, was caught up in a court intrigue. The sheer
emphasis on doctors at the court seems to be a distinctive feature of this
generation; perhaps Alexander's heirs took heed of his example and
resolved to take better care of their own health. Surely, more philosophers
are to be found than in the previous generation's courts, but the peripatetic connection to Macedonian courts is of course long-lived, and it is in
this court context that we find Demetrius and Strato. The Megarian
connection is intriguing, if perhaps tenuous. And the Cyrenaics drop by –
how could they not pass through nearby Alexandria? Indeed, the massive
presence of Cyrene is the only remarkable feature of the map of origins of
the cultural figures of early Alexandria.
     Fraser must have overreached:[134]

> [Among] those eminent in literature and the sciences in Alexandria we
> notice a preponderance of persons originating from the Ptolemaic empire
> and associated regions (excepting Cyprus, the poverty of which in intellec-
> tual matters is conspicuous), particularly Cyrene, Cos and Samos. So
> marked is the preponderance of persons from these cities in both literature
> and science that, without neglecting the role of the individual, the general-
> ization may be hazarded that the intellectual achievement of Ptolemaic
> Alexandria was based on them.

We see that about 10 percent of the attested early cultural figures of
Alexandria come from Cyrene and about another 10 percent from Cos

---

[133] Athenaeus 51a.     [134] Fraser (1972: I.307); echoed by Green (1985: 157).

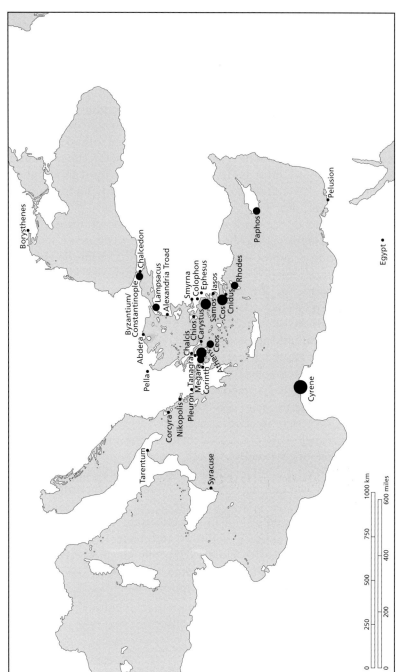

Map 14   Origins of authors in early Alexandria

and Samos taken together. Putting this map side by side with the post-Chaeronea map, we see that there is nothing surprising about the low numbers of Cypriots, and nothing inherently surprising about the large numbers of individuals from islands *such as* Cos or Samos: the islands/Asia Minor region formed the base of Alexander's entourage, as well. The absence of Athens is indeed striking (even the philosophers are mostly Megarian and Cyrenaic) – but this once again agrees well with the overall contours of post-Chaeronea intellectual life other than philosophy. Nothing distinctive: we remain with the Cyrene phenomenon, which therefore must be understood as a strictly regional phenomenon.[135] One wonders: to a Cyrenaic, was Alexandria at all "remote", at all an "alibi"?

Are the contents of the work of generation one at all distinct from those of earlier scientists? (We should rightfully concentrate on science, for this generation is almost devoid of poetry.) Other than the geographers, we see a few remarkable achievements: the first systematic astronomical observations by the Greeks; Euclid's *Elements* (perhaps); the bold new turn in medicine led by Erasistratus and Herophilus. But would it be far-fetched to detect, in this group of intellectual achievements, a descriptive, perhaps even a "geographical", tendency? Let me illustrate the point briefly: I shall return to discuss it in the following chapter. Now, this geographical tendency is fairly obvious in the astronomical case. Indeed, one attractive hypothesis is that Timocharis and Aristyllus were gathering materials for the construction of a celestial globe.[136] If so, they were in effect commissioned – surely, by the court – to produce a *map*. Is it not logical that, having produced all those surveys of Meroe, one's attention would at some point be drawn even further, into the sky? To briefly add a fantasy: is it an accident that the more senior of the two astronomers got the more *southerly* portion of the sky (see note 90 above) – the mapping of an exotic, astronomical Aethiopia? Now, Herophilus and Erasistratus were first of all medical practitioners in the Hippocratic tradition, and many of their contributions can be understood in this context (clinically, the most striking was Herophilus' emphasis on the phenomenon of the pulse: von Staden, 1989: section VII.4; theoretically, the most striking was Erasistratus'

---

[135] For the recruitment sources of the Ptolemaic kingdom – literally, in the terms of the origins of mercenaries – see Bagnall (1976: 88 n.40) – "heavy representation of Asia Minor and the islands".
[136] See n.90 above: Goldstein and Bowen (1991: 105–6).

broadly "mechanistic" program of biological explanation, original in its contents but true to the spirit of earlier medicine and philosophy: von Staden, 1997). Where they stand out from earlier – and later – medical practice is in their sustained anatomical project, involving apparently the description of the entirety of the human body,[137] based on bodies – dead or alive – supplied by the kings, presumably in Alexandria.[138] This is sometimes ascribed to peripatetic influence – a subject to which we shall return below.[139] A project such as this would have to depend on royal goodwill and to reflect royal interests: was Soter a peripatetic? Or was he, in general, interested in knowing what's out there? Perhaps we may put it like this: the court experience of the post-Chaeronea age – focused on getting the *phainomena* first,[140] on surveying one's world – overlapped with new epistemological tendencies; and so a king in Alexandria had geographers describing voyages up the Nile, astronomers constructing globes, physicians producing works in anatomy. Another way for us to think about the end of Alexandrian anatomy, then: it was never a self-motivated scientific program, in which dissection was perceived as essential to the doctor as such. Rather, it was a specific royal commission. Once the anatomical survey was considered complete, there was no point retracing it – and no new commissions. Nor did later astronomers, prior to Hipparchus, accumulate further observations of the fixed stars in the manner of Timocharis and Aristyllus.

[137] The case that Herophilus' project was explicitly that of mapping could be bolstered if we could argue that (1) Herophilus adopted the ordering principle de capite ad calcem and (2) that this was an original decision. (Then, we would see Herophilus as engaging in a new type of project, aiming at comprehensive coverage as a key goal of anatomy and introducing explicit principles to sustain this goal of comprehensiveness.) Von Staden (1989: 154–5) tends to support (1), though he emphasizes that this must be a tentative conclusion; it might be added that the later popularity of this ordering principle seats well with the assumption that Herophilus himself – certainly one of the key models in ancient anatomy – used it (for some of the later history, see Flemming, 2007: 253–4). For (2), certainly several treatments in the Hippocratic move in a downward direction (to an extent, *Affections*; *Mochlicon* and *Places in Man* even more so; but not *Fractures/Joints*).

[138] This use of the human body is by far the most commented upon aspect of Hellenistic medicine; the most useful treatment remains von Staden (1989: section VI.1); compare Nutton (2004: 131–2). There is virtually only one reliable source, which is only fairly reliable, however: Celsus, *Medicine* I. intr. (translation by von Staden, 1989: 187): "Herophilus and Erasistratus, they say, did this in the best way by far when they cut open men who were alive, criminals out of prison, received from kings." (Why "kings"? As Lloyd, 1975, points out, it is much more economic to envisage a single program of human vivisection in Alexandria rather than multiple ones in several courts; so, a program begun under Soter and continued by Philadelphus? Or perhaps we should not read too much into Celsus' rhetorical prose – in which contrasts are relished, between life and death, between *criminals* and *kings*.)

[139] See, e.g., Vegetti (1998).

[140] So, Herophilus: von Staden (1989: 125–6, with discussion in 117–24).

Could Euclid's project fit in the same kind of endeavor? Within Greek mathematics he presents a paradoxical figure. From Hippocrates of Chios, via authors such as Archytas, Theaethetus, Menaechmus and then the other major Hellenistic figures, authors in the Greek exact sciences are almost always mentioned for their specific, original contributions – unless, that is, they are essentially lost to us and remain just as a mere name.[141] But Euclid is extant – in a massive corpus, large parts of which must be genuine, and which appears to be mostly derivative. He is remembered primarily for a project of *surveying past knowledge*. That he was content to do that suggests, to my mind, a good stipend, as well as a "geographical" – courtly – post-Chaeronea mindset. The best evidence for his nature as a scientist comes, perhaps, from an author 100 years younger: Apollonius. Imagine a book with 181 propositions, each of which is but a variation on the same problem, taking its various cases one by one.[142] This is Apollonius' *Cutting off of a Ratio*. The problem (stated in the abstract; it is an abstract problem) is as follows: given two points on two separate lines, to draw a line from a certain point (which is not on the two given lines) that cuts through the two given lines and creates segments – bounded by the produced cutting line and by the two given points – such that the two segments stand to each other in a given ratio. Apollonius goes on to solve this, as the two lines are parallel or fail to be parallel; if the latter, according to the relative position of the point of intersection, each case produced through both analysis and synthesis.[143] Whether or not pedagogic in character, the treatise proceeds through the logic of the exhaustive survey: not only a problem, divided according to each of its many cases, but also a solution, presented through all its parts – analysis, diorism and synthesis. This forms something of an exception within Apollonius' corpus but may be seen as a reflection of several works from Euclid's generation. We may start with a work extant, once again, only in Arabic – but plausibly attributed to Euclid: the

[141] Consider Theodosius: an author of works in spherics which are perhaps primarily derivative, he is also credited by Vitruvius (IX.8.1) as the inventor of a new type of sundial; or Autolycus: his own treatment of spherics need not have been original, but he is also known for cogent, original criticisms of Eudoxus' astronomy (Simplicius, *In DC* 504).

[142] The judgement of Hogendijk (1986: 224): "Long and dreary."

[143] The best treatment of this treatise is by Saito and Sidoli (2010: 595–608). The text is otherwise largely neglected by modern scholarship, because it is known only through Arabic translation (so that, indeed, there is room for some concern regarding its precise presentation), and because of its somewhat anomalous structure. As Saito and Sidoli insist, however, this anomalous structure must be seen as revealing. They point out that this text heavily relies on analysis, presented in much fuller detail than elsewhere, thus suggesting it is something of a pedagogic exercise, setting out to display the practice of analysis.

*Division of Figures*, once again, is a survey of various cases of a type of problem, thus a very close antecedent indeed to Apollonius;[144] it is quite possible that the Euclidean works merely attested in Pappus – the *Porisms* and the *Surface Loci* – proceeded, similarly, through the survey of mutually related problems.[145] As pointed out by Hogendijk, the slight hints we have for works such as the *Porisms* suggest a more creative – and more difficult – author than that of the *Elements* (and, indeed, it is probably this very difficulty which made such works largely disappear). We find, then, that Euclid dedicated much of his energies, and especially his more creative work, to the project of the *comprehensive survey*. Very little is known about any of Euclid's contemporaries, if indeed any can be safely dated. But the strongest historical figure – Aristaeus – seems once again to have been the author of a treatise dedicated to the surveying-of-a-problem.[146]

So much for mathematics. And then, what about medicine itself? Not just the body, but medical *knowledge*? Medical knowledge, in the late fourth century, was already varied and contradictory. It could not be summed up into a single deductive sequence in the manner of the *Elements*. In the field of medicine, then, the equivalent project to Euclid's *Elements* would have been collection of the available works. Sure enough, we find that, in all likelihood, it was at this historical juncture that the Hippocratic corpus was formed. Herophilus, already, has started on the project of Hippocratic commentary.[147] Whether the bodies of criminals, or

---

[144] Archibald (1915).

[145] The slight indications we have for the *Porisms* (for which one usually starts from Simson's heroic effort of reconstruction; see Tweddle, 2000) are summed up in Hogendijk (1987): what we find are different sources, providing variations on the same problem with slightly different conditions.

[146] The most extended discussion of Aristaeus is Knorr (1982). Knorr's conclusions are extreme, though not impossible (so, for instance, he suggests that there was not one but two authors named Aristaeus, later conflated by our sources). This merely serves to remind us how little we actually know. The key question is the nature of Aristaeus' contribution to the theory of conic sections. Some evidence suggests he wrote works directly in that theory; other evidence suggests he surveyed problems in the manner of other surveying works mentioned above. The compelling core of Knorr's reconstruction is to make Aristaeus' contribution a study of various constructions solving problems, out of which the conic sections emerge. A surveying work in the manner of Euclid – which provides some materials for the later mathematics of Archimedes and Apollonius.

[147] Von Staden (1989: 427–42); the collection of Hippocratic texts as a medical endeavor is well attested from Bacchius onwards (von Staden, 1989: 484–500), and this is sometimes taken to represent a decline in the quality of medical research and perhaps the influence of philology on medicine: the library taking over the dissection room (so Sluiter, 1995: 194, echoing remarks already made by von Staden). What does seem to emerge from the evidence is that, by the time of Herophilus' pupils, an assumption was already in place that a Hippocratic collection (not necessarily identical with ours) existed. The most economic assumption, in my view, is that this collection was put in place, then, in Alexandria's first generation. For a recent, authoritative survey of the problem of the formation of the collection, with references, see van der Eijk (2015a: 20–4).

Hippocrates' body of works: the medical authors of Soter's court produced *surveys*.

Alexandria of generation one did not stand out from the entire generation preceding it. Nor did it stand out, in its intellectual climates, from other, contemporary courts. As mentioned above, court physicians must have been present elsewhere; we have noted above the presence of geographers and historians together with the other diadochi. Hieronymus of Cardia served Antigonus I; Megasthenes and Patrocles served Seleucus I; Ophellas, ruler of Cyrene, was an author himself. The parallels are easy to find but they bring out an obvious asymmetry in sheer numbers. And, indeed, here, above all, must be found the originality of Soter's Alexandria.

I was careful to speak of "generations", an imprecise term; indeed, my "generation one" is certainly longer than generations two and three, as it stretches in theory from about 320 to about 280. In practice, its members were prominent in Alexandria mostly over the last two decades of Soter's reign; many of the authors of generation two had already begun their activities in the first years of Philadelphus. The division by years is thus not as sharp as the distinction into generations might suggest; and, clearly, members of generation one could in many cases survive to witness the brilliance of generation two. As a further consequence, the overall quantitative trend is not so much of long-term stability (as suggested by the numbers of generation one, 27, or generation two, 25) but, rather, of a gradual build-up, the number of cultural figures active in Alexandria growing from the 300s to the 270s, only then reaching a plateau. If we concentrate on the more precise among our dates, we find:

> *c.* 305 (Demetrius of Phaleron in exile), *c.* 295 (Philadelphus gains his tutors, Philitas and Strato), 294 (Timocharis' earliest dated observation), 293 (the Erasistratus romance), 283/2 (later date for completion of Pharos), 280 (execution of Chrysippus, dated observation by Aristarchus), 276 **to the 260s** (several Arsinoite poetic allusions: Callimachus, Theocritus, Hedylus hence Ctesibius, Posidippus), 275–274 (the Pompe: Philicus), *c.* 270? (Zenodotus engaged as tutor to Euergetes? Alexander of Pleuron found in Pella?), 268 (apparent earliest likely date for Colotes' dedication of a treatise to Philadelphus)

The impression is clear: generation one was in place mostly from the mid-290s onwards, joined about a decade or two later by generation two. The consequence is an incredible density of attested cultural figures active, mostly in Alexandria, around 280.

Are there precedents in previous courts? In a sense, there are: as noted above, Alexander's retinue is known to have contained about a dozen known cultural figures; in the most expansive reading of the sources, Dionysius I had well over 15 known cultural figures associated with his court. Syracuse did not get its Fraser, and so this is surely an undercount (then again, many of the names associated with Dionysius could well be figments of later apocryphal traditions). Still, it might be of some use to compare Alexandria's generation one with a list of the court of Dionysius I, once again simply reiterating Sanders' list from pages 280–1 above. Here are two salient comparisons.

**Generic composition of courts**

|  | Dionysius I | Soter |
| --- | --- | --- |
| Performance (poetry and speech making) | 53% | 4% |
| Non-performance | 47% | 96% |

**Cities of origin**

|  | Dionysius I | Soter |
| --- | --- | --- |
| Athenian origins | 60% | 11% |
| Non-Athenian origins | 40% | 89% |

This calls for very little explanation. Dionysius I's world was dominated by contemporary Athenian performance. Soter's world still displayed various asymmetries: philosophy was even more Athenian than a century earlier, and drama, to the extent that it was a living presence – above all, in comedy – was equally focused in Athens. But the canon was now closed, and cultural life already thrived in the specialized genres, where place no longer mattered. Hence, being "elsewhere" mattered less. A geographer or a medical author in Alexandria, in the early third century, was not in any important sense "away from Athens".

They were not "away from Athens"; which made it easier to be, indeed, *in Alexandria*. Neither Dionysius nor Alexander had a major concentration of authors-belonging-to-a-city. Dionysius I attracted visitors whose cultural horizons were fixed away from Syracuse. Alexander's retinue was a campaign and never "resided" anywhere. Dionysius was powerless to construct a new Athens: individuals might be for sale but poetics are formed by structural forces beyond any single individual's control. But, by the time of Soter, the poetics were already altered and culture had become mobile. The expedition settled.

The argument, then, is quite simple. Since the specialized genres did not have any particular spatial attachment, they could go anywhere, and so would tend to concentrate in the one place which attracted most, by the simple logic of network effects. Now, we may borrow Scheidel's (2004: 15) table of lower and upper estimates for the sheer size of the population of Alexandria through the period that interests us.[148]

| Date | Lower | Upper |
| --- | --- | --- |
| 330 | 5 | 5 |
| 300 | 66 | 101 |
| 270 | 148 | 230 |
| 240 | 230 | 359 |

In all likelihood, Alexandria's population then stabilized at a level not far above that of the middle of the third century (Scheidel, 2004: 17). The three generations of this section span, then, the years of Alexandria's growth. And we may now note the significance of their central inflection at about the year 280. By this point the city of Alexandria had reached a population of well over 100,000, a significant number not only in decimal but also in historical terms. At about the year 300 – when intellectuals began to congregate in Alexandria – the city was about the same order of magnitude as Athens and Syracuse at their highest.[149] Two decades later Alexandria was already by far the biggest Greek center. It is probably not an accident that, at just that time, its culture went through a transition, from the standard (if bigger) government sector of the post-Chaeronea courts, to a new cultural synthesis that expanded the logic of the specialized genres of the court, via scholarship, into poetry itself.

For now, all of a sudden, there was a major concentration of cultural figures residing within a single place, that place being *other than Athens*. Someone – Callimachus? – sensed the significance of this new development, the reconstitution of earlier *audiences* making possible the reconstitution of earlier *poetics*. The old cliché, so often discussed, resisted, repeated – as if Callimachus and his generation mark the transition to a new, non-

---

[148] The estimates are derived from comparative assumptions, so that the lower estimate is based on the growth of Edo, the upper one on that of London. As Scheidel goes on to explain, the lower bound is probably much closer to the reality.

[149] Morris (2005: 15–18).

performative literature – has it, in a way, upside down; it is in error not just because performance would always remain salient but because it studies literary history in a narrow, belletristic sense. Thus, Callimachus appears to follow on the heels of Pindar and Euripides – Plato and Menander offering, perhaps, a halfway house leading to Callimachus' final, alleged, non-performativity. The actual literary world occupied by Callimachus was made of a wider array of genres other than the belletristic, and for 50 years, already, performance had been marginal to most Greek literary practice. Callimachus emerged from a world of historians, philosophers, geographers, physicians and mathematicians. He himself, after all, was primarily a grammarian.[150] The canon has been closed already, you see. And then – in Alexandria, a new development: a sufficiently powerful *local* audience. A revolutionary, nearly archaic development, the springboard to Callimachus' revolutionary, nearly archaic poetics.

The typical "geographic" impulse of the post-Chaeronea generation was extended, in Alexandria's generation one, into fields such as anatomy, astronomy and geometry. It was most natural to produce this kind of surveying, non-performative work within the specialized genres. At some point the extension was made: one could survey the lands, the sky, the human body; one could collect Hippocrates; put together past achievements in the exact sciences – so why not survey the literary field itself, the already established canon of the performative genres? And then, finally, we have this typical Alexandrian combination: a surveying of the literary field, combined with an original poetic agenda that revives archaic forms in new ways, emphasizing the variety of one's endeavors. In a formula, we can sum up as follows. It is sometimes considered that Alexandria brought about the closure of the canon of performance, but it was the other way around: the much earlier closure of the canon of performance made Alexandria possible. It reshaped the nature of the relation between author and audience, making authorship gravitate to the specialized disciplines, where locality hardly mattered, which in turn made the creation of new centers – and so, the finding of new audiences – even more difficult. With fewer local concentrations, the only way to build any cultural practice was through a network of communication. Hence, a new model of centrality, based on a unique center surrounded by an unstructured cluster, wherein, crucially, the specific character of the central city – other than its very centrality – did

[150] And so, as a grammarian, he was primarily perceived (Acosta-Hughes and Stephens, 2012: their original emphasis on this point emerges from their original attention to Callimachus within a wider, not just literary, context).

not matter. It could have been anywhere else, but, for the time being, Alexandria was the biggest city, with the most generous patronage. It would therefore remain, for long enough, the center of the specialized genres.

In the following chapter I will try to spell out this formula through the detail of Alexandria's cultural achievement. Meanwhile, I turn to consider how Athens, at the same time, became its own, distinct, cultural center through its own, distinct, logic of post-canonicity.

## 3.4   The Road to Athens

To understand Alexandria, we needed to follow the overall spatial trajectory of ancient science. For Athens, we need to do the same for philosophy. In section 3.4.1, I follow the longue durée of philosophy in the Mediterranean in the archaic and classical eras: here, space *always* mattered. The question is not exactly why philosophy developed an institutional center, in the Hellenistic era, but, rather, why Athens should have retained this unique role: I discuss this in section 3.4.2. The rise of the philosophical schools involved a routinization of charisma: which was possible only with Athens, with its residual charisma of Socrates and, in general, of public performance. Philosophy – as well as new comedy, yet another Athenian staple – went through a *routinization* of charisma, and so survived, within the same institutional pattern, for almost two centuries.

### 3.4.1   Before Athens: The Rise of Philosophical Spatial Organization

Before Athens. . . This is already ground we have covered, after all. Looking for the rise of the brand-name author in the archaic world (see section 2.3.3 above), we have compared poetry to wisdom and considered the rise of famous wise men.[151] Philosophy, we noticed, echoed its poetic counterpart by a gap of a generation or so: the major moment of the formation of the poetic tradition, at around the turn of the seventh century, was answered by the rise of Milesian philosophy near the middle of the sixth century. The lyric repertoire was expanded in the second half of the sixth century – and, a few decades later, a number of central figures emerged in philosophy. The processes are parallel, and they are broadly similar in scale – as well as in

---

[151] For the fundamental parallelism between sages and poets – both, at this stage, performative – see Martin (1993). Tell (2007), in particular, pursues this further, considering the role of the performance of wisdom in the Panhellenic games. (We note how wisdom-as-performance implies, already, a spatial dimension.)

their geographic reach. It is perhaps best to be as inclusive as possible in constructing such a list, as our information is so limited. Map 15 lists the earliest figures of Greek wisdom, up to and including Parmenides (and including the Seven Sages).

This is indeed reminiscent of the spread of lyric poetry. The Aegean Islands are well represented: two wise men, Cleobolus and Pittacus, are from Rhodes and Lesbos, respectively, while two atypical Presocratic figures, Pherecydes and Cleostratus, are from Syros and Tenedos, respectively; Pythagoras, finally, was born in Samos. The Seven Sages include three mainland figures: Solon, Chilon and Periander, from Athens, Sparta and Corinth, respectively. Of course, the "Seven Sages" are political no less than intellectual figures, and so their map resembles better the map of archaic power (early power, apparently, sometimes had the connotation of wisdom: the very early form of the connection, noted in section 2.3.1 above, between social and cultural prominence). Asia Minor of course remains crucial, not only with the three Milesians but also with two other very well known figures (Heraclitus and Xenophanes, from Ephesus and Colophon, respectively – the latter essentially a poet rather more than a sage), as well as one final sage (Bias of Priene) and another atypical Presocratic (Metrodorus of Lampsacus). The west comes as something of an afterthought: Pythagoras travels there and Parmenides is active right at the end of this early period; once again, this echoes the lyric pattern, where activity is centered on the Aegean with only two notable poets from the west. So, the geography of early Greek wisdom is essentially that of early Greek poetry – with the major difference that *some kind of regional specificity does emerge*. Philosophy – unlike poetry – developed the Milesian phenomenon, one not only of continuity within a single city (which is perhaps comparable to the role of Lesbos or Ceus in lyric poetry) but also of a distinctive local "tradition".

Following Parmenides, philosophy takes off and a new geographical regime emerges (see Map 16).

In this "Socratic" era – the two time nodes –450 and –400 – the 50 attested philosophers are best divided into three: those with some kind of documented attachment to Athens, of which there are 14; those with some documented connection to the west (Magna Graecia and Sicily), of which there are 18; and the "other" 18. Now, when authors have a documented connection to Athens as well as some other city, the locations of those *other* cities are similar to those of the "other" categories and are largely of the "Aegean" kind, seen, for instance, in archaic poetry or in the map of mathematics in the classical era (which is indeed not much different

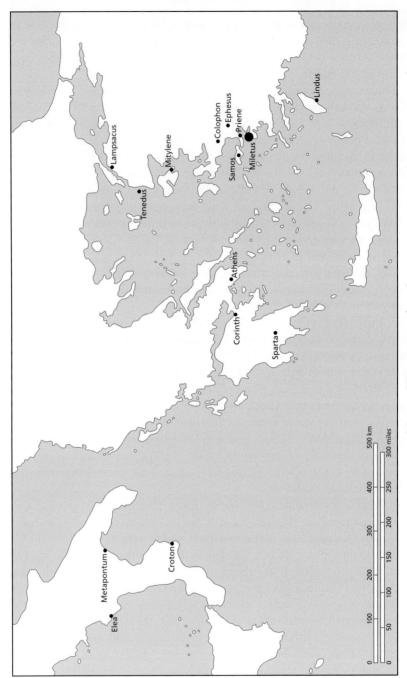

Map 15    Wise men in archaic Greece

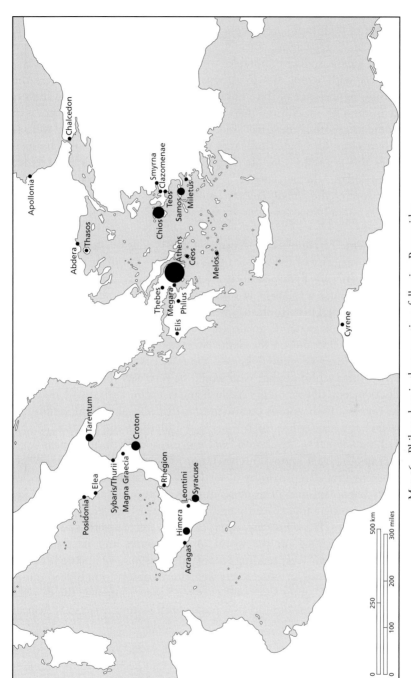

Map 16   Philosophers in the generations following Parmenides

from that of philosophy in that era – I shall return to this below). Cyrene makes a small appearance, merely suggesting its much more significant future; Chios is suddenly notable, with four names (of course, this is a major city with strong ties to Athens in this period). One notices the surprising significance of the "Thracian" area, usually not of such importance in most of our cultural maps: Diogenes of Apollonia, Anaxagoras of Clazomenae, both Protagoras and Democritus of Abdera (as well as Thrasymachus of Chalcedon; and note also Thrasyalces of Thassus). Perhaps this is a reflection, once again, of the area's strategic importance in the period of Athenian apogee.[152] What is perhaps more significant is the near-erasure of the Ionian center. Leucippus was perhaps from Miletus; there was also a Diogenes of Smyrna; that's all. Once again: the *transiency* of centers.

The theme of regional concentration emerges again, however, in the west. The majority of the western philosophers – 12 out of 18 – are likely "Pythagorean"; no Pythagorean is attested elsewhere. Of the remaining, Zeno is of course a follower of his compatriot Parmenides; Gorgias and Euthydemus are both "sophists", who do, however, engage directly with Parmenidean dialectic; Empedocles had his own, strange, hybrid of Ionian-style reflections on the elements, mixed with a gospel of salvation. Otherwise, close to nothing is known about Idaeus of Himera (what we do know suggests a philosopher who would fit very well the Aegean world), while Alcmaeon of Croton is a medical and scientific author who does not strike one as a Pythagorean by any means; that several ancient authorities nevertheless consider him such[153] perhaps underlines the fact that, at this period, merely being "of Croton" was suggestive of Pythagoreanism.

Perhaps this well-known interpretation should not be pressed too far, but there is after all a proximity of sorts between Parmenides, Empedocles and "Pythagoreanism", all three tending away from the world of appearances, suggesting a higher reality with its promise of salvation. In short, at around 450 BCE philosophy diverges into two separate clusters, the Aegean concentrated on the world of appearances and its underlying material causes, the west tending to deny the existence of apparent reality or to turn away from its value: a very well known observation indeed (more on this below). Slightly less familiar is the observation that the distinct clusters of belief correlate, up to a point, with distinct practices. Aegean

---

[152] The geopolitical significance of this area for Athens' dominance over the Greek world has been well known since de Ste. Croix (1972).
[153] Zhmud (2012: 121–4).

philosophy is that of "modern" prose authors. Thus, even the Aegean representative of Parmenides – Melissus – takes it as his business to restate Parmenides' philosophy (originally in hexameter) in prose form. Ion of Chios was a poet, a successful tragedian as well as a lyric poet (and, all round, a rare example of a single figure representing several genres). He also was a philosopher – but his philosophy was written in prose. There seems to have been a generic expectation, then, that poetry is not useful for philosophy. Not so in the west, where Empedocles, at least, did produce a belated epic – however lame – on his philosophical subject.[154] This brings up a related point: Empedocles' epic was likely his *unique* work.[155] It appears that Philolaus, too, was the author of one work alone,[156] and it is no less likely that Zeno's paradoxes emerge from a single work written to buttress the arguments of his master.[157] As for other "Pythagoreans", it is not at all clear how many writings they produced, their record being transmitted more through testimony and anecdote.[158] In the Aegean, however, philosophical authorship explodes, whether in the form of writing or in speeches. There are exceptions, of course (Socrates would end up as the most important philosopher of his age, never having "authored" a single work), but the writing of *many* prose works is the distinctive invention of the later fifth century (I return to this in Chapter 6, pages 634–5), and it is with philosophy, in this time and place, that Greece produces its first mega-prolific prose author – Democritus. In broad outline, then, the west is a place where philosophers engage with the other-worldly and do so through poetry or, in general, through sage-like,

[154] Aristotle famously denigrated Empedocles as a poet (*Poetics*, 1447b17–20), which is not self-evident based on the quality of his extant fragments. Hardie (1995: 207) suggests this might have been merely polemical ("You might think him a good poet, but I do not"). Perhaps the more standard account (e.g. Newman, 1986: 38–45) is to see here Aristotelian genre theory, objecting to the very category of the "didactic epic": the point is that, in Aristotle's time, such a genre had not yet come to be (I return to discuss this in the following chapter), so that Empedocles appeared to Aristotle as inappropriately trying to repurpose an archaic form for a modern purpose.

[155] Osborne (1987) first recognized that the two titles attested in the ancient literature, "On Nature" and "Purifications", probably refer to a single work; most scholars now believe that the papyrus find (Inwood, 2001) corroborates this interpretation.

[156] Huffman (1993: 12–16). There is an ancient tradition ascribing three books, but it is obviously a later invention.

[157] Kirk, Raven and Schofield (KRS) (1983: 264). Once again, the *Suda* ascribes more works. The general point is that the ancient tradition that filters our information on the pre-Socratics took it for granted that authorship, as such, standardly involved the writing of many books.

[158] Which gives rise to debate, in the scholarship, as to the very nature of their activity. I thus argue, for instance in Netz (2014a), that Eurytus' philosophy, such as it was, consisted of public performances of calculation upon the abacus!

performance-based cultural life, while Aegean philosophers engage with this world and identify as prose authors.

We find a "normal" system, with more variation within it, with a single center (the Aegean around Athens); and a "marked" region, with much less internal variation but with marked difference from the "normal" system (the west). The marked region functions as a loose geographical network and is not concentrated on any city (all we can really say is that it is more south Italian than Sicilian; but this is a matter of degree, and Sicily is represented in Pythagoreanism – and it is also the home of Empedocles). The west looks backwards, and so its very topology is that of the loose network of archaic poetry: it neither looks to Athens nor develops an Athens of its own. It still displays the image of wisdom as a performance encapsulated in one's life or perhaps one's single work; it has not given up poetry, yet. And it evokes figures of the past – for Pythagoreans, already by then, were "Pythagoreans". At this point of time, being away from Athens was also being away from the world, away from the present.

So, a spatial duality. This, to repeat, is hardly news for the study of ancient philosophy, so that KRS, for instance, structure their discussion under the three headings "The Ionian Thinkers" (the early stage, preceding Parmenides), and then the near-contemporary "Philosophy in the West" and "The Ionian Response".[159] Nor were KRS original: the observation is ancient and is succinctly presented by Diogenes Laertius himself. In the introduction to his *Lives of Philosophers* – of which I concentrate on I.13–17 – Diogenes Laertius produces the classification standard for such introductions. The most basic division (the two "archai" of philosophy) are the Ionic and the Italian. This Diogenes sets out in terms of genealogies, from Thales and Pherecydes (a Samian; the genealogy operates via Pythagoras), respectively, leading all the way through Greek philosophy (the Italic genealogy, though, moves through Parmenides and then on to Democritus and finally Epicurus – that is, Diogenes' genealogies are regional only as a matter of *origin*).[160]

---

[159] Slightly a misnomer, as "Ionian" means different things in the two stages. First, it refers to the geographical region of Ionia; then, to the ethnicity (which I prefer to consider in regional terms, as "Aegean").

[160] For a very able discussion of this idea in Diogenes Laertius and its afterlife in the reception of Greek philosophy, see Sassi (2011). Sassi's own purpose is the opposite of mine – to point out the constructedness of such categories, hence (in a move typical of contemporary scholarship) their artificiality. (In particular, ancient readers tended to distinguish much more between Eleatics and Pythagoreans: that's indeed a fair observation.) In the conclusion of her argument (39), she points out the absence of institutional continuities: thus, she seems to suggest, we should envisage early philosophy as an unstructured set of singletons (my terms! Her discussion on this follows closely on

All this, to note that, perhaps, Diogenes Laertius' geographical intuitions make sense! This is important for what comes next. Diogenes, in the spirit of variety that animates his history, offers not one but many alternative classifications. First among the genuinely fine-grained classifications is the one by cities: Elians, Megarians, Eretrians, Cyrenaics. Once again, he may be at least partly right! Here, in fact, we have moved into a new historical, and geographical, arrangement. As the fifth century gives way to the fourth, philosophical space becomes even more marked.

By "Elians" Diogenes means Phaedo of Elis and his followers. Among those are Menedemus, apparently, originally of Eretria and apparently mostly residing there; he and his followers, if any, are the "Eretrians". The evidence is confined to a few anecdotes, mostly from Diogenes himself.[161] Three names are mentioned in Elis in the generation immediately following Phaedo himself: Anchypilus, Moschos and Plistanus.[162] As for Eretria, this "school" essentially means Menedemus himself together with his friend Asclepiades of Phlius.[163] Both friends went first to study at Megara, where, finally, the contours of a genuine school emerge: Euclid of Megara's philosophy is known in some detail and Stilpo, his follower, is a significant figure in his own right.[164] Cyrene, finally, is even more significant: Giannantoni (1990: part V) covers nine individuals who all seem to follow the same philosophy. Perhaps we should parse the notion of a city school with some care: the evidence for Elis and Eretria, taken on its own, could perhaps be seen as an anachronistic extrapolation, based on the presence of a single charismatic individual (for Eretria, more so). And yet, in Megara and Cyrene the concentrations are remarkable and the most obvious point of comparison is that of Plato's contemporary "school" in Athens. Plato – like Phaedo, Euclid and Aristippus – depended on Socrates' charisma, and had a number of followers surrounding him, in

that of Laks, 2005.). But this is precisely the fact calling for explanation: even without institutions, an east/west stylistic distinction did come to define fifth-century Greek philosophical practice.

[161] Diogenes Laertius II.125–44; the definitive study is Knoepfler (1991).

[162] The evidence is surveyed in Giannantoni (1990–1: III). Anchypilus and Moschus: DL II 126 but also Athenaeus II.44; Plistanus is reported only in DL II 105 but he is explicitly mentioned as Phaedo's heir. In a generation later, we hear of Alexinus, Eurylochus and Pyrrho – whose diverse persuasions seem unrelated to those of Phaedo, however.

[163] Haake (2007: 177–81): likely a political no less than a philosophical life? Giannantoni (1990–1: I.497) also notes the very obscure Pasiphon of Eretria; it is perhaps interesting to note that the very obscure historical source Diodorus of Eretria – Jacoby 1103, apparently antedating Aristoxenus – is quoted for a piece of information regarding Pythagoras: was he a contemporary philosopher?

[164] The school is the subject of Giannantoni (1990–1: II). Seven individuals are now known not merely to have been associated with the Megarian school in this generation but also to have been native Megarians. There must have been several dozens more of whom we do not know, suggesting that a substantial fraction of the city elite pursued philosophy: a harbinger of the future of Athens.

this case much better documented: I count at least 12 philosophers active in direct relation to Plato (though perhaps also in direct competition: this list includes such names as Eudoxus and Aristotle). Starting at 335, there would be at least two "Athenian" or "Platonic" schools, the one run by Xenocrates and that run by Aristotle (it is only then that "schools" begin to assume a genuine, institutional sense; see section 3.4.2 below). At around this time we also have some indications of an active school of philosophy in Lampsacus, headed by Epicurus (I count at least nine Epicureans known to have been related to Lampsacus in some form; it was also, at the same time, the origin of the major peripatetic Strato – the transfer of this Epicurean school to Athens would mark the beginning of a new philosophical system, firmly centered on Athens). Nor is the survey complete: we must recall again the transient astronomical center of Cyzicus, criticized by Epicurus for its reliance on astronomical instruments, and known to have had at least six mathematicians active in the fourth century. A minor mathematical school, we noted: and now we can put this in the wider context of local philosophical traditions in the fourth century. The point is that, in this context, the notion of a city school – even when only one individual is now seriously attested (as is the case with Eretria) – seems more plausible. Perhaps there is nothing anachronistic about the notion of a local intellectual tradition, based in a city, in the fourth century: this is how philosophy was then pursued.

So, perhaps seven attested "school cities" in the fourth century: Elis, Eretria, Megara, Cyrene, Athens, Lampsacus, Cyzicus.[165] But, with so many – could we not have missed some more? We see even more evidence for geographical clustering in the mere locations of philosophers. The following cities have not been mentioned above but still show two or more attested philosophers during the fourth century (numbers in brackets): Abdera (3), Chalcedon (2), Ephesus (2), Heraclea Pontica (5), Lesbos (5), Miletus (2) Phlius (2), Scepsis (3), Syracuse (4), Tarentum (2), Teos (2). At this point it becomes useful to ask if any philosopher in the fourth century is uniquely attested to his city. I repeat the precise question: how many cities are there for which (1) there is an attestation of a philosopher attached to the city, but (2) only one. It turns out that there are exactly *five* such cities. The curve of distributions has a very short tail and, remarkably, there are more cities attested with two individuals! Such short tails suggest, in and of themselves, that philosophical activity was not highly dispersed.

[165] It is also at this point that the epigraphic evidence for local connections between city and philosopher begins to emerge; for a systematic review of this source of evidence, see Haake (2007).

But let us consider the precise detail: here are the geographically hapax fourth-century philosophers.[166]

- Diogenes of Smyrna. All we know is that he was a disciple of Metrodorus of Chios (see below) and a teacher of Anaxarchus of Abdera. Was he merely born in Smyrna, but active in Chios and/or Abdera?
- Pamphilus of Samos. Epicurus' first teacher, he was a "disciple" of Plato, and – active in Samos – could well have been, just like Epicurus himself, an Athenian.
- Metrodorus of Chios: known to have been the "disciple", in some sense, of Nessas of Chios (whom I date to the fifth century). This, then, is an illusion of a hapax created by an arbitrary chronological cut-off.
- Diodorus of Aspendus, Xenophilus of Chalcidice. Two hapaxes together – an oxymoron! But they are also both Aegean Pythagoreans.

The last observation is telling: an anomalous philosophical creature, less defined, apparently, by its association with a school. The remaining three all belong to another fifth-century tradition – Democritean – in this case, closer to its historical roots (returning all the way to Abdera). It seems that one could practice philosophy in isolation, here and there, in the fourth century, but that such a pursuit would be rare and anachronistic. In lyric poetry we noticed a centrifugal pattern, no center ever emerging. In fourth-century philosophy we see something of a scatter, once again – but this represents not the absence of geographical structure but its proliferation. A new kind of system, then: neither that of a single center (as we saw in some "pure science" contexts) or of two (as we saw in the sciences that attract patronage) but, instead, a *polycentric* system.

Map 17, then, is the map of the centers – the many places where more than a single philosopher is attested.

Let us begin with the continuities. First, the west lives on. In Tarentum, both Lycus and the (much more important) Archytas are well described as "Pythagoreans"; the same is true of Damon and Phintias (but do they even exist?), as well as Hermodorus of Syracuse (as for Monimus, his Syracusan attachment is merely that of the city of origin of a slave: he was made a philosopher, and a free man, in Athens). Aristoxenus of Tarentum, a critic of Pythagoreanism for sure, nevertheless dedicated himself to the field most closely associated with Pythagoreanism, that of music. We did notice above

---

[166] For the biographical evidence, I refer for all authors to the DPA.

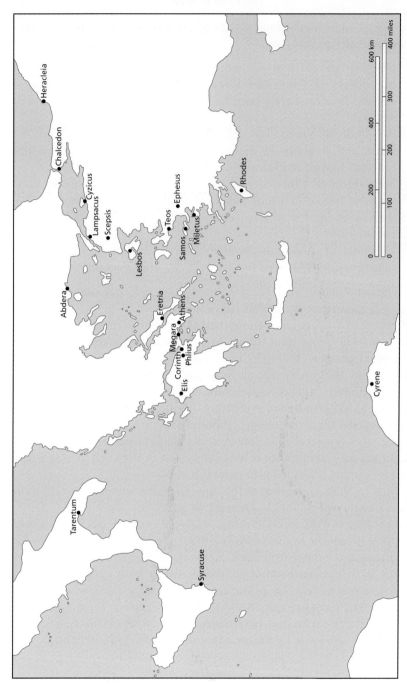

Map 17   Philosophical centers in the generations following Socrates

that the curious appearance of eastern Pythagoreans was an anomalous event. So Pythagoreanism survives, and survives as a western phenomenon. Still – looking backwards.

There are continuities in the east, too. Many of the fourth-century schools derive from late fifth-century developments; there, the system was (like the one we saw in Map 1) that of a single center in Athens with considerable scatter. (Perhaps the normal system, in which patronage matters less and the network effects matter more?) This continues into the fourth century, in spite of the rise of many centers. We find many individuals with Athenian connections, which of course has always been rightly assigned to the influence of Socrates. And so: Elis, Megara, Cyrene and Athens itself are foreshadowed in the system of the late fifth century, through the figures of their founders. In addition, we may note the survival of an older center. We mentioned Chios; we may also note Abdera, where Anaxarchus and Bion appear to have been, in some sense, followers of Democritus (so: perhaps yet another "school"?). But it is probably no more than an anecdote that two (unrelated) individuals are associated with Miletus, that birthplace of philosophy, and in general we should also note the ways in which the new philosophical map does *not* depend on its predecessors. The north Aegean area now reverts to its (more typical) marginal position; most important, the Aegean Islands recede in importance (Lesbos is an important recruitment ground, especially for the Peripatos). The major centers all come as a surprise. The most important city other than Athens is distant, somewhat isolated Cyrene. The Hellespont emerges as a leading center – four centers, or five, if we also count the related Heraclea Pontica. And what would have been most evident – certainly to Diogenes Laertius himself – would be the significance of the mainland outside Athens, with Phlius, Elis, Eretria and Megara. This is hard to parallel in any other cultural map. This – I note in passing – is a direct consequence of polycentrism. In a system with powerful unique centers, places near the center cannot develop any centrality of their own: any individuals active near the center would inevitably be attracted to that unique place. But, as the system becomes polycentric, the operating forces are reversed: now the position near the most important centers is favorable: the energy of the main center may leak out of it. The local mainland schools are started by teachers with close Athenian connections, and they maintain those relationships. (I return to this in the following chapter, on pages 378–80.)

As we put together the three maps, 15 to 17 (let us say "Presocratic", "Socratic" and "post-Socratic"), we notice that there is little overlap, and even this is qualified: in a map, we find the seeds of its heirs (the Presocratic Pythagoras, suggesting the flowering of the "West" in the Socratic age; Socrates' followers – and their various post-Socratic schools): the continuity of the "West" as a phenomenon comes closest to an exception – though here, too, the fourth century is no more than a rump of the fifth. That Athens remains, as well, means nothing – no cultural map of those centuries avoids Athens – and it is more important to note that it is central, in the fifth and the fourth centuries, in radically different senses. From the focus of a center/scatter model, it becomes yet another city hosting schools. Very much the first – among equals.

In the choice of spaces, change is almost random, chaotic motion through the entirety of the Greek-speaking world – the usual transiency of traditions. Other changes appear to be meaningful. One main theme is the *growth of spatial organization*. At first the Milesian phenomenon (marking a particular place in an otherwise fairly unstructured Aegean system); then the east/west divide (a sharp divide across the entire Greek-speaking world); and then a philosophy organized according to cities – that is, maximally structured by space. At the same time, we note a *growth of absolute numbers*: 16 attested figures (very generously defined) in the first map; 50 in the second; 129 in the third. The consistency of the rate of growth is intriguing in and of itself. Philosophy was on a trajectory. That it reflects an objective rise in the number of philosophers (and not just a subjective rise in our knowledge of them) is likely, and I will return to discuss the general question of the ratio of attested to actual individuals in Chapter 5; it is likely that our attested numbers, if anything, under-report the actual growth.

Likely, the two types of growth – scale and structure – are correlated. With more individuals, more structure becomes possible. Beneath a certain threshold of scale, the random appearance of talented individuals overrides any spatial structure. As that threshold is crossed, it becomes natural to expect individuals engaged with that particular cultural endeavor to spread more or less equally everywhere, and then – if space matters at all – they would gravitate to one another, and be influenced by one another, in the ways that give rise to spatial structure. At a certain, even higher threshold of scale, one can even have multiple such centers.

Scale matters, and so does genre. What we find is that, in philosophy, space *does* matter. Each successive stage in the growth of philosophy is more spatially organized – and it is also more spatially organized than any parallel cultural form. There is no archaic equivalent to the Milesian group of philosophers. In the fifth century we see several spatial arrangements, typically in the form of an Aegean centered on Athens (the medical system is duopolic, however). Philosophy goes further and creates the contrast between east and west, one which carries – uniquely! – consequences in terms of the cultural contents themselves. And finally, in the fourth century, other fields simply maintain the Athens-centric model of the fifth century itself. It is then, indeed, that the tyranny of Athens over Greece is firmly established – not, however, in the field of philosophy, which instead develops a plurality of city traditions. Spatial organization grows everywhere – philosophy remaining a step ahead.

Why does space matter in philosophy? Or, to step back, why does it matter at all? In a way, this is hardly a mystery: the spatial is *social*. To the extent that a cultural practice is premised on face-to-face interaction between individuals, it will tend to develop spatial organization. And so, the spatiality of Greek literature derives from the social practices of performance and reperformance. In archaic poetry, the social institution is replicated across the Greek-speaking world, and so spatial organization is minimal; when the institution of performance gains a canonical focus in Athens, this is replaced by the model of a center, Athens.

Neither patronage nor prestige determines the philosophical spatial organization. Rather, philosophy is a case to itself, based on a special kind of performance: the interaction of discourse, of individuals conversing together. Thus, the audience which philosophers require is especially meaningful: that of *other philosophers*. From this, the heightened spatial organization of philosophy flows in an obvious way. Above all, we see this in the remarkable extent to which all of Greek philosophy can be understood in terms of specific responses, be it with the Aegean philosophers offering rivaling naturalistic accounts of the material world; the set of authors responding to Parmenides' challenge; the many responses to Socrates; or the debates internal to Athens (Isocrates and Plato, Aristotle and rival Platonists) and external to it (Aristotle and the Megarians; Epicurus against the Platonists). Indeed, one main reason why we know the contents of ancient Greek philosophy so well, down to the doctrines of individual, minor authors, is that this habit of specific responses made Plato and especially Aristotle preserve so much of the detailed philosophies of their predecessors. You note that I do not provide secondary literature to this claim (the role of debate in early Greek philosophy), which is, frankly, undebatable! Once again, we might add a little perspective to the evidence by considering what may count as *exceptions* to the rule. Here, then, are the pre-Hellenistic philosophers whose activity is not known to arise from any of the known philosophical conversations.[167] These are as follows.

- Three authors, perhaps to be understood within literary culture: Damon, Diagoras, Ion[168] – all active in Athens and expressing themselves mostly in music or (in Damon's case) about music.
- An author who is perhaps to be understood purely within the culture of the exact sciences: Oenopides of Chios.
- Two authors whom we cannot place in terms of their "responses", simply because of our ignorance: Thrasyalces of Thassus and Lycophron (whom we cannot even localize).

Early philosophy was defined by a handful of debates. To be more precise: the very identity of a "philosopher" emerged from the setting of active debates. The handful of counter-examples above are mostly illusions created by our ignorance, but one counter-factual is worth pursuing. We see, above, the names of a few poets. And, indeed, it is not impossible that, here and there, poets expressed views that ended up characterized by later scholarship as "philosophical", without them belonging to any philosophical tradition. For a concrete example, consider the evidence for religious skepticism, such as it is, in early Greek thought. This is mostly a few poems by Xenophanes and a dramatic monologue (by Critias? Euripides?). While this has been often taken in modern scholarship as a chapter in the history of philosophy,[169] most scholars today consider such passages as examples of religious-philosophical thought which happened to end up in a purely literary context. This, I suggest, is invalid. Such poetry functions primarily not as a debate against other thinkers. Xenophanes sings against the received epic canon, and, most fundamentally, he sings – as most surely did the actor of the Sisyphus fragment – *against his audience*. Greek literature is often motivated by a sense of a strong, personal voice, rising

[167] I take these to be, roughly in order: what Aristotle ultimately understood as the conversation concerning material causes; Pythagoreanism; responses to Parmenides; and responses to Socrates, Plato and other local leaders of philosophical "schools". I also put aside, as a special case, sophists who engage with the culture of performance and patronage.
[168] But it seems that Ion's claim to being a philosopher – his triagmos – could well have been more cosmological in character, and so more directly in dialogue with other early philosophers. (Three principles? Brisson, s.v. DPA, 865–6.)
[169] Lesher (1978): "Xenophanes' Scepticism"; Kahn (1997): "Greek Religion and Philosophy in the Sisyphus Fragment". The tone of such articles (extracting particular points of doctrine out of poetry) is typical of most of modern scholarship into these texts. It is perhaps telling that the most comprehensive study of ancient atheism is by a literary scholar (Whitmarsh, 2016). There were certain questions of morals and values that the Greeks kept bringing up – only not so much in the context of what ends up as the philosophical genres.

adversarially, but in poetry this is most typically triggered by an *occasion of performance*.

Philosophy was different. What philosophy did was create a debate, even apart from such occasions, even apart from such audiences, merely through the continuous stream of authors explicitly arguing against each other. The debate, as it were, functioned in lieu of the occasion. Thus, a certain set of major open debates constituted an alternative site for generic identity: the debate, itself, as the setting. In a way, then, space could have been elided: it was not about a local occasion. And yet: a cultural practice all modeled by debate would strongly invite its practitioners to debate, directly, with each other – as soon as this became feasible. And this, in turn, was a function of scale.

We can set out the early history of Greek philosophy in a nutshell as follows. Philosophy arises from the principle of debate. Because, at first, the density of philosophers is fairly small, debates are mostly "virtual", though there are isolated cases of a local tradition based on face-to-face responses: Miletus, Elea, Pythagoreans in the west. As soon as a certain scale is reached, however, the density is such that face-to-face responses become more frequent, and so come to be understood as the unmarked mode of philosophizing; at this point the sociology flips, with local traditions becoming the norm. This transition forms the passage from Presocratic to later philosophy, and it is appropriate that the figure defining the transition, Socrates himself, had his entire career based on the performance of face-to-face conversation. The sociological transition has obvious consequences in terms of the contents: Presocratic philosophy carries few presuppositions, making instead a fresh start with radical claims requiring little context. (This is the philosophy of a virtual debate, arguing against the views of those not present.) Later philosophy would typically take for granted a certain framework (the one assumed by the local, face-to-face conversation from which it arises) and offer a more nuanced contribution within such a framework. So: the context of an active debate framed the genre of philosophy, giving rise to what we may call a "thematic lock" (you would have to discuss certain questions, because they were already raised by others, and so, to make your mark, you had to argue against *them*). As the context of debate became more spatially concentrated, thematic lock intensified, and one tended, now, to stick with specific questions of doctrine within an established framework. (This was what people were doing, all the time, around you.)

This spatial sociology of early Greek philosophy is decisive for the growth of the genre, and we shall return to it in the following chapter.

But, so far, we have found nothing surprising, in terms of space itself: we still have many – transient – centers. We did learn why, in philosophy, spatial concentrations would come naturally, and so we may begin to understand why spatial organization, in philosophy, would be the most tenacious. And yet, the argument so far could equally explain a polycentric Hellenistic philosophical Mediterranean. In other words, we still need to explain Hellenistic Athens.

### 3.4.2   Foundations of Athens

From archaic times to the fourth century BCE, philosophy was often driven by powerful personalities. It was the culture of performance – brought about even more vividly, more directly, through the enacted life, the charged challenge. Pythagoras, Socrates and Diogenes: objects of marvel and reverence; Heraclitus, Parmenides – indeed, even Plato: masters of paradox. And it was the charismatic presence of such individuals that gave rise to powerful local responses and, then, to traditions of debate. So much – for centuries.

And then, at some point not later than the early third century, Athens was the site of four fixed philosophical institutions. The identity of the philosophical leader, usually, mattered less. School doctrines and practices mattered more. It was through these institutions that philosophy gained a unique, many-generational spatial stability, through most of the Hellenistic era.

Something deep had changed. To understand how, we need to locate this transition precisely, in space and time. This is made possible only thanks to a relatively recent historical interpretation. Let me explain. There used to be a view according to which the institutional basis for the Athenian schools went back to a deliberate act by Plato, who, around the year 387, set up a learning institution – the Academy – on the model of a religious institution (or, *as* a religious institution).[170] Based on this

---

[170] Von Wilamowitz-Moellendorff was perhaps the first to set out (1881: 263–91) an account of the philosophical schools, beginning with Plato's foundation of the Academy, as institutions of a religious type. Usener (1884) took up that model, and described the philosophical schools of the fourth century as sites of deliberate intellectual division of labor, making possible the foundation of the various sciences (in other words, Usener fell for the image of Plato as the architect of science, a fiction of ancient Platonic propaganda: see Zhmud, 1998; it is also easy to deconstruct Usener's historically specific, Humboldtian ideology of learning and education). Unfortunately, while debunked by more recent scholarship, the image of fourth-century philosophical schools as fully established institutions is a standard presupposition even of much of sophisticated contemporary scholarship (e.g., Wallach, 2001: 64: "Plato established the Academy as a community of

assumption, it was natural to understand the later growth of philosophical schools in Athens as imitations of Plato's successful initiative. Then, over a generation ago, it was pointed out that there is no evidence for any institutional significance to Plato's so-called foundation of the Academy and that, in general, the evidence suggests a very minimal institutional footprint for any philosophical practice in fourth-century Athens.[171] All that happened circa 387 was that Plato moved to a villa in a suburban part of the city, an area rich with gardens famous for their association with the hero Akademos; naturally, therefore, he was often seen there together with his friends. As Dillon points out, the terms of Plato's will do not refer to a school (Dillon, 2003: 31): "It is not even clear whether the school was the sort of entity which one could bequeath to anyone." More: there is no doubt fourth-century Athens witnessed antagonism between Plato and Isocrates,[172] the two routinely described by modern literature as the founders of rival schools;[173] but this, too, goes beyond the evidence: Isocrates, for sure, was active as a teacher,[174] but he did not institute a school having an impersonal existence separate from that of Isocrates the person, and no one taught in "Isocrates' school" following his death (yet another

---

learning..." Or Allen, 2010: 13: "By 383 [Plato] had returned to Athens and opened his philosophical school, the Academy... This means that [he generated] a philosophical reputation that could justify opening a school.").

[171] In the order in which this historiographical revolution was achieved, see Lynch (1972), for the nonreligious character of the Lyceum and its minimal institutional antecedents; Glucker (1978), for the lack of institutional continuity in the tradition of the academy and the exceptional character of the Hellenistic institution; and, above all, Dillon (1983) (elaborated in 2003: chap. 1), for the key fact: there was no property associated with an institution such as "Plato's Academy". There was no institution of which Plato acted as head (a passage in the *Vita Marciana* 11 seemed to many scholars, on its face, to state that Aristotle had arrived in Athens when Eudoxus, temporarily, filled in for Plato as head of the Academy; Waschkies, 1977: 34–58, was the first to show that in fact this passage arises from a textual corruption of a reference to the Athenian archon. Indeed, no one was the "head" of "Plato's Academy" when Aristotle arrived in Athens, because there was nothing to be the head of.).

[172] The polemic was oblique; for an example of how it may best be teased out of a particular document – in this case Isocrates' *Antidosis* – see Nightingale (1995: 26–40); for a broad survey, see Rutherford (1995: 63–6) (the general question of Isocrates and his contemporaries is the theme of Eucken, 1983). The modern interpretation of Isocrates and Plato as the heads of rival schools was epitomized in volume III of Jaeger's *Paideia* (1944 [1939]: chap. 2), where it is described as (46) "the first battle in the centuries of war between philosophy and rhetoric".

[173] So a recent important collection mentions, as if in passing, that "Like Plato...Isocrates founded a school in Athens" (Depew and Poulakos, 2004: 2), which of course is correct if we remove any institutional meaning from the term "school".

[174] For an attempt to reconstruct Isocrates' teaching, see Johnson (1959); this project is feasible because Isocrates' own work is replete with references to his practice of teaching – in marked distinction from Plato, where we see only the evidence for Plato's views about others' – or Utopia's – teaching.

single-generation phenomenon, then).[175] On the one hand, there was an aristocratic author of Socratic dialogues who cultivated a group of like-minded friends in walks through the gardens near his villa; on the other hand, there was a citizen hard on his luck who became a speechwriter, then a private teacher of rhetoric. So much for "schools" and such was the institutional setting of intellectual life in mid-fourth-century Athens.

The historical question, which has not yet been fully tackled by the literature, arises thus: how do we explain the rise of the philosophical schools in Hellenistic Athens, *against* the background of such loose antecedents?

Let me briefly pursue the main course of events, as I see them. First, it is not as if intellectual life was *formless*, already in the middle of the fourth century. Dillon (2003: 10–13), for instance, looks to Aristotle's *Topics* as evidence for an established structure of exchange among Plato's associates: this is a valid exercise, and it reminds us that there certainly was a social reality – even if not an institutional reality – to Plato's group. People did associate, around him, and there must have been certain common routines in the garden of the Akademos at around 350 BCE. Middle comedy has a Plato figure engaged in other absurd philosophical practices (clearest of all: a group congregates and tries to define a pumpkin;[176] but the evidence should not be pushed too far. Would Plato, stylus in hand, gazing at his wax tablet, be good comedy material?). But it needs to be emphasized that even the Hellenistic Academy itself, late into its history, was marked for its limited endowment as an institution:[177] it was never *founded*.

Plato died in 347. Our sources speak of Speusippus – son of Plato's sister – as, in some sense, Plato's "successor" (so, e.g., Diogenes Laertius IV.1). Nothing is known about the social significance of this "succession", and, seeing that no property changed hands – and no official institution was at stake – we should pause to consider just what did happen in 347.[178]

---

[175] Antiquity preserved substantial biographical information on Isocrates – one of the canonical authors – and so we have also lists of his alleged pupils, some of whom became important rhetoricians and teachers of rhetoric in their own right (Engels, 2003): when we can form a judgement, e.g. for Philiscus of Miletus (Jacoby 337B), we find authors who are free agents, teaching in their own name and not as continuators of an Isocratean institution. This – even though Isocrates' "school" was, if anything, much more meaningful as a pedagogic practice than Plato's.

[176] Epicrates fr. 10. For a survey of "Plato", the comedy figure, see Chroust (1962: 100); the prominence of this figure, as noted on p. 208 above, could reflect Plato's canonical status already in his lifetime.

[177] This is clarified in O'Sullivan (2002: 258–60) (following on the discussions by Glucker and Dillon; see n.171 above).

[178] This event is something discussed in the literature based on the anachronistic and very misleading assumption that this was a Hellenistic-type succession to a formal scholarchate; then the question naturally arises: *why not Aristotle?* (See, e.g. Chroust, 1967a.) Such questions are quickly dissolved as soon as we understand that the Academy, at this point, is *not* an institution.

Luckily, we can do this because we have a somewhat clearer sense of the events following Speusippus' own death in 339 – thanks to a surprisingly specific account in Philodemus' *Academica* 6.41–7.14. We learn there that the "young" – following Speusippus' death – voted for his replacement, and that Xenocrates won over Menedemus and Heraclides Ponticus.[179] If we take this account seriously, we should notice that Speusippus is not involved in the process at all: it seems to be a response to his demise, not any "succession". Once again, no property is involved (the "young" do not have any control over that). The implication, I believe, is clear enough: what we find is that a group that followed Speusippus in the study of Plato decided, following upon Speusippus' death, to continue in their Platonist pursuits, and they asked Xenocrates to stand as their new teacher.

Now, it is not unreasonable to suggest that Speusippus' death was something of a crisis, calling for a more explicit response from the group associated with Plato's memory. I explain: Speusippus' attraction as a teacher certainly resided in his blood relation to Plato. He still carried some of the master's charisma, in hereditary form. With Speusippus gone, however, the link to Plato (and, through him, to Socrates) was severed, and the meaning of the group was revised. Around the year 339, then, we see a new development: an Athenian *quasi-institution*, dedicated to the teaching of Plato's philosophy *at a remove from personal charisma*. It is probably significant that Xenocrates was the first *systematizer* of that philosophy (see page 385 below): this, after all, was what a school needed. It still had no property, only a tentative scholarch and just the very beginning of the formulation of a school doctrine. But it did rely on the power of the past (these are also the years of Lycurgus' project, Athenians self-consciously celebrating their city as a site of memory; see page 198 above). And more than just the power of the past: it had the power of space, not in the sense of *owning* any real estate (which, as noted above, is doubtful until the end of the *third* century) but in the very notion of an "academy": Plato and a particular place came to be mutually marked through the many years of Plato's residence there. Significant, perhaps, that this was suburban: there were few non-Platonic associations. What the Academy had – the requirement for its foundation – was hallowed ground. (Once again: Lycurgus' program, too, involved the

---

[179] The passage is, papyrologically, very sound. I follow Gaiser (1988: 465–9) in taking its strange and precise details as confirmatory of basic validity (so a recent discussion, Watts, 2007: 115, through which see more references).

hallowing of such spaces as the Theater of Dionysius as sites of continued, active memory.)

Xenocrates was chosen by his students. Aristotle needed no one to elect him. Under my account, when Plato died there was no philosophical institution, no school, for Aristotle to associate with; so he moved on, in the search of institutional foothold elsewhere. Specifically, he sought *patronage* (the rise of the government sector is right around the corner): we remember his association with Hermias of Atarneus; and then, a promotion: royal patronage in Macedon (for all this, see pages 280–1 above). Aristotle could have joined the great expedition to the east. He did not – forgoing, as it were, his *Beagle*.[180] Instead, at the appropriately mature age of 49 – an elder statesman, now – in the year 335, he went back to Athens to found an institution. In this case, the evidence of the will, as well as the clear implication of the surviving esoteric works, is of a specialized and regulated institution, with its property, hierarchy and fully structured projects.[181] It was not any kind of return to a previous Academic practice, however, and of course it did not represent any effort to recapture Plato's charisma. If it was a rival to Xenocrates' group, it signaled this not by institutional imitation but by institutional difference. Indeed, it is tempting to see here the imprint of those patronage years in Pella. Philip's Macedon was a new experiment in the specialized state, with its

---

[180] Pliny thought Aristotle did join Alexander – hence, in fact, his trove of biological knowledge (*Natural History* VIII.7.44) – but this is clearly an Imperial-era author imposing his own contemporary assumptions regarding the nature of cultural patronage. (For the debunking of Pliny, see Romm, 1989.) Bigwood (1993: 551–2): "Alexander's Indian expedition may have revolutionised Greek knowledge of the East. However, there is no trace of this in Aristotle's zoological writings."

[181] The Lyceum's "mapping" projects may be seen in the collection of 158 constitutions – most, perhaps, compilations of lore (so, convincingly, Toye, 1999), and so maybe more in the spirit of Greek geographical writing than the hard-core social science model of the *Athenian Constitution*; the Peplos must have been an even looser collection of mythical material (Gutzwiller, 2010), while some other projects, such as the lists of victors (Bosworth, 1970: 408–9), must have been very spare *pinakes*: the *didaskaliai* belong of course in this last tradition. Aristotle even anticipated the Alexandrian mapping of the body in his *anatomai* (Stückelberger, 1994: 76; Lennox, 2012: 301 n.1); this lost work of course underlines the extent of Aristotle's surveys of living organisms – which, furthermore, fit in a comprehensive project of knowledge and contemplation. The surveying project is of course in line with the contemporary turn towards geography. None of this directly implies institutionalization, but the sheer scale of the projects implies a division of labor; further, all of this fits within what was certainly a course of studies (whatever its intended level or the size of its classes); Jackson (1920) engaged in the project of teasing out the trivia of Aristotle's lecture room from his comments, and his observations (there must have been a brass sphere!) are striking in their cogency: these texts do emerge from a real-life performance within an institutional framework – as is suggested, after all, from the very texture of the extant corpus (more perhaps a seminar than a set of lectures? So I argue in Netz, 2001.). In general for Aristotle's school experience, see Natali (2013: chap. 3).

planning, scale and ambition.[182] Could this be the *inspiration* for the Lyceum? I suggest, that is, that we could perhaps turn upside down a standard story – as if Alexandrian authors such as Callimachus implemented, for Macedonian patrons, a peripatetic program.[183] What if the innovation of the Peripatos had been exactly the reverse: that it implemented, in an intellectual sphere, the exciting innovation of a Macedonian state organization? Impressed by "Big State", Aristotle could have tried "Big Science". At any rate, the first clear institutionalization of philosophy is that by an outsider, metic, quasi-Macedonian; it appears as if an institution, in this case, could have been required just because other forms of social capital were lacking: routine, instead of charisma.

Two further caveats. First, Aristotle's will makes clear that, at his death in 322, there was no formal entity such as "the school": the peripatetic school, such as it was then, was not yet impersonal (the will is highly personal and it involves Aristotle's own property, own family).[184] It was Aristotle's sheer energy drawing people and projects together. Second, Aristotle brought those people and projects together around a specified type of space. He could have moved into his private accommodation and then taught in the undifferentiated space of the city (shall we meet today at Theophrastus'? At Aristotle's? Go meet our friends at the Academy? Or hang out near the walls?); he could have built a private institution of learning, secluded behind walls. Instead, he had his activities associated with a well-known space, right next to the city wall, physically distant from the Academy but functionally analogous to it: the Lyceum, with its gymnasium – a place of public confrontation (which Socrates, too, used to frequent; and which Lycurgus, very recently, had enlarged).[185] The Academy was not yet an institution; but it already defined the manner of situating oneself: imitating Plato, or Socrates, by spatial proximity, carving out something of the space of Athenian memories.

Aristotle left town as the Macedonian–Athenian hostility flared up again in 323; the striking fact is that the school did not decamp with him. Theophrastus remained as a teacher and as the leader of a course of research – indeed, enormously successful in that role. At this point the

---

[182] For a succinct account (necessarily, involving a great amount of inference) of the terms of Macedon's rise, see Ober (2015: 278): the image shared by Ober and many contemporary historians is of Philip's Macedon rapidly rationalizing and modernizing its army and bureaucracy in deliberate imitation of Greek models.

[183] "In Egypt the main factor in the new scientific attitude to literature and to all branches of natural study was...the influence of Peripatetic thinkers" (Fraser, 1972: I.305–6; see the significant, learned endorsement in Glucker, 1998: 312–13).

[184] This has been observed already by Chroust (1967b).     [185] Lynch (1972: 15).

Lyceum must have already obtained some kind of identity transcending that of either Aristotle or Theophrastus.[186] A little later, when Xenocrates died in 314, the Academic group, once again, did not disband and the master was replaced by his much younger acolyte, Polemo (was Polemo among the youth who chose Xenocrates? In the year 269 Polemo would die, succeeded by his rough coeval Crates; was Crates, too, among the same founding group?).[187]

And all the time, as we have noted, philosophy was everywhere in the Aegean: much more of it than just the Platonic-Aristotelian tradition. Indeed, there were many other philosophers in Athens itself; and there is no evidence that any of them were active in the context of a school institution. Theodorus of Cyrene was in Athens probably in the 310s and the 300s, his presence marked by the provocation of atheism.[188] Crates of Thebes probably plied the same streets of Athens – engaging in the Cynic performance of philosophy-as-shock. This was charismatic philosophy, of a kind that most directly appealed to Socrates' example (so, Long, 1996a). The very identity of a "philosopher" was still fluid.[189] Indeed, the city would be attractive to the enemies of Platonism, as well. Epicurus, an Athenian citizen, grew up in Samos and established a city following, originally in Lampsacus. In the final years of the century he moved to Athens[190] – a roughly 35-year-old leader with his band of acolytes: a charismatic figure whose appeal had obvious religious resonance.[191] In his case, though, institutionalization did not arise from any *posthumous* routinization of charisma. Epicurus himself founded the school as a place governed by prescribed social attitudes and doctrines. No more than a few

---

[186] The terms of Theophrastus' own will – much later, of course – take for granted the school as an institution, and it seems plausible that a genuine institutional foundation was achieved sometime between 317 and 307, the years of Demetrius of Phaleron's ascendance (so, O'Sullivan, 2002).

[187] I envision the early Academy, then, as a roughly generational event, led for many years by those who personally knew, if not Plato, then at least Xenocrates: the bond of personal charisma. This link would be cut following Crates' own death in the 260s. The new scholarch, Arcesilaus, would now assume the headship of the Academy and remake it – pivoting away, so to speak, from Xenocrates.

[188] See Winiarczik (1981); for his atheism, he was persecuted – a rare case of a persecution for impiety that might have been motivated by actual religious concerns (though O'Sullivan, 1997, argues that here, too, political considerations – directed against Demetrius of Phaleron, Theodorus' patron – could have been at play).

[189] In the immediate aftermath of Demetrius of Phaleron's fall in 307, Sophocles, son of Amphiclides, passed a law to banish all the "philosophers". This is open to rival interpretations, but the broad brush, the lack of specific institutional detail, is perhaps telling (for this episode, see Haake, 2008).

[190] Epicurus' move took place in 307/306, or 305/304 (Dorandi, 1999a: 43): not an important difference, and, either way, what is most striking is the proximity to Zeno's move to Athens.

[191] The nature of the early Epicurean Garden as an institution – indeed, something like a spiritual commune – is relatively clear. For an account, see Clay (2009).

years later another foreigner would establish his own presence: Zeno of Citium. We are told that he first followed Crates of Thebes. At some point he became his own man, by picking his own space. Cynics are not supposed to settle down, but Zeno was a different kind of Cynic, and he would return again and again to just one place – and that, perhaps the most celebrated public space of the Athens of his time, the Stoa of the Paintings (more than other places, this was a space of the city's memory, dominated by the monumental painting of the Battle of Marathon: here, as elsewhere, the Stoa leveraged the memory of the past, the sense of the canon: more on this below). When exactly did that happen? General surveys give the date of 301, working back from Philodemus' precise archon year dating of Zeno's death (262/261), Persaeus' statements that Zeno died aged 72 and came to Athens aged 22 (DL VII.28; the likelier age at death among those offered in antiquity: Dorandi, 1999a: 38); and then, the very vague and weak claim in DL VII.2 that Zeno studied for ten years (with Stilpo and Xenocrates, at that). In fact, there likely was never a moment in which Zeno said: "Enough studied! Now I found my own school!" He was around certain well-known Athenian characters long enough to become a character himself, already at an early age; at some point, going to the Painted Stoa, one would expect to find Zeno there, discoursing with his followers: yet another place, another band of talkers.[192]

The Stoa would emerge gradually,[193] just as did the schools as a whole. Some of the historical moments we have surveyed were more deliberate: Aristotle's move into the city in 335; Epicurus' own move, some 30 years later. Other key moments involved no more than the choice, less remarkable at the time, to stay put, to remain associated with a place: Speusippus and others returning to the region of the Academy; the youth deciding to stay there following upon Speusippus' death, asking Xenocrates to lead them; Theophrastus, continuing Aristotle's projects; Polemo picking up

---

[192] And there, the bands cap: at four groups. I do not try to offer an account of this closure, but it is reasonable to suggest (following Collins, 1998: 81–2) that such a number ought to cap at some point for, as it were, game-theoretical reasons: debate is meaningless with too *few* views on offer but then it tends to consolidate with no more than a few well-charted options on display, and so it avoids having too many views. The number of views has to be just right, and Collins estimates this at three to six – a number which refers to the entire cultural system, however.

[193] Eventually the school would be refounded, becoming newly systematized and much more formal, at the hands of Chrysippus. This is analogous to (and roughly contemporary with) Arcesilaus' refoundation of the Academy, and once again is a mark of the passing of the old guard. In Cleanthes we see a leader who was among the early band of Zeno's followers, rather like Polemo and Crates vis-à-vis Xenocrates. With Cleanthes gone, the school pivoted in a new, more formal direction, turning old charisma into new routine (we will note in on p. 399, n.144, the rather Prussian nature of Chrysippus' institutionalization).

where Xenocrates left off; Cleanthes, then Chrysippus, firming up their attachment to Zeno, following his death.

At the background of our survey was the Weberian *routinization of charisma*. Weber himself understood this process to arise from the problem of *succession*.[194] We should not push this too far: Weber thought primarily through the examples of kingship and the Church, in which charismatic authority presided over large social forces. The end of charismatic authority would entail a genuine crisis, so that there would *have* to be found some way to routinize charisma. In our case, the end of charismatic authority would entail a crisis only to the close band of followers, and the most natural outcome of the end of charismatic authority would be simply for the small group to peter out. Weber's question is: how come a charismatic mode of authority can be transformed into its opposite in a bureaucracy? This is certainly relevant for us, but our main question is slightly different: why here, and not before, would the crisis of succession give rise not to the dissolution of the social group but to its cementing in routinization? Why continuity, just now?

A causal account will have to be speculative, but several observations are fairly solid, concerning the timing and nature of this continuity. The routinization of charisma that created the Hellenistic philosophical schools took place from the 330s to the 260s. It happened mostly as local responses to crises of succession: followers staying put and making a deliberate choice to cling to a past. And we may note one repeated feature of all these moments of continuity: they involved an attachment to a particular place that evoked the memory of a charismatic individual. As already suggested above, this is in fact an attitude typical of contemporary Athens, where the communal sense of identity was more and more based on the charismatic presence of the canonical figures of the past, enshrined in the key, iconic locations of the city. The Athenian philosophical routinization of charisma was of a piece with the culture of post-canonical Athens.

The argument is that routinization took place in Athens, from the late fourth century through the early third, because this was the Athenian thing to do. If our argument involves Athenian practices as a whole, we should bring in the full context. And so, a detour: alongside the dour philosophy of the schools, Menander's escapades. Comedy, in fact, was the major cultural practice to thrive in Athens through all those years. How to account for this combination?

---

[194] The locus classicus (in English translation) is Weber (1978 [1921]: 246–54).

Menander was active from 322 to 292 – that is, during the central years of the formation of the schools. He was also, as we recall, an author of the central canon, clearly established already early in the third century itself. Bear in mind that the central, small-library Hellenistic canon did not include the orators. (In the third century BCE Demosthenes and Aeschines belonged, rather, to the big-library, erudite canon.) Seen from the perspective of the early third century BCE, then, Menander was by far the most successful author to have emerged since Euripides himself – one among many authors, in a field which, Csapo emphasizes, had by now a very strong Mediterranean following. Let us step back to consider the geography. The following maps are adapted from Csapo (2010: 102, tab. 3.1). Map 18 shows the sites of theaters attested to about 370 and Map 19 shows those attested to about 340 BCE itself; Csapo also notes a great many different locations in Attica: 15 about 370 BCE, nine about 340 BCE!

Csapo emphasizes the rise of career opportunities for actors, but it should be added that, through the fourth century, those careers are mostly at or near the city of Athens (a proliferation in Attica; theaters are also set up in those central Greek cities which are in direct competition with Athens) – or far from it, above all in the west, where theater is an indigenous phenomenon.

And yet there might be the first inkling of a truly global proliferation already in the 340 stage of the map – at about Menander's date of birth – with a few more places which are neither very near nor very far from Athens: Lemnos, Samos, Thebae Phthiodites, Philippi, Cos; this begins to be more like a normal map of the Greek poleis. Frederiksen (2002: 93) has a chart breaking down the identified ruins of Greek theaters by region, and there we see the predicted dominance by Asia Minor, a more muted presence for the west – and yet also a major presence for central Greece.[195] This evidence is mostly much later. We have moved from the biographical timescale of Aristotle, Epicurus and Menander into the archaeological timescales of theater remains, mostly of the Roman era and, anyway, misleading (we do not have evidence for the wood structures, which might have been more important at the time). And yet, even in our Roman-era evidence – when there is genuine internationalization of theater – the special connection of the art with its origins in Attica is not yet eroded. Through the fourth century Athens grew into a theater district; by the early third century this was the most significant form of art for all

---

[195] Of 251 ruins, nearly 100 are from Asia Minor; about 20 from the west; and about 70 from central Greece.

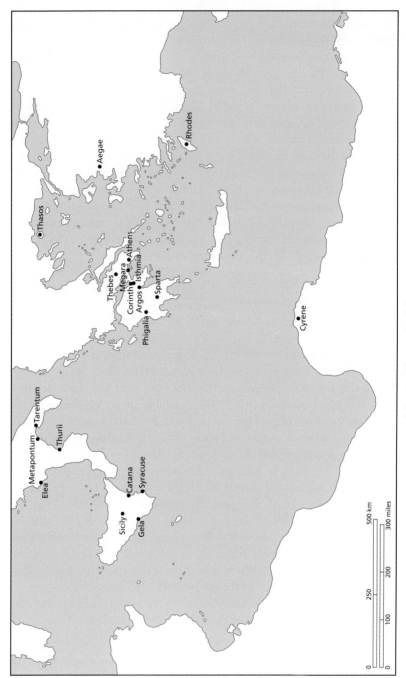

Map 18   Theaters built by 370

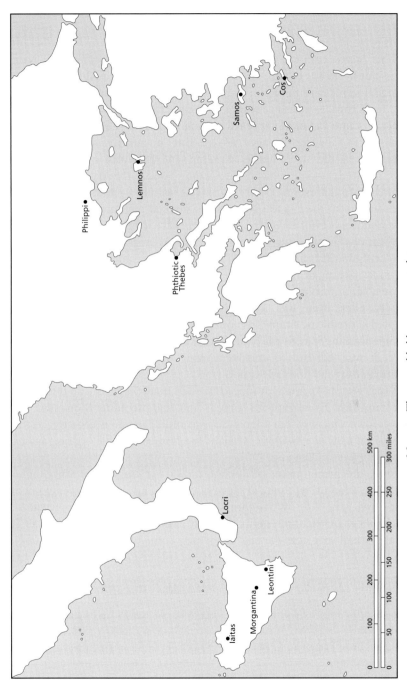

Map 19   Theaters added between 370 and 340

Greeks, centered on Athens not only as a cultural memory but also as a vivid presence.

This meant comedy, because the canonization of tragedy, as it were, froze it out. Already by the 340s, as we recall, Astydamas could not compete on equal terms with the canonical authors, and in the period that interests us – from the late fourth century to the early third century – Euripides, in effect, became the contemporary leading tragedian (I shall return to the evidence in Chapter 5, pages 561–4). But in comedy, as noted above, Aristophanes did not reign as supreme, and the form was much more alive. Indeed, as emphasized by Csapo (2000), the typical feature of comedy through over a century – from its beginning in the middle of the fifth century to the late fourth – was its marked malleability as a genre. It was a subversive form, of the new; naturally, it had relatively few fixed conventions (even a single author, such as Aristophanes, could therefore display significant variety).[196] The sheer variety of comedy and its tendency to renew itself made it possible for it to survive in active form, even against its own canonization.

Menander, then, was active in a world in which Athenian comedy reigned supreme as, simply, the only major form of literary performance. Geographically, it was still Athenocentric, but already ubiquitous; culturally, it was still full of creative energy, but within a cultural setting dominated by the dramatic canon.

What was the comedy produced by such dualities? It is true that we do not know how heterogeneous comedy was, just preceding Menander. But the point is precisely that Menander was unlike previous comedy, in that he was, in fact, *homogeneous*. Menander's form was stable – going against the very grain of comedy.

Frye, the great master of "new criticism", thought that, in general, literature relies on repeated, archetypal forms. This, in fact, fitted comedy best (Frye, 1957: 163): "What normally happens is that a young man wants a young woman, that his desire is resisted by some opposition, usually paternal, and that near the end of the play some twist in the plot enables

---

[196] In the extant plays, we see an early Aristophanes directly engaged with concrete political realities, contrasted with the two last extant plays, *Assemblywomen* and *Wealth*, in which the political contents are mere generalities. This has been typically invoked as indicative of the transition from old to middle comedy (e.g. Sommerstein, 1984: 314). Csapo's (2000) contribution is to point out that there was always a great deal of synchronic variety among comedies, some political, others not, some based on invective, others eschewing it. The division into "old", "middle" and "new" comedy – a later construct – is therefore misleading, not in the sense that comedy did not change but, to the contrary, in the sense that it kept being heterogeneous (which explains, of course, how change was possible; see pp. 216–17 above).

the hero to have his will." Frye thinks of this as timeless archetype but in fact this model emerges (in an even much more restricted range of plots) with Menander, was then copied by Latin drama and through its influence informed early European comedy, so that we now think of it as "archetype". It seems that practically all of Menander's comedy was confined to such plots! But the plot-templates were not at all the single fixed elements, around which variety revolved. Zagagi is succinct (1994: 15): "[C]onvention in plot, characters, situations, performance and costumes is of the essence." Or we may quote at greater length a more recent, sophisticated, semiotic analysis (Petrides, 2014: 116–17; the reader is referred to the original, where the many footnotes point to the rich literature on Menander's conventionalism):

> By "standardization" we refer to the process whereby New Comedy, via the intermediary Middle Comedy, crystallised standard systems of signs including: structured parameters of plot, with defined actants and conventional resolutions; stock character types, associated with typical costumes, premises of acting (movements etc.), and to a certain extent even a type-specific type of language; specific genera of masks; a new arrangement of space. . .a steady number of no more than three actors; and the marginalization of the chorus.[197]

As Petrides continues to note, this "standardization" goes hand in hand with what he calls "hybridization", specifically of comedy with tragedy. This, once again, goes back to a widely noted feature of Menander's comedy, which strikes moderns for a certain "fairy tale" quality, especially with the nearly obligatory recognition scenes: a girl discovers her true father; a soldier, long considered dead, arrives on the scene. . . What is to us "fairy tale" was to the ancient audience, of course, *myth*, and this is the key way in which this comedy is a hybrid of comedy and tragedy: Menander takes the contours of mythical plots – which were the typical theme of tragedy – and turns them into comedy, not by the direct parody of myth (which was often used in previous comedy, especially so-called middle comedy) but by creating fictional stories that echo the conventions of myth within near-realist settings. This combination of myth and realism demands a certain abstraction: the scene must be a diluted version of actual

---

[197] There is a controversy concerning the extent to which the tragic convention of the unity of time (established in the plays of Sophocles and Euripides) also held for Aristophanes (Hunter, 1979: 28–9): this is part of a general question, about the extent to which fifth-century tragedy and comedy marked themselves as genres *against* each other (Taplin, 1986). Germany (2014) argues that Menander adhered closely to the unity of time, which would make his comedy, once again, more conventional – and more "tragic".

city life (usually located, then, at a vaguely suburban setting); the protagonists, too, have been somewhat bleached of personality, and became the "characters", now defined by a system of masks.[198] The study of Menander's system of masks has been invigorated by Wiles (1991),[199] who notes (71): "Menander did not write his plays around specific actors whom he knew well, as Molière did. . . Rather, he wrote for the masks that were the characters of his plays." This, too, harked back specifically to tragedy (previous comic masks were about the body, phallus and all; in new comedy, the mask became an expression of a position within a tale). To quote further from Wiles, once again with a note that is now routine in the scholarly literature (68): "New Comedy. . .owes more to Euripides than it does to Old Comedy." Surely, this must be central to our account of Menander. Quite simply, his audience went to the theater, in the first place, because they were in thrall to Euripides. Indeed, the presence of this canonical past was so overpowering that it all but precluded contemporary tragedy: a new tragedy would painfully pale, in comparison with the past. Comedy remained, then; it is therefore unsurprising that this comedy would end up resembling, to the extent allowed by its generic constraints, the drama of Euripides.

We can form a sense of the impact of new comedy from Latin drama, of which we have a substantial survival: 21 plays (some fragmentary) in the Plautine corpus as well as the six extant plays by Terence. Those of Terence are nearly translations of Greek new comedy (four – the majority, as we would expect – from Menander), but even the Plautine corpus evidently has at its base the adaptations of Greek models, if let loose onto a much more self-conscious, farce-like stage.[200] It is hard to say how typical, among the many local adaptations of new comedy in the Hellenistic era, was the city of Rome. What the evidence of Latin drama shows is the extent of

[198] It has been suggested that Menander's characters have already arrived at the absolute genericity of the commedia dell'arte, with a small stock of named characters circulating between the many plays (MacCary, 1970): perhaps exaggerated, but certainly the overall tendency to which Menander's plays led.

[199] We can study these masks, thanks to an explicit report by Pollux (*Onomasticon* 4.143–54) with which we may decipher the many depictions of comic space surviving through the archaeological record (see p. 142 above): a semiotic matrix surviving through the centuries of Menander's performances. Conventions, repeated for centuries.

[200] For an overview, see Slater (2000). It is likely enough that the theatrical self-reflexivity of the Plautine corpus reflects local, Italian traditions of improvisation and farce; it is also possible that, at a certain distance from the weight of the Athenian canon, drama could move away from Euripidean expectations (Terence was somewhat later and more literary: in the middle of the second century he already points the way to a Latin culture working within the constraints of the Greek canon itself). Most basically, Latin drama acutely experienced its status as translation – a marking of the artificial which is especially effective for comedy (Feeney, 2016: 141).

influence. New comedy was written for an international audience – which probably has something to do with its stock, abstracted quality.

In the case of comedy, then, we find two factors leading to growing routinization: the heavy presence of the canonical past – and the growing geographical reach. The two work together: the growing geographical reach of Hellenistic comedy could have led to a splintering into local traditions, had there not been a clear center in the Attic theater district. Then again, the survival of the Attic center was certainly a consequence of Athens' cultural association as the place of dramatic performance par excellence. The topology of Greek theater was that of a powerful center, surrounded by a cluster – with consequences for the content of the art.

Comedy mirrored philosophy in its turn towards the routine: it took an Athenian form of shocking performance, marked by diversity and surprise, and turned it into a conservative genre following very fixed practices. In philosophy, too, we have already noted the significance of the past: the way in which certain Athenian groups made the deliberate choice to stay put in the same place, to cling to the memory of the same charismatic figure, echoing the staying of the Platonic group, in the Academy, and ultimately harking back to the unique Athenian charisma of Socrates. What about the geography of philosophy, though? While new comedy was still very much an Athenian genre, its tendency, in the Hellenistic era, was to spread away from the center. Athens was exporting actors. At the same time, however, it was *importing* philosophers, and the years that saw the foundations of many theaters, across the Mediterranean, saw the end of the philosophical schools everywhere but Athens. The resulting pattern, however, was – once again – that of a center (in which philosophy was pursued) and a cluster (from which philosophy was recruited).

The comparison with comedy helps to reorient our discussion from its Weberian roots. Sure enough, the process of the formation of the Hellenistic schools was that of the routinization of charisma, and so, with Weber in mind, we might have concluded that the process was driven by the crises emerging from the deaths of the founders. But, in fact, philosophers have been dying in Greece since time immemorial, with no school ensuing. And, we now see, comedy went through a process of routinization, quite analogous to that of philosophy, in the same years and in the same place, whereby the deaths of charismatic authors necessarily meant less since an institution was *already* in place.

The same years, the same place: and so, the roots of the process must have something to do with time and space. Let us look, first, at space. We have seen theaters, built across the Mediterranean – with Attica remaining the major theater district; and we have seen more and more philosophers being recruited – into four spatially defined schools.

The spatial pattern of philosophy is produced by recruitment: it is a set of vectors, motioning into the city of Athens. It helps, now, that we may compare between schools.

The following contrast is especially stark: the cities of origins (other than Athens) for the Stoa, and for the Peripatos, during the period from 300 to 100 BC (to make this comparison more robust in quantitative terms, I look first to a wider time-frame).

Maps 20 and 21 are, quite simply, the maps of the Aegean, against the Mediterranean. We do find Alexandria and Tyre in the peripatetic map; but these are few and late names (Sotion, Ariston and Diodorus). Otherwise, we find central and traditional places: the coasts of Asia Minor, the islands, the mainland.[201] The map of the Stoa, on the other hand, has 30 names from outside the old Aegean core – which is 60 percent of the 50 individuals in the list for whom a non-Athenian connection can be identified. This, of course, is well known in qualitative terms: Zeno came from Citium, Chrysippus from Soli, and in general there is a special connection between the Stoa and the Cypriot/Syrian/Cilician area; but its geographical reach extended further, to places such as Mesopotamia, non-Greek Italy, possibly Carthage.[202]

Different schools, different relationships to the space of the Mediterranean. Let us now extend the comparison, bringing in the remaining two schools, the Epicurean and the Academic schools.

Here the Epicurean school largely matches the Peripatos, though perhaps less so: of the 28 Hellenistic Epicureans for whom non-Athenian connections can be established, eight come from beyond the Aegean core. The Academy has 75 Hellenistic philosophers localizable beyond Athens; 24 of these range beyond the core. We see a sequence forming the following.

Aegean              –              Mediterranean
Peripatos   Garden   academy   Stoa

---

[201] An anecdote in Aulus Gellius (13.5) has Aristotle, on his deathbed, asking for wines from Lesbos and from Rhodes, tasting both and preferring the one from Lesbos, from which his followers deduced that Theophrastus, not Eudemus, should be his heir (Gottschalk, 2002: 26): the reference to Aegean wines evokes a sense of space that goes back to archaic times (a good summary of the evidence is based on Athenaeus: Brock and Wirtjes, 2000: 464–5).

[202] Shaw (1985: 21): "Stoicism was propagated by 'outsiders', by Hellenized Anatolians, Cypriots, and Syrians, or by Greeks who lived in peripheral borderlands." See also Richter (2011: 58).

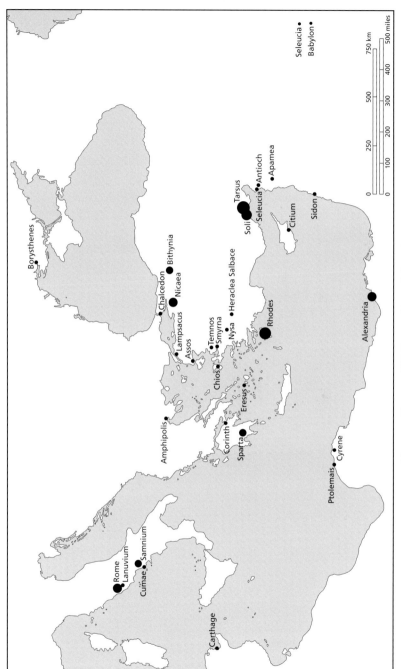

Map 20   Origins of Hellenistic Stoic philosophers

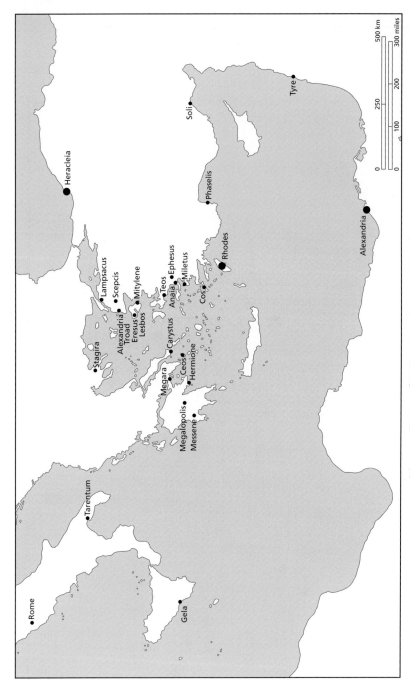

Map 21   Origins of Hellenistic peripatetic philosophers

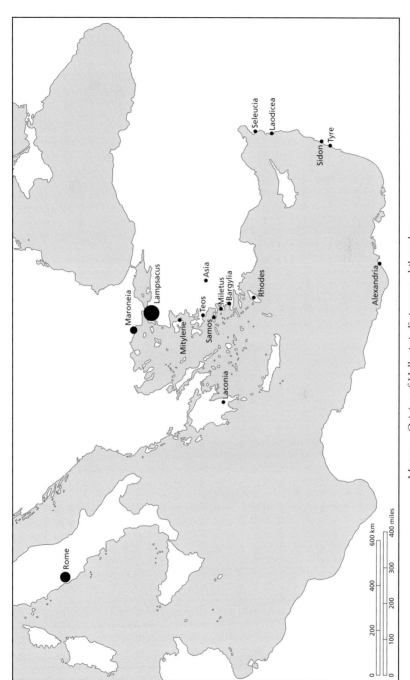

Map 22   Origins of Hellenistic Epicurean philosophers

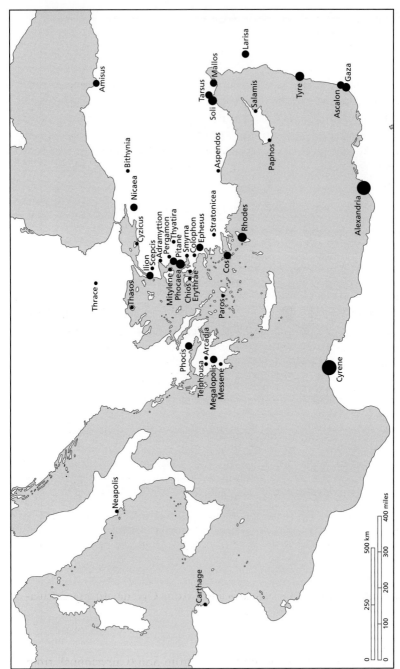

Map 23   Origins of Hellenistic Academic philosophers

The absolute numbers are interesting as well. Judging from sheer numbers, the Academy stands out, the other three schools clustered together (the Stoa somewhat more significant, the Garden less so; surprising to us, in view of the later Italian reception of Epicureanism). Perhaps not too much is to be made of this contrast, as the bias of our sources is hard to account for (but, then again, is the low number of attested Epicureans not significant, given what is in fact our favorable prosopographical position, based on Philodemus' papyri?). At any rate, the numbers, seen in the chronological detail, ring true. Consider just the beginning of the Hellenistic period (300 to 250),

Peripatos 29    Academy 19    Garden 18    Stoa 14

against its closing (150 to 100):

Peripatos 8    Academy 55    Garden 12    Stoa 34

We begin with the four schools roughly balanced (perhaps important for their eventual survival: early on, a tetrapoly was established). Clearly, however, the Peripatos is especially successful (or, perhaps more precisely, the influence of the Peripatos is claimed for many intellectual figures of the era: as we will note on page 378, note 84, many names are of individuals whose association with the Peripatos is less than certain). A century and more later the main story is that of the near-total collapse of the Peripatos; the Academy and the Stoa break out of the pack.

Now, the growth of the Academy is specifically a mid-second-century BCE phenomenon – and it is precisely at this period that the wider geographical reach of the Academy can be verified. The Academy has exactly one individual from beyond the Aegean core before 150 BCE – indeed, the not inconsequential Crantor of Soli. In the two temporal nodes of 150 and 100 BCE, 23 out of 51 individuals in the Academy localizable outside Athens are from beyond the core – which is not at all distinct from the Stoa's 30 out of 50. The Academy becomes successful as it attains the Stoa's Mediterranean pull, which, once again, starts with the very leaders: the Academy becomes successful through the influence of Carneades, from Cyrene. In my calculations above, I count Cyrene as old core (it is a classical established polis and participates more than its share in the center formations of the fourth century). For the old core, however, it is as distant as it could get. And so we see: from Citium (Zeno), from Soli (Chrysippus), from

Cyrene (Carneades); this is how Athens becomes a major force, in pulses in the early third century, the late third century, the middle of the second century. The Garden, the Peripatos, thoroughly Aegean schools, remain behind – especially the Peripatos, the most Aegean of the schools, which indeed goes through a crisis early in the Hellenistic period and does not recover.

This pattern is not easy to account for, neither externally, in terms of the political trajectories of the schools, nor internally, in terms of their doctrines. Politically speaking, the Peripatos would seem to profit most from the Macedonian ascendancy – and indeed it did so, briefly, right at the end of the fourth century. Intellectually, a case can perhaps be made, somehow, for the adequacy of the Stoa to the times (a cosmopolitan philosophy for a cosmopolitan age!)[203] – but, then, what about Carneades' success? Was Skepticism the right thing for the middle of the second century? In general, Greek philosophers sought political paradox more than political accommodation; as is well known, the foundational text of Stoic political theory advocated, in some sense, incest and cannibalism.[204] It was not *that*, as such, or *Skepticism*, as such, which made the Stoa, or the Academy, so successful. And, at any rate, it is probably a false exercise to look for the intellectual category that included Chrysippus and Carneades but excluded Strato and Epicurus.

No; and, so, the basic correlation begins to look less tautological and more as the relevant proximate explanation. Hellenistic philosophical schools have been successful to the extent that they have successfully attracted students from a distance, especially from beyond the old Greek core.

Since very few philosophers come from Alexandria (as we shall return to note below), and since exotic origins such as Carthage, the "Samnites" or Babylon are ultimately rare, distant recruitment typically means the north-eastern corner of the Mediterranean, the Cypriot/Syrian/Cilician area mentioned above. This area also made a contribution, as we noted above, to both medicine and mathematics. The one field in which this area is markedly under-represented, in the Hellenistic

---

[203] A simplistic connection made already by Tarn (1948); made somewhat more promising by Shaw (1985). But Stoic cosmopolitanism harks back to Diogenes the Cynic, a resolutely fourth-century figure; it accommodated the realities of Hellenistic monarchies no more and no less than it did those of the classical polis (Brown, 2006).
[204] This was Zeno's *Republic*; see, e.g., Hook (2005: 32–9).

era, is grammar – the Alexandrian field par excellence. And so, a complementarity: on the one side, the Stoa at Athens, a very successful Hellenistic institution, bringing people from the new lands into the central city of the old core; on the other side, the profession of grammar at Alexandria, a very successful Hellenistic practice (with something of an institutionalized foothold, in the Museion?), bringing people from the old core into the central city of the new lands. The Stoa was the Greek world, folded outside in; grammar was the Greek world, folded inside out.

This is a suggestive way of describing the nature of Athens' pull, but it does not yet explain it. There is nothing surprising about the agglomeration of philosophers: as we have seen in the previous section, philosophical space was always the most structured. Thus, it is natural that there should be schools, and it is only natural that many of them should be in Athens. The one question, really, is why all of a sudden, at about 300 BCE, philosophical schools cease to be founded anywhere else. Which, once again, may be paralleled by comedy: why did the proliferation of many theaters, in the Hellenistic era, not correspond to the rise of many local schools of comic authorship?

With comedy, the answer clearly has something to do with the power of the literary canon's association with Athens (there is, in fact, a qualified exception – at a certain remove from the gravitational pull of Greek literature, that is, in *Roman* comedy). This is suggestive, so let us now turn to philosophy. Here, the question boils down to the following: why did Zeno not found a school in Citium?

This has several answers. To begin with, the Stoa was an interpretation of Socrates in the light of Diogenes (so, for instance, Schofield, 2003). Sinope, Diogenes' city of origin, was distant: it is further away from Athens than was Citium.[205] Diogenes gave up his citizenship – to become, after all, a dog. To have moved from a distant place to a place marked by its past was the closest a Greek could do to renounce his association with any particular polis. Would-be philosophers came to Athens – as Plutarch said[206] – seeking the quiet which is not to be found in one's native city. Athens was "quiet", already; that is, its cultural resonance overrode its politics.

---

[205] Orbis calculates the route, in June, as taking 11 days from Sinope, ten days from the Pedalion promontory (from Alexandria 9.8 days, from Carthage 9.9: ten summer days from Athens is, indeed, rather far).
[206] *On Exile* 605b.

But more than this: Zeno – not more than a moderately prolific author, as we shall note on pages 389–90 below – wrote one book on Greek education, one on the reading of poetry and five on Homer.[207] All this, by a Phoenician! I am not saying this to denigrate him (I was born 300 miles south-east of Citium; and my English is much worse than Zeno's Greek). But, surely, he set out to *make a point*. No one, we found, would take him to Alexandria's Library as a Greek grammarian, so he went to the most Greek place and out-Greeked them all. That was something you could do only in Athens: acting as if it was immaterial what your origins were, since you were living "the Greek education": within the Greek canon, in the space where one could imagine it most directly – within a handful of courtyards in Athens.

Philosophy and comedy both produced a Mediterranean web: the entire Mediterranean was ready for them. But they also both remained anchored to Athens. And, by now, we can easily see how the two hang together. Philosophy and comedy differed from tragedy, rhetoric and (rhetorically inflected) historiography, in that they survived mostly as living forms into the Hellenistic era. But, like them, they were fundamentally performative genres, kin to the literary canon. For various reasons, directly or indirectly attributed to political transformations, the other elements of the performative genre lost their vitality. Philosophy and comedy were, then, *the canon that remained*. In a formula, in the Greek context:

Performance – politics = (philosophy, comedy)

Remaining – in the shadow of a frozen canon. No contemporary practice could really rival the power of the past and no local center could really rival that of Athens. And so: in both comedy as well as philosophy, cultural practices not only remained Athenian but also became much more deeply anchored within a sense of the past. And it is for this reason that Zeno did not set up a school in Citium: it did not have a past, and, at this point, the past mattered most.

Let us conclude by looking, once again, at the two centers – Hellenistic Athens and Alexandria – side by side. They are both

---

[207] He did not, in fact, write a commentary on Hesiod's *Theogony* (Algra, 2001: 563–5); nevertheless, enough by him on this work survived to give rise to such an impression. His original philosophy did not look much different, to future readers, from commentary on the canon.

surprising, remarkable developments, going against the grain of much previous Greek history. And now we can see why: they were both heirs to an upheaval.

Within a few decades poetic realignment went together with political realignment. A culture of performative experiment was displaced by the culture of the entrenched canon. A dispersed system of poleis with Athens at its core was displaced by few monarchic centers, marginalizing Athens. (Both happened together because, even beforehand, poetics and politics had been brought together – in Athens.) Now, the closure of the canon sent creative activity into the specialized genres, which naturally organized themselves around whatever would end up as the central node in the network of cities; politically, this could no longer be Athens, and, in fact, it ended up being Alexandria. And then in Athens itself: its canon established, the city's past cultural associations would have been much more powerful than any contemporary associations of the actual city in Attica. And, indeed, having fallen from its political centrality, Athens gained something of the character of a Delphi or an Olympia. Hence, it could become a site for cultural activity, the most purely "Hellenic" place: hence the attraction for figures such as Zeno.

We noted that the routinization of charisma, in the case of Hellenistic philosophy, should not be explained merely on the basis of the deaths of charismatic philosophers. But perhaps we have looked at the wrong crisis altogether? What mattered was not the death of any individual philosopher or comic author but, rather, the political crisis of Imperial, democratic Athens. It was the death of this city – not that of Plato or of Aristotle – that gave rise to a new need for a new anchoring of cultural practice in impersonal institutions. And so: the crisis of the city, answered by the routinization of charisma. Routinization, unsurprisingly, gives rise to routine and the new systems of Athenian performance – the philosophical schools, Menander's comedy – would now remain stable for many generations. We shall pursue the consequences of this new type of philosophy – philosophy as school routine – in the following chapter.

But, even before that, note the precise combination, with the two responses we have now seen – in Athens and in Alexandria – to the same crisis. Athens' failure and the rise of monarchy gave rise not to a new, homogeneous state ideology but to its very opposite: the rise of even greater, more marked cultural variety, because this crisis was marked by the gap it created between cultural and political centers. The argument of the following chapter is that this duality had important consequences in cultural practices, of lasting significance: most importantly, Athens and Alexandria set philosophy apart from science – making the latter, in a sense, possible.

CHAPTER 4

# Space in Action
## When Worlds Diverge

I begin by looking at the two worlds – that of Athens, as against that of Alexandria – in the third century BCE.

More than previous chapters, this is "normal" cultural history. I survey the contents of cultural trends, and do not just count them (although I do do this, mostly in broad brushstrokes – preserving, in this sense, something of the "statistical" tendency of this book). Specifically, I discuss the nature of culture in Alexandria and in Athens, and try to explain their separate routes, based on the structural background provided in the preceding chapters.

In addition, more so than in previous chapters, I touch on topics close to my main area of expertise – and, indeed, close to topics on which I have already published. *Ludic Proof: Greek Mathematics and the Alexandrian Aesthetic* (Netz, 2009) argues for a distinct alignment of science and poetry in Alexandria in the third century. Especially in the descriptive section 4.1, I revisit arguments made there, expanding the argument (which, in Netz, 2009, focuses mainly on the exact sciences) to consider Hellenistic/ Alexandrian civilization as a whole. This is followed, in section 4.2, by a parallel account of the literary practices of Hellenistic philosophy. With this in place, I proceed to show the bifurcation of the two. Briefly put: the main argument in section 4.3, "The View from Alexandria", is that Hellenistic scientists cared little for philosophy; the argument in section 4.4, "The View from Athens", is that Hellenistic philosophers cared little for science (this is also the most detailed section in this chapter, and the one closest to traditional intellectual history). Finally, in section 4.5, I present the moment of transition at around the year 100 BCE, when a synthesis, of sorts, of Athens and Alexandria did take place – and I account, in section 4.6, for the piecemeal, eclectic nature of this realignment. The net result of all this is twofold. First, as the Mediterranean kaleidoscope shifted and reshifted in the third millennium of the Hellenistic and early Roman eras it reinforced the pluralism of Greek civilization. We see, then, how the coming of monarchies failed to bring a unified ideology: variety, instead, accumulated. Second, the Hellenistic moment, with its bifurcation of science and philosophy, was especially important: an era of flourishing science also saw an autonomous science – or, quite simply, *science*, in something like the modern sense. The practices of Herophilus and Erasistratus, Archimedes and Apollonius of Perga were very distinct from those of Plato and Aristotle; they anticipated, in a real sense – in fact, as direct inspiration – those of Harvey and Galileo. This might be antiquity's most lasting legacy.

## 4.1   Alexandria: A Literary Survey

The following section is indeed a survey, proceeding somewhat haphazardly from theme to theme – which is appropriate for Alexandrian civilization, not just as a matter of a literary tribute but because *such* was this culture. Its many facets were all interconnected, but they were not powerfully centered, no single central practice driving all others. Canonicity, after all, was already qualified.

### 4.1.1   Alexandria: General Comments

Having written a whole book on the style of Hellenistic mathematics (Netz, 2009), I feel entitled to a mere set of bullet points. And so: in that book, I identify several stylistic strands in Hellenistic mathematics.

(1)   A fascination with big numbers. (Thus: Aristarchus, wrote a treatise on "The Sizes and Distances of the Sun and the Moon" – showing that they are bigger, and further away, than you would think! Or Archimedes – counting, in his *Stomachion,* the number of combinations made possible by a child's game.)

(2)   These big numbers are surveyed in such a way, however, as to suggest the limits of surveyability as such; they are ironically undercut (so, even in the last-mentioned treatise by Aristarchus, the use of upper and lower bounds is puting the exercise into question).

(3)   A telling of the mathematical content based on the poetics of surprise – raising expectations so as to quash them later and, in general, leaving questions, intentionally, unanswered (the example from which I start in Netz, 2009, was *Spiral Lines*; the most significant example is Archimedes' intentional sending out of false results so as to trip up his readers; see now Netz, 2017c).

(4)   An emphasis on the combination of seemingly unrelated fields and results, creating a "mosaic" surface, with elements often at a certain tension with each other (most significantly, this gives rise, with Archimedes, to the birth of *mathematical physics*).

(5)   The growth of a more personal writing style (and, thus, introductory essays become more and more discursive).

(6)   In general, the incorporation of literary references into mathematics (for which a prime example is the one I started from on page 13 above: Archimedes' allusion to Pindar in the *Sand-Reckoner*; an especially interesting case is that of Apollonius – attested through the commentary by Pappus, *Collection* Book II – using a hexameter line as the springboard for an exercise in calculation).[1]

The various stylistic strands cohere around the related themes of surprise and variety. Such observations correspond, then, to what we usually assume concerning Hellenistic poetry itself. Scholarship has always emphasized the *poikilos*, varied character of this literature, especially its hybridization of genres (see Kroll, 1924: chap. 9; for a historicized reading, see Barchiesi, 2001), a theme never abandoned by more contemporary scholarship but, rather, widened to encompass other features, above all an alienation in space ("Alibis", the title of Selden, 1998: 289: "Callimachus of Cyrene wrote for a society of displaced persons") and in time (the main theme of Fantuzzi and Hunter, 2004, is the insistent archaizing of Hellenistic poetry).[2] For us, at this stage of the argument, all this is familiar: here is a culture self-conscious about its relative position, in terms of genre, space and time. The canon was entrenched, recently, as Athenian; accordingly, Alexandrian poets turn back to pre-Athenian forms and reinsert themselves as the rivals to the canonical archaic authors, inflecting epic and lyric with the sensibilities of drama and those of the specialized genres. Self-consciousness is kin to irony, to playfulness. Minute, erudite knowledge of the legacy of literature and myth, presented within a diction that prides itself on very precise imitations of archaic voices – all this extends the irony

[1]   For all of this, see Netz (2009): chapter 1, "The Carnival of Calculation" (17–65), is about the reach for big numbers; in chapter 2, "The Telling of Mathematics", pages 66–91 are about the poetics of surprise, while pages 92–114 are about the presence of the author; chapter 3, "Hybrids and Mosaics", is mostly (115–60) about the combination of seemingly unrelated theoretical strands, and pages 160–73 are about the turning of science to literature.

[2]   As ever in contemporary scholarship, some of the literature does wish to discard such interpretations more radically, most notably Cameron (1995). While useful on many points of detail, such scholarship does not really do much to displace the obvious, large-scale features of Hellenistic literature (and it suffers from a lack of attention to Alexandrian literature beyond poetry).

in a well-defined way: towards a mock-pedantic voice that becomes, finally, the most natural literary idiom of Alexandria. The claim of Netz, 2009, then, is that this overall stylistic trend of Alexandrian literature was answered by that of Hellenistic mathematics (which, in turn, serves to confirm our impression of Hellenistic culture as a whole: a significant segment of our evidence, brought to bear on this question).

But why, after all, should science and poetry display a similar aesthetic? In Netz (2009) I largely bracket this question. I note, towards the end of the book (238–40), that science came later. In the terms of section 3.2 above, the generational event of Hellenistic poetry was initiated around 280 BCE, while the generational event of Hellenistic mathematics was initiated around 250 BCE. They overlap – and so Archimedes, the main spring of Hellenistic mathematics, writes to Eratosthenes, who is in the "response" generation of Hellenistic poetry (he is counted among my Alexandria, generation three, on page 295 above: the generation of Callimachus' echo). But if those gears are engaged, it is poetry that moves mathematics. Thus, my summary (Netz, 2009: 240): "It is a simple and straightforward assumption that authors, writing in the Greek Mediterranean between the mid-third and mid-second centuries, could have had their aesthetic sensibilities shaped by their readings of Callimachus, Theocritus, or Apollonius of Rhodes." But this surely won't do, at least not on its own. For now it is obvious to us that the Mediterranean in the middle of the third century presented multiple aesthetic possibilities. One need not have become Alexandrian; one could have remained, instead, Athenian. Was Alexandrian poetry, in fact, rather than Athenian philosophy, the model for Hellenistic science? And, if so, why? This is our question for this chapter. And, to repeat once again: it is an important question, worth expanding a chapter on. For, I would argue, it was the precise configuration of cultural forces in the Hellenistic era that made the variety of Greek culture give rise to our modern science.

And so: we may begin with the finer-grained picture of Alexandrian culture, developed in the preceding chapter. On pages 284–7 above, we have noted the rise of what I called a "government sector" in the post-Chaeronea generation. As the performative canon was closing, it became more natural to reach for cultural status through non-performative writing. For this, Athens was no longer the obvious center; status could be obtained, instead, through royal courts. Court-commissioned culture (or culture akin to that which was, at the time, commissioned by courts) had a surveying, "geographical" tendency, and this was the typical cultural product of

Alexandria's first generation. As discussed on pages 304–5 above, however, as Alexandria grew in size and in self-confidence, this geographical impetus was transformed into a subtle renewal of past, performative culture. It is this which we now need to describe, in greater detail. What was original about Hellenistic culture? As noted already: the thread is all bundled up together, and we may pick it up in many places. Geography – the animating theme of the early third century – remains a useful starting point.

## 4.1.2   Alexandria: Vignettes

Around the year 305 Dicaearchus was commissioned by monarchs (Macedonian, Ptolemaic, or both) to measure the height of mountaintops. Dicaearchus also gave a measure of the size of the Earth. His *Survey of the Earth* (*periodos gēs*) perhaps included a geometrically conceived map and certainly included an entire set of estimated geographical distances.[3] All this seems to us, perhaps, par for the course for a geographer, but, in fact, this was all quite unprecedented. I have argued on pages 300–1 above – speculatively – that the mathematics of Euclid's age took a "geographical", surveying turn. What we now see is that geography, in the same age, took a mathematical turn. I count 26 authors cited by EANS as geographers, active prior to Dicaearchus. The writing of this group – which includes most writings emerging from the expeditions of Alexander's era – seems to have been dominated by a Herodotean, ethnographic impulse.[4] We find, then, that the specific project of doing geography *by numbers* emerges at the

---

[3] For Dicaearchus' geographical program, see Keyser (2001). If part of Dicaearchus' point really was to argue for the perfect sphericity of the Earth, measurement of the size of the Earth went hand in hand with measurement of the height of mountains (the – correct – claim being that relatively low mountains were but a minor detail on a huge and near-perfectly spherical Earth).

[4] Among the better-known authors in this group are, for instance, Ctesias of Cnidus and Callisthenes of Olynthus. The emphasis of such authors seems to be on exotic detail, which is in some tension with the homogenizing nature of mathematical geography. There were certainly antecedents to a more mathematical geography, traces of which can be found, for instance, in Pseudo-Scylax – which mixes, unsystematically, lengths of travel with explicit measures of distance (but, then again, number and calculation are typically Herodotean and not yet mathematical; note, however, that Shipley, 2012, is more optimistic about the intellectual ambitions of Ps.-Scylax and suggests he might have been, simply, the same as Dicaearchus!) – as well as some comments in the Aristotelian corpus (e.g. *Meteor.* 362b19–25, *de Cael.* 298a15–18, both containing mathematical measurements of geographical distances). The fragmentary evidence suggests that the techniques of mathematical geography were all available throughout the fourth century – but were never made the basis for a systematic study before Dicaearchus himself. (Thus, even Eudoxus' geography, extensively cited by later authors – Lasserre, 1966, frr. 272–372 – is now known only for its ethnographic, rather than its mathematical, details, and he is remarkably missing from the strictly geometrical discussions of Strabo's Book II. It is often assumed that this geography must have been innovative in its use of mathematics – e.g. Engels, 2007, 548 – but this might be an anachronistic generic interpretation on our part.)

same time as post-Chaeronea patronage. Not just numbers, of course: all
such measurements – of the height of mountaintops, of the Earth as a
whole, of distances within the Earth – involve optical and astronomical
principles and so lock together geography and the very practices of the
exact sciences. This entanglement is typical of the third century:
Eratosthenes, so Strabo would note, was mathematical in geographical
things, geographical in mathematical things.[5] Eratosthenes himself was
responsible for the most famous measurement of the size of the Earth,
not by any means a pursuit unique to him.[6] Thus, a very obscure
Dionysius, son of Diogenes, has confirmed Eratosthenes (as did
Posidonius, rather later).[7] Xenagoras, near the end of the third century,
measured the height of Olympus for the kings of Macedon;[8] Aristocreon,
Bion and Dalion all apparently preceded Eratosthenes, and all gave measures of Aethiopian distances (so, likely, they did so in an Egyptian
context?); both Sosicrates and Hieronymus of Cardia gave measures of
Crete, another area of Ptolemaic interest, though Hieronymus is known to
have served other monarchs instead. Both Ophellas and Pytheas himself
might have incorporated some mathematical and astronomical knowledge
into their geography.[9] In fact, just as it is hard to show for any pre-
Dicaearchean geographer a specific mathematical interest, it is hard to
argue for any immediately post-Dicaearchean geographer that he could
have written a purely ethnographic survey. It was an age when mathematicians mapped; and the geographers became mathematical.[10]

[5] *Geography*, II.1.41. To be clear, this is an ironic critique, the thrust of the aphorism being (from
Strabo's perspective) that Eratosthenes does neither well. But the point remains that Eratosthenes
sought the mathematical/geographical crossover – to an extent censured by later authors (for the
overall question of the cultural place of geography, see Clarke, 2001).
[6] Though perhaps Eratosthenes was an especially sophisticated measurer: Carman and Evans (2015)
argue that he could have been interested in finding bounds on the size of the Earth, based on the
assumption of a finite-distance Sun!
[7] Taisbak (1974): the thrust of Posidonius' measurement was to reproduce, not to criticize,
Eratosthenes' measure.
[8] Ziegler (1967: 57–63), based on the one testimony we possess: Plutarch, *Life of Aemilius* 15. This
measurement was expressed in the poetic form of an epigram, and the overall thrust – bringing "holy
Olympus" under precise measurement – has the typical mock-epic undertones of Hellenistic
science.
[9] I do not know of a synthetic study of geographic measurement in the early third century BC; for the
authors mentioned in this paragraph, see EANS s.vv.
[10] A speculative yet powerful example of mathematics reaching out to a geographical metaphor can be
found in a work by Eratosthenes' contemporary – Archimedes. The latter's masterpiece of mathematical
physics, *On Floating Bodies*, is dedicated to an absurdly difficult comprehensive survey of a problem in
the conditions of stability of a certain object immersed in liquid. The conditions of stability turn out to
depend on the weight of the immersed object. Archimedes finds, in the final proposition II.10, that,
depending on that weight, certain results are arranged symmetrically: the heaviest and the lightest case
behave the same as each other; the second heaviest and the second lightest behave the same as each other.

So, our quick glance at geography has brought in, already, the theme of the mixing of the genres. It also brings in the theme of *big* things: mountains; the Earth (part of the attraction, perhaps, of geography?). And then, one could measure the heavenly bodies as well. Aristarchus offered a measure of the sizes and distances of the Sun and the Moon, once again extending a project first attempted by Eudoxus and, once again, launching a minor Hellenistic genre. Pheidias (Archimedes' father) after him, as well as Archimedes himself and then Hipparchus, all offered measures of the sizes and distances of heavenly bodies.[11] Much of our knowledge derives from Archimedes' *Arenarius*, his only work known to have been dedicated to a monarch, and also a study in gigantic numbers. So, in line with what we see from geography: great sizes of Earth and sky were considered appropriate fodder for royal patronage. And of course, in general, the age of Hellenistic monarchies is the age of gigantism. I have mentioned, in Netz (2009), that this was the age of the Pharos and the Colossus, and indeed we know somewhat more about technical authors, in this age of royal patronage, partly because it is an age of massive monuments. So the temple of Apollo in Didyma, but also many of the new developments in mechanics; Diades' *Wall-Borer*, as well as Epimachus' *Helepolis*, seem to have been remembered primarily because of their sheer size;[12] the same of course is true for Archimedes' feat in launching the giant ship, the *Surakosia*. "Give me where to stand, and I shall move the Earth!" (pages 157–8 above), he said, as he did *that* – echoing, that is, recent measures of the Earth and the cosmos even while producing a mechanical feat of gigantism. Gigantism was its own point, as we have noted for the *Helepolis*. The *Surakosia*, too, surely was an overkill of a ship rather than a breakthrough dreadnought. The craze for the military elephant – sending

---

The results involve the object standing up, or inclining, and so there is a certain pun involved in Archimedes' referring to such conditions, in the preamble to II.10 (Archimedes *Palimpsest* 127v col. 2.14), as *klimata*, a word meaning both "inclinations" and – within mathematical geography – "zones". The term refers, in Archimedes, not to any particular inclinations of the objects immersed in the liquid but, rather, to its conditions of weight. Thus, the metaphor is clear: there is a conceptual arrangement going symmetrically around a center, which is that of conceptual "zones", akin to the zones into which mathematical geographers such as Eratosthenes have divided the Earth.

[11] Van Helden (1985) surveys the main pre-Newtonian estimates of cosmic sizes; our knowledge derives primarily from Ptolemy, whose use of past calculations can be seen through a more recent study: Carman (2010). The emphasis of recent literature, such as Jones' studies on both the Keskintos and the Canopic inscriptions (Jones, 2005; 2006), is on the extent to which ancient astronomical parameters could have been informed by the properties of the numbers as such, seeking meaningful – and big – numbers.

[12] EANS s.vv. Vitruvius' survey of Diades' machines (X.13.3–8) emphasizes large numbers; the *helepolis* was, famously, too big for its own good: Rowland (2016: 448).

Ptolemaic kings to hunt for African elephants and thus promoting Aethiopian explorations[13] – appears as something of a blunder, Hellenistic monarchs investing in a military proposition whose main justification was that of sheer scale; a cultural obsession, dooming armies?[14]

We started from geography, and we were led in two directions: on the one hand, towards measurement and mathematics; on the other hand, towards size and big numbers. The two are clearly connected – measurement and size do go hand in hand – but are also in tension. Measurement implies, to us, the austerity of an exact science; fascination with size suggests a certain exuberance. Something of a paradox, then, within Hellenistic culture. Let us pursue this further, expanding our view from geography into its allied field of history. Now, it is perhaps not so remarkable that Hellenistic authors compiled exotic information, perhaps of a "literary" character: Herodotus did so already. But, then again, for that very reason, Greek historical writing came to be marked, early on, by its debate concerning the exotic and the literary – Herodotean exoticism implicitly repudiated, perhaps, by that other canonic historical author, Thucydides.[15] Much of the ethnographic and geographical data amassed by the Alexander expedition appears to have been of a sober, descriptive character, but already Cleitarchus may have emphasized, in his history of the expedition itself, its more marvelous aspects. Perhaps significantly, he could also have been one of the early historians to have settled in Alexandria.[16] Alexandria did not establish itself as the unrivaled center for historical writing, as we shall return to note below; all the more remarkable, then, that some of the most significant historians associated with the city were marked by a more "literary" and "sensationalist" inflection. The literary style of Hecataeus of Abdera – certainly a central figure of the first generation of Greek historians in Alexandria – is difficult to pin down, as knowledge of his work is so heavily mediated. That he ranged

---

[13] Casson (1993).

[14] Elephants are extremely difficult to breed in captivity and are never truly tamed. Outside south Asia their cost/benefit as war animals is truly prohibitive. "Unlike the tank, an elephant is made of flesh and blood and resents becoming an animated pin cushion" (Glover, 1944: 262); and so, when facing sustained resistance, they simply turn back, causing havoc among their own ranks. Only one major power of the Hellenistic world – Rome – made the correct assessment and avoided the elephant (it must have helped that none were available in Italy); of course, this major power decimated all its rivals, so putting an end to the experiment of the Mediterranean war elephant.

[15] Packman (1991), repeating a common view in the literature, criticized, for instance, by Keyser (2006); whether a valid critique of Herodotus or not, what matters for us is that this type of contrast between historians was conceptualized in antiquity itself.

[16] Prandi (1996: 66–9). Was Cleitarchus in fact a more "sensational" historian? We cannot tell, but it is at least significant that such was the ancient verdict (Hammond, 1991: 411 n.48).

widely, in a geographical sense, is obvious – from Egypt to the Hyperboreans; the exotic element could easily tend towards the novelistic, and it is common to understand Hecataeus' work on the Hyperboreans as a travel novel (geography, again);[17] such, for sure, was Euhemerus' history, of the same generation.[18] Later on, the most significant "serious" historian associated with third-century Alexandria came to be criticized precisely for a sensationalist, specifically "tragic" tendency: such, at least, were the terms in which Polybius criticized Phylarchus.[19] So, perhaps, Alexandria as the city of a more belletristic historiography[20] (and why should Alexandrians not infuse Herodotus with tragedy? Apollonius was infusing Homer, after all, with tragedy, as well.).

Whether or not Phylarchus was a dramatist-historian, Alexandria was certainly the site of *paradoxography.* The one historical author writing on third-century Alexandria itself to have survived in some substantial (if mediated) form was Callixeinus – author of "On Alexandria", remembered especially for the description of the *Pompē*, Ptolemy Philadelphus' triumphal procession famous for its outré extravagance. It appears that the history of the city, in this author, became a catalogue of its marvels – lingering on a major episode in which the city and court, themselves, engaged in the accumulation of a marvel catalogue. The history and geography of Alexandria *were* paradoxography.[21] Once again, this genre of historical writing could have had antecedents in the fourth century (though Giannini, 1965, doubts the titles ascribed to Ephorus and Theopompus, *paradoxa* and *thaumasia*, respectively). Most likely,

---

[17] Warren (2002: 151–9) is a philosophically motivated discussion. Much of the literature concerning Hecataeus concerns his possible position (and, by implication, that of Greeks of his time) towards non-Greeks such as Egyptians and, potentially, Jews (for a recent treatment, see Dillery, 1998).

[18] Winiarczyk (2013).

[19] Schepens (2005); Vanhaegendoren (2010), going against the grain of current scholarship, takes this characterization of Phylarchus as a "tragic" historian at face value and identifies the tragic modes of his historiography. But it is very hard to know how much weight to give to Polybius' undoubtedly biased account (the many fragments are mediated almost entirely through paradoxographic tradition or, most often, through Athenaeus; is there anything to learn from the fact that such sources saw Phylarchus as useful to their purposes?).

[20] The other author often cited as perhaps a "dramatic" historian – once again, a misleading label, but with antecedents in the ancient reception itself – was Duris of Samos (see Baron, 2016, for a recent discussion: Duris as a *Herodotean* historian – which, to him, means *vivid, detailed and mimetic*). Certainly not a resident of Alexandria – indeed, he was a ruler of Samos! – one may only speculate concerning his relations with the Ptolemaic court (for an overview of the evidence, see Gattinoni, 1997: chap. 1).

[21] For Callixeinus, see Rice (1983). He is known through Athenaeus – and Athenaeus stands out among our extant authors in the extent to which he includes memory of early Alexandria, and not just of Athens, within his Imperial reconstruction of a Greek past (Thompson, 2000). Athenaeus' memory was paradoxographic, and it was as such that Alexandria memorized itself from its very beginning.

paradoxography as a genre began properly only with Callimachus, and among Giannini's datable authors – no more than 12 – seven can be assigned to the third century, in varying degrees of certainty; the rest are later still.[22] Callimachus' *mirabilia* was, among his overall corpus, a minor work[23] – but by the major literary figure of the city, and one which was continuous with Callimachus' overall project: as noted above on page 305, he was engaged primarily with the survey of the literary past (in the *Pinakes*) as well as of the antiquarian details of myth and ritual (in the *Aetia*): so, why not collect the more literary-marked, more myth-like elements from historical writing? The emphasis is on the collection and appreciation of individual items within a literary cabinet of curiosity. Even the big numbers accumulated by geographers and astronomers, after all, were such isolated marvels; literally, indeed, they measured *mountain peaks*. But the notion of a "cabinet of curiosities" is somewhat misleading. I have noted in Netz (2016: 289–94) the curious tendency of ancient mirabilia to concentrate on liquid marvels (the strange behaviors of rivers and beverages) – and suggest that the context for this could have been, simply, sympotic. The collection of mirabilia extracts, from the sobriety of history and geography, the tidbits useful for polite, inebriated conversation.

Let me now offer a parallel to the Hellenistic mirabilia: a close parallel, indeed, as we move from the merely described marvel to the marvel produced. Mechanical devices are sometimes ascribed to Archytas,[24] and Ps.-Aristotle approaches the field of mechanics as marvelous,[25] but such sources are so dubious and minimal as to suggest that, in the fourth century, there was no systematic effort to *produce* mechanical marvels as such. Of course, there was plenty of mechanical effort, remarkable in its close association with named authors. This is the era of the engineer in the

---

[22] These are: Callimachus, Philostephanus, Myrsilus, Nymphodorus; likely also Archelaus, Antigonus of Carystus as well as Ps.-Aristotle. It is remarkable that Myrsilus and Nymphodorus, who likely did not have an Alexandrian attachment, were authors of local wonders (Lesbos and Sicily, respectively). The collection of wonders from across the oikoumene was a typical mapping, Alexandrian project.

[23] But a real one nonetheless: for succinct defenses of the historicity of the ancient genre of mirabilia, see Vergados (2007: 737 n.2) and Prioux (2009: 122–3).

[24] See Huffman (2005: 571–9), and the discussion (28–30): likely a misattribution from a work by another, anonymous author (who – DL VIII.82 – "learned from Teucer the Carthaginian" – likely a Hellenistic author?).

[25] In the sense of the surprising effects of technē (does it or does it not overcome nature? See Schiefsky, 2007, for the debate.); the actual devices covered are all mundane, with the exception of the engaged wheels dedicated at a temple – paradoxical in their opposite motions (*Mech.* 848a19–25)! (Andrew Wilson suggests that dedicating wheels at a temple is in fact attested archaeologically and is specifically *Egyptian*, and so this treatise is, likely, from Ptolemaic Alexandria: personal communication.)

service of government. But such engineers would without exception produce war engines. Objects of wonder, all right: mechanical elephants, we
may now say. But practical they were. Of the 47 mechanical authors I
count from antiquity, I can assign a specific field of activity for 42. Of these,
two-thirds appear to have been strictly war engineers. Authorship of
theoretical mechanical devices was a rare pursuit, we find: mostly, a
generational event, associated with the Hellenistic era.

This tradition has very little to do with practical mechanics. Recall the
epigram by Hedylus, preserved in Athenaeus' 497d–e:

> Come, lovers of strong wine, and behold the *rhuton*
> In the temple of the venerable Arsinoe, dear to the West Wind:
> It represents the Egyptian dancer Besas, who trumpets a shrill
> Blast when the stream is opened up, allowing the wine to flow.
> [H]onor this clever invention of Ctesibius –
> Come, young men! – in this temple of Arsinoe.

This apparently is an epigram on an artifact produced by the master
mechanician of Alexandria, Ctesibius. Liquids, again! Indeed, the devices
in question are, specifically, "pneumatic" – based on liquids in motion –
and our main sources are two treatises on pneumatics: by Philo of
Byzantium (whose *Pneumatics* is extant only via the Arabic translation),[26]
perhaps a contemporary of Archimedes; and by Hero of Alexandria, likely
an Imperial-era author. What we find in these two treatises is, in
Drachman's phrase, "parlour-magic".[27] Tybjerg (2003: 444 n.5) neatly
summarizes the negative reaction that this has met from many past scholars, with Peter Green the pithiest and the most dismissive of ancient
pneumatics, writing disparagingly of "a collection of elaborate mechanical
toys, curiosities, the subsidized exotica of an authoritarian regime" (Green,
1990: 478). Tybjerg herself points out the place of wonder, as a *philosophical*
concept, in Hero's self-presentation as a scientist-philosopher (which
perhaps fits this Imperial-era author better than it fits Philon). What is
most important for us is to note the significance of marvel devices for
ancient Hellenistic audiences. Drachmann's reference to "parlour-magic"
was apt, but it still tends to understand ancient pneumatics through the
prism of modern practices, modern expectations. Tybjerg's emphasis on
wonder brings us closer to the ancients. What we should now add is that
the wonders of ancient pneumatics were directly continuous with Greek

---

[26] Carra de Vaux (1903); Prager (1974).
[27] Drachmann (1948: 46–7) is especially useful, refuting an attempt to recover a philosophical kernel
from Philon's devices of marvel.

*natural* wonders. Callimachus collected tales about the strange behaviors of liquids in nature; and Ctesibius made such liquids behave strangely, by art. Hedylus, producing an appropriately symptotic epigram, is not a lucky witness: this is what such devices were *for*.

The parallelism is very close indeed. The collection of literary mirabilia emerged in Alexandria as a variation within a more "sober" practice of history and especially geography. The production of mechanical mirabilia emerged in Alexandria as a variation on a more "sober" practice of military engineering.

We find a proportion:

Geography:marvels::mechanics:wonder devices

This expands on the paradox noted above. On the one hand, a rational impulse to survey and to map; on the other hand, a fascination with the extraordinary and the marvelous. What we begin to notice is how the extraordinary is *nested* within the sober survey. Recall: the basic trajectory we noted for Alexandria in section 3.3.3 was from the "government sector" – accounting for the spirit of the "mapping", comprehensive survey – into a more original cultural composition. This was made, we now note, by preserving the mapping attitude – and injecting, into it, the extraordinary. The map – brought into the symposium.

This seems to be a general theme, going beyond just the pair of mechanics and historiography. Once again, without repeating in detail the arguments made in Netz (2009), we should recall the significance of surprise, which might perhaps qualify even as *marvel*, in the Hellenistic exact sciences. Archimedes, in his pure mathematics, engaged with ad hoc, playful objects (a spiral, a parabola, an arbelos – and so many more), seemingly unmeasurable and yet minutely measured: a ludic study that will ultimately give rise to the calculus. In his mixed science, Archimedes created toy universes of planes hanging on a balance, of liquid spheres (his own response to the liquid marvels of Ctesibius) – and, through the radical idealization of such impossibilities, he paved the way to mathematical physics.

Certainly, in Hellenistic medicine, marvels as such are less significant. Herophilus and Erasistratus could have described medical monstrosities; they concentrate, instead, on normal anatomy. This is infused by the extraordinary, however, at the level of the medical *language*. Of course, almost nothing survives of Hellenistic medicine, directly. Even authors such as Herophilus and Erasistratus – fairly well attested by later sources – are known not through quotations but through references to individual pieces of doctrine: testimonies rather than fragments. Had they expressed themselves in arresting phrases, would not more have remained? On the other hand, such testimonies that we have do suggest a language expressive at the level of verbal choice. The writings were rich with metaphor, often of a striking (typically, surprisingly humble) character. I have surveyed Herophilus' anatomical nomenclature in Netz (2009: 158–9): one bone is a "weaver's shuttle"; an organ is the "twelve-fingered" (a measure of size, this: our duodenum); several parts of the brain/skull are "stylus-shaped", "lambda-shaped", "pharos-shaped", "reed-pen-shaped"; membranes are "net-like", "cobweb-like", "grape-like" or "coats"; the female pudendum can be like "the head of the octopus or the upper part of a windpipe".[28] This may be further corroborated from Erasistratus, for whom we have mostly evidence for physiological theory rather than anatomy: the growth of the embryo explained as like that of "a sieve, a rope, a bag, or a basket";[29] nerves are plaited, once again, "like a rope";[30] the heart contains a "three-barbed" (tricuspid; shades of Herophilean-like nomenclature, here) valve;[31] the liver found, in one patient, to have the hardness of a rock (like the pudenda described by Herophilus?).[32]

We are reminded of the evidence on pages 144–5 above concerning the remarkable treatise title: common to comedy – and to Hellenistic science and scholarship. Naming and mapping are related projects, and so Hellenistic doctors surveyed the body, and named it. This once again has parallels elsewhere in Alexandria: mathematical authors surveyed intellectual fields – and, as they were doing so, they introduced names. The "belly ache" (Archimedes' *Stomachion*) or "fast delivery" (Apollonius' *Okutokion*). Apollonius invented a type of sundial – and named it "the Spider Web", *Arachne* (this is directly reminiscent of medical terminology).[33] Conon, famously, named a feature among the fixed stars "the Lock of Berenice" (see Gutzwiller, 1992, on the reverberation of this episode into poetry; but

---

[28] In Netz (2014b), I argue that the anatomical term "clitoris" could be another piece of Hellenistic nomenclature, deriving from an elaborate mythical-literary sexual innuendo. (The term literally means "the little Cleitor thing"; Cleitor was a village known for a fountain whose waters were such that, having tasted them, one could no longer enjoy wine.)

[29] *Nat. Fac.* II.3 Kuhn.II.87. What is at stake, for Galen, is the argument that organs grow by having additions to them throughout their extent, as opposed to an Erasistratean doctrine according to which growth is, as it were, "on the edges". It is possible that all of this is from Galen, not from Erasistratus, though Galen does frame the argument as if it were Erasistratean.

[30] *Nat. Fac.* II.6 Kuhn II.96: the "rope" is here much more clearly Erasistratean, and the proximity to the previous image (see previous note) makes it more likely that the previous mention, too, was triggered by an expression in Erasistratus himself.

[31] Galen, *PHP* VI.6.6.3.    [32] Caelius Aurelianus, *Morb. Chron.* III.124.

[33] *Architectura* IX.8.1. The reference is uncertain (and just how original was Apollonius?), but the metaphor readily suggests the kind of radial arrangement one could naturally trace on time-measuring devices (to us, the astrolabe would be the most obvious example, with its own rete or net).

note, throughout, the humble, mock-epic tone of such scientific names). By making the act of naming deliberate, one makes it ironic: and so Diodorus Cronus (active, as we recall, in Alexandria's first generation) named one of his slaves Allamēn, a grammatical connector, to show, precisely, the arbitrariness of naming. This was part of a larger project of Diodorus: philosophy as a kind of catalogue of marvels. His modus operandi was not simply to refute his opponent in conversation, but to do so while promulgating a particular set of paradoxes, at least two of which – naturally – came to have marked, vivid names: the "Veiled", the "Horned".[34] Callimachus himself recognized Diodorus as a peer and celebrated him in an epigram marked by the confusion of sign and signified: "[T]he Cronos (lit., the old fogey) is wise."[35]

Of course Callimachus knew about signs: he was a grammarian, surely the key activity of Alexandrian intellectuals from his time on. The aim in this practice is to collect and survey canonic literature (although Callimachus' *Pinakes* involved, in some sense, the totality of literature),[36] all the while emphasizing its idiosyncrasies, mastering the individual characteristics of authors and of works. Already Philitas' *glōssai* – the foundational work of Alexandrian grammar – was a collection of rare words (the mirabilia, as it were, of lexicography).[37] Surveying archaic texts, Zenodotus marked certain lines – literally, by an added symbol of the obelus, a skewer (yet another homely metaphor), a horizontal line set

---

[34] Diogenes Laertius contradicts himself, first asserting that Euboulides invented "Liar, Disguised, Electra, Veiled, Sorites, Horned and Bald" (II.108: shades of Menander here), then assigning (II.111) "Veiled" and "Horned" to Diodorus Cronus. Euboulides, unlike Diodorus Cronus himself, seems to have written philosophical treatises (Goulet, 2000: 246) which one could mine for the contents; thus, that a paradox is attributed to him does not imply that it was so named by him. Aristotle, who does refer to a particular argument, in a concise manner, as "third man" (*Metaph.* 990b17, 1039a2, 1059b8, 1079a13, SE 178b36, 179a3), never mentions any of those names ("sea battle" is not used by Aristotle as a name of an argument, and is instead the stock example taken for an argument); nor does Epicurus, from whose response to the Megaric authors we do have a few fragments. The first author known to have responded to such paradoxes in their named form was likely Chrysippus (or, at least, we can say that later librarians classified some of his works as explicitly referring to such terms: *DL* VII.196–8; Theophrastus' list includes one treatise title referring to the "liar": *DL* V.49). In short, it seems quite possible that the practice of attaching sharp, memorable names to paradoxes originated with Diodorus Cronus, even if many of his paradoxes were based on those of his predecessors, whether Eleatic, Megarian or Dialectician.

[35] There is a series of modern studies dedicated to this epigram, trying to discern the precise philosophical doctrines of Diodorus lampooned by Callimachus (most recently, as far as I can tell, Kurzová, 2009; key studies are Sedley, 1977, and White, 1986). Likely enough, the epigram is written based on a close, personal knowledge of Diodorus' philosophy: an Alexandrian poet, mockingly aware of a half-mocking Alexandrian philosophy.

[36] Witty (1958).

[37] The sources: Spanoudakis (2002: 347–403); Bing (2003) for discussion (336: "Was he interested in the lack of uniformity, in semantic dissonance itself?").

next to strange lines,[38] marking in this way the literate, meta-linguistic character of the new pursuit:[39] the principle with which we are already familiar, the comprehensive survey pursued not so as to homogenize a field but so as to mark its idiosyncrasies: *this* line stands out.

It is not surprising to see the grammatical mode in other Alexandrian disciplines. The evidence that Herophilus himself engaged in Hippocratic commentary is far from certain, but it remains possible that he studied rare words in the Hippocratic corpus, in the spirit of Philitas.[40] And then, as noted on pages 253–4 above, the single-generation event of the anatomy of Herophilus and Erasistratus gave way to at least two distinct groups active in Alexandria, Herophileans and empiricists, both pivoting away from Herophilus' anatomy (with or without questioning his very dogmatism), and both emphasizing grammar as a central literary form for the medical author. Already, in the middle of the century, we find Bacchius[41] as well as Philinus[42] engaged in the writing of commentaries, and the interpretation of rare words, in the Hippocratic corpus. At about the same time Mnemon of Sidon created a complex system of annotating the third book of the Hippocratic *Epidemics*, an annotation whose interpretation (and putative authorial status) would explode into a major controversy in the second century.[43] The much later prevalence of the commentary as intellectual form, largely in the context of late ancient education (to which I return in section 6.5.3 below), should not mislead us. The emphasis on rare words in the Hippocratic corpus suggests that the medical commentary of the third century served not medical teaching in the strict sense but, rather, was continuous with the contemporary practices of grammar, approaching Hippocrates in the manner of the literary canon. (Which is, of course, suggested by the very formation of the Hippocratic corpus, likely enough, early in the Hellenistic era).[44]

We recall Callimachus' water marvels, Ctesibius' water devices: let us now consider Herophilus, approaching his patients with a water clock. He touches their body, synchronizing the motions of two liquids, the water discharged from the clepsydra, the blood in motion through the arteries. This was Herophilus' major clinical innovation, and one that

---

[38] Pfeiffer (1968: 115); but the evidence is all from the Imperial era.
[39] It has been customary to see Zenodotus as a textual critic who excluded repetitions; van Thiel (1992) suggests he was merely marking parallels, vigorously opposed by Schmidt (1997).
[40] Von Staden (1989: 74–6, 429–32).
[41] Certainly in some sense a "Herophilean": von Staden (1989: 484–500).
[42] I return to the question of Philinus' project on pp. 404–5 below.
[43] Von Staden (1989: 501–2).
[44] We know surprisingly little about the circumstances of the corpus. See p. 301, n.147.

came to define all later Greek medicine: the arteries pulsate, and
Herophilus noted that this pulse has diagnostic and prognostic significance.[45] So, what's a Hellenistic author to do? Of course, to produce a
comprehensive survey of types of pulse. Galen insists that Herophilus'
fully elaborated system had four parameters, rhythm, magnitude, speed
and vehemence (*rhythmos, megethos, tachos, sphodrotēs*), and it seems clear
that already Herophilus was engaged in the project that took up so much
of Galen's work: a catalogue of the various combinations according to the
given parameters (as against a further classification of clinical subjects,
especially in terms of age), together with a statement of the diagnostic and
prognostic consequences of each deviation from the norm established
through such catalogues. Moreover, as we have by now come to expect, a
few aberrant types of pulse are named through piquant metaphor: "gazel-
ling", "anting".[46] So far, familiar mapping. But whence the parameters? I
would not put too much weight on the potential scientific resonance of
"magnitude"[47] and "speed",[48] and "vehemence" is clearly a biological
category. The category of "rhythm" must have been deliberately modeled
on *music*, however. This is not a trivial detail: rhythm leads the series of
parameters listed by Galen, and was apparently the one put to most
clinical use. The water clock was there, measuring time; and the human
body was understood as a rhythmic organism. As Aratus was rendering
the stars in poetic terms – so Herophilus was rendering the body in
musical terms. Dilation and contraction of the artery were explicitly
understood in terms of *arsis* and *thesis* (T.183), terms of dance – raising
and lowering the foot – and hence of musical theory – stressed and
unstressed metrical units; different rhythms were described, in
Herophilus' system, specifically as different *metrical* forms: as we grow,
so does our pulse rhythm, trochee to spondee, "based on the scansion by
feet of the grammatical art".[49] Von Staden cogently argues that none of
this should be seen as a direct debt to the music theoretician,

---

[45] The evidence and discussion are in von Staden (1989: 322–61, 262–88), and the matter was recently
discussed in detail in Berrey (2011: chap. 4), from which my discussion derives.
[46] T. 170: Marcellinus is explicit that the term itself is a Herophilean coinage.
[47] A central technical term in Greek geometry, a study of "magnitudes"; typically, objects are
compared according to their "magnitude" or "multitude".
[48] The connection is thin: that Eudoxus' main theoretical contribution to astronomy was titled "On
Speeds". But, then again, why should the observation of fixed bodily movements not bring to mind
an astronomical association?
[49] T 177 16–17.

Aristoxenus.[50] Herophilus' achievement could not be reduced to mere dependence on a past author. No: he made the body musical, and, since musical structure was essential to Greek performative poetry, Herophilus made the study of the body analogous not exactly to music theory but, more to the point, to Alexandrian grammar.[51] And so we have brought them all together: the water marvel; the comprehensive survey; the performative canon.

Medicine – turned to commentary, inspired by "philology". Not quite what happened with mathematics: in this field, after all, no single past author was set up as canonical.[52] And yet, mathematical authors did discuss words – in their *definitions*. Russo (1998) has pointed out – as a criticism – that some of the definitions in Euclid's *Elements* I are mathematically inert. His solution is to suggest these could have been later, spurious additions of, perhaps, the early Imperial era.[53] But what if the definitions are there not just to prepare for an axiomatic process but also to engage, directly, with mathematical *words*? Apollonius of Perga, once again reverting to a Euclidean practice, made words, as such, of concern, devoting the beginning of his *Conics* to a renaming and redefinition of the conic sections, coming up with the names, still standard today but resonant, in the third century, with strangeness: "deficiency", "fitting-ness", "excess" (ellipse, parabola and hyperbola).[54]

Mathematicians – however briefly, acting like grammarians? This might seem far-fetched, until we recall the general phenomenon of scientists

---

[50] Arguing against a long line of interpretation, see von Staden (1989: 278 n.134); Berrey (2011: 35–41) argues that Herophilus' reliance on the concept of the "primary time-unit" may derive specifically from Aristoxenus, hence showing a more direct dependence.

[51] At least from Varro on, the rhythmic structure of the pulse could also be transposed to the key of harmony (so that a rhythm of three out of four is 4:3, a fourth!) and then provided with a neo-Pythagorean meaning, a transposition that would remain with Western medicine through the Middle Ages and beyond (Holford-Strevens, 1993). Clearly, Herophilus had no similar Pythagorean inclinations – or else he would have been severely criticized by Galen (neither, of course, had Aristoxenus. Music, to Herophilus, connoted the literary, not the philosophical.

[52] The so-called commentary by Hipparchus to Aratus – the earliest "commentary" extant through the manuscript tradition – is dedicated to a literary text and is not a commentary but, rather, a critique. The *Suda* reports a commentary by Theodosius on Archimedes' *Method*, which *could* then be a second-century commentary on a very recent work, but are we sure that this was indeed by a Hellenistic Theodosius? (I return to this question on p. 761 below.)

[53] Not merely a radical intervention in our text but also put in serious doubt by Posidonius' fr. 47, whose simple reading, in my view, is that Posidonius took the claim that the diameter bisects the circle (certainly inappropriate in the context of mathematical definitions) to be part of the text of Euclid.

[54] Eutocius, *in Apol.* Heiberg 168.17–179.24 asserts, based on Geminus, that the more "general" conception of the conic section (implied in the terminological change) was due to Apollonius; Pappus, *Collection* VII.30, states specifically that the terminology itself was original to Apollonius.

turning towards literature, or, then again, poets turning towards science. I
have surveyed this in Netz (2009: 160–99). Of course, Eratosthenes – "a
mathematician among geographers, and yet a geographer among mathematicians" (Strabo II.1)! – was himself poet, scientist and grammarian.
Very little survives from Euphorion (librarian to an Antiochus, not a
Ptolemy),[55] and yet this tiny corpus contains a very complicated pun on
a sophisticated mathematical term, the "perfect number".[56] We may
further recall a certain Apollodorus of Cyzicus, author of an epigram on
Pythagoras' mathematical discovery[57] (Callimachus, too, in *Iambus* 1,
narrates Pythagoras' mathematical activity).[58] A certain Perseus discovered
certain speiric curves (thread-like or rope-like; a metaphor favored by
Erasistratus as well, we recall), whereupon he wrote an epigram (did he
inscribe his curves and set them up as a dedication?):[59]

> Finding three lines on five sections
> Perseus, honoring these [the gods?], propitiated the daimones.

Advanced geometry – propitiating daimones, poetic! But, of course,
science as a whole is poeticized, in this Alexandrian moment. I count
(modifying the data in EANS 1030–2) 58 Greek authors of poetry in the
subject areas of the specialized genres.[60] Most belong to one of these two
distinct categories.

- 24 Hellenistic authors, whose quality of verse suggests they could have
  been motivated primarily by poetic ambition. A substantial group –
  seven out of the 20 – dedicated at least part of its output to astronomy
  and meteorology, the Aratean fields – and also those for which myth
  and science could most readily be invoked side by side.[61] A similarly
  sized group is of authors who wrote poetry, of a grammarian or
  historical character, directly on the variety of myth and ritual, a
  literature of which the most famous example was Callimachus'

---

[55] For a survey, see Kolde (2006).
[56] Lightfoot (1998): the limbs (of Dionysus?) are cut off in such a way that they are equal to the whole
  and so are "perfect"; the pun involves *melos* and *meros*, "limb" and "part" (in the technical
  arithmetical sense), *teleioi* (perfect) and *telestai* (initiated in the mysteries).
[57] Netz (2009: 196–8).   [58] Netz (2009: 194–5).   [59] Proclus, in *Eucl.* 112.
[60] The term is a bit wider than "didactic epic", since not all such poetry was written in epic meter; the
  sense of "didactic" would have to be taken ironically in many cases. I also exclude archaic
  antecedents (Hesiod, Homer, Xenophanes) as well as the classical authors who followed directly
  on the epic model (Cleostratus, Parmenides, Empedocles).
[61] Other than Aratus himself: Anacreon, Dionysius of Corinth, Diophil (EANS 269), Eratosthenes,
  Hegesianax, Sminthes.

*Aetia.*[62] Variety remains essential and the last third is of poets each
with his own, sometimes multiple, themes.[63]

- 20 authors, mostly of the early Empire, writing in one of the following
fields: medicine (more than half this group, with 14 authors, of whom
no fewer than 12 wrote specifically on medical pharmacology) and
astrology (six authors). These are the service industries of antiquity,
and the overall impression is that the authors' professional identity, in
this group, typically was that of an astrologer or a physician, rather than
of a poet – poetry serving, in this case, to bolster one's claim to elite
status. This, then, belongs in the wider field of Greek culture as a status
signifier within the expanding elites of the Imperial era: more on this, in
the next part of the book, section 6.3.

Of the remainder, we may note a few subgroups. Chronologically tucked
in between the two groups, we find three authors of geographical poetry
from the first century BCE: Dionysius of Athens, Pausanias of Damascus
and Alexander of Ephesus; the use of iambic trimeter by the first two
suggests, at the very least, a different kind of poetic ambition from that of
the authors of didactic epic.[64] In the iambic poetry of Nechepso and
Petosiris' manual of astrology – late second century BCE – we see the
emergence of a new service industry; see pages 464–5 below. Just later
than the second group there was a boomlet of more ambitious poetry on
the specialized genres near the end of the second century CE: so the two
Oppians, as well as Nestor of Laranda[65] (though this boomlet does not
signify a relative rise in the frequency of expository poetry: there was

[62] Archelaus and Zenothemis wrote on marvels; not in EANS is Nicander the Elder, who I suppose to
have been the author of various geographical-mythical works, rather like the *Aetia*, and not
distinguished by EANS' entry from the younger Nicander; see Jacoby 271–2; and Rhianus,
Demosthenes of Bithynia and Musaeus of Ephesus, with strictly "historical" poems (an hybridization, as I see it: the most typical genre of prose, history, turned into verse); and also Phanocles, with
an *Aetia*-like collection of homoerotic lore.
[63] Other diverse poets are as follows. Apollodorus, noted above, is cited as a "calculator" (was he a
mathematician, then?) and for an epigram on Pythagoras. Nicias, Theocritus' friend, wrote
epigrams that brought in his medical erudition. Menecrates of Ephesus may have preceded
Aratus, and his "works" may have still been more directly in the Hesiodic mold; others have written
on diverse biological subjects, perhaps with a touch of the "marvel": Nicander is the clearest
example, but we may also mention Dionysius of Philadelphia, Caecilius, Pancrates of Alexandria,
Pancrates of Argos and the author of P.Oxy. 1796; perhaps we should also mention Posidippus,
though his engagement with, say, "Stones", is at a great remove from any meteorological science.
[64] Two later geographical authors use poetic form: Ps.-Apollodorus and Dionysius of Alexandria.
[65] The remaining authors are various exceptions to the classification above: Noumenius, perhaps
genuinely a medical author of the Hellenistic era; the author of the *Ars Eudoxi*, perhaps genuinely an
astronomer? Maximus, as well as the author of the *Praecepta Salubria*, were late ancient authors; the
dates of Ammon (the astrological poet) and of Posidonius of Corinth are hard to establish.

simply more writing then, in general, and more of it remaining extant; see pages 704–5 below). What is evident is that the writing of poetry on the subject areas of the specialized genres explodes in the third century BCE, without having any genuine antecedents in the previous century and a half (the very rise of prose, as we noted on pages 233–4 above, coinciding with the rise of the specialized genres). And this, of course, is not just a quantitative observation: among the works of poetry, engaging with the subject area of the specialized genres, are Callimachus' *Aetia* as well as Aratus' *Phaenomena*. With such works, we seem to get near the essence of Alexandrian civilization.

### 4.1.3  Alexandria: A Formula

Are we getting near the essence? Let us look for the formula; and I start by noting: we do not find in Alexandrian culture just the hybridization of genres, as such. Much more specific, we find the mutual infusion of literary modes of *varying degrees of performativity*, hence varying degrees of canonicity.

I review our examples, somewhat changing the order.

Mathematics, the least performative of all genres, engaged directly with poetry.

Medicine, closer to the performative, turned not so much to poetry but, rather, to a somewhat meta-literary or "grammarian" emphasis. There is Herophilus turning to music (the key component of the performative genres), and in general an interest in metaphor and verbal invention, in the early generation of Alexandrian medicine; Herophilus' heirs imitated grammarians directly and so treated Hippocrates as if he were Homer.

The complex of history/geography can be seen as both performative and specialized. Appropriately, it was infused twice, in both directions: through the marvelous, utopian and the "belletristic" (so, a case of a "specialized", factual science – made more literary); and through the emphasis on mathematical geography (so, a case of literature – made more scientific).

Poetry itself gave rise to two new, aligned developments: the invention of grammar as a kind of meta-poetry; and a new kind of poetry, which often took the specialized genres as its subject matter.

We can spell out precisely how grammar, and technical poetry, are analogous – and why it is exactly these that the Hellenistic era creates. Each transforms, in one of the two possible directions, the specialized (or the performative) via the performative (or the specialized), as follows.

Grammar = specialized genre (performative genre)
>    (that is, the literature of the performative genres,
>    brought under the scrutiny of the specialized genres)

Technical poetry = performative genre (specialized genre)
>    (that is, the literature of the specialized genres, brought
>    into the form of the performative genres)

This, then, is certainly *one* principle of Alexandrian civilization: the specialized and performative, infused into each other.

We may bring this together with the more specific analogy noted above:

Geography:marvels::mechanics:wonder devices

And, in general, what we find are the various combinations of the two themes of the comprehensive survey – with the idiosyncratic, often by the same author, even within the same work. The principle, once again, is finally very simple: the comprehensive and the idiosyncratic, together.

The analogy is direct:

> the performative genres    are infused    into the specialized genres

much as

> the idiosyncratic        is infused     into the comprehensive

Because, after all, the sense of the idiosyncratic comes out of a detail (marvel, or myth – that is, an element with poetic resonance) that is made to fit within a systematic survey that, at this historical stage, is suggestive of a prose, specialized work.

The many details seem to fit in some overall structure, and we need, now, to put them in space. The following, I find, is the most instructive. The following two maps put poetry, and history, side by side. The first, Map 24, presents 46 localizable non-dramatic poets of the third century;[66]

---

[66] Map 24 was produced through a word search on the BNP (made by Amy Carlow), with terms such as "verse", "poetry", "lyric", "epic", "comedy", "tragedy", etc., giving rise to a dataset of about 1,000 ancient authors, from which one may cull various subsets; for the purpose of the map above I have also checked the dataset against OCD as well as Cuypers' Hellenistic Bibliography, and was able to add in this way a handful of poets. The list is not exhaustive but has all but the truly obscure names (and so perhaps nearly all the datable and localizable authors). Adding in more minor authors from the Supplementum Hellenisticum would tend to bring in authors for whom we often assume an Alexandrian connection. This map, then, is perhaps slightly biased against Alexandria.

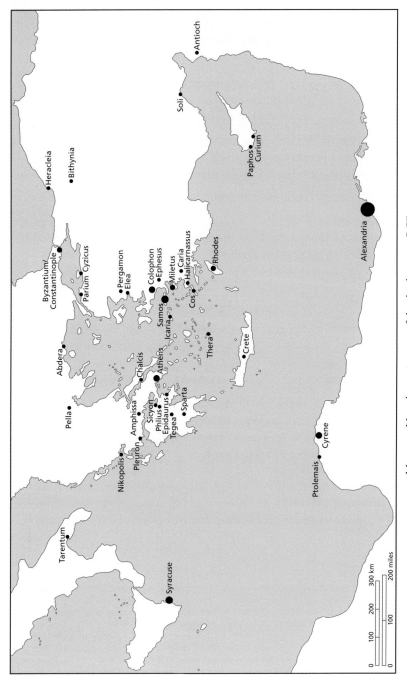

Map 24  Non-dramatic poets of the third century BCE

the other, Map 25, presents 45 localizable third-century historians who are already on the New Jacoby.[67]

Map 24 is Alexandria-centric – though what is evident to us, at this stage, is the weaker attachment of poetry to Alexandria compared to that of the sciences (let alone of philosophy to Athens). There is no "poetic school" established in Alexandria, and note in particular that some of the significant authors associated with Alexandria had a very strong attachment to other locations: so Theocritus (counted here as partly "Alexandrian" because of his encomia and several of his locales, but surely above all Syracusan), but also Posidippus; while both Aratus and Euphorion had their royal patronage away from Alexandria.

Still, the clear center of gravity, in poetry, was in Alexandria. History is different. Map 25 is our only third-century map to show something like a duopoly of Athens and Alexandria, though the main feature is not the dominance of any particular city but, rather, the *lack* of any such dominance. History, in the third century, was fiercely local. This is a sample, based on the New Jacoby; even an expansion into the full Jacoby would increase substantially the places – from 35 to perhaps 50 to 60 cities? And these are just the attested historians! The impression is that, in the third century, at least 100 cities, perhaps considerably more, had their own historian.[68] The authors surveyed here mostly collected local anecdotes of myth and ritual, producing their comprehensive surveys – of a particular location. The few authors we note here of a more narrative, political history, perhaps of a more rhetorical character, include Demochares and Timaeus, both writing early in the century, in or about Athens (hence the hint of a duopoly). This is the last gasp – for the time being – of a performative tradition of historiography, written, nostalgically, by Demosthenes' nephew, Demochares – and also, anachronistically, by a western Greek, writing on the west (the west is late, even at this late stage: compare my observations on western philosophy, on pages 310–11 above). Otherwise, history tends to be non-performative, and truly local.

---

[67] I have produced this set for Map 25 by searching "third century BC" in Jacoby Online, and then culling the information on all the individual historians (preserving only those I consider, albeit largely following the Jacoby entry of course, to have been active in the third century and to have been genuine authors). I count 51 individuals, of whom 45 have at least a likely localization (a high ratio, for a good reason: these are mostly *local* historians). In the following discussion, as I mention individual historians, readers should refer to the New Jacoby for references.

[68] Ober (2015: 32) counts 173 bigger cities of size 4 to 7. Size 4 is estimated by him to average 17,000 population; size 3 is estimated to average 7,000 population. The implication is that most cities of 10,000 population or more would have had, in the third century, a local historian. I return to discuss the enormous spread of ancient historiography in Chapter 5, pp. 598–604.

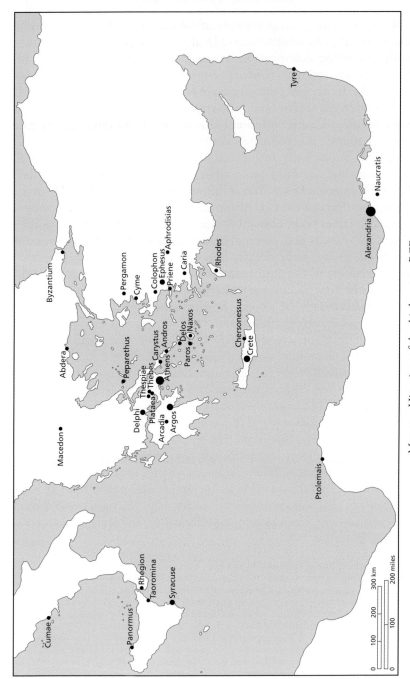

Map 25    Historians of the third century BCE

We may compare the explosion of local historiography in the third century to the previous explosion of local *philosophy*, in the fourth century. In the preceding century local identities were formed by a discursive practice of public debate. In the third century local identities were formed by a written practice of the collection of local, archaic lore. Fourth-century local identity was *in* the city; third-century local identity was *about* the city. Fourth-century local identity was imitation of Athens; third-century local identity was imitation of Alexandria.

Because, you see: the *wide-ranging survey of local information* seems to have been an Alexandrian specialty. Agias and Derkyllus wrote on their Argos; Demeas on Archilochus of his native Thasos – making Demeas a harbinger of things to come, the *patriot-grammarian*; Eparchides wrote on his island – most likely, Icaria (but what could he find to write about this island? Or was this the point?). Calixeinus did write on Alexandria itself, but most Alexandrian authors avoided, in fact, this rich subject. In the third century the thing was to write about local, archaic traditions.

To our two opposites infused, then, we may add a third one, characteristic of Alexandrian civilization. The formula is now extended:

the performative genres     are infused     into the specialized genres

much as

the idiosyncratic          is infused     into the comprehensive

and as

the local                  is set         within the Panhellenic

Through this section, I have surveyed many vignettes of literary practice, summing them up into neat structuralist oppositions. The abstraction is misleading. People do not navigate the world by binary vectors; they see opportunities, they make choices. Around the year 280 Callimachus saw an opportunity: to create works of great, Panhellenic ambition. It was not so obvious, at the time. After all, he was active away from Athens, primarily identified as an author in the specialized field of grammar. And, even so, what could he write? Definitely not tragedy, of course not speeches. For comedy, one would have to move to Athens – right? History in the grand Herodotean or Thucydidean manner was forgone (what would one write it on? The Ptolemies?). Socratic dialogues? Well, if anyone could write them, it would have to be the philosophers in Athens (but, then again, even they had stopped doing so). So, no: somehow, one would have to revive the very old forms. Because any of the new forms of performance were associated with Athens.

But – the point is – this suddenly seemed possible, because there was no clear reason not to. It was not as if a nod to the epic tradition would appear out of place, in a literary scene dominated by new forms. The literary scene was no longer dominated by the new forms: they could no longer be made. On the other hand, Alexandria had a big enough audience, on its own: even if away from Athens, Callimachus could strike out, on his own.

But what would the theme be? To be Panhellenic, it could not be about Alexandria, even less about any particular place or tradition. It would have to take them all, surveying them. But carefully: the most likely outcome of an effort to survey past literature would be a work strictly in the specialized genres, not "past literature" but "present grammar". Callimachus, the master grammarian, had to guard against this, especially in this more ambitious, literary work. He, more than others, would have been aware that the Telchines might accuse him of not being enough of a poet, not truly conforming to the models he elevated but merely gesturing at them. So, what should one do? How to recap past literature, without becoming meta-literary? How to reflect on past Hellenism so as to become Hellenic and not meta-Hellenic?

What was required was a meta-literature which was at the same time simply literary, a meta-Hellenic approach which was at the same time simply Hellenic. And what could sustain such a project was precisely the duality – inherited from the Greek literary system itself – of the performative as against the specialized. Meta-literary but literary? Meta-Hellenic but Hellenic? What was required, then, was a specialized genre, infused by the performative; a comprehensive survey, infused by the idiosyncratic. Which is how we may account for the making of Callimachus' *Aetia*, the work that, above all else, defines its generation.

In the previous chapter, we noted the rise of Alexandria as a kind of centrality-by-default, simply due to the manner in which (non-epichoric, specialized) genres would tend to agglomerate. What we now note is that, even as the performative canon became closed, performativity remained, and remained as the most resonant force in the Greek literary field. The center by default of Alexandria was a center for non-epichoric, specialized genres; and it became truly effective – not a mere concentration, but a genuine driver of culture – as it found how to suffuse the two together, the specialized and the performative.

The plurality of many genres, many places, all interconnected in a kind of loose mosaic, was thus essential to the Alexandrian literary paradigm. Little wonder that Alexandria did not produce a single monolithic ideology. But all this is just one half of the story. One pole, away from Athens, recreated a culture based on the principle of variety. The other pole, Athens, had a literary practice based on distinct principles. The burden of the argument of the following sections is this: to identify the principles of Athenian literary practice; and then, from the combination of the two, those of Athens and those of Alexandria, to account, finally, for the interaction – or lack thereof – between the two.

## 4.2   Athens: "Beneath Literature"?

### 4.2.1   A Contrast: Outside Athens

The literary practice of Hellenistic philosophy in Athens is best seen through a contrast: with that of Hellenistic philosophy, *elsewhere*. The following is a list of (1) those third-century philosophers, (2) likely active mostly *not* in Athens, (3) whose character as authors can be discerned through the surviving evidence. This is not a long list; of almost 150 philosophers attested for the third century, the great majority are very obscure, Athenian or both. The rest form a diverse, and yet meaningful group. We may further classify them as follows. First, we note several very early third-century philosophers (most reaching their acme, it seems, towards the end of the fourth century), who perhaps were engaged primarily in disputatious display, some of them avoiding writing altogether:

> Diodorus Cronus[69]
> Philo ("Megarian")[70]
> Alexinus of Elis[71]
> Menedemus of Eretria[72]

---

[69] We met Diodorus Cronus in *Alexandria*, on p. 297, n.87, and p. 362 above – a lively proponent of sharply marked paradoxes and, in all likelihood, not a written author. Originally from Iasus, he did certainly pass through Athens; that he had some connection to Megara, too, is more doubtful (Sedley, 1977).

[70] We do not have any genuine references to Philo's biography other than the constant attachment of his name to that of Diodorus Cronus. Unlike his teacher, he did write, and, among his few attested works, one stands out: a dialogue with Diodorus' five *daughters* for protagonists – their good education was a well-known scandal in antiquity (Goulet, 2012a: 438–9).

[71] The most sustained study is Schofield (1983), focusing on his debate against Zeno. The impression is of an author who (34) "simply relished dialectical debate for itself"; a Diodorus-Cronus-type author but one who did collect some of his disputations in writing.

[72] Perhaps originally of the philosophical school in Elis (denied by Kyrkos, 1980 [a study in modern Greek: my understanding of its contents is based on references by other scholars], but reaffirmed by Knoepfler, 1991: 173), and certainly active through most of his life in his native Eretria, where he was an eminent citizen whose political career involved several embassies and stays in various courts. Listed by Diogenes Laertius as a philosopher who avoided writing, and not so much the author of significant doctrinal developments: rather, it appears, an elegant disputer.

Pyrrho of Elis[73]
Hegesias of Cyrene[74]
Stilpo of Megara[75]

In the case of Stilpo, we find a figure who is remembered as much for his logical fireworks as for his moral standing; Hegesias is remembered for his paradoxical ethics. This brings us to a small group of somewhat later authors, who address not so much logical as moral concerns (most often, with a "Cynic" tendency), and engage in more elaborate, and distinctly original, written forms:

Bion of Borysthenes[76]
Menippus of Gadara[77]
Timon of Phlius[78]

---

[73] Another philosopher who avoided writing and was remembered as attached to his native Elis, with the major exception of his participation in the Alexander expedition; famous, of course, for his powerful denial of all assent.

[74] A Cyrenaic, Hegesias was probably active in Alexandria, where he was banned by a certain Ptolemy – for his all too successful advocacy (in dialogue form) of suicide (Goulet, 2000: 528–9).

[75] It is somewhat less clear in Stilpo's case that his activity really extended significantly into the third century. At any rate, it does seem clear that he was indeed attached primarily to Megara; besides engaging in dialectical debates he was also reputed as the author of philosophical dialogues (DL II.120), though one should not neglect Diogenes Laertius' opposite claim (I.15) that Stilpo was among the philosophers who wrote nothing.

[76] Somewhat younger than the authors above, in that he probably died between 246 and 239 (Kindstrand, 1976: 5–6). He certainly spent time in Athens as a young man, but his career through the third century was that of an itinerant and court philosopher (Kindstrand, 1976: 12, 14–16). He may not have written himself, his "lectures" being written down instead, but these "lecture notes" did not belong to the classroom; rather, the fragments suggest an author engaged in a highly marked rhetorical display (34–49).

[77] The city of origin is the only distinctive element in a biography which otherwise appears as a pastiche of the generic Cynic biography; an author such as Menippus may not have expected his biographers to take their task seriously. One has to express the worry that even the claim that he was of Gadara is based on a single witness, Strabo XVI 2.29; a sober source, for sure, but the precise mention is of "Meleager and Menippus the serio-comic author". Meleager was Menippus' follower, in some sense, and certainly was from Gadara: could Menippus' attachment to Gadara, too, be yet another, very late element in the pastiche of his biography – in the manner in which Diogenes Laertius misunderstood one of his references, and considered Meleager and Menippus to be contemporaries (Goulet, 2005: 385, 387)? It remains likely that this was an author of the third century (old enough to have been a byword, by Meleager's youth: AP VII. 417.4, 418.5–6), and that he was not associated with any other major city: perhaps an itinerant poet, perhaps indeed of Gadara. Both Meleager and Varro thought of their works as "Menippean" (in modern times the term came to mean an entire genre, with famous Bakhtinian implications; see Relihan, 1984). Menippus' stylistic innovations are secure even though not much more remains of his work than of his life: he combined prose (of various kinds) with poetry, the serious with the comic.

[78] The reconstruction in Clayman (2009: 20–1) is of an itinerant author, familiar with monarchs, who spends his last years (in the middle of the third century) in Athens. It is thus less clear that this was a *non*-Athenian author, though the report of the years spent in Elis and the Hellespont is suggestive (Diogenes Laertius IX.109–10: the connection to Pyrrho in Elis appears real enough, and there is no obvious reason for a story about teaching in the Hellespont to develop as biographical fiction).

Teles (of Megara?)[79]
Cercidas of Megalopolis[80]

Finally, two authors who were not primarily philosophers:

Euphantus of Olynthus[81]
Eratosthenes of Cyrene[82]

The two above cannot easily be classified according to "school", hence our willingness to think of them primarily as non-philosophers. I would argue the same, however, for three authors who were in various degrees of likelihood "peripatetic" and yet not primarily "philosophers":

Much more remains of his works than of those of Menippus, and it is well understood that he saw himself as a follower of Pyrrho and that, while he did not mix prose and verse in the Menippean manner, he did write both prose and verse, both very accomplished; also, we notice the same combination of the serious and the comic, in this case specifically the parodic. *The Sylloi*, in fact, is entirely Alexandrian in character, a witty comprehensive survey of past and present philosophy, in a manner that maximally marks the various entries.

[79] Once again, the biography of this Cynic (?) author is extremely vague; the few references in his work suggest he was active in Megara in mid-century. His stylistic originality, or lack thereof, is much debated, for which see Fuentes-Gonzalez (1998); Fuentes-Gonzalez comes down to emphasize his originality. Undoubted are the "rhetorical" aspects, perhaps of a more demotic character (of a "sermon"?).

[80] Cercidas' attachment to Megalopolis – of which he became a lawgiver – is undoubted; through his political activity we may date him to the second half of the third century (we do note, however, once again, a close relationship to the courts: a necessity of course, at this point, for any political actor). He was also a poet, in a variety of iambic genres, their moralizing character (and specific attacks on Zeno) suggestive of a "philosophical" identity, perhaps specifically Cynic, perhaps less determinate (Goulet, 1994: 276–9). Williams, 2006: 352–4, argues convincingly that Cercidas, at the very least, adopted for himself the metaphor of a "dog".).

[81] The biographical essay in the New Jacoby is the most extensive treatment of this enigmatic, and yet distinct figure: born in Olynthus – i.e. before 348 (or perhaps not long afterwards, when his family could still be recognized as "Olynthian"?); a tutor to an Antigonus; the author of histories on contemporary and political, perhaps also ethnographic and religious, themes; finally, a successful tragic author too. The only attested work likely to have been of a philosophical character was an "On Kingship" addressed to Antigonus, his pupil, wildly popular according to Diogenes Laertius (II.110): a sermon, then, and hardly a disputatious Megarian display piece.

[82] He was undoubtedly born in Cyrene and died in Alexandria; that he passed through Athens and for a considerable time, is well attested, but, certainly, his enormous productivity is associated with Alexandria, where he was probably royal tutor and definitely royal librarian. He may well be considered the leading figure in the culture of the second half of the third century. We know the extreme range of his overall writings, in genre and in content; we know that he made much fewer contributions to philosophy, a few of which are likely in the form of rhetorical exercises, others in dialogue form (Goulet, 2000: 207–8). One of these – a dialogue, perhaps the *Platonic?* – is somewhat better known. The impression is of a literary polished work which, at the same time, emphasizes fairly advanced mathematics as relevant for the understanding of Plato (see Vitrac, 2006: was there an entire mini-treatise on proportion theory inserted into this dialogue?). It is striking, indeed, to find this reading of Plato – suggestive of the Imperial era, with its more Pythagorean Platonism (from which, admittedly, our sources derive) produced in the era of Arcesilaus' Academy.

Praxiphanes of Lesbos[83]
Chamaeleon of Heraclea[84]
Clearchus of Soli[85]

To sum up: an interesting group of individuals for sure, with the following characteristics.

*Geography*

A significant subset of the authors – those, in a word, who are obviously "philosophers" – are constrained within a small range: mainland Greece, not far from Athens. Stilpo, Pyrrho, Menedemus and Cercidas are deeply committed to their native Megara, Elis, Eretria and Megalopolis, respectively; Diodorus Cronus, Alexinus, Timon and Teles all had varying, and varyingly attested, relations to Megara, Elis and Phlius. Bion ranged far and wide (as did Timon), and Menippus can hardly be placed; yet Bion died in Chalcis and Menippus reportedly died in Thebes (in novelistic circumstances, for sure, so perhaps the detail is misappropriated from his writings; Timon, too, is reported to have spent time in Thebes). So, the band is mapped in Map 26.

Elis and Megalopolis are more distant but Megara, in particular, is literally within walking distance of Athens, which surely is related to the surprising tenacity of its philosophical engagement. In the third century it simply did not make sense to be a philosopher far from Athens: Euphantus

[83] Sometimes referred to as "peripatetic" and occasionally mentioned as "pupil" (or, once, "friend") of Theophrastus, he is most often described by later authors simply as "grammarian". While a work "On Friendship" is securely attested, the bulk of his work was in literary criticism. Born in Mytilene (was he then, truly, Theophrastus' younger friend?), he was then active mostly in Rhodes; he was honored in Delos between 270 and 260 BC. His writings included at least a couple of dialogues featuring authors of the literary canon (Plato and Isocrates; Thucydides and several poets): a grammarian's version of the Socratic dialogue.
[84] Chaemaeleon changes his colors: sometimes a philosopher, perhaps writing in dialogue form; mostly author of biographies of literary authors of a grammarian and novelistic bent (so, even the single reference to him as peripatetic – Tatian, *Ad Gr.* 31.2.8 – is about *Homer*). Any visit to Athens is purely conjectural, and the author is shown consistently as Heraclean, representing his native city in an embassy to Seleucus Nicanor, just after 281 BC (Photius cod. 224). Praxiphanes and Chamaeleon together now have a Theophrastus volume dedicated to them – Martano, Matelli and Mirhady (2012) – the industriousness of modern scholars of the Peripatos tending to claim, for the school, even such marginally attached figures, who should better be seen, I suggest, as free agents in the Alexandrian Mediterranean.
[85] Unlike Praxiphanes and Chamaeleon, our sources insist on referring to Clearchus as a peripatetic and a pupil of Aristotle; perhaps this has to do with the appearance of Aristotle as a character in one of his dialogues. He was primarily an author of dialogues, with a strong historical emphasis tending on the marvelous – and an attachment to a mathematical Platonizing that seems strangely out of place for a peripatetic. His geographical range is famous: he certainly was in Ai Khanoum at the beginning of the third century. If indeed "Arcesilaus" was the title of one of his dialogues, he lived through not a few decades of that century, making it more difficult to see him as a pupil of Aristotle.

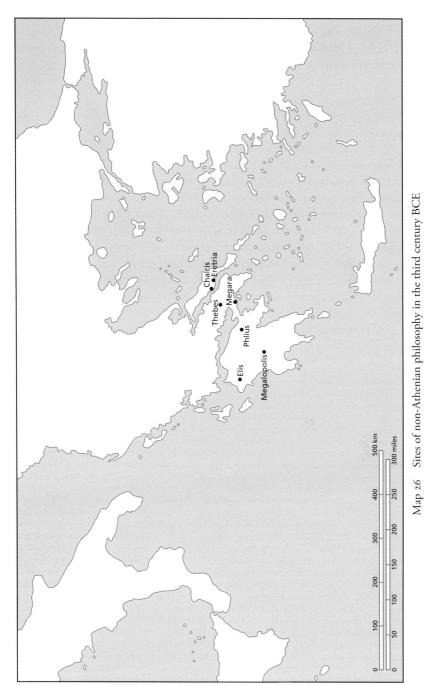

Map 26   Sites of non-Athenian philosophy in the third century BCE

and Eratosthenes, Praxiphanes and Chamaeleon, all perhaps philosophically trained, did not have the same attachment to central Greece and engaged in philosophy only marginally.

## Doctrine

I would argue that none of those authors should be classified within the four major Athenian schools, though this of course would be controversial for the three authors conventionally considered peripatetic. Indeed, Cynics and Skeptics – who make up the bulk of this group – made it their goal to criticize all established opinion; Alexinus was remembered for his criticism of Zeno. Those represented as having studied in Athens at all are reported to have studied across the schools, refusing an attachment to any school in particular.[86] Now, it is not as if the adherents of the four major schools all necessarily had to spend the bulk of their lives in Athens,[87] and yet we find no solid evidence, before the end of the third century itself, for either (1) a philosopher coming to uphold the doctrines of one of the four schools, without having studied such doctrines in Athens, or (2) a philosopher formed by one of the four schools – and then establishing a subsidiary campus, as it were, in another city (commonplace, as we will notice below, in the first century BCE).[88] Inside Athens, one developed the schools'

---

[86] Bion: Kindstrand (1976: 10–11); Eratosthenes: Goulet (2000: 194–7).

[87] So, for instance, how much of his life did Hieronymus of Rhodes spend in his native city – where he was sumptuously buried? (See White, 2004, for a collection of the sources, and Matelli, 2004, specifically for a discussion of his relation to the two cities; his funerary stone from Rhodes, the key evidence, is reproduced in Fortenbaugh and White, 2004: 476–80.) Demetrius of Phaleron as well as Strato had their Alexandrian sojourns but their identity was strictly Athenian. Ecedelus and Demophanes, both pupils of Arcesilaus, became professional revolutionaries in the middle of the third century (involved in coups against tyrants in Sicyon, Megalopolis and Cyrene, in the last city supporting Demetrius, likely a fellow-student of Arcesilaus: Walbank, 1967: 223–4): but was their identity that of Academic philosophers?

[88] The earliest counter-examples are: (1) Artemon and Philonides: a couple of passages in PHerc. 1044, *Life of Philonides* (frr. 7, 33), can be reconstructed as follows: following his early training as a mathematician (in Pergamon and in Caunus), Philonides drifted and fell, in some place away from Athens, under the influence of a certain Artemon, an Epicurean teacher (indeed, author of a commentary To "On Nature", so he displays a genuine school attitude towards a school founder); Philonides then breached etiquette, somehow, by beginning to teach Epicureanism himself. Philonides would be an elder statesman in Seleucid politics in 175–50, so this episode takes place in the late third century; the category of a "teacher" is precarious, in this episode, so perhaps nothing like a "school": Glucker (1978: 131–2) sees here freelance teachers; (2) Epicrates of Heraclea, honored in Samos at around 200 BCE (epigraphic evidence: IG XII.6.1 128) as a "peripatetic". The most substantial discussion is Scholz (2004: 331–6), but I have to differ. The decree implies a lengthy stay, and its conclusion – not discussed by Scholz – endows upon him city rights. Quite possibly, then, we see here a citizen of Heraclea who re-established himself later in life as a member of Samos' civic life – contra Scholz (2004: 335) saying that "it must have been at least several months, if not a full year or more". This is important, since Scholz's general point is that third-century philosophers often became wandering scholars, for which the only examples are Epicrates himself, Aristippus of Cyrene

project. Outside Athens, one drifted away from philosophy altogether – or spent a life criticizing Athens.

## Style

Most of these authors aimed for stylistic distinction, often through original, marked departures: the performance of dialectical prowess by the first authors in my list who *eschewed* writing; the various combinations of rhetoric, prose and verse, from Bion and Teles, through Cercidas and Timon, all the way to the truly outré innovations of Menippus; the wide generic reach of Euphantus and Eratosthenes – so that Eratosthenes' major contribution to philosophy, the *Platonicus*, could well have taken the form of a *literary dialogue* infused with *technical, mathematical* discussion. Such a combination came into its own many centuries later, with Galileo. In the third century it carried a specific, Alexandrian meaning: the performative, infused by the specialized genre. All three – Eratosthenes, Praxiphanes and Chamaeleon – were grammarians who were also, possibly, the authors of philosophical dialogues (the last may be true of Stilpo, as well, and is certainly the case for Clearchus). If Stilpo's dialogues were "cold" (Diogenes Laertius II.120),[89] Clearchus' were flamboyant. Hegesias' attested dialogue could have been serious in intention, however macabre its claim and its consequences (see note 74 above); surely, Philo's dialogue must have been intended as a piquant showpiece, figuring as it did five women who mastered Megarian dialectics.[90]

### 4.2.2 *A Contrast: Before Athens*

Or have we pre-judged the question of style? We have, after all, looked for those philosophers whose character as authors can be recognized from the extant evidence. Would this not create a bias, then, for those philosophers whose form of authorship was especially *marked*? Is this why we have come up with so many Cynic authors? What if we were looking simply for the

---

(who was a fourth-century figure!) and Bion of Borysthenes ("to the best of my knowledge, these are the only cases in the literary tradition that deal with the phenomenon of wandering philosophers in Hellenistic times": Scholz, 2004: 330). Of course, wandering scholars were a major phenomenon of third-century cultural life, but, in philosophy, the wanderers would be foreign to the four Athenian schools. (For wandering as a specifically cynic occupation, see Montiglio, 2005: chap. 8.)

[89] But he must have been an effective disputationist; Chrysippus asserts that he gained, in his lifetime, a huge fame for his wisdom, *alongside Menedemus* (Plutarch, *De Stoic. Repug.* 1036F) – both, so Chrysippus, now considered stale.

[90] See n.70 above. That women, philosophizing, should have been shocking to them is shocking to us; but it was.

style of philosophy, as such, in the third century BCE: would we still find any meaningful geographical distinctions? The problem, of course, is that so much of the style of philosophical authors from within Athens has to be inferred. And so, for this purpose, too, we require a contrast, now not in space but in time. To see in better relief the style of third-century philosophers from Athens, we should first of all compare it with the style of *fourth-century* philosophers.

Variety should be emphasized, once again: there were many centers, and it would be rash to generalize. But so much is clear: the most canonical figure, for such fourth-century philosophical authors, was surely Socrates. Socrates died, as we have noted on pages 233–4 above, at exactly the moment when prose was established as a means with which to carry the vividness of performance. While Socratic dialectics never disappear (and reappear occasionally, as we just noted, even in the third century), Socratic philosophers are marked by a typical fifth-to-fourth-century transition, from performance to prose: from the dialectical tournaments alone to the written, imagined Socratic dialogue. In the generation of Socrates' acquaintances, Hirzel (1895: 99–271) went through the following authors of dialogue:

> Alexamenus,[91] Simon, Glaucon, Simmias, Cebes, Crito, Aristippus, Euclid, Phaedo, Antisthenes, Aeschines, Xenophon, Plato.

Of those 13 apostles, some may be the mere illusion caused by later forgeries (what is more natural, than to foster pseudepigraphic dialogues on the figures known through Plato's own dialogues?),[92] but most are genuine. Nearly certain are Aristippus, Euclid, Phaedo, Antisthenes, Aeschines, Xenophon, Plato: seven authors who, together, form the backbone of philosophy in the first half of the fourth century. The only important philosophical contemporary of Plato who certainly did *not* write dialogues was Archytas (so: yet another case of a western holdout in matters of style; cf. pages 310–11). By the middle of the century the dialogue form had come to be associated especially with the figure of Plato (a canonical author and –

---

[91] Since Diogenes Laertius (III.48) contrasts the claim that Alexamenus was the inventor of dialogue with the alternative that the inventor was Zeno of Elea, one might consider him an author of dialogues of a non-Socratic character; but the other testimony to Alexamenus, Athenaeus XI 505C, explicitly refers to his writing "the first Socratic dialogues": a small detail but relevant to the large point, that the very notion of the dialogue form was to make a particular form of Athenian performance – Socratic debate – come alive on the written papyrus.

[92] For example, the extant *Pinax* – attributed to Cebes by Diogenes Laertius (III.62) – is surely apocryphal, perhaps Neo-Pythagorean; the same is probably true for the two other non-extant dialogues that Diogenes also attributes to him ("Seventh Day" – Neo-Pythagorean from the title already; "Phrynichus"): Goulet, 1994: 248–51. (More on Simon, on pp. 592–3 below.)

unlike Xenophon – the author of dialogues *only*). The writing of dialogues now seemed to be associated primarily with those philosophers brushing against Plato's influence, such as his immediate follower Philippus – likely enough the author of the *Epinomis*;[93] we may also add Aristotle, Speusippus[94] and Heraclides Ponticus,[95] all known, in their own lifetime, perhaps primarily as the authors of dialogues. Perhaps, at this point, the dialogue form was already like-Plato, rather than like-Socrates, and so, further away from Plato, it appears that already Euboulides, while probably a written author as well, distinguished himself primarily in oral disputation, by recreating the sense of performance of the original Socratic impetus.[96] Bryson – perhaps active a little earlier, and also apparently a flamboyant disputer – was counted by Diogenes Laertius among the philosophers who did not write books (I.16). We see already outlined one of the models of third-century philosophy outside Athens. Another model, out-Socrating Socrates himself, was that of Diogenes of Sinope – revivifying the figure of the performative philosopher through a performance of maximal estrangement and, I would say likely, through no writing – as the writings ascribed to him could very naturally arise pseudepigraphically.[97] In the following generation Crates was (perhaps) an author in verse,[98] and, if so, distinguished himself sharply from contemporary philosophers. This combination of life as performance art and as stylistic experiment would remain essential to the future of Cynicism; unlike Crates, however, future Cynics would be active primarily away from Athens.

Philosophy as performance and, specifically, the charisma of Socrates were maintained through three-quarters of a century in vivid practices of speech and act. Of course, what was at stake was not some kind of academic pursuit but, instead, the examined life – a maximal intensification of one's engagement with one's life and one's words, enacted through elegant, detailed elaborations of speech, debating life's burning questions, or enacted through extreme public acts. Through those years – between the two deaths, of Socrates and of Aristotle – art, verbal and performative, kept charisma suspended, awaiting its coming into routine.

---

[93] Tarán (1975: chap. 1).
[94] The evidence depends on Diogenes Laertius, and so is weak; see discussion in Tarán (1981: 198–201).
[95] Gottschalk (1980: 6–11): a clearer case, as we have evidence for the literary embellishment of the dialogues.
[96] Muller (DPA, s.v. Euboulides, 246); see n.34 above.
[97] Goulet-Cazé (DPA s.v.) is optimistic considering the authenticity of his writings but concedes that they were doubted already in Hellenistic times. If genuine, his writing would certainly be very marked stylistically.
[98] See Noussia (2006) for the tragedy associated with the early Cynics.

### 4.2.3   The Routinization of Socrates

This, indeed, is what we gain by our account above – pages 322–30, bringing to their logical conclusion the studies of Glucker, Lynch and Dillon – according to which the rise of philosophical schools was a routinization of charisma, begun not before the second half of the fourth century and completed only as the third century began.[99] We have emphasized that what was routinized, above all, was performance as such. Until the late fourth century this could still be preserved in written form: Athens, as a literary-performative site, was still active. With this understood, we then find a direct correlation between school routinization and the erosion of the form of dialogue. Two complementary modes of preserving past charisma: through the vividness of the charismatic philosophical figure, presented through the written dialogue; or, later on, through the formation of school practices, which replace the need for such charisma.

We can envisage art and routine side by side in Aristotle himself: on the one side, the elegant prose of the dialogues;[100] on the other, the quasi-administrative business of case-by-case contemplation.[101] Aristotle's so-called esoteric works were surely not meant to be hidden,[102] but they were internal *working documents* – their antecedents, if any, being such internal technical documents as the Hippocratic *Epidemics*. Presumably, many in-members of the group had access, and could make copies, and eventually such works were collected; but the question of what to collect, and how to categorize such a collection, perplexed ancient readers – as it does the modern scholars who wade through the confusing evidence.[103] There would be few antecedents – but more than a parallel: for if, in Aristotle, working school documents exist alongside the normal dialogues of a

---

[99] Notice that this is the opposite of the old picture, as if the schools begin with Plato, and at 387 at that; under such a picture, the heyday of the writing of dialogues coincides with the beginning of the project of the Athenian philosophical school, and thus the writing of dialogues comes to be seen (absurdly) as the hallmark of a school!

[100] "A river of flowing gold" (Cicero, *Acad.* 2.119).

[101] The extant Aristotelian school texts are, quite simply, not a river of flowing gold. In Netz (2001) I emphasize their rough, piece-by-piece structure.

[102] "So-called" because Aristotle never refers to the extant corpus as "esoteric", simply referring to, presumably, the published dialogues as "exoteric" (see Boas, 1953: a discussion prompted by the notorious Straussian program – mounted on the basis of a misunderstanding of the notion of the ancient "esoteric" – to ascribe hidden views to past philosophers).

[103] See Lord (1986) for a more recent statement of a problem discussed earlier (but perhaps more convincingly) by Chroust (1962); the key facts are: (1) that there were rival ancient catalogues of Aristotle's school texts; (2) a clearly exaggerated story – but how exaggerated? – told of the loss and rediscovery of the bulk of the corpus in the Hellenistic period; (3) from the first century BCE onwards interest in Aristotle's writing grew and eventually eclipsed that in any ancient philosopher other than Plato; I shall return to discuss this relative fame, below.

Platonizing philosopher, Xenocrates seems to have been a much more thoroughgoing school writer. Diogenes Laertius reports the count of 224,239 lines or roughly 400 papyrus rolls – about ten times the Platonic corpus itself. If we assume that a rather larger proportion stems from the duties of the master following Speusippus' death – say, three-quarters of the corpus produced during Xenocrates' 25 years of tenure? – we must assume that, in those years as scholarch, Xenocrates produced a roll about once a month. This suggests not so much polished prose as a course of studies which the list of titles, a litany of *peri*, tends to confirm: "On Temperance", "On the Power of Law", "On the Republic", "On Holiness" – citing at random (DL IV.12) a sequence of four out of 159 books reported to have been classified (at least, by future librarians) simply as "On" this or that. Above, we have reconstructed the styles of various authors, based sometimes on tiny indications; but even such small references as we have for Teles, say, or for Philo the Dialectician, already suggest a portrait of the author. For Xenocrates, we have an enormous catalogue and no sense of authorial style at all. We remain with a comment by Diogenes Laertius – Plato, encouraging Xenocrates "to sacrifice to the Graces" (DL IV.6), presumably to propitiate them for his sins: clearly a forged chreia. This is the remark of future readers, exasperated by the literary gap between the master and his expositor.[104] It is likely that the few titles that do suggest the content of a dialogue[105] were not literary masterpieces, but at any rate the point is that they comprised only a tiny section of Xenocrates' output – and that none of this mattered to his students, who, after all, chose him. They didn't take him as a stylist. Of course, loss was in part a matter of doctrine: from Arcesilaus onwards, school doctrine was no longer that systematized by Xenocrates. Here was a vast corpus, not exactly "internal" (it survived for future readers to catalogue and count it), that could make sense only as doctrine, not as literature. The doctrine repudiated, the literature was easily cast aside.

The Platonist group of philosophers was the first to give up the dialogue form. Little is known of the following generation of Academics (those who suffered the most from Arcesilaus' takeover), but we do know that Polemo wrote many works (DL IV.20), with one title (perhaps) alone attested (Clemens, *Strom.* VII.6.32, "The Books on Ordering One's Life According to Nature" – doesn't make you run to the bookstore), and that Crantor,

---

[104] As pointed out by Dillon (2003: 97), this remark was understood by ancient readers to refer to the written style, even though in context it mentions Xenocrates' demeanor; indeed, since such anecdotes are late inventions, what could they refer to other than the writing?

[105] "The Arcadian", "Callicles", "Statesman", "Archedemus or on Justice": Dillon (2003: 97 n.29).

finally, was responsible for a new development: the philosophical commentary, on Plato's *Timaeus*.[106] This turning of the Timaeus into an object for commentary is telling. The practice seems to be distinct from that of the medical commentary in Alexandria, which was inspired by grammatical concerns and seems to have involved much care for Hippocratic lexicography (page 363 above). The memory of Crantor's commentary survived for its views concerning Plato's doctrines, and the implication is that Crantor, himself, did not produce a running commentary, attuned to textual matters, but, instead, discussed key questions of doctrine raised by the dialogue.[107] The literary, in such a commentary, is turned into a depository of doctrines. Little wonder the Academics did not engage with that literary form, the dialogue: Plato's dialogues ceased, in a sense, to *be* a literary form for them, because, enshrined as school text, they now became a source from which to establish one's philosophical allegiance. Plato was canonized as a literary author everywhere, in the early third century, *other than* at the Academy at Athens – where his function was not literary but doctrinal.

The Academy would not be revived as a center of elegant *writing*, but it did revert to style, in mid-century: and away from the doctrinal. We recall the near-Athenian group of early third-century authors, typically eschewing writing, stretching from Eretria to Elis; with Arcesilaus they gained, as it were, an Athenian beachhead (or perhaps the other way around: the last few remaining bastions of extra-Athenian philosophical life in the near-Athens band collapsed, in mid-century, into Arcesilaus' Academy). Timon characterized Arcesilaus as a composite of Menedemus, Pyrrho and Diodorus Cronus;[108] Diogenes Laertius related an anecdote that reveals sympathy, perhaps, to Alexinus.[109] From Arcesilaus to Carneades, the Academy would display to the world primarily the spectacle of dialectical wit. The sophisticated arguments of those authors did survive in their subtle detail, however, and this is thanks to other, prolific authors.

---

[106] Proclus, *In Tim.* I. 76.
[107] See, e.g., Niehoff (2007: 167). This of course would always remain largely true of the philosophical commentary: a feature we should see as remarkable, against the background of grammarian commentary.
[108] Diogenes Laertius IV.33; apparently a variation of the same idea was taken up by Ariston of Ceos, the peripatetic (replacing Menedemus by the necessary Plato).
[109] A follower of Alexinus failed to reproduce correctly an Alexinian argument, whereupon Arcesilaus recalled how Philoxenus the musician, on hearing certain bricklayers singing his songs off-key, trampled their wet bricks: "You ruined mine, I'll ruin yours!" The attitude implied, I think, is one of sympathy to Alexinus as a professional colleague. (DL IV.36; Alexinus is obscure enough for one to suppose the anecdote could have had a historical kernel.)

Clitomachus – born Hasdrubaal – "inherited" Carneades by writing more than 400 rolls, once again the Xenocrates–Theophrastus range (so according to DL IV.67. A scholarchic output: Clitomachus would, indeed, eventually succeed Carneades at the scholarchate). Apparently, then, the rolls set out in writing a reflection of Carneades' spoken discourse. Of the two, Carneades was born in 214 and started teaching the 28-year-old Hasdrubaal in the year 159 – so we need to imagine that Carneades' long old age (he died 30 years later, in 129, aged 85) was accompanied by a steady stream of Carneadic literature from the pen of the pupil. Could the same have been true for Arcesilaus himself and, say, someone such as his successor, Lacydes?[110] Arcesilaus and Lacydes, Carneades and Cleitomachus – could these be two pairs dividing between them discourse and writing, charisma and routine? It is typical to the worldview of the later middle Academy that the discourses, not the writings, would be celebrated, hence the relative obscurity in which the later figures languish. And yet, perhaps we should think of Lacydes, certainly of Cleitomachus, as the – paradoxical – systematizers of Skepticism.

Just think about it: 400 rolls – on the impossibility of certainty! Such was the philosophical literature of Hellenistic Athens. "Zeno wrote many books, Xenocrates[111] more, Democritus more, Aristotle more, Epicurus more, Chrysippus more" (DL I.16). This sober assessment covers the two founders of the Stoa and the effective founders (I would argue) of each of the other

---

[110] Pythodorus wrote down Arcesilaus' lecture notes, if this is the correct meaning of the tattered bottom of a Herculaneum column (P.Herc. 1021 XX.43–4: Dorandi, 1991b: 156); I find unlikely the notion that Arcesilaus' philosophy remained primarily in oral form all the way down to Cleitomachus (so suggested, e.g., by Schofield, 1999a: 324 n.5): just what did rank-and-file Academics do? It is, rather, that Cicero, our main source, knew the Academy mostly via Cleitomachus. Nothing of substance is known of Lacydes' writing (he did write, though: *Suda* s.v.); Diogenes tells us (IV.59, the source for most of our knowledge) that he was *philoponos* from youth – in this context, this could mean the writing of many books, but he seems to have been known to future biographers, if at all, through comic anecdotes; so, perhaps, *philoponia* as a mark of poverty (compare Cleanthes: DL VII.168). Still, he is enigmatically said, by Diogenes and by the *Suda* (not independently?), to have initiated (*katarxas*) the New Academy, which, contra Glucker (1978: 235), I find an odd Greek expression, if what is meant is that he got the Academy a new piece of property. True, he does appear, from our meager evidence in Diogenes and Philodemus, mostly as a fundraiser (the substance of Philodemus' account, though, has been lost in column XXI). Glucker finds this statement, if meant in its natural philosophical sense, "astonishing" (234), and, admittedly, we do not think of Lacydes as the founder of a new philosophical tendency. But, if indeed he was the most substantial author setting Arcesilean philosophy in writing, he would certainly appear important to his contemporaries – arguably, the refounder of the new Academy, it having gone through its period of flamboyant, Scythic existence under Arcesilaus (P.Herc. 1021 XXI.39: Dorandi, 1991b: 156; the reference, once again, is to real estate, but the sense of having come down to stability could well resonate in other ways as well).

[111] The manuscript's reading, "Xenophanes", is an obvious error – reminding us, once again, of Xenocrates' future oblivion.

schools, omitting, however, the Peripatos' second founder, Theophrastus. The latter had 232,808 lines counted, according to Diogenes Laertius (V.42– 50), remarkably similar to Xenocrates: the number of the teacher-system-atizer.[112] Once again, a handful of the works might have been dialogues (Hirzel, 1895: 317), but the balance, in Aristotle, between school documents and "exoteric" works has now been lost: the school documents, with Theophrastus, *were* the works. We noted above the authors, brushing against Theophrastus' teaching and then going on to pursue their own literary careers elsewhere and away from philosophy; but the close followers of Aristotle who remained most committed to his philosophical methods stayed also closest to strict theoretical prose. Aristoxenus experimented – in the direction of even more austere, more precise "Elements".[113] And Strato, in the following generation, worked hard until he could top his master by 100,000 lines: 45 titles are mentioned by Diogenes Laertius (V.59–60), and in this case it is clear that no literary embellishment is intended anywhere: it was all morning, never afternoon.[114]

Epicurus may have written a "Symposium" (but he did not dilly-dally about Eros, or the muses, dedicating the work instead to wine-drinking matters: an exemplum of atomistic conviviality).[115] His enormous output consisted of red-blooded pedagogy, the lectures of *On Nature* (that, alone, twice the collected works of Plato) reading, for once, just like *lectures*. "The main style of argument throughout the surviving fragments is likely to seem remarkably sparse, abstract, theoretical and impersonal in tone."[116] The epistles are lectures delivered by writing, explicitly designed to help those to whom the entire lecture course is too difficult; indeed, a repeated pattern among Epicurus is the explicit recycling and re-explanation, at

[112] This vast production went together with vast teaching commitments (and concerns, with which one easily sympathizes: Glucker, 1998: 300–1).

[113] I discuss the specific sense in which the "Elements of Harmonics" owes a debt to mathematics in Netz (2017a).

[114] See p, 144, n.98 above. White (2010), the best survey of Hellenistic philosophical school writing, rightly takes Strato as his model for the genre. Much later, a minor counter-example might be that of Ariston of Ceus, for whom see Fortenbaugh and White (2006); the list in DL VII.163, of works attributed to Ariston of Chios but in fact mostly by Ariston of Ceus (see n.127 below), contains "dialogues", within the specification of any titles; Cicero granted the works of this philosopher – in an otherwise critical context – a certain grace and elegance, so perhaps we should imagine a burst of more literary activity in the Peripatos at around the end of the third century or the beginning of the second.

[115] Hirzel (1895: 363–4). Book 28 of *On Nature* was in dialogue form, so that, instead of Epicurus' usual voice – a single author, speaking from his lectern – the text was a mimesis of a teaching environment with teacher and follower. To me, this appears fundamentally as a teaching text (Asper, 2007: 320–2: generally more optimistic about Epicurus as a prose writer; compare Clay, 2009: 21).

[116] Sedley (1998: 107); and read the entire discussion of style (104–9).

various levels, of the same claims; he was, after all, simultaneously founder and systematizer: charisma and routine. It is clear that Epicurus' followers imitated his approach to writing – as to all else – which we may corroborate with the (tiny) papyrus fragments from Herculaneum from Metrodorus, Carneiscus, and Colotes among the immediate followers;[117] less survives in Herculaneum from the next 150 years of Epicureanism (other than a substantial survival from Polystratus)[118] but, as the evidence – perhaps Epicureanism itself – picks up in the second to first centuries, we find enough evidence for Demetrius Lacon and of course for Philodemus himself that allows us to say that Greek Epicureanism, at least, remained true to its prosaic origins. We find again and again the same tone of pointed, almost exasperated polemic, arranged in predetermined structure:[119] sentences that are long not for the sake of an elegant period structure but merely because every last objection, qualification and alternative detail must be put in. Sarcasm provides the only note of grace – a feature that goes back, of course, to Epicurus himself. This is all remarkable, as Philodemus, unlike all his Epicurean predecessors, was an accomplished poet. But the genre of the Epicurean prose treatise was, at this point, entrenched. "Initially great expectations were aroused that their contents [sc. of the papyri of Herculaneum] might unlock the secrets of antiquity, but. . .the books in the library are mostly restricted to Epicurean philosophy." This sublimated sigh of disappointment from Fowler (1999: 210) is shared by most readers familiar with the finds from Herculaneum (excluding, of course, the scholars of Hellenistic philosophy) – and, indeed, little in what survives, elsewhere, from ancient literature prepares us for the character of those 1,000 rolls. Herculaneum is a core sample of a particular cultural form, otherwise nearly entirely lost: that of the schools of Hellenistic Athens; and what we find – stunningly, for Greek literature – is a form that strives to be as little marked as possible as verbal art, a text reduced, as far as possible, to the propositional contents of its writing.

Zeno is mentioned in Diogenes' list as the author of many books, but this is an exaggeration in the context of Hellenistic polybiblia (the list strives to include founders of schools; and Zeno is the first in the list for a

---

[117] The evidence is summed up in Dorandi (1995: 173–4). We may further confirm our impression of Colotes, in particular, through Plutarch's extensive rebuttal (Kechagia, 2011). A similar style is suggested for Hermarchus, too, based, in his case, on Egyptian papyri (Obbink, 1988).

[118] Fitzgerald, Obbink and Holland (2004: 9 n.40). The fourth scholarch, Apollodorus "the tyrant of the Garden", wrote more than 400 books: DL X.25.

[119] Philodemus chooses his opponents (one or many), then sums them up one by one, criticizes them one by one and, finally, sums up both the positions of the adversaries as well as his own correct position: Janko (2000: 191–2; see also the clear statement in Woodward, 2009: 11–12).

reason, the least prolific among prolific authors). All routinization of charisma is rife with tension, but it was especially paradoxical to pursue Zeno's project, the routinization of cynicism. Dogs abhor culture; they do not write. Zeno loved brevity; a joke quotes his advice for authors: "Use, as far as possible, *short syllables.*"[120] No poetry, then, with its obligatory longa! Crantor wrote a commentary on the *Timaeus*, thus reducing it to a depository of doctrine: Zeno, perhaps at about the same time, took down Plato's *Republic* to a single book, apparently free of literary embellishment, the mere statement of – antinomial – doctrine. The catalogue of Zeno's books in Diogenes Laertius, likely incomplete but not by much,[121] suggests no more than a few dozen rolls (of the 20 titles – a round number?[122] – only two, "Books of Homeric Questions" and "Refutations", are explicitly said to be multi-volume books). Is it the case that the *only* subject on which Zeno wrote expansively was Homer? "Contrast the Athenian Epicurus, who rejected Homer as part of his radical program to abandon all *paideia*... The Cypriot *arriviste* Zeno could not have been more different..." (Long, 1992: 48). Long goes on to explain the Stoic use of the epic poets: in part, it was for substantial philosophical reasons;[123] in part, it was an exercise in Hellenism. (And so, Long – striking a note that I followed on page 346 above – emphasizes the cultural value for such a display of Hellenism for the outsider.) Hence Zeno's attention to poetry; but was he an elegant author, himself? There were surely no dialogues by Zeno; one title, however, is "Memorabilia of Crates". Perhaps Zeno approached this difficulty, the routinization of cynicism, by putting his philosophical hero not on the vivid stage of the dialogue but as the subject of a more historical, Xenophonic treatment.

Sedley (1999: 151–2) suggests that the Stoic avoidance of dialogue could have been grounded in their substantial psychology: a dialogue argues via *exempla*, addressing faculties other than the rational, whose significance

---

[120]  DL VIII.20.
[121]  For suggested titles outside the Diogenes list, see RE, Zenon (2) col. 90 – though the one non-generic title there, "Commentary on Hesiod's Theogony", is a modern fabrication (Algra, 2001: 563–5).
[122]  Cleitomachus and Apollodorus both had "more than 400", the square of 20; Cleanthes, as we shall note below, had 50, another round number. One would normally dismiss such counts, but Diogenes' bibliographic sources are genuine enough, and, if anything, when verifiable (in Aristotle's case) the lists appear to *understate* the author's output.
[123]  In particular: etymology, as well as the interpretation of myth, could be used to discover archaic views on gods and nature. The Stoa was committed to a project of recreating a new, naturalized theology; recovery of such pristine views of gods, and nature, was therefore urgently needed. (As Long emphasizes, however, the Stoics did not subscribe to an allegorical interpretation of Homer, as if he were crypto-Stoic.)

was denied by orthodox Stoics. And so, treatises based on direct, rational argumentation. Indeed, the extreme rationalist reduction of humanity, essential to Stoicism, ill suits literary art of any form. But since when do form and content have to fit comfortably? Had the Stoics been inclined to this kind of literature, what was to stop them from the writing of dialogues advising against the writing of dialogues? (But that was Plato's specialty: the making of fodder for future deconstructionists.) In fact, a few authors within the Stoic sphere did write dialogues: Herillus stands out (a heterodox, for sure; was the very writing of dialogues a mark of insubordination?),[124] but, according to the *Suda* s.v., a certain Hermagoras of Amphipolis also had written three or four dialogues: that he is said to have been a pupil of Persaeus, and that his dialogues have appropriate literary titles such as "Dog-Hater", provide the specificity which suggests a legitimate source. Persaeus himself seems to have authored another *Memorabilia*-type work, this time on Zeno himself (but also another, on Stilpo).[125] So, the literary production of the third-century Stoa would have been slightly more colorful than that of Epicureans or of Academics, perhaps because, in the Stoic case, there was – as yet – no Epicurus, no Xenocrates, setting the tone of systematizing school prose. Even so, the credible titles we have of Persaeus (with the Memorabilistic exception noted above), of Ariston of Chios, of Sphaerus,[126] and even of Dionysius Metathemenus (a genuine renegade Stoic, for once) suggest straightforward systematic philosophy.[127] Surely, this would characterize Cleanthes, what with a 50-strong title list conserved by Diogenes Laertius (round numbers, again), and six more noted by Goulet (1994: 412) – almost all "on" or "against".[128] Cleanthes was a systematizer to Zeno's foundation,

---

[124] The meager literature on this meagerly attested Stoic concentrates on the extent of the originality of his doctrines (e.g. Ioppolo, 1985). DL 165–6: works short in lines (Zeno would have approved of *that*) but full of *dunamis*; tantalizing titles, "Midwife", "Teacher", "Hermes", "Medea"; one notes the influence not only of Socratic dialogue but also of drama itself.

[125] That the dialogues ascribed to him by Diogenes Laertius VII.36 are in fact a memorabilia is argued in Goulet (2012a: 242).

[126] See Cicero, *Tusc. Disp.* 4.53, for a sense of Sphaerus' prose in action: three lugubrious definitions of courage in succession. (Apparently, Cicero tells us, definition was Sphaerus' forte.)

[127] DL VII.36, 173, 167, respectively; I take it that Panaetius and Sosicrates were right (DL VII.163) and that the list ascribed to Ariston of Chios was mostly confused with that of Ariston of Ceus, the peripatetic philosopher.

[128] Cleanthes' systematization of Zeno's philosophy repeatedly returned to Zeno's device of appealing to poetry as philosophical testimony. It is in principle possible that some of the epigrammatic material scattered through the testimonies could be from Cleanthes' own hand (but the passage adduced as a key example for this – Galen *PHP* V.6.35 – would read much more naturally if it were Posidonius' original observation, that a certain verse from drama would fit well a philosophical point independently made by Cleanthes); the *Hymn to Zeus* is clearly Cleanthes' own contribution,

not canonized as such merely because he was so massively upstaged by Chrysippus.

Diogenes' source for the quip in I.16 considered Chrysippus to hold the record for philosophical prolixity, and a mere fragment of that philosopher's catalogue – an entire library – comprises 14 Laertius pages (VII.189–202).[129] There seems to be a tight relationship between being a leading Athenian Hellenistic philosopher and being a prolific author. Chrysippus, the most significant philosophical leader of Hellenistic Athens, was also the most prolific author of antiquity. The list of writings is striking in many ways, giving up even on the pretension of a title as such; instead, one has richer description of the themes discussed in a given roll (or set of rolls), as well as the mention of addresses (pupils responsible for writing down the notes? Or more in the manner of Epicurus: souls that need to be saved?).[130] One thousand five hundred rolls circulating around the Stoa, perhaps without as much as a title; producing a catalogue would indeed have been urgent. But what did it look like, before the catalogue, while the rolls were still being produced? Epicurus wrote out his lectures on nature;[131] Pythodorus wrote down the lecture notes for his master Arcesilaus; Chrysippus' output could represent some development along those lines: perhaps lecture notes written down by students on a continuous basis,

---

perhaps not a testament to poetic genius and yet an indication of a certain poetic ambition. It is wrong, however, to consider it on par with the Hellenistic revival of archaic poetry (contra James, 1972). It is debated how to interpret the original context of the poem, but a recent extended discussion concludes that "in view of the centrality of prayer. . .a religious setting seems more likely than merely a literary one" (Thom, 2005: 13). One envisions, then, Cleanthes, the scholarch, producing a religious ceremony: this is occasional poetry with its limited ambitions.

[129] The catalogue was meant to cover logic, ethics and physics, in order, but it is cut short in the middle of the ethical section. An interim calculation by the author of the catalogue states that there were 311 rolls on logic alone (DL 198; for some fun with those numbers, see Barnes, 1996: 173–4). Those rolls stand for 157 treatises (summing up the titles in the list DL VII.189–99, and adding the extra 39 logical works mentioned in summary form in 199 itself), so on average between two and two and a half rolls per treatise; the fragment of the catalogue for ethics has 97 rolls for 39 works, however, so definitely about 2.5 rolls per treatise. Chrysippus' overall treatise count was 705 (DL VII.180) which would imply, then, over 1,500 rolls. It comes as a surprise to hear he was reported to die at the tender age of 73; we find about one roll for a bit less than two weeks of his adult life, or a treatise every month. "500 lines a day" was the ancient exaggeration: "Tons of material, bad style" (to paraphrase DL VII.181). For the sources of the catalogue, see Barnes (1996).

[130] There is a clear correlation between the length of works and their tendency to get a named addressee: about two-thirds of the single-roll works and a third to a half of the works with two to six rolls are non-addressed, but none of the works with seven rolls or more. Perhaps addressing a work was a way of putting a seal to it, while the non-addressed works were more trivial, or even unfinished (for general discussion of Chrysippus' practice within the larger context of addressing one's works, see Wietzke, 2014: chap. 2).

[131] Indeed, these were even dated as they were being written down! See the overview in Asper (2007: 317–18).

perhaps the master continuously addressing this or the other among his followers. Text may have been dissolved, it appears, into the life of the studying community. The many fragments collected by von Arnim (over 200,000 words in the TLG text – immense for a fragmentary author) are mostly heavily mediated, but a very substantial papyrus fragment (P.Herc. 307, *SVF* II.298a) survives from Herculaneum,[132] while Galen's fierce critique of Chrysippus (*Doctrines of Plato and Hippocrates*, especially Book III) adds up – perhaps, a back-handed compliment to Chrysippus' own practice of extensively quoting from his sources – to a nearly continuous citation of half a papyrus roll (the various fragments are collected by von Arnim *SVF* II.879 ff. and summed up in II.911).[133] This is not the same as our knowledge of Epicurus (for whom we have three extant short treatises quoted verbatim by Diogenes Laertius, as well as very substantial papyrus survival, especially of the major work, *On Nature*). The papyrus survival, at least, is not random: it was kept in Herculanum for a reason (otherwise, of course, this library had very little non-Epicurean philosophy), and it is indeed possible that this was Chrysippus' most substantial work on logic.[134] In general, the style itself is not that distant from that of Epicurus. We find the same colloquialisms, suggestive of a lecturing style;[135] if anything, the text appears to be even more numbing, even less discursive, than Epicurus': Epicureanism, as it were, without the

---

[132] Several other Herculaneum papyri likely by Chrysippus provide smaller continuous stretches of prose. (P.Herc. 1038, 1421; perhaps both from *De Providentia*; also P.Herc. 1020. For Chrysippus' survival in Philodemus' library, see Fitzgerald, Obbink and Holland 2004: 11 n.46.) Other papyrological survivals are dubious and small (Goulet, 1994: 360–1). P.Herc. 307 itself is titled "Logical Questions, I", and it seems to agree with the final title mentioned in Diogenes Laertius' list: 38 books (so, Chrysippus' main logical work?). The extant papyrus takes about an entire roll, from which several snatches of sense can be glimpsed, often not more than several sentences long. Sufficiently many of them remain, however – 216 non-lacunose lines in Cronert's text (which is slightly over-optimistic, however; Marrone, 1984, improves, mostly by adding a handful of lacunae instead of Cronert's confident readings).

[133] A physical title, it is not found in Diogenes Laertius' list, but it is attested (*SVF* II.55, a testimony also transmitted via Diogenes Laertius: *SVF* II. 55) to have been at least two books long. I believe this may represent the bulk of the original Chrysippean text. It is more difficult to say how significant, or typical, *De Anima* was in Chrysippus' physics.

[134] Atherton (1988: 419) suggests that this might come from mere private notes: but would this be out of place in such a massive, school-based production?

[135] There is a single occurrence of νὴ Δία in both *SVF* 298a (*Col.* 12.13) and 911 (*SVF* II.259.22); Chrysippus disarmingly noted himself, regarding his propensity for boundless citation: "They will say that this is the garrulity of an old woman, or perhaps of a schoolmaster who wishes to list as many verses as possible under the same thought" (*SVF* II.907; translation from De Lacy, 1981: 197). The "garrulity", *adoleschia*, is the same root Epicurus himself uses – in the very same tone of self-disparagement – referring to his lecture course (Sedley, 1998: 104, uses "chat", instead: "Let that be enough chat. . . I have now finished chatting to you.").

sarcasm.[136] The typical mode of Chrysippus' writing, I would venture to suggest, is propositionalization: that is, he takes a subject and quickly finds propositions that could be asserted about it, which he then either supports or refutes via other constructed propositions – such as "and if someone were to state such arguments. . ."[137] or "some say it [the governing part] is located in the chest, some in the head".[138] To make the examples somewhat more substantial and vaguely "sampled", I go by through Plutarch's *Stoic Self-Contradiction*, which has the advantage of quoting verbatim from a wide range of Chrysippus' writings (tr. Cherniss, 1976):[139]

> Citation 1 (1033 C–D): "All who suppose that the scholastic life is especially incumbent upon philosophers seem to me to make a serious mistake. . ."
>
> Citation 2 (1035 A): "Now I believe in the first place, conformably with the correct statements of the ancients, that the philosopher's speculations are of three kinds, logical, ethical, and physical. . ."
>
> Citation 3 (1036 A): "For while that practice is incumbent upon those who in all matters observe suspension of judgement and is conducive to their purpose, it is, on the contrary, incumbent upon those who inculcate knowledge in accordance with which we shall live consistently to instruct their pupils in the principles and to fortify them from the beginning to end by destroying the plausibility of the opposite arguments. . ."

---

[136] Chrysippus did say that Archestratus' *Gastronomy* was the mother-city of Epicurus (Athenaeus 104a: the passage continues to note that Archestratus is indeed the Theognis – or Theogony? – of all gastric philosophers, a meta-meta-ironic comment added, I suppose, by Athenaeus himself). That's not very biting (for a genuine Stoic attack on Epicureans, see Cleomedes, *Lectures on Astronomy*, II.1; is it an accident that nothing of this kind is attested for Chrysippus himself?).

[137] P.Herc. 307 I.26–8, translation from Sedley (1984: 314). This turn of phrase (*eipoi tis an*) is common enough in extant direct quotations from Chrysippus – see also *SVF* III. 359, 476, 479; as we have in the order of 10,000 words in direct quotation, four occurrences is frequent enough to merit attention (Plato, extant in the order of 500,000 words – and the most frequent user of this phrase prior to Chrysippus – has 32 occurrences, which is about an order of magnitude less than Chrysippus' frequency, then).

[138] *SVF* II.911 259.3–4, *PHP* III.1 K.V. 252. Recall Chrysippus' self-deprecating note that "they will say" – again, the verb *phēmi*, obviously very common: "Whether they *say* that distress and anxiety and suffering are not pains" (*SVF* II.911 261.8–9; *PHP* III.7, K.V. 335; De Lacy, 1981: 213); "In keeping with this we *say* that some people vomit up their impressions" (*SVF* II.911 259.41–2; *PHP* III.5 K.V. 292; De Lacy, 1981: 205).

[139] My method is simple: I looked for an example from each Plutarch page; typically there were several explicit citations per page (none in 1034), of which I took – I admit – the most salient to my argument. I am cherry-picking, to make the argument clear; but my cherry-picking was severely constrained and could hardly manufacture the result (anyway, the rejected citations are usually almost as good!).

Citation 4 (1037 B): "Even when they have a definite apprehension it will be possible to argue to the contrary..."

Citation 5 (1038 D): "For, if it is held to be a good but not a goal and if the fair too is among the things that are of themselves objects of choice, we could preserve justice by maintaining that the fair and just is a greater good than pleasure."

Citation 6 (1039 D–E): "Such an assertion [*logos*] is self-contradictory and also least effective as exhortation. For in the first place by indicating that it is best for us not to be alive and in a sense requiring us to die it would exhort us to do something other than to philosophize..."

Citation 7 (1040 C): "For if it is held to be a good and not a goal and if the fair too is among the things that are of themselves objects of choice, we could preserve justice by maintaining that the fair and just is a greater good than pleasure."

Citation 8 (1041 A): "Every right action is a lawful act and an act of justice; but what is done in accordance with continence or endurance or prudence or courage is right action; consequently it is also an act of justice."

Citation 9 (1042 E): "For even with the following one has enough to assert that good and evil things are perceptible."

Citation 10 (1043 C–D): "For, holding fast to this let us again consider the proposition[140] that he will go campaigning and dwell with princes."

It is evident that Chrysippus spent much of his writings going through the analysis of potential logical structures, set out in explicit propositional terms, but always qualified by their potential proponents – such as "it is believed that..." and "from which follows that...". And, indeed, he was explicit about it – as well he should have been, spending so much of his life discussing logic and dialectic in a classroom!

There seems to be some emphasis on the simplicity and clarity of the propositional content – with some very simple indirect clauses, such as "it is sufficiently clear that people have been brought from the outset to the view that *our governing part is in our heart*", "it is reasonable that *that to which the meanings in this go and out from which discourse comes is the sovereign part of the soul*" (still *SVF* II.911; De Lacy, 1981: 173, 131,

---

[140] To clarify: the word "proposition" is Cherniss' (valid) addition in translating Plutarch's text (which has, simply, *hoti*).

respectively), "it is not reasonable to claim that *the divine is the cause of shameful things*" (*SVF* II.1125 – said by Plutarch to be a direct quotation) and "We say that this follows from that, *the sage does not opine*" (P.Herc. 1020; *SVF* 131 21–2).

Bobzien (1998: 236–9) surveys the three sources we have from Cicero, Gellius and Plutarch for Chrysippus' views on fate and determinism. It is clear that our sources draw on several distinct works by Chrysippus, but they display a recurring pattern of a counter-claim, summed up by Chrysippus, and then refuted. (This is reminiscent of the structure found in Philodemus' works.) And indeed Gellius, whose reliance on the original works by Chrysippus is the most direct, is quite clear: the key operation was to reduce his opponents' claim to a well-articulated propositional content. This was: "*If there were providence, there would be no evils*" (*SVF* II.1169; Gellius, *N.A.* VII.1). The opposing view being crystalized into a proposition, this then is attacked and refuted. One's impression is that this, at least, is among Chrysippus' standard modi operandi.

On pages 448–53 below I discuss extensively the key example for Chrysippus' engagement with mathematics (his objections to Democritus' indivisibles-like geometry), and I conclude that Chrysippus approached this subject, once again, by analyzing Democritus' claims into a logical skeleton, consisting of a well-articulated, propositional statement, which then was resolved in strictly logical terms. This type of approach is clearest, in fact, with Chrysippus' engagement with medicine. The basic strategy of Chrysippus' *De Anima* II – in which Chrysippus attacked the Hellenistic deviation from Zeno's cardiocentrism – was to propositionalize. Here we see much more of the detailed texture of Chrysippus' text, and we find that the tendency to propositionalize is seen in every step along the way (not just in the grand strategy of reducing one's opponent to a refutable, well-articulated proposition). Everything available to Chrysippus' attentive, retentive mind was turned into logical assertions. "But my heart swells with bitter anger" (*Il.* 9. 646); "no such thought is in my chest" (*Od.* 17.403). So, as consequences: affections and cognition are deduced to be located in the heart (De Lacy, 1981: 179, 185, respectively). Single words, in proverbial usage, are propositionalized as well (so, the single word *akardion*, "heartless", is taken to imply that "the heart is assumed to be the seat of affections": *SVF* II.902; De Lacy, 1981: 193), and, much more wonderfully, even gestures – Chrysippus moving into ethnographic mode – are taken to carry meaning: "Women. . .if a remark does not go down with them, they often move their finger to the region of the heart and say that it does not go down there" (*SVF* II.911 259.38–41; De

Lacy, 1981: 203). It is clear that Chrysippus' text was bulging with citations, and apparently they were there with this purpose in mind: to marshal the entire range of Greek culture (above all, of course, the canon) as an arsenal of propositional claims.[141]

It is clear why Chrysippus would like to turn his opponents' claims into well-articulated propositions: he was drawing them into the field in which he reigned supreme. He was, after all, the inventor of propositional logic!

The papyrus fragment of "Logical Questions" does not seem to cite any passages. But then, of course, its very subject matter is propositionalized already. The text is arranged as a set of claims about what follows, or does not follow, from stated propositions, some of them in a meta-language ("There are plurals of plurals"); then they use linguistic and logical terms, but most typically they are set in the object language. Then, they become stripped of anything beyond pure propositionhood. Chrysippus' original contribution to Greek literature was with phrases such as these.

"It is day" (five TLG results prior to Chrysippus; 103 in Chrysippus himself).

"Dion walks" (of course, no occurrences prior to Chrysippus; seven in Chrysippus himself, whose testimonies include the name "Dion", itself, 71 times).

The object language discussed in Chrysippus' logic appears to be made primarily of sterilized propositions of this type. In P.Herc. 307 I count 26 of these, such as (von Arnim's pagination):

"Dion, Theon is" (102.18);

or

"This one walks, if he does not sit down" (108.23–4);

or

"This, if not that" (109.17–18).

One evident feature of the catalogue of Chrysippus' logical works is his extensive engagement with discrete logical problems: about a fifth of the attested titles discuss solutions to puzzles, often those that had an

---

[141] I take Fronto, *Epist.* II 14–16 ("Don't read Diodorus and Alexinus, but Plato, Xenophon and Antisthenes... Read Chrysippus: you will find there rhetorical tools") to mean, in effect, "Read *even* Chrysippus himself – and you will find there rhetoric". In fact, the emphasis in Fronto's discussion of Chrysippus' style seems to be on the sheer amplification through repetition and variety: which is indeed what we glimpse through the few fragments.

entrenched name (so, perhaps, from the early third-century tradition of disputatious display; see page 362, note 34, above. Five titles are dedicated to the "liar" alone.). It is apparent from the remains of P.Herc. 307 that this, at least, was structured as a miscellany of individual problems and solutions, as the very title, "Logical Questions", implies. Propositional logic as such – to us, the pride and glory of Stoic logic – is of course well developed, but less so than the more basic level of terms and propositions considered independently of inference. Barnes counts 35 rolls on arguments, 46 rolls on more elementary propositional forms: "Chrysippus devoted as much paper to the elements of arguments as to the arguments themselves – and here his work has no parallel in the Peripatetic tradition" (Barnes, 1996: 178). In sheer *SVF* fragment counts, the ratio is even starker: 95 fragments on the elements of argument (*SVF* II.136–230) to 39 on argument, excluding solutions to sophisms (*SVF* II.231–69). Chrysippus perceived the universe through a filter of propositional content, and so he invented, from scratch, an entire science analyzing what propositional content *is*. On the other hand, he did not care much for rhetorical embellishment, and in fact he explicitly believed that rhetoric, properly, was no more than dialectic.[142] It should be understood that, for the Greeks, rhetoric was the main structuring principle of prose style, and so to state that rhetoric should be dialectic is, essentially, to say that prose style is reducible to logic. Apparently that's how Stoics were understood to express themselves: drily and logically.[143]

There was a certain variety of philosophical literature in Athens. Theophrastus and Strato produced more dockets of research in the tradition of Aristotle's case-by-case contemplation project – while Epicurus concentrated on the written teaching of his doctrine. Among Epicurus' followers, one could read more entertaining terms of abuse, heaped at the opposition. Arcesilaus was exciting in argument, his followers perhaps distilling this into a philosophical statement of a more theoretical character; other teachers appear to us, from our distant viewpoint, to have been deadly dull. But, in fact, Chrysippus attracted many students, and, overall, the difference in style between the various schools is quite constrained. In the Epicurean papyri, we have to work our way through the detail of the philosophical argument so as to decide which the positive portion of Epicurean doctrine is, which the quoted passage of doctrine to which the

---

[142] See Atherton (1988) for Stoic rhetoric.

[143] Our evidence comes mostly (though not entirely) through Cicero, whose disdain for Stoic rhetoric is pervasive: according to him, the first Stoic who was also an effective speaker was Cato the Younger (Stem, 2005)!

Epicureans object. The language itself provides no clues: the same frequent
*gar*s (at the expense of other, more vivid particles), long composite verbs
and nouns striving for precision, complex but unrhetorical sentence structure. And the same would be true for the way of life, too. Arcesilaus did
become a favorite character in jokes, and in all likelihood was a witty
speaker. But even he did not engage in outré behavior.[144] Stoics, the
admirers of Diogenes, did not walk about naked; Academics, the admirers
of Socrates, did not stay up the night, meditating. They were teachers; they
stuck to the code.

Literary practices in the Hellenistic philosophical schools in Athens were
largely stable and homogeneous, always related to the reduction of literary
texts to a core of doctrine, an extraction of a bare propositional structure.
This was the point of giving up on almost any pretense to literary grace.

Alexandrian literary practice, I argued on page 373 above, was characterized by the infusion of a comprehensive survey with the spirit of detail. It
was *within* literature, while also being *above* literature. We recall Pyotr
Trofimov, in Act 3 of the *Cherry Orchard*, patronizingly declaring that he
and Anya are "above love" (*vyshche lyubvi*) – to which Ranevskaya replies,
magnificently, that she is then, as it happens, *beneath love* (*nizhe lyubvi*). So
it was with Alexandria and Athens. Alexandria was above literature. Athens
was *beneath literature*.

It will not do to say that Athens gave up on style simply because it
was more technical, more specialized. In fact, the most typical thing of
Alexandrian literature is its graceful literary elaboration of the specialized and the technical, whether into didactic poetry or into ludic
proofs. And, in general, any retreat from style should be seen as
surprising: the philosophers in Athens had exactly the same education
in the literary canon – and in rhetoric – as all intellectuals elsewhere.
They all highly valued literary grace. Athenian Hellenistic philosophers
deliberately marked themselves with their stylistic abstemiousness. For,
indeed, philosophical literature itself, we noted above, tended to be
much more embellished – prior to the third century, away from
Athens.

Specifically, style recedes as the school comes in. Surely, this correlation
has some causal meaning. Once again, I develop grand structural oppositions, but there is no need to think in such abstract terms. The

[144] Cleanthes on Arcesilaus: "Never mind what he says; he acts just fine" – to paraphrase the beginning
of a joke (Arcesilaus: "Stop flattering me!" Cleanthes: "No flattery intended; I point out your
inconsistency!" – from DL VII.171). Chrysippus kept to exactly the same timetable every day
(shades of Kant, there): Philodemus, *Ind. Stoic* XXXVIII.1–7.

philosophers in Athens, digging into strict doctrinal positions, retreating, as it were, into mere propositional content, represent something quite simple: they talk, incessantly and without exception, with each other – and with no one else.

I pointed out on page 321 above the tendency of philosophy to become gripped by its thematic lock: questions are discussed because they have been discussed already, and thus can effectively function as frames for debate. This thematic lock, I noted, intensified with growing spatial concentration. In Presocratic philosophy, one debates distant and unknown figures and one goes back to the very basic questions. Is change possible? What is the world? As philosophers tend to aggregate together in single cities, debate comes to be more local, and more presuppositions are given: one debates within more established terms. In the Hellenistic schools, spatial concentration is maximal, and so is the thematic lock. One debates, now, the minutiae of school doctrine, no more. My colleagues should know: under maximal thematic lock, questions that seem, from the outside, arid, indeed hardly motivated, could attain, in the debaters' minds, supreme significance, because it is here, around such questions, that you and your friends – having spent years together, studying and teaching in precisely the same setting – finally differ.

And so: routine. The loose centrality of Alexandria brought together many disciplines, speaking to each other in a kind of generic koine, always marked, however, by literary inventiveness: because one's audience was so wide, one could assume little beyond the rhetoric of speech. The opposite was true in Athens, with its extreme spatialization. Speech became logical, stripped of rhetoric: "beneath literature", then.

Speaking widely, or speaking to one's colleagues: there is a difference. Once again, we, contemporary scholars in the humanities, should know. How does this difference play, then, in terms of the dialogue between Athens and Alexandria, themselves?

## 4.3   The View from Alexandria: What Did Alexandria Know about Philosophy?

Whatever the reason: Hellenistic Athenians wrote *a lot*. One of the fixed features of cultural life in the Mediterranean through the third and second centuries BCE was the stream of new writings from Athens, all of them setting out, in various terms, the doctrines of the four schools. How did Alexandrian culture respond to this literature? In what follows, I try to answer this question, discipline by discipline.

### 4.3.1 The Exact Sciences

Here, we may be brief. While arguments for the influence of philosophy on Hellenistic mathematics were sporadically offered in the past, there is, in fact, very little in those highly technical mathematical texts to suggest any engagement with philosophy.[145]

The written structure of Greek mathematics emerges from such practices as the lettered diagram and technical language, which seem to arise without any deliberate planning, let alone philosophical inspiration.[146] Scholars have long toyed with the idea of having the axiomatic apparatus of Greek mathematics correspond to philosophical strictures, above all those of Aristotle's *Posterior Analytics*;[147] this connection, tenuous at best, loses any meaning when we realize that the structures of axiomatic apparatus in Hellenistic mathematics are in fact varied, and typically much simpler than those of Euclid's *Elements* Book I,[148] But, considering the chronology, even Aristotle as an influence on mathematics – let alone any later Hellenistic philosopher – is a stretch; the creation of deductive mathematics preceded him, and the key theme in the history of Greek mathematical form was stability (this, after all, is why I started writing this book). Nothing of substance changed in the deductive form of mathematics through the Hellenistic period, with or without philosophical influence.

What about the contents? Not only do Hellenistic mathematicians not respond to the new philosophies of the Athenian schools; they even turn their backs on the more obviously mathematical concerns of

---

[145] Wilbur Knorr argues, in a series of essays from the late 1970s (especially 1975; 1980; 1982; 1983) leading to his major book (1986), *The Ancient Tradition of Geometrical Problems*, for the independence of ancient mathematics from philosophy, showing throughout that various features of the mathematical practice are best understood as responses to internal mathematical considerations. In fact, the bulk of the extant evidence for Greek mathematical practice comes from the Hellenistic era; is it possible, then, that Knorr's thesis is essentially right – but for a particular period?

[146] Netz (1999a): my main point there is to understand the logic of Greek mathematics in terms not of its axiomatic but of its deductive structure (not what makes treatises as a whole logically sound but what makes individual claims perceived as necessary and general: which must be the operative question for the special position of mathematics within the space of Greek genre). This deductive structure is also cognitive, rather than purely logical, and depends on certain textual practices. I claim that such practices emerged, organically, early in the fourth century. Netz (1999b) specifically argues that the most explicit statement of Greek mathematical textual practices – the scheme of Proclus' division of the mathematical proposition into parts – was a late reflection, rather than an early prescription; the counter-argument of Doxiadis and Sialaros (2013) relies on an earlier dating of Ps.-Hero's *Definitions* 137 (usually considered a Byzantine addition to the text; the authors wish to suggest it could be due to Hero himself), which I find implausible.

[147] The locus classicus is Lee (1935).    [148] Mueller (1991).

fourth-century philosophy.[149] A single example suffices. Central to the engagement of science and philosophy, through the Pythagorean-Platonic tradition, was music theory: the key example of a philosophical question (whence harmony?), mathematically solved (numbers!). The Hellenistic era sees an eclipse of mathematical music. The only attested piece of mathematics dealing with music theory, in this period, is that of Eratosthenes, perhaps in the context of his *Platonicus*:[150] within an idiosyncratic return to Platonic dialogue (see page 381 above), an idiosyncratic return to Platonic-inspired mathematics. A unique exception to the rule: the field that brought mathematics and philosophy together – music – seems to disappear in the Hellenistic era (see page 467, then, for music's return, in a very different cultural environment).

It is certainly false to see, say, an influence of Epicurean minima, or of Epicurean infinities, in Archimedes' indivisibles and counting systems:[151] Archimedes' indivisibles are of a lower dimensionality than the objects they constitute – quite un-Epicurean[152] – while his *Sand-Reckoner* does not, in fact, engage with infinity at all.[153] What ultimately motivates authors such as Serres – who made the supposed Epicureanism of Archimedes central to his historical project – is of course the fact that atomism ended up so crucial to the scientific revolution. So, it looks as if atomism *should* matter to a mathematically inspired science. But in fact this was precisely a modern – original – combination. Epicurus, after all, attacked science and, in particular, attacked the making of astronomical models – among Archimedes' most celebrated achievements![154]

In the ancient context, it would make more sense to look for the influence of philosophical *continuum* theories on the exact sciences. Indeed, a few (very mediated) cases are suggestive. Galen asks himself a sensible question: what does one's muscle do when the arm is extended

---

[149] There is a separate question, having to with Euclid's possible response to Platonism; see especially Knorr (1980: 194); Proclus explicitly claimed that Euclid was a Platonist, in *Eucl.* 68.20 Friedlein, but at any rate the very project of the commentary to Euclid is meant to subsume him within the corpus of Platonic knowledge. I am not sure this was a silly claim to make but at any rate I treat Euclid as, effectively, heir to the fourth century more than a Hellenistic author.

[150] Vitrac (2006).

[151] I mention this only because this is seriously proposed by Serres (2000 [1977]: 13–15). Serres, like me, writes about many things he knows well but not enough; it is sobering to find how little, in such cases, one actually knows.

[152] Perhaps in tension with continuum theories, too, whether peripatetic or Stoic – if he took indivisibles to be the potential end points of division. I return to this on pp. 450–1 below.

[153] Netz (2003).

[154] For Epicurus' attacks on fourth-century astronomical models, see Sedley (1976); for Archimedes' model within its historical context, see Evans and Carman (2014). I shall return in the following section to the question of Epicurean (and Skeptical) views of mathematics.

and kept steady? Does it *do* anything at all?[155] This calls, in his view, for Stoic tonos theory, and von Arnim cited some parts of his ensuing discussion as a fragment of Chrysippus (*SVF* II.450). In particular, Galen asks further why a bird, suspended in air, does not fall down: is it not because it is moved up by its own motion, as much as the weight of its body moves it down?[156] This kind of canceling out of the forces is the basic mechanism of Archimedes' statics, and so this passage becomes intriguing: did Archimedes pick up a scientific concept from the Stoa? It is likely, however, that the example of the bird is Galen's own.[157] There is no Stoic mathematics here at all, but the background to this doctrine, in the Stoic theory of *tonos*, merits a brief detour: we see here how the Stoa brushes against, but never quite reaches into, science. The issue arises from a very different problem from that in which Galen brings it to use. From the basic tenets of the Stoa it follows that the existence of any entity – even the inanimate – requires its pervasive and never-ending permeation by active, material principles (say, pneuma). Why, then, do things appear to be stable? The Stoic answer seems to be that the various intervening forces counteract against each other, throughout; not necessarily simultaneously canceling each other out, but sufficiently counterbalanced so as to maintain apparent stability. (Perhaps, then, in fact, everything *slightly vibrates*: always dances, in appropriately Heraclitean fashion.) This is not a model of two vectors canceling each other out but, rather, of two overlying pieces of matter.[158] The key difference from Archimedes is not just the much vaguer approach of the Stoics but a precise, technical detail: Archimedes' model treats a rigid body as reducible to its center of the weight (the counteracting forces then understood in terms of vectors, indeed, passing through the centers of the weight of the rigid bodies, and of the Earth). Such a reduction of a body to a single point goes against the grain of the Stoa's holistic approach to physics.[159] Now, it is not as if the science of physics has to treat problems in terms of centers of the weight only, and Sambursky (1959) was right to be excited about the modern ring of such Stoic notions as the stretching, mutual

[155] *On Muscular Movement*, IV.400.   [156] *On Muscular Movement*, IV.402.
[157] This is acknowledged even by Sambursky (1959: 32–3). I am not aware of scholars since him picking up this episode as an example of potential interaction between science and philosophy: it is useful, then, mostly as a counter-example. When Stoic-like notions strike us as mathematical-like, it takes a Galen to mediate them!
[158] While the theory has to be pieced together from fragments, scholars tend to think that, at its base, lies the Stoic need to provide a fully materialistic account of the soul. This becomes then a special kind of matter, distributed throughout the body (Inwood, 2014: 63–6).
[159] In general, for the essential "holistic" approach of the Stoa, see Gill (2006).

permeation and the wave-like behavior of material continua.[160] Indeed, it was certainly within the ability of a scientist such as Archimedes to take such concepts and to make out of them a study of phase transitions, of chemical reactions, of airwaves. He did not, and neither did anyone else in antiquity. Instead, authors in the exact sciences in the Hellenistic era mostly concerned themselves with radical physical abstractions that relied on reduction to geometrical models based on lines and points, which simply did not lend themselves to any of the cosmologies then available.

### 4.3.2   Medicine

With mathematics, there might have been less room for influence by philosophy: the deductive method perfected in the early fourth century was too effective to be replaced; Hellenism, in mathematics, did not signal a break. Medicine, much less stable in its methodologies, could have been a more fertile ground for philosophical influence. Indeed, we are presented with a striking coincidence: just as Arcesilaus pivoted away from Xenocrates and Polemo, taking with him the entire Academy, Philinus of Cos was pivoting away from his own teacher, Herophilus.[161] The dating is in fact very vague, but it is likely that, of the two, Philinus was somewhat younger.[162] Arcesilaus advocated *epochē* or suspension of judgement; Serapion – likely echoing Philinus – advocated *empeiria* (first-hand experience – hence the eventual name of the "sect": *empeirikoi*), *historia* (in this case the accumulated fruits of the past experience of one's predecessors; in other words, medical tradition) and "transition of

---

[160]  This respected study by Sambursky remains, in fact, the one sustained effort to bring together Hellenistic philosophy and mathematical physics. It is also anachronistic through and through, though it does remain a useful reference point for its clear presentation and good survey of the evidence (for an early, and rare, critical review – Sambursky was universally liked at a personal level and respected for his wide culture – see Stannard, 1961).

[161]  See Chapter 3, n.122, above for Philinus' date; we rely on Erotian, who seems to imply (*Voc.* 31.12– 16) that he was contemporary with Bacchius, hence the middle of the century (von Staden, 1989: chap. 14); see following note.

[162]  Arcesilaus certainly died in 241, at the stylized but inherently likely age of 75; so, likely born not much later than 316 (Goulet, 1989: 328). Philinus was probably, indeed, Herophilus' direct pupil, so, all in all, likeliest to have been younger by about a generation or 30 years; applied to von Staden's guess that Herophilus was born between 330 and 320 BC (1989: 36), we may center the curve of probable Philinian years of birth at 295; see also Pellegrin (2006: 678). To suggest the influence of Pyrrho – that hermit of Elis – is, on the other hand, extremely unlikely; through the Aenesideman revival of Skepticism, he would indeed be an influence upon later medicine – but this belongs to a different cultural climate (see sections 4.5 to 4.6 below).

the similar" (analogy).[163] The question of the relationship between medical "empiricism" and philosophical skepticism is of course difficult,[164] but it is obvious that the basic structure of empiricism, even if we extract a general "epistemology" out of its – strictly medical – methodological statements, was very different from that of Arcesilean skepticism. Above all, the motivation for early empiricism appears to have been *clinical*. These are the authors who wish to emphasize the individual knowledge of the doctor, irreducible to book learning but dependent upon autopsy – and upon tradition; to emphasize that the value of medicine is in its clinical achievement, not in its scholarly production. And so: the emphasis is on the methodology of *practice*.[165] These – *empeiria* and *historia* – are very different from *epochē*, and the fact that much later authors – from Celsus onwards – explicitly equate medical empiricism with philosophical skepticism is an interesting indication of later transformations, on which more in sections 4.5 to 4.6 below. Meanwhile, in the third century BCE itself it appears at least possible that medical methodological debate could be conducted purely within the terms of medical research, no reference being made to epistemological debates in philosophy. (To be clear: my point is not that the evidence shows lack of philosophical influence on early medical empiricism. Our evidence is certainly too meager to support such a strong claim.)

So much, then, is warranted for the methods of medicine. For the contents of medical theory, the obvious contact with contemporary philosophy is that of the model of pneuma – a case of medicine seeming to precede philosophy, however; I return to this problem in the following section. But, then, there are several non-contacts: several dogs, refusing to bark. The connections between medicine and philosophy, in the fifth and fourth centuries, are complex: thus, we have in fact plenty of antecedents for methodological and metaphysical discussion among the medical authors, suggesting an awareness and interest in contemporary

---

[163] For the medical tripartite ("tripod") epistemology, see von Staden (1975: 191–2); by this time Academic *epochē* would certainly have been established and diffused in written form. It is not clear if the first group of Philinus' followers referred to themselves as "Empiricists" but one of them – Apollonius (of Antioch) – is cited as the *empeirikos* by Demetrius Lacon, so the adjective must have been current for the latter group of such medical authors, at least around the beginning of the first century (Berrey, 2014b: 147).

[164] For a philosophically motivated discussion of the epistemology of early empiricism, see Frede (1990). The issue is complicated, to repeat a point from n.162 above, by the tight connection between Imperial-era Pyrrhonian Skepticism and medicine; see Allen (2010).

[165] This is the key observation of Berrey (2014b).

philosophy.[166] From the very beginning both philosophy and medicine engaged with the ultimate constituents of bodies; at least from the fourth century onwards they both emphasized value as explanatory of nature. How does this compare to the Hellenistic era? Indeed, through the classical era – and then, once again, in the generations leading up to Galen – the need to develop *some kind* of humor theory was perhaps as entrenched a medical theoretical practice as any; it would remain so for 2,000 more years (a very specific version of humor theory would become enshrined as medical gospel, following Galen; before that, debate was the rule).[167] No one in Alexandria seems to have denied the existence of some humors but Galen was impatient with how little the Hellenists studied them: Erasistratus, he found, wrote nothing at all on black bile, and very little on yellow bile (and there, Galen quotes verbatim: Erasistratus' main claim is that it is unimportant to inquire about the *origins* of yellow bile).[168] Von Staden (1989: 244–7) rightly rejects Kudlien's radical claims (1964: 8) that Herophilus directly denied the medical significance of the humors, but he concedes that we find in Herophilus no positive contributions to the study of the humors, and, especially among the Herophileans, no evidence that they even subscribed to them. Medicine – no longer engaging with the ultimate constituents of the body?

Similarly, it is difficult, now, to find any evidence for doctors arguing for the ultimate *usefulness* of the parts of the body. Galen often complained about his predecessors, and so there is no special lesson to be learned, perhaps, from his complaint that much is lacking in previous writings on anatomy; for our purposes, we are especially intrigued to find that, according to him, past authors neglected to show the *use* of the study of anatomy, instead haphazardly throwing in all the bits and pieces they knew.[169] No

---

[166] So the debate against "hypothesis" in the Hippocratic *On Ancient Medicine* (though Schiefsky, 2005: 11–14, 120–6, suggests that we might see here not philosophical influence but, rather, the home-grown epistemology of a medical author); see, in general, Longrigg (1989). Later still, van der Eijk (2000: II.xxv) speaks of Diocles' "philosophical sophistication" and "methodological awareness".

[167] Nutton (2004).      [168] Galen, on Black Bile, K. V.123. See, in general, Nutton (2005: 118).

[169] The critique as a whole is in Galen, *On Anatomical Procedures* II.1–3, K. II.281–91; he actually emphasizes that the display of teleology is not the major aim of anatomy, and a fault of his immediate predecessors (so, van der Eijk, 2000: II.32), who studied anatomy mainly for the sake of settling theoretical questions. In the one strictly historical passage, however, K. 282.7–10 (in which Diocles is mentioned, and the reference must be to the early tradition of anatomy), the complaint is that such authors did not display *chreia* – by which is meant either usefulness for clinical practice, physiological teleology or both – but, instead, were purely descriptive. Even though Diocles is the only author mentioned by name, Galen surely would have had in mind (to the extent that any historical reference was genuinely intended) the works of Herophilus.

use – that is, no teleology? Perhaps so: there is no "teleology" in von Staden's (1989) index. Why should there be? The pulse theory as well as the anatomy are purely descriptive, and there is little theory at all among later Herophileans. Erasistratus, famously, repeatedly provides accounts that seem to imply an understanding of the body on the model of mechanical devices (the pumping heart, the canals of digestion, the rope-like nerves: Berryman, 2009: 198–200), but, as Berryman emphasizes throughout, when ancient authors turn to their own mechanical sciences, this need not be projected into the modern debate between modern "mechanical" and "teleological" philosophies. Erasistratus seems to have provided accounts based on the model of mechanical devices which could therefore have been, among other things, non-teleological accounts, but there is nothing in Galen's extended polemic against all this to suggest that Erasistratus himself presents his accounts as arguments against teleology. With an author such as Galen, the argument from silence is not mean-ingless: his two chief targets in *On the Natural Faculties* – to mention one prominent discussion of teleology – are Erasistratus and Asclepiades, and, of these two, Erasistratus is cited repeatedly for specific theories about body processes, but it is Asclepiades who is also censured for an overall philoso-phical approach: "According to Asclepiades, nothing is in sympathy with anything else in its nature, all substance being divided into unattached elements. . ." (K. II.39). The impression, then, is that Hippocratic authors – and, then also, much later authors from Asclepiades onwards – all tie their theories of the human body into theories of body as such, and ultimately with metaphysical and even ontological questions such as the ultimate constituents of the body and its functional account. But not so much in between – in Hellenistic Alexandria. We seem to glimpse a more descrip-tive, less metaphysical theory of the body.

Indeed, theory seems to have been neglected in a more fundamental manner: medicine was not further studied (as it briefly was, in the fourth century) within a context one can consider, vaguely, as "biological". That is: there would be no further study of *animals*. "I do not think it is an overstatement to say that the next work that can be called a biological treatise [after Aristotle and Theophrastus] . . .is Albertus Magnus' *De Animalibus*, in the twelfth century of the Christian era" (Lennox, 1994: 7). Lennox points to a mystery: the early Peripatos created an immense research program in zoology and botany, providing a database, the method for augmenting it and an entire range of open questions, as well as claims open to criticism. This then just stays untouched for centuries. In a sense, we have yet another example of our generational events – in this case, the master-and-pupil pair of Aristotle and Theophrastus. But the problem runs deeper, since, after all, the early Alexandrian approach to medicine clearly could have been extended very naturally to the study of biology in general. We do have the report of an experiment, by Erasistratus, with a bird as subject – but this poor bird is a generic living creature, no more.[170] Galen referred to Herophilus' views on the position of the liver in the hare, but this goes to prove our point: Herophilus, so Galen, stated that a left extension of the liver is rare among humans but not among animals, "but he mentioned only the hare, and left it to us to examine the other animals"[171] – did he have a hare at hand for dissection? Or is it a brief mirabile inserted within the anatomical survey?[172] In short, for the Alexandrians, medicine was a clinically minded study of man, and animals were largely irrelevant. Here is a case when the scientific culture of Alexandria refused to consider the Athenian contributions *to science itself*. Nor, indeed, would the biological research program be revived by later authors: the Imperial-era revival of Aristotelianism tended in a logical, metaphysical and in general "Platonizing" direction, and perhaps for this reason marginalized Aristotle's biology.[173] (Galen's anatomy, while thoroughly anthropocentric, would involve, as a matter of practice, some element of comparative zoology, however: it was based, after all, on animal dissection.) Hence Lennox' observation of a 15-century gap. Lennox himself accounts for this in philosophical terms: in the Hellenistic world, some were skeptics, while those who were not would be "studying various plants and animals as an adjunct to various arts, such as medicine" (Lennox, 1994: 22). But this merely restates the puzzle – and restates it in an unlikely form. Of course we find that Herophilus and Erasistratus, relative to Aristotle, became much more focused on the human organism; but they did so in the context of a project that, to future medical authors, would be impressive precisely because of its wide, empirical horizons. One almost wonders, then, if Herophilus and Erasistratus could not have avoided zoology

---

[170] The bird is weighed, caged, starved to death; the combined weight of her emaciated body together with her excreta is less than the original weight, hence something else was lost (anon., *Lond.* XXXIII 44–51). It is an open question whether this was in fact not a pure thought experiment, and at any rate it is clear this is not part of a study in *zoology* (von Staden, 1975: 179–81). Erasistratus certainly engaged in some animal vivisection, however: Galen II K. 648–9, CMG V.4.1.2 p. 446 De Lacy).

[171] Von Staden (1989: 182–3, fr. 60b 19–21).

[172] In fr. 289 Erasistratus comments upon his own observations of the human brain and mentions in passing the similarity to all animals, "deer or hare or others": is this an actual dissection program, or random observations – "a sportsman's sketches", as it were?

[173] See Rashed (2007) for the manner in which Alexander of Aphrodisias – *not* a Neoplatonist – attached metaphysics to logic, rather than to biology.

precisely because it was so obviously Aristotelian? The point is merely suggested by the evidence, but we should ponder it. In the fifth and fourth centuries the discussion of quasi-philosophical questions would not mark one necessarily a philosopher. Establishing their identity as physicians, Hippocratic practitioners did not mind what we now identify as Presocratic flourishes. My suspicion is that, in the third century, this might have been harder: specifically philosophical concerns would mark one, I suggest, precisely *as a philosopher*. Perhaps, because philosophical concerns were now so clearly associated with particular places, particular schools?

### 4.3.3    The Thinness of Contact

The evidence is limited, but it certainly does not suggest that the sciences in Alexandria were engaged in any type of systematic response to contemporary philosophy in Athens. Now, this is probably not because the philosophy of Athens was simply unknown. Athens and Alexandria were certainly aware of each other, and indeed there was, after all, a considerable traffic between the two.[174] And yet, how many philosophers even traveled to Alexandria? There were several active, for sure, in Alexandria's first generation – a larger-than-usual entourage of a Macedonian court, no more and no less: Demetrius of Phaleron (an exile) and Strato (peripatetics, both); but also Diodorus Cronus, as well as Cyrenaics; Stilpo is mentioned in the context of a Ptolemaic encounter (Diogenes Laertius II.115: though did that encounter take place in Megara?). It is not as if Alexandria resisted philosophy. But, then, as soon as its specific cultural character was established, philosophers became scarce. The first generation moved away or died, and then – almost nothing.

One theme in our sources is the coyness of philosophers in front of kings: the latter keep requesting the philosopher's presence, advice and education, the philosopher himself resisting and sending, perhaps, his adjutant. This may all be chreiai, playing with the figure of the philosopher

[174] This is true, first of all, at the most basic political level. A weak power, Hellenistic Athens feared most its stronger neighbors, and was eager to rely on the goodwill of a distant superpower. Thus, through the Hellenistic era, the Ptolemies often acted as the patrons of an independent Athens – that independence occasionally broken, however, by more direct Macedonian control (Habicht, 1992). Remarkably, Athens was at its most directly dependent upon Alexandria from the 280s to the 260s – that is, exactly during the years when, in cultural terms, the two cities become set in original, divergent ways.

as against power.[175] Perhaps: at any rate, later chreiai had to work with this, the *absence* of contact. Zeno, we are told, refused to go to Pella, and sent Persaeus and Philonides of Thebes instead (DL VII.9); Cleanthes, in his turn, refused to go to Alexandria; he assigned Chrysippus, who also declined (so all first scholarchs get their royal invitations). Sphaerus went ahead instead (DL VII.185); his tiny Laertian biography consists (other than a list of works) of two Ptolemaic anecdotes.[176] Both are surprisingly tense and serious. Ptolemy tricks Sphaerus by presenting him with toy pomegranates, which the philosopher proceeds to try and eat – humiliating in particular for a Stoic who argues that the wise do not opine (so far, familiar ground: Alexandrian marvels, the joke of the parasite). But then Sphaerus responds at length, with no hint of irony – as if the anecdote comes from a serious philosophical context – distinguishing between different interpretations of this event as philosophical example. The next anecdote is even more troubling: a certain Mnesistratus accuses Sphaerus of denying that Ptolemy is a king (presumably, according to Sphaerus' philosophy, only he who is wise, and philanthropic, may be called such).[177] Sphaerus replies: "Such being Ptolemy, he is a king as well" – a witticism of sorts, finally (the response is ambiguous: either "because Ptolemy has, in fact, the requisite character, he is indeed king" or "to the extent that Ptolemy *would* have the requisite character, he *could* be king" – but as yet he is not). In both anecdotes, Sphaerus threads an anxious needle. Little wonder philosophers did not show up at Alexandria. But, of course, not too much is to be made of this tiny speck of evidence, and, instead, the emphasis should be on how small it is: if post-Strato philosophers went to Alexandria, they did so very rarely – and very late in the century – while practically no Alexandrian is known to have sought philosophical learning in Athens.[178] Athens did not partake of Alexandria's pomegranates.

---

[175] For the tendency to remember cultural figures, as opportunity presents itself, in the circuits of kings, see Wietzke (forthcoming).

[176] DL VII.177, referring to Philopator; scholars consider this an error for Euergetes (Goulet, 1994: 410), as Cleanthes was dead by Philopator's ascendancy, but, since it is easy to see how the tale of Cleanthes being invited, and having declined, emerges out of Stoic propaganda, I am not sure the case is clear. Sphaerus is said to have gone to Alexandria when well advanced in *logoi* (already a prolific author?). Perhaps we are to imagine a contemporary of Chrysippus, *retiring* to Alexandria in his old age (Sphaerus also spent some time in the court of Cleomenes of Sparta, who ruled from 235 to 222 BC).

[177] Murray (2007: 19–20).

[178] We do hear, in Diogenes Laertius, of a certain Posidonius of Alexandria, among the "other philosophers" who studied with Zeno (DL VII.38; the name is not in the parallel list in Philodemus' *Index Stoicorum*). The adjective *alexandreus*, without qualification, could mean only "of the Alexandria in Egypt", but one has to make a note that "Alexandria Troas" could have been misunderstood by a reader who, like us, knew nothing of the Posidonius involved (the Troas

And yet: if not people, then surely their texts? There is no doubt that philosophical texts circulated, early on, outside Athens, some of them reaching very far indeed: among the most spectacular finds is the early Hellenistic impression left on a brick, in present-day Afghanistan, by an Aristotle dialogue. This is perhaps a freak event; in Egypt itself, however, there is a reasonably sized group of Ptolemaic philosophical papyri. Excluding school exercises of moralistic contents, we find 20 potential Ptolemaic philosophical papyri of unknown authorship (CEDOPAL, "Philosophie", –300 to –100),[179] which compares very well with the same search, unrefined, for +100 to +300: a bare count of 171.[180] The total numbers of *all* literary papyri from the same time frames are 489 against 4,103, so the first impression is of incredible stability – about 4 percent philosophy in both samples! This should be seen, however, against the overall tendency of Ptolemaic papyri to be more specialized (more dominated, that is, by the big library; see page 40 above; it is very typical that, among Ptolemaic philosophical papyri, the major group is the unknown author, while, among Imperial philosophical papyri, the major group is Plato). Philosophy belongs to the big library par excellence – it figures prominently in the few big-library catalogues we possess, as we noticed on pages 75–7 above – so in fact we see, if anything, evidence for a certain increase of interest in philosophy in Egypt, from the Ptolemaic to Imperial eras (it is very likely that the Ptolemaic big libraries in Egypt stocked a bit more on minor performative literature, those of the Imperial era a bit more on philosophy; while small libraries – more numerous in the Imperial era – included no philosophy at all). But this all depends on some very small numbers, and the key lesson from Egyptian papyri is that philosophy, after all, *was* known. The contents are worth considering, however: of the 12 published, non-Plato Ptolemaic fragments of philosophy, three are dialogues,[181] one a utopia setting out an ideal

certainly furnished several philosophers, including the fourth scholarch of the Peripatos – i.e. likely a contemporary of our Posidonius).

[179] Eleven are not catalogued by Mertens–Pack (M–P) by author (though many suggested attributions have been made in the past), six are Plato, two Theophrastus and one – doubtful – Chrysippus.

[180] Eighty-eight Plato, 60 unattributed (though I did not attempt to read through the entries and cull out the overcounts; also: ten Aristotle, two Antiphon and one each associated with Antipater of Tarsus, Aristoxenus, Chrysippus, Cornutus, Empedocles, Epicurus, Favorinus, Hermarchus, Hierocles, Posidonius and Ps.-Pythagoras).

[181] M–P 2593, 2584.01, 2587.01. Among the unidentified prose fragments, three – M–P 2812, 2842, 2845.8 – could perhaps be dialogues as well. In the most extensive count, we find 12 Hellenistic fragments of philosophical dialogues from Egypt (that is, excluding the freak find of Ai Khanoum), of which only half are Plato: the distribution between canon and secondary authors is typical of the Ptolemaic big libraries, while the overall presence of the genre suggests its importance as a literary

city[182] (so, perhaps, rather like Hecataeus? This is not the typical fare
of the Hellenistic philosophical schools); Theophrastus' *Characters*
belongs in this category, of philosophical works related to a more
literary interest. Two are straightforward scientific fragments;[183]
maybe this is the context in which we should mention a critique of
Plato – perhaps from the early Peripatos?[184] The remaining four
papyri are all ethical in character. One is a tiny fragment which
seems to discuss pleasure (but it is not clear if it is a good or a bad
thing),[185] another survives extensively enough for us to know that it
was strange: it starts off considering whether pleasure is a good, then
whether storks do right to feed their parents, then veering off (in the
same treatise?) to discuss the proper attitude of followers to their
masters; "dialectical" philosophers and a certain Menedemus are
mentioned; we seem to envisage a wide philosophical space beyond
Athens alone.[186] Finally, two fragments, M–P 2575 and 2576,[187] are
likely from the Epicurean school. It should be remembered that
Epicurus' corpus may have been the largest, preceding Chrysippus,
and his *On Nature* could have been among the longest works ever
written. It is useful that the papyri are provenanced, one to Hibeh,
the other to Oxyrhynchus; so, not the same library. Epicurus was
known, though of course to only a few very sophisticated readers, in
Ptolemaic Egypt.

What about Chrysippus? Surely we should be able to find some fragments, from such a corpus? Not quite – though one fragment is suggestive.
P. Par.2, dated to the first half of the second century BCE, is a very legible

medium: a major form of prose in this time and place (when we find somewhat fewer histories and
speeches). Philosophy, as performance, was more alive than the political speech; more on this below,
p. 498.

[182] M–P 2570.1, interpretation as utopian due to West (1983); it could also be a documentary (or
historical?) text discussing a real city!

[183] A study of water, attributed to Theophrastus (M–P 1499), and a study of optics (M–P 2579). The
last, P.Louvre 7733 inv., is a substantial fragment that allows us to form a clear sense of its program.
It deals with optical illusions; there are many claims for paternity in the literature; see Bett (2007)
for discussion and a survey of past literature. Even if the authorship is Athenian, and philosophical,
the subject matter is technical and we do not need to imagine that the papyrus was collected by a
reader especially interested in philosophy.

[184] P.Hibeh 184, discussed in Sedley (2011); previously considered as a school exercise, Sedley finds here
a serious engagement with Platonic doctrine, from a critical angle; while Sedley stops short of saying
that, the overwhelming likelihood, then, is of an early peripatetic text. The main interest seems to
be in argumentation as such, so, perhaps, a "logical" text.

[185] M–P 2602.2; discussion in Carlini (1978: no. 15). The few surviving words do settle that this is a
piece of philosophy.

[186] M–P 2586.01: Richter (1997).     [187] CPF I.1.51.10–11.

papyrus with 15 extant columns, 13 of which are complete; we seem to have the middle part – the bigger part? – of an entire roll. The surviving columns all repeat exactly the same pattern: framing a piece of poetry that takes the form of a negative statement, such as

I know not what to do, I have two minds (Sappho fr. 51),

within a complex inference schema:

> If Sappho denied, as follows: "I know not what to do, I have two minds", there exists a certain positive proposition opposite to "I know not what to do, I have two minds". Indeed. There does not exist a certain positive proposition opposite to "I know not what to do, I have two minds", indeed; Sappho did not deny, as follows: "I know not what to do, I have two minds."

The clearly legible portion of the roll contains 27 passages that offer trivial variations on this schema. It is possible that the last, fragmentary column finally moves to make some kind of comment on the pattern as such, but more likely the same schema just rolls on and on. The papyrus was attributed early on to Chrysippus, for a good reason: the contents are obviously logical, and surely Chrysippus' writings dominated ancient logic, above all in the second century BCE. The subject matter – negated sentences and their inferences – certainly fits Chrysippus' interests. And yet it is hard to fit the scant evidence this papyrus presents with any genuine logical program in Chrysippus.[188] It does not appear, in fact, as a contribution to logic at all. It is a genuine contribution to scholarship, however. The use of Sappho is typical: the passages chosen are extremely sophisticated, six from lyric poets (Alcman, Anacreon, Ibycus, Pindar and two of Sappho), one from the *Cypria*, one from Thespis and one from Timotheus; six passages of tragic adespota. The only mainstream canonical author is Euripides, of course, with eight fragments (four identified and four from unknown plays; a handful of passages cannot be classified at all). This is two notches above Chrysippus' normal range of the epic poets. But it is worse than this: Chrysippus has good reasons to cite the epic poets (or, occasionally, drama), to provide evidence for doctrines widespread among contemporary or (even better) archaic humanity. Thus, the use of citations is most relevant in ethics and physics, where we do indeed find it in spades. But it is for a reason that such citations are absent from logic. There, as we

---

[188] Cavini (1985) is a sustained effort to squeeze philosophical significance out of this papyrus, concluding that it was probably not by Chrysippus; Barnes (1986: 94) responds skeptically: "This conclusion goes, I think, some way beyond the evidence. I am reluctant to believe that Chrysippus – rather than some schoolboy – penned the thing." But, clearly, this was a bookroll, and a distinguished one at that.

saw on page 397 above, Chrysippus is the inventor of the synthetic, sterilized sentences such as "Dion walks" or "It is day" that, by their utmost simplicity, act as some kind of schematic representation of *sentence in general* (thus, a little of the functional analogue of the use of P in modern propositional logic). On the other hand, a sentence such as "I know not what to do, I have two minds" is, as a logical example, plain awful. It is not even clear what the scope of negation is (is it "know" or "know what to do"? Does "I have two minds" need to come under the scope of the negation? All this would be crucial for Chrysippus' system, in which the distinction between simple and complex propositions is paramount.).[189] In terms of logic, the poetry is counter-productive, and so we must assume this roll was produced with goals other than logic in mind, even though it was clearly produced on the model of Chrysippus' logic. Whether this roll – or its contents – was produced in Athens or in Egypt, we find, then, that the one trace we find by Chrysippus in the soil of Hellenistic Egypt hijacks Chrysippean logic for the purposes of Alexandrian philology.

It is dangerous to use P.Par. 2 as a piece of evidence for "the reception of Stoic logic outside Athens". A single piece of papyrus is but a single throw of the dice. What the evidence clearly shows is that philosophical works related to the teaching of the Athenian schools did circulate outside Athens; that they did so in reasonable and yet small numbers – the occasional collection by several truly expansive big libraries (direct allegiance to philosophical schools, outside Athens itself, being perhaps less common in the third and second centuries themselves). But what P.Par. 2 prompts us to ask is, what did the owners of such expansive libraries make of their philosophical collections? Would they not read them to fit other, non-philosophical agendas? In fact, the case of P.Par. 2 is very reminiscent of that of the other early, documented second-century response to Chrysippus from outside Athens – Hipparchus' combinatoric calculation. Our evidence for this derives from Plutarch, who – critical as ever of the Stoa – was eager to pass on a report according to which Chrysippus' claim – that the number of conjunctions from ten assertibles exceeds a million – was refuted by the mathematician Hipparchus, who instead determined the correct numbers: 103,149 (if negation is avoided), or 310,954 (if negation is allowed).[190] Bobzien (2011) argues that this may well be unfair, and that,

---

[189] One of the innovations of Chrysippus' logic was the formulaic language of particles, designed to make complex propositions transparent for logical analysis; see, e.g., Ebert (1993).

[190] *Stoic. Repugn.* 1047c–e, *Quaest. Conv.* 732f–33a. The second number is reported by the manuscripts as 310,952, but this is certainly an error, as a calculation that gives rise to the first number 103,149 also gives rise to the second number as 310,954. (The first number was identified as a meaningful

with the correct Stoic assumptions concerning the nature of propositional combination, the number does indeed turn out to be above a million: to get his refutation, Hipparchus had first creatively to misunderstand Chrysippus. The more natural reading, according to which "more than a million" merely gestures at an order of magnitude, would involve Hipparchus in a more interesting creative misunderstanding, taking the Chrysippean statement at a face value it was never meant to carry.[191] Everything in what I have to say here is mediated via multiple layers of speculation; such is often the case in the interpretation of the early Stoa. But, so far, I have suggested that P.Par. 2 displays a transformation and misreading of Chrysippus, as if in his many citations his real interest was in the scholarly, philological survey as such – as if Chrysippus were Callimachus; and that Hipparchus' combinatoric study displays a transformation and misreading of Chrysippus, as if his gestures towards orders of magnitudes were motivated by an interest in actual calculations of the seemingly unbounded – as if Chrysippus were Archimedes. We see Chrysippus read, outside Athens, *as if he were outside Athens*. And this is the argument I wish to outline: not that Athens was unknown throughout the Mediterranean. Of course it was known, its works circulating and its schools beckoning. But the works of those schools were read, away,

---

combinatorial number and in a sense a "correct" answer by Stanley, 1997, reporting an observation by Hough; the second number was understood immediately afterwards by Habsieger, Kazarian and Lando, 1998; for substantial contributions since, see Bobzien, 2011, and references therein; the most significant is Acerbi, 2003.) That this is reminiscent of P.Par. 2 (simple propositions, combined and negated) is not an accident: Stoic logic was the study of *what makes a proposition*.

[191] Bobzien specifically finds the number 4,978,688 based on her reconstruction of Chrysippus' meaning in "conjunctions from ten assertibles". Her reconstruction is ingenious and revealing – for displaying the cavalier way in which Hipparchus treated actual Stoic logic. And yet I find it highly unlikely that Chrysippus produced an actual calculation. Had he done so, then why did he not publish? And, if he had, would it not have been apparent to Hipparchus' readers that the only reason he came up with different numbers was because he based himself on different assumptions, and thus his contribution did not count as refutation at all? (Chrysippus was not publication-shy; indeed, he probably would not waste time on intellectual work that did not lead to publishable results. I find it unlikely – contra Bobzien, 2011: 182–6 – that Hipparchus' knowledge of Chrysippus could be merely mediated. Chrysippus' works would have been easy to come by in the second century BCE, and an author of a work dedicated to pointing out an error in Chrysippus would take the trouble of checking the original. Hipparchus' formulation of a problem was a natural way of turning it into a well-defined mathematical problem, and no peripatetic mediation was required for that.) Bobzien considers the option of "a million" as a mere hyperbolic expression, presented to her by Alexander Jones, who also suggested parallels in Plutarch (see Bobzien, 2011: 164, and n.17), and she resists it on the cogent grounds that Greek did not use thousands and their powers for hyperbolic numbers but, rather, myriads and their powers. While cogent, this argument is not so forceful, once we consider what the alternatives were. Why did Chrysippus not say "myriads"? Because he felt, intuitively, this might be too small. Why not "more than a myriad myriads"? Because he felt, intuitively, this would be too big.

differently from how they would have been read at home; encountering a different audience and filtered by a different poetics.

### 4.3.4    A Close-Up: Aratus

Hipparchus' most famous creative misunderstanding was not that of Chrysippus, but of Aratus: in his commentary to him, he read him as if he were not a poet but a mathematician-astronomer – and criticized him as such.[192] But was it a case, perhaps, of Hipparchus, once again, misunderstanding a *Stoic*? Indeed, I have left till last the star witness. The main burden of my argument, so far, was the absence of Athenian philosophy from Alexandrian science. But Alexandria, after all, was primarily not a place of science but of poetry.

It is a rare study of Aratus that does not mention the Stoa. His extant poem – the *Phaenomena* – took as its starting point two prose works that were transformed to become Aratus' own composite imitation of Hesiod's *Works and Days*: Eudoxus' *Phaenomena*, and Theophrastus' *On Signs*. It is already evident that Aratus took works by philosophers associated with Athens, the one sui generis associate of Plato (perhaps, in some sense, the founder of a school in Cyzicus), the other Aristotle's heir at the Peripatos. So, Athens is not avoided; nor is there any preference for a particular school. Perhaps, indeed, this is just what one had available to work from. If so, then, why the literature's emphasis on the Stoa? This goes back to ancient interpretation and to some genuine biographical details. Aratus' trajectory was from Soli to Pella, and both city of origin as well as court were entangled with Athens. Cilicia was, as we noted above, a recruiting ground for the Stoa:[193] Chrysippus, too, would come from Soli, and, more to the point, we hear of an Athenodorus of Soli, very likely Aratus' own brother, as a Stoic.[194] At the court of Pella Aratus would surely meet – among many others – Persaeus, and ancient tradition had envisioned the poet as the pupil of the philosopher;[195] nevertheless, the sources are at their most insistent in connecting Aratus with another pupil of Zeno, Dionysius of Heraclea.[196] A letter from Aratus to Zeno was accepted as authentic by

---

[192] I sum up the account suggested in Netz (2009: 168–71).
[193] Or for Alexandria, of course: in general, draw in your mind a rectangle with the corners, clockwise, as Athens, Cilicia, Alexandria and Cyrene. Cilicia and Cyrene are interesting in their co-proximity, as it were, to *both* major centers of the third century.
[194] *Vita* I.6: Aratus had a brother called Athenodorus; DL VII.38: according to Hippobotus, Athenodorus of Soli was among Zeno's (minor) pupils.
[195] *Vita* IV.20: Aratus studied with Persaeus in Athens and they traveled together to Pella.
[196] *Vita* I.8, IV.19: Aratus studied with Dionysius; DL VII.167: Dionysius admired Aratus.

the author of *Vita* I, against one Apollonides nicknamed Cepheus (who ascribed the letter to an apparently well-known forger, one Savirius Pollo).[197] I am surprised that a few modern scholars have chosen to follow the author of the *Vita*, rather than Apollonides,[198] but recently the letter has been indeed usually considered a forgery, perhaps on a par with the inscriptions said by Diogenes Laertius to have been erected in Athens – on Antigonus' orders! – to celebrate Zeno, most recently also shown to be ahistorical.[199] At least some authors, then, influenced by the Stoa, were intent on showing the high esteem in which the court at Pella held Zeno: the paradox of the king admiring the cynic. And yet the sources are also equivocating, in a sense: Dionysius of Heraclea, after all, was nicknamed "the renegade", for having quit the Stoa for the sake of a philosophy – Cyrenaic or Epicurean – that took the body more seriously than the Stoa did (suffering from disease, he concluded that pain, after all, was not an indifferent).[200] Diogenes has this Dionysius studying with Heraclides Ponticus, Alexinus and Menedemus; then Zeno, then in touch with Aratus, then becoming a Cyrenaic. The theme is that of many-stranded connections outside Athens, and, sure enough, we hear of his good style:[201] so, perhaps, a little more like Eratosthenes or Bion, rather than, say, like Chrysippus. The biographical details, then, do not force us to think of Aratus as a Stoic, though likely enough he knew the school well, and, even more clearly, the school came to know and admire him, whether in his own lifetime, or in the posthumous glorification of the school's founder.

If not the biography, what of the poem? Scholarship on the question of Aratus' Stoicism takes its start from Zeus: the first 18 lines of his *Phaenomena* are, formally, a hymn to the deity, obviously a response to Hesiod's own invocation in the first ten lines of *Works and Days*. Hesiod's anxious invocation of the gods' capriciousness is transformed, however, in Aratus, to pure celebration, with the god omnipresent and ever-blessing, sanctioning in this the ubiquity of natural signs – the poem's theme (whether among the fixed stars – the first part – or among weather phenomena – the second). In this, Aratus differs not just from Hesiod but also from his contemporary, Callimachus, who, in his own *Hymn to*

---

[197] For this entire episode, see Martin (1998: xv).

[198] So Goulet (1989: 323), relying on Martin (1956: 192); by 1998 Martin had changed his mind (1998: xv).

[199] Until recently considered genuine, but Haake (2004) proves quite clearly that those are likely forgeries, and a piece of Stoic propaganda.

[200] We rely on Diogenes Laertius, VII.166–7.

[201] DL VII.167: "Few-lined books, but full of *dunamis*."

*Zeus*, in conclusion, supplicates in front of the same capricious god as Hesiod's (lines 84–95: some kings get more from Zeus, some less; lucky we to live under Ptolemy!). As observed in note 128 above, we do have extant a hymn to Zeus by Cleanthes. And there, finally, we find a pantheistic, entirely benevolent deity, analogous if not identical to that of Aratus.

That much is clear, then. There was a variety of third-century attitudes towards Zeus, and Aratus' was much closer to Cleanthes' (if not identical to it) than to Callimachus'. Consider this together with Aratus' attested biographical relation to the Stoa, and it begins to appear likely that the poet was indeed, in some sense, a Stoic; such is the standard assumption in the literature, and I do not seek to deny it. But what, then, not for the person, Aratus, but for the poem, the *Phaenomena*? Effe (1977) seeks to argue that the *Phaenomena*, as a whole, should be understood as a versification of Stoic philosophy, meeting with swift rejection from authors such as Kenney (1979: 71): "In the body of the poem, however, it does not seem to me that Aratus succeeds in keeping the real, Stoic message present to the consciousness of the reader to the extent maintained by Effe." Or, as Kidd sums up (1997: 12): "Aratus' higher purpose is literary rather than philosophical". Others, in most detail Gee (2000: 70–90) and Hunter (1995; 2004: 238–42),[202] do pursue a project such as Effe's. I usually do not wade into such controversies, preferring to cover, in my synthesis, views on which there is either consensus or little discussion at all: one does not wish to make one's overall argument a hostage to particular scholarly debates. And yet this is the crux for the influence of Hellenistic philosophy on Hellenistic poetry; the debate, therefore, must somehow be resolved. I turn not to the literary scholars but to a historian of astronomy, Alexander Jones (2003: 333): "This [referring specifically to the weather signs section], in the hands of a later Stoic, could have been rich material for a discourse on causation and *sumpatheia*, but poetic expression furnishes the only substantial difference between Aratus' treatment and Theophrastus' *De signis*."

Here is the general methodological issue concerning *influence*. How should we judge if a text X was under the influence of Y? All we have are but two points, and it is impossible to establish correlation, let alone causation. The points can be multiplied, however, if we are able to consider not only the actual two points but also the entire set of potential

---

[202] For a recent survey of the debate, with further references, see Van Noorden (2015: 171 – her cautious position shown in her saying that "the most productive commentaries emphasize the plurality of cultural frames") and Cusset (2011: "Les rapports d'Aratos avec le stoïcisme se révèlent finalement être assez minces").

possibilities to which they belong. We should consider (1) the entire potential space of alternative texts to X (how could it have been written otherwise? What were the choices made by the author?); and we should also consider (2) the entire space of possible influences such as Y (what could have influenced this work other than the suggested influence under discussion?). Then it becomes possible to argue that (1), of all the potential ways text X could have been written, none displays so clearly the influence of Y as the actual text X; or that (2), of all possible influences on text X, none is as manifest in the actual text as influence Y itself. I am not sure Gee – throughout her impeccable display of literary scholarship – did consider explicitly enough the potential spaces against which correlations should be measured. Her argument boils down to three grounds of detecting Stoic influence: (1) the divinity of the stars, (2) universal sympathy and (3) Stoic theory of language. In (1) the space Y of alternative influences has not been fully considered; there is nothing distinctively Stoic about the divinity of the stars. For (2), Gee supports her case through the proem alone; this, then, does not add anything to our discussion of the poem. By (3) seems to be meant, essentially, the fact that Aratus reflected upon language and the acts of naming. Of course, Stoics would do that as well, but so would anyone whose business involved language: once again, then, a failure to consider space Y. Nowhere does Gee even stop to consider the space X of alternative potential texts which, as Jones points out, makes it unlikely Stoicism was a major concern for the composition of the poem: one could have written so many more Stoic poems! As for Hunter (2004: 238–42), this is explicitly based on the honorable sentiment that, seeing that Aratus *could* have been a Stoic, why not try and see what in his poem *could* present such influences? No harm indeed, but such an emphasis makes us lose the real explanandum. The question is not "What's Stoic about the *Phaenomena*?" but, rather, "How come, if indeed Aratus was sympathetic to Stoicism, there is so little about his poem which is Stoic?".

So: let us elaborate, then, on space X – the likely alternatives to Aratus. How could one go about writing a *Phaenomena* that is *more Stoic*? Jones must be right to emphasize *sumpatheia*, but, at an even more basic level, what I would expect above all from a specifically Stoic poem about nature is an emphasis upon the unity and shared cosmos of all. This is precisely the thrust of Cleanthes' own *Hymn to Zeus* – and this, remarkably, is absent from Aratus' poem. It is not even said, anywhere, that the stars are permanently fixed in a sphere. Aratus' manner is to refer not to the sphericity of the heavens as a whole but to the circling motions of individual elements within the sky: emphasizing flux rather than durability. His entire strategy is analytic, proceeding from one constituent to the next, never arguing even for the continuity of the sky. The planets are mentioned purely as an exception; even larger-scale structures – the four circles of the zodiac, the equator and the two tropics – are presented as isolated elements and not as constituents within a sphere. Heavenly and meteorological signs are not presented as one continuous whole, and within the meteorology, of course, atomic individuation rules, just as in the sky. All this is easy to understand in the light of Aratus' likely sources, and it all suggests an interest in versifying prose surveys – but no special interest in inserting any particular ideology into them. The key point, however, is that all this evidently works in terms of poetry: the sheer variety is as charming to us as it was for ancient readers, and it was surely intentional (and not a faulty execution, as if Aratus set out to write a Stoic poem but ended up, constrained by his prose sources, with the sheer mosaic of a double catalogue!). Bénatouïl shrewdly observes (2005a: 140) that "[l]e Zeus d'Aratos est dans les détailes", referring to the hymn itself as well as to the manifestation of divine goodwill throughout the poem. The point of Cleanthes' hymn was to unify the universe via the presence of Zeus; the point of Aratus' poem is to spread Zeus across the universe into the discrete bits of individual signs. Both, of course, obey the same logic of one-over-many; but the implicit theology works in opposite directions.

Why should that be? Once again, I am not trying to deny that Aratus was a Stoic. But, Stoic or not, he ended up with a poem which was, at the very least, much less Stoic than one could wish for; not, perhaps, to Cleanthes' liking. But very much to *Callimachus'* liking, which must have mattered more. Aratus may have had his philosophy, but he was primarily constrained by his poetics. That poetics – of the literary survey, the catalogue, the comprehensive, synoptic view that, even so, foregrounds its details – would override, for a Hellenistic poet, writing in the court at Pella, any other ideological commitment.

A clarifying example, then. My argument, once again, is not that of some biographical accident, as if people in the Athenian and the Alexandrian spheres no longer conversed, as if some ideological preference made it impossible for one group to learn from the other. Rather, we see a decisive divergence of poetics, so that texts produced within the Alexandrian sphere, even those responding to Athenian culture, would *deflect* the Athenian. Such would be Athens, read by the Hellenistic Mediterranean: ever-present, and yet ever-distant; filtered via the reception of diverging poetics. How, then, would be the Mediterranean, in Athens?

## 4.4 The View from Athens: What Did Athens Know about Science?

### *4.4.1 General Observations*

So far I have discussed the influence of Athenian philosophy on extra-Athenian practices. Now I turn to discuss the influence of extra-Athenian practices (in particular, science) on the philosophy of the Hellenistic schools. The evidence should become a little more helpful. The scarcity of second-order observations in Hellenistic mathematics, the scarcity of evidence *tout court* for Hellenistic medicine and the style of Hellenistic literature all combine to make it inherently difficult to show the influence, or lack thereof, of philosophy on any of them. It is, therefore, perhaps unsurprising that we came up with nothing in the preceding section. As against this, the evidence for scientific influence on philosophy should be easier to establish: Hellenistic philosophy is known only through mediated sources, but it is, after all, a matter of doctrine, not style, which we now try to establish; and our mediated sources, while often opaque, are abundant enough.

The key piece of the argument, then, should come now. I claim, finally, that the category of "science" has Hellenistic origins because, then, science and philosophy decidedly diverged. So, this merits a more detailed discussion. The following section is the closest that I come, in this book, to traditional intellectual history. Readers more interested in general cultural history may take the hint, and skim through some of the more detailed argument through this section. The main empirical observation I make – that, prior to Posidonius, the Stoa had little interest in science – is not exactly controversial, but neither has it been argued as such by past scholarship; and, since it is so central to my overall interpretation, I do need to address the evidence in greater detail than usual.

The point is important! "Science" – having its roots in antiquity? We, historians of science, are proud of our recent achievement in recognizing the historicity of the category itself. We now insist that the word – and also the entire set of social practices surrounding it – emerged through the nineteenth century, in a process in which "science" cleaved away from "natural philosophy".[203] Another recent important claim is that the

---

[203] Schaffer (1986), in an elegant argument, details the new narratives of genius and scientific discovery at the turn of the eighteenth century – leading to "the end of natural philosophy and the invention of modern science". The emphasis on the historicity of the category "scientist" coincided with the rise of Whewell (the author of the term) as a canonical figure in science studies; Yeo's (1993) study of Whewell, whose main title is *Defining Science*, can simply assert that "[Whewell's] life spanned the period of transition from natural philosophy to what we now recognize as modern science".

"natural philosophy" of the scientific revolution was also, in turn, embedded in the theological debates of the Middle Ages that preceded it.[204] We end up with a picture of a clean break around the year 1800 – yet another of those Foucauldian elaborations. In about 1800, science is born. Before that – an era in which "science" is more or less a misnomer for a field permeated by philosophical and theological concerns.

Let us once again pick as our example Lindberg (1992), which is perhaps the best recent survey on pre-modern science. Chapter 1 is about the Presocratics and Plato; chapter 2 is about Aristotle; chapter 3 is about Hellenistic philosophy. The mathematical sciences come in chapter 4, or on page 85: so the implication is that "science" begins with philosophy. All of this, in fact, simply repeats Lloyd (1970), whose volume I has only two chapters, out of nine, dedicated to "science" in the strict sense, on the Hippocratics and on astronomy; the main theme of the chapter on the Hippocratics, as well, is the problematization of the demarcation of medicine and philosophy (though, to be fair, Lloyd ends up finding a genuine demarcation in the context of practice). That volume is titled, after all, *Early Greek Science: Thales to Aristotle*. This, in turn, goes back to Sarton (1952), *A History of Science*, volume I: *Ancient Science through the Golden Age of Greece*, with chapters such as "Philosophy and Science to the Death of Socrates", "Mathematics and Astronomy in Plato's Time", "The Natural Sciences and Medicine in Aristotle's Time" – philosophical figures serving simultaneously as chronological landmarks and as historical explanations. And thus, as noted above, when a modern historian tries to recover ancient physics (the field, after all, most closely associated with the scientific revolution), he goes back, specifically, to the theories of the *Stoa*.[205] Scholarship simply tends to take for granted, then, that science and philosophy were largely indistinguishable throughout antiquity. Stated as simply as that, this is plainly wrong. There was a clear boundary between ancient genres; at the same time, the interest that philosophers had in science could vary, in time and place. Let us survey this background.

To begin: one of the earliest types of Greek non-performative authorship, indeed, was the writing of "On Nature"", in which concerns that we would call "philosophical" mixed freely with "physical" or "biological" speculation; at this stage, however, as noted on pages 228–9 above, the identity of the practitioners was not that of a "philosophical author" but of a "wise man", authorship being one facet of a lived practice of sagehood. Only at the very end of this tradition do we find, perhaps, a single

---

[204] Funkenstein (1986).      [205] I refer, of course, to Sambursky (1959).

exception: Democritus, extending the interests of "Presocratics" to a project of prolific prose authorship. It is not clear how we should place early "mathematical" texts such as those of Hippocrates of Chios,[206] and the medical Hippocratic texts certainly set out often enough to claim a specific identity for the medical practitioner (a point already emphasized, as noted above, by Lloyd). At any rate, the figure of the prose author emerged clearly only in the early fourth century (see page 637 below). As soon as it did, so did distinct specialized prose genres, associated with their own practices and groups of practitioners. I emphasize: there was never a stage in which there was a clearly defined role of the "prose author", which was not yet that of the author in a particular field. There was an early role, of the sage (where prose authorship was non-existent or marginal), and then later roles, of philosophers, medical authors or mathematicians; but the intermediate role, of the "natural philosopher", an author who engages equally with what we now call "science" and what we now call "philosophy", is very rare. In a way, we learn, once again, of the centrality of the category of genre.

So, through the fourth century, one group of authors referred itself directly or indirectly to the charisma of Socrates (or, in a less common western variation, to that of Pythagoras), with almost all authors in this group reviving that charisma – at least in some of their writings – through the vehicle of dialogue. This is what we call, at this point, "philosophy". Another group of practitioners charged money for healing; their writing would be related, in themes and in arguments, to the emerging canon of "Hippocratic" texts. This is what we call, at this point, "medicine". Finally, a group that was less clearly distinguished sociologically (often interacting, at this stage, with philosophers) was the most marked stylistically, employing a highly specialized form of writing based on the lettered diagram and on a limited, technical vocabulary of formulaic phrases. This is what we call "mathematics". Between the three groups there already was, in sociological terms, fairly little overlap.

So, never a "natural philosophy" as an established type of authorial identity. And yet, that the genres – and the authors who produced them – were clearly demarcated does not mean, of course, that intellectual boundaries were shut tight or that Sarton, Lloyd and Lindberg, writing on fourth-century science and philosophy, are fundamentally wrong. The

---

[206] I set out the question mark in Netz (2004a), pointing out the possibility that the original text by Hippocrates was not demarcated as specifically "mathematical", especially if indeed (as I think the textual evidence makes likely) his works did not yet employ the lettered diagram. (See, however, Bodnár, 2007: 14 n.39; I look forward to his detailed argument.)

relevant fact is that key philosophical authors (though not all, and not in all their writings) did evince mathematical as well as medical concerns. Plato's *Timaeus* was a composite, the first part reflecting mostly mathematical texts (in music and in astronomy), the second reflecting mostly medical texts. As noted on page 250 above, there is no need to doubt that many mathematicians were in fact in contact with Plato, including the three fourth-century individuals whose contribution is most clearly known to us (Archytas, Eudoxus and Theaetetus); the school in Cyzicus may well be a later reflection of this contact (at least, we have the record of both Eudoxus' interaction with Plato, and Aristotle's with Callippus). It is clear that many of the philosophers who engaged closely with Plato[207] – most significantly, the founder of the Academy (as I would characterize him), Xenocrates – emphasized this aspect of Plato's teaching.[208] While Aristotle staked his philosophical independence on the denial of such metaphysics, his school texts would be shot through with references to and imitations of the medical and, especially, the mathematical genres,[209] the most obvious

---

[207] Not necessarily strictly "Platonists": Heraclides of Pontus was an author of philosophical dialogues – and of astronomical speculation (Gottschalk, 1980: chap. 4).

[208] The works with five or more books are: *On Nature*; *On Dianoia* (the division of Plato's line to do with mathematics); *Physical Lectures* (same as *On Nature?*); *On the Mathemata*; *On Geometry*; *On Astronomy*. Non-scientific are: *On Wisdom*; *Theses* (could these, however, not be theses on nature?); *Dialectics*; and "mathemata concerning style", whatever that was. We know little about the detail of Xenocrates' metaphysics (for a sense of the difficulties, see Dillon, 1985), but it is clear enough that it was closely related to the *Timaeus*, if anything even more "Pythagorean", in some sense reducing the universe to numbers.

[209] Mathematical examples are dominant in the *Posterior Analytics* (Barnes, 1975: 70 n.32. Ierodiakonou, 2002, points out that biological examples are more common in the *Prior Analytics*, but this is slightly misleading, as "biology" was not a category relevant to Aristotle's audience, while the terms of Aristotle's examples, such as "man", "horse", "mortal", of course relevant to his project – which we perceive as "biological classification" – would have been perceived as belonging to the wider project of "division", of logical or metaphysical import). Aristotle's own deployment of arguments from the mathematical genre is surveyed in Vitrac (2002), though Vitrac argues persuasively that the most extensive of those arguments – the *Meteorology* passage concerning the rainbow – is in fact mostly a late interpolation. Aristotle's books engaging directly with mathematics and medicine are now lost (other than the likely pseudo-Aristotelian *Mechanica* and *Indivisible Lines*) but – rather brief – treatises are attested in the lists, on the following fields (referring to Goulet, 1989: 424–34, lists by Diogenes Laertius and Hesychius): medicine (two books, DL 110=H 98; perhaps also H 167), astronomy (one book, DL 113=H 101), optics (one book, DL 114=H 103, perhaps also H 173, two books), "mathematics" (one book: what was that? DL 63=H 53) and music (one book: the practice, the scientific theory, or just "culture"? DL 116=H 104). How much of this fairly meager count was pseudepigraphic, as well? (The Arabic tradition knew also a treatise on the pulse, surely apocryphal; Goulet, 1989: 434.) Aristotle's very original project of biology is seen by us as kin to medicine, which, to us, is closely related to or perhaps subsumed under the life sciences; but I am not sure this connection would be evident at all to ancient readers, to whom Aristotle's project of seeking causes of animal phenomena would appear simply as a massively exaggerated version of one particular facet of the traditionally philosophical study of nature.

being the use of letters to represent objects; did they refer to diagrams?[210] Indeed, Aristotle did not stray from Plato all that far, and, in particular, he was perfectly willing to provide his own mathematical accounts of physical phenomena.[211] Obviously, the Aristotelian interest in the sciences would be a distinguishing feature of his school, including such authors as Eudemus, Aristoxenus and Dicaearchus, not to mention Theophrastus and Strato themselves. All of this could mean no more than that a particularly influential author of Socratic dialogues came under the spell of the mathematical genre and that his influence extended to his immediate associates. And yet there seems to be a more robust correlation, between location and intellectual project – yet one more version of this constant theme of Athens against the rest. An interest in mathematics, by authors whose identity is philosophical, was precisely Athenian. Elsewhere, authors perpetuating the Socratic charisma remained much closer to Socrates' own model of disputation on values – so that they concentrated on what we would call logic, or on ethics, but did not engage with science – or, indeed, with the questions of "nature" in the old fifth-century sense.[212] Epicurus – heir of the Democritean tradition but much more attuned to the debates of Athenian philosophers, a critic of Cyzicus, first and last an Athenian himself – is an interesting interim example, confirming the correlation: in between Athens and the rest, he was also in between the sciences and their avoidance. He did revert to the construction of grand cosmological models – and spent, after all, much of his energies worrying about mathematics, if in a negative sense.

---

[210] On this *More Geometrico* aspect of Aristotle's writing, see Netz (2017a).

[211] See, in particular, Sorabji (1972).

[212] Already the ancients ascribed to the Cyrenaics the position that ethics alone is the proper study of philosophy; see Tsouna (1998) for a brief statement and minor qualification (some logical concerns, even physical ones, could sneak in if they could be seen as subdivisions of ethics); the same seems to hold for Phaedo of Elis (Goulet, 2012a: 285). Megarian and/or *dialektikoi* performers (as well as Menedemus) seem to have discoursed in a direct imitation of Socrates, with perhaps a more evident emphasis on the theory of compelling argument as such (it is telling that here we have a group of individuals referred to by their style and subject matter – "dialecticals" – rather than a city). Cynics, obviously, did not bother with the specialized genres. There was a tradition, however, almost entirely obliterated by the hazards of transmission, traced back to Democritus (retracing this tradition is the key theme of Warren, 2002). Once again, however, natural philosophy seems to have receded in significance: Anaxarchus of Abdera wrote, perhaps, on kingship; his teacher, and the direct follower of Democritus – Diogenes of Smyrna – is virtually unknown but the extended piece of physical doxography ascribed to him belongs, in fact, to Diogenes of Apollonia (Laks, 1983). Nausiphanes of Teos, finally, might have maintained certain pieces of Atomistic doctrine, but the key theme of this tradition is the direct transition from Democritus to Pyrrho, from Atomism to Skepticism: these authors are not the proponents of new, original cosmological models but the critics of claims to certainty.

It is the precision of this correlation that forces us to look for Athens as such, rather than for Plato, as the proximate cause for the divergence in philosophical projects. So let us restate our observation: that, the further one was from Athens, the more the route was blocked, for Socratics, to engage in non-Socratic pursuits. Which is, in fact, obvious: elsewhere, philosophers had only their philosophical project with which to perpetuate Socrates. In Athens, the charisma lived on through the power of the place itself, and so the lived practice of philosophy could be much more flexible. Away from the central space of a cultural practice, it could be maintained only in the narrowest form: the logic of provincialism.

Reflecting upon the specialized sciences was the mark of sophisticated, Athenian philosophy, in the age just prior to the formation of the Athenian schools. This goes beyond the age of Plato and Aristotle themselves. Zeno, for sure, would emphasize Greek literature more than Greek science; but his basic project, after all, was routinizing the *Cynic* interpretation of Socratic charisma. He took a philosophy produced away from Athens, one that rabidly disdained all fruits of cultural specialization, science of course included. For such a project, Zeno's innovation can be seen as an Athenaization: Cynicism, fused with a study "On Nature". Already, in Zeno's time, the Stoa was characterized by its insistence on a unique view of nature, as simultaneously *material* and *divine*. Whether or not the precise formulation was already Zenonian, or originated with Cleanthes, it was in accordance with that nature that the Stoics, famously, exhorted us to live.[213] The actual testimonia on Zeno's own physics are at a surprisingly elementary, even naïve, level (so, the basic theory of the eclipses is put forward as if it still required elucidation:[214] this, from an author wedged, chronologically, between Callippus and Aristarchus!). So, if more

---

[213] It is not in fact obvious that, because the end is to live consistently with nature, it is a part of philosophy to study nature in detail: White (1985) suggests an account for why this should have been the case, as early as Zeno. It is a pity that the evidence on whether "consistently with nature" is a Zenonian formulation is contradictory, but it is standardly assumed in the literature that, even if the phrase was by Cleanthes, it would be a correct interpretation of Zeno's own phrase, merely "consistently" (see Striker, 1991). While the precise formulation is indeed distinctively Stoic, the sentiment is very widespread in antiquity, if not universally, each philosophy and each individual picking up their own version of "living according to nature" (a good example is Lehoux, 2012: chap. 2 – a study of Cicero's "according to nature").

[214] DL VII.145, *SVF* I.119. Zeno also proposed a startlingly implausible proposal concerning comets, as if they came about through the ad hoc coming together of some stars' rays (Seneca, *Nat. Quaest.* VII.19.1, *SVF* I.122). Seneca presents this theory as if it rendered comets as mere optical illusions, which would tend to undermine, then, our ability to discern geometrical patterns in the night sky. Overall, the materialist emphasis of Zeno's philosophy was in some ways incongruous with the geometrical idealization required by mainstream Greek astronomy, and was, then, not exactly unlike Epicurus'.

"Athenian" in its very attention to physics, the Stoa of the first quarter of the third century was also at the greatest remove from actual science. The Epicureans, the enemies of science, knew their enemy well; it may have been at this time that Crantor produced a commentary to the *Timaeus*; Theophrastus, and then Strato, strayed little from Aristotle's project of the contemplation of natural causes. True, at least the Academy could have begun to drift away from Xenocrates' close engagement with the mathematical science: whatever the significance of Crantor's work, Polemo himself, and then Crates, the scholarch, seem to have perceived their task, already, as primarily ethical.

Long and Sedley (1987: 2) exaggerate somewhat when they assert that, "if Aristotle could have returned to Athens in 272 BC, on the fiftieth anniversary of his death, he would hardly have recognized it as the intellectual milieu in which he had taught and researched for much of his life".[215] In fact, he would have found an Athens still under the spell of Socrates, still fusing it with a theory of nature as understood by the specialized genres. He would have been dismayed, if hardly surprised, by what he would consider the superficiality of Plato's direct heirs; amused by that of Zeno's Stoa. But in Strato he would have found a worthy successor, in Epicurus a worthy rival. Something had drifted away, a certain direct awareness of science, sometimes even a certain sophistication had been lost; but no real break, yet.

Let him come back five years later, though! And now, indeed, Arcesilaus is perhaps already head of the Academy, Lyco head of the Peripatos. (Epicurus, also dead, was replaced by Hermarchus: hardly his equal but perhaps not so distant from Epicurus' own practices.) Suddenly Zeno's naïve science remained as the most positive engagement of Athenian schools with the specialized genres. To some extent, what we see here is the coincidence of a generational turnover: Crates and Strato happened to die at about the same time, both old remnants, witnesses of the moment of the routinization of the schools. In these two, older schools, a new generation was no longer bound by the founders (the Garden and the Stoa – losing their immediate founders, Epicurus and Zeno, through the same decade – did not undergo a similar transformation). But why did the generational shift have to be so abrupt, and why should it go, broadly speaking, in the same direction?

---

[215] To do so, they exaggerate Strato's specialization: it becomes evident from Sharples (2011) that Strato's interests were more catholically Aristotelian, ranging from metaphysics, via psychology, to the animal world. They also push Arcesilaus' accession to the head of the Academy to before 272.

In the case of Arcesilaus, our evidence is positive. We have noted on page 386 his character as more akin to those of the near-Athenian philosophers, engaged with unwritten disputation on ethics and (especially) logic, arguing indeed against the possibility of scientific knowledge. That this goes so blatantly against the tradition from Plato's *Timaeus* through Xenocrates' systematization is a well-known conundrum: what did they have in mind, nominating him as scholarch?

In the case of Lyco, our evidence is mostly negative. His election to the scholarchate is one of the strangest of all: Strato had to go out of his way to defend it; the scholarch was only 30 years old.[216] The remaining 44 years of Lyco's life would be filled by his beautiful voice echoing through the porticoes of the Lyceum, his immaculate dress shimmering. Such, at least, is what posterity would recall of him: nothing else remains.[217] And yet, at the end of those 44 years, the Lyceum was thriving.[218] This contrasts with the other relevant observation (for which see Sandbach, 1985) that the influence of Aristotle himself was waning in the Hellenistic era. Of course: it was waning *in the Lyceum itself*. Strato must have picked Lyco for the same reason the Academy had picked Arcesilaus: because there was a need for someone who could dispense with the great figures and speak elegantly, instead, of the good life.

Even some Stoics felt a similar need. Among the more prominent followers of Zeno, Ariston of Chios was distinguished for his denial of any value in anything other than virtue or vice, including, specifically, denying the value of physics or logic.[219] He led his own school at the Cynosarges – so, effectively, a case of an author pivoting away from his master; in this case, though, the rebellion was seen off by the main school of the Stoa, and Ariston's pivot did not outlive him; the new power of the

---

[216] It is hard to see how to escape the explicit, detailed chronological statements in Diogenes Laertius V.68, especially as they make sense of Strato's apologetic words ("I chose him because, of the rest, some are old, others uninclined to learning [*ascholoi*]": Diogenes Laertius V.62). The markedness of this choice should be emphasized. Among the 13 scholarchs whose age at beginning of their scholarchate can be given, the average age is 52.5; the youngest, other than Lyco, was Carneades, at age 47 (and clearly a charismatic genius). This of course fits our observations from p. 181 above concerning the significance of old age for ancient cultural achievement.

[217] Voice: Diogenes Laertius V.65–6. Dress: Diogenes Laertius V.67. He was always considered a nonentity, so modern scholars, naturally, root for him. Fortenbaugh and White (2004) gamely try to squeeze some philosophical significance for him, and yet we remain with four fragments, 9–10, 12–13 (9: "Grief is occasioned by small things"; 10: "The end is true joy of the soul"; 13: "Salt is dug up with good- or foul-smelling" – undoubtedly an ethical metaphor; while 12 is an extended harangue against excessive drinking. Note that fragment 11, referring to Lyco's "speech rich in style" (*oratione locuples*), may well have referred to his sweet voice rather than to the quality of his writing.

[218] Mejer (2004, esp. 278–9): Lyco had plenty of followers and associates.

[219] Diogenes Laertius VII.160.

school, in action. Not that Cleanthes himself was much more of an author on nature than Zeno was, before him: if he expanded the brevity of Zeno into a comprehensive system, he did this by writing mostly on ethics.[220] And yet – such, in fact, was the Hellenistic school closest to science. On this school, then, we need to focus our attention. In what follows I consider this by genre. I begin with medicine, and then I move on to the specialized genre most associated with philosophy, in post-Platonic Athens: mathematics.

### 4.4.2 The Stoa and Medicine

Nothing remains, directly, of Stoic Hellenistic writings. But two of the most prolific authors of antiquity have dedicated considerable effort to badmouthing the Stoa, and their corpora are largely extant: Plutarch, and Galen. The circumscribed evidence those authors provide for the early Stoa's knowledge of medicine has some value, then, not only positively but also for its evidence from silence. Let me explain with an example from Plutarch, *Stoic Self-Contradiction* 1047C–E. Plutarch begins by quoting Chrysippus, in paraphrase and then verbatim:

> In the Physical Questions he [Chrysippus] has exhorted us to remain silent on matters requiring scientific experience and research if we have not something surpassingly manifest to say "...in order", he says, "Not to make surmises either like Plato's that the liquid nourishment goes to the lungs and the dry to the belly or other errors that there have been like this."[221]

---

[220] Von Arnim interpreted the list in Diogenes Laertius VII.174–5 as divided neatly into three parts: physics, first 14 works; ethics, the next 31; and then five on logic. In fact, this seems to over-interpret what we can tell based on the first 14 titles, which seem like a more mixed group. It contains all five titles referring to previous authors (two positive, on Zeno's physics and on Heraclitus; three negative, against Democritus, Aristarchus – but see below n.232 – and Herillus; obviously some are physical in character, but already von Arnim found the reference to Herillus surprising); five works that perhaps operationalize archaic literature ("Archaiologia", "On the Gods", "On the Giants", "On the Wedding Song", "On the Poet" – i.e. on Homer. Undoubtedly, such appeal to archaic knowledge would emphasize its capacity to transmit cosmological truths, but the organizing principle here is not that of "physics" as such.). Of the rest, some are of physical content – "On Time", "On Perception"; one is likely physical – "On Impulse"; "On Art" is more difficult to classify. So, definitely Cleanthes wrote something on physics, but hardly ever on physics as such, instead producing, alongside his main ethical project, a few commentaries, critiques and summaries of archaic views, which could have supported Zeno's own views on nature. This tendency, to preserve the master's cosmology without adding to it, is the same as that of Hermarchus vis-à-vis his own master, Epicurus – the difference being that the Epicurean legacy, in cosmology, was so much more substantial than the Stoic.

[221] Translation from Tieleman (1996: 192), with the exception that I translate *kreitton kai enargesteron* as "surpassingly manifest", taking the comparative to have an intensive meaning and the *kai* to be epexegetic. The point is that Chrysippus does not advocate merely to remain silent in the face of a

Plutarch then goes on – as is his wont in this treatise – to find an example when Chrysippus did the very thing against which he advocated. That is, Plutarch now needs to find examples when Chrysippus made pronounce-ments on a matter requiring "scientific experience and research", even though he had nothing "better and clearer" to say. And what does Plutarch come up with? The testimony on Hipparchus' counting of con-junctions. Chrysippus claimed there were more than 100 myriad conjunc-tions, whereas – gasp! – people with real scientific experience and research – Hipparchus – had shown that there were about ten, or 40 myriads, depending on how you count them (as discussed on pages 414–15 above).

As self-contradictions go, this is very feeble. What I would argue, as an argument from silence, is that, had Plutarch had readily available to him an original medical pronouncement by Chrysippus, on the lines of Plato's views of nutrition, he would certainly have used it. Now, Plutarch did not go through the several million words Chrysippus had written on physics, and he must have missed some claims (in particular, perhaps Chrysippus' views on the heart, to which I turn in a moment, could have furnished somewhat better examples, though, as we shall see, Chrysippus was quite circumspect there). But the clear impression is that it would have been very difficult to cull a medical doxo-graphy out of Chrysippus' writings. This is explained by Plutarch's own quotation: Chrysippus was, in fact, not self-contradictory, and, having expressed a plausible methodological principle – that a philosopher should best avoid specifically medical matters – he in fact did.[222] The example Plutarch came up with, then, had to be internal to philosophy: Plutarch took a Stoic pronouncement in logic, and misread it (following on Hipparchus' original, intentional misreading) as a pronouncement in mathematics.

Let us consider, then, the most celebrated case, which is not only the most we know of Chrysippus and medicine but in fact the most we know of Chrysippus *tout court*. As pointed out on page 393 above, through Galen's prolixity, and his sheer polemic viciousness, we have extant some-thing like the bulk of the second half of the first book of Chrysippus' "On

given scientific claim, relative to which we have the comparative *kreitton kai enargesteron*, but, rather, that we should remain silent simply when the matter requires scientific experience and cannot be settled based on the surpassingly manifest; Plato went wrong in his very wading into such territory, not just in arguing against, say, some Hippocratic position (where indeed, as Plutarch notes, he could easily find support for his views; in fact, almost certainly the view was *not* Plato's own). Incidentally, note once again the propositionalizing impulse in Chrysippus, here applied, in a critical mode, to Plato.

[222] When Chrysippus did get to the heart, he prefaced his discussion by explicitly stating his ignorance of anatomy (his actual contribution, as we will see, followed from Homer and was conceptual in character): Galen, *PHP* I.6.13.

the Soul", in which the Stoic philosopher did, in fact, argue for a thesis concerning the human body: that the heart is the location of the mind. Why did he go there at all? Should this not have been best avoided? Indeed, Chrysippus did not so much come to the debate concerning the location of the mind, as he got, in Sedley's apt phrase, stranded there like "religious zealots defending the Genesis account".[223] In a passage whose naïveté rivals that of his account of eclipses, Zeno proved that the seat of the mind was near the heart, since speech travels through the windpipe.[224] Hence, Stoics would be stuck with this particular piece of medicine. Now, our evidence for Zeno's passage derives – where else? – from Galen, *PHP* II.241. This in turn derives from Chrysippus, and the entire passage in which Galen picks up the treatment of this passage, and its later Stoic restatements by Chrysippus, and then picks it apart, going through its methodological and medical deficiencies, is extensive – II.240–58. It is also glaring for its uniqueness. There is no other physiological Stoic argument dissected through *PHP*. All we find, implied for Chrysippus' intervention, are: a methodological comment in line with that cited by Plutarch (*PHP* I.143); a couple of observations of disagreement among medical authors, one referring explicitly to Praxagoras (*PHP* III.253, I.145); and, finally, a cogent but purely epistemological observation: the claim of a relation between the head and the mind is granted, but still this is logically consistent with the governing part being in the heart (*PHP* II.254–5). The cavalier treatment of physiological doctrines as mere hypotheticals is telling: Chrysippus never engages, in fact, with medicine. There is nothing here remotely resembling Aristotle's creative problem solving, and, instead, a turn away from medical argumentation. And, so, the entirety of the reminder of Galen's attack on Chrysippus is dedicated to Chrysippus' attempt to extract the location of the mind from the endoxic, in which context we find Chrysippus' huge accumulation of especially Homeric quotations (see pages 396–7 above).

Tieleman[225] further refers to *PHP* II.196–7, which I quote from De Lacy's translation (1981: 125–7):

> For the present it is enough for me only to make this further statement, that if speech were produced when pneuma in the lungs is somehow shaped by the heart's pneuma and then imparts this shape to the pneuma in the windpipe, speech would not immediately be destroyed when certain nerves have been cut in the neck or head.

---

[223] Sedley (1998: 69).    [224] Sedley (1998: 68–70); Hankinson (1991: 214–15).
[225] I refer to Tieleman (1996: 189–95), a compelling overview that informs my summary of medicine in Chrysippus.

Tieleman cautiously notes (1996: 194) that this is unlike the verbatim passages, and that "we should not make too much of this single sentence", but, if anything is to be made, it should be as an argument from silence: why should Galen not quote and dissect in detail such an argument, providing a positive Stoic physiology, had he had such an argument available to him in his source? He surely would not have flinched from such a refutation, and, indeed, the discussion of Zeno's argument concerning the windpipe occupies Galen extensively. And why not attribute and cite this claim properly, in this explicit context of the *PHP*? The likely conclusion, then, is that *PHP* II.196–7 is not some unattributed piece of Stoic doctrine but, instead, is precisely Galen's own attempt to construct, on his own, the view the Stoics would have held, had their doctrine assumed the shape of an explicit *physiological claim susceptible to anatomical testing by experiment*. The negative impression, from *PHP* taken as a whole, is that the closest the Stoics ever came to such explicit physiology was Zeno's argument concerning the windpipe. Ever since then, it was all logic, epistemology, ethnography, Homer.[226] To borrow Hankinson's understatement (2003: 309), "Some philosophers paid less attention than they usefully might have done to the staggering advances in medical knowledge taking place at the time."

Now, surely, the animating principle of Stoic physics was the combination of strict materialism with the pervasive, active presence of God. This was expressed, at least since Chrysippus onwards, in the language of pneuma or breath (everything is matter, which is sustained, however, by a particularly fine form of matter, *pneuma*, which organizes it and so allows rational principles to structure mere matter). Thus, the Stoics ended up with this term, *pneuma*, of a medical resonance, as a cornerstone of their philosophy. Indeed, medical authors held specific, and distinct, views on pneuma, which came to be seen as allowing various, specialized forms (not only one "breath" but a variety of fine matters). Most famously, Erasistratus developed a theory that the arteries carried not blood, but pneuma.[227] All this, to return to Hankinson's judgement, "is of only limited relevance to the Stoics' pneuma",[228] which did not respond to any of the specific medical theories

---

[226] In this I differ from Tieleman, who sums up Chrysippus' project in "On the Soul" as an attempt to produce a persuasive argument based on "common notions, popular parlance, science and poetry" (1996: 288). Chrysippus did indeed rely on common notions, popular parlance and poetry, but he mentioned science only to the extent required for the setting up of a *cordon sanitaire* surrounding the philosophical discourse and preventing the need for any further scientific mentions.

[227] Garofalo fr. 109; for Herophilus on pneuma, see especially von Staden (1989: 252–67). An overview on Hellenistic medicine and the soul is Annas (1994: chap. 1).

[228] Hankinson (2003: 300).

of the era and was, rather, a philosophical extension of the lay notion of "breath": the untroubled usage of the term "pneuma" once again suggests, if anything, the lack of concern regarding the potential medical ramifications of one's philosophy. (Much later, in the Roman era, a medical sect known as "pneumaticists" would carry an obvious Stoic imprint; we shall return to this later synthesis on page 464 below.)

Of course, there were stray comments in the Chrysippean corpus regarding pretty much anything. He noted, for instance, that "even the beasts have been endowed with *oikeiosis* for their offspring, commensurate with the need, to the exclusion of fish, as their spawn is nourished by itself".[229] The quote is from *On Justice*: a note made in passing, no more committing Chrysippus to a particular biological doctrine than his "hundred myriad" committed him to a particular combinatoric doctrine. Or, during a conceptual discussion on types of mixtures, medical drugs (apparently, considered at this level of generality, of "medical drugs" as such) are thrown in as an example;[230] this implies no actual discussion of pharmacology – or, indeed, anything beyond lay experience. Or Chrysippus' comment from *On Ancient Physics* (that is, a treatise dedicated to the extraction of truth on nature from archaic literature), preserved as a Homeric scholion: women give birth with ease on nights of full moon, not so on moonless nights (*SVF* II.748). This is not scientific obstetrics; this is Chrysippus reconciling popular lore with Homeric sentiments regarding Artemis. In Diogenes Laertius' survey of Stoic physics we find, indeed, nothing that can count as medicine (other than obviously philosophically motivated theories regarding, say, the nature of the soul, or of perception) – until the very end, when we come upon a theory of the sperm.[231] A more general connection between sperm and (of course) pneuma is ascribed to Chrysippus; a much more specific theory – that the sperm is pangenetic, only the male is generative – is attributed to Sphaerus. Here, finally, we come across a Stoic pronouncing on a matter which would call, so one would think, for "scientific experience and research". Is it a mere coincidence, then, that this is nearly the only piece of doctrine we can now associate with Sphaerus? That it is, in fact, the only doctrine, in Diogenes Laertius' summary which he assigns to Sphaerus? One almost concludes that Sphaerus stood out, among the early Stoa, in engaging directly with medical speculation (was Chrysippus rebuking him, then?). And is it a coincidence, then, that Sphaerus is also the only early Stoic philosopher known to have been active in Alexandria?

[229] Plutarch, *De Stoic. Repug.* 1038b.    [230] *SVF* II.473, 154.17.    [231] Diogenes Laertius VII.159.

### 4.4.3   *The Stoa and the Mixed Exact Sciences*

The Stoa's engagement with the exact sciences began badly enough – to the extent that it did[232] – with Cleanthes' attack on Aristarchus. The clearest piece of evidence is from Plutarch: *On the Face in the Moon*. Lucius, speaking for the Academy, had just reported, rather disrespectfully, the Stoic doctrine according to which the Moon combines fire and air (the detailed texture of the combination accounts for the face in the Moon), a report to which Pharnaces the Stoic objected with some vehemence. Thereupon (923A)[233] "Lucius laughed and said: 'Oh, sir, just don't bring suit against us for impiety as Cleanthes thought the Greeks ought to lay an action for impiety against Aristarchus the Samian on the ground that he was putting in motion the hearth of the universe because he sought to save phenomena by assuming that the heaven is at rest while the earth is revolving along the ecliptic and at the same time is rotating about its own axis.'"[234]

---

[232]  I wish to add this qualification, since I find a key piece of evidence problematic. We know about Cleanthes and Aristarchus through (1) a passage in Plutarch, to which I turn below, and (2) an entry in Diogenes Laertius' list of titles, *pros aristarchon* (DL VII. 174). Now, the entry immediately following is *pros hērillon*, and this sets one mind's working: two of the main polemic exchanges Cleanthes was engaged in were with (1) Ariston of Chios (e.g. Schofield, 1984) and with (2) Herillus. It is perfectly plausible, then, that Cleanthes could have authored a *pros aristōna*. So, what would a sophisticated reader, aware of some version of Plutarch's anecdote but no longer familiar with the early disputes of the Stoa, make of a title such as that? Would he not be tempted to read automatically *pros aristarchon* instead? I know that such gratuitous emendations are abhorrent to many contemporary classicists, and, indeed, I would never recommend changing the text. But in fact Diogenes' text is replete with such errors (we noted a very similar case from I.16 in n.111 above: the more familiar Xenophanes substituted for the somewhat more obscure Xenocrates). The doubt, I think, is real, and should at the very least temper our willingness to draw any conclusions from the title.

[233]  Helmbold's translation, 1957.

[234]  Russo and Medaglia (1996) raise a number of good points, forgotten by the literature: that it is not entirely clear how the example of Cleanthes' attack against Aristarchus is meant to be relevant here; that there is no obvious reason for a Stoic to object to a theory that elevates the Sun (Cleanthes' ruler!); that, indeed, the text relies on an emendation. Their ultimate solution – that in fact Aristarchus attacked Cleanthes and not vice versa – is, I find, textually untenable (the text does read Aristarchus in the nominative, Cleanthes in the accusative; Plutarch's text as standardly restored is appropriately elegant and involved, however, in a way that makes such an error easy to account for; while Russo and Medaglia's suggested alternative requires the assumption of other, somewhat less persuasive corruptions, and ends up with a text which is considerably less elegant and, frankly, makes little sense. In particular, it is natural and expected that, when Aristarchus is first introduced into a work by Plutarch, he should be qualified as "of Samos": to distinguish him from his far more famous namesake, antiquity's greatest grammarian.). The relevance of Lucius' reference is clear enough: do not attack me with the vehemence with which Stoics are known to have attacked, when the issue had to do with astronomy. And, finally, Russo and Medaglia are absolutely right that Stoicism could easily accommodate heliocentrism. But Cleanthes would fiercely object to anything that denied views explicitly expressed by Zeno – which surely encompassed geocentrism.

First of all, note that the passage from "because he sought. . ." onwards is in the spirit – permeating the dialogue as a whole – of throwing about playful erudition, over and above what is immediately required; it is quite likely, then, Plutarch's own addition to what he found in his sources concerning Stoic physics, representing his own understanding (surely a valid one) of whatever he remembered, or quoted, from some source independent of the subject of the conversation at hand.[235] What he cited, or remembered, should have looked as follows:

> Cleanthes thought the Greeks ought to lay an action for impiety against Aristarchus the Samian on the ground that he was putting in motion the hearth of the universe.[236]

Now, in general, as noted on pages 165–7 above, our evidence for ancient authors is littered with chreiai – those passages of the author-in-action, the canon made flesh; a brief verbal performance summing up the very idea of the cultural figure as such, striking out against some other figure. Cleanthes was quite prone to generate such chreiai: von Arnim did not bother with a separate heading for Chrysippus' apophthegms (of which there are but a few; I count five in Diogenes Laertius); Zeno has 332 *SVF* entries, of which 56 are apophthegms; Cleanthes has 157 SVF entries, of which 23 are apophthegms – almost the same ratio as his much more famous master. In short, then, I find it very likely that Plutarch is reflecting an apophthegm of which only the end – the comeback – is preserved by his report, which, in rough structure, went as follows:

> [When asked what he thought of Aristarchus' doctrine], he said that the Greeks ought to lay an action for impiety against him, as he was putting in motion the hearth of the universe.

An apophthegm works through surprise: you thought the speaker should have remained speechless; and yet he manages to come back with a

---

[235] Bénatouïl (2005b), who offers the best treatment of the context of this episode (emphasizing, for instance, that Cleanthes could have seen in Aristarchus' a representative of *Strato's* position), errs, I think, in putting too much weight on this passage. He suggests that Cleanthes could have objected to the hypothetical character of Aristarchus' model (2005: 216–17): this is possible, but the sole directly relevant evidence is the words "sought to save phenomena", which Plutarch could be adducing, as I suggest, from a source different from that with which he takes his Cleanthes anecdote. I add finally an observation due to Görgemanns (1970: 95–6): that Lucius' emphasis on Aristarchus' "saving phenomena" was intended to stress that Aristarchus' actual project rendered Cleanthes' criticism moot (Aristarchus never intended this as *more* than a hypothesis) – adding to the sharpness of Lucius' snark. *Cleanthes did not get it.*

[236] That the "hearth" in question refers to the Earth, not the Sun (surprising for us, as the Sun is more fiery – right?) is a traditional Greek identification; see the discussion in Bénatouïl (2005: 211–12).

vengeance. Here, Cleanthes is supposed to be impressed, or annoyed, by Aristarchus' model (perhaps even to like it: it is, at first blush, more favorable to the *Sun*, after all, so powerfully championed by Cleanthes). Cleanthes is then surprising and ruthless in his response: the theory is to be brushed off entirely, as being a non-starter *for religious reasons*.

The sentiment itself is reasonably Stoic – indeed, as suggested above, specifically Cleanthic. The Stoic interest in the cosmos was based on its divine character (just as that of the Epicureans was based on their denial of such a character). Cleanthes specifically considered the Sun as the ruler of the cosmos (Chrysippus after him, as well as Posidonius, assigned this role to the *ouranos*, which I take to be the sphere of the fixed stars: DL 139; prudently, it would appear, as the position of the fixed stars is not in contention). Thus the Sun, for him, would be in some sense the ultimate divine. Cleanthes would have to develop an account within which Zeno's cosmological model was the only one appropriate given the divinity of the Sun; hence, any critique of such a model would be, for Cleanthes, a critique of the true theology of the stars – which is wittily expressed in the chreia as an observation concerning the attribution of motion to the Earth.

Whoever put together the story cited by Plutarch did a creditable job: it is a good summary of the kind of response Cleanthes could have produced to Aristarchus' heliocentrism. If indeed this story was invented to distill a treatise "Against Aristarchus" by Cleanthes, we gain genuine historical insight: Cleanthes had in fact produced a treatise that responded to Aristarchus rather in the manner in which Chrysippus responded to Herophilus and Erasistratus, above all so as to defend Zeno, and perhaps not so much through detailed astronomical critique as through theological objections (likely, in fact, relying upon myth and upon archaic literature). Then again, perhaps there was no "Against Aristarchus", or perhaps the story was invented with scant knowledge of the contents of such a work; in which case, we learn that Cleanthes may, or may not, have responded to Aristarchus in historical fact. Either way, it remains clear that Stoic responses to contemporary astronomy were distant and dismissive, relying, in all probability, on no concrete scientific content beyond those of Zeno's dicta that one set out to defend.

The role of actual physical science for the Stoa was in fact qualified for good philosophical reasons. That the universe displays rational order is the underlying assumption of the Stoa's basic requirement, of life consistent with nature. The animating principle of the world's rationality is not grounded in any particular scientific theory, however, but, rather, in the

principle of a living, divine presence.[237] Hence, for the early Stoics, the
sense of the world as a rational *cosmos* was predicated not upon one's proper
understanding of Eudoxus' "Astronomy", or of Archytas' "Harmonics",[238]

---

[237] For a survey of the foundations of Stoic theology, see Meijer (2007); within this rich field, a key
passage is Cleanthes' fragment *SVF* I.528 (Cicero, *De Nat. Deor.* II.13–15): four causes bring the gods
to our mind: foreknowledge; the fitness of the Earth for human life; terrifying natural phenomena;
and the order and beauty of the universe. The last one must be compared with *SVF* III.1009
(perhaps reflecting later sources, but, once again, a long and detailed passage), in which the beauty
of the cosmos is referred not only to its regularity but also to its colors, for instance, or size. The
fundamental point in all of this is that the religious impulse towards the universe is not inferred by
the Stoics from some kind of scientific observation; rather, it is the starting point to their entire
endeavor.

[238] Here I flatly deny an argument put forward by no less than A. A. Long. This, then, is to be a long
footnote. In his article "The Harmonics of Stoic Virtue" (Long, 1991; collected in Long, 1996b:
chap. 9), Long argues that the Stoa's notion of correct ethical life was that of acting harmoniously,
the sense of harmony emerging from a Pythagorean understanding of the musical scale. Three key
pieces of evidence are adduced. (1) Stobaeus, who quoted Zeno's definition of the End in the briefer
version "living consistently", and added an explanation, namely "living in accordance with a single
and concordant rationale [or ratio: *logos*] – since those who live in conflict are unhappy" (*SVF*
I.179). This *heis kai sumphōnos logos* undoubtedly resonates with Pythagorean music theory. None
of our other sources to the Stoic End (Cicero, Philo, Diogenes Laertius) ever reflect any such gloss,
however. Clearly, Stobaeus depends on a later historiographical tradition, as he continues immediately to the well-known discussion on the reason why "consistently" was expanded to "consistently with nature", and on later Stoic definitions of the End, all the way down to Antipater; the
prudent assumption is that this gloss comes from this kind of historiographical context, and does
not antedate Posidonius. (2) Ariston said, in a striking turn of phrase, that it is hard to struggle
against "the whole tetrachord: pleasure, distress, fear, desire" (*SVF* I.370; incidentally, I am not sure
why it is taken for granted this is Ariston of Chios and not his peripatetic namesake). "Tetrachord"
here has the meaning probably of "many things that, taken together, are even more powerful than
each taken on its own"; it certainly does not have the meaning of "a well-tuned thing", as it refers,
after all, to negative affections. The only reason to take this as evidence for harmony as a model of
correct ethical conduct is if one assumes that the only reason Ariston could have had for picking up
this metaphor was as an inversion of a standard, positive use of "tetrachord". I see no reason for that
assumption. (3) There is a definite Stoic doctrine – this is by far Long's stronger point – according
to which virtuous actions must be perfectly virtuous in all their parts, which is sometimes expanded
as "containing all the numbers" (the various passages, from Cicero, Seneca, Marcus Aurelius,
Diogenes Laertius and Stobaeus, are in Long 1996b: 210–12). In Diogenes Laertius VII.100 this is
specifically presented as a theory of the *kalon*, the noble, defined as "having all the numbers required
by nature, or being perfectly symmetrical". This finally is expanded and assigned to Chrysippus
himself by Galen, *PHP* V.425–8, as an overall theory of analogy in which bodily beauty and health,
as well as the soul's nobility, are all correlated to each other, each separately understood in terms of
numbers and of measurements. Finally, this passage refers to Polyclitus (*PHP* V.426), and, as Long
admits, the reference likely goes back to Chrysippus himself. Now, Polyclitus famously asserted
that the "well-made" (*eu*) comes about from many numbers, and this was understood by our source
(and Chrysippus' contemporary) Philo of Byzantion (Marsden, 1971: 106, 50.4–12) as follows: that
one must be precise in everything or else the "well-made" is lost – i.e. exactly the ethical point
Chrysippus wishes to make here. The natural interpretation, then, is that the Stoic doctrine of the
requirement of ethical perfection referred sometimes to "all the numbers", with Polyclitus in mind.
Such indeed was the interpretation put forward in Dyroff (1897: 352–4), and Long tries to resist this
(1996b: 221–3) by arguing that (i) Polyclitus refers to "many numbers", not "all numbers" (but Philo
of Byzantion, at least, understood "many numbers" to mean exactly what Long wishes to get out of
"all numbers"; while a TLG search of extant musical authors fails to yield references to "all

but upon one's proper understanding of Homer's *Iliad* (as embodying, that is, archaic and true knowledge of the divine). Little need to engage with the exact sciences, then.

Once again, the negative evidence is not trivial. Strabo, a proud Stoic, refers extensively (if mostly polemically) to past authorities, especially in the first two books dedicated to theoretical geography, as well as to some features of astronomy related to this endeavor. Some of those past authorities were indeed related to the philosophical schools, in varying ways: these are Dicaearchus (from the early generation of the Peripatos), Eratosthenes (that renegade Athenian-become-Alexandrian) and Posidonius – finally, a Stoic of a later generation (to whom I shall return in section 4.5.1 below). Strabo repeatedly criticizes Posidonius, so he is not averse to criticizing fellow Stoics; and he would surely have been

numbers" in the sense required by Long. There is a reason why Long himself (1991: 109) could adduce only a musical passage referring to "all the ratios" (Aristides Quintilianus I.22) and not to "all the numbers": music theory engaged with ratios such as the hemiolic (half-as-much-again) or the epitritic (a-third-as-much-again), which were not numbers; Polyclitus, who started from a given module, actually had his statue constructed from numbers – the essential point being that, for the Greeks, fractions were not numbers), and (ii) Polyclitus referred to *summetria*, while the Stoa referred to *sumphōnia*, so they must have had in mind a musical, not a visual, metaphor – which I think hits the wrong note in more than one way: (1) The Stoics use both, and both not too often (*summetros* in the relevant sense occurs four or five times: *SVF* III.83, 87, 462 = *PHP* IV.340, and perhaps 489; all aside from the long *PHP* passage referring explicitly to Polyclitus; relevant references to *sumphōnos* are seven, in *SVF* III.4, 69, 87, 144, 262, 264, 293 [I ignore *SVF* III.392, whose musical language is clearly due to Philo himself] – hardly a meaningful difference; but the key point is that when *sumphōnos* is used instead of *summetros* this is because it carries a different meaning, not because it carries a different metaphorical field of associations: *sumphōnos*, but not *summetros*, has the specific meaning of "being in friendly agreement" which, unsurprisingly, is a meaning sometimes required by the Stoa). Long of course admits the speculative nature of his interpretation, and one could argue that I merely point out that the links in the chain are each weak – but surely the chain taken as a whole is stronger? But what I argue is that each of the pieces of evidence provided by Long weakly argues, if anything, against the presence of music as a central metaphor among the early Stoics. Zeno's definition of the End could naturally be expressed with musical terms; Zeno avoided them. Ariston's fragment, if it is relevant at all, suggests that "tetrachord" was not entrenched as a reference to a "well-tuned thing". And the references to "all the numbers" show that, when they did consider proportion and order, Stoic authors as early as Chrysippus paid attention to Polyclitus at least as much as they did to music. I suggest that Long was wrong. How come? I think his underlying thought must have been as follows. Clearly, order and rationality matter enormously to the Stoa. And, no less clearly, the Greek theory of harmonics provides a supreme example of rational order. Hence, it would be surprising if the Stoa did not appeal to music theory as a central model. In light of this basic assumption, even weak arguments seem to gain force, as they reflect what is otherwise a likely enough result. Taken in this way, Long's argument is indeed persuasive. But the shoe is on the other foot: it would indeed be surprising if the early Stoa appeared not to pick up harmonics as a central model – and, therefore, the fact that our evidence does not suggest that it did is, indeed, surprising. But we should confront this surprise so as to not lose sight of the truth towards which it points: the early Stoa, it appears, was marked by a surprising distance from science – even from the kind of science that could best have supported its basic tenets.

happy to cite an agreement with other Stoic authorities. He never does: this makes it likely that, even if early Stoics did make any geographical pronouncements, these were not of a systematic, scientific character.[239] But, then again, this would be the kind of matter that requires scientific experience and research. . .

I can trace the following pieces of doctrine, related to the exact sciences, associated expressly with Stoic authors earlier than Posidonius (but ignoring purely cosmological or meteorological doctrines, such as those related to void, or to fire).

(1) Cleanthes claimed (*SVF* I.506) that the shape of the Moon was cap-like (*piloeidēs*), (*SVF* I.507) the stars cone-like (*kōnoeidēs*). I can only guess he imagined the stars and the Moon to be somewhat under the influence of the Sun. Whatever is behind this theory, it is designed from cosmological speculation, not geometrical astronomy.[240]

(2) Chrysippus assented to a standard, basic cosmology with a spherical Sun (*SVF* II.652: and so presumably also all the other bodies), circular motion in the heavens, and motions towards and away from the center in the sublunary realm (*SVF* II.527). (He also repeated Zeno's account of eclipses, *SVF* II.678, and assented, in *SVF* II.693, to a model of the passage of the year that, if anything, antedates geographical astronomy: summer, for instance, is when the Sun heats the most! To be fair, the entire ascription of this detailed account to Chrysippus rests on an interpretation of a lacuna in Stobaeus.)

(3) He also provided the basic account of the terms "rising" and "setting" in the course of his *physical art* (*SVF* II.683).

(4) Finally, he had an optical theory where sight is cone-like, its base on the object seen (*SVF* II. 866–7. This theory further elaborated, in the usual Stoic manner, on the material constituents of such sight and its relation to the soul's pneuma).

---

[239] So, Geminus, *Elements of Astronomy* 16.21: some of the "ancients" (among whom Cleanthes is named) claimed that the tropics were occupied by the ocean. This is followed by the observation that Crates, in his Homeric geography, shared the same view and produced it in his globe. Strabo does criticize Crates at length, so why not Cleanthes? But, then again, Geminus, too, expands in much greater detail on Crates and merely cites Cleanthes briefly. It is quite possible, then, that Cleanthes' geographical claim was an isolated comment made in passing, in the pre-scientific manner of the "ancients", a piece of cosmology rather than geography – unlike Crates' claim, inscribed within a treatise of largely geographical subject matter (the *Wanderings of Odysseus*) and entrenched in a globe (for Crates' globe, see Bilić, 2012).

[240] Russo's attempt (2004 [1996]: 257–8) to connect this with modern reflections on the slightly non-spherical shapes of heavenly bodies is, of course, hopelessly anachronistic.

We see in Stoic philosophy an inordinate capacity for cosmological elaboration, the basic doctrines of divinity, materialism and continuity brought
to surprising conclusions, together with a complete avoidance of any piece
of doctrine related to the exact sciences, other than those which are
perfectly non-controversial (or were enshrined already in Zeno's model).

This is not to say that the elaborations of doctrine are meaningless. They
are indeed quite subtle. So let me turn to this, the chief glory of Stoic
physics (DL VII.158):

> We hear when the air between the sonant body and the organ of hearing
> suffers concussion, a vibration which spreads spherically and then forms
> waves and strikes upon the ears.[241]

We are struck by this doctrine, above all for its non-trivial scientific truth.
If we assume, however, that this is indeed the gist of the Stoic theory of
hearing (and that it is by Chrysippus), we find that it marks, in the Greek
context, a turning *away* from the available scientific debate. The problem
structure for the Greek science of acoustics can be described as follows: a
preliminary question arising from the fact of pitch – (1) what is the physical
reality underlying the quality of "high" and "low" pitch? And then the
central question: (2) what explains the observation that certain pitch
combinations, but not others, harmonize?[242] In short, we once again
come across a possible argument from silence: could it be that the Stoa
did not contribute anything to this research program? An argument from
silence – but perhaps not an entirely meaningless one, for, after all, our
ancient doxographies could well have been interested in reporting Stoic
views on pitch and harmony. On the other hand, it is easy to see how the
reported Stoic discussion of sound does emerge, from specifically Stoic
concerns. As Løkke (2008: 42) points out, the doxography in Diogenes
Laertius is an account not of sound but of hearing: it belongs to the
philosophy of mind. The Stoic account of hearing, in this doxography,
follows directly on the account of vision (which appears to have been – as is
so often the case in such philosophies of mind – the one paradigmatic case
on which any significant attention was expended). Vision was explained in
terms of a stretching through the air, because what mattered to the Stoics

---

[241] There is only one more piece of evidence, Ps.-Plutarch, *Plac.* IV.19.4, a brief doxography that cites
the Stoic view on sound; here the emphasis is on how transmission of sound works in the absence of
void (the implication is that it is straightforward to understand transmission in terms of actual
bodies in motion, but that this assumes that there is a void through which those bodies might move:
hence, a continuum forces some kind of "wave" account).

[242] This statement of ancient harmonic theory is not meant to be controversial. For an overview of the
scientific research program, see Barker (2007) and Creese (2010).

was the necessity, simultaneously, of materialism and continuity. (Descartes would be forced upon his own wave-like theory of vision, based on the same logic.)[243] Chrysippus in all probability produced his lectures through massive amplification, more and more examples and parallels added throughout. Obviously, then, he would provide an account of hearing parallel to that of vision, and made the explicit claim that hearing was based not on particles, moving through void, but on the air itself as a medium, set in motion as a whole.

If such indeed was Stoic acoustic theory, then it amounted to no more than a minimal statement of the manner in which hearing is possible, in a universe assumed to be material and continuous. That is, Stoic acoustics amounted to no more than a *conceptual, negative* observation based on cosmological first principles. This minimalistic interpretation can in fact be supported by one of our more sustained pieces of evidence for the relatively early Stoa. Very substantial fragments of Philodemus' *On Music* are extant, and the bulk of Book IV is dedicated to a polemic against the treatise on the same subject by Diogenes of Babylon (Chrysippus' pupil, and heir as scholarch). This is extensively reported across more than 50 columns, and then refuted along some hundred more, all of it now meticulously edited in Delattre (2007). We stand here on a ground almost comparable to that which Galen provides us for Chrysippus on the soul.

What we find, then, is amazingly little. A very strong emphasis on traditional views on music's ethical impact, a tradition that clearly precedes even Plato himself;[244] comparisons between the study of music and that of poetry; an attention – what else, from a Stoic author? – to traditional forms of music. The most "scientific" moment is when Diogenes grants that harmonics contains many "definitions, divisions and demonstrations" (col. 48.23–5), but, then again, he never finds it important to detail any. Barker concludes that Diogenes represented a tradition separate from either the Aristoxenian or the Pythagorean, and contrasts this with Philodemus (Barker, 2001: 369–70):

---

[243] See, e.g., Smith (1987: 13–19). The point is not to claim any Stoic influence on Descartes (see, however, Barker and Goldstein, 1984) but, rather, to emphasize that the very terms of the question would make a superb logical mind – whether that of Descartes or of Chrysippus – hit upon the same broad metaphysical account (the difference being, of course, that, in Descartes' time, this logical argument interacted with a living *scientific* research program).

[244] Woodward (2009) ends up emphasizing precisely this traditionality of Diogenes, emerging with clearer finality, now that Delattre's edition is available.

> Philodemus. . . [recruits Aristoxenus] as an authority. . . What it makes clear
> is that Philodemus, writing in Italy in the first century BC, could assume
> that his readers would recognize Aristoxenus without question as the fore-
> most authority in musical matters. . . [T]he context of Diogenes' work was
> evidently quite different in that respect.

Barker continues cautiously: perhaps this is because Aristoxenus' authority
was not established, for Diogenes (he does write during a bad patch for the
reception of peripatetic science); perhaps the Stoa had doctrinal reasons to
avoid that authority. But the point seems to me rather different, and in line
with what we see throughout regarding the early Stoa: a tendency to avoid a
reliance on particular scientific doctrine and the treatment, instead, of
matters of scientific concern through a more distant, conceptual prism, the
one that goes back to early philosophical speculation.

Perhaps the following comparison would be useful. I have mentioned
above Sambursky (1959), a book titled *Physics of the Stoics*. It is useful to
set this side by side with Mates' (1950) book, *Stoic Logic*. The two
contributions are nearly contemporary, and also similar in broad outline.
Mates shows how one could make better sense of the attested logical
theories of the Stoa by comparing them with logical achievements of the
late nineteenth century. Sambursky sets out to recover a Stoic physics
based on force fields, a physics suggestive of modern ethers and waves.
There the similarity ends. Mates (1950) can be said to be the foundation
of the contemporary scholarly practice of studying Stoic logic: articles
published on the subject today regularly formalize terms and arguments
with the symbolism of contemporary logic and take it for granted that
Chrysippus developed a "propositional logic" different in detail but
similar in character to that taught today.[245] Sambursky's 1959 contribution, on the other hand, is now rarely used by scholars of ancient science
and philosophy,[246] and, if it is cited today, it is mostly by studies of later
science, looking at the potential of a Stoic influence on early modern
scientists.[247]

---

[245] For a distinguished example, consider Bobzien (1996): Stoic logic – asserted to be specifically rather
like contemporary *relevance* logic.
[246] This is not to say that Sambursky is explicitly repudiated anywhere (see n.160 above: his anachronism was seen as mostly innocuous for his immediate readers in the 1950s, and more recent
scholarship simply does not engage directly with his precise problematic). Even an enthusiastic
proponent of Hellenistic science such as Russo – never shy of anachronism – does not try to make
much out of the Stoic field of forces. When he does mention Sambursky – e.g. Russo (2004 [1996]:
202) – this is to criticize him for not admitting the ancient "genuine" physics!
[247] So, for instance, Barker (2008): the crucial insight is that the Stoa could provide a respectably
ancient alternative to *Aristotle*.

In the tradition of Sarton or Koyré, both Mates and Sambursky look for a history of ideas in which humanity gradually reveals new conceptual possibilities, with little attention paid to institutions of learning, even less to genres of writing. From such a perspective, it makes sense to look for the conceptual field of ideas concerning body and space and extract them away from the contexts of practice and writing in which they were originally produced. From other perspectives, of course, such an exercise seems historically misleading, and it is therefore a telling observation that Mates' project seems still so meaningful. This is because Chrysippus' practice and genre of logic were indeed directly comparable to those of modern logicians. In his logic, he developed an original tool, which he taught and set out in extensive writing. The emphasis was on the unit of the proposition; the writings proliferated with intensive attention to detail and precision. In short, a recognizable logician: perhaps, more so than any other ancient author. Mates gets that *right*.

But Chrysippus just was not a physicist, and Sambursky is, quite simply, *wrong*. The study of nature, in the "physics" section of his output, emerged not out of the project of setting out a physical theory of the universe but, rather, out of the project of responding to early and contemporary philosophical statements on nature, in ways that tended to support core Stoic doctrines (especially those enshrined in the few extant, relevant assertions by Zeno), everything created, once again, through the technique of proliferated writing produced through attention to detail and precision, once more centered around the proposition. Doctrinal claims were propositionalized, analyzed, refuted if non-Stoic, supported if deemed Stoic, all done at a purely conceptual level. The very conceptual nature of school philosophy in Athens made a science of logic possible and, at the same time, made a science of physics impossible.

### 4.4.4   Mathematical Notes

So much for physics, or, to put this less anachronistically, for the mixed exact sciences in the Stoa of the third century.[248]

---

[248] The following section moves away from my typical, more impressionistic, broad-brush treatment to something approaching the standard classicist article: "Chrysippus' Knowledge of Mathematics". I have no ready literature to quote on this, and so I have to provide my own. Generalist readers may of course skip this (Chrysippus is hard going at the best of times; and I discuss Chrysippus *and mathematics*). Specialist readers, please bear with me: this, indeed, is the crux of the argument for Hellenistic Athens' avoidance of Hellenistic Alexandria.

Otherwise, the period is marked above all by the achievements of pure mathematics – potentially, at least, more suitable for the conceptual filter of Hellenistic philosophy. It is tempting for historians of thought to posit such connections: with our fragmentary evidence, we reach for any source of insight, and so beckons the synchronic dimension: they were contemporary, so surely they were influenced by each other; surely one can be used to elucidate the other! In a series of studies, now over a century old, the great German papyrologist Wilhelm Crönert argues for the existence of an entire school of Epicurean mathematicians around the second century BCE (Crönert, 1900; 1907a; 1907b). These were Philonides, Protarchus and Basilides of Tyre (early second century), and Demetrius Lacon and Zeno of Sidon (late second century to early first century). The claim should have been seen as shocking, as, after all, Epicurus argued in very clear terms against the very practice of the exact sciences, but Crönert's philological prowess – new readings from the Herculaneum papyri, brought together with rarely noticed pieces of Hellenistic prosopography – was instantly compelling, and the fact of Epicurean mathematicians was taken for granted through the twentieth century. In fact, Crönert was almost certainly wrong. Key to his identification is the observation that Hypsicles, in his introduction to what is now known as *Elements* XIV, mentioned two contemporary mathematicians, Protarchus and Basilides; and that it was known that there was both an Epicurean Protarchus and an Epicurean Basilides active at the same time. In fact, Tepedino Guerra (1980) has revealed a more precise chronology for one of these Epicureans – Basilides – and as a consequence we now see that it is unlikely that the two Epicureans, Basilides and Protarchus, were in fact contemporary. This identification was probably mere coincidence.[249] Remaining are Philonides, mentioned as a geometer in an introduction to Apollonius' *Conics* II; the same as another Philonides, an Epicurean? (I have argued in Netz, 2017b – see there for references – that likely, not: the language of Apollonius' introduction, as well as other suggestive evidence, leads me to believe, instead, that the geometer mentioned there was the father of the Epicurean – so they do come close!) As for the remaining, later, examples of Demetrius Lacon and Zeno of Sidon, it has been always noted that their engagement with mathematics was almost certainly polemical (Vlastos, 1965; 1966, argues otherwise, in a claim rightly dismissed by more recent scholarship). I have argued in Netz (2015) – see this for more references –

---

[249] This argument was first made in Netz (2015), and the reader is directed there for more references (note my caution on p. 263 above, a passage I wrote originally before realizing crönert's mistake).

that they did not merely criticize geometry but, instead, tried to prove its impossibility – as an Epicurean should. In short, we find that, of course, there were no Epicurean mathematicians. (It remains intriguing to notice the renewed attention to mathematics – if polemically – among Epicureans at the end of the second century; I shall return to this below.)

But what about Stoic mathematicians? In fact, there is very little to go by for Chrysippus' *awareness*, even, of any mathematics, contemporary or otherwise. Only two passages are even remotely relevant.[250] I will take them in turn, in detail: the second, in particular, brings out an important contrast.

Our first piece of evidence is from Proclus's *In Euclidem* 395.13–18 (Morrow, 1992, slightly revised):

> Well then [*d'oun*], Chrysippus, so Geminus tells us, likened theorems of this sort to the Ideas. For just as these [the *Ideas*] embrace the generation of an indefinite number of particulars within definite limits, so also in these [i.e. theorems of this sort] an indefinite number of cases are comprehended within definite places.

To be clear: what we have here is a fragment (perhaps) from Geminus, including a testimony on Chrysippus.

The context is as follows. The fragment comes from Proclus' commentary to *Elements* I.35. This proposition asserts that "parallelograms which are on the same base and in the same parallels are equal to one another". Proclus first notes that such theorems are "locus theorems" and explains the concept, still familiar to us from contemporary mathematical usage (so: theorems identifying the set of geometrical objects satisfying a given property). Proclus then sets out a sophisticated account of locus theorems, complete with examples from conic sections. Following that, he proceeds to the passage above.

---

[250] Mansfeld (1983b: 66) mentions that "Cic., Fat. 15, in a Chrysippean context, quotes the theorem, 'the greatest circles in a sphere bisect one another'", as an argument for Chrysippus' positive knowledge of mathematics. In fact, however, the context in Cicero is a Chrysippean argument concerning the *logical structure* appropriate for stating claims of *divination*. In the argument mounted against Chrysippus, Cicero builds the reduction considering the extension of the same logical principle for statements from other arts, such as medicine or geometry. This critique clearly goes beyond the Chrysippean original, so that the passage can be used, if anything, negatively. (But note that, even for the paradigm statement taken for the case of divination (*Fat.* 12), "[i]f (for instance) a man was born at the rising of the dogstar, he will not die at sea", nothing in Cicero's language suggests this is from Chrysippus himself, and in fact the clear astrological significance suggests, if anything, that Cicero takes his own, more contemporary and therefore more vivid example of divination, instead of Chrysippus' likely pre-astrological example. Thus this passage likely has no bearing at all on the scientific examples used by Chrysippus.)

In a maximalist interpretation, this could have been read as Proclus finding in Geminus a very sophisticated Chrysippean awareness of advanced geometry, the statement "theorems of this sort" at the head of the fragment referring back to the sophisticated locus theorems mentioned in the preceding paragraph.[251] But this would probably be wrong, as can be seen even on grammatical grounds: the "well then", *d'oun*, introducing this passage, likely means here "back to our main subject", bracketing the preceding discussion of advanced locus theorems.[252] By "theorems of this sort" is meant not locus theorems in the sophisticated sense, then, but – going back to the lemma of Proclus' commentary – theorems for which *Elements* I.35 may be taken as an example.

A likely account for the origin of our passage, then, is that Proclus strung together two distinct comments on *Elements* I.35 ("used two sources", as scholars of a previous generation would have put it). One was mathematical (its author unknown: but perhaps Geminus, too?): it located I.35 within the context of locus theorems. The other, philosophical, was certainly from Geminus. The question then becomes: what was the philosophical point made by Geminus himself?

Now, what are the characteristics of *Elements* I.35 that Geminus would find relevant to Chrysippus' philosophical needs? This is explained well by Caston (1999: 199) (who follows Stephen Menn). In a theorem such as *Elements* I.35, the statement is clearly general, holding for an indefinite set of cases. We are not tempted to hypostatize the object of the theorem, however. There is no single object, the "parallelograms which are on the same base and in the same parallels". A single formula applies to an indefinite plurality of cases, without there being a corresponding single object over and above the many cases. This indeed corresponds well to Chrysippus' (broadly nominalist) understanding of universals.

And so, when Geminus states that Chrysippus likened "theorems of this sort" to the *Ideas*, this, if anything, suggests that the decision to tie Chrysippus' statement precisely to I.35 was made by Geminus himself. It

[251] So, Knorr (1986: 371 n.19): "The fact that a philosopher like the 3rd-century Stoic Chrysippus should find such a useful metaphor in the geometers' locus, while earlier philosophers do not mention it, suggests to me that this notion of locus was relatively recent in the 3rd century BC."
[252] For the particle, see Denniston (1950: 463–4). I note immediately that Proclus appears to return to the same topic of locus-theorems, in the paragraph following that on Chrysippus, in which he notes that this is the first locus-theorem in the *Elements* and is to be distinguished from others in Book III. But his train of thought is not: "Here is what I have to say on locus-theorems (a bracketed note on Chrysippus)." It is: "This theorem is a locus-theorem; also, there is a relevant note on it by Chrysippus, as reported by Geminus. Now, having made those two introductory remarks, let me move on to comment on the place of this proposition within Euclid's project."

was Geminus' observation that I.35 belonged to the class of theorems that could serve to illustrate Chrysippus' philosophical point. Indeed, it would be strange to have Chrysippus bringing in an example of the level of granularity of I.35, which is therefore best understood as Geminus' own contribution. Or, put more positively: a basic claim stated in the most general, conceptual terms would fit well with Chrysippus' practice as a whole.[253] That basic claim likely involved the nature of the generality of propositions. Its purpose would be to turn upside down a piece of Platonic ontology. Plato took mathematics as a key example for why one should assume the existence of universals answering to general claims. Chrysippus in response noted that even in mathematics no such assumptions of separately existing universals are required. As a result, of course, mathematics would therefore lose its paradigmatic ontological position. This example would show, then, not Chrysippus inspired by contemporary mathematics in his philosophy but, rather, Chrysippus explaining why Plato was wrong to pay so much attention to mathematics.

The account I propose, then, sees a gradual inflation of this passage. Chrysippus made a general claim concerning *theōrēmata*. Geminus noted that *Elements* I.35 fits this claim very well.[254] Proclus, finally, put this observation by Geminus into the context of a treatment of locus theorems in general (in this, he might have followed Geminus' lead already).

To be clear, the above is one possible, minimalist interpretation. I have produced some arguments against a more liberal reading of Proclus – as if Chrysippus was in fact actively engaged with the advanced mathematical

[253] To be precise, it is no more than a likelihood that Chrysippus' argument even mentioned *mathematics* specifically. What he did have to say would likely indeed refer to *theōrēmata*, but these do not at all entail mathematical "theorems" in Greek authors in general or in Chrysippus in particular. The word is hard to translate but it never loses its original sense of "object of contemplation", and so can mean, roughly, any unit of theoretical reflection. (So, a couple of Chrysippean titles refer to "theorems" in logic.) DL 175, a genuine Chrysippean fragment, is most suggestive when it says that "the *theōrēmata* of the virtues are common" – i.e. the same kind of theoretical knowledge required for making the correct decision in courage, or in prudence. But does this entail the existence of a super-virtue comprising all virtues, to which, directly, such *theōrēmata* apply? Could this, after all, be the context in which Chrysippus made his statement on the relationship between *Ideas* and general *theōrēmata*? I find this possible – in which case Geminus would be original in bringing to bear not just *Elements* I.35 but even mathematics as such.
[254] I ascribe to Geminus a certain creativity in his interpretation; effectively: "When Chrysippus asserts that *Ideas* are like *theōrēmata*, he has propositions such as *Elements* I.35 in mind." But this is absolutely benign by the standards of Posidonian reconstructions in the history of philosophy, for which see Ju (2013). In general, I repeatedly suggest that Roman-era sources for early Stoicism could take general claims concerning the sciences and fill them in with precise scientific examples. This is not my begging of the question; rather, it relies on the independent evidence – to which we will soon turn – that, indeed, in the Roman era and beyond, many philosophers did bring into their philosophy some detailed scientific knowledge.

concept of a "locus theorem" – but nothing I have said would make such a reading impossible. That I find such a liberal reading hard to believe is because, if it is assumed, such a case would be so isolated.[255]

To confirm this, we need to turn to the second relevant piece of evidence for Chrysippus and mathematics.

We are drawn back to Plutarch for yet another substantial polemic. We find ourselves in the midst of *On Common Conceptions*. The Stoa – so the dialogue starts – claims that Chrysippus was there as the academy of Arcesilaus – newly made skeptical – argued against the common conceptions of humanity. The Stoa, then, presented itself as – by the standards of the time – a "common sense" philosophy.[256] For an academic such as Plutarch it becomes important to respond, then, by demolishing any of Chrysippus' claims to common sense. He should be seen as counter-intuitive to the point of being unreasonable. Most of the ensuing discussion is in ethics, but some of it is physical (none logical), involving very broad questions in the constitution of matter. Typically, Plutarch finds fault with claims having to do with the nature of parts and of continuity, and it seems likely that this would emerge, in Chrysippus, in the context of his polemic against atomism, an active force in his contemporary Athens. Plutarch largely ignores this Epicurean context (would that muddy his basic dramatic setting, pitting the Stoa against the Academy?), but he does mention the specific polemic target of one of Chrysippus' arguments, perhaps because this target is a more distant source and so more interesting for a scholar such as Plutarch. This is Democritus.

The argument of Democritus with which Chrysippus took issue appears, in Plutarch's retelling, as a puzzle. This takes the cone (and perhaps also the pyramid) as an example[257] (1079E):

[255] Long and Sedley (1987) feel compelled to cite this passage, which they fit within their treatment of "continuum"; but then all they find to say about it is that it (I.50) "represents a very rare Stoic excursion into philosophy of mathematics". Their general verdict there – that "in the Hellenistic age philosophy and mathematics had become widely separated disciplines" – is the starting point for my exploration here.

[256] Plutarch's work is formally a dialogue, beginning with this pro-Chrysippean claim as a problem for a Platonist; this problem is hammered away through the progress of the dialogue. We note incidentally the ease with which an ancient philosopher such as Plutarch could read an Athens of three centuries earlier – as a living context of debate. We also note the validity of this starting point, as against Plutarch's eventual conclusion: within the terms of third-century Athens, the Stoa was the most "scientific" – such as it was – of the philosophies on offer.

[257] The example of the cone is ascribed by Plutarch explicitly to Democritus, in *Comm. Con.* 1079E. Immediately preceding that, Chrysippus' account of an analogous problem with the pyramid is very briefly mentioned in 1079D. It seems almost certain that Plutarch refers to a single discussion in Chrysippus, having to do with both cone and pyramid. Chrysippus (1) could have responded to a passage in Democritus in which only the cone was mentioned, and then added his own example of

> Look at the way in which he [Chrysippus] attacked Democritus, who had raised – in a concrete and vivid fashion – this difficulty: if a cone is cut by a plane parallel to the base, how should we conceive of the arising surfaces of the segments – equal or unequal? For if they are equal the cone is then uneven, possessing notches and rough points; but if they are unequal, the segments are equal and the cone would appear to have the property of a cylinder, composed of equal, and not of unequal circles.

Is this a fragment close to Democritus' own formulation? This is how this passage is usually taken, but only Sedley (2008) seems to have taken this assumption to its logical conclusion, namely that the dilemma is intended to be wrong on both its horns, so that the conclusion is that a cone cannot be cut parallel to its base, from which follows atomism. This seems too powerful, however (as this would be an argument for making anything an atom: Sedley embraces this and proposes that, effectively, the cone is just an example of a solid), and to ignore the context of Democritus' mathematical contributions concerning the cone and the pyramid. Since it is in fact very helpful for the geometrical reasoning of the kind Democritus was likely to assume to argue that cones are in fact indistinguishable from rectilinear solids, it is prima facie likely that Democritus did take the first horn of the dilemma as valid. This may be supported by 1080A, in which (according to one emendation of the text) Chrysippus mentioned the "rough edges he [Democritus] suspected to be around the cone". The arrangement of Democritus' argument as a two-horned dilemma suits well Chrysippus' purpose, however, as his own contribution would be precisely

the pyramid, or he (2) could have responded to a passage in Democritus having to do with both cone and pyramid. Now, (i) it is striking that the two examples on offer are precisely those of the cone and the pyramid, as Democritus is famously attested for having found the volumes of precisely those objects (Heiberg 1910 4.5, 1913 430.2, now revised in Netz et al., 2011: 297). Further (ii), there is a ready explanation why Plutarch should wish to dissociate the problem of the pyramid from Democritus. This is because the problem of the pyramid directly invokes the difficulty of comparing adjacent lines in a triangle. (When a triangular pyramid is cut parallel to its base, the resulting touching triangles at the cut are either equal or unequal, and so too are the touching sides of such triangles. Chrysippus explicitly asserted that such sides are neither equal nor unequal.) Plutarch later on, in 1080G, would present the impossibility of comparing the size of lengths as a key step in a reductio (if circles cannot be compared, neither can their circumference, so not lengths either; and, if lengths cannot be compared in size, neither can the other dimensions, hence neither can solid bodies) – which is presented as an absurd consequence of Chrysippus' resolution of Democritus' problem of the cone. This sense of a refutation by reductio would have been muted had the key statement been seen not as Plutarch's clever deduction but as a direct statement from Chrysippus. Putting (i) and (ii) together, I find option (2) above the likelier. There are two consequences. First, it then becomes likely that Democritus had produced a single treatise on the pyramid and the cone, containing both philosophical reflection as well as mathematical demonstration. This is an interesting comment on the state of the prose genres in the late fifth century BCE. Second, it looks as if Chrysippus did not introduce any mathematical examples of his own, taking the problems as presented in Democritus and then subjecting them to pure conceptual analysis.

that: both horns are wrong. We find that Plutarch could have been quite close to a Chrysippean source; and that Chrysippus' likely move was one of propositionalization (of course), in this case transforming an argument in Democritus into the terms of Chrysippus' propositional logic.

And still: the argument by Democritus does discuss explicitly the slicing of a three-dimensional object into its two-dimensional components. This is striking, if anachronistically, from the perspective of the third century. For then, works by Archimedes would take up this very theme. One – for which we do not have a title – was merely reported by Pappus;[258] the other is known through the Archimedes Palimpsest, and it is usually referred to as the *Method*:[259] we may refer to the two taken together as Archimedes' *Method*-like works. In the operations of the *Method*, one takes typically "all the circles" in, for instance, a cone, so that the comparison of two adjacent circles is not an issue at all.[260] There is nothing in Archimedes' approach to suggest how he would have gone about resolving Democritus' puzzle, and, given the epistemic caution with which the *Method* as such is presented, this mathematical tour de force is completely orthogonal to any philosophical position. The emphasis is, instead, on the tour de force itself: on the surprise of the results and the convoluted objects produced by Archimedes' new measurements; on the paradoxical bringing together of the mathematical and the physical (for Archimedes typically relies on the consideration of the separate planes as lying on a *balance*; in the case of the *Method*-like study of the spiral, he brings together, surprisingly, spirals and cones – objects which appear, at first glance, quite unrelated). The emphasis is on the sheer variety of the display and the very enigmatic character of the *Method*-like works. In Pappus, it is characterized as "amazing",[261] and such was probably Archimedes' intention: a clear example of ludic science.

No philosophy, then, in Archimedes. It should have provided grist to the philosophical mill, however. Here is rich material that goes well beyond Democritus' own cone, giving rise to significant puzzles in the metaphysics of the continuum. Our first observation, then, is that nothing in

---

[258] *Collection* IV.21–5; see Sefrin-Weis (2010: 230–6) and Netz (2017c: 181–6).

[259] For a popular account of this treatise and of its intriguing survival, see Netz and Noel (2007, esp. chaps. 6–8). Another usage of a similar technique is in Archimedes' *Quadrature of the Parabola*, propositions 1 to 18.

[260] Cones produced out of circles parallel to the base are ubiquitous, turning up in all the proofs offered in *Method* 2–9 (Heiberg's numbering: in fact, all the solid proofs aside from the two new results), as well as, possibly, in the passage preserved in Pappus' *Collection*. Archimedes seems to imply that underlying his entire project of measuring curvilinear solids is the idea of considering the cone as constituted of circles parallel to the base.

[261] *Thaumastē: Collection* IV.30 234.3.

Chrysippus' treatment seems to imply any recognition of such new developments.[262] His problematics seem to be constructed entirely out of the terms of Democritus' argument, mediated through the particular concerns of a Stoic philosophy.

To see this, let us now consider Chrysippus' solution. Plutarch's report on this (1079 F) is:

> He says that neither "the surfaces are equal" nor "are unequal", but that "the bodies are unequal", together with[263] "neither the surfaces are equal nor are unequal".

We note the propositionalization of the problem – veering from physics to logic. The main claim is clear enough: it is a *category error* to relate surfaces by "equal" or "unequal". This must mean that, according to Chrysippus' *conceptual* analysis, a relation such as "equal" properly holds only between bodies and does not hold between surfaces. So, as ever – the conceptual analysis of the elements of propositions.

Plutarch must have been especially attracted by the apparent koan-like absurdity of Chrysippus' assertion that "neither 'the surfaces are equal' nor 'are unequal'". Indeed, in this case, Plutarch's position was well founded. Plutarch's goal was to argue that Chrysippus was not an adherent of the common conceptions, and, indeed, on this ultimate ontological question, Chrysippus' metaphysics was not common-sensical at all: strict materialism (surprisingly) often ends up with deeply non-common-sensical consequences, as happens here. Our tiny fragments do not do justice to what was likely, in Chrysippus' lost writings, a rich and subtle analysis. But one thing seems clear: the emphasis of Chrysippus' account was on the unique ontological status of *bodies*, understood in a restricted way as three-dimensional, material objects, and radically different from objects of other dimensionality.

This emphasis is grounded, as usual, in the few metaphysical clues Stoics could find in Zeno's own writing. Zeno was a materialist in the vein of

---

[262] Everything from this point on depends on this (far from ironclad) argument from silence. Our evidence comes from a prolix, name-dropping, math-loving discussion by Plutarch. Would he really pass over a mention of Archimedes, had Chrysippus made one? Perhaps; my inclination is to assume he would not, and the argument rests on this inclination.

[263] The Greek τῷ in Plutarch seems to mean that the bodies being unequal is constituted by, or is a consequence from, the surfaces being neither equal nor unequal. This seems nonsensical, and is likely to be a misrepresentation by Plutarch or a textual corruption (both problems, frequent in this treatise). I take this τῷ to be, effectively, a conjunction, ultimately distilling the claim that there is no contradiction between (1) surfaces being neither equal nor unequal and (2) the associated bodies being equal or unequal.

fifth-century Ionic philosophy, delineating a cosmology in which (positively) fire is all-permeating while (negatively) nothing calls for explanation
in extra-bodily terms: striking against both Plato and Epicurus, deliberately archaizing. And so: it's all bodies, all permeated by fire. It is the need
to flesh out this meager yet undeniably Zenonian doctrine that animates all
of Stoic physics.

Zeno's strict materialism got interpreted by his successors – quite
naturally – as a doctrine in which anything that participates in the physical
chain of causes is a body.[264] Further, it is typical of the subtlety of
Chrysippean metaphysics that non-bodily objects are understood in a
variety of ways: some as fully real and yet incorporeal (so, lacking in causal
efficacy: for instance, voids), some as mere conceptual constructs (so, as we
have seen above, universals). This subtlety, together with the limitations of
the extant evidence, means that it is difficult to judge which precise path
Chrysippus took in the case of surfaces, lines and points. He could have
judged them to be incorporeal, and yet fully existent ("subsistent" is the
technical term: so, Robertson, 2004) or he could have judged them to be
mere fictions (so, Nolan, 2006).[265]

Either way, Chrysippus' claim would have to be that the relations
"equal" and "unequal" held only between corporeal objects – that is, *bodies*.
Since surfaces are not bodies, they are neither equal nor unequal to each
other. Chrysippus took Democritus' challenge, arranged it in neat logical
terms as a dilemma – and then resolved the dilemma into meaninglessness.

It is resolved, and *no more*: we learn nothing about the cone, and in fact
it becomes quite difficult to understand how one should go about studying
the properties of this or any other geometrical object. It is not made of
atoms, it is truly curvilinear, so Democritus' Lego (if this understanding of
his geometry is correct) will not do. But what is the status, not of the many

---

[264] Long and Sedley (1987: I, section 45) provides the evidence which, for once, is unequivocal:
     materialism was the core Stoic doctrine.
[265] I will not go any further into this debate, except for explaining a little more Nolan's argument, as its
     consequences, if true, would be especially significant for the relation between philosophy and
     mathematics in the Stoa. It should be remembered that another core Stoic doctrine was that of the
     universal pervasiveness of fire. This drop of dogmatic wine was expanded by Chrysippus into an
     entire ocean of the metaphysics of *blending*. When two pieces of matter blend, both are preserved,
     and yet there is no place where both cannot be found. Nolan takes this, together with Chrysippus'
     explicit statements that there are no ultimate parts – everything is divisible, always – to reconstruct a
     mereology that, in spatial terms, has solids but no lower dimensionalities. The parts of a spatial,
     three-dimensional object are other, *smaller* spatial, three-dimensional objects – turtles all the way
     down. (This is the theory of David Lewis' "gunk" (Lewis, 1991), ultimately dependent on A. N.
     Whitehead, from whom Nolan takes his cue). While the evidence will always be insufficient to
     support any such confident interpretation of Chrysippus, there is an attractive Stoic model here, in
     which everything is bodies, the parts of bodies, too, always being bodies.

Archimedean circles constituting the cone, but of a polygon inscribed inside the base of the cone, as in the treatment of the cone in Euclid's *Elements*? Greek mathematics only rarely speaks of solids, almost always deriving the properties of the objects it studies (two- or three-dimensional) from the relations of lines and points. But Chrysippus quite clearly thought it was wrong to assert that this line is greater than that – so he denied the very basic type of claim made in the course of Greek mathematics. So, for instance, the first proposition of the *Elements* sets up an equilateral triangle and is all about arguing that three given lines are equal to each other. For Chrysippus, all these statements are a *category error*! Perhaps Chrysippus even thought (if we follow Nolan, 2006) that there is no such thing that has no part – contradicting the first sentence of Euclid's *Elements*! Under this more radical (and yet plausible) account, it becomes impossible even to assert the *existence* of points. Either way, the Chrysippean model would posit an asymmetry between three-dimensional and lower-dimensional bodies, emphasizing the ontological priority of the former over the latter – as alien to the practice of Greek geometry as could be.

It is possible to construct an atomistic geometry just as it is possible to construct a point-free geometry without ultimate parts (in fact, both would collapse into a similar discrete, algebraic space). It is not as if geometry has to be the way it is. But Greek geometry was. Neither atomistic nor point-free, it operated on the assumption – captured well by Aristotle – that bodies are divisible anywhere, such divisions picking up planes, lines and points that are geometry's true subject matter. Archimedes' daring experiment of the *Method* enriched the range of possibilities available to anyone interested in producing a new metaphysics of the continuum, but even the *Method* remained committed to continuity and, if anything, emphasized its foundations in low-dimensional entities. Whether or not it was Aristotelian, Greek geometry was always neither Epicurean nor Chrysippean.

Had Chrysippus directly denounced geometry, this would have created at least some tensions for future, mathematically minded Stoics (on which more below), and would surely have been picked up by the enemies of Stoicism. We can say with some confidence that he did not. Of course: it was not Chrysippus' project to deny the validity of the arts. Plutarch was quite right that Chrysippus presented his philosophy as true, ultimately, to humanity's common conceptions.

And yet we find that, through separate routes, the strict materialism of both Epicurus and Chrysippus leads them to postulate a reality governed by a structure in genuine tension with that projected by Greek geometry.

While Epicurus drew from this the conclusion that geometry should be confronted as false and misleading, Chrysippus drew no such conclusion.

It is a real possibility that Chrysippus did develop a positive account – functionally equivalent to that of Aristotle in *Metaphysics* M3 – explaining how the fictions or incorporealities of mathematics could be valid and explanatory of the physical world; an account now lost.[266] It is also possible that Chrysippus produced no such account and that the gap between his metaphysics of mathematicals, and the practice of mathematicians, was left as no more than an implicit tension, to be tacitly ignored by future, mathematically inclined Stoics. I am not sure how to judge between these two options, but the following should be observed, emerging from our discussion so far. Chrysippus' corpus was intensive rather than extensive: multiplied not by ranging everywhere, in the manner of the Peripatos, but by a minute engagement, through a massive reamplification of given points, with a (relatively restricted) set of philosophical questions dictated by the core questions of doctrine. That something is a philosophical problem from our perspective, then, does not prove that Chrysippus resolved it. We have lost the catalogue of Chrysippus' physical writings, so we do not know if it contained any titles engaged directly with mathematics. And yet, many titles are known through other sources (see the extensive list in von Arnim 1905, III.195–205). No mathematically related titles are reported. Plutarch refers, just prior to the Democritean discussion (1078E), to Chrysippus' *Physical Questions*; just following it (1081F), he refers to *On Void* and *On Parts*, the latter apparently a long work (in at least five books). Such titles are typical of the physical Chrysippean titles, and, likely enough, the discussion of the Democritean challenge took place within a more general physical context, Chrysippus' more immediate concern being not with mathematics as such but with the nature of physical objects: most likely, indeed, within the study of parts. A reasonable scenario is that, within a work on parts, Chrysippus would explain how the parts of a body were themselves bodies (rather than surfaces, lines

---

[266] Robertson (2004: 170–1) sketches a possible account (one based on Robertson's own model, however, in which the geometricals are incorporeals and yet subsistent; a similar account would be harder to pull off starting from Nolan, 2006, in which points no longer exist). In my mention of *Metaphysics* M3 I refer to the fact that Aristotle – in his eagerness to deny Platonist ontology – often denied the existence of separate mathematical objects over and above those of the physical world. In a few places, most prominently *Metaphysics* M3, he proposed an account of the ontology of mathematics that makes the science valid even though its subject matter is ultimately physical. (The literature on this is wide, but there is no recent treatment that pulls it together; most of it can be traced through the literature that refers back to Lear, 1982.) The ontological challenge posed by Chrysippus' account of geometry is more serious, but not insurmountable.

or points) and would then also spend considerable time in attacking an account by Democritus, presenting it as a paradox and explaining how the paradox emerges out of a misunderstanding of the metaphysical observation produced by Chrysippus.

For Chrysippus, then: why take up Democritus' cone? Because Democritus was an Atomist, and so arguments of his would naturally provide fodder for argumentation concerning the fundamental constitution of matter.

And, on the other hand – why engage with Archimedes? There was nothing in Archimedes' *Method*-like works (or indeed in his more traditional works) open to a Chrysippean analysis. No meta-mathematics, and especially no clearly defined metaphysical propositions: instead, a surprising variety of concrete results, their overall meaning intentionally left enigmatic.

Chrysippus had a hammer – the conceptual analysis of propositions – and he managed to find many nails: ready-made philosophical arguments, waiting to be analyzed. But in the works of Archimedes there were no such nails to be found: it was all mercury-like, with nothing for Chrysippus' hammer to hit. And so the two, Chrysippus and Archimedes, never did make contact.

Here, then, is the central contrast of the third century. Its two greatest minds, Archimedes and Chrysippus, were nearly precise contemporaries.[267] It is so tempting to imagine them in dialogue! In one passage attested from the works of Chrysippus – and through an entire array of extant works by Archimedes – we can see their two minds trained on the very same object. They are close – both, riveted to a circle in a cone. And then – no contact made between the two. Chrysippus looks at this circle, and sees an opportunity to turn a past argument into a paradox and then to resolve it. Archimedes looks at the same circle, and sees an opportunity for a variety of enigmatic surprises.

At issue was not just individual temperament but, rather, the different cultural practices as well. One was the propositionalizing, a-literary pursuit of conceptual analysis; the other was the catalogue of surprise. Above all, we see Chrysippus within the grip of the philosophical thematic lock: what calls for discussion is previous, analyzable, philosophical argument. And so the Stoa, like all the other schools, digs further and further, back into philosophy, away from the other genres.

---

[267] Chrysippus died in 206, Archimedes six years earlier; both were old men at their death.

### 4.4.5   Interim Conclusion

Because of the way in which space and canon were woven together, being in a different place entailed a different attitude towards the past. In Athens, tradition was paramount. One belonged to a school; clung to a very narrow slice of the past; emphasized one's adherence to the stablest element of that past – the core doctrine of a philosophy. More and more, one would be locked into the same conversations, with the same group of people. Elsewhere – which meant, in practice, mostly in Alexandria – one surveyed the past so as to inject it with a sense of the new. Genres were mixed; surprise was valued above all.

And so, the two simply had little use for each other. The philosophers, clinging to their own tradition and de-emphasizing style and surprise, had no need for scientific innovation – and provided no fodder for the Alexandrian experiment. As philosophy's thematic lock deepened, it had less to offer to others; little wonder that others had little use for it. As emphasized on page 423 above, the genres of philosophy, and of science, were always distinct – and yet, prior to the third century, had often been in dialogue. By the time we reach Chrysippus and Archimedes, the ties had been severed. Whatever one knew of the other did not matter for one's current activity as a philosopher – or as a scientist.

There are consequences for the separation of the ways. A mathematical science that does not commit itself to philosophical interpretation may be more willing to engage with objects whose only significance is internal to mathematics. There is no wider cultural discussion of parabolas, for instance – objects known and studied only by mathematicians. It is quite possible, as Knorr suggested in 1982, that the conic sections were invented in the fourth century as a tool for the study of proportion – proportion itself being a shared cultural concept and one of significance to philosophers. In what was a typical move for the third century, such objects as the conic sections, having become objects of study in their own right, were studied not for the sake of some other, widely shared concept but for the sake of advanced – spectacular – knowledge itself. It is around the study of such specialized objects that Archimedes and his generation advanced the studies that eventually gave rise – almost two millennia later – to calculus.[268] A parallel observation is that a mathematical science

---

[268] I argue for a variation of this thesis (Netz, 2018) as a contrast with Chinese mathematics: because Chinese mathematics is always formulated in reference to canonical objects such as the cube and the pyramid, enshrined in the mathematical canon and in imperial examinations (that is, becoming part of official state practice), even when authors such as Liu Hui approach problems of

independent of philosophical interpretation may be more willing to make ad hoc, radical assumptions in the application of the exact sciences to the physical world, allowing the construction of a fully mathematical model. One need not worry about the philosophical correctness of one's assumptions, as long as the mathematical exercise continues to dazzle and impress. Thus, by eliding the question of physical interpretation, Archimedes may construct his toy universes of planes hanging on balances, of objects reduced to their centers of gravity, and so construct the first effective mathematical physics[269] – the one that would serve as the direct inspiration to Galileo and beyond.[270] Finally, while the works themselves in this instance have been lost, it does seem the case, as already noted on pages 406–9 above, that the leading generation of Alexandrian medicine tended to elide the more obviously philosophical questions of ancient medicine – the constitution of the body, the value of its parts – and instead emphasized a research program that allowed results to be judged by the practitioners themselves: a more empirical study of anatomy and physiology, which would provide the seeds for what was best in Galen's science – and made Harvey possible.[271]

And so: I try to explain throughout the survival of a pluralistic system of cultural practices, across the ancient Mediterranean. The emphasis of this book is on pluralism as such, and in this sense the duality of Athens and Alexandria is significant in and of itself. The Mediterranean, even in the age of monarchy, failed to develop a single, monolithic ideological system, in part, of course, because the site of the canon – Athens – was distinct from the site of power – above all, Alexandria.

Thus we get pluralism, which takes, specifically, the form of dualism. But, in this case, the duality gains a deeper meaning. It is not just "more than one". By being apart, one may, sometimes, develop more fully. Specifically, medicine and mathematics developed autonomously from philosophy. They thus develop their own, autonomous research programs which, being self-derived, are also more productive. This is not the nineteenth century, and science is neither an institution nor a profession. This I do not deny. If one wishes to reserve the term "science" for the nineteenth

---

sophisticated measurement of the type studied by Archimedes, and advance them in ways suggestive of calculus, such results remain marginal because they do not develop a sustained study around objects of the level of complexity of the conic sections.

[269] I argue this in Netz (2016): the physical world of Archimedes' *Floating Bodies* is difform (liquids and solids behaving distinctly) in a radical way, driven by mathematical necessities: a mathematical model, avoiding questions of physical ontology, and for this reason effective.

[270] Laird (1991).    [271] Wear (1983).

century, then this remains a valid choice. But something new does emerge, and it is, indeed, decisive for the scientific revolution.

This is now all told as the epos of enlightenment: Let There Be Science! Above, I have told it, in terms perhaps more appropriate to the age of Menander, as a comedy of errors. Chrysippus and Archimedes, so close, and yet as if unaware of each other. . .

And yet we know about this episode, because Plutarch was aware of *both*. Indeed, this philosopher is not only one of our two key sources for Chrysippus (alongside Galen) but also our most prolific source for Archimedes' life, as of so much else in Hellenistic science. Eventually, Hellenistic philosophy and Hellenistic science – together with Hellenistic literature – did come to be read together. We now turn to this eclectic synthesis.

## 4.5    Coda to Hellenism: When Worlds Converge

We have discussed so far variety – but also stability: through the third and second centuries practices in and outside Athens remained largely the same – and remained dual. The main theme we will now survey is synthesis, which gives rise to more, not less, diversity. Athens and Alexandria came together – in a cacophony of eclectic variations. The specific timing, and form, of the Greco-Roman encounter ended up not solidifying a monolithic Greek tradition but, instead, splintering it further.

The following series of vignettes is long,[272] and so it calls for more structure. Following this introductory section 4.5.1, bringing in the main figure in our cast – Posidonius – I move on in section 4.5.2 to the sciences. Section 4.5.3 returns to philosophy (in which the most obvious transitions take place) and 4.5.4 goes beyond science and philosophy to literary practices in general. Section 4.5.5 begins, once again, from Posidonius, and tries to explain this moment of the early first century BCE – the coda to Hellenism.

---

[272] I try to provide an outline, synoptic picture of culture in this century. There is no consensus to rely upon and so I need to provide more detail on my own (we need a monograph on the overall shape of first-century BCE Greek culture; in the absence of one, the following section is a kind of micromonograph). I follow, of course, many previous studies. In particular, there is an important tradition of study of the growing awareness of Greek culture among the Romans, whose capstone remains Rawson (1985); there is also outstanding literature on the transformations of philosophy, often concentrating on doctrinal transformations, though, since Glucker (1978), and more recently, especially in the work of Sedley (see Sedley, 2003), more attention has been paid to changes in philosophical practice.

### 4.5.1   Exhibit Number One: Posidonius

Posidonius, the leading Stoic philosopher of his era, was – it is now generally agreed – orthodox in his Stoicism (see the brief summary in Algra, 2014: 305). And yet: he was an original. Beginning with his space: Posidonius did study with Panaetius in Athens, but his own school was definitely in Rhodes (it may well be that, in this, Posidonius in some sense followed Panaetius: Rhodes was Panaetius' native city, not Posidonius').[273] And Posidonius, most importantly, strayed away from the institutional practices: "Stoic philosopher, scientist and historian," is how Kidd's entry in the *Oxford Classical Dictionary* begins. And was there anyone, before him, who could fit the same description? Remember our observation concerning the intensive, rather than extensive, nature of Chrysippean prolixity: many words, constrained in genre. Posidonius wrote widely: a massive *History* in 52 books,[274] studies in geography, contributions that clearly related specifically to the exact sciences (a positive contribution to astronomy,[275] a polemical stand in support of Euclid's *Elements*),[276] even a study in tactics: we will return to characterize this oeuvre on pages 501–4 below. The commitment to history writing implies a literary ambition, and it is a trope (starting from Cicero, well positioned to make such a judgement) that Posidonius was a remarkable stylist.[277] What is more, this new set of practices *stuck*. Geminus is among the few authors interested in the

---

[273] The *Suda*, s.v. Posidonius, names him as the successor to Panaetius, which seems to imply a Panaetian school in Rhodes (in which case, the spatial innovation would be Panaetius'). Whether or not Panaetius had a formal school in his native city, it is often conjectured that Posidonius – native of Apamea in Syria – ended up in Rhodes because of his master's connections there (see, e.g., Sedley, 2003: 32–3).

[274] A Stoic who was also a historian was definitely a novelty. How about a historian who was also a Stoic? Was Polybius Stoic? We now usually say he wasn't, but see Brouwer (2011) for the debate, as well as a moderate resolution: not a Stoic, Polybius nevertheless could on occasion use Stoic ideas. I will return to the comparison between Posidonius and Polybius below.

[275] Measurement of the Earth, a very Hellenistic endeavor suggesting a concern with large scale; see discussion in Taisbak (1974).

[276] For a recent discussion, see Verde (2013). These two episodes are far from exhausting Posidonius' forays into the exact sciences; see in general on that Kidd (1978).

[277] This seems to be not just a feature of the history writing but also of the more philosophical writings directly related to doctrine: so, the various ethical virtues are said to hang together as if "from a single chord" (Edelstein and Kidd F150a); a question of cosmological optics is considered through a vivid thought experiment: does the Sun's size appear affected by the medium? How big would the Sun appear if everything appeared to us through the super-power of Lynceus, who could see through walls? (Edelstein and Kidd F114.) It is clear that extended quoted passages such as in Galen's *PHP* IV (Edelstein and Kidd F164–5), are structured by neat binary structures, considerable periods neatly resolved: "[I]n which the suppositions are often equal, and the infirmity; but the affections are neither from an equal source, nor become equal" (from F164, *PHP* IV.5.35). This is elegant, rhetorical Greek.

exact sciences known to have been active – likely – in the first century BCE. He most likely produced an epitome of Posidonius' meteorological writing: I thus take him to be a follower of the Stoic.[278] This is significant, since he is attested as an author of scientifically inflected philosophy: the epitome of Posidonius mentioned above but also, crucially, "On the Order of the Mathematical Sciences", apparently a many-book study of the various fields of the exact sciences from a philosophical, meta-mathematical perspective. This may well have been the most ambitious philosophical discussion of mathematics by *any* philosopher since at least the fourth century BCE. Now, we do not have Geminus' epitome of Posidonius. But we do have a treatise on tactics by an Asclepiodotus, who was apparently active in the middle of the first century, and probably the same as the philosopher who serves as the source of some of Seneca's testimonies on Posidonius; the conclusion is that here, too, we have a follower of Posidonius who pursued the master's endeavor, producing at least one strictly technical treatise.[279] Right at the end of the first century, of course, we have the unambiguous case of Strabo, who self-identified as a Stoic philosopher – and dedicated his career to the writings of geography and history.[280] Needless to say, all this would become commonplace in the Roman era, with Arrian, both a Stoic and a historian (as well as tactician!), Seneca, a Stoic and a literary figure, Musonius, with his elegant apophthegms, and Cleomedes, who used technical astronomy as part of his teaching of Stoic philosophy: in short, it is hard to find a post-Posidonian Stoic whose generic range did not extend beyond philosophy.

It is not that all future Stoics would be Posidonian, or that Stoicism became Posidonianism. The positive Posidonian contribution to philosophy, as such, remained somewhat specific to him and to his immediate followers (yet another generational event, it appears). Consider, for example, logic. The evidence is minimal and mediated, but there is something of

---

[278] Simplicius, *In Phys.* 291.21–2. I find it curious to deny that the author of an epitome of Posidonius – and the one author known to have ascribed to Chrysippus a statement in the philosophy of mathematics (pp. 445–7 above) – would not be a Stoic. And yet, Geminus' Stoic allegiance is debated, largely because Geminus' only extant work, *Introduction to the Phaenomena*, does not show any considerable philosophical considerations at all; but, then again, it is a narrowly defined, elementary piece of astronomical education (Cleomedes' analogous work is written for the purpose of teaching Stoic philosophy; but that of Geminus is clearly written for the purpose of teaching *astronomy*.) Finally, some views expressed by Geminus were sometimes construed by past scholars to be in tension with Stoic orthodoxy. This type of exercise is infinitely elastic. For an overview, see Evans and Berggren (2006: 23 ff.).
[279] This is the extant *Tactics*, on which more on pp. 501–4 below. For the identification (standard, and uncertain), see, e.g., White (2007: 40).
[280] Dueck (2002: 62–9).

a scholarly consensus regarding its interpretation. We have extant Galen's *Institutio Logica*, a survey of all logical systems in 19 brief chapters. Galen covers Aristotle's syllogism; he then moves on to Chrysippus' logic of propositions; and then finally, near the end, he adds three chapters on a different kind of logic – the logic of relations. There are enough indications to make us suppose that this last one was due to Posidonius: so, a major original contribution. This contribution is restricted, however: it is clear that, even after Posidonius, Stoic logic was understood to be, simply, the logic of propositions.[281] The Stoa was stamped by Chrysippus, and no one could ever replace that stamp.

There is one more remarkable feature to Posidonius' logic of relations that we need to mention: the logic of relations – unlike those of Aristotle and Chrysippus – is directly relevant to mathematics. Indeed, most of the examples adduced by Galen (in all likelihood following Posidonius) were mathematical.[282] Stoic logic – the field in which Chrysippus made his most remarkable contribution – was brought, all of a sudden, directly face to face with the discipline which Chrysippus himself ignored: mathematics. And so, in general: certain *combinations* that were avoided prior to Posidonius (philosophy and science, philosophy and literature) now became natural. Here's the sense of a pivot.

Posidonius, as mentioned above, apparently studied with Panaetius, who in turn died in 110/109. Posidonius was also certainly alive in 60, probably in 51. We do not need the ancient testimony that he died old (84 years old, specifically?):[283] this is to be expected. Let us say that he was born not later than around 130 BCE. We note, then, that around the year 100 a young Stoic set out on a new course for a Stoic philosopher, going beyond the literary forms and genres associated with past Stoics; and that likely around the year 80 BCE – perhaps even a little before that – this upstart became the most respected Stoic philosopher alive; changing, from now on, the very meaning of what it was to live as a Stoic.

The goal for the following sections 4.5.2 to 4.5.4 is to look for more parallels. We see a transformation in cultural practice, based on new spaces, away from Athens/Alexandria – and a new combination of the traditional Hellenistic

---

[281] I discuss all of this in Netz (2018).

[282] Quite elementary, however: "Theon has twice as much as Dion; but Philon in turn has twice as much as Theon; therefore, Philon possesses four times as much as Dion" (Galen, *Institutio Logica* 16). The Dion–Theon schematic language might be inherited from Chrysippus; that two times two equals four is a Posidonian contribution.

[283] The source is unreliable; see the discussion in Bar-Kochva (2010: 339), and also for the chronological questions in general.

elements associated with these two centers. How far can this formula be extended? How did it enhance the pluralism of the specialized genres?

### 4.5.2    *Coda to Hellenism: The Sciences*

We turn to Asclepiades of Bithynia. Rawson (1982) has shown – interpreting a reference in Cicero's *De Oratore* (I.62) – that he was dead by 91 BCE. On the other hand, scholarship has tended to take as historical the report that Mithridates Eupator (reigned 120–63) invited Asclepiades to his court. Asclepiades' death was therefore likely nearer 91 than 120 (the invitation took place following 120; the longer Asclepiades lived after 120, the more likely it would be for such an invitation to have taken place; so, reasoning backwards, and in Bayesian fashion, we are led to a somewhat later date of death). Let us say, then, that Asclepiades died *c.* 100 BCE. He was old by then (though not a Methuselah),[284] so a life roughly from about 175 to 100 is likely enough. As usual, we assume a position of pre-eminence at a mature age, so we should say that, at about 120 BCE, a new kind of doctor dazzled the Roman elite.

What was new and what was dazzling? This is especially difficult to ascertain. Our sources emphasize a philosophy of matter otherwise associated with Heraclides of Pontus – a fourth-century philosopher! (See Gottschalk, 1980: chap. 3.) Such archaisms aside, modern scholars have noted the clear influence of Epicurean, Atomistic ideas; Vallance (1990) stands out in downplaying them; see Leith (2009; 2012) for recent statements of the more mainstream position, confirming Asclepiades' specific debts to Epicureanism. "Debts" and no more: clearly, Asclepiades' main identity was that of a physician, not of a philosopher (and, whatever Epicurean-inflected theories Asclepiades may have entertained, he was not an orthodox Epicurean; but – especially with this sect – one was either an orthodox or not a member of the sect at all). Hostile sources doubted Asclepiades'

---

[284] Polito (1999) notes that Asclepiades could have been the son of a certain Andreas, and that the same could have been the Herophilean doctor of the third century BC (d. 217). He does not try to explain away the evidence for the invitation issued at some point later than 120 BC, arguing instead that this is consistent with the evidence, otherwise, that Asclepiades died at an old age. I do not engage in polemic as such, and I mention this only for the general methodological lesson. In such arguments, what matters are not *possibilities* (which is what is implied by our usual language of "ante quem" and "post quem") but *probabilities*. We know that Asclepiades died sometime between 120 and 91; to have him die just in the range 120 to 117 has prima facie no more than a 10 percent probability. To have him die at the age of about 96 to 100 is possible, but by about two orders of magnitude less likely than dying in any of the ages 70 to 95. It is therefore prima facie about 1:1,000 probable that Asclepiades was born before 217. Thus, any evidence suggesting that he did is overwhelmingly likely to be misleading. It was a different Andreas.

medical credentials, but, then, their charge was not that he was a philosopher masking as a doctor but, rather, a failed rhetor![285] He clearly was noted for his public eloquence (which is why he was mentioned in the *De Oratore* to begin with). Finally, his therapeutics were marketed – the term seems appropriate – as non-traditional, as well as pleasant.[286] Now, we know little about medical practice between the first Alexandrian generation and that of Asclepiades himself, but the little we do know on, say, the Empiricists, or on Herophilus' followers, suggests a medical tradition pursued distinctly from philosophy. Sometimes we find a textual, almost grammatical practice; sometimes a traditionalist veneration of Hippocrates.[287] It is clear that Asclepiades pivots away from such a tradition, cultivating a new fad that obtains its authority not from the tradition of Greek medicine but from the wider Greek cultural currencies of rhetoric and philosophy. This, once again, sticks – not as the fad for Asclepiades himself (which need not have outlived him) but as a Roman penchant for Greek medical fads. Themison was considered by the ancients as a pupil of Asclepiades, but not too much faith should be put into this for either doctrinal or chronological purposes. Probably he was active, indeed, in the first century BCE.[288] Clearly, he presented himself, once again, as an innovator, though in this case it is hard to know which was his innovation, which that of later Methodist followers. The one clear thing is that Methodism stands in a peculiar position in both epistemology and the ontology of the body: in some ways quasi-skeptical, in other ways insisting that all maladies are related to a few basic bodily conditions. If not explicitly philosophical, this is certainly a reflective, meta-medical doctrine.[289] So, once again, medicine – in a philosophical

---

[285] Pliny XXVI.7.12–13.
[286] Celsus III.4.1, Caelius Aurelianus, *Acute Diseases* I.15.126, Pliny XXIII.22.38; innovation is the key theme of the extended passage by Pliny on Greek medicine and Rome which begins with Asclepiades.
[287] For this interpretation of Hellenistic medicine following the generation of Herophilus, see section 4.3.2 above, though, clearly, the tradition of medical rhetorical performance is continuous; see Dana (2007: 200–2) for a second-century inscription honoring a doctor from Cyzicus who excelled in his speeches in Istros (*Bull. Ep.* 1958 no. 336 brings several parallels).
[288] We have a statement that a certain Eudemus was his pupil (Caelius Aurelianus, *Acute Diseases* 2.219), and this Eudemus is probably the one who died in 31 CE, victim of court intrigue (the type of event always useful for medical chronology: in this case we rely on Tacitus, *Hist.* 4.3, 11), which is, strictly speaking, incompatible with Themison being a pupil of Asclepiades. Probably, in one or both of these cases "pupil" is not to be taken literally, and Themison's activity can be put anywhere in the first century BCE.
[289] For a recent discussion of the Methodist epistemology (arguing that its weird ontology follows, in a way, from its weird epistemology), with an overview of the literature on the subject, see Webster (2015).

vein? Later on, ancient tradition as well as modern scholarship saw Thessalus, in turn – a first-century CE physician – as a follower of Themison, and here we are firmly within the territory of what Galen enshrined as the "medical sect" of Methodism; by this time the medical marketplace would have many other variations of new-fangled medicines based on diverse teachings, whose source was outside the medical tradition itself: starting from astrological lore,[290] or even from Stoicism itself (this is the important new development of Pneumaticism).[291]

So, an Asclepedian pivot in medicine, preceding the Posidonian one in philosophy: offering, in this case again, a new *combination* of science with philosophy – one that, in many variations, will be characteristic of much future medicine.

Put medicine aside: new combinations allow for sciences that are new altogether. To understand this era, surely we should make sense of the rise of astrology. As usual for the first century, our firmest foundation is in Cicero: he not only criticizes astrology at length but also reports that some of his contemporaries trust in it.[292] This gives credence to stories in Plutarch, who has his Romans, from as early as Sulla, rely on Chaldean astrologers.[293] All this contrasts sharply with the world of Polybius, in which there is no astrology – not even as a proper target for Polybian derision: as arguments from silence go, this is fairly dispositive.[294] Now, for his philosophical discussion of astrology Cicero does turn to Posidonius, but in this philosophical tradition the mode of divination under scrutiny seems to be more generalized star lore rather than the specific science of astrology.[295] With Posidonius, then – as usual – we seem to be on the *cusp*. The earliest text often adduced for a Greek science of astrology is a pseudo-epigraphic work – or set of works – that circulated in antiquity under the names of Nechepso and Petosiris – figures

---

[290] For an overview, see Nutton (2008).    [291] Stannard (1964).    [292] *Div.* II.99.

[293] Sulla 37. To my knowledge, Plutarch does not impute the same kind of trust in astrology to earlier Romans.

[294] Writing on Mediterranean political history from the vantage point of the Roman elite, Polybius should have been able to tell us about astrology in the kind of contexts for which we have Cicero's and Plutarch's reports for the late Republic – and which are absolutely commonplace for the Principate. But, more than this: he was especially interested in the question of the theoretical knowledge required for military art, including astronomy, even mentioning the problem of being able to account for eclipses! (So as to quell superstitions among the troops: Bowen, 2002: 87–9.) And yet: no mention of astrology!

[295] Augustine, *De Civitate Dei* V.2: Posidonius believed that one could account for similarity in the train of the diseases between twin brothers (a stock example in ancient discussions of determinism), based on their being born under the same constellation.

not so much invented as remolded, by a Greek author, from genuine Demotic sources.[296] This may well have been, for ancient astrologers, the key written reference point, at least prior to Ptolemy's *Tetrabiblos* (though it continued to circulate much later).[297] When did this begin to circulate? The very centrality of this text may argue for a relatively early origin. It is perhaps not very damaging that it is not attested in our extant sources prior to the first century CE[298] – how many works, likely to cite this, survive from earlier centuries? – but it should be emphasized that the key argument for the dating of the work (which is typically given as "*c.* 150–120 BCE") is no more than the historical universe it imagines: a Mediterranean of warring, independent Greek states.[299] This could be a reflection of contemporary realities – or, more likely, a deliberate archaizing trope (we will note a very similar archaizing choice in Asclepiodotus' *Tactics* on page 504 below). Now, the extant literature of Greco-Roman astrology does combine Babylonian techniques with a sophisticated understanding, specific to Greek astronomy, of calculation of positions on an oblique ecliptic.[300] It most likely derives from literate, sophisticated sources, and the very popularity of astrology in late Republican Rome suggests the credentials of high culture. It is likely enough that some astrological texts did circulate already early in the first century BCE, but a firm date cannot be given. All we can say is that there was probably no *Greek*, literate astrology at about 125 BCE (there surely were "Chaldeans", though – of whatever actual ethnicity – practicing their craft), but that this Greek, literate astrology was significant already by about 75 BCE (though it did present itself then – as it would always go on to do – as a "Chaldean" or "Egyptian" science). We are looking, in other words, for another major transition point not far from the year 100. I put the rise of astrology side by side with Posidonius and Asclepiades, for all of whom the key theme seems to be the merging of science and philosophy (the merger approached, as it were, from opposite directions). This, then, seems a plausible key to the rise of astrology. The Greek practice of the exact sciences – now firmly set within a wider purpose: cosmological and ethical. Astrology combines Greek mathematics with a

[296] Heilen (2011: 23–31), largely based on research by Ryholt (2002; 2011), sums up the evidence for the Demotic background.
[297] Boll (1908: 106) calls it "the astrological bible".
[298] For an extensive list of testimonies and fragments, see Heilen (2011: 32–4).
[299] Goulet (2005: 606–7).   [300] Jones (2003: 339–40).

kind of wisdom. This case is different from those of Asclepiades and of Posidonius in that the wisdom in question was not Greek.[301]

Astrology appears. What happens otherwise in the exact sciences? Not much – which is, once again, an important pivot. Now, as argued above, Greek culture generally was produced in generational clusters, and one of our key cases was that of advanced mathematics, created primarily through two generational events, the one surrounding Plato's Academy, the other surrounding Archimedes (see pages 250–2 above). And yet: near the turn of the second century we witness a sharper drop, not so much a decline as an extinction event. Of course, this should be qualified with a view to the limitations of our evidence. While enough Hellenistic mathematicians are known to have been active around Archimedes or immediately following him, a few are hard to date, so that it is mostly a probabilistic argument that makes us assign little-known authors such as Dionysiodorus, say, to the same post-Archimedean generation. And, at any rate, we do have one very important author in the exact sciences who certainly was active in the *second* half of the second century: Hipparchus. The corpus attested for Hipparchus is enormous, almost entirely astronomical,[302] almost all lost with the exception of one work, a critique of Aratus; but, to have anything at all extant, from this era, is quite an achievement. When precisely was Hipparchus' era of activity? We have astronomical observations reported by Ptolemy: those from 147 to 127 are explicitly said to be by Hipparchus while others, from 162 on, are said to have been reported by Hipparchus and so may or may not be by him personally. Jones (1991) improves on these rough data by assigning the observations to possible treatises, and he deduces a series of treatises, each focused on a particular astronomical problem, from after 146 to after 127. When we say that 127 was the post quem for Hipparchus' death, there is quite a lot packed into that "post". We do not know how many years elapsed between Hipparchus' last publication and his death. We do not know if his

---

[301] This is not to say that the success of astrology was merely sociological. To the contrary, as emphasized by Lehoux (2012: chap. 7), ancient astrology worked precisely because it did succeed in marshaling the epistemic resources of the Greek exact sciences – to an extent, indeed, I would say, *supplanting* them with a new combination of science and wisdom.

[302] For a list of attested *titles*, see Lehoux, s.v. Hipparchus, in EANS; but it is especially important to note a possible contribution to optics which we can no longer assign to a title (Aetius 404.3–8); among the extant titles we can also mention a study in bodies carried down by weight – comparable to Archimedes' works in mathematical physics? – and a ludic engagement in combinatorics, ostensibly targeting Chrysippus (Acerbi, 2003). More closely related to astronomy were a substantial study that effectively founded the science of trigonometry (Sidoli, 2004) and contributions to geography. The overall picture is of an author contributing to a full range of the exact sciences, and obviously the model for Ptolemy (though – still Hellenistic in this regard – Hipparchus still seems to have omitted music).

last publication was astronomical and, if so, whether it was based on new, original observations (this is naked-eye astronomy; did elderly astronomers rely on younger friends?). We do not know how many years would pass between Hipparchus' observations and his publication of them; we do not know if the observations quoted by Ptolemy were even among the latest ones he could find within the Hipparchian corpus. In short, it is very unlikely that Hipparchus died at around 125 BC. A rather later date is more likely, perhaps around 110 BC. We should imagine him, then, a contemporary of Panaetius.

And then – we cannot assert with any conviction, for anyone later than Hipparchus and prior to the Imperial era, that his main identity was as an author in the exact sciences. Posidonius, Demetrius Lacon and Zeno of Sidon – authors of the generation that interests us in this section – were all philosophers who commented (positively or negatively) on mathematics. Later on, as noted above, on page 460, note 278, it is almost certain that Geminus' identity was that of a philosopher.[303] The Antikythera mechanism was lost at sea at about 60 BCE,[304] but we are not sure how long before that it was made (at any rate, a similar device was commissioned by Posidonius,[305] and so we cannot deduce, from the piece of bronze found in the Antikythera shipwreck, a mathematical patron).[306] The next stirring of any original mathematical work is possibly from Thrasyllus, a scholar who made his living as a court astrologer to Tiberius and who could – we have no certainty here – have contributed to mathematical harmonics; perhaps part of a generation of authors who returned to cultivate this field following what could have been a long, Hellenistic hiatus.[307] It is, in fact, only deep in the Imperial era – mostly, from late first century onwards –

---

[303] A more obscure author, Diodorus of Alexandria, seems to have been active in the first century (he is cited by Eudorus of Alexandria), and is quoted for various observations, of a philosophical nature, on the stars; he is also reputed to have written an analemma, so a more technical work related to astronomy or perhaps to geographical astronomy. It has been traditional to see in him a Stoic, and so we see perhaps a follower of Posidonius, more directly engaged with mathematical practice: a Geminus-like figure. If anything, then, this shows, once again, the enduring influence of Posidonius – but, still, not an example of an author whose primary identity is that of a mathematician. See Goulet (1994: 782–3).

[304] Tselakas (2012).

[305] Freeth (2002) suggests that the Antikythera mechanism could simply be the one commissioned by Posidonius: it is this train of thought that originally led recent scholars to posit that the mechanism could have contained planetary motions (and not just the motions of the Sun and the Moon).

[306] The Keskintos inscription, another documentary piece of evidence for theoretical work in astronomy, is comparable in that it was dated on paleographic grounds to between roughly 150 and 50 BC, in that the date of its inscription is essentially an ante quem for the date of producing the science that it represents and in that its location – Rhodes – as well as its contents – a philosophically inflected interest in planetary numbers – are continuous with the evidence for Hipparchus, Posidonius, the Antikythera mechanism and Geminus (Jones, 2006).

[307] Barker (1989: chap. 9).

that significant engagement with the exact sciences is visible again:[308] we shall return to discuss this return in the following part of the book. But the clear impression is that the exact sciences had to *return*, following a *gap*.

In this case, then, the important pivot is constituted not so much by Hipparchus himself but, once again, by the generation following him: for some reason, the class of 100 no longer turned to the exact sciences, as if contribution to this field – the glory of the Hellenistic era – was no longer meaningful. This happened alongside the rise of this new phenomenon – philosophers dabbling in mathematics; and of the new "mathematical" wisdom-practice of astrology. The implication seems to be that, all of a sudden, the exact sciences could carry a meaning *only* if they were made to be attached, somehow, to wisdom and philosophy in general. It is thus not surprising that, when mathematics did return, in the Imperial era, it was similar neither to that of the first, "Platonic" generation of advanced mathematics nor to that of the second, "Archimedean" generation. It was, instead, most similar to that of Hipparchus. Contributions to pure, advanced geometry in the manner of Archimedes were almost entirely avoided, and the identity of an author in the exact sciences was fixed, instead, around the mixed sciences. The dictate of the age: combine – or perish.

The following should be noted. With Ptolemy, the major task of the mathematical astronomer is to find a combination of geometrical models and numerical parameters that predict the positions of planets. This is an exercise that combines observation (based on instruments), geometry, trigonometry and calculation, and it will define astronomical science all the way down to Kepler and beyond. It has been traditional to see this project as emerging at least as early as Eudoxus (if not before him), whose school in Cyzicus had produced three-dimensional models (not merely geometrical but likely also mechanical) that mimic the motions of the planets. In a series of publications from the early 1980s onwards, Goldstein and Bowen have argued against this interpretation (see especially Goldstein and Bowen, 1983; and 1991). Their claim is that there is no evidence for the

[308] It was customary to date Heron to the middle of the first century CE, based on a discussion of the observation of a lunar eclipse. Sidoli (2011) points out the abstract nature of this discussion, so the observation is best understood as a thought experiment with its numbers simply made up: thus, no dating possible. We are left with the mere impression that Heron must have been an author of the Imperial era. Somewhat more securely dated authors emerge with Theon of Smyrna, Menelaus and Nicomachus, all active in the generation immediately preceding Ptolemy himself, near the turn of the first century CE.

precise instruments, observations and calculations required for this type of planetary theory prior to Hipparchus himself; these emerge in response to the influx of Babylonian data at around the time of Hipparchus and later, and represent the precise numerical tools (such as the division into degrees) that such data carried. Eudoxus and his school, it was argued, could have engaged in a merely qualitative, cosmological study of the sky.

Goldstein and Bowen did not do much service to their cause by their insistence, sometimes shrill, on the argument from silence – for a field as little documented as early astronomy! Indeed, to obtain the silence they required, Goldstein and Bowen also had to downplay the evidence for the roots of Ptolemaic models in Apollonius[309] and for the roots of the Antikythera mechanism in Archimedes.[310] Furthermore – to go a bit deeper into the sociology of the field – the spread of the personal computer during the 1990s made it much easier for historians to produce detailed calculations and animations. As a consequence, it became possible to play with the meager suggestions we have for Eudoxus' model in precise, numerical terms, and to provide new interpretations: one of the more active fields, recently, in the study of early Greek astronomy (beginning with Mendell, 1998; and Yavetz, 1998). Against this background, skepticism concerning Eudoxus seems less attractive, and scholars today are mostly unskeptical regarding early astronomical models and calculations.

It should be said, however, that Goldstein and Bowen have a point. Astronomical models, calculations and observations were produced prior to Hipparchus but they are never attested as the full Hipparchus–Ptolemy complex (instead, we find evidence for a few theorems in Apollonius, a mechanical model in Archimedes). This is a matter of foreground and background. It is possible that the specific nexus of observations, modeling and calculations was, previously, a secondary pursuit for mathematicians otherwise engaged – perhaps even for Hipparchus himself (who likely produced isolated studies, not a single comprehensive account in the manner of Ptolemy). In the Imperial era, however, this nexus certainly became the central mode of astronomy, which in turn became the central field of the exact sciences (with table making very much brought into the fore). What we see, then, is that Hipparchus pursues mathematics differently from his predecessors; that, in the generations following him, the very identity of the mathematician becomes marginal to non-existent; and that, as this

---

[309] Bowen (2001: 821–2).
[310] Goldstein and Bowen (1991: 106) (written when scholarly attention to the Antikythera mechanism was still sparse).

identity becomes reconstituted, it is based on a Hipparchic template, moved even further away from previous models of mathematical authorship.

Astronomy would eventually become central to the identity of the author in the exact sciences: and, specifically, an astronomy of a certain kind, in which mathematical knowledge is marshaled, above all, so as to provide *a system of the universe*. For indeed – and here, in direct contradiction to the Hellenistic tradition – Imperial-era authors in the exact sciences would be marked by *philosophical* interests. Hardly surprising, seeing that, perhaps, during the hiatus of the first century BCE and later, the exact sciences survived precisely as a practice embedded within philosophy. And so we will have, in the Imperial era, Theon of Smyrna and Nicomachus – authors whose identity is philosophical no less than mathematical – and then Hero, and Ptolemy, would present themselves as at least quasi-philosophers.[311] This is parallel to the development of medicine, through the various post-Asclepiadean fads detailed above, mostly marked by new combinations of medicine and natural philosophy – all the way to Galen, the supreme doctor-philosopher. Science, a distinct practice, was born in Hellenistic Alexandria. But, in the Roman era, it would go on to be subsumed, more than it ever had been beforehand, within philosophy. "Natural philosophy": born, now.

To be clear: what I emphasize is a transition in professional identities. There was astronomy, prior to Hipparchus; but the identity of the scientific astronomer, dedicating his life to calculating the skies so as to determine the form of the cosmos, was perhaps suggested for the first time by Hipparchus himself, perhaps crystalized no earlier than the Imperial era.

Alongside this, then, we should note the rise of yet another professional identity: the *geographer*. We require, once again, a sense of the deep history of the discipline. Indeed, geography had been an important thread running through the Greek historiographical tradition, ever since Herodotus. There were also, it appears, much more technical manuals (so, perhaps, not quite "literary"), recounting routes and harbors; the earliest extant – Pseudo-Scylax – goes back all the way to the fourth century. And, indeed, starting then, with the rise of the post-Chaeronean government sector, we see an enormous explosion in writing of a geographical character.[312] None

---

[311] For Hero, see Cuomo (2002) and Tybjerg (2003). For Ptolemy, there are more studies; Feke (2009), specifically, is a study dedicated to his identity as a philosopher.

[312] I count 45 authors contributing to "geography", widely understood, around the years roughly 300 to 250 (this includes six authors who are surely Hellenistic but cannot be dated more precisely, who therefore likely – but not certainly – belong to this group). I count, in all, 169 authors in this group in antiquity *as a whole*. (This list is fairly solid: the sources are the New Jacoby – which already covers all the geographical authors – and EANS.)

of this is extant but almost all, as noted on pages 353–4 above, appears to be Herodotean ethnographic and even historical works (so, for instance, Megasthenes, writing on India). A handful of more technical navigational surveys are attested as well (Ophellas, king of Cyrene, wrote a periplous of the Atlantic; but about all we know is that Strabo disliked it).[313] In this early generation, Dicaearchus stands aside from these, bringing in a scientific approach to geographical questions, and, as noted on pages 353–4 above, this new approach will be typical for several later Hellenistic writings in geography; thus, with Dicaearchus, mathematical geography is created. But it is likely that Dicaearchus' *identity* was that of a philosopher. A couple of generations later the first author to cut the tie to the Herodotean tradition and to produce a "geography" – meaning both the title (perhaps, *geographika*?) and the principle of a synchronic survey organized spatially, and explicitly not ethnographically or historically – was Eratosthenes.[314] He is often referred to as the founder of the discipline, which is a fair assessment: but of course in his case, too, geography was a single element within a much broader literary project. At any rate, Eratosthenes was not so much a beginning but an end. In this field, as elsewhere, the following century was relatively fallow (a more marked decline, in this case, given the great early Hellenistic production). I count 12 authors contributing to geography in the late third century and through the second – mostly, it appears, the authors of scholarly-grammarian works who collected topographic observations related to the study of the canon. We find less evidence for Herodotean historians (Agatharchides being the one exception). There are two other contributors to geography of much greater significance: Hipparchus is a remarkable mathematical geographer; Polybius is a political historian who also produces a geography which is closer to Eratosthenes' than to Herodotus.

From Strabo's vantage point, there appear to be four outstanding Greek geographical authors after Herodotus, and into the second century: Dicaearchus, Eratosthenes, Polybius and Hipparchus. Their identities, respectively, were: a philosopher, a wide-ranging scholar, a historian and a mathematician. The first Greek geographer – the first literary author whose professional *identity* was built around writings of a "geographical" character – was Artemidorus of Ephesus, I would argue.

Here is what we know of Artemidorus. He wrote a book titled, perhaps, "Geography" or "Geographical Descriptions". This ran to 11 books and covered the entire world. It was very widely cited by later authors from

---

[313] Strabo XVII.3.3.   [314] For the evidence, see Roller (2010).

Strabo to late antiquity (Marcianus of Heracleia, perhaps in the fourth century CE, produced an epitome of the work).[315] He was evidently among the most important authorities on geographical information in antiquity.[316] If he does not count among Strabo's major authors – those who are most frequently discussed in his introductory books – this is probably because Artemidorus did not comment so much on broad theoretical concerns, limiting himself to the geography alone.[317] Indeed, it appears that he wrote little else; the one potential exception is the title "Ionian Commentaries", mentioned once by Athenaeus (111d), which could simply refer to the segment of the "Geography" covering Ionia. Now, Strabo reports that Artemidorus participated in an embassy to Rome in the Olympiad years of 104 to 101 BCE. This suggests a considerable degree of prominence in those years; on the other hand, a book such as his would take many years to finish. The publication of Artemidorus' "Geography" cannot be put many years before or after 100: so, squarely within our group of scholars.

And then: geography, of course, "sticks". In the first century BCE I count 39 authors contributing to geography. Fewer, perhaps, than the early Alexandrian pace. But, still, these are significant contributions. We have Posidonius himself; two extant pieces of geographical didactic poetry, for which see page 367 above; most importantly, this tradition leads up to Strabo himself, who proves that, by the end of the century, the authorial identity of "geographer" is clearly established. In this case, it should be clear: the tradition from Artemidorus to Strabo and beyond did not add much to the theory of geography, compared to authors such as Eratosthenes, Hipparchus or Posidonius. What it did was to construct a particular combination into a new mode of authorship. No theoretical innovation: but a new literary practice, which amounts, in some sense, to the rise of a new science. This science lies at an intersection: historical, mathematical, philosophical, occasionally grammarian. For this very

---

[315] The evidence is surveyed in Stiehle (1856); he identifies 156 fragments, mostly of course from Strabo and Stephanus of Byzantion, but I count a total of 18 authors citing Artemidorus, beginning as early as Diodorus Siculus.

[316] Famously, there is even a papyrus find, an outlier document: an aborted manuscript that seems to contain the beginning of the work with an incomplete map (the most remarkable aspect: if genuine, could it be that Artemidorus was a pioneer in this respect as well?), with some remarkable drawing inserted in the workshop when this failed piece of papyrus became scrap paper (perhaps). The authenticity is usually conceded but, rightly, debated. (The starting point for discussion of the papyrus' images – the key to its nature – is Elsner, 2009.)

[317] In Strabo's descriptive geographical books 3 to 17, Artemidorus is apparently the third most frequently cited author (following Homer – of course – and Ephorus: Johannes Wietzke, private communication).

reason, it never assumed its own identity previously, subsisting merely as the extra activity of authors otherwise engaged. But now is an era of intersections; the identity of the geographer, therefore, comes into its own.

A combination that gives rise to a new science. I move to yet another example, when a new science may be created, conceptually – in this case, though, without a real break in professional identities. We turn, then, to Dionysius Thrax.

This author has one work extant to his name – by which we mean that medieval manuscripts assign a work titled "Grammatical Art", to an author, "Dionysius Thrax". Enough is known of an author of this name to place him historically: a pupil of the greatest grammarian of antiquity, Aristarchus of Samothrace – who, in turn, clearly died as an old man, an exile from Alexandria, not much later than the accession of Ptolemy VIII in 145 BCE (a fraught moment in Alexandrian history: we shall revisit this in the following part of the book).[318] It appears that the activity of Dionysius Thrax took place mostly in Rhodes, following this exile. In broad terms, then, here is another author somewhat preceding the class of 100. So much for date and place. As for the extant work, almost nothing is known. It is, indeed, if the ascription is correct, the first attested work in the West in the field of grammar: a study of the formal properties of language.

Di Benedetto has shown (Di Benedetto, 1958) that the treatise, as found in medieval manuscripts, is almost certainly not by Dionysius Thrax and is likely mostly a late ancient compilation. It is agreed that this observation has important historical consequences.[319] What consequences, precisely, remains controversial, however.

So, again: to the longer historical context. The tradition we think of as "grammar" or "philology" emerged in the first generation of Alexandria as the collection and critical study of the canon. It is also clear that, alongside their critical reflections on the canonical texts, Alexandrian scholars noted regularities and anomalies of linguistic usage. It is hard to find any evidence, however, for any study whose subject matter is linguistic structure as such. The old view, as if Alexandrian scholars were always, among other things, "grammarians" in the sense of, effectively, linguists,[320] saw a continuity with a philosophical past (Plato's Cratylus, Aristotle's *De Interpretatione*) as well as a philosophical present (Chrysippus' logic with

---

[318] The main evidence is in Athenaeus IV 184BC; see discussion in the New Jacoby, s.v. Andron of Alexandria (246).

[319] For the status quaestionis, see Law and Sluiter (1995).

[320] So, in passing, Lyons (1968: 9) – a canonical text of modern linguistics, blaming the Alexandrian grammarians for inventing *prescriptive* grammar!

its supreme attention to verbal detail). The traditional dating of Dionysius Thrax' grammar served, then, in this model, to indicate the kind of grammatical work produced in early Alexandria itself (whose loss would not be so surprising, as, after all, no prose is extant from the early grammarians!).

Following the studies by Di Benedetto, however, the evidence for early Alexandrian philology came into sharper focus. Contemporary scholars recognize that, very likely, *all* the early grammarians did was to write on literature; *never* on language.[321] (That this puts them apart from preceding and contemporary philosophy is, of course, as we now come to expect: the worlds of Alexandria and Athens diverging, that of Athens moving, precisely, *beneath literature* – into Chrysippus' abstract study of propositions and significations.) The question then becomes: when *did* grammar, in the strict sense, emerge? Supporters of an early date point to the fact that, even though the text now transmitted by Thrax is indeed likely a mishmash of interpolations,[322] the *beginning* of the extant treatise is, in fact, ascribed, on ancient authority, to Thrax himself (so that *some* of what is being mishmashed in this transmitted text is early indeed);[323] that, while the grammatical papyri – of which we have substantial fragments – do not show clear remnants of Thrax' text in its current form before late antiquity, we do have fragments of this type of theoretical grammar from the first century BCE onwards;[324] and that we have some indications that grammarians of the first century BCE did contribute to grammar in the strict sense.[325] In short, we are left without a firm date. We may revert to our formulation concerning astrology, but stating it even less precisely. The science of grammar, in the narrow sense, was probably very rare, and quite possibly non-existent, around 150 BC. It was also, probably, a standard part of grammatical practice around 50 BCE. Yet another pivot around the class of 100, with a significant caveat of "plus or minus". And perhaps the need for a caveat is not a mere accident of the survival of our evidence: the transition would not necessarily have presented itself in such stark terms to ancient readers, as, after all, ancient grammatical authors would always remain – above all – scholars of the canon. It was perhaps less significant to them that

---

[321] For the traditional view, see Pfeiffer (1968: 202–3); in this tradition, an important place is given to an assumed episode of a debate concerning abstract grammar between Alexandria and Pergamon; see p. 254 above. I have described the actual, literary practice of Hellenistic grammarians on pp. 362–3 above.

[322] That it is marked by interpolations is beyond doubt, and is, indeed, as expected, as the work – extensively used in the classroom – also attracted an enormous body of scholia; see Montana (2011).

[323] Sextus Empiricus, *Adv. Math.* I.57.    [324] Wouters (1979).

[325] Indeed, Siebenborn (1976) locates one of the origins of normative grammar with authors such as Tyrannion and Tryphon, active in Rome in the middle of the first century BCE.

such authors also tended now to engage with a new genre, the grammatical art – obviously an ancillary, classroom genre, pursued on the margins of one's studies in Plato or Homer. Grammar did not take over scholarship in triumph; it slipped in, undetected. To us, by now, the significance is clear: Alexandrian scholarly practice – now transmuted, with the Athenian ingredient added of a philosophy of language; and, from the mix of scholarship and philosophy, linguistics is born.[326]

### 4.5.3   *Coda to Hellenism: Philosophy*

In looking at science, we kept returning to philosophy: marking, above all, its escape from Athens and into the many Alexandrian disciplines. We should take a wider look at the massive sea change taking place within philosophy as a whole.

The beginnings, indeed, are small. We have noted on page 410 above the absence of Hellenistic philosophers from Alexandria; not only the absence of a philosophical tradition in Alexandria, but the absence – even more puzzling – of philosophers in Athens of Alexandrian origins. As noted by Levy (2012: 291), this seems to change among the generation of the pupils of Carneades. Zeno of Alexandria had a privileged position, writing down Carneades' notes; other reported pupils of Carneades, of Alexandrian origins, include Antipater, Demetrius, Nicostratus, and Sosicrates. This is not yet a significant *over*-representation (the *Index Academicorum* XXIV, on which we rely, lists nearly 30 individuals; and, obviously, at this point Alexandria was by far the biggest concentration of educated Greeks), but what we learn is that Alexandria, all of a sudden, ceased to be *under*-represented in Athens, at least at this particular school. Perhaps we can explain this as a function of political unrest in Alexandria itself (as we have noted above concerning the history of grammar, scholarship made much of reports of the anti-intellectual repressions by Ptolemy Physcon, who reigned from 145 to 116; I return to this episode in the following part, on page 651). But this type of account, at least as far as Alexandria's relationship to the Academy is concerned, is made considerably less likely by the consideration that we also hear of another pupil of Carneades – Zenodorus of Tyre – setting up a school in Alexandria itself, the first of its kind (Levy, 2012: 291)! If Academic philosophers came from Alexandria to Athens to

---

[326] Luhtala (2005: 4) (an argument that begins with the consequences of di Benedetto's work): "It can be concluded that grammar interacted definitely with philosophy during the first two centuries A.D."

flee Physcon, how come they went from Athens to Alexandria at just the same time? No: we see something stirring in the cultural background: Alexandria and Athens, somewhat less incompatible.

Carneades was scholarch in the years 160 to 128. His pupils would have been young at about 150 BC: we envision them reaching an important status on their own in the final decades of the second century BCE. These are the coevals of Asclepiades of Bithynia, but, at this stage, their originality is strictly geographical, and nothing else is known about the distinct philosophy, if any, of any of their number.

This changes, however, with Antiochus of Ascalon. As is often the case with the figures and movements discussed in this section, little is known and much is debated; Glucker (1978) has turned previous scholarship upside down, without having created a new consensus; the authors of the essays edited by Sedley (2012) are often in disagreement among themselves. As usual, what little is known depends on our interpretation of mediated sources (once again, mostly in Cicero); once again, the stakes are high. A major transition seems to take place. The following facts seem clear. Antiochus' life was within the range 135 to 66 (so, definitely a member of the class of 100; roughly, Posidonius' coeval).[327] We hear about his involvement, twice, with Lucullus, a major Roman political figure, first in Alexandria, when Lucullus is a legate there, in the year 87;[328] and then in the eastern campaign of 73 to 66.[329] He was also the head of his own school in Athens, from sometime before 79 till his death, though always travelling in embassies[330] (presumably related to his position as Lucullus' client). At some point in his career Antiochus chose to present himself as a proponent of "the Old Academy", by which he meant that he turned away from the skepticism of the Academy and returned to some version of Plato, the dogmatic philosopher. The story relayed by Cicero suggests that this new turn took place sometime before 87, but not too long beforehand.[331] We can be quite precise, then. Around the year 90 a 40-something-year-old

---

[327] Birth at around 135 to 130 is found by a reasonable deduction by Hatzimichali (2012: 10–11); death not long before 66 is assured by the reference to death in Mesopotamia, in Lucullus' campaign, and a written report of an event that took place in 69.

[328] The key scholarly debate concerns the significance of this meeting in Alexandria: was Antiochus, then, if briefly, an Alexandrian figure? Did he leave his mark in that city? Probably not, concludes Glucker (1978: 90–8) (saying that Antiochus merely passed through Alexandria, for the immediate needs of his political patron). Alexandria will change, philosophically; but this change has deeper underlying causes than the new philosophy of a single individual.

[329] Hatzimichali (2012: 28).

[330] Hatzimichali (2012: 25). The school did not have a lasting influence (28).

[331] Hatzimichali (2012: 11–16).

philosopher in Athens deviates sharply, all of a sudden, from the teaching of his school, the Academy, founding, eventually, a new school based on Platonism in the dogmatic sense. Scholars are right to study this episode with keen attention. Nothing quite like this had been happening for perhaps as long as two centuries – not, that is, since Arcesilaus' own turning away from dogmatic Platonism.

This, indeed, goes together with the rise of new philosophical centers – once again, not seen for so long! We have noted already Zenodorus of Tyre setting up a philosophical school in Alexandria, likely of the orthodox, Carneadean variety, towards the end of the second century. But the field may be significantly expanded, and Sedley (2003) documents the rise of new philosophical centers near the beginning of the first century. We have already mentioned Posidonius' activity in a school at Rhodes, quite likely within an institution already founded by Panaetius. Sedley notes another school in Rhodes, this time Epicurean, certainly active before 70 BCE (2003: 33),[332] as well as Demetrius Lacon's own Epicurean school in Miletus (33–4) (perhaps going back to Protarchus? The dates and the institutional practice parallel Panaetius/Posidonius.). Philo of Larissa was active in the 80s in Rome. The last scholarch of the Academy itself – so, a major figure – he seems to have written, away from the old center, works that deviated, once again, from the old orthodoxy: suggesting, against Academic skepticism, that knowledge is in some sense possible.[333] Further, at the time Antiochus sojourned through Alexandria, the peripatetic philosopher Staseas of Naples was in some sense the teacher of the future consul of 61 BCE, Piso Frugi.[334] So: in the last few decades of the second century it became possible for philosophy to take root outside Athens; in the first few decades of the first century it became commonplace.

---

[332] Sedley points out the willingness of the Rhodian school to deviate from positions held by the Athenian "center", but, even so, the question at stake – whether rhetoric is a technē or not – could have been reasonably debated within the bounds of orthodox Epicureanism. What we see, then, is not the rise of a new, heterodox school. Heterogeography is not heterodoxy. We do see the rise of a new Epicurean, orthodox school *independent of Athens*. This is comparable more to Panaetius, in Stoicism, than to Antiochus, in the Academy; and, in general, the very appeal of Epicureanism was always so dependent on the charisma of Epicurus, his doctrines so carefully and explicitly laid out, that Epicureanism would never deviate as much, doctrinally, from its Hellenistic origins as other schools did.

[333] Brittain (2001: chap. 3). The evidence is scanty but what seems consistent among our sources is that, while the transition was subtle, it was self-conscious: apparently Philo sought, or was immediately perceived to be seeking, to reposition Academic skepticism – specifically, in the new setting of Rome.

[334] Staseas and Piso Frugi; see Syme (1960).

We noted Antiochus, pivoting away from the skepticism of the
Academy, back to a reading of Plato as a dogmatic philosopher with
positive doctrines. But skepticism is not thereby removed from the
Greek philosophical scene. To the contrary: at apparently just that time
(or perhaps a little later) a new skepticism is put forward, by another
philosopher, who grounds it, for once, in the writings of a genuine
Skeptic. We recall Pyrrho and his pupil Timon. Active in Elis, Phlius
and Megara – that is, outside Athens, but not too far away – in the years of
the formation of the philosophical schools, in the late fourth century and
early third BCE (that is, when the Academy was still dogmatic). Such
philosophers were physically, doctrinally and stylistically removed from
Athens. Pyrrho wrote not at all, Timon wrote satirical verse; their views,
such that they could be pinned down, were radically negative. They were,
so to speak, epistemological cynics. As is true in general, such practices of
the early third century BCE had no continuity (except, that is, in sharply
modulated form, in the school practice of the Academy from Arcesilaus to
Carneades and their followers: a respectable Skepticism, now). We should
appreciate, therefore, the sharp break produced by Aenesidemus. He
decided to pick up the ancient traditions of Pyrrho and Timon – that is,
to restart from a tradition which was at this point a two-century-old piece
of antiquarianism. Apparently, he revived a more radical Skepticism (not
merely debunking certainties but advocating that one should never assent
to any claim at all. Modern scholars are properly puzzled: can the Skeptic
live his Skepticism?).[335] And he did this, in contrast to his antique predecessors, in fully fledged philosophical form: an eight-book treatise of
"Pyrrhonian discourses". (We may perhaps judge the style, based on the
assumption – none too wild – that it could have been broadly similar to
that of the extant works by Aenesidemus' follower Sextus Empiricus: lucid
but unadorned philosophical prose.) When and where did this take place?
The evidence for Aenesidemus is difficult, but it was brought together
convincingly by Decleva Caizzi (1992). Eusebius quotes a passage by a
certain peripatetic author, Aristocles of Messina: Aenesidemus "yesterday,
and the day before, tried to revive [Pyrrhonism] in Alexandria".[336] This is
not as helpful as it seems, because we are not sure when Aristocles was
active, or what "yesterday, and the day before" actually means. But it does
establish that Aenesidemus was active in Alexandria, perhaps for the bulk
of his active career. It is worrisome, then, that Diogenes Laertius refers to
him as "of Cnossus" (*Life of Timon* IX.116), while Photius refers to him as

---

[335] The title of the article by Burnyeat (1980).     [336] Eusebius, *PE* XIV.18.29.

"of Aegae" (*Bibliotheca Cod.* 212 170a41). Now, Photius actually reads and sums up Aenesidemus' *Pyrrhonian Discourses*, and he begins by a note on the dedication. The work was addressed to a Lucius Tubero, and Decleva Caizzi's original observation is that, since Photius probably drew his biographical information strictly from the book itself, the reference to "Aegae" could have been related to the dedication – that is, Aenesidemus could have recalled his meeting with Lucius Tubero in Aegae (in Aeolia). Now, the only Lucius Tubero who was prominent enough to justify Aenesidemus' terms of dedication was a legate in Asia from 61 to 58 BC, a Pompeian whose career ended with the ascendancy of Caesar. This finally allows us to reconstruct Aenesidemus' context with some clarity. Born in Cnossus in Crete, he was active mostly in Alexandria. He was sufficiently prominent as an intellectual to gain the acquaintance of a Roman legate in the years 61 to 58 and to dedicate to him, a few years later, a major philosophical work. We envision, then, an author born around 100 BC or perhaps a little earlier, pursuing a radically new philosophy in Alexandria from perhaps the 60s onwards. This, once again, sticks. Diogenes Laertius ends his life of Timon by mentioning an ancient debate: was there a continuous succession of Pyrrhonism, from Pyrrho himself all the way down (*Life of Timon* 115–16; see Dorandi, 1999a: 46–7; see also page 247 above)? We know the answer to this: the evidence concerning Aenesidemus is unequivocal, and, clearly, the proposed succession from Timon to Aenesidemus was a fiction (Diogenes is clear enough that this was understood by some authors in his own time, as well). Nevertheless, there is no reason to doubt the basic outline of a succession from Aenesidemus to Sextus Empiricus and beyond (Diogenes has seven generations following Aenesidemus). At the very least, we find that many authors later than Aenesidemus identified themselves as Pyrrhonists. A new philosophy created, from the dusty remains of satires by Timon of Phlius, around 60 BCE. For at least a quarter of a millennium thereafter Skeptics succeeded in living their Skepticism.

Aenesidemus went *back*. So did Antiochus, of course, going back to the doctrines of Plato. Ariston and Dion of Alexandria (together with Cratippus of Pergamon) moved to another past authority. Perhaps originally followers of Antiochus himself, they came to identify themselves as *peripatetic* philosophers.[337] We find a pattern – Athenian school allegiances frozen for a couple of centuries – now melting in the Alexandria of the first half of the first century BCE. Eudorus of Alexandria engaged in a similar

---

[337] Goulet (1989: 396–7).

kind of revival, in his case reaching back to an even more distant – and mostly apocryphal – past. Now, already Posidonius was greatly interested in the figure of *Pythagoras*, finding in him an ancient figure who could lend authority to positions claimed by Posidonius himself: this was of a piece with the standard Stoic move of an appeal to archaic authority, however, essentially in support of canonical school doctrine.[338] Eudorus – not a Stoic – seems to have moved beyond that: to him, Pythagoras was, directly, a source of philosophical doctrine. His precise philosophical identity and background have been subject to debate, and even his date is not clear (Strabo's account, however, in XVII 790 C, suggests that he was a contemporary of Ariston of Alexandria, so – once again – a figure of the first half of the century). Here we have therefore a major figure, author of many works, ranging from science (the reference by Strabo is to a treatise on the Nile) through philosophical commentary (commentaries are attested on both the *Timaeus* and Aristotle's *Categories*) to original philosophical works. The few details we have of his doctrines closely resemble the pseudepigraphic Pythagorean writings that are obviously hard to date and yet could also have emerged in the first century BCE,[339] of which perhaps the more significant were ascribed to Archytas. Now, to go back to Pythagoreanism, specifically to Archytas, could imply an interest in the exact sciences, and indeed there is much about number metaphysics (the "one" and the "dyad" as principles, etc.), but, unlike the authors in the Posidonian tradition, we do not see in Eudorus or in the Pythagorean pseudepigraphic writings any traces of the exact sciences developed in the Hellenistic era. The mathematics is no less archaizing than the philosophy, and it is, if anything, reverse-engineered from Platonic works such as the *Philebus* and the *Timaeus* (literally so, in the case of the pseudepigraphic work ascribed to Pseudo-Timaeus, which is the supposed Pythagorean "original" of Plato's dialogue: Baltes, 1972). Instead of trying to combine the philosophy of their own time with the science of their own time, Pythagoreans of this era looked back through the mist of the ages and tried to intuit, through the works of Plato, the pristine past when science and mathematics still went hand in hand. Doctrinal radicalism went together with minimal stylistic ambition. As Centrone sums this up (2014: 320), "The basic material betrays a scholastic origin: the subjects discussed are presented in a plain and schematic way, with a marked

[338] Ju (2013).
[339] For Eudorus, see Bonazzi (2013); for the pseudepigraphic Pythagorean works of the first century, see Centrone (2014), who is cautious concerning the dating.

tendency towards classification and systematization. Expositions tend to be pedantic, and often consist of monotonous enumerations of cases." This recalls the Hellenistic schools. But in one respect we see a significant, and, indeed, almost a unique innovation: the authorial attitude of pseudepigraphy. As noted on page 108, note 27, above, most works now titled, by modern scholars, as "pseudo-" were transmitted with their authorship inadvertently confused; or, occasionally, these were rhetorical exercises that perhaps were never intended to fool anyone; sometimes, indeed, these could be genuine forgeries produced for mercenary gain. But the category of the pseudo-author as such is extremely rare and marginal in a literary field marked by the striving after authorial status.[340] As Pythagoreans presented themselves in the first century BCE and beyond, what they emphasized was not only their own individual status as authors but also, and even more importantly, their role as expositors of an ancient, alien tradition. It seems possible that their greatest success was as aliens, in the city of Rome. At least, we have some indications (slight, and controversial) of a fully fledged Pythagorean circle headed by Nigidus Figulus – a Roman aristocrat, a contemporary of Cicero – in the city of Rome. The evidence for this is indeed problematic, but it is clear that Pythagoras was a major presence for Roman authors from Cicero to Ovid and beyond. His specifically *Italian* origins could have been part of his appeal.[341] We are reminded of Sallustius' *Empedoclea*[342] – indeed, of the central role of Empedocles in Lucretius' own poem,[343] of Horace's homage to Archytas,[344] of the strangely central role of a Pythagoras (Empedoclean-inflected?) in Ovid's *Metamorphoses*.[345] Eudorus may have been active in Alexandria; but the reinvention of Pythagoreanism had also something to do with a new, western tilt to the Mediterranean. It was also one of the more lasting innovations of this era.

---

[340] There is a significant body of pseudepigraphic works in the Judeo-Christian tradition, which is of course marked by a different understanding of authorship; this parallel sheds some light on the Pythagorean pseudepigrapha, which evoke their own claim of charismatic inspiration (it is remarkable, however, that most are ascribed not to Pythagoras but to more mundane authors).

[341] For an entry point into the literature on Imperial-era Pythagoreanism, see Flinterman (2014). The geographical emphasis on Italy is discussed on page 347.

[342] We are not sure who this Sallustius is, or what his *Empedoclea* were. We know only that Cicero compares the work, in passing, with Lucretius' *De Rerum Natura*. Apparently, then, a hexameter epic on Empedoclean topics (or an adaptation of Empedocles' poem: the evidence is *Q. Fr.* 2.10 (9).3; see Cowan, 2013, for a recent discussion).

[343] See, e.g., Garani (2007).

[344] There is no scholarly consensus on the interpretation of Horace's *Ode* I.28; authors such as D'Angour (2003) suggest it directly reflects Pythagorean themes. It certainly invokes Archytas as an Archimedes-like figure.

[345] Hardie (1995).

Much more obscure, but perhaps more telling, is the figure of Potamon of Alexandria. At some point in the first century BCE – probably later than the authors mentioned above – this author carried, with pride, the flag of "eclecticism".[346] It would be an exaggeration to say we know the contents of Potamon's philosophy.[347] It is interesting to see that, in the one context in which he is cited significantly (in Simplicius' commentary to *De Caelo*), what we find is primarily explications of mathematical details in the writings of Plato and Aristotle.[348] Specifically, Potamon used geometrical diagrams – unlabeled, however, with letters – in his philosophical writings. Once again, then, an experimental philosophy goes together with an experimental philosophical form of writing. It is not clear that any future philosopher called himself an "eclectic", and, in general, the labels of philosophical allegiance survived the upheaval of the first century (that is, the names of the schools largely remain as before, and remain as the major labels a philosopher could carry). But the innovation, of referring to mathematics for the explication of philosophy, will stick: already from the first century CE we have extant Theon of Smyrna's "Mathematics Useful for the Understanding of Plato". The extended mathematical passage, inset within the commentary to Plato or Aristotle, is commonplace, as early as our first evidence for the new format of the commentary as such (which might go back as early as the first century BCE): the *Anonymous Commentary to the Theaetetus*.[349] This brings us to one of the key innovations in philosophical writings in the era – that of commentary. On this subject, too, I wish to emphasize the inherent variety, in this regard, between the schools.

Of course, Crantor had already written a commentary to the *Timaeus*; but this was more of an isolated event. The negative evidence is significant. We have substantial reports on the writings of the Hellenistic schools, and they are marked by the *absence* of commentary on the masters. This was at the same time as medical authors were beginning to produce their own creative work in the form of commentary to Hippocrates. As noted on page

---

[346] Runia (1988) has identified an inscription from Ephesus that seems to praise "P[otamon], the eclec[tic] philosopher"! The name is reconstructed – confidently – from a single Pi (the stone is likely of the Imperial era: this is consistent with the statement of the *Suda*, that Potamon was active before and after Augustus; in general, for the problems of identification and date, see Hatzimichali, 2011: chap. 3).

[347] Hatzimichali (2011: chap. 4) heroically tries to squeeze some meaning out of the very brief account in Diogenes Laertius, I.21. Perhaps "eclecticism" meant just that – box-checking philosophy in which various catchphrases, from the various philosophical schools, are brought together.

[348] Hatzimichali (2011: chap. 5).

[349] Sedley (1995). The mathematical passage is at xxix.42–xxxi.28.

363 above, the medical commentary may well represent the influence of Alexandrian philological practices, and so the marginal position of the Hellenistic philosophical commentary is yet another example of the gap between Athens and Alexandria. And then, in the first century BCE, this gap begins to close.

Now, in late antiquity, the reasons for which we will get to in section 6.5.3 below, commentary became the dominant cultural form. We are thus tuned to see, in the first stirrings of this medium, hints of things to come. In the first century BCE, however, and throughout the Imperial era, the role of philosophical commentary is more qualified. Let us begin with the following table of peripatetic authors, from the age of Andronicus of Rhodes down to the end of the second century CE (that is, excluding Alexander of Aphrodias and his contemporaries).

### Roman-era peripatetic philosophers

| Commentary attested | Some work attested, but not commentary | No work attested |
|---|---|---|
| Andronicus | Nicolaus of Damascus | Athenaeus |
| Boethus | Aristocles of Messenia | Cratippus |
| Ariston | Aristocles of Pergamon | Menephylus |
| Athenodorus (but Stoic?) | Agathocles | |
| Alexander of Aegae | Cailianus | |
| Apollonius of Alexandria | Alexander Damas. | |
| Adrastus | Aristotle Myti. | |
| Aspasius | Eudemus Perg. | |
| Herminus | | |

We have a number of individuals obscurely attested – some of Galen's acquaintances mentioned as peripatetics, another philosopher known only through inscriptions, etc. – for whom we cannot say what form their writings took. Otherwise, from among the 12 authors for whom we can form some concrete sense of the contents of their writings, it is only for three that no commentary is attested. Two of these are Nicolaus of Damascus, whose main identity was that of a historian (and from whom we do have a *paraphrase* of some Aristotelian writings), and Aristocles of Pergamon, whose main identity was that of a rhetor. The writings of the authors in this group fared very badly (the only work that comes anywhere *near* extant is, indeed, the paraphrase by Nicolaus – surviving in the single mutilated manuscript of a Syriac translation!), and we likely know only a fragment of their works. The implication is that, starting with Andronicus of Rhodes,

practically any author who wished to be identified as a peripatetic philosopher wrote commentaries on Aristotle. Indeed, it seems significant that
practically all authors have attributed to them a commentary, specifically,
on the *Categories*[350] (though, it should be emphasized, we have also attested
some commentaries on other Aristotelian works). To be a follower of
Aristotle, in these centuries, meant, to begin with, to teach the *Organon*.

   We find some evidence for the writing of commentary by the followers of
Plato, as well, but this is quantitatively as well as qualitatively different.
Eudorus did write on the *Timaeus* (but he wrote on Aristotle's *Categories* as
well; as would Nicostratus, too, two centuries later, yet another Platonist
joining in this Aristotelian practice). Philo's commentaries were biblical.
Gaius, perhaps early in the second century, may have written scholia on
Plato. It is only in the middle of the second century CE that we find more
substantial evidence for commentaries by Platonists: surely Calvenus Taurus
(*Republic*, *Gorgias*, *Timaeus*), Aelianus (*Timaeus*), perhaps Cronius
(*Republic*), Atticus (several commentaries). Dillon (1971) reconstructs some
evidence for commentary work by Harpocration, and there are traces of a
commentary by Galen (again on the *Timaeus*). Of course, we do have a
survival, on papyrus, of the *Anonymous Commentary to the Theaetetus*, which
might be as early as the first century BCE:[351] this should give us pause. Even
so, authors in the Academic tradition would normally write mostly in other
forms: we have extant general handbooks or introductions (Theon of
Smyrna, Apuleius, Alcinous, Albinus: so this was the more typical form of
introductory teaching), as well as free-form essays (Cicero, Philo, Plutarch,
Maximus of Tyre; the same will still be true even in Plotinus' age). In the
Platonic tradition, commentary becomes the natural form of writing only in
late antiquity itself. It may also be somewhat different in character from that
of the Aristotelian school. The main target for Platonic commentary – true
to its early antecedent, by Crantor – always remains the *Timaeus*. This must
imply a different type of work from that of the Aristotelian commentaries to
the *Categories*. A commentary on the *Categories* invites close interpretation
and explication of basic philosophical ideas: the isagogic practice par excellence. It belongs to the classroom. A commentary on the *Timaeus* invites a
more original scientific and metaphysical exercise and envisions a more
sophisticated readership. Indeed, we do not have commentaries on those
of Plato's works that were usually understood in antiquity to be

---

[350]  For this tradition of commentary, see Griffin (2015).

[351]  Tarrant (1983) and Sedley (1995) argue for an earlier date for the commentary, but this is a
     controversial position (see summary of the literature in Bonazzi, 2008: 598 n.1). Perhaps the base
     probability, given the evidence discussed above, is for a later date?

"introductory" (such as the *Alcibiades*)[352] until late antiquity itself. And so: Aristotelians wrote commentaries, and taught; Platonists wrote essays and general surveys, and only occasionally zoomed in on the interpretation of individual passages within individual works.

In the remaining philosophical traditions commentary and edition activity seems to have been marginal – indeed, nearly non-existent. The exceptions are few. Athenodorus, a Stoic as well as a librarian at Pergamon (and an old man in the year 67/66), produced an edition of Zeno's *Republic* from which he removed the more outré proposals (such as having women in common). We envision a philologer-philosopher, active away from Athens at about the beginning of the first century. But his proposal was ultimately rejected by other Stoics (imagine the peripatetics, refusing to utilize Andronicus' edition!), and, indeed, it is not a very philological exercise at all: it is a philosophical doctrine masked as edition.[353] Still, it remains an important fact that Demetrius Lacon seems to have turned to philological as well as lexicographic techniques in his interpretation of Epicurus' writings.[354] Otherwise, we have very few traces of commentaries to Epicurus or to Chrysippus[355] – a major omission that perhaps accounts, in part, for the near-total disappearance of these philosophies in late antiquity. The negative evidence for the Epicurean school is meaningful, since, in fact, this is precisely what we would have expected to find among the Herculaneum papyri. Perhaps, because Epicureans found a different and complementary way of engaging with the philosophical past? I refer to the historical and biographical treatments of the philosophical schools, which are first attested in the Herculaneum papyri.[356] This innovation, once again, stuck. Apollonius of Tyre wrote biographies of Stoic philosophers[357] and, in

---

[352] Mansfeld (1994: 1).    [353] For this episode, see Schofield (1991: chap. 1).

[354] Puglia (1988); Roselli (1990). The evidence comes primarily from Demetrius' own writings, surviving in fragmentary form among the Herculaneum papyri; the negative evidence, that previous Epicureans did not engage in such practices, is not overwhelming but, given the evidence we do have of a rising interest in grammarian technique among philosophers at this time, we may perhaps assume that Demetrius was indeed original. At any rate, in Demetrius we have grammar as an occasional technique, but never a running commentary or an edition.

[355] The *Suda* notes that a certain Stoic philosopher, Aristocles of Lampsacus, wrote a commentary on Chrysippus' "How to Say and Think Each Thing" (s.v. Aristocles), but this author may well be identified as a pupil of Chrysippus (DPA, s.v. Aristoclès de Messine), and so the sense of "commentary" is more that of a "study". (More, then, in the manner of Crantor writing on the *Timaeus*.) Epictetus remarks pejoratively on such teachers of Stoicism who interpret Chrysippus' words (*Diss.* I. 17.16–18, III.21.6–7). This is taken down from Epictetus' spoken teaching and is clearly meant to denigrate the spoken teaching of others.

[356] Sedley (2003).

[357] Goulet (1989: 294). This author is mentioned by Strabo as "recent" (a loose category) and may have been used by Philodemus himself: in all likelihood, a contemporary of Philodemus.

Philodemus' direct tradition – of writing on authors across all the philosophical schools – we have, attested, Arius Didymus (whoever he may have
been),[358] as well as Diogenes Laertius, extant. Remarkably – the main
observation of Sedley (2003) – such histories of philosophy all end in the
middle of the first century. Partly, this may be Philodemus' own influence;
but, above all: there is a sense that philosophy has pivoted away (or "ended",
in Sedley's term: I return below to explain my different perspective on this
transition).

As noted above (page 143), Thrasyllus – rather later in the first century
BCE (or even early in the first century CE) – arranged and catalogued the
text of Plato, in what must have been seen as a philological, grammarian-like
exercise. Now Alexandria has consolidated the texts of the literary canon –
which includes Plato himself. Thus, Thrasyllus' edition of Plato probably
had Hellenistic, Alexandrian antecedents.[359] This, then, should be contrasted with the one case we have of a genuine grammarian-philosopher:
and so we return, once again, to Andronicus of Rhodes.[360] His activity may
indeed be seen as the starting point for the entire project of Aristotelianism –
as grammar, and, hence, as commentary.

Andronicus' quest for the Aristotelian text is romantically told by
Strabo, in details that have come under scrutiny by modern scholars.
Strabo, for various reasons, tended to exaggerate the significance of
Andronicus' edition, making it into a *rediscovery* of works that had previously been *lost*. This account – not long ago seen as historical truth – is
now rejected by Aristotle scholars (see, e.g., Barnes, 1997: Aristotle's
esoteric works were never entirely unknown). But the important thing is
not what Andronicus discovered but, rather, what he invented: a new
attitude towards a philosophical text. He consolidated the text of the
esoteric works by Aristotle, produced a new edition and published a
catalogue. In a word, he acted in the manner in which Alexandrian
grammarians consolidated the texts of literary authors. Apparently, no
one before him had done the same with any non-literary work.
Andronicus, indeed, took the most unliterary component of the
Aristotelian corpus – the fully fledged school works – to give them the

---

[358]  He used to be identified with the Alexandrian Stoic Arius, active in Augustus' court; this has been
      vigorously denied by Göransson (1995). If Göransson is wrong (and the argument is one of
      probabilities), then we have a correlation: when Epicureans and Stoics become engaged in the
      scholarship of philosophy, they do so less with commentary and edition, more in history and
      biography.
[359]  The relative role of Alexandrians and Platonists in the early editions of Plato is debated; see Solmsen
      (1981).
[360]  For discussion of the activities of Thrasyllus and Andronicus, see Hatzimichali (2013).

full literary treatment.[361] According to another strand in the ancient tradition, the new edition by Andronicus relied on work by Tyrrhanion, the Alexandrian grammarian, who catalogued Sulla's collection – the spoils of war – in the city of Rome.[362] It is hard to tell how the two versions could – or should – be reconciled, but the implied parallelism, between philosopher and grammarian, is telling. The grammarian-like activity of the writing of commentary would become enshrined, from this moment on, as the hallmark of a new Aristotelianism: a stylistic departure as remarkable as the doctrinal departure of Antiochus.

The dating of Andronicus has certainly been debated – some wishing to make him active late in the first century – but this is mostly because of Cicero's silence concerning him. (This silence would be truly remarkable only had Andronicus been the actual discoverer of Aristotle's works: which indeed we need no longer believe).[363] The edition of Aristotle's complete esoteric works is a massive endeavor, and we can imagine Andronicus launching it well before his death. And so, yet another pivot, perhaps not much later than Antiochus, that of course sticks: Aristotelianism would remain grammarian-like, focused on textual teaching, and will indeed, through Thrasyllus and later commentators, come to influence Platonism as well.

Aristotelianism as a textual/teaching philosophy, begun by Andronicus at about the time that Platonism, as dogmatic philosophy, was revived by Antiochus. I note a transition in literary practice, among Aristotelians; a transition in doctrine, among Platonists. But let us not forget that the same Antiochus was creative, once again, not only in the contents of his philosophy but also in his *style*. The work in which Antiochus set forth his opposition to Skeptic Platonism, *Sosus*, was in dialogue form: undoubtedly an intentional move, dramatizing the sense of a return to Plato. As noted above, only a handful of philosophical dialogues are attested from the Athenian schools, and by Antiochus' time the form could well have been moribund for over a century – was it most recently produced in Alexandria,

---

[361] The Aristotelian corpus was transmitted into the Middle Ages almost entirely without the diagrams and anatomical drawings which are clearly assumed by the logical, physical and biological works (for the absence of diagrams from the medieval text of Ps.-Aristotle's *Mechanics*, see van Leeuwen, 2016). The diagrams must have been lost at some authoritative stage along the way. It seems to me likely enough – if a speculation – that the author who had the means, as well as the motive, to remove the diagrams was Andronicus himself, presenting in this way a more literary Aristotle. (That is: had the diagrams survived through his edition, who would be the later editor with sufficient independent authority of removing them all? See pp. 146–7 above for the non-literary character of illustrations.)

[362] Plutarch, *Life of Sulla* 26.1.      [363] So, Gottschalk (1990).

by Eratosthenes? The new innovation – we come to expect this – sticks. Very soon Antiochus' follower, Dion of Alexandria, wrote a sympotic work, so probably a dialogue. This is attested by Plutarch (*Quaest. Conv.* 612DE), in his own sympotic writings, and of course Plutarch was a major author of philosophical dialogue: the form is extant from Cicero and Philo as well, themselves Platonists of various shades. Partly under the influence of Cicero, the form became enshrined in Latin prose, reaching beyond the philosophical domain: so Tacitus, a historian writing a dialogue on rhetoric, Varro, a scholar writing a dialogue on agriculture... In fact, dialogue, having been reinvented by the Platonic philosopher Antiochus, is now reincarnated as a form only marginally attached to philosophy, let alone to Platonism. Lucian's dialogues are free from philosophical allegiance; sympotic writing becomes purely sympotic – or purely textual – in Athenaeus' strange work of semi-drunken quotations, the *Deipnosophistae*. Plato's own dialogues used to belong to philosophy – but also, and perhaps primarily, to the literary canon. The revival of the dialogue form did not belong to one or the other but signaled, instead, a much more open-ended spectrum between literature and philosophy, a spectrum made open as philosophy ventured out of Athens.

Even Philodemus – the sober Epicurean philosopher – was well regarded as a poet, author of (non-philosophical) epigrams. Who, among previous Epicureans, could claim as much? But, soon after him, a Roman author would make Epicureanism the subject of his *didactic epic*! Lucretius' *De Rerum Natura* is the epitome of first-century BCE innovation. Looking back, it seems unaware of any philosophical developments within Epicureanism later than the master's *On Nature*;[364] but it also seems unaware of the divisions of a Hellenistic past, separating philosophy from poetry. As noted already, the didactic epic harks back to its obvious antecedent in Empedocles (we recall Sallustius' contemporary effort, of an Empedoclean epic in Latin), but also surely to the archaic didactic epic and its Hellenistic revival (whatever else Lucretius was ignorant of, he could not have been unaware of Aratus).[365] The poem hews closely to its prose source of Epicurus' *On Nature* – with, perhaps, one of the few original contributions being the tale of the Athenian plague, which is doubly original. It subjects an Athenian historical subject matter to the hexameter meter of wisdom and myth (of course, the poetization of history is much less

---

[364] So, Sedley (1998).
[365] Aratus was one of the central figures of the Latin reception of Greek poetry; Gee (2013: chap. 4) discusses the evidence for his influence, specifically, on Lucretius.

surprising in Latin); and it brings a description, suggestive of Thucydides, hence of the Hippocratic medical tradition, into the philosophy of Epicurus (who had no more interest, in his own writing, in medicine than in mathematics). But Lucretius' main theme, after all, is the fear of death: why should he not bring in all the disciplines touching upon it, philosophy – as well as medicine?[366] Lucretius' poem is aware of its Hellenistic poetic antecedents, but it is quite distinct in attitude and achievement, earnest throughout its wordplay, subjecting all its many vignettes to the sense of an accomplished whole. The result is inspiring precisely because of the sense of poetry, infused by a serious, even a noble, sense of purpose.

In general, it is typical that, with the poetry of the Latin golden age, scholars are comfortable detecting the echoes of philosophy[367] (and the record, on the poets' own philosophical engagement, is considerable).[368] A mere decade or so later than Lucretius' death, L. Varius Rufus wrote a hexameter poem, *De Morte* – now almost entirely lost – which could well have been the rendering, into poetic form, of a prose work by Philodemus. It is clear that the two, the Epicurean philosopher and the Roman poet, were familiar with each other: Athens and Alexandria, in a literary collaboration.[369] But they are but two members of a wider, well-documented circle: it included, famously, Vergil himself, as well as Horace.[370] Lucretius, then, was not a fluke. The synthesis of poetry and philosophy was the key theme of the Roman golden age.

We linger on the description of first-century philosophy: it is here that the pivot is the most apparent, and, indeed, it has been sufficiently recognized in the literature. Frede sees a watershed (Frede, 1999: 782): "In each case we are led back to the end of the second century BC... [T]here seems to emerge at just this point in time a certain pattern which comes to shape the philosophy of the first century BC and, beyond it, the philosophy of the early Empire." Even more significant is the observation by Sedley (2003): he detects an attitude – among the ancients themselves – to treat the middle of the first century as "end of history" in philosophy. At this stage of the argument this sense of an "end of history" reminds us of the Greek attitude towards their *literary* past. In some ways, what we see is that, around the middle of the first century, philosophy came to be treated

---

[366] For this interpretation of Lucretius' themes, see Segal (1990).

[367] Garani and Konstan (2014) carries a title, typical of an entire branch of the study of Roman poetry: "The Philosophizing Muse: The Influence of Greek Philosophy on Roman Poetry".

[368] See the collection of papers Armstrong et al. (2010).   [369] Hollis (1977), Gigante (2004).

[370] Yona (2015).

analogously to the way the literary canon had been for several centuries already. We recall the evidence from the portraits – so many of them emerging from the Italian villa, the site of the first-century Italian reception of Greek culture. There, a philosophical canon was arranged alongside and in rough parity with the literary canon. The event of the middle of the first century BCE was not quite simply the canonization of philosophy but, rather, the doubling of the canon, its extension to a parallel form, from literature into philosophy.

To quote now from Sedley (2003: 41):

> These people [such as Philodemus] were, after all, better placed than anybody to appreciate the massive gulf that separated their former philosophical life in their school's Athenian headquarters from their new life, one of teaching their discipline and its history to a local clientele, while continuing to study the school's treasured scriptures.

Back in Athens, one would have immersed oneself in the detail of intra-school dispute; Philodemus still did a fair bit of that. This is the thematic lock of the Hellenistic school (see page 400 above). But his other face – perhaps put up for a Roman readership? – was that of the author of a wide-ranging history of philosophy, encompassing all the schools. He presented, to a Roman audience, Greek philosophy as a kind of literary heritage. To be a philosopher, in Hellenistic Athens, was to be a zealot of one's school. But the reading of the canon is inherently a matter of being able to range across its width. It is the collection of the big library. Philodemus, of course, was still fixed in his Epicureanism (the philosophical position which will remain the most stable, through the Imperial era). Many other philosophers would be eclectic, not merely in the presentation of other people's philosophy but in the development of their own philosophy. One brings together Plato and the Stoa; Aristotle and commentary; philosophy and science; and, above all, philosophy and literature – that is, Athens and Alexandria.

### 4.5.4    Coda to Hellenism: Literature

I argue that the main theme of the pivot is the rise of new combinations – which is what Hellenistic literature has always prided itself on! The change here would be subtler. And yet, there are ways to emphasize the role of *combining*. Meleager was famous for an *Anthology*; he should be seen as a prime member of this class of 100. First of all, chronologically. The evidence for him depends on Roman poets (who likely responded to poems he collected) who in turn can be dated with precision – Romans, even poets, often engage in datable political careers – and also on Greek poets (whom he cited) who left an epigraphic mark, also dated with some certainty. Alan Cameron may therefore conclude with some certainty (Cameron, 1993: 56): "The *Garland* cannot have been published more than a year or so before 100 or after 90 BC." Meleager wrote an anthology (collection of flowers: "Garland") of epigrams, representing different poets as "flowers", selecting from their poems, intertwining them in meaningful ways: an original work of great subtlety. As Cameron points out, this was a first. All the evidence we have for previous collections of short poetry involves poems by a single author; scholarly surveys; or collections produced for largely didactic purposes (Cameron, 1993: 5–12), a conclusion supported by papyri finds since). This is indeed surprising: what else can one do with such short verse, in a book culture, if not collect it? We have noted this omission in Part I above, on pages 18–19: it marks, indeed, the domination of the Greek literary scene by the figure of the author. Which underlines Meleager's originality: he set out for no less than a reinterpretation of authorship. The spirit of the anthology is close to Alexandrian scholarship – the survey, in which the sense of individual voices is not muted but, rather, amplified through its piquant juxtapositions. As noted above, Roman poets may well have reacted to this new work almost immediately (by writing their own poems, however, not their own anthologies), and the production of anthologies of short verse became a major genre. It surely stuck: the work was copied, another anthology produced by a Philip in the early Imperial era (Cameron, 1993: 56–65), and then yet others were made in later centuries and well into Byzantine times, ultimately surviving as the now extant *Greek Anthology*. This first-century BCE innovation – rather like that of Aristotelian commentary – suited well the textual practices of late antiquity and the Middle Ages. Once again, we should not be misled by future glories: at this point, it is a very successful, but rather strange, innovation. And, against the background of new combinations that give rise to new identities, of eclecticism in philosophy, its significance is perhaps just that of *combination*. Potamon brought together many philosophers; Meleager many poets.

Meleager's anthology, as well as its heirs, is an erudite affair, structured around the collection of many names. It is thus easy to date. The *Anacreontea*, by contrast, are predicated on imitation and the erosion of authorial status: their date is thus much more difficult. But they may well form the closest contemporary parallel to Meleager. The *Anacreontea* are a series of 60 short poems, now extant as a small appendix inside the Codex

Palatinus Gr. 23, from which the "anthologia Palatina" itself derives. Their early modern readers considered them to be, indeed, by the archaic poet Anacreon, but scholarship quickly concluded they had to be later imitations, put together in our Byzantine manuscript as a collection based on previous collections – exactly analogous to the *Anthology*. Martin West (1993) has detected four layers, dating likely from the first century BCE to the sixth CE: an interpretation which is now the consensus position.[371] Throughout this period, then, we have Greek poets engaging in the imitation of Anacreon's poetry, emphasizing love and wine, suggesting the context of the symposium but bleaching away the cultural specificity of the Greek sympotic rituals. There is clearly an interest in imitation as such – assuming the voice of a past poet – and in collection as such – putting short verse together.[372] These are all typical attitudes towards the canon. What was found disappointing by many generations of readers is precisely the generic quality, the author reduced to the minimal idea of how an Anacreon should be like. We recall the many extant Anacreon portraits: from the first century BCE on; bland representations of Greekness were set up and collected in villas, sometimes in stone, sometimes in song.

The same principle – anthologizing, reducing the element of authorship – has parallels in prose, as well. We can begin with a work which is even (remarkably, for this age) extant: Parthenius' "Sufferings of Love", a collection of 36 brief love stories of mythical and historical subjects, apparently drawn mostly from prose sources such as history, retold by Parthenius.[373] The entire collection is self-deprecatingly presented by Parthenius to Gallus – the well-known Latin poet (hence our dating: 52 to 26 BC) – as a *hupomnēmation*, "small handbook", no more than prose "material" for Gallus to transform into his verse. This is not quite the same as an anthology (Parthenius does not merely set out to cull out and order love stories), but probably, with prose, one had to do more (we are reminded, indeed, of the histories of philosophy, perhaps invented at the same time, and at the same Greek/Roman intersection, by Philodemus). This turn has more ample Hellenistic antecedents (already Callimachus' paradoxography was not that different), and more parallels: Photius could still read another collection of love stories, by a certain Conon, apparently only a little

---

[371] To identify an important layer of the *Anacreonta* in the first century depends, ultimately, on a certain understanding of the character of this period as a whole. A circular, yet valid exercise: it is good that we rely on an authority such as West.

[372] There is now some scholarship on this poetics of imitation and arrangement – perhaps in tune with a post-modern sensibility; see Rosenmeyer (1992) and Baumbach and Dümmler (2014).

[373] My discussion is based on Lightfoot (1999).

younger than Parthenius himself. Perhaps most striking is the very use of the prose introduction and dedication and the reference to the book as a "handbook": this is the treatment of literature as a technical subject matter, one poet handing another a tool for one's work.

Parthenius (and Conon) are closer to Meleager's practice of anthologizing, but considerably later in time. Aristides, author of the *Milesiaca*, was surely active very early in the first century. Our evidence is much more problematic, but the work is of some consequence. It is reported that it was paraphrased into Latin by Sisenna, that it was found on the body of a Roman following the Battle of Carrhae.[374] Not surprising to find this in a soldier's knapsack: it was a collection of mostly pornographic stories,[375] assumed to be set in Miletus (famous for such things in antiquity: places carried their meanings), perhaps recounted in the first person by Aristides. Sisenna died in 67 BC, so the Roman reception is in this case very early – as was that of Meleager's poetry. (Thus the overall impression: such Greek works are written at the very least with an awareness of a potential Roman audience.) We are reminded of Menippean satire, and it is generally assumed that Apuleius and Petronius – the Latin heirs to Menippus – also relied, directly or indirectly, on Aristides (whether or not his own book involved the same Menippean combination of prose and poetry). We do not know of Greek authors reviving this form – but Menippus himself was surely imitated by the Roman Varro, around the middle of the century, who wrote – the first to do so, perhaps, after more than two centuries! – a satire that combined prose and verse of various meters. Parthenius had few pretensions (or he pretended to have few); Aristides clearly understood his contribution as in some sense of a "low" genre. But such collections of love stories, such Menippean works, would have a significant legacy. It is remarkable that the geographical focus of Parthenius (as well as of Conon) was mostly in Asia Minor,[376] as of course was that of Aristides; we are reminded of the geographical focus of the ancient novel. This, of course, has many fathers, and emerges in its fully fledged form only in the first century CE. The anthologies of love and sex, produced in the first century BCE, merely suggest the possibility of such a new generic leap. The main themes are of a capacious narrative, within whose convolutions

---

[374] Plutarch, *Life of Crassus* 31–2.
[375] A potential papyrus fragment, P.Oxy. LXX. 4762, involves a donkey (May, 2009).
[376] Lightfoot (1999).

many subplots can reside; and a related generic openness, a prose that opens to poetic themes, on the one hand, and to historical and even technical exposition, on the other hand.

But perhaps we should look not so much at the origins of the novel but, rather, at its ecological niche. Something has opened up, allowing for a new belletristic genre. This surely owes something to a winnowing down of other generic possibilities. In the first century BCE we see, quite simply, something approaching a hiatus in *poetry*, as such. There are altogether 90 authors in the TLG, dated in any likelihood, at least through parts of their career, to the first century BCE.[377] Of course, we know that the TLG is not exhaustive. It does tend to emphasize authors of a more literary character; hence it is significant that we have here only 15 "belletristic" authors (by which I mean poets, or pre-novelistic authors). The comparable numbers for the same exercise, this time with the second century BCE, yields 131 authors, of whom 34 are "belletristic". The quantitative difference seems real enough (from 26 percent to 17 percent), but the qualitative observations are more significant. The 15 TLG belletristic authors from the first century BC are as follows.

| | | |
|---|---|---|
| Alexander 0401 | Comic | 1 BC |
| Batrachomyomachia 1220 | Parod. | 2/1 BC |
| Blaesus[378] 1227 | Comic | 2/1 BC |
| Boethus 0146 | Epigr. | 1 BC/1 AD |
| Butas[379] 2611 | Eleg. | 1 BC |
| Erycius 2653 | Epigr. | 1 BC? |
| Harmodius 0720 | Trag. | 1 BC |
| "Ninos" 1804 | Narr. fic. | 1 BC |
| Parthenius 0655 | Myth. | 1 BC |
| Polemaeus 0625 | Trag. | 1 BC |
| Pompeius Macer[380] 0346 | Trag. | 1 BC/1 AD |
| Pompeius Macer Junior 1631 | Epigr. | 1 BC/1 AD |

[377] This is looking just at authors whose date is given within two centuries (so, either the second or first century BC [2/1 BC], or the first century BC or first century AD [1 BC/1 AD]), even with a question mark. (In the most expansive sense, the TLG counts 221 authors in this century, but such results are massive overcounts, including any chronological range that happens to coincide with the given century: thus, one of the results is the "Homerica", ranging from the fifth century BCE to the tenth century CE.)

[378] Born in Capri, of Oscan origins (so the name suggests); the fragments suggest the influence of Rhinthon, and Rawson (1985: 103) tends to assign him to the third century. The TLG may well be simply wrong here.

[379] Freedman of Cato the Younger; the attested poetry is on Roman *Aetia*: Horsfall, 1991: 206.

[380] A Roman; White (1992) is adamant, however, that he ought to be understood as a Latin, not Greek, poet.

(*cont.*)

| | | |
|---|---|---|
| Priscus[381] 2641 | Epic. | 1 BC/1 AD? |
| Sostratus[382] 2694 | Poeta | 1 BC? |
| Theodotus 0816 | Trag. | 1 BC |

We can fit about half these authors within the evident trends noted so far: three epigrammatists (clearly a TLG undercount), Parthenius and (perhaps) a parallel figure in Sostratus; the novel "Ninos" (optimistically dated by the TLG to the first century BCE). The *Batrachomyomachia* may well be an earlier Hellenistic work. Remaining are a few authors identified as "tragedians", of whom practically nothing is known. A few further, even more obscure first-century tragedians are noted by Snell (1971: 309–11), but they derive almost exclusively from epigraphic sources – that is, occasionally, a person is honored as a "tragedian". (An author? An actor? Perhaps, the craft in question may have been that of pantomime: more below.) Obviously, the list is incomplete, based as it is on the TLG, which requires actual texts: Cicero, after all, defended the *poet* Archias.[383] In general, it is certain that occasional poetry went on being composed and performed. The most important study of the social setting of Greek poetry in the Roman era as a whole is Hardie (1983, esp. chap. 2). He is correct to emphasize the inscriptional evidence for itinerant poets, but his account is vitiated by a desire to fit the evidence within an unbroken chain leading from the earliest archaic rhapsodies to the Byzantine "wandering poets" studied by Cameron (1965) (on which, more on page 56 above). It is indeed true that public performance of poetry would always remain part of the Greek cultural vocabulary,[384] but, against this background, the following discontinuity is even more remarkable. Hardie (1983: 17–21) notes how the epigraphic evidence –

---

[381] A Roman, executed by Tiberius for reciting potentially subversive poetry: Shotter, 1969.

[382] O'Hara (1996) suggests identifying him with a grammarian from Nysa, attested – of course – for teaching Roman patrons, in the second half of the first century BC. The attested poetry – just like the attested prose – is mythographic in character. As noted by O'Hara (1996: 208), a rather Parthenius-like figure. The identification is uncertain; without it, the attribution to the first century collapses.

[383] Archias was clearly a major cultural presence, seeking high-level Roman patronage: Wiseman (1982); some sense of the literary skill that made the patronage possible is suggested by Cicero's tribute to it: Nesholm (2010). Remarkably, it appears that he wrote epic poetry in praise of contemporary Roman political achievements. This is poetry-for-patronage in a very direct sense, for which there are not many antecedents.

[384] It was indeed constitutive to the educational process: Mitchell (2006).

which is fairly extensive[385] – has the itinerant poet arrive at the city, sing its encomia and then receive, in turn, his commemoration in stone. This evidence is *all* from the third and second centuries BCE, however (Hardie, 1983: 21). "The poetic eulogy of cities disappears from the inscriptions after the second century B.C." – perhaps because, Hardie goes on to suggest, "[i]tinerant display orators may. . .have been enjoying the first taste of the popularity. . .which led to the movement known as the Second Sophistic". Arguing for continuity, Hardie might have hit upon an important semiotic break: somehow, around 100 BCE, the currency of poetry was no longer fully valid for the traffic of praise.[386]

Something had changed, qualitatively. Indeed, let us put our survey of TLG poets of the first century next to those of the preceding, second century. Even there, a similar survey yields 34 poets, including such authors as Bion and Moschus, the Bucolic poets, or Nicander, the author of (among other things) didactic epic. Lyric poetry, tragedy and especially comedy are all attested sufficiently to suggest an active (if, of course, already shrunken) literary scene. The overall contours of the genres are essentially the same as in the canon.

At some point between the second and first centuries something broke entirely. Greek literary figures are now almost entirely scholarly figures, perhaps producing mythographic surveys, perhaps lending their voice to the wit of epigram. But this is just that: lending one's voice. Only a handful seem to carry, as primary identity, the badges of "lyrical poet", "epic author"; even the "comedian" or the "tragedian", as an identity, seems to have become a merely local identity. This result is shocking, but it seems real enough. Just as the entirety of the exact sciences disappears, at the beginning of the first century BCE – to survive, if at all, as an added string to the philosopher's lyre – so does the entirety of poetry quasi-disappear at the same time. Its voice is now heard as a string added to the scholar's lyre. Of course, this is less of a clear transition: the identities of the grammarian and the poet have long intermingled. But it is, if anything, more remarkable as a transition. Mathematics was always a rare pursuit, and it is conceivable that sheer bad luck could have nearly wiped it out for a period.

---

[385] Nineteen Hellenistic inscriptions counted in Hardie (1983: 206), who says (207 n.26) that "completeness is not claimed".

[386] During the Imperial era authorship seems to expand, and, with it, there is also some more activity in poetry (though drama, at least, is almost entirely dead). But this will come when rhetoric is growing even more and the overall ratio between poetry and rhetoric very clearly flips to the latter's advantage, during the Roman era. A traditional view – which the data confirm. (On all this, see more on the counting of the authors of the various genres in Chapter 5.)

But poetry is essential to a culture's identity: it is almost incredible that it could be lost. But, in a way, it was, with the important ecological consequences suggested above: in the absence of poetry, Greeks could proceed to create the novel. And was it not the same absence – of Greek *poetry* – that made possible the creation of the Latin mirror canon? It is one thing to write in the shadow of Callimachus. But imagine Roman authors as the *contemporaries* of Callimachus; would this not have inhibited their writing? Romans proceeded to the creation of their own ambitious lyric and epic poetry – when no such ambitions were any longer expended on the Greek original. And so, from the ecological vacuum, two new developments: two ways of literature, not-being-Greek-poetry. On the one hand, the novel; on the other hand, Roman poetry. It is from these two that modern European literature emerges. For a reason: the two suggest, in their two distinct ways, how – with the Greek canon as a given – new, fully ambitious literature may yet be written.

For, of course, the canon remains. Indeed, in real ways, it is expanded: the relatively minor field of rhetoric now becomes codified along the lines of other, canonical literature. Eventually, the re-emergence of rhetoric would be the central cultural phenomenon of Greek life, declamations reanimating the city squares of the Greek east. This phenomenon – the Second Sophistic – belongs mostly to the second century CE, but it seems to be the culmination of a longer tradition of Atticism, in which the style and language of Attic orators is made to be the touchstone of refinement.[387] So: once again, turning back towards a past. And, indeed, this was invented as a reaction to a supposed intermediate, decadent era of "Asiatic" speech. What "Atticism" means is not merely that the canon is to be revered but that, right up to now, it has not been revered properly (we recall Antiochus, going back to Plato and condemning his heirs in the Academy). It is obvious that this is all invented – "Asianism", constructed by newly made "Atticists".[388] When, and why, this construction? Our earliest evidence is from Cicero, who represents Atticism as a debate internal to Latin rhetoric of the 50s and 40s. In this, "Atticism" is of course not a matter of Greek dialect but of style; and, among the canonical orators, only a handful are considered truly valuable (the most austere, Lysias, is marked especially for veneration). Cicero – attacked as not enough of an Atticist – defends himself by invoking Demosthenes – i.e. a more traditional form of the

---

[387] For the rise of Atticism, I rely on Wisse (1995) and O'Sullivan (1997), whose relatively recent proposal seems to have become the consensus opinion.

[388] So, already, von Wilamowitz-Moellendorff (1900).

canon. Later on, Greek scholars active in the city of Rome in the 30s to the 20s (Caecilius – a Greek from Sicily – may have been the first;[389] the somewhat later Dionysius of Halicarnassus is still extant) promulgate their own version of Atticism, this time with the entire range of the Attic orators taken as models; from the time of those critics onwards the Greek tradition of Atticism is uninterrupted. The implication of this evidence – that Atticism was first a Roman, only later a Greek passion – was resisted by all scholars prior to Wisse (1995), perhaps because of a prejudice that influences should not run in such directions. In fact, as Wisse makes clear (1995: 77), the negative evidence from Cicero – his failure to cite *Greek* Atticists – is meaningful. It is only natural that, around the middle of the first century BCE, it should be Romans, more than Greeks, who would be interested in oratory, and the fundamental point is that, for them, Athens' fall from political power hardly mattered. To them, Athens never was a *political* site.

Now, Roman authors such as Cicero did not try to show that *all* Greek canonical orators adhered to their own preferred standards; they picked and chose from the past, making this their model, that their enemy. Their interest, in other words, was in living oratory, not in the canon as such. Greek grammarians, coming a decade or two later (when political positions, too, would have been altered), capitalized, then, on the Roman renewed interest in the rhetorical canon, now representing this entire segment of the Greek canon as worthy of veneration: producing, as it were, their own anthology of the rhetorical canon. A Roman rhetorical moment reanimated Greek rhetoric; and an entire genre rose in significance. Very soon afterwards even the small libraries of the Nile would make sure they had their Demosthenes (see pages 37–8 above).[390]

Rhetoric rises: somewhat, as noted above, at the expense of tragedy. But of course this remains central to the Greek literary system, and comes, in a sense, to be performed again – though in a radically new way.

I refer to the rise of pantomime: sweeping through the literary practices of the Mediterranean much as astrology swept through its scientific practice. Once again, our evidence is meager. Around 80 BCE Aulus Aemilius

---

[389] On him, see O'Sullivan (1997).

[390] The outline presented here is revisionistic, in its emphasis on the invented nature of "Atticism". It is also conservative – indeed, Philostratean – in its claim that rhetoric receded in importance through the Hellenistic era and rose again in the Roman era. Recent scholarship – what else? – tends to support the revisionist claim and to deny the conservative one. There is of course substantial qualitative evidence for the rise of Imperial-era rhetoric, and, by now, we can see that the evidence of the papyri is at least suggestive. Why do we get so much more Demosthenes, in Imperial papyri? (We return to count ancient orators on pp. 588–96 below.)

Sextus Zosimus – gymnasiarch in Priene – arranged a festival whose crowning moment was a performance by Ploutogenes, a "pantomime".[391] This is the first that we explicitly hear of pantomime in the Greek world – and also the last, until the following century. By then, however, we have substantial evidence for the rise of pantomime as a major cultural form in the city of Rome, perhaps at the time of Octavian (one source speaks specifically of the year 22 BCE), perhaps even earlier.[392] It appears clear that, already by this point, pantomime had become the central form of literary performance; it will remain so for centuries to come, in the Greek east as in Italy itself.[393] Now, this was not exactly a *silent* form. The actor, to be sure, remained silent, dancing and expressing the action as it unfolded. But he was typically accompanied by a choir, whose background singing provided the "libretto". The subjects were typically drawn from myth, and so, typically, they were those of tragedy. Once again, we are reminded of Parthenius. In pantomime, dramatic dialogue was stripped away, and in its place all the emphasis was put on characterization and plot. This is a medium of solo performances, the audience's response triggered by an appreciation of virtuoso achievement. It is a *panto*mime in that the solo dancer was able to imitate all the characters, all the actions, in his own body – becoming, as it were, a moving, pulsating anthology of tragedy.[394] This is how the canon was now performed, marking the single individual who embodied, in himself, the virtuosity of many combinations.

The pantomime master, presenting in his body a strange combination – above all, it appears, for a Roman audience. We may consider such pantomimists alongside other Greek artists, now producing the *depicted*

---

[391] Inschr. von Priene 113 63–6; see Robert (1930: 114–17). For Zosimus, see Kennell (2013: 229–30). I am not sure what is to be made of his cognomen; Robert suggests that the pantomime in question could also have Italian associations, and he suggests a parallel (Robert, 1938: 11–13) in another pantomime from about the same time, found in an inscription from Delphi: Klio 17 (1921) 177,161 [2]; this depends on heavy restoration, however.

[392] The evidence for the explosion of the popularity of pantomime in Rome is discussed in Jory (1981).

[393] The papyrological evidence for the popularity of mime in Egypt is abundant; see Swiderek (1954). Turner (1963) is left wondering: did tragedy even survive in Roman Egypt, as a form of performance? It did, of course: but, now, secondary to mime.

[394] In general, Lucian was clear: the pantomime actor/dancer should be an expert in the dramatic and epic canon. It was a form of performing the canon. Pantomime is often seen as a bridge between high and low culture (it strikes modern tastes as somewhat more "vulgar" than canonical tragedy, perhaps because text was less central; certainly, its audience was wide). This, I believe, is wrong. In pantomime we see, instead, once again, the homogeneity of subject matter between all forms of cultural expression. Pantomime was quite unlike modern vaudeville, and, exactly like the ancient novel (see p. 87 above), it disrupts our tendency to apply to antiquity the categories of Bourdieu's literary fields. For the ancients, the canon was one, all culture organized around it. For general surveys on the art of pantomime, see Lada-Richards (2007) and Hall and Wyles (2008).

body – and this, too, shows a remarkable combination! And so, we need to look at our evidence for Greek portraiture. I glance, briefly, beyond literature and into art: this will allow us a closer look at the social, and political, context, which we may need for the following section. This, indeed, derives mostly from Italy and begins primarily in the first century BCE. As Roman patrons commissioned portraits of the canonical Greek authors, they also accumulated portraits of *themselves*; it is here that we find an original transformation.

Late Republican portraiture is characterized by the style of "verism". This is marked by an emphatically naturalistic representation of (typically, old) facial features – literally, warts and all – of a kind which is only very distantly approached by the realistic tendencies of Hellenistic art. In most cases, however, such faces are mounted on nude, idealized bodies, of the type associated with the artistic representation of myth. Art history, ever formalistic, always had a hard time accounting for such transitions in style. Richter (1955) suggests, essentially, that verism was born as Greek artists were struck by the strange faces of Roman people (!). Kaschnitz von Weinberg (1926) has suggested that the facial features of verism go back to the specifically Roman tradition of the death mask, a superficial resemblance that undoubtedly emphasizes the strong naturalism of portraiture in the veristic style: it was indeed comparable to a genuine copy of the facial features (but this type of account cannot explain why verism arises at the time and place that it does). Richter, in a sense, has it right: it is clear that veristic portraits were produced primarily by *Greeks*, for *Romans*. Thanks to Tanner (2000), we now have a fuller account of this moment of Greco-Roman encounter, and we can understand verism as a reflection of the conditions of Roman patronage. The fundamental point is that such portraits were often commissioned by Greek cities, to honor their Roman patrons. They arise from the social circumstances of the Roman patronage relations with the east. There, the nude body suggested a quasi-religious veneration of the patron as savior; the detailed face suggested the gravitas of a Roman aristocrat.

Let us take Tanner's lead: his account is compelling, for the overall nature of cultural encounter for the first century BCE. In this case, the artist brings forward a culturally specific skill, for which the Roman dedicatee, or patron, relies on the Greeks. The artist does not simply recreate, for this new Roman authority, the same art he would have produced for Greeks, however. Instead, the artist reaches out and seeks a new combination from among his arsenal of culturally available techniques – one that will be effective for the specific encounter. This, in turn, becomes the leading style for active artists. Greeks, then, transforming *themselves* for Roman consumption. From now on, verism – the way in which Greekness is played out for Roman patrons – becomes, quite simply, the major way in which Greek artists practice their art. As we saw with the rise of rhetoric, in the preceding section: Romans, effectively, changing Greek culture itself. We tend to think of transmission as a transitive process – the transmitter providing something to the transmittee, remaining himself unchanged. But it is in fact reciprocal, and the transmitter, himself, gets changed. And so, with art: Roman patronage did not simply collect a given Greek practice. Greek civic authorities, Greek artists, subtly transformed themselves, as they approached the Roman patron. Rome, captivated by Greece, ended up capturing its cultural mistress.

### 4.5.5 When Worlds Converge: Towards an Account of the First Century BCE

Tanner's theory of verism is suggestive: surely, the main plot of the century was that of Greeks, transformed by their exchange with Romans. Let us see how far such an account may be extended. I shall begin with a closer look at Posidonius – the emblematic and, quite simply, the most influential author of the era. Following that, I will try to sketch some possible generalizations, based on the evidence as a whole.

A closer look on Posidonius: this brings us back to Asclepiodotus' *Tactics*. Let me explain how. We have the mere name of this author, from a Florence manuscript collecting several ancient tactical works.[395] An author of this name is cited by Seneca, for information in natural philosophy, and he is said to have been a student of Posidonius. Further, there was a treatise on tactics by Posidonius himself, now lost.[396] Finally, Asclepiodotus' treatise is in fact merely the first of an entire series of Roman-era Greek tactical treatises (another practice that "stuck"), mostly extant, all so closely related as to force the postulate of a common source. In these works, past authorities are mentioned as sources, none later than Posidonius. The likeliest account, then, is that we have here a tradition largely shaped by Posidonius' lost treatise, closest to Posidonius with Asclepiodotus himself.[397]

---

[395] Laur 55.4 132v–142v, an early minuscule Byzantine manuscript later copied by several Renaissance hands.
[396] Edelstein and Kidd (1972–99: II.333–5).
[397] The other extant treatises are by Aelian (who is dated by the addressee of his treatise, Trajan) and by Arrian, the second-century author, as well as an anonymous glossarium militare. The various treatises are nearly identical, that of Asclepiodotus being more compressed, however; all appear,

A curious text. It is about historical material: but it turns away from history. Not a single anecdote is recounted. This is quite possibly an original turn in the genre of tactics,[398] and, in general, we see here a combination of distinct approaches, and so probably some insight into Posidonius' *eclecticism*.

A history: away from history. The only sense that war is made by historical people, not by abstract tokens, is the occasional reference to ethnics – the central type under discussion is "Macedonian"; certain formations are "Scythian" or "Thracian" (VII.3), certain movements are "Cretan" or "Persian" (X.15). The discussion as a whole has an abstract air. The treatise is structured by an overarching conceptual taxonomy: the arrangements for war are landed or naval (we are to discuss just the landed), which are then either footed or mounted, each further subdivided. Once the conceptual analysis reaches the military units themselves, they are discussed in a similar taxonomic, terminological vein (hence the use of ethnics to characterize the different taxa). At this taxonomic level, we see a "philosophical" approach to the historical material of warmaking. The terminological emphasis makes this into an almost grammarian work, however, almost a kind of lexicographic aid to the reading of historical works to do with war. Was this indeed one of the work's functions?

And then, another genre, which allows us a glimpse into the combination most typical to Posidonius. Within each basic term the discussion is always framed in the most quantitative terms. As war, so history: made philosophical, grammatical but, above all – mathematical.

This takes two main forms. For the hoplite phalanx, the author is engaged primarily with the numbers to be deployed within given units, especially concerned to make sure that the numbers will be divisible by two: hence, everything is governed by the powers of two, and the ideal phalanx is declared to have $16,384 = 2^{14}$ soldiers. Chapter 2 is almost entirely given over to the various divisions arising out of this number. In chapter 3 the parts of the phalanx are arranged by military valor, and we are told that the rightmost fourth of the line should be composed of the

---

therefore, like different recensions of a single source (so, Stadter, 1978: 117–18). Wrightson (2015) is non-committal on the identity of the source, while Eramo (2010: 150–1 n.80) suggests that the lost source could be by Posidonius or by Polybius. This coyness is in fact entirely due to the reaction of contemporary scholarship to the "Panposidonianism" of past generations. In fact, there is little reason to doubt that this treatise, with its extreme impracticality, could not be in Polybius' style. Let's get real: this is Posidonius.

[398] Aeneas Tacticus' is the only extant earlier tactical work (possibly as early as the fourth century BC); it is made up entirely of historical anecdote.

best soldiers, the leftmost and second leftmost should be composed of those who follow, and the worst should stand as the second rightmost, as in this way the right and the left are balanced ("the geometers say"): clearly, a reference to a:b::c:d ➜ ad = bc. Further numerical discussions involve the gaps between the soldiers in the phalanx as well as the lengths of the spears they carry – all indeed directly comparable to the numerical discussions in architecture (chapters 4 to 5). Later follows a very abstruse discussion (chapter 7) of the geometry of cavalry formations, which are of course more complex than the purely rectangular phalanx. It is in this context that diagrams are added in great profusion, typically lettered (each letter, in this case, standing for an individual horseman). Once again, the author touches briefly on terminology; and then the most substantial discussion in the treatise (chapter 10) involves motions – typically rotations, either of each individual separately or of formations as a whole. Once again, this discussion is carried through extensive reference to diagrams. This brings in a type of geometry which is not usually discussed in explicit terms in Greek mathematics, and it makes apposite, if trivial, observations: for instance, that following three for-ward quarter-rotations it is more convenient to return to the original position via one further forward quarter-rotation than by three backward quarter-rotations (X.9). Chapter 11 combines, in a sense, the discussions of formation and of motion, to discuss formations in march – once again, of course, considered via lettered diagrams.

The language is spare throughout, and very reminiscent of mathematical terminology: not the language of a Greek mathematical proof but, above all, of a Greek mathematical definition. Indeed, the text lacks any argu-ment and is, instead, a series of statements, mostly of a terminological or conceptual character. (The overall use of language could equally fit, then, in a philosophical or even a grammatical context.) The diagrams, too, do not serve in an argumentative but in an explanatory role. For this reason, one does not manipulate the labels within the text, but merely point to them in the diagram. Hence, the very logic of the diagrams is distinct from the mathematical one: most obviously, one often has the very same letter repeated over and over again (standing, in this case, for a horseman or a hoplite, repeated time and again).

We see mathematization which is obviously just that – a *move* in the generic space that nods towards mathematics without actually invoking it. Words such as "thin veneer" come to mind, but perhaps we should not be too harsh on Posidonius: all we have is an epitome, not necessarily a first-rate one.

In general, what is the purpose of this thin mathematization? In fact, we are puzzled by the purpose of such treatises as a whole. Surely not a practical manual. Remarkably (and the sure sign this treatise does not go back specifically to Polybius), Romans are not in evidence at all. Everything is archaizing, perhaps literary in function, at any rate meant to evoke the sense of a Greek world. Mathematization must have been part of this vague Greek evocation: it is in this point of history an exotic genre. It is also specifically resonant of Greekness, however: one of the things "Greeks do". They form phalanxes; they produce arguments concerning geometrical figures.

So, is this what the combinations of the first century do? Provide a sense of Greekness by bringing together various strands of such aspects of cultural practice that are considered most Greek?

Let us pause and consider: why should Posidonius have written a work such as this? Indeed, why write a *Tactics* to begin with? We need to consider, then, the full range of his writings. These were very substantial, but also more restricted than is sometimes implied by the broad-brush characterization of Posidonius as a "polymath".[399] His writings are primarily those that could fit most naturally within the three divisions – physics, ethics and logic – of Stoic philosophy. To these we should definitely add a massive engagement with both history[400] and geography.[401] Otherwise, however, there is little recorded activity. Posidonius certainly responded to an Epicurean attack on Euclid's use of his starting points,[402] which implies a closer engagement with the exact sciences than that of any past Stoic author. But it was not a contribution to mathematics as such and, instead, should be seen as a volley sent from one philosophical school against another. The *Tactics* may well be the only work we should add to the list above. He did not write on medicine (Galen quotes him extensively: for his

---

[399] A commonplace. Taisbak (1974) calls him a "Stoic philosopher and polymath", Evans (2005: 340) "the Stoic polymath, Posidonius" and Castellani (2013) the "Stoic polymath Posidonius of Apamea in Syria".

[400] We have a credible report of the *Histories*, a narrative history in 52 books (continuing Polybius into Posidonius' own time); other, stand-alone, historical monographs are possible. (For an extended discussion of the *Histories*, see Clarke, 1999: 154–70.)

[401] "On the Ocean" would have been a substantial work, and there are several reports of mathematical geography by Posidonius; in general, Strabo takes Posidonius as one of the few major authors with whom he repeatedly contends, alongside Eratosthenes and Polybius. (For an extended discussion of the work "On the Ocean", see Clarke, 1999: 139–54.)

[402] I survey this in Netz (2015: 287–95), emphasizing how Posidonius' contribution is narrowly defined by its purpose as a response to Zeno of Sidon.

philosophical views about the soul, see note 277 above). He did not write on grammar (indeed, for a Stoic, he seemed to have relatively little to say on language as such; all we find is a tendency to look for etymologies).[403] We end up with a philosopher who also wrote on history, geography and tactics.

The vague appellation "polymath" is unhelpful, and in fact we can be much more precise. What we see in Posidonius is, precisely, *a Stoic philosopher who also wrote on the topics covered by Polybius*. Polybius, as we recall, was a political figure of Megalopolis who was exiled by the Romans to Italy after the Battle of Pydna (168). Exiled, a private citizen, he then embarked on his career as an author; a familiar path for ancient historians from Thucydides onwards. He stands out as the first Greek whose works we have extant, to have his worldview shaped by the encounter with Rome and with Romans. Indeed, he wrote on three topics: history, geography and tactics. The three, for him, went closely together. The function of all was to provide information for better military and political decisions, which also call, in more general, for a wide education, specifically in the exact sciences (with which Polybius showed a certain familiarity – not very deep – but on which he never wrote directly).[404]

Posidonius began his histories specifically from the point where Polybius left them off: was this significant?[405] Or consider their geographies. For Polybius, our evidence derives almost entirely from Strabo, and what we find there is the trace of a debate. Apparently, Polybius engaged in a critique of the major past geographers (Dicaearchus and Eratosthenes), concerning a particular aspect of the geography of the Mediterranean, namely the size of its western part. We have here a Greek geographer looking, distinctly, to the west. Something similar seems to be the case for Posidonius, as well. Map 27 shows the places mentioned in Posidonius' geographical fragments.

The emphasis on the western Mediterranean is obvious (and familiar); it should be added that Posidonius' major geographical work, "On the Ocean", would have to be primarily about the Atlantic, so the map, if anything, tends to underestimate Posidonius' pull to the west. We note the relative absence of places outside the oikoumene – no

---

[403] Strabo I.2.34.    [404] I discuss this in Netz (2002a: 210–13).
[405] Nock (1959: 4) notes that such continuations do not necessarily imply any reverence, and yet, in this particular instance, it seems independently likely that Posidonius' choice does represent some recognition, and more, towards his predecessor.

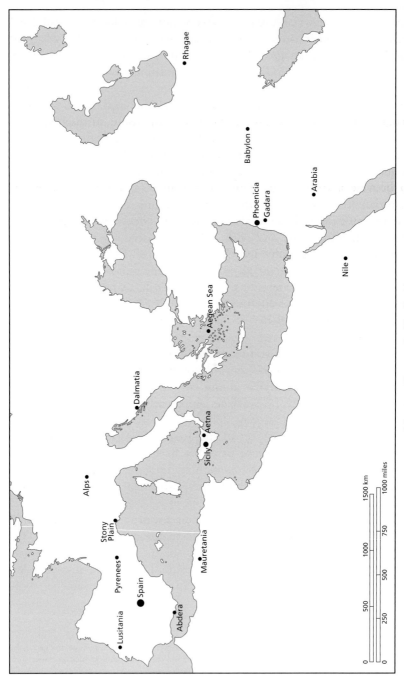

Map 27   Sites studied by Posidonius

Herodotean engagement with Scythia or Asia (a single place in today's Iran, mentioned in the context of a seismological anecdote);[406] to the south we have only the obligatory Nile. Posidonius was a Syrian, residing in Rhodes; we do in fact see a minor cluster, in the map, in Syria and Phoenicia. The map, in short, is that of the western Mediterranean – as seen by a Syrian. Indeed, several of Posidonius' geographical comments claim autopsy, and the standard account of his career is that, after having made a certain name for himself, Posidonius undertook a long tour of the west – likely this was in the 90s – establishing, upon his return (or inheriting), a school in Rhodes, then to become a truly major figure. His eminence was reflected by the company he kept: Pompey, visiting twice; Cicero, a close friend;[407] but it is inherently likely that such Roman contacts would go back at least to his tour of the west.

The suggestion presents itself, and is in fact entirely uncontroversial, that the salient feature of Posidonius' career was its attunement to a Roman audience. He began his life by travelling the well-trodden path from Syria to the Athenian Stoa. A typical Hellenist, so far. But then he went further, made significant Roman contacts, remade himself. And thus he added, to his Stoic triad of physics, ethics and logic, the three Polybian disciplines of history, geography and tactics. The body was the Stoa; the face was Polybius; and the combination was a kind of philo-sophical verism, a new combination of Greekness presented to one's Roman patrons. A Stoic, his eye trained on Rome, and an entrepreneur of Hellenic eclecticism.

Let us see how the case of Posidonius fits within the overall set of vignettes surveyed in this section. In the following table, each event is considered as an encounter between Greeks and Romans. This is first considered in terms of an encounter, for which I note the *location*, and the evidence for a *Roman presence*. This is also considered in terms of eclecticism, and I note the specific combination of *elements of Greekness*. In all, the table sums up the section, now arranged (to the extent possible) chronologically.

---

[406] Edelstein and Kidd (1972–99: III.305–6 [F233]): Rhagae – named after its frequent earthquakes?

[407] Posidonius' biography may be pieced together from many testimonies (Edelstein and Kidd, 1972–99: II.T1–39); it is typical of the life, but also of our sources, that many of them derive from Roman sources or relate to the western Mediterranean.

| Name, date[408] | Location | Greco-Roman encounter | Elements of Greekness |
|---|---|---|---|
| Panaetius, 130 | Athens, Rhodes, Rome | Dedicates to Q. Aelius Tubero, a client of Scipio Aemilianus? | A traditional Stoic; marked by turn to Platonism? |
| Asclepiades of Bithynia, 120 | Bithynia, Rome | Active in the city of Rome. | Medicine and philosophy. |
| Petosiris-Nechepso, 100 | Egypt, Rome? | The origins are obscure but it is clear that it is Romans who drive the explosion of interest in astrology in the early first century BC. | Cosmology and the exact sciences. Unique in that it brings in specifically a non-Greek wisdom, understood primarily as "Egyptian". |
| Meleager, 100 | ? | Immediately received in Rome; but little sense of context. | Not a combination of diverse genres, but a combinatorial attitude towards the genre of epigram. |
| Aristides, 100 | Unknown | Translated by Sisenna, reportedly popular in Rome. | "Milesiaca", a prose anthology, suggestive of the future of the novel: fiction – and prose. |
| Artemidorus of Ephesus, 100 | Ephesus, traveled very widely | Embassy to Rome, no indication that this was significant. | Herodotean geography and a more mathematical approach (adding maps?) – solidified to a new practice of "geography" as an authorial identity. |
| Demetrius Lacon, 100 | "Laconia", Athens, Miletus? | Dedicates to Nero, Quintus. | Orthodox Epicureanism; but some interest in grammarian techniques. |
| Philo, 90 | Larissa, Athens, Rome | Spends his last years in Rome; Cicero's teacher. | Turns the Academy from Carneadic skepticism to a softer fallibilism. |
| Posidonius, 90 | Apamea in Syria, Rhodes, the western Mediterranean | Visit to Rome; visited in Rhodes by Pompey and Cicero; dedicates to Q. Aelius Tubero. | Stoic philosophy – and the Polybian package. |

[408] I look for a moment when the career began to be influential, or displayed an important transition, preferably both. I round to the nearest ten, and, as usual, throw in a guess even when there is little chronological evidence.

(*cont.*)

| Name, date | Location | Greco-Roman encounter | Elements of Greekness |
|---|---|---|---|
| Antiochus, 90 | Ascalon, Athens, Alexandria | Repeated encounters with Lucullus in the east. | The Academy brought back to dogmatism; return to the dialogue form. In all: philosophy, and the Plato of the literary canon. |
| Archias, 90 | Antioch, Rome | Poetry dedicated to Marius and to Lucullus, becomes a Roman cause célèbre. | Greek poetry – on Roman historical subjects. |
| "Dionysius Thrax", 80 | ? (The new transition is essentially anonymous) | It is clear that, around 80 or so, there begins an influx of grammarians into Rome, perhaps correlated with the rise of the new grammatical technē? | Literary scholarship and philosophy. |
| Ploutogenes, 80 | Priene | Could the name suggest an Italian origin? | The first evidence we have for pantomime as a substantial medium. |
| Andronicus, 70 | Rhodes, Athens | Maybe some contact with Tyrranion, working with Sulla's library at Rome; but this evidence might be spurious. | Peripatetic philosophy – and the grammarian practices of edition and commentary. |
| Aenesidemus, 60 | Cnossos, Aegae, Alexandria | Dedicates to Q. Lucius Tubero. | Pyrrhonian Skepticism – revived in the terms of Athenian school philosophy. |
| Varro, 50 | Rome | Roman; studies in Athens with Antiochus. | Very wide-ranging and prolific scholarly activity; two generic innovations stand out: revival of the Menippean satire; the mixing of science and history in the *Hebdomades* (illustrated biographies). |
| Cicero, 50 | Rome | Roman; several stays in the Greek-speaking world, and important contacts with Greek intellectuals. | Significant for the history of the Academy as well as of rhetoric. Perhaps his most important influence on the overall transition is his paradigmatic role in |

*(cont.)*

| Name, date | Location | Greco-Roman encounter | Elements of Greekness |
|---|---|---|---|
| | | | the rise of rhetoric as "Atticism". |
| Sallustius, 50 | Rome | A Roman author, responding to Greek philosophy and poetry. | "Empedoclea": reviving philosophical hexameter. |
| Anacreontea, 50 (put in mid-century as no better dating is possible) | Not authorial | Could easily fit in the culture of the Roman villa; but nothing more can be said. | Another example of anthologizing as an authorial form. |
| Lucretius, 50 | Rome | A Roman author, responding to Greek philosophy and poetry. | *De Rerum Natura*: an Epicurean didactic epic (with a touch of canonical Athenian history). |
| Philodemus, 50 | Gadara, Athens, Rome, Naples | Piso was his patron; addresses several prominent Roman figures and (together with Siro, another Campanian Epicurean) an influence on Roman poets. | An Epicurean – and a poet; also, a pioneer of the biographical history of philosophy. |
| Eudorus, 40 | Alexandria | If we take him as emblematic of Neopythagoreanism as a whole, one of its main exponents is the Roman Nigidus Figulus. | Platonism infused by Neopythagoreanism; related to the overall phenomenon of pseudo-Pythagorean writings; himself a varied philosopher, more "scientific". |
| Potamon, 40 | Alexandria | No Roman contact known. | Explicitly an "eclecticist". |
| Parthenius, 40 | Nicaea? Rome | Dedicates to Gallus. | Poetic themes – anthologized in prose, in a "small commentary". |
| Caecilius, 40 | Caleacte, Rome | Unknown; but certainly active in Rome. | May be the first Greek to make Atticism – and rhetoric – foundational to the literary canon. |

(*cont.*)

| Name, date | Location | Greco-Roman encounter | Elements of Greekness |
|---|---|---|---|
| Pylades and Bathyllus, 30[409] | Alexandria, Cilicia, Rome | A specifically Roman phenomenon. | Pantomime made into the central form of dramatic performance. |

Not too much should be made of the chronological details: so many of the dates are questionable, or arbitrarily reduced to a given decade. In broad outline, however, we do see a trajectory of the cultural forms in which the encounter is most notable: earlier are the more practical realms of geography, medicine and astrology. Next, there is a broad pattern of a change coming through philosophy. Finally, the transitions are more literary in character, along the way preparing the ground for the Latin golden age. (There is perhaps even an uncanny reflection here of the generations of Alexandria, which gives some credence to this overall pattern: could there be structural reasons why patronage should evolve in such a direction, from the more practical to the more symbolic?) In most of these developments we see new packages of Greekness: in the manner of Posidonius, bringing together elements of Hellenic heritage and emphasizing such elements that would be of interest to a Roman audience. We see the rise of the disciplinary identities of astrologer and geographer and the disappearance of the pure mathematician: is it an accident that the first two are useful for the governors of an empire, that the last is not?

It is perhaps suggestive, at any rate, that philosophy does not seem to lead the way. While the change in philosophy is the most conspicuous, my point throughout has been to locate it within a wider sea change. This is significant, for a precise reason: it allows us to discount one of the accounts on offer for the transformation.

It was perhaps only following Glucker's *Antiochus and the Late Academy* (Glucker, 1978) that scholarship came to recognize the extent of the rupture of the first century. Let me explain. Prior to this study, histories of philosophy often had strung together (1) Ammonius, Plutarch's teacher and a Platonic philosopher in Athens, (2) the establishment of

[409] Jory (1981: 148); the date usually given, 22, is unreliable – and apparently too late for the explosion of interest in pantomime.

philosophical chairs in Athens by Marcus Aurelius and (3) the Neoplatonic school in Athens in late antiquity, all taken without much reflection as evidence for institutional *stability* across the ages. This is clearly wrong, not only in the sense that this is a very poor showing for seven centuries but because we can positively show, for all the three above, that they are unrelated, as institutional events, to the Hellenistic Academy (Ammonius is not head of an "academy" and there is no institution implied; Marcus Aurelius as well as the Neoplatonic school fill a pre-existing institutional void. In all of this I rehearse points forcefully made by Glucker, 1978.). Glucker was therefore the first to see the full significance of the rupture – strictly within the terms of the Athenian history of philosophy. Thus, he could not but relate all this to a momentous event in the political history of Athens and its schools. In the first Mithridatic War, many Greek cities supported the Kingdom of Pontus against Rome. Among those cities was Athens. The details are confusing,[410] but we can extract a clear core. Philosophers were central to the political life of Athens at the time (hardly surprising). Athenion, a peripatetic, or Aristion, an Epicurean – or both – were among the leaders of the fight against Rome. They are represented – in our unsympathetic sources – as tyrants. It appears likely that the decision to choose sides against Rome went together with local strife: rebellion and civil war, led by philosophers. Worst of all, Athens was still, even at this time, strategically important. Athens chose Mithridates in 88; Sulla laid siege to it in 87; it fell, and was viciously pillaged, in 86. Athens and its philosophers lay prostrate, and so it would be a tempting conclusion that the Mithridatic War cut off the Athenian schools. This would be a very direct way of accounting for the historical transition of the first century BCE, in terms of a Greco-Roman encounter: the Romans, essentially, destroying a preceding Greek culture, for another to rise and replace it. This account is tempting – but likely wrong.

The first empirical observation is that at least the Garden was certainly active, apparently intact, in later decades[411] while the Stoa was at least likely to be active, though perhaps in a somewhat fragmented form.[412] Indeed, why not? 86 was a terrible year in Athens, but so were 415 and 406, 338 and 322. (Even prior to that, the city was burned to the ground in 480.) Those

---

[410] The evidence (rich and difficult: a long passage by the very reliable Posidonius, transmitted to us in very tendentious paraphrase by Athenaeus; plus a few other passing notices) is summarized and analyzed in Bugh (1992).

[411] Dorandi (1995: 45).

[412] We have mentions of two teachers – scholarchs? – Dardanus and Mnesarchus (Goulet, 1994: 613–14).

were Athens' centuries of glory; even after 322 (which did mark a political end, of a sort) Athens' cultural dominance, if anything, only solidified. In general, military catastrophe would periodically visit most ancient cities. For many individuals this was a calamity, but for the city this almost always was a disturbance, not an end. The next year the fields were sown again; the same stock of land and people would serve to recreate the same civilization. At the eye of political storms, Athens of the fifth and fourth centuries went through several such cataclysms, and thrived through them all. The much-reduced city of the Hellenistic era had less cause to be sacked, and so less experience of military catastrophe. It also had fewer material resources on which to fall back, but, conversely, it had even more of a cultural legacy to draw upon. Its role as a magnet for philosophy had been detached, centuries ago, from the fortunes of the city as a political agent, and if Romans now viewed it with suspicion – so what? Clearly, the sack of 86 would have been a hiccup in the history of the philosophical schools, *had there been a real cultural need for them*. The fundamental point is that there wasn't.

For the exodus from Athens pre-dated 86. Panaetius, perhaps, and Posidonius – almost certainly – were established in Rhodes by the late second century and early first. At the same time, Demetrius Lacon was probably teaching Epicureanism in Asia Minor; Antiochus was in Alexandria in time for the *Sosus* affair of 87. But, even at a more basic level: we have seen enough evidence for significant cultural transition outside philosophy, taking place at about the same time. The end of the philosophical schools cannot account for the rise of astrology, or for the end of poetry as a key cultural identity and of advanced mathematics; it cannot account for the rise of the grammatical technē or for Meleager's (surely, earlier) anthology, for Artemidorus and for pantomime. The underlying roots of such a shift ought to be found in more fundamental causes. Indeed, perhaps the historical account should work, at least in part, in the opposite direction. The Athenian philosophers involved in the First Mithridatic War are curiously insignificant. We hear of an "Athenion", of an "Aristion". Nothing is known on the *philosophy* of any of these. This, at a time when the history of philosophy is relatively well reported, even if in severely fragmented form (Sedley's "end of history" was yet to come). It is completely possible, in a word, that by the year 88 the philosophical schools in Athens were *already* shrunk, no longer intellectually vibrant, no longer a focus for Mediterranean cultural life. That much is clear: it was not Sulla wot done it.

86 is simply too late, too specific.[413] But, even more broadly: the story is not about Rome, as such – that is, not about Rome's direct political ascendancy. For this, clearly, happened much earlier, with little in the way of discernible consequences. Let us recall the basic historical outline. Roman domination of the eastern Mediterranean began in 197 BCE, when the decisive Roman defeat of the Seleucid Kingdom, at the Battle of Cynoscephalae, proved that no power could stand against a Rome no longer distracted by its Punic adversary. Polybius saw the process as finished by 168 BCE, when the Romans put an end to the Kingdom of Macedonia. Following 146, Corinth – one of the most powerfully symbolic cities of Greek memory – was destroyed, the whole of core Greece turned into a Roman province; when Asia Minor became a Roman province in 133, this merely confirmed a Roman control that had now been established for generations. The next major political events surrounding Roman control of the Greeks were, indeed, the Mithridatic Wars, from the 80s to the 60s (which may indeed have been even more destructive than Rome's previous military engagements in the east), and then the end of the Ptolemaic Kingdom in 30 BCE, conventionally (and misleadingly) taken as the milestone concluding the Hellenistic era (323 to 30 and all that: this nonsensical periodization badly confuses our understanding of the history of the first century BCE). Two points emerge. First, the period that interests us most – near or just prior to 100 BCE – is, as far as the narrative of Roman conquest is concerned, among the least eventful. Second, the major moment of this conquest is located in the first half of the second century, or perhaps near its middle. This is, as far as the narrative of Greek culture is concerned, among the least eventful. (It is a moment of conservative lull: I return to discuss this as a phenomenon of scale, in section 6.1.2 below.) The two watches – politics and culture – are curiously misaligned.

But it is not as if politics c. 100 BCE was *boring*! The decisive moment of the Greco-Roman cultural encounter took place while the internal strife,

---

[413] It does not help to widen our perspective just a little, to the First Mithridatic War as a whole. Rawson's classic study, *Intellectual Life in the Late Roman Republic* (1985), makes the presence in Rome of Greek exiles from that war into a major cause of the growth of Roman knowledge of the Greeks (7–9); this is simply unconvincing (there are shades here of the vulgar account of the Renaissance as a consequence of the fall of Constantinople in 1453). Posidonius' stature could well precede the wars; he stays at Rhodes; he is a key figure of the transition. It was perfectly possible to go to Rome even beforehand; it was perfectly possible to go elsewhere even afterwards. The one flaw in Rawson's account, as a whole, is that it is written from the perspective of the city of Rome, itself. But, early in the century, changes were already afoot; and they were afoot elsewhere.

about to bring the Roman Republic to its end, came to the boil. And this, indeed, must also be part of the account for this encounter.

Starting with the Gracchi, political ascendancy in Rome was no longer assured. The fight was on. By about the year 100, at the latest, Marius' example opened the doors of an arms race. Now began the centrifugal pull of the first century – Roman generals seeking opportunities to increase their glory and their power, reaching out for ever-expanding networks of foreign patronage, conquests, triumphs, armies; an escalation that, ultimately, could be resolved only by a winner-takes-all resolution. Within this context, the acquisition of a particular type of patronage – contact with Greek cultural figures – served to signal one's prominence, in yet another arms race of paideia. This arms race escalated to the point that several major figures presented themselves, directly, as men of letters (most spectacularly, Cicero and Caesar); this arms race got resolved, finally, into the golden age of Latin literature.

Now, of course, Romans knew Greeks and Greek literature even well before Cynoscephalae. As they went along their unlikely project, of constructing their own Latin literature, they did so in direct imitation of Greek models, already in the late third century BCE; in fact, they did so precisely, and *surprisingly*, as a mirror of a Greek legacy (as we now can follow, precisely, thanks to Feeney, 2016 – and understand, thanks to him, how surprising that was). So, the point is not that Greek emerges into the Roman consciousness, all of a sudden, around the year 100. No: the point is the precise way in which Greek culture was *used*, changed, around the year 100. A springboard for one's own literary project (mostly, dramatic) – for over a century. And then, all of a sudden, a much more wide-ranging engagement. And this likely means something about the new functions to which Greek intellectuals, and Greek legacies, could be used, in the cultural context of the late Republic.

This is a vast subject: as I sketch my account, let me introduce it, once again, with the aid of the vignette. Here is Cicero, quoting from Homer. Higbie (2011) mentions how, in his letters to Atticus, Cicero would frequently return to the same line (Il. 6.442):

> I hesitate before Trojan men and Trojan women with their trailing dresses.

Often it would be enough to cite but a couple of words and the sense would be clear: Cicero, telegraphing hesitancy in the face of an uncertain political decision. As Higbie (2011: 379) points out, this quotation was a kind of "private aphorism" shared between Cicero and Atticus. Indeed, the use of the Homeric quotation is, in Cicero, directly correlated with the familiar exchange. In his public writings, Cicero hardly quotes Homer, and does not refer to scholarship; these often show up, however, in the letters. Higbie herself sees here an effect of genre and of audience expectations (as if the point is that the more general writings would have to appeal to a wider audience and so could no longer assume the requisite knowledge on the part of the readers). It seems pertinent to bring in, as well, the precise function of the epistolary. This, as explained by Wilcox (2012), was the vehicle of friendship: the place where the gift-relationship of exchange was used to form relationships between Roman public figures. And so, we see the easy-going familiarity between Cicero and Atticus – the shared aphorism acting, then, as a bond of solidarity.

Then again, we may see related effects, in more fraught political relations. One of Cicero's major rivals was Clodius Pulcher, the patrician – and yet populist politician. So much set them apart: in their correspondence, tension is always close to the surface. Here is how Cicero tries to smooth such tensions – for instance, as follows (*Ad Fam.* III.11.5):

> But if the letter was, as you say, not well expressed, you may be sure I did not write it. Just as Aristarchus denies the authenticity of any Homeric line which he does not like, so I would request you (being in jocular vein), if you find any piece of writing not well expressed, not to believe I wrote it.

Or as follows (*Ad Fam.* III.7.5–6):

> If you think otherwise, you will not go wrong if in order to appreciate the difference between *eugeneia* and *exochē*,[414] you were to study with a little more attention what is said on this subject by Athenodorus, the son of Sandon. But to return to my point, I should like you to believe that I am not only your friend, but a very great friend of yours... If it is your object, however, to make it appear that you are less bound to further my interests in my absence than I strove to further yours, I release you from that anxiety:
>
> > Others are by my side
> > To honor me, and most of all, wise Zeus.[415]

As pointed out by Macleod (1979: 17–18), Cicero's rhetorical strategy, in such passages, is complex: he creates a bond, and at the same time asserts his own worth vis-à-vis his aristocratic superior. There is some element of "We both know our Homer" – and a little bit, too, of the "I know Homer

---

[414] In context, these are philosophical terms, in Greek in the original: noble blood as against spiritual excellence.
[415] Homer, *Il.* I.174.

better" (and, for sure, "I know *Greek philosophy* better"!). But the fundamental point is that, as Cicero considers how to defuse a tense encounter, he transforms and sublimates it to the safer, cultural sphere, in which the two are closer to friendship. And it is this sublimation of political friendship, precisely, which informs Cicero's philosophical writings, as well.

As we recalled above, these are set in dialogue form – now transformed into a model of polite conversation between elite members: literary activity is projected as the ideal form of sociability between equals (Hanchey, 2009). Further, this is projected into Rome's *political* past, the fictional protagonists taken from among Rome's illustrious historical leaders. It was in these dialogues that Cicero created the fiction of a "Scipionic Circle" (as if mid-second-century senators were engaged in conversation concerning Greek philosophy!): this was never understood, not even by the author, as historically accurate (Zetzel, 1972). This choice may have served various purposes for Cicero, but, surely, among other things the result was to have Roman strife become twice removed: from the present to the past; from the political to the philosophical. This is a transformation from the world of affairs into the world of leisure, from res publica into otium. As Stroup (2010: chap. 1) emphasizes, otium becomes marked in the late Republic as a site for cultural production; as Hanchey (2013) points out, otium becomes not so much the antithesis of political life as its idealization: an alternative Rome, where strife is transcended.

The observation we make is that, at around the last generation of the Republic, leisure came to be organized around cultural production, understood in the terms of a Greek literary tradition. This was particularly significant, as it was through such shared arts of leisure that the Roman elite could construct its friendship. The arts of otium served in the formation of amicitia, which, of course, was anything but politically neutral: the networks of amicitia were crucial to the accumulation and maintenance of political power. And thus: through the arms race of the Roman elite, in the late Republic Greek culture came to matter. You needed Greek culture, not so as to show it off but so as to maintain the networks of amicitia with your peers.[416] The Greek client, in such a Greek–Roman encounter, supplied

---

[416] My emphasis on amicitia, as a key to the understanding of Roman literary patronage, is in itself unoriginal – and so unproblematic. Already Starr (1987) has emphasized the basis of Roman literary exchange within networks of friendship, and the observation that the contact between Roman political figures and Greek scholars was perceived through a Roman lens of amicitia and/or the patron–client relationship is commonplace. The small twist I offer on this account is to emphasize the role Greek learning would have, not for the interaction between Greeks and Romans but for the interaction between Romans themselves – which surely must have mattered more. The question is: what were Greeks good for? And my answer is: they were good to talk about. (Gold, 1985, for

something vital. What was required was precisely the full package of Greekness: not a professional pursuit of an isolated practice that would have put one at a remove from the networks of friendship but, rather, a generalized familiarity with a broad range of culture. This is the point of view of the collector. Anthologies will come in handy.

But there is more to this. You do not want to stand aside, in an isolated pursuit. But you do want to be distinctive, to make your own claim for position in a competitive social setting. And so, advantage, both for Greek purveyors of culture and for Roman patrons, resided in the new. A striking feature of the table on pages 508–10 above is that no two combinations are the same. This is partly an artifact of how I construct it: I look for examples of new turns, and so do not record authors who merely repeat the examples of their predecessors. But, in fact, it is not obvious that many such repetitions can be found. Siro strikes us now as another Philodemus, engaging with poetry as well as with Epicureanism around the villas of Campania.[417] But is this not simply because so much less is known about Siro than about Philodemus? Whenever our evidence is sufficient to cast any light on an individual in this group, we glimpse some unprecedented, unparalleled project. It is this desire – to produce one's own, distinctive, combination – which marks the true eclectic, as opposed to the mere polymath.

I sketch an argument analogous, in broad structural terms, to Tanner's (2000) account of verism (see pages 500–1 above). A new combination by Greek practitioners – because this is what makes them useful for Roman patrons. And, thus, the specific needs of Roman patronage transform Greek culture itself.

It was crucial for Tanner's argument that the new type of art was produced not just in Italy but in fact, primarily, in the Greek east itself. Indeed, it seems significant that this is where the Greco-Roman encounter now takes place. Consider the contrast with the second century. Romans, as noted above, did know their Greek then – and did meet Greek intellectuals. But this was primarily within the city of Rome itself. Polybius, of course, was effectively a prisoner in Rome. Then we have the anecdotes concerning the year 155, when Carneades, Critolaus and Diogenes –

---

instance, a classic account of a Roman–Greek case of patronage – Pompey and Theophanes – ultimately ends up suggesting that Theophanes was useful for Pompey as a political actor of significance in his home city of Mitylene. It is this account I wish to resist. No: Theophanes was important for Pompey because, as his ghostwriter, he let Pompey play his bit in the arts of otium and so thicken his networks of *Roman* amicitia.)

[417] Sider (1997: 15 ff.).

scholarchs in the Academy, Peripatos and the Stoa, respectively – were sent to the Roman senate by the city of Athens to argue in a dispute with Oropus. The elaboration of this anecdote – as if it involved a substantial philosophical contact between the scholarchs and a Roman public – is due to an anachronistic dressing-up by first-century sources, who imagine the conditions of later patronage (Powell, 2013). The actual historical event took place in the city. We also know that Tiberius Gracchus had Greek tutors, Blossius of Cumae a Stoic philosopher, Diophanes of Mitylene a rhetor. We have some traces in our sources for the claim that Blossius influenced the program of the Gracchi (the evidence is discussed by Nicolet, 1965: 142–58), though this seems to arise, if anything, from sources hostile to the Gracchi: look how bad they were – they were even influenced by Greeks![418] What grabs our attention is the geography: Diophanes the orator did come all the way from Mitylene, but Blossius' origins in Cumae are probably not an accident. We may put this together with the three philosophers in 155, with Polybius: at this point, Greek intellectuals mostly *happen upon* a Roman contact. You are sent on an embassy; taken hostage; live nearby. Panaetius, a little later, does seem to reach specifically for a foothold in Rome; he does obtain a patron in Scipio Aemilianus; he does dedicate works to Quintus Aelius Tubero. But, with him, we already reach the table above: we begin to sense the tensions of a Roman polity less in equilibrium; we begin to see the stirrings of a new turn in Greek culture. What we do not see, yet, is the evidence for a Roman, reaching for the Greeks. Once again, it was Panaetius who had to come to Rome.

Posidonius, finally, would surely visit Rome early in his career; but, later on, it was Pompey who came to visit him in Rhodes. Antiochus' Roman encounters took place in the east, as, likely, did those of Demetrius Lacon and of Aenesidemus. Once again, not too much is to be made of the small chronological details, but the broad-brush picture seems clear. At the moment that the Greco-Roman encounter really takes off, at about 100 BC, it takes place mostly in the east, and it is only later, in the second half of the century, that it comes back to the city of Rome. This has parallels in the cultural pulse of Latin culture, as well. It is only in the middle of the century that the city of Rome became a major site, and the Latin language a major vehicle, of cultural life.[419] This is simply the political pulse of the first century. First the centrifugal impulse, the systole, in the first half of the

---

[418] Shaw (1985: 45–6).
[419] The main theme of Rawson (1985), whose first sentence reads: "The first great intellectual flowering at Rome came in the fifties and forties B.C."

century, the ever-widening campaigns of conquest, threatening to tear the republic apart; followed by the centripetal impulse, the diastole, as central control is established, and then re-established, firmly anchored in the city of Rome, during the third quarter of the century. This is why the geography of culture, over the decisive first half of the century, is so confused, the old centers of Athens and Alexandria losing ground but no other place becoming a genuine alternative. Everything is dictated by the Greco-Roman encounter; and, through those decades, the Romans are on the move.

Map 28 is the map of cultural life in this era.[420] As explained in footnote 420, this map if anything exaggerates the significance of Athens and of Rome. But, even so, this is a Mediterranean without a clearly defined center. Partly this is because centrality has been diluted, divided three ways when once it was divided merely two ways. But it seems that the very attractive power of the centers has been attenuated. Many of the locations cited are mere sojourns. Posidonius passes through Athens; Philo of Larissa passes through Rome; Antiochus passes through Alexandria. (Even Varro, it should be remembered, produced much of his output in exile.) So, it will not quite do to sum this up as "a tale of three cities" – Rome, added to Athens and Alexandria. It has become, somehow, less of a tale of cities, at all.

Cities used to provide the social markers for Greek cultural figures. You became prominent via your standing in a city. The city of Athens acquired a particular meaning, associated with the canon, and so authors away from Athens produced their own sense of a vivid presence via the alternative form of authorial networks, which, in turn, tended to be constructed around Alexandria. Hence the duality of the Athenian/Alexandrian Mediterranean. But now a new currency of status suddenly began to pour into the east: that of Roman patronage. The Hellenistic authorial networks were now locked into Roman circles of patronage. Aenesidemus met Tubero at Aegae, Antiochus met Lucullus at Alexandria, Posidonius met Pompey in Rhodes. What mattered in such meetings was not Aegae, Alexandria, Rhodes but Tubero, Lucullus, Pompey. The Hellenistic

---

[420] Map 28 aggregates the evidence for authors in the four genres of philosophy, medicine, geography and grammar, in the two temporal nodes –100 to –50, which is, effectively, those for whom the center of their career fell into the period –125 to –25. A map more limited in time to the actual first half of the first century would surely have a lower relative number for Athens (much more important in philosophy around the years 125 to 100 than later on) as well as for Rome (much more important, in all fields, in the years 50 to 25 than earlier). Only Alexandria would remain as a very qualified center.

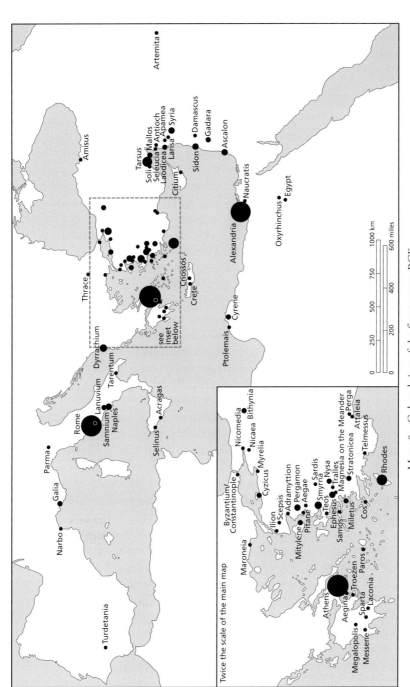

Map 28   Cultural sites of the first century BCE

Twice the scale of the main map

1000 km
750
500
250
0

600 miles
400
200
0

**Main map labels:**

Turdetania
Galia
Parma
Narbo
Rome
Lanuvium
Sammium
Naples
Tarentum
Dyrrachium
Selinus
Acragas
Thrace
Amisus
Artemita
Tarsus
Soli
Seleucia
Mallos
Laodicea
Antioch
Larisa
Apamea
Syria
Sidon
Damascus
Gadara
Ascalon
Citium
Naucratis
Alexandria
Crete
Cnossos
Cyrene
Ptolemais
Oxyrhinchus
Egypt
see
inset
below

**Inset map labels:**

Byzantium/
Constantinople
Maronea
Nicomedia
Nicaea Bithynia
Cyzicus Myrelia
Scepsis
Ilion
Adramyttion
Pergamon
Mitylene
Pitane
Aegae
Sardis
Teos
Nysa
Smyrna
Tralles
Magnesia on the Meander
Samos
Ephesus
Stratonicea
Miletus
Cos
Attaleia
Perga
Telmessus
Rhodes
Athens
Aegina
Troezen
Sparta
Paros
Laconia
Megalopolis
Messene

system of meanings involved cities, and networks; with the influx of
Roman patronage, networks got detached from cities. Romans were itinerant within the eastern Mediterranean. They pass there in their procon-
sular terms, or through their campaigns, never establishing themselves in a
particular place. The place remains external: in Rome. They thus do not
produce a new spatialization internal to the Greek world; they attenuate
the significance of Greek spatial distinctions.

And this, finally, made eclecticism even more acceptable. It would have
been strange for an Epicurean, writing in the Garden for Greek readers, in
the third or second centuries BCE, to engage extensively with Alexandrian
grammarian techniques. When reading an Epicurean, one would imagine
him in a school in Athens, living the philosophical life by engaging with
propositional contents. Grammar was what one did in Alexandria, surveying the literary canon from the bird's-eye view. There would be a certain
solecism, then, in a grammarian-Epicurean; and we do not have evidence
that there were any, in the Garden in Athens itself. But, when Demetrius
Lacon writes in Miletus, dedicating his work to Roman readers, such
perceptions are less salient. The thematic lock is loosened.

And so, starting around the year 100 BCE, Roman patronage pours into
the eastern Mediterranean, calling forth the entrepreneurs of eclecticism.
The Hellenistic polarities lose their meaning; space itself ceases to be the
key explanatory principle of Greek culture. An appropriate point, therefore, at which to conclude this part of the book.

Let us finally pause and consider the significance of the first century, and
its entrepreneurial eclecticism, for the broad narrative of the pluralism of
Greek cultural life. As it were, the impulse of Greek democracy now
dodged its second imperial bullet. The first was the coming of
Hellenistic monarchies. They could not remove the canon of democratic
Athens, primarily because performance was so essential to Greek poetics,
Athens such a good fit for this performativity. Hence, the end of democracy failed to undo the canon, and, instead, froze it in position. More than
this: the frozen presence of the canon, together with the continued significance of Athens as an actual physical center, created the bipolarity of
the Hellenistic Mediterranean. The plurality of the polis of letters was
extended by redoubling. It was now an Athenian canonical polis of letters –
and then also a bifurcation of Athenian schools, on the one hand, and an
Alexandrian literary and scientific culture, on the other hand.

Little wonder, then, that this two-layered, as well as bifurcated, set of
pluralities made possible such a rich set of combinations and recombina-
tions. There was so much to choose from: anthologize the epigram; insert

maps into your Herodotean geographical surveys; make a didactic epic out of Epicurus. Why not? But the crucial thing is that all this happened while a monolithic, imperial order was descending upon the entire Mediterranean. How come, then, that we have such a diversity? How was the second monarchic bullet dodged? The answer is very simple, in terms of Roman political history and its synchronization with Greek culture. The key moment of contact happened while the Republic was at its most vital, most overtly in the grip of internal conflict – indeed, when it came closest to mimicking an actual democracy. The pluralism of Greek eclecticism, through the first half of the century, corresponded with a vital, pluralistic Roman politics.

When monarchy was in fact established it did, of course, call forth an imperial ideology. But at this point it was inevitable that it would be based on a Greek model, giving rise to the Roman mirror canon. This must have been meant, among other things, as the ideological instrument of a monarchy. But it was always meant – not just by us, but already by ancient authors and readers – to be appreciated intertextually, within the terms of its sophisticated combination of Greek sources. It did not replace the plurality of the Greek edifice but merely filled it with yet another set of echoes.

There are, in short, two reasons why the Augustan age did not create the literary instruments for a true ideology of monolithic empire. First, it was not the Augustan age that produced the Greco-Roman encounter. It was, instead, the previous, hyper-republican age that did so (and this, too, for a reason: because it was the centrifugality of the late Republic that thrust the Roman networks of amicitia upon Greek culture). Second, the Augustan age did not erase Greek culture so as to replace its legacy with a new, Roman one. Under the unstated terms of the Augustan pact, Roman elites gave up their power so as to keep their otium, which, at this point, was already Greek. Left with no other choice, they withdrew from the political battle. At this point, that was the one thing the Roman elites would not give up: their Greek grammarians.

# PART III

# *Scale*

The argument of the book so far often concerned the *relative* distributions of culture. My claims took such forms as: the top authors in performative genres were much more frequently copied than were the rest; Demosthenes became much more popular in the Roman era; there was more medicine in Alexandria, more philosophy in Athens; more mixed activity in the first century BCE relative to the second; there was a rise in the post-Chaeronea "government sector"; a trend in the Greco-Roman encounter, from the more practical towards the arts of the literary canon. These are all statements about the differential clustering of cultural activity in space and time. Culture, not homogeneously distributed: concentrated at certain places, fluctuating through time.

Relative distributions reveal a lot – but only so much. There is one historical account to be told, if we assume that there were, at a given time, 20 philosophers in Athens, two in Alexandria. There is another one, if we assume that there were 300 in Athens, in Alexandria 30. In some ways, the two accounts are similar: they are both about Athenian dominance in philosophy. But the nature of cultural life in the two cities, Athens and Alexandria, would be very different under the two accounts. Do we need to imagine lonely Alexandrian philosophers, having only the same old faces to quarrel with? (No wonder they might move to Athens). Was Athenian philosophy the affair of a few artisans – or was it a genuine industry?

I started this book in Chapter 1 on a statistical note, counting papyri and comparing such counts among each other and with other measures. It was only gradually, through Chapter 2, that statistics were built into historical consequences. But then, even as I turned to drawing maps in Chapter 3, these were always very close to a historical interpretation, and much of our discussion in the last few chapters took the form of a chronologically ordered historical account of Greek literary practices, from the formation of the canon to the coming of the Romans. It is now time to study culture under the Roman Empire and beyond.

And so: the history of ancient literary practice in the Roman Empire and then, especially, into late antiquity is ultimately to be explained, I believe, through the terms of scale. We thus need to introduce a new kind of statistical tool. In Chapter 5, "A Quantitative Model of Ancient Literary Culture", our chronological account is, as it were, paused. The basic assumption is "static": I look at a synthetic category, "the population engaged with (mostly) Greek culture up to the year 200 CE", and try to count it.

Once this tool has been established, the following chapter reverts to history. In Chapter 6, "Scale in Action", I first look back on the classical and Hellenistic eras, enriching our account of the rise of the canon and of the changing fortunes of Hellenistic culture – and then march on, suggesting an account of the qualitative nature of Imperial and, in particular, late ancient literary practices – in terms of the scale of authorship.

The Greek polis of letters preserved a pluralistic ethos through the many political transformations of the ancient Mediterranean, dodging the bullets of monarchic consolidations by Hellenistic and Roman Empires, partly because the culture in charge of the polis of letters always remained *big enough*. It had less luck with the demographic collapse of cultural life in late antiquity, and, if the polis of letters survived, it did so in much-qualified form, now as a canon understood to be much more monolithic.

CHAPTER 5

# A Quantitative Model of Ancient Literary Culture

The scale of ancient culture involves several different quantities. First, there is the size of the audience; then, the number of authors. (Note that this is a study of ancient *literary* practices: we engage primarily with books. So, by "audience" I mean primarily "book owners", while by "authors" I mean primarily those having a book to their name.)[1] Finally, there is the scale of the distribution of the object itself, what I think of as the ancient "bibliosphere" – the total amount of literature circulating on papyrus. This chapter looks at all such questions but its primary task is counting the number of authors.

The scale of ancient culture may also be gauged through many different approaches. It was argued in detail in Chapter 1 that the literary papyri may be used as a fairly random sample for the relative frequencies of authors in circulation. In section 5.1, I will try to repurpose this evidence for a much more difficult task: estimating the absolute number of book rolls in circulation in antiquity. This serves as a preliminary check on the scale of authorship. The main discussion is distributed between sections 5.2 and 5.3. In section 5.2, I bring in arguments having to do with the number of ancient authors as a whole; in section 5.2, I zoom in to consider the number of authors active in the individual genres. Section 5.4 unpacks the results and somewhat adds to their probability by relating them to the wider numbers of ancient demography, and section 5.5 concludes with a few methodological notes.

---

[1] I do not wish to spend time on definition for its own sake, but in fact it is clear that the category of the "author" cannot be as neat as that. The performative always remained a central facet of ancient culture, and so there was always a certain number of individuals who left their mark, in a manner analogous to that of book-authors, by sheer performance: early on, many poets; later on, philosophers and sophists. I consider these as "authors" (when counting philosophers, I do not exclude Arcesilaus or Peregrinus Proteus; when considering Second Sophistic rhetors, I count all the inscriptions and do not try to gauge how many had their performances recorded in writing for posterity). This does not change the numbers substantially, as, in fact, by the Hellenistic era at the latest, most genres had become almost entirely written.

Methodology will be at the background of this chapter throughout, and, indeed, I ask a lot from my readers. Because I wish to avoid, as far as possible, any trace of circular reasoning, my strategy is to move from the very uncertain to the somewhat more probable arguments (thus, each added argument is meant to be independent from those preceding it, in the hope that, in such a way, even individually weak arguments might tend to lend support to each other). And so: bear with me. Especially to begin with. We count papyri; we rely on thin reeds.

## 5.1  First Route: From the Papyri

This first approach takes the longest to follow – involving the most deductions – and is also, as a consequence, the most tenuous. Still, let us not throw away any potential information. Based on the evidence concerning the survival of papyri, I attempt first to build a model of the distribution of literary papyri in antiquity; based on this, I try to look at the implications of such a model for the number of authors.

### 5.1.1   Counting Papyri

I begin – as one should, counting ancient things – with Keith Hopkins. I quote again his observation (Hopkins, 1991: 133 n.2), cited already on page 27 above, that the census returns from Egypt may be suggestive for estimating the fraction of ancient papyri that survives:

> Consider the following: the Romans conducted 17 censuses of the Egyptian population by households in 14-year intervals between A.D. 19 and 257.[2] If the average household size was 5 persons, and the population is deliberately estimated low at 3.5 million, and we have less than 1,000 surviving census returns, the survival ratio is c. 1:12,000. Of course, this is only a rough estimate, a cautionary tale – adjustments would have to be made for documents of different value. . .

Hopkins himself does not proceed to extrapolate any further numbers: the point of the exercise, for him, was indeed as a "cautionary tale" and no more (he mistakenly thought, as noted on pages 27–8 above, that such a small survival ratio vitiates the statistical significance of the distribution among papyri). We should go through this more slowly.

---

[2] There are in fact 18 events, going in 14-year intervals from 19 to 257 (Hopkins makes a common mistake).

The evidence for the ubiquity of the census is firm and confirmed by the extant returns themselves.[3] (The distribution of the evidence is not homogeneous, but it remains broadly consistent with the patterns of documentary papyri as a whole: more from the Fayoum than from elsewhere,[4] considerably more from the second century than beforehand or afterwards).[5]

Hopkins seems to measure this against the population of the province of Egypt as a whole. The valid comparison is against the population of Upper Egypt (from which our papyri derive), which likely was a little more than half that of the province as a whole.[6] If we take 5 million for the population of the province as a whole at the peak (unlike Hopkins, I look for central values, not for upper or lower bounds; I choose a round number, perhaps a little on the high side),[7] this would mean a population in the Nile Valley of about 3 million at the peak, but perhaps a little more than 2.5 million on average. The number per declaration is in fact a little higher than five (declarations were based on the unit of the house and included lodgers). Hobson (1985) finds an average of 7.3, and so we may conclude that about 400,000 houses in the Nile Valley had to produce census returns every 14 years from 41 to 257 – i.e. slightly fewer than 7 million declaration events.

It is very unfortunate for our purposes that, apparently, a single declaration event could have resulted in multiple declarations. We even have a handful of cases when several copies of the same return were preserved together and addressed to different authorities.[8] It is likely that a return

---

[3] Bagnall and Frier (1994: chap. 1). (While the literature on the demographic implications of the census documents is now very significant, our discussion can mostly rely on the details of the distribution of the documents as such, somewhat independently of their contents; for this, I will rely mostly on the authoritative Bagnall and Frier study.)

[4] Bagnall and Frier (1994: 7) have 184 Arsinoite returns out of 300, or about 60 percent; from Habermann (1998: 154) it seems that the percentage of all documents from the Arsinoite nome, during the first three centuries CE, was about 40 percent. The difference is meaningful, but not overwhelming.

[5] Bagnall and Frier (1994: 8) show in graph form that this is partly better represented than the third, comparatively speaking; as can be seen from Habermann (1998: 154), this may be driven by the trend of the evidence from the Arsinoite nome (which indeed peaks in the second century). The numbers from the first century are especially low: we have a single return from 19 and 47, two from 61 (we also have only one from 257). Bagnall and Frier (5) suggest that the year 19 belongs to a previous census system. It is perhaps best excluded from consideration, then, which brings us back into Hopkins' 17 events.

[6] The argument in a nutshell is that a little over half the land under cultivation was in the Delta, but that along the Nile itself density of population must have been higher (Bowman, 2011: 320–2, sums up some of the salient scholarship).

[7] Rathbone (1990). This estimate is respected but is also controversial (so, for instance, the implications of Mueller, 2006: III.chap. 2); lower estimates go down as far as 3 million or so.

[8] Bagnall and Frier (1994: 19); such forms are preserved together because they were never submitted.

would have at least two copies – for the central nome administration and for the village administration; perhaps also another for one's personal files – which would not be universal, however, given that most declarants were illiterate.[9] The last point is the most reassuring. Illiterate households would produce the minimum number of declarations, and so it is unrealistic to expect, on average, anything *much* higher than that minimum (which is, indeed, perhaps, two?). The numbers – up to this point rather robust – now begin to be quite hazy, but a total of 15 million census returns filled may serve as our round value, understanding that, if anything, the number might be somewhat higher (bear in mind, however, that we chose a high estimate for the size of the population; the number is perhaps not *very* much higher).

The comparison between documentary and literary papyri is potentially worrisome, and Hopkins is cautious, saying that "adjustments will have to be made for documents of different value". The difference in the process of discard is important. Roman-era literary papyri fragments were produced primarily by deliberate discard of rubbish; documentary fragments were produced more often by the loss of archives (pages 34–5 above). Since the processes are different, it is possible that one or the other might be more conducive to preserve the papyri. There is no obvious reason to see the one or the other as inherently more likely to survive, and it is perhaps useful to make a comparison with another case, when some quantitative comparisons can be made.

The discard process of literary papyri of the Ptolemaic era was very different from that of those of the Roman era (Ptolemaic papyri survive much more often through their recycling in mummy cartonnage;[10] Roman-era papyri are more typically found in rubbish dumps, of course dominated by that of Oxyrhynchus). While this difference is not the same as that between literary and documentary papyri, the discard processes are distinct, and so it is useful to see if a distinct avenue of discard gives rise to a different fraction of survival. Now, the two sets of papyri are roughly an order of magnitude apart – that is, there are about ten times more Imperial-era literary papyri than Ptolemaic-era literary papyri. So, were Ptolemaic papyri about ten times less likely to survive? This would certainly be very wrong. It is clear that there had to be more Roman-era literary papyri *originally*. Populations grew; the material circumstances of the elite may have improved

---

[9]  Bagnall and Frier (1994: 20).
[10]  This still rests on a number of early spectacular finds: while since much updated, the most rewarding reading remains Grenfell and Hunt (1906: introd.).

overall;[11] above all, this elite became much more Hellenized through these centuries (I will return to discuss this below, on pages 643–4). This indeed is directly implied, as argued on page 40 above, by the qualitative difference in the nature of collections in the Ptolemaic and the Roman eras (more sophisticated – so, likely, less frequent – in the Ptolemaic era). But this consideration does not exhaust the difference. The Roman era was longer. Finally, the main fact is that an accident – of Oxyrhynchus' archaeology – meant that all its pre-Roman papyri were lost to rising water levels. Since Oxyrhynchus accounts for about a half of our evidence for literary papyri, we should accordingly reduce the difference in survival, *due to the distinct routes themselves*, by a factor of two, for this reason alone.

We expect Roman-era papyri to be more plentiful several times over. And we note that the accident of Oxyrhynchus' survival should augment this ratio of survival by another 2:1. When combining these two considerations, then – the difference in the original numbers, and the accident of Oxyrhynchus – we find that we should expect the number of found Roman-era papyri to have been twice-several-times over the number of found Ptolemaic literary papyri. This is not very different from about 1:10, then. While, of course, no real precision is possible on this question, what we can say is that, in this particular case, a discard process did not give rise to an obviously different *rate* of survival, *due to the discard process itself*.

This kind of consideration adds a dollop of credibility to what may be seen as inherently likely: that the loss of papyrus is fundamentally a matter of the elements. It is a story of water and wind, sand and fire. It is a broadly similar tale told anywhere in the Nile Valley, and so, to this extent, it is possible that, as a first approximation, literary and documentary papyri survive at a similar rate. In what follows, I will go on to assume that this is the case (while admitting that this big assumption adds quite a bit to our error bar).

Hopkins' (1991) figure of "less than a thousand" census returns looks strange in the face of the 300 returns identified by Bagnall and Frier (1994),[12] but the point is well taken. If our purpose is to estimate, based on the fate of the census returns, that of literary papyri, then it should be borne in mind that a considerably larger fraction of the documents remains unpublished. Once again, the number is hazy: we do not have a catalogue

---

[11] There is a debate concerning the comparison of economic performance in Egypt between the Ptolemaic and Roman eras, though this concerns mostly the causes for (modest) economic growth, not so much its very existence; see Monson (2012).

[12] In Hopkins (1980: 303) he correctly reports 270 returns published then. "More than 300" is Scheidel's (2001: 118) formulation.

of the *unpublished* papyri of the world, and all we have to go by is the vague sense of papyrologists that there are plenty of them.[13] Instead of Hopkins' obviously exaggerated 1,000, meant as an upper bound and as a round number, I will go for a lower round number. If we assume that documentary papyri are twice less likely to have been published than literary papyri, we can look at about 750 "surviving" census returns. This, out of 15 million such returns originally produced: the implied survival ratio then is 1:20,000, even worse than Hopkins', though not much different from his: a reasonable, round, starting point. In my tale of papyrus against the elements, I suggest that the evidence of the census returns implies that a given piece of papyrus has a 1:20,000 chance of surviving through 2,000 years. Better put: of the total amount of papyrus committed to writing in Greco-Roman Egypt, it appears that about 1/20,000th has survived.[14]

This indeed is but a first step for our reconstruction. But the very word "survived" needs to be qualified. Hopkins did commit one major error, as in fact he failed to compare like to like. It does not tell us much about the chance of a literary roll leaving some trace when we are told that one out of 20,000 census returns did. This is because, as we noted on page 20 above (then for the sake of the *internal* comparison between literary rolls), the size of the original artifact matters as well. What survives are so many square inches of papyrus, and the more of those you have, the higher your chances of survival. The average literary roll was, in fact, much bigger than the average census return. The latter took the form of a single sheet (so that sometimes, in bureaucratic contexts, separate census returns could be glued together to form booklets, with each sheet/return given a numeral value.[15] This means that a literary roll had several times more chances to go through the same lottery of survival than a census return did. In fact, about 20 times more.[16] This finally allows us to deduce a survival ratio, for literary papyri in the Nile Valley, of about 1:1,000.[17]

---

[13] Rathbone (1991: 1) estimates that there were about 450 published documents from the Heroninos archive – and perhaps about 600 then unpublished. How far can this be generalized?

[14] The term "surviving" is slightly misleading, as we have effectively considered *excavated* papyri. It is plausible that many more await excavation; and that development in the Nile Valley has destroyed many others that were still unexcavated during the great era of papyrus hunting, in the late nineteenth century and early twentieth.

[15] Bagnall and Frier (1994: 19–20).

[16] Skeat (1982) (following on Lewis, 1974: 55): the standard roll size was 20 sheets. There is some debate concerning the variability of such size in practice, but this matters to us less, as it is fairly uncontroversial that the 20-sheet roll would have been at least common. (To equate the document with a single sheet is no more than a useful simplification.)

[17] This slightly simplifies the probabilistic calculation (to have 20 goes at a one in 20,000 chance is not the same as a one in 1,000 chance), but the difference, with these parameters, is trivial.

A round number; and surrounded by fat error bars. In ascending order of ignorance, we are uncertain about the number of households in the Nile Valley; the relative frequency of the edition of literary and documentary papyri; the significance of the differential discard paths of Roman-era literary and documentary papyri; and the average number of copies per census return. Each of these can sway the result by tens of percentage points either way, but the central result remains likelier than higher or lower figures (errors do not have to enhance each other; they could, equally, cancel each other out, which is why distributions of probabilities are bell-shaped). I would venture to suggest that, based on the argument thus far, the survival ratio of literary papyri was less likely to go below 1:500 or above 1:2,000 than it was to be within that range.

How plausible is this range? Let me quickly bring in some more evidence – tenuous though it is – for the ancient distribution of papyrus. Consider, first, the economic end. Even a million roll equivalents produced annually would cost, as stationery, something like 20 million denarii or 2 million sesterce (HS)[18] – compared to total annual GDP in the Mediterranean of, say, 20 billion HS, of which something on the order of 10 percent came from Egypt.[19] The papyrus industry would constitute, then, about one-tenth of a percent of the Egyptian economy: not absurd, for what was, after all, noted as a significant Egyptian product. In fact, we do have suggestions of up to 1,000 rolls being bought at a time, tens of thousands or more roll equivalents harvested annually in single locations.[20]

---

[18] Bagnall (2009a: 55): seven rolls ≈ artaba of wheat in the fourth century CE (it is conceivable that in the Roman era papyrus prices could have been somewhat lower; see n.338 in the following chapter), or one roll ≈ 4 kg. As an order of magnitude, a kilogram of wheat is estimated to cost less than half a sesterce (see summary in Scheidel and Friesen, 2009: 7).

[19] Scheidel and Friesen (2009: 14). As another comparison, Lewis (1974: 132) finds a consistent relation between the price of a single roll as stationery and a day's laboring wages: the roll was worth a little more than a day's labor. A million rolls, as stationery, then translate into perhaps a couple of million days of subsistence, or about 10,000 annual subsistences, in an Egypt which had an economic output of about 10 million annual subsistences or more: once again, we derive about a tenth of a percent of the economy. This calculation ignores the non-stationery uses of papyrus (manifold, but apparently economically less significant), as well as the added value of scribal work (irrelevant for the many documentary papyri, and often, perhaps, produced outside Egypt).

[20] The Zeno estate could acquire more than 1,000 papyri at a time (Lewis, 1974: 101). Constantine endowed a single church in Rome with an annual supply of 11,200 sheets of papyrus, or perhaps 500 roll equivalents: in a time, and place, distant from the heyday of papyrus (Davis, 2000: 20). Lewis (1974: 108–10) sums up the contracts for two papyrus plantations. In one of them, the lessees undertake to pay 600 armful-loads of papyrus (in the sense of stalks, apparently) as well as 5,000 drachmas annually. 5,000 drachmas is the market cost of thousands of finished rolls (as stationery: see again Lewis, 1974: 132), so that, to make any profit, the plantation was surely expected to turn out much more than that. In the other contract, 20,000 armful-loads of papyrus stalks were merely the payment of interest on the loan making it possible for the lessees to operate the plantation; this papyrus document (BGU 1180) is literally from a mom and pop shop, a husband-and-wife team

This may then be tested against the implication of our argument above, for the total number of ancient documents. We can compare the 300 census returns published in 1994 to the roughly 17,000 documents mentioned in Habermann (1998: 157). Census returns appear, then, to occupy 2 percent of the documents produced in Roman Egypt, through the era of the Roman census. If indeed there were 15 million such census returns, the central value we get is 750 million documents produced at that time at the Nile Valley alone, or, very roughly, 3 million documents annually. This apparently mind-boggling number comes down to about 150,000 roll equivalents used for documents annually in the Nile Valley, through the Imperial era – which, we now note, is far from absurd. Or consider quickly a few *types* of documents. Depauw (2015: 68) counts 577 deeds of sales in Demotic alone (ranging across over a millennium). Palme (2009: 365) finds a total 170 sales of slaves (in all languages) and (361) a total of about 2,450 private letters, in the Ptolemaic and Roman eras. Is it reasonable to multiply such numbers by well over[21] 20,000 to get to the "total original number"? This implies that, on average, every year saw the production, in the Nile Valley, of tens of thousands of Demotic documents related to *all* sales; tens of thousands of documents (in any language) related to the sale of slaves; and a few hundred thousand private letters. There are many questions surrounding such numbers – how many documents would be produced by a single sale, for instance? – but the orders of magnitude, once again, are not patently absurd.[22]

So, let us take up the implication of the Hopkins (1991) calculation more seriously: a survival rate for literary papyri of between 1:500 and 1:2,000. . . Can we improve on this?

We may compare papyrus to other materials. Take Panathenaic amphorae – produced to be distributed as prizes in competitions whose

---

undertaking to harvest a particular marsh. The conclusion is that a very modest operation could involve the cutting of many tens of thousands of stalks of papyrus annually – hardly surprising, as this was a year-round product. Lewis (1974: 102) ends up simply stating that millions of rolls were produced annually. For all this, remember that we are looking at a plant-based product (what is more, one that essentially grows wild, with no special effort required for irrigation and manure). When we think of writing surfaces as scarce, what comes to mind is the Middle Ages, with writing on the skins of valuable animals. The papyrus reed was no cow: you didn't need to feed it. Eventually, writing would take off – first in the Islamic world – when animal-based parchment was replaced by plant-based paper (Bloom, 2001).

[21] "Well over" because many documentary papyri are still unpublished.

[22] For instance: assume that 10 percent of total population in antiquity were slaves (Scheidel, 1997: 158) and you have on the order of a few hundred thousand slaves in Upper Egypt. Since each sale would give rise to multiple documents (see the overview in Depauw, 2015), tens of thousands of documents concerning the sale of slaves, annually, implies that perhaps a few percent of all slaves were sold in a given year.

schedules are fully known, so that their survival ratio is known. This survival ratio stands at roughly 1:100, which is standardly taken to be representative for ancient pottery as a whole.[23] Duncan-Jones (1974: 360–2) finds that certain inscriptions from Roman Africa could survive at a rate as high as 5 percent, though he considers this exceptionally high relative to inscriptions as a whole (there are various reasons why Roman African inscriptions are particularly well attested).[24] The rate of survival for inscriptions overall must have been closer, once again, to 1 percent. Now, pottery and inscriptions are as close as ancient artifacts come to indestructibility. Papyri – thin organic surfaces – are, in the long run, extremely fragile. (Indeed, they survive at all only under very special circumstances). It just doesn't seem right that our rate of witness for Roman-era papyri in the Nile Valley should be so close to our rate of witness for Athenian *pottery*. This argument suggests that, if indeed the rate of survival of literary papyri is between 1:500 and 1:2,000, it is perhaps likelier to be on the higher side within this range.

Further, bear in mind that literary papyri from Oxyrhynchus survive at a rate several times higher than that of literary papyri elsewhere.[25] A high rate of survival for the valley as a whole implies a crazy rate of survival for Oxyrhynchus: 1:500 in the valley as a whole implies, perhaps, a ratio of survival as high as 1 percent in Oxyrhynchus? (This city would have its

---

[23] Shanks (2004: 44); Johnston (1987) slightly lowers Cook's (1959) estimate of 1 percent survival.

[24] A couple of comparisons. (1) 488 fourth-century decrees of the Athenian assembly are now extant as inscriptions, out of a total of perhaps 30,000 decrees passed through that century. We do not know how many of the passed decrees would be inscribed, in how many copies (it is significant, however, that the extant decrees do not fall obviously into some small subset of the passed decrees: was the practice of inscribing quite widespread, then?). The rough ratio of 1 percent – in one of the best-studied archaeological sites anywhere – is suggestive (data from Hedrick, 1999: 393, based on Hansen, 1987: 108–13). (2) There are now about 7,000 to 8,000 published Roman milestones, for about 70,000 miles of Roman road (Kolb, 2004: 137–41). It is clear that many milestones could and were set up, over time, in a single location (indeed, small forests of milestones are sometimes still to be found *in situ*: for an illustration, see Sauer, 2014: 9, fig. 1). New milestones could be set up to commemorate the repair of the road or simply as propaganda, marking events such as the instalment of a new emperor. Sauer argues that the latter would have been the most frequent cause (hence the domination of our record of milestones by the third century CE – the period of maximal imperial turnover). If so, the number of milestones should indeed greatly exceed the number of miles, and our 7,000 to 8,000 published monuments once again may well be in the range of roughly 1 percent of the original population.

[25] The city likely had a population in the low tens of thousands (Bowman, 2011: 345), out of a valley that could have had an urban population in the high hundreds of thousands, if not a million (the high urbanization of the Nile in antiquity is well known: perhaps approaching one-third?). It was surely more sophisticated than many other smaller and more distant settlements (one important case is shown by Morgan, 2003), but, even so, it could not have more than about 10 percent of the literary papyri of the valley; it now accounts for about one-half of the edited literary papyri with known provenance. So, its papyri had about five times the rate of survival of those of other cities?

literary papyri extant in the same frequency most other places have kept their inscriptions, their pottery!) Perhaps the city does present to us such a miracle of survival. The main reason to doubt this, however, is that, in such a case, we should have been able to reconstruct with better clarity the detail of individual libraries. One percent is a very large sample, which already implies a certain granularity. But, in fact, our evidence is very frustrating in this regard: it is extremely hard to piece it together like this. The individual finds, even when they seem to come from similar eras, are hard to put together into collections (Houston, 2009: we have discussed this evidence on page 33 above). This is more consistent with a thinner survival.

In short, it is likelier that the rate of survival of literary papyri was about 1:1,000 to 1:2,000.

What would that imply for the total number of Greek literary papyri discarded in antiquity in the Nile Valley? As noted above, the number of genuine book scroll papyrus fragments is about 5,000. The implied total number of literary papyri produced in the region is therefore more than a few million and perhaps as high as 10 million. This is the total for antiquity as a whole, and what matters for the book as a social reality is the number of books "above ground" at a given time. As noted on page 43 above, a literary roll might be normally curated for as long as a century: a stylized but plausible rate. This would mean that we can derive a preliminary rough estimate of the fraction of books in circulation at the peak, from among the total ancient production of rolls in the Nile Valley, by applying the fraction of rolls produced in the peak century, the second century CE. In fact, about a third of all literary papyri are dated in rough terms to the second century. Many of these are dated more vaguely, to the first to second centuries or second to third centuries; and we probably undercount, as noted above, Ptolemaic papyri. In short, it is not too far off to suggest that about a quarter of all ancient papyri would circulate simultaneously at the peak. This means that we need to envision the Nile Valley hosting, at the peak, somewhere between 1 million and 2.5 million rolls.

We may advance this further. One of the most reliable features of the statistics of literary papyri, as we noted, is their relative distributions between (well-attested) works and authors. At first glance, it appears that about one-quarter of all ancient papyri were copies of the *Iliad*. This is an overcount: some of these derive from the educational process, and some of these might have been discarded more frequently because of heavier use (now that we have moved to considering the number of papyri at a given time, this becomes a factor again). Let us say that about one-fifth, then, of the papyri circulating at the peak were copies of the *Iliad*: so, between 200,000 and 500,000 *Iliad* rolls. It is harder to estimate the number of rolls in a given collection. Some libraries would have had multiple copies (see page 41 above), while quite a few might have had just a selection – perhaps only the first book. The two would tend to cancel each other out, though boorish collectors of just a few books must have been more numerous than the owners of multiple copies, and the average could well be somewhat lower than 24 rolls.[26] At this point we are close to finding 10,000 to 25,000 book-owning households in Upper Egypt at the peak. Now, this is a Nile Valley with perhaps some 3 million people, or a little more than 600,000 households.[27] We now see a Nile Valley in which between 1.5 and 4 percent of all households owned books. I will return to discuss the sociology of this in section 5.4, but this percentage immediately suggests we have not been crazy to pursue the Hopkins calculation. The number is perhaps high – and it does carry consequences for the sociology of the book – but it is not beyond the bounds of plausibility.

To be precise, we have found an inverse relation between sociology and archaeology. The lower the penetration of the book (sociology), the higher the survival ratio of papyrus (archaeology). The alternative which could prima facie make historical sense – namely, a substantially lower rate of book owning (say, in the range of half a percent of all households?)[28] – would tend to imply an uncomfortably high survival rate for literary papyri: half a percent of book-owning households translates most naturally into a survival ratio for literary papyri as high as 1:250![29]

---

[26] I make the stylized assumption that the *Iliad* would indeed typically occupy 24 physical rolls; this seems a good central value to take, and is in fact the clear rule among published papyri. I have looked through all the papyri for *Iliad*, Books 1 to 6, in Pack (1965) (this kind of non-sample survey is still easier to do on a print resource). While a certain number of Homeric papyri (mostly from the schoolroom context) are selections from across several books, there were, in this selection, zero papyrus rolls that run over from one book to another (P.Lit. Lond. 5, for instance – the rare counter-example, running from Book 2 through all of 3 to the beginning of 4 – is in fact a codex; so is P. Bodm. 1, with Books 5 to 6).

[27] Here we should consider households, not houses: that you own books does not make your lodgers into intellectuals; Bagnall and Frier (1994) find an average household size of between 4.3 and 5.0.

[28] This would be the implication of Bagnall (1996: 103): "It is doubtful that the audience for [the literary] authors exceeded a few thousands in all of Egypt in any period."

[29] As noted in the beginning, I try and move from weaker to stronger arguments. Thus, the argument for a survival ratio for literary papyri of about 1:1,000 has been developed first based on (1) a refinement of the Hopkins calculation, and only then based on (2) – a combination of (2a) sociology (a ratio in the thousands produces an implausibly high number of books) and (2b) archaeology (a ratio in the hundreds produces an implausibly high rate of survival). I have presented (1) the Hopkins calculation first, and spent much more time on it, because it requires much more nuance. But in fact (2) – which does not require all that much elaboration – is also the stronger of the two.

We may move further and consider not just book ownership as such (that is, the number of small libraries) but the number of truly educated – that is, to return to the concept introduced on page 40, the number of big libraries. As noted on pages 24–5 above, Plato must have been something of a sine qua non in the big library. On the other hand, the kind of small library owners who had perhaps some books of the *Iliad* and a few other canonical works would have been very unlikely to own the complete works of Plato. The ratio between the frequency of the *Iliad* and of the complete works of Plato can be taken as a rough estimate of the relative numbers of small libraries and big libraries. Now, even the *Phaedrus* (which must have circulated beyond the "collected works" of Plato) had about 5 percent of the penetration of the *Iliad*; the collected works of Plato had perhaps a half to a third of that (see pages 20–4 and 118–21 above for the details of this calculation). The number of households containing the *Iliad* was estimated above at about 10,000 to 25,000; so, we find a few hundred big libraries in the Nile Valley at the peak. The number could not have been much smaller than that. As noted above, Oxyrhynchus held perhaps a tenth of the intellectuals of the valley. Johnson has documented, from the papyri themselves, circles of readers who sat together to study, in scholarly fashion, the works of the literary canon.[30] Such Plutarchean communities are easy to imagine with the city holding a few dozen collectors of big libraries, much more difficult to understand if their numbers were considerably smaller.

And, so, the outlines of a plausible model for the libraries of the Nile begins to emerge. The valley might have had, at the peak, about a million or two book rolls, maybe a little more; a few hundred big libraries, the kind that we associate with the truly learned; many thousands, perhaps even as many as 20,000, households (about 4 percent of the population, or 10 percent of the urban population) identifying as book owners.

"Big" and "small" libraries are abstractions, and so far in this book have been used as qualitative terms, describing a library's relation to the canon. Let me try and clarify what these mean in practice – and in concrete numbers. Libraries in the high thousands of rolls no doubt existed, even in the Nile Valley, but they were quite rare, even at the peak; libraries of tens of thousands of books should have been considered shockingly big; in fact, this is the order of magnitude that our sources imagine for exceedingly large private libraries.[31] The royal library in Alexandria is imagined at an

---

[30] Johnson (2010: chap. 9).
[31] The *Suda* believed that the grammarians Tyrannion as well as Epaphroditus (s.vv.) owned libraries of 30,000 books, and Isidore of Seville, *Etymologies* 6.6, reports the same number of books for the

order of magnitude above that: our sources, none earlier than the Imperial era, mention figures of between 400,000 and 700,000 rolls[32] – a number which interests me right now, once again, only from the point of view of implied perceptions. The purpose of such numbers is to make your jaw drop. Such numbers are read by the owners of big libraries – the people who own about a thousand books and have heard of their superiors owning even 10,000 or so. The royal library of Alexandria was supposed to be *much more than that*. Suppose, then, that the average big library would have about 1,000 rolls,[33] and the median rather fewer; many "big libraries" would have then no more than a few hundred rolls, already continuous with the more affluent "small library", which had, say, both the *Iliad* and the *Odyssey* together with a good representation of the other canonical authors, with perhaps 100 rolls altogether. Needless to say, I imagine a continuous curve of frequencies, "big" and "small" used as my own conceptual terms of aggregation and not implying any bimodal distribution. But note how the numbers work together. Hundreds of big libraries, with 1,000 rolls on average each: this accounts for somewhat fewer than a million books; and then well over 10,000 small libraries, each with a dozen books on average, maybe a little more: this accounts, again, for less than a million. Is this roughly how we may put together a complete distribution of books in the Nile Valley, at the peak, totaling to somewhere between 1 million and 2.5 million?

So far, I have been speculating about the valley. But speculation should not stop there!

The Upper Nile had perhaps a population of 3 million, and so about 10 percent of the entire population of the Greek-reading Mediterranean at the Imperial peak. The baseline calculation would be simply to multiply the numbers obtained by ten to derive the total distribution of ancient Greek libraries at the peak. This is certainly wrong, in two opposite directions. (1) Papyrus was an important part of the culture of the Nile,

---

library of Pamphilus of Caesarea; the *Historia Augusta*, Gordian 18.2, reports that Serenus Sammonicus' library comprised 62,000 books. It hardly needs pointing out that such numbers are stylized (in all the cases quoted above, we have scholars fantasizing about the size of previous scholars' libraries), but such numbers provide us with a sense of the order of magnitude for such fantasies.

[32] Bagnall (2002: 351–2). Seneca (*De Tranq. Animi* 9.5), perhaps reflecting Livy, implies that the library had merely 40,000 books – i.e. pushing it back to the level of a supremely lavish private library, which might be part of the point (he castigates the library as being merely for the sake of ostentation, in the context of criticizing private luxury).

[33] We have discussed on pp. 75–8 above the papyrus fragments of library catalogues, studied in Otranto (2000). At least two of these – nos. 15 and 17 – seem to imply a library of several thousand rolls: definitely a rarity, then, in the Nile Valley, but not anything unheard of.

and so it may have been simply culturally entrenched in ways it has not been elsewhere in the Mediterranean. (It was also certainly cheaper, though this effect was probably weak.)[34] This argument holds especially for the small libraries, and it stands to reason, then, that across the Mediterranean there were less than ten times the small libraries of the upper Nile, or fewer than a quarter of a million. (2) Even big libraries would have been more natural on the Nile than elsewhere, but these must have been primarily metropolitan. Once again, Egypt was prosperous: economically, the Nile Valley was not a backwater. Culturally, though, it was, and the truly great would gravitate away, to the centers of Alexandria, Asia Minor and Italy. (The greatest of the residents of the Nile Valley – the Apion family, admittedly already in Byzantine times – were absentee landlords, based in Constantinople.)[35] The number of big libraries in the Greek-reading world, at the peak, was certainly more than ten times that in the Nile Valley, and so more than just a few thousand.

We should pause to consider, in particular, Alexandria. Rich as any ancient city, other than Rome: papyrus, abundant; books, the foundation of elite identity. Now, the urban population of the Nile Valley taken together was two to three times greater than the population of Alexandria, and this must mean that the number of books held in private big libraries, in Alexandria, would have to have been at least greater than that of the Nile Valley (two to three times greater incidence of big libraries in Alexandria is a minimal assumption, and this ignores the likely bigger size of an Alexandrian bigger library). And so, a million or so books in Alexandrian big libraries is a very prudent, low estimate. It is this observation which makes the "Library of Alexandria" such a canard. There was a royal Library in Alexandria, but there wasn't a single "Library of Alexandria". There always have been *libraries* of Alexandria. Johnstone

---

[34] Freight costs were given by volume. We now interpret Diocletian's Edict to imply the cost of freight for a Modium Kasternsis – 13.9 l. – at 1 denarius per day (Scheidel, 2013a; Arnaud, 2007). This is about 1/36th of a day of unskilled labor (Allen, 2009: 3). This Modium would surely hold dozens of rolls, so we will need to transport a single roll for about 1,000 days to make its freight cost equal to one day's unskilled labor, which should be on the order of 10 percent of its price. Freight for normal travel times is therefore a trivial element of cost. The cost at a distance would be higher, simply because of the transaction costs along the way; but in fact costs of papyrus recorded in Egypt and in Delos were not far apart (Lewis, 1974: 76). The fundamental fact is that there was little discernible effort, throughout antiquity, to introduce papyrus, commercially, nearer its potential markets (there was always some Syrian production; the Arabs would eventually bring the production of papyrus into Sicily: Lewis, 1974: 19). Had the price been much higher away from the source, it would have made economic sense to bring the source closer.

[35] Wickham (2005: 248); for the growth of the family, see Ruffini (2008: chap. 2).

has looked into the evidence for Hellenistic library foundations, concluding (Johnstone, 2014: 349):

> [T]he evidence of libraries at various sites around the Mediterranean in the second century is more consistent with a model of diffuse, if syncopated, development than with the traditional hierarchical story.

And this, pushed downwards all through the social ladder and further in time, is my claim for the distribution of books throughout antiquity. It may well be that in Alexandria's early days the single collection of the king dominated all else, but, generally, most books in the city were held by private citizens, and the royal library was simply a *primus inter pares*. At the peak there were many hundreds – more? – of big libraries, some of them very substantial, holding between them many hundreds of thousands of rolls containing literature *outside* the central canon. If you got to know the right people in Alexandria, you could read Jacoby's historians, Snell's tragedians – before they became fragments. "Getting to know the right people": and we envision a cultural life defined not only by royal patronage but also by elite networks.

And then, across the Mediterranean as a whole: fewer than a quarter-million small libraries; more than a few thousand big libraries. The two numbers are still related, though we may assume that, across the Mediterranean as a whole, the fraction of big libraries among the total number of libraries was higher than it was on the Nile. (This is especially obvious in the case of Italy, where the big library must have dominated and where, indeed, we have our single case of such a big library surviving, in the Villa dei Papiri). Further, already the number 25,000 for small libraries on the Nile was on the high side, so we should probably look for a number significantly lower than a quarter-million. How about 100,000 small libraries and 10,000 big libraries? I take this to be my order of magnitude.[36]

### 5.1.2    Beyond Papyrus: A First Stab at the Number of Authors

We may now turn from the implications of the libraries in terms of readers to the implications of libraries in terms of authors. We have a model with perhaps as many as 10,000 big libraries (or perhaps fewer) and 100,000 small libraries (or perhaps more). The question that interests us is the number of truly minor authors – the kind of authors who do not show up,

---

[36] This has obvious implications for the familiar questions of ancient literacy. I do not aim to address those questions here, but I return to such broad considerations on p. 609 below.

individually, at all often in the papyrus record but who, taken together, occupied a significant fraction of the big libraries.

There were, in 2011, 76 hapax fragments among our literary papyri – that is, papyri that are the unique identified witness to their author (and only about 100 authors that have more than one witness). I also estimated on page 86 above that there could be a total of 950 fragments by minor authors if we include the adespota, which I noted on page 85 was probably a generous estimate (since the number of annotated adespota would then be surprisingly low, as minor authors tend to acquire more annotations). I also noted that this agrees well with the (tiny sample of) extant titles, of which about a fifth are the unique witness to their author. I suspect that the practice of attaching titles to rolls would be most common in big libraries, however, so that the estimate of a fifth is once again an overestimate. Indeed, even the estimate of 950 minor author papyri among the adespota does not remotely mean 950 hapax papyri. Surely, many of those minor authors are currently unassigned but would yield, once perfectly identified, several multiple witnesses. We have plenty of unidentified medical fragments: how many are by Herophilus? Of the minor poetry – how much is in clusters of several papyri each, for various minor lyric poets? How many fragments of minor prose are really various fragments of some mammoth historical works that we now consider lost? There is no way of fixing this number precisely, but it is clear that the total number of hapax among the papyri is well short of 1,000 and is measured in the hundreds (conversely, the number of non-hapax authors is truly not about 100 but is, instead, in the low hundreds). We estimate that about 2,000 of our papyri are from big libraries. So, if about 400 of these are hapax, we find that about 20 percent of the ancient big library was of authors who survived at a rate of one hapax and below. (This may be an underestimate for the Mediterranean as a whole, since the really big libraries of Alexandria and of the Italian villa could have had more of those truly minor authors.)

Now, a hapax papyrus represents, on average, an author whose entire circulation in the Nile Valley, throughout antiquity, was about 1,000 to 2,000 rolls, or some 250 to 500 circulated simultaneously at the peak in the Nile Valley alone. (This, I note, is a relatively safe conclusion.) We are looking here at big libraries, which are under-represented for the Nile, so as we extrapolate to the Mediterranean we now look at *more* than 2,500 to 5,000 rolls at the peak across the Mediterranean. This stands for authors who are fairly minor, which once again serves to underline that our numbers are at least not implausibly small and, if anything, are rather high. (Do we really think there were 2,500 to 5,000 rolls in circulation for

Empedocles? For Menelaus? Of course, they were lucky, in that a single roll by each does survive; but they suggest the *kind* of authors we are looking at.) Depending on the precise survival ratio we choose, we will adjust accordingly this threshold, which is the cutoff point between the somewhat more frequently copied authors of antiquity – a few hundred authors, each on average circulating with more than 2,500 to 5,000 total rolls at the peak – and the somewhat less frequently copied authors of antiquity. Those would comprise X authors, each on average circulating with fewer than 2,500 to 5,000 total rolls at the peak.

The value of X would provide us with the number of authors in circulation under the Antonines. Unfortunately, this cannot be recovered through this simple calculation; some extra constraint must be brought in.

The way to go about the estimate of X is as follows. The total number of rolls in the big libraries across the Mediterranean would be, according to our model, perhaps about 5 to 10 million. Of these, we say that about 20 percent, or a little more, are by the minor authors: 2 to 4 million rolls, to be divided by authors who each have fewer than 2,500 to 5,000 rolls on average. If all the authors in this category are right at the threshold, the central value we get for the number of authors is roughly 1,000. This can be taken as a reasonable estimate (central value, with a big error bar surrounding it) for a *lower boundary*. For, surely, the number of authors would have been higher, since the average authors would have *fewer* than the maximal threshold, and instead there ought to have been a distribution whereby more and more authors would be found with fewer and fewer rolls.

It is here that our estimates hit a block. The reason is that there is nothing with which to estimate the size of the lower tail. A distribution in which there are 10,000 authors with exactly one roll each and a distribution in which there are 100,000 authors with exactly one roll each are nearly indistinguishable. Under one scenario, the single-roll authors would take less than 1 percent of the entire circulation of minor authors; under the other, they would take a few percentage points. There is nothing to say which is closer to the truth; but the difference between them involves a tenfold explosion in the size of our universe of ancient authors!

There is no way to eliminate this uncertainty, but we can simply cut away this statistical tail. What I would suggest is that we should concentrate on the category of *authors in meaningful circulation*.

Since many ancient works were in multiple rolls, and many authors had more than a single work in circulation, it follows that even ten rolls in circulation, at a given time, would very often mean no more than a single copy of a given work. Absent perfect catalogues, perfectly shared, such a work would need extraordinary luck to belong to any kind of cultural conversation, and so would be *effectively* lost. I thus define having at least a few dozen rolls as the threshold, only above which an author is meaningfully extant. (In fact, since this is not a print culture, perhaps the difference between "a private copy" and "a published work" is at around this quantitative threshold?)

This suddenly makes our estimate, of the number of rolls in circulation by minor authors, much more meaningful. We look at a range between a few dozen and a few thousand, on a downward-sloping curve. The average, therefore, must certainly be around a few hundred. And so, if indeed there were a few million rolls by minor authors circulating at the peak, this then yields *about 10,000* as a central value for the number of authors effectively known to the cultural elite.

It might appear as something of a magic trick that we can produce such an estimate, based on the evidence of the survival of papyrus rolls from Upper Egypt. What this estimate stands for, once again, is a set of correlations and constraints. If indeed we assume much fewer than 10,000 authors in effective circulation, at the peak, this implies that the total number of rolls by such minor authors would have to be much less than a few million, and so the fact that several hundred rolls by such minor authors are currently published, from Upper Egypt alone, is very remarkable, implying either that papyri survive in surprisingly high frequency or that a surprisingly large fraction of all ancient big libraries were in Upper Egypt. On the other hand, if we imagine much more than 10,000 minor authors in effective circulation, this would imply a very large number of big libraries, which begins to be unlikely on more general sociological grounds.

This is as far as the evidence of the papyri themselves can lead us. Central values, with enormous error bars attached. Are these values plausible? Is it likely that the second century CE would know, effectively, 10,000 authors? Let us turn to an alternative route to estimating the scale of ancient culture.

## 5.2 Second Route: From the Set of All Authors

In this section my goal is very simple: to find the size of the set of all authors, active before 200 CE.

The most basic question is: how many of this set are currently attested? This is in principle answerable with precision (of course, conceding the fuzziness of the definition), but for our purposes it is enough to arrive at a rough estimate. Here are some starting point: EANS has almost exactly 2,000 entries. The *Dictionnaire des philosophes antiques* (DPA), now finished, has about 4,000. The New Jacoby has a little more than 1,000 entries. (We can immediately see how restricted TLG is, with fewer than 2,000 ancient authors.) All those numbers cover late antiquity as well, but, more importantly, EANS, DPA and Jacoby are all, by design, an overcount of the genuinely attested authors. The DPA includes (which is to be commended) pretty much any ancient figure whose tombstone named them a "philosopher", any known pupil of a philosopher, any apocryphal Pythagorean – indeed, any figure whose biography might be of interest to a student of ancient philosophy. I have sampled DPA, going in "skips" of 20 pages (looking for the author beginning after the start of the selected page). Forty-four out of 141 entries thus sampled could qualify as "genuine philosophical authors (even if non-writing), active before about 200 CE". I will therefore assume that there are about 1,200 attested philosophers in the period which interests us. Overcounting in EANS is substantial, as well. It mentions, in particular, hundreds of "pharmacologists", which were often names attached apocryphally, almost as a mnemonic serving to identify the various concoctions. Another source of overcount is produced by overlap, which is best addressed through EANS: many of its entries are philosophers (engaged in natural philosophy); many others are in Jacoby (especially the geographers). A similar sample (now with skips of ten pages) finds 25, out of 73 authors sampled, who are genuine scientific authors, neither in DPA nor in Jacoby, active before about 200 CE. This is about 35 percent, and I will add 700 scientists to the 1,200 philosophers. There is some overcount in Jacoby (as some modern scholars sometimes wonder whether this or that historian's name may not be an invention of unscrupulous compilers), but this is relatively minor, and most of Jacoby's entries are genuine historians, neither scientists nor philosophers. In addition, the great bulk of these historians antedate late antiquity (I find, in the searchable portion of Jacoby, which has some 800 authors, no more than 98 historians from the third to sixth centuries). I will add 900 historians, to obtain a total of 2,800 authors attested via DPA, Jacoby and EANS.

   At this point I also sampled the original Pauly–Wissowa, looking for any figures who could be identified as "ancient authors prior to 200 CE", checking for all whether or not they are among the authors of DPA/EANS/Jacoby. (I took many volumes haphazardly from the shelves, and then went through them by "skips" of 50, going in no particular order among the volumes until I reached a sample of 100.) Fifty-eight of the 100 taken were indeed within DPA/EANS/Jacoby, 42 were outside them. This is perhaps a slight undercount, as I found in P.–W. five authors who were doctors, attested via inscriptions, who likely enough were not authors and so, rightly, should *not* have been included in EANS (I will return to this epigraphic evidence on page 583 below. The remaining 37 were: 19 poets, 7 grammarians, 11 orators). As 2,800 is 58 percent of about 4,800, I conclude that there are roughly 5,000 authors prior to late antiquity attested in P.–W. This is probably not very far from the actual number of authors we should consider currently "attested" (P.–W. might miss a few authors, but the count also must, as noted above, include some spurious cases. All my numbers are based on small samples but a result within 10 percent or so of the correct value – which my samples roughly provide – is good enough for the purposes of this study.).

This number – roughly 5,000 – is among the most solid we have, and it, in itself, carries consequences. If we assume, for instance, that there were 10,000 authors prior to 200 CE, we end up with the incredibly high ratio of attestation of about a half! True to my methods, however, I wish to start from the weaker arguments and build gradually. And so I put this aside for the time being and proceed to another, more complicated argument.

Some accounting identities, first. Some pre-200 authors were active before the Imperial era – and almost all of them in the four centuries between –400 and 0. (I will return to discuss in section 6.1.1 below the rise in scale through the fifth century, from a very low base.) The rest were active in the first two centuries CE. So, two categories: the pre-Imperial, effectively through four centuries; the Imperial, through two.

Now, it is extremely unlikely on general historical grounds that the frequency of authors went down from the pre-Imperial to the Imperial era. On the other hand, it is quite unlikely that the frequency of authors went up so much from the Hellenistic to the Imperial era that it more than doubled. (All this is a matter of our general understanding of the cultural history, and is discussed in detail in the following chapter.) If so, the conclusion is that, roughly: not more than two-thirds of authors prior to late antiquity, but no less than one-half, were pre-Imperial. This, too, is a useful, fairly solid observation.

Now, in the previous section I touched on a different number: the number of authors circulating at a given time. For obvious methodological reasons, I do not wish to rely here on the results of the previous section. But let us see how we may proceed with such calculations independently. As a simplification, we may think of the number of authors in circulation in the second century CE as the aggregate of two components: Imperial-era authors and those pre-Imperial authors who were still in circulation.

The number of Imperial-era authors would be perhaps a third (perhaps more) of the total pre-200 authors; of these, a relatively large fraction would be in circulation through the second century CE.

The number of pre-Imperial authors would be perhaps two-thirds (perhaps less) of the total of all pre-200 authors; of these, a somewhat smaller fraction would be in circulation through the second century CE.

We begin to develop a few equations; let us see if we may put any concrete parameters into them. One basic value to consider is that of pre-Imperial authors still in circulation in the second century CE. As it happens, we do have some evidence with which to calculate this value. A main theme of this era is its explicit, naming engagement with its cultural legacy. Two corpora are especially big (and are also very well served by their indices). I count in the index to Athenaeus' *Deipnosophists* (Olson, 2012) 824 figures I would count as "authors".[37] In the index to Plutarch's *Moralia* (O'Neill, 2004) I count 463 such figures. (I count only authors active up to and including Plutarch's own time, though this does not matter, as Athenaeus hardly mentions Imperial-era figures.) Now, if you pick 100 balls out of an urn, mark them, drop them back, mix thoroughly and then randomly pick 100 again – and then, among these, ten are found to be marked, you know that there are about 1,000 balls in that urn. (Notice that, for this calculation, it matters only that one of the pickings was random; it does not matter how the first one was constructed.) There are 244 authors shared by both the *Deipnosophists* and the *Moralia*. The simplest application of the calculation implies that Athenaeus and Plutarch had access to an urn with about 1,100 balls: had they mentioned authors in a truly random fashion, we could use this evidence directly to conclude that, in the second century CE, there were 1,100 mentionable pre-Imperial authors. As a matter of fact, they mention authors non-randomly, which means that the calculation may serve as a lower bound. So, surely, rather more than 1,100 pre-Imperial authors known in the second century. Can we get any nearer to a random sample?[38]

To some extent, the two corpora have their biases of selection, which do corrupt them as evidence (both share an interest in the history of music,

---

[37] This avoids actors and those merely listed as players on a musical instrument; many of these would in fact have been authors. I do count the handful of unwritten philosophers.

[38] It should be emphasized that the concrete route through which the selections were made is in and of itself immaterial. That Athenaeus had access to Larensis' library, and that Plutarch built his own in Chaeronea, are simply our way of describing how they dipped into the urn, picking out their balls. The question is different: to what extent were the biases, informing the formation of such collections, correlated (positively or negatively) with each other?

which makes them pay an inordinate amount of attention, in particular, to the poets of the new music of the late fifth century and early fourth; Plutarch is more "scientific", Athenaeus of course emphasizes the gastric and the frivolous),[39] but, overall, their interests are comparable, and comparably universal,[40] so that this corruption, while real, is fairly minor. The *Moralia* and the *Deipnosophists* mostly trawl the same seas, but they plumb different depths. The *Moralia* is a normal corpus of Imperial-era paideia, occasionally trying its hardest to be jolly, but overall a sober display of the author's enormous cultural capital. It cites abundantly, but with decorum, and Plutarch's goal is to mention the authors *worth mentioning*. It is thus "higher" in the sea (and so its selection is in fact, while extensive, most definitely not random). Athenaeus often trawls much nearer the bottom, reveling in the lowbrow and the frivolous. Thus, Athenaeus comes much closer than Plutarch to a truly random sample of what one could find in the big libraries of the Imperial era. Being random is, for Athenaeus, part of the point.

It is useful to note that, apart from Homer (whom Athenaeus does revere), the topmost literary canon, while of course well noted, is somewhat less significant in this work. I count (this is hard to do with precision) 26 mentions and citations of Demosthenes in Athenaeus and 145 in Plutarch's *Moralia*; 109 mentions of Euripides in Athenaeus; 347 in the *Moralia*.[41] In general, it is clear that the curve of frequencies of author mentions in Athenaeus has a long tail. About 450 authors were mentioned by Athenaeus exactly *once*. Here we finally reach a useful category for our purposes. Those 450 authors are mostly deeply obscure, and our

---

[39] Plutarch has one author named Seleucus: an astronomer who may have been the only one in antiquity to uphold Aristarchus' heliocentric hypothesis. Athenaeus has two: one wrote "amusing songs", the other – what else? – wrote on fishing.

[40] It should be emphasized that Athenaeus does not have any less interest in philosophers, for instance, than does Plutarch. Their difference is real, but it hardly matters to us: both Plutarch and Athenaeus mention philosophers, but they mention them differently. Plutarch is often (not always) interested in the doctrine of such philosophers; Athenaeus is interested strictly in the piquant stories surrounding them. It is typical that the group of "interesting" philosophers of the early era of the Athenian schools, active mostly outside Athens (section 4.2.1 above), is very well represented among the 244 authors shared by both Plutarch and Athenaeus: I note Alexinus, Aristippus, Bion, Cercidas, Clearchus, Diogenes (of course), Menedemus, Pyrrho, Stilpo and Timon. The absence of Diodorus Cronus from Athenaeus is puzzling (Diogenes Laertius knew a lot about him, so it is not as if the philosopher's memory had been effaced by Athenaeus' time). This is a good example of something irreducibly random about Athenaeus; a randomness which is, in fact, most useful to us.

[41] Driscoll (2016: appendix I) compares the frequency and function of Homer citations in Plutarch's *Moralia* to those of Euripides and the Lyric poets. Even in Plutarch, one finds a much larger incidence of Homer, and a tendency to use the non-Homer authorities, as Driscoll calls this, for "color" (rather than for substantial claims).

understanding of Athenaeus' project suggests that he cited them simply because he *could*. I would suggest we may look at them as proxy to the authors whom Athenaeus chose to cite *almost* at random.

Let us go back to the table listing authors according to number of papyrus fragments (pages 15–17 above). There, we find 46 authors with four fragments or more, which form indeed the indispensable core for both Plutarch and Athenaeus: only three of these are not among their shared 244 authors.[42] Nine out of 13 pre-Imperial authors counted in 2011 with three papyrus fragments are mentioned by both Plutarch and Athenaeus, as are also seven out of 13 – once again – pre-Imperial authors with two papyrus fragments. The internal difference is merely suggestive, but we already see a certain drop from the truly canonical authors. I count 54 pre-Imperial authors with exactly one identified papyrus fragment, and, of these, 20 are among those mentioned in both the *Moralia* and the *Deipnosophists*. So far we have counted 79 shared authors, out of the total of 244. These are already many of the authors frequently mentioned by Athenaeus (among the authors attested in the papyrus record, only one – Alcidamas – is cited by Athenaeus exactly once). Surely, the layer of the "core", inevitable authors to whom Athenaeus frequently returned was somewhat larger than this. But this core was certainly smaller than the 244 authors shared with Plutarch. Indeed, among those 244 authors, 45 are cited by Athenaeus once only. The names we find are intuitive. Looking at the list, I find 33 who are quite obscure (You ask yourself: "*Hagnon* who?") – though, of course, they would have to be somewhat meaningful to be mentioned by Plutarch (Hagnon, it turns out, was among the students who transcribed Carneades' lectures). Of course, this might be a little of an overcount: some authors cited once only were important, but unlucky. But, clearly, some of those cited a handful of times by Athenaeus would also have been very obscure, and simply cited more than once merely because they had a handful of juicy quotable bits. All in all, then, using "cited once by Athenaeus" as a proxy for "cited at random" is at least a possible short cut. To emphasize: the argument here is not primarily statistical but historical. It represents an interpretation of Athenaeus, as an author who deliberately sought to cast his net as wide as possible and so mentioned authors – beyond the several hundred he simply had to quote – more or less at random.

---

[42] These are: Euclid (over-represented among the papyri because of his educational use), Philo of Alexandria (marginal to the civilization of paideia and, at any rate, barely pre-Imperial), and – drumroll please – Apollonius of Rhodes, inexplicably absent from the *Moralia* (but not a major presence in the *Deipnosophists*, either: I count five mentions or citations. See p. 117 above for Apollonius' qualified position in the canon.).

A short cut. Where does it lead us? We are left now with 450 "random" Athenaeus citations, as well as 463 Plutarch citations; but obviously we need to remove, from the Plutarch number, the 199 authors whom he both shares with Athenaeus and whom Athenaeus cites more than once (the 199 scholarly must-have authors, so to speak): since we removed them from the Athenaeus list, there is no way for Athenaeus to coincide with them, in principle.

And so, we removed a little over 250 balls from the urn (the Plutarch mentions, once we removed the 199 shared by Athenaeus and cited by Athenaeus more than once). We marked them and put them back. We gave the urn to Athenaeus and he shook the urn not perfectly, but fairly well, and then got out 450 balls – those authors whom Athenaeus cites exactly once. It turns out that exactly 10 percent of these were marked; exactly 10 percent intersect with the original Plutarchean selection. Therefore, the Plutarchean selection of a little over 250 authors is likely about 10 percent of the original universe of mentionable authors, available in the second century.[43] This would suggest a little over 2,500 authors available for citation in the second century. Now, even here, it is something of an exaggeration – though perhaps not much of one – to make Athenaeus truly random; I would take this still as a lower bound, though one perhaps not far from the real number. (Notice some consequences: the *Moralia* quotes something approaching a sixth of the authors available, Athenaeus something approaching a third – a good sense of the encyclopedic reach of the respective projects.)

In all this, I put aside the question of the extent to which Plutarch and Athenaeus rely on extant works, and not on intermediary sources that conveyed authors who were, in fact, no longer in circulation by the second century CE. In other words, 2,500 is a *lower bound* (because Athenaeus' citations are not truly random) for an *upper bound* (because Athenaeus' citations are sometimes mediated). The number of pre-Imperial authors in circulation in the second century CE was somewhat fewer (but by how much?) than – 3,000? 4,000? . . .

Our parameters are still very loose, and so I set the number aside, once again, as it would be helpful to bring in even more equations. I therefore turn to another massive citer: Photius. This ninth-century patriarch of Constantinople liked to read, and to show off his reading. At his time,

---

[43] This is not a comparison between Plutarch's library and that of Athenaeus. This is an extrapolation from Plutarch's citations, assuming that Athenaeus' authors mentioned once only can be considered as a random sample of all the authors then available. For this consideration, the absolute size of Athenaeus' total library is immaterial, and all that matters is its randomness.

being well connected in the capital meant you could get hold of pretty much all books in circulation, and so we are very lucky to possess the public version of his reading diary, known as the *Bibliotheca*. This runs to 268 entries, a diverse work of roaming curiosity.

And so, we have discussed above the question: which fraction of pre-Imperial authors were circulating in the second century CE? Let me now ask a distinct question: which fraction of pre-200 CE authors were circulating in the ninth century CE? The answer is: about 80 of Photius' entries are prior to 200 CE. A small sample and not quite a random one – but, still, our clearest view of the libraries transmitted into Byzantium. At this point we have come so close to the current transmission that we may simply compare Photius against the works that are *now* extant. In fact, the fraction of Photius' works that can still be read today through the manuscript transmission is strongly dependent upon genre. The early Christian works seem to be all preserved: perhaps because they were better curated, perhaps because, in this field, Photius made sure to display his reading of the more important books. This is surely the case for rhetoric, for which Photius clearly made an effort to read the ten classic orators of critical reception (who, for reason of their canonicity, are all more or less transmitted now) – though he did also have access to Dionysius of Aegae and to speeches by the Emperor Hadrian, now no longer extant. History, as always, is a wide field, difficult to canonize. Exactly half the 28 pre-200 histories read by Photius can now still be read; but, surely, this still represents some effort on Photius' part to read the more important works (he has Herodotus, and several works by Josephus Flavius; he does not bother to record his reading of Thucydides and Xenophon, however). In prose fiction, Photius has seven entries, three of which are still extant (Heliodorus, Lucian and Achilles Tatius), four are now merely reported – tantalizingly! – by Photius' *Bibliotheca* (Iamblichus, Lucius of Patrae, Antonius Diogenes and – I would count him here – Conon). Further, it seems that in some areas Byzantine scholars decided to make do with their own epitomes – and this must be the reason why we no longer have any of the grammatical works still read directly by Photius. The statistical value of this dataset is limited but it seems clear that Photius could have had the possibility, at least, of reading considerably more pre-200 authors than we now possess; but not *that* many more. A ratio of 1:2 or 1:3 is suggested, by these data, as a lower bound, which may indeed not be too far off the mark. Since about 200 pre-200 authors are still transmitted, we find that there were more than 500 pre-200 authors, but probably well fewer than 1,000, circulating in the ninth century.

I now add another relationship. If we compare the attrition in circulating authors between (1) Hellenistic-to-Imperial, or the pre-Imperial era to the second century CE and (2) ancient-to-Byzantine, or the second century CE era to the ninth century CE,[44] it is clear that the (2) ancient-to-Byzantine rate of attrition must have been quite a lot higher than the (1) Hellenistic-to-Imperial rate. This is for many reasons of general cultural history, which I will return to discuss in the following chapter, but it should be obvious that the ancient-to-Byzantine transition involved several transformations in the medium of writing, political catastrophes and a major cultural upheaval, none of which is at all comparable to the Hellenistic-to-Imperial transition, and that – quite simply – the final four centuries of the first millennium were not that distant, in time, from the second century CE. As noted in note 44 above, however, the terms in which this problem are set are somewhat to the disadvantage of the ancient-to-Byzantine transition. All we can say, then, is that the fraction surviving from the second to the ninth centuries CE was rather less than that surviving from pre-Imperial times to the second century.

Some kind of constraint, then: but not a very powerful one. So, let us go on to consider more directly the rate of attrition from the pre-Imperial era to the second century CE. I will do this by a closer look at two limiting cases.

The best starting point is classical tragedians. We have already looked at this group on pages 203–4 above, considering the process of admission into the canon. Our conclusion there was that canonization happened in the classical era itself, made by the audience's reception, and that this was reflected in the absolute domination of performances in the Great Dionysia by a few leading authors.[45] One consequence of this is that the

---

[44] In this comparison, note that I compare slightly different transitions. In the Hellenistic-to-Imperial transition, I compare the totality of works in circulation at some point during the last four centuries before 1 CE to those in circulation in the second century CE. In the ancient-to-Byzantine transition, I compare the totality of works in circulation in the second century CE *itself* to those in circulation in the ninth century. This means that the gap between the two transitions is less significant than it would otherwise have to be, since a good number of Hellenistic authors would have been lost through the Hellenistic era itself.

[45] From here on I will refer to these as "Dionysia". The discussion here relies on the evidence we have and so we must extrapolate from the main festivals; the assumption is that the main authors of the main events would dominate, early on, in rural performances as well. Thus, it is hoped that we have not lost a major group of authors who performed *only* rurally. Conversely, it is sometimes impossible to prove that a particular classical playwright performed in the Dionysia (though, in fact, only a handful of the tragedians mentioned by Snell appear not to: so, for instance, Dionysius of Syracuse). At any rate, with or without this qualification, this exercise is helpful as a study of the

group of authors who performed at the Dionysia was limited. The well-attested activity of the Dionysia lasted almost exactly a century and two-thirds (from about 490 to 320), during which time the theoretical maximum number of playwrights was slightly fewer than 500, or slightly fewer than 1,500 tragedies.[46] The actual number of tragedians participating in the Dionysia would have had to be substantially smaller. We can note the following.

- There are 85 *known* tragedians who were likely to perform in the Dionysia in the years 490 to 320.[47] Sixty of these are attested through the literary tradition, 25 are known only epigraphically.[48] Thirty-three authors are attested with fragments.[49]
- Of the 29 tragedians whose victories in the Dionysia are epigraphically recorded, one or two at most are not known via the literary sources.[50] It is safe to conclude that no more than a handful of victories were won by authors outside the 60 known via the literary tradition.
- The literary tradition recounts the fuller details of several competitions, always because one or more of the three tragedians participated in them. If we remove the three tragedians themselves, we have left 14

---

upper bound of attestation. Surely the participants of the Great Dionysia are among the best attested of all ancient authors!

[46] During several years there was no festival: so, apparently, 479, 478 and 404 (Snell, 1971: 4, 11). A certain number of performances included two plays only, but three was clearly the norm; especially from the year 386 onwards, it appears that some performances were revivals of old plays, though, once again, original productions appear to remain the norm.

[47] Of Snell's 95 tragedians of the fifth and fourth centuries I remove Thespis, Plato, Dionysius of Syracuse, Polyidus (wrote dithyrambs only), Diogenes of Sinope, Philiscus, Crates, Python, Heraclides Ponticus and Phanostratus.

[48] Many of the epigraphic-only attested tragedians are known through Lenaea inscriptions, but I will take it as prima facie evidence for a likely performance in the Dionysia as well. This counts only dated tragedians. Snell (1971: 319–25) cites 16 further authors (201 to 216 in the catalogue). A few of these might be fictitious or based on confusions of names in our sources (203, 205, 207, 208, 210, 213) and a couple must be Hellenistic (204, 206). Of the remaining eight, only one is attested epigraphically, three have fragments, and the statistical likelihood is that the bulk are classical. Including these in our totals, in slightly reduced number, we then should count, perhaps, more than 90 attested classical tragedians, of whom about 65 are attested in the literary tradition, about 35 with fragments.

[49] Snell (1971) includes titles in his count of fragments, but I ignore these, looking at cases where the text is actually cited.

[50] The clear case is Menecrates (Snell, 1971: 154), IG II² 2318 l. 118. A certain ]ippus is found as a one-time winner in IG II² 2325 I l. 14 (Snell, 1971: 85). Already Snell suggests this could be the same as the Nothippus of Snell (1971: 144); there is also a Gnesippus in Snell (1971: 144–5), both witnessed via the literary tradition. The base probabilities make such an identification likely.

tragedians mentioned, 11 of whom are also known independently, through other sources in the literary tradition.[51]

- The best evidence are the full didascalia inscriptions, providing the names of all participants in the Dionysia. They are almost entirely lost, and the little we possess from the years 341 and 340 has four authors, of whom one is otherwise unknown.[52]
- I went through the list of attested classical tragedians trying to generate a low estimate of the number of plays they produced. This means that, for an otherwise unknown tragedian, I have assumed one trilogy – three plays – and looked at the evidence for those who are known to have participated more than once case by case, usually assuming only slightly more than the performances attested; and that I pared down substantially some (not all) of the high numbers thrown about by the *Suda*.[53] The total I obtain is 1,080 plays, of which almost exactly 1,000 are by authors known via the literary transmission.[54]

All the evidence coheres around roughly 300 plays written by "dark matter" tragedians, which implies substantially fewer than 100 "dark matter" tragedians. I will assume 75 such tragedians (in a stylized way, for instance 50 of them competing once, 25 competing twice), so that the total number of the classical tragedians who participated in the Dionysia should be around 160, or roughly a third of the theoretical maximum: this is inherently likely.[55]

---

[51] The evidence is in Snell (1971: 43–9). These are (underlining those otherwise unknown): <u>Aristias</u> and <u>Polyphrasmon</u> (lost to Aeschylus), Euphorion (won against Sophocles and Euripides), Philocles (won against Sophocles), Iophon and Ion (lost to Euripides), Xenocles, Acestor, Dorilaus, Morsimus, Melanthius and <u>Nicomachus</u> (won against Euripides) and Theognis (lost together with Euripides and that aforementioned competition). Note that, generally speaking, these authors are mentioned because their victory should surprise the reader ("What – Xenocles beat Euripides? *Xenocles??*"). This list then has a bias towards the obscure.

[52] Known are: Astydamas (won both times), Aphareus and Timocles. Euaretos is otherwise unknown but, remarkably, participated both times (less surprisingly, he lost both times: second place and then third place). This shows that some of the otherwise unknown authors could have participated more than once.

[53] Cleophon, for instance (Snell, 1971: 246–7), has 10 attested titles and was sufficiently well known to have been frequently mentioned by Aristotle; I assign him 15 plays. I reduce Astydamas from the 240 plays assigned to him by the *Suda* to 90 (Astydamas absolutely dominated the Dionysia – as we saw – from 371 to a year later than 340; the same *Suda* entry assigns him 15 victories, which is possible. While in the shadow of the three tragedians, Astydamas was very well known in antiquity and this suggests a large corpus, which we may well set at the level of Euripides.). Throughout, I seek numbers that are low, but not unreasonably so.

[54] This does not include the undated tragedians (see n.48 above). These might add about 30 plays by authors known through the literary tradition.

[55] As noted on p.204, n.223, above, this implies a single debutant, on average, for every competition: reasonable, given a sociological setting that favors the established leaders of the profession. This was

Many of the literary testimonies are contemporary or near-contemporary. In particular, comedy is the genre that makes fun of the tragic, and tragic authors were routinely the butt of jokes in comedy; some of these get quoted by later authors – hence our knowledge of some of the more obscure tragedians. Some testimonies imply merely an acquaintance with the didascalic lists (which surely did survive into Imperial times: in terms of the mere attestation of the name, close to 100 percent of classical tragedians were still known, six or seven centuries after their performances, no matter how obscure). In short, literary testimonies generally do not imply survival of the works into the Imperial era. The case is very different for fragments. These are invariably from the Imperial era or later (many are from Byzantine-era sources such as the scholia, which have been culled, however, from Imperial-era grammarians: I return to discuss the formation of scholia, in general, on page 769 below). Some could be mediated, but in general there is no compelling reason to suppose that a grammarian, or an encyclopedia author of the Imperial era, quoting a tragedy by name and the name of the author, did not have the play available. The number of authors for whom we have fragments – 33 – can therefore be taken nearly as a lower bound for tragedians whose works survived into the Imperial era. The outcome is that *at least* 20 percent of the classical tragedians were in circulation in the Imperial era. This was, of course, a distant time; but right at the core of scholarly collection. This number must be substantially above the average rate of survival for pre-Imperial authors into the Imperial era. (On the other hand, the very centrality of tragedy for scholarship suggests that our lower bound is, perhaps, not far from the actual number: there was a very powerful incentive to quote minor tragedians.)

Tragedy is one limiting case in which the pre-Imperial was very likely to survive into the Imperial era. Let us now consider the opposite limiting case: pure mathematics. As noted on page 468 above, no genre interested the Romans less. Furthermore, even in their heyday, the exact sciences were certainly never copied in great numbers, and so were particularly liable to be lost. We have, however, ten to 12 pre-Imperial authors in the exact sciences extant *now* who therefore, obviously, must have been in

not *Athens' Got Talent*. (Why have that single debutant, on average, at all? Assuming a creative longevity of 20 years for a debutant tragedian, there would be 20 established playwrights available to perform in any given year; even the most skillful would sometimes be plagued by writer's block; surely, some of those 20 moved on to other things. To make sure one had access to enough talent to sustain annual performances, it was crucial to train new talent. This is an example of the general principle of the Athenian democracy, emphasized by Ober, 2008: *human capital, built via participation in public tasks*.)

circulation in the second century CE.[56] Otherwise, our testimonies to pre-Imperial mathematics are almost entirely from late antiquity and beyond, and it is only rarely that we can show that such references imply an unmediated acquaintance with the author's work.[57] We have attested about 20 pre-Imperial mathematical authors later than Eudemus' history (taking "mathematics" in a wide sense), only a handful of whom appear to have been known to late ancient readers in book form.[58] We end up with fewer than 20 mathematical authors for whom the likelihood is that they survived in book form into the Imperial era. A lower boundary, of course. There could have been more who were simply lost between the Imperial era and Pappus' time, and some more who were unlucky enough to escape the attention of the late ancient commentators. But we are looking at a group that was intensely valued by readers from late antiquity onwards, and our survival of late ancient mathematical commentary is significant. There probably were not that many mathematicians known, other than these.

On the other hand, the number of mathematicians in antiquity could not have been very high, either. This is primarily because mathematical activity was so clustered. We have noted this phenomenon, emphasizing

---

[56] These are: Autolycus, Aristarchus, Euclid, Archimedes, Apollonius, Philo, Biton, Theodosius, Hipparchus, perhaps Hypsicles (if indeed he was Hellenistic; see Netz, 2015), perhaps Geminus (if indeed we should see him as an author in the exact sciences; see p. 460, n.278, above). Diocles, now extant only in Arabic, must have been transmitted through the Imperial era.

[57] Posidonius' response to Zenon of Sidon included explicit geometrical proofs and so should count as a work in the exact sciences. Even if our evidence from Proclus is mediated – and it does not appear to be – this work certainly circulated in the Imperial era. Theon of Alexandria knew a work by Zenodorus on isoperimetric figures (*Commentary to Ptolemy's Almagest*, Rome 355–79; Knorr, 1989: III, chap. 10, offers a very complex account of the interrelations between the various treatments of isoperimetric figures now extant in our manuscript tradition, identifying several late ancient reflections of the text by Zenodorus – which makes it more likely, perhaps, that this text was still extant in the Imperial era). On the other hand, Eutocius' knowledge of Archytas' solution to the problem of finding four lines in continuous proportion is explicitly said to depend on the interim authority of the (early) historian Eudemus – as appears to be true of Proclus' knowledge of the early history of mathematics – and, in general, no author preceding Eudemus is cited, by our extant sources, in a way that suggests familiarity with the author's original work (to sum up with Zhmud, 2002: 276: "Practically every mathematician that is known to us from the time of Thales to the second third of the fourth century does appear in Eudemus' fragments"). The absence of any mathematical fragment by Eudoxus or Theaetetus is especially glaring: the late antique mathematical authors (in the case of the first) and the commentators on Plato (in the case of the second) would surely have leapt at the opportunity of quoting such works, if available even in mediated form (it may be, however, that Eudoxus was simply unlucky in that Eutocius did not understand his source for him; see Netz, 2003. But, even then, I envision a mediated fragment, misunderstood precisely because it was taken out of context!).

[58] I count in this group: Aristotherus, Aristyllus, Charmandrus, Conon, Ctesibius, Demetrius of Alexandria, Dionysodrus, Dositheus, Eratosthenes, Hippias (author of *Quadratrix*), Hipponicus, Nicomedes, Nicoteles, Perseus, Pheidias, Thersydaeus, Timocharis, Zeuxippus. Underlined are the eight whose fragments imply, at varying degrees of probability, some survival of the work itself.

the two main mathematical half-century clusters: that of Archytas, and that of Archimedes. These two half-centuries take up, in sheer chronological terms, more than a quarter of the period in which pre-Imperial mathematics was produced. They must have represented, therefore, a much higher concentration of mathematical activity (the first century, in particular, as noted could have been nearly barren of mathematics). Let us assume, modestly, that each of the mathematical clusters represented about a quarter of all pre-Imperial mathematical authors, the two taken together representing a half. Now, the second cluster, that of Archimedes, is well attested, and, thanks to the habit of written introductions, we have a glimpse of its sociology. We definitely see a buzzing network of mathematicians in written communication, but it is also evident that they rely on such written communication across cities (more than on communication within the city), and, famously, Archimedes implies a rather small group of active mathematicians (I have discussed this in detail in Netz, 2002a). This is simply inconsistent with a group of contemporary mathematical authors much larger than about several dozen, or, let's say, about 100 authors, as the absolute maximum for the entire half-century: and so, inconsistent with more than 400 pre-Imperial mathematical authors. If indeed 20 or so of these survived into the Imperial era, this provides a rate of survival of 5 percent. I am not convinced myself that the number of mathematicians could have been much higher, and, if anything, it is likelier that 20 is too low an estimate for the number of mathematicians surviving into the Imperial era in book form. Five percent, as a rate of survival, is therefore likelier to be an undercount than an overcount.

This begins to be useful. If indeed mathematical authors survived into the Imperial era at a rate of about 5 percent or even higher, while tragedians survived at a rate probably not much higher than 20 percent, the conclusion is that the likeliest range for the overall survival of all pre-Imperial authors into the second century CE was about 10 to 20 percent – which seems reasonable enough on the face of it (the half-life of an author, under this calculation, is between one and two centuries).

We have now assembled six pieces of the puzzle.

> The evidence from the extant manuscripts and Photius strongly suggests that about 500 to 1,000 pre-200 authors circulated in the ninth century (but perhaps closer to 500 than to 1,000).
> The evidence from Plutarch and Athenaeus suggests, with some confidence, that something on the order of 2,000 to 4,000 pre-Imperial authors circulated in the second century CE.

As a matter of logic, the total number of authors circulating in the second century CE would be composed of these 2,000 to 4,000 authors, as well as (a good fraction of) the authors active in the Imperial era itself.

On general historical grounds, it must be the case that between one-half and two-thirds of all pre-200 authors were pre-Imperial.

Also on general historical grounds, the rate of attrition from the pre-Imperial era to the second century CE must have been considerably less than the rate of attrition from the second century to the ninth century.

Finally, the evidence from the tragedians, as well as from the mathematicians, suggests that the rate of survival from the pre-Imperial era to the second century CE could have been in about the range of 10 to 20 percent.

We now have enough pieces to complete the puzzle; nothing is as yet certain, however, because the pieces are all so elastic. Almost any reasonable number of the set of all authors before 200 CE can be made to fit within the parameters above. Some such numbers demand more violence to the parameters, however (they demand, that is, that we consistently adopt values near the tails of the distribution of probabilities), while others are closer to central values. It is possible in principle to address such problems with statistical tools, looking for a regression that optimizes the different parameters. This would merely beg the question, however: which parameters matter more, which elasticity is the likeliest? Instead, I shall now offer a central value reconstruction, and discuss the difficulties that would ensue from its alternatives.

Let us start from the Athenaeus/Plutarch result, which I take to imply that, most likely, there were about 3,000 pre-Imperial authors circulating in the second century CE. Together with our observations concerning the overall rate of attrition from pre-Imperial times to the second century, this suggests that there were about 20,000 pre-Imperial authors; this would also imply somewhat more than 10,000 Imperial authors, most of whom (but not all) would be in circulation in the second century itself, so that, together with the 3,000 pre-Imperial authors, there were a little more than 10,000 authors in circulation in the second century, of whom about 5 percent were still in circulation at the time of Photius (a rate of attrition considerably worse than the 15 percent rate from the pre-Imperial era to the second century CE). This central scenario ends up with a total of over 30,000 pre-200 authors.

How would a lower combination look? We can get down to a total of 15,000, by having fewer than 10,000 pre-Imperial authors, perhaps about 2,000 authors known to Athenaeus, for a total of roughly 6,000 authors circulating in the second century CE, about a tenth of whom were known to Photius. Note here that the rate of survival from the Hellenistic to the

Imperial era is surprisingly high, that it does not drop by all that much into the ninth century and that the number of authors known to Athenaeus becomes very low indeed.

A larger combination might look as follows. For us to have 60,000 authors, we will need about 35,000 pre-Imperial authors, of whom perhaps 4,000 were known to Athenaeus; together with perhaps 15,000 Imperial-era authors still extant by Athenaeus' time, we have about 20,000 authors circulating in the second century CE, about 3 percent of whom were still known to Photius. Now, the rate of survival from the Hellenistic to the Imperial era is very low, while the number of authors known to Athenaeus is made to be very high.

Finally, could we get to about 100,000 authors? This would demand about 60,000 pre-Imperial authors, of whom no fewer than 5,000 ought to have circulated in Athenaeus' time; and so, more than 25,000 authors in total circulating in his time, of whom only a small fraction survived in circulation into the Middle Ages. This is already a very unlikely reconstruction, implying a very steep rate of attrition from the pre-Imperial era to the Imperial era, and assuming an incredibly high number of authors still circulating in Athenaeus' time.

One conclusion of the preceding section was that the number of authors in effective circulation at the peak was on the order of 10,000. We have now done a little better, bringing in various considerations of relative distributions of the total set of authors: and we can say that the central value for the number of pre-200 authors was perhaps about 30,000, though it could (somewhat less easily) be half or twice that – but hardly less than half or more than twice. We have also already noted the possibility of better precision, made possible by the consideration of specific genres, whereby the detail of the evidence can hint at likely numbers – as we did, just now, for classical tragedy, and for pre-Imperial mathematics. In what follows, I will try to extend this discussion to cover the entire range of ancient genres, trying to come up with a fuller demographic model of authorship before 200 CE.

## 5.3　Third Route: From the Genres

Our ability, such as it is, to reconstruct the number of (classical Athenian Dionysia-performing) tragedians results from the specific institutional setting. The rules constrained the number of participants and stipulated documentation. In general, however, ancient genres did not rely on institutions; but philosophy, with its Athenian schools, is something of an exception. To a certain extent, what we do in this section, then, is construct a demographic model for poetry – based on a series of deductions starting from tragedy (as well as comedy); and construct a demographic model for prose – based (much more weakly) on a series of deductions starting from philosophy. More generally, our method is simple: when estimating the numbers of authors in a particular field, we look first for the number of attested authors, and then try to project the current rate of attestation.

We will consider the genres one by one. The main poetic genres are tragedy, comedy and the "rest", which is best treated separately for archaic and for later verse. The main prose genres were philosophy, history, grammar, speech and "science"; the last is best treated separately as medicine, mathematics and diverse technical manuals. We need also to take account of the separate genre, particular to the Imperial era, of prose fiction.

Even before we set about the individual estimates we may form some sense of the relative frequencies. As usual, it is helpful to take a comparison. I bring in two sets of numbers. First, I return to the set of authors mentioned by *both* Athenaeus (this time selecting those authors cited *more than once*) and Plutarch's *Moralia*. This is a good enough approximation of the set of fairly significant authors known to the second century CE. I compare this set against Diogenes Laertius' list (discussed on page 128 above) of homonymous authors – which is the best approximation we have for a *random* set of ancient authors. Above, I have used it to point out how often a Greek author would have been characterized by his genre. Now we consider the genres themselves.

| | Athenaeus + Plutarch | Diogenes Laertius' homonyms |
|---|---|---|
| Poetry | 74 (37%) | 25 (16%) |
| Tragedy | 15 (7%) | 3 (2%) |
| Comedy | 17 (8%) | 6 (4%) |
| Archaic poetry | 21 (10%) | 0 (0%) |
| Later verse | 21 (10%) | 16 (10%) |
| Prose | 125 (63%) | 126 (84%) |
| Philosophy | 58 (29%) | 31 (20%) |
| History | 39 (19%) | 32 (21%) |
| Grammar | 7 (3%) | 11 (7%) |
| Rhetoric | 10 (5%) | 30 (20%) |
| Medicine | 7 (3%) | 13 (8%) |
| Mathematics | 3 (1%) | 5 (3%) |
| Various technical | 0 (0%) | 4 (3%) |
| Prose fiction | 1 (0%) | 0 (0%) |

Both sets have their biases. The intersection of Plutarch and Athenaeus clearly has more philosophers (which, after all, was one of Plutarch's key identities). That of Diogenes' homonyms is not entirely random, either, and should be suspected for collecting more of the better-known authors (while Demetrius of Magnesia – Diogenes' main source – could have tried to be near-exhaustive, he would still have relied on sources that themselves were affected by cultural bias). And yet: we may compare the percentages in the two lists, and work with the following assumption. Both lists display a certain set of biases towards the more culturally visible. The Athenaeus/ Plutarch set does this more, the Diogenes set does this less. Therefore, we can assume that the real fraction of a given genre was likely "even further than Diogenes". If the Diogenes fraction is higher than the Athenaeus/ Plutarch one, it is likely that the real fraction was even higher; if the Diogenes fraction is lower than the Athenaeus/Plutarch one, it is likely that the real fraction was even lower. Applying this logic, we find as follows, all as rough, first indications.

(1) Poetry as a whole has about 15 percent in the Diogenes list, nearly 40 percent in the intersection of Athenaeus and Plutarch. We know enough of the cultural context to assume there indeed ought to have been a significant cultural bias favoring the mention of poetic authors, and so, had the Diogenes list been truly random, it probably would have had even fewer than 15 percent poets.

(2) About 20 percent of the authors in the Diogenes list belong to various technical fields (medicine, grammar, mathematics and various technical works), but fewer than 10 percent of the authors mentioned by both Athenaeus and Plutarch. We know enough of the cultural context to assume there ought to have been a significant cultural bias limiting the mention of technical authors (relative to other fields), and so, had the Diogenes list been truly random, it probably would have had even more than 20 percent technical authors.

All of this, of course, is a mere set of suggestions, based on very small sample. I put this, then, as no more than a potential reference point – and move on to discuss the evidence for the genres, directly.

### *5.3.1 Poetry*

**Tragedy**

We have extrapolated, based on the 85 relevant authors in Snell (1971), 160 poets who might have participated in the Dionysia. Even for the classical era, this is but a subset of the total number of tragedians who might have participated in other festivals only (for Dionysius of Syracuse, for instance, we have a literary report of participation in the Lenaea, not the Dionysia)[59] or even, in a few cases, been already purely "literary" tragedians (if indeed any early cynic wrote tragedies – see page 383, note 98, above – surely these were not produced?). Even so, there is no doubt that most tragedians aimed to participate at the Dionysia, and it is perhaps prudent not to assume many more than about 200 tragedians in the classical era. As this era comes to a close, drama becomes a wide Mediterranean phenomenon. Without its institutional anchor in Athens, we lose our ability to make firm counts. It is clear, however, that the writing of new tragedy (unlike that of comedy) becomes much less common already in the third century. Thirty-five authors are reported by Snell for the third century (beginning with Phanostratus: Snell, 1971: 263, catalogue nos. 94–128). This is probably an overcount of the actual set of attested authors, however. Snell (1971: 281, 284) plausibly suggests identifying away five of these (catalogue nos. 107 = 102, 109 = 98, 110 = 105, 111 = 122, 124 = 68 – so, perhaps classical?). Catalogue no. 126 is from an inscription and amounts to a single doubtful kappa. Several of the mentions, while fuller, are still tenuous: an inscription, or a single epigram, may or may not imply that a particular person was honored as the author of tragedy (so: catalogue nos. 95, 113 to 115, 117, 120 and 121). Of the 12 noted so far, perhaps no more than three or four should count as tragedians of the third century. Of the remaining, nine are those mentioned (one or two, perhaps, through scribal confusion) in the various lists of the "Pleiad" (catalogue nos. 98 to 106). Sositheus and Alexander of Aetolia have fragments; Lycophron, incredibly, is extant. They were called "Pleiad" for a reason. It was a remarkable feat: even though they were away from Athens, they still managed to attain some stature, as *dramatists*, in their own lifetime.[60] But it is clear that, in general, one could no longer count on tragedy to gain fame. The Pleiad were active early in the third century, in an Alexandrian court that trafficked in the symbols of literary glory past. At the same time, we find a handful of Athenian holdouts: Phanostratus (catalogue no. 94), Astydamas III (catalogue no. 96), perhaps also Moschion (an Athenian, and a significant presence, known through many fragments: likely, the Athenian star who outshone the Pleiad itself). There are only a handful of pieces of evidence

---

[59] Diodorus Siculus 15.74.1.

[60] For the overall context of Hellenistic tragedy, see Sens (2010). His overall approach is to take Lycophron's *Alexandra* as, possibly, revealing of the style of Alexandrian tragedy as a whole: if so, it ought to have been a highly literate affair, and, so, unsurprisingly rare.

for any tragic authorship even later than that. Demetrius of Tarsus, and Bion following him, wrote satyr plays in a new style (these are catalogue nos. 206, 204: Snell, 1971: 319–20; undated by Snell, these are almost certainly Hellenistic); but, otherwise, no one ought to be brought back from the list of undated tragic authors, and, going further into the second century BCE and beyond, as noted on pages 494–6 above, the numbers steadily diminish together with the genre – as a creative endeavor – as a whole.

There is no doubt that the distance of time accounts for the loss of so much early third-century tragedy outside Athens. A single fragment from Tebtunis (P.Tebt. 695) provides us with three names that are otherwise entirely unknown: Amymon of Sicyon, Democrates of Sicyon and Moschus of Lampsacus (catalogue nos. 123 to 125). The number of plays of the first are lost, but 20 and 30 are ascribed in the fragment to Democrates and Moschus, respectively: this is a list of significant authors (for this reason, it is almost certain they are *not* classical, for, otherwise, we would have heard much more about them). But the passage of time cannot account, to quite the same extent, for the loss of tragedy from the first century BCE (this comes very close to the ever-citing Imperial era), and this absence must rather be assigned, instead – as noted above – to a cultural transition away from the writing of long verse form as a central cultural medium. The broad implication of the evidence is that, at least for tragedy, this transition is already beginning within the third century itself.

Taking this into consideration, we may suggest as follows. As tragedy lost its anchoring in Athens, it likely expanded in respect of the number of authors, even though much fewer were preserved. If, in the fifth and fourth centuries, about 90 attested authors stand for about for 200 active authors, then the 15 to 20 authors genuinely attested for the early part of the third century probably could stand for a great many dozens of authors. For the remainder of antiquity the evidence is extremely thin: an ambiguous inscription there, the odd report of a playful Roman composition of drama. Most of those attestations could be spurious. The reality was that, in a dramatic practice dominated by revivals of the classics,[61] here and there an author (an actor, perhaps?) was commissioned to produce a new work. Most important: the field remained as visible as any: a public practice, taking place in a public theater (hence the survival of

---

[61] See Nervegna (2007) for recent discussion. (The total domination of later theater by revivals is not in doubt, and the question debated by scholarship is how far such revivals kept to original scores, instead of producing various condensations; ultimately, of course, mime, an essentially compressed form, would nearly replace tragedy; see pp. 498–9 above.)

inscriptions), with an attentive audience: it should be an attested phenomenon. The 70 or so post-classical authors of Snell (1971) therefore cannot
stand for more than a few hundred genuine authors of tragedy (= individuals whose main identity was that of a tragic author). In sum, the number
of Greek tragedians in antiquity as a whole was probably not significantly
above 500, and the 200-odd names in Snell (1971) represent a ratio of
attestation of 1:2.5 to 1:3.

Tragedy, as noted, was surely among the best-attested genres of all. This
ratio – say, 1:2.5 – can therefore be taken as a strong upper bound for the
aggregate ratio of attestation for authors as a whole. That is, it is really as
certain as can be that the aggregate ratio of attestation ought to have been
considerably lower than 1:2.5. If 5,000 authors are attested overall, there
ought to have been considerably more than 12,500 authors in antiquity.
Would 20,000 be enough? 25,000? Perhaps; but 15,000, we can now note,
definitely appears rather low.

## Comedy

Here I merely make a few comments, comparing the evidence with that of
tragedy (we have already made general observations concerning the overall
trajectory of comedy, on pages 330–7 – the efflorescence of Menander's
comedy – and pages 494–5 – comedy's gradual, post-Menander decline).

Comedy is well reported, but in ways distinct from those of tragedy. We
do not rely on institutional cues so much – and indeed the genre, to
a certain limited extent, did escape the constraints of the Athenian institution. Even with the excellent didascalic evidence for tragedy, however –
and with the appetite of late scholars for its quotation – nothing is quite as
attested as comedy. If I count correctly, the *Poetae Comici Graeci* (Kassel
and Austin, 1983–2001) has 266 comic authors. Even though we have
a substantial body of inscriptions, here the great bulk of sources is that of
citations. Comedy was piquant – and valued, in the age of Atticism, as
evidence of Athens' colloquialisms.

The central period of Athenian comedy can be taken to be 450 to 280,
exactly the same length as the central period we surveyed for tragedy. The
150 or so comic authors attested for this period must have been attested at
least as well as their tragedian counterparts: so, these could stand for about
300 originally active.[62] This is reasonable: the number of comic authors at

---

[62] Starting in an early period, there was a long tradition of Doric comedy in the west. Eleven
playwrights are cited; the genre – both comic and exotic – did attract the attention of ancient
scholars, so the numbers could not have been much higher. At any rate, this genre cannot expand
our number of comic authors substantially (for a survey, see Kerkhof, 2001; as Rusten, 2006,

this period must have been greater than that of tragic authors, since the opportunities for comic success were more open-ended, especially towards the end of the period.

About a third of our authors are attested for later dates, now mostly via inscriptions that are either in Athens or that mention an Athenian author. Such later authors had less of a chance to be remembered by posterity, and so the real fraction of post-third-century comic authors was not a third of the ancient total but, rather, higher than that. Still: once again, it is clear enough on broad cultural terms, that original comic authorship declined through the Hellenistic era, especially through the second century. It would be strange if the number of post-classical comic authors greatly exceeded that of the classical authors; and, while the evidence from inscriptions is less complete than that for tragedy, comedy, as a form of theatrical performance, did give rise to much epigraphic activity.

Having 300 authors over 170 years of the classical era implies perhaps three dozen authors active on average per generation. The likely story, on cultural grounds, is for the number to go up until the age of Menander, and then to go down continuously. Certainly, it is hard to imagine more than a couple of dozen authors active simultaneously in what appears to have been the fairly derivative drama of the second century, let alone the first. If so, we may well envision, for the little more than ten generations of pre-Imperial but post-classical comedy, something on the order of 300 post-classical Attic authors; and we should expect a rather lower number of extra-Attic, post-classical authors, to which we need to add the smattering of Imperial, Doric and Latin comic authors. We end up with roughly 750,

emphasizes, whatever comic traditions preceded Athens they certainly seem to go into steep decline as Athens' hegemony is established – a clear case of Athens usurping the position of the stage of Hellas. Doric comedy thus belongs to the constrained field of archaic, mostly unwritten poetry; see more below). Above, I have completely ignored Latin drama, which was also very active for about a century and a half, from the later third century to the early first. (Many surveys: a recent summary in Lowe, 2007: chaps. 4–6). A fragment by Volcacius Sedigitus (Courtney, 1993: 93–4) provides a canon (!) of Roman comedy (apparently, the more significant genre, as would be expected from the overall survival of Menander's comedy as a Mediterranean force), with no fewer than ten figures. These are cited elsewhere, and include the two extant authors, Plautus and Terence. Only a handful are reported from elsewhere (if I understand this correctly, Courtney, 1993, lists eight early authors of early Roman drama – among other forms of poetry – extant now in fragmentary form). It is perhaps telling that the key figure, Plautus, is the subject of a debate concerning the very nature of authorship (the extreme – but by no means maverick – position is that of Marshall, 2006: Plautus as the producer, supplying his actors with outline-plots which they fill up with improvisation!). The figure of the author does not emerge powerfully from the evidence, and it is not clear that many Romans, in the years 250 to 100 BCE, sought to make a name for themselves as the authors of published comedies. It is possible, then, that here we have (just as we have in Athens in the same years) a formidable tradition of performing *technitai*, without a significant authorial trace. No more than a few dozen authors, perhaps?

or perhaps a little more, comic authors: a guess – based on the strong foundations of the comparison to tragedy, as well as on the Imperial era's penchant for quoting an Attic joke.

Guesses. Precise numbers, such as "500 tragedy", "750 comedy", should not mislead. But it is hard to get to substantially different numbers without assuming, essentially, that drama remained, throughout the post-classical era, a thriving field of original writing. This goes against the evidence – as well as against the basic logic of the relationship between the institutional realities of classical Athens, the rise of drama and its later fossilization. It is our understanding of canon – as generated through the first part of this book – that makes the numbers above, ultimately, credible.

**Archaic Poetry**
How many lyric poets were effectively knowable in antiquity? The number of attested authors is, of course, fairly small. The TLG reports some 20 authors in the genre of epic in the eighth to sixth centuries, but all this means is that, of the corpus of epic poems circulating in the Archaic era, the sixth and fifth centuries decided to assign most to "Homer" or to "Hesiod", while the certain number that remained anonymous gave rise, with the fullness of time, to various inventions of authorship (see discussion on pages 97–8 above). Otherwise, the TLG reports 27 poets in these centuries. Terpander is counted as an author, because there are fragments attributed to him. This, once again, is likely fiction (see page 220, note 262, above), while other fictional early poets, such as Arion or, of course, Orpheus, are not counted by the TLG. I count, through West (1999), a total of 36 non-epic poets likely to have been active before the middle of the fifth century who are now attested (this is the rare category in which even the TLG is near-exhaustive).

How does this number compare to the number that would have been effectively knowable throughout antiquity itself? Surely it would have been bigger, but perhaps not by much. I count the following cases in which a single fragment now remains: Apollodorus, Asius, Cydias, Echembrotus, Lasus. I also count four poets who were likely historical figures and who are attested without any fragment: Myrtis, Polymnestus, Sacadas and Xanthus. A full three-quarters of the known early lyric poets, then, are attested with two fragments or more. The tail of this distribution is telling in its short-ness. The point is that, had we had access merely to the top of a much larger set, we would have seen a much larger group of authors who were "just at" the selection threshold and so would be represented by one or zero frag-ments. The dominance of our group by multiply cited authors suggests

Third Route: From the Genres

that our sources cited as many as they could – which, in fact, the evidence clearly supports: from Plato and all the way down, citing lyric poetry was a standard way of displaying one's culture. This genre should be attested well: it was widely quoted by the classical sources – those, indeed, of the extant canon itself. Perhaps not many more than about 50 named archaic lyric poets – but well fewer than 100 – could have been known, then, in classical antiquity itself.

What does this mean? Perhaps that such was the number of archaic lyric poets, committed to writing through the fifth century. With a few rolls on average for each poet (one guesses that many could have been accommodated in a single roll),[63] by the end of the century the Greek world would possess an archive of a little more than 100 rolls of lyric poetry. Epic – with "Homer", "Hesiod", and a handful of smaller collections – had somewhat fewer rolls, though perhaps bigger ones on average. The totality of the heritage of archaic poetry, committed to writing in the classical era, was perhaps between half a million and a million words.

What is the "half-life" of an oral text? What is the limit of the potential size of the oral archive? Our initial assumption might be that such numbers are low: the audience would forget particular poems, and not many could be known simultaneously. If so, it could be, at the extreme, that the Greeks had an entirely different poetic corpus in each generation, only a handful of poets transmitted. The classical library of early poetry would represent, then, no more than the final snapshot of a rotating literature. But it is clear from the evidence of Sanskrit literature[64] that Greek archaic poetry operated well below the sheer cognitive limits of oral transmission. There is no significant recency bias in the transmitted corpus (Pindar is very significant, and Bacchylides could well have been less famous had he been less recent; but Archilochus and Sappho, not to mention "Homer" and "Hesiod", were truly archaic. In general, for the chronological distribution, see again page 221, of course a very speculative exercise; it does show a modest – but no more than modest – bunching from the middle of the sixth century to the middle of the fifth.). The basic logic of oral transmission is traditionality, and it would be truly astonishing had there been

[63] I have calculated a little more than 5,000 words on average per poetic roll on p. 22, n.34, above; but the average would have to be lower for the truly minor poets, who could indeed be remembered for no more than a handful of poems, even back then.

[64] The *Mahabharata* alone – the largest of them all, but merely one of many Sanskrit oral compositions (Brockington, 1998: 2–4) – has about 150,000 lines, which are much longer than those of Greek verse, however: in English translation, these end up as well over 2 million words.

many fads – poets whom "everyone knew" at the year 550 BCE, forgotten by the year 500 BCE.

The flip side of this positive result concerning survival is a negative result concerning ancient incidence. The number of poets obtaining widespread fame was small. In the table on page 221 above, to which I have just referred, I could easily fit up to three or four poets even in the more intensive later decades. If, indeed, we know about a half of all the poets who did gain widespread fame, we find that, through the first 100 years of the rise of the named author, there was a new brand author name made every two, three, perhaps even more years: a rare event. This may perhaps be correlated with the absence of any marked spatial hierarchies in archaic culture, as discussed on page 246 above. Because the numbers involved were so small, it was hard for any local traditions to form. Once numbers got somewhat higher, a certain local tradition did gain in meaning: a peculiar variety of choral poetry, in Athens at the turn of the sixth century – which ultimately became "tragedy". Poetry got larger, and so, for the first time, it had a *center* – soon to upend its system as a whole. I shall return to discuss the consequence of scale, in the following chapter, section 6.1.1. For the time being we simply note that, compared to Attic drama, the number of archaic poets making their name known was vanishingly small.

### Other verse

This category may appear like a disordered "none of the above", but we can quickly cut to the counting. A central vehicle of poetry in the Hellenistic and Roman eras was epigram, to which many poets (who may have formed their identity mainly through other forms) made contributions.[65] "Author of epigrams", then, is as good a proxy as we may get for "post-classical poet". Now, as noted on pages 490–1 above, from about 100 BCE on there was a continuous tradition of anthologizing epigrams.[66] Here, then, we

---

[65] I did not try to study this systematically, but I looked at a "random" list of ten third-century poets – of whom five are known to have written epigrams (known: Rhianus, Simias, Theocritus, Theodoridas, Tymnes; not known: Phoenix, Rhinthon, Sopater, Sotades, Timon). It is striking that, in this list, most authors known to have written epigrams did not have their main authorial identity as that of an "epigrammatist" (marginal in the corpus of Rhianus and Theocritus; Simias was primarily a scholar) and that we know about epigrams mostly for the better-known poets; also, we notice that, in this early era, dramatic poetry is still something of a presence. The likelihood is that (1) had we known their full corpora, we would find that, even in the third century, most poets also wrote epigrams; and (2) the likelihood that a poet wrote epigrams went up through the centuries. We end up with the conclusion that, likely, the bulk of Hellenistic and Imperial poets wrote epigrams, at least as a side pursuit. Hence the usefulness as proxy.

[66] The basic historical parameters for the various layers of anthologies are thoroughly discussed in Alan Cameron (1993), which I follow for the dates and the composition of the corpus (this basic outline –

have something of a probe for the measurement of poetic production. Meleager's prooemium mentions 47 names of authors woven into his garland, of whom 42 appear to be post-archaic; remove Plato, and the remaining 41 are likely all Hellenistic. Meleager is explicit in that he has included poems by more authors than those mentioned by name in the prooemium, and I count 20 more such authors in Gow and Page's index (1965: 718–19). We thus have a total of 61 likely Hellenistic epigrammatists known from Meleager alone. Often all we have is a handful of epigrams on a generic subject: these authors should have been quite anonymous. So, for instance, we have two epigrams by Artemon: in one he falls in love, in the other he praises the beauty of a certain boy. There are also several Hellenistic literary figures called "Artemon": the epigrammatist may or may not be the same as any of them, or of any other. It should be seen as surprising, then, that so many of the 61 Meleagrian epigrammatists are likely identifiable as otherwise known poets. There are only seven ambiguous cases – including, indeed, Artemon's – as well as 13 cases for which we cannot even find a likely namesake (a certain Carphyllides, for instance, is known only as an epigrammatist conserved by Meleager). But 41 of the 61 Meleagrian authors would have been known even without the tradition of the anthology. Since at least some of the seven ambiguous cases should in fact be identified with known authors, we may say that three-quarters of the poets used by Meleager would have been attested even without him. This would suggest a fantastically high rate of attestation for Hellenistic poetry.

This needs to be qualified, in two ways. First, later authors, to some extent, cite anthologized poets precisely *because* they were chosen by Meleager. Three-quarters is therefore a high upper bound on the fraction of Meleagrian poets who would have been attested *had there been no Meleager*. Second, Meleager's choice was not random: he chose the poets he liked, presumably the better and better-known poets. So three-quarters is an *upper bound twice over*. But, then again, neither was Meleager's choice completely constrained by past judgements. The sheer size of his anthology becomes significant: at over 60 poets, at least, this was hardly a choice of the obvious, established poets, and in fact his interest was clearly in variety, in and of itself, while his choice of poems was dictated, likely enough, by considerations of overall *thematic* structure (whatever his *anthologia* was, it was not "The Oxford Anthology of Hellenistic Verse": it did not seek

unlike many individual claims made by Cameron – does not, in fact, diverge from previously established opinion).

representation as such).[67] Some element of randomness must be assumed, then, after all. Three-quarters means *something* – though it is hard for us to say quite what.

Hard to quantify, on this basis. What the fraction of attestation for Meleager's poets does underline, however, is that Hellenistic poets were not neglected by later reception – which is indeed obvious to begin with. They would have to be less well attested than classical tragedians, but, clearly, they were better attested than prose authors: the poetic forms favored by Alexandrian poets were, after all, eminently citable, often striving at verbal precision and a certain wit. Surely fewer than 40 percent – fewer than the tragedians – should be attested. But how many fewer than that?

The *Supplementum Hellenisticum* counts 152 authors of poetry in the Hellenistic era. The dramatic ratio of attestation, of perhaps 1:2.5, would imply 400 poets, which may be seen as a very distant lower bound. On the other hand, we may consider the implications of higher numbers, for what must have been the most significant concentration of poetic work through the era. While the evidence is not quantitative in nature, the overall impression of the trajectory of Hellenistic culture is real enough (and the facts of the erosion of drama are clear enough): that it remains likely there was more poetic activity in the third century than in the second, likely most of it in the generation of Callimachus. Of the roughly ten Hellenistic, pre-Meleagric generations, that of Callimachus could well have been responsible for a third of all poetic production, which was also very clearly concentrated in Alexandria. It is a very modest assumption, then, that about a tenth of all Hellenistic poets were Callimachus' contemporaries, residing in the same city. If so, there certainly had to be well above 40 – providing already a glimpse of Callimachus' audience. By this crude calculation, 1,000 Hellenistic poets translates into 100 contemporary poets in Callimachus' Alexandria, a genuine birdcage of the muses. This is possible but, to my mind, already suggestive of something of an upper limit. If indeed we cap the number of Hellenistic poets at 1,000, we end up with a ratio of attestation of about 1:6, significantly lower than that of the dramatists (perhaps too different from that of the dramatists?). All in all, then, I will put down the range of 750 to 1,000 poets. This range implies that, had Meleager's choice been truly random, we would have expected to

---

[67] This is the theme of Gutzwiller (1997), who finds, for instance, ring structures in the topics with which epigrams engage. The point is that such thematic structures would suggest a choice based not on authors but on themes, which would necessarily expand one's choice of poets beyond the most established.

know, independently, of about ten to 12 of his poets; with a much larger number of Hellenistic poets than 1,000, we would have expected to know, independently, of only a handful, which is already in some tension with our ability to identify so many of Meleager's poets. For the moment, I move on, and note that this (like the guesses above, for the tragedians and the comedians) has more elasticity upwards: it is hard to envision a much better rate of attestation for Hellenistic poets, and so anything approaching a few hundred Hellenistic poets is truly surprising. But our arguments that such poets should be capped at about 1,000 are much weaker.

Next, we may note that the *Garland* of Philip, representing the production of epigrams in roughly the century and a half following Meleager, has 51 poets. Almost none are independently attested, and it is perhaps not a coincidence that the one relatively secure identification, of Argentarius, is with an author who is otherwise known only for his prose (a rhetorician). The gaze of posterity was lifted away from this group, which means that the rate of attestation ought, indeed, to have been lower. But it does remain noteworthy that so few names can now be associated with the Greek poetry of the era. Among epic authors, for instance, the TLG can now identify, in the three centuries from 100 BCE to 200 CE, exactly three authors, straddling three consecutive letters: Naumachius, Oppian and Pancrates. Poetry remains attested from the inscriptional evidence (for which see Merkelbach and Stauber, 1998–2004), but this is the occasional, non-authorial use of poetry, and the overall sense is that Greek poetry, as such, lost much of its cultural currency as the maker of authorship. We have noted a "blip" in the first century BCE (pages 494–5 above), and, under the high Empire, not much changed (poetry would make a qualified comeback only later on, in late antiquity). In other words, we now begin to employ, for poetry as such, the kind of argument we used above for tragedy (in the late third century onwards) and for comedy (from the second century onwards). While the rate of attestation must be abysmal, the fact that so few poets are mentioned, and with so little apparent interest, suggests that the activity, as such, must have become less common. It is quite possible that most of the poets selected by Philip were prose authors who made the occasional contribution to poetry in the form of epigram.

In fact, the number of later poets is surprisingly bounded from both ends. On the one hand, the overall impression is that the frequency of poets, in the era of the *Garland* of Philip, was indeed below that of the third and second centuries BCE. Thus, the number could not have been higher than in the hundreds. On the other hand, there is no sense that Philip scraped right at the bottom of the barrel: the epigrams are professional enough, and, if anything, are even more constrained in formal terms.[68] This, once again, suggests that Philip ought to have had a few hundred authors to choose from.

The simplest assumption is that the frequency of post-Meleagric poetry went down, and the prudent assumption is that it did – but not by *all* that much. We had 750 to 1,000 poets for the 200 years of the Meleagric era, and so we can put down 500 poets for the 150 years covered by Philip's anthology. This leaves us with a reasonable rate of attestation – a little above 10 percent – dependent, now, on the sheer accident, really, of the survival of Philip's *Garland*. We may add 500 more to round off the Imperial era (assuming the same rate in the years 50 to 200 CE as in the years 100 BCE to 50 CE: as good a guess as any). The overall conclusion is that there were fewer than 2,000 poets between the years 300 BCE and 200 CE.

What remains unaccounted for is a period and set of genres that are hard to quantify: the poetry of the years 450 to 300 BCE. As noted above, on pages 547–8, it is a period for which the true aficionados of music have an intense interest, the moment when Greek song flourished most. The logic of oral traditionality was cast aside in favor of experiment, allowing a much wider variety of performances and forms.[69] I assume that the repertoire in the year 450 BCE had not many more than 50 poets; a couple of generations later it surely had hundreds. Compared to the archaic era, this was a moment of revolutionary explosion. But it is prudent to assume that, compared to the Hellenistic era, it was not all *that* much more active. LeVen (2014: 22–42, tabs. 1–3) includes a total (by my count) of at most 136 distinct poets of this era of new music (for some of whom we have only an inscribed piece of poetry without the name of the author). This, in fact, is not that different in scale from the *Supplementum Hellenisticum*. Perhaps the best we can do is to assume that Greek poetry in the years 450 to 300 was somewhat more common than in the years 300 to 100. We assumed above slightly fewer than 1,000 Hellenistic poets, through two centuries; the number in the preceding 150 years could not have been very far away from 1,000, once again.

We may put together some round numbers. We guessed 1,000 pre-Hellenistic poets, 1,000 post-Hellenistic poets, not more than 1,000 in

---

[68] Lausberg (1982: 37–44): no more than eight lines!
[69] The field has only recently been recognized for its significance: the major monograph is LeVen (2014).

between. In short – with some error bars – we end up guessing that there were 3,000 "other" poets, perhaps slightly fewer, up to 200 CE. Add in the dramatic poets and you have a little over 4,000, which entails, however, considerable overlap (many authors of tragedy and comedy also contributed to other verse forms).[70] Four thousand, then, for the number of Greek poets prior to late antiquity.

Putting aside the precise numbers, it is useful to consider the overall ranking, from the most numerous to the least, among the categories surveyed here:

Other poetry > comedy > tragedy > archaic

What immediately jumps out is that this ranking is, neatly, the converse of that of canonicity (where archaic poetry ranked above tragedy, tragedy above comedy, all these ranked above all other, later poetry). This is in a sense surprising – would not a culture produce more of that which it more highly valued? – but a moment's reflection shows why this result is to be expected. When we count the number of authors in a given genre, we measure its replicability across time and space: the ability to pick up a given work and do something different-but-like-it. A truly frequent genre throughout antiquity is one that could have been recomposed-with-variations anywhere, at any time. But what the Greeks valued and canonized was precisely the aura of the performative, understood as maximally situated: a work, understood to be joined to a particular imagined performance – indeed, even to a particular author. Following their canonization, Homer, in a sense even Sappho, simply could not be replicated-with-a-difference. The imagined performance became, simply, specific to that powerful sense of a particular work/author. Tragedy was replicable to a large extent – but only within the terms of a particular Athenian ritual; new comedy became pan-Mediterranean but was always perceived as belonging to Athens. The most replicable form, reproducible with one's new twist at any symposium, was also the most trivial: the epigram. This consideration, conversely, makes our numbers the more plausible, certainly for their lower bound. It is hard to see how the combined number of dramatists was much lower than 1,000 plus; and it is hard to see how the number of other poets could not have been substantially more than

---

[70] Nearly all the attested classical lyric poets, for which see LeVen (2014: 44–7), were also active as tragic authors, though this perhaps reflects, to some extent, the conditions of attestation: we hear mostly the gossip of later generations, who would be interested primarily in stories about the tragedians.

that of dramatists. And, thus, it is, overall, hard to see how there could have been much fewer than 4,000 poets in antiquity prior to 200 CE.

The same, finally, is true for poetry, as against prose, as a whole. To write poetry would always be to pick up some choice of genres that carried specific local and temporal meanings. It was always a constrained choice, and, generally speaking, it was prose genres, not poetry, that were the more readily available for replication. An observation, then: there ought to have been rather more prose authors than poets, through antiquity. This is indeed the conclusion drawn already from the adespota papyri, and the trend of papyri from the better attested to the least attested, as noted on page 18 above: it is clear that the great bulk of minor literature, preserved on papyrus, was in prose. Now, based on the comparison of Plutarch and Diogenes' list of homonyms, I suggested, on page 561 above, a more specific number: poets, likely, constituted less than 20 percent of all authors, perhaps substantially less.

I admit once again: the bounds I put on the numbers of poets are fairly weak, especially upwards. While the number of poets in antiquity could not have gone much below 4,000, it could perhaps have been somewhat higher: in truth, we do not have strong arguments against this. But note: even if we assume somewhat fewer than 4,000 poets, a total of all authors of 15,000 (poetry *and* prose) appears too low, as the fraction of poets, then, becomes too high: and this, with a modest assumption concerning the number of poets. Our arguments so far, weak as they are, already suggest a total of rather more than 20,000 authors, perhaps significantly so, before 200 CE.

*5.3.2    Prose*

**Philosophy**

About 30 percent of the authors shared by Plutarch and Athenaeus are philosophers, as are 20 percent of Diogenes' homonyms. But both numbers are "wrong", in different ways. Plutarch, obviously, had a special interest in philosophy, so the 30 percent must be inflated. As for Diogenes, his homonyms were selected relative to philosophical authors (he would provide a biography of Socrates, say, and then add a note on other people called Socrates). In general, we may think of Diogenes as taking a set of homonyms off the shelf (indeed, as noted on page 128 above, scholars assume he largely worked off a previous work by Demetrius of Magnesia), and choosing from them a certain subset: that of authors whose names coincide with Diogenes' philosophers. In counting Diogenes' homonyms, I of course did not count the subjects of the biographies (otherwise, of course, our numbers would be infected by the bias of Diogenes Laertius' selection of philosophers as his subjects). This introduces another subtle bias against philosophy, however: in each list, the number of philosophers I find is one fewer than that of the list available for Diogenes to choose from. A figure of 20 percent in Diogenes, then, is a slight undercount. Not that it matters much in such a small sample, but we end up noting that the "true" number in both lists is somewhere between 20 percent and 30 percent. This is consistent with another fact: that philosophers form about a quarter of all attested authors. Everywhere we look, we find the same level of roughly a quarter. And yet it does remain clear – from Athenaeus and Plutarch, as well as from the very existence of Diogenes Laertius' work – that philosophy was an appropriate field for the display of one's paideia.[71] To some extent, then, philosophers ought to be over-represented in our lists. And so: the true number, *less* than a quarter of the total? Perhaps, all this begins to suggest some constraints.

We may once again use the probe of the top citator of the field. Meleager surveyed Hellenistic epigram; Diogenes Laertius surveyed philosophy (with no more than a handful of exceptions: pre-Imperial, or, more precisely, before Sedley's 2003 "end of history"). I went through the index nominum to Dorandi's edition of Diogenes Laertius, comparing it against the DPA available to me in 2015 – i.e. all the way down to and including the letter "R" (this is already the bulk of the work, however; 41 out of the 49 pages of Dorandi's index). Extrapolating, it seems that Diogenes cited about 500 fully fledged philosophical authors, for about 150 of whom he is the sole witness. As we recall, there are about 1,200 fully fledged philosophers attested before late antiquity. Thus, the comparison to Meleager is more than structural. Meleager's work covered at least about 30 percent of the total number of authors known in his field in his survey; Diogenes' covered about 40 percent. About 75 percent of the authors in Meleager's survey would have been known without him; the same is true for about 70 percent of the authors in Diogenes' survey. The effect that we noted above for Meleager does not repeat for Diogenes, however. Authors included in Meleager's list would thereby gain a greater chance of being cited by later authors other than Meleager himself; Diogenes Laertius did not have the same effect. (Meleager occupied a pivotal role in the cultural

---

[71] This indeed is obvious from our wider understanding of cultural history; see, in particular, the evidence on pp. 64–5 above, concerning portraits, and the presence of philosophers among TLG citations.

memory of epigram, while the much later and very derivative Diogenes Laertius did not have any comparable impact.)[72] Further, Diogenes Laertius had a little of the Athenaeus in him, and certainly was a fan of the trifling anecdote.[73] While the subjects of the biographies were mostly chosen on the basis of perceived importance, the other names mentioned in passing were there simply because they were available for entertaining citation. I count 82 subjects of biography, so a little over 15 percent were chosen based on their importance! Of course, Diogenes was dependent on a tradition that tended to preserve the more important names. The straight calculation based on the pattern of his citation (implying a little over 1,500 ancient philosophers) is, of course, a massive undercount. But this already begins to suggest that the number of ancient philosophers was not that large: had there been many more, would we not expect more surprises among Diogenes' names?

We may say a little more, in this case, thanks to the institutional form that philosophy, occasionally, took. This may provide some plausible upper bounds, considering the concentrations of philosophers in space and time.

While philosophy was always a central cultural practice, it is clear that it was even more central in pre-Imperial times (we shall consider in more detail the relative expansion in other, non-philosophical specialized genres, during the Imperial era, on pages 663–7 below). It is also clear – as abundantly shown in Chapter 3 – that for two centuries – a full third of the *entire* period surveyed here – almost all philosophical activity took place in Athens. Roughly speaking, then, perhaps a half or more of all philosophers before late antiquity, but certainly not much *fewer* than a half, must have been active in the Athenian schools in the years 300 to 100 BC.

Indeed, we have reported some astronomical numbers of students: 2,000 is the number reported for Theophrastus, which must be hyperbolic – and is surely some kind of a limiting figure.[74] At any rate, what we

---

[72] Perhaps no impact at all. He is first cited in the sixth century, albeit rarely, by Byzantine historical encyclopedists (Hesychius, fr. 7; Stephanus, *Ethnica* 4.133.1 [for the term "Druids"]). The significant observation is that late ancient philosophical commentators do not seem to need him for their histories of philosophy. Better sources were still available through late antiquity; by the sixth century – when this begins to change – the survival of philosophy is already set.

[73] The chreia, specifically, is among Diogenes Laertius' key tools: Kindstrand (1986). (It is almost as if the chreia, to Diogenes, is like poetic citation to Athenaeus.)

[74] Diogenes Laertius V.37. Mejer (1998: 21), following Regenbogen 1940, col. 1358 (RE, s.v. Theophrastos), believes the number refers to the students throughout Theophrastus' teaching career, which translates to an incoming class size of about 40, which is in fact perfectly plausible. (Had they had 2,000 students *simultaneously*, surely they would have moved the Lyceum to a bigger location.)

are looking for is not the number of youngsters sitting at Theophrastus' feet but the number of individuals on a par with the minor philosophers mentioned by Diogenes Laertius, the type of person who would be counted as a "philosophical author". We have some indications for this type of group for the case of Chrysippus. A group of individuals closely associated with him is attested both in a list of disciples, preserved in the *Index Stoicorum*, and in the set of the individual addressees of Chrysippus' works, preserved through Diogenes Laertius' catalogue of the works, both fragmentary. The catalogue by Diogenes covers perhaps a half or more of Chrysippus' original works, in which are found 43 named addresses.[75] Chrysippus' works are often addressed more than once to the same individual (unless, that is, we are misled by homonyms: but the duplication is substantial, with 93 works addressed to the 43 individuals; both Metrodorus and Aristocleon have nine works addressed to them. Data from Wietzke, 2014: 145.). The likelihood, then, is that the full catalogue would have enumerated more than 43 addressees, but substantially fewer than twice that: the number cannot be far from 60 to 70.

The *Index Stoicorum* – a fragmentary papyrus – now preserves 19 names for the disciples of Chrysippus. What matters to us is that 11 of these 19 are among the 43 named addressees of Diogenes' catalogue.[76] If 11 out of 19 coincide with a subset numbering 43, the most probable number for the entire set has to be 74, which is in the ballpark of what might have been the entire set of addressees in Chrysippus' entire catalogue. It is in fact likely that the author of the list preserved via the *Index Stoicorum*, or one of his sources, could have relied on the catalogue of books, or some of its versions.[77] The evidence is no more than suggestive, then, but it does conjure up a group of active philosophers, surrounding the master, with many dozens – a hundred, even – through the lifetime of an exceptionally successful philosopher.[78] This certainly strikes one as historically plausible.

The implication is that, through Chrysippus' activity in the Stoa, he had every year, on average, some three to four future philosophical

---

[75] DL VII.189–202. For the discussion of this catalogue and of Chrysippus' addressing practices, see p. 392, n.129, above; the starting point for the analysis is, as always, Wietzke (2014: chap. 2).

[76] P.Herc. 1018, Dorandi (1994: 98, col. 47). Calculation from Wietzke (2014: 157) (with a small correction).

[77] If we number the 11 authors shared by the two lists by the order of appearances of the names in the *Index Stoicorum*, then they appear in the catalogue in the following sequence: 10, 1, 2, 3, 4, 5, 6, 7, 9, 8, 11.

[78] In Theophrastus' will, ten individuals are mentioned as those who should co-own some of his bequeathed school property: something like an inner circle (DL V.53). Theophrastus must have had, through his lifetime, a considerably higher number of disciples.

authors coming to study with him (his intake, so to speak, of grad students).[79] Perhaps several Stoic philosophers, in the generation following Chrysippus, were not among his students; but, if ever a philosopher dominated a school, it was at this moment – and surely most philosophical schools were less active than those of Chrysippus. Surely, then, the number of Chrysippus' students is our best guess of the (upper bound on) the size of a cohort. So: three to four per year? Multiply the number by four (for the four schools), and then by 200 (for the years 300 to 100), and you have an absolute upper bound on the number of authors associated with the Athenian philosophical schools in their heyday. This upper bound is calculated at 2,400 to 3,200, and we are entitled to say that, in all likelihood, there were fewer than 3,000 such authors. Based on the argument above, concerning the fraction of this group among all ancient philosophers, we find that the total number of philosophers in antiquity prior to 200 CE indeed probably did not exceed 6,000.

If we assume fewer philosophers, we end up with an even higher rate of attestation. For instance, if we push the number of philosophers all the way down to 4,000, we end up with a ratio of attestation which almost approaches that for dramatic poets, which is already very unlikely. The plausible range for the number of ancient philosophers, then, is fairly narrow. Fewer than 5,000, and the rate of attestation begins to be uncomfortably large; more than 6,000, and Athenian schools begin to be uncomfortably crowded. In what follows, I will take the number 6,000, with the understanding that it might be generous.

We begin to build a sense of the plausible rates of attestation. The upper bound on the number of philosophers is found completely independently from the dramatists (in the lower bound, I did refer to the number of dramatists). This therefore makes for a useful comparison.

The rate of attestation I found for drama was about 1:2.5; it certainly could not be much better, though perhaps it could be worse (our upper bound on the number of dramatists, as on poets in general, is not so hard and fast). The rate of attestation I now find for philosophers is about 1:4 to 1:5. I repeat: I find *independently* that the rate of attestation for dramatists cannot be *better* than 1:2.5, and that the rate of attestation for philosophers can hardly be much *worse* than 1:5. And this combination is *as it should be*. The rate of attestation for philosophers surely should be, on general

[79] Chrysippus was scholarch for roughly 25 years (Dorandi, 1999a: 38, 40), but surely took on disciples even before that.

historical grounds, somewhat worse than that for dramatists. And so I find that each rate of attestation is in fact constrained in a fairly narrow band, each reinforces the other's likelihood, and the two, combined, can be used as a baseline for the kinds of rates of attestation we should see elsewhere.

The number of philosophers also has wider implications for the total number of authors. I suggested above that the number of philosophers ought to be less than a quarter the number of all authors. "Less than a quarter" – by how much? Even taking the large factor of two, I find that philosophers had to occupy more than 10 percent of ancient authorship – a number which seems, on general historical grounds, like a reasonable *lower* bound. What I find, then, is that the figure for the total number of ancient authors was not likely to exceed 60,000. In short: poetry provides a likely lower bound (more than 20,000); philosophy provides a likely upper bound (fewer than 60,000); and the closeness of the two tends to inspire some confidence in the guesses, as they accumulate.

## The Sciences

This is a composite category: not an ancient genre. As noted above, I have probed EANS to find about 700 authors who were genuine "scientists" (which also means that they were not primarily philosophers or historians). In a more expansive sample, I find there (five-page skips, always counting only authors before late antiquity): 73 medical authors, 48 authors in the exact sciences and 33 authors in various technical fields. Each category requires a brief qualification.

For medical authors, my numbers might be a little short, because I dismiss, for reasons explained above, authors to whom only a single recipe is ascribed: a few of those must have been genuine medical authors, after all.

The exact sciences are taken widely to include not only authors in the diagrams-cum-formulaic language genres of mathematics as such but also authors on machines of any kind (but excluding those who were mostly practising architects, which I count as "Others"), as well as astrologers. (Those "extended" categories of mathematics account for 13 out of my 48.)

Various technical fields: among the authors counted by EANS, these include authors on such topics as stones, fish, animals, gardening, agriculture... These range from quasi-historical compilations of curiosities to genuine technical manuals. EANS ranges far and wide, but not all that far, all that wide. It would include Athenaeus' authors who specialized in catching fish, but not those who specialized in *cooking* them. If I were to include the more mundane manuals omitted by EANS, the category of the technical author would be somewhat expanded.

The sample above suggests about 350 (or a little more) attested medical authors; 200 (or a little fewer) attested mathematical authors; and about 200 (if we extrapolate for the few categories excluded by EANS) in the various special technical fields. Indeed, I have relied in my maps in Chapter 3 above on a named list I have produced of ancient medical authors (almost all prior to 200 CE) which had 275 entries (counting only those who can be dated and located). My named list of mathematical authors from Netz (1997) (now slightly expanded by EANS; this looks at mathematics in a more narrow sense) has 142 entries. We find that the total, then, of 750 attested "scientific" authors seems about right.

Taken together, this amounts to a substantial fraction of attested authors from antiquity: about 15 percent. It is obvious that, as a group, they are under-attested, and so they likely formed, originally, more than 15 percent of total authors (unless, that is, some other category is even less represented: more below). Let us try to refine such numbers.

Mathematicians, I have noted above, on pages 555–8, must have been the least favored by Roman reception. But the argument relies, in fact, on a converse observation: that the mathematicians must have been highly favored by later, late antique and Byzantine transmission (see page 74 above). Both sides of the equation are important: on the one hand, there was no Imperial-era author interested in producing a "Lives of the Mathematicians". On the other hand, what was available at the end of the Imperial era must have been especially well reported. In many of the fields we survey there is one outstanding prosopographic resource, typically from the Imperial era, from which many of the names are compiled. In the case of mathematics we have several, mini-prosopographic, late antique resources: Pappus, Proclus and Eutocius. I shall return to discuss Pappus in more detail on pages 760–5 below, for his construction of an entire community of past mathematicians. This indeed contrasts with Oribasius, another fourth-century author whose compilation – in this case medical – was primarily an epitome of a single author, Galen (pages 765–6 below). In the case of mathematics, more than that of medicine, there seems to have been a late antique interest precisely in preserving the array of available mathematical knowledge. Which indeed is easy to explain in general historical terms: as Neoplatonism came to epitomize pagan thought, knowledge of the mathematical past suddenly came to be on par with knowledge of the philosophical canon itself. The Romans lost a great deal of mathematics; what they did preserve, however, was largely preserved by later generations.

It is possible to apply the same kind of calculation used in section 5.2, pages 547–50, to the overlaps of citations between the three late antique authors Pappus, Proclus and Eutocius. I have pursued this calculation in Netz (1999b: 282–3), suggesting that there were perhaps about 300 mathematical authors knowable in principle to late antiquity (meaning "mathematics" in a stricter sense). This is about double the number still available to us. To recall, I also suggested on pages 555–7 above that there could hardly have been more than 400 pre-Imperial mathematical authors, and Imperial-era contribution could not have been more intensive than that (mathematics, in the Imperial era, begins to gain its later significance, but surely never approaches the flourishing of the Archimedean moment). We reach about 600 mathematical authors prior to 200 CE or slightly fewer than that, about half of whom, once again, were still knowable in principle to late antiquity. The conclusion is that mathematicians in the strict sense could be attested at a rate of about 1:4. This might seem like a surprisingly high rate, which underlines the crucial role that late antiquity plays in such rates of survival. The bare result – of some 600 mathematicians in the strict sense – is not at all surprising: it has philosophers outnumbering mathematicians by an order of magnitude, which is definitely consistent with our general historical understanding. Indeed, it has been suggested above that for much of the period surveyed – from the late second century BCE to the Imperial era – mathematics could more or less cease to exist as an authorial identity. But even in the generations of Archytas and of Archimedes there were many more philosophers than mathematicians (these were also the generations of Plato, and of Chrysippus).

While pure mathematicians are probably very well attested, the same conclusion likely cannot be extended to engineers and astrologers, whose (combined) attested number now is about a third of that of the strict mathematicians: probably, originally, their numbers were rather higher than that, especially in the Imperial era. And so, to conclude, if we say that the number of mathematicians (in the wider sense) prior to late antiquity was about 1,000, perhaps a little more, we are likely not wrong by much.

For medicine, we possess no prosopographic compendium. The issue, in fact, runs deeper, and merits a brief general comment.

In general, we have a very large group of individuals attested from antiquity, and, ultimately, this goes to an ancient habit: *mention people's names*. This, indeed, is related to the centrality of the author as a literary vehicle, discussed in Chapter 2. Now, I have made a stab at studying this habit of mentioning names, as follows. I went into my departmental library, took off the shelves all the Greek Loebs and read a single core sample: pages 80, 82, and 84 (in the case of multi-volume authors, I read volume II; in the event of there being several authors in a volume, if an author began on page X I read pages X + 20, X + 22 and X + 24). I then counted and classified all the proper nouns, to a total of 73 authors and 915 proper nouns (or about 12 per author). The results were modest and largely predictable: there were many mythical names in poetry, many place names in historical prose, many individual names in works of a "scholarly" character. Here, however, is the somewhat surprising set of authors whose core sample yielded no more than three proper nouns (which means that, in the experience of reading, one hardly comes across any names).

> Scientific: Hippocrates, Aeneas Tacticus, Asclepiodotus, Onasander, Oppian, Galen, Ptolemy.
> Philosophical: Plato, Aristotle, Theophrastus, Philo, Epictetus, Marcus Aurelius, Plotinus.
> Rhetorical: Antiphon, Lysias, Dionysius of Halicarnassus, Libanius.

No field is as characterized by the absence of the proper noun as science. Instead, this is typically engaged with its proprietary object language – triangles, diseases, fish – so as to avoid humans altogether. The same is sometimes true of philosophy as well, which sometimes (not always) has the same concentration with its object language. Finally, rhetors may occasionally indulge in pure purple prose, in which people are neatly forgotten. And yet: the strict avoidance of proper names is proper to science.

The point is that this is true even for *Galen*. His texts have been recently mined for their vivid impression of a Roman embodied encounter, in studies such as von Staden (1997), Barton (2002), Gleason (2009) and Mattern (2008; 2013). This is made possible not exactly because Galen engages in extensive name-dropping but because his corpus is so huge that even the very infrequent mentions of specific individuals add up to a useful picture. The recent historians mentioned above do have to resort, after all, to the same restricted set of vignettes, and the relative fame of such vignettes obscures the reality that the corpus of Galen is more than 99 percent made up of the object language of medicine.

Specifically, there was no deliberate attempt on Galen's part to preserve the memory of past medical authors. He was no Diogenes Laertius, no Meleager – not even a Pappus. Thus, our usual probe (comparing an author who cites widely and somewhat unselectively against the field as a whole) will no longer do. Galen cites about 150 medical authors, for only 29 of whom is he the unique source.[80] This does not have the same consequence as the similar exercise for Diogenes Laertius and Meleager, because Galen did not seek the variety of Meleager, the rich texture of Diogenes. All we learn from this exercise is that there were about 100 or so medical authors in Galen's time whose citation Galen considered essential.[81] And, as noted above, the late antique reception – which ended up canonizing Galen – was not interested in medical authorship as such. The total number of extant Greek medical authors prior to late antiquity, other than Galen and the Hippocratic corpus, is six: Apollonius of Citium, Dioscorides, Rufus, Soranus, Aretaeus and Aelius Promotus. The first survives as a commentary to Hippocrates, the second because he became established as the canonical herbalist. The other four were lucky to have a few of their works survive (it helped, probably, that they were relatively late – as of course was Galen himself, coming right at the end of the Imperial era; more on this on pages 704–7 below). This is all brutally selective; the absence of any strictly Hellenistic author is especially striking. In short, all we can say, based on such evidence, is that the ratio of attestation, for medical authors, was probably well below that of all other fields so far surveyed.

Indeed, it is likely that there were, compared to the other sciences, many medical authors. I believe I find 928 mentions of the title "doctor" used in Greek inscriptions,[82] as against 12 uses of a significant title associated with the exact sciences, "astronomer".[83] The whole question of the meaning of professions, in their appearance in inscriptions, is of course complicated.[84]

---

[80] I adapt this from a survey made by Paul Keyser (private communication), in which he finds 178 EANS authors known only through Galen's citations; the great bulk of these, however, are the pharmacologists I dismiss in my survey of ancient medical authors. (I do count four pharmacologists in this list as genuine "authors": Alcimion, Aphrodas, Diophantus of Lycia, and Publius of Puteoli). I am deeply grateful to Paul Keyser for sharing this work with me.

[81] Many of the 29 strictly medical authors cited by Galen only are his immediate contemporaries and peers: so, his teacher Aeficianus and Maecius Aelianus, his Erasistratean opponent Martialius, etc. In short, there are only a handful of minor prior authors for whom Galen is our sole witness. He had no patience for the minor.

[82] These are the PHiSearches for ιατρ (1,242), minus the searches for ιατροκλ (317) and for διατριβ (97).

[83] These are the PHiSearches for αστρονομ (2) and for αστρολογ (10).

[84] I will use Puech (2002) below, on p. 592, for estimating the numbers of rhetors; see also Chaniotis (1988) for historians, which testifies precisely to the rareness of "intellectual" inscriptions, however. For added context, it is helpful to see a few more PHiSearches: ποιητη + ποιητον, 216; φιλοσοφ 172; ρητωρ/ρητορ, 166; σοφιστ 88; τεχνιτη + τεχνιτον, 66; φιλολογ 61; ζωγραφ 54; σχολαστικ 54; καθηγη 38; παιδαγ 30; γεωμετρ 16; μηχανικ 11; μαθηματικ 3.

But the evidence reminds us of an obvious observation: the profession of the physician was respected in antiquity, much more than that of the mathematician. It makes sense, then, that there would be considerably more medical authors than mathematical authors. If so, there should have been many more than 1,000 medical authors prior to 200 CE.

To be clear: our goal is to isolate a very select group: medical authors, going for the marked, elite status of authorship. Now, in general, the profession of the physician, as we noted, entailed a certain status. Certainly sought after, it was not extremely common. It was, apparently, always difficult to find physicians, of any kind, anywhere outside the cities (Lang, 2012: 220). Cohn-Haft (1956: 53) has argued that the evidence of the inscriptions concerning "public physicians" suggests that cities, in general, struggled to gain even a single reputable doctor. Nutton (2004: 155) cites the case of Myania and Hypnia, two small towns teaming together to hire a single physician between them. As Nutton goes on to note, the physicians encountered at such inscriptions, let alone the papyri, are still best understood at the level of craftsmen. But even such numbers would have to be quite constrained: there were probably, at any given time, no more than a few hundred Greek cities with any physicians, and, while bigger cities had many more than one, it is likely that the great majority, even at the peak, never had more than a few dozen.[85] This suggests something between many hundreds to, at most, a couple of thousand individuals recognized as physicians, even at the peak. But how many of these had the status we now associate with "authors"? We may consider Nutton's (1977) survey of those recognized in the inscriptions as *archiatri*. This apparently is a more exalted category than that of the "public doctors" studied by Cohn-Haft, perhaps representing physicians whose status was considered sufficient for the exemptions from civic duties (see note 85). Here we consider a group of perhaps several hundred individuals at the peak. Of the 94 individuals of Nutton's catalogue, two are definitely of authorial status (no. 42: Statilius

[85] *Digest* 27.1.6.2 preserves a well-known rescript by Antoninus Pius to the province of Asia, limiting the numbers of members of elite professions who may claim exemptions from civic duties (a much-sought-after privilege, and the subject of a tug-of-war between professionals – who wished to see such exemptions as flowing automatically from their status – and the state – which wished to limit such exemptions; for medicine specifically, see Lewis, 1965). The numbers cited by Antoninus Pius are specified for physicians, rhetors and grammarians (both of the latter understood as teaching professions, but likely envisioning those who cater specifically to the elite), in a scale from largest to smallest cities, as follows: 5/3/3, 7/4/4, 10/5/5. It is remarkable that, in a city such as second-century CE Pergamon, an emperor could expect to limit the number of exempt physicians to ten! Likely enough, in practice there were more, and rather more who sought such a status; but this is consistent with a few dozen physicians, even in such a center.

Attalus; no. 54: Apollophanes of Seleucia). This should be considered against the background of our low attestation of medical authorship, and, surely, if all ancient medical authors were attested, we would find that more of the *archiatri* were also authors. On the other hand, there is something remarkable about the fact that none of the many medical inscriptions refers to any medical doctrine, let alone any authored work, by the physician who set it up.[86] As is made clear from Galen – the most prolific physician of them all! – status depended on the network of acquaintances obtained through the successful treatment of the elite.[87] Publication must have helped, but books provided no short cuts. The art remained long. And, so, the evidence is suggestive: likely enough, even many *archiatri* could have been non-authors. The book was not some kind of a thesis, required for one's advanced diploma. It seems that a physician became an author not just because he wished to become recognized as a physician. Perhaps he did so because he wished to be respected *not just* as a physician but also as an author (which, once again, is patently the case with Galen). At any rate, when we estimate the numbers of medical authors, we likely consider a subset of *archiatri*, a group that, even at the peak, would likely have numbered in the hundreds.

Lots of "likelies", there: time to bring in another angle. The following argument – weak as it is – appears to me the strongest we can muster: namely that it would be surprising if the number of medical authors was not well lower than that of philosophers. This is not just a tautological restatement of the fact that many more philosophers are attested than physicians. Rather, the observation is that medicine, qualitatively, never behaves with quite the same established, institutional solidity of philosophy. I have used the very concentrations of philosophers in Athens as an argument why the number of philosophers should be capped at some level. But this argument may be reversed: institutional continuity should be correlated with a certain scale, and the lack of such continuity, in medicine, suggests that it simply never had the numbers. As noted in \*\*\* above, medicine is characterized by generational events; even Herophilus and Erasistratus never quite manage to leave behind a coherent, continuous

---

[86] The most "literary" reference in any medical inscription is that of Serapion, IG II² 3631, 3796, 4544: it is a poem celebrating the medical profession, produced by a medical author who wished to mark the literary pedigree of his second-century CE Athenian family (I return to discuss this on pp. 677–9 in the following chapter). No one ever set up a theoretical medical inscription, in the manner of the astronomical inscriptions (such as the Keskintos inscription: p. 467, n.30 above) or of Diogenes of Oenoanda's philosophical inscription (p. 662 below).

[87] This is described in a lively way in Mattern (2013: chap. 7).

tradition. As Massar (2010) documents, the basic institutional unit, throughout antiquity, remains that of the personal, master–student pair – out of which is composed the social networking of physicians (who refer regularly to their master or even, on occasions, to fellow disciples of the same master). It may be seen as a mark of the dearth of biographical anecdote in medicine, but it is remarkable that Massar keeps citing very small networks: her most extensive is that of the pupils of Chrysippus of Cnidus, numbering three (Massar, 2010: 175–6): Aristogenes, Chrysippus of Rhodes, Metrodorus (remarkably, each gets his own royal patron).[88] There is nothing to suggest the kind of grouping around, say, the Stoic Chrysippus. It is true that Galen puts much rhetorical emphasis on the role of the medical authority as teacher,[89] and, just for this reason, it is all the more remarkable that one of the few things about which Galen does not brag is *the number of his students*. If ever an argument from silence could carry weight, it would be here. Had ancient doctors regularly competed for the size of their student body, so would Galen. His failure to do so suggests that the implication of Massar's evidence is indeed correct and that Greek medical authors did not develop around them a very

[88]  Indeed, more invested in the quest for patronage, physicians would tend to disperse more than their philosophical counterparts. This might be seen to explain the lack of impersonal continuities; but why not have permanent schools, near the main seats of patronage? On this relative dispersal of medicine, there are some suggestive indications among the papyri. Of the library catalogues studied by Otranto (2000), two, nos. 15 and 17, are especially large (as noted on pp. 76–7 above), and it is intriguing that no. 17, for sure, but also possibly no. 15, could have been a combined philosophical-medical library. The very number of medical fragments is noteworthy: about 300, of which about a half are genuine book rolls and not merely artifacts of the educational process (whose numbers, as explained in section 1.2.4 above, would tend to be greatly inflated. The numbers I cite here were calculated in 2011, and in this field rather many have been published since.). This means that about 5 to 10 percent of all non-canonical books in circulation in Upper Egypt could have been medical in content. Finally, the Hippocratic *Aphorisms*, a smallish work, has six fragments: maybe a fluke, and possibly a number inflated by the relatively quick discard of such a frequently consulted work. And yet it suggests, as noted in the table on pp. 20–4 above, that perhaps, once again, some 5 to 10 percent of all book owners in Upper Egypt owned the *Aphorisms*. What all this seems to imply is that a relatively large fraction of the leisured elite in the Nile Valley was composed of medical practitioners, which is indeed plausible: more than other professions, medical practitioners had a reason to be dispersed, since, after all, wherever there were reasonably sized cities one could make a living – whereas, in other pursuits, the only place in which to pursue one's ambition would be a more metropolitan center. There must have been plenty of Messieurs Bovary out there in the boondocks. It might be added that the most obvious case of a Greek text finding its way into Jewish tradition is found in the first-century CE Rabbi Trafon's (or Tryphon's) saying in *Pirke Avot* II.15 – "The day is short and the work is long" – clearly a variation on the first Hippocratic *Aphorism*. Of all Greek forms of knowledge, Hippocratic medicine traveled the furthest.

[89]  This is the subject of Boudon-Millot (1993). Galen himself also emphasizes that he preferred medical practice to teaching (*On My Own Books*, 15), and, while he certainly wrote several works "for beginners", it is clear that even his Hippocratic commentary (in the explicitly titled commentaries and elsewhere) was motivated by doctrinal rather than strictly pedagogic issues: arguing for Galen's position as the correct expositor of Hippocrates (Lloyd, 1991: chap. 17).

large entourage of students, noted upon by themselves and by their contemporaries, in the manner of the Athenian philosophical schools.

Let us bring together, then, the arguments produced so far.

The number of medical authors was likely much higher than the number of authors in the exact sciences, which itself was probably about 1,000.

The number of medical authors was likely lower than that of philosophers, which itself was probably at about 6,000 or even fewer. (It was also rather lower than that of the *archiatri*-level physicians, who could have numbered no more than a few hundred at the peak.)

The 275 attested medical authors must represent a very low rate of attestation, compared to other prose fields such as philosophy or the exact sciences (in which I envision a ratio of attestation of about 1:4 to 1:5).

These arguments, taken together, imply a likely number of medical authors before 200 CE of about 3,000 to 4,000, with a rate of attestation at about 1:10 or somewhat worse.

Medicine is our entry point into the truly technical, badly attested disciplines, and for this reason it is especially useful if we can cap the number of ancient medical authors: this puts some kind of a bottom for the rate of attestation as a whole, for it seems likely that medicine is among the worst attested of all fields.

I have argued, with varying degrees of confidence, that the best-attested fields could have been represented at the rate of about 1:2.5, while other, relatively well attested fields, such as Hellenistic poetry, philosophy as a whole or the exact sciences, could have been attested at the ratio not much better than 1:5. With medicine, a fairly badly attested field, I have now developed an argument that it was attested at a ratio not much worse than, say, 1:10; likely enough, better than 1:15. The emerging band of the rate of attestation as a whole is thus, in a way, well defined. Apparently the mechanisms of attestation were, to some extent, robust across the fields; the bottom did not simply fall off. Perhaps this was the power of ancient cultural memory, as such: commemorating, in the aggregate, about 10 to 20 percent of all names.

But, if the band of attestation is indeed fairly well defined, this has implications for the total size of the original population. Roughly put: if 5,000 names are attested, at an average rate of 10 to 20 percent, there ought to have been 25,000 to 50,000 authors originally. This is the closest that our upper and lower bounds have come so far.

To this, let me add a droplet of an argument. Medical authors are about 3 percent of the intersection of Athenaeus and Plutarch, but almost 10 percent of the authors in Diogenes' homonyms. These numbers are very small, but the indication that medical authors constituted, perhaps, 10 percent or more of all ancient authors is suggestive. Together with the assumption of 3,000 to 4,000 medical authors this is once again consistent with a number somewhere in the 25,000 to 50,000 range. Our numbers, if nothing else, are coherent.

Finally, a quick word on the various technical fields. One might think that we should finally pass even lower than the normal band of attestation. In fact, the various technical fields did fine, in a sense, just because they were minor: the more encyclopedic of our authors took an interest specifically in such fields. Thanks to Athenaeus, we probably have a very thorough record of ancient writing on fish and the culinary arts; Pliny is rather thorough for many minerals, plants and animals.[90] I will simply assume that this category must have been less well attested than mathematics, but better attested than medicine. Perhaps the 200 or so attested authors stand for about 1,500 authors prior to late antiquity, though the number could very easily be as high as 2,000. At any rate, we should expect this number to be well below that of the medical authors. Put together 1,000 mathematicians, perhaps 1,500 to 2,000 authors in the various technical fields and 3,000 to 4,000 medical authors, and we have 5,500 to 7,500 authors in "science". More than the philosophers – but not by much.

**Rhetoric**

Authorship in rhetoric is diverse, as the discipline itself zig-zagged through its ancient career – a protean genre that straddled the ancient duality of performance, literary as well as political.[91] Roughly speaking, we may distinguish four main attested categories.

---

[90] It has now become standard in the scholarship to see Pliny's project as "imperial", the accumulation of universal information as a counterpart to concrete control over Rome's world (Murphy, 2004; Riggsby, 2007). This bodes well for exhaustiveness, though, as Doody (2009) points out, the modern reference to the work as an "encyclopedia" is anachronistic. While highly rational in the order of the book (most famously, and most useful for us, in the summarium of Book I, with its list of facts and authorities used throughout the work), Pliny owes most to the tradition of mirabilia, and is committed above all to the detailing of surprising facts. Pliny's collection was expansive – just like that of Athenaeus – precisely to the extent that it was *irr*esponsible.

[91] The genre is also the one in which authorship is harder to characterize. The writer of a technē, or of circulated speeches, is definitely an "author". Teachers who did not commit anything to writing are not. But what about public speakers who gained fame but somehow did not get their speeches copied down and circulated? Suppose their speeches made an impact: was their status, on a par with written rhetors, in doubt? How are we even to know how many of the attested rhetors got into circulation? I am just not sure about any of this, and would simply assume that anyone, say, at the level commemorated by Cicero's *Brutus* should count as an "author". This may make our counting a little too expansive.

(1) "Classical" (= up to 300 BCE) political figures, those attested being primarily Athenian (we also have attested a number of teachers of rhetoric or "sophists" from this era).

(2) Roman political figures, mostly from the end of the Republic.

(3) Teachers of rhetoric from about 300 BCE to about 50 CE, mostly (but not entirely) Greek.

(4) The authors of the Second Sophistic, mostly (but not entirely) Greek.[92]

I produced numbers for all those categories through several routes, trawling, so to speak, with various nets. The one I could apply everywhere – but also the most porous – was based on searches of *Brill's New Pauly*, looking for the terms "rhetor", "orator", "sophist", "teacher of rhetoric" and "declamator". With those basic searches, I found:

70 Classical Greek, mostly political rhetors;
72 Roman political orators;
33 Hellenistic/early Roman-era rhetors;
76 Second Sophistic authors.

For three of these categories I could produce alternative sources that had, so to speak, denser nets. For the classical Greek rhetors I can also refer to Mark Pyzyk's database (Pyzyk, 2015), produced through his actual reading through all the entries of *Brill's New Pauly*. He counts 205 figures, a number about three times higher than the one obtained through the search function. It might seem strange that so many rhetors are not labeled as such in their Brill entries and so escape my automated search, but Pyzyk rightly makes the decision to apply the label "rhetor" to any political figure who was likely to pursue his career at least in part through public speeches. Pyzyk's number is therefore perhaps something of an overcount: many of those political figures should not count as "authors". Still, even for a field as central as classical politics, *Brill's New Pauly* is not a truly exhaustive survey.

---

[92] This division omits one category: Imperial-era Roman orators. Tacitus' claim (dialogue on *Orators* 1) that their number was much smaller than that of their Republican counterparts is of course a clichéd sentiment, required for Tacitus' own rhetorical needs (and, at any rate, ambiguous: is the decline in question at all quantitative, and not merely qualitative?); and yet the claim is inherently plausible, largely for the reasons implied by the dialogue itself: the rise of the profession of the orator was associated with the political conditions of the late Republic (Brink, 1993). Even more significant is Tacitus' implication that, instead of "orator", one more recently speaks of "advocates"; indeed, the decline of the profession of the Roman orator was associated with the rise of the profession of the Roman lawyer, which became a central authorial identity. I discuss this in detail on pp. 664–5 below, and here I shall merely note that there were certainly many hundreds of Roman legal authors in the Imperial era, possibly even more.

Probably, then, there are about 200 attested classical rhetors, perhaps slightly fewer.

For Roman figures we may expand the survey through various additional resources, but I limited myself to only one, which is especially full and useful: Cicero's encyclopedic history of Roman oratory, the *Brutus*, whose prosopography is fully catalogued in Sumner (1973). Sumner counts a total of 221 entries, albeit starting in the mists of Roman history. If we limit ourselves only to authors active from the middle of the second century onwards, which I will define as those born from 200 BCE onwards, we reduce the number to 196. This is truly near-complete for the rhetors up to and including Cicero's time, but it does omit a substantial number of post-Ciceronian Roman orators, attested mostly through the works of Seneca the Elder. The last one mentioned no fewer than 120 rhetors, both Roman and Greek – the unique source for many of these.[93] The total number of attested Roman orators is probably about 250. Once again, we find that searches through the BNP pick up about a third to a quarter of the actual attested number.

For Second Sophistic authors, we have an extraordinary resource in the PGRSRE. I count there 219 second-century authors (including authors who straddle the first and second centuries). There are also 34 authors from the first century itself (excluding authors who straddle the first century BCE/first century CE). Further, there are also 30 authors who straddle the second and third centuries, as well as 43 who cannot be dated at all. A great many of these must have belonged to the category "Second Sophistic authors, active mostly prior to 200 CE". (I return to discuss the evidence and its interpretation in the following chapter, pages 717–19. In all this, I ignore "rhetors" attested through court documents on papyrus where the reference is definitely not to authorial figures.) The full attested number of Second Sophistic rhetors, then, is a little over 300, which once again, however, involves some overcount as a good many of these would have used the title "rhetor" without any genuine claims to authorship (even in the qualified, oral sense of "notable speaking practitioners of the rhetorical art"). It is not surprising that my search through the BNP yielded such a small fraction: many of these are obscure figures, mentioned in passing, the nearly anonymous picked up by the extremely exhaustive survey of the PGRSRE.

I do not have similar prosopographic resources for Hellenistic rhetors (the one exception is that Seneca the Elder throws a little light on the very late

---

[93] Edward (1928: xl).

generation among this group – a generation which already begins to take the shapes of the Second Sophistic). The relative stability of the fraction obtained through my rough search count becomes useful. The simple extrapolation, from the 33 found through those BNP searches, implies 100, or perhaps somewhat more, Hellenistic rhetors attested from antiquity.

At any rate, it seems safe to conclude that, overall, something in the range of "more than 800 rhetors" are attested from before 200 CE.

At this point, we need to calculate the rate of attestation – which is complicated by the diversity of the category. Political actors, in Athens and Rome, are extremely well attested. We did lose a few names. Aristotle, in his *Rhetoric*, provides examples of metaphorical language used by orators. Most come from the usual suspects (Pericles, Leptines...), but the last name mentioned is "Lycoleon, in defense of Chabrias" (*Rhet.* 1411b6). This use of the name "Lycoleon" here is, amazingly, a hapax in Greek literature. And so: a classical rhetor, known entirely through a single metaphorical usage. But this must be balanced against a substantial overcount: our evidence counts as rhetoricians many practical political speakers whose work never circulated in writing, was never considered an example of spoken authorship. The rate of attestation for these political rhetors – about half my survey! – must be very high, then.

The authors of the Second Sophistic are a more "literary" lot, and our sources for them are more precarious. As will be noted below, in section 6.2, our biographic evidence for the Imperial era, especially its later parts, is surprisingly thin. Philostratus, specifically, does not aim at the rich variety cherished by Diogenes Laertius, and he constructs instead a much more constrained circle of the leading Sophists: no more than a few dozen are reported via this, our main biographical source of evidence, and I count only 14 "minor" names brought in incidentally by Philostratus.[94] Otherwise, we often rely on the epigraphic evidence, which is indeed plentiful and, once again, may well suggest an overcount (since the title of "rhetor" seems to have become, in this epigraphic context, something of a political honorific that did not need to imply concrete authorship, written or spoken).

[94] He explicitly says he won't discuss Soter, Sosus, Nicander, Phaedrus, Cyrus, Phylax because they are too minor (605; he says the same for rhetors "between the two sophistics", as it were, on pages 510–11). Rufinus is mentioned as a teacher of Hermocrates (608), Aurelius and Cassianus are mentioned as instigators of a quarrel between Aspasius and Philostratus (627), and it is then noted how trifling they are: the last-mentioned has only one student, Periges, and Marcianus is mentioned in the context of an intrigue involving Heraclides (613). Amphicles is brought in within anecdotes concerning Philagrus (578) and Herodes (586), Ardys in an anecdote about Isaeus (513), Megistias in a more lengthy anecdote concerning Hippodromus (618–19). This sums up Philostratus' minor authors.

Finally, for Hellenistic rhetors our evidence is simply non-existent. I suspect that this is, indeed, because the discipline was not the focus of intense contemporary interest and was considered by later, rhetoric-crazed generations, mostly obliquely and pejoratively. The rate of attestation for this group may well be as low as that for the more obscure technical genres, which is perhaps as such authorship should be understood: it is quite possible that what we consider, here, is mostly authorship in the genre of the rhetorical technē. Obviously, rhetoric never receded from the educational curriculum; indeed, Diogenes Laertius, in his list of homonyms, has five authors of rhetorical technē – an Archelaus, an Aristotle (not a mistake for the philosopher?), a Bion, a Heraclides and a Simon – most likely, this derives from Demetrius of Magnesia and so attests a Hellenistic tradition).

The one clear observation, on general historical grounds, is that a very significant fraction of pre-200 rhetorical authors must be those of the Second Sophistic. This era covered about a quarter of the period up to 200 CE, and, if so, it must have represented well over a quarter, perhaps even about a half, of all ancient rhetors.

Let me add a couple of observations. I count in Puech (2002) 256 inscriptions that identify a person as "rhetor" (or "sophist"), from the Second Sophistic era of the late first century CE through the early third century (for the following discussion, it would be a waste of information, to ignore post-200 inscriptions). These cover 152 individuals: 109 with a single inscription each, 43 with more (up to 16 inscriptions – the number accumulated by Lollianus: Puech, 2002: 327–36). Now, the survival ratio of Roman-era inscriptions is probably on the order of 1 to 2 percent (see page 535 above), so, during the Second Sophistic, there were something on the order of 15,000 to 25,000 inscriptions recognizing an individual as a rhetor. Among the extant inscriptions, the top 30 percent of the individuals (with more than one inscription each) are responsible for about 60 percent of the inscriptions. This is not a very steep distribution – which is surprising, as the setting up of monuments can be taken as an excellent proxy for wealth, and, as in this age, of extreme inequality (for which, more below), one would have expected a steep curve characterizing the distribution inside the top elite itself.[95] Indeed, there is no doubt that many of the single-inscription individuals had in fact spectacular careers and were merely

---

[95] If I understand Nutton's survey of *archiatri* preserved on inscriptions correctly, he has 82 such *archiatri* (a number are reported by papyri), of whom only four have multiple inscriptions (this is not easy to establish from Nutton's, 1977, data through no fault of Nutton: he has set this up as a survey of *archiatri*, not of inscriptions relating to them. The four exceptions are L. Gellius Maximus, T. Statilius Crito, T. Statilius Attalus and C. Stretinius Xenophon, all pursuing not

unlucky in the survival of their inscriptions (Hadrian of Tyre, for instance, who followed Herodes Atticus as chair of rhetoric in Athens, and then became secretary *ab epistulis* to Commodus in Rome, is among those with a single Puech inscription, no. 128). Thus, quite a few of the single-inscription Puech authors must have had 50 to 100 inscriptions or even more. They were celebrated by cities; they dedicated monuments; they became part of the highest political orders, all recorded for posterity. And it is entirely possible that someone such as Lollianus – a senator – would leave many hundreds of inscriptions or even more. At the other end of the scale, even the most modest figures could easily leave – at this, most fecund age of the epigraphic habit – more than a single inscription. For every milestone there could be a stone: you could set up an inscription upon the death of those near you; relatives could leave one for you, upon your own death; any success at all could be recorded – recovery from illness, successful visit to a city and, of course, the setting up of a new building.[96] In for an inscription penny, in for an inscription pound. In other words, there needn't have been a long tail of individuals with just a single inscription; the number could have bottomed down, largely speaking, at a few stones (in other words: perhaps those who really had no more than one stone mentioning their name were below the level of the honorific "rhetor"?). With the many hundred inscriptions of the top members of the elite, then, the *average* would have to be well above a few stones, and so it is very likely that the average was at least on the order of ten inscriptions per inscriber. Taking this number literally, we find a maximum of about 1,500 to 2,500 Second Sophistic rhetors or a maximum, for the ratio of attestation, of about 1:5 to 1:8, which is in fact likely in itself (worse, but not by much, than that of philosophers). This in itself is something of an upper bound, since, as noted above, quite a few of the inscriptions use the title merely as an honorific, while it is hard to see how a fully fledged Second Sophistic rhetor of any significance could have spent his life without at least a few monuments mentioning his name.

As Bowie (2004: 68) notes, the Second Sophistic was fairly concentrated: mostly in Asia Minor, but, even more specifically, fame was to be obtained in one of the five major centers: Athens and Rome, of course (but these were more in the nature of a sojourn, the places in which to cash in on your success), and then the three Asian centers (which is where most aspiring

only a medical but also a political career). Socio-economically, the physicians were a rung or two below the rhetors. As Nutton (1971: 262) observes, it appears that no doctor ever entered the Senate.
[96] For a survey of the great variety of contexts feeding the Roman epigraphic habits, see Woolf (1996).

rhetors must have spent more of their careers): Smyrna, Pergamon and Ephesus. Something on the order of 2,000 pre-200 Second Sophistic rhetors would imply about 250 active simultaneously, on average; but everything suggests a higher figure in the second half of the second century CE (400? 500? I shall return to discuss this on pages 666–7 below). The densest city among the big three would have maxed, perhaps, at something like a fifth of this total. We push near to 100 rhetors at the authorial level, all active simultaneously in a single city. This verges on the absurd (which is perhaps right for the Second Sophistic).[97] The calculation is similar to that concerning the number of philosophers, on page 578 above, and it is based on a similar logic: the Second Sophistic, like philosophy, was concentrated (but to a somewhat lesser extent) in time and place – which means that very large total numbers would imply very high local concentrations.

Next, we return to the comparison between Athenaeus + Plutarch, and Diogenes Laertius. Rhetoric is fairly rare in the intersection of Athenaeus + Plutarch (5 percent), quite common in Diogenes Laertius (20 percent). It can be seen how Athenaeus + Plutarch are perhaps biased for poetry, and also, in other ways, for philosophy and for history, all of which would tend to reduce the representation of rhetoric; 5 percent is therefore probably too low, even if the 20 percent in Diogenes Laertius could simply be a statistical fluke. But, overall, the fraction of ancient authors who were rhetors was probably no less than 10 percent, perhaps more. While we have not yet established the overall number of all ancient authors, we already know that it is in the (low) tens of thousands, and so we expect to have the number of rhetors at the thousands.

If indeed there were about 2,000 Second Sophistic rhetors, this would imply perhaps 4,000 rhetors in all. For this, we would also bring in 1,000 political rhetors in the heyday of public speech in the Greek and Roman worlds, combined (ratio of attestation 1:2.5, comparable to the Attic dramatists, who, indeed, were similarly the focus of a city's attention);[98] and 1,000 Greek rhetors and authors of rhetorical technē in the interim (ratio of attestation 1:10, or that of a technical genre). Since this is probably

---

[97] Also, bear in mind: Antoninus Pius aimed to cap the number of rhetors exempt from civic duties, in the biggest cities, at *five* (see n.85 above). Brunt (1994: 26) cuts through this: "The prestige of a Polemo or Herodes was obviously untypical. The great majority of sophists ignored by Philostratus himself were probably men of little repute resident in small towns." But such an assumption would, if anything, cap the total number of elite, author-level rhetors even lower.

[98] By our calculation, then, Roman rhetors were more than 10 percent of all ancient rhetors, perhaps (especially if the Jurists are brought in) close to 20 percent. I shall return to this broad calculation below.

also the best place to count Roman legal authors (see note 92 above; I will return to count them in the following chapter, on pages 664–5), and since these should add at least a few hundreds, I sum up this category as "likely more than 4,000".

Little is safe about any of the numbers. But this much is notable already: the emerging numbers are surprisingly low, lower than those for philosophers, comparable to the technical profession of the medical author. Was rhetoric not one of the defining practices of antiquity?

The simple point is this: if indeed we believe in an account in which Greek rhetoric, as a defining authorial identity, declined following its Attic heyday, to recover fully only in the Second Sophistic, then there is nothing surprising about an *aggregate* low number of rhetors prior to late antiquity. This is of course Philostratus' explicit position, which, for this very reason, is often contested. It is something of a scholarly cliché, to point out Philostratus' deficiencies as a historian and to deduce the existence of a mostly unattested, but highly active tradition of rhetoric through the Hellenistic era.[99] It is indeed easy to deconstruct, more generally, the prejudices of Imperial-era authors – from Dionysius of Halicarnassus down to Philostratus – who, in order to make themselves "Atticists", had to invent a kind of Middle Ages separating them from the classical past. Furthermore, it is clear that rhetoric did remain, throughout, a cornerstone of Greek education, and we have the Ptolemaic papyri of rhetorical exercises to prove this (see page 212 above). And yet, the very low numbers of attested post-classical Greek rhetors is an important piece of evidence, bolstered by the clear evidence of the Ptolemaic papyri, in which, indeed, even though rhetorical education is reasonably well attested, rhetoric as a whole – including canonical figures such as Demosthenes! – is essentially missing. The argument that Imperial-era authors mislead us by their bias has its limits. Surely, the Imperial era valued its *own* rhetoric. But, even more fundamentally, the Imperial era was, simply, obsessed with rhetoric

---

[99] Already Blass (1865) has collected the evidence for Hellenistic rhetoric (but without much optimism concerning its extent); already von Wilamowitz-Moellendorff (1900) has brought in such scraps of evidence to refute Philostratus' account (a typical move of the erudite scholarship of his time: the minor, employed so as to tear down the evidence of better-known sources). This is the beginning of a long tradition. Brunt (1994) refers to "the bubble of the Second Sophistic"; Kremmydas (2013) is a collection of essays setting out to rehabilitate Hellenistic rhetoric. In this scholarly tradition one detects not only a prudent caution concerning Philostratus' testimony but also an ideological bias. Scholars from von Wilamowitz-Moellendorff down to Brunt have resisted, above all, the idea that the most productive age for Greek rhetoric could have been after the end of political freedom (This is how I read Brunt, 1994: 46: "If it is right to speak at all of a Greek renaissance in the second century, it can hardly be found in sophistic oratory; conditions were such that no new Isocrates or Demosthenes could arise." This is straight out of Tacitus!).

as such. That Imperial-era authors mention so few Hellenistic rhetors – even if only to denigrate them – is therefore a strong argument that, in fact, there were not that many to mention. And we can easily fit this within the broader pattern, seen in the preceding part of this book: in the Hellenistic world, performance was spatialized. Hence, the performative genres typical to classical Athens did not transfer well – as creative endeavors – to the wider Hellenistic world. Philosophy and (to a lesser extent) comedy survived, in Athens; tragedy withered. So, apparently, did rhetoric. Tragedy would remain, as revivals performed in the theaters; and rhetoric, too, would remain, as exercises performed in the classroom. But maybe, in fact, we should trust what the ancients tell us: there was little rhetorical creativity in the Hellenistic era. Let us turn, then, to grammar.

**Grammar**

Grammar is much simpler than rhetoric. The generation of Callimachus created a well-defined and well-respected category of the "grammarian", and this became one of the most consistent forms of literary production. At least in qualitative terms, there is less of an ebb in activity in this field, even during the second century BCE, compared to other fields (more on this on page 651 below); grammar adapted naturally to the Roman era (inventing, along the way, the grammatical technē; see pages 473–4 above) and enjoyed Roman patronage from the first century BCE on. In all this, it never lost its attachment to Alexandria. (In the Hellenistic era, Alexandrian grammar was complementary to Athenian philosophy; in the Roman era, Alexandrian grammar was complementary to Asian rhetoric: Bowie, 2004: 70).

I have surveyed grammar in the BNP, similarly to my survey of rhetoric (reading, in this case, the entries generated by searches for "grammar", "grammarian", "scholar", "scholarship"). I have found 138 authors prior to late antiquity.[100] As soon as one moves into late antiquity, of course, one can turn to Kaster (1988), an outstanding survey of all the individuals known as grammarians from the middle of the third century CE through the middle of the sixth century (as Kaster emphasizes, these are mostly teachers – a category considerably wider than "grammatical author"; more on this on page 733, note 185, below). His total is 281, of whom only a negligible number are from the second half of the third century – which indeed will be important for our discussion in the following chapter. Kaster

---

[100] The online Lexicon of Greek Grammarians in Antiquity currently has, by my count, 137 entries, a number surprisingly close to my count based on the BNP.

does have, however, about 100 individuals from the *fourth* century, which in general is the best comparison we can find, in terms of attestation, for the second. (In general, I will argue below, on page 708, the somewhat less active fourth century is in other ways better attested – this is the century of Libanius! – and the two factors roughly cancel each other out.) My BNP survey finds 30 grammatical authors from the second century, which is within the ballpark of Kaster's 100 (bearing in mind, as always, that my survey of the BNP is designed as an undercount). I will assume that we have about 300 to 400 grammarian authors attested prior to late antiquity.

Which rate of attestation does this represent? We have no "Lives of the Grammarians". Explicit citation formed the very ethos of the field, however. In Erbse (1983: index I) (testimonies included within the scholia vetera to the *Iliad*) I count no fewer than 128 names of ancient grammarians – a number very close, naturally, to that of the grammarians found through the BNP search. (This number does not include the many quotations from historians, as well as from other poetry, embedded within the scholia.) I have read all the pages of the scholia vetera to the *Iliad* in Erbse's edition whose page number divides by 100: a total of 28 very short pages (about 15 to 20 lines, usually a handful of glosses). Fifteen of these – a bare majority – include at least one explicit quotation naming an ancient grammatical authority. Read through the scholia, then, and every few glosses you will come across a cited authority. To be clear: the same is no longer true for the grammatical technai, which, instead, are as devoid of proper names as any other technical literature. And, indeed, these grammatical technai form the bulk of the ancient grammatical literature which is still extant in authorial, treatise form. As noted on pages 473–4 above, however, such was not the typical form of ancient grammatical writing, which instead was that of the commentary, made precisely of small, citable units of text, forever being recycled. This practice of repeated citation would tend to preserve many names in circulation, and indeed ended up forming the massive collections of scholia we now possess: citation, becoming its own textual identity.

As noted on page 276 above, about 40 percent of the grammarians I surveyed had known Alexandrian connections – a significant under-count, as the geography of attested grammarians is only patchily known. Likely, most well-known grammarians were active, for at least part of their career, in Alexandria. It may well be that the absolutely minor grammarians could be located further away from the metropolitan center, but it should be emphasized, once again, that I am considering here the category of the grammatical author – that is, the very top stratum of ancient grammarians (and certainly not the local schoolteachers). This discipline, then, had an unparalleled connection to a single city (as noted on page 254 above, no enduring rival center ever developed, even Pergamon remaining as no more than a generational event). Let us say that 40 percent or more of all grammatical authors were active in Alexandria. If I take a generation of scholarly activity, schematically, as 20 years, then there were more than 20 such generations between Callimachus and the end of the second century CE; and so we may suggest that roughly 2 percent of the total number of pre-200 grammarians would have been active, at any given time, on average, in Alexandria. The number must have fluctuated somewhat, and so the peak can be put, roughly, at 3 percent. A rate of attestation of the grammarians, along the lines of obscure technical fields, will give rise to 3,000 to 4,000 authors. But even 3,000 pre-200 grammatical authors implies something like 100 active in the same city, at the same time, at the peak. Such a number is comparable to what we found for the Hellenistic philosophical schools or for the Second Sophistic rhetors of Ephesus: once again, a spatially concentrated cultural activity would have to be somewhat constrained. Perhaps we need to think of grammar, after all, as fairly well attested, given its practice of citation, and so we should assume not more than 2,500 grammatical authors. Indeed, both Diogenes Laertius and the intersection of Athenaeus and Plutarch have rather fewer grammarians than rhetors – but they both have grammar at a rate nearly identical to that of medicine. This is suggestive: the two service industries – the healing of the body, the healing of the text – could well have been more or less on par. Now, the number offered above for grammar would be somewhat lower than that of the medical authors – but medicine had more than a century of intensive activity before it was joined by grammar. I will stay with 2,500 grammarians. I admit, however, that I have no right for such precision, my number offered as a tribute to the science of the minutely precise.

## History
Our evidence for grammar does not lend itself to certainty, precisely because the evidence is so undifferentiated: a great mass of citations in scholia, written by a group of somewhat self-effacing authors. The same is doubly true for history, a discipline massively attested in fragmentary survival, the least marked of all ancient genres; indeed, as noted above (page 129, note 63) concerning the overall division into genres, history, to a large extent, was

seen as simply the default form of prose. Historians, of course, gained some foothold within the canon, and as such they could gain their own individual attention with works such as Plutarch's *On the Malice of Herodotus*, but those are the exceptional treatments of canonical authors. Generally speaking, the study of historians was not a field of ancient historiography, and we have no "Lives of the Historians". For grammar, we could use geographical concentration as some kind of bound on the number of grammarians. History, to the contrary, as noted on page 371 above, is the spatially dispersed field par excellence. It is the one field that did not acquire, in the Hellenistic era, any central pole, either in Athens or in Alexandria, multiplying instead with the proliferation of many local histories, presumably many of them produced locally. Once again, this is a practice which was not even concentrated in time but was, rather, fairly stably produced throughout antiquity (in this case, beginning well in the fifth century itself). All we can say, then, is that the ratio of attestation must have been very poor. The New Jacoby has about 900 Greek historians prior to late antiquity (in a sense that encompasses geography), while the *Fragments of the Roman Historians* has about 100; a nice, round group of 1,000 attested historians.[101]

Consider the pattern of fragments. I went through a sample of Jacoby with 75 historians,[102] counting the number of authorities citing each fragmentary historian – trying to gauge, in such a manner, the precariousness of the transmission.[103] Of the 75 historians in my sample, nearly two-thirds are cited certainly (43) or possibly (4) by no more than one citing authority. Recall how, above, the fact that so few archaic poets had a single

---

[101] Latin historians are probably well attested relative to the Greek: so, fewer than 10 percent of historians prior to 200 CE wrote in Latin. This should be put alongside our observation from p. 594, n.98, above, that about 10 to 20 percent of rhetors prior to 200 CE wrote in Latin. Since the fraction of Latin-language philosophers, grammarians, and scientific authors was vanishingly small in the years before 200, we find that overall authorship in Latin was indeed quite marginal, in all likelihood less than 10 percent: fewer than 1,000 rhetors, fewer than 1,000 historians, fewer than 1,000 of all the rest? These, of course, are much more concentrated in the first century BCE (when, especially late in the century, Latin was after all a major vehicle), and so, otherwise, Latin literature was truly no more than a rare pursuit, a statistical afterthought that a later, Latin West, starting in late antiquity itself, would gradually make into its own canon.

[102] I took off the shelf the volumes of the old Jacoby (for such samples, print versions are more convenient) and read through all the historians whose number divided by ten, albeit avoiding the placeholder entries used by Jacoby for anonymous historians on a given topic; I did so until I had 75 entries, which was near the end (my last entry is no. 830).

[103] I suggest that the significant factor is not the number of *fragments* but the number of *citing authors*. If an author is cited once by Stephanus of Byzantium, but nowhere else, we conclude that he is now attested thanks to (at best) a single copy reaching the Byzantine author. Twelve citations by Stephanus would yield the same conclusion, perhaps with a higher chance that the work itself, not just an epitome, survived.

fragment was used to argue that we may not have lost that many. A significant loss would have predicted a longer tail, a larger group of low-attestation figures. Conversely, with history we do find a set with apparently a very long tail, and the conclusion is that this is likely cut from a much larger original set.

Interestingly, this tail does not derive from the limit of a gradual curve but, rather, from an almost bimodal distribution. In my survey, there are 13 historians cited by two to four authorities, and then 15 who are cited by six authorities or more, typically in the range of about ten: there are quite a few historians who were cited by several of the major citing authorities for historians such as Eusebius, Stephanus of Byzantium, Athenaeus, Plutarch, and then also by several of the collections of scholia. Qualitatively, the result is clear. There was a certain circle of more central historians, who could get cited often, perhaps becoming something like standard authorities in their particular fields and thus preserved in a good number of big libraries. Beyond that inner circle, however, are authors whose circulation was always minuscule, whose survival was always a matter of chance – so that what we now see is no more than a tiny fraction of such minor historians.

Let us dig a little deeper into this pattern of citations. In general, while citations of past authorities were not an essential part of the ancient historical ethos – so that we may have a rate of attestation worse than that for the grammarians – historians did provide useful stores of information for grammarians and grammar-like authors. Thus, many of the authorities cited by Athenaeus are historians; especially useful for Jacoby was Stephanus of Byzantium, a sixth-century grammarian whose *Ethnica* is now extant in epitome. This immense lexicon of geographical proper names proceeds alphabetically, providing information – with authority cited – for each entry. Quite a few of those authorities are, naturally, from the literary canon, but the great majority are historians (or grammarians who, preceding Stephanus himself, collected geographical information). In the index to Meineke's (1849) edition I count 250 historical authorities, which I believe to be the major single source for the names of ancient historians. And yet, it was, in the main, not thanks to authors such as Stephanus that Jacoby could produce his wide collection of fragments. I now zoom in on the same small sample of sources of citation in Jacoby, now considering only the historians for whom we have but a single citing authority (excluding papyrological and epigraphic sources). The citing authorities, arranged now chronologically, are as follows.

| Source | Century | Number of historians (in sample) for whom authority |
|---|---|---|
| Apollonius Paradox. | 2 BCE | 1 |
| Polybius | 2 BCE | 1 |
| Hyginus | 1 BCE | 1 |
| Strabo | 1 BCE | 1 |
| Vitruvius | 1 BCE | 1 |
| Pliny (Elder) | 1 CE | 2 |
| Plutarch | 1 CE | 4 |
| Aelianus | 2 CE | 1 |
| Athenaeus | 2 CE | 6 |
| Diogenes Laertius | 2 CE | 1 |
| Lucian | 2 CE | 1 |
| Libanius | 4 CE | 1 |
| Scholia Aristophanes | LA | 1 |
| Scholia Apol. Rhod. | LA | 1 |
| Ps. Plutarch | LA | 2 |
| John Malalas | 6 CE | 3 |
| Stephanus of Byz. | 6 CE | 2 |
| *Suda* | 10 CE | 5 |

The number in the sample is now really tiny: 35. Nor should we pay too much attention to the division between centuries, in particular the contrast between Hellenistic and Imperial-era sources (obviously, there should be fewer Hellenistic sources, since so much more literature has been preserved from the Imperial era). What is of some interest, and of some significance even in such a small sample, is the contrast between early (up to and including the second century CE) and later sources. Twenty of the 35 single-fragment Jacoby historians surveyed here are known through authors active in the Hellenistic or the Imperial era; only 15 of the 35 survive through later sources. Even of those 15, most are due to evidently derivative compilations, not the sources' familiarity with the original work itself (this will often be true for the scholia, Ps. Plutarch, *Suda*, likely also Stephanus of Byzantium himself). When Byzantine grammarians come on the scene, this is already too late. Stephanus does recur again and again in Jacoby – but this is mostly among the fragments of historians who have other citing authorities. What he had available to him in full, original form, must have been primarily the inner circle.

The impression, then, is that, already by the fourth century CE, the great bulk, even of those historians dimly visible through Jacoby, must have been lost. Indeed, the argument on page 551 above would suggest that the milieu of Photius possessed no more than several dozen ancient historians. The fourth century must have possessed many more: but, once again, perhaps not much more than the inner circle range of a couple of hundreds.

In short, we have but a small fraction of all ancient historians. How small? All we can say, perhaps, based on the rates of attestation seen so far, is that it would be surprising if the rate of attestation for history was at all better than 1:10. Thus, the simplest assumption is: 10,000 historians, or perhaps more.

Diogenes Laertius' homonyms have three prominent groups, each with about a fifth of the total: historians, philosophers and rhetors. In the intersection of Athenaeus and Plutarch, history comes second to philosophy (which of course is central to Plutarch) but is far above rhetoric. All in all, the fifth in Diogenes Laertius must be an undercount, and something like a third, even perhaps more than that, of all ancient authors being historians is therefore quite possible.

So this is where all ancient authors were hiding.

I will try to be even more specific than that. Jacoby has divided his survey into categories, going through various forms of historical monographs in entries 1 to 296 and then covering, in the remaining entries 297 to 856, the various histories of "Städte und Völker" – that is, regional and local histories. Now, quite a few historians prior to late antiquity are extant, and within that category we have *zero* local historians, perhaps one regional historian.[104] Admittedly, there is no obvious tendency for historians 1 to 296 to get more citing authorities than those of historians 297 to 856.[105] But this is because the context in which minor historians get cited is precisely for "color", for local detail: and so we find, for instance, Plutarch, reaching in his bookshelves for details on Egyptian gods, as he writes his treatise *On Isis and Osiris*; finding there, among many other sources, a certain historian Hermaeus, whom he cites for two statements concerning Egyptian divine names. Thus a Jacoby entry is made (no. 620). And so, we still have a good number of minor local historians attested. Flukes of survival, all. The

---

[104] I count these 14 extant authors (ignoring a few minor geographical authors, none of whom is a regionalist): Herodotus, Thucydides, Xenophon, Polybius, Diodorus Siculus, Strabo, Dionysius of Halicarnassus, Appian, Josephus, Arrian, Plutarch, Suetonius, Pausanias, Cassius Dio. Josephus, perhaps, comes closest to a "regional" historian.

[105] Eight out of 26 non-local historians, in my survey, have more than a single citing authority; as well as 17 out of 49 local and regional historians. It is clear that some regional historians could become the standard authorities for a particular region and thus survive well through antiquity and beyond (consider, for instance, Berossus, for Babylon: historian no. 680).

likelihood remains that an even larger fraction of the original histories were local in character.

To the extent that this argument is correct, we should conclude that local historians would have had to constitute well over a half of the truly minor historians who are now entirely lost. I believe that we should imagine thousands – six or seven; eight or nine; more? – of local historians, mostly chroniclers of their own cities, of whom nothing is now known, not even to the readers of Jacoby.

Here is the dark matter, or our blindest spot. Throughout the preceding part of the book I have emphasized the spatial character of ancient civilization, how culture was rooted in its places. What we have to some extent lost is the extent to which culture was made locally, from a place, about the place. This was not necessarily the most sophisticated form of writing, and we may have lost it for a reason. The positivist historians of the nineteenth century practiced quellenforschung as a way of making sense of the literary historical evidence for antiquity. We now deride their lack of attention to authorial agency,[106] but it is at our peril that we give up on the intuitive understanding of the Mommsens of the past. Ancient historiography really did involve the making of new books by the compilation of past books. Let us consider the numbers involved. We estimate several thousand local histories, in a Mediterranean that had about 1,000 Greek "cities", many of them no more than villages. Many of the local histories would be regional rather than city-based, but, still, we need to assume that there were a few thousand truly local histories, dedicated to a few hundred cities:[107] about ten local histories per city, through antiquity, on average. Even a medium-sized city would have a new history every few generations – for which there would be ample material from all those previous histories. History could be compiled from past histories, simply because there was so

---

[106] For a history of quellenforschung, see Most (2014): the field emerged out of the need to reconcile inconsistencies within texts (originally, most pressing in biblical studies) and was, through the nineteenth century, simply taken for granted because of its superficial resemblance to the Lachmannite method of textual criticism (whereby the genealogical method is indeed most secure, since new manuscripts are to a meaningful extent produced by near-mechanical copying of old manuscripts!). Thus, the long reign of quellenforschung went without much reflection on the concrete conditions of the production of ancient works, so that, as soon as scholarly interest moved to the understanding of individual works within their context, so did interest in quellenforschung wane. I suggest that we should consider the possibility that original, creative work in antiquity, particularly in the very prolific historical fields, could very well have relied, quite often, on fairly mechanical copy-and-paste procedures.

[107] Sixty-two cities from the Greek core, alone, have their own local histories attested in Jacoby. Most of the lost local histories would have covered the same central group again and again, but it is certain that the original number of cities covered by a history must have been in three figures, at which point one would have reached into the truly minor cities.

much of it. *syggrapheus*, "putter-together of writing", was one of the words used by Greek to refer to historians (sometimes, more generally, this referred to "prose authors", or even to "writers"; see page 129, note 63, above). History, quite simply, was the default form of writing, and it was literally a *compilation*, the bringing together of information so as to create a new history. It was both the easiest as well as the most unmarked form of authorship. The contrast is telling. Today the default thing to do as a writer is to write about oneself; in antiquity the default was to write about one's city.

In this case, we lack the means to produce any specific numbers. I think it is safe to say that the number of ancient historians could not have been substantially lower than 10,000. There is no clear way to bound the number from above, however, and it is with this category that our numbers are most elastic.

## Prose Fiction

The default form of ancient writing was not about an individual but about a city. And so, indeed: the ancient *novel* was late, never became truly central, and it is in fact extremely rare among the extant works from antiquity, with just *seven* extant novels (five Greek, two Latin: but this under a narrow definition of the genre). It is extremely rare that a single author is even *attested* for more than one novel; but how would we even know? The biographical tradition for novelists is tenuous, closer to that of technical literature than to that of canonical, performative literature. Often the names of our authors are, in this case, no more than the titles affixed to medieval manuscripts.[108] The very nature of authorship is in question, and modern scholars sometimes wonder if some of the names we do possess could not be *noms de plume*.[109] The best we can do, then, is to count novels – which presents its own difficulties. In a wider sense, fictional letters or myth-like histories should also count as "prose fiction": so, "letters of Hippocrates", the "Acta Alexandrinorum", the *Alexander Romance*. Each of these existed, already in antiquity, in multiple forms (Selden, 1994, sees this fluidity of form, often crossing cultural boundaries,

---

[108] Apuleius is the only author of an extant novel (in the strict sense) who is also known to be extant otherwise: but, even so, only a single novel is extant. In a wider sense, Parthenius is a well-attested author of an extant prose fiction (see p. 492 above), and several of Lucian's extant works are prose fictions; "The hunters of Euboea" is sometimes used as a title for an inset novella within Dio Chrysostom's' seventh *Oration*.

[109] So, the name "Petronius" attached to the *Satyricon* could well be a misattribution, or a *nom de plume*, based on the identity of Nero's courtier (Henderson, 2010).

as essential to the genre – a view which of course ultimately derives from Bakhtin, 1981 [1975], who was the first to celebrate the novel form precisely for its open-endedness, and to ground that openness in antiquity itself). We must recognize that authorship here changes its meaning, so that the number of authors – in the sense of historical persons who engaged for part of their career in the creation of prose fiction – was probably somewhat greater than the number of novels.[110] But this should not be exaggerated: many of the works of prose fiction (such as the seven transmitted "novels" in the strict sense) seem to belong to more stable narratives; those that are most plastic were probably transmuted by authors whose main identities were established otherwise (I shall return to this below).

In the widest sense of the word, then, I count 47 attested novels and novel types.[111] In this case, attestation must be abysmal. It would be surprising if the ratio of attestation was not significantly worse even than 1:10. Thus, the number of the authors of prose fiction prior to late antiquity could hardly have been fewer than about 1,000.

It is clear that authorship of the novel was strongly concentrated in space and time. The novel arose, perhaps, in the first century BCE (I count Parthenius' "Sufferings of Love", for which see page 492 above, as one of my 47 novels; the question of the "origins of the novel" is highly contentious and need not detain us here), but it is clear that authorship had proliferated in the second century CE, perhaps parallel to the rise of the Second Sophistic, and, together with it, as already noted above, this was a phenomenon primarily located in Asia Minor. We therefore probably need to assume no fewer than 500 authors of prose fiction in Asia Minor through the second century, or, on average, five new authors joining

---

[110] What is a "novel" and what is a "novel type"? In a sense, all five extant Greek novels follow the same type (lovers, separated and rejoined), but they are sufficiently distinct in their treatments to count as distinct novels. The many variations present within the Acta Alexandrinorum theme – or within the *Alexander Romance* theme – do not qualify, in my judgement, in quite the same way: I see them as a case of multiple, dispersed authorship for a single novel. I also count groups of fictional letters by the same author as a single "novel", which of course stretches the term. Such definitional questions are important, but for our purposes they are purely semantic. But it should be clear that many – perhaps most – ancient novels were indeed distinct, separate works, carrying at least the identity of a clear title (for whose conventions, see Whitmarsh, 2005).

[111] Bare list, with authors (when available) followed by novel types (when authors are not available): Achilles Tatius, Alciphron, Antonius Diogenes, Apollonius of Tyre, Apuleius, Aristides, Pseudo-Callisthenes, Chariton, Dio Chrysostom, Heliodorus, Iamblichus, Iambulus, Lollianus, Longus, Lucian, Lucius of Patrae, Pseudo-Lucian, Melesermus, Parthenius, Pescennius Festus, Petronius, Xenophon/Acta Alexandrinorum, *Aesop's Life*, *Alexander Romance*, *Antheia*, *Anthia and Habrocomes*, Apollonius of Tyana, *Araspes, the Lover of Panthea*, *Calligone*, *Chion's Letters*, Chione, Daulis, *Dictys and Dares*, Herpyllis, *Joseph and Aseneth*, *Letters* (seven major types), *Metiochus and Parthenope*, *Ninus and Semiramis*, *Sesonchosis*, *Tinouphis*.

the genre, there and then, annually. Now, in the middle of the eighteenth century – before the numbers begin to climb – there were about 20 new novels published annually in Britain and Ireland, but certainly fewer *debut* novels (the publication of novels at this point was mostly anonymous, so that this fraction cannot be known for certain).[112] As in so many other ways: the Roman era, at its peak, was hovering near the cusp of a modernity it would fail to reach.

The numbers do need to be qualified in one major sense. There is a very plausible story to be told that at least some authors of prose fiction identified themselves as rhetors or sophists. Writing novels could have been another facet in the life of many second-century prose authors in other genres.[113] We may begin to double-count, then. And so: time to sum up.

### 5.3.3    A Calculation of the Genres

We have counted the following.

| Poets | 4,000, as follows: |
|---|---|
| Tragedy | 500 |
| Comedy | 750 |
| Other verse | 3,000, with some overlap |
| (1,000 pre-Hellenistic, 1,000 Hellenistic, 1,000 post-Hellenistic) | |

| Prose | 29,000–30,500 or more, as follows: |
|---|---|
| History | 10,000 or rather more |
| Philosophy | 6,000 or fewer |
| Science | 5,500–7,000 |
| (3,000–4,000 medicine, 1,500–2,000 "other" technical, 1,000 exact sciences) | |
| Rhetoric | 4,000 or more |
| Grammar | 2,500 |
| Prose fiction | 1,000 |

---

[112] Data on the eighteenth-century British novel: Raven (2006).

[113] A possibility raised already in antiquity. Philostratus mentions a debate (*Lives of the Sophists* 524) as to whether or not the Sophist Dionysius of Miletus was the author of an otherwise unknown *Araspes, the Lover of Panthea*. We are equally perplexed: was the Heliodorus whose memory is preserved in Philostratus' *Lives* 32 also the author of the *Aethiopica*? Was Achilles Tatius the author not only of *Leucippe and Clitophon* but also of the extant, and rather "sophistic", survey of astronomy (of all things) ascribed by its manuscripts to the author of the same name? (How common could this name combination be?) Then again, Xenophon of Ephesus, according to the *Suda* (s.v. Xenophon Ephesios), also wrote what must have been a historical work on his city.

This adds up to 33,000 to 34,500 or more, with a modest amount of double-counting. As noted on page 133 above, the identity of the "scholar" invited an engagement with many fields, and this would have been visible especially in the category of the "grammarian". Many of these could have written works that we would also call "historical", and, of course, many would have been poets as well. In general, the authors of "other verse", especially as we move to later eras, were often epigrammatists, whose main identity could be in any genre of prose.[114] As noted just now, some of the authors of prose fiction could have been primarily rhetors (and so, in general: in the post-classical era "fine" literature was often the pastime of authors who formed their identity primarily through contributions to the specialized genres, in the sense that includes rhetoric). We should deduct about 1,000 to 3,000 from any totals, and so we end up with "more than 30,000". Many of the numbers are uncertain, none so much as that for the historians. There could be 10,000 of them, or about a third of the total; but it is still within the realm of the reasonable that there could have been, say, 20,000 of them, or about a half of the total. What we can definitely say is that the calculation, based on the individual genres, suggests a number between 30,000 and 40,000 – which is very consistent with the numbers emerging from the preceding sections. Let us consider, in greater detail, the historical context of such numbers.

### 5.4    Observations on Cultural Scale in Social Setting

In section 5.1 we produced numbers for the cultural audience – owners of books, schematically arranged by big and small libraries; in sections 5.2 to 5.3 we zoomed in on a much smaller category, that of the cultural protagonists – the book authors. The sets of numbers should be related to each other, and to wider social realities. And so, I introduce a model, following on the work of Scheidel and Friesen (2009: 76). This model starts from the demography of the Roman Empire (which is, in broad outline, surprisingly non-controversial), to develop a sense of the economic and social strata, focusing – as is usually done and as is most useful for our own purposes – on the peak of the Imperial era.

The Roman class system was mostly based on a sequence of political castes or "orders", with the senators (a defined body of households) at the top, possessing great wealth as a consequence of their political power, and

---

[114] Argentarius was an orator; Diogenes Laertius is best understood as a historian; Philodemus surely should count primarily as a philosopher.

the equestrians behind them, defined by a property qualification which was very substantial (400,000 HS or something on the order of 500 mean annual wages).[115] Beyond those come the decurions, mapping roughly into local elites (schematically, these were defined as a certain number of individuals in each city: something of a local, mini-senate). These definitely belonged to the leisured elite, if leading a much less opulent lifestyle than their senatorial and equestrian counterparts. As Scheidel and Friesen insist, it seems clear that the leisured elite, in this modest sense, extended somewhat beyond the formally defined decurional order.

The Senate at its peak was formally defined as 600 households, a number to which Scheidel and Friesen add more than 20,000 households of the equestrian order. This group stands for the uppermost elite, leading the truly lavish life of the Roman villa. About half of these belong to the Greek half of the empire (though the very top elite would certainly consume Greek culture, regardless of their ethnic identity): so, let us say, well over 10,000 opulent households, belonging to the sphere of Greek paideia.

Scheidel and Friesen further estimate the number of households of decurional or comparable wealth at 195,000 to 260,000. Here we may perhaps begin to ignore Italy, and so the strictly Greek eastern Mediterranean comes down to less than half that, or perhaps 80,000 to 120,000 households belonging to the modestly leisured, Greek-speaking elite.

This estimate is not uncontroversial, with other scholars looking for a somewhat smaller leisured elite, more concentrated at the top, but the range of controversy is not that large: it is clear that there would be thousands in the first group (the richest who defined themselves by Greek paideia), tens of thousands in the second (the merely well-off Greeks). Obviously, those groups coincide very well with my estimates from section 5.1 for the numbers of big and small libraries, respectively. I suggest that, at the peak of the Roman Empire, most (though perhaps not all) equestrian households in the eastern part of the Mediterranean (but to some extent also in Italy) would have owned a large collection of Greek literature.[116] Meanwhile, at least in the Greek-speaking world, even

---

[115] Scheidel and Friesen (2009: 12). There used to be a debate as to whether or not the equestrian order was defined purely by wealth; see Wiseman (1970) (this would hardly matter for our purposes, as Scheidel and Friesen's figures derive from considerations of reasonable wealth distribution, instead of the less reliable explicit reports, from antiquity, concerning the numbers of equites).

[116] The mean annual income in this group is estimated, by the same authors, at above 40,000 HS. Assuming a century's survival for a book, a family would have to buy ten rolls a year ("This year we

individuals with very modest claims to elite status would try to have, among their belongings, the tokens of paideia: at the very least, a few rolls of the *Iliad*.[117]

If book ownership was as constitutive to elite identity as such numbers imply, this is at least in some tension with excessively pessimistic, primitivizing views of the place of literacy in ancient society.[118] Conversely, this is also an observation on the scale of the groups aspiring to some kind of elite status. A truly closed caste system, in which essentially everyone other than the senatorial and equestrian elite is shut out, is inconsistent with the distribution of the tokens of paideia suggested here. And so, we may note that the literary papyri of Upper Egypt form a meaningful social document. Their large number and their bottom-heavy distribution (suggesting their origins, mostly, in many small libraries) are consistent with a fairly high rate of book ownership, at least in this region.

It remains true that a book-owning class of as many as 4 percent of the Nile Valley appears surprisingly large. Was Egypt as literate as that? But, even if I wish to resist an overly archaizing view of ancient literacy, I do not ask to modernize it either. Societies with a truly modern level of literacy show a considerably higher penetration of the book. The gold standard is seventeenth-century England: indeed, it is estimated that it had more than 1 million vernacular Bibles in circulation.[119] Coincidentally, the population of pre-industrial England – estimated at roughly 5 million – was about the same as that of Roman Egypt. Multiple ownership of the Bible must have

get the *Republic*") to achieve the thousand rolls of a good big library; this would cost perhaps a couple of hundred HS – very well within reach; see n.121 below. The point is of deep consequence: the fact that one could curate books for long periods made them effective stores of ostentation.

[117] The mean average annual income in this group is estimated at 9,000 HS or more. A nice set of the *Iliad* would not be a negligible expense (many hundreds of HS?), but it would be a very rare expenditure, made once in a lifetime.

[118] Harris (1991) – now something like the traditional view – was written to debunk earlier views that literacy was widespread in Greco-Roman antiquity. As Harris points out, previous scholars were vague and non-quantitative, and so it is hard to say how radical his claims were even in 1991. His conclusion – of about a 10 percent literacy rate – does not strike me as very low. (That this is so may be a mark of Harris' success.) It is certainly the case that antiquity did not possess mass literacy; but it does seem to have had what we may call "mass elite literacy" (Temin, 2006: 147: "The upper classes were educated in Rome, as were most urban slaves. Literacy appears to have been universal for any Roman in a managerial role and may have extended to skilled workers as well."). In general, elite status was always closely entwined, from the classical era onwards, with the culture of the book. It seems that scholarship has more recently swung in this, more positive estimation of Greco-Roman literacy, perhaps because this has been more often considered, recently, through the comparative study with other ancient civilizations. "Within the larger comparative perspective we have just been considering, the Roman elite of the middle Republic now appear unusual in their degree of literacy..." (Feeney, 2016: 196).

[119] Konkola (2000: 15–18). A million Bibles printed between the early sixteenth century and the middle of the seventeenth century is a conservative lower bound.

been common, but the simple conclusion is that most seventeenth-century English households possessed a Bible (even if they could not read it). Papyrus rolls were no doubt more expensive than their equivalent seventeenth-century printed books.[120] But this only partly accounts for the wider spread of the Bible relative to the *Iliad* (since one could own an *Iliad* even by collecting a handful of rolls – a much less significant investment than a complete Bible).[121] Egypt was nowhere like Shakespeare's England. A level of penetration of about 4 percent of households was achieved in England probably as early as the 1530s, and the suggestion is that book owning in Egypt, under Marcus Aurelius, might have been *at most* comparable to that in England under Henry VIII. Put more generally: why own the Bible; why own Homer? In early modern England, the Bible was salvation; in the Greek-speaking Mediterranean, Homer was education. Salvation mattered, ultimately, to about 100 percent of seventeenth-century English households. The implication of the argument so far is that about 1.5 to 4 percent of the population of the Nile Valley, during the Roman era, cared for the display of their paideia. This does not strike me as so absurd.

We can make a few more quantitative comparisons to get a better handle on the significance of the numbers. First of all, a certain subset of the

---

[120] The question of the cost of the ancient book has been discussed primarily in terms of the cost of papyrus (this is related to the question of the transition from roll to codex; I return to this below, n.338). There used to be a view, entrenched in much of the literature, that papyrus was expensive – successfully demolished, in my view, by Skeat (1995), based on evidence from Egypt. The writing surface for a document could cost as little as one-fifth of an obol (Skeat, 1995: 90)! The question of prices outside Egypt remains open (this is Harris' strongest claim: Harris, 1991: 195), but see n.34 above.

[121] The price of an early seventeenth-century Bible is estimated to have ranged from 4 to 14 shillings – so, 48 to 168 pennies, or about 24 to 84 loaves of bread forgone. From Bagnall (2009a: 55–7), I calculate that a complete Bible in Egypt in the fourth century AD would have cost about 4 to 16 solidi, or roughly about 1,000 to 4,000 loaves of bread, labor excluded (10 solidi get you 82 artabas of wheat, with each artaba making between 33 and 36 kg. of bread: Scheidel, 2010: 431 n.13). But this is the entirety of the Bible, with some 130,000 lines: about eight *Iliad*s, or, with allowance for poetry's layout, perhaps about five *Iliad*s. An ancient *Iliad* would thus cost between 200 and 800 loaves of bread. The price for an English Bible of the lower range would buy you the first three rolls of the *Iliad* (low quality). Clothing is a more direct comparison than food (famously, in antiquity they are a store of value as well as a prominent marker of status). From Allen (2009: 5) I calculate the minimum price for clothing for a single person at the equivalent of 30 loaves of bread – once again comparable to a cheap English Bible or a few rolls of the *Iliad*. Notice, however, that from Diocletian's price edict it appears that high-end clothing cost at least two orders of magnitude more than the most basic clothing. The owner of a fancy cloak spent on it about as much as it would take to acquire many hundreds of (admittedly, low-quality) rolls. A minimal piece of clothing and a fancy one: like a small library and a big one. The *Iliad* was not a necessity, and, of course, was not bought by the masses; but there is nothing unlikely about as many as the top 4 percent being able to afford it.

makers and consumers of culture would be engaged in teaching – those whose work was the cultural reproduction of the elite. How many were there? Second, authors were recruited from a certain set of individuals with the access to authorship. What was this set and which fraction, out of this set, was recruited?

First, the size of the education labor force. It is not very helpful to compare the elite with the number of grammatical or elementary teachers – as the scope of such education could have been somewhat wider than the elite, even in an expansive sense, and since its teachers would be socially much lower than the class of authors.[122] Nevertheless, the teachers of rhetoric – providing advanced education, the polishing up required for high status – catered to a group very tightly related to the leisured elite, and their ranks were quite closely related to (if of course larger than) those of rhetorical authors.[123]

To assess the number of teachers of rhetoric, then, it would be good to have a sense of the number of their potential students. We can certainly look for upper boundaries. If we suppose that the bulk of the Greek-speaking, male decurional class (100,000 individual adults?) went to rhetorical school at age 14 and stayed there on average for less than two years,[124] we may have perhaps something on the order of 5,000 students enrolled at a rhetorical school (this, at the demographic peak).[125] This is in the nature of an upper bound, and we do not have anything to indicate, seriously, the size of each individual class (though you always assume, in the discourse

---

[122] The relatively low status of the grammarian-teacher is the main theme of Kaster (1988), admittedly focusing on late antiquity; but Cribiore (2001) paints a similar picture, broadly speaking, for antiquity itself, saying (54): "It is important to realize that a teacher's lack of dependability was often due to his usually precarious financial and social position."

[123] As will be evident, my understanding of rhetorical education in antiquity depends on Cribiore (2007).

[124] There was a theoretical expectation of five years of schooling (Cribiore, 2001: 56–9), but few completed such courses (and no diplomas depended on this). The reality was much shorter (Cribiore, 2007: 179–83, is a discursive survey of short educational careers; the full catalogue she provides, 323–7, of lengths of schooling that can be reconstructed for many of Libanius' students shows, by my calculation, 11 students for less than a year; 14 for a year to two; 19 for two to three years; seven for three to four years; three for five years or more. Those who left could have gone to other schools, but Libanius must have been among the more successful teachers. As Cribiore explains, the point is that you left when you got yourself something better to do.).

[125] Precise reconstruction of ancient age structures might be a chimera (Scheidel, 2001) but for our rough purposes the calculation is obvious and straightforward: those aged precisely 14 were about 3 to 4 percent of the adults. A quick comparison: ancient rhetorical education had a social role perhaps not unlike that of university education in early modern Europe, and Oxford and Cambridge – holding a near-monopoly – each had, at any given time, something between 1,000 and 3,000 students on different occasions in the sixteenth and seventeenth centuries (O'Day, 2009: 80). As noted above, early modern England had about a fifth of the population of the Greek-speaking Roman Mediterranean – but it was also, on the whole, rather more literate.

surrounding education, students performing in front of each other:[126] so, at least a small group). Surely something on the order of 1,000 teachers would be up to the task of educating those students. This is at the peak, and there may therefore have been, in the Hellenistic era, no more than a few hundred teachers of rhetoric. Now, even the truly elite sophists of the Imperial era engaged, in some sense, in teaching (the coveted top position was that of the chair of rhetoric in Athens!), and yet there must have been many teachers of rhetoric, too obscure to be considered, even in their own eyes, as authorial "rhetors".[127] A thousand *teachers of rhetoric*, at the peak, is therefore doubly an upper bound for the number of *authorial rhetors* at the peak. This agrees well with the few hundred rhetorical authors, at the peak, deduced on pages 588–96 above.

Now, a word concerning the ratio of elite to authorship. The implication of roughly 30,000 authors prior to 200 CE is of roughly 1,000 authors active simultaneously, on average. This would make the overall group of authors about 1 percent of the entire leisured elite (or even a little more, since about 100,000 Greek-speaking members of the leisured elite is an estimate for the demographic peak). Is this reasonable?

First of all, it bears repeating that authorship correlated most directly, indeed, with the *leisured* class. This needs to be emphasized. It is rare that we have any reliable information on the social and economic background of any cultural figures (which is, of course, significant in and of itself: an elite background could be taken for granted). Simon the Shoemaker, described in our sources as an associate of Socrates and one of the early authors of Socratic dialogues, would be, if genuine, the clearest case of an author of relatively modest background. It is partly for this (good!) reason that some scholars are skeptical. Shoemakers were the kind of people of whom Socrates would speak (hence, it is easy to imagine the rise of a fictional Socratic shoemaker); were they the kind of people to write *on* Socrates?[128] Or we may consider Aeschines the Socratic. A chreia preserved

---

[126] It seems as if at least one standard teaching environment was that of a fairly large room – larger than the usual ancient living room – which could have accommodated many pupils in lectures and, further, would have been used by the students themselves for declamation, always one of the hallmarks of rhetorical education (Cribiore, 2007: 44–7, citing in particular archaeological finds).

[127] So, for instance, Titus Flavius Aelianus Artemidorus (Puech, 2002: 148–9), specifically honored by the city of Amyzon for the teaching of rhetoric (as well as of philosophy). Such teachers would have generated fewer inscriptions on average, and so it is not surprising that Puech's records are mostly of "rhetors" in a more elevated sense.

[128] Thus, a likely enough scenario is that the dialogue by Phaedo, titled Simon, had a shoemaker as its central protagonist; which in turn spawned a pseudepigraphic tradition of writing dialogues from the point of view of that Simon, who eventually coalesced into a fictional philosopher, presented by Diogenes Laertius as genuine (see Kahn, 1996: 9–11); Diogenes' biography is in II.122–4; naturally,

by both Seneca (*De Benef.* I.8) and Diogenes Laertius (II.34) has him tell Socrates that he, Aeschines, was poor[129] and so could give him no other gift but himself ("But no, that's the greatest gift," replies Socrates.). The biographical tradition on Aeschines[130] reveals a figure of contention: how close was he to Socrates? Did he steal his dialogues? Even his father was in dispute; Plato's evidence in the *Apology* (33e) is decisive (the father's name was Lysanias). But others in antiquity nevertheless claimed that Aeschines' father was "Charinus, the sausage-maker" (DL II.60). This provides a hint to the source of the tradition concerning Aeschines' poverty. The picture of the indigent urchin, making his sausages with whatever scraps come his way, belongs in the varied stories of plagiarism to which Aeschines was subjected.[131] He probably was not rich, but, as with the case of Simon, we are at the mercy of a biographical tradition that valued vividness of persona more than it did accuracy – more, indeed, then it valued the very existence of its subjects. We can note that, among the other early Socratics, Antisthenes was attacked not for poverty but for having a Thracian mother,[132] while Aristippus was taunted for his allegedly luxurious lifestyle (obviously concocted out of his genuine philosophical attachment to hedonism).[133] The story on Phaedo was that he was sold to slavery and was forced to become a male prostitute! Perhaps to render this even more salacious, Diogenes Laertius begins by telling us that Phaedo was from a noble family in Elis (DL II.105). Nothing of substance is known about Euclid of Megara's biography, and it is only for the two remaining genuine authors of Socratic dialogues that we have firm biographical evidence. These two are Plato and Xenophon, however – and with them we already

---

the historicity of Simon is subject to a debate – into which, remarkably, even archaeological finds are brought as witness! See Sellars, 2003, and references therein). Curiously, the Mishna knows a second-century CE Jewish rabbi, Yohanan Ha-Sandlar, literally, "John the Shoemaker": in this case, too, the name might be misleading (is it possible that Ha-Sandlar, "the Shoemaker" is a corruption of Ha-Alexandroni, "of Alexandria"? Rosenfeld and Menirav, 2005: 208 n.91), but it belongs to an entire list of such artisan-rabbis (Ayali, 1987: 100–1, 143–51); the cultural setting of rabbis in Palestine was truly different.

[129] *Penēs*: could well mean "not a member of the liturgical class" (the very top elite of a few hundred families): Ober (1989: 195).

[130] Diogenes Laertius II.60–4. As is often the case, we have practically nothing else, but Diogenes is very inconsistent and so provides us with the sense of the tradition as a whole.

[131] This emphasis on Aeschines, always in need of cash, also goes together with another tradition, which can be read to mean that he composed speeches and taught rhetoric for pay (DL II.63) – inherently possible, though it should be remembered that no fewer than four of his namesakes, recorded by Diogenes, were rhetoricians (one of them, of course, the canonical rhetor, Demosthenes' enemy).

[132] Diogenes Laertius VI.1.

[133] "Why do you pay 50 drachmas for a partridge?" "Well, would you pay an obol for it?" "Sure" "Fifty drachmas for me are like an obol to you" (DL II.66).

get near the very top of the Athenian elite. I dwell on this Socratic group because it emerges from the most egalitarian moment of ancient history, and because it also shares an ideology that puts the qualities of the mind above worldly advantages. Where can we find non-elite authors, if not here?[134] But it is not merely that we cannot ascertain the presence of the non-elite, even in this group. The point is, rather, that, even here, alleged material needs – even the very practice of charging fees for one's services – were routinely deployed as *slurs*.

Among other things, the Socratic tradition served as the Greek conduit for the habit – universal to all cultures – to reflect critically upon wealth and to develop some variation of the "puritanical complex".[135] Later philosophers would make such material abnegation into the basis of their philosophy. *Becoming* poor was possible; Diogenes the Cynic gave up his wealth. In his case, the biography is entirely novelistic, but it is significant and perhaps even trustworthy that he is said to have had some wealth to give up (the son of a banker, no less).[136] Half a millennium later Lucian's own novelistic invective against a contemporary cynic known as "Peregrinus Proteus" begins with a biographical crescendo of vices (adultery, the rape of a boy, then parricide); what is interesting to us is that Peregrinus is imagined to have escaped from the charges of rape by paying off the family of the raped boy, to the tune of 3,000 drachmas.[137] What we find are, so to speak, "champagne cynics".[138] There is no expression in Greek philosophy of a critique of wealth, coming from outside the elite.[139] Finally, the only group for which authorship was a vehicle for social mobility was that of Greek freedmen, serving powerful Roman masters – especially grammarians and historians.[140] It is typical that this emerges

---

[134] Evidence for *elite* authors is easy to find. The philosopher Philo's brother was said to be the richest man in Alexandria (Josephus Ant. XX 100). The doctor Crinas of Massalia left 10 million HS in his will (Pliny, *N.H.* XXIX 9). The wealth of Pliny the Younger is estimated at about 20 million HS (Duncan Jones, 1982: 17–23).

[135] Goody (2009: chap. 6).        [136] DL VI.20.

[137] Lucian, *On the Death of Peregrinus* 9. Admittedly this is a theme of Lucian, who makes his cynics into Tartuffe-like figures (Theagenes, a cynic associate of Peregrinus, is said to have made 15 talents from moneylending *after* having become a cynic: *On the Death of Peregrinus* 30). Perhaps the one solid fact is that even a cynic would have to survive somehow: you could give up your wealth and still prosper only if you had the compensating social contacts.

[138] This is not necessarily the mark of invective. Demonax, a Cynic who was something of a mentor to Lucian, is said by him to have come from a very substantial family – but to aspire even higher, to philosophy (Lucian, *Life of Demonax* 3).

[139] De Ste. Croix (1981: 425–41) is eloquent on this absence, which extends, in his view, even to Christianity.

[140] In these non-performative genres, the status embodied by the author can be somewhat elided. We noted above how grammarians sometimes emerge from the rank of freedmen, p. 276, n.49; for

within antiquity's least egalitarian context: such scholarly freedmen represent not the power of scholarship to transcend social boundaries but, rather, the power of Roman wealth to bestow the requisite authorial status even upon the more marginal members of their households.

We touch upon a historiographical cliché: the disdain of the ancient elites towards labor.[141] In fact, the rise in authorship can be seen as yet another expression of the rise of a specialized economy in classical Greece, one that made labor highly visible.[142] Socrates, for sure, was keenly aware of this new world of crafts, a recurring theme of his discourse in both Plato and Xenophon.[143] Perhaps it is wrong to extrapolate from Plutarch's comments against the "banausic" to a universally shared ideology. In truth, ideologies are rarely shared universally, and what was common to most Greek authors was, more simply, the fact that, even though they were familiar with the world of labor, they still viewed it from a certain distance.

The reality is simple and well known. To become an author one had first to have rare privileges: a childhood of education, an adult life spent in a writing for which there was no commercial market. Further, and somewhat less obviously, we need to recall our conclusion from section 2.3.1 above: absent the market, the very *existence* of one's work as a social reality would depend upon its status. You needed someone to accept the work: so, authors needed to position themselves within well-defined social networks. The group of authors therefore simply had to be a specially defined subset of the leisure class.

And, indeed: once the option of authorship becomes at all available – why not avail oneself of it? The possession of books was a marker of status; the writing of them, generally speaking, was even more so. We may begin by noting that even political rulers quite often wished to become authors. A few quick examples: Dionysius of Syracuse, as noted in note 45 above, produced a tragedy; Ophellas, king of Cyrene in the late fourth century, wrote a geographical treatise; Attalus III, the last king of Pergamon in the

---

history, see Cornell (2013: 334), who cites at least six cases of freedmen writing history praising their erstwhile masters. (Slavery was social death; freedmen were antiquity's ghostwriters.)

[141] De Ste. Croix (1981: 274–5); as he points out, such views need not have been shared by the non-elite, an observation amplified by Cuomo (2007), who goes on to qualify (chap. 3) this historiographical cliché: workers, in antiquity, were very happy to present themselves as such.

[142] The evidence for Athens is discussed in Ehrenberg (1951) – based on comedy – and, more recently, Harris (2002); it is often noted that we do not have comparable evidence outside Athens, which makes the invention of prose authorship and prose genres stand out as examples of specializations whose *sources* are non-Athenian!

[143] The use of the craft analogy by Plato's Socrates is very well known; Roochnik (1996) is a detailed study. (For some of the evidence for Xenophon, see Roochnik, 1996: 8 n.21, 19 n.6.)

latter part of the second century, wrote a treatise on agriculture; Cleopatra VII, the last queen of Egypt in the second half of the first century, is said to have written a treatise on medicine (or was it on "cosmetics"?). Juba II was installed by Augustus as king of Mauretania, near the end of the first century; he is well remembered for his historical works, cited by Pliny among others. A somewhat depressing list, often of the rulers of kingdoms in descent, turning in solace to literature. But in ascendant Rome, too, significant political figures often sought the status of the author, beginning with Cato the Elder, and then through central figures such as Sulla, Cicero and Caesar (as we will note on pages 657–8 below, the writing of history, especially, became – in the late Republic – almost a required badge of elite status). This was continued by a long list of emperors who wished to be remembered for their literary accomplishments, beginning with Augustus himself (author of the *Res Gestae*!) all the way down (in our period) to Marcus Aurelius. Royal patrons, even when not seeking to become authors themselves, sought the presence of authors in their court – a practice that became routine in the late fourth century (see section 3.3.2 above) with the end of the Athenian dominance. Desirable and accessible (to the elite), it is possible that post-classical authorship operated not far from the point of saturation: whenever the right skills, inclinations and circumstances combined, one would become an author. But many people did not have the facility with words; were too philistine; or were too preoccupied with business, a military career, political intrigue.

Now, let me make a quick contemporary comparison. Authorship was prestigious in the twentieth century, as well – indeed, felt by many to be supremely self-fulfilling; many among the educated possess the intellectual resources, as well as the leisure – in retirement, if not prior to that – to write. What is the contemporary ratio of authorship? The numbers are not readily available, but we may make some inferences.[144]

(1)   The Bureau of Labor Statistics estimated that there were 129,100 "writers and authors" and 1,267,700 "post-secondary teachers" in the United States in 2012 (searches through www.bls.gov/ooh). The precision is absurd but it suggests the order of magnitude. The "post-secondary teachers" are a large group that includes many who never become authors, but it may be compared with the number of PhD

---

[144]   It is a little surprising, but in fact librarians do not keep track of authors, counting, instead, books. It is thus easy to find the numbers of new books published in a given year, but I did not find ready sources for the number of contemporary authors. Below, then, I offer some pointers to those figures.

degrees awarded annually in the United States: in the academic year 1999/2000 this number was 106,494; in 2009/10 this number was 140,505 (https://nces.ed.gov/fastfacts/display.asp?id=72). The millions of individuals granted a PhD are a considerably larger group than those who pursue writing and teaching for a living – as our graduate students soon find out. "Writers and authors" is a smaller group whose main occupation is writing. The many individuals with a "normal" career who just happened to publish a book would not be counted in either rubric.

(2) The number of "new titles" published in the United States early in the twentieth century hovered at first between several thousands and a little over 10,000, then rose gradually to be counted in the tens of thousands annually, but this has jumped early in the twenty-first century to reach about 200,000 "new titles" annually, a development usually ascribed to the spread of the personal computer (Greco, 2013: 35–6). It seems that a very recent trend towards self-publishing, in particular, allows even greater numbers.[145] Now, a "new title" does not mean a debutant author (a certain number of titles are translated, and a great many are new titles by established authors). The annual number of debutant authors in the United States rose through the twentieth century from the many hundreds, rising gradually to the thousands and finally jumping more recently to the tens of thousands. This, in fact, is consistent with the estimate of over 1 million authors active today.

(3) What is the denominator against which such numbers should be assessed? For the modern equivalent of the "leisured elite", I will take the college-educated. While many books are written by individuals of lesser educational attainment, in the past few decades especially a college education has become, in the United States, nearly a necessary condition for aspiring to any significant cultural status, perhaps our best approximation, then, to the mere book owners of a handful of *Iliad* rolls in the Nile Valley. Now, the number of bachelor's degrees conferred annually in the United States rose from tens of thousands, early in the twentieth century, to over a million in the last couple of decades, and is now approaching

---

[145] From Bowker's report on self-publishing in the United States from 2008 to 2013 (http://media.bowker.com/documents/bowker_selfpublishing_report2013.pdf): "A new analysis of U.S. ISBN data by ProQuest affiliate Bowker reveals that the number of self-published titles in 2013 increased to more than 458,564, up 17 percent over 2012 and 437 percent over 2008." (Reassuringly, Bowker goes on to suggest the numbers might finally be stabilizing.)

2 million (see http://nces.ed.gov/programs/coe/indicator_cvc.asp
and www.census.gov/hhes/socdemo/education/data/cps/historical
for detailed data going back to 1940; overview in Snyder, 1993: 67).

We find, then, that through the twentieth century the ratio of college-
educated Americans to American authors was indeed about 1:100 – the
ratio broken, perhaps, with the rise of the personal computer. These are
substantial numbers. When your degree is conferred, look around your
graduating class: one in 50 is going to write a book! And yet, even now,
even with the personal computer: no more than a small fraction of those
who can write do write. In any event, this comparison suggests that
a substantially higher number of ancient authors would imply
a surprisingly high propensity to write books, among the educated.
I envision perhaps about 1,500 authors, at the peak. Anything higher, at
about 2,000 to 3,000 authors active simultaneously, and we reach
a fraction of authorship comparable to the world of the PC.

While the comparison of sheer numbers is telling, and helpful for the
sense of the emerging limits, the social realities underlying authorship in
antiquity, and in the contemporary world, are of course starkly different.
This is, in particular, the conclusion of the argument from Chapter 2,
pages 189–94, concerning the absence of ancient *graphomania*. As modern
book culture came to be defined by a market for books, it became natural
for authors to seek validation from the market directly, thus instilling the
hope, in any would-be authors, that their fame is just a single best-seller
away. In this sense, authorship, today, is open to a wide social stratum,
defined by education. Such was not the case in antiquity, when books
gained audiences through the position of their authors. Thus, it was simply
absurd, absent the requisite social capital, even to try. Ancient authorship,
then, was not equally distributed among the social strata but was, instead,
much more concentrated near the top. The examples cited above of rulers
who chose to become authors, of prominent Roman politicians who did
the same, were not sheer anecdotes. Many, perhaps most, of our authors
could well have had an income comparable at the equestrian level, so that,
in this group, the incidence of authorship was not around a single percent
but perhaps nearer to 10 percent. This already seems to push at the limit of
the distribution of skills and even beyond (surely, some of those books
must, indeed, have been ghostwritten: see note 140 above).[146] It seems

---

[146] There is surprisingly little direct evidence for ghostwriting in antiquity: van der Blom (2011: 557–9);
it was generally frowned upon, which makes the paucity of the evidence even more curious: why
was this accusation not thrown about more regularly?

likely, at any rate, that a very substantial fraction – most? – of those who could both write and command an audience for their writing did so. The canon had established an exalted identity, "the author," which, throughout antiquity and beyond, would always remain a prize, coveted by many. In this, too, we are the heirs of the Greeks.

## 5.5  Coda: By Way of Methodology

It is easy to imagine the critique of this chapter, going through my arguments and puncturing them, one by one, to conclude: "Wish that we could; unfortunately, we cannot really know how many authors there were in antiquity."

Let me engage for a moment with this response. I do not disagree with its underlying call for precisely delimiting the border between the knowable and the unknowable. I claim that such a response is simply wrong about the position of this border, ultimately because it does not understand the nature of probabilities precisely. Let me explain.

My critic would, of course, agree we can say *something*. The attested 5,000 authors are a hard fact of sorts (my critic would object to my statistical projection of this number, but, if, at least, I went and read every bleeping article of the RE, I could ultimately convince even my most skeptical critic). In addition, at some point, I imagine I could find a number sufficiently absurdly high for any critic to agree that it was above the number of ancient authors. Let us say 500,000 authors.

I could get my critic, then, to agree that the number of ancient authors was above 5,000 and, let us say, below 500,000. His point would be that we are not entitled to say anything beyond those limits of our certain knowledge. Our knowledge is entirely summed up in the statement:

$$500,000 > n > 5,000$$

This algebraic expression does not represent our knowledge precisely, however. This is because our knowledge is a knowledge of probabilities. With this in mind, the above position translates into meaning the following: if we were to plot a graph of the probabilities of the numbers of authors, this would form a horizontal straight line between the values 5,000 and 500,000, falling off sharply at those boundaries; something like this figure.

5,000                              500,000

This is evidently false. It is true that we can rule out fewer than 5,000 authors and more than 500,000. The zero probabilities above and below those points are justifiable. But it should be obvious that it is simply wrong that all numbers in between 5,000 and 500,000 are equiprobable. Surely there is sometimes evidence that, while not ruling out a particular number, or proving conclusively that a certain number is correct, makes certain regions of the graph more likely, others less likely. It is morally certain that, when all this evidence is aggregated, we will have a curve, and not a straight line. Indeed, it is extremely likely, in this case, that, when all information is processed, we will find a distribution of the probabilities in the form of a peak surrounded by two tails.[147]

There is certainly room for debate concerning the precise position of the peak, as well as concerning the steepness of the descents from the peak to the tails. Of course I welcome such a debate: getting this debate started, indeed, is the whole point. I know I have traced but a rough opening. I was the first to try and clear a path through this jungle – doing so in the hope that others might yet turn it into a highway.

What I wish to emphasize, by way of concluding this methodological interlude, is that knowledge of probabilities is a form of knowledge – indeed, the only form of knowledge open to us, as historians and simply as humans. This is why I resist the skeptics, who puncture evidence to pronounce "We cannot really know" when, in fact, there are probabilistic arguments to be made, and so knowledge to be had. The proper task of the historian, as I see it, is to assert the truth when it can be asserted. Which means *exactly* the same thing as asserting probabilities when they can be asserted. And, since "We cannot really know" ultimately boils down to a resistance to any probabilistic claims, it ends up as a counter-productive retreat from any assertion. "We cannot really know" is not an admission of ignorance; it is a destruction of knowledge. I now close the methodological parenthesis.

---

[147] There are circumstances in which a multimodal curve is conceivable. Indeed, this would often emerge in discussions of chronology, which are precisely analogous. Suppose we know that an ancient mathematician was attested by Geminus. This provides us with a "terminus ante quem": he must have been active prior to about 50 BCE. Suppose he also directly uses a result by Hippocrates of Chios; this would provide a "terminus post quem": he must have been active after about 450 BCE. Many historians would stop at that and say "We can only say he was active somewhere in between 450 and 50 BCE", and would resist any further attempts to make the date more precise. This in effect implies a flat curve of probabilities in between 450 and 50, and this approach, once again, is surely wrong. In fact, since we know independently that there was much more mathematical activity at certain times in antiquity, the distribution should be understood as a bimodal curve with two peaks at around 350 BCE and 200 BCE.

The argument marshaled so far in this chapter suggests that the probabilities, for the number of authors prior to 200 CE, are almost entirely contained within the range from 20,000 to 60,000. While a smaller or larger number is possible, it would also be genuinely surprising. This range perhaps corresponds to something such as 90 percent of the probabilities, if not even more than that.

This is a range of 40,000 possibilities, no more, and the central segment (30,000 to 40,000) occupies a quarter of that, *even without any added considerations of probabilities*. In fact, I did produce in section 5.3 fairly suggestive arguments in favor of the segment between 30,000 and 40,000. It is thus very reasonable to assign it *considerably more than a quarter* of the probability; I would say even in excess of a half.

My claim, then, is that it is more likely than not (more than 50 percent probable) that there were between 30,000 and 40,000 authors in antiquity. The range from 22,500 to 45,000 has a probability well in excess of that (it occupies practically all of the reasonable downwards tail, as well as a good chunk of the upwards one). Let us say that it has about 75 percent probability. I think this is what we, as ancient historians, mean when we pronounce a historical claim "likely".

I therefore claim that "likely there were between 22,500 and 45,000 authors prior to 200 CE".

With about 30 generations for the pre-200 era, the range from 22,500 to 45,000 translates, on average, to 750 to 1,500 authors working simultaneously. I think it is reasonable to translate this range, more qualitatively, into "about 1,000 authors, or perhaps somewhat more".

I conclude that there likely were, in the era from the late fifth century BCE to 200 CE, about 1,000 authors active simultaneously, or perhaps somewhat more, on average. This is the kernel of historical fact which I will take, moving on from this statistical chapter into the historical consequences of the following chapter.

Before I conclude, I note another substantial result: the finding that, likely, about 1:5 to 1:9 of all ancient authors are now attested. Let me finally comment on the meaning of this value.

I suppose most of us harbor, to begin with, two assumptions: (1) that there were relatively speaking few books in antiquity, what with this being an *ancient* culture; and (2) that ancient culture is mostly lost, what with its being so distant and lost in the mists of time. These are two ways of expressing our deeply entrenched sense that *antiquity is far away*. The reason I think many of us harbor these assumptions is that I know I used to harbor them, myself, before working on this book. Only now, having engaged in this quantitative exercise, have I come to notice that these two assumptions are in fact *inconsistent*.

If, indeed, we are to assume a society with but few authors and books, then the overall size of written culture ought to be small, and so there would be few books to preserve, few authors to know. It should be immediately obvious, then, that a Greece with few books would be a Greece we know very well, because, in fact, there are massive amounts of text and of attested authors now known.

Conversely, if we assume that ancient culture is effectively lost, almost all authors and works now forgotten, then we also need to assume – given the scale of what is in fact still attested – that this was in fact an astronomically large civilization.

What we find, instead, is that ancient civilization had many books, many authors; and that it is also largely – though not entirely – known. Antiquity is *not* all that far away.

Of course, in some ways it is. In particular, we really no longer know a great deal of the *contents* of ancient culture. In the most general terms, what is "knowing" an ancient figure? Take an example: we could tell, based on the literary sources alone, that there was a Greek epigrammatist (some of his epigrams extant!) who was also an Epicurean philosopher, active in Italy in the first century BCE, called Philodemus. Would we have "known" Philodemus, then? It is only thanks to the chance discovery of the Villa dei Papiri that we can begin to form a sense of the vast range of his achievement. Even so, all that remains is fragmentary. Before the papyri, Philodemus was both lost and present, depending on the level of granularity with which he was studied. He was almost entirely lost – to a scholar *of Philodemus*. (And he often remains more lost than found, to the scholars whose interest is truly focused, in the detail of a particular work). To a scholar interested in ancient cultural life at a more coarse-grained level, Philodemus was broadly known even prior to the discovery of the papyri. So, ancient culture is lost, in most cases, for the study of individual authors; it survives, to a large extent, for the study of its broad contours.

Let us say, then, that 5,000 authors are attested out of 30,000. It is true that we know only a sixth of the authors, and that we know almost all of them only for the purposes of a broad-brush study. But this means that we know of *almost everyone worth knowing*.

I will explain. Knowing one-sixth of the authors does not mean that we know the top author, then author number seven, then author number 13, losing all those in between. No: clearly, the authors who are still attested tend to be the ones who were more important already back then. Neither is it the case that we have precisely the 5,000 "top authors" from antiquity, losing the names of everyone from, so to speak, 5,001 on down. No: we have a very thick representation at the top, which begins to thin out at some point; then we have mixed representation, until we hit a few sporadic authors, very low on the ancient ranking. To get a handle on the significance of our loss, it makes sense to ask: who is *the top lost author from antiquity?* Let's call him Leipon.

Leipon was likely to be active in a low-attestation field, in which even quite important authors would be more likely to fall through the cracks. The best options, then, would be history, medicine or the novel.

If Leipon were a historian, we would first imagine him as the author of a local history: surely the local would be the more readily forgotten? For all the top 20 cities surveyed in Ober (2008), however, we have at least one attested author of a local history. Had Leipon written on a city even as important as, say, Sicyon, he would have to have been merely the no. 2 historian of that city. Going outside Ober's 20, there are a number of medium-sized cities of some importance we might consider: for instance, how about Colophon, in Asia Minor? Home city of Nicander, protagonist and victim of several wars, surely someone in antiquity wrote its history – and yet, none is known: so is this, maybe, Leipon? But this is hardly impressive, and perhaps history is not such a promising field after all. Attestation of historians was sparse, but discerning: it was clear as to which the important events and localities were, who their important chroniclers were. The thousand historians collected by Jacoby include, I suggest, the top 200 to 300, and the rest were perhaps equally forgettable.

We need a field that is not merely sparsely attested but also capriciously so. That is, we need a field in which tastes change enough so that someone can be considered important, and then fall out of favor and eventually out of memory. Both medicine and the novel fit this better, and Leipon should be found here (he could still be a historian, but perhaps a historian of contemporary events, of great interest to his contemporaries, less so to future generations? More on this on pages 681–3 below). Leipon may have been the leader of a medical fad (later than Pliny, but well before Galen: so, late first century CE), which could have been the toast of all of Rome as long as he was alive. For a brief while he could have been the most celebrated medical author in the entire Mediterranean; and yet, we could fail to know a single thing about him (even though, unaware, we could even now have a few papyrus fragments of his works!). Or he could have been the author of a massively successful novel, one that, for a decade, *everyone* read. It might have been a masterpiece; we can never tell.

This, then, is the limit of our knowledge: we do not know the fads, the ephemeral. This underlines the significance of what we do know: by and large, we know the constants.

We can now be precise about the nature of our knowledge of ancient culture. We have truly lost much of the detailed contents. We have also lost even the trace of some passing fads. What we do know, truly well, is the broad contours of the constants. A lot has been lost. But there is no submerged Atlantis, entire swaths of ancient culture of which no trace survives.

Classical scholarship is the discipline of close reading par excellence, and this is part of the reason why we tend to think of ancient civilization as mostly lost. But, if we approach ancient civilization from a distance, interested now not in the detail of Philodemus' debates with fellow-Epicureans but with the contours of a career – genres, locations, connections – he would still be there, with or without a Vesuvius. The pattern of attestation of ancient culture would make sure that such a figure, at such a level of detail, would still survive.

This is one claim, then, of this chapter. For the purposes of studying scale, space and canon, ancient civilization is fundamentally extant, making a book such as this one possible. Let us move on, then, to study scale in action.

CHAPTER 6

# *Scale in Action*
## *Stability and Its End*

The preceding chapters suggested some absolute numbers for a well-defined span considered mostly as a whole: antiquity, from Pericles to Caracalla. I have implied so far that, century by century, the number of authors did not fluctuate by much. Helpful, for our purposes; but also surprising, and of course in need of qualification.

The reason for the stability is simple. We can see here the interaction of two forces, largely canceling each other out. On the one hand, Greek civilization reached out and gradually Hellenized most of the elites of the eastern Mediterranean (and some of those of the west, in particular in Italy, even if their language remained Latin). On the other hand, Greek civilization of the early fourth century was, compared to other pre-modern societies, by far the most egalitarian. This implies a greater rate of participation of both audiences and authors. (I shall return to this below, when commenting upon the rise of cultural activity in the fifth century.) The civilization of the Imperial era was considerably less egalitarian – in fact, was probably marked by shocking inequality and stratification. Now, the overall size of the Greek world, in demographic terms, was at least (but not much more than) 7 to 8 million in about 350 BCE.[1] The "eastern Mediterranean plus" region, which participated in Greek culture 500 years later, had about 30 million people.[2] The base expanded by a factor of three to four. The idea is plausible that stratification tightened by about a comparable factor. This is the basic outline of ancient cultural stability. It goes without saying that the two processes were not precisely synchronized. There ought to have been ups and downs: Hellenization progressing at a faster, or slower, rate than inequality. The two processes syncopate, and, in

---

[1] This is taking the lower end of Hansen's (2006) estimate – the most respected, and yet usually treated as somewhat optimistic – of 7.5 to 10 million Greeks in the middle of the fourth century.
[2] Scheidel (2007: 48): about 25 million in the eastern part of the Empire; about 10 million in Italy and Sicily.

section 6.1.2, I note the potential significance of such syncopation for the rhythm of ancient culture.

Section 6.1, touching on the historical ground covered already, moves somewhat more rapidly. In section 6.1.1, I revisit the growth of the Athenian canon and its surrounding literary system, through the perspective of the rapid rise in scale through the fifth century BCE; in section 6.1.2, I touch on the possibility that, following the cultural heyday of Hellenism in the third century BCE, the second century, especially its early part, went through something of a trough.

Following that comes the main task of this chapter. In the previous part of the book I have studied the Hellenistic era, and the coming of the Romans, in terms of an opposition based on space: a duality between Athens and Alexandria, formed and dissolved. In this part, I study the Imperial era, and late antiquity, in terms of an opposition based on scale: the number of authors, reaching, perhaps, a peak in the second century – followed by a third-century collapse. Sections 6.2 to 6.3 discuss the Imperial era, sections 6.4 to 6.5 discuss late antiquity. In both cases, I start with a detailed consideration of the numbers, followed by a cultural account. Section 6.2 is a study in the scale of the second century CE; section 6.3 follows with a qualitative account of culture in the era (this is selective and superficial: the goal is not to provide an account of Imperial-era culture but to produce supporting arguments for the quantitative account, as well as for the following account of late antiquity). Section 6.4 is a study in the scale of the third century CE; section 6.5 is more expansive, providing a qualitative account of culture from the third century and through its transformation into the culture of late antiquity (for late antiquity, the qualitative account is much more detailed, as this is the goal of my quantitative discussion).

## 6.1   Scale before Rome: The Rise and Wobble?

### *6.1.1   The Rise*

I have argued on pages 566–8 above for the relatively small numbers of archaic authorial names. Poets and sages gained fame, one by one, for generations – slowly.

This clearly changed with Athens. Here is the outline. I have suggested on page 556 above that one of the distinguishing features of Athens (as eloquently argued by Ober, 2008) was its explicit *training for skills through participation*. The city manufactured public performance as a reliable, repeated practice – and it trained a cohort of citizens as tragic authors, adding, a generation later, two more cohorts: rhetors and comic authors. This concentration of experienced dramatists and speakers (Athens' version of poets and sages) was, as we can see, unprecedented, an outcome of an unprecedented public dedication to widespread public skills. Partly because this was unprecedented, but mostly through the sheer political power of Athens, these new cohorts gained recognition across the Greek world.

For the following discussion, I rely on the database compiled by Mark Pyzyk, who, as mentioned on page 589 above, has read through the entire *New Pauly* and tabulated information for all the Greek individuals there recorded by name from the fifth and fourth centuries BCE.[3] Of these 1,331 individuals, a large minority is of what I call "authors" (the bulk of the remainder known purely for political and military exploits). This database is organized by Pyzyk into six chronological "boxes" of a third of a century each, and I will study the breakthrough in scale of the Greek literary system through four of these boxes: the second and final thirds of the fifth century (in Pyzyk's terms, "5.2", "5.3"), the first and the second of the fourth ("4.1", "4.2"). I will mostly aggregate numbers, but for the earliest – and smallest – of the four studied here, 5.2, it is worthwhile looking at the names themselves. These may be organized as follows:[4]

## Athens 39[5]

Performative (33):
Tragedy (14): Achaeus, Aristarchus, Carcinus, Euripides, Gnesippus, Hieronymus, Ion, Iophon, Morsimus, Neophron, Nicomachus, Patrocles, Philocles, Sophocles.

---

[3] As noted in the discussion on pp. 589–90 above, Pyzyk's numbers are something of an undercount, since he relies on *Brill's New Pauly* (and not on the original RE, which effectively did aim at exhaustive coverage of cultural figures), though this may not be very significant: when I compared my own counting, based on search functions within the NP, as against (1) Pyzyk's direct reading of the BNP, (2) Cicero's *Brutus* and (3) PGRSRE, the numbers rose by a similar factor of three in all cases, even though (2) appears to be near-exhaustive and (3) surely is. The conclusion is that, at least for some purposes, we do not lose much information on the classical era by relying on the *New Pauly*, and I will mostly ignore this caveat.
[4] Dating people is hard. Is it correct to put Euripides, for instance, as Pyzyk does, in this box rather than the following one? Then again, which evidence should you trust? (Is Corinna even a genuine poet?). I usually leave Pyzyk's judgements in place, as they follow those of the *New Pauly* closely and so represent "the consensus of scholarship". I do remove the following three authors to box 5.3: Melanippides of Melos, Xeniades of Corinth and (more importantly) Herodotus of Halicarnassus (see the discussion on p. 231, n.282, above concerning the "publication" of Herodotus' history).
[5] I count here authors whose main locus of activity was Athens: so, Ion of Chios (and I count him as a tragedian), as well as Anaxagoras.

Comedy (10): Aristomenes, Callias, Crates, Cratinus, Diopeithes, Ecphantides, Euphornius, Hermippus, Pherecrates, Telecleides.

Rhetors (9): Andocides, Callias, Critias, Dionysius, Diopeithes, Ephilates, Myronides, Tolmides, Thucydides.

Non-performative (6):

3 architects (Ictinus, Callicrates, Metagenes), 2 "philosophers" (Anaxagoras, Damon), 1 geographer (Phileas).

**Outside Athens 19**

A western hub (10): "philosophers" – Empedocles of Acragas, Zeno of Elea, Menestor of Sybaris, Lysis of Tarentum; Croton: Archippus, Cylon, Mnesarchus, Myia.[6] Others (both Syracuse) – Philoxenus, poet; Corax, rhetor.

Ionian "philosophy" (3): Diogenes of Apollonia, Melissus of Samos, Protagoras of Abdera.

Medical authors (2): Heraclides of Cos, Euryphon of Cnidus.

Female lyric (3): Praxilla of Sicyon, Telesilla of Argos, Corinna of Tanagra.

None of the above (1): Polyclitus of Sicyon.

Several observations emerge. First, indeed, writing is not central to this expansion of culture. Many of these performers, sages or practitioners need not have resorted to writing at all, or, even if they did, they still were the authors of a single book (Anaxagoras, Empedocles, Ictinus, Polyclitus). The assumptions of cultural memory are still those of the archaic era.

Second, even while memory works through the spoken word, the system of genres is already revolutionized. Any major lyric poet emerging at this point would stand a good chance of being remembered by future generations: we are right at the cusp of the moment of the active commemoration of lyric by Plato and his generation (see page 215 above). It is therefore striking to see that, effectively, no major lyric poet did emerge.[7] It may even

---

[6] Skepticism is in place for this group in particular: later scholarship may have felt an urge to invent a continuity between archaic Pythagoreanism and that of the late fifth century. For a survey of the history of early Pythagoreanism, very optimistic in its assessment of the sources, see Zhmud (2014); the names he singles out as somewhat more visible to the historical record are either earlier than the middle of the fifth century (Hippasus and Alcmaeon, the generation immediately following Pythagoras) or, likely, somewhat later, Hippo and Menestor.

[7] West (1993: ix): "I have taken 450 as the notional limiting date because the poetry of the succeeding period is somewhat different in character, more self-conscious, less spontaneous in feeling and expression; there are no major figures among its poets." Such categorical claims – pertaining even to quality – are suspect to contemporary scholarship (and LeVen, 2014, does bring back into the focus the significance of post-450 poetry). But West has a point: something in the cultural commemoration

be significant that we have three female lyric poets: away from Athens and its new competitions, a form that already became archaic and, so, marginalized – that is, more inviting for marginal authors. Not so much Sappho's daughters as her orphans.

Finally, we note, once again, the early spatialization of philosophy (see page 318 above), as well as that other breaking of symmetry – around Syracuse. (This, too, involved a tradition of drama, in "Doric comedy", for which see page 564, note 62, above; the attested authors in this genre, perhaps the genre as a whole, are earlier). But we also note, once again, the absence of any other localization. The only important center is that of Athens itself.

Now, we can in fact extrapolate some absolute numbers for the city of Athens. The process of the competitions would eventually train (as argued on pages 626–7 above) about 20 experienced poets, in tragedy and comedy each, active at the same time. The attested numbers for rhetors are comparable, and it is reasonable to suggest that Athens also possessed, by the time of Pericles, no more than about 20 individuals who were sufficiently prominent and experienced in public speaking as to be called "rhetors".[8] The number of remaining non-performative authors was probably not big, and so we can safely say that there were fewer than 100 – but surely many dozens of – "authors", active in the Athens of Socrates' youth, shaping his understanding of the examined life. Such was Socrates' world: bustling with the masters of public speech – punctured by a single book: Anaxagoras'.

We note along the way two kinds of absolute numbers. There is the number of ten to 20 individuals, pursuing the same activity, in tragedy, comedy and rhetoric. We find that "20's company": as practitioners of a certain kind of activity accumulate at a given location, they cross a certain quantitative threshold at some point, creating a meaningful identity. (Is there a comparable scale effect, with the rise of the Hellenistic philosophical schools? Mathematical generational events? Medical sects? Alexandrian poets?) On the other hand, we notice the number of "not much fewer than 100". This is also the number at which we capped, in the preceding chapter, many kinds of activity (philosophers at a given school at its

---

did break down, at this point; as suggested on pp. 232–3 above, it is absurd not to note that this transition is contemporary with the rise of a new, Athens-centered form of performance, capturing wide attention.

[8] Hansen (1984) argues the number of ten to 20 in the middle of the fourth century, while Ober (1989: 108) suggests that this might be on the low side. The size of the political class in the middle of the fifth century might have been smaller, but notice also that we are still in an era when generals were also expected to be accomplished orators (this may have changed in the post-Periclean era as the two careers diverged: Ober, 1989: 119–21).

peak, any concentration of Second Sophistic rhetors, grammarians in Alexandria...). At the level of the many dozens of authors, an ancient city would have felt absolutely buzzing with cultural activity. Twenty's company; 100's a crowd. Athens, by the middle of the fifth century, was already crowded.

Turning now to the contemporary authors, outside Athens, these two points are clear. First, their density must have been much lower than that of Athens. This city had about 4 percent of the entire Greek population of the time; and so, the Greek world surely had much fewer than 2,000 authors at the time.

Second, their attestation must be terrible. This must be emphasized: it is not merely that future attention, for this period, is focused on Athens. It is also that we are looking at an extremely early point in time – books would have to survive for five centuries to reach the relative safety of the name-dropping Imperial era. Worse: it is still a moment with few books, and so a moment much more dependent on the activation of cultural memory. And in point of fact the middle of the fifth century is not extremely well documented, not even for Athens: it is the gap between Herodotus and Thucydides. The extant works from this era are all tragedies (or perhaps a few medical works), genres that avoid contemporary names; even from comedy we have no more than a few fragments.[9] Authors, in this period, do not get a chance to get piggy-backed on the names of others. But it surely is the case that there would have been more authors, in this time, even outside Athens, than in previous generations. The Athenian democratic experiment was far from unique, and there were many other local cultures of public speech.[10] Non-Athenian authors are a third of the attested group for this era. If we assume there were about 80 authors active simultaneously in Athens, the – absurd – assumption of an equal attestation inside, and

[9] The only significant comic survival from this era is that of Cratinus, with 514 (generously defined) fragments and testimonies; almost all are tiny excerpts of a line or two at most, supplying no historical milieu.

[10] There are some indications of a tradition of comedy not only around Syracuse but also in Megara (see Rusten, 2006). Democracy was a widespread phenomenon, only partly explained through Athens' direct influence. The evidence is set out in Robinson (2011, esp. chap. 4). The main result is that, through the classical era, dozens of cities took part in the democratic experiment, though these took off mostly from later in the fifth century, and, even then, a great many cities were democratic only for stretches of a few decades at a time. If Athens, with its highly entrenched democratic culture and its huge size – by Greek standards – never had more than ten to 20 rhetors, it seems likely that younger, smaller cities would have had their political life dominated by no more than a handful of able speakers. Still, the sophists catered for *someone*; multiply a handful of rhetors across several dozen states... It is reasonable that, even by the middle of the fifth century, there were more rhetors outside Athens than inside it.

outside, Athens would imply 120 authors across the Greek world, which must therefore be a very low bound. Many fewer than 2,000; considerably more than 120.

A ratio of attestation of about 1:10, we found, is fairly low by the standards of antiquity as a whole, and so our 18 attested non-Athenians can easily stand for 150 to 300 authors or thereabout, for the entire middle third of the fifth century – or a little fewer than this active simultaneously. So: fewer than 100 active simultaneously? Or up to 300? Either way, add this to the Athenians and we end up envisioning a Greek world with a few hundred authors, active simultaneously, already by the middle of the fifth century. (Now – nearly all forgotten, in particular those outside Athens: because the first generation of a truly large authorial culture was also the last generation of a truly oral culture of memory.)

The picture forming is that the revolution in scale must have taken place, already. It had nothing to do with writing,[11] everything with the example of Athenian democratic culture.

I provide the evidence for numbers over the following century in table form, using, for my chronology, the same Pyzyk rubrics.

| Chronological unit: | Second third, fifth century | Third third, fifth century | First third, fourth century | Second third, fourth century |
|---|---|---|---|---|
| Performative Athens | 36 | 112 | 49 | 61 |
| Non-performative Athens | 6 | 12 | 16 | 28 |
| Outside Athens | 19 | 48 | 34 | 51 |

To make sense of the numbers, we need to bear in mind that this period is very well attested – which makes it not less but *more* subject to bias. What really jumps out is the sheer number of individuals attested for Athens in

---

[11] This point needs to be emphasized – and clarified. What I mean is that the genres in which the numbers explode involve performance: drama, rhetoric, the sage-like life of philosophy. That the multiplication of memory would involve, already by now, writing remains likely, and, of course, the basic technology of writing has now been widespread for many generations – which is precisely the historical point I am making. There are two writing-related breakthroughs in ancient Greece: the introduction of writing as a widespread tool – the writing breakthrough; and the explosion of more-written genres of prose writings – the prose breakthrough. There was also a scale breakthrough in the middle of the fifth century. The scale breakthrough came much later than the writing breakthrough (how early was that? Powell, 1991, puts it at an extraordinarily early moment, perhaps even the eighth century! But even the most cautious studies, such as Thomas, 1992, find the technologies of writing firmly in place through the archaic era itself.). It came well before the prose breakthrough. The scale breakthrough does not derive from the technology of writing but, rather, from the institution of democracy.

the late fifth century BCE, which comes down in particular to the combined evidence from Aristophanes, Thucydides, Plato and Xenophon. The
extant rhetors of the fourth century do not provide quite the same amount
of cultural prosopographic information, and in general we see a certain
retreat from the day-to-day realities of the city of Athens itself in the later
Athenian authors (this would be most evident, eventually, in new comedy).
This was perhaps a mark of Athens' success: early Athenian authors write in
the city, for the city, but later Athenian authors already know that they
write with all of Greece glancing over their shoulders.

It is also notable that, through the end of the fifth century, performative
authors continue to dominate Athenian culture. This is, indeed, the
generation that cements Athens' place in the canon as a performative
center (stage A of Athens' canon, in the terms of Chapter 2, page 231).
Once again – we look for the prose breakthrough, the time and place
genres less dominated by performance begin to be significant. And this
does not appear to be late fifth-century Athens.

And yet: it is especially for Athens that our numbers are biased. How to
get a sense of the overall development? The best way to think of the
numbers overall is in terms of non-Athenian authors, much less at the
mercy of Athenian attestation. And, there, the conclusion appears to be
that the growth in numbers is real. Almost all the 48 non-Athenians of the
late fifth century would still have been attested had Thucydides,
Aristophanes, Xenophon and Plato all been lost.[12] Further, eight of the
48 non-Athenian authors were, specifically, non-Athenian politician/rhet-
ors, a category that is completely unattested in the early fourth century
(whose political history is known with less personal detail; also, our view of
public life begins to be dominated by the "general", somewhat oversha-
dowing the "rhetor"). Remove those so that you have only authors in
comparable categories of attestation, and we find 40 in the late fifth
century, 34 in the early fourth and 40 in mid-century (of the 51 individuals
in the bare count above, 11 are once again "rhetors"/politicians: our picture
of political history – moving into the age of Demosthenes – becomes filled
once again with more detail). The stability of the numbers stands out, as
does their contrast with the numbers from the middle of the fifth century.
The simple reading of the evidence is that the number of authors did rise
substantially during the final decades of the fifth century, then stabilized or
perhaps grew more slowly through the fourth century itself.

---

[12] The exceptions are two "rhetors" – that is, political figures – recorded by Thucydides: Archias of
Camarina and Ptoeodorus of Thebes.

This of course would make sense in terms of our broad, qualitative understanding of classical culture. We know that there was a Sophistic movement, that there were the Hippocratic authors. . . As we connect the dots, a picture emerges. In the last third of the fifth century Athenian culture was still entirely dominated by the performative practices of drama and speech.[13] But, elsewhere, culture moved into prose. Here – outside Athens! – is the prose breakthrough. Removing the "rhetors"/politicians as well as a handful of poets from the 48 non-Athenian authors of the late fifth century, we have 35 remaining non-Athenian, non-performative authors, a group quantitatively as well as qualitatively different from their Athenian counterparts – or, indeed, from any preceding Greek civilization.[14] We have here the sophists, indeed (seven, in this list), as well as a number of medical authors, many of them clustered in Cos and Cnidus (nine doctors, five from Cos/Cnidus). There is also a series of more "scientific" authors, ranging from Philolaus, the Pythagorean philosopher, to Oenopides, the astronomer and geometer from Chios (I count here ten figures, perhaps with some concentrations in south Italy – and in Chios): this is still broadly similar to the groupings of philosophers from the previous generation. But

[13] Even the 12 non-performative authors mentioned for Athens are an overcount. There was one major prose author in Athens at the time: Herodotus, who occupies a unique position between prose and performance (as well as between Athens and its Ionian periphery). Otherwise, we find here a couple of authors who point towards rhetoric as a profession, going beyond the "rhetors" of the preceding era (Lysias, Antiphon) – so, still, close to the performative practice of rhetoric. And then: five figures known purely through association with Socrates and likely not authors in their own right (for instance, Eryximachus, the physician of the symposium!); the master architect Mnesicles (was he an author? The BNP also adds Philocles, who need not be even a major architect). The only remaining, apparent non-performative authors of Athens of the time were the two "mathematicians" Meton and Euctemon. (I remove Thucydides and Xenophon to the early fourth century, to which their careers as historians belong; it is deeply surprising that more Athenians did not write, at this point, the history of their Athens – an argument from silence that is especially eloquent for this well-attested moment. While the question of the emergence of Atthidography is complicated, our – very substantial – evidence truly begins only in the fourth century. For an overview, see Harding, 2007). Note also that, against this evidence, it is perhaps John Philoponus' testimony that Hippocrates of Chios was active in Athens (*In Phys.* 31.3–6). Philoponus recounted a story – based on a line in Aristotle, as well as on Philoponus' own vague impression – that could well have been shaped by many centuries of later Greek cultural perception that "it all happened in Athens". We trust Philoponus, because this seems right to us, for the same vague reasons. But it did not, yet: non-rhetorical prose, at this stage, was almost entirely extra-Athenian.

[14] It is natural, and appropriate, for classicists to study cultural developments not from broad statistical observations but from the close readings of texts. This creates a very strong bias to study the phenomenon of the rise of prose from the writings of the extant prose authors: Plato has been central to many such studies since Havelock (1963) (to say nothing of Derrida!); Goldhill (2002) pays close attention to Thucydides, for instance (and even Kurke, 2011, is, after all, a study of *Aesop*!), and the consequence of this methodology is a misleading Athenocentrism. In fact, the prose breakthrough occurred outside Athens, and it is mostly its later rippling through Athens itself which we now study among our canonical authors ("stage B" of Athens' canonization, in the terms of Chapter 2, p. 231).

the remaining group is perhaps the most significant: nine historians, each from a different city.[15] (The broad spatial patterns of cultural life are already in place: poets, scientists and philosophers are spatially organized in different ways; historians are more dispersed.)

The great bulk of all authors attested for this period are Athenians; the great bulk of non-performative authors are non-Athenians. Further, at this point the numbers of such non-performative authors become very substantial, to the extent that entire genres, and centers, take shape. We finally also have clear evidence for individuals who dedicate their lives to the writing of many prose works – Democritus being the clearest case.

Two observations are called for. First, it is true that the projected few hundred non-Athenian prose-authors would contain "sophists", some of whom could have taught without writing,[16] as well as a number of old-school sages who, once again, could have avoided books (Eurytus, for instance, almost certainly *performed* his strange Pythagoreanism);[17] some of the medical practitioners would be famous even without committing their experience into writing. But we do have after all the Hippocratic corpus – mostly a product of this generation (and, in its extant form, a mere fragment of the medical production of the time). The nine attested historians could very well stand for many dozens of lost authors, many of whom – given their genre – could have written works of multiple rolls. In short, there were at the very least many hundreds of prose rolls, probably more (types, not tokens), produced around the Greek world during the

[15] These are Agathocles of Cyzicus, Damastes of Sigeum, Evagon of Samos, Glaucus of Rhegium, Hellanicus of Mitylene, Philistus of Syracuse, Thibron of Sparta, Thrasyalces of Thasos, Xenomedes of Ceus. Other than Hellanicus, these are very minor figures, and it is easy to imagine that the rate of attestation for this group is in fact very low. It would be of course extremely telling if indeed – as is still the standard opinion (Ruschenbusch, 2003) – it was Hellanicus, from Mytilene, who was the first to write a history of Attica!

[16] But did they? It seems telling that the earliest evidence for the writing of rhetorical technai – the most written form of rhetorical education – emerges not in Athens but in Syracuse, with Corax and Tisias (Kennedy, 1959). We routinely – and correctly – emphasize that the defining feature of the sophists was not written theory but, rather, lived practice – that of teaching professionally, for a fee (see, e.g., Corey, 2002). It would be natural, then, to have testimonies for sophists who taught, without showing any interest in writing per se. In fact, it is very rare that we have any knowledge of any sophist, however obscure, without an indication that he also wrote (Lycophron, so Aristotle tells us – fragment 91 – *egrapse* a particular view; even Hippias, the seemingly hyper-performative jack of all trades, was known to posterity through his written production, the collections of lists in the Aristotelian manner – Plutarch, *Numa* 1; Athenaeus XIII 608F. The single exception is Xeniades of Corinth, known only through several mentions of his strange doctrine – everything is false! – by Sextus Empiricus; the testimony is so vague as to be consistent with either a written or non-written tradition.). It seems that, even back then, the prominent sophistic teacher would seek to be marked out through writing.

[17] Netz (2014a: 173–8).

final decades of the fifth century. By this point the accumulated Attic dramatic repertoire – at this time the bulk of the poetic repertoire – must have had fewer than 2,000 dramas. Even under a very wild scenario, in which most drama did end up in written circulation,[18] we find that at some point, late in the fifth century, prose had probably overtaken poetry (once again: in types, not tokens).

Let us pursue the numbers a bit further. The implied corpus is of a few thousand roll types of prose alone, and so perhaps several hundreds of thousands of rolls in total, produced over a few decades – that is, not much below several thousand, or perhaps even 10,000, rolls produced annually. Assuming that a certain fraction of these were copied and sold commercially, we need to assume a book trade that sells something between several hundred to a few thousand rolls annually; assuming that about 10 percent of this commerce takes place in Athens (see below), we need to assume several dozen to several hundred rolls sold, annually, in the city. Now, since bookselling is recognized, by the late fifth century, as a fixture in the Athenian landscape,[19] such numbers are not only plausible but, in fact, seem to be on the low side: even assuming that the "booksellers" actually sold many other goods as well (my own university "bookstore" sells sweaters, mostly), would they not manage to sell, on average, at least one book a day? So: ancient book culture is already in place; it would continue to rise (by perhaps as much as an order of magnitude) into the Roman peak, but it is already at a very substantial level.

This brings me to the second point. I use in my calculation the value of about 10 percent of all books consumed in Athens. It is in fact this assumption that makes it possible to draw, from the fact of an Athenian bookselling market, the conclusion of a large book-making practice across the Greek world. This in itself might leave eyebrows raised. Indeed, I revisit the evidence for bookselling in Athens; this is in fact well-known terrain, often brought up for the study of ancient literacy. This, in turn, is typically pursued through an implicit a fortiori argument: recognizing that our evidence is predominantly Athenian, the argument then becomes that, if literacy in Athens – "the school of Hellas" – even in the late fifth century,

---

[18] Kovacs (2005) may be consulted for the standard pessimistic position, expressed earlier by Burns (1981: 381): books with drama were available, but rare.
[19] The evidence is summed up in Woodbury (1974: 354–5 n.15), the key passages mostly from comedy: tiny fragments with the word "bookseller": Aristomenes 9, Nicophon 19, Theopompus 77, extant precisely because grammarians were interested in the word as such; even more significant is Eupolis, fragment 304, in which the speaker wends his way through the market, passing the stalls selling garlics and onions, to reach the place where books are sold; finally, of course, there is Socrates in the *Apology* (26d–e), referring to the books of Anaxagoras, readily available for sale.

was limited in range and significance, surely this must be even more true of the Greeks as a whole (so Harris, 1991: 65). The implicit assumption is then, perhaps, this:

> Fifth-century book culture would have been concentrated, above all, in Athens.

It now appears to me that this presupposition is false. Obviously, books mattered more in Athens than in some rural, outlying parts of the Greek-speaking world. But the simple evidence from the rise of the prose genres, considered above, suggests the opposite of that: at first, book culture could have been more important in the other major cities, away from Athens' *performative* school of Hellas.

And yet: our evidence is Athenian, and so our numbers must be at least as biased in favor of Athenian authors. Let me work this backwards. If we allow that a third of all authors in this period were active in Athens (which seems like an upper bound: ten times more frequent!), and that there were 750 authors all told through the last third of the century, we end up with 250 Athenian authors, and so their ratio of attestation becomes about 1:2. This is not impossible: almost all the attested Athenians are dramatists, rhetors and the group surrounding Socrates; the attestation, for such persons, can be near-complete, if not beyond! (We might be overcounting Athenian authors by calling so many prominent politicians "rhetors", so many friends of Socrates "philosophers".) But the rate of attestation for Athens could hardly have been much higher than 1:2, and Athens' fraction of all Greek cultural production could hardly have been much higher than 1:3. Some 750 authors, then, seems close to a *minimum* for the era as a whole. And so: a few hundreds of mostly prose authors, active simultaneously, outside Athens, all quite badly attested, near the end of the fifth century.

As explained above, our evidence for the fourth century cannot compare with that for the late fifth century. The absolute numbers go down. What keeps going up, however, is the number of non-performative *Athenian* authors: prose has become the vernacular, the self-evident form of expression. (As it were: the Greeks discover that, for 40 years, they have been speaking prose.) These Athenian, prose writers are, in the terms of Chapter 2, page 231, "stage B": the authors who complete the Athenian canon. A Thucydides, a Plato, a Xenophon, an Isocrates. In Athens' moment of political defeat, these authors pick the performances of a previous generation, noted everywhere across the Greek world – those of a Socrates, of a

Pericles, of an entire tradition of rhetoric – and leverage them into new forms now explicitly based on writing.

But of course prose expands everywhere. This is also the moment of philosophical city traditions, suggesting a plurality of concentrations (see pages 313–18 above). With Diocles of Carystus, we see established the figure of the medical author (no longer hiding behind the non-authorial anonymity of previous medical practitioners);[20] with Archytas at the latest, the genre of the exact sciences achieved its final form.

Let us sum up the possible numbers. We started out with a dramatic explosion: from a few dozen poets and sages around the Greek world, in the late sixth century, we move to perhaps 250 authors active simultaneously around the middle of the fifth century, about a third of whom were in Athens (almost all, primarily, masters of the spoken word). The numbers could rise further, perhaps substantially, as authors around the Greek world take up prose as an alternative to Athens' centrality, and, indeed, there could hardly be fewer than 750 authors through the final third of the century. By the end of the century we might have as many as 500 authors, maybe more, active simultaneously, many of them now prose writers in the full sense. As this practice is taken up by Athens, its own cultural production can expand beyond dramatists and rhetors, which in turn pushes up the numbers overall. Indeed, the Greek population as a whole rises measurably through the fifth and fourth centuries.[21] It is reasonable, then, that we should have considerably more than 500 authors active simultaneously by the middle of the fourth century. Here, we may begin to gain insight from the conclusions of the preceding chapter. There, we found that the number of authors, active simultaneously at any point prior to 200 CE, was about 1,000, or perhaps a bit more. This is directly comparable to "considerably more than 500". And, indeed, our overall sense, based on the evidence from cultural history, is that the middle of the fourth century obtained, at the very least, the *average* scale of ancient culture (if not above that). It was as rich and productive a period of Greek civilization as any. If so, the attestation is in fact especially poor, which, as we will return to note

[20] Van der Eijk (2000: I.vii–viii) emphasizes the unique nature of Diocles as the earliest author emerging, from our evidence, with his own identity. This is presented primarily as a matter of the survival of fragments and testimonies, but, with 20 works now credited to him, it seems likely there were not many like him, even in his own age!

[21] Morris (2004) comes down on the more optimistic side of the ranges proposed by Scheidel (2003): the Greek rate of demographic growth, through the archaic and classical eras, at about 0.4 percent per annum. This translates into roughly a doubling over two centuries, but, no less important, it also translates into about 10 percent growth over the mere 20 years of a short generation. Cultural practices changed – within a visibly expanding universe.

in the following section should not come as a surprise: we are in an early era, far away from Imperial memory; and Athenian commemoration is already less active.

Let us review the order of events suggested in this section.

First there was an expansion of scale occurring in Athens (and in its cultural parallels and epigones) during the first half of the fifth century. This expansion was driven not by technologies but by institutions. Prose writing was, as yet, marginal; what was central was the communal commitment to expanded public performances. Next there was a response, in the following generation, across the Greek world, which took the form of prose writing. My interpretation of this is that, seeking a Hellenic audience in a world that was already dominated by Athens' performances, non-Athenian authors had to resort to alternative means of broadcasting their work. The option of writing was always there: it became more attractive when local performances outside Athens lost their potential Panhellenic significance. So, a second best: prose writing also made possible the rise of new genres, however, and did lead to a significant expansion of literary production. Finally, as prose genres became established, they were picked up and pursued alongside the old performance traditions, even in Athens itself. This happened in the first decades of the fourth century. At this point the literary system as a whole was established in the forms, and scales, that would last for the remainder of antiquity, until about 200 CE.

I would imagine that an account of the rise of Greek literature in the classical era, focused on the technology of writing, would have looked like this:

Technology → genre

That is, a particular technological input (the rise of writing) gives rise to new genres, and thus a new form of culture.

The model developed here pushes technology lower in the causal flow. It is a more layered model; it also considers how causation can turn into self-reinforcing cycles:

Social setting → scale →
(Technology ↔ genre ↔ scale)

A new social setting gives rise to a shift to a bigger scale, which then drives a self-reinforcing cycle whereby technology sustains new genres, which in turn sustain larger scales.

I do not propose that this is the universal form of cultural history. This is simply a model of the rise of the literary culture of classic Greece. What needs to be emphasized at this point is that the system stabilized as the shift is made complete: a system of genres, and their technologies, in which writing is by far the most common, canonical performances by far the most valued; sustained by a flow of authors sufficient to the task of maintaining the same genres, through the same technologies.

In the following two sections, I will concentrate on the overall stability of the system, even while looking at the evidence for potential contraction in the second century BCE (section 6.1.2) as well as potential expansion in the Roman era (sections 6.2 to 6.3). Following that, I move to the third century CE, when the long stability of the classical system may finally have been disrupted (sections 6.4 to 6.5). I will then return, at the end of section 6.5, to this causal mechanism involving society, technology and scale.

### 6.1.2   Wobble?

I have argued on page 612 above that ancient authorial culture scaled with the size of the leisured class:[22] a strong assumption, but, ultimately, also the simplest hypothesis.

Estimating the size of this class is a difficult question in its own right, but here at least we can rely on comparative evidence and on a priori economic considerations. The salient facts are that the Roman Empire was a typical, pre-modern non-egalitarian society, whereas the democratic poleis of the classical Greek world were, relatively speaking, quite egalitarian – but without doing away with social and economic distinction. This position – relative egalitarianism – could make a larger class with access to leisure possible.[23] As pointed out above, it is hard to define the "leisured class", but

---

[22] In what follows I need to define what I mean by "leisured elite" more precisely. The narrow, technical meaning of the term would refer to those who may live entirely off their rents and therefore need not engage in any profession at all. This is too narrow a term for us, since obviously a somewhat larger fraction had access to education and to the social capital required to be recognized as an author: a fuzzy category that will only partly come into the focus through our discussion.

[23] To explain: prior to the technological advances of the twentieth century, a completely egalitarian society would have to be universally brutish. "If there had not been a sufficiently wealthy minority, no one would have been able to worry about anything other than survival" (Piketty, 2013: 416). Such a society would have a zero-sized leisured class. On the other hand, a completely unequal society could have, at the extreme, only a handful of leisured individuals (such conditions were nearly approached in some well-documented early modern European cities: Scheidel, 2017: 225–7 – conditions that inspired an extremely well funded patronage of specialized craftsmanship; see, e.g., Boström, 1994. I shall return to discuss in section 6.3 below the relation between inequality and patronage.). The calculation is complicated but the simple stylized fact is that, given a society's purchasing power per capita, there is an optimum level of equality defined by this level – the one at which the largest leisured class is produced. Given contemporary conditions, this would likely be complete egalitarianism (if social arrangements could be obtained that in fact spread current wealth

a good first shot at it would be to assume that it also included, beyond the absolutely rich, dominant citizens, a subset of the middling range, of citizens who were not massive landholders and yet lived well above subsistence level. As Ober shows, this middling range was significant in classical Athens (and so, likely, in classical Greece as a whole) but was much narrower in almost all other pre-modern civilizations. The calculation obtained in Ober (2015: 97) finds that the "decent middling", in fourth-century Athens, covered between 42 and 58 percent of the population as a whole (a denominator that includes non-citizens, and even slaves!). This contrasts with the number for the peak of the Roman Empire – which Ober obtains based on Scheidel and Friesen (2009) – of between 6 and 12 percent among the "decent middling". The size of the fraction of all individuals living above subsistence therefore shrinks by a factor of roughly five to seven times. (The fraction of the absolute elite is, obviously, tiny in both Athens and Rome – a little over 1 percent.) This is an overestimate (since fourth-century Athens was probably somewhat more egalitarian than the Greek average), and it does not directly measure the size of the "leisured class" as such. And yet other numbers are suggestive for a similar result. Sparta, in particular, had, in theory, a much sharper distinction between "haves" and "have-nots", all the citizens – in theory, once again – possessing equal rights and wealth.[24] As its egalitarianism shrank, so did its citizen body. The leisured elite in Athens could correlate with its authorial body; in Sparta, it correlated with its standing army. Numbers (which are far from certain) suggest a fairly rapid collapse. A few numbers, some attested, some conjectured, are summed up in the following table.[25]

equally, probably everyone would enjoy enough leisure to be able to participate in culture). Given pre-modern conditions, the optimum level of inequality is, of course, short of complete egalitarianism (complete egalitarianism would then lead, as noted above, to a complete lack of leisure), but it is also surely above the Augsburg levels. It is possible that, among pre-modern societies, the one that came closest to the leisure-producing optimum was classical Athens (did it, actually, occupy that optimum?).

[24] I bypass quickly in this discussion the question of the roots of Greek egalitarianism. While these may be associated with democracy, it is clear that, most fundamentally, they derive from the realities of hoplite warfare, requiring a significant commitment from an entire citizen body. Thus, one of the least democratic states – Sparta – could nevertheless be, early on, relatively egalitarian (among its citizen body), simply because it was the most militarized. This is significant to us, since the erosion of democracy following the end of the fourth century went hand in hand with the erosion of citizen-hoplite warfare.

[25] Scheidel (2017: 133) (based on Hodkinson, 2000).

| Year | Number of citizens (based on the standing army) |
|---|---|
| 480 | 8,000 |
| 418 | 4,000 |
| 371 | 1,200 |
| 240s | 700 |

This collapse represents not only changing economic conditions but also the costs of endless wars, as well as Sparta's ultimate military failure. Thus, the rate implied here between maximum and minimum – roughly 1:10 – represents something of a distant upper bound on the overall contraction of the "middling" class in Greece as a whole.

The implication of all this is that the fraction of the "leisured class" in classical Greece should have been several times higher than that in the Roman peak. In the preceding chapter, on page 608, I took Scheidel and Friesen's (2009) estimate of the size of the decurional-and-equivalent class to derive about 100,000 adult men of leisure in the Greek-speaking world, or half a million individuals in households possessing leisure. To have a similar number in the mid-fourth-century Greek-speaking world, we will need to have about 5 percent of the population as a whole or more possessing leisure (recall Hansen, 2006, mentioned in note 1 above, finding – optimistically – 7.5 to 10 million individuals in the Greek-speaking world), or perhaps 10 percent of the population in the more egalitarian Attica. Now, 10 percent of the Athenian population makes about 30,000 individuals in leisured households, or perhaps 6,000 adult males. This is in fact a significant number in Greek democracy. This may have been the quorum required for important votes in the assembly;[26] this was also the size of the subset of the citizen body, from which juries were selected by lot.[27] In short, this is what the Athenians themselves expected their reliable, politically active citizen body to be, which is perhaps the best proxy we may have for what I mean by "possessing leisure". To have the free time to produce speeches, you must have had, first, the free time to listen to them.

This, then, is the outline of an argument: the rise in scale, from the middle of the fourth century BCE to the second century CE, of the

---

[26] So, ostracism? See, e.g., Sinclair (1988: 67).
[27] Hansen (1991: 167). Clearly, "6,000" is here chosen as a round decimal – natural, also, given that the habit of counting by multiples of three, not only of two and five, is common (because of the ultimately sexagesimal – Babylonian – roots of the Greek monetary system). Still, it was the round number chosen as closest to the realities of Athenian political life.

population living in mostly Greek-speaking areas could well have been about the same order as the contraction of the fraction possessing the minimum leisure required to participate in culture, the two processes thus canceling each other out.

This does not mean that the leisured class was always stable. Two observations stand out.

First, its rise until the middle of the fourth century is obvious. Through the archaic period and into the heyday of Greek democracy, the size of the Greek-speaking population keeps rising, from perhaps about 3 million to about 7.5 to 10 million;[28] so did the reach of democracy. If we assume that the Greeks were never as inegalitarian as the Romans – and yet gradually became even more egalitarian – we may assume, perhaps, that the fraction of the moderately leisured class, say, doubled between the archaic and the classical eras. We thus find that, from about 650 BCE to about 350 BCE, the size of the Greek-speaking leisured elite could have grown by a factor of five, or well above that. Among other things, then, the spectacular growth of the Greek authorial class into the middle of the fourth century goes together with a substantial growth in the size of the leisured class.

The argument may be extended, based on the spatial observations from the preceding part of the book. Remember that, in the archaic period, no city really breaks out as much larger or richer than the rest, presenting instead more of a continuum between large and small. Cities are capped in the thousands. Thus, the absolute concentrations of adult males of the leisured elite, in any given city, was, even in fairly big settlements, counted in no more than the many dozens. This, to repeat, represents not the authorial class but, more or less, the *audience*. Little wonder that the symposium mattered so much; that they had no poetic "schools". And we may begin to note how a much bigger city, empowering a much larger fraction of its citizen body, would break into a different cultural scale altogether. If the scale of the leisured class as a whole grew by a factor of well over five, then the rise of scale of the Athenian state, together with its exceptional egalitarianism, would mean that the scale of the maximal-sized leisured class grew by a factor of many dozens. And thus culture, in the middle of the fourth century, operated in an entirely different world from that of the archaic era.

Now let us consider the converse to this rise in egalitarianism. How do you get from A to B – from an abnormally egalitarian Greek society in

---

[28] Hansen (2006) sums up what has become nearly a standard view; starting from Morris (2004), scholarship has focused more and more on the remarkable growth of the Greek world from the archaic and into the classical era.

which about 5 to 10 percent belong in the leisured class, to a normally inegalitarian eastern Mediterranean society in which about 1.2 to 1.7 percent belong in the leisured class? The two figures we have, from the two ends of the process, are guesswork – based on the two points at which numbers can be generated at all. In between, our knowledge of the reach of Greek culture, as well as that of the basic economic parameters, is much murkier. I will now therefore briefly touch on the broad trajectories of Hellenization, and of egalitarianism, from the classical to the Imperial era.

When considering Hellenization, in this context, what matters to us is not the adoption of Greek costumes or language by large swaths of the population. We are looking instead at the extent to which members of local elites chose to participate in Greek literary culture, whether in Greek or (especially in Italy and especially from the first century BCE onwards) in their own language. This, then, is not so intractable, and the best way to approach this question is directly: through the evidence of the authors themselves. A very simple question: how many authors come from non-core Greek lands? Now, we may exclude authors of Alexandrian origins, as, in this case, the kind of evidence we typically have – an author being active in Alexandria – usually tells us nothing about their origins. But we may still look at authors from the "Levant" or the eastern edge of the Mediterranean – from the southern Anatolian shores to Sinai. This evidence typically involves origins, and, while many of those authors, once again, might have been "ethnically Greek", they present, in aggregate, our best measurable proxy for authors from the new lands of Hellenization. Here, then, is the number of authors from the Levant in philosophy, medicine and the exact sciences, combined, for the temporal nodes from 300 to 100 BCE (I look at the fields more open to non-Greeks; see the discussion on page 277 above).

| 300 | 250 | 200 | 150 | 100 |
|-----|-----|-----|-----|-----|
| 5 | 5 | 10 | 15 | 14 |

The numbers are small, and we should use them only as very broad guides. First – as we knew already from the single example of Zeno of Citium – Greek authorship reached the Levant early on. Second, such authorship was rather more noticeable in the second century than in the third. This is, in fact, much more pronounced in relative terms: the total number of authors counted for this exercise in the temporal nodes 300/250 is 190; in the temporal nodes 200/150 it is 90. (The downwards trend is of course meaningful in and of itself, to which we will get soon below.) This group becomes genuinely significant in the second century BCE (almost 30 percent from the Levant!). This is a very distant upper bound, however: we are looking at the more foreign-friendly fields, and, more importantly, many of those authors were in fact "ethnically Greek", whatever this may precisely mean. And in fact this group never became central, and the old cities of the Greek core – together with Alexandria, with its unique trajectory of cultural demography – remained the mainstay of Greek culture.

We see, then, a modest Hellenization of the east, much more noticeable in the second century BCE than in the third. This pales into insignificance, however, compared with the Hellenization of the west in the first century BCE. The numbers of Italian authors joining the Greek literary tradition (typically, in their own Latin language) was very significant, and in some of the decades late in the first century BCE such authors could have constituted (very briefly) even the majority of all Greek-inspired culture in the Mediterranean: for all this, see page 519 above. While such numbers do seem to recede later in the first century CE, the overall contribution of Italy to Mediterranean authorship remains significant in future centuries, and it is added to the contribution of an east whose elites, by now, have become fully Hellenized; at this point a Roman-inflected Hellenization – so, Romanization – begins to filter further west. As we will note on pages 732–4 below, this process is extended much further in the Imperial era, and even more so, apparently, in late antiquity. The entire Mediterranean is fully Hellenized/Romanized – about 700 years after Alexander the Great. The fundamental point is made by Wallace-Hadrill: this entire process truly gains steam near the end of the first century BCE, as the Hellenic/Roman acculturation of the entire Mediterranean is finally buttressed by the realities of a Roman imperial power, now fully Hellenized.

I will not try to provide exact numbers, and so what matters to us is the overall arc of Hellenization, which may be stylized as follows.

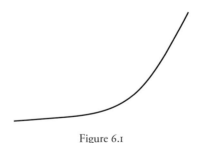

Figure 6.1

The curve starts out, moving upwards, accelerating from the first century BCE onwards: a process that took place, roughly speaking, from about 350 BCE[29] to 350 CE.

Moving on to the size of the leisured elite, we have even less evidence to work with. I assume, however, that the egalitarianism of Greek cities correlated with their democratic constitutions, and so we may take the constitutional trajectory of Greek cities as a proxy for such egalitarianism. Of course, even this history is partly obscure. At a broad level, we know that the Greek world does become monarchic at the end of the fourth century, and that the new monarchies outside the Greek core are owned by small groups of warlords. In the Greek core itself, and to some extent within the new cities founded by the warlords, these monarchies do recognize the independence of their subject cities – a recognition whose precise significance is a matter of historical debate.[30] We also know that, in many cities, democratic constitutions did survive the political collapse of

---

[29] It should be remembered that the Hellenization of inland Asia Minor already seems to have begun by the fourth century itself. It should be clear that I employ an outdated terminology, implying a single-dimensional spectrum between non-Hellenic and Hellenic, and a rather passive transition from one to the other, while current scholarship is more interested in the way in which people, actively, construct their own multifaceted identity. Thus, if scholarship once looked at the "Hellenization of Caria" in the middle of the fourth century, today one seeks various models of creolization: so, Hornblower (1982), as against Henry (2013). Bear in mind, then, that my concern is not with identity politics but with a rather more specific question: what is the range of individuals who could be drawn into the Greek-style authorial system? And, for this, once again, the best way is to look, directly, at the individuals themselves. In the fields of science and philosophy, the first individuals to emerge in my database from *original, inland* Carian cities are Cydias of Mylasa, a late Hellenistic Herophilean, and Hermogenes of Alabanda, a late Hellenistic architect (while technically inland, Alabanda is in fact very near the coast). Later Hellenistic foundations in inland Caria include the early Hellenistic foundation of Stratonicea (Menestheus of Stratonicea was an author in pharmacology, active in the late Hellenistic or early Roman eras; Metrodorus of Stratonicea was an Epicurean who switched – very rare! – to the academy, lured by Carneades: late second century BCE, then) and the second-century foundation of Aphrodisias, which becomes a major cultural center; in my list are Adrastus (philosopher, second century CE) and Alexander (philosopher, second to third centuries CE), but even more important is Chariton, the novelist, and in general, the city seems to have played a role in the culture of the Second Sophistic. An Apollonius of Aphrodisias was an early Hellenistic historian, perhaps hailing from the Carian city before its Hellenistic refoundation. There are a number of later historians writing on Caria, noted by Jacoby, either unlocated or located to sites on or near the coastline, beginning with the fourth-century Scylax of Caryanda. In general, coastal Caria was always a very significant area for cultural recruitment, and it suffices to note that *Halicarnassus* was located there. What this brief exercise shows, once again, is that culture moved inland only gradually. It will only be in late ancient times that cultural recruitment will get all the way inland into Cappadocia. The curve is not linear; it starts nearly flat, and accelerates very slowly.

[30] In general, there is no doubt that pre-modern states, in general, would leave much room for city autonomy. These were "thin" states, with very small bureaucratic apparatuses. (So, Strootman, 2011; Ober and Weingast, in Ober, 2015: 321–8, propose a formal argument predicting that the compromise of royal, elite and popular interests found with the city ceded a moderate amount of control and maintained some level of democracy informally, because it was not worth it to anyone, not even

Athens in the late fourth century (including, of course, Athens itself, even if its institutions never regained their participatory intensity). Even such democracies gradually lose their meaning, most surely by the end of the second century BCE.[31] At this point, then, Greek political realities would be nearly as oligarchic as they would be by the second century CE, and the assumption must be that most of the economic transition, as well as towards inequality, happened at this time: so, a transition taking place mostly (though of course not entirely) from 300 to 100 BCE.[32] Once again, I will not try to date or quantify this any more precisely, and simply point out that the shape of the curve can be stylized as follows.

to the king, to engage in war, but, at the same time, the elite had to accommodate popular interests so as to maintain its defensive stance towards the king.) Once again, I am not sure how such formal considerations would be expressed in actual interactions, had the Greeks not possessed, already, the cultural vocabulary of the network of free cities. Ma (2003) emphasizes the continuing place of the autonomous city, especially as a diplomatic entity, expressed with more or less symbolic acts (ambassadors exchanged between cities, decrees by one city mentioning another; indeed, our evidence, mostly epigraphic, is biased towards such symbolic gestures). The symbolic realm was constituted, after all, by the memory of an era with many cities, structured around Athens. Yet again, the polis of letters, a symbolic survival with some real consequences.

[31] Hamon (2009) is a useful survey of current scholarship on the survival of democratic institutions into the Hellenistic era. The current consensus is that democracy was widespread in the third century, if of course more important in the Aegean core than elsewhere in an expanding Hellenic world, and that it gradually lost its meaning in the Hellenistic era. The two interlocking areas of debate are as follows. (1) The chronology of the decline: beginning as early as in the third century, or only in the second? (2) Its aetiology: a Greek, spontaneous erosion of equality, or a Roman-imposed oligarchy? Dmitriev (2005) is an argument for the spontaneous model, but, then again, this is a case of both/and rather than either/or. It is striking that the Athenian epigraphic habit, which certainly emerges with democracy, does collapse dramatically at the end of the fourth century (Hedrick, 1999: 392). The *stakes* for democracy, certainly, declined. At any rate, it is clear that the many new cities founded and populated in the Hellenistic era, always growing in numbers, were considerably less democratic than their counterparts in the old Greek core (see, e.g., Gagarin, 2013: 232–3). Thus, even apart from the erosion of democracy in the old cities, the gradual demographic shift from old to new areas kept diluting Greek democracy.

[32] This, if anything, is an extremely slow-moving process of disegalitarianism; one of the key takeaways from Scheidel (2017) is the rapidity with which economies "snap back" from the more egalitarian exceptions into the historical norm of near-maximal inequality: it takes no more than a few decades (as, indeed, we have all witnessed in our own lifetimes). The clearest verifiable proxy for the ancient case is that of Sparta, noted on p. 641 above: here, egalitarianism was completely dead already by the middle of the third century. This, above all, makes it inherently unlikely that democracy had not already begun to retreat by the third century: to assume this, we will need to argue either (1) that economic inequality remained frozen for centuries (from the fifth through the whole of the third) at such low levels that they have no historical parallel, and that it did so for generations after the military regime that made such egalitarianism possible was over, or (2) that sheerly political institutions could maintain their egalitarianism, for several generations, in the face of growing economic inequality. We cannot really rule out either of these, as the evidence, even for the political history, let alone the economic history, of the Hellenistic city is so sparse. Barring such evidence, the prior should be clear: most likely, the third century saw a rise in inequality.

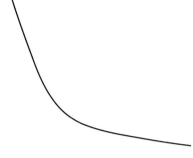

Figure 6.2

Democracy (and, with it, egalitarianism) keeps receding, much of this frontloaded early in the process of the overall transition from fourth-century Greece to Roman-era Mediterranean.

I have two stylized curves, and, while, once again, no precise dating or quantification is possible, the shape of their combination is in fact obvious. In the first (Figure 6.1), the rise was backloaded; in the second (Figure 6.2), the decline was frontloaded. The combination, then, will have to take roughly the following form.

Figure 6.3

I predict that, at first, as the reduction of Athens reverberated through Greek society, the size of the moderately leisured class must have plummeted, at this early stage compensated only to a modest extent by the recruiting of new elites from the east. It was only later, as the fraction of the leisured class stabilized, that the demographic bleeding stopped, and then, simultaneously, as the Roman and other elites joined in the making of Greek culture, that the process reversed itself, the size of the leisured class now getting back, roughly, to its late classical heyday, possibly even reaching above that.

Let us now test this prediction against the evidence – which, once again, we should not take at face value: as usual, we need to correct our raw numbers for their bias.

As noted above, our main witness for classical civilization is the intensive naming of the Imperial era. To be remembered today you have, generally speaking, first of all to have been remembered by the year zero. The obvious consequence should be that the bigger your BCE number, the less likely it is that you will be remembered. Now, this is not the first impression left by the evidence, in which we notice a significant group of archaic authors and then, of course, the massive cultural memory of the classical era. The active effort to commemorate these eras was more powerful than the sheer passage of time. To estimate the chronological contours of this effort of cultural memory, let us look again at the group of authors mentioned in Plutarch's *Moralia* as well as (more than once) in the *Deipnosophists*. This divides chronologically as follows.

| Archaic | −5 | −4 | −3 | Later |
|---|---|---|---|---|
| 25 | 40 | 78 | 36 | 33 |

It is certain that there were many more authors active in the fourth century than in the fifth, and of course many more active in the fifth century than in the archaic era; so the rise in numbers through the first three rubrics represents a gradually *shrinking* effort of cultural memory. Following that we hit the memory cliff, and it is certain that there was less of an effort to remember post-classical names.[33]

Even this is true only as far as the performative genres and, to a lesser extent, philosophy are concerned; otherwise, we do not see an effort to preserve, in particular, the early archaic and classical contributions.[34] We may consider once again the example of the exact sciences. As pointed out above, on pages 250–1, these flourish in two separate generational events, that of Archytas and that of Archimedes. Here the contrast is clear. The generation of Archytas left practically no direct fragments (the bulk of what is now known seems to have been available to our sources only indirectly, via Eudemus' history, a compilation *c.* 300 BCE).[35] As noted on pages 555–7

---

[33] The exact position of the memory cliff, of course, need not align with the boundaries of centuries; perhaps it should be dated to about 270 BC, following the generations of Menander and Callimachus. Eratosthenes is the only later third-century poet in this group, as against Menander, Philemon, Callimachus, Theocritus, Aratus, Philitas of Cos, Alexander of Aetolia and Euphorion, all active early in the century. Poetry was declining; but was it declining *that quickly*? By a factor of *ten*?

[34] Thus, even when there was an effort to preserve an early non-performative "canon" of sorts – that of the Hippocratic corpus – there was no concurrent effort to remember its authors.

[35] See Zhmud (2002) (who emphasizes that in fact little is known of Eudemus' work, and yet it seems clear it is the pre-eminent source for the ancient knowledge of pre-Euclidean mathematics). The one exception may be Archytas' work on music, which might have been available for Porphyry to consult, directly in his commentary to Ptolemy's *Harmonics* (fr. 1, Düring 55.27–58.4). This may well have been preserved for its philosophical rather than its scientific interest.

above, the generation of Archimedes is remarkably well preserved, even today. This is despite the fact that the first century BC surely did not engage primarily in the preservation of mathematics (see pages 467–8 above). The conclusion must be that being active at around 200 BCE was much better, in terms of future preservation, than being active at around 350 BCE.[36]

Let us now bring in the wider range of the non-performative genres. The New Jacoby lists, in raw form, the following numbers of historians.

| Fourth century | Third century | Second century | First century |
|---|---|---|---|
| 124 | 165 | 125 | 117 |

This, to recall, is among the least actively commemorated genres (more like mathematics than like poetry), and thus the effects of the sheer passage of time must be paramount. Let us suppose that the rise from the fourth century to the third represents precisely this effect. If so, we would have expected, other things being equal, more than 200 historians in the second century, more than 250 in the first. Thus, if the ratio of the fourth century to the third implies stability, the ratio of the third to the second and then to the first implies freefall: more than halving the number of Greek historians?

A count of medical authors (in a restricted sense) based on EANS gets the following numbers, now arranged by 50-year nodes.

| 350 | 300 | 250 | 200 | 150 | 100 | 50 |
|---|---|---|---|---|---|---|
| 15 | 13 | 20 | 10 | 16[37] | 12 | 21 |

Here the numbers are too small to allow any strong conclusions. (It is always worrisome when such results are sensitive to the way in which you

---

[36] While the case of the exact sciences is one of the clearest, it is a little confusing for a modern reader, because to us it is perhaps unsurprising that earlier (and, therefore, "out-of-date") works will be cast aside. There is very little indication that this is how ancient science operated: partly because it did not build up, layer upon layer, in the modern manner, rendering earlier iterations obsolete, and instead progressed more "sideways", adding more within the same, or competing, research programs (Netz, 1999a: 237–8); partly because its ideology of scientific progress was complicated by an ideology of a reverence towards the past (out of a reverence for the past, I will simply refer to Bury, 1932: his argument is outdated but his conclusion – that the idea of a monotonic, simple march towards progress is a modern invention – remains valid). Thus, the growth of science led to the accumulation of results put side by side, not to the replacement of past results by the most recent one.

[37] The concentration in this node is an illusion: I gave three Hellenistic medical authors, whose dates cannot be ascertained otherwise, the date "150 BCE ± 100", and I gave four authors who can be dated only to the second century the date "150 BCE ± 50", all of which I report here simply as "150 BCE".

aggregate by chronological boxes.) What is clear is that the rise in the first century itself should at least in part be due to better attestation: it is here, in fact, that we have our earliest extant non-Hippocratic work, by Apollonius of Citium. The conclusion is that there was more scientific medical activity in the early third century BCE than in the later Hellenistic period, but not much else is clear.

The evidence for philosophy is partly comparable.

| 350 | 300 | 250 | 200 | 150 | 100 | 50 |
|-----|-----|-----|-----|-----|-----|-----|
| 42  | 83  | 42  | 45  | 51  | 61  | 34 |

The main contrast here is with the sheer drop at about 50 BCE (these numbers, it should be noted, include Roman authors). Some of this is the "end of history" in the commemoration of earlier philosophy, discussed in Chapter 4, pages 489–90. Philosophy was remembered – up to the end of its Hellenistic career. But this is also a reality, not just a selective filter. The Athenian schools engaged in the mass production of philosophers, which ceased not much later than around 100 BCE. This mass production began at about 300 BCE, and indeed here, as with medicine, we see a moment when numbers rise substantially – followed by a drop. The drop from about 100 to about 50 may be explained by "the end of history". But the rise from 250 to 100 is very modest, given that the historical sources to the later commemoration of philosophy were active already in the first century and thus directly proximate to the late second century BCE. With this in mind, the reported uptick could reflect, if anything, a decline in real numbers.

With the non-performative genres, we have something to work with: these are among the most active fields of the Hellenistic era. Poetry and rhetoric are different. In the preceding chapter, while counting poets, I have pointed out the gradual decline in the size of poetry: first tragedy (meeting its cliff in the third century), then comedy (collapsing, perhaps, through the second century) and then in verse as a whole (with the possible exception of the occasional form of the epigram), which was sharply reduced by the end of the second century. To this, of course, we need to add the case of rhetoric, where I have argued on pages 595–6 above that we must take seriously the prima facie evidence for a substantial reduction in the numbers of rhetors around 300 BCE. This is all controversial, admittedly, but the fact remains that we have very few poets and rhetors attested for the second century BCE (for the first century BCE, of course, we have many – in Latin).

There is of course a significant exception: grammar, which emerged early in the third century and then rose through much of the Hellenistic era. But there was in fact an ancient tradition for, at the very least, a momentary weakness in Alexandrian scholarship. This was presented as the consequence of the contingent dynastic history: Ptolemy VIII Euergetes II emerges, in this tradition, as the villain who expelled the intellectuals of Alexandria in the year 145.[38] Surely, there were grammarians to expel then – including no less than Aristarchus of Samothrace, perhaps the most famous grammarian of antiquity. My database of Greek grammarians is of an especially low quality (based, as noted on page 596 above, on a cursory search through the *New Pauly*), and is biased to the truly famous. But its chronological contours are clear.

| 300 | 250 | 200 | 150 | 100 | 50 |
|-----|-----|-----|-----|-----|-----|
| 6 | 10 | 12 | 20 | 13 | 9 |

This seems like a genuine area of growth (though probably exaggerated by the growing proximity to the Imperial era), reversed, however, in the middle of the second century, with clear contraction following that. So: once again, the arrow points downwards, even if its downward turn emerges somewhat later, in this, quintessentially Hellenistic tradition.

Let us dwell briefly on the qualitative observations suggested by the mention of a luminary such as Aristarchus of Samothrace. Grammar stands out, in fact, in its second-century *qualitative* peak. Let me go through the evidence quickly, with the broadest brush. We may line Aristarchus side by side with other great figures of the Hellenistic era, such as Chrysippus, in philosophy; Archimedes, in mathematics; Herophilus and Erasistratus, in

---

[38] The story is told, for instance, by Fraser (1972: I.86–7, 121, 467–8): Euergetes II "provided the rest of the Greek world with a welcome supply of trained teachers and practitioners in many fields". (Shades, here, of another famous myth – the fall of Constantinople, 1453, prompting the Renaissance). That there was much political disturbance in Alexandria in the middle of the second century BCE is clear enough. The notion that this had far-reaching cultural consequences is entirely dependent on a single passage (!) in Athenaeus (*Deipnosophists* 184bc). This passage could perhaps be seen as a fragment from a genuine historian, Menecles of Barca, as this is the name dropped right at the front of Athenaeus' passage (and so this becomes Jacoby, FGrH 270, F9), but in truth this is an extended authorial comment on the cultural glory of Alexandria, put by Athenaeus in the mouth of his Alexandrian speaker, the musician Alceidas, and one which is obviously intended as hyperbole. (In this telling, all Greek culture was in ruins right after the Wars of the Diadochs; it was saved only in Alexandria; then re-exported to the entire Mediterranean following the crisis of Euergetes II – all of which was meant as a contrast to the tranquil continuity of Greek musical culture prior to its Hellenistic disturbances. The hyperbole is most evident in that philosophy is mentioned, without any reservations, as one of the fields re-exported from Alexandria following 145.)

medicine; and the great poets and scholars, from Callimachus to Eratosthenes. The point is obvious: all these other luminaries are from the third century. Outside grammar, the first half of the second century is especially barren. This era – between Chrysippus and Carneades – appears to have been the one when the Athenian schools were at their most stagnant. Following the generation of Archimedes, nothing of significance is seen in the exact sciences before Hipparchus.[39] We have a very hard time figuring the shape of history writing, in the generation just preceding Polybius; or of poetry, in the generations separating Eratosthenes from Nicander. The medical "node" I have for the year 150 BCE, such as it is, is of such figures who can hardly be dated securely – and of whose contributions to science little can be formed. There is no theoretical innovation we can date to the entire era between Philinus of Cos (founder of empiricism, active second half of the third century?) and Asclepiades (see page 462 above: active near the turn of the second century?). Surely, the early second century is a badly attested period; but why should the first half of the second century be worse off than the second half of the third? This late third century was not some kind of focus of cultural memory in the manner of classical Athens (the memory of Alexandria, if anything, focused on its *earlier* years) – and it was the more distant period. And yet enough is known of the late third century to make us form the picture of a brilliant scientific peak of the non-performative genres. The overall impression of a decline, on all fronts other than grammar, near the beginning of the second century is probably not an accidental construct of our evidence. Could it represent, then, at least among other things, the trough predicted above? The Greek cities now produced much smaller cohorts of leisured citizens: non-Greeks from the east only beginning to contribute to Greek culture in significant numbers; non-Greeks from the west remaining, at this point, no more than distant observers. And, when Greek-inspired civilization took off, again, towards the end of the second century and beyond, this would be thanks to authors such as Posidonius, the Syrian from Apamea, and Cicero, the Italian from Arpinum.

This brief account is based on two assumptions. The first is that the authorial class scales fairly directly with the size of the leisured elite. The second is that cultural achievement, in a qualitative sense, is closely related to the size of the authorial class. I have discussed briefly the first of those assumptions, on pages 612–16 above, but, obviously, we do not have the statistics to prove it. We have to be even more speculative with regard to the second.

---

[39] I have my doubts concerning the dating of Hypsicles, for which see Netz (2015); in any event, he is a minor author.

This, of course, is at the very heart of the project of this book, and I imagine many readers are offended by its very emphasis on mere numbers. Indeed, genius is elusive, and, by its very nature, rare: so it *should* be unpredictable. In fact it is not. The stubborn fact of the history of culture is its localization: particular forms of human expression are invariably concentrated, becoming much more refined and successful at a few particular times and places. Hence, space and canon. It should be added, now, that genius is at the side of the biggest battalions. We can form some judgement as to the relative scales, at different points in time, and the conclusion is that the great cultural achievements surveyed in this book all emerge from moments of *growth* – classical Athenian drama, philosophy in the age of Plato, Alexandrian medicine, the generation of Archimedes, Cicero's oratory and Horace's poetry. All these authors were active in generations for which we can argue with great confidence that the number of authors active in their respective fields was much higher than it had been in the previous generation.

To offer a final speculation, then: perhaps the correlation is not so much with the absolute numbers involved as with the trend line. Cultural production tends to higher achievements in periods in which more and more people engage with it. And, conversely: even starting from high numbers, there could be something demoralizing and deflating about a field that shrinks, even moderately. Fewer new voices, a shrinking audience... This must be disheartening; professors in the humanities should know. Was the first half of the second century a little like that?

## 6.2   To the High Empire: A Quantitative Introduction

The preceding two sections studied the dynamics of scale: how it grew, wobbled, grew again, in the half-millennium before Augustus. In this and the following sections, I am looking at scale, once again, in a more static way, trying to develop a model for the later part of the second century CE. This will sometimes involve considerations for the first two centuries as a whole, which in many ways can be seen as a historical unity (further, we are forced to cast our net wide: the evidence, as I will emphasize, is surprisingly sparse). The importance of this model lies, once again, in a dynamic consideration. In the remainder of this chapter, I will concentrate on the question of the decline in scale through the third century, and on its consequences. To understand this, then, we need to set, first, a baseline for such a calculation, right before the decline sets in. We also need to suggest an account of how scale was sustained through the Imperial era itself – so as to account for later transformations.

Indeed, the first thing to recognize is the significant challenge imposed by the evidence. We have relied throughout on the tendency of Greek authors to construct their cultural past as a polis of letters, fully populated by many diverse individual citizens. This tendency expands significantly in the Roman era (we have noted the rise of the histories of philosophy, in particular, on pages 485–6 above; and of course we have relied extensively on the evidence from Plutarch and Athenaeus, masters of the symposia of cultural commemoration). As I shall return to note in the following section, the habits of commemoration subtly shift in the following centuries: from the third century onwards we see much more remembrance of things *present*, a closer engagement with the proximate past (while, of course, maintaining the memory – and the works – of the core canon). The consequence is that the Imperial era remembers the past: but who now remembers the rememberers?

This intersects with the growing proximity of the Imperial era to the decisive moment for the survival of works into the manuscript tradition: the transition from roll to codex in the fourth century. It would have been easier for papyrus rolls to wait a century or two for their material upgrade (as did those of Athenaeus, or of Plutarch) than it would have been for them to wait three, four or five centuries (as did the rolls of Juba, Posidonius or Phylarchus). We saw a similar logic operating for attestation – for which one key, I have argued, must have been proximity to the Imperial era. Proximity to the fourth century CE must have acted similarly for the survival of works. I shall return to calculate this effect more rigorously in the following section, on pages 704–10, but, for the time being, it is enough to sum up these basic two observations in a qualitative way.

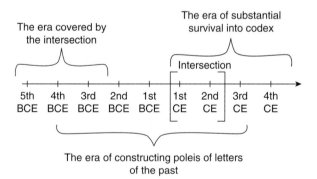

The Imperial era is the intersection of two eras: that in which extensive commemorations of Greek cultural history were produced (classical through Imperial); and that from which works have a higher chance of survival into codex (Imperial through late ancient). This intersection is our source of light for deeper antiquity. It casts its light backwards, however, onto the past, and so it commemorates primarily the almost half-millennium from Pericles to Augustus. As we move into the Imperial era itself, our knowledge no longer derives from extensive commemoration but is, instead, mostly, the more random outcome of contemporary mentions.

What does this mean for the number of the attested? I shall begin by looking at the evidence for the two most significant prose genres, philosophy and history.

Here are the raw numbers for (more securely identified) philosophers.

| 0 | 50 | 100 | 150 | 200 |
|---|---|---|---|---|
| 13 | 32 | 31 | 43 | 22 |

The simple reading of such numbers is of considerable growth (if from a very low nadir) through the first two centuries, reversed around the end of the second. (This possible reverse is the subject of the following sections, and I shall put it aside for the moment.) The number for 150 CE is respectable, but is at the normal level for philosophy from 350 through 100 BCE.

The raw numbers from the New Jacoby are as follows: first century CE, 74; from the second century CE, 69. This suggests perhaps a plateau, at a rather low level of attestation. (For the preceding four centuries, the comparable numbers had three digits.)

The evidence from the fragmentary historians in Latin shows a very distinctive pattern.[40]

| −150 | −100 | −50 | 0 | 50 | 100 | 150 | 200 |
|---|---|---|---|---|---|---|---|
| 3 | 13 | 38 | 24 | 23 | 11 | 1 | 2 |

Here we see a clear decline into and through the Imperial era.[41]

---

[40] I read through Cornell (2013), removed authors in Greek (to avoid double-counting with Jacoby; but this consideration hardly matters for the period that interests us) and added such authors from appendix I (excluded by Cornell's strict definition) who would have been included by Jacoby. Even so, the set we find is somewhat more restricted and more "political" than Jacoby's, which somewhat skews the evidence (it seems that the purely "antiquarian" historians would have been less rare in the Imperial era).

[41] The absolute numbers of attested historians are somewhat smaller than those for the Greek fragmentary historians, however, and there are reasons to think that Roman fragmentary historians of the first century BCE are comparatively well attested, so the absolute size of this group must have been smaller, and its fluctuations matter less.

I will start with a detailed consideration of the group of philosophers attested from the peak, and then generalize to the even more difficult case of historians, both Greek and Latin.

Here, then, is how we come to know about the philosophers whose center of activity is known to have been from about 125 to 175 CE.[42]

Sixteen who are now known through the two main conduits for evidence of philosophy in the era:

nine through their association with Marcus Aurelius;[43]
seven through their mentions by Galen.[44]

Thirteen who are known through their contacts with non-philosophical traditions:

eight through the testimony of extant "sophists";[45]
five through their brushes with Christianity.[46]

Fourteen who survive variously:

six through inscriptions;[47]
five (only!) through the philosophical tradition;[48]

---

[42] This is surely an undercount, as some individuals are harder to date (how about Alcinous/Albinus, for instance?). Note, however, that we refer to those whose center of activity fell within this temporal node: a qualification that excludes, for instance, Demonax and Oenomaeus. Note also that, in this eclectic era, the identity of "philosopher" is hazier. I avoid individuals whose main identity was not that of a philosopher: so, for example, Favorinus, in my counting is a rhetor; this of course is debatable.

[43] Alexander of Seleucia, Apollonius, Bacchius, Basilides, Cinna Catulus, Claudius Maximus, Rusticus, Sextus of Chaeronea and the emperor himself. Some of these are mentioned by Marcus Aurelius, some are mentioned by the historiographical tradition surrounding him.

[44] Alexander of Damascus, Antisthenes, Antonius, Eudemus of Pergamon and Glaucon are creatures almost entirely of Galen's works (see also p. 583, n.80, above); also known through Galen (but fairly well known also through the later tradition of Aristotelian commentary) are Aristotle of Mytilene and Aspasius.

[45] Two are mentioned by Philostratus, because of their involvement in the lives of sophists: Aristocles of Pergamon (converted from philosophy to rhetoric) and Pancrates of Athens; two who are mentioned by Aelius Aristides (Capito, Evaristus of Crete); two who are mentioned by Aulus Gellius (Calvenus Taurus, Hierocles: both are major figures who might have remained known otherwise; Hierocles even survives on papyrus). From Lucian we have the names of the cynic philosophers Proteus Peregrinus and Theagenes of Patrae.

[46] Aristides of Athens converted to Christianity, Athenagoras is known as a philosopher who was also a Christian apologist; Celsus and Crescens polemicized and persecuted Christians, respectively. (Eusebius' citations of Diogenianus are more of a fluke: he had nothing especially to do with Christianity.)

[47] Cornelianus, Heraclides and Zosimus of Athens, Maximus of Gortyna; and then Diogenes of Oenoanda and his friend Dionysius of Rhodes. (A few others, known through the literary tradition, are attested by inscriptions as well; as I will return to note below, this is the high point of the Greek epigraphic habit.)

[48] Two, Herminus and Nicostratus, remembered primarily through the tradition of Aristotelian commentary; Cronius and Aelianus, as well as the much more significant Numenius, would be recalled by the Platonist tradition, in particular starting with Porphyry.

three extant, though they perhaps should not be counted: Arrian (primarily a historian), Apuleius (primarily a "sophist"), Ptolemy (primarily an author in the exact sciences). I have made the judgement call not to count Galen here as "philosopher", but he, too, of course, was an author who left behind extant philosophical works, even while noted primarily for his non-philosophical careers.

What emerges from the above is that the philosophers of this period are known to us *by accident.* Philosophers sometimes crossed the paths of others – an emperor, a doctor, sophists, saints. Philosophers could leave their name on stone. But philosophy itself did not invest any active effort into the remembrance of this period, and, in general, our evidence is remarkable for its *contemporaneity.* We do not see here the later memory of the second century by authors of the fourth, fifth and sixth centuries.

And yet: the Imperial era, if not so much remembered, is *preserved.* The extant contemporary or near-contemporary sources are sometimes very substantial (as in Galen and – effectively launching the extant tradition of the Aristotelian commentary – in Alexander of Aphrodisias). Some are quite chatty, as with Lucian, Aelius Aristides, and Aulus Gellius. It is remarkable, then, how few names they provide, usually no more than a couple each, only a little more even in the Galenic corpus. Antiquity was just not very good about *contemporary* names.

Who remembers the rememberers? Even more directly, then: who historizes the historians? Truly, no one: the "Lives of the Historians", as I noted on page 599 above, was never an ancient genre, and commemoration for this genre is truly random.

What we are considering right now is the survival of historians of the Imperial era. This raises questions, in particular, concerning the case of Latin-language history – which is something of a special case, however, that follows its own path, for specific, historical reasons. This calls for a brief detour.

Literary life exploded in Rome in the first century BCE, following on its politics: a significant part of all cultural production took the form either of speeches or of political history.[49] Literature, in other words, was one field among many of senatorial competition. (I touched on pages 514–22 above on the way in which this competition impacted upon the culture of the Mediterranean as a whole.) This competition was brought to a close through Imperial domination. The Augustan policy – less consistently pursued by

---

[49] Almost all the historians in this set are from the senatorial order, or (less often) freedmen from the households of senators (see p. 615 above); knight-historians such as Atticus are very rare.

emperors immediately following him – was not to shut culture down but, instead, to embrace and centralize it; hence the golden age of Latin literature. (Of course, this quick statement sums up a large field of scholarship, not without its controversies, which I will here avoid.) The trend is clear: a decline of the more overtly political forms of expression. Fewer rhetors (see page 589, note 90, above; but also more jurists; see pages 664–5 below). And also fewer historians. For the most part, this should be explained not just in terms of an unnatural decline through the first century CE[50] but, rather, in terms of an unnatural explosion in the first century BCE. Authorship was always a problematic fit with the Roman senatorial ethos. As the era of the civil wars was over, not a few must have been relieved to lay down not only their swords but also their pens.

With this understood, let us now look at the set of extant historical authors (broadly construed) from the Roman era.[51]

| | −50 | 0 | 50 | 100 | 150 | 200 |
|---|---|---|---|---|---|---|
| Greek | Diodorus Sic. | Dion. Hal. | Peripl. M.E. | Plutarch | Appian | Cassius Dio |
| | | Strabo | | Josephus | Arrian | Athenaeus |
| | | | | | Aristodemus | |
| | | | | | Dion. Perieg. | |
| | | | | | Dion. of Byz. | |
| | | | | | Pausanias | |
| | | | | | Polyaenus | |
| Latin | Caesar | Livy | Lucan | Tacitus | Suetonius | |
| | Sallust | Velleius. Pat. | Valerius Max. | Curt. Rufus | Ampelius | |
| | Nepos | Pomp. Trog. | Pomp. Mela | Florus | | |
| | Cicero[52] | Seneca Sr. | Pliny Sr. | Frontinus | | |
| | | | | Silius Italicus | | |

[50] There must have been some active suppression: overt political activity was not only dangerous (as perhaps it always has been) but also futile. Sometime under the reign of Tiberius Cordus inserted a praise of Cassius into a political history, likely of the Triumviral period; put to trial for this offense, he committed suicide (Cornell, 2013: 498–500). But one could still write antiquarian or more geographical histories, and, indeed, a good many of the authors recorded for the first century are of this non-political kind – found now mostly in Cornell's appendix of more antiquarian authors (15 out of 37 of Cornell's historians from the first century CE are antiquarian, as opposed to eight out of 51 for the first century BCE). Many of these first-century CE non-political authors are known through the witness of Pliny the Elder, so in a sense this represents a bias in our evidence; on the other hand, Pliny himself can be seen as part of this shift, from political to more natural, less threatening histories.
[51] I will define "extant" as "surviving in parchment form into Byzantium, and now directly legible, even if severely lacunose". This includes Aristodemus but excludes, for instance, Cephalion, known only through Photius' report (*Cod.* 68).
[52] Cicero is here strictly for the extant *Brutus*, a cultural history of Roman rhetoric.

The numbers are small and should not be analyzed for their node-by-node detail. In broad contour, we do see a transition from Latin to Greek: as expected. We also note that this is a major group – more than 30 authors, many of them very bulky. Together, they constitute a significant fraction of the literature extant from antiquity. State ideologies – from Constantine all through the Middle Ages (and beyond) – rested on the ascendancies of Rome and of Jerusalem; their histories had to be preserved.

And now, finally, what I see as the most significant observation, in terms of the demography of historians. We may compare the two trajectories, for fragmentary and for extant historians, from the two last centuries BCE to the two first centuries CE. The contrast is very simple. In the last two centuries BCE we have more fragmentary historians, and then their numbers go down sharply in the first and second centuries CE. The number of extant historians, on the other hand, rises sharply into the first and, even more, into the second century.

Fragmentary historians ↓ extant historians ↑

At first glance this is surprising. You would think that both sets – fragmentary historians and extant historians – are subsets of the same original set, of all historians, and so should scale similarly. But, of course, this is hardly a mystery. Once again: the extant historians do not provide us with any information on their contemporaries, hence they do no give rise to a larger set of fragmentary historians. This effect is indeed even more marked for history than what we found for philosophy. Of the 69 historians that the New Jacoby lists for the second century CE, *three* are known via reports in contemporary or near-contemporary historians.[53] Nor do historians piggy-back on their non-historian contemporaries to be commemorated in quite the same way in which philosophers piggy-backed on non-philosophers. In general, historians are mentioned (only when they are lucky) as they are recycled – for their language (by later grammarians) or for their information (by later historians). The language of Imperial-era historians, Greek or Latin, interested no grammarian. What they needed to survive, then, were many

---

[53] Athenaeus cites Pancrates (*Deipnosophists*, XV.21 677d–f: while this is a New Jacoby entry, the Pancrates in question wrote a poem on Hadrian, and he is more a panegyrist than a historian) and Aristomenes of Athens (*Deipnosophists*, III.82 115a–b: this one was an Athenian actor of the old comedy who also wrote on ancient Athenian rituals!), and Philostratus tells us that the sophist Anteius Antiochus was also the author of a history (*Lives of the Sophists* 570). Just as in the Latin case, discussed below, the handful of historians commemorated for this era were not primarily historians. There are 16 historians who are dated by the New Jacoby to "before the second century CE" based on their citation in this century, mostly by Athenaeus; the probability is that they are almost all Hellenistic.

later historians to cite them: an absence that begins to suggest, already, the contours of a transition, following the Imperial era.

Of the three (!) fragmentary *Latin* historians of the second century CE, one is Apuleius, and another is Septimius Severus, which once again is reminiscent of the pattern of survival of the philosophers: remembered primarily not as historians but, respectively, as a rhetor and as an emperor. The remaining one is indeed an individual whose main persona as an author was as historian. This is Marius Maximus, distinguished for being the only author cited by the *Historia Augusta* for this period, whose name we now take to be authentic. There is no more than a tiny thread of historical writing in Latin from late antiquity that covers the Imperial era, and that of very inferior quality. The *Historia Augusta* invents the historians it cites, while later authors such as Aurelius Victor simply elide such citations altogether. (It is for a reason that the "Kaisergeschichte" is, to us, anonymous.)[54]

In short, then, the raw numbers of fragmentary, Imperial-era historians must be very misleading. Should we trust, then, the evidence of the numbers of extant authors? Here we do see rising numbers. These must be biased by the effect mentioned above, however: of chronological proximity to the transition from roll to codex in the fourth century CE. The case of the histories of Alexander provides a good example. Here is a favorite theme for ancient historiography (and prose writing more generally). It is a subject early enough, and the tradition of historical writing on Alexander started right at the beginning, with many eyewitness accounts (see pages 286–7 above). It has accumulated many authors. Jacoby lists nearly 40 fragmentary authors (nos. 117 to 153) whose main focus is on Alexander's expedition, a number which excludes many other authors whose histories would provide significant information on Alexander (for instance, Theopompus of Chios, the main author on Philip; or the historians of the diadochs, all lost). In short, there must have been many histories of Alexander circulating through parts of antiquity – perhaps as many as hundreds. And yet our evidence for

---

[54] "Kaisergeschichte" is the name of a work whose existence was postulated by Enmann (1883) as the common source explaining the close similarities between two historical works from the late fourth century that could be shown to be independent from each other. It has later been shown to be heavily used by other late ancient historians (see discussion in Burgess, 1995, who argues, in turn, for a mid-fourth-century date for this work, and suggests a possible identification). The point for me is not the precise identity of the author but the very fact that we need to reconstruct it. Here is the historical work that was practically, in its time, the key reference work in political history, heavily used by an entire generation of historians, many of whom are extant. And yet – nothing is known of the identity of the author! Such were the habits of attestation, among ancient historians. This has the paradoxical consequence that the heavy citation practice of the *Historia Augusta* is, in fact, one of the key features that mark it as inauthentic.

the campaign rests primarily on Curtius Rufus, Plutarch and Arrian, all from the late first century CE to the middle of the second. The only significant, earlier source is Diodorus Siculus. This is suggestive: perhaps the period between Curtius Rufus and Arrian was simply the latest one of extensive historical writing, hence the one most likely to survive into codex. The considerable survival of Imperial-era historiography may represent, then, a recency bias; the collapse of fragmentary historiography may represent a transition in the pattern of citation.

The argument so far can be summed up as follows. There were particular events that did limit authorial activity, for certain periods, in particular genres. The closing of the Athenian schools made for a first century BCE that was intellectually innovative but also smaller in the scale of its philosophical production. The Principate did manage to exercise a cooling effect on the writing of political history in Latin. But, overall, the transition from the Hellenistic to the Roman era concerns the level of attestation, not the level of ancient practice. The fact that more is extant does not mean that more was produced. But there is no real reason to think that any less was produced – *pace* the evidence of the fragments. Activity in the main prose genres must have been very significant, and perhaps comparable to that of earlier peak periods.

And yet, the fact remains: our attestation for the bulk of production in the traditional prose genres of history and philosophy in the Imperial era is so low that we cannot even tell how bad it is. For once, our statistics come up short. And it is precisely *statistics* that comes up short. I explain: we have many extant authors for the first century CE and, even more, the second century. There is thus ample room for traditional scholarship, based on the extant sources. At the same time, our knowledge of second-tier Imperial-era philosophers and historians is much less detailed than for previous centuries. A few dozen authors attested for each century, for each genre, all heavily influenced by the biases of a few sources. Can we rely on Pliny the Elder, and reconstruct a more "paradoxographical" school of Roman history, immediately preceding him? Was Greek history in the second century concerned more with regional and ethnic subjects, perhaps more "geographical"?[55] I am

---

[55] Abydenus, Pseudo-Manetho, Pancrates of Egypt, Antonius Julianus, Judas and especially Bardesanes are historians of "ethnic" subjects from the second century (should we also count Tacitus? Josephus, a little earlier, certainly belongs to this group.). But this may well represent specifically Christian interests in the Jews – and in universal chronologies subsumed under a single sacred history. Millar (1969: 14) states: "Local histories apart, the pagan historiography of the second and third centuries took broadly three directions: scholarly rewriting of periods of the classical, and sometimes the Hellenistic, past; massive compilations of Roman history up to the present; and a remarkably flourishing historiography of the most recent past, chiefly related to the reigns of Emperors, or, more specifically, to the wars fought by them." This relies mostly on the impression

not sure we have the relevant sources to answer such questions. For instance, it is occasionally suggested that Epicureanism recedes in the Imperial era, and one points to Diogenes of Oenoanda as the rare counter-example:[56] he is the only Epicurean philosopher, definitely identified as such, in his era. When making such assertions, we are unreflectively relying upon the evidence as a reliable sample. But suppose, for instance, that 10 percent of Imperial-era philosophers were Epicureans – which would mean that it did remain a respectable group. Suppose, further, that the combined bias of our handful of major sources (Seneca, Plutarch, Galen, Marcus Aurelius, the Aristotelian commentary tradition: none an Epicurean) would be to reduce the expected percentage, *before random sampling effects*, to 3 to 4 percent. We have only a few dozen philosophical authors securely attested by the literary tradition. Getting zero, in such a small sample, when we expected 3 to 4 percent would not be a remarkable result.[57] If so, the inscription of Diogenes of Oenoanda is not a bizarre accident: it simply reminds us that, for this period, inscriptions are almost more reliable – for statistical purposes – than are literary sources (more below). And one further thing we can no longer deduce from such limited, biased samples: the chronological division. The internal evidence of history and philosophy is consistent with either a plateau or, perhaps, a rise into the second century CE.

We have very little to go by, then, as we try to extrapolate absolute numbers. Earlier we assumed, for the period of a little more than six centuries preceding 200 CE, about 16,000 authors in both history and philosophy (a misleading precision). If we simply assume that this roughly obtained for the second century CE, then there should have been about 2,500 historians and philosophers active – as against a little more than 100 whom we have attested. Assume a somewhat smaller group (as, after all, the Hellenistic schools are no longer

---

of the *extant* works; his entire third category derives from Lucian's "How History Is to Be Written", an essay that condemns historians of a contemporary Parthian war, distinguishing at least ten authors (some by name, some by description of the contents of their work). This unique source looms large within the statistics of historians attested for the second century CE; it may be entirely fictitious (Jones, 1986: 63–4, 161–6); even if real, this is exactly the type of biased source that renders such small samples meaningless.

[56] See, e.g., Erler (2009: 46–7). (Diogenes was a second-century CE citizen of Oenoanda – a Lycian, inland city, definitely not a cultural metropolis – who acquired something like an entire piazza to carve on its walls his epitome of Epicurean philosophy; he is now known entirely through this massive epigraphic find.)

[57] We do not in fact get zero; rather, we get a few fractions, as there are several Epicureans performing in Plutarch's dialogues and some possible – but uncertain – historical figures (Xenocles, Alexander, Zopyrus – as well as a doctor, Boethus – also a mathematician! For a brief discussion, see Gordon, 2012: 156–7.). Many Romans in the late Republic were sympathetic towards Epicureanism without assuming the identity of an "Epicurean philosopher", and a handful of such figures are still attested from the Imperial era. Castner (1988) counts 22 in the late Republic, five in the Imperial era. The decline in this case may well be attributed to the bias of our testimony (as our leading source for this prosopography is Cicero).

active, Latin political history is curtailed) and we find a ratio still rather worse than 1:10 (the overall average we imply here for historians), though not *much* worse. In short, the argument leads us to believe that cultural production in history and philosophy, in the Imperial era, was at a level comparable to that of the preceding centuries, if perhaps somewhat below its peak levels (which were: in philosophy, in the Hellenistic era; in Latin history, in the first century BCE; and in Greek history, who knows?).

Let us consider more genres. Medicine, I argued, was a substantial genre, and its ups and downs are significant. Looking at my restricted database, of relatively securely attested medical authors, I find the following distribution.

| 50 | 0 | 50 | 100 | 150 | 200 |
|----|----|----|-----|-----|-----|
| 21 | 33 | 37 | 25 | 23 | 5 |

That the node at 150 is not more substantial is at first glance surprising, but we should remember that Galen, after all, does not mention that many authors, and confronts but a few contemporary ones (see pages 582–3 above. I discard, in this database, the many authors cited purely for pharmacological recipes: it is only for this group that Galen's attestation is significant – though, even here, most are not contemporaries.). Once again, perhaps the trend line from the first century CE to the second is not significant (the first century is certainly somewhat inflated by the accident of the survival of Pliny the Elder), but in this case what stands out is the sheer absolute numbers. Here, unlike history or philosophy, the Imperial era is the one for which *more* authors are attested. The highest number attested for any period prior to the Roman era – the heyday of Alexandrian medicine, in 250 BCE – is merely 20. Given what we have seen for the attestation from the Imperial era – and seeing that Galen, in fact, does not raise the numbers of attested medical authors substantially – the likelihood is that we should take this evidence at face value: more medical authors now. This chimes with some more evidence. Here are the comparable figures for a few other groups.

| | 50 | 0 | 50 | 100 | 150 | 200 |
|---|----|----|----|-----|-----|-----|
| Grammarians[58] | 9 | 17 | 12 | 18 | 9 | 3 |
| Astrological authors | 3 | 5 | 4 | 7 | 8 | 0 |
| Mathematicians | 0 | 0 | 1 | 6 | 5 | 2 |

---

[58] A significant group, for which I have a sketchy database (p. 596 above): the numbers are significant undercounts, and I can only hope this does not contaminate my data too much.

Astrology was invented not long before our period, and it was only gradually that the writing of astrological handbooks became a recognized form of authorship; it is not surprising that the numbers rise. I argued on pages 467–8 above that mathematical authorship effectively ceased around 100 BCE but we do see it revived – and apparently especially in the second century CE, when Ptolemy was the towering figure. The numbers attested are below those for the generations of Archytas or of Archimedes, but, once again, who bothered to remember the generation of Ptolemy in its prosopographic detail? As for grammar, here once again we find numbers that are slightly below the earlier Alexandrian peaks. That Alexandrian peak, we recall (page 651), was achieved late compared to other Hellenistic achievements – in my temporal node of 150 BCE. There I find 20 grammarians: comparable with the higher numbers found at some of the nodes of the Imperial era. The overall impression, then, is that the central fields of scholarship, from medicine to grammar, did see a growth from the late Hellenistic era to the Roman era, though, once again, it is hard to prove an overall direction of growth, or otherwise, from the first to the second century CE.

Such growth remains plausible. Medicine, astrology and grammar are the typical Greek "service industries" (as I will note below, the exact sciences, too, may acquire in the second century something of this character). These are the fields in which, broadly speaking, Greeks earn their professional status in the east and then cash that status into Roman patronage: the Galenic route. It makes historical sense that such fields will grow into the Roman era; I shall return to this below.

I have estimated the total numbers of authors in the technical fields surveyed above – from medicine to grammar – at roughly 8,000 to 10,000. Given the evidence above, it is reasonable to assign a quarter or so of such authors to the second century CE: once again, a figure of 2,000 to 2,500 authors through the century, or 500 active simultaneously at the peak, seems reasonable.

Certainly, growing state patronage explains the following pattern. I now turn to a field which is in some sense almost a creation of the Roman era: jurists. Here is a suggestive outline.[59]

| −50 | 0 | 50 | 100 | 150 | 200 | 250 |
|---|---|---|---|---|---|---|
| 9 | 6 | 6 | 8 | 12 | 9 | 2 |

[59] Methodologically, this list is very weak: I searched the New Pauly for "jurist" and noted all the individuals, hence the small numbers. The broad historical outline is sufficiently clear in this field, however, in which, indeed, there is a continuous historical self-awareness from the early Principate down to Byzantium.

This table should be taken together with that of the fragmentary Roman historians, and in particular against the evidence for Roman orators (almost entirely concentrated, as noted on page 590 above, in the late Republic and the Augustan era). The business of the state intersects, in the late Republic, with the Greek practices of authorship, and so speech, history – and also, to some extent, legal theory – become fields of activity for the senatorial elite. As the emperors take control of the business of the state, speech and history are muted or perhaps deflected away from politics, but legal theory continues to be cultivated: if the orator is an actor on the state's stage, and the historian is the state's critic, the jurist is more obviously the state's servant. He is of more use, then, to a state that no longer values free actors and free critics. As usual, transitions of scale can be detected also at the institutional level, and it is in this era that we see the emergence of *schools* of jurisprudence, the Sabinian and the Proculian – first-century CE creations that lasted well into the second.[60] This has the result, perhaps, of an even more intensively cultivated intellectual practice (thus the peak at about 150). In this case, then, we have fairly clear evidence for growing state patronage accounting for the growth of an intellectual practice. The numbers presented here are based on the weak evidence of searches through the New Pauly – and are already quite meaningful. The reality of two rival schools strongly suggests a marked presence, with, perhaps, many dozens of authors active at the same time in the city of Rome.

Within Roman cultural life, the jurists, to some extent, plug a hole left by the decreasing orators; in Greece, of course, there is no hole to plug. The period is marked above all by the eruption of rhetoric. Here, finally, we see evident growth in numbers of authors. We have begun to look at the chronological distribution of rhetorical authors already on pages 588–96 above, since, in this genre, we really have to distinguish between different epochs. Something clearly shifts during the Imperial era: the question is, how much to read into our evidence, with its two biases of Philostratus' *Lives of the Sophists* and of the inscriptions.

---

[60] For a survey, see Leesen (2009) (who argues, persuasively, that the schools should be understood as institutions of law based on state patronage, and not as theoretical centers: the heads of schools granted specified prerogatives of authoritative legal statement by the emperors). Our evidence for the schools as institutions derives mostly from the late second-century author Sextus Pomponius, who composed a kind of brief prosopography of the discipline, as an introduction to his *Enchiridion*, now extant as *Digest* I.2.2.47–53. This historical survey proceeds to the reign of Hadrian; it is thus harder to determine the later history of the schools. It should be noted that, while our *institutional* grasp of jurisprudence fails us, our attestation remains strong, thanks to the frequent citations of individual jurists by later compilations – jurists whose activities are often datable thanks to historical references in their opinions.

First, to the epigraphic evidence. I have counted those inscriptions in Puech (2002) that allow meaningful dating, within this period. This division is as follows (following Puech's chronological categories).[61]

| I | I/II | II | II/III | Early III | Later (up to and including the sixth century) |
|---|------|----|--------|-----------|-----------------------------------------------|
| 5 | 10 | 61 | 30 | 28 | 21 |
| 3% | 6% | 38% | 18% | 17% | 13% |

In my category "Early III" I have avoided the handful of individuals who can be dated to late in the third century (such as Marcus Junius Minucianus: Puech, 2002: 353–6). My remaining set is those who were active in the first third of the century. The preceding category, "II/III", bifurcates into authors whose dating is very difficult (hence can be anywhere within this range) and those whose dating is very precise – and precisely straddles the centuries. Many of the authors in the category "II", as well, can be dated precisely, and almost always they can be dated to the second half of the second century, often late in it. The net result is that, likely, not much less than 75 percent of the rhetors attested epigraphically can be dated to roughly 150 to 230 CE, a great many of those to the period 180 to 210 CE.[62] Obviously, this effect is built, in part, from the concentration of the epigraphic habit in this period.[63] But this might miss the

[61] I ignore the evidence from coins and the graffiti of the Valley of the Kings; these are interesting, but their pattern of survival is distinct from that of inscriptions.

[62] For comparison: Nutton (1977: 219–26) has a list of 80 individuals attested epigraphically as *archiatri*, discussed on pp. 584–5 above. Of these, 23 are clearly dated to outside the second century CE or early third century CE, but in this case there is less of a concentration on the very late second century/very early third century. The impression of this evidence is that elite physicians were only somewhat over-represented in the second century CE, relative to the frequency of inscriptions.

[63] MacMullen (1986) remains the only thorough quantitative survey of the chronological distribution of inscriptions in the Roman east. In Lydia, the custom was to put exact dates on epitaphs, which allows us to date precisely 405 documents. MacMullen provides a rough bar graph, which I read off numerically to mean that something like 55 percent of the inscriptions date to the same period of 150 to 230 CE. I shall return below to the question of the epigraphic habit as a whole, but it should be noted that the literature, following on MacMullen's pathbreaking work, has emphasized the importance of regional variation in the contours of such chronological distributions. Indeed, Puech's inscriptions range very widely, from Asia Minor and central Greece, but also from Rome and elsewhere. The superposition of the different chronological waves should result in a somewhat "flatter" distribution, and the likelihood is that, overall, across Puech's area, weighted by the number of inscriptions per region, the original total distribution of all inscriptions was such that *fewer* than 55 percent were from the central period 150 to 230 CE (though perhaps not by much). The bare numbers of Puech's distribution imply an overconcentration of rhetors by a factor of 1.5 in the period 150 to 230 CE; but this is, for reasons explained in the text, an undercount of this concentration.

point, which is that the two processes – growing numbers of inscriptions and growing numbers of rhetors – are in fact correlated.

It is conceivable that the epigraphic habit and the declamatory habit could well have sprung from similar sources. (This claim is essential to the argument of this chapter, and so I shall return to elaborate on this argument in the following section.) Let us suppose, then, that we trust the evidence of the inscriptions broadly and assume that most rhetors of the Second Sophistic were in fact active during the period from 150 to 230, many of them in the period 180 to 210. I have suggested on page 593 above that there were about 2,000 rhetors active in the Second Sophistic as a whole, which would imply, then, perhaps more than 1,000 in the period from 150 to 230, quite a few hundred in the central years straddling the centuries. There could well have been, then, something like 300 rhetors – possibly more – active simultaneously at the peak (which, judging from Puech's numbers, may well have come right at the turn of the century; I shall return to this in the following section).

We can barely date the authors of prose fiction – indeed, we often fail to name them! But the simplest assumption is that their chronological contours match those of the Second Sophistic as a whole, and my guess above was for prose fiction at about half the rhetors. The error bars on all of this are considerable but my central assumption, therefore, is that, at the peak, the number of authors in both rhetoric and prose fiction could have exceeded 300 and could perhaps have been not that far from 500.

The number 500 is useful, in that it is not unlike the numbers mentioned above for historians and philosophers taken together, and also for the various cultural "service industries" taken together. The rough outline of culture implied, for the late-Antonine (post-Antonine?) peak, looks as follows:

- one-third "traditional prose", historians and philosophers;
- one-third the prose of the service industries, from medicine to law;
- one-third the Second Sophistic.

The set as a whole can easily make 1,500 authors, active at the same time; perhaps as many active together as the Mediterranean has ever seen. This quantitative statement is no more than a guess, and a generous one at that. Mainly so as to make it somewhat more plausible, I turn to add a few remarks of a more qualitative nature.

## 6.3 To the High Empire: Patronage and the Quest for Status

I accounted above for two factors in the long-term trend in the numbers of authors citing: demography and economics. The numbers of potential authors rose as more local elites participated in Hellenized culture; the numbers of potential authors shrank as social narrowing reduced the relative size of the elite. How do such forces continue to work through the first two centuries CE?

There is clearly some demographic growth – most of it in the less populated, especially western parts of the Empire.[64] There we also find significant Latinization, and the expected outcome should be a gradual transition of the center of gravity of cultural life, through those two centuries, from east to west, from Greek to Latin. Indeed, several important figures of this era have roots in the trans-Italian west: Seneca, from Spain; Tacitus and Favorinus, from Gaul; Apuleius, from Africa. But in fact the thrust of culture in this era is away from Italy, eastwards: the small evidence we have for history and philosophy is heavily Greek; the doctors, astrologers and grammarians who serve the elite, get their training in the east; the Second Sophistic is a phenomenon of Asia Minor – and, if it recruits elsewhere, this seems to be primarily in the Levant (see pages 732–3 below for a somewhat later period). This is in contrast to the first century BCE, whose trend was so clearly towards Latin, towards the city of Rome. A geographical paradox, then: as demography moves west, culture moves east. But this paradox is not hard to resolve: culture was never really made Italian.[65] As I pointed out in the preceding section, the flowering of culture in Latin was driven by the heightened political competition of the senatorial class during the late Republican era (and its peaceful resolution under Augustus). This was a temporary valorization of Latin, as a cultural vehicle. As Imperial power descended on Rome, normalcy returned, Latin was remarginalized. The emerging Latin-speaking elite in the west gained prominence, then, primarily through political and military service (while the topmost elite in Italy remained enmeshed within *Greek* culture). This put a cap on the potential growth of culture in the Imperial era (besides having important consequences for the future cultural history of the Mediterranean, by creating local traditions, in the Latin-speaking world, of a more militarized elite: more below, on page 723).

---

[64] Frier (2000: 814).
[65] Indeed, in a world ruled by the Latin language, Greek culture was newly valorized as an alternative space, for Greek speakers: one of the main themes of Whitmarsh's interpretation of the Second Sophistic.

The question of the performance of the Roman economy in the Imperial era is contested. It is obvious that this was, by pre-modern standards, an extraordinarily successful state, integrating a very large population and sustaining unprecedented urban centers. Classical antiquity, as a tourist attraction – monuments, statues, aqueducts – was mostly made under the early emperors. Optimists see economic growth through the first two centuries; pessimists see a spurt of growth in the first century BCE (as the Empire was made), followed by a more stable economy (so, for instance, Wilson, 2009, and Scheidel, 2009b, speaking, respectively, for optimism and pessimism). At any rate, overall growth would surely be very modest by modern standards. This remains consistent with the growing splendor of urban centers, so evident in the archaeological record – if it is assumed that such gains as there were in the economy went almost entirely to the urban elite. This indeed is made necessary, once again, by considerations from first principles. Political structures were non-egalitarian; peaceful conditions favored the accumulation of capital; and in fact there is plenty of evidence for the concentration of extreme wealth during the Principate.[66]

From the economy – back to cultural demography. And, once again: consider first the very broad, bird's-eye view. To recall, I have speculated above that the rise in Roman authorship, in the first century BCE, could have reversed the retreat in scale of the late Hellenistic era. The obverse of this observation is that, as Latin authorship retreated, in turn, early in the first century CE, the overall scale of authorship would slide as well. Indeed, this is the moment when the traditional field of philosophy was still at its nadir (following the end of the Athenian schools), while the typical sophistic genres of the second century CE were merely beginning their ascent. The early first century CE, then, may well have been a period with somewhat less authorial activity.

The claim in the preceding section that the number of authors could have reached something like an all-time peak near the end of the second century CE is conjectural. But what it implies, then, is that the numbers rose relative to the early first century.

Let us now begin to bring the economy and cultural demography together. As noted on pages 657–8 above, a large fraction of Roman authorship in the first century BCE, in Latin oratory and in history,

---

[66] Scheidel (2017: 51–8). The largest recorded fortunes owned by Romans of the late second century BCE – at the time that Roman patronage was sufficiently powerful to begin to reshape Hellenistic culture – stood at a few million sesterces. Two centuries later the largest recorded fortunes (now, invariably found at or near the Imperial court) stood at several *hundreds of millions* sesterces.

came from the senatorial elite itself – a set of genres, and so a class of authorship, that largely disappeared under the Principate. There would always be senatorial authors, but the bulk of authorship came from the sub-senatorial, Greek-speaking elite. We should now see this as a surprising outcome. The argument is that the social base for authors – the sub-senatorial, Greek-speaking elite – was still expanding, in the face of growing accumulation of wealth by the Roman senatorial class – indeed, above all by the Imperial court itself.

Once again, I will go through several examples before suggesting an account. I begin with Nicomachus, in his preface to the *Manual of Harmonics*:

> Though [harmonics] is in itself complex and difficult...and though I especially, because of the restlessness and hurry of a traveller's life, am unable to devote myself... Nevertheless, best and noblest of women, I must arouse my greatest efforts, since it you who have bidden me at least to set out the major propositions for you in simple form...[67]

Such a preface – reminiscent of Renaissance prostrations before princes – is in fact rare in antiquity (the conventions of polite address were set in the early Hellenistic world and are much more restrained; and, indeed – Wietzke, forthcoming – the very act of dedicating to royalty was not that common). We see a significant noblewoman (an emperor's wife?)[68] addressed by someone who at least presents himself as a humble teacher. It is not clear what Nicomachus' travels entailed. The most accomplished sophists were also the most itinerant, and we do not need to imagine a teacher wearily peddling his learning across many cities. But there is something remarkable about the contents of Nicomachus' works themselves. He is usually dated to late in the first century CE,[69] and, as noted above on pages 467–8, there is not much evidence for mathematical activity in the two centuries preceding him. His main surviving work was an *Introduction to Arithmetic*, which would eventually reach canonical

---

[67] Translation from Barker (1989: 247–8).
[68] McDermott (1977) is correct to point out that she may be Plotina Augusta, Trajan's wife, though there is no positive support for this identification. The vague reference is essential, the last remnant of a certain decorum.
[69] Nicomachus cited Thrasyllus – Tiberius' astrologer – and was in turn, so it is reported, translated by Apuleius (EANS s.v.). Dillon (1969) and Criddle (1998) attempt more precise dates, based on the report (see following footnote) that Proclus considered himself a reincarnation of Nicomachus, which – together with specific assumptions concerning Neoplatonist theories of incarnation and numerology – could be used to define the gap in years between Nicomachus' death and Proclus' birth.

status, certainly for Neoplatonist philosophers[70] (he himself did seem to subscribe to some kind of Pythagoreanizing philosophy).[71] And, in fact, it is not clear what the antecedents for such an introduction could have been. It is a book that sets out various classifications of numbers (odd and even; square. . .) and their ratios, sometimes with a certain sophistication as well as erudition, but never any proof. The extant Greek mathematical tradition does not engage in such purely descriptive surveys (and is very much structured around geometrical, rather than arithmetical, problems).[72]

Let us step back, then, to consider Nicomachus' position within the traditions of Greek mathematics. Asper (2009) has referred to "the two cultures of mathematics in ancient Greece", one theoretical, the other practical. This is correct, but needs to be qualified: the evidence for so-called practical mathematics does not suggest a continuous tradition of a literary genre but, rather, that it emerges from non-literary papyri. Indeed, it emerges almost entirely from the school context. There, schoolchildren were submitted to various problems, sometimes in applied geometry, sometimes more directly arithmetical, such that, given certain parameters (expressed in numerical form), one had to find, for instance, areas and volumes.[73]

Further, in practical calculations the Greeks relied on the manipulation of concrete tokens, moved on the surface of the rudimentary ancient abacus.[74] Such manipulations were never made part of theoretical

---

[70] Four commentaries are extant: by Iamblichus, John Philoponus and Asclepius of Tralles, as well as an anonymous one. As noted above, it is believed – based on Cassiodorus and Isidore – that Apuleius had already translated Nicomachus into Latin (Tarán, 1969: 5). In fact, the one extant Latin translation or adaptation is that by Boethius. An early translation by Apuleius – if it is to be believed – could perhaps suggest that Nicomachus' campaign of patronage was successful; it need not imply a specific ascendancy of Nicomachus within the Platonist firmament (nothing suggests such a central role, at the time, for any single philosopher). As is well known, Proclus considered himself as the reincarnation of Nicomachus (Marinus, *Vita Procli* 28), though this should be qualified: Nicomachus is very rarely quoted by Proclus without any superlatives (I find one citation by name: *In Tim.* II.20.25–6. For the contrast to the authorities most valued by Proclus, see the very precise quantitative study by Lankila, 2008. It seems clear that even Proclus perceived Nicomachus as a mere mathematical, not a philosophical, authority.).

[71] Dillon finds a place for Nicomachus among his "Middle Platonists" (Dillon, 1977: 352–61). Besides works that more clearly belong to the teaching of exact science, he also wrote on numerology and on Pythagoras, so that – as noted below – he certainly, at the very least, sought the status of a philosopher.

[72] This may be true primarily for the Greek mathematics of the generation of Archimedes, less so for the mathematics of the generation of Archytas. But I have suggested on p. 556, n.57, above that, perhaps already by Nicomachus' time, the mathematics of the generation of Archytas could have been mostly lost.

[73] For a survey of mathematical education and the papyri, see Sidoli (2015).

[74] The pervasive role of token manipulation in ancient numerical practice is described in Netz (2002b). The ancient abacus is best described in Schärlig (2001).

mathematics (which, even when it did discuss arithmetic, did so at an abstract level, ignoring the practice of calculation) – until, that is, Nicomachus. In the *Introduction to Arithmetic* we see the representation of concrete tokens brought into the text itself, with a new kind of mathematical diagram representing numbers with dots (that is, each token was represented, in diagrams, by a dot, these dots being arranged together to represent arrays of tokens).[75] We see, then, that Nicomachus brings within theoretical writing practices which were associated with the classroom and with practical calculation: concrete numerical values and the representation of numbers with tokens/dots.

And so, Nicomachus' preface to the *Manual of Harmonics* is perhaps telling: the work could have come from the classroom ("introduction" or *eisagogē* suggests as much: it is the term for the teacher, leading his pupil). We may see in Nicomachus, then, something like a schoolteacher – someone whose main identity is in the teaching of mathematics – using authorship so as to secure a higher status (comparable, perhaps, to that of a "philosopher"?) – all to be validated, perhaps, through elevated patronage. A speculative scenario, for sure: but worth pursuing a little further. As noted above, elite, literary Greek mathematics had generally nothing to do with exercises such as Nicomachus'. Geometrical objects, generally, were not provided numerical parameters, and there were no explicit calculations of elementary measurements. The one major exception, however, is in the work of Hero of Alexandria.[76] The substantial corpus now surviving under the name of Hero is a composite, some of it certainly the accretion of later, Byzantine layers. At its core are a series of competent works in mechanics. This puts Hero in the same interface between the practical and the theoretical – albeit one that previous authors in the "government sector" had occupied since the late fourth century BCE. What is more original,

---

[75] This system of dot representations gave rise to a fundamental misapprehension in the scholarly literature. Because of the overall Pythagorean flavor of Nicomachus' writing, it was customary, until recently, to identify here a special variety of Greek mathematics of a "Pythagorean" kind, so that under this account it was the early "Pythagorean" philosophers who used the dot diagram to study arithmetic, a practice lost but still attested by the late Pythagorean Nicomachus. The first substantial reconstruction of such Pythagorean mathematics is Becker (1936), and even Knorr (1975: chap. 5) offers a variation of such a reconstruction. Such interpretations, I believe, are made untenable in light of Netz (2002b); I try to argue this in Netz (2014a), especially by showing how the evidence for Eurytus – perhaps the strongest example of token manipulation as practiced by early Pythagoreanism – changes its meaning once the pervasive nature of the practice is understood.
[76] Neugebauer (1938) believes that Hero can be dated precisely to 62 CE, based on an astronomical observation. Sidoli (2011) points out that this is a mistake on Neugebauer's part: the parameters used in the observation were ad hoc numbers produced for the sake of a theoretical calculation (typical, indeed, of Hero's style as a whole: he avoided abstract arguments and instead used numbers as examples). Still, there is no reason to doubt that he was active in the Imperial era.

however, are the *Metrica* and *Stereometrica*, two works that present series of problems in, essentially, the form we otherwise see in the educational mathematical papyri (concrete calculations, with concrete numerical examples). Another work, the *Definitions*, is once again suggestive of the classroom, summing up a long series of definitions of mathematical objects. Hero, we find, was not just an engineer, seeking patronage for his mechanical skills; he was also a teacher of mathematics, seeking to elevate the status of his profession. Indeed, it has been noted recently that, in his mechanical works, Hero claimed a particular philosophical value to mechanics.[77] We see, then, a similar thrust: from the applied services, such as teaching and engineering, to a more elevated status of authorship – indeed, with a specific claim to philosophical status.

The date of another important mathematician – Diophantus – is once again difficult to ascertain.[78] He is famous for a complex achievement, now only partly extant (some of it only in Arabic), the *Arithmetica*. Unlike Nicomachus' *Introduction*, Diophantus eventually reaches very difficult problems that would eventually inspire important paths to modern mathematics (including, famously, Fermat's Last Theorem). It should be made clear, then, that Diophantus, once again, sticks throughout to concrete arithmetical examples. While he states general arithmetical problems, those are, as before, akin to schoolroom practice.[79] Further, they are always represented and solved in the terms of given numbers – for instance (I.10): "Let the number which is added and taken away from each number be set down, [namely] one number. And if it is added to 20, result: one number, 20 Monads." (The number 20 here is an arbitrary choice of a precise numerical value.) This is Diophantus' way of

[77] Cuomo (2002); Tybjerg (2003).
[78] He is cited by Theon, an author of the fourth century CE. Tannery produces an argument (1912 [1896]) that would have placed Diophantus in the late third century, but, as Knorr (1993: 183–4) shows, this was based on a false emendation of a Greek text (Tannery emended a sentence by a late Byzantine scholar to state that Anatolius, a late third-century author, took a text based on Diophantus, made it somewhat different and dedicated it to Diophantus. In fact, the simple reading recovered by Knorr is that Anatolius produced a text based on (the well-known) Diophantus and dedicated it to a *different* Diophantus. Tannery's error lingered through the twentieth century, as did Neugebauer's concerning Hero, dispersing two authors away from their rightful places: given base probabilities, likely, could they both belong to the peak of the second century CE? Knorr briefly entertains the possibility that Hero and Diophantus were contemporaries (1993: 184), to reject it in favor of another construction whereby some works by Hero were reassigned to Diophantus (a possible conjecture). He does correctly identify the pedagogic strain shared by several works ascribed to those authors (185).
[79] Høyrup (1990: 84 n.30): Diophantus I.24–5 is best understood as an abstraction from a schoolroom exercise concerning the price of a horse! (Diophantus' method is to avoid the concrete examples of the schoolroom, but to preserve the concrete numbers.)

writing, roughly, X + 20. And, indeed, while this example avoids symbolism, he not only relies, systematically, on a set of symbol abbreviations but also makes them the central theme of his introduction. Those symbols are of a scribal nature,[80] and so Diophantus ends up with a set of schoolroom exercises, expanded into dizzying sophistication – and explicitly based on attention to scribal practice, further accentuating, in practice, the relation to education. Here is an author who starts from the schoolroom – pushing all the way up to Fermat.

Ptolemy reached even higher – to the sky. With him, we reach the most significant author in the exact sciences from the Imperial era, and so it is natural to think of him as primarily a theoretical author who may have dabbled in the practical. In fact, in his introductions, he makes claims for the philosophical significance of mathematics – directly comparable to those Hero makes on behalf of mechanics.[81] But what did such mathematics mean to Ptolemy himself? We do not know what Ptolemy's main identity was – that of an astrologer or that of a theoretician. The point, at any rate, is that Ptolemy blurred such borders. Both his theoretical works on astrology, the *Tetrabiblos* and his *Handy Tables*, belong to the tradition of the astrological manual, but, in this tradition, they would have stood out for their theoretical sophistication. A move, then, higher on the ladder of literary status: from the practitioner's manual to the theoretical survey. The same move is found globally in Ptolemy's work as a *philosopher*. The various Platonizing, Pythagorean and even Aristotelian strands in Ptolemy's worldview have often attracted the attention – and irritation – of scholars.[82] (It is indeed hard to pigeonhole Ptolemy into a clear philosophical box: typical of this era of authors, flaunting their own singular identities.) The one powerful indication we have for Ptolemy's self-presentation to his audience is in the fact that only some of his works are dedicated to an individual. These are all dedicated to the same individual, an otherwise unknown Syrus (Tolsa, 2013, has argued that this might be a Hellenization of the Roman name Sura, perhaps the prefect of Egypt?), and these are precisely Ptolemy's astronomical works. Nothing surprising in this, really: Ptolemy probably enjoyed patronage as an astronomer, which probably also involved astrology. But, even for a theoretical astronomer, the claim of philosophical authority is

[80] This is the argument of Netz (2012).    [81] Feke (2014).

[82] Taub (1993); and compare two recent dissertations: Feke (2009) and Tolsa (2013). But it is not clear that Ptolemy's reach towards philosophy should be understood primarily at a theoretical level. It was also a social move, staking a position in the cultural sphere, and perhaps the key, to him, was the sheer literary appeal of philosophy: thus Wietzke (2016), showing Ptolemy's competent *literary* allusion to Plato.

remarkable, and suggests the quest for even higher status. Indeed, he not only claimed such status but (if we trust the manuscript's ascription of the work) he was also the author of a small philosophical work, *On the Criterion*.[83]

We are reminded of Galen, who famously argued "The Best Doctor Is Also a Philosopher" – the title of one his treatises – and wrote himself on such philosophical topics as logic (see page 461 above). No less famously, the *Digest* starts with the claim that jurisprudence is the "true philosophy", a sentiment ascribed to Ulpian but apparently widespread in the writings of the Roman jurists.[84] Schoolroom mathematics, mechanics, astronomy/astrology, medicine, law[85] – again and again we see, during the Imperial era, the authors of the cultural service industries claiming for themselves a more gentlemanly status. In Nicomachus, Hero and Diophantus, we see the schoolmaster, chasing authorial status. In Ptolemy, Galen, Ulpian and (again) Hero, we see the author of a more lowly service industry (engineering, astrology/astronomy, law, medicine) chasing the status of a "philosopher". Chasing up the status ladder – which seems to be the very context for the re-emergence of the exact sciences as an area of authorial activity. After all, throughout the earlier Roman era astrologers cast horoscopes, schoolmasters taught arithmetic, engineers designed machines. Spurred by the chase for status, some of these practitioners – perhaps especially during the second century CE – sought an entry into the more elite world of authorship.

This would cast light on several other examples. In Latin, we note Vitruvius, chasing after the highest patronage.[86] We can add the entire genre of the agrimensores, or "land surveyors". Here once again are practitioners, masters of a skill in applied mathematics. The profession of agrimensores was established at the latest by the first century BCE, a practical endeavor of the concrete measurement of concrete lands, symbolized by physical tools: the surveyor's cross, the measuring rod (Morris,

---

[83] For a recent discussion – which takes the authenticity for granted – see Schiefsky (2014).

[84] Honoré (2010a): the scholarship of this passage starts from a sense of perplexity: what even is the legal function of such statements? They serve, instead, a rather straightforward social function, one that can be paralleled in many other service professions.

[85] To clarify a contrast – and a continuity: the status claim of a philosopher, by specialized authors in the high Imperial era, would have been impossible without the breaking of the boundary between science and philosophy, produced in the first century BCE. That breaking of the boundary, in the late Republican era, did not result in a new claim for status, however: the insistence on the status of a philosopher is the typical new twist of the high Empire, and typical of its status consciousness.

[86] Nichols (2009), perceptively, puts Vitruvius side by side with Horace: both seeking status, while fashioning a persona of self-abnegation.

2016: 20). It is only from the second century CE onwards that we have manuals – displaying, to varying degrees, their theoretical aspirations – of the technique of land surveying.[87] A technical practice – chasing after status via authorship.

Another example, now in Greek, is more specialized – but for that reason also more remarkable. I pause, then, to discuss Mesomedes, and I step back for some background.

Ancient poetry was primarily sung, and purely instrumental music was the rare exception: thus, music and poetry were nearly synonymous.[88] Further, the Greeks invented a musical notation, known now primarily through documentary sources. A relatively abundant group are the papyri: mostly rough in presentation, these suggest a professional use rather than a published "text".[89] The inscriptions include a (first-century CE?) epitaph, probably for a professional musician, in which a small composition is included;[90] and a commemoration set up by the Athenian technitai of music, in the year 151 BCE.[91] Otherwise, there is no ancient literary evidence on this rather remarkable practice, prior to late antiquity[92] – not even from music-crazy authors such as Plutarch and Athenaeus – and the overall sense is that before us is a specialized, technical lore that did not become part of the literary reception of poetry and its music. The notation of music was a tool, used by the practitioners, and knowledge of musical

---

[87] The authorial position, in this case, has a curiously modern twist. While selections of Latin land-surveying works had been printed beginning in the late fifteenth century (Bluhme et al., 1848–52: II.76–8), modern reception was determined by Bluhme et al.'s (1848–52) publication of a critical edition of a group of such works. This was Lachmann's last work (its second volume published posthumously: Timpanaro, 2005 [1963]: 102), and, in its reception by the classical profession, the edition, taken collectively, had a more powerful authorial status than that of each individual author in it. Thus, we came to think of such texts as belonging to a generic *corpus agrimensorum*, while individual authors such as Balbus, Siculus Flaccus and the two Hygini recede, in the perception of the modern classical profession, into a semi-authorial status, mere titles attached to works whose main identity is the generic "agrimensores".

[88] A standard observation (true of lyric verse, above all; less so for iambic and hexameter, though they too emerge often from musical performances). For a brief survey of Greek music, as found mainly through the evidence concerning poetry, see, e.g., Comotti (1989: chap. 2).

[89] Pöhlmann and West (2001). As noted on p. 47 above, it could well have been the very practical use of the papyri that partly accounts for their availability in the archaeological record: a technical tool, frequently handled and frequently discarded.

[90] DAGM 23: this is the Seikilos epitaph, perhaps roughly contemporary with Mesomedes.

[91] DAGM 20–1. I put aside the inscription from Epidaurus (DAGM 19; see West, 1986), perhaps from the third century CE: a text whose function is more difficult to determine (and, indeed, is hard to square with any musical notation at all! Compare Hagel, 2009: 280–1.).

[92] We are fortunate to possess the late ancient treatise on music by Alypius – written when this notation was perhaps no longer in practical use – which describes the notation in detail, as an essentially antiquarian exercise; this treatise makes it possible for modern scholars to interpret the documentary evidence: Mathiesen (1999: 593–607).

notation was no more widely disseminated in antiquity than was the knowledge of, say, the mechanical production of musical instruments. In particular, poetry, in antiquity, was disseminated without its accompanying melody: text, without musical notation.

With this in place, let us finally bring in Mesomedes himself. A freedman of Hadrian, and so a fairly rare example (as pointed out by Whitmarsh, 2004) of an author emerging from beneath the elite.[93] He was a Greek poet (this pursuit, as so many, seems to emerge, somewhat, from its earlier near-moribund state). Some of Mesomedes' poems are extant; three are accompanied by musical notation, and, in this, are unique *in the entirety of the manuscript tradition*. The implication is that Mesomedes published a notated book of poetry. Mesomedes' identity, then, was clearly that of the service industry – servant, indeed, to the emperor! Likely enough, we should think of him as a working musician, a Haydn to his Esterházy. What he did, however, was to seek, from within this service position, the more elevated status of an author. Practiced music – as published poetry. And so, once again, a technical practice, seeking admission into the world of the elite, relying on the device of authorship sanctioned by patronage: the same formula we have already seen with Nicomachus, repeated again and again across the genres of the cultural service industries.[94]

So far we have relied on the evidence of the texts themselves and extrapolated, on that basis, the trajectories and ambitions of cultural figures. But, then again, we can often see the records left by the authors themselves, through their pursuits. I will take just one example, remarkable only in the vivid detail it supplies for authorship and status. This is the Sarapion monument. In the Athenian temple to Asclepius, by the late second century, there stood a remarkable, multi-generational assemblage of inscriptions and dedicated monuments.[95] We have three phases of dedication: Sarapion himself, dedicating a tripod for his victory in a poetry contest from about 113 to 116 CE;[96] his grandson, Quintus Statius, setting

---

[93] Though I would still insist – see p. 615 above – that such examples display not so much the ability of authors to gain status, upwards, as the ability of mighty patrons to bestow status, downwards. For Mesomedes' poetry, see now Regenauer (2016).

[94] Specifically, the publication of a book marked by technical notation, which was previously used only in technical, informal settings, is perhaps comparable to Diophantus' explicit use of arithmetical/scribal abbreviations (p. 674 above).

[95] Just like the monument itself, the evidence was put together through the heroic work of generations of archaeologists and epigraphers. This work is summed up in Geagan (1991), followed here; for the literature beginning in Oliver (1936), see there page 145, note 2.

[96] Geagan (1991: 153). No other element can be as securely dated (for the poetic contest of 113 to 116, we actually have a literary source in Plutarch!), but the later inscriptions seem to belong to the middle to later second century CE.

up a statue of Sarapion; finally, a statue of Quintus' own son, named Quintus Statius Themistokles, set up by yet another family member (Titus Flavius Glaukos). Two of the dedications in this series – the tripod and the statue of Sarapion – were accompanied by a complex inscriptional program, including a unique poem dedicated by Sarapion himself – and a paean, dedicated by Quintus Statius.

The original monument celebrated a literary victory. The choice of the temple of Asclepius for such a dedication was very untypical, and Geagan (1991: 153–5) suggests that this might be related to the comparatively open, "democratic" character of the precinct, and, so, one that was open to individuals from outside the central elite. Another aspect is the association of this temple with intellectual pursuits.[97] All of this fits with a picture of Sarapion as an outsider (of course, relative to the elevated society of monument-setters). We do not know about any aristocratic connections he may have had at this point, and, indeed, perhaps he was not an Athenian citizen at all. As an author he certainly aimed to make his mark, and the monument stands out with its unique inscription, a philosophical panegyric to the profession of medicine.

Not that Sarapion himself was a physician (the subject matter of Sarapion's poem may have been suggested by the setting): his grandson identified him as a "poet and a Stoic philosopher". This grandson, Quintus Statius, set up his own monument as the lifelong priest to Asclepius: having first used this temple to secure a toehold in the Athenian status scheme, the family, two generations later, now governed it. Quintus Statius was now able to marry well: his own son, Quintus Statius Themistokles, portrayed in the last monument in this series, was already a celebrated member of the elite, belonging (through the mother's side) to the family of the consul, Claudius Agrippinus, and of the Asiarch, Claudius Themistokles. This final statue of Quintus Statius Themistokles was set up, as mentioned above, by yet another family member, Flavius Glaukos, who explained that he put this statue next to "our common grandfather" Sarapion – the spatial proximity thus constructed, between Sarapion and his great-grandson Quintus Statius Themistokles, serving as a pretext for the claim of a proximity in lineage, between Quintus Statius Themistokles and Flavius Glaukos himself. To cap it all, Flavius Glaukos referred to himself as "poet and rhetor and philosopher", echoing the titles already bestowed by

[97] Geagan (1991: 154) counts, in the same precinct, up to (some cases are uncertain) five inscriptions honoring physicians (naturally), six honoring philosophers, three honoring rhetors, one honoring a historian and two honoring "teachers" more generally.

Quintus Flavius on Sarapion. The family came up; they did not forget how. It was always the same, through the second century: cultural excellence, a currency convertible with status.[98] "In the happy epoch of the Antonines, performance in oratory or letters led notoriously to public honor" (Syme, 1982: 181).

Culture – for the sake of political currency. So far we have looked at the cultural service industries, for which perhaps this equation is more obvious. But the same is true for cultural activity more generally. Beginning with Vespasian, certain categories were excused from certain obligations to the cities in which they resided (and thus were relieved from the significant financial burden of providing liturgies). Philosophers of certain renown were included among those categories, surely by the time of Marcus Aurelius if not before that.[99] From the extension of such benefits to a fixed number of prominent teachers is but a short step to providing a fixed position for such figures (which, of course, was an occasional practice in medicine from early times).[100] Elite members across the Empire were vying, in this era, for the formal attributes of status: priests of the emperor's cult; Asiarchs; above all – senators and consuls[101]... Such fixed

---

[98]  The Serapion monument is a single, vivid example; we may put this in a wider context, for instance via Morgan (2014), a systematic survey of the Imperial-era honorific inscriptions from Aphrodisias (of which there are 206, honoring 183 individuals: this is a sizeable sample). Morgan (2014: 117–24) observes that, beginning in the first half of the second century, one of the themes of such inscriptions begins to be the commemoration of the success of elite members in athletic and cultural performances. Serapion may have started his family on its career with his literary triumph; the same may have been true also in Aphrodisias, or perhaps notable elite members merely cemented their standing with a literary or athletic victory. Either way, we find the same need to express one's status in public through competitions that display one's mastery of a shared Hellenic culture.

[99]  See the discussion on p. 584, n.85, above. By one account, such lists of tax-exempt intellectuals were first promulgated under Vespasian, with philosophers at first excluded; included by Hadrian; excluded again by Antoninus Pius; finally, included by Marcus Aurelius (so, Bowersock, 1969: 30–42) – all paralleling the overall attitude of the emperors to the authorial elite. For an argument that favors the early inclusion of philosophers, see Copete (1993); Nutton (1971) argues that Pius did not curtail immunities for intellectuals in general; Millar (1983: 78) wisely sums up that this was a disputed area of Roman law. Immunities of this type were highly valued and thus formed a major arena for patronage in their own right.

[100]  I have mentioned on pp. 584–5 above the category of *archiatri*, and the related category of the "public doctor" (Cohn-Haft, 1956; Nutton, 1977). There was a long tradition for some of the Greek cities to identify certain individuals as publicly recognized, medical authorities; this category may have overlapped, in the Imperial era, with the grant of imperial privileges, such as tax exemptions.

[101]  "In Asia Minor we can see, in several cases, the following advancement, within the same family: father, provincial high-priest → son, eques → grandson, senator" (Camia, 2008: 40). As with the case of the Serapion monument, we see a pattern of concentration of elite status, elevated through the generations, and often (though not always) cemented through Roman titles, leading in some cases all the way up to the top Roman elite (for this final crucial development – the Imperial recruitment, beginning in the first century CE but much expanded in the second century, of Greeks into the senate, see Birley, 1997; the seminal study is Syme, 1958: 504–19). Elite status becomes a rare

positions began to enter the authorial pursuits themselves. It was certainly already by the Flavian era that teachers of rhetoric, in Rome, were provided direct Imperial patronage.[102] Did the Flavians follow, or create a precedent for other, municipal foundations? At some point near the middle of the second century there was certainly a chair of rhetoric in Athens. It was probably Marcus Aurelius who instituted another chair: an Imperial one, and thus much more coveted.[103] We also know that Marcus Aurelius instituted at least four chairs, in Athens, for philosophy – one for each Hellenistic school.[104] Lucian's *Eunuch* – written shortly thereafter – is the first Academic novel, a dialogue discussing the quarrel over one of the chairs.[105] This must be emphasized. Rhetoric was already linked, as noted above, to the network of official recognitions, and its successful exponents were exactly those enjoying city and empire-wide honors. One made oneself a famous rhetor precisely so as to be up for attention for such positions as priest, eques, senator. So much for rhetoric. And now, perhaps, eight chairs in philosophy. . . This may not sound like a large number for a "philosophy department", but under my scenario from the previous section – *optimistic*, based purely on the assumption that philosophers at this point are badly attested – there could have been something like 200 active philosophers at a time. Eight magnificent prizes, dangled in front of a group with some 200 members: this would be meaningful indeed. Even within rhetoric – in which there were many other, *political* prizes – squabbling for the Athenian Imperial chair structures much of the action

---

commodity, confined to a few families; and it becomes ever more intertwined with Roman patronage, ultimately that of the emperor itself. Status is not so much gained and displayed but also, perhaps even more, conferred from above.

[102] Suetonius (Vespasian 18) asserts that Vespasian created two positions, for the teachers of Greek and Latin rhetoric, respectively, with the fantastic remuneration of 100,000 sesterces; Jerome, *Chron.*, Migne XXVII col. 460, asserts that Quintilian was the first holder of such a chair, though he dates this foundation to Domitian's reign.

[103] Avotins (1975). This paid out 40,000 sesterces, or a little less than 1 million sesterces in wealth: just short of the senatorial threshold (the holders of such a chair – the most magnificent rhetors of their generation – would have to be wealthier than that. This was the final accolade of status, with a nice income added on top.).

[104] Oliver (1970: 80–5) (not a very lucid presentation, but the key details are clear enough, with significant evidence from both Lucian and Philostratus). The philosophy chair paid, according to Lucian (*Eunuch* 3), 10,000 drachmas – somewhat less than the chair of rhetoric but still a nice job if you could get it (indeed, one wonders if Lucian's nice round number is not thrown in as a mere illustration).

[105] The subject for the quarrel is said by Lucian to be "the other peripatetic chair" (*Eunuch* 3), hence the modern interpretation that there could have been *two* chairs for at least some of the sects. (On the other hand, isn't it simply a narrative need, to make the chair *minor*, and the competition for it even more comical?)

of the *Lives of the Sophists*.[106] Lucian's *Eunuch* brings to mind a similar mindset, among the philosophers: the pursuit of philosophy, now conducted with an eye to Imperial patronage.[107]

So much for philosophy. As for history, we are once again at the mercy of the evidence from Lucian – always keen to laugh at the learned. "How History Is to Be Written" is in the form of a letter, condemning a new "plague" – this is written shortly after 166 – of recent histories on the recent war against the Parthians. As noted in note 55, this is our most substantial source for the names and descriptions of historians from the second century as a whole – and those are most likely fictitious! There are only three facts we can take out of this novelistic exercise.

First, there surely were at least several histories written just on this war, or otherwise Lucian's humor falls completely flat. By implication, there ought to have been many histories written on the many wars conducted through the Imperial era.

Second, it should be noted that, out of all these contemporary histories, not many are attested and only one is fully extant: Josephus' *Jewish War*, obviously extant thanks to its interest for Christian historians.[108]

Third – to follow an important observation by Kemezis (2010: 289–90) – Lucian's main complaint against the historians is telling: they fail, in that, unlike the classic historians (above all, Thucydides), they unduly flatter their subjects as well as their audiences.

---

[106] Avotins (1975). Philostratus mentions, for nine of his sophists, that they held the Athenian chair (Avotins, 1975: 315; this would be over a quarter of Philostratus' subjects). This is probably a complete list of the holders of at least the main chair (if indeed there was more than one) for the years 174 to 220 (Avotins, 1975: 324; notice the short average tenure: the chair was won by the most prominent rhetors, thus the oldest: you enjoyed it, on average, for no more than four years. This was not about the quality of education: this was a supreme marker of status, for the most status-conscious profession of a most status-conscious era.).

[107] In a footnote, we may mention a set of authors that is extremely well attested and is in some ways akin to philosophy: the Christian apologists of the second century CE (see, e.g., Young, 1999). From the time of Hadrian to the early third century – but not before or after that – a new genre of Christian writing emerged, of works formally addressed to the emperor and seeking to enlighten him concerning the superiority of Christianity. It is clear that such works were not meant as actual legal petitions, and so the dedication to the emperor should be understood as a literary device, one which, to us, is somewhat surprising: what has Jerusalem to do with Rome? The practice falls into place if we fit it within a cultural context in which literary works, in general, aimed, above all, for Imperial favor: the gravitational pull of the Imperial, reaching well beyond the social sphere that could actually conceive of Imperial interaction.

[108] This is to some extent a matter of the chance of very late, post-Photius Byzantine transmission: Arrian's *Parthica* – a history of Trajan's wars – did survive to be read by Photius (*Bibl.* 58). But Arrian was among the most successful historians of the entire century – the "younger Xenophon", as Photius put it: how many of his less famous colleagues survived to be read in Byzantium? (Note also that Herodian is excluded here, somewhat arbitrarily, as a "third-century" author.)

Now, Kemezis contrasts Lucian's treatment of the historiography of the war with the historiographical comments made by Lucian's contemporary, Fronto. In letters to the emperor Verus, Fronto discussed plans for his own potential history of the war, which – written by a courtier – was supposed to be a (sober) panegyric. It never came to be written (Fronto died not much later, from the plague). But this reminds us of yet another gap in our evidence. As noted on pages 659–60 above, there are practically *no* histories in Latin attested from the second century CE. As noted above, this is a puzzling lacuna – and, while the very absence of attestation makes it difficult for us to provide any generalizations, we have to base our account of second-century historians on the fact that they are lost.

Kemezis (2010) structures his argument as an account as to why there was no contemporary or near-contemporary history under the Antonines – as if the problem was one of production. But, clearly, the problem was one of survival. The pattern that we do find is that contemporary or near-contemporary history under the Antonines was not preserved by later generations. But, as noted on page 658 above, it is not as if the medieval era avoided the historical writing produced by the Imperial era: to the contrary, the Imperial era seems to be much likelier to be extant: it is only that, among such works of history, non-contemporary histories predominate. The conclusion, then, is that the selective bias took place early on: already, in the Imperial era itself, non-contemporary histories were transmitted more frequently than the contemporary ones. Let us note the actual examples. Many of the extant historians from the Imperial era write on geographical themes (from Strabo to Pausanias) or on a remote Greek past (so, Curtius Rufus and Arrian). Putting aside Cassius Dio (who may survive by the sheer virtue of his date; more below, on pages 704–7), there are only a handful of extant historians dealing with themes directly related to the political experience of the Empire. According to my argument above, these are the authors who were favorably selected by readers in the generations immediately following their own lifetimes, unlike all other historians (who were fairly soon neglected). These are: Plutarch, Tacitus and Suetonius.

What is typical of this group (small, but significant in our reconstruction of Roman history) is that it did, in fact, find a way to avoid Lucian's critique. Authors on themes that either were near-contemporary (with Tacitus and Suetonius) or directly reverberated with contemporary history (with Plutarch) managed yet to write on empire with a certain critical, "Thucydidean" distance (in Tacitus' case, indeed, with a clear subversive undertone). Even so, this was possible only thanks to the avoidance of the actually contemporary. The task was thus relatively manageable: under the Flavians, to write about the Julio-Claudians (as Tacitus did), and then, under the Antonines, to write about the Flavians (as did Suetonius). But there had to be plenty of historians writing about the dynasty under which they still lived, and the most fundamental fact is that almost none of them are now even *attested*.

This is no more than a guess, but, in the absence of evidence, guesses ought to be hazarded: might readers have objected precisely to the necessarily flattering tone of such historians? Even if popular contemporaneously, such works would be discreetly tucked away when the reign was over, put to the fire when the dynasty fell out of favor: for, indeed, such Orwellian *damnatio memoriae* is in fact well attested.[109] The result of this process was paradoxical: the history of the Empire was ultimately left to be written by its vanquished. And not such an improbable paradox, in the end. Lucian, it turns out, provides us with the clue to its solution. Because the elite was so much beholden to the tradition of the polis of letters – of Thucydides, Herodotus, Xenophon – it was precisely in political history that one could *not* construct a state ideology, based on an unquestioned supreme ruler. History was assumed to do something different: the record of debate and of political strife. The few who managed the balancing act of an ironic distancing under empire, of "doublespeak", succeeded;[110] the rest were ephemeral. Here, the Empire was powerless against the canon.

But, ephemeral as they were, the point is that there must have been plenty of them. I am erecting an edifice on no more than guesswork; but how else may one reconstruct the dark matter? And so, here is my proposal: that a significant part of the historiographical production of the second century – that which we have entirely lost – was the historiography of praise of contemporary emperors, geared directly for Imperial patronage.

As, indeed, must have been true for literature, as such. Juvenal, in the seventh *Satire*, bemoans the state of the contemporary literary scene, its

---

[109] The term is modern, but the practice was widespread and systematic. It was primarily about the more public forms of memory, and it is especially well attested in marble. There are extant many portraits of emperors, now found in mutilated form because their subjects were posthumously condemned (a full survey is provided by Varner, 2004). There is no specific report of the burning of books simply because they praised fallen emperors, though the burning of seditious books is attested, as well (Krevans, 2010: 208 n.38). But, even without the fire, how much effort was put into the copying of panegyrics to the condemned?

[110] Once again, shades of Orwell, made necessary by the study of empire. I refer to Bartsch's (1994) study of the praise of the emperor by the intellectuals of the era, "Actors in the Audience: Theatricality and Doublespeak from Nero to Hadrian". Once again, Bartsch emphasizes the ironical stance of our extant authors.

authors cast low, its patrons missing. His first line offers a contrast – and celebrates the one patron Rome still boasts:

> Et spes et ratio studiorum in caesare tantum
> On Caesar alone hang all the hopes and prospects of the learned.

This is, of course, Juvenal's own piece of doublespeak, and the ironic sigh is understood. It is also – as good ironies must be – somewhat true. Literary culture drifted, more and more, into the orbit of patronage; poetry subsisted in the tension between the tropes of autonomy and realities of dependence.[111] Under the Antonines, if not before, the Roman emperor was established as indispensable to this vertical, downwards-trickling network.

Indeed, this network trickled all the way down, encompassing ultimately the entirety of Roman society. We recall Sarapion, whose family we know so well. But there are so many individuals we now know, from this peak moment of the Roman Empire! For the very same reason that we know Sarapion: we have the inscriptions.

Is it the case, perhaps, that the chase after status was pervasive, throughout antiquity – indeed, throughout history – and that it is simply better attested in the second century CE, with its more ample inscriptions? I have referred to this problem on page 666 above, when considering the evidence for the number of rhetors in the second century (so often attested epigraphically). Ever since MacMullen (1982) we have been aware of the fact that the frequency of inscriptions – the "epigraphic habit" – is an independent variable and cannot be reduced to, say, economic forces. Instead of deducing the number of inscriptions from the Roman economy, then, we need to refer it to some cultural factors. Elizabeth Meyer (1990) concentrates on funerary inscriptions, pointing out that they are dedicated by family members, who use such occasions to proclaim themselves (while it is not a funerary inscription, we are reminded of Flavius Glaukos advertising his shared ancestry with Quintus Statius Themistokles). More specifically, she points out that in the province of Africa[112] inscriptions peaked in the second century, when many Africans – but not all – enjoyed Roman citizenship. The epigraphic habit, then: a reflection of the chase after the specific status of a *Roman citizen*. (Thus, with Caracalla's universal grant of citizenship in 212, we could expect the habit to subside.) This is compelling

---

[111] Roman (2014); see page 336 for Juvenal's seventh *Satire*.
[112] Those inscriptions are especially well preserved and well edited (see p. 535 above). For this reason, they served as the key evidence used for MacMullen (1982), so that Meyer (1990) could naturally take them as her point of reference.

and certainly suggestive. But there are many other forms of status displayed in the inscriptions as a whole, besides citizenship as such (see immediately below); and is the year 212 truly the decisive turning point for the epigraphic habit? The most ambitious treatment of the problem of the epigraphic habit, in general, is by Woolf (1996), who tries to range across the entire stock of documents, funerary and non-funerary, from the urban centers and from the military context. His conclusion is, accordingly, more general as well: inscriptions were not specifically about the display of Roman citizenship. Rather, more generally, they reflected, according to Woolf, an anxiety about social mobility – the gap between the rich and the poor was so wide; mobility was, at the very least, cast as a *possibility*.[113] As Woolf concedes, however, such a general statement loses the explanatory power of Meyer's specific account, since, after all, there is no obvious sense in which anxieties about social mobility rose and dropped sharply along with the fate of the epigraphic habit.

What is perhaps more helpful, from our perspective, is to consider the epigraphic habit as the general expression of an authorial habit. After all, to inscribe is, literally, to write – and in public! Inscription uses a medium more widely accessible than that of the formal bookroll (though still constrained by cost and by norms of social access). The simple meaning of the rise of the epigraphic habit is that, through the first two centuries, there must have been many individuals, heretofore silent, who now made the transition into public writing via the medium of the inscription. It was a status step upwards, using what access to public visibility one had. And, in fact, we can document precisely those first-generation inscribers. Mouritsen (2005) studies a particular case, that of Italian funerary inscriptions (based on the evidence primarily from Ostia and Pompeii). Our first glimpse is at Pompeii, where, early in the first century CE, the local elite creates an epigraphic precedent. In the middle of the century we can follow this new fashion trickling down, so that it tends to become associated with freedmen (this would fit Woolf's model of social mobility). From the late first century CE onwards our evidence comes primarily from Ostia, and there we see an epigraphic habit heavily dominated by freedmen. It appears as if, by this point, funerary inscriptions have trickled down so far that the elite might actually avoid them.[114] Notice that, in Ostia, the *ingenui* – born to freedom from freedmen

---

[113]  Woolf (1996: 35): "Debate over actual rates of social mobility. . .continues, but for present purposes the reality is immaterial, since it is perfectly clear. . .that anxieties about social mobility occupied a significant place in the collective imagination."

[114]  All of this fits directly with Wallace-Hadrill's (1994) model of fashion in Roman material practices and, more generally, with theories of symbolic capital and difference; Mouritsen (2005) relies

parents – are much less frequent in the funerary evidence. The medium of the funerary inscription, in Ostia, belongs to first-generation inscribers, and to them *primarily*. But all this does not mean that the elite dropped out of the epigraphic habit. In fact, elite inscriptions proliferated here – as everywhere else – precisely in the second century CE. In this case, these are the inscriptions of the *collegia*, often translated as "guilds",[115] structured according to type of economic endeavor but apparently manned not so much by low-level artisans as by employers and property owners: "chambers of commerce", perhaps. Men of property proclaimed their worth, in guild buildings visible throughout the city,[116] and then reaffirmed this worth in public writing.

The play of fashion and status was enacted differently in different environments, but, everywhere, it was enacted with greater intensity through the Imperial era, and especially through the second century CE. And, so, different groups reached for new forms of expression. Freedmen set up individual inscriptions. Magnates proclaimed their membership in guilds and, of course, displayed their beneficence. And also, at the same time: practitioners in the service industries – teachers, engineers, astrologers – sought a more literate identity, became authors; gentlemanly authors in mathematics, medicine and jurisprudence dared to call themselves "philosophers". Everywhere, an upwards push for status: produced by the pressure of the inflation of symbolic capital.

What was the point of all this display? Let us move back to consider, finally, something of the historical setting of the Imperial era. Ever since Saller (1982) it has been recognized that, in this era, the role of patronage increased. Vertical dependency relations, going, more and more, all the way up to the emperor himself, were paramount. This is evident in the most basic material level. The transfer of cash and goods from the topmost elite to lower economic strata constituted a significant (though now very hard to quantify) fraction of economic life. Famously, a significant fraction of the population of the city of Rome subsisted directly on state-supplied grain.[117] Such handouts were by no means limited to the city of Rome, and,

specifically on an account of funerary habits following a cycle of elite ostentation, which is imitated by the non-elite to the extent that eventually the elite adopts restraint in its funerary costumes (Cannon, 1989).

[115] Hermansen (1982: chap. 2) is an old and somewhat optimistic overview. As he notes (62), smaller craftsmen (such as butchers or barbers) are not represented in the inscriptions.

[116] The high visibility of such so-called "guild houses" (scholae) – prominent in the urban fabric – is the theme of Stöger (2011: chap. 8).

[117] Perhaps a third directly, another third indirectly (Erdkamp, 2005: 257)? The question is debated in the literature within the context of the overall nature of the Roman economy: was it fundamentally an administrative or a free-market economy? Lo Cascio (2006) points out that this is a misleading

indeed, some of the prevailing institutions of the Roman Empire were the perpetual foundations: endowments created by members of the elite, the interest on which paid, typically, for feeding local populations. This is especially well documented through inscriptions in the west, primarily in Italy, and the implication of this evidence is that such foundations had a significant economic footprint.[118] During the second century CE an entire Italian system of such foundations was added, locally mediated but emanating ultimately from the emperor. This system – the *alimenta* – started with loans, with landholdings as collateral, from the emperor to local elites. Out of such loans, local foundations were to be set up to feed children, the entire operation understood, officially, as an imperial project designed to support population growth.[119] The need felt by local elites to provide funds to their communities is a pervasive theme in ancient history, but there is some evidence that this became even more powerful through the Imperial era. We have mentioned grain distribution in Rome, which, of course, was just one part of the equation of bread and circuses. Those circuses – generally, public entertainment provided at private expense – seem to have multiplied, and risen in cost, through the Imperial era. In particular, gladiator shows or *munera* played no part in the civic life of the Greek cities of the first century BCE, were introduced early in the first century CE and

formulation, in that the "state" is not impersonal: it stands, in the Roman Imperial case, for the goodwill of a single individual, the emperor. A free-market economy – with a massively wealthy individual, acting as its backstop-philanthropist (my formulation, not Lo Cascio's!).

[118] A back-of-the-envelope calculation: the foundations attested via inscriptions in the list produced by Duncan-Jones (1974: 171–84, nos. 638–755) add up to capitalization of almost exactly 15 million HS. Using, as a heuristic, our basic assumption of survival of inscriptions at 1 percent, and abstracting away from biases in this survival, we should assume perhaps a total of 1.5 billion HS invested, in Italy, in charitable foundations (given the abstraction we ignored, this is perhaps best seen as a ceiling). This should be compared with the estimated imperial GDP of 17 to 19 billion HS (Scheidel and Friesen, 2009: 73) = imperial capital of roughly 100 to 150 billion HS = Italian capital of roughly 20 to 30 billion HS. The implication is that several percent of total wealth was invested in such charities – remarkable but not absurd (see the following note).

[119] The best description and interpretation remains Duncan-Jones (1974: 288–319). His conclusion is that that program should indeed be understood (this is, in fact, controversial in the literature) as essentially philanthropic, rather than a system for providing cheap loans. Further, the scale of the foundations was such that they have to be understood as providing support to a wide swath of the population and yet not feeding all of the poor. Woolf (1990) is right to point out that, in all likelihood, the program did not even target, directly, poverty as such, but even so there is no question that it was a progressive transfer (perhaps from the elite to a subsection of the population that, thanks to such subventions, could maintain a precarious hold on a certain respectability: a middling segment, dependent on the patronage of the elite?). Above all, as Woolf emphasizes, the system of the *alimenta* represents an ideological project, the concentration of patronage in the figure of the emperor. Finally, it should be noted that, in principle, the loans were at 8 percent the land value. This provides a ceiling to the value of the foundations (not all land was put as collateral to such loans, and not all capital was landed, though most was), which suggests, once again, a total value in the range of a few percent of total capital.

were absolutely essential to civic life by the second century CE. This growth was driven by an evident inflationary logic: cities competing against each other, magistrates competing against their predecessors. Through the second century local elites were struggling with the need to have their cities stage ever larger games; a law from 177 CE introduced price controls (always the best mark of inflationary pressures). Our own gaze as modern spectators is riveted on these performances, so foreign and yet so titillating, but the ancients themselves cared even more about another type of titillating spectacle: chariot races – a fixed element of Roman urban culture from the first century BCE on. Surely the construction, across the Empire, of the huge circuses necessary for the Roman chariot race happened only during the Principate and perhaps mostly from the second century CE onwards (chariot racing, more than many other Imperial fashions, throve well into Byzantine times). Indeed, circuses are distinctive, in that they are a form of monumentality that emerged in the Imperial era and then never retreated: they became culturally entrenched, and monumental scale was, in this case, a functional necessity. Generally speaking, however, the second century formed a peak in monumental architecture. This should be mentioned here, since, after all, most of this building was public in character. Stoas, temples and baths were funded by the topmost elite and enjoyed, once again, by a much broader swath of the population. The broad outline of this architectural history is uncontroversial: following an Augustan "classicizing" era of more austere forms, later Julio-Claudian building programs became more "baroque", utilizing the capacity of cement-based concrete to bring together a variety of curved and more ambitious shapes (MacDonald, 1982: chaps. 1–2; Ball, 2003). Later developments involved primarily the multiplication of monumental architecture and a further rise in scale through the second century, especially under Hadrian but well into the entire Antonine period (Thomas, 2007). The basic logic is clear: as inequality set in through the Imperial era, more and more wealth trickled down as discretionary spending. It is indeed certain that there was a gift economy, constituted by direct handouts from the elite members to their inferiors. No more than tiny indications survive, and no quantification is possible, but the ideology of the institution of Roman patronage must have made this pervasive. "Romatius Firmus, Pliny's family friend, received a gift of 300,000 sesterces which quadrupled the value of his estate and gave him the equestrian census... Metilius Crispus obtained a commission as a centurion with Pliny's support and also received 40,000 sesterces to purchase the necessary equipment" (Saller, 1982: 123). Such anecdotes remind us of a much more fundamental fact about Imperial society: the most valuable commodity was status, a position in the Imperial political ladder, which was definitely also of clear economic value.[120] Now, political status – at this historical juncture – was driven entirely by one's position in the network of patronage. The very Latin word *suffragium* – a key observation of de Ste. Croix (1954) – originally signifying, under the Republic, something like "popular vote", came to mean, in the Imperial era, nearly its opposite: the whim of elite members and, above all, of the emperor. This account, proposed by de Ste. Croix (1954) and then greatly amplified by Saller (1982), is now a consensus interpretation, succinctly put forward by Garnsey (2010: 45):

> Political patronage now operated within a pyramidal structure: the emperor was at the top, with a chain of dependence leading down from him. The final arbiter was the imperial will. However, in practice the emperor was in no position to choose personally anyone much beyond his own entourage. He necessarily leaned on the counsel of the people closest to him, friends, top officials, and other courtiers. Subimperial patronage was absolutely essential in the bringing forward of the next generation of aristocrats and administrators.

Within such an economic-political setting, it is only to be expected that authorial practice would be organized around the quest for patronage. But the point is more than just the crass observation that a handbook of arithmetic could have been motivated by the desire to gain an Imperial post as a teacher, that a brilliant rhetor wished, above all, for political goodwill from his superiors that would raise him up the political ladder. The point is that social life, as such, was infused by the values of a patronage-system to such a degree that, of course, having obtained any status at all, one would wish to display it by the granting of one's own patronage: an attractive hypothesis put forward by Wietzke (2017). The ancient author could have presented himself, at least on occasion, as a kind of benefactor – his literary work a kind of monument erected on behalf of his fellow

---

[120] The judgement of de Ste. Croix (1981: 382) is straightforward: becoming a member of the political elite gave one considerable latitude in exploiting its subjects. We need to add, in view of Saller (1982), that, with the revenues from such exploitation of their inferiors, elite members could then decide to hand out gifts to some others. Exploitation and gift, both covered under the same umbrella of elite discretion. Exploit (nearly) at will; and then, at will, show liberality. Needless to say, status could matter in all sorts of way, all across the ladder. Consider the act of manumission: an owner granting his slave the status of freedman. As emphasized in the literature ever since Wiedemann (1985), the assumption of manumission as being granted as a matter of course was a mere ideological construct. Slaves worked hard to get free. But, when they did, they did so at the whim of their masters, now become their patrons. Steps up along the ladder – always predicated on the goodwill of one's superiors.

citizens. Wietzke produces his argument on general grounds, but it is perhaps not an accident that his key example is that of Ptolemy. In the late Empire everything was enmeshed within patronage, a two-faced institution: looking upwards, to benefit from one's superiors, and then turning downwards, to display one's position by providing benefit further down. And, so, perhaps a dual motivation for literary production. A competition for the attention of the uppermost elite; a display of one's elevated position. Either way: literary production, in the late Imperial era, appears to have been entangled within the ideology, and practice, of patronage.

Let us stop to take stock. My ultimate goal has been not the interpretation of culture as such but, rather, the qualitative understanding of culture, as a stand-in for the hard data (which we tend to lack) for demography. Here is what I need, then. I have argued, in the preceding section, for two claims: (1) that the number of authors in the high Empire might have been rather high; and (2) that such authors would have been concentrated in certain fields, rhetoric as well as what I call "the cultural service industries". The cultural panorama provided in this section serves to support these two claims, in part by showing their interrelatedness. If indeed literature became entangled within the ladder of political and economic patronage, we would expect to see more individuals striving for the status of the author, more of them concentrated in the fields of patronage par excellence. We have started out with a picture of the Imperial era, with a growing concentration of power among the very top elite, the sub-senatorial class perhaps put under a certain pressure, and we wondered how such pressure could be compatible with a growing authorial field. We can now understand this authorial growth as the direct consequence of the pressure. The relative power of top elite became overwhelming, and so the only route to success lay, indeed, in patronage: "*Et spes et ratio studiorum in caesare tantum.*"

Authorship was impelled by a buoyant force pushing it upwards, closer and closer to Imperial patronage. The group to expand most was that of rhetors – that is, authors whose very cultural practice was tied together with the political. Physicians, grammarians, jurists, astrologers and antiquarians sought patronage as professionals. We have lost the court historians, but they surely existed; even the philosophers, near the end of the century, quickly floated up towards the Imperial patronage of the Athenian chairs.

I envision a rich, expanding culture – but also a top-heavy one: the buoyancy of Imperial and senatorial patronage pushed everything to its dependency, at a point not far from the Imperial apex. Top-heavy; hence, unstable?

## 6.4    The Scale of Authorship in the Third Century

I study a traditional question: the nature of the crisis of the third century. That this was a century of overall collapse used to be uncontroversial.[121] More recent scholarship has veered away from this understanding, for several reasons: because an *Annales* attention to material continuity makes one focus on such aspects of history, in which crisis is less evident; because the very word "crisis" (which carries with it the shadow of another word: "decline") suggests the historiographical error of teleology – nay, anachronism; quite simply, because anything uncontroversial is – to the restless hordes of contemporary scholars – an invitation for controversy.[122] I will address such general questions as little as I can. My central response to this historical controversy is to emphasize the narrow scope of my question: I study, to begin with, strictly the scale of authorship. This is one aspect of the historical process, among many, and I would specifically argue that it is one of the aspects in which the third century saw a genuine crisis.

### 6.4.1    The Authors of the Third Century: Attestation

My main task is almost prosopographic: counting authors. Whom should I count? During its very earliest generations, some – though by no means all – Christian authorship was based on its own, distinct cultural practices – circulating in specialized book forms[123] and, for several generations, almost entirely pseudonymous.[124] Through the second century a few fully Hellenized elite members of the authorial class began to embrace Christianity (few indeed they must have been: this is a very well attested group). Figures such as Justin the Martyr are already, clearly, "authors" in the sense studied in this book.

---

[121] For a sense of this pre-revisionist history, see Alföldi (1967): a study of the *world crisis* of the third century!

[122] For a survey of the historiographic debate as a whole, see Liebeschuetz (2007). Optimistic views concerning the third century (or, rather, critiques of the pessimistic views) have been offered, especially by Witschel (1999) and, later, a body of work that emphasizes the scope, and limits, of archaeological evidence: in the Latin west, it is found by the archaeologists, life goes on (this is related to my point concerning the approach of *Annales*-like history, which tends to find continuities, not dislocations; I return below to Rathbone, 1991, on p. 732 below. But, surely, the major background to such revisionism is the figure of Peter Brown, who, since 1971, has revived interest in late antiquity as an era that was not only creative and interesting but also long, and porously bordered. Against this new – and well-justified! – understanding of late antiquity, it became less attractive to introduce it with a "crisis" (this is related to my point concerning the teleological, anachronistic implications of the notion of "crisis").

[123] I shall return in on p. 781 below to mention the tight relationship between Christianity and the codex form – a well-known observation first made central by Roberts and Skeat (1983).

[124] Gamble (1995: 107).

(Especially in the second century, these are the "apologists" mentioned in on page 681, note 107, above: not only are these "authors" but also – like everyone else! – they are moved, by the buoyant force of patronage, to seek the emperor himself). During the third century the number of such attested authors rises significantly. At the same time, there are even more non-traditional Christian writings entering circulation: apocryphal sayings, visions of apocalypse, circulating anonymously, subsisting outside the main circuit of "literature". Such texts I still exclude, just as I did not count anonymi, in my survey of authorship prior to 200 CE.[125] (The phenomenon of Judeo-Christian apocrypha does carry its own historical significance; I return to discuss this on page 740 below.)

Further, there do begin to arise, through the third century, more clearly defined institutions of the Church, and there are therefore several individuals recorded as producing writings, strictly within this institutional setting and for its institutional purposes: they speak to their congregations, send letters on the affairs of the Church. These are the narrowly episcopal authors. In some ways they should be seen as more akin to Roman public officials (who would also have had to speak in public, and would have had to issue their own edicts) than to authors in the sense studied in this book. I do not exclude such authors, but I find it important to set them aside and count them separately: the eventual rise in narrowly episcopal authorship would be significant.

This, then, is the meaning of the authorship of the title of this section. It does not mean "pagan". It means authors who use their name, and write primarily in their own name, for their own career, rather than producing works for an impersonal institution. I completely exclude anonymous Christian writing; and I produce two counts, with and without episcopal writing. It should be emphasized straight away, however, that such choices have little impact on the overall results. Christian writing, even in the third century, was not yet a decisive part even of attested authorship, let alone of authorship as such (the Christian episcopal authors are, obviously, over-attested in our sources).

With this clarified, I move to the prosopography. In what follows I start, first of all, with a catalogue of attested traditional authors of the third

[125] Recent scholarship moves away from the term "apocrypha", in the context of Judeo-Christian literature, because it suggests, to a theological audience, the meaning of "heretical" (Reed, 2002). The distinction we require, however, is not between apocrypha and canon but between apocrypha and the authorial – the point being that Judeo-Christian apocrypha were distinguished from contemporary mainstream Greek literature precisely in that they maintained the authorial stance of the essentially pre-authorial Hebrew Old Testament (p. 101 above).

century. The catalogue excludes what I called "episcopal" authors, and so these are noted in a footnote.[126] The catalogue is surely not exhaustive; but likely I have not overlooked many. We have at our disposal some remarkable pieces of scholarship. Aside from the usual sources in the DPA, EANS, Jacoby and PGRSRE, of most relevance to us is Brisson (1982) (a prosopography of Porphyry's *Life of Plotinus*, a source which I will consider further below), as well as Janiszewski (2006) (an even fuller survey than Jacoby's, for the historians of the period 250 to 400 AD), Jones, Martindale and Morris (1971–92) (for the years 260 and following) and Kaster (1988) (for the second half of the third century). It is significant that, in fact, the last three mentioned sources hardly add any names to our list, beyond the major dedicated prosopographies of culture.

As I sort the authors into their "decades", what I have in mind is the period in which the author's name was "made", sometimes based on a dated significant work, sometimes based on political recognition, sometimes based on the author's age (as argued on pages 178–89 above, I consider age 50 as more appropriate than the 40 standardly taken as the "acme"). The authors noted for a decade are those who would have been prominent then. This is important for the interpretation of the data, as they contain a certain "lag". There is an entire series of important figures whose names were made very early in the fourth century,[127] and so they may have been born not long after the middle of the third century and probably embarked on the authorial life in the last few decades of the third century. All these authors are omitted from my list (which shows an especially low number for the last decades; what this means is a very low rate among our attested authors, of implied entry into the authorial life during the third quarter of the third century). Conversely, the relatively many authors (compared to what comes later) attested for the first four decades would have embarked on their own careers roughly from about 180 to about 220 CE.[128]

---

[126] Alexander of Jerusalem, Beryllus, Gaius (210), Geminus, Heraclas (230), Cornelius, Cyprian, Dionysius of Alexandria, Novatian (240), Pontius (250), Coracion, Gregory Thaumaturge, Nepos, Tryphon (260), Archelaus, Malchion, Paul of Samosata, Victorinus (270), Pierius, Meletius (280), Lucianus, Phileas (290).

[127] Lactantius and Iamblichus are obvious examples, each carrying an entire set of authors attested together with them, who are usually taken to be their near-contemporaries.

[128] Further, an author may be active for decades after their name was "made". Alexander of Aphrodisias addressed *On Fate* to Septimius Severus and Caracalla, who co-reigned during the years 198 to 209; it appears that he was then already in possession of a chair. Thus, the chair would have been gained, more likely, even before the end of the second century, and I consider him a man of the 190s. It is quite possible, given Alexander's output, that he remained active for decades more. Hermogenes, born perhaps around 160, made his name as a wunderkind (this is rare in our corpus). He thus belongs, once again, to the late second century, even though many of his extant works were likely

Obviously, there are many decisions one must make. So, for instance, there is a reasonable suggestion in the literature that the alchemist Zosimus should be dated to the 270s, based on his reference to Mani;[129] I am not sure that the Mani argument is decisive, and in view of the overall scarcity of authors active in this period I prefer to assign Zosimus (as many other scholars do as well) to the early fourth century. My caution on such questions produces an overall bias against the third century, but in fact such cases of genuine doubt are rare. I believe Knorr (1993: 183–4) refutes Tannery's reconstruction of the date of Diophantus (see note 78 above) decisively; in addition, the view that Cassius the Iatrosophist was an early third-century CE author is a simple error, unfortunately entrenched in the literature.[130] The most fundamental point is that there are, as we will immediately see below, many more authors attested for either the first and second centuries, or the fourth and fifth centuries, than for the third century, and thus the likelihood is that an otherwise undated, post-Hellenistic author would *not* be from the third century: an application not of circular but of – sound – probabilistic reasoning (see page 620 above).

Finally, I do use inscriptions – but I avoid the evidence from papyri. The "intellectuals" revealed in them – a physician here, a lawyer there – were probably not "authors" to begin with but, usually, more local practitioners. Even more significantly, the chronological pattern of the survival of papyri is *primarily* an archaeological construct: we have more second- and third-century papyri, mostly because of the water levels in Oxyrhynchus (as well as what we may refer to as the *documentary habit* of the Roman Empire in Egypt, which has little to do directly with authorial practices). The survival of inscriptions is different in kind: the chronological patterns are driven almost entirely by the epigraphic habit: they exhibit the varying rates in which inscriptions were actually set up (and, much less, the varying rates in the *survival* of inscriptions from different centuries – at least through the range of centuries that interests us). This epigraphic habit is, I believe, not unrelated (see pages 684–6 above) to the authorial practice itself, and so its evidence should be recorded.

---

written early in the third century. Galen himself – who anyone would normally classify as an author of the Antonine era – was active well into the following century.

[129] Letrouit (1995: 46); it is my impression that Letrouit stands alone in finding this argument decisive.

[130] Szabat's survey of iatrosophists (PGRSRE 404–15) has 26 figures, all of them – other than Cassius himself – dated to the fourth century and later. The error emerges from the similarity between the problems studied by Cassius the Iatrosophist and those studied in Ps. Alexander's *Problems*, which then led some past hasty compilers to put Cassius alongside Alexander himself (see Manetti, 2012).

And, with this, to the list.[131]

## 200s (24)

| | | |
|---|---|---|
| Aelius Apollonius | Athens | Rhetor |
| Apollonius | Athens/Naucratis | Rhetor |
| Aristaeus | Athens | Rhetor? |
| Aurelius Athenaeus | Tyana Ephesus | Rhetor |
| Aurelius of Tyre | Tyre | Rhetor |
| Bardaisan | Edessa | Variety |
| Basilicus | Nicomedia | Rhetor |
| Cassius Dio | Nicaea (Italy) | History |
| Clement | Alexandria | Church |
| Cornutus | Prusa/Cyzicus | Speeches? Poetry? |
| Diogenes Laertius | Nicaea? (Asia Minor is likely) | Grammarian/historian? |
| Heraclides | Lycia | Rhetor |
| Hippodromus | Larissa Thessaly/Athens | Rhetor |
| Iulius Paulus | Rome | Jurist |
| Jude | Alexandria | Church |
| Marcianus | Athens | Rhetor |
| Megistias | Smyrna | Rhetor |
| Mnesaius | Athens | Rhetor |
| Nestor | Laranda | Sophistic epic (lipogrammatic) |
| Ps/Hyginus | ? | Military, geometry |
| Serenus Sammonicus | Rome | Animal paradoxography, poem |
| Tertullian | Carthage | Church |
| Tryphoninus | Rome | Jurist |
| Ulpianus | Tyre/Rome | Jurist |

## 210s (13)

| | | |
|---|---|---|
| Aelianus | Rome/Praeneste | Animal paradoxography |
| Anonymous | Alexandria? | Teacherly text on astronomy? |
| Claudius Minucianus | Athens | Rhetor |
| Florentinus | Traveled widely | Georgics |
| Iulius Africanus | Jerusalem, traveled | Encyclopedia |
| Messius | Rome | Jurist |
| Oppian | Apamea | Didactic, hunting |
| Peitho | ? | Geometry |
| Philiscus | Larissa Thessaly/Athens | Rhetor |

[131] I do not footnote this list; arguing for each and every date would quickly become a small monograph, which I, instead, leave as a black box underlying my argument, as it were. I recognize that this is a methodological flaw, and if readers open the hood of my argument and detect a consistent bias in my choice of dating, skewing the chronological pattern, then this is a valid criticism; all I can say is that I have tried hard to judge each case on its own.

(*cont.*)

| | | |
|---|---|---|
| Philostratus Elder | Lemnos/Athens | Rhetor |
| Pom. Corn. Lollianus | Smyrna | Rhetor |
| Serenus | Antinoöpolis | Geometry |
| T. Flav. Menander | Ephesus | Rhetor |

## 220s (18)

| | | |
|---|---|---|
| Aelius Antiochus | Asia Minor? | Rhetor |
| Aemilius Macer | Rome | Jurist |
| Ammonius Saccas | Alexandria | Philosophy |
| Annianus | Thyateira | Rhetor |
| Asinius Quadratus | Antium (Italian) | History (but "sophist" somehow) |
| Athenaeus | Naucratis/Rome | Grammar of a sort |
| Aurelius | Rome/Ionia/Cyzicus | Rhetor |
| Aurelius Septimius Apollonius | Antioch Meander, Sardis? | Rhetor |
| Charidemus | Aphrodisias | Rhetor |
| Claudius Saturninus | Rome | Jurist |
| Eragatianus Menodorus | Perge | Rhetor |
| Fronto | Athens | Rhetor |
| Herennius Ptolemy | Athens | Rhetor |
| Herodian | ? | Historian |
| Hippolytus | Rome | "Philosophy" (anti-heresiology) |
| Lysimachus | ? | Philosophy (Stoic) |
| Modestinus | Rome | Jurist |
| Themistocles | Athens? | Philosophy (Stoic) |

## 230s (20)

| | | |
|---|---|---|
| Aelianus | Miletus | Philosophy (Stoic) |
| Alexander | Lycopolis | Philosophy (perhaps Platonist?) |
| Anon. 1128 | Cappadocia/Rome | Rhetor |
| Aspasius | Ravenna | Rhetor |
| Cassianus | Ionia/Athens? | Rhetor |
| Censorinus | Rome | Grammar, exact sciences |
| Cornelianus | Lebadia | Rhetor |
| Ctesias | Aphrodisias | Rhetor |
| Democritus | Athens? | Philosopher |
| Euclid | Athens? | Philosopher |
| Licinius Rufinus | Rome | Jurist |
| Lollianus | Prusa and much more | Rhetor |
| Nicagoras | Athens | Rhetor |

*(cont.)*

| | | |
|---|---|---|
| Origen | Alexandria | Philosophy to Christianity |
| Philippus | Edessa | Astro-anthropology |
| Pisander | Laranda | Sophistic epic (history) |
| Proclinus | Troas | Philosopher |
| Rufinus | Athens | Rhetor |
| Serapion | Alexandria | Rhetor |
| Valerius Apsines | Gadara, Athens | Rhetor |

## 240s (15)

| | | |
|---|---|---|
| Agapetos | Athens | Teacher of rhetoric, rhetor? |
| Ammonius | ? | Philosophy (peripatetic) |
| Annius | ? | Philosophy (Stoic) |
| Anon. 1129 | Egypt | Rhetor |
| Athenaeus | ? | Philosophy (Stoic) |
| Cl. Rufinus | Smyrna | Rhetor |
| Gaianus | Athens/Berytus | Rhetor |
| Heliodorus | ? | Philosophy (peripatetic) |
| Herminus | ? | Philosophy (Stoic) |
| Medius | Athens? | Philosophy (Stoic) |
| Musonius | ? | Philosophy (Stoic) |
| Philostratus Lemnos | Lemnos/Athens | Rhetor |
| Phoebion | ? | Philosopher (Stoic) |
| Ptolemy | ? | Philosophy (peripatetic) |
| Theodotus | ? | Philosophy (Platonic) |

## 250s (12)

| | | |
|---|---|---|
| Amelius | Rome | Philosophy |
| Anon. 1132 | Antioch | Rhetor |
| C. Iulius Romanus | Italy (Rome?) | Grammarian |
| Dexippus | Athens | Historian |
| Firmus Castricius | Rome | Philosophy |
| Herennius | Alexandria | Philosophy (Platonic) |
| Maior | Arabia/Athens | Rhetor |
| Marius Plotius Sacerdos | Rome | Grammarian |
| Origen | Alexandria/Rome | Philosopher |
| Olympius | Alexandria | Philosophy (Platonic) |
| Paulinus | Scythopolis/Rome | Physician/philosopher |
| Plotinus | Alexandria/Rome | Philosophy |

## 260s (20)

| Anatolius | Alexandria/Laodicea | Philosophy, exact sciences |
|---|---|---|
| Apollonius | Athens | Grammarian |
| Aspasius | Tyre/Athens | Rhetor, historian |
| Callietes | Athens | Philosophy (Stoic) |
| Callinicus | Petra/Athens | Rhetor and much more |
| Cassius Longinus | Athens | Philosophy, grammar, rhetoric |
| Demetrius | Athens | Geometer? Philosophy |
| Diophanes | Athens | Rhetor |
| Eubulus | Athens | Philosophy (Platonic) |
| Gargilius Martialis | Mauretania | Horticulture |
| Iunius Minucianus | Athens | Rhetor |
| Lupercus | Berytus | Grammarian |
| Metrophanes | Lebadia?? | Rhetor |
| Metrophanes | Phrygia | Rhetor, historian |
| Nicostratus | Trapezus | History |
| Philostratus | Athens | Historian |
| Philostratus Younger | Athens | Rhetor? |
| Pigres | Philadelphia | Rhetor |
| Tleoplemos | Athens | Rhetor? |
| Zethus | Rome/Arabia | Physician/philosopher |

## 270s (5)

| Eustochius | Alexandria/Rome | Physician |
|---|---|---|
| Genethlius | Athens/Petra | Rhetor |
| Herennius Dexippus | Athens | Rhetor |
| Theodosius | Rome? | Philosophy? |
| Zoticus | Rome | Poet, critic |

## 280s (7)

| Andromachus | Neapolis (Samaria), Athens, Nicomedia? | Rhetor |
|---|---|---|
| Cleodamus | Athens? | Philosophy? |
| Nemesianus | Carthage | Poetry (hunting, cp. Oppian) |
| Pamphilus | Berytus/Caesarea | Various, but above all Church |
| Paulus | Mysia? Athens | Rhetor |
| Porphyry | Tyre/Rome/Athens | Philosophy |
| Torkouatos | Trebenna | Rhetor |

**290s (5)**

| | | |
|---|---|---|
| Apsines | Athens | Rhetor |
| Gregorius | Nicomedia | Jurist |
| Helladius | Antinoöpolis? | Poet |
| Menander | Athens | Rhetor |
| Soterichus | Oasis (Libya) | Poet (historical themes, epic) |

The broad picture is clear enough, as can be seen in the figure.

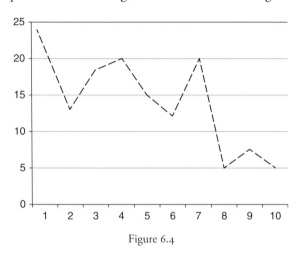

Figure 6.4

One's first impression is of overall resilience into the middle of the century, followed by a sharp drop in the final third. But it would be a mistake – based on such slender, subjective numbers – to tell a story of a local decline in the 210s, a local rise in the 260s. Smooth away these anomalies and a more likely story is one of a fairly stable number into the 230s, though perhaps slightly declining; followed by a sharper decline. To stylize, we get Figure 6.5.

Let us be clear about one thing: we are looking at an arbitrary chronological window. What we would need to know above all is the process through the decades that straddle the second and third centuries, from about 150 to 240 – and we are hampered by scholarship that categorizes its evidence in the broad category of the "century". It would have been best to expand this study and to classify the attested authors of the second and the fourth centuries by distinct decades, as well. The entire point, however, is that this would also have become prohibitively difficult, since there are *so many more of them*. I shall return to this question below, but one qualification must be added immediately. The

Figure 6.5

PGRSRE has about 30 authors classified as "II/III century" whom I was unable to assign to a particular decade (mostly, these are merely dated epigraphically), as well as more than 40 authors who are completely undated, of whom at least 20 should be assigned to this "II/III category". Probabilistically (as I shall note below), a third of these, perhaps slightly fewer, surely belong to the early third century: let us count these as 15. But there are surely more such authors who in fact belong to the third century, and whom I omitted from my survey because I have decided – erroneously – to assign them to the second century. To take an obvious example, I have excluded Sextus Empiricus (Annas and Barnes, indeed, believe he was a second-century author);[132] there is a certain probability that I am wrong on this. Such cases will add, then, let us say, about ten more authors.[133] Adding, then, 25 more authors to the third century would further unbalance our graph. Those will be added almost entirely to the first few decades of the century – indeed, mostly right at its beginning. The figure contains about 140 authors but it misses about 25, most in the first and second decades. Its "true" shape, then, may be stylized as a relatively elevated near-plateau, followed by, at first, a noticeable decline and, then, nearly a freefall.

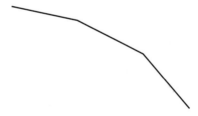

Figure 6.6

---

[132] Annas and Barnes (2000: xii). The argument is a little fantastic, if credible (there is a pseudo-Galenic text that mentions Sextus; pseudo-Galenic as it is, however, this may well be the text Galen *himself* famously referred to as falsely attributed to him: Galen, *On His Own Books*, K. XIX.8–9, from which it follows that a text that circulated when Galen was in his old age – but very much alive – included a reference to Sextus).

[133] Of course, I might have been wrong about some of the authors I did assign to the early third century, and a few of them might have reached their acme in the late second century, instead. Nevertheless, since there are many more authors I assign (unlisted) to the late second century than ones I do assign (listed) to the early third, the probability is that correction of the error, in and of itself, would make the numbers higher in the early third century.

This is the shape produced when episcopal authors are excluded (a valid exercise, as it shows how the dislocations of conversion may have impacted authorship in those genres that were typical for the second century CE). Bringing such authors in, however, the graph, once again, is subtly transformed. More of the episcopal authors are found near the middle of the century, blunting the decline somewhat.[134]

Now, instead of a sharp drop from 240 onwards, we see in Figure 6.7 a gradual decline through the century as a whole, gradually accelerating – which, in and of itself, seems plausible. This, then, is the raw evidence of attestation. This observation – concerning the pattern of attestation – should be fairly uncontroversial.

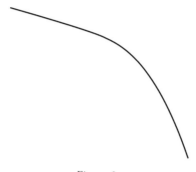

Figure 6.7

### 6.4.2 The Authors of the Third Century: Interpretation

What does this decline in the number of attested authors imply, in terms of the *actual* numbers of authors originally active in the third century itself? It is possible, of course, that authorship remained the same, while attestation fell. So, is it perhaps the case that, as the century wears on, our sources, simply, thin out?

Let us look more closely, then, at our sources for the third century. We have two main non-Christian clusters of evidence. One we have seen

---

[134] I am not sure if this should really carry all that much significance statistically, however – and, so, all the more reason, perhaps, to ignore, for the purpose of some calculations, the evidence for the episcopal authors – since episcopal authors are likely to be considerably better attested than the pagan authors. Thus, three more episcopal authors in a decade are "worth" only as many as, let's say, one non-episcopal author, for the purpose of trying to extrapolate the original numbers of actual authors.

already: the combined evidence for rhetors, gained from inscriptions as well as from Philostratus. The other important cluster of evidence we have is that for philosophy, seen from the Plotinian circle. We have Porphyry's many mentions of philosophers of his time and of the recent past; most significantly, Porphyry also cited in full an introductory passage from Longinus' *On the End*, whose goal was to provide a comprehensive history of the philosophy of Longinus' youth. Taken together, this amounts to an extremely rich and contemporary prosopographic source, covering the years from the 220s to the 280s (but waning after the 260s). Finally, for the last few decades of the century we have no comparable sources (though we still have Eusebius, for Christian authors).

Eunapius – a mid-fourth-century author – explicitly claimed that there was a hiatus in what he calls "philosophical" practice immediately following the reign of Severus[135] (that is, for the last two-thirds of the third century), and so his own *Lives of the Philosophers* concentrated on a couple of generations up to and including his own. Similar considerations hold for other fourth-century sources such as Libanius, for rhetoric, and Oribasius, for medicine. Ausonius provides us with a snapshot of Burdigalia (Bordeaux) for the early fourth century. Our evidence from the fourth century, in the form of authors who provide significant prosopographic information, is plentiful. It is engaged, however, specifically with the recent past. (This trend towards the near-contemporary, beginning already with Philostratus, is significant in and of itself: I shall return to discuss this below.) It remains noteworthy that all these authors from Eunapius to Ausonius seem to have so little to tell us about the latter part of the third century, and yet: one story we can tell of the third century, then, is of the life-supporting machines of attestation being gradually cut off. Inscriptions and Philostratus cut off at about 230 to 240; Porphyry and Longinus cut off at about 260 to 280. So, perhaps there were more authors, later on in the century, without us knowing that?

But this would be the wrong metaphor. The pattern of the extant sources is not some kind of arbitrary implements thrown in from the

---

[135] *Lives of the Philosophers* 455: "The genus of the Best Philosophers extended as far as Severus." Following a brief survey of a few third-century authors, then, Eunapius begins his narrative proper with Iamblichus. Compare with Longinus' introduction to *On the End*, quoted by Porphyry, *Life of Plotinus* 20: "There have been in our time, Marcellus, many philosophers, especially in the early part of our life; I say this because at the present moment there is an indescribable shortage of philosophy." Indeed, such litanies concerning the third century are so common (collected by Alföldy, 1974; compare de Blois, 1984) that scholars may be tempted to dismiss them as tropes; in fact, if decay in scale were so fast as suggested here it could well have been visible, and would have been commented upon, at the time. No trope, then, but reality?

outside: they are, themselves, part of the historical reality. There ought to be some significance in the fact that we have many more contemporary sources for the late second century CE (and, to some extent, the early third century) than for the later third century.

To begin with, and to repeat a point made on page 685 above, we should not simply dismiss the temporal concentration of the inscriptions: they reveal the fact that authors wished to be broadcast. Benefactors of the second and third century CE could have decided to set up monuments celebrating the gods, the traditions of their city, its past illustrious members. Instead, they set up monuments celebrating themselves. What we witness here is not merely an epigraphic habit but an *auto*-epigraphic habit (such that, even in funerary inscriptions, the dedicator of the stone is advertised no less than the deceased individual!).

The same logic obtains, in fact, for Philostratus himself. It should be emphasized just how remarkable this source is, in that its *primary* interest is in the recent past to the contemporary. As noted above, the very substantial survival of works from the Imperial era does not, in general, provide us with a significant prosopographic advantage for this era. This is because, name-dropping as they are, our sources from the first two centuries tend to drop names – but past names (classical and Hellenistic) – while maintaining a certain allusive attitude towards the nearer past and hardly ever mentioning their contemporaries.[136] Philostratus' *Lives of the Sophists*, indeed, is in parts an auto-historiographical project, as it celebrates Philostratus' teacher, Proclus, as well as members of his family – the work applying the logic of a dedicated honorific inscription to papyrus. The point is that this was not unique to Philostratus: as noted above, both Longinus and Porphyry, later in the third century, produced similarly auto-historical works, which would remain as a central feature of historiography for the following centuries; in a word, this is the era of the *hagiography*. This is not an accident: there were genuine cultural shifts that contributed to a late ancient turn towards a cultural historiography of the near-contemporary. I shall return to explain this, as a cultural

---

[136] It is interesting that, among the extant literature, the nearest parallels seem to come from rhetoric: above all Cicero's *Brutus* (a history of rhetoric from its foundations down to Cicero's own day), but also the introductions to Seneca the Elder's *Controversies*. But the history of philosophy by Philodemus was written not much later than the *Brutus* – and also reached not so far from the present (we do not know how close it got to Philodemus' own time; but it certainly was not written from the deep temporal distance of Diogenes Laertius). It is possible, however, that, compared with the literature written in the two centuries preceding him, Philostratus was among the closest to a contemporary cultural history. The revival of histories-of-the-near-present is a marked feature of the third century, *compared with the high Empire*.

phenomenon, below, in section 6.5.2, but the consequence for the pattern of attestation should be spelled out now already. If anything, the third (and later) centuries are *well* documented. Recall the chart from page 654 above, concerning the brief intersection – during the high Empire – of significant survival into codex, as well as the construction of the poleis of letters of the past. We may now add another, complementary era: that of the histories of the near-present.

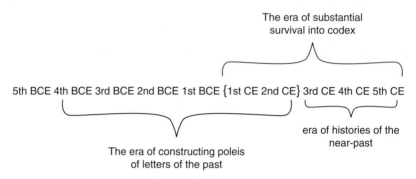

The high Empire was an era which survived substantially into the codex – but which did not set out to document itself. This is no longer true for late antiquity, which, first epigraphically and then hagiographically (taking "hagiography" in a wide sense), was fully invested in its own commemoration. Thus, the level of attestation should in fact rise, as we move from the high Empire into later antiquity.

But not only that: survival into codex should not be seen as a flat function, rising all of a sudden into the high Empire and then plateauing. It is much more plausible to see this as a rising curve. Let us follow this argument through its consequences.

We begin, indeed, with what may be the clearest pattern of them all: the amount of extant literature drops dramatically, early in the third century.

The following is what I hope to be a near-complete list of extant authors active roughly from the years 150 to 225 (I include authors extant via epitome).

| | |
|---|---|
| Aretaeus | Medicine |
| Galen | Medicine |
| Julius Africanus | Encyclopedia |
| Sextus Pompeius Festus | Encyclopedia |
| Ampelius | Encyclopedia |
| Aulus Gellius | Encyclopedia |
| Artemidorus | Divination |

(*cont.*)

| | |
|---|---|
| Polyaenus | Tactics |
| Aelianus of Praeneste | Paradoxography |
| Cleonides (weak dating) | Music |
| Ps. Hyginus | Agrimensor |
| Serenus | Mathematics |
| Ptolemy | Exact sciences |
| Antiochus of Athens (date uncertain) | Astrology |
| Vettius Valens | Astrology |
| Achilles Tatius | Astronomy |
| Anonymous "Commentary to Ptolemy" | Astronomy |
| Cleomedes (weak dating) | Astronomy/philosophy |
| Hermias | ~Philosophy/rhetoric (Church) |
| Tertullian | ~Philosophy/rhetoric (Church) |
| Athenagoras | ~Philosophy (Church) |
| Apollonius of Ephesus | ~Philosophy (Church) |
| Theophilus | ~Philosophy (Church) |
| Justinus Martyr | ~Philosophy (Church) |
| Irenaeus | ~Philosophy (Church) |
| Clement | ~Philosophy (Church) |
| Minucius Felix | Philosophy (Christian dialogue) |
| Albinus | Philosophy |
| Philippus (Bardaisan's pupil) | Philosophy |
| Hippolytus | Philosophy |
| Marcus Aurelius | Philosophy |
| Alexander of Aphrodisias | Philosophy |
| Sextus Empiricus | Philosophy |
| Diogenes Laertius | Philosophy/history |
| Pausanias | Geography |
| Phlegon (but maybe earlier?) | History |
| Aristodemus | History |
| Cassius Dio | History |
| Herodian | History |
| Athenaeus | Grammar/history |
| Fronto | Grammar |
| Hephaestion | Grammar |
| Aelius Herodian | Grammar |
| Moeris | Grammar |
| Phrynichus | Grammar |
| Hermogenes | Grammar/rhetoric |
| Pollux | Grammar/rhetoric |
| Rufus | Rhetoric |
| Aelius Aristides | Rhetoric |
| Herodes Atticus | Rhetor |
| Lesbonax (weak dating) | Rhetor |
| Anonymous Seguerianus | Rhetoric |
| Apsines | Rhetoric |
| Papinian (qualified) | Jurisprudence |

*(cont.)*

| | |
|---|---|
| Ulpian (qualified) | Jurisprudence |
| Iulius Paulus (qualified) | Jurisprudence |
| Lucian | Prose fiction (comico-philosophical) |
| Antoninus Liberalis | Prose fiction (myth) |
| Babrius | Fiction, poetry (fables) |
| Achilles Tatius | Novel |
| Longus | Novel |
| Oppian | Didactic poetry |
| Ps. Oppian | Didactic poetry |
| Serenus Sammonicus | Didactic poetry |

Some of the names here are questionable (so, for instance, we do not have any evidence that Cleomedes was active late in the second century and not, say, several decades earlier).[137] On the other hand, the very strong concentration of authors in this period suggests that, other things being equal, hard-to-date works are somewhat more likely to originate from these years. In some ways, then, this is an undercount of the concentration of extant literature in the late Antonine to Severan eras (so, for instance, I do not count here Hero, Diophantus or Hypsicles – see page 444 above: just a few of the authors in the exact sciences who, possibly, *could* have been active in these decades).

We have here 63 authors, or over a third of all post-classical Greek authors (as is typical of the second century, the great majority of these authors wrote in Greek). This ratio is made even starker when we consider the sheer bulk of the extant works. About 7.5 million words of Greek survive from the third century BC to the first century CE; more than 10 million words survive from the second century alone.

The preliminary conclusion is that there was, in fact, a substantial flourishing of authorial activity late in the second century CE, which is, of course, what I have argued in section 6.2 above. But this argument needs to be refined. It is likely that there were more authors active in this period than in previous periods, but it is certainly not the case that a third of post-classical Greek authors were active in the years 150 to 225 CE, or that more

---

[137] The references to Epicureanism clearly suggest a date in the first two centuries; since in general we see more evidence for interest in the exact sciences picking up in the second century CE, there is something of an inherent likelihood that he was more a second-century than a first-century author. To suggest, then, that he was active later rather than earlier in the century is a matter of mere probability.

Greek words were written in the second century CE than in the previous four centuries combined. The preponderance of the later years most likely represents a selection bias for recency: later works survived better, presumably because of their greater proximity to the pivotal moment for the survival of ancient works – the transition from roll to codex in the fourth century CE. Whatever our hypothetical "half-life" estimate for ancient papyrus rolls, it is clear that, to survive into codex, works from Hellenistic times would typically have had to be copied several times, and even those from early Imperial times would have been unlikely to survive directly into the fourth century. As we move into the second century CE, however, especially towards its end, it becomes perfectly plausible that a lucky, well-curated roll could have made it safely into the middle of the fourth century CE. The fact that not only many authors but especially more *bulky* authors tend to survive from this late period is especially suggestive: the recency bias I suggest operates on rolls, not on authors. The argument is indeed obvious: is it at all likely that so much of Galen would have survived had he been active any earlier than he did – that is, further away from the codex? (Imagine for a moment Galen and Chrysippus swapped in chronological position; then imagine a universe in which Galen is known only through innumerable quotations by later medical authors, Chrysippus through a shelf-full of edited volumes.)

And so we return to the claim that the probability of survival into codex was likely to represent a gradually rising curve, which, we can now see, is both (1) reasonable on first principles and (2) apparently vindicated by the evidence for the survival into codex of works from the second century CE.

Now consider the extant authors of the period from 225 to 300 CE. By my – admittedly cautious – count, these are as follows.

| | |
|---|---|
| Censorinus | Grammar (numerology) |
| Gargilius Martialis | Horticulture |
| Anatolius of Laodicea | Church work, chronology |
| Commodianus | Didactic poetry (Church) [doubtful dating] |
| Methodius | Philosophy (Church) |
| Marius Plotius Sacerdos | Grammar |
| Menander Rhetor | Rhetoric |
| Philostratus the Elder | History/rhetoric |
| Philostratus the Younger | Rhetoric |
| Porphyry | Philosophy (exact sciences) |
| Plotinus | Philosophy |
| Origen | "Grammar"/Church |
| Alexander of Lycopolis | Philosophy |

The years 150 to 225 have 62 extant authors; the following 75 years have 13.[138] Once again, counting literary survival by authors is, in fact, generous towards the later period. The TLG counts about 1.5 million words from the third century CE, more than 10 million for the preceding one – and, again, many of the extant works of the third century are from its earliest part. Thus, the number of words surviving from 225 to 300 seems to be almost an order of magnitude lower than that of the preceding 75 years.

Compare this now to the fourth century, from which entirely unlikely hoards of works survive – 18 million words of Greek! – which must have something to do with the proximity to the codex, which becomes widespread, indeed, through this very century.

It might be suggested that so much is preserved from the fourth century not because of any recency bias but because this is the century from which Christian literature – of obvious interest to medieval readers – emerges on a much larger scale. This is not entirely false: there was certainly some Christianity bias, as I will note below (and as we have observed already through the evidence from Photius: see page 551 above), in the survival of works from antiquity. Still, let us avoid the naïve, "enlightenment" assumption, as if late antiquity and the Middle Ages were biased against the achievements of classical antiquity. I have noted on paegs 69–75 above the survival of the ancient literary ranking into Byzantium: if they liked it in Oxyrhynchus, they liked it in Byzantium. The Middle Ages did not shun the pagan. This becomes clear as we consider some of the extant works themselves: it is from this fourth century, for instance, that we have the corpus of the pagan Libanius, with its incredible trove of contemporary prosopographic information; we have an enormous survival of explicitly pagan works from Neoplatonists such as Oribasius, Eunapius and, ultimately, the major Neoplatonist philosophers. But it is true that a more rigorous approach to the recency bias should pay attention to the generic composition of works across the centuries. Let us consider such qualifications.

First, we see no evidence for any "mini-canonization" of, specifically, the latter part of the second century CE. The most likely way this would manifest itself would be through a tendency to preserve the speeches of the generations of rhetors celebrated by Philostratus' *Lives of the Sophists*. This was a huge corpus, as we consider something like 1,000 authors, the most prominent of whom must have been enormously prolific. (It is not clear how many of them

---

[138] Adding episcopal authorship would bring the number of extant authors to 18 (by adding Cyprian, Gregory Thaumaturge, Novatian, Pamphilus and Victorinus; as noted above, these authors were even more likely to survive into codex, for reasons of genre).

were even committed to writing – which is part of the point, however: was there even a significant effort to achieve *that*?) It is quite likely that their original output amounted to tens of thousands of speeches. In fact, the *only* corpus of Second Sophistic speech to survive substantially is that of Aelius Aristides. A considerable amount of the survival of "rhetoric" from this era is of rhetorical theory (from the sophisticated Hermogenes to the banal works of Apsines and the Anonymous Seguerianus). Little survives even from Herodes Atticus. (Indeed, it is striking that we do have a few more survivals from the Second Sophistic, from a somewhat *earlier* period: Dio of Prusa, and Favorinus. Indeed, we can now see in the evidence of the papyri that, quite possibly, the most successful Imperial-era author could have been Plutarch! No special canonization of the later second century, then.) But, of course, there was no such mini-canonization, hard as Philostratus tried. The canon was closed by the end of the classical era; it would not be opened again.

The conclusion becomes that the ratio of the scale of surviving works from the second and third centuries is best approximated by multiplying two factors: the recency bias; and the actual original ratio of the scale of works produced.

To begin with, I did argue above that there were somewhat more authors active in the second century CE than in prior centuries. We will not be too far off the mark if we assume that the number of Greek words written between 300 BCE and 100 CE was about three times (rather than four times) the number of Greek words written between 100 CE and 200 CE. In fact, as noted above, the Greek words surviving from the period 300 BCE to 100 CE are about three-quarters of those surviving from the period 100 CE to 200 CE. Thus, our best first stab at the size of the recency bias is that, over two and a half centuries, it reduces survival by a factor of four. This is in fact very consistent with a half-life of the papyrus roll of about a century.

Now, there are more than one and a half times more words surviving in Greek from the fourth century CE than from the second. Factoring in the recency bias, this should mean that, originally, the literary output of the fourth century was about one-half of that of the second. Factoring in any further Christianity bias, we need to assume an even smaller fourth-century literary output. One-third? One-quarter? One-fifth? There is a considerable latitude with such estimates, but their overall direction is clear and inherently plausible: the fourth century had, originally, a very lively literary culture, but also significantly smaller (in Greek, at least) than that of the second century. At least the assumption of a consistent recency bias accords with the facts of the survival from the fourth century.

The net outcome of all this is that the third century, in turn, *must be over-represented in our sources, relative to the second century.* I emphasize: I am not saying that "the third century should have been over-represented", expressing surprise over the fact that it is not. I am asserting that, in all likelihood, the third century *is*, in fact, over-represented. The few authors we do have are more than we *should* have. And, if the extant corpus collapses, between 150 to 225 and 225 to 300, by a ratio of something around 1:5 (authors) to 1:6 (words), this must mean that, in the original literary output, the collapse was even more marked, at a rate considerably more than 1:5. This, once again, makes sense, as we compare this now with the fourth century. It is historically plausible that authorship rose, perhaps to a significant extent, from the third century CE to the fourth. Which means that the third must have produced *much less* than the second.

To return, then, finally, to those life-supporting machines: it is true that the sources for attestation gradually disappear through the third century. But the more salient points are (1) that these are, to begin with, exceptionally rich sources (this is the argument above concerning the auto-prosopographic nature of Philostratus and the Plotinians); and (2) that the third century has only itself to blame for the loss of such sources. The sources die out because authorship does.

What is most important is that the transition is not merely quantitative. What we see is a qualitative change affecting certain genres; and this, in turn, makes us trust our evidence better – and begins to suggest the outlines of a possible account.

I have provided a long list of 63 extant authors from the years 150 to 225, partly because, otherwise, you may not have believed me that there were so many of them. But, more to the point, what such a list brings out is the sheer generic variety of authorship in the later second century CE. This changes rapidly as we move into the third century, now considering not only the extant works from this era but even the much wider list of attested authors provided at the top of this section.

Serenus of Antinoöpolis may have been active in the 210s.[139] An astronomical observation dates an anonymous work, misleadingly referred to as a "commentary" on Ptolemy, to the same decade.[140] The next time we meet anyone whose identity is clearly that of "an author in the exact sciences" is with Pappus and his generation – dated to the years

---

[139]  The evidence is most clearly set out in Auffret (2014) (I do not share his optimistic reading of the name Serenus based on the two letters "SE..." in an inscription from Antinoöpolis, however).

[140]  Jones (1990: 3–4).

surrounding 320 CE.[141] In the intervening years we do have, of course, Porphyry himself, who was all-round brilliant and did display the mathematical fluency of specialized education in the exact sciences – and yet clearly was no mathematician (the same is true of Anatolius of Laodicea). The strongest candidate is "Demetrius the Geometer": a fragment from Porphyry puts an author of that name in Athens, in 263; Proclus describes the same person as a teacher of Porphyry (was he *merely* a teacher?) – and quotes him for a specifically *Neoplatonic theory*. Was he really active as a mathematician – or did he carry that sobriquet as a way to distinguish him from other Demetrii?[142] The argument from silence is telling: mathematics was so crucial to Neoplatonism; how come we do not hear of *more* mathematicians, through the Plotinian circle? (Did those new Platos not seek out their new Archytae, Theaeteti, Eudoxi?)

Demetrius was a "geometer", in some sense, drawn into the Plotinian orbit. We hear similarly of two physicians close to Plotinus: Eustochius and Zethus. We have no indication that either of them was a medical author. We have no convincing evidence for any other medical activity for an *entire* century! This is a truly remarkable hiatus, as there is no earlier parallel to any such hiatus in the history of medicine.[143] There are several hard-to-date medical compilations, such as, for instance, that of Cassius the Iatrosophist, which in the past used to be assigned erroneously to the early third century (see page 694 above). Some of these may well derive from the fourth century, but the earliest extant post-Galenic securely dated medical author is Oribasius. He is dated through his close political association with Julian the Apostate:[144] so, rather younger even than Pappus. Oribasius – like Pappus – relies on past works which are explicitly cited (a feature to which I shall return below), and his citations range from classical antiquity up to his staple source, Galen, then jump to several near-contemporaries.[145] In fact, we have some more biographical data from Eunapius, who refers to near-contemporary doctors because of their

---

[141] For the evidence and a plausible synthesis, see Cuomo (2000: 6).

[142] EANS, s.v. Demetrius (Math.), where it is suggested that this might be the same as s.v. Demetrius (Music): the suggested identification is made less likely, I believe, in light of the enormous frequency of the name.

[143] This hiatus has been noted already: Kudlien (1968) (writing at a time when the overall crisis of the third century was not yet put into question, Kudlien does not see the hiatus as all that puzzling; he further tends to believe that Galen became so dominant in his own lifetime as to curtail future elaborations – a view which seems to be undercut by the evidence of Galen himself).

[144] Baldwin (1975). It is through Oribasius – member of a fanatically pagan circle – that the most significant survival of all ancient authors has been arranged: that of Galen. So much for any Christian biases in the survival of works from antiquity!

[145] For Oribasius' sources and his use of them, see van der Eijk (2010) (also below, pp. 765–6).

"rhetorical" nature (it is for a reason that Cassius was called "Iatrosophist": this is indeed typical of late ancient medical authors as a whole, who tended to display not just their scientific knowledge but also their general paideia). The earliest medical author in this group is Zeno of Cyprus, a teacher in Alexandria, and we have also the names of some of his pupils (Ionicus, Magnus of Nisibis, Theon – as well as Oribasius himself).[146] A few are mentioned in the correspondence of Libanius, closing a circle of attestation. Zeno of Cyprus' students belong to the middle of the fourth century, and Zeno himself can therefore be dated to the early fourth century CE, perhaps a contemporary of Pappus, in the same city: the time, and place, for what seems like a new beginning following a long hiatus.

There was not strictly speaking a "hiatus" in grammar as such. It is remarkable, however, that the extant grammarians from the era – Censorinus and Plotius – are both Latin. In general, Latin authorship rises in relative significance from the third century (one can say it achieves parity with Greek grammar only with the work of Donatus, the fourth-century commentator on Vergil – through whose hands the Latin tradition of an *Ars Grammatica* receives its lasting, medieval form).[147] This is for a rather obvious reason: as the bonds of the Mediterranean are loosened, regional cultures become more prominent. The re-emergence of Latin as a major literary vehicle is, then, analogous to that of, say, Syriac (this is also the age of Bardaisan). So, eventually, more *Latin* grammarians; but the drop in the numbers of attested Greek grammarians through the third century is very marked indeed. From Athenaeus, all the way down to the fourth century, we find only two figures whose main identity is clearly that of a Greek grammarian. These are: an Apollonius, brushing against the Plotinian circle; as well as Lupercus of Berytus, known to the *Suda* s.v. (This is only slightly better than the exact sciences.) Kaster finds about 100 (!) grammarians in the fourth century, of whom no more than about 15 are attested by papyri alone (which I ignore in this context). The fourth century is certainly over-represented in this regard, but, qualitatively, it once again presents a new beginning. For mathematics, we have the name of Pappus, and, for medicine, we have the name of Oribasius – both fourth-century authors who drew heavily on traditions culminating in the second century. For Greek grammar, we do not have a similar name, but this is because the important work of excerpting and collecting is now

---

[146] The evidence for the group of Ionicus, Magnus of Nisibis, Theon and Zenon is summed up s.vv. PGRSRE.

[147] Irvine (1994: 56–9).

preserved anonymously as the "Four-Man Commentary", an epitome of Aristonicus, Didymus, Aelius Herodian and Nicanor which is also standardly taken to be from the fourth century (and which is deduced from the scholia to the famous Homer manuscript, Venetus A).[148]

Our evidence is much clearer for jurisprudence, as, in this case, the very act of compilation has been amply documented. Here is what Justinian put in motion in the 530s: more than 1,500 (ancient) books, by 38 authors, were assigned to several committees whose responsibility was to excerpt – with explicit citations – the most important observations.[149] This collection must have represented at least the bulk of the more respected extant works in jurisprudence. The major authors in jurisprudence would be politically active, and their transmitted legal views often imply the political circumstances of their times of writings. Hence, these 38 authors cited by the *Digest* can generally be dated. They date, in fact, from the Republican era to the fourth century. Several of these are cited so extensively that they can be considered as "extant", in epitome form. Three of these are from the late second century or right at the beginning of the third: Papinian, Ulpian and Iulius Paulus. No other later legal author is cited extensively and none dates from the final two-thirds of the third century; but two are from the early fourth century: Hermogenianus and Charisius. Once again, then: a visible hiatus.

The corpus of extant astrological literature is not large, and, even there, many of the works do not include explicit horoscope calculations. When they do, however, such horoscopes allow very precise dating.[150] The last datable horoscope included in the work of Vettius Valens was cast in the year 173. The earliest datable horoscope included in the work of Firmicus

---

[148] For an accessible overview, see Nagy (1997: 103–5). The history of scholia involves not only the question of when compilations of past scholia were made but also when they were inscribed as marginalia. The classic treatment of this question is Wilson (1967), bolstered since by the evidence studied by McNamee (1995; 1998; 2007); this has been taken to be mostly a late ancient phenomenon (against Zuntz, who definitely did believe in the formation of collections of scholia in late antiquity, but preferred to delay their marginal placement to a later, medieval development; still followed by Montana, 2011). The seemingly technical debate hides a fundamental question of overarching interpretation: just how close were the cultural practices of late antiquity to those of the Middle Ages? In general, for the history of scholiography, see Montana and Porro (2014), especially for the important reminder that scholia are not distinctive to grammar and are, instead, found across the disciplines (especially the exact sciences: Acerbi, 2014). Teaching was everywhere, defining the authorial life.

[149] I follow the synthesis in Honoré (2010b).

[150] This rests on the assumption that the horoscopes provided by way of example are "real", their data derived from astronomical calculation and not just thrown together for the sake of example: not always a safe assumption.

Maternus was for a birth in 303 and was probably cast in 337.[151] I believe
that the manuscript transmission does not include any evidence for elite
astrologers active in between the two dates.[152]

The evidence from the horoscopes is, of course, weak, given the small
numbers involved. But it is suggestive. Astrology is the clearest case of a
"service industry". Indeed, on page 667 above, I produced a rough model
for the second century, divided into three equal parts – the service industries, rhetoric, and the two venerable genres of history and philosophy. We
find that the first of these collapsed almost entirely early in the third
century.

Rhetoric and philosophy, in particular, remained. It is a much more difficult
question, however, as to how to account for our evidence concerning these
fields: for rhetoric, the evidence might be skewed against the later third century
(because Philostratus, and the inscriptions, cease); for philosophy, the evidence
might be skewed favorably for the later third century (because of Porphyry). I
tend to take Longinus' statement that there were more philosophers active in
his youth at its face value.[153] Indeed, I find it intriguing that the tradition of
commentaries on Aristotle, culminating with Alexander of Aphrodisias – who,
I believe, made his name right before 200 – is not *directly* continued by any
later authority.[154] Just as we see a hiatus in the various service industries, so,
after all, we should pay attention to the dramatic closing of the tradition of the
Hellenistic schools. For once, the evidence is uncontroversial: the Stoics and
the Epicureans (as well as the Cynics and the Skeptics) are not attested beyond
the very beginning of the third century.[155] Philosophy remains robust, in the

---

[151] Heilen (2015): see page 273 (for Vettius Valens), 330 (for Firmicus Maternus). There are also a
couple of horoscopes included in an anonymous commentary to Ptolemy's *Tetrabiblos* (Heilen,
2015: 273–4, 277), which Jones (2010: 43 n.58) identifies as ad hoc concoctions.

[152] Hephaestion – a fifth-century author – reports a horoscope for Porphyry, which he derived not
from a previous astrological handbook, however, but from Porphyry's own works (Heilen, 2015:
234). There are a great many astrological papyri for this period, found in Heilen (2015: 274–88), but
the chronological nature of this series, as noted above, is misleading. Astrology went on; what we no
longer see is astrological book authorship.

[153] Porphyry, *Life of Plotinus* 20: 17–20.

[154] This is significant, because we have a very substantial survival of Aristotle commentaries, which
often refer back to past commentary. Thus, we have a sense of a continuous tradition up to and
including Alexander of Aphrodisias (with figures such as Adrastus, early in the second century, or
Alexander's teacher, Herminus). What we do not find are references to Aristotle commentaries –
other than those emerging from the Plotinian circle – between Alexander and Themistius (middle
of the fourth century).

[155] While uncontroversial, it is hard to prove a negative. Scholars are cautious, accentuating the
positive; e.g., Gill (2003: 33): "Stoicism continued as an active philosophical force for at least
the first two centuries A.D." Caution should not obscure the remarkable fact of a sea change: the
diversity of philosophical schools, maintained by the Greeks all the way from the archaic era, comes
to an abrupt halt at about 240 CE.

third century – but it changes. And such changes tend to carry a quantitative meaning; indeed, a *spatial* meaning.

Throughout this part of the book dedicated to scale I have largely ignored space. My main theme here is the Roman era – when the opposition of Athens and Alexandria receded so that culture came to be somewhat less determined by space. And yet the transition of the third century brings space back. Culture, so to speak, is reduced – and is thereby concentrated. The following two maps present the recorded locations for (1) authors reaching prominence through the years 200 to 240 (Map 29) and (2) authors reaching prominence through the years 240 to 300 (Map 30).

Consider Athens. It was responsible for a little over 20 percent of the recorded locations in the years 200 to 240; it was responsible for a little over 35 percent of the recorded locations in the years 240 to 300. Both values are very substantial, but with the second one we are already not too far from the potential ceiling on spatial concentration (This is because it is likely that, with fuller evidence, we would have an even larger fraction of the authors recorded in the more central locations; see page 243 above). I have not tried to produce a similar map for the second century, but it is clear that the rise of Athens was related to the foundation of the Imperial chairs in the 170s (see page 680 above); thus, the trajectory leading to Athens' return to cultural domination in the late third century must have begun a few decades previously.

Another, correlated transition involves Asia Minor. This was responsible for about 25 percent of the recorded locations in the years 200 to 240; and for only about 10 percent of the recorded locations in the years 240 to 300. This, even as the Empire was becoming unmoored from Rome, the emperors spending most of their time now in cities closer to the east – indeed, often in the Asian city of Nicomedia: prior to the foundation of Constantinople, as close to a capital as the Empire now had.[156] Once again, it is fairly likely that this cultural transition, away from Asia Minor, extends a trend from the second century itself; then, of course, Asia Minor must have been even more dominant, with its special position for the Second Sophistic.

Asia Minor is the center, in the Greek-speaking portion of the Empire, for the rise and fall of the epigraphic habit – which rises, and falls, through the same years. It represents the investment of local elites in civic patronage, and thus we may easily account for both developments – the receding

---

[156] Nicomedia became especially significant as Diocletian's capital: it was there that the bleeding of the third century was finally halted. For the itinerant emperors, see Averil Cameron (1993: 8); for Nicomedia's place in the late ancient imagination, see Kelly (2003: 595).

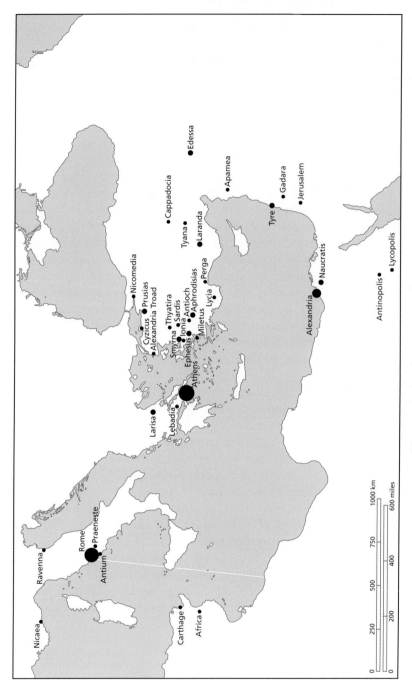

Map 29  Authors between 200 and 240 CE

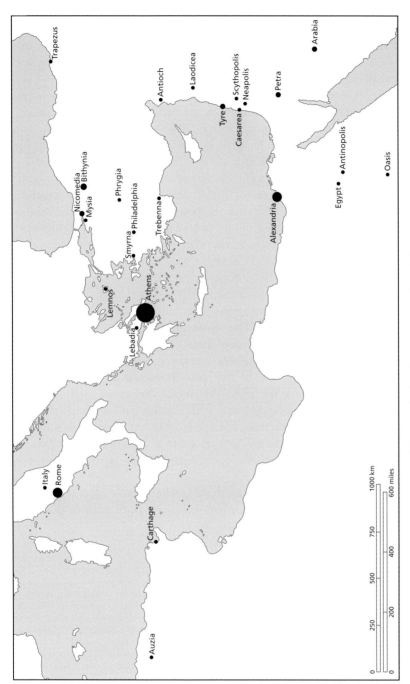

Map 30  Authors between 240 and 300 CE

of the service industries and the receding of Asia Minor – as expressing, in two different ways, the receding of local cultural patronage. This, in a nutshell, both *describes* the retreat of the authorial practice and also *explains* it. I shall expand on this argument-in-a-nutshell below.

Now let us turn to study the trajectory of rhetoric, surely the key for the cultural demographic transition from the second century to the third. I have mentioned the difficulty of studying the second century in the same detail. It is too big! But, in fact, this can be done for rhetoric, specifically, thanks to the survey of PGRSRE.

I find 35 rhetors in the first four decades of the third century – a period for which we have the resources of Philostratus together with an expansive epigraphic habit. This figure *excludes*, however, such rhetors as can be assigned a date (usually on epigraphic grounds) only of the "second/third" centuries, of whom there are 30; it also excludes the other 43 who cannot be dated at all.[157]

At the same time, I find in PGRSRE 219 rhetors in the second century as well as 343 rhetors in fourth century.

Based on this, we may probabilistically assign the less securely dated rhetors, and I place 15 more in the early third century, 35 more in the (mostly late) second century. The numbers then become: second century, more than 260; early third century, about 50.

Now, let us qualify the sheer numbers for centuries. The bulk (though by no means all) of our prosopography of rhetoric in the fourth century derives from the enormous corpus of Libanius, with its chatty web of correspondence with contemporaries and its active auto-prosopographic practice. What this Libanius effect means is that, certainly, we do not have any evidence for a rhetorical practice in the fourth century *richer* than that of the second. It is the sources that expanded, not the practice.

The second century does not have a comparable advantage in its sources over the early third century, however. Both periods possessed

---

[157] All these numbers derive from my own reading of the evidence and not from the mere title and date provided by PGRSRE. Thus, there are some figures assigned by this resource to the "II/III centuries", meaning not that they cannot be dated with any greater precision but that their careers straddle the year 200; in such cases I decided on the key decade of the careers, and assigned the authors accordingly. (It is thus natural that the borderline cases tend to be based on epigraphic sources: this is when all we have is an inscription that does not provide a clear historical context, which we date, essentially based on the inscription itself, to the two centuries.) The choice by PGRSRE to provide a rough date for some authors, and to leave others undated, is somewhat arbitrary. Many of the 43 undated authors are attested epigraphically and so, likely, are also from the second to third centuries. I will assume – cautiously – that the total number in this "II/III centuries" rhetors group is about 50.

an epigraphic habit (indeed, the epigraphic habit is weaker early in the second century). Philostratus does mention many rhetors of the second century but, as noted above, on page 702, he seems to have no bias against his contemporaries (see further pages 742–4 below). In short, the comparison in the number of rhetors between the second and the third centuries seems to be real enough: not a matter of changing sources but of changing numbers.

The average per-decade number of attested rhetors for the second century as a whole is 26 – but it is surely above that in the final decades of the century. The average for the first four decades of the third century is 12.5. The number of attested rhetors is roughly halved – and then some – between the end of the second century and the beginning of the third century. And, so, it seems clear that decline sets in well before the year 240.

This must have been true for cultural demography in general. The simplest argument, indeed, comes from the consideration of the numbers as a whole. I have suggested on page 667 above that there could have been, at the peak, about 1,500 authors active at the same time, or in a given 20-year window. If we assumed that the early third century still saw culture at the peak level, then we would need to have about 3,000 authors active through the years 200 to 240. Allowing for a sharp drop thereafter, we would still need to assume 4,000 to 5,000 authors active through the century as a whole.

Looking just at the traditional, securely dated authors of the table above, we find about 140; adding in the less securely dated, as well as the "episcopal" authors, we get to roughly 200 attested authors from the entire century. This, under the optimistic scenario above, would be an extremely low rate of attestation: about 4 to 5 percent. This compares, based on arguments earlier in the book, with about 5,000 attested authors from the preceding six centuries, or about 15 percent attestation (assuming a little more than 30,000 active authors). Even with some latitude with such numbers, we find that to assume that numbers were stable *into* the third century is to assume that, while authors remained, attestation sharply collapsed.

But, in fact, as I reiterate through this section, the mechanisms of attestation for the century are robust. Philostratus and the inscriptions; then the Plotinian circle; then Eusebius (and we need to mention him, since to get to 200 attested authors we must bring in all named Christian authors, who are remarkably *well* attested). And we are so much nearer the codex! Surely our attestation is better than for the Imperial era, with its much weaker auto-prosopographic practices. In aggregate, the simplest assumption is that the attestation of the third century was not much lower than that of the preceding six centuries. And, if so, it is hard to see how there could have been much more than about 2,000 authors active throughout the century. This is impossible to achieve, unless the numbers begin, even early in the century, at a somewhat lower level.

A rough model, of course. But what we find is that it is hard to construct a plausible path in which cultural activity remains at peak level till about 240 then suddenly collapses. In all likelihood, the picture is of gradual decline (already set into motion, perhaps, late in the second century), accelerating through the century.

A more fundamental observation is that, even aside from literary activity, it is hard to find any measure of activity in the Roman Empire that peaks at the year 230. True, it is then that the epigraphic habit nearly fades. But this practice does not move, in fact, in a plateau – culminating with a cliff at 230. Rather, we see a normal bell curve, rising up to about the year 200 or thereabouts and then beginning to retreat. (For whatever it's worth, the graphs of MacMullen, 1982: 242–3, peak in the 190s to 200s.) A somewhat later peak is provided by civic munificence. Zuiderhoek (2009) documents that the dedications of major monuments declines fairly sharply – starting, however, in the 220s. (This coincides, in fact, with the end of attestation for the "service industries"; see pages 711–14 above: the same people, building monuments, hiring elite physicians?) Wilson (2011: 164–6) provides the statistics (1) for building inscriptions, (2) for those related to waterworks in north Africa (a good proxy for investment in infrastructure, as this series of inscriptions is especially well preserved) and (3) for infrastructure projects as a whole. The first peaks in the 180s; the following two in the 200s to 210s. All this follows on clear evidence for the impact of the Antonine Plague of the 160s and the 170s. Scheidel (2002) argues for a demographic impact comparable to that of the fourteenth-century Black Death; Duncan-Jones (1996) argues for an overall economic shock during the same decades (for instance, it is sometimes possible to date bricks based on their stamps – so, an even more effective proxy for building activities – and these seem to show a retreat during the plague, with only a minor revival thereafter). In short, the proxies for general economic activity peak at different points, from the middle of the second century to the very early third century, but what they never do is to peak nearer the middle of the third century. This, at the very least, encourages us to trust our evidence further, and to postulate that the decline in the scale of authorship should be set, at the latest, early in the third century.

Now, my survey is based on the decades in which authors "gained prominence". It is a survey of middle-aged intellectuals. Their more youthful selves, enthusiastically embarking on the life of learning, should be dated to 20 years previously. Now, it is quite possible – indeed, likely – that the fraction of individuals embarking on the authorial life who actually eventually gain prominence about 20 years later would vary historically. I am sure that around 240 quite a few would-be scholars gave up on that pursuit, retiring to their estates: there was no *point*. But it is also likely that some of the effect indeed lags. Surely, the rise of authors – making their names through the early years of the fourth century – reveals something not about the year 300 but, rather, about the year 284 (or a bit thereafter), when political conditions finally stabilized – and more young people of ambition set out to prepare for a life of cultural achievement. But, conversely, what we seem to find is that, already in Galen's lifetime, fewer individuals set out to become doctors; already in Alexander's lifetime, fewer individuals set out to become peripatetic philosophers; already in Serenus' lifetime, fewer individuals set out to become mathematicians; and, already in Philostratus' lifetime, fewer individuals were setting out to become rhetors.

Let us try, finally, to put some more precise numbers on this. The parameters are as follows.

I have argued that the number of authors in the second century could have reached, at some point, something probably close to an all-time peak. (So, close to 1,500 authors active simultaneously?)

I have also argued that the number of authors through the third century as a whole (both Christian and pagan) probably adds up, very roughly, to about 2,000.

Finally, the overall evidence points to gradual decline, gradually accelerating.

Of course, precision is impossible, but I find it useful to try and turn these parameters into concrete numerical terms: this makes it possible to draw a picture in one's head. Let us say, conservatively, that the number of authors active simultaneously through the last two decades of the second century was about 1,250. If we consider 20-year-long generations, we can fulfill the parameters with a series such as this.

Active in the years 200 to 220: 900
Active in the years 220 to 240: 700
Active in the years 240 to 260: 300
Active in the years 260 to 280: 150

Active in the years 280 to 300: 250

Is this a plausible approximation? As it stands, the series might still
appear a bit arbitrary. Let us then recall, in somewhat more detail than we
have had so far, the surrounding history.

This surrounding history is something of a train wreck.[158] First, as
noted above, the Antonine Plague came to the Mediterranean in the years
165 to 180, perhaps with some ferocity.[159] Further, the Roman Empire –
such a successful builder of institutions in so many other ways – never
produced clear mechanisms of dynastic stability.[160] (Perhaps because,
created in stealth out of a senatorial ideological caste, it never did form a
coherent imperial ideology.) The Antonines (ruling from 96 to 192)
managed exceptionally well in this regard; with the Severan emperors,
such luck ran out. Septimius Severus was installed in 193, and his own
dynasty – lasting for 42 years – was marked by brief reigns cut short by
violent death, by the tenuous legitimacy of child emperors and, as a
consequence of all this, by recurrent civil war. Finally, in the year 235,
what started out as yet another succession crisis turned into a decades-
long upheaval – with a repeated pattern of regional breaks from the
Empire – achieving a return to relative stability only with the accession
of Diocletian in 284.

Already, from the middle of the second century onwards, one can
detect price inflation, measured in a very gradual debasement of silver
(not gold) coinage. This inflation was low by our standards (about
1 percent a year), but would still be felt, over a period of decades, in an

---

[158] I return below, on pp. 726–7, to discuss the sense in which this is contested by revisionist historians.

[159] So, Duncan Jones (1996) and Scheidel (2002). The key argument is biological: if indeed this was a
major epidemic hitting a virgin population, we should expect its effect to be catastrophic. Since it is
to be expected that, with growing Eurasian contacts, such epidemics should hit at some point; and
since the evidence, such as it is, can support such an interpretation, our prior should be that the
Antonine Plague was, well, pretty bad. Skeptics (e.g. Greenberg, 2003, and Bruun, 2007) have to
offer, primarily, the valid observation that our positive evidence for such catastrophic impact is, as
usual for antiquity, incomplete (making it possible to argue, specifically, that our most significant
evidence – for mortality and population in well-documented Egypt – could be contaminated by
local, climatological effects; see the discussion in Elliott, 2016, and references therein).

[160] Romans recognize adoptive sons as equal members of the family, so that an emperor had in effect a
rather free hand in designating his preferred successor – if, of course, within the traditional
structures of a family (Hekster, 2001); further, the very first serious crisis of succession had revealed
what Tacitus called the Arcanum Imperii: that emperors could be made away from Rome – that is,
made by the choice of the military (Haynes, 2003: 112). And so, as it were, each new emperor had to
*achieve* greatness, and then, in turn, was tasked with the complex problem of engineering, well in
advance, the family and military structures requisite for the desired succession. The wonder, if
anything, is that, through the second century, succession functioned fairly smoothly.

ancient economy with its very low growth rate and without the modern apparatus of funded public debt. Emperors during the Severan era attempted various monetary reforms, but without success; trust in coinage dramatically collapsed in the year 238, with much higher inflation persisting through the remainder of the century, stabilized only by Diocletian's reforms in 303.[161] All of this suggests, at least, serious pressures on the economy.

Such dislocations, of monetary failure and of civil war, would be dwarfed by yet another massive epidemic (the "plague of Cyprian") hitting the Mediterranean in 249, abating only by about 270.[162]

The two following observations speak more directly to the history of cultural patronage. First, the year 235 presents a rupture in Imperial style. Emperors came, originally – naturally enough – from the long-established land-owning senatorial elite of Rome, and so they were heirs to the Hellenized traditions of the first century BCE; later on, the net was cast wider, encompassing Italy more broadly as well as the elite Italian diaspora along the shores of the western Mediterranean. At the same time, as will be recalled (page 668 above), through the Imperial era large areas were Romanized without being quite Hellenized. From north Africa to Britain to Pannonia there were many cities and villas where Latin was spoken, baths built, coins circulated – and where social status was rather less dependent upon paideia than in the Greek-speaking east. These areas also encompassed the regions of maximal friction with the nomads of the steppe, and so, also, these were indeed the regions of recruitment for the best-trained soldiers. In some parts of the Empire, then, soldierly reputation, and *not* paideia, served as the route to social status – and those came to be more and more significant in the army itself. The army, in turn, particularly in times of crisis, was the guarantee of Imperial succession. It was only a question of time, then. From the year 235 on – until the very end of antiquity – emperors would come mostly from a single network of north Balkan military commanders.[163] The soldier-emperors never renounced paideia, and it remains (as we will note below) a crucial token of elite status,

---

[161] Wassink (1991).
[162] Harper (2015). The evidence for the Antonine Plague is relatively substantial (and yet – doubted by some scholars!), but, in comparison, the evidence for that of Cyprian is extremely meager, and Harper has to make heroic efforts to prove the significance of the outbreak – a mark, once again, of the massive erosion in literary output between the second and the third centuries. In the third century even plagues go nearly unrecorded!
[163] Scheidel (2013b).

but we have, from this point onwards, much less evidence of direct Imperial patronage of culture.[164]

Second, and finally, we should mention a local event – important in this century in which culture, once again, became more concentrated. The context was the constant border raids by nomadic tribes (the experience, indeed, that shaped the new Balkan soldier-emperors). While most such raids were repulsed, a few were not, and an especially daring one by a Gothic tribe, the Heruli, reached, in the year 267, as far as the city of Athens itself. Literary sources allege – and excavations confirm – the complete destruction of the city;[165] this is when Longinus decamps from Athens to Palmyra, and a chapter closes in the history of ancient culture.

The simplest statement, then, is that, with all the external pressures, there is nothing surprising about a reduction in the scale of authorial culture, and especially nothing surprising about a nadir around the years 267 to 284.

A much harder question is: just when does decline set in? Is it the 160s? The 200s? Even closer to the middle of the third century? I have argued throughout for a relatively early onset, but this effect would be subtle and, so, hard to detect with our sources. Does it matter, ultimately? One can suggest various accounts, and, in the context of general economic and political history, the choice is significant, since different dates imply different causes. A biological or environmental aetiology would lead us to look for an effect noticeable from the middle of the second century onwards. A dynastic or political aetiology would lead us to the end of the second century, or perhaps even later; a purely material or economic aetiology would certainly push us to later in the third century, and perhaps make us doubt the very sense of a "crisis". The choice of dates implies a choice of causes, which implies an overall philosophy of history.

But I would like to step back – in this vein of the philosophy of history – and question this very centrality, in such models, assigned to the efficient cause.

The turn towards the efficient cause is especially evident with the more recent interest in environmental history. Often this takes the following approach: you pick up a historical crisis for discussion – and then look for the external environmental event that best correlates with it. The economy, we find, went bust. And, so, the environmentalist historian turns to ask: what happened to cause this? Was it a series of earthquakes? A new

---

[164] Syme (1988: 362): "The martial rulers who issued from Illyricum and 'saved the sum of things' lacked care for 'humanitas,' according to the famous verdict of Aurelius Victor ([De Caesaribus] 39.26)."

[165] Thompson (1959).

epidemic? Climate change? One always looks for the *tool*. What was the specific identity of the specific hammer, the one that dealt the blow?[166]

But sometimes the identity of the hammer matters less than what it ends up hitting. Hit metal and it will bend, even strengthen. Hit sandstone and it will crumble. To predict the outcome of a hammer blow, what really matters is the fracture lines.

And, here, the account of the preceding two sections, 6.2 and 6.3, becomes relevant. I have argued that the authorial culture of the second century CE became top-heavy, more and more dependent upon patronage from an ever-diminishing circle of the very highest elite – indeed, even the patronage of the emperor itself. Even the Hellenistic era had more than one center, and what mattered most was the network and institutions made by the authors themselves: a network defined by Archimedes, a school defined by Chrysippus... Such an authorial practice would be less vulnerable to external shocks, and, indeed, the Athenian schools took off even as Athens, as a political and economic center, began its decline; Alexandria's fortunes as an intellectual center were only very indirectly tied to the strength of the Ptolemaic dynasty. This culture could withstand hammer blows. Not so much so, perhaps, the authorial culture of the high Empire: dependent as it became on the patronage of a small elite, any shocks that took away from such patronage would have significant repercussions. Imperial-era culture was vibrant, indeed prolific – but already hollowed out by the corrupting effect of patronage, or, in the final analysis, by the corrupting effect of extreme inequality.

My model of the late second century had the authors divided three ways roughly equally, between the "service industries", rhetoric (and practices with similar sociological bases – supported by similar groups of authors and consumers – which, I suspect, covers the novel) and the two traditional fields: history and philosophy. If declining numbers indeed represent declining patronage, we should see this first in the service industries, then in rhetoric, last in philosophy. And, indeed, we see fields such as medicine and the exact sciences – even (Greek) grammar – cut entirely as early as near the beginning of the third century, while rhetoric is still quite robust. By the middle of the century cultural life is dominated by the two fields – the only two to remain attested in any numbers – of rhetoric (nowhere near its numbers at its peak) and philosophy; and then, of course,

---

[166] A caricature: and often, of course, the conclusions of environmental history are simply correct. For a good (and eager) overview of the range of historical crises attributable to the environment, see Brooke (2014).

the Church. We need to assume, then, at the lowest point, a few dozen philosophers; a few dozen rhetors; a few dozen Church authors – and, besides these, no more than a few isolated individuals.

This, then, is the suggested account. To gain more confidence in it, we need to repeat the work of section 6.3, now for the third century and beyond: showing how the newly formed authorial culture reveals, precisely, a retreat from patronage. This is part of the task, then, for the following section, 6.5. But, before I get there, a note on how my proposal is, in fact, consistent with more optimistic accounts of the third century. I recall my hypothetical numbers.

> Active in the years 200 to 220: 900
> Active in the years 220 to 240: 700
> Active in the years 240 to 260: 300
> Active in the years 260 to 280: 150
> Active in the years 280 to 300: 250

With these, I wish to resolve two apparent tensions.

(1) On the one hand, the entire context of the early third century is suggestive of decline (in the archaeological record of gradually diminishing epigraphic activity and building activity, and in the overall pattern of dynastic crises). On the other hand, this is also a lively period of cultural life: reading Philostratus, one does not have the impression of a thinly populated culture. But, if we assume that the final decades of the second century were a peak period, the puzzle disappears: even with moderate decline, the early third century could very well have been culturally active at a rate close to the average of antiquity up to 200 CE as a whole.

(2) It should be added that ancient culture as a whole was so thick with literary activity that – even following a *major* decline – authorial production would be on some measures quite healthy. Even at the lowest point of the crisis of the third century, with as few as 150 authors active simultaneously, there could have been something like, say, several dozen new works sent out every year – a new book issued *more or less on a weekly basis!* Puech (2002), highly skeptical of the notion of a decline in the third century CE, points out that (7) "l'époque de Longin, de Plotin et de Porphyre n'a pas forcément été un vide culturel". Of course it was not empty; it was just much less full. Janiszewski (2006) is titled *The Missing Link*, and it sets out to prove that Greek pagan historiography survived through the years 250 to 400 CE. He finds 42 well-documented authors (though most of them are attested from the fourth century) and concludes

that (431) "contrary to popular opinion – in the second half of the 3rd and in the 4th century there were many active historians". Of course there were. Indeed, there were probably many dozens of unrecorded historians, active through the crisis of the third century.[167] Authors such as Puech and Janiszewski make an important observation, as this sheer survival puts into context the *continuity* of cultural practices before and after the third century. It is not as if, in the fourth century, anything had to be reinvented entirely from scratch. Rather, it is that, through the third century, everything has been subtly transformed, forever.

Once again, as in section 6.3, we should bring in the qualitative nature of the transformation of culture in late antiquity – so as to expand on our meager quantitative evidence. But now, in what follows, the qualitative discussion assumes a bigger meaning than that. My ultimate point would be that a transformation in scale gave rise to a transformation of the nature of canonization as such – in a sense closing, in a sense bringing into relief, the entire pattern of an ancient, pluralistic Mediterranean. So: for a more extended, qualitative analysis.

### 6.5  Late Antiquity and the New Equilibrium

A couple of hundred authors? When all's been said and done, this is just not a very strong presence on the ground. The last time we saw such small numbers of authors was in the middle of the fifth century BCE; since then, however, geographic horizons have expanded. By the later decades of the third century CE authors are literally spread across the Mediterranean. We hear of a Nicostratus of Trapezus (today's Trabzon) writing a history of the years 244 to 260 (Janiszewski, 2006: 92–6); we have extant a work in horticulture by a certain Gargilius Martialis, likely identifiable with an author known from an inscription from the 260s, in Auzia (near today's Algiers). Stanford's Orbis tells me that "the fastest journey from Auzia to Trapezus in July takes 49.3 days, covering 4839 kilometers". (But why would you undertake such a journey – and in the unsettled conditions of the 260s?) Authors such as Nicostratus and Gargilius lived at the same time but,

---

[167] Perhaps the historiographical problem has to do simply with the tendency to think of culture, in general, in qualitative rather than quantitative terms. Averil Cameron (1993: 11) asserts, concerning the third century, that " cultural activity flourished... The philosopher Plotinus continued to lecture... Dexippus...wrote a history..." Then (14): "This is just to give a preliminary idea of the richness of the available literary material. Not surprisingly, it took some time to flower, given the apparent dearth of writing in the third century..." There is confusion about what we mean by culture "flourishing": a single Plotinus – or hundreds of minor authors?

effectively, in separate worlds. These are, of course, just the extreme points on Map 30 above, but what is evident in general in the map is the erosion of the mid-level centers of Asia Minor: a single congregation in Athens, and otherwise – the scattering of all remaining cultural life. This is the context of fragmentation, within which Latin grammar emerges as a major field of study (see page 712 above). As it were, as the network becomes thinner, Latin authors are left to fend for themselves. This bifurcation, in particular, will have important consequences (see page 788 below).

Almost everywhere, the form of the author's life would be swamped by other forms of self-expression and social promotion. In particular, I will argue, while there are fewer authors, there are still many teachers. There are the exceptions – a few locations where the authorial life would still be pursued – but these would now be marked as such: self-conscious circles of like-minded intellectuals.

In what follows I consider the two effects in turn. section 6.5.1 discusses the swamping of the authorial by the non-authorial; then section 6.5.2 discusses the appearance of self-conscious authorial circles. These sections also serve to show how, in qualitative terms, the culture of the third century moves away from patronage, thus complementing the quantitative claim of the preceding section, 6.4. The overall consequence of the swamping of the authorial by the teacherly, and of the rise of the self-conscious circle, is a culture of the teacherly circle. In section 6.5.3 I discuss the most important consequence of the culture of the teacherly circle: the rise of *commentary*. I then conclude, in section 6.5.4, with an account of how – following the dislocations of the third century – a new equilibrium was formed, lasting through late antiquity and beyond.

### 6.5.1  *Stability in the Scale of Non-Authorial Culture*

In my census of third-century authors, I have avoided the evidence of papyri (while still using that of inscriptions). We have them primarily from the second century, somewhat fewer from the third, mostly for archae-ological reasons having to do with the conditions of survival. It is thus wrong to take the numbers of papyri and to conclude, say, that Egypt was culturally more active in the Imperial than in the Ptolemaic era. Furthermore, epigraphically attested cultural figures, and papyrologically attested cultural figures, are an apples-to-oranges comparison. In inscriptions we see prominent citizens who may well have authored books, and at any rate had wide audiences. The rhetors of the inscriptions mostly do belong to the "authorial class", or are at least not too distant from it. In papyri, we see provincial practitioners who had much more modest ambitions. Now it is time to note that, while the apples disappeared, the oranges remained. In papyri, the transition from the second century to the third is far less significant.

Kaster's catalogue of grammarians only begins in the middle of the third century. He does find a reasonable number of grammarians attested papyrologically (which means, then, *teachers* of grammar): one from the middle of the century; eight from around its end.[168] Or take Cribiore's catalogue of educational ostraca and papyri, a more ample and therefore more reliable proxy for education. We find there 95 documents that may be assigned to the second century, 94 that may be assigned to the third.[169] This in fact at first glance suggests a *rise* in the intensity of educational practice from the second century to the third, as, overall, there are rather more documentary papyri from the second than from the third,[170] but perhaps the more important observation is that *literary* papyri do not decline very significantly, either. CEDOPAL has the following series for the central periods of the survival of literary papyri.[171]

| Date | Number of fragments |
|---|---|
| 101–150 | 2,193 |
| 151–200 | 1,963 |
| 201–250 | 1,365 |
| 251–300 | 1,657 |

---

[168] Kaster (1988: 469–70).

[169] The catalogue is in Cribiore (1996: 173–284). This involves a certain double-counting, as I count papyri dated to "II–III AD" under both second and third centuries; this accounts for about half the entries.

[170] Habermann (1998: 157) counts more than 8,000 documentary papyri in the second century, nearly 6,000 in the third; overall numbers would have gone up since then, but the ratio is safe. The decline in documentary papyri is partly concentrated at the end of the century, when the hand of the state began to be slightly lighter even in Egypt (the census was discontinued, as we recall, after 266): Habermann (1998: 153). But, otherwise, bear in mind that the main source of evidence for the dire demographic and economic consequences of the Antonine Plague is these very Egyptian documentary papyri. It is in the face of such pressures, undoubted at least at the local level, that Egyptian papyrus-making continues essentially unabated. (Skeptics concerning the Antonine Plague usually admit the force of the evidence from Egypt but provide it with alternative, local explanations; see n.159 above.)

[171] Once again, this involves substantial double-counting. The numbers drop massively into the fourth century, now a result not so much of changing archaeological context as of changes in the materiality of writing; more below, pp. 789–93.

There isn't a credible narrative of reading culture in provincial Egypt wobbling in the early third century, with a recovery at the end; rather, we see random variation (probably driven by archaeological luck) around a stable core. The trend line might be genuinely pointing downward, ever so slightly – there would be nothing surprising about that – but the point is that it moves, down, only *slightly*. In the educational ostraca and papyri, we see people keep learning their canon; in the literary papyri, we see people keep collecting it.

Indeed, the same can be found across the "service industries" as a whole – considered at a level beneath that of authorship. As noted above, the extant astrological treatises contain no horoscopes dated to the third century. But among the papyri the third century may well have been the peak century for the casting of horoscopes.[172] A close comparison is that of the medical papyri: about half are strictly tools of trade (medical prescriptions, for instance), and as such are directly comparable to horoscopes; these also include, significantly, a group of educational medical texts such as catechisms or definitions (for discussion of this group, see Hanson, 2010). The remaining fragments are from medical books, but a good fraction of these, too, could come from the libraries of medical practitioners. If so, the chronological distribution of medical papyri can be seen as a rough indication of the chronological distribution of practicing doctors in Upper Egypt. There, we have the following.

| 101–150 | 151–200 | 201–250 | 251–300 |
|---------|---------|---------|---------|
| 87      | 70      | 66      | 69      |

This should be compared to the small table on the preceding page above: it is evident that the medical papyri are within a narrow range of about 4 to 5 percent of overall literary papyri.

Not a few documents directly attest to professions (in a census entry, a receipt for a debt, or court proceedings, one may note not only the name but also the profession of the person involved).[173] The numbers seem meaningful and plausible: so, for instance, "barber" is only rarely applied

---

[172] See the cautious discussion in Jones (1999: 5–8): the total number of datable astrological papyri – both horoscopes and more theoretical texts – reaches a maximum in Oxyrhynchus at the end of the third century.

[173] This distribution certainly should not be extrapolated to reconstruct the structure of professions: just as with inscriptions, so with papyri, the choice to note a profession as part of a person's identity is a matter of status and context.

as the title of a profession, but it is a relief to find five in the second century, four in the third. There are 25 shepherds in the second century, 32 in the third; 5 butchers in the second century, 11 in the third; in all likelihood the number of shepherds and especially of butchers did go up, as, with the relief of Malthusian pressures following the plagues, more cattle were tended, more meat consumed.[174] If so, it makes sense to look at the cultural professions. So far in this book I have not discussed, for instance, the profession of the "flute player", but, whatever the vicissitudes in the numbers of elite *poets*, there were still people out there, singing and dancing and playing an instrument. In the papyri published by 1987 there were 11 under the category "flute player" (*aulētēs*) attested for the second century CE, nine for the third.[175] From the same source, take "doctor" (*iatros*): 32 attested for the second century, 19 for the third (a real decline? Or does this scale with the lower number of documents published from the third century? Or just a random outlier result?). We may go higher on the social scale – but still, probably, not quite at the level of the "author" – by considering the category of *archiatri*, studied in Nutton (1977) (the evidence in this case, noted on pages 584–5 above, comes partly from inscriptions, and so it has a bias for the turn of the second and third centuries). In Nutton's catalogue, I count 17 from the second century, 22 from either the second or the third and 17 from the third century. (There are also six dated for the "third or fourth" century.)[176]

I go back to the data from Harrauer (1987). Another, low-level intellectual line of work was the "interpreter" (*hermēneus*), a kind of paralegal profession: we have 12 from the second century, eight from the third. In general, attested professions often have a chronological pattern related to the specifics of political and economic history, as well as to the fine-grained structure of the survival of papyri. This is probably how we need to explain the pattern for advocates – which is what, in the papyrus evidence, is meant by "rhetors". At first glance, it is striking that these are indeed considerably more frequent in documents of the second century than of the third:[177] is it here, perhaps, that we find a sub-authorial profession, collapsing through

---

[174] Scheidel (2002; 2010); I return to note this in n.338 below.

[175] The professional data are from Harrauer (1987: 50–173).

[176] The main argument of Nutton (1977) is that this category, as a whole, seems to rise in significance through time, as, from the second century onwards, the label is invoked to seek tax exemption. Still, the data certainly do not suggest a decline in the number of notable physicians, going into the third century – this, even while medical *authorship* seems to have collapsed entirely following Galen.

[177] Harrauer does not aggregate the data for this profession – perhaps because it hardly ever shows up in economic documents but is attested only through court proceedings – but the data can be put together from PGRSRE. I find 90 rhetors, attested purely papyrologically, from the second century,

the crisis of the third century? Probably not: the title "rhetor" appears almost always in the specialized context of the summary of a court case; this happens to be especially well documented in the Arsinoite nome; and we happen to have, for purely archaeological reasons, a higher number of documents from the second century from the Arsinoite nome than from the third.[178] Finally, we are not surprised to find eight under "teacher" (*didaskalos*) from the second century, eight from the third. We can now see how this stability stands to reason. There was a change, through the third century, in the scale of, say, grammarian *authorship*. But there is no reason why this should have been reflected in the scale of the *teaching* of grammar. Kids still went to school, it seems.

In all of the above I rely on the quantitative evidence of the papyri, in particular the documentary ones. To repeat: does this carry any meaning at all? There are serious problems in principle with such a use of the evidence (see page 694 above), but, then again, the route of survival for second-century papyri was not qualitatively different from that of third-century survival; prima facie, their absolute numbers do matter, a little. But even more important is the qualitative impression left by the documentary papyri. They definitely imply a major response to the Antonine Plague (or, at the very least, some other effect, local to Egypt; see note 159 above). But, as Rathbone (1991) has insisted – and this has subsequently become the standard position – they do not reveal any major collapse through the third century. Life went on locally, as it always did. The economy, at least, remained stable. This begins to suggest to us the grounds for revisionism concerning the crisis of the third century. And so, once again: the kids still went to school.

So, let us look for paideia, outside Egypt. The merely local grammarian-teachers, of the kind traced via papyri, are usually not attested directly in the literature transmitted from antiquity. But we can infer their existence, from that of their pupils. Prohairesius was born in Armenia or in Caesarea of Cappadocia in, perhaps, 276 CE. The next we hear, he is the best pupil of rhetoric in Antioch: soon thereafter he would move to Athens to become the leading rhetor of his age, and, eventually, Eunapius' own teacher.[179] There had to be high-quality grammar education to be had in the 280s, in remote

---

and only 46 from the third (the problem of double-counting is trivial in this case, as documentary papyri, especially court documents, are usually well dated).

[178] Why are more court cases recorded for the Arsinoite nome? Perhaps because, in this more far-flung region, court cases could have been settled more locally. I am grateful to Uri Yiftach-Franko for sharing with me this hypothesis, which should not be taken as more than one possible account, however; he suggests this question should be pursued further (private communication).

[179] Prohairesius' origins are not certain, but are at any rate at the furthest eastern reaches of the Anatolian mainland; the evidence is surveyed in PGRSRE 310–11.

Cappadocia.[180] Indeed, Prohairesius joined in Athens a markedly cosmopolitan society, with many of its members coming from the eastern frontiers: Maior from "Arabia", Genethlius from Petra, Andromachus from Neapolis in Samaria (PGRSRE nos. 73, 413, 645). Next to the sophists – the saints. Hilarion was born in Thabatha in the year 291: even as a child he was sent to Alexandria to further his education in grammar, following his beginning in his place of origin – a small village in Palestine.[181] St. Hilary of Poitiers is late and unreliable but many of his writings survive. He is attested as a major political figure in the year 356, and so was likely born very early in the century; clearly a native of Poitiers, it is no less clear that he had a thorough grammatical and rhetorical education. Nothing surprising about that: from Ausonius we get a glimpse of intellectual life in Burdigalia and its surroundings from the early fourth century onwards. His *Professores* is a collection of obituaries in verse of the teachers associated with Ausonius' native city. I count a total of 31 individuals, almost all active as teachers of rhetoric or grammar. (One of them, indeed – Anastasius – left for *Poitiers*).[182] Now, Ausonius himself was a figure almost straight out of Philostratus, a teacher of rhetoric from a rich, well-connected family – who became, himself, a member of the Imperial court (as a tutor, however: this is the age of the teacher).[183] He then made his name as an author as well as political figure (eventually obtaining a consulship). Among his subjects, Delphidius comes closest to Ausonius himself in authorial as well as political ambition (Delphidius produced epic poetry [*Prof.* V.10] and sought Imperial patronage, albeit unsuccessfully).[184] But most of the *professores* strike us as, essentially, schoolteachers.[185] My point is that, obviously, such could be found – in spades – in early fourth-century Burdigalia, and the city was unique

---

[180] This nice romantic vignette is complicated by some additional information. First, it is possible (but far from proven) that Prohairesius' own father, Pankratius, was a rhetor in his own right (PGRSRE s.v.). Likely enough a member of the topmost elite would be trained at home: perhaps, simply, by his father? Second, Proairesius' own teacher in Athens – Iulianos (PGRSRE s.v. 543) – already was in some sense a "Cappadocian", though, in this case, we do not have a similarly detailed biography. But both complications simply push the chronology a generation earlier, and we are reminded of the point made above: Hellenization – with its cohorts of Greek teachers – did not contract in the third century but went on expanding into eastern Anatolia and the Caucasus. (Through the fourth century, of course, this would become one of the main areas of recruitment for Greek Christian civilization, with the Cappadocian fathers of the Church.)

[181] The only relevant source is Jerome, *Life of Hilarion* 1.

[182] See discussion in Kaster (1988: 241).

[183] Teachers might reach even higher, in this milieu: Flavius Eugenius, a teacher of grammar and rhetoric at the court, would, in the years 392 to 394, claim the very throne of the Western Empire (Socrates, *Church History* V.25.1)!

[184] See Sivan (1993: 361): Delphidius acted on the main stage of the political history of his times.

[185] So, for instance, in a shared obituary on three teachers of Greek (*Prof.* 9), Ausonius mentions that two of them were his own teachers – and apologizes, looking back, for being such a bad pupil! Victorius, praised for his good memory, died while still a *subdoctor* – that is, not yet a teacher

only in its chronicler. We may go back to Egypt: sometime in the 250s Paul the Hermit escaped persecution, fleeing to the desert of Upper Egypt. He gave up everything – including his good education ("both Greek and Egyptian", suggestive for his ethnicity.[186] During the 230s and 240s, we learn, Greek grammar was valued in the Thebaid. Of course: it was the mark of Hellenization.). This is written by Jerome, anxious to find in Paul an echo of himself, the ascetic polymath. Jerome was active later in the fourth century but it is noteworthy that the foundations of his own – unsurpassed – education were laid in his native town of Stridon, "in Dalmatia, not far from Pannonia";[187] a glimpse of Balkan grammar in the first half of the fourth century. Priscillian of Avila (we are now in central Iberia), another contemporary of Ausonius and Jerome, was condemned for his ascetic theology. Writings attributed to him imply – and our sources affirm – a deep rhetorical training: one source specifically blames Priscillian's heresy on foreigners, including the rhetor (his teacher, then?) Helpidius.[188] Or back to the Anatolian heights: in Phrygia, we have attested the rhetor Metrophanes, likely active in the late third century. Certainly an author (we know him through titles in the *Suda*), he was clearly above all a master of a school of rhetoric (the titles are mostly technical, including one of the earliest examples of rhetorical commentary: PGRSRE no. 705). A little to the south, in the small city of Trebenna – on the borders of Lycia and Pamphylia – we find Torquatus, a late third-century rhetor attested, in the old-fashioned way, with an inscription. Most likely, another local school of rhetoric (PGRSRE no. 1057)? Eusebius tells us of the martyrdom of Aedesius and Apphian: born to the very highest Lycian elite in the 280s, they must have had superb education back home. We catch up with them as they study in Berytus. They convert in the 300s – bad timing, as it turns out – and they are executed in the persecutions of Maximinus II.[189] In fact, many *Lives of Saints* start out rather like Philostratus' *Lives of the Sophists*, setting out the high birth, wealth and education of their subjects – to turn them upside down. The saints could have had it all – that's the point; but they gave it all up for Christ. In

himself (*Prof.* 22). Those are humble people (Kaster, 1988: 101 – "a middling group of men, with the balance perhaps tipped more obviously toward the lower end"). The scholarship on Ausonius' *Professores* often refers to the "university" of Bordeaux, detecting, for instance, the intrigue surrounding *chairs* (Green, 1985, and references therein: by "chair" we mean perhaps no more than tax-exemption). This is wildly misleading if anything like a modern university is understood: Ausonius' subject is, quite simply, the people who taught, for a living, the offspring of the Burdigalian elite.

[186] Jerome, *Life of Paul* 4.    [187] Jerome, *Vir. Ill.* 135.
[188] Sulpicius Severus II. 46.2–3 (see Van Dam, 1985: 92–3).
[189] Eusebius, *Martyrs of Palestine* 4.2–5.

Philostratus' time, but no less so in Ausonius' or Jerome's time, one of the conditions for "having it all" was good education. Paideia still mattered. And it did so everywhere. This is the significance of the evidence considered so far: the teaching of grammar in Cappadocia, Petra, Neapolis, Gaza, Poitiers, Bordeaux, the Thebaid, Dalmatia, central Iberia, Phrygia, Lycia... There is no tendency, for the intellectuals educated in the third century, to have had their origins, primarily, in the metropolitan cities. If anything, the clear tendency is for education to spread further out, to reach right to the borders of empire. Here is how Peter Brown describes the conditions of power and paideia through late antiquity: "In every province with which the imperial administration had to deal, its representatives met a group of persons who claimed, on the basis of their high culture, to be the natural leaders of society. [...] The ideal of the cultivated governor, the carefully groomed product of a Greek paideia, was a commonplace of the political life of the Eastern Empire" (Brown, 1992: 37–8).

Brown's key point is that this paideia was never dethroned, and, instead, was simply merged into a Christian ideal. Once again – stability, rather than upheaval. This is where revisionism concerning the notion of a third-century crisis is at its strongest: in fact, I am not aware of any scholar arguing for the contraction of the circle of paideia through the third century. The argument of this section, then, is quite uncontroversial. I did need to go through the argument for the survival of paideia, however, so as to bring out the contrast: we have clear evidence for the survival of paideia – even while we also have clear evidence for the contraction of *authorship*.

We may perhaps begin to see how the two could be true, simultaneously, based on the discussion so far. We see how the Roman state, and its elites, were tested; and yet, life went on. We may translate this into the terms of the sociology of culture, as follows: even as discretionary senatorial patronage declined and then nosedived, the demand for paideia survived, and, indeed, continued to expand; all in all, values stayed the same, and paideia remained the surest mark of status, all the way down to Dioscorus of Aphrodito, who, as we recall (see page 190 above), in the sixth century, as head of his village, still collected Menander, still tried to have himself noticed by his superiors through the composition of poetry. It was this cultural conservatism which preserved the canon. Even this will be severely disrupted, eventually – especially in the west[190] – through the sixth and seventh centuries; but not in the third.

A collapse in discretionary senatorial patronage, together with a continued practice of paideia. What does this mean in terms of broader

---

[190] Wickham (2005: 158).

cultural practice? This implies a collapse in new cultural *production* – even while the *transmission* of culture hums along, uninterrupted. My suggestion would be, then, that, at some point in the third century, the practice of culture became nearly identified with the practice of transmitting culture. To be interested in X meant, now, to be interested in collecting books on X. To be a practitioner of X meant, now, to be the teacher of X. This paramount role of book teaching will have enormous consequences. I will spell out such consequences in sections 6.5.3 to 6.5.4. But, first, we also need to bring in the other main feature of this late ancient transition: the rise of self-conscious cultural circles.

### 6.5.2    The Rise of the Self-Conscious Circle

My goal in this section is to document a new cultural attitude: whereby legitimacy for a cultural practice emerges not from outside, "vertically", from patronage but, instead, from within the practice itself: a circle of learners, validated through a shared history and a shared life of teaching – their following of a master through canonical texts.

To do so, I first point out the social fact of validation in such self-conscious circles; and then provide a closer sense of how culture would be experienced, in such endeavors. There are only a handful of examples for us to study in depth. But, what we do find represents, consistently, a sea change from the second century. In general – as we have done to some extent already while showing the persistence of paideia – the evidence for the third century is so meager, that for the fourth century so plentiful, that we must, throughout, glance forward. We will need to return to this, and consider the stability from the third to the fourth century, in the following sections.

And so, the sociology: moving away from patronage. Which, indeed, we have seen already! We recall, for instance, Aedesius and Apphian, mentioned on page 734 above: Lycian noblemen, giving up on their legal careers around 300, so as to join the Christians of Caesarea. They were not the first to join this group in such a way: the earliest such case was of Gregory, a Cappadocian who, a young man on his way to study law in Berytus, met in the same Caesarea the founder of the city's cultural circle of Christian scholars – Origen. Gregory converted, gave up Berytus, eventually went back home to be a bishop and became well known as Saint Gregory Thaumaturge.[191] Giving up law – to become a wonder-maker! In other words, elite pagan converts at

---

[191] Van Dam (1982: 272–3). We have no indication of the mechanics of conversion, other than the usual transition, as noted on p. 734 above: from the expected life of Paideia, to Christianity.

this point give up a career path that would have brought them the benefits of a political career and, instead, retire to a more local community, seeking to be validated by fellow Christians. My point is that this is not unique: intellectuals, in the third century, begin, somehow, to validate themselves; patronage becomes less central to their identity.

For the example is more striking still: just why was Gregory on his way to *Berytus*, of all places? Now, the teaching of law was always centered, obviously enough, on the city of Rome, with its schools – atypically, institutionalized during the Imperial era itself – of Sabinus and Proculus (see page 665 above). It is all the more surprising to see this local continuity broken, so sharply, early in the third century. Throughout late antiquity we find repeated references that take it for granted that the one place in which to study Roman law – in Latin! – was Berytus.[192] Our first indication is indeed from the life of Gregory himself. The argument from silence is of some value: had Berytus been central to the teaching of law much earlier, we would have expected to find traces of this in the *Digest*, as well as in the *Lives of the Sophists*. We learn, then, that at some point early in the third century the teachers of law could gain their authority through their sheer prestige, creating a center of learning at a certain remove from Imperial patronage (if closer to the origins in the Levant of many contemporary scholars, however). The service industry of law would now become normalized. Just as one used to study medicine in Alexandria, and only then come to practice at Rome (see page 278 above), so, through late antiquity, lawyers would be trained in Berytus to practice at Constantinople.

We do not have much direct evidence on this transition: there are no "Lives of the Lawyers" (it would, after all, remain a service industry, even if its teachers could somehow validate themselves in a kind of separate campus town). And yet, we have noted already – as a feature of our evidence – the auto-prosopographic habits of the third century. It is time now not only to count this habit but also to try to understand it: and so we turn, once again, to a more qualitative survey. Our sources are less abundant, and so we end up returning, time and again, to the same well-documented circles: following some more general comments, I will offer a more detailed look at a few of the usual suspects – and pivotal authors! – of this century, namely Porphyry, Origen and Eusebius.

---

[192] The literary evidence is surveyed in Collinet (1925: 26–54). As the Empire moved east, Latin remained for centuries the language of government, giving rise to such cultural activity as Latin grammars, translated into Greek – and the teaching of Roman law, in the east. Beirut was in this sense a natural choice, because, as a Roman colony, it was one of the most densely Latin-speaking cities of the eastern Mediterranean. For a general survey, see Hall (2004).

We must start from philosophy, the most significant genre continuing into the third century. I have argued that, in the Imperial era, even philosophy must have been influenced by the competition for patronage. Indeed, intellectuals remained enmeshed within the elite even in the third century. The evidence is not decisive, but Plotinus was active in Rome and perhaps was in some contact with emperors.[193] Longinus is found – near the very end of his life – at the court of Zenobia in Palmyra; but this may represent a response to genuinely difficult political circumstances: so, seeking patronage, not so as to gain validation but simply for physical protection.[194] The tragic tale of Longinus and Zenobia was played out during the same years, on a smaller scale, in the west: Porphyry moved away from Rome because of more personal troubles, and was hosted, away from the intellectual center, in the more provincial settings of the Sicilian city of Lilybaeum, by a certain – otherwise unknown – Probus: once again, this is patronage as a *substitute*.[195] A substitute for what?

The young Porphyry read a poem in public; Plotinus commented: "You have proved yourself a poet, a philosopher, a hierophant!" Porphyry must have carried this memory with him throughout his life; he cited it as a key moment of his "Life of Plotinus" (15.4–6). But this is just an anecdote illustrating the supreme power, in this generation, of a master over his pupils. The outpouring of writings around the Plotinian circle emerges precisely because philosophers now define themselves – and struggle for relative status – through rival interpretations of the master.[196] Even before

[193] Indeed, just because intellectuals in the high Empire were closely intertwined with the affairs of the court, it was natural for past scholars to suggest the same for the Plotinian circle: so, Alföldi (1967: 228–311). Edwards (1994) is perhaps a little too eager to debunk what evidence we have, but I follow him, in that the evidence for the contact between Plotinus and any emperor is far-fetched; indeed, even among senators, the evidence we have is for a few "converting" to Neoplatonism (Porphyry, *Life of Plotinus* 7.29–46), not of particular senators treating Plotinus as their client. Plotinus' most practical involvement in politics was in his harebrained plan to set up a new philosophical city, Platonopolis (Edwards, 1994: 146–7); of course, nothing came of it.

[194] The fact of the matter is that Longinus got to Palmyra, in all likelihood, following the destruction of Athens in 267 – following a long career as a self-sufficient intellectual away from Imperial centers. His role in Zenobia's court is not well documented, and the tale, according to which he had major influence on her diplomacy, is based on the *Historia Augusta* (which may well have been concocted by self-aggrandizing court clerks). For a brief discussion, see Brisson, DPA, s.v. Longine, 120–1.

[195] I see no real reason to doubt the account, provided by Plotinus himself, that he decided to leave Rome for reasons of mental health (for the episode and the evidence, see Ahonen, 2014: 228–31).

[196] It goes without saying that Porphyry's career's capstone was the edition of the works of Plotinus. Amelius, his major rival for the title of foremost pupil, was earlier a follower of Numenius – and he wrote on the difference between them, besides producing 100 books (!) of scholia to Plotinus' lectures – but these were beside various specific works of explication and polemic, several of which were a defense of Plotinus against Longinus (Brisson, 1982: 66). Indeed, the bulk of the attested work by Longinus himself was in the form of polemic against Plotinians (Brisson, DPA, s.v. Longine, 123–4), or commentary to Plato (indeed, the evidence might be biased by our sources,

that, Plotinus' own work emerges from a similar environment of rival dependency on a master: the decisive influence on Plotinus was his teacher in Alexandria, Ammonius Saccas, a philosopher who avoided writing – indeed, a philosopher who was shrouded in secrets. The one clear testimony we have concerning him is that Herennius, Origen (the Platonist) and Plotinus himself were joined in a pact not to reveal Ammonius' doctrines – much of the history of mid-third-century Neoplatonism revolving, then, around the various breaches of the pact.[197] It becomes impossible to say with any certainty what Ammonius' secret doctrines were: he did not write, he meant to keep his views secret, his pupils kept tiptoeing about that secrecy. The only thing clear about all this is the role of secrecy itself. So, for instance, Pythagoreanism is now reinvented as a major philosophical tradition – and onto this past are projected the contemporary habits of secrecy, with a new model of early Pythagoreanism divided into the *mathematici* and *acusmatici* (the first, not the latter, fully initiated).[198] The meaning of the terms shifts as the story gets retold: a story of a secret carries meaning – as the story of a secret divulged, of a renegade follower. Hippasus is cast into this role,[199] and, so, a famous tale is born: Hippasus, betraying the secret of the discovery of the irrationals, punished![200] It seems possible that the hermetic corpus, too, emerged through the second and third centuries – and, so, yet another case

which mostly come from the Plotinian circle). Polemic was always essential to Greek cultural life, produced as it was within the shadow of the polis of letters. What is so striking is the centrality of contemporary polemic, with named near-coevals; it is from this context that much of the Christian polemical literature of the era survives: and so, Origen, and Celsus (Chadwick, 1953); Eusebius, and Porphyry (Barnes, 1994). Plotinus himself does avoid mention of his near-contemporaries: but this is because he writes under complicated school duties towards his own dead master, Ammonius, as I explain immediately below (O'Brien, 1994: 125).

[197] Our only source is Porphyry, *Life of Plotinus* 3.22–35. And then again: Porphyry may well intend to mislead us, as suggested in O'Brien (1994), an entertaining and plausible account.

[198] This division is first mentioned by Clement of Alexandria, somewhat older than Ammonius Saccas; it becomes entrenched with Porphyry, and then is foundational to Iamblichus' history of Pythagoreanism (Zhmud, 2012: 174).

[199] Thus, the very terms *mathematici* and *acusmatici* are redefined in terms of followers of the original Pythagorean doctrine, as against the new version by Hippasus (Burkert, 1972: 194).

[200] Burkert (1972: 455–61); Fowler (1999: 295–6): the specific story of the discovery of the irrationals as a secret doctrine, divulged by Hippasus, is found fully only in Pappus, though some version of it was known already to Iamblichus. Finally, in twentieth-century scholarship it was standard to project a "crisis of foundations" precipitated by this discovery, so that, once the secret of irrationals was out, mathematics was paralyzed until Eudoxus produced his new axiomatization of proportion (the first important critique of this version is Knorr, 1975: 41–3). This obviously projected onto the past the experience of the crisis of mathematical foundations in the early twentieth century, so that we have projection twice over – first Ammonius Saccas and Plotinus, then Frege and Russell – successively projected upon Pythagoras and Hippasus. (It should be added that the notion of Pythagoreanism, as revolving around a secret, has deeper, perhaps historically valid roots, in the ancient tradition of mystery cults, for which see, e.g., Netz, 2005; this is obviously the context for Plutarch's version of the secrecy, *Numa* 22).

of "secret doctrine": but, obviously, this corpus is not easy to date (secrecy has consequences).[201] What is reasonably clear from the texts themselves is that they emerge from a didactic context, their secrets conveyed to a few select followers (and so, in this sense, are comparable to the Plotinian milieu)[202] – "small, informal circles…gathered round a holy teacher".[203] To be quite precise, much of the literature of the century takes the form of "spiritual guides" (see Valantasis, 1991). Between Hermeticism, Neoplatonism, Gnosticism and other varieties of Christianity, one may argue that it is in this century that the "New Age" shelf begins to form. This is literature, addressed to an individual – and moving away, to an extent, from the classical model of the author. It should be noted that the third century was probably the best for the production of apocrypha. A lot has to do with the trajectory of Christianity. In the first and second centuries Christianity was almost negligible (though Christian writings from these centuries are, relatively speaking, very likely to survive or at least to be attested). By the fourth century the great bulk of Christian writing was fully assimilated into mainstream Greek forms, and so was also authorial. But, in the third century, Christianity in its many varieties was sufficiently widespread – but had not yet significantly normalized its authorial practices. Thus, in the third century Christian apocrypha are significant within the literary survival: among the 127 third-century authors counted by the TLG, 53 are non-authorial, 28 of whom are Christian.[204] So, not just Christianity; or, more precisely, Christianity is part of a wider feature of the century. When pronouncing hieratic secrets, a secret identity – implying an even higher authority for one's pronouncements – is more powerful than the merely named individual. And so, there were now entire libraries devoid of any recognizable "authors": one such was found, indeed, in Nag Hammadi, assembled in the fourth century out of materials completed by the third (Robinson, 1984). Against this background, it may perhaps become significant that Longinus, recounting the history of philosophy in his lifetime, sees a significant division into two types of philosophers: those who wrote and

---

[201] The standard dating of the *Hermetic Writings* is from the late first to the late third centuries CE (Fowden, 1986: 11), although it is only for the first treatise, the Poimandres, that a date as early as the late first century is widely suggested (though even that, quite as likely, is second century: Jackson, 1999: 104 n.26).

[202] So, Van den Kerchove (2012). Indeed, how else could "secret doctrines" be used?

[203] Fowden (1986: 193).

[204] The TLG numbers as a whole are inflated by some bad attributions and by the normal overcount (which makes any author "from the third century onwards" count here). Those for non-authors are an undercount, since some of the categories (such as the "Corpus Hermeticum") represent, in fact, more than a single writing event.

those who did not.[205] He ends up naming, I believe, 25 authors, of whom nine are definitely said to have been non-writing.[206] Did, indeed, something like a third of the philosophers of the third century eschew writing? This model of philosophical authorship was of course always available, and employed by some of the major figures, from Socrates through Arcesilaus and Carneades to Epictetus. And yet, probably not a third! These are not statistics (the numbers are small and perhaps misreported, as explained in note 206; and then, it is hard to construct a control group: no one set out to provide us with comparable information on *minor* philosophers, earlier). But it makes sense: philosophers, in the third century, turn away from the broadcasting of one's name via the named work addressed to a patron, concentrating much more on the master–pupil relationship.

And this is clearly the case for the contents of the philosophy. It moves in an other-worldly direction. Rogatianus, the senator-become-Platonist mentioned above, gave up the trappings of political power (Porphyry, *Life of Plotinus* 7.31–46). This is an anecdote, but it is typical of Neoplatonist doctrines: "Plotinus was...a Plato without politics" (De Blois, 1994: 172).[207] The secret doctrines entertained by the masters of the third century all involved the invisible hierarchies of vast cosmic orders: good and evil, ladders of emanation. My point is not that such doctrines could form some kind of escape from a political world turned upside down. My point is just that they no longer were of much use to a political patron. What mattered most now were not patrons but teachers. Which is why terms such as "Neoplatonism" begin to acquire meaning – unlike the comparable appellations for groups of so-called Imperial-era "Middle Platonists". In the Imperial era isolated philosophers sought patronage, vertically, and so did not form distinct groups. In the generation of Plotinus we begin to see a group whose main identity was horizontal,

---

[205] Porphyry, *Life of Plotinus* 20.25–104. It is perhaps more than a literary trope that Longinus himself sees the distinction as between those who seek to enlighten only those surrounding them at present and those who seek to enlighten future readers as well.

[206] Longinus initially mentions 11 non-writing philosophers, and then qualifies this by saying that some of those did write, however inconsequentially, and he names two examples; hence my count of nine. Clearly, the qualification extends further, so the correct number must be no more than nine; and yet, equally clearly, the passage assumes that the non-writing philosopher was a major feature of the intellectual landscape: so, not many fewer than nine.

[207] O'Meara (2003) seeks to recover a political philosophy of Neoplatonism: indeed, a scheme as all-encompassing as such a philosophy will hardly fail to have ramifications for political theory as well, but O'Meara is reduced to the Neoplatonist interest in the notion of the king, as divine. (That many of the commentaries they produced touched upon works that originally were political does not show that they had a political theory to contribute; it shows that they were stuck with a philosophical canon which they could not replace.)

shaped not by patronage but by the interactions between the philosophers themselves: a philosophical, *doctrinal* identity.

The proposed hypothesis is that a self-validating, self-conscious circle reflects a certain turn away from (or simply the absence of) patronage. The most obvious earlier parallels are, indeed, from outside the traditional Greek genres: that is, such parallels are found where patronage was rare to begin with. Christian authors did, in the second century, address emperors, which, I suggested above, may be read not simply as apologetics – literally seeking the emperor's goodwill – but also as an attempt to participate in a wider culture defined by patronage. But, even so, true charisma, to Christians, was carried by saints, not senators. The worship of masters became quite explicit, in the Christian context, as early as by the second century, as a cult of saints. From that time onwards documents surrounding such masters begin to be accumulated; by the third century Eusebius (if not others before him) has created, out of such material, new literary genres: Christian historiography made of *Acts of Martyrs, Lives of Saints*.[208] With the lives of saints, a cultural practice becomes validated through a chain of past practitioners, to which the dominant political powers act as mere obstacles.

Such chains of validating masters are now everywhere. Take, for instance, *Pirke Avot*, or *The Sayings of the Fathers*, a tractate of the Jewish Mishna (and so produced right at the beginning of the third century), composed of sayings of Jewish sages, arranged chronologically down to the milieu of the redactors of the Mishna themselves.[209] I suggest, then, that Rabbi Yehuda HaNasi – who did not have an emperor to validate his literary project – projected himself, instead, as heir to a chain of sages. At about the same time as Rabbi Yehuda HaNasi, Alexander, patriarch of Jerusalem (died 251), composed his own succession-list of his see, counting – so, inventing? – the remarkably round number of exactly 30 bishops (exactly half Jewish, half Greek).[210] There would be several parallels to this in Christian literature, and episcopal succession lists could have become an established genre from the second century onwards, culminating in Eusebius' (extant) lists.[211] And now we may return to traditional Greek authorship: for instance, take the chain of transmission of Skeptic philosophy preserved by Diogenes Laertius. This

[208] Barnes (2010: chap. 2); these genres then become distinctly authorial – and very widespread – in the fourth century: Krueger (2011).
[209] For the historical setting of the tractate, see Tropper (2004) (for the date and milieu of writing, see chapter 3).
[210] Grant (1980: 49–51).
[211] Williams (2005), arguing for the various polemical motivations animating the construction of the various lists. In the second and third centuries groups acting outside traditional structures of patronage asserted themselves by composing their own, immediate histories.

chain leads all the way down to Sextus Empiricus; it has no other parallel in Diogenes' *Lives*, whose chains otherwise end with the first century BCE (Sedley's "end of history"; see pages 489–90 above). It seems clear that Diogenes had access to a contemporary work that validated contemporary Skeptic philosophy through such a chain.[212]

We should push briefly into the fourth century, to consider Iamblichus – who similarly produces a chain (almost certainly fictitious) of Pythagorean scholarchs following the master's death (*The Pythagorean Life* 265–6). In general, it should be emphasized that this treatise by Iamblichus is not some kind of variation on Diogenes Laertius, offering a series of anecdotes for the reader's entertainment. It is a serious piece of ideology, the introductory part of Iamblichus' major work, *On Pythagoreanism*. About to lead the reader on his spiritual journey towards the Pythagorean life, Iamblichus first offers, as a programmatic note, a piece centered on Pythagoras himself (the title, *On the Pythagorean Life* – not "On the Life of Pythagoras" – is meaningful).[213] The many names dropped are there not for the sake of anecdote, then, but for the sake of evoking a central image, necessary so as to turn one into the true pupil of Iamblichus himself: the master, surrounded by followers. The named chain of scholarchs is overshadowed, indeed, by the named school: a cascade of 218 names of Pythagoras' alleged followers, unleashed right at the end of the treatise (section 137). This list plays a major part in scholarly attempts to reconstruct the history of early philosophy, and, indeed, Iamblichus did not invent it from whole cloth.[214] Perhaps a few of the names are "real", of individuals who would have considered themselves as "Pythagoreans", in the generations following upon the master. The point is that the key image evoked by the list clearly belongs not to the sixth and fifth centuries BCE but, rather, to the third and fourth centuries CE: once again – the master, surrounded by a circle of followers. What we learn, then, is that this, by now, has become the central image of learning. Such circles are from now on further attested, further imagined. Eunapius' *Lives of the Sophists and Philosophers* is,

---

[212] Skepticism concerning this succession list can be traced back to Glucker (1978: 352–3); see Polito (2007: 338).

[213] Staab (2002: 35–6) (and see Staab, 2002, more generally, whose interpretation I follow closely).

[214] Zhmud (2012: 111–19). To be clear: since Iamblichus clearly relies on sources for at least some of the names, it is plausible in principle (but impossible in practice?) to try and recover some sense from his list. I am not saying such scholarship, addressing Iamblichus' list more positively, is entirely misguided; but that we should also remember that it is, after all, somewhat anachronistic.

essentially, a survey of the transmission from a single individual – no other than Iamblichus himself – leading, in a couple of generations, to Eunapius' own time:[215] the tree developing to encompass not only philosophy but also rhetoric and medicine, both fields in which Eunapius himself had training – the biographies, as a whole, culminating with Eunapius' own teachers: "*The Lives of the Sophists and Philosophers* represents Eunapius' understanding of his own family tree" (Watts, 2005: 338). All later Neoplatonist philosophy would emerge from similar circles actively projecting their identity through the praise of central, founding figures.[216] Of course, such pagan efforts pale next to the massive flowering of the biographical tradition in Christian authors, from Eusebius onwards. This, above all, will be taken up, in Latin, by Jerome – who produced, in his *De Viris Illustribus*, a survey of Church authors from the gospel all the way down to Jerome's own teachers – culminating (with somewhat unchristian lack of humility) with Jerome himself, including a full accounting of *his writings to date* (shades of Galen, there). Indeed, auto-prosopography quickly morphs into a kind of collective biography. Apsyrtus of Clazomenae (was he active early in the fourth century? Or much earlier, around 200?) wrote on the care of horses – a medical work verging on the military-technical manual. It is written in an epistolary form, addressing 60 individuals (some soldiers, some doctors), invoking a late ancient horse-loving community;[217] this model in turn was imitated by Pelagonius – he has 35 letters – another hippiatric author, this time composing in Latin, and now quite clearly from the middle of the fourth century.[218] We are reminded of the *Professores* – Ausonius' collection of poems on the teachers of Burdigalia – or his *Parentalia*: his collection of poem-epitaphs on all the deceased members of his immediate family. This already verges on the directly autobiographical. We find such works soon enough: Libanius' so-called first *Oration*, and of course Augustine's *Confessions*. The autobiography emerges from the auto-prosopography, as cultural narratives become folded into a single life – a Bildungsroman

---

[215] Following some introductory remarks and a fairly cursory look at the Plotinian circle itself, the biography of Iamblichus is at 457–61; all later figures are related back, directly or indirectly, to Iamblichus himself. See Athanassiadi (2010: 132).

[216] Hence, Neoplatonist hagiography: Marinus' *Life of Proclus* is more in the nature of an isolated panegyric, but Damascius' *Life of Isidore* broadens, once again, to provide the full panorama of a school (O'Meara, 2006: my perspective is different from his, as I see this biography-of-a-school as the natural form for the era).

[217] McCabe (2007: 122–55).          [218] Fischer (1981).

in which the individual, himself, performs the chain of succession along the path of professional (in Libanius' case) and spiritual (Augustine's) growth.

Augustine, Libanius! We are already pushing ahead... Still in the fourth century (in all likelihood), we should also note the *Historia Augusta*. This forged history proclaimed six invented *authors* – and then relied, for its arguments, on no fewer than 36 fictional source historians.[219] Since these are fictional, it is interesting that such, exactly, was the number chosen. It is not a silly number to choose. This scale is somewhere between that of the *Pirke Avot* – in which I count 54 sages – and that of Longinus' history of contemporary philosophy – in which I count 25 philosophers: between the 60 horse lovers of Apsyrtus and the 35 of Pelagnius. This number compares well with the 31 teachers of Ausonius' *Professores* or the 30 bishops counted by Alexander of Jerusalem; it is, in fact, precisely the same as the 36 authors of Philostratus' *Sophists*. We often find the same scale, that of a few dozen figures – the number required, perhaps, as big enough to project an entire society.

My argument is that, in the teacherly circles of the third century, such groups begin to function as an *alternative* to surrounding social realities. This sounds likely enough, in principle. But is this, in practice, what such circles do? We need to understand, in detail, the cultural lives of such teacherly circles.

We have, as noted, but a few such circles surviving in our extant sources, but, for those that we do have, our evidence is surprisingly rich: they are auto-prosopographic (because these are circles) but, also, they are quite simply prolific (because these are teacherly). In sheer bulk, we are reminded of the Hellenistic schools of Athens. I will emphasize our two major sources: the Christian teacherly circles of Caesarea (first that of Origen, then that of Pamphilus and Eusebius) and the Platonist teacherly circle seen in the works of Porphyry. Origen comes first, but for the sake of this discussion I believe that it is best to treat them as contemporary: neither gave rise to the other; both came about through similar cultural contexts. I will begin with the pagan author, as his corpus – because of its subject matter – is easier to compare with past Greek literature. I hope this choice, to put Porphyry first, does not mar my historical account: I return to this below.

And so we make a new start: with Porphyry.

---

[219] Cornell (2013: 650–1). The details of the authorship of the *Historia Augusta* are widely debated, but this debate involves the precise date and motives for the forgery (see Cameron, 2010: chap. 20, for recent discussion): the roughly late fourth-century date, and the very fact of forgery, are clear enough.

Eleven works are extant – a substantial survival in and of itself – but the most recent list of Porphyry's works (Goulet, 2012b: 1301–11, 1350–74, 1408–19) counts up to 77 works attested via the Greek tradition alone (there are more attested in translation only).[220] A few of the 77 are spuria and some probably are duplicates – the same work attested under various headings – but this catalogue is assembled without the benefit of a Diogenes-Laertius-like catalogue and is based on citations by later authors and by Porphyry himself: it has to be far from complete. So, as a minimum, Porphyry wrote well over 100 works – of which many were substantial.[221] Let us count the words. More than 300,000 are extant (a large part of the extant Greek literature of the third century). The works now extant in full, with the exception of *On Abstinence from Meat* (four books), are all single-book treatises. The indirect tradition reports, in 16 cases, the number of books in the original work, however. Of these, only one is a single-book treatise; the average is a little over six books per treatise. Surely, the bias was to report the number of books for longer treatises – but it also appears clear that there was a certain bias to preserve the brief and more introductory works (this is evident with the case of the commentaries to the *Categories*, which I will mention a little further below). The extant works, then, likely represent much less than 10 percent of Porphyry's output, and it is certain that he authored several million words. We are looking at a production perhaps comparable to the Galen/Chrysippus range.

Once again, this kind of authorship always demands a functional account – what could those millions of words be *for*? – and, once again, the evidence is clear. Porphyry's life project was to turn an audience towards philosophy and then to lead it along, through the reading of a philosophical canon.

We may begin with the *Ad Marcellam* (G 1308 55), formally a letter to his wife, beseeching her to study philosophy while Porphyry, her husband, is away... As Whittaker (2001) points out, this is a protreptic intended for the wider audience of elite female readers, who, at this point, were seen as

---

[220] In the following, when first introducing a work by Porphyry, I will refer to it in parenthesis by its number in the list in Goulet, 2012b: G, followed by a page number and then the work number (the entry provides three series, each, unfortunately, separately numbered – general works, commentaries to Aristotle, commentaries to Plato). The evidence for translation is discussed in Goulet (2012b: 1447–68).

[221] The case is somewhat speculative, but it has been plausibly argued by Chiaradonna, Rashed and Sedley (2013) that the commentary to the *Categories* of which a fragment survives in the Archimedes Palimpsest is, in fact, the lost *Ad Gedalium* by Porphyry, and that in its original form this would have run to 200,000 words. This was divided into seven (hefty) books; one can only surmise what the length was of the lost, 15-book *Against the Christians*.

in danger of becoming converts to Christianity. Indeed, an important part of Porphyry's output was in such *polemical protreptic*, including what could well have been his longest work, *Against the Christians*, in 15 books (G 1302 11; but also: a treatise against Zoroaster! G 1304 28). But, clearly, the key protreptic/isagogic work by Porphyry is his *Life of Plotinus* (G 1310 59), occupying, in Plotinus' corpus, a role comparable to that occupied by the *On the Pythagorean Life* in the corpus of Iamblichus. But there is a difference: whereas Iamblichus' biography of Pythagoras makes use of many elements of the legends of Pythagoras, thus weaving together a fully fledged historical work, Porphyry's *Life of Plotinus* expressly avoids the individual Plotinus: the very first words of the *Life* assert that Plotinus felt ashamed even to be in a body (thus preparing the reader for the dearth of biographical material), the bulk of the treatise involving, entirely, Plotinus as a philosophical teacher. This account of Plotinus revolves around a duality – the written and the oral[222] – and around a pattern: Plotinus' interactions with other philosophers and with his followers.[223] The two are both emanations of the same principle of teaching. Teaching creates the philosophical network; teaching is the oral; it is merely mediated through writing (Plotinus demanded the reading of all the commentaries but relied, himself, on Ammonius' spoken doctrines;

---

[222] In general, Porphyry keeps interweaving judgements on Plotinus as writer and as teacher in person (chapters 8–9, 13–14). The key episode of the pact of secrecy, which effectively launches Porphyry's narrative, is forced into the duality of teaching and writing – intimating, apparently falsely, that the pact allowed oral but not written expositions of the secrets: 3.32–4 (O'Brien, 1994: 120); the key testimony that nearly completes Porphyry's narrative is Longinus' preface to *On the End*, or the brief history of near-contemporary philosophy cited above (chapter 20), which is explicitly about the bifurcation of philosophy into oral teaching and writing. The dialectic of writing and the oral was made to be part of the very schoolroom experience: demanding that the students read all the commentaries, Plotinus then expounded without reference to the texts, relying merely on Ammonius' oral teachings (14.10–16). A small but telling example is 13.3–5: Porphyry mentions that Plotinus was liable to make certain mistakes in speech, and he immediately notes that he made the same mistakes also in writing (this, indeed, serves to underline Porphyry's role as an editor and why, as an auditor, he is especially well prepared for the task: which underlines the nature of Porphyry's project, to make Plotinus' lived presence as a teacher survive into writing).

[223] This, once again, begins with the pact in chapter 3; is immediately followed in chapter 4 by Porphyry's arrival at Rome, to find Amelius there by Plotinus' side; chapter 7 is a longer exposition on the followers; this leads to his various interactions, and so to the account of Plotinus as teacher and writer. Vignettes include Plotinus' interactions with Porphyry himself (chapters 15, 17–18); the interactions gradually emerge outside the school: there is a mention of an attack, as if Plotinus plagiarized Numenius, refuted from within the school (chapter 17); then, of course, the passages from Longinus (chapters 19–20); and, finally – this is a dossier with ever more impressive letters of reference – an oracle by Apollo on Plotinus (chapter 24). The biography begins by recanting the body and ends on the divine – passing through a school, located within a wider philosophical discourse.

Porphyry's own role was to make Plotinus' spoken teaching endure as writing).

And so: having turned into the philosophical life, this, as envisioned by Porphyry, would always involve *close textual study*. This might begin with Aristotle's *Organon*, for which we have substantial remains of Porphyry, and for which, indeed, his influence would be the most lasting. He wrote at least three commentaries to the *Categories*, two of which are extant. One is very elementary, the famous "Introduction" to the *Categories* (G 1350 1). This of such a historical importance that the title *Isagoge* – Greek for "introduction" – now is often reserved for just this work! The other is written in the format of catechism, always a giveaway for elementary teaching context (G 1351 2). The third one, "To Gedalius" (G 1353 3), was massive – now available only in small fragments – but, likely enough, it was transmitted into Byzantium and survived into the thirteenth century.[224] The multiplicity of works on the same topic, once again, suggests the educational context (as Cribiore, 2001, emphasizes, the typical structure of ancient education was spiral, leading its readers in ascending steps through the same canon). In this case, the reading of the *Categories* may have led into Aristotle's *Organon* as a whole (commentaries by Porphyry attested for all the works there), into much more by Aristotle (commentaries attested for *Physics, Ethics* and at least *Metaphysics Lambda*, perhaps also *De Anima*. It is very likely that many other Aristotelian treatises were commented upon as well, and there is even a suggestion of some kind of commentary on Theophrastus!).[225] We also have attestations for commentaries on seven of Plato's dialogues, surely an incomplete list (G 1357–74 1–7).[226]

Above all, this ascent would all lead into Plotinus. Porphyry's great work was the edition of Plotinus' lectures in the *Enneads* (G 1304 24). *The Life of Plotinus* was issued, as noted already, specifically as an introduction to the *Enneads*, ending with bibliographic notes on the structure of Plotinus' teaching as organized by Porphyry – and then, right at the end, it noted the

---

[224] It was then palimpsested; see preceding note.

[225] The remaining Aristotelian commentaries are G 1355–7 4–11; the commentary to Theophrastus is attested by Boethius (Smith, 1993: fr. 167) and must be, once again, on a treatise of logic.

[226] There is a debate, not so much concerning the very existence of a commentary by Porphyry to the *Parmenides* (G 1358 3) but concerning the identification of that commentary with a palimpsested fragment, read in the National Library of Turin (Kroll, 1892) before its destruction by fire in 1904 (this is reminiscent of the *Ad Gedalium* and the Archimedes Palimpsest – though the Turin Palimpsest was apparently extremely early: sixth century?). The arguments, all suggestive, not dispositive, lean on the doctrines espoused in the fragments (Goulet, 2012b: 1358–71), to which one should add the argument from base probabilities: given the sheer bulk of Porphyry's corpus and its impact, an otherwise unidentified Byzantine text is much likelier to be by him than by, say, some unknown follower of Numenius.

many further works Porphyry produced to surround this publication. These pedagogic tools included writings in three distinct genres: commentaries, summaries, and arguments[227] (G 1304–5 33–5, *Life of Plotinus* 26.29–37). We notice once again the many-layered structure of commentary, similar to Porphyry's handling of the *Categories*: one would surely approach the *Enneads* again and again, at different levels. The *Enneads* themselves are very substantial (more than 200,000 words), and it is hard to believe Porphyry treated them any less thoroughly than he treated Aristotle: these commentaries alone must have accounted for a substantial fraction of his entire corpus, a fraction now entirely lost. On the motivation for all this, Porphyry is quite explicit (*Life* 26.30–2): "Because the companions urged us to write on those <passages> that they themselves have deemed worthy of clarifying to themselves" – such is the teacherly circle. The teacher in this case is Plotinus, his followers in implicit competition for the status of *the teacher of the teacher's doctrines*.[228]

As noted, there were different *levels* of teaching. Among the extant works we find a brief treatise titled "Auxiliaries to the Perception of Intelligible Natures" (G 1308 53), a concise work; as a consequence of its concision, a highly difficult one as well. It sets out a particular piece of Plotinian doctrine in the form of theses. This does not seem to belong to the body of elementary commentary to the *Enneads* mentioned in the *Life*, but it may be instead a stand-alone piece of more advanced teaching, the commentary-teaching verging, in the most sophisticated level, into original restatements of the master's position: this seems to be the context of the corpus of original contributions to philosophy (which, for most other philosophers, would have appeared as very large in and of itself), of which a few are extant.[229] Scholarship on Porphyry often seems disappointed that such works do not seem to add anything significant to Plotinus' thought, or, indeed, anything substantial at all (just where is

---

[227] The last term is *epicheirēmata* – not otherwise attested as the title of philosophical commentary (Brisson, 1982: 321–2). The word was, at the time, important especially for the teaching of rhetoric, and one can perhaps see here Porphyry applying the tools of rhetorical teaching to the study of philosophy.

[228] This competition is not a mere inference but is, indeed, directly attested: there was a debate between Porphyry and Amelius concerning the correct teaching of Plotinus, which even gave rise to its own treatise, G 1304 30; Amelius' own commentaries to Plotinus, we recall (n.196 above), ran to 100 books.

[229] Especially on the nature of the soul: *Ad Gaurum* (G 1308 54), and so also, effectively, *On Abstinence from Meat* (G 1301 5). We recall how Plotinus shrank from his own body, and the entire Neoplatonic project is one of learning, as progress, from body to soul; the thematics of the nature of the soul recur in many attested works, which I will not cite here in full.

Porphyry's originality?),[230] but this is not their purpose, and we read such works out of context, because we do not possess the commentaries on the *Enneads*. Porphyry's stand-alone philosophical essays are simply excursus in his grand project of teaching Plotinus' philosophy, and the lack of originality here does not tell us that Porphyry failed as a creative philosopher; it tells us that, by the time we get to Porphyry, to be a philosopher meant to be a teacher of philosophy.

Or, indeed, more generally: to be an intellectual meant to be a *teacher*. One of the surprising features of Porphyry's output was his engagement in the teaching of many subjects. His life project became something like a university. It is least surprising that Porphyry also wrote traditional commentary to Homer (of course, turning Homer into a Neoplatonist);[231] he was addressing, after all, pupils trained by grammatical education. His skills as a grammarian were formidable. The "Philological History", a major work in five books (G 1302 14: a substantial extract is preserved by Eusebius),[232] was a survey of literature (hence, "history") that proceeded by noting innumerable cases of plagiarism in ancient literature. The remarkable feature of this work is its extensive practice of textual collation: Porphyry always arranges texts: Plotinus' treatises by *nines*,[233] ancient texts collated. . . Even more remarkable is the application of commentary to rhetoric. Attested is a commentary on Minucianus' *Art* (G 1304 21), which could well be the first commentary on a rhetorical work in the technical tradition: even the teaching of rhetoric, understood now on the model of textual exegesis.[234] Even more original was Porphyry's practice of

---

[230] Strange (2007: 17): "[I]t is much less clear to what extent Porphyry can be considered an original contributor to the development of ancient philosophy." The Stanford Encyclopedia of Philosophy (http://plato.stanford.edu/entries/porphyry): "This is Plotinus' philosophy, which Porphyry shares, in broad outline. . . There are, however, some differences in terminology. . ." Barnes, as usual, is honest, and brutal (Barnes, 2003: xii): "[D]espite his vast learning and his unusual critical acuity, Porphyry had a weakness for fudge."

[231] The centrality of the canon was such that some of this grammarian work even survives: we have extant an allegorical commentary to the Cave of the Nymphs passage in the *Odyssey* (G 1307 52); attested is a similar work, *On Styx* (G 1306 46 – as well as a question on Pindar! G 1303 16). Just what was the attested work on Homer's helpfulness for *Kings* (G 1303 17 – ten books!)? More significantly, we also have some parts of the much more substantial, and even more grammarian-like, "Homeric Questions" (G 1306 47; also "Grammatical Problems": G 1304 23). Finally, the attested title (titles?) on *The Philosophy of Homer* (G 1302 12) is perhaps best understood as a protreptic: from grammar – into philosophy.

[232] *Praep. Evang.* X. 3.

[233] Indeed, one further feature of the *Life of Plotinus* that brings out the relationship between school teaching and textual order is the various orders implied by the text: not only the established order by nines, but also an order according to the chronological account (chapters 4–6).

[234] For Porphyry's originality, see Heath (2003: 146–8). The clearest antecedent for such a rhetorical commentary comes from nearby – we have attested a commentary on Hephaestion, by Longinus. It

commentary to the exact sciences. Extant are a sophisticated commentary to Ptolemy's *Harmonics* (G 1310 56), as well as an introductory work on Ptolemy's main work in astrology, the *Tetrabiblos* (G 1310 57); attested are, in general, introductory works to astronomy (G 1304 22: did he write a commentary on the *Almagest*, then, as well?). Porphyry thought that Platonists should know about music, about the stars. And so the most natural thing for him to was to seek appropriate texts on those subjects and write commentaries about them. It is noteworthy that Porphyry spent so much time on writing commentary on *recent* authorities: Plotinus, above all; but also Minucianus, in rhetoric, and Ptolemy, in science.[235] Porphyry was actively *constructing* near-canons.

There is nothing very surprising about Porphyry never trying actively to deviate from his master's philosophy. This was just as he thought it should be, and, indeed, he thought *Aristotle* never deviated from Plato's philosophy – and so Porphyry wrote a massive work to prove that ("On Plato's and Aristotle's Sect Being One and the Same", in seven books: G 1301 8; on the same topic, perhaps the same work: G 1305 37). There was one true philosophy, expressed most importantly by that canonical author, Plato, but also seconded by Aristotle. It was probably with such claims in mind that Porphyry wrote his history of philosophy (G 1302 10), from which there are several fragments but from which also may derive the extant *Life of Pythagoras* (G 1310 58). This may well have been yet another work structured by chain of succession – leading in this case from Homer to Plato (Goulet, 2012b: 1330–1).

The picture we have of Porphyry is clear enough: he is a teacher, very capable in the teaching of rhetoric and grammar as well as the exact sciences, but above all a teacher of philosophy. Texts to be taught are the starting point of the teaching; texts are the medium of teaching, as Porphyry produces his own new works as a multi-layered structure of

---

should be noted that Metrophanes of Phrygia, according to the *Suda*, wrote a commentary to Hermogenes; this author is hard to date but he was roughly Porphyry's coeval. It is not so much that Porphyry was an innovator: he belonged to a time marked by the sudden prevalence of commentary. It also seems that Porphyry wrote himself a work in the tradition of the rhetorical technē (G 1307 48), and there are further works attested of a generally rhetorical character (G 1307 49: a collection of questions relating to rhetoric; should we count here the attested proem to Thucydides – G 1303 19 – as grammatical or rhetorical in character?). The most important of these works is "Against Aristides" (G 1303 20 – seven books!), likely a polemic against Aelius Aristides' own defense of *Rhetoric* against Plato's *Gorgias* (Pernot, 2006), which explains why this should have become such a substantial work: this was Porphyry's major work of protreptic, addressed to the pupils of rhetoric.

[235] It is not clear which Minucianus was the subject of Porphyry's commentary (traditionally, this was assumed to be Iunius Minucianus, Porphyry's coeval! Heath, 1996, argues this was Claudius Minucianus, born about 60 years earlier).

commentary. This entire project assumes a community of shared belief, and, indeed, it projects a view of intellectual life as fundamentally settled – there being a single, unified true doctrine, which, moreover, is uniformly proclaimed by a group of main authorities.

This is a cultural practice which is organized entirely around the teaching of a specialized canon; approaching it on a textual level; treating it as established doctrine. So much should be uncontroversial.

I also believe that, within the literary tradition surveyed so far in this book, this is nearly unprecedented. Epicureanism had a doctrine; it was not a textual practice (commentary and textual edition was marginal to Epicureanism, if at all practiced; see page 485 above). In the Imperial era Aristotelianism nearly became a textual practice; it was much less doctrinal and the piecemeal nature of Aristotelian contemplation accorded well with lemma-by-lemma commentary. Earlier than Porphyry the medical veneration of Hippocrates had textual and doctrinal elements, but these never become so dominant in the career of any medical author (the "medical author" had not yet collapsed – surely not by Galen's time – into "the teacher of medicine"). What is especially noteworthy is the centrality of edition and commentary to one's own creative life. This is a new type of authorship, which I have elsewhere labeled "deuteronomic" (Netz, 1998b; 2004b): the making of texts which are essentially second-order, dependent on previous texts; this is a type of writing that will continue to be dominant, now, for centuries to come – in some ways, all the way to the end of the Middle Ages.

And so, how important was Porphyry? I am reminded of a figure we met in the second part of this book: Posidonius. Porphyry and Posidonius are not often brought together, but at some broad structural level they are analogous: authors who are epoch-making not in the contents of their writing but in their literary practice. And so: scholarship always sensed that there was something dramatically new about Posidonius, and so tried to detect his Stoic "heterodoxy". In fact, there is very little evidence of this, and he subscribed to doctrines within the range available to all Stoics. Nevertheless, Posidonius marks a decisive turning point in terms of his literary practice, in that he was a major philosopher active away from Athens, bringing together activities of the "Alexandrian" and "Athenian" Hellenistic eras, and producing all this in the context of Roman patronage. This combination would define cultural life for over three centuries (see pages 501–7 above).

At the end of those three centuries it would be Porphyry – another Greek-speaking Syrian – who would mark yet another, decisive turn.

Modern scholarship, once again, is disappointed by Porphyry's lack of originality, but, in this case, it is precisely this avoidance of the original, authorial statement, in favor of the teacherly, deuteronomic attitude, that sets the course for an entire era.

But it should be added immediately: Porphyry was not the first. I start out with him because it is worthwhile to note the rupture, in cultural practice, taking place within the system of genres surveyed throughout this book. But now I have to go back in time and note a Christian author, Origen. Born in Alexandria near the end of the second century (and gaining there a thorough paideia), Origen seems to have belonged to a circle of Christian believers/ scholars active in that city (recent scholarship tends to believe this was not a formally structured "school").[236] Political entanglements with both Church and Empire had him landed, finally, in Caesarea in the early 230s. Settled there, ordained as a priest and finally allowed to teach as he saw fit, he completed there, during the following 20 years, an epic textual project.[237] Having presented Porphyry's project in detail, I can describe that of Origen more concisely. The best evidence is Eusebius, and Nautin (1977: 242–60) has reconstructed a Eusebian list of 77 works – by sheer accident the same number as those we may now ascribe to Porphyry (this is not the complete set of all works attested, however, and the ancient reports of the number of the works by Origen are, literally, incredible).[238] The similarity does not end there. Porphyry arranged and published the words of Plotinus, in six *Enneads*. Origen arranged the words of *God*, in six columns of writing – the famous Hexapla text of the Bible published in parallel, in six languages! Porphyry commented on the canon he had assembled: Aristotle, Plato and his own version of Plotinus (but also Minucianus and Ptolemy!). Origen produced a massive commentary on at least a major selection from the Bible (likely enough, his goal was to produce a complete set of commentaries – but it

---

[236] The evidence beginning with Eusebius assumes a fully fledged institution; Bardy (1937) is the first to have pointed out that this is an anachronistic reading, inserting the conditions of the late third century a century earlier – not simply because later sources might be anachronistic but specifically because Eusebius is committed to unbroken, and homogeneous, chains of succession. A rupture in Christian teaching practices would be anathema to him! (See Dawson, 1992: 219. Van den Hoek, 1997, offers to revive an account more sympathetic to Eusebius' report: see 59 n.1 for a survey of the literature in the twentieth century; see also DPA s.v. 809.)

[237] The fullest recent biography is Nautin (1977), titled *Origène: Sa vie et son œuvre*. For a brief overview, see Martens (2012: 14–19), the subtitle to whose book is *The Contours of the Exegetical Life*. Life and work, life and exegesis; in fact, Origen is never presented to us in any form other than the author of exegesis, a life folded, by himself and then by his biographers, into a textual, deuteronomic practice.

[238] Rufinus, *De Adulter. Libr. Orig.* 15.1–5, cited a source claiming to have read 6,000 books by Origen; Jerome responded, *Contra Rufinum* II.22, that not even a third were recorded in the full catalogue by Eusebius (a full catalogue now lost to us).

was cut short by death). Porphyry's teaching was multi-layered, the same work subjected to commentary at various levels. So was Origen's teaching, from whom are attested scholia, fully fledged commentaries, advanced works on the principles of exegesis and also homilies – that is, explicitly pedagogic works (but conceived at a truly elementary level) addressed to the congregation of Caesarea. This last detail is crucial, and provides a sense of the nature of Origen's project as a whole. It is, as explained by Torjesen (1985), one in which pedagogy becomes salvation. Everything is geared towards Origen's hearers, who are redeemed through their learning of the Bible.

While we do have testimonies (mostly through Origen himself) for earlier exegetical Christian works, these appear to have been isolated works (never the defining project for any individual author), or even simply the exegetic comments embedded within works whose main format was not that of commentary.[239] Something has changed, then, in the age of Origen.

And yet I start with Porphyry rather than Origen; for this there are many reasons, among them that Origen simply was not that influential in his own time. He was active in Caesarea, not a backwater by any means, but also not a metropolitan center such as that of Alexandria, Rome or Antioch. And his position within the Christian Church (in itself a minority sect), in sheer political terms, was always precarious.[240] There is a direct continuity from Porphyry, via Iamblichus, to later Neoplatonism, but with Origen it is harder to trace continuities.[241] Origen was by no means neglected: he was widely known (and even cited, it appears – many years after his death! – by Porphyry himself), but it seems that there could have

---

[239] I rely on the summary in Fürst (2011); it is not controversial. It should be noted, though, that scholars of Christian commentary take it for granted that Christians merely borrowed from a clearly established practice of pagan commentary. To the contrary, I would argue that it was very rare, prior to the third century, to have one's life project defined by commentary (unless, that is, one was a grammarian): even Aristotelians typically committed more effort to original philosophical work, and commentary was never central to the other schools (see 482–7 above, and my remarks there on the place of commentary to Hippocrates in the medical tradition prior to late antiquity). Origen may well have been the first to lead the exegetical life.

[240] Origen has been caught, on more than one occasion, in the crossfire of the struggle for authority between the Alexandrian Church (from which he emerged) and the Church of Palestine (where he eventually found his foothold). Not only had he never reached the rank of a bishop; even his late ordination to mere priesthood became the subject of a political clash between the Churches (see, e.g., Cain, 2006: 728–9; Holliday, 2011, has a full survey of the evidence, though her interpretation envisages a Church more rigidly structured than was probably the case in the early third century).

[241] The most significant of Origen's pupils may have been Gregory the Thaumaturge – who, upon completion of his studies, left Caesarea to return to the life of the Church in his native region of Pontus (in fact, we have his "Address of Thanksgiving to Origen"; authorship has been questioned, but see Barnes, 1981: 329 n.39).

been no active school in Caesarea when Origen died – broken by Roman torture – in the year 254.[242]

Teacherly circles beget texts; and then texts can beget teacherly circles. Pamphilus of Berytus was, likely, a mere child when Origen died. His type is by now familiar: a Christian, born with the advantages of the elite – wealth and paideia. His paideia formed his passion: the textual study of the Bible. His wealth made it possible to pursue this passion by amassing a huge library, with Origen's own works at the center of this collection. At some point Pamphilus, too, settled in Caesarea and taught there. By far his most important pupil was Eusebius, born in the 260s. In the year 309 – during the last spasm of anti-Christian persecution – Eusebius saw his teacher and adopted father, Pamphilus, die a martyr's death. Through the remaining 30 years of his life Eusebius completed one of the most significant corpora of antiquity, and – this being the fourth century – much of it is still extant (more than a million words), and in a textually unmediated form. For Eusebius wrote, so it appears, directly for the codex.

His project, as prolific as those of Porphyry and of Origen, was even more explicitly textual. As with Porphyry, the corpus fits together if considered as an overarching program: protreptic, isagogic, teacherly.[243] I have often referred above to Eusebius' historical works, which clearly function as validating succession chains leading to the Christianity of his own generation (TLG 002–004, 020, 022, 025; more are attested, as for instance the *Life of Origen*: Photius Cod. 118). Eusebius' own polemical protreptic works were extensive. They include an anti-pagan work, the extant *Praeparatio Evangelica* (TLG 001), which was designed, at least in part, as a response to (and is thus our main extant source for) Porphyry's *Against the Christians*.[244] Besides this response, Eusebius also wrote a

---

[242] The negative evidence is decisive, since we now move into the orbit of the auto-prosopography of Eusebius, and if he could have presented a continuous tradition of teaching in Caesarea he would surely would have done that. Instead, for biographical information on the young Origen, Eusebius has to rely on anonymous "old men" – never on a chain of teachers leading up to Eusebius himself (Nautin, 1977: 20–1). Eusebius' own mention and his actual link to the Caesarean past was Pamphilus. Born in Berytus not earlier than the 240s, then a student in Alexandria before establishing himself in Caesarea (Photius, *Cod.* 118 93a22–3), Pamphilus certainly did not study directly with Origen. The circles of Origen, and then of Pamphilus/Eusebius, can be seen as yet another example of generational events (see section 3.2 above).

[243] It is important, then, to approach him at the level of the entire corpus. For Eusebius – well studied, and yet not the subject of anything comparable to the DPA's magnificent entry on Porphyry – I will identify works by providing their number in the TLG *Canon of Greek Authors and Works* (this covers only extant and fragmentary works, however).

[244] The standard view in the literature used to be that the *Praeparatio Evangelica* simply was a refutation of Porphyry's *Against the Christians*; Morlet (2011) argues that its project should be understood more broadly, as directed against pagan anti-Christian polemic as such: all the more, a

massive work specifically in refutation of Porphyry; there is also another extant polemical protreptic, *Demonstratio Evangelica* (TLG 005), set up against the Jews. The multi-layered project, with different books often repeating and varying similar arguments, is now an established feature of the making of such a corpus. Porphyry's argument against Christianity was historical and grammarian, showing how alien Christianity was to the best traditions of all past civilization. Eusebius, in reply, produced his own grammarian-historical project, in which he criticized all past mistakes by citing and commenting upon them. His polemic has almost the flavor of a grammarian study (or commentary) of theological error (and becomes, for us, an important source for philosophical fragments).[245] Indeed, the central work of Pamphilus and Eusebius remained – following on that of Origen – the edition and commentary to the Bible. Extant are an Isaiah commentary (TLG 019 – over 150,000 words) and a commentary on the Psalms (TLG 034 – about 300,000 words), nearly half the extant corpus.[246] But the significance of the commentary project goes beyond the mere counting of commentary works. Eusebius – in the tradition of Greek grammar – went on to provide interpretative context: a geographical onomasticon (TLG 011); a study of biblical measures (TLG 018); above all – a chronography (TLG 040: also serving in the refutation of Porphyry's own, chronographic argument against Christianity).[247] There were also isagogic works, preparing for the study of the biblical text: various "problems" – a typical title of the educational series – survive in fragmentary form (TLG 028–032), as does the "General Elementary Introduction" (TLG 023–024). As in Porphyry, then, we see a vast, many-layered structure: the protreptic to

mirror to Porphyry's project. If genuine, the *Contra Hieroclem* would be another, minor, polemical-protreptical work (TLG 017; but see Hägg, 1992).

[245] This Christian, grammarian protreptic has an antecedent, of sorts, in the *Stromateis* of Clement of Alexandria, written a century earlier; Inowlocki (2011: 208), comparing Eusebius both to Clement and to his contemporary Athenaeus, notes the absence of the playful from Eusebius, who instead "deals with citations in a far more orderly manner, organizing his material according to clear and definite purposes". Authors such as Clement and Athenaeus used paideia within a culture of patronage, and so maximized individual effect; Eusebius was, instead, bookish and teacherly.

[246] There are fragmentary attestations for more commentaries on the Old Testament (Proverbs, Song of Songs, Jeremiah, Ezekiel, Daniel; the situation is less clear for the New Testament; the TLG chose to count a few of those as numbers 012 and 035 to 038). These derive from catenae – mosaic collections of commentary notes from various previous commentators – that, in future centuries, often end up supplanting the original commentaries: the textual grammarians of the Bible becoming, in turn, subject to textual-grammarian processing (more on this on p. 771 below).

[247] Christians were in the habit of citing the Book of Daniel to prove the prophetic powers of the Bible; Porphyry, quite rightly, pointed out that the book must have been written after the events prophesied, and, as part of this argument, produced a chronography of world history – to which Eusebius responded with his own chronography (see Croke, 1983).

the study of a textual corpus; and then the texts produced for the reading of that text: introductions, commentaries and interpretative handbooks. Johnson's statement (referring especially to the comparison between Eusebius' "General Elementary Introduction" and Porphyry's "Philosophy from Oracles") is a plausible summary (Johnson, 2011: 118): "What is shared by the two is the common understanding of what they were attempting to do as educators." This is what education meant: making texts, for texts: a deuteronomic project.

Eusebius' commitment to the ordering of texts, as such, was much more thorough – indeed, more interesting – than that of Porphyry. As emphasized by Grafton and Williams in their magisterial study from 2006, *Christianity and the Transformation of the Book*, what was remarkable about Origen's *Hexapla* was its explicit reliance on tabular arrangement – thus making the physical structure of the page itself contribute to its meaning;[248] and it was in this respect, in particular, that Eusebius went further than his predecessors. His most remarkable formal innovation was book two of his *Chronicle*. In the first book, Eusebius argued in detail for the primacy of Jewish and Christian history, by the construction of a set of synchronous events between biblical and Greco-Roman histories, and those of the ancient Near East. In the second book, this synchronicity was presented in the form of the timeline table, each column representing the events in a particular "kingdom" in diachronic sequence (arranged by decades), each row being the synchronic alignment of co-dated events in the different kingdoms. This form is by now familiar to us, but, as Grafton and Williams emphasize, such work would appear, in context, as a radical innovation.[249] In some ways, this was continuous with Eusebius' larger pattern of historical and grammatical work. Eusebius stands out, in his historical works, in his ample use of citation. He often turns his history from narrative into a more purely textual mosaic of original documents (even though his account of martyrs, in particular, shows a very lively

[248] When they assert (Grafton and Williams, 2006: 17) that it was "perhaps the first book – as opposed to official documents – ever to display information in tabular form", they of course forget for a moment the tabular practice of ancient astronomy (Jones, 1999, passim), preserved above all in Ptolemy (who has a tabular star catalogue, as well as numerical tables used for astronomical calculations – see Sidoli, 2014 – a practice extended by Ptolemy to music and optics as well). Ptolemy can do this, however, because he writes in the exact sciences, always based on the visual tool of the diagram; thus, his text is understood to be textual and non-performative. Origen's radical departure in the *Hexapla* is the treatment of a canonical, performative text – the Bible – as if it were a textual artifact whose value resided in the codex itself: a choice suggestive of the distinctive cultural practice of Christianity (see below, p. 781).
[249] Grafton and Williams (2006: 172–5).

narrative skill: he was pedantic by *choice*). In the *Chronicle* the mosaic was reduced to an even more abstract pattern. Narrative history – rendered into a textual, then almost purely a visual, tool. Remarkably, Eusebius did the same with the most performative works of the Christian canon itself. The narratives of the Gospels were numbered by him into sections – so that tables could now set out the correspondences between the four Gospels. (Indeed, these – purely numerical – tables directly resemble those of astronomy.) And even the Psalms – the main piece of Christian liturgical performance – became subject for grammarian-textual analysis, with Eusebius' *Pinax* setting out, in tabular form, the speakers of the various Psalms.[250] Near the end of his life Eusebius finally turned to the central editorial work of presenting a text of the Bible. This was ordered by the newly Christian emperor – Constantine. Imperial patronage, now returning to touch the teacherly circles that originated in its absence. No longer a mere pedagogic document, this edition was on a significant scale (50 copies of the entire Bible?), and lavish material: Eusebius explicitly ordered to use parchment. It is a tantalizing possibility that this work may now be consulted directly, in either of the two manuscripts of the fourth-century Bible that are still extant.[251] We enter the world of parchment, and the air of the medieval library will permeate all the works to be studied from now on.

The intimations of the Middle Ages are real enough, and Grafton and Williams may be granted their references to a Caesarean "scriptorium". I suppose that, when they say that, "[l]ike a great German professor, Eusebius relied on assistants" (2006: 214), they are mostly being cute, but here and there one has the sense that they conceive of Eusebius as primarily a research scholar, a kind of freelance grammarian. In fact, our knowledge of Eusebius' life in the key years of his literary activity (that is, after Pamphilus' death) is limited. We see the political figure – the bishop of Caesarea, in correspondence even with the emperor (Origen could only dream of such status) – and we can work out the sequence of the works from their internal references, but anything else about Eusebius' own living practice has to be surmised. Eusebius did not have another Eusebius as his biographer (Jerome, who comes closest, relies entirely on Eusebius' own works). The best way to understand Eusebius' own understanding of his mission, then, would be through his own portrayal of the ideal Christian

---

[250] Grafton and Williams (2006: 195–8).
[251] Grafton and Williams (2006: 216–21). The manuscripts are the *Sinaiticus* and the *Vaticanus* B, the major manuscripts of the Gospels (Skeat, 1999; see the skeptical remarks in Parker, 2012: 73–4).

master – that of Pamphilus: much as Porphyry's *Life of Plotinus* is the best guide for the understanding of his own project. This portrayal of Pamphilus we have in multiple forms (if often mediated and fragmentary): the biography is no longer extant, but the *Martyrs of Palestine* more or less is (we have Greek fragments, and a fuller Syriac version); the same material is also covered in the *Historia Ecclesiastica*. Pamphilus clearly emerges as the master of a small circle of ascetic learners, living around their text: the Bible.[252] The trajectory of Caesarea begins with Origen's commentaries – and leads to Constantine's edition of the Bible. Eusebius was not a German professor. He was a biblical teacher.

Let us take stock of the historical trajectory, as suggested by these three vignettes of Origen, Porphyry and Eusebius. I apologized early on for starting from Porphyry, chronologically not the first. But indeed this should hardly matter. It would be preposterous to suggest that Porphyry's literary practice was formed in response to that of Origen. Then again, when we get to Eusebius we can no longer doubt the enormous presence of Porphyry, who was indeed the subject of direct refutation by Eusebius. And yet, Eusebius mostly followed on a project initiated by Origen and expanded by Pamphilus (who, himself, was Porphyry's near-contemporary). To connect the two sets of literary practice, the Christian and the pagan, in this direction or the other, would indeed be to commit the fallacy of *post hoc, ergo propter hoc*. Origen preceded Porphyry, who preceded Eusebius. But it was not because of Origen's biblical scholarship that Porphyry produced his massive systematization of Neoplatonism, nor was it because of that systematization that Eusebius invented his new textual apparatuses of the codex. And, if so – if a historical lineage is to be denied – similarities have to be understood in terms of shared environment. It was the third century. Patronage, as well as authorship itself, receded; cultural life was restructured through the small circles surrounding teachers; and, so, there was the creation of a new type of literary project: the protreptic to learning and its guidance through extensive commentary.

Before moving on, a word on the structure of my argument. For the Imperial era, and then for the third century, I provided an argument based on social/economic setting, its cultural interface, the resulting scale and the ensuing sociology of cultural practice (from which I derive, for late antiquity, a qualitative account of cultural production).

---

[252] Penland (2010); cf. Urbano (2013: 148–9).

Imperial era
massive inequality → patronage → large scale → "cultural service industry"
Third century
political/economic crisis at the top → erosion of patronage →
collapse of scale → teacherly circles → commentary ("deuteronomic") culture

The causal explanation goes from the material to the cultural. My account also proceeds chronologically, from the second century to the third. But my evidentiary arrows point in all directions. The evidence for the collapse in scale in the third century is part of the evidence for a larger scale in the second century; the qualitative nature of culture in both eras – the thing, after all, for which we have the most direct evidence – serves to support the claims for the social setting which made such culture possible. The evidence is limited: you make use of what you have, promiscuously.

Use what evidence one has: and so, indeed, I have already begun to look ahead, into the fourth century. But the point, once again, is not just one of evidence. What makes the transformation of the third century so important is that it *stuck*. A new cultural stability was formed, supplanting, in a way, the one seen throughout the book.

The remaining two sections document, first, the centrality of commentary culture in late antiquity (6.5.3) before concluding with, second, an account of the (relative) stability of late antiquity and the Middle Ages (6.5.4): the third century, then, as an appropriate conclusion to this book's narrative.

### 6.5.3   Late Antiquity: Teacherly Circles and the Rise of Commentary[253]

In our discussion of the third century we have emphasized, naturally, those fields in which evidence is more abundant – so, philosophy and Christian commentary. But the impact of the third century would be primarily as a hiatus: it could have been felt even more acutely in fields that had less continuity (and, so, less probability of stability via sheer inertia). It is especially useful, then, to see how the fields, left mostly barren through the third century, flourish again in the fourth.

---

[253] The central claim of this section – that authorship, in late antiquity, was pursued primarily through commentary – is not controversial (see, for instance, the sources cited in Montana, 2011: 114–15 n.25). The fact bears repeating, and it is worth emphasizing – as I shall do through this section, and as, I believe, is not usually emphasized – just how different this was from authorial culture up to 200 CE.

And so it is appropriate to take, as our starting point, the transformation of the exact sciences. I will follow the traditional dating of Pappus to about 320 (not much hangs on this for our purposes; he was surely a fourth-century author). If so, this marks a major turning point in the history of mathematics: no previous mathematicians were remotely like him.

There is very little in the mathematical culture, at any point prior to Pappus, suggestive of commentary or of what I call "deuteronomic culture". While mathematicians often refer to previous authors, they do so in their more discursive passages, and do so by distinguishing themselves critically from their predecessors. Menelaus aimed to improve on Theodosius, perhaps on Hipparchus – but did so implicitly;[254] Hypsicles, more explicitly, emphasized how much he improved upon Apollonius (as well as upon Aristaeus).[255] The one fully extant mathematical treatise, prior to Pappus, which is standardly labeled a "commentary"[256] – Hipparchus on Aratus' *Phaenomena* – has in fact nothing to do with commentary and is simply an extended critique of the poet by the astronomer;[257] it is impossible to say what the form of Theodosius' own alleged commentary on Archimedes' *Method* was:[258] nothing else of the kind is suggested for any other advanced work in mathematics, but, given all the surrounding evidence, the simplest account is that Theodosius criticized Archimedes. (The *Method* was a risk-taking work, right at the edge of the pre-calculus; there was a great deal to criticize, if one so wished, about its mathematical rigor.)[259] Now, Euclid's *Elements* did become, to a limited extent, part of the educational syllabus, and so the authors discussed in section 6.3

[254] So implicitly that we are left unsure as to Menelaus' actual originality (Sidoli, 2004; this may well have been the intention, Menelaus seeking to emphasize, as far as possible, his own achievement), which brings out how little authors such as Menelaus cared about their presentation of their indebtedness to the past.

[255] Netz (2009: 93–6) (in which I still take it as settled that Hypsicles was a Hellenistic, not an Imperial author. I am now less sure; see p. 444 above.).

[256] As noted in n.140 above, there is an anonymous astronomical treatise extant in fragmentary form from the early third century, which refers to yet other previous treatises, including one by Artemidorus (to which this is the only attestation). Both the anonymous fragmentary treatise and that by Artemidorus have been described by some past scholarship as "commentary to the Almagest", but that by Artemidorus is a critique while the anonymous treatise is merely an introductory survey of astronomy. (For all of this, see Jones, 1990.)

[257] Netz (2009: 168–71): that this is not a commentary is made even clearer by this subject matter, as, in fact, as a canonical poet, Aratus had gained grammarian commentaries already by Hipparchus' time – entirely different from Hipparchus'!

[258] The *Suda*, s.v. Theodosius (Θ 1443): "Philosopher. He wrote Spherics in three books, a Commentary on the summaries of Theudas, On Days and Nights [in] two [books], a Commentary on the Method of Archimedes, Specifications of Houses in three books, Investigatory summaries, Astrological matters, On Habitations."

[259] Of course, another account could be that the *Suda* confused two Theodosii, of whom the commentator was much later (I put this in a footnote so as to reduce the risk of being charged for my circular reasoning; but, in truth, this is the account I find the likeliest).

above – teachers, seeking the status of elite authors – could write on Euclid in a more sophisticated manner; and this is the context for the one likely example of mathematical commentary preceding late antiquity, which is Hero's commentary to Euclid's *Elements* (now extant only in Al-Nayrizi's mediated Arabic version; Hero's definitions, clearly belonging to the same project, are extant in Greek in a form heavily mediated in medieval Byzantium. The many transformations of such texts are telling: Hero's writings were heavily transformed by a reception that needed a more evidently "teacherly" text.).[260] Previous mathematicians tended away from the discursive and metatextual, emphasizing the textual closure of proof.[261] Thus, even Ptolemy – who is much more "philosophical", and so much more discursive – is really very spare in his metatextual statements, bringing in a very small group of cited authors and generally remaining very close to the technical material at hand, thus frustrating his many scholars today, who, as noted on page 674 above, cannot really place him as a thinker.

With Pappus, however, mathematics becomes entirely metatextual. His text brings in an entire mathematical society – the by now obligatory 30 or so cited authorities.[262] This is not auto-prosopography, in the sense that Pappus does not detail much recent mathematical work (because, I suspect, there was so little). Nonetheless, Pappus does provide us with a clear sense of a contemporary setting.[263] There is the protreptic element, in this case persuading the students of philosophy that they should study mathematics instead. And there are clear references to the context of teaching. An extant treatise (Book III of the so-called *Collection*) is dedicated to a critique of a rival teacher, Pandrosion.[264] She taught mathematics – so Pappus complains – in ways

---

[260] See pp. 672–3 above for Hero's relation to mathematical pedagogy (for Al-Nayrizi, see Bello, 2003).

[261] This is one of the themes of Netz (1999a: chap. 3).

[262] See p. 745 above: I count 33 in Pappus.

[263] The definitive account of Pappus in his context is Cuomo (2000), which I largely follow here. For the elements of anti-philosophical protreptic, see chapter 2; for the rival teacher Pandrosion, see chapter 4; for the episode of Euclid and Apollonius, see pages 196–9. (While Pappus does not confront rhetoric as directly as he does philosophy, Bernard, 2003, has shown the rhetorical background assumed in Pappus' project.)

[264] There is no question that this is a female name, which makes her nearly unique, though with one important parallel: the famous Hypatia, yet another female teacher of mathematics active in Alexandria later than Pappus and Pandrosion (she was killed in 415; her father, the mathematical teacher Theon of Alexandria, is dated astronomically to the 360s – was there more or less continuous teaching of mathematics in Alexandria through the fourth century?). Eunapius, *Lives of the Sophists and the Philosophers* 466–71, tells us of Sosipatra, yet another contemporary female scholar (a Platonist philosopher, apparently), perhaps consciously having the more famous Hypatia in mind (Penella, 1990: 61–2). Authorial status was always at least suggestive of the performative, and so was not available to women, as long as performance was understood to be public (women could be imagined as performing in the closed, aristocratic circles of the archaic symposium,

wrong not merely in terms of geometrical but also in terms of historical decorum, in that her procedures did not conform to established, canonical classifications of problems. Pappus' detailed critique, long on examples, seems to put on display not just mathematical correctness but, I would suggest, Pappus' views concerning the correct way of *teaching* mathematics ("There; *that's* how one should teach!"). When discussing Apollonius, Pappus was scathing – criticizing Apollonius for acting impolitely towards Euclid, even though Apollonius himself had studied with Euclid's own pupils! Surely Pappus had no specific knowledge of the teaching relationship between Euclid and Apollonius: he was imposing, on the Hellenistic past, his contemporary understanding of a teacherly circle. Of course Hellenistic mathematicians would criticize each other heavily; Pappus would need a different construct, of a mathematical canon that could be harmonized together, always following the same, established rules. Hence Pappus' explicit engagement with classifications and definitions: problems should be solved in particular ways, according to their type as plane, solid and linear problems (a classification which may well be original to Pappus); proofs should be presented in the modes of analysis, or of synthesis (such practices precede Pappus, but his explicit definition may be original). The structures of Greek mathematical texts begin to be defined – because they begin to be taught in a school environment.[265]

Practically everything attested for Pappus is a variation on the theme of mathematical commentary. We have from him the remains of a commentary on Ptolemy's *Almagest* (from books V and VI),[266] as well as an Arabic version of a commentary on Euclid's *Elements*, book X (this is Euclid's theory of irrationals, a particularly opaque project; this surely did not form part of Euclid's reception in the elementary classroom). Of the seven books now extant (sometimes only in mutilated form) from among his so-called *Collection*, only one was an explicit commentary (Book II, a

---

however). Perhaps with this least performative genre of mathematics – with the new, textualized understanding of teaching – gender barriers could, for once, be overcome.

[265] I pass all of this briefly: the way in which "deuteronomic" writings impose greater structure and unity on mathematical practice has been the main theme of Netz (1998b; 2004b), and I have described Pappus' classifications, specifically, in Netz (1998b: 271); Pappus' originality with regard to the method of analysis and synthesis has not been generally considered in the significant literature on the subject, which often simply takes Pappus as its guide, as if he was heir to a continuous tradition of reflective commentary on mathematical practice; I have been skeptical concerning this in Netz (2000a). Recent scholarship that tries to locate the significance of ancient analysis within the terms of ancient mathematical practice itself (Saito and Sidoli, 2010; 2012) does not conform to the classification produced by Pappus himself.

[266] About 60,000 words are extant, from the commentary on two out of 13 books: the original would surely have gone into hundreds of thousands of words.

commentary on a lost, abstruse work by Apollonius). Pappus' preferred mode in this collection was the making of ad hoc textual canons produced out of a compendium of ancient works. In Books VI and VIII he produced compendia of astronomy and of mechanics, respectively; in Book VII he produced a compendium of the procedure of analysis; Books III, IV and V were more varied collections arranged by themes (in Book III, Pandrosion's false teaching provides Pappus with an excuse to survey solutions to a certain problem; in Book IV, Pappus classifies problems and solutions in a gradual ascent, as described by Sefrin-Weis, 2010; in Book V, the theme is provided by the solids of Plato's *Timaeus*: appropriate to a protreptic, addressing philosophers). Besides all of this, a discursive *Geography* by Pappus is attested – in a very mediated form – in Armenian translation.[267] The most natural way to understand this is as the vestiges of a commentary, or perhaps re-edition, of some sort, based on Ptolemy's own *Geography* (which was not discursive – and whose geographical indications are indeed assumed in the Armenian text).[268] Everything in Pappus' project is about edition, definition, classification and compilation. Bernard sums this up neatly (EANS s.v.): "Pappos' scientific contribution consisted not in any substantial innovation but in the way he used, organized, and compared an impressive mass of scientific texts." This is surely correct – and reminiscent of the somewhat exasperated judgement made of Porphyry by his modern scholars. We do not have Pappus' precise biography, but the few hints we possess, taken together with the corpus, suggest an intellectual project similar to that of Porphyry: seeking followers and leading them in the reading of a newly formed mathematical canon.[269]

---

[267] Hewsen (1971).

[268] Hewsen (1971: 189) translates the Armenian redactor introducing the passages based on Pappus thus: "We thus begin after the Geography of Pappus of Alexandria, who followed the circuit of the particular map of Claudius Ptolemy, beginning his measurements from the Torrid Zone to the north and south."

[269] Pappus is better understood than the few other authors we have in the mathematical fields from late antiquity; but it should be noted that nearly all the texts known from late antiquity in the exact sciences seem to belong to similar projects, producing commentaries and compendia. A typical product is the small compendium to Optics, by Damianus of Larissa (Schöne, 1897: 2–22). More substantial are Theon's commentaries to Ptolemy, and perhaps his re-editions of Euclidean works; the commentaries and re-editions by his daughter, Hypatia, are lost (for Theon and Hypatia, see s.vv. EANS). With Theon and Hypatia we are already moving into a cultural setting in which the teaching of the exact sciences is folded into the teaching of Neoplatonist philosophy (Porphyry, already, led the way there). The bulk of the extant work in the exact sciences from late antiquity belongs in this tradition: Proclus' extant commentary to Euclid's *Elements* I (and the lost one by Simplicius), Marinus' commentary to the *Data* and finally – now emerging with much greater mathematical competence and ambition – Eutocius' commentaries to Archimedes and to Apollonius.

We note the emphasis, in Pappus, on collecting and arranging works (the astronomical works, the works "on analysis"). This is the teacher, the broker of texts – and also, quite simply, the collector. Book teaching as well as book collecting continued, through the third century, as elite cultural patronage collapsed: part of the background to the very textual, library-making project of Caesarea. Just as Pamphilus was eager to create a Christian library, Pappus was creating a mathematical library.

A generation later we see Oribasius creating a *medical* library. Compared with Pappus, we have a richer – though by no means unequivocal – picture of Oribasius' life. He belonged simultaneously to a small intellectual circle of friends, and to the world of Imperial patronage. Such were the special circumstances of Julian's court.[270] As noted on page 711 above, it is only with Oribasius that we begin to find evidence for medicine after Galen. What does it look like?

Several works are ascribed to Oribasius,[271] but the only safe attributions are, indeed, the medical works.

(1) An *Epitome of Galen* (in 25 books, apparently!) addressed to Julian the emperor (now known only through its introduction, quoted by Photius: *Cod.* 216).

(2) *The Medical Collections*, an epitome, arranged by subject matter, of all useful medical authors (! – in 70 or 72 books), which – according to Oribasius' introduction – was also, incredibly, addressed to Julian (was the entire work completed in less than two years?).

Extant are also the following.

(3) A nine-book epitome of *The Medical Collections*, addressed to Oribasius' son Eustathius (who, himself, obtained the status of *archiatros*: so, is this the epitome used for actual medical education?).

(4) A four-book epitome of *The Medical Collections*, addressed to Eunapius (was this intended for the amateurs?).[272]

[270] As a young man, Julian the Apostate attached himself to the Neoplatonist circle – ultimately traced to Iamblichus – which is the main subject of Eunapius' *Lives of the Philosophers and the Sophists*; as he got closer to power, the living members of this circle became part of the court (these historical facts are fairly uncontroversial; see, e.g., Bowersock, 1978: 28–9). Oribasius became a subject of a biography by Eunapius (*Lives of the Philosophers and the Sophists* 498–9), and dedicated to him one of his own works; he was also a physician – and more – to Julian (see Baldwin, 1975, who suggests (89–90) that the doctor could have become a full political actor, complicit in the plot that brought the apostate to the throne).
[271] See, in particular, Janiszewski (2006: 382–90) for the evidence concerning Oribasius as a historian.
[272] Eunapius describes a scene in which Oribasius advises, correctly, against the treatment proposed by a group of doctors, as "the author of this work is not unknowledgeable in medicine": not a

The very layering – an epitome, epitomized in turn according to audiences – is reminiscent of the layers of commentary found in authors such as Origen and Porphyry. Oribasius also assumes, to an extent, something like a canon, and something like a master – the person, and corpus, of Galen;[273] but it is noteworthy that his project is of epitomizing, not of commentary. In the few cases in which we see him speaking for himself, in the introductions, he addresses in a more Imperial fashion – indeed, even to the emperor himself. Patronage, you may say, took over. Or, perhaps, the other way around: what we find is that, by the second half of the fourth century, even a patron such as an emperor would ask not for the embellishment of original work but, instead, for a textual, nearly pedagogical compilation. The assumptions of the teacherly circle have taken over. We never find the likes of Galen from later in antiquity, and the genre of medicine, hitherto diverse – indeed, often nearly literary in its style and intended audiences – is from now on reduced to compilations in the manner of Oribasius (of which there are two more extant examples)[274] and, much more frequently, commentaries in the narrow sense (on Hippocrates, but even more on Galen). As with compilations, the extant evidence derives mostly from a considerably later date (not earlier than the fifth century; most, in fact, seem to derive from the years 550 to 650). They do, of course, derive from a well-defined school context which seems to be almost confined to Alexandria.[275] The Arabic tradition

---

physician himself, but an amateur (*Lives of the Philosophers and the Sophists* 504–5). There was also a one-book epitome (so, Nutton, 2004: 302).

[273] This is a cliché of the scholarship (so, for instance, Grant, 1997: 15, talks about "preoccupation with and reverence for Galen. . .his master"), and it is often suggested that Oribasius could have been attracted to Galen because they both came from the same city, Pergamon (Baldwin, 1975: 87). Van der Eijk (2015b: 197) emphasizes that Oribasius quotes authors who were severely criticized by Galen, suggesting an attitude different from that of the unquestioning follower. Oribasius' compilations are, generally speaking, so undiscursive that we are left in the dark concerning his basic approach.

[274] By Aetius and Paul of Aegina, both much later Byzantine authors; for the genre of the medical compilations a whole, see van der Eijk (2010).

[275] Extant are commentaries by Asclepius, John and Palladius, all of Alexandria; and Stephanus of Athens – born there but teaching in Alexandria – as well as commentaries attributed (much less securely) to Gessius of Petra, "Petra" once again being merely his birthplace (for all, see s.v. EANS). There likely was, in the city, something like an established medical faculty: "Much more than, say, Beirut with law, Alexandria became synonymous with doctors and medical studies" (Duffy, 1984: 21). We see a similar development with philosophy, which is perhaps how we should understand the archaeological findings of an institution of teaching, in Alexandria, from the early Byzantine period: Derda, Markiewicz and Wipszycka (2007); Cribiore (2015: 157–8). As cultural life became strictly associated with the practice of teaching, there emerged something akin to the institution of a university.

knows a collection it refers to as the"Summaries of the Alexandrians", a set of commentaries on canonical works by Galen; these are a form of teaching with careful attention to visual-textual aids, with many tabular and diagrammatic representations of the contents, including the use of branching tree diagrams for the representation of intellectual contents (it was late ancient medical education, then, apparently, that had invented Porphyry's tree).[276] We may have a glimpse of the very late tradition of medical commentary in a sixth-century papyrus codex; the extant text (the *Aphorisms*) contains a set of scholia.[277] In this case, it is clear that the tradition extends much earlier, since we have fragments of two different papyrus codex commentaries to Hippocratic works, both dated by their most recent editors to the late third century or early fourth.[278] Remarkably, these are already codices (the teacherly context may explain this early adoption of the medium), and – alongside a commentary on Thucydides – are the earliest of the commentaries on codex now known.[279]

Of course, commentary has grammarian origins; and grammarian it mostly remains. We have just noted the two medical commentaries, now extant as fragments of codices from late antiquity. Otherwise, *all* late ancient commentaries surviving on codex are on the central canon (Thucydides, as noted above; and then Callimachus [two], Aristophanes [two], Demosthenes, Homer and Euripides). And yet, in the fourth century, the teaching of mathematics and medicine in Alexandria is well attested; so where are the grammarians? They are still there – but they seem to have become, strictly speaking, teachers, no longer seeking to mark themselves as, primarily, grammarian *authors*. I have argued above that we no longer find grammarian authors in the third century, and pointed out that we can, nonetheless, reconstruct the presence of the teachers of grammar – throughout the Empire – from the implications of the biographies of the well educated. This remains true in the fourth century as well. This time, however, we can plot this with the aid of a much more expansive set of sources (which allow us to reconstruct not just the presence of grammarian-teachers but even their names and something of their

---

[276] Unless, of course, these are introduced by the Arabic tradition; see the careful discussion in Savage-Smith (2002: 122–5), who is ultimately inclined to a late ancient, Greek origin.

[277] P.Ant. 3. 183. For an analysis of the origins of this text, and more observations on medical commentary on papyrus, see Andorlini (2000).

[278] P.Ryl. 3.530; P.Flor. 2. 115.     [279] Stroppa (2009).

biographies).[280] On the other hand, we have nearly no traces of original grammarian authorship in the fourth century.[281]

The fourth-century grammarian whose identity we can understand most clearly is Palladas, an author of epigrams heavily represented in the *Palatine Anthology* (AP).[282] These are the poems of a frustrated schoolmaster. Indeed, in general, teachers of grammar who wish to make a name for themselves now do so not so much in their new works of *grammar* but, rather, in (more or less occasional) poetry; the obvious parallel, in Latin, is that of Ausonius (see page 733 above). Perhaps this might be the background against which we need to understand the rise of a new tradition of poetry in late ancient Egypt (see page 190, note 181, above). Meanwhile, in the fourth century itself, the only possible counter-example – that is, the only credible case of a grammarian authoring a grammarian treatise – is the poorly dated Theodosius,[283] author of an extant "Introductory Canons to

---

[280] I went through all the fourth-century grammarians listed in Kaster (1988) (references are to Kaster's catalogue numbers). Ammonius (Kaster 10) and Helladius (Kaster 67) taught the Church historian Socrates. Cleobulus (Kaster 32) and Didymus (Kaster 46) taught Libanius, who also mentions Eudaemon (Kaster 210), probably a grammarian-teacher, and further singles out the good grammatical education of Harpocration (Kaster 226), as well as of yet another Eudaemon (Kaster 55): if at all grammarian, these last two certainly were not the authors of original commentaries (they might have been rhetors, though). Isidore of Pelusion sent letters to two teachers of grammar: Agathodaemon (Kaster 3) and Ophelius (Kaster 109). Diocles (Kaster 206) might have been, at most, a teacher before becoming a monk; Apollinarius (Kaster 14) is referred to by historical sources as a grammatical teacher and as the father of a heresiarch of the same name. (Yet another Helladius, Kaster 227, was definitely a poet rather than a grammarian; finally, I do not list the fourth-century grammarians attested on documentary papyri, who are all, of course, teachers.) Even in Alexandria, the grammarians have become the teachers of grammar – which is, of course, the general conclusion of Kaster (1988), with its emphasis on the "mediocrity" (in the social sense) of the late ancient grammarian.

[281] Perhaps already early in the fifth century we find two individuals who are attested (both by the *Suda*) as authors of more ambitious, original contributions. Both taught first at Alexandria and then at Constantinople. One is Orus (Kaster 111: a large corpus of "grammatical" – not commentary – work); the other is Horapollon (Kaster 77: commentaries on Alcaeus, Homer, Sophocles). There is something of a Byzantine authorial tradition from this point onwards (see, in general, Matthaios, 2015: 266–73), but it should be noted that this group – Byzantine grammarians – must be among the best-attested groups of individuals from antiquity. The *Suda*, our central source on this group, knows them well: it is, in fact, their direct heir. So, even the few we do find are probably not a small survival of a much larger group. (Incidentally, there is no reason to date Seleucus of Emesa [Kaster 253] to late antiquity: in all likelihood this is an author of the Second Sophistic.)

[282] Of Palladas' epigrams, perhaps 150 are extant, easily the best preserved of all the poets of the *Anthology* (this is recency bias in action). Just which precisely were his poems, and how they got to be copied into the AP, is debated; see Lauxtermann (1997) (arguing, against Averil Cameron, 1993: 78–96, that Palladas' collection did not survive directly into Byzantium). Palladas has been traditionally dated to the late fourth century; Wilkinson (2009) suggests he could be an early fourth-century author instead – the contemporary of Pappus rather than of Hypatia.

[283] Kaster 152. He can be dated only if we assume that he is identical with another grammarian Theodosius (Kaster 151), who is mentioned in a letter by Synesius (Hypatia's student and friend). But, in fact, Theodosius is as common a name as one could find in late ancient Alexandria.

Verb and Noun Declension" – a comically teacherly title, and, indeed, this work is no more than an epitome of the rules of inflection, taken out of Dionysius Thrax.

In fact, it is a bit misleading to represent this text by Theodosius as so unusual. The only thing special about this grammatical epitome is that it happens to have a genuine name attached to it. (Compare the case of Dionysius Thrax' *Techne*, whose authenticity was debunked by Di Benedetto, 1958 [see pages 473–4 above] – that is, a nameless epitome, circulating in late antiquity, received a misleading title with a misleading authorship.) We reach here a central feature of the transformation of Greek grammar into late antiquity and Byzantium. While the ancient grammarians are reasonably well attested as names, they are also among the least-preserved authors of antiquity. This is not because the ancient literary commentary was useless to Byzantium but, to the contrary, because it was too useful. The literary canon continued to be valued and, above all, studied, and so ancient grammar was not so much transmitted, in a passive way, but, rather, used and reused in forms most useful for the process of teaching. For this reason, a considerable fraction of ancient grammar is now extant on the margins of the canonical works, as fragmentary scholia.[284] The most important are those to Homer, and it has long been suspected that our key piece of evidence for ancient grammar – the sophisticated set of scholia preserved in the Venetus A codex of the *Iliad* – derives from a compilation that took four major Imperial-era commentators (Erbse, 1969: xi–xii) and turned them into a single epitome (this, indeed, is reminiscent of both Pappus and Oribasius). This hypothetical work – titled by modern scholarship the *Viermännerkommentar* – is certainly early Byzantine, perhaps as early as the fourth century. We do not know: the absence of the named author(s) responsible for such compilations makes it harder to date and to place such activity. We do not know who the grammarianist Oribasii were. But activity – of a new, non-authorial kind – went on.

But, surely, the most typical attitude towards literature became more, not less, grammarian-like. Grammatical education, traditionally, was meant to lead the student from reading to performance. Grammarian reading processes were a ladder to a performance-based outcome. And performance, indeed, was the semiotic implication of the papyrus roll, the

---

[284] For the vexed question of the history of scholiography, see p. 712, n.148, above; enough to recall that most scholars, today, see the collections of scholia as mainly a late ancient development (with or without their placement as marginalia).

self-effacing medium that did not seek attention to itself, encouraging its reader to consider, instead, the implied projected performative experience.

One could, occasionally, transpose performative poetry into the codex format, but this was when one did not try to experience it by projecting its performativity but, instead, sought merely to *study* it. Our evidence is tiny, but it is suggestive. We have two early codices of Euripides: P.Oxy. 47.3321, a fragment of *Phoenician Women*, is dated to the late second century or the early third century; P.Berol. 13217, a parchment (!) codex of the Cretans, dated by Cavallo to the third century (previous editors assigned earlier dates). These two are by far the earliest of Euripides on codex. Carrara (1994: 47) has noted concerning P.Oxy. 47.3321 that the only obvious parallel to this version of Euripides, in terms of its text, is a private copy (P.Oxy. 47.3322), and the impression one gets is that this codex, too, could be some sort of schoolmaster's collection; it is interesting that P.Berol. 13217 carries marginalia. The canonical performative text could have, occasionally, been brought to the codex – when it was reduced to the schoolmaster's tool of trade.

This is indeed the clear implication of the very pattern of survival of the canon into early Byzantium and beyond. The most obvious example is the archaeological survival comparison between Menander and Aristophanes (number of fragments by date, in either papyrus or parchment).

|          | Menander | Aristophanes | M/A ratio (rounded to 0.5) |
|----------|----------|--------------|-----------------------------|
| 200–250  | 30       | 5            | 6                           |
| 251–300  | 30       | 8            | 4                           |
| 301–350  | 9        | 11           | 1                           |
| 351–400  | 10       | 10           | 1                           |
| 401–450  | 6        | 20           | 0.5                         |
| 451–500  | 7        | 16           | 0.5                         |
| 501–550  | 5        | 4            | 1                           |
| 551–600  | 2        | 9            | 0                           |

Obviously, the samples are tiny, but the overall picture is clear – as is its historical meaning. Aristophanes was never in the small-library canon, and it seems that acquaintance with him was always of a more "literary", mediated nature. Mosaics showing scenes from Menander's comedies are fairly common in Imperial villas,[285] while Aristophanes is never attested

---

[285] See Csapo (2010: chap. 5); an archaeological survey is in Gutzwiller and Çelik (2012: 580).

visually later than the classical vases.[286] In short, scholars assume that there was no performance tradition of Aristophanes, while Menander – perhaps even more than Euripides – was the byword for performance as such. On the other hand, it is clear that ancient scholarship, especially from the Imperial era onwards, engaged closely with Aristophanes' text,[287] as the best witnesses to "genuine" Attic speech[288] and as an intriguing interpretative puzzle (since the jokes require so much historical context).[289] Perhaps these two authors, Menander and Aristophanes, can be taken, then, as indices for two uses of canonical literature: as the launchpad for the projection of imagined performances; or as the target of scholarly, teacherly engagement. The archaeological survival tells the story of imagined performances as dominant through the end of the third century; the fourth century is balanced between the canon as performance – which is still very much alive – and the canon as teacherly document, which now emerges to occupy center place; from the fifth century onwards the Greek canon is an object of study; and, by the sixth century, the Byzantines are already, in this respect, our contemporaries.

Reducing ancient commentaries into collections of scholia is, in a sense, a reflection of the basic practice of the self-consciously textual, the "deuteronomic": taking old texts and transforming them into new ones. (The same practice will become widespread with biblical commentary as well, for which the collections of scholia are referred to as "catenae": once again, because of the popularity of this form, many early commentaries, from Origen onwards, are no longer directly available.)[290] This is expressed even in literary form, in the genre of the cento. A cento is a poem constructed out of previous "source" poetry. The rule of the game is that one is allowed to write only with complete lines or half-lines from the source poetry, rearranging them to form one's own poetry. Naturally, the ideal source should be big (so as to possess sufficient material) and canonical (in composing a cento, one's source must be readily available to memory;

---

[286] See p. 197 above.

[287] The most significant corpus of scholia, other than that of Homer (Dickey, 2007: 28–31).

[288] The most restrictive of the Atticist lexicographers – Moeris – relied on Aristophanes alone among the dramatists (avoiding all the tragedians! See Strobel, 2009: 102.). In this Aristophanes was favored simply as the most significant representative of old comedy, which, in general, enjoyed enormous scholarly attention (to the detriment of middle comedy, which remains, for this reason, entirely neglected in our sources). Even Galen wrote commentaries on old comedy (*On My Own Books* XIX.48 K)!

[289] Readers complained (Plutarch, *Table-Talk* 712a): you need a grammarian for each reference!

[290] See McNamee (1995: 406) and references therein; the catenae (in the narrow sense of collections of scholia excerpted from past commentaries, whether or not adjusted to the margins of main texts) seem to emerge through the fifth century.

this is aside from the obvious semiotic and cultural meanings of the canon). As a consequence, nearly all centos are based on either Homer or Virgil. The genre was not invented in late antiquity; there are traces of the cento technique from earlier than that: Hellenistic? Late Republican? Surely, Imperial.[291] But, aside from the second-century CE Latin cento of Hosidius Geta, all the extant centos – and there are plenty – are from late antiquity.[292] As noted there might be a certain bias for the preservation of centos, but, even so, the extent of the late ancient corpus of such works is remarkable, and it suggests that at least a large minority of late ancient poets experimented with the form. It was thus not some kind of novelty experiment but, to the contrary, one of the marks of poetic ability: to be able to produce, deuteronomically, new texts from old. Literature as teacherly book excerpting/collecting, rebrokering the canon.

The habits of excerpting-and-collecting are everywhere. We recall Oribasius, and his medical epitomes. Indeed, laymen do not need much theory; give them the remedies. Marcellus "the Empiricist" (a modern nickname), probably a citizen of Burdigalia from the turn of the fourth century, is the author of *De Medicamentis*. A generation later than Ausonius, he belongs to the same literary circle (and mentions some of the dramatis personae of Ausonius' grammarian world): he does *not* identify himself as a physician and is best understood simply as an encyclopedist – and, like Oribasius, an author emerging from the court (he was apparently in the service of the emperor Theodosius I). The work is formed primarily by a collection from past medical authorities (especially Scribonius Largus, a first-century Roman physician who wrote in Latin), excerpting just the remedies to various ailments, organized according to body part (obviously, from head to toe).[293] A similar encyclopedic project

---

[291] Quintilian, *Inst.* 6,3,96, reports that Ovid wrote a cento using the verses of a fellow poet, Macer (a parody? A compliment?). He could well have come across this idea independently, but, then again, it is likely enough that such a practice could have Hellenistic antecedent. Perhaps all that is involved in such cases, however, is merely short-form, occasional poetry assembled from famous lines, which is well attested in the second century (Rondholz, 2012: 5–13). It clearly belongs to the world of rhetorical exercise. The first attested full-scale cento (Virgil ➜ Medea), by the second-century Hosidius Geta, is extant, which is not surprising: there is a very large corpus of surviving centos – 16 in Latin alone! (McGill, 2005). This is the kind of literature that would very naturally be transmitted when it is professional grammarians who do the transmitting.

[292] The non-Christian Virgil tradition – the core of our evidence, with 12 examples – is surveyed in McGill (2005); Sandness (2011) studies Christian centos from the perspective of their specific function for Christians (so as to accommodate the pagan canon within a Christian worldview), while Usher (1998) is a study of the Greek cento by Eudocia – written with a highly optimistic view of the extent to which the cento form still carried the resonance of Homeric performances.

[293] Its introduction is a small anthology of seven letters by medical authorities (one is reminded of the use of the letter form in contemporary veterinary medicine): so, another evocation of a small circle

is that of Epiphanius (active in Constantinople near the end of the fourth century), caring for souls rather than bodies: his *Panarion* (literally, *Medicine Chest*) is an encyclopedia of the refutation of all past heresies.[294] Excerpting is the useful thing to do. Cetius Faventinus produced an epitome of Vitruvius (removing all the rhetorical flourishes and adding some more practical information), and he was in turn among the (several) authors epitomized by Rutilius Palladius, who wrote on agriculture, excerpting materials from past authors and then arranging it, in books 2 to 13 of his massive compilation (which was arranged according to the months in which information becomes useful: Vitruvius, gradually transformed into an almanac). The dates are difficult to establish for either excerptor. The conditions assumed by Palladius (a secure Roman west) cannot be later than the early fifth century; Faventinus must be earlier than Palladius; he is also familiar with concrete-based architecture. Both are now usually assumed to be fourth-century authors – in which century they will be accompanied by a great many Latin epitomators.[295] Especially in the field of history: Aurelius Victor, a major political figure (a governor of Pannonia, later prefect of the city of Rome) wrote the *Historiae Abbreviatae*, composed by stringing together thumbnail biographies of the emperors; almost immediately this was turned, by an unknown author, into the *Epitome de Caesaribus*, an even shorter handbook of Roman history arranged by rulers. And then: Eutropius' history was commissioned – per the dedication – by the emperor Valens (we are reminded of Julian, whom Oribasius portrays as the commissioner – not merely the dedicatee – of his compilation: clearly, at any rate, Eutropius did serve in the court as *magister memoriae*). Titled *Breviarium*, this is truly short: it covers the entire history of Rome, from the foundation of the city to the author's own days, in about 20 words per year. Festus was Eutropius' immediate follower as *magister memoriae* – and produced his own *Breviarium*, this time arranged in a thematic order.[296] It is probably at about this time that Justinus' epitome of

---

of authorities (in the year 512 this idea will be visualized in the famous image of seven medical authors with Galen in their center: Vienna Cod. Med. Gr. 1 3v). In general for Marcellus, see the especially thorough entry s.v. EANS.

[294] Kim (2010): the *Panarion* is a collective biography of heresiarchs, a kind of inverted mirror image of the many Christian auto-prosopographic works from Eusebius onwards, but, this time, conceived as a medical analogy. While precise dating is impossible, the medieval genre of the *Physiologus* (a Christianized encyclopedia of exotic animal lore, excerpted and organized according to animals) could well have its roots in a similar context (Scott, 1998).

[295] The best introduction remains Plommer (1973).

[296] For this series of authors, see Bonamente (2003) (who suggests that the emphasis on brevity may derive from exigencies of the political careers of such authors! Indeed, those historical epitomes are remarkable for their miniature scale: no Oribasius, there.).

Pompeius Trogus was written.[297] Clearly, the making of Latin epitomes was a major form of the late fourth century, and it is this fact that has led past scholars to assume that the (extant) epitome of Livy, the *Periochae*, is also from the late fourth century: a sound probabilistic argument, though, in this case, it has to be admitted that epitomes of Livy's *Ab Urbe Condita* were produced even earlier (it is definitely a very big work).[298]

Such historical digests are already reminiscent, in both form and function, of the famous legal *Digesta* itself. Here we see the court directly commissioning the production of epitomes. The need for a legal epitome of some sort would appear self-evident to us, but it seems that through most of antiquity lawyers had to rely on capacious libraries and a powerful memory (it is for a reason that the law school was institutionalized so early).[299] Collections of law appear only in the late third century: the *Codex Gregorianus* and the *Codex Hermogenianus* were both produced under Diocletian and were apparently expanded periodically through the fourth century, then expanded yet again on a much larger scale, early in the fifth century, into the *Codex Theodosianus*. All these are collections of law as produced by emperors, not collections of legal theory as produced by lawyers: such a collection was envisaged by Theodosius but achieved only by Justinian. To recall (page 713 above): about 1,500 rolls by 38 legal authors were divided into three subcommittees, which read through them and excerpted the passages that were seen as relevant precedent for future legal practice; the entire compilation, in 50 books, was produced in three years, from 530 to 533[300] (we are reminded of Oribasius, producing 70 or 72 books of medical epitome, in less than two years; was it committee work in his case, too?). As emphasized by Turpin (1987), none of this is produced out of sheer intellectual curiosity: these are all administrative documents produced for the state. This brings us back to the case of the historical

---

[297] Syme (1988).
[298] Begbie (1967: 337). Generally, for the ancient condensing of texts, see Horster and Reitz (2010): their examples from before late antiquity are usually of a grammarian character, such as the hypotheses to drama. This is an interesting parallel (and reminds us of the manner in which late antiquity involved, in a sense, a grammarization of culture as a whole), but we should note that such examples involve not the turning of a text to another but, rather, the addition of a paratext to a text that, in itself, remains stable.
[299] Our lawyers primarily deal with the drafting and parsing of written documents such as contracts. The ancient world was different. The law handled interactions that happened in a face-to-face world – contracts did not have to be written – and it was administered in a face-to-face setting (the law court, after all – even more than the public forum – was the prime habitat of rhetoric!): Riggsby (2010: 87–97).
[300] For an account, see Honoré (2010b).

epitomes, written in the court: we are by now indeed removed from the world of teacherly circles and back into the world of state and patronage. Within a literary system based on practical teaching, however, even history and the law – the areas of political debate par excellence – become deuteronomic, reduced to the making of new texts from old texts.

Books remain, above all, the instruments of teaching. The third-century practice sticks: each field is now a field of teaching, hence in need of a canon with its commentaries. We recall Porphyry, producing a commentary on Minucianus – possibly the first commentary on a rhetorical treatise. Porphyry led the way, but it would be other authors who would make it into the canon. Metrophanes, another third-century author, wrote a commentary on Hermogenes: this choice was preferred by posterity. Already Sopater, Iamblichus' pupil, had written another commentary to Hermogenes, and such commentaries accumulated through the fourth century until a well-defined canon of rhetorical teaching was formed, probably in the generation following Libanius (that is, right at the end of the century): this consisted of the *Progymnasmata* by Aphthonius (probably a late fourth-century work, and so the final addition to the canon) together with four works by Hermogenes. All rhetorical education would now be organized around this canon, with many commentaries produced on it. This should be emphasized: the rhetorical technē, as noted on page 592 above, was a very prolific genre, with hundreds of teachers of rhetoric trying to stand out through their own, original rhetorical curriculum. Ancient rhetoric was the field pitting individuals against each other, extemporizing, debating – and teaching according to their own, individual lights. It took a major transition – the transition to late antiquity – to turn this field into a *canon*.[301]

Porphyry's choice of Minucianus, as the canon of rhetoric, was a false start; Porphyry would be very effective in his own field of philosophy, however, defining it for many centuries to come. Iamblichus' project appears to have been very similar to that of Porphyry, and, indeed, it would be otiose to survey late ancient philosophical commentary further, as the case of philosophy is so clear, Porphyry's stamp so powerful. Between Porphyry and the Renaissance practically all philosophy around the Mediterranean would be a synthesis of Plato and Aristotle, pursued in teacherly circles whose main activity was the study of texts – primarily

---

[301] For an account of the canon of the teaching of rhetoric, see Kennedy (1980) (the main outline on page 185).

those of Aristotle – with commentaries.[302] We now take this stability for granted, but it was in fact in radical contrast to the ever-shifting pluralism of philosophical debate from Parmenides to Plotinus. Even the Athenian Hellenistic schools were, from time to time, sites of considerable experiment. (All schools, other than the Garden, went through major doctrinal and formal transformations through the third century and then again around the end of the second century; and there were four of them, not one!) Nor was this stability a matter of institutional continuity, not even among the philosophers of late antiquity. The continuity in the tradition of, say, Ammonius Saccas–Plotinus–Porphyry–Iamblichus was intellectual rather than institutional, each individual in this chain teaching separately, with different groups, in different locations.[303] In the late fourth century one could probably have found more than a single teacher of Platonism in Alexandria: likely Theon and his daughter Hypatia;[304] Eunapius, as noted above, reports several threads for Iamblichus' followers in the fourth century,[305] but there were other Neoplatonist teachers, as early as the fourth century.[306] There was a school in Athens from Plutarch to Damascius (over a century of various schools of institutional continuity, then, covering the long fifth century). The teachers of philosophy in Alexandria of the fifth century were, of course, in contact with the school in Athens and often studied there:[307] there was now, perhaps, a single network of pagan philosophy. But the institutions are well attested and are distinct. The persistence of content and form across those many reincarnations (which would, of course, go on into the Middle Ages) is a case of the persistence – so often witnessed in this book – not of institution but of

---

[302] A few useful surveys (just the three main linguistic traditions, and just for Aristotle): Falcon, s.v. Commentators on Aristotle, Stanford Encyclopedia of Philosophy (https://plato.stanford.edu/entries/aristotle-commentators/#Oth). For the Latin tradition, we have the database http://hiw.kuleuven.be/dwmc/al/editions/index.html#database. For Arabic, see Adamson (2012).

[303] Plotinus studied with Ammonius Saccas in Alexandria and then taught at Rome. Porphyry passed a major part of his career in Lilybaeum, and, if he did return to Rome, this was following a hiatus after the death of Plotinus. Iamblichus, Porphyry's follower, had his own school at Apamea, and then, as Eunapius states (*Lives of the Philosophers and the Sophists* 461–2, trans. Wright 1921): "When Iamblichus had departed from this world, his disciples were dispersed in different directions."

[304] Were Theon and Hypatia more like Pappus, or more like Porphyry? Their teaching of Ptolemy is extant, and a wider project of the editing and commenting upon the mathematical canon is attested as well (n.269 above). And yet the sources consistently refer to Hypatia as a *philosopher*, while the teaching of the mathematical canon is attested for many bona fide late ancient philosophers from Porphyry to Simplicius.

[305] Summed up in the stemma of Iamblichus' Diadoche (Goulet, 1989: 77): five distinct followers to Iamblichus.

[306] For the many schools of Alexandria in the fourth century, see Watts (2006: chap. 7).

[307] For a brief survey of the two schools, see, e.g., O'Meara (2003: 19–30).

genre. There was by now a well-defined canon, a well-defined manner of approaching it as a textual artifact.

The format of the commentary becomes well established, across many disciplines and, most importantly, within Christianity itself. Now, it should be emphasized that, through the fourth century, as the political power of the Church is expanded, so is the political aspect of Christian authorship: many Christian authors now are episcopal, and their written activity is now often occasioned directly by their institution. A considerable amount of this political engagement is "horizontal", addressed to the authors' peers within the Church as well as to political authorities. This activity produces, above all, the great corpora of Church letters, but also the documents occasioned by, for instance, the preparation and the wrapping up of synods.[308] At the same time, a large part of the activity of the episcopal author is addressed "vertically", to his community, which is now clearly understood as a community of learners, the teacherly circle writ large onto a city congregation (it is this understanding that distinguishes episcopal authors from the past political figures of the Mediterranean city). There would be the crash course – every year during Lent – preparing neophytes for their baptism (in the fourth century we have extant Cyril of Jerusalem's catechetical writings, produced for this course).[309] Above all, these authors *preach*: teaching week by week over many years. This can give rise to vast corpora (not even Porphyry taught that much, to so many): the TLG canon counts 411 works ascribed to John Chrysostom (admittedly, some might be spurious). The bulk of these are *homilies* – that is, fairly brief speeches taking a biblical passage as their starting point and drawing out its lesson. This is rhetoric, brought into the institutionalized teaching of the Church and understood through the teacherly mechanism of commentary. (Indeed, series of homilies can form a continuous commentary: Chrysostom took 67 homilies to cover Genesis, for instance.) The word of god, being used for teaching an entire community; little wonder that god is understood, in turn, as a *teacher*.[310] By the fourth century biblical exegesis was almost an obligatory genre for any ambitious Christian author: to be a Christian author was to be a teacher of Christ. Origen's Caesarea ended up shaping a Christian Mediterranean. Didymus the Blind had his own teacherly circle in Alexandria in the middle of the fourth century, with a massive oeuvre; as usual, most is lost, but several hundred

---

[308] For the political realities underlying such episcopal authorship, see Rapp (2013).

[309] Doval (2001) discusses the authenticity of these documents; Lages (1971) brings in Armenian documents that reveal the institutional setting for such teaching.

[310] See Rylaarsdam (2014), a study of Chrysostom's project as "divine pedagogy".

thousand words remain (arguably, this is the most ambitious grammarian project of that time and place).[311] Alexandria is central; but there are now such circles everywhere. There has been a tendency in the modern literature to divide early biblical exegesis into distinct camps ("the Alexandrians" are more allegorical, "the Antiochians" are more literal) – perhaps a simplistic construct.[312] Indeed, the practice of commentary tends to make the text, which you broker to your students, into a unified, monolithic source, from which all tensions are expunged.[313] But biblical exegetes, addressing each other, are still mostly polemical.[314] Greek habits die hard.

After all, the centrality of commentary as a cultural vehicle is not distinctively Christian. This has been plotted down to the basic generic properties. Hadot (1987) (expanded by Mansfeld, 1994; 1998) has recorded, in particular, the presence of a very specific introductory format, in which a teacher brokering a text would first go through a list of questions to be settled concerning it: so, for instance, its theme, utility, or more specifically textual questions such as authenticity, position in the corpus and subdivision into chapters. Her fundamental observation is that this system can be found not only in philosophical commentary but also in biblical commentary going back to Origen. The tendency of scholars such as Hadot and Mansfeld is to account for shared features, in a common origin, and so they deduce, from this coemergence of the genre of commentary among both Christians and pagans, the existence of prior (Hellenistic?) canons of commentary. In fact, there seems to be no evidence for such hypothetical origins,[315] and the near-simultaneous rise of the genre of commentary, in both pagan and Christian contexts, should be seen in the terms of a shared original late ancient development.

Let us pause to describe the development more precisely. We have seen two types of literary practice: commentary in the narrow sense; and, in the more general, practices that are more "textual": writing a cento, reading Aristophanes rather than Menander, producing epitomes. Such textual practices are often similar to commentary in the narrow sense, in two different ways: they often involve a close engagement with a source-text;

[311] Layton (2004). [312] Young (2003).
[313] We recall the harmony of Aristotle and Plato, emphasized by Porphyry and assumed, in different ways, by most philosophers in the centuries following. For the Christian assumption of the unity of the Bible, see Young (1997: part I).
[314] Indeed, these biblical exegetes were trained, specifically, in the dialectical techniques of rhetoric: Mitchell (2005).
[315] Mansfeld (1994; 1998) points to various introductory comments from extant Hellenistic and Imperial works, such as Apollonius' *Conics* or Galen's auto-bibliographic treatises. As I have argued in Netz (2000b), such comments are very different in character from those in late ancient commentaries: they have nothing to do with brokering a text to a circle of learners.

and they are often produced with an eye to an educational purpose. The two are interrelated, because education, in antiquity, did involve a close engagement with a source-text. It was the education of the grammarian, brokering the canon. Thus, we can sum up and say that, from the fourth century onwards – but beginning, as we saw, already with Porphyry, and indeed even with Origen – cultural life changed, to become more like teaching.

Throughout the book, I emphasize the role of the Greek canon in shaping cultural practice. As long as literature was understood primarily in terms of performance, the centrality of the canon made practitioners seek to become more like the individuals performing through the canon: authors set out to become, themselves, protagonists in the imagined polis of letters. Hence the seeking after a distinct, polemical voice, engaging critically with a handful of antagonists. The centrality of the canon made one wish to be like Socrates, like Demosthenes (but in a specialized genre, in which authorship was more open). It appears as if the canon kept its centrality in late antiquity, but that this centrality changed its meaning: performance receding in favor of the text itself, perhaps because of the foregrounding of the education as a context. Authors set out to mark themselves out, now not in their implied similarity to the protagonists of the canon but, instead, as being the master brokers of canonical texts, teachers leading along a group of followers.

In sections 6.5.1 to 6.5.2 I explained the rise of this attitude, in the specific setting of the crisis of the third century: very few authors, immersed in a sea of paideia; with patronage receding, they validate themselves, instead, through their self-understanding of a small society of learners. Hence the teacherly circles. The stability of the new cultural practice serves to support my argument, in that it shows that something deep did snap, through the third century. And yet it is also a difficulty for my account: the wider setting changed considerably into the fourth century – and yet the habits of the third century remained. Why was this, and, in general, how do we account for the stability of a new cultural mode, into late antiquity and beyond? Before I conclude this chapter, and this book, we need to understand this: the closure of antiquity.

### 6.5.4 *The Equilibrium, Punctuated: Into the Middle Ages*[316]

The cultural practice described in this section was induced, I argue, by the specific circumstances of the third century; but then it persisted, even when

---

[316] In part, this final section (even more than the preceding one) looks into evidence pertaining not only to the fourth century, but much further beyond – the fifth century and well into the Middle

those circumstances disappeared. In this section I begin by delineating a
model to account for this type of persistence, and then proceed to provide
some data in the model's support.

For the sake of my explanatory model, I finally need to bring in
Christianity. But we need to be clear about its precise position in the causal
network. Late antiquity was not made by Christianity; but Christianity was
part of what made late antiquity *stick*.

Chronologically, after all, it all begins with Origen: in Caesarea, barely
ordained; somewhat marginal, even within the Christian world. Origen
began his own literary project under the Severans, at a time when the likes
of Philostratus still conceived of cultural life in terms of Imperial chairs,
Imperial favors. But he was far away from patronage, to begin with.

We can add a little more to this. Teaching, in antiquity, always was
conceived as a triad: a *master*, brokering a *canonical text* to a small circle of
*pupils*. This is the reality underlying the stability of the canon, witnessed in
the first chapter. Paideia was about getting to a fixed point: knowing
Homer, Demosthenes, Menander well. It is thus natural that the more
cultural life was organized around the model of teaching, the more it would
be organized around the model of brokering canonical texts, its texts
assuming, then, the role of canon, and becoming ever more crucial as
textual artifacts.

Christianity, in this sense, was *ahead of the times*: it already was in
possession of its own new canon that went beyond the classical canon itself.

Even more. This much is known: by the end of the second century, at
the latest, the principle was established that Christians would keep their
canonical texts in the form of the codex.[317] (This is certainly true for Upper
Egypt, from which our – papyrological – evidence derives; but, as always,
there is no reason to think this region was exceptional in its book habits.)
The most fundamental thing about the codex was that it was *different*: so,
the new scripture was unlike Homer.[318] Difference also carries a meaning
through its similarities: if the Christian scriptural text was unlike canonical
Greek literature, it was more like the collections of documents (in which
codices could be made of individual tablets, or of individual papyrus

---

Ages. I hope my readers will not object – in fact, I suspect they will be relieved – if I handle this
material more cursorily. This final section already anticipates the more bird's-eye view of the
following coda.

[317] The association of Christianity with the codex is well known and long debated; the best recent
summary is in Bagnall (2009b: chap. 4).

[318] A semiotic preference: the convincing argument of Hurtado (2006: 69–70).

documents strung together),[319] or more like other subliterary products, such as practical manuals,[320] or even books of magic.[321] The papyrus was invested with the culturally valued practice of performance; the codex did not carry this baggage, and instead suggested a mere tool for the storage of writing. It was less performative, more "textual". As Bagnall puts this in his account for the rise of the codex (2009b: 83): "The performative character of reading became less relevant to the range of material finding expression in book form in the Imperial period." This asserts itself first with Christians, and their scripture, and becomes more widespread only later. And we can now see why. Of course, the Christian canon included superb narrative and poetic passages that were in fact performed in Christian liturgy. But such performance did not constitute the main value of this canon, which was valued, instead, as a scripture to be learned – and, indeed, worshipped. Christianity quite naturally was the cultural practice of a teacherly circle – organized, we now see, around texts that were approached in a more "textual", non-performative manner. And so, it was ready. As patronage receded, as teacherly circles predominated, the cultural practices of the Church – until then marginalized – came to be much more mainstream.

It was a period of "Christian"-ization – by which I mean not the fact that more individuals became Christians, but that non-Christian, "mainstream" authors assumed cultural practices that until then had been Christian-like.[322] And so, naturally, especially in the arts of the book, Christianity would come first. In possession of no investment in papyrus culture to write down, it could proceed, very quickly, to Origen's *Hexapla*, to Eusebius' *Canon Tables*. To be clear: this is not an argument to *explain* the rise of Christianity, a multidimensional process. I do not make the absurd claim that the collapse of senatorial

---

[319] Gamble (1995: 49–71) sees the origins of the Christian book habits directly in this documentary "notebook".

[320] Those are very extensively documented; see the updated version of Roberts and Skeat (1983), maintained electronically by Kraft (http://ccat.sas.upenn.edu/rak/courses/735/book/codex-rev1.html, chapter 12), in which the main categories of the early, non-Christian codex are in astronomy (this is explained by the role of tabular information) and in Homeric scholia.

[321] These are the comparisons marshaled by Bagnall (2009b: 83–8): the Roman comparanda are well known, and it is Bagnall's contribution to bring attention to magical papyri and other manuals.

[322] Miron (2010: 412) points out that Jewish literatures were always hybridizations of distinct, marginalized traditions (the many traditions of Yiddish come to mind) and that, in a paradox, post-national and post-colonial European literatures of the late twentieth century tended to assume similar formal characters to that of historically Jewish literature – Europe becoming "Judaized". This is the sense in which I suggest that third-century culture, as a whole, became Christianized. First, Origen; Porphyry comes later.

cultural patronage led to a collapse in the scale of authorial culture, which led to the rise of the teacherly circle, which led to the rise of Christianity. What I suggest is this: that the new cultural climate, structured more around the teacherly textual practices of new canons, less on original, performative practices inspired by classical literature, would have made Christianity somewhat more congenial to the learned. Giving up paideia, for Christ, was a colossal effort, tearing one's ego – one's pride in one's mental accomplishment – away from oneself. But it was still doable.

Imagine becoming a Christian, when you desire the kind of life exhibited in Philostratus' *Lives of the Sophists*. Then, compare this to becoming a Christian, when you desire the kind of life exhibited in Porphyry's *Life of Plotinus*. Which is easier? The most celebrated case – that of Jerome – comes to mind. He recalls in his *Letter* 22 how he was tortured – literally – in a dream, confronted by a heavenly judge: you are a Ciceronian, not a Christian! And why? Because, of all his possessions and earthly entanglements, the one thing he could not give up was his library (giving up family, he explains, was hard; gourmet food, even harder; but giving up a library – impossible!). And so, under the force of the dream, he made a vow not to read pagan literature. As Adkin (1995: 84) observes, "The question to ask is not whether Jerome may have quoted pagan authors less frequently after his dream, but rather to what extent his citations from the Old Testament increase... Since Jerome specifically states that it was above all the uncouthness of the prophets which put him off, his quotations from these books deserve particular attention." And, indeed, Adkin proceeds to show: this was the genuine consequence of the dream conversion. From the master broker of a pagan canon, Jerome became the master broker of a Christian canon, uncouthness be damned. The performativity of the literature cited now mattered less, and this, indeed, was a rough transition. But it was, after all, a transition within the same way of life, substituting one citable canon for another. Perhaps, then, yet a tiny drop in the bucket of explanations for the Christianization of the Roman Empire. When the cultural elite finally converted in substantial numbers (which would happen only through the fourth century), this would be in a cultural world already defined by teacherly circles.

The important observation for us, however, is not that the practices of teacherly circles benefited the rise of Christianity:

Teacherly circles → Christianity

but, rather, that Christianity is an example of the way in which the practices of teacherly circles could have given rise to a culture that would, in turn, further sustain the practices themselves:

Teacherly circles ➜ (culture produced by teacherly circles) ➜ teacherly circles

Specifically, following several generations whose culture was dominated by teacherly circles, there were two main cultural models on offer: Christianity and Neoplatonism. And, not surprisingly – since both thrived through the culture of the teacherly circle – both assumed that culture was a matter of masters, brokering a specific canon; literature was a matter of text, rather than performance; indeed, it was carried, more and more, by the codex, which in its very form suggested the attitudes of the teacherly circle. And, if this is how culture and literature were understood, then this made authors and their followers *expect* the practice of the teacherly circle.

I add another detail. Second-century civilization was shared across the entire Mediterranean; less so in the fourth. Even if the two main parts of the Empire were still politically tied together, they certainly did come apart, culturally, through the third century: the fragmentation we have noted on page 712 above. Thus, there is, in fact, important cultural growth during the fourth century, in Latin, which, at long last, catches up (above all, it constructs its own apparatus of grammar).[323] In many ways each linguistic area became, through the third century, its own cultural sphere, and, once again, it would be unrealistic to expect that omelette to unscramble itself. As conditions improved and political structures across the Mediterranean got partly re-established, there were now something like two cultures within a single Empire. Indeed, especially through the fourth century, on top of this third-century-induced linguistic fragmentation there was also a religious fragmentation: the two lanes, of Christian and of pagan literature, proceeded somewhat separately.[324] Borders could be

---

[323] In a sense, a familiar observation (Conte, 1994: 621: the fourth century sees a "literary flourishing that is one of the most impressive in the history of Rome"; Vessey, 2014, in particular, argues against the traditional, heavily classicizing view – which gets it entirely upside down! – as if Latin literature somehow declines after 200 CE!). Note indeed that, while there was a continuous tradition of Latin literature from its beginnings, it was also almost always – all the way down to the end of the second century – pursued within the shadow of Greek literature and (with the potential exception of the late Republic/golden age) very small in scale of authorship (p. 668 above). The fourth century, then, may be the first when Latin literature is at a comparable footing to the Greek. (To simplify, I ignore in this discussion the rise of other, smaller linguistic traditions.

[324] Among the most important insights of recent scholarship is the need to see pagan and Christian cultural developments in late antiquity together. I do not wish that we go back to a time when the two were studied separately, and, indeed, my claim is meant to be true for both together! During the fourth century both Christians and pagans were conditioned by similar social conditions,

porous (Libanius' rhetoric, in his *Orations*, does not occupy a different universe from that of John Chrysostom in his *Homilies*: the first was probably the latter's teacher!).[325] But the fact remains that more genres were introduced, and so literary coverage had to be stretched wider, and so became thinner. Didymus the Blind was a biblical grammarian; and, so, there was one less grammarian to study Homer. (The fundamental point, then, is that one was, after all, grammarian of one or the other: Jerome's choice.) And, so, the Mediterranean hosted four cultures, whereas, beforehand, there had been one. Each culture's scale, then, was capped at a quarter-Mediterranean. In this respect, too, scale just could not bounce back precisely to that of the second century.

So far the model, in its general form, is really not all that surprising. The fourth century did not revert to the second century, because its setting was distinct: the fourth, unlike the second, happened against the background of the third.

In this book, I have described a long period of stability, following the rise of the canon early in the fifth century BCE, punctuated by the crisis of the third century CE, which, in turn, produced another long period of stability. This is a model of punctuated equilibria.[326] And, in a way, for historians trained on the *Annales*, it is the punctuation, not the equilibria, which calls for explanation: practices, we now know, have many ways of entrenching themselves. And yet it is important to look at the precise ways in which cultural practices did stabilize during the fourth century. My argument is that authorial book culture became locked, in several ways, into a scale that was substantially smaller than that obtaining prior to 200 CE.

To see this, let us first consider the scale of authorship during the fourth century.

Two things are clear to begin with. First, this scale was above that of the later third century. Second, it was below the level of antiquity from 400 BCE to 200 CE. The last observation rests on the argument – discussed on pages 704–10 above – for recency bias.

---

among which, indeed, is the very fact that each group had to contend with a world occupied not only by itself but also by its complement. One led one's life – on a hemisphere.

[325] Carter (1962: 358). In general, religious coexistence in late ancient Antioch should not be romanticized, but, as the clear-eyed study by Sandwell (2007) shows, the two lanes, surely, did cross each other.

[326] A term from evolutionary biology. The classic statement in Gould and Eldredge (1977: 115): "Phyletic gradualism was an a priori assertion from the start. . . A punctuational view of change may have wide validity at all levels of evolutionary processes."

Let us start with medicine. In the fourth century we do find more medical authors than we do in the third – clearing a nearly non-existent bar. The evidence derives from a few sources. Above all, Eunapius – extant – provides our testimony for an entire group leading up Oribasius (see page 711 above: this yields Zeno of Cyprus, Magnus of Nisibis, Ionicus of Sardis and Theon of Gaul [?]). Then we hear, from Marcellus "the Empiricist" – extant – about several physicians among his recent fellow citizens of Burdigalia: Siburius, Eutropius and Julius Ausonius. To these we may add a few isolated individuals. Pelagonius, author of a *Veterinary Art*, may come from a similar background, and he, too, is extant (in fragmentary form). The fourth-century physician Theodorus Priscianus is directly extant, and he mentions his teacher, Vindicianus, who is extant as well. From the corpus of the Cappadocian father of the Church Gregory Nazianzus we surmise that his brother, Caesarius, was a successful physician in Constantinople. Finally, among the authors cited by Oribasius (who is of course extant), Philagrius must be recent, hence almost certainly a fourth-century author. This adds up to 14 attested fourth-century medical authors (exhausting EANS: if not quite the entirety of the evidence, then not far from it). How would our evidence look, however, had this group been transposed into the second century? Our prosopography depends on six extant authors, four of whom were specifically medical authors. It is certain that most of those authors are extant just because they were active in the fourth century: authors such as Pelagonius simply did not survive from earlier centuries. One has to have an enormous proximity to Byzantine manuscript transmission to have this breadth of authors, of such capaciousness, survive. We notice further the auto-prosopographic habit, expanding the numbers of attested authors (especially through Eunapius and Marcellus). Imagine, then, that the same cast was subject to the strains of attestation of the pre-200 world: much less of a tendency to mention authors near in time, many fewer surviving works. . . Put fourth-century medical authors in the second century – and you would probably possess now, in datable form, the names of no more than a handful. There are about 50 individual physicians attested in the same way in the second century, of course partly (but not entirely) because of Galen's presence then. But so many more second-century medical authors have been lost! All in all, then, it seems likely that the number of medical authors was considerably lower in the fourth century than in the second.

We have a small group of astrologers known from the fourth century: Andreas of Athens, the "Astrologus of 379", Firmicus Maternus, Maximus and Paulos are all known because their works are extant (often, now, in heavily mediated form); otherwise, historians mention a certain astrologer named Heliodorus, active in Antioch under Valens and involved in political intrigue. Once again, such names depend on the survival of extant works, which is a matter of the recency bias of the fourth century. Surely, far fewer of these works – hence, of these names – would have survived had they been active in the second century.

Finally, as noted on pages 767–8 above, there is essentially no report, from the fourth century, of Greek authorial activity in grammar (though there is much more, of course, in Latin grammar); and, as noted on page 713 above, nearly none in jurisprudence.[327]

In short, then, the "service industries" return in the fourth century – but in a qualified way. There are certainly now centers (perhaps, above all, Alexandria) where they are taught, and this teaching sometimes involves the writing of books. But the overall number of authors appears to be considerably below that of the second century, particularly if we concentrate on Greek authors alone. This is significant, in particular, to the extent that the "service industries" can act as proxies for cultural patronage. It appears that, in the second century, one produced speculative work "on spec", whose range was in principle unlimited, hoping to raise one's status and in this way to open doors for potential patronage. Now, however, authorial activity has become constrained with the generic expectation that one should write teacherly works – handbooks, epitomes, commentaries – severely narrowing the space for potential publication.

Clearly, most authors would be active in fields other than the service industries – above all, rhetoric. The number of attested fourth-century rhetors (a category which includes many teachers of rhetoric, however) is extremely large, but, as noted on page 718 above, the recency bias is obvious in this case. The total is 343 rhetors, but, by my count, without the witness of Libanius, only 121 would still be known.[328] Libanius' evidence is an aberration even within the standards of the fourth century (almost 1 million words, put to massive auto-prosopographic use). This corpus is something of a literary Pompeii, from which we may recover all sorts of

---

[327] Or consider the exact sciences: Pappus and Theon are extant from the fourth century (as is Hypatia, to the extent that Theon's commentary on the *Almagest* was in fact co-edited with her). Otherwise, the only individually attested mathematician (in the sense of one's main identity) is Pandrosion, Pappus' rival in the teaching of mathematics (but did she in fact author books?). This: compared to the case of authors in the exact sciences of the second century, from Menelaus to Cleomedes. Given the recency bias, this suggests to me a somewhat less active fourth century, but the overall numbers are small and the latter century does, after all, have some work in the exact sciences.

[328] I rely on PGRSRE, which is, thankfully, thorough concerning sources of attestation. In my count of 121 names, I include authors attested to "III/IV" or "IV/V", as long as they likely were active at least in part in the fourth century.

aspects of the daily life of culture (and, like Pompeii, still not fully excavated: we need more Libanius scholarship badly). It is near-certain that, had he lived in the second century, only a fraction of this corpus (if any at all) would have survived, and, certainly, we would have known far fewer of Libanius' rhetorical acquaintances.

This compares to 219 rhetors attested to the second century – or roughly 250, if we include the share of "II/III" rhetors who were likely active in the second century. Now, the second century, itself, is uniquely served by epigraphic evidence, and I count 53 rhetors attested purely epigraphically. Let us remove these, as well, to get to something like an equal field. And, now that we've handicapped both sides, we have roughly 200 on the second-century side (the attested, even without inscriptions), to roughly 125 on the fourth-century side (the attested, even without Libanius).

Now, it is not as if Libanius would have *exhausted* the recency bias in favor of the fourth century. Many of the names attested from the fourth century come from corpora that are comparable to those of Libanius, if less prolific and less rhetoric-centered (once again, the corpus of Gregory Nazianzus stands out: attesting a single doctor – and plenty of rhetors!). In sum, it is a reasonable guess that the overall ratio of second- to fourth-century rhetors was above 2:1. This, when rhetoric is probably one of the fields that recovers the most through the fourth century (the field, after all, of paideia)! This, finally, brings us back to the very elementary calculation on pages 709–10 above: with about 17.5 million words from the fourth century, and about 10.5 million from the second, and with a recency bias, between the two centuries, which may be independently estimated to have been on the order of 1:5, it is plausible that the Greek literary output of the fourth century was about one-third that of the second.

On page 721 I proposed a path for the number of simultaneously active authors, going down from a second-century peak of about 1,500 (including Latin: but, in the second century, this was marginal) to a third-century nadir of about 150. It seems plausible to suggest a recovery to a midpoint in the fourth century, with perhaps as many as 500 Greek authors active simultaneously at the peak (near the end of the century).

There are two important qualifications to this number. First, the above calculation refers to *Greek* authors. It is clear that the number of Latin authors in the fourth century was significant, perhaps nearly on a par with the number of Greek authors. If we add them in, then we find that the number of authors active, at the peak of the fourth century, across the entire Mediterranean, was perhaps nearly on a par with the average prior to 200 CE. Authorship did bounce back, then, if only later in the century

(and, then, briefly: more on this below). This agrees with the intuition of
the scholars of late antiquity: it was, for a moment, a busy Mediterranean
culture, expanding once again.

But, even if there were, say, 800 or so authors active across the
Mediterranean in the year 390, no more than 200 to 300 among them
still manned each of the old generic rubrics of "Greek rhetoric", "Greek
philosophy", "Greek medicine", etc. This is the effect noted on page 784
above: the expansion into the new genres of the Church, and into the new
genres of Latin, was also a *thinning*. The Mediterranean had been bifurcated earlier, between Athens and Alexandria; but, then, each took over its
own set of genres, so that each genre became not less but more concentrated. The new double bifurcation of the fourth century was a doubling
and quadrupling of the genres, spreading them out – even geographically!
Latin history was produced in Constantinople,[329] just as Latin law was
produced in Berytus (see page 737 above) – and as Greek medical texts
could well have been produced, at this point, in Gaul.[330] The emperors still
bound the Empire together, in rather concrete ways: there was a network
that bound together, say, Ausonius and Libanius, passing through their
shared correspondence with members of the Imperial entourage (both
corresponded with Symmachus, for instance).[331] And yet: if Marcellus
circulates a collection of remedies in Burdigalia, does this add to the energy
of the medical community surrounding Oribasius in Constantinople?

It is worth considering, then, the consequences of having 200 to 300
Greek authors spread across the traditional genres. Of these, perhaps half
were rhetors: and we are left with no more than a few dozen Greek
philosophers, a few dozen Greek authors in the various "service industries".
And this – at the peak of the fourth century. The numbers are above the
nadir of the third century, which means that more genres once again
become attested. But there were simply not enough to maintain many
communities. Even in the more robust conditions of the late fourth
century, there were still not enough philosophers to maintain more than
a single main tradition of philosophy. Under such conditions, one would

---

[329] In general, travel through the Empire was constant, and many authors straddled the east/west
divide. Ammianus Marcellinus, who referred to himself as a Greek, in all likelihood from the east,
concluded his career – and wrote his Latin history – in Rome (Libanius, *Letter* 1063). In many other
cases we lack such biographic precision; but Eutropius, at least, appeared like an eastern Greek
speaker who wrote his historical epitome in the city of Constantinople (in general, for this
phenomenon, see Geiger, 1999).

[330] Which is where Oribasius may have produced his single-volume epitome of Galen: Nutton
(2004: 302).

[331] Ausonius–Symmachus: Green (1980: 191); Libanius–Symmachus: Sogno (2017: 175).

expect generic traditions to merge, and we see this in practice: the exact sciences, in particular, were very poorly manned, and so they became consolidated, effectively, into philosophy. Little wonder there was little theoretical speculation in medicine: there were no more than a handful of medical authors in any given place, even in Alexandria itself. So, why bother with theory? Who would you quarrel with, save the ghosts of the past?

The account offered here is that the recovery of the fourth century did not transform a small literary culture into a big literary culture, because, instead, it transformed a small literary culture into four small literary cultures. This is perhaps best seen in terms of the history of the book, and, so, we need to go full circle, to the point from which we started this part of the book, at the beginning of Chapter 5. Having counted the papyri rolls that produced the peak of the second century, we should now count the parchment codices that produced the Middle Ages.

Well, then: when we last checked on the entire universe of books in circulation, we estimated perhaps 10 to 15 million literary papyrus rolls across the Mediterranean, at the peak of the second century CE – when they were indeed almost all rolls, almost all papyrus; and, also, almost all non-Christian. All three features would change – together, since all three were intertwined – in a process taking place largely around the fourth century.

Let us start by considering the percentages (rounded to the nearest 5-percent mark) of Christian content, of codex and of parchment, among "literary" fragments in Egypt, from the third to the seventh centuries (the counts were taken from LDAB searches, Egypt only, strict dating).

| Century: | Third | Fourth | Fifth | Sixth | Seventh |
|---|---|---|---|---|---|
| Christian | 10 | 45 | 60 | 75 | 90 |
| Codex | 20 | 70 | 90 | 80[332] | 75 |
| Parchment | 0 | 25 | 55 | 55 | 50 |

---

[332] The decline in the percentage of the codex in the final two centuries is a statistical aberration: in the sixth century many of our "literary papyri" are the individual poems on single sheets from the archive of Dioscorus of Aphrodito, so, essentially, documentary rather than literary (see p. 191 above); the absolute numbers of literary documents from the seventh century are already considerably lower (about 200, compared to about 400 to 500 from each of the preceding three centuries), of which many are educational, with a large group of ostraca.

Historical processes do not proceed step-wise, the nines of history's speedometer all turning to zeros. If we extrapolate the data to continuous curves, we find that most books in Upper Egypt were already in the codex form early in the fourth century; most books carried Christian content, at some point later in that century; and, well before the middle of the fifth century, most of our fragments derive from parchment.

We have, certainly in the third century but, to a lesser extent, also in the fourth, implausibly many books with Christian contents. Bagnall (2009b) states this problem forcefully (but refrains from offering more than hints towards a solution).[333] Perhaps we should note that Christians, more than others, created communities of learning organized around canonical texts.

As noted above, the rise of the codex certainly correlates with the rise of Christianity. The codex was the preferred form of Christian books, so, obviously, the more Christian books there are, the more codices there will be as well; but, as I noted on page 781 above, the correlation might run deeper, as the new attitude towards the book – not a springboard for performance but a focus for learning – became more widespread among Christians as well as non-Christians. The codex became dominant early in the fourth century, but – given the conservative nature of artisanal practice – attitudes could well have shifted even before that: the evidence from book form suggests a new attitude towards the book was established already by the late third century.

Now to parchment. Here our evidence is subject to a couple of modifications. I have argued in section 1.3 that, in general, we should trust the evidence from Upper Egypt as indicative of the Mediterranean as a whole, but this is surely false as soon as rival media to papyri began to proliferate. Egypt always had been – and would remain for centuries – associated with papyrus.[334] Hence, it would be very strange if it were not lagging in its adoption of parchment.[335] On the other hand, the evidence above is somewhat skewed in favor of parchment. The statistics above are from

---

[333] What he emphasizes at the end is the specifically marginal position of newly enfranchised Christian elites, who would therefore feel an acute need to assert their status: Bagnall (2009b: 66–9).

[334] As is well known, production of papyrus in Egypt continued well into the eleventh century (Sijpstein, 2009: 453). The sheer numbers of Arabic papyri are staggering – perhaps 150,000? – though a direct comparison to the numbers surviving from Greco-Roman antiquity is, at least, misleading, given the different routes of archaeological survival. What this evidence does tell us quite clearly is that, throughout the first millennium, Egypt never ceased to be awash with papyrus.

[335] Note also that the codex form may have originated with the practices of the Roman state, and so, to a certain extent, might have been more prevalent in the city of Rome itself (Bagnall, 2009b: 87). If so, Egypt could have been a slow adopter of the codex, as well, at least compared to Italy, or perhaps the west as a whole; but this effect must be much weaker compared to the effect of the papyrus' relative dominance in Egypt.

LDAB, which counts all "books" (and much more), regardless of transmission. CEDOPAL counts more strictly such books that emerge in the field of "papyrology", which excludes books found in libraries. There, the dominance of parchment does appear to come, in Egypt, a little later.[336] We are left with considerable uncertainty concerning the transition from papyrus to parchment, but these two points seem clear: the transition from roll to codex was earlier and more fundamental, achieved early in the fourth century; outside Egypt, at least, the transition from papyrus to parchment may have followed not much later.[337]

At the margins, costs matter. As noted on page 610, note 121, above, parchment (as a writing surface) would be, at this time, about two or three times more expensive than papyrus.[338] No less importantly, codices were less "modular". Papyrus rolls were comparable in scale to a modern pamphlet, and so one could buy Homer "in installments" – one roll at a time. At a pinch, the first book would do – hence the proliferation of *Iliad*, Book I, in the evidence of the papyri (see page 45 above). It was the book that defined the small library. The majuscule codex would be the equivalent of perhaps five rolls, and you couldn't buy a "fifth of a codex":[339] so, it was a more

[336] There, indeed, the papyrus codex remains rather more common than the parchment codex, right into the Muslim era (42 papyrus codices from the seventh century – and only 21 parchment codices).

[337] There is a small number of very early medieval books on papyrus now extant through library transmission: so, for instance, CLA 3.304, a sixth-century Latin translation of Josephus, probably produced in Milan! (Rather more papyrus documents are preserved through archival transmission: the major group, the Ravenna papyri, are edited by Tjäder 1955; 1982.) By far the great bulk of the early medieval books now extant through the manuscript transmission are on parchment, however, which does not seem to have much to do with parchment's longevity: papyrus, as attested by ancient libraries (p. 43, n.83, above) as well as by the handful of hardy survivors, such as Milan's Josephus, could have made it as well. Apparently there were not that many papyrus books to begin with in medieval Italy.

[338] Bagnall (2009b: 57) emphasizes that (based on the data available for late antiquity) the different costs of parchment and of papyrus would have made less of a difference compared with the (fixed) costs of scribal labor: for the composite of labor and material, the gap between parchment and papyrus is significantly reduced, to no more than about 20 to 50 percent, depending on the quality of writing (this calculation ignores the cost of a cover, required in a codex but not in a roll). It is very likely (Scheidel, 2002; 2010) that, as Malthusian pressures were relieved following the demographic shocks from the second century onwards, (1) labor became somewhat better compensated and (2) meat consumption rose (which should correlate with a more abundant supply of parchment, as well). Bagnall's point is that a parchment book would not cost that much more than a papyrus book: there might have been economic reasons bringing the two costs closer together in late antiquity.

[339] I count 62 specimens of Homeric material on parchment. Only three of these include Book I of the *Iliad*, and, of these, two are clearly from extensive books that covered the entire *Iliad* (one is the Ambrosian *Iliad*; the other is a ninth-century commentary from the monastery of St. Catherine in Sinai, on the early books of the *Iliad*, LDAB TM 117953). There is only one fragmentary survival of Homeric material of which only Book I is extant – a sixth- to seventh-century find from Egypt, P. Pisa Lit. 16. It is true that the numbers are small and that, in the codex form, the beginning and the

significant investment. The model produced above, on page 537, for book circulation at the peak of the second century requires book ownership to be common even among a local, decurional elite which, at the lowest levels, would find it hard to acquire more than a handful of rolls. A bound parchment codex would therefore be beyond their means. In general, this implies a gradual migration of the book up the social ladder through the fourth and fifth centuries. Now, to be clear, we do not see, in Egyptian books of the Byzantine era, a return to the big-library model of the Ptolemaic era (in which a larger fraction of books are rare and scholarly). The share of Homer, for instance, among non-Christian books, is stable,[340] implying that a stable fraction of the books comes from the context of ordinary paideia; this is indeed consistent with our overall understanding of cultural life in late antiquity. This could be squared with a migration of books up the social ladder, however, if we assume that libraries are impoverished *across the board*. Even the large libraries become smaller,[341] while the truly modest book owners retreat from the book market. Dioscorus of Aphrodito may have owned an Isocrates, a Menander: a very elementary small-library collection. Imagine a person similarly invested in the display of his own paideia, from the second century CE. Would he not have had a bigger library?

It seems reasonable that, in aggregate, the Roman Empire of the third and fourth centuries was less rich than that of the second; and that books were somewhat more expensive. Thus, it should be expected that the overall circulation of books declined from the second century onwards; and this, in fact, is what the evidence suggests.[342]

---

end of the book are the more vulnerable; but the greater prevalence of Book I was among the strongest statistical features of the survival of Homer on papyrus, and the disappearance of this effect, consistent as it is with arguments from first principles, is therefore telling: likely enough, in the world of the parchment codex, Homer was no longer retailed significantly as single books, but, instead, as entire epics.

[340] There are 1,031 Homer fragments from a total of 4,207 in the years 100 to 300 AD; and 197 from a total of 1,343 in the years 350 to 550 (when this total of 1,343 is about half Christian).

[341] Eusebius' episcopal library in Caesarea must have been among the greatest of his era: the equivalent of the metropolitan, grammarian libraries of the high Empire. Eusebius' enormous corpus is produced with great bibliographic care, so much so that Carricker (2003) has been able to reconstruct an implied partial catalogue of the library. This has about 400 books (many of which, of course, were the equivalent of several rolls). Even bearing in mind that this is just a partial list, the emerging library seems to be more comparable to the handful of big libraries attested papyrologically from Upper Egypt (Otranto, 2000; see pp. 75–6 above). Was a metropolitan library of the early fourth century the equivalent of a major provincial library a century or two earlier?

[342] It is dangerous to put too much weight on the chronological series of literary papyri, as this corresponds to a large extent on archaeological survival. Still, it is worth mentioning that the number of papyri drops by about 50 percent from the third century to the fourth (having already fallen somewhat from its second-century peak), then to remain stable for three centuries (Habermann, 1998: 157).

So, how many books made? As usual, the variables are very elastic, but, for once, as we move closer to the world of the medieval codex, we may begin to bring in evidence beyond that of Egyptian papyri. Buringh (2011) is an outstanding study of the rate of book production in the Latin west through the Middle Ages (ultimately, this is based on statistical extrapolation from a comparison of the number of manuscripts reported from catalogues with that of manuscripts more recently extant): he comes up with the following rates for the early centuries (262: total production through each century).

| | |
|---|---|
| Seventh century | 11,000 |
| Eighth century | 44,000 |
| Ninth century | 202,000 |

So, about a hundred annually in the Dark Ages, rising to a couple of thousand annually in the Carolingian era. This is perhaps optimistic for the ninth century.[343] Indeed, there are about 100 parchment codices surviving as "papyrus fragments" from fifth-century Upper Egypt (when that region may have nearly caught up the culture of the parchment codex). By the usual assumptions (a 1:1,000 rate of survival, a 1:10 rate of Upper Egypt to overall Greek book production), this implies, as an upper boundary on the order of magnitude, 10,000 books produced annually,[344] rather higher than Buringh's numbers for the Carolingian era. The conclusion that there were several thousand codices produced annually in the Greek-speaking world, through the more settled years of late antiquity, is plausible.

But, more than this: books carry with them (as you will be aware, having read so far) an opportunity cost. Reading one, you do not read another; producing one, you do not produce another. The size of the class of new books produced in late antiquity will be determined by two variables: not only the number of all books produced but also the fraction, among them, of new books. How much of the making of codices, in late antiquity, would consist simply in transcribing the past?

[343] The mechanism I would suggest is that Carolingian manuscripts were generally of higher quality compared with late medieval manuscripts, and so especially valued, and so extra steps would have been taken to guard them; hence, their survival rate might be somewhat better than the one predicted from a simple statistical extrapolation. Cisne (2005) relies on a tiny subsample to derive an implausibly small number of Carolingian-era manuscripts (25,000; notice that roughly 7,000 are extant!), but his methodology does suggest that these manuscripts seem well curated.

[344] Upper boundary: because the rate of survival ought to be rather better than that for earlier papyrus (admittedly, the fraction of book production concentrated on the Nile ought to be smaller).

I have assumed, somewhat on the optimistic side, that there could have been 10 to 15 million papyrus rolls at the peak; and I have noted that the number might decline, but certainly not dramatically, through the third century. Let us say, then, that at the time of the conversion of Constantine there were somewhat fewer than 10 million Greek rolls across the Mediterranean. To turn them all into majuscule codex would take slightly fewer than 2 million codices, and, assuming, as usual, roughly 1 percent annual attrition, a stable population would require the annual making of something in the order of 20,000 Greek codices. (The transformation into codex, then, was, in all likelihood, at a rate considerably below replacement levels, to begin with.)

So, just what was transcribed into codex? There are now extant almost 500 palimpsests (often very fragmentary) whose inferior script was produced during the early Middle Ages (I refer to script in majuscule, generally speaking, dated to before about 800 CE). Now, palimpsests – somewhat surprisingly – do not seem to have any particular "anti-pagan" biases in their choices of works to be recycled (as will be noted, recycled texts are mostly Christian, and most often biblical: these are the texts one in principle would need most; they were recycled because they were in some way no longer usable, as artifacts, *apparently regardless of their contents*). These are, therefore, a smaller but potentially less biased sample, for our purposes, than the *transmitted* books from the early Middle Ages, of which we possess a great many – 1,800 from the Latin side alone[345] – a dangerous sample, as, in this case, survival might be biased towards such books that would be exceptionally valued through the centuries.[346]

Among Greek palimpsests, the inferior scripts break down as follows (first absolute numbers, followed by rough percentages).[347]

[345] A famous catalogue of genius, due to E. A. Lowe: the 12-volume *Codices Latini Antiquiores*.
[346] As a control on this, I went through the CLA, classifying a sample of all the early medieval Latin manuscripts that survive through library transmission. The results are: New Testament, 15; Old Testament, three; liturgy, ten; other Christian, 64; lit. non-Christian, two; tech. non-Christian, six. Naturally: the books needed for monastic life were the ones to survive on monastic shelves (note that this massive category of "Other Christian" is made mostly of commentaries; it also has a few regulae).
[347] These numbers are calculated before the publication of the recent trove of findings from St. Catherine. In this collection of palimpsests – mostly small fragments – the inferior script is, nearly without exception, either Christian or *medical* (Claudia Rapp, personal communication). A big find, its consistency is, in fact, worrying. Do we face something like a single cache, potentially contaminating our evidence? If we do admit this evidence, however, it would tend to make the Greek material closer to the Latin.

| New Testament | Old Testament | Liturgy | Other Christian | Literary non-Christian | Technical non-Christian |
|---|---|---|---|---|---|
| 61 | 34 | 6 | 27 | 10 | 10 |
| 40+% | 20+% | 5–% | 20–% | 5+% | 5+% |

The parallel results for Latin are as follows.

| New Testament | Old Testament | Liturgy | Other Christian | Literary non-Christian | Technical non-Christian |
|---|---|---|---|---|---|
| 29 | 32 | 37 | 118 | 31 | 54 |
| 10% | 10% | 10+% | 40% | 10% | 15+% |

On both the Christian and non-Christian sides, Latin is less focused on the literary canon and has more specialized literature; it also has less Christian literature overall. Perhaps the Latin survival represents a more erudite, big-library survival. The major urban centers of the west all went through many catastrophes through the early Middle Ages.[348] In the Greek east, however, book collections had a somewhat better chance of surviving peacefully into the later Middle Ages, and did not depend so much on a few lucky survivals. In general, the more widespread smaller, parochial libraries would be more Christian, as well as more canonical. If so, original conditions could have been even more skewed to canonical literature than the palimpsests suggest.

We find that the earliest codices, unsurprisingly, were predominantly (80 to 90 percent, if not more) Christian. On both the Christian and non-Christian sides, they would contain somewhat more canonical than specialized literature (biblical and liturgical, in the Christian case; the literary canon, in the non-Christian case). The most remarkable thing is that, even in these small samples, we find multiple manuscripts from a few central authors. Among non-Christian Greek authors, we have two Platos, two Menanders – but also two Galens (more, once the St. Catherine's evidence is fully processed). Among Christian Greek authors, we have four manuscripts of Gregory Nazianzus, five of John Chrysostom, two of Basil of

---

[348] I am not saying that western Europe was desolate through the early Middle Ages – a point of view which contemporary scholarship has by now overcome. Once again: life went on. As Pounds (1994: 44) points out, "If the town of Trier was destroyed four times, it is evident that there must have been some degree of recovery between each act of destruction." But it is also evident that Trier was not a safe place for ancient books.

Caesarea and two of Ephraim of Syria. In Latin (for which more palimpsests have been identified), multiple manuscripts are of course better
attested: 13 Augustines![349]

The evidence shows, quite clearly, the domination of the late ancient
library by Christianity and by the central canon. Here, above all else, the
sheer extension of culture – to encompass Christianity, and not just the old
pagan canon – mattered most. Effectively, the rise of the Christian canon
meant that there was an even larger body of literature that had to be copied
in massive numbers – but this, while the old canon was still maintained
with all the care required for the canon. It *still* was paideia. In short – the
conclusion of this long excursus – there would likely have been no more
than hundreds of majuscule codices produced, annually, dedicated to
anything outside the (pagan and Christian) canon – and even much of
this would have been *old* non-canonical works! Spread this among several
hundred authors... The conclusion is that becoming an author implied
the making of very few physical books; perhaps, in many cases, authors
produced a single, unique artefact?

In the world of papyrus, writing was based on an assumption of multiple
readers. This was writing so as to broadcast one's cultural status in front of
a wide elite. In late antiquity this is over. Books are now essentially unique
documents: for one's immediate circle of readers (a teacherly circle) or for a
major patron. Commentaries – and epitomes.[350]

My argument, emphasizing that which, in principle, may be counted,
did not seek out causes and consequences. In fact, these might be confused.
It is not the case that some kind of external force made scribes in the fourth
century produce fewer books, so that new authors would have to limit
themselves to a handful of copies and to the teacherly circle. Rather, it is
that, because literature receded into the teacherly circle, the production of

---

[349]  Buttenwieser (1942) – still the most informative treatment of this question – counts the extant pre-
1300 manuscripts for several popular classical Latin authors. She reports 370 Priscian, 223 for Lucan,
slightly fewer than 70 for Pliny the Elder, 250 and 169 manuscripts for Horace and Statius,
respectively.

[350]  The numbers suggested above have consequences for textual criticism: the implication is that, for
non-canonical works (in the wide sense of a canon that includes any educational use), the number
of late ancient copies would have been rather small, so that it is quite likely that our medieval
manuscripts indeed derive, in many cases, from a single late ancient archetype. I mention this
because I believe this is the common intuition among textual critics and because, indeed, I believe
this is the implication of the relative stability of most manuscript traditions: the reconstructed
stemmata imply, then, among other things, fairly constrained book-copying activity in late
antiquity. This is not often commented upon, perhaps because scholars assume – falsely, in my
view – that circulation in a small number of copies was natural throughout antiquity (p. 622 above).
Typical circulation in a few copies may have been, I suggest, a *new* development of late antiquity
and of the book culture of the codex.

fewer copies became more natural. This becomes, in turn, part of the explanatory context, however. The authorship of the teacherly circle did not seek out larger audiences and imaginary performances, and so it emphasized more the unique, written product, the focus of learning attention: a document, nearly. And so the codex became more natural, and this – the codex – was harder to produce and, by its very nature, did not envision a large number of copies. And so, once again: a practice, entrenched, sustaining itself.

To sum up, then, why did the omelette not unscramble itself? Why did the fourth century not revert to the practices of the second? I have outlined several possible answers. First, a qualitative answer: through the third century a new cultural model – that of the teacherly circle – came to occupy center stage. A new rise in scale could not undo this transformation. Second, a quantitative answer: even though numbers did spring back, to some extent, in the fourth century, they did so in conditions that had already been shaped by a culture that expected to be spread thin, that expected small circles of readership. Literary practices would be spread over a quadrupled cultural field (Christian and pagan, Greek and Latin); they would be conveyed through the more restrictive medium of the codex, perhaps already that of the parchment codex. And, so: the quantitative and the qualitative – in a new equilibrium.

In the conclusion to section 6.1.1 above I paused to reflect on the explanatory model provided for the literary developments of classical Greece in the late fifth century BCE. Not a simple consequence of the technology of writing, of course: and, yet, it is clear that writing – and the new prose genres it made possible – was crucial. I suggested the following explanatory outline (quoting from page 638 above):

"The model developed here pushes technology lower in the causal flow. It is a more layered model; it also considers how causation can turn into self-reinforcing cycles:

$$\text{Social setting} \rightarrow \text{scale} \rightarrow$$
$$(\text{Technology} \leftrightarrow \text{genre} \leftrightarrow \text{scale})$$

A new social setting gives rise to a shift to a bigger scale, which then drives a self-reinforcing cycle whereby technology sustains new genres, which in turn sustain larger scales."

I do not suggest that a single explanatory model should fit all different events in cultural history, and, indeed, even these two events do not fit the model in quite the same way. But the structural resemblance is real. Once again, social setting impacts on scale, which in term determines a stable system of technologies and genres that go hand in hand with a sustained scale.

In the fifth century BCE the unique event of the rise of democracy gave rise – through an expansion of scale – to a stable combination of a writing-based culture with prose genres and a large scale. In the third century CE the unique event of the crisis of patronage gave rise – through a reduction of scale – to a new stable combination of a codex-based culture with the genres of the teacherly circle and a smaller scale. By these two events, antiquity was bookended.

I have given a complicated account for why a new equilibrium was achieved, why late antiquity did not revert to the practices of the second century. Perhaps this is over-thinking it. Material circumstances for culture were indeed on the mend, through the fourth century, and in the 360s or the 370s scale might have been restored nearly to the high Imperial level. Had fortune been kinder, perhaps a different kind of equilibrium might ultimately have been formed. It was not. The Empire never truly recovered from the catastrophe of the Battle of Adrianople.[351] In the west, complete disaster had struck already in the fifth century: the Roman west was replaced by Vandal Africa, Gothic Italy, German Gaul. Culture was eroded to the point that, by the sixth century, paideia was no longer sought by the political elite (remaining, however, as an ecclesiastic pursuit).[352] In the east, the fifth century was better contained (though, already by then, the scale of cultural life was probably well below the peak of the fourth century); but, then, the pressures of the sixth and seventh centuries – certainly the plague of the sixth century (worse than the Antonine and Cyprian Plagues?),[353] perhaps climate change,[354] and finally the Muslim conquests – brought the civilization of late antiquity to a close in the east, as well. Small scale was forced, by external circumstances.

But, in other ways, stability was more powerful than such external pressures imply. The Church formed itself, especially through the third century, as an institution of book learning; and so the books continued to be copied. We recall how Origen started on a new teacherly project; how his teaching gave rise to texts; and then how those texts, in and of themselves – following a hiatus of a couple of decades – gave rise to another teacherly circle, that of Pamphilus and Eusebius. This third-century Caesarean drama would be repeated, writ large, across the Mediterranean. Again and again, the teacherly texts bequeathed by late

[351] As realized even by contemporaries: Lenski (1997).    [352] Wickham (2005: 158).
[353] Horden (2005).    [354] Brooke (2014: 342, 351–3).

antiquity would be picked up and give rise, again, to new, active centers of learning: Baghdad, Cairo, Constantinople, Bologna. Teacherly circles turned into the institutions of textual learning of the medieval universities. Commentaries, encyclopedias, summaries multiplied. So, after all, indeed, a very long equilibrium: even longer, in fact, than that of the classical papyrus book.

The new equilibrium of late antiquity and the Middle Ages was, in a way, the negation of literary culture prior to 200 CE. It was now a culture premised on the notion of a single, unified truth: not because it was Christian (its truth, mostly, preceded Christianity) but because it was deuteronomic, based on the harmonized teaching of canonical texts. Late antiquity turned each field into a canon, and made those canons cohere with each other: an Aristotelian-Platonic canon, which was, on the one hand, made consistent with Ptolemy, on the other hand, with Galen. Eventually, Thomas Kuhn would, mistakenly, interpret this as the ancient "paradigm". And so, a proper end for this study. My entire point is that antiquity possessed a literary canon – but no scientific paradigms. It was a world of debate and pluralism, throughout, because, up to the third century CE, it never did manage to develop a non-literary canon – and, when it did, so to speak, this was already too late.

I started this book with Geoffrey's question – how to account for the long-term cultural influence of the Greek democratic tradition. I now return to this question in the Coda.

# Coda to the Book

To repeat the question with which we started: we understand the distinctive nature of the Greek legacy, as a consequence of the democratic polis. And yet, democracy, in antiquity itself, was no more than an episode in a mostly monarchic Mediterranean. How to reconcile these two?

This book has tried to answer this question by following a series of contingencies that served, in turn, to preserve a literary canon shaped by classical, democratic Athens.

(1)  Canons are shaped by shared expectations for what literature is supposed to do. For our purposes, what mattered most was the centrality of performance to ancient poetics. And so: in appreciating works that are understood primarily as performative, it helps to have a sense of place. Athens' democracy was hyper-performative. Its places were broadcast and made familiar, hence making the appreciation of this city's literature – once made canonical – even more effective. Later (non-democratic, hence less performative) centers could not rival it. And so, an Athenian literary canon remained.

The historical consequence of this Athenian-based literary canon was the formation of what I call the polis of letters: the understanding of cultural life as being based on strong individuals, cast together as groups characterized by oppositions. The point is not that the Athenian canon preserved the ideology of democracy through its contents; rather, that it inspired the practice of radical debate in its shape.

(2)  In the aftermath of the formation of the Athenian literary canon, cultural practices had to measure themselves against the canon, and against its places. Inside Athens, what mattered most was the preservation of the past, in a manner abstracted away from politics (hence new comedy, and, above all, philosophy). Outside Athens, new centers formed at a distance from the expectations of performance,

foregrounding different genres and different attitudes to literature and ending up, in many ways, as "meta-literary" (this happened, above all, around Alexandria as the center). The monarchic civilizations of the Hellenistic world witnessed, then, not a unification of a single monarchic ideology but, to the contrary, a bifurcation into two radically different cultural styles.

(3)   The opposition between Athens and Alexandria receded in significance as Mediterranean culture came under the gravitational pull of Roman patronage. The transition happened through the last century of the Roman Republic, and it took place against intense senatorial competition. (Even later, as monarchic stability was achieved in Rome itself, the patronage of Greek culture would always remain, as among the constrained fields for the expression of aristocratic Roman values.) The tendency of this transition, then, was not towards the creation of any single model but, rather, towards the production of many eclectic syntheses, each Greek intellectual putting on offer, for his own patron, his own version of Hellenism – all marked, however, to a greater or lesser degree, by the coming together of traditions that, beforehand, had been pursued separately in Athens or in Alexandria.

The historical consequence of the Hellenistic bifurcation of Athens and Alexandria, followed by its Roman varied syntheses, was the sheer proliferation of variety. By the Roman era the cultural repertoire had expanded to the full combinatorial potential of many genres and many agendas. Greek culture, we noted, always remained marked by debate; through the centuries it became even more marked by pluralism.

These are, then, the historical contingencies that made a monarchic Mediterranean give rise to a culture marked by debate and pluralism.

Something did change in late antiquity. I argue that a collapse in elite patronage led to a collapse in the scale of authorial culture, and to its move away from the model of patron and author (which made authors seek the most distinctive cultural expression possible, the one obtaining maximal affect) to the model of the teacherly circle. Authors became the brokers of well-defined canons in their respective fields; and the attitude of the teacher made authors into the masters of new defined canons – selecting and harmonizing. Within each field separately: a Christian canon, an Aristotelian-Platonic canon, a Galenic-Hippocratic canon, a Ptolemaic-Euclidean canon; and more and more, all, together: a single Christian-(or Muslim-)Aristotelian-Galenic-Ptolemaic "paradigm", which would be bequeathed to the Middle Ages and which will serve as the foil to the scientific revolution.

And yet. . . Late antiquity did indeed manage, one way or another, to sew together a single whole out of the huge variety it had available. But the crazy quilt was still there. It was, ultimately, very easy to see the gaps, to exploit them. We may recall this briefly (skipping the separate, and fascinating, story of the many episodes of debate within Islamic civilization, very often taking their cues from ancient tensions). And so: beginning with the high Middle Ages, we find authors mobilizing pagan philosophy against Christian theology – and vice versa: Plato against Aristotle against Plato; Archimedes against both. The humanists mobilized the literary canons against the philosophical and scientific canons of the schools. And why not? The expectation of debate was there, too: easy to read and tempting to imitate. At some point, everyone – so, for instance, Copernicus (starting from Ptolemy), Descartes (from Apollonius), Harvey (from Galen) – noted the *explicit* debates enshrined in the scientific canon, and proceeded to pick up the polemic at the point at which it was left off by the ancients. By which point it was already modern science: essentially, you may argue, the *revival* of an ancient set of debates.

More than this. I have presented late antiquity so far as something of a correction of an aberration. So many societies follow the same principle: they achieve political unity and then mirror it by ideological unity. For a long while the Greeks did not, but this, finally, was resolved by late antiquity, the Greeks folded into "normal" history. Under this story, the Mediterranean is unique only in that it took so long for it to achieve its ideological unity – so that, before the achievement of an eirenic synthesis, so much variety and contention were already packed in as to render that intellectual peace into no more than a ceasefire.

This is valid, as it goes. And yet I think we are still missing an important part of the argument. I may have started with one question, regarding the role of debate and pluralism in the legacy of ancient culture. But, throughout this book, more has been added to this question, and I think it may now be framed somewhat differently – and so as to reveal more in the way of continuity through the cultural history of the Mediterranean.

Let us take a step back. Why does the question even matter? The answer is, I suppose, because there is a good case to be made that the cultural developments of early modern Europe play a pivotal role in world history. Our world is defined by the Industrial Revolution, or, more generally, by modern science; and also by modern ideologies, such as (among others) nationalism, secularism and, one hopes, democracy. However Eurocentric such a statement might appear, it also remains quite obviously true.

To this extent, then, it is important to understand why these cultural developments took place at all, and why they took place, specifically, in western Europe, at the time they did. So much is clear.

What is somewhat less obvious to modern historians, but, I think, really should not be controversial at all, is that – at least to a certain extent – these developments could take place in early modern western Europe because, at this time, and at this place, the cultural legacy of the ancient Mediterranean was available, ready to be deployed so as to launch modernity. This, then, is the point of this book. (The question remains as to why the launch had to take place just then and there, in just the way it did; but this is *not* the point of *this* book.)

I argue that the path leading to early modern cultural developments began in antiquity; the fork in the road, perhaps, taken already by the time of Athens' demise. And the argument of the last few paragraphs suggests directly one way in which this might be the case: namely that the ancient expectation that culture should be marked by debate, together with the entire panoply of ancient cultural pluralism, taken together, gave rise to an early modern culture of debate and pluralism which, in and of itself, led to cultural growth. (I put aside the question of why debate and pluralism, as such, should be culturally beneficial: these we mostly take for granted, now, for reasons which Popper – and Darwin – made sufficiently plausible.)

I think this captures a large part of the truth, but perhaps not all of it. Before concluding, I wish to highlight another way – perhaps even a more essential one – in which the precise formation of the classical legacy, as highlighted in this book, served to open specific possibilities, exploited within European history. And in this sense, perhaps, we can also do justice, finally, to late antiquity itself.

In truth, there is something rather bizarre about the notion of late antiquity supplying the Confucian-like state ideology hitherto lacking around the Mediterranean. The authors of late antiquity did not, in any way, emerge from within the state! These are not Confucian courtiers: to the contrary, the synthesis of late antiquity was produced from the margins. In the third century it was Christians, prosecuted by pagans, who led the way to a new project: culture, as the brokering of a specialized, textualized canon. In the fourth century, in turn, this project was completed and extended to all disciplines – by Neoplatonists, prosecuted by Christians! Late antiquity was made by *outsiders*, all the way – beginning with Origen and ending with Hypatia. Tortured by the state, killed by its mob: such were the makers of the canon of the West. And we have seen why it had to be this way: it was culture, after all, as made in late antiquity by the *removal* of patronage.

But, in this, late antiquity was, after all, of a piece with earlier eras. The entire point is that there was never a Western Confucius. Throughout – even when cultural patronage did become, on occasion, more significant – the Greek legacy never took the form of a culture made to fit the needs of the state. Monarchs and senators added luster to their courts or enriched their own otium by having, for friends, poets and philosophers. But Alexandria needed no political philosophers, while Rome took in too many, of all stripes and varieties, none becoming the state philosopher. Of course: Greek culture *already was* a culture of debate and variety, it had already *assumed* the conditions of the polis of letters. And, so, it just wasn't a very good fit for the single ruler. States cannot just manufacture their ideologies, engineer-like: they engage – as does everyone, in history – in cultural bricolage, making do with what is already available. Antiquity was stuck with a legacy to which a monarchic state ideology was a bad fit; so monarchs found other uses for culture.

I started this coda by outlining a response to the question concerning the role of democracy for the legacy of antiquity: a role which seems, at first glance, puzzling, given the *political* failure of ancient democracy. This response takes the form of a "but". True, I admit, democracy failed, politically. But it succeeded *culturally*. Because antiquity was so performative, democracy with its hyper-performativity continued to dazzle. And it was this cultural success, I argue, that mattered most. This is one valid argument, outlined above.

I now wish to add to this "but" argument another argument, an "*and*" argument. Yes, democracy failed politically. And, yes, it succeeded culturally. And it is precisely this *combination* – political failure *and* cultural success – that ultimately matters.

Combine political failure and cultural success – and you drive a wedge between politics and culture. All ancient monarchical civilizations, then, were stuck with a cultural canon whose core emerged from a civilization whose political assumptions were drastically different from those of their own. And thus the canon persisted: culture, marked by the purely literary polis of letters, somewhat less relevant to the actual state.

In this sense, finally, we can see late antiquity as *continuous* with earlier eras. With patronage receding, culture was reorganized *all the more* around the library. It took the teacherly attitude towards the literary canon –

everywhere. At this point it became, in fact, somewhat less important that this canon had, initially, been formed around the Athenian polis of letters (indeed, the canon was expanded to include both scripture as well as the central scientific and philosophical texts now made canonical: all this expansion tended to dilute, so to speak, Euripides and Demosthenes). But the new practices of late antiquity were still path-dependent, we now see, upon the early gap between the cultural and the political order. Culture fit the state to the extent that the display of paideia mattered, and not as the expression of state ideology. It was a luxury, discarded by soldier-emperors; picked up by teachers.

And so, quite simply, the emerging monolithic canon was not the ideology of the state. It became, instead, the ideology of the *Church*. And, so, we notice a very long arc of continuity, in a basic duality: culture – and power. Throughout antiquity, from the moment of Athens' fall, we see a certain remove: cultural figures occasionally enjoy political patronage, but culture is defined by a past alien to current monarchies, and so the interactions between cultural figures – what they talk about, how they talk – are all mostly autonomous from the state.

Now, it is recognized that among the central institutions of early modern Europe is *civic society*. We find there the social arena of cultural debate, pursued away from the state: elite members, pursuing their own agendas, through their own social networks – drinking their own coffee – regardless of what goes on inside courts. At this point in our argument, this now appears as, perhaps, predictable. Why should early modern Europe *not* have a civic society? My argument, by this point, should be obvious. The role models for a civic society were provided by the polis of letters. Its discursive possibilities were provided by the variety of ancient literary genres. All of them: bequeathed from antiquity and *preserved* through the Middle Ages; throughout, culture was largely an autonomous enterprise. Sure, to become the civic society of the seventeenth and eighteenth centuries, culture had to free itself, partly, from the Church. But this was simple, seeing that it never had been part of the *state*. And so, the polis of letters, starting on the path that would lead to modernity – because the autonomy of culture matters so much – because it is there that debate may flourish. The modern coffee house – made possible, ultimately, by the ancient symposium. A long path. Arguably, determined by the political failure, together with the cultural transcendence, of the city of Athens.

# Bibliography

Aaker, J. L. 1997. Dimensions of Brand Personality. *Journal of Marketing Research*, **34**(3), 347–56.

Aaker, J. L., and Schmitt, B. 2001. Culture-Dependent Assimilation and Differentiation of the Self: Preferences for Consumption Symbols in the United States and China. *Journal of Cross-Cultural Psychology*, **32**(5), 561–76.

Acerbi, F. 2003. On the Shoulders of Hipparchus. *Archive for History of Exact Sciences*, **57**(6), 465–502.

2014. Types, Function, and Organization of the Collections of Scholia. *Trends in Classics*, **6**(1), 115–69.

Acerbi, F., and Del Corso, L. 2014. Tolomeo in Laurenziana: Il primo papiro della Psephophoria (PL II/33). *Analecta Papyrologica*, **26**, 37–73.

Acosta-Hughes, B., and Stephens, S. A. 2012. *Callimachus in Context: From Plato to the Augustan Poets*. Cambridge.

Adamson, P. 2012. Aristotle in the Arabic Commentary Tradition. In C. Shields, ed., *The Oxford Handbook of Aristotle*. Oxford, 645–64.

Adkin, N. 1995. Jerome's Use of Scripture before and after His Dream. *Illinois Classical Studies*, **20**, 183–90.

Ahbel-Rappe, S. 2010. *Damascius' Problems and Solutions Concerning First Principles*. Oxford.

Ahonen, M. 2014. *Mental Disorders in Ancient Philosophy*. New York.

Alexander, A. R. 2010. *Duel at Dawn: Heroes, Martyrs, and the Rise of Modern Mathematics*. Cambridge, MA.

Alföldi, A. 1967. *Studien zur Geschichte der Weltkrise des 3. Jahrhunderts nach Christus*. Darmstadt.

Alföldy, G. 1974. The Crisis of the Third Century as Seen by Contemporaries. *Greek, Roman and Byzantine Studies*, **15**(1), 89–111.

Algra, K. 1999. The Beginnings of Cosmology. In A. A. Long, ed., *The Cambridge Companion to Early Greek Philosophy*. Cambridge, 45–65.

2001. Comments or Commentary? Zeno of Citium and Hesiod's *Theogonia*. *Mnemosyne*, **54**(5), 562–81.

2014. Posidonio, testimonianze e frammenti. *Gnomon*, **86**(4), 300–7.

Allan, W. 2014. The Body in Mind: Medical Imagery in Sophocles. *Hermes*, **142**(3), 259–78.

Allen, I. 2010. Pyrrhonism and Medicine. In R. Bett, ed., *The Cambridge Companion to Ancient Scepticism*. Cambridge, 232–48.

Allen, R. C. 2009. How Prosperous Were the Romans? Evidence from Diocletian's Price Edict (AD 301). In A. Bowman and A. Wilson, eds., *Quantifying the Roman Economy: Methods and Problems*. Oxford, 327–45.

Alty, J. 1982. Dorians and Ionians. *The Journal of Hellenic Studies*, 102, 1–14.

Andorlini, I. 2000. Codici papiracei di medicina con scoli e commento. In M. O. Goulet-Cazé, ed., *Le commentaire entre tradition et innovation*. Paris, 37–52.

Annas, J. E. 1994. *Hellenistic Philosophy of Mind*. Berkeley, CA.

Annas, J. E., and Barnes, J. (eds.) 2000. *Sextus Empiricus: Outlines of Scepticism*. Cambridge.

Archibald, R. C. 1915. *Euclid's Book on Division of Figures: With a Restoration Based on Woepcke's Text and on the Practica Geometriae of Leonardo Pisano*. Cambridge.

Ariely, D., and Norton, M. I. 2009. Conceptual Consumption. *Annual Review of Psychology*, 60, 475–99.

Armstrong, A. H. 1967. Plotinus. In A. H. Armstrong, ed., *The Cambridge History of Later Greek and Early Medieval Philosophy*. Cambridge, 195–268.

Armstrong, D. 1995. The Impossibility of Metathesis: Philodemus and Lucretius on Form and Content in Poetry. In D. D. Obbink, ed., *Philodemus and Poetry: Poetic Theory and Practice in Lucretius, Philodemus, and Horace*. Oxford, 210–32.

Armstrong, D., Fish, J., Johnston, P. A., and Skinner, M. B. (eds.) 2010. *Vergil, Philodemus, and the Augustans*. Austin, TX.

Arnaud, P. 2007. Diocletian's Prices Edict: The Prices of Seaborne Transport and the Average Duration of Maritime Travel. *Journal of Roman Archaeology*, 20, 321–36.

Arthur-Montagne, J. 2016. Parodies of Paideia: Prose Fiction and High Learning in the Roman Empire. PhD dissertation, Stanford University.

Forthcoming. *Through the Eyes of a Child: The Boy Viewer in Imperial Ecphrastic Treatises*.

Asper, M. 2007. *Griechische Wissenschaftstexte: Formen, Funktionen, Differenzierungsgeschichten*. Stuttgart.

2009. The Two Cultures of Mathematics in Ancient Greece. In E. Robson and J. Stedall, eds., *The Oxford Handbook of the History of Mathematics*. Oxford, 107–32.

Athanassiadi, P. 2010. Canonizing Platonism: The Fetters of Iamblichus. In E. Thomassen, ed., *Canon and Canonicity: The Formation and Use of Scripture*. Copenhagen, 129–41.

Atherton, C. 1988. Hand over Fist: The Failure of Stoic Rhetoric. *The Classical Quarterly*, 38(2), 392–427.

Auffret, T. 2014. Serenus d'Antinoë dans la tradition gréco-arabe des *Coniques*. *Arabic Sciences and Philosophy*, 24(2), 181–209.

Avotins, I. 1975. The Holders of the Chairs of Rhetoric at Athens. *Harvard Studies in Classical Philology*, **79**, 313–24.

Ayali, M. 1987. *Po'alim ve-Umanim: Melakhtam u-maamadam be-sifrut chazal.* Tel Aviv.

Bagnall, R. S. 1976. *The Administration of the Ptolemaic Possessions outside Egypt.* Leiden.

   1996. *Egypt in Late Antiquity.* Princeton, NJ.

   2002. Alexandria: Library of Dreams. *Proceedings of the American Philosophical Society*, **146**(4), 348–62.

   (ed.) 2009a. *The Oxford Handbook of Papyrology.* Oxford.

   2009b. *Early Christian Books in Egypt.* Princeton, NJ.

Bagnall, R. S., and Frier, B. W. 1994. *The Demography of Roman Egypt.* Cambridge.

Bakhtin, M. M. 1981 [1975]. *The Dialogic Imagination: Four Essays by M. M. Bakhtin*, ed. M. Holquist, trans. C. Emerson and M. Holquist. Austin, TX.

Bakola, E. 2010. *Cratinus and the Art of Comedy.* Oxford.

Baldwin, B. 1975. The Career of Oribasius. *Acta Classica*, **18**, 85–97.

Ball, L. F. 2003. *The Domus Aurea and the Roman Architectural Revolution.* Cambridge.

Baltes, M. 1972. *Timaios Lokros über die Natur des Kosmos und der Seele.* Leiden.

Bang, P. F. 2008. *The Roman Bazaar: A Comparative Study of Trade and Markets in a Tributary Empire.* Cambridge.

Barbet, A. 1987. La diffusion des Ier, IIe et IIIe styles pompèiens en Gaule. *Cahiers d'archéologie romande*, **43**, 7–27.

Barchiesi, A. 2001. The Crossing. In S. J. Harrison, ed., *Texts, Ideas, and the Classics: Scholarship, Theory, and Classical Literature.* Oxford, 142–63.

   2007. *Carmina: Odes* and *Carmen Saeculare*. In S. J. Harrison, ed., *The Cambridge Companion to Horace.* Cambridge, 144–62.

Bardy, G. 1937. Aux origines de l'école d'Alexandrie. *Recherches de science religieuse*, **27**(1), 65–90.

Bar-Hillel, M., Maharshak, A., Moshinsky, A., and Nofech, R. 2012. A Rose by Any Other Name: A Social-Cognitive Perspective on Poets and Poetry. *Judgment and Decision Making*, **7**(2), 149–64.

Barker, A. 1989. *Greek Musical Writings: Cambridge Readings in the Literature of Music.* Cambridge.

   2001. Diogenes of Babylon and Hellenistic Musical Theory. In C. Auvray-Assayas and D. Delattre, eds., *Cicéron et Philodème: La polemique en philosophie.* Paris, 353–70.

   2007. *The Science of Harmonics in Classical Greece.* Cambridge.

Barker, P. 2008. Stoic Alternatives to Aristotelian Cosmology: Pena, Rothmann and Brahe. *Revue d'histoire des sciences*, **61**(2), 265–86.

Bar-Kochva, B. 2010. *The Image of the Jews in Greek Literature: The Hellenistic Period.* Berkeley, CA.

Barletta, B. A. 2001. *The Origins of the Greek Architectural Orders.* Cambridge.

Barnes, J. 1975. *Aristotle: Posterior Analytics: Translated with a Commentary.* Oxford.

1986. Editor's Notes. *Phronesis*, **31**(1), 92–100.

1996. The Catalogue of Chrysippus' Logical Works. In K. Algra, P. W. van der Horst and D. T. Runia, eds., *Polyhistor: Studies in the History and Historiography of Ancient Philosophy.* Leiden, 169–84.

1997. Roman Aristotle. In J. Barnes and M. T. Griffin, eds., *Philosophia Togata*, vol. II: *Plato and Aristotle at Rome.* Oxford, 1–67.

2003. *Porphyry: Introduction: Translated with an Introduction and Commentary.* Oxford.

Barnes, J., and Griffin, M. T. (eds.) 1989. *Philosophia Togata*, vol. I: *Essays on Philosophy and Roman Society.* Oxford.

1997. *Philosophia Togata*, vol. II: *Plato and Aristotle at Rome.* Oxford.

Barnes, T. D. 1981. *Constantine and Eusebius.* Cambridge, MA.

1994. Scholarship or Propaganda? Porphyry against the Christians and Its Historical Setting. *Bulletin of the Institute of Classical Studies*, **39**(1), 53–65.

2010. *Early Christian Hagiography and Roman History.* Tübingen.

Baron, C. A. 2016. Duris of Samos and a Herodotean Model for Writing History. In J. Priestley and V. Zali, eds., *Brill's Companion to the Reception of Herodotus in Antiquity and Beyond.* Leiden, 59–82.

Barthes, R. 1977. *Image, Music, Text*, trans. S. Heath. London.

Bartman, E. 2001. Hair and the Artifice of Roman Female Adornment. *American Journal of Archaeology*, **105**(1), 1–25.

Barton, T. S. 2002. *Power and Knowledge: Astrology, Physiognomics, and Medicine under the Roman Empire.* Ann Arbor, MI.

Bartsch, S. 1988. *Decoding the Ancient Novel: The Reader and the Role of Description in Heliodorus and Achilles Tatius.* Princeton, NJ.

1994. *Actors in the Audience: Theatricality and Doublespeak from Nero to Hadrian.* Cambridge, MA.

1997. *Ideology in Cold Blood: A Reading of Lucan's Civil War.* Cambridge, MA.

Bastianini, G., Carlini, A., Cavini, W., Decleva Caizzi, F., Funghi, M. S., Linguiti, A., Manetti, D., Most, G. W., Sedley, D. N., and Tulli, M. 1995. *Corpus dei papiri filosofici greci e latini: Testi e lessico nei papiri di cultura greca e latina*, part III: *Commentari.* Florence.

Battistoni, F. 2006. The Ancient Pinakes from Tauromenion: Some New Readings. *Zeitschrift für Papyrologie und Epigraphik*, **157**, 169–80.

Baumbach, M., and Dümmler, N. (eds.) 2014. *Imitate Anacreon! Mimesis, Poiesis and the Poetic Inspiration in the Carmina Anacreontea.* Berlin.

Becker, O. 1936. Die Lehre vom Geraden und Ungeraden im neunten Buch der Euklidischen *Elemente*: (Versuch einer Wiederherstellung in der ursprünglichen Gestalt). *Quellen und Studien zur Geschichte der Mathematik, Astronomie und Physik*, **3**, 533–53.

Beecroft, A. 2010. *Authorship and Cultural Identity in Early Greece and China: Patterns of Literary Circulation.* Cambridge.

Beer, J. 2004. *Sophocles and the Tragedy of Athenian Democracy.* Westport, CT.

Begbie, C. M. 1967. The Epitome of Livy. *The Classical Quarterly*, **17**(2), 332–8.

Bell, H. I. 1944. An Egyptian Village in the Age of Justinian. *The Journal of Hellenic Studies*, **64**, 21–36.

Bello, A. L. (ed.) 2003. *The Commentary of Al-Nayrizi on Book I of Euclid's Elements of Geometry: With an Introduction on the Transmission of Euclid's Elements in the Middle Ages*. Leiden.

Bénatouïl, T. 2005a. Les signes de Zeus et leur observation dans les *Phénomènes* d'Aratos. In J. Kany-Turpin, ed., *Signes et prédiction dans l'Antiquité*. Saint-Étienne, 129–44.

2005b. Cléanthe contre Aristarque. *Archives de Philosophie*, **68**(2), 207–22.

Benner, A. R. 1949. *The Letters of Alciphron, Aelian and Philostratus*, trans. F. H. Fobes. Cambridge, MA.

Bennett, A., and Royle, N. 2016. *An Introduction to Literature, Criticism and Theory*, 5th edn. London.

Beresford, A. 2009. Erasing Simonides. *Apeiron*, **42**(3), 185–220.

Berkowitz, L., and Squitier, K. A. 1990. *Thesaurus Linguae Graecae: Canon of Greek Authors and Works*, 3rd edn. Oxford.

Bernard, A. 2003. Ancient Rhetoric and Greek Mathematics: A Response to a Modern Historiographical Dilemma. *Science in Context*, **16**(3), 391–412.

Berndt, T., 1881. *De ironia Menexeni Platonici*. Münster.

Berns, G. S., Capra, C. M., Moore, S., and Noussair, C. 2010. Neural Mechanisms of the Influence of Popularity on Adolescent Ratings of Music. *NeuroImage*, **49**(3), 2687–96.

Berrey, M. S. 2011. Science and Intertext: Methodological Change and Continuity in Hellenistic Science. Doctoral dissertation, University of Texas, Austin.

2014a. Chrysippus of Cnidus: Medical Doxography and Hellenistic Monarchies. *Greek, Roman and Byzantine Studies*, **54**(3), 420–43.

2014b. Early Empiricism, Therapeutic Motivation, and the Asymmetrical Dispute between the Hellenistic Medical Sects. *Apeiron*, **47**(2), 141–71.

Berryman, S. 2009. *The Mechanical Hypothesis in Ancient Greek Natural Philosophy*. Cambridge.

Bett, R. 2007. Sceptic Optics? *Apeiron*, **40**(1), 95–122.

Betz, H. D. (ed.) 1992. *The Magical Papyri in Translation*. Chicago.

Biba, O. 1979. Schubert's Position in Viennese Musical Life. *Nineteenth-Century Music*, **3**(2), 106–13.

Bigwood, J. M. 1993. Aristotle and the Elephant Again. *The American Journal of Philology*, **114**(4), 537–55.

Bilić, T. 2012. Crates of Mallos and Pytheas of Massalia: Examples of Homeric Exegesis in Terms of Mathematical Geography. *Transactions of the American Philological Association*, **142**, 295–328.

Bing, P. 2003. The Unruly Tongue: Philitas of Cos as Scholar and Poet. *Classical Philology*, **98**(4), 330–48.

Biraschi, A. M. 2005. Strabo and Homer: A Chapter in Cultural History. In D. Dueck, H. Lindsay and S. Pothecary, eds., *Strabo's Cultural Geography. The Making of a Kolossourgia*. Cambridge, 73–85.

Birley, A. R. 1997. Hadrian and Greek Senators. *Zeitschrift für Papyrologie und Epigraphik*, **116**, 209–45.

Bischoff, B. 1965. Panorama der Handschriftenüberlieferung aus der Zeit Karls des Großen. In B. Bischoff, ed., *Karl der Große: Lebenswerk und Nachleben*, vol. II: *Das geistige Leben*. Düsseldorf, 233–54.

Blanchard, A. 1989. *Les débuts du codex*. Turnhout.

Blass, F. 1865. *Die griechische Beredsamkeit in dem Zeitraum von Alexander bis auf Augustus*. Berlin.

Bloom, J. 2001. *Paper before Print: The History and Impact of Paper in the Islamic World*. New Haven, CT.

Bluhme, F., Lachmann, K., Rudorff, A. A. F., Momsenn, T., and Bursian, E. (eds.) 1848–52. *Die Schriften der römischen Feldmesser*, 2 vols. Berlin.

Blum, R. 1991. *Kallimachos: The Alexandrian Library and the Origins of Bibliography*. Madison, WI.

Boas, G. 1953. Ancient Testimony to Secret Doctrines. *The Philosophical Review*, **62**(1), 79–92.

Bobzien, S. 1996. Stoic Syllogistic. *Oxford Studies in Ancient Philosophy*, **14**, 133–92.
  1998. *Determinism and Freedom in Stoic Philosophy*. Oxford.
  2011. The Combinatorics of Stoic Conjunction. *Oxford Studies in Ancient Philosophy*, **40**, 157–88.

Bodnár, I. M. 2007. Oenopides of Chius: A Survey of the Modern Literature with a Collection of the Ancient Testimonia, Preprint 327. Berlin.

Bodson, L. 1991. Alexander the Great and the Scientific Exploration of the Oriental Part of His Empire: An Overview of the Background, Trends and Results. *Ancient Society*, **22**, 127–38.

Boll, F. 1908. *Die Erforschung der antiken Astrologie*. Leipzig.

Bolling, G. M. 1940. Zenodotus' Dehorning of the Hornèd Hind, and the Text of Homer. *Transactions and Proceedings of the American Philological Association*, **71**, 40–4.

Bomgardner, D. L. 1992. The Trade in Wild Beasts for Roman Spectacles: A Green Perspective. *Anthropozoologica*, **16**, 161–6.

Bonamente, G. 2003. Minor Latin Historians of the Fourth Century AD. In G. Marasco, ed., *Greek and Roman Historiography in Late Antiquity: Fourth to Sixth Century AD*. Leiden, 85–125.

Bonazzi, M. 2008. The Commentary as Polemical Tool: The Anonymous Commentator on the *Theaetetus* against the Stoics. *Laval théologique et philosophique*, **64**(3), 597–605.
  2013. Pythagoreanising Aristotle: Eudorus and the Systematisation of Platonism. In M. Schofield, ed., *Aristotle, Plato and Pythagoreanism in the First Century BC: New Directions for Philosophy*. Cambridge, 160–86.

Bone, R. G. 2006. Hunting Goodwill: A History of the Concept of Goodwill in Trademark Law. *Boston University Law Review*, **86**(3), 547–622.

Bonner, S. 1977. *Education in Ancient Rome: From the Elder Cato to the Younger Pliny*. London.

Booth, W. C. 1961. *The Rhetoric of Fiction*. Chicago.

Borges, J. L. 1962 [1947]. Averroes' Search. In *Labyrinths*. New York, 148–55.

Bosher, K. 2014. Epicharmus and Early Sicilian Comedy. In M. Revermann, ed., *The Cambridge Companion to Greek Comedy*. Cambridge, 79–94.

Bosman, P. 2006. Selling Cynicism: The Pragmatics of Diogenes' Comic Performances. *The Classical Quarterly*, **42**(1), 93–104.

Boström, H. O. 1994. Philipp Hainhofer: Seine Kunstkammer und seine Kunstschränke. In A. Grotte, ed., *Macrocosmos in Microcosmo: Die Welt in der Stube: Zur Geschichte des Sammelns 1450–1800*. Opladen, 555–80.

Bosworth, A. B. 1970. Aristotle and Callisthenes. *Historia: Zeitschrift für Alte Geschichte*, **19**(4), 407–13.

Boterf, N. 2017. Placing the Poet: The Topography of Authorship. In E. J. Bakker, ed., *Authorship and Greek Song: Authority, Authenticity, and Performance*. Leiden, 80–98.

Boudon-Millot, V. 1993. Médecine et enseignement dans l'*Art médical* de Galien. *Revue des études grecques*, **106**, 120–41.

2007. Un traité miraculeusement retrouvé, le *Sur l'inulité de se chagriner*: Texte grec et traduction française. In V. Boudon-Millot, A. Guardasole and C. Magdelaine, eds., *La science médicale antique: Nouveaux regards: Études réunies en l'honneur de Jacques Jouanna*. Paris, 73–124.

Bourdieu, P. 1993 [1983]. The Field of Cultural Production, or: The Economic World Reversed, trans. R. Nice. In *The Field of Cultural Production: Essays on Art and Literature*. New York, 29–73.

Bowen, A. C. 2001. La scienza del cielo nel periodo pretolemaico. In S. Petruccioli, ed., *Storia della scienza*, vol. I: *La scienza antica*. Rome, 806–39.

2002. The Art of the Commander and the Emergence of Predictive Astronomy. In C. Tuplin and T. E. Rihll, eds., *Science and Mathematics in Ancient Greek Culture*. Oxford, 76–111.

2013a. *Simplicius on the Planets and Their Motions: In Defense of a Heresy*. Leiden.

2013b. Three Introductions to Celestial Science in the First Century. In M. Asper, ed., *Writing Science: Medical and Mathematical Authorship in Ancient Greece*. Berlin, 299–329.

Bowersock, G. 1969. *Greek Sophists in the Roman Empire*. Oxford.

1978. *Julian the Apostate*. Cambridge, MA.

Bowie, E. 2004. The Geography of the Second Sophistic: Cultural Variations. In B. McGing and J. Mossman, eds., *Paideia: The World of the Second Sophistic*. Berlin, 65–83.

2009. Wandering Poets, Archaic Style. In R. L. Hunter, ed., *Wandering Poets in Ancient Greek Culture: Travel, Locality and Pan-Hellenism*. Cambridge, 105–36.

Bowman, A. 2011. Ptolemaic and Roman Egypt: Population and Settlement. In A. Bowman and A. Wilson, eds., *Settlement, Urbanization, and Population*. Oxford, 317–57.

Bozzolo, C., and Ornato, E. 1980. *Pour une histoire du livre manuscrit au Moyen Age: Trois essais de codicologie quantitative*. Paris.

Branham, R. B., and Goulet-Cazé, M. O. (eds.) 1996. *The Cynics: The Cynic Movement in Antiquity and Its Legacy*. Berkeley, CA.

Braudel, F. 1979 [1967–79]. *Civilization and Capitalism: 15th–18th Century*, 3 vols., trans. S. Reynolds. New York.

Braund, D. 2000. Learning, Luxury and Empire: Athenaeus' Roman Patron. In D. Braund and J. Wilkins, eds., *Athenaeus and His World: Reading Greek Culture in the Roman Empire*. Exeter, 3–22.

Bravo, B. 2001. Un frammento della *Piccola Iliade* (P.Oxy. 2510), lo stile narrativo tardo-arcaico, i racconti su Achille immortale. *Quaderni urbinati di cultura classica*, **67**, 49–114.

Bréchet, C. 2007. Vers une philosophie de la citation poétique: Écrit, oral et mémoire chez Plutarque. *Hermathena*, **182**, 101–34.

Breebaart, A. B. 1967. King Seleucus I, Antiochus, and Stratonice. *Mnemosyne*, **20**(2), 154–64.

Brink, C. O. 1993. History in the "Dialogus de Oratoribus" and Tacitus the Historian: A New Approach to an Old Source. *Hermes*, **121**(3), 335–49.

Brisson, L. 1982. *Porphyre: La vie de Plotin*. Paris.

Brittain, C. 2001. *Philo of Larissa: The Last of the Academic Sceptics*. Oxford.

Brock, R., and Wirtjes, H. 2000. Athenaeus on Greek Wine. In D. Braund and J. Wilkins, eds., *Athenaeus and His World: Reading Greek Culture in the Roman Empire*. Exeter, 455–65.

Brockington, J. L. 1998. *The Sanskrit Epics*. Leiden.

Broggiato, M. (ed.) 2001. *Cratete di Malo: I frammenti*. Baltimore.

2014. Beyond the Canon: Hellenistic Scholars and Their Texts. In M. Giordano, ed., *Submerged Literature in Ancient Greek Culture: An Introduction*. Berlin, 46–60.

Brooke, J. L. 2014. *Climate Change and the Course of Global History: A Rough Journey*. Cambridge.

Brooks, P. 1981. Introduction. In T. Todorov, *Introduction to Poetics*. Minneapolis, vii–xix.

Brouwer, R. 2011. Polybius and Stoic Tyche. *Greek, Roman and Byzantine Studies*, **51**(1), 111–32.

Brown, E. 2006. Socrates in the Stoa. In S. Ahbel-Rappe and R. Kamtekar, eds., *A Companion to Socrates*. London, 275–84.

Brown, P. 1971. *The World of Late Antiquity: AD 150–750*. New York.

1992. *Power and Persuasion in Late Antiquity: Towards a Christian Empire*. Madison, WI.

Browne, G. M. 1976. The Origin and Date of the *Sortes Astrampsychi*. *Illinois Classical Studies*, **1**, 53–8.

Brunt, P. A. 1994. The Bubble of the Second Sophistic. *Bulletin of the Institute of Classical Studies*, **39**(1), 25–52.

Bruun, C. 2007. The Antonine Plague and the "Third-Century Crisis". In O. Hekster, G. de Kleijn and D. Slootjes, eds., *Crises and the Roman Empire*. Leiden, 201–19.

Bugh, G. R. 1992. Athenion and Aristion of Athens. *Phoenix*, **46**(2), 108–23.

Burgess, R. W. 1995. On the Date of the Kaisergeschichte. *Classical Philology*, **90**(2), 111–28.

Buringh, E. 2011. *Medieval Manuscript Production in the Latin West: Explorations with a Global Database.* Leiden.

Burkert, W. 1972. *Lore and Science in Ancient Pythagoreanism.* Cambridge, MA.

1992. *The Orientalizing Revolution: Near Eastern Influence on Greek Culture in the Early Archaic Age.* Cambridge, MA.

Burns, A. 1981. Athenian Literacy in the Fifth Century BC. *Journal of the History of Ideas,* **42**(3), 371–87.

Burnyeat, M. F. 1980. Can the Sceptic Live His Scepticism? In M. Schofield, M. F. Burnyeat and J. Barnes, eds., *Doubt and Dogmatism: Studies in Hellenistic Epistemology.* Oxford, 20–53.

1982. Idealism and Greek Philosophy: What Descartes Saw and Berkeley Missed. *Royal Institute of Philosophy Supplements,* **13**, 19–50.

Burton, J. B. 1995. *Theocritus's Urban Mimes: Mobility, Gender, and Patronage.* Berkeley, CA.

Bury, J. B. 1932. *The Idea of Progress: An Inquiry into Its Origin and Growth.* Mineola, NY.

Buttenwieser, H. 1942. Popular Authors of the Middle Ages: The Testimony of the Manuscripts. *Speculum,* **17**(1), 50–5.

Cain, A. 2006. Origen, Jerome, and the *Senatus Pharisaeorum. Latomus,* **65**(3), 727–34.

Calame, C. 2004. Identités d'auteur à l'exemple de la Grèce classique: Signatures, énonciations, citations. In C. Calame and R. Chartier, eds., *Identités d'auteur dans l'Antiquité et la tradition européenne.* Grenoble, 11–39.

Cameron, Alan. 1965. Wandering Poets: A Literary Movement in Byzantine Egypt. *Historia: Zeitschrift für Alte Geschichte,* **14**(4), 470–509.

1980. Poetae novelli. *Harvard Studies in Classical Philology,* **84**, 127–75.

1992. Genre and Style in Callimachus. *Transactions of the American Philological Association,* **122**, 305–12.

1993. *The Greek Anthology from Meleager to Planudes.* Oxford.

1995. *Callimachus and His Critics.* Princeton, NJ.

2010. *The Last Pagans of Rome.* Oxford.

Cameron, Averil. 1993. *The Later Roman Empire: AD 284–430.* Cambridge, MA.

Camia, F. 2008. Imperial Priests in Second Century Greece: A Socio-Political Analysis. In A. D. Rizakis and F. Camia, eds., *Pathways to Power: Civic Elites in the Eastern Part of the Roman Empire.* Athens, 23–41.

Cannon, A. 1989. The Historical Dimension in Mortuary Expressions of Status and Sentiment. *Current Anthropology,* **30**(4), 437–58.

Capel Badino, R. 2010. *Filostefano di Cirene: Testimonianze e frammenti.* Milan.

Carlini, A. (ed.) 1978. *Papiri leterari greci.* Pisa.

Carman, C. C. 2010. On the Determination of Planetary Distances in the Ptolemaic System. *International Studies in the Philosophy of Science,* **24**(3), 257–65.

Carman, C. C., and Evans, J. 2015. The Two Earths of Eratosthenes. *Isis,* **106**(1), 1–16.

Caroli, M. 2007. *Il titolo iniziale nel rotolo librario greco-egizio: Con un catalogo delle testimonianze iconografiche greche e di area vesuviana.* Bari.

Carrara, P. 1994. Sull'inizio delle Fenicie di Euripide. *Zeitschrift für Papyrologie und Epigraphik*, **102**, 43–51.

Carriker, A. J. 2003. *The Library of Eusebius of Caesarea*. Leiden.

Carter, M. J. 1999. The Presentation of Gladiatorial Spectacles in the Greek East: Roman Culture and Greek Identity. Doctoral dissertation, McMaster University, Hamilton, ON.

2003. Gladiatorial Ranking and the "SC de Pretiis gladiatorum Minuendis" (CIL II 6278 = ILS 5163). *Phoenix*, **57**(1/2), 83–114.

Carter, R. E. 1962. The Chronology of Saint John Chrysostom's Early Life. *Traditio*, **18**, 357–64.

Cartledge, P. 1998. City and Chora in Sparta: Archaic to Hellenistic. *British School at Athens Studies*, **4**, 39–47.

2003. *Spartan Reflections*. Berkeley, CA.

Casson, L. 1993. Ptolemy II and the Hunting of African Elephants. *Transactions of the American Philological Association*, **123**, 247–60.

Castellani, V. 2013. The Image of the Jews in Greek Literature: The Hellenistic Period. *The European Legacy*, **18**(4), 502–6.

Castner, C. J. 1988. *Prosopography of Roman Epicureans from the Second Century BC to the Second Century AD*. Frankfurt.

Caston, V. 1999. Something and Nothing: The Stoics on Concepts and Universals. *Oxford Studies in Ancient Philosophy*, **17**, 145–213.

Cavallo, G. 1996. Veicoli materiali della letteratura di consumo: Maniere di scrivere e maniere di leggere. In O. Pecere and A. Stragmaglia, eds., *La letteratura di consumo nel mondo Greco-Latino*. Cassino, 11–46.

1997. Qualche annotazione sulla trasmissione dei classici nella tarda antichità. *Rivista di filologia e di istruzione classica*, **125**, 205–19.

Cavallo, G., and Capasso, M. 1983. *Libri scritture scribi a Ercolano: Introduzione allo studio dei materiali greci*. Naples.

Cavini, W. 1985. *Studi su papiri greci di logica e medicina*. Florence.

Centrone, B. 2014. The Pseudo-Pythagorean Writings. In C. A. Huffman, ed., *A History of Pythagoreanism*. Cambridge, 315–40.

Chadwick, H. 1953. *Origen: Contra Celsum*. Cambridge.

Chaniotis, A. 1988. *Historie und Historiker in den griechischen Inschriften: Epigraphische Beiträge zur griechischen Historiographie*. Wiesbaden.

Charlesworth, M. P. 1937. *The Virtues of a Roman Emperor: Propaganda and the Creation of Belief*. London.

Chiaradonna, R., Rashed, M., and Sedley, D. N. 2013. A Rediscovered Categories Commentary. *Oxford Studies in Ancient Philosophy*, **44**, 129–94.

Christes, J. 1979. *Sklaven und Freigelassene als Grammatiker und Philologen im antiken Rom*. Wiesbaden.

Chroust, A. H. 1962. The Miraculous Disappearance and Recovery of the Corpus Aristotelicum. *Classica et Mediaevalia*, **23**(1/2), 50–67.

1967a. Aristotle Leaves the Academy. *Greece and Rome*, **14**(1), 39–43.

1967b. Aristotle's Last Will and Testament. *Wiener Studien*, **80**, 90–114.

1972. Aristotle's Sojourn in Assos. *Historia: Zeitschrift für Alte Geschichte*, 21(2), 170–6.

Cisne, J. L. 2005. How Science Survived: Medieval Manuscripts' "Demography" and Classic Texts' Extinction. *Science*, 307, 1305–7.

Clark, J. 2001. *Dioscorides and Antipater of Sidon: The Poems*. Wauconda, IL.

Clarke, J. R. 1991. *The Houses of Roman Italy, 100 BC–AD 250: Ritual, Space, and Decoration*. Berkeley, CA.

Clarke, K. 1999. *Between Geography and History: Hellenistic Constructions of the Roman World*. Oxford.

Clay, D. 1994. The Origin of the Socratic Discourses. In P. A. Vander Waerdt, ed., *The Socratic Movement*. Ithaca, NY, 23–47.

  2009. The Athenian Garden. In J. Warren, ed., *The Cambridge Companion to Epicureanism*. Cambridge, 9–28.

Clayman, D. L. 2009. *Timon of Phlius: Pyrrhonism into Poetry*. Berlin.

Clayton, P. A., and Price, M. (eds.) 1988. *The Seven Wonders of the Ancient World*. London.

Coale, A. J., and Demeny, P. 1966. *Regional Model Life Tables and Stable Populations*. Princeton, NJ.

Cohn-Haft, L. 1956. *The Public Physicians of Ancient Greece*. Northampton, MA.

Coleman, K. M. (ed.) 2006. *Martial: Liber Spectaculorum*. Oxford.

Collinet, P. 1925. *Histoire de l'École de droit de Beyrouth*. Paris.

Collins, R. 1998. *The Sociology of Philosophies: A Global Theory of Intellectual Change*. Cambridge, MA.

Comotti, G. 1989. *Music in Greek and Roman Culture*. Baltimore.

Compton, T. 1990. The Trial of the Satirist: Poetic *Vitae* (Aesop, Archilochus, Homer) as Background for Plato's *Apology. The American Journal of Philology*, 111(3), 330–47.

Conte, G. B. 1994. *Latin Literature: A History*. Baltimore.

Cook, R. M. 1959. *Die Bedeutung der bemalten Keramik für den griechischen Handel*. Berlin.

Cooper, C. 2002. Philosophers, Politics, Academics: Demosthenes' Rhetorical Reputation in Antiquity. In I. Worthington, ed., *Demosthenes: Statesman and Orator*. London, 224–45.

Copete, J. C. 1993. Ut philosophus. *Athenaeum*, 81(1), 276–9.

Corey, D. 2002. The Case against Teaching Virtue for Pay: Socrates and the Sophists. *History of Political Thought*, 23(2), 189–210.

Cornell, T. J. (ed.) 2013. *The Fragments of the Roman Historians*, vol. I: *Introduction*. Oxford.

Courtney, E. 1993. *The Fragmentary Latin Poets*. Oxford.

Coventry, L. 1989. Philosophy and Rhetoric in the *Menexenus. The Journal of Hellenic Studies*, 109, 1–15.

Cowan, R. 2013. Of Gods, Men and Stout Fellows: Cicero on Sallustius' *Empedoclea. The Classical Quarterly*, 63(2), 764–71.

Creese, D. 2010. *The Monochord in Ancient Greek Harmonic Science*. Cambridge.

Cribiore, R. 1996. *Writing, Teachers, and Students in Graeco-Roman Egypt.* Durham, NC.

2001. *Gymnastics of the Mind: Greek Education in Hellenistic and Roman Egypt.* Princeton, NJ.

2007. *Libanius the Sophist: Rhetoric, Reality, and Religion in the Fourth Century.* Ithaca, NY.

2015. School Structures, Apparatus, and Materials. In W. M. Bloomer, ed., *A Companion to Ancient Education.* Chichester, 149–59.

Criddle, A. H. 1998. The Chronology of Nicomachus of Gerasa. *The Classical Quarterly,* **48**(1), 324–7.

Croke, B. 1983. Porphyry's Anti-Christian Chronology. *The Journal of Theological Studies,* **34**(1), 168–85.

Crönert, W. 1900. Der Epikureer Philonides. *Sitzungsberichte der Akademie der Wissenschaften zu Berlin,* **61**(2), 942–59.

1907a. *Kolotes und Menedemos.* Munich.

1907b. Die Epikureer in Syrien. *Jahreshefte des Österreichischen Archäologischen Instituts,* **10**, 145–52.

Csapo, E. 2010. *Actors and Icons of the Ancient Theater.* New York.

2014. The Iconography of Comedy. In M. Revermann, ed., *The Cambridge Companion to Greek Comedy.* Cambridge, 95–127.

Csapo, E., and Slater, W. J. 1994. *The Context of Ancient Drama.* Ann Arbor, MI.

Cunliffe, B. W. 2002. *The Extraordinary Voyage of Pytheas the Greek.* New York.

Cuomo, S. 2000. *Pappus of Alexandria and the Mathematics of Late Antiquity.* Cambridge.

2002. The Machine and the City: Hero of Alexandria's Belopoecia. In C. J. Tuplin and T. E. Rihll, eds., *Science and Mathematics in Ancient Greek Culture.* Oxford, 165–77.

2007. *Technology and Culture in Greek and Roman Antiquity.* Cambridge.

Cusset, C. 2011. Aratos et le stoïcisme. *Aitia: Regards sur la culture hellénistique au XXIe siècle.* https://journals.openedition.org/aitia/131.

Cuvigny, H. 2009. The Finds of Papyri: The Archaeology of Papyrology. In R. S. Bagnall, ed., *The Oxford Handbook of Papyrology.* Oxford, 30–58.

D'Angour, A. 2003. Drowning by Numbers: Pythagoreanism and Poetry in Horace *Odes* 1.28. *Greece and Rome,* **50**(2), 206–19.

Dana, M. 2007. Éducation et culture à Istros: Nouvelles considérations. *Dacia,* **51**, 185–209.

Daston, L. 1998. The Academies and the Unity of Knowledge: The Disciplining of the Disciplines. *Differences: A Journal of Feminist Cultural Studies,* **10**, 67–86.

Daverio, J. 2000. One More Beautiful Memory of Schubert: Schumann's Critique of the Impromptus, D. 935. *The Musical Quarterly,* **84**(4), 604–18.

Davies, M. 1988. Monody, Choral Lyric, and the Tyranny of the Hand-Book. *The Classical Quarterly,* **38**(1), 52–64.

Davis, R. (trans.) 2000. *The Book of Pontiffs (Liber Pontificalis): The Ancient Biographies of the First Ninety Roman Bishops to AD 715.* Liverpool.

Dawson, D. 1992. *Allegorical Readers and Cultural Revision in Ancient Alexandria.* Berkeley, CA.

De Blois, L. 1984. The Third Century Crisis and the Greek Elite in the Roman Empire. *Historia: Zeitschrift für Alte Geschichte,* 33(3), 358–77.

1994. Traditional Virtues and New Spiritual Qualities in Third Century Views of Empire, Emperorship and Practical Politics. *Mnemosyne,* 47(2), 166–76.

De Jonge, C. C. 2008. *Between Grammar and Rhetoric: Dionysius of Halicarnassus on Language, Linguistics, and Literature.* Leiden.

De Lacy, P. 1981. *On the Doctrines of Hippocrates and Plato/Galen: Edition, Translation and Commentary.* Berlin.

De Marcellus, H. 1996. "IG" XIV 1184 and the Ephebic Service of Menander. *Zeitschrift für Papyrologie und Epigraphik,* 110, 69–76.

De Polignac, F. 1995 [1984]. *Cults, Territory, and the Origins of the Greek City-State,* trans. J. Lloyd. Chicago.

De Solla Price, D. 1976. A General Theory of Bibliometric and Other Cumulative Advantage Processes. *Journal of the American Society for Information Science,* 27(5/6), 292–306.

De Ste. Croix, G. E. M. 1954. Suffragium: From Vote to Patronage. *British Journal of Sociology,* 5(1), 33–48.

1972. *The Origins of the Peloponnesian War.* London.

1981. *The Class Struggle in the Ancient Greek World: From the Archaic Age to the Arab Conquests.* Ithaca, NY.

De Vaux, C. 1903. Le *Livre des appareils pneumatiques et des machines hydrauliques par Philon de Byzance.* In *Notices et extraits des manuscrits de la Bibliothèque Nationale et autres bibliothèques.* Paris, 27–235.

Decleva Caizzi, F. 1992. Aenesidemus and the Academy. *The Classical Quarterly,* 42(1), 176–89.

Deichgräber, K. 1930. *Die griechische Empirikerschule: Sammlung der Fragmente und Darstellung der Lehre.* Berlin.

Deitz, L. 1995. "Aristoteles imperator noster. . ."? J. C. Scaliger and Aristotle on Poetic Theory. *International Journal of the Classical Tradition,* 2(1), 54–67.

Delattre, D. 2007. *Philodème de Gadara: Sur la musique, Livre IV.* Paris.

Delcomminette, S., d'Hoine, P., and Gavray, M. A. 2015. *Ancient Readings of Plato's Phaedo.* Leiden.

Denniston, J. D. 1950. *The Greek Particles,* 2nd edn. Oxford.

Depauw, M. 2015. Sale in Demotic Documents: An Overview. In É. Jakab, ed., *Sale and Community: Documents from the Ancient World.* Trieste, 67–80.

Depew, D., and Poulakos, T. 2004. *Isocrates and Civic Education.* Austin, TX.

Derda, T., Markiewicz, T., and Wipszycka, E. (eds.) 2007. *Alexandria: Auditoria of Kom el-Dikka and Late Antique Education.* Warsaw.

Di Benedetto, V. 1958. Dionisio Trace e la *Techne* a lui attribuita. *Annali della Scuola Normale Superiore di Pisa,* 27(3/4), 169–210.

Dickey, E. 2007. *Ancient Greek Scholarship: A Guide to Finding, Reading, and Understanding Scholia, Commentaries, Lexica, and Grammatical Treatises.* Oxford.

Dickie, M. 1998. Poets as Initiates in the Mysteries: Euphorion, Philicus and Posidippus. *Antike und Abendland*, **44**, 49–77.

Diels, H. 1887. Leukippos und Diogenes von Apollonia. *Rheinisches Museum für Philologie*, **42**(1), 1–14.

Dijksterhuis, E. J. 1987 [1938]. *Archimedes*, trans. C. Dikshoorn. Princeton, NJ.

Dillery, J. 1998. Hecataeus of Abdera: Hyperboreans, Egypt, and the "Interpretatio Graeca". *Historia: Zeitschrift für Alte Geschichte*, **47**(3), 255–75.

    2005. Chresmologues and Manteis: Independent Diviners and the Problem of Authority. In S. I. Johnston and P. T. Struck, eds., *Mantikê: Studies in Ancient Divination*. Leiden, 167–231.

Dillon, J. M. 1969. A Date for the Death of Nicomachus of Gerasa? *The Classical Review*, **19**(3), 274–5.

    1971. Harpocration's "Commentary on Plato": Fragments of a Middle Platonic Commentary. *California Studies in Classical Antiquity*, **4**, 125–46.

    1977. *The Middle Platonists: 80 BC to AD 220*. Ithaca, NY.

    1983. What Happened to Plato's Garden? *Hermathena*, **134**, 51–9.

    1985. Xenocrates' Metaphysics: Fr. 15 (Heinze) Re-Examined. *Ancient Philosophy*, **5**(1), 47–52.

    2003. *The Heirs of Plato: A Study of the Old Academy (347–274 BC)*. Oxford.

Dillon, S. 2006. *Ancient Greek Portrait Sculpture: Contexts, Subjects, and Styles*. Cambridge.

Dirven, L. 2007. The Emperor's New Clothes: A Note on Elagabalus' Priestly Dress. In S. G. Vashalomidze and L. Greisiger, eds., *Der Christliche Orient und seine Umwelt*. Wiesbaden, 21–36.

Dmitriev, S. 2005. *City Government in Hellenistic and Roman Asia Minor*. Oxford.

Doody, A. 2009. *Pliny's Encyclopedia: The Reception of the Natural History*. Cambridge.

Dorandi, T. 1991a. *Ricerche sulla cronologia dei filosofi ellenistici*. Berlin.

    1991b. *Filodemo: Storia dei filosofi: Platone e l'Academia (PHerc. 1021 e 164)*. Naples.

    1994. *Filodemo: Storia dei filosofi: La stoà da Zenone a Panezio (PHerc. 1018)*. Leiden.

    1995. Report: La "Villa Dei Papiri" a Ercolano e la sua Biblioteca. *Classical Philology*, **90**(2), 168–82.

    1999a. Chronology. In K. Algra, J. Barnes, J. Mansfeld and M. Schofield, eds., *The Cambridge History of Hellenistic Philosophy*. Cambridge, 31–54.

    1999b. Organization and Structure of the Philosophical Schools. In K. Algra, J. Barnes, J. Mansfeld and M. Schofield, eds., *The Cambridge History of Hellenistic Philosophy*. Cambridge, 55–64.

    2007. *Nell'officina dei classici: Come lavoravano gli autori antichi*. Rome.

Dougherty, C., and Kurke, L. (eds.) 2003. *The Cultures within Ancient Greek Culture: Contact, Conflict, Collaboration*. Cambridge.

Doval, A. J. 2001. *Cyril of Jerusalem, Mystagogue: The Authorship of the Mystagogic Catecheses*. Washington, DC.

Doxiadis, A., and Sialaros, M. 2013. Sing, Muse, of the Hypotenuse: Influences of Poetry and Rhetoric on the Formation of Greek Mathematics. In M. Asper, ed., *Writing Science: Medical and Mathematical Authorship in Ancient Greece*. Berlin, 367–409.

Drachmann, A. G. 1948. *Ktesibios, Philon and Heron: A Study in Ancient Pneumatics*. Copenhagen.

Driscoll, D. 2016. Acting the Exegete: Homeric Quotation and Interpretation in Imperial Literary Symposia. Doctoral dissertation, Stanford University.

Dueck, D. 2002. *Strabo of Amasia: A Greek Man of Letters in Augustan Rome*. London.

Duffy, J. 1984. Byzantine Medicine in the Sixth and Seventh Centuries: Aspects of Teaching and Practice. *Dumbarton Oaks Papers*, **38**, 21–7.

Duncan-Jones, R. 1962. Costs, Outlays and Summae Honorariae from Roman Africa. *Papers of the British School at Rome*, **30**, 47–115.

  1965. An Epigraphic Survey of Costs in Roman Italy. *Papers of the British School at Rome*, **33**, 189–306.

  1974. *The Economy of the Roman Empire: Quantitative Studies*. Cambridge.

  1994. *Money and Government in the Roman Empire*. Cambridge.

  1996. The Impact of the Antonine Plague. *Journal of Roman Archaeology*, **9**, 108–36.

Düring, I. 1957. *Aristotle in the Ancient Biographical Tradition*. Stockholm.

Durrani, O. 2002. Editions, Translations, Adaptations. In J. Preece, ed., *The Cambridge Companion to Kafka*. Cambridge, 206–25.

Dyroff, A. 1897. *Die Ethik der alten Stoa*. Berlin.

Ebert, T. 1993. Dialecticians and Stoics on the Classification of Propositions. In K. Döring and T. Ebert (eds.), *Dialektiker und Stoiker: Zur Logik der Stoa und ihrer Vorläufer*. Stuttgart, 11–127.

Eckhardt, G. M., and Bengtsson, A. 2010. A Brief History of Branding in China. *Journal of Macromarketing*, **30**(3), 210–21.

Edelstein, L., and Kidd, I. G. (eds.) 1972–99. *Posidonius*, 3 vols. Cambridge.

Edmunds, L. 1997. The Seal of Theognis. In L. Edmunds and R. W. Wallace, eds., *Poet, Public, and Performance in Ancient Greece*. Baltimore, 29–48.

Edward, W. A. 1928. *The Suasoriae of Seneca the Elder*. Cambridge.

Edwards, M. 1994. Plotinus and the Emperors. *Symbolae Osloenses*, **69**, 137–47.

Effe, B. 1977. *Dichtung und Lehre: Untersuchungen zur Typologie des antiken Lehrgedichts*. Munich.

Ehrenberg, V. 1951. *The People of Aristophanes: A Sociology of Old Attic Comedy*. New York.

Elliott, C. P. 2016. The Antonine Plague, Climate Change and Local Violence in Roman Egypt. *Past and Present*, **231**, 3–31.

Elsner, J. 2009. P. Artemid.: The Images. In K. Brodersen and J. Elsner, eds., *Images and Texts on the "Artemidorus Papyrus"*. Stuttgart, 35–50.

Engels, J. 2003. Antike Überlieferungen über die Schüler des Isokrates. In W. Orth, ed., *Isokrates: Neue Ansätze zur Bewertung eines politischen Schriftstellers*. Trier, 175–215.

2007. Geography and History. In J. Marincola, ed., *A Companion to Greek and Roman Historiography*. Oxford, 541–52.

Enmann, A. 1883. Eine verlorene Geschichte der römischen Kaiser und das Buch de viris illustribus urbis romae. *Philologus*, 3(supp.), 337–501.

Eramo, I. (ed.) 2010. *Siriano: Discorsi di guerra*. Bari.

Erbse, H. (ed.) 1969. *Scholia graeca in Homeri Iliadem (scholia vetera)*, vol. I: *Praefatio et scholia ad libros A–Δ continens*. Berlin.

(ed.) 1983. *Scholia graeca in Homeri Iliadem (scholia vetera)*, vol. VI: *Indices I–IV continens*. Berlin.

Erdkamp, P. 2005. *The Grain Market in the Roman Empire: A Social, Political and Economic Study*. Cambridge.

Erler, M. 2009. Epicureanism in the Roman Empire. In J. Warren, ed., *The Cambridge Companion to Epicureanism*. Cambridge, 46–64.

Eucken, C. 1983. *Isokrates: Seine Positionen in der Auseinandersetzung mit den zeitgenössischen Philosophen*. Berlin.

Evans, C., and Jasnow, B. 2014. Mapping Homer's Catalogue of Ships. *Literary and Linguistic Computing*, 29(3), 317–25.

Evans, J. 1998. *The History and Practice of Ancient Astronomy*. Oxford.

2005. A Greek Textbook of Astronomy: *Cleomedes' Lectures on Astronomy: A Translation of The Heavens* (Book Review). *Journal for the History of Astronomy*, 36(3), 340–2.

Evans, J., and Berggren, J. L. 2006. *Geminos's Introduction to the Phenomena: A Translation and Study of a Hellenistic Survey of Astronomy*. Princeton, NJ.

Evans, J., and Carman, C. C. 2014. Mechanical Astronomy: A Route to the Ancient Discovery of Epicycles and Eccentrics. In N. C. Sidoli and G. Van Brummelen, eds., *From Alexandria, through Baghdad: Surveys and Studies in the Ancient Greek and Medieval Islamic Mathematical Sciences in Honor of J. L. Berggren*. Berlin, 145–74.

Fakas, C. 2001. *Der hellenistische Hesiod: Arats Phainomena und die Tradition der antiken Lehrepik*. Wiesbaden.

Fantuzzi, M., and Hunter, R. L. 2004. *Tradition and Innovation in Hellenistic Poetry*. Cambridge.

Farrell, J. 2002. Greek Lives and Roman Careers in the Classical Vita Tradition. In P. Cheney and F. A. de Armas, eds., *European Literary Careers: The Author from Antiquity to the Renaissance*. Toronto, 24–46.

Febvre, L., and Martin, H.-J. 1958. *L'apparition du livre*. Paris.

Feeney, D. 2016. *Beyond Greek: The Beginnings of Latin Literature*. Cambridge, MA.

Feke, J. A. 2009. Ptolemy in Philosophical Context: A Study of the Relationships between Physics, Mathematics, and Theology. Doctoral dissertation, University of Toronto.

2014. Meta-Mathematical Rhetoric: Hero and Ptolemy against the Philosophers. *Historia Mathematica*, 41(3), 261–76.

Finglass, P. J. 2012. The Textual Transmission of Sophocles' Dramas. In K. Ormand, ed., *A Companion to Sophocles*. London, 9–24.

Finkelberg, M. 1998. *The Birth of Literary Fiction in Ancient Greece*. Oxford.

Fischer, K.-D. 1981. The First Latin Treatise on Horse Medicine and Its Author Pelagonius Saloninus. *Medizinhistorisches Journal*, **16**(3), 215–26.

Fittschen, K. 1991. *Zur Rekonstruktion griechischer Dichterstatuen*. Berlin.

Fitzgerald, J. T., Obbink, D. D., and Holland, G. S. (eds.) 2004. *Philodemus and the New Testament World*. Leiden.

Fleming, S. J. 1999. *Roman Glass: Reflections on Cultural Change*. Philadelphia.

Fleming, T. J. 1999. The Survival of Greek Dramatic Music from the Fifth Century to the Roman Period. In B. Gentili and F. Perusino, eds., *La colometria antica dei testi poetici greci*. Pisa, 17–29.

Flemming, R. 2007. Galen's Imperial Order of Knowledge. In J. König and T. Whitmarsh, eds., *Ordering Knowledge in the Roman Empire*. Cambridge, 241–77.

Flinterman, J. J. 2014. Pythagoreans in Rome and Asia Minor around the Turn of the Common Era. In C. A. Huffman, ed., *A History of Pythagoreanism*. Cambridge, 341–59.

Flory, S. 1980. Who Read Herodotus' Histories? *The American Journal of Philology*, **101**(1), 12–28.

Foertmeyer, V. 1988. The Dating of the Pompe of Ptolemy II Philadelphus. *Historia: Zeitschrift für Alte Geschichte*, **37**(1), 90–104.

Ford, A. L. 2011. *Aristotle as Poet: The Song for Hermias and Its Contexts*. Oxford.

Fornara, C. W. 1971. *Herodotus: An Interpretative Essay*. Oxford.

Fortenbaugh, W. W., and White, S. A. (eds.) 2004. *Lyco of Traos and Hieronymus of Rhodes: Text, Translation, and Discussion*. New Brunswick, NJ.

2006. *Aristo of Ceos: Text, Translation, and Discussion*. New Brunswick, NJ.

Foucault, M. 1977 [1969]. What Is an Author?, trans. D. Bouchard and S. Simon. In D. Bouchard, ed., *Language, Counter-Memory, Practice: Selected Essays and Interviews by Michel Foucault*. Ithaca, NY, 113–38.

Fournet, J. L. (ed.) 2008. *Les archives de Dioscore d'Aphrodité cent ans après leur découverte: Histoire et culture dans l'Egypte byzantine*. Paris.

Fowden, G. 1986. *The Egyptian Hermes: A Historical Approach to the Late Antique Mind*. Princeton, NJ.

Fowler, D. H. F. 1999. *The Mathematics of Plato's Academy: A New Reconstruction*, 2nd edn. Oxford.

Franco, C. 2003. *Senza ritegno: Il cane e la donna nell'immaginario della Grecia antica*. Bologna.

Fraser, P. M. 1969. The Career of Erasistratus of Ceos. *Rendiconti del Istituto Lombardo*, **103**, 518–37.

1972. *Ptolemaic Alexandria*, 3 vols. Oxford.

Frede, M. 1987. The Empiricist Attitude towards Reason and Theory. In R. J. Hankinson, ed., *Method, Medicine and Metaphysics: Studies in the Philosophy of Ancient Science*. Edmonton, 79–97.

1990. An Empiricist View of Knowledge: Memorism. In S. Everson, ed., *Epistemology: Cambridge Companions to Ancient Thought*. Cambridge, 225–50.

1999. Epilogue. In K. Algra, J. Barnes, J. Mansfeld and M. Schofield, eds., *The Cambridge History of Hellenistic Philosophy*. Cambridge, 771–97.

Frederiksen, R. 2002. The Greek Theatre: A Typical Building in the Urban Centre of the Polis? In T. H. Nielsen, ed., *Even More Studies in the Ancient Greek Polis*. Stuttgart, 65–124.

Freeth, T. 2002. The Antikythera Mechanism: Challenging the Classic Research. *Mediterranean Archaeology and Archaeometry*, **2**(1), 21–35.

Frier, B. 1982. Roman Life Expectancy: Ulpian's Evidence. *Harvard Studies in Classical Philology*, **86**, 213–51.

2000. The Demography of the Early Roman Empire. In P. Garnsey, D. Rathbone and A. Bowman, eds., *The Cambridge Ancient History*, vol. XI: *AD 70–192*. Cambridge, 787–816.

Frye, N. 1957. *Anatomy of Criticism: Four Essays*. Princeton, NJ.

Fuentes-Gonzalez, P. P. 1998. *Les diatribes de Télès: Introduction, texte revu, traduction et commentaire des fragments*. Paris.

Fujita, M., and Thisse, J.-F. 2002. *Economics of Agglomeration: Cities, Industrial Location, and Globalization*. Cambridge.

Funkenstein, A. 1986. *Theology and the Scientific Imagination from the Middle Ages to the Seventeenth Century*. Princeton, NJ.

Fürst, A. 2011. Origen: Exegesis and Philosophy in Early Christian Alexandria. In J. Lössl and J. W. Watt, eds., *Interpreting the Bible and Aristotle in Late Antiquity: The Alexandrian Commentary Tradition between Rome and Baghdad*. Farnham, 13–32.

Gagarin, M. 2013. Laws and Legislation in Ancient Greece. In H. Beck, ed., *A Companion to Ancient Greek Government*. New York, 221–34.

Gaiser, K. 1988. *Philodems Academica: Die Berichte über Platon und die Alte Akademie in zwei herkulanensischen Papyri*. Stuttgart.

Gallagher, C. 2006. The Rise of Fictionality. In F. Moretti, ed., *The Novel*, vol. I: *History, Geography, and Culture*. Princeton, NJ, 336–63.

Gallo, I. 1980. *Frammenti biografici da papiri*, 2 vols. Rome.

Gamble, H. Y. 1995. *Books and Readers in the Early Church: A History of Early Christian Texts*. New Haven, CT.

Garani, M. 2007. *Empedocles Redivivus: Poetry and Analogy in Lucretius*. London.

Garani, M., and Konstan, D. (eds.) 2014. *The Philosophizing Muse: The Influence of Greek Philosophy on Roman Poetry*. Cambridge.

Garnsey, P. 2010. Roman Patronage. In S. McGill, C. Sogno and E. Watts, eds., *From the Tetrarchs to the Theodosians: Later Roman History and Culture, 284–450 CE*. Cambridge, 33–54.

Gattinoni, F. L. 1997. *Duride di Samo*. Rome.

Gavrilov, A. K. 1997. Techniques of Reading in Classical Antiquity. *The Classical Quarterly*, **47**(1), 56–73.

Geagan, D. J. 1991. The Sarapion Monument and the Quest for Status in Roman Athens. *Zeitschrift für Papyrologie und Epigraphik*, **85**, 145–65.

Gee, E. 2000. *Ovid, Aratus and Augustus: Astronomy in Ovid's Fasti*. Cambridge.

2013. *Aratus and the Astronomical Tradition*. Oxford.

Geiger, J. 1999. Some Latin Authors from the Greek East. *The Classical Quarterly*, **49**(2), 606–17.

Gentili, B. 2006 [1984]. *Poesia e pubblico nella Grecia antica: Da Omero al V secolo.* Rome.

Germany, R. 2014. The Unity of Time in Menander. In A. H. Sommerstein, ed., *Menander in Contexts*. London, 90–105.

Giannantoni, G. 1990–1. *Socratis et Socraticorum reliquiae*, 4 vols. Naples.

Giannini, A. 1965. *Paradoxographorum Graecorum reliquiae*. Milan.

Gianotti, G. F. 2005. Odisseo mendico a Troia (PKöln VI 245). In F. Crevatin and G. Tedeschi, eds., *Scrivere, Leggere, Interpretare: Studi di antichità in onore di Sergio Daris*. Trieste, 225–32.

Gibson, R. K., and Steel, C. 2010. The Indistinct Literary Careers of Cicero and Pliny the Younger. In P. Hardie and H. Moore, eds., *Classical Literary Careers and Their Reception*. Cambridge, 118–37.

Gigante, M. 1995 [1990]. *Philodemus in Italy: The Books from Herculaneum*, trans. D. D. Obbink. Ann Arbor, MI.

  2004. Vergil in the Shadow of Vesuvius. In D. Armstrong, J. Fish, P. A. Johnston and M. B. Skinner, eds., *Vergil, Philodemus, and the Augustans*. Austin, TX, 85–99.

Gill, C. 2003. The School in the Roman Imperial Period. In B. Inwood, ed., *The Cambridge Companion to the Stoics*. Cambridge, 33–58.

  2006. *The Structured Self in Hellenistic and Roman Thought*. Oxford.

Gladhill, B. 2012. The Emperor's No Clothes: Suetonius and the Dynamics of Corporeal Ecphrasis. *Classical Antiquity*, **31**(2), 315–48.

Gleason, M. W. 1995. *Making Men: Sophists and Self-Presentation in Ancient Rome*. Princeton, NJ.

  2009. Shock and Awe: The Performance Dimension of Galen's Anatomy Demonstrations. In C. Gill, T. Whitmarsh and J. Wilkins, eds., *Galen and the World of Knowledge*. Cambridge, 85–114.

Glover, R. 1944. The Elephant in Ancient War. *The Classical Journal*, **39**(5), 257–69.

Glucker, J. 1978. *Antiochus and the Late Academy*. Göttingen.

  1998. Theophrastus, the Academy, and the Athenian Philosophical Atmosphere. In J. M. van Ophuijsen and M. van Raalte, eds., *Theophrastus: Reappraising the Sources*. New Brunswick, NJ, 299–316.

Gmirkin, R. E. 2008. *Berossus and Genesis, Manetho and Exodus: Hellenistic Histories and the Date of the Pentateuch*. London.

Gold, B. K. 1985. Pompey and Theophanes of Mytilene. *The American Journal of Philology*, **106**(3), 312–27.

  1987. *Literary Patronage in Greece and Rome*. Chapel Hill, NC.

Goldhill, S. 2002. *The Invention of Prose*. Cambridge.

Goldhill, S., and Osborne, R. (eds.) 1999. *Performance Culture and Athenian Democracy*. Cambridge.

Goldstein, B. R., and Bowen, A. C. 1983. A New View of Early Greek Astronomy. *Isis*, **74**(3), 330–40.

1989. On Early Hellenistic Astronomy: Timocharis and the First Callippic Calendar. *Centaurus*, **32**(3), 272–93.

1991. The Introduction of Dated Observations and Precise Measurement in Greek Astronomy. *Archive for History of Exact Sciences*, **43**(2), 93–132.

Goldstein, R., Almenberg, J., Dreber, A., Emerson, J. W., Herschkowitsch, A., and Katz, J. 2008. Do More Expensive Wines Taste Better? Evidence from a Large Sample of Blind Tastings. *Journal of Wine Economics*, **3**(1), 1–9.

González, P. F. 1998. Teles Reconsidered. *Mnemosyne*, **51**(1), 1–19.

Goody, J. 2009. *The Eurasian Miracle*. Cambridge.

Gorak, J. 1991. *The Making of the Modern Canon: Genesis and Crisis of a Literary Idea*. London.

Göransson, T. 1995. *Albinus, Alcinous, Arius Didymus*. Gothenburg.

Gordon, P. 2012. *The Invention and Gendering of Epicurus*. Ann Arbor, MI.

Görgemanns, H. 1970. *Untersuchungen zu Plutarchs Dialog De facie in orbe lunae*. Heidelberg.

Gottschalk, H. B. 1980. *Heraclides of Pontus*. Oxford.

1990. The Earliest Aristotelian Commentators. In R. Sorabji, ed., *Aristotle Transformed: The Ancient Commentators and Their Influence*. Ithaca, NY, 55–82.

2002. Eudemus and the Peripatos. In I. M. Bodnár and W. W. Fortenbaugh, eds., *Eudemus of Rhodes*. New Brunswick, NJ, 25–37.

Gould, S. J., and Eldredge, N. 1977. Punctuated Equilibria: The Tempo and Mode of Evolution Reconsidered. *Paleobiology*, **3**(2), 115–51.

Goulet, R. (ed.) 1989. *Dictionnaire des philosophes antiques*, vol. I: *Abam(m)on à Axiothéa*. Paris.

1994. *Dictionnaire des philosophes antiques*, vol. II: *Babélyca d'Argos à Dyscolius*. Paris.

2000. *Dictionnaire des philosophes antiques*, vol. III: *D'Eccélos à Juvénal*. Paris.

2005. *Dictionnaire des philosophes antiques*, vol. IV: *De Labeo à Ovidius*. Paris.

2012a. *Dictionnaire des philosophes antiques*, vol. V a: *De Paccius à Plotin*. Paris.

2012b. *Dictionnaire des philosophes antiques*, vol. V b: *De Plotina à Rutilius Rufus*. Paris.

Gow, A. S. F. 1965. *Machon: The Fragments*. Cambridge.

Gow, A. S. F., and Page, D. L. (eds.) 1965. *The Greek Anthology*. Cambridge.

Gowler, D. B. 2006. The Chreia. In A. J. Levine, D. C. Allison Jr. and J. D. Crossan, eds., *The Historical Jesus in Context*. Princeton, NJ, 132–48.

Grabiner, J. V. 1981. *The Origins of Cauchy's Rigor in Calculus*. Mineola, NY.

Grafton, A., and Williams, M. 2006. *Christianity and the Transformation of the Book: Origen, Eusebius and the Library of Caesarea*. Cambridge, MA.

Grant, M. (ed.) 1997. *Dieting for an Emperor: A Translation of Books 1 and 4 of Oribasius' Medical Compilations with an Introduction and Commentary*. Leiden.

Grant. R. M. 1980. *Eusebius as Church Historian*. Oxford.

Graziosi, B., 2002. *Inventing Homer: The Early Reception of Epic*. Cambridge.

Greco, A. N. 2013. *The Book Publishing Industry*. London.

Green, J. R. 1991. On Seeing and Depicting the Theatre in Classical Athens. *Greek, Roman and Byzantine Studies*, **32**(1), 15–50.

Green, P. 1986. The New Urban Culture: Alexandria, Antioch, Pergamon. *Grand Street*, **5**(2), 140–52.

    1990. *Alexander to Actium: The Historical Evolution of the Hellenistic Age*. Berkeley, CA.

Green, R. P. H. 1980. The Correspondence of Ausonius. *L'Antiquité classique*, **49** (1), 191–211.

    1985. Still Waters Run Deep: A New Study of the Professores of Bordeaux. *The Classical Quarterly*, **35**(2), 491–506.

Greenberg, J. 2003. Plagued by Doubt: Reconsidering the Impact of a Mortality Crisis in the 2nd C. AD. *Journal of Roman Archaeology*, **16**, 413–25.

Greenberg, N. A. 1958. Metathesis as an Instrument in the Criticism of Poetry. *Transactions and Proceedings of the American Philological Association*, **89**, 262–70.

Greenspan, P., Heinz, G., and Hargrove, J. L. 2008. Lives of the Artists: Differences in Longevity between Old Master Sculptors and Painters. *Age and Ageing*, **37**(1), 102–4.

Grenfell, B. P., and Hunt, A. S. (eds.) 1906. *The Hibeh Papyri*. London.

Griffin, J. 1977. The Epic Cycle and the Uniqueness of Homer. *The Journal of Hellenic Studies*, **97**, 39–53.

Griffin, M. J. 2015. *Aristotle's Categories in the Early Roman Empire*. Oxford.

Griffith, M. 1983. Personality in Hesiod. *Classical Antiquity*, **2**(1), 37–65.

    1990. Contest and Contradiction in Early Greek Poetry. In M. Griffith and D. J. Mastronarde, eds., *Cabinet of the Muses: Essays on Classical and Comparative Literature in Honor of Thomas G. Rosenmeyer*. Atlanta, GA, 185–207.

Griffiths, F. T. 1979. *Theocritus at Court*. Leiden.

Grossberg, L. 1987. The In-Difference of Television. *Screen*, **28**(2), 28–46.

Guillory, J. 1993. *Cultural Capital: The Problem of Literary Canon Formation*. Chicago.

Gutzwiller, K. 1992. Callimachus' Lock of Berenice: Fantasy, Romance, and Propaganda. *The American Journal of Philology*, **113**(3), 359–85.

    1997. The Poetics of Editing in Meleager's *Garland*. *Transactions of the American Philological Association*, **127**, 169–200.

    2004. Seeing Thought: Timomachus' Medea and Ecphrastic Epigram. *The American Journal of Philology*, **125**(3), 339–86.

    (ed.) 2005. *The New Posidippus: A Hellenistic Poetry Book*. Oxford.

    2010. Heroic Epitaphs of the Classical Age: The Aristotelian Peplos and Beyond. In M. Baumbach, A. Petrovic and I. Petrovic, eds., *Archaic and Classical Greek Epigram*. New York, 219–49.

Gutzwiller, K., and Çelik, Ö. 2012. New Menander Mosaics from Antioch. *American Journal of Archaeology*, **116**(4), 573–623.

Haake, M. 2004. Documentary Evidence, Literary Forgery, or Manipulation of Historical Documents? Diogenes Laertius and an Athenian Honorary Decree for Zeno of Citium. *The Classical Quarterly*, **54**(2), 470–83.

2007. *Der Philosoph in der Stadt: Untersuchungen zur öffentlichen Rede über Philosophen und Philosophie in den hellenistischen Poleis*. Munich.

2008. Das Gesetz des Sophokles und die Schließung der Philosophenschulen in Athen unter Demetrios Poliorketes. In H. Hugonnard-Roche, ed., *L'enseignement supérieur dans les mondes antiques et médiévaux: Aspects institutionnels, juridiques et pédagogiques*. Paris, 89–112.

Habermann, W. 1998. Zur chronologischen Verteilung der papyrologischen Zeugnisse. *Zeitschrift für Papyrologie und Epigraphik*, **122**, 144–60.

Habicht, C. 1992. Athens and the Ptolemies. *Classical Antiquity*, **11**(1), 68–90.

Habsieger, L., Kazarian, M., and Lando, S. 1998. On the Second Number of Plutarch. *The American Mathematical Monthly*, **105**(5), 446.

Hadot, I. 1987. Les introductions aux commentaires exégétiques chez les auteurs néoplatoniciens et les auteurs chrétiens. In M. Tardieu, ed., *Les règles de l'interprétation*. Paris, 99–122.

Hagel, S. 2009. *Ancient Greek Music: A New Technical History*. Cambridge.

Hägg, T. 1992. Hierocles the Lover of Truth and Eusebius the Sophist. *Symbolae Osloenses*, **67**, 138–50.

2010. Canon Formation in Greek Literary Culture. In E. Thomassen, ed., *Canon and Canonicity: The Formation and Use of Scripture*. Copenhagen, 109–28.

Hall, E., and Wyles, R. (eds.) 2008. *New Directions in Ancient Pantomime*. Oxford.

Hall, J. M. 1997. *Ethnic Identity in Greek Antiquity*. Cambridge.

Hall, L. J. 2004. *Roman Berytus: Beirut in Late Antiquity*. London.

Hammond, N. G. L. 1991. The Various Guards of Philip II and Alexander III. *Historia: Zeitschrift für Alte Geschichte*, **40**(4), 396–418.

Hammond, N. G. L., and Griffith, G. T. 1979. *A History of Macedonia*, 2 vols. Oxford.

Hamon, P. 2009. Démocraties grecques après Alexandre: À propos de trois ouvrages récents. *Topoi*, **16**(2), 347–82.

Hanchey, D. P. 2009. *Cicero the Dialogician: The Construction of Community at the End of the Republic*. Austin, TX.

2013. Otium as Civic and Personal Stability in Cicero's Dialogues. *The Classical World*, **106**(2), 171–97.

Hanink, J. 2014. *Lycurgan Athens and the Making of Classical Tragedy*. Cambridge.

Hankinson, R. J. 1991. Galen's Anatomy of the Soul. *Phronesis*, **36**(2), 197–233.

2003. Stoicism and Medicine. In B. Inwood, ed., *The Cambridge Companion to the Stoics*.Cambridge, 295–309.

Hansen, M. H. 1984. The Number of *Rhetores* in the Athenian *Ecclesia*, 355–322 BC. *Greek, Roman and Byzantine Studies*, **25**(2), 123–55.

1987. *The Athenian Assembly in the Age of Demosthenes*. Oxford.

1991. *The Athenian Democracy in the Age of Demosthenes: Structure, Principles, and Ideology*. Norman, OK.

2006. *The Shotgun Method: The Demography of the Ancient Greek City-State Culture.* Columbia, MO.

Hanson, A. E. 2010. Doctors' Literacy and Papyri of Medical Content. In M. Horstmanshoff, ed., *Hippocrates and Medical Education.* Leiden, 187–204.

Harbsmeier, C. 1999. Authorial Presence in Some Pre-Buddhist Chinese Texts. In V. Alleton and M. Lackner, eds., *De l'un au multiple: Traductions du chinois vers les langues européennes.* Paris, 221–54.

Hardie, A. 1983. *Statius and the Silvae: Poets, Patrons, and Epideixis in the Graeco-Roman World.* Prenton, UK.

2005. Sappho, the Muses, and Life after Death. *Zeitschrift für Papyrologie und Epigraphik,* **154,** 13–32.

Hardie, P. 1995. The Speech of Pythagoras in Ovid *Metamorphoses* 15: Empedoclean *Epos. The Classical Quarterly,* **45**(1), 204–14.

Hardie, P., and Moore, H. (eds.) 2010. *Classical Literary Careers and Their Reception.* Cambridge.

Harding, P. 2007. Local History and Atthidography. In J. Marincola, ed., *A Companion to Greek and Roman Historiography.* Oxford, 180–8.

Harker, A. 2008. *Loyalty and Dissidence in Roman Egypt: The Case of the Acta Alexandrinorum.* Cambridge.

Harper, K. 2015. Pandemics and Passages to Late Antiquity: Rethinking the Plague of c. 249–270 Described by Cyprian. *Journal of Roman Archaeology,* **28,** 223–60.

Harrauer, H. (ed.) 1987. *Corpus Papyrorum Raineri.* Vienna.

Harris, E. M. 2002. Workshop, Marketplace, and Household: The Nature of Technical Specialization in Classical Athens and Its Influence on Economy and Society. In P. Cartledge, E. E. Cohen and L. Foxhall, eds., *Money, Labour and Land: Approaches to the Economies of Ancient Greece.* London, 67–99.

Harris, W. V. 1991. *Ancient Literacy.* Cambridge, MA.

Harrison, S. J. (ed.) 2007. *The Cambridge Companion to Horace.* Cambridge.

2008. The Sophist at Play in Court: Apuleius' *Apology* and His Literary Career. In W. Riess, ed., *Paideia at Play: Learning and Wit in Apuleius.* Groningen, 3–15.

Hatzimichali, M. 2011. *Potamo of Alexandria and the Emergence of Eclecticism in Late Hellenistic Philosophy.* Cambridge.

2012. Antiochus' Biography. In D. N. Sedley, ed., *The Philosophy of Antiochus.* Cambridge, 9–30.

2013. The Texts of Plato and Aristotle in the First Century BC. In M. Schofield, ed., *Aristotle, Plato and Pythagoreanism in the First Century BC: New Directions for Philosophy.* Cambridge, 1–27.

Havelock, E. A. 1963. *Preface to Plato.* Cambridge, MA.

Haynes, H. 2003. *The History of Make-Believe: Tacitus on Imperial Rome.* Berkeley, CA.

Heath, M. 1996. The Family of Minucianus? *Zeitschrift für Papyrologie und Epigraphik,* **113,** 66–70.

2003. Porphyry's Rhetoric. *The Classical Quarterly*, **53**(1), 141–66.

Heath, M., and Lefkowitz, M. 1991. Epinician Performance. *Classical Philology*, **86**(3), 173–91.

Heath, T. L. 1921. *A History of Greek Mathematics*, 2 vols. Oxford.

Hedrick, C. W. 1999. Democracy and the Athenian Epigraphical Habit. *Hesperia: The Journal of the American School of Classical Studies at Athens*, **68**(3), 387–439.

Heilen, S. 2011. Some Metrical Fragments from Nechepsos and Petosiris. In I. Boehm and W. Hübner, eds., *La poésie astrologique dans l'Antiquité*. Paris, 23–93.

(ed.) 2015. *Hadriani genitura: Die astrologischen Fragmente des Antigonos von Nikaia: Edition, Übersetzung und Kommentar*. Berlin.

Hekster, O. 2001. All in the Family: The Appointment of Emperors Designate in the Second Century AD. In L. de Blois, ed., *Administration, Prosopography and Appointment Policies in the Roman Empire*. Amsterdam, 35–49.

Henderson, J. 2010. The *Satyrica* and the Greek Novel: Revisions and Some Open Questions. *International Journal of the Classical Tradition*, **17**(4), 483–96.

Hendrickson, T. 2013. Poetry and Biography in the *Athēnaiōn Politeia*: The Case of Solon. *The Classical Journal*, **109**, 1–19.

Henry, O. (ed.) 2013. *4th Century Karia: Defining a Karian Identity under the Hekatomnids*. Paris.

Herington, J. 1985. *Poetry into Drama: Early Tragedy and the Greek Poetic Tradition*. Berkeley, CA.

Herman, G. 1986. *Ritualised Friendship and the Greek City*. Cambridge.

Hermansen, G. 1982. The Stuppatores and Their Guild in Ostia. *American Journal of Archaeology*, **86**(1), 121–6.

Hewsen, R. H. 1971. The Geography of Pappus of Alexandria: A Translation of the Armenian Fragments. *Isis*, **62**(2), 186–207.

Hickey, T. 2012. *Wine, Wealth, and the State in Late Antique Egypt: The House of Apion at Oxyrhynchus*. Ann Arbor, MI.

Higbie, C. 2011. Cicero the Homerist. *Oral Tradition*, **26**(2), 379–88.

Hirzel, R. 1895. *Der Dialog: Ein literarhistorischer Versuch*. Leipzig.

Hobson, D. W. 1985. House and Household in Roman Egypt. *Yale Classical Studies*, **28**, 211–29.

Hock, R. F., and O'Neil, E. N. 1985. *The Chreia in Ancient Rhetoric: The Progymnasmata*. Atlanta, GA.

(eds.) 2002. *The Chreia and Ancient Rhetoric: Classroom Exercises*. Leiden.

Hodkinson, S. 2000. *Property and Wealth in Classical Sparta*. London.

Hoepfner, W. 2003. *Der Koloss von Rhodos und die Bauten des Helios: Neue Forschungen zu einem der Sieben Weltwunder*. Darmstadt.

Hogendijk, J. P. 1986. Arabic Traces of Lost Works of Apollonius. *Archive for History of Exact Sciences*, **35**(3), 187–253.

1987. On Euclid's Lost Porisms and Its Arabic Traces. *Bollettino di storia delle scienze matematiche*, **7**(1), 93–115.

Højte, J. M. 2005. *Roman Imperial Statue Bases: From Augustus to Commodus*. Aarhus.

Holford-Strevens, L. 1993. The Harmonious Pulse. *The Classical Quarterly*, **43**(2), 475–9.

Holliday, L. 2011. From Alexandria to Caesarea: Reassessing Origen's Appointment to the Presbyterate. *Numen*, **58**, 674–96.

Hollis, A. S. 1977. L. Varius Rufus, *De Morte* (Frs. 1–4 Morel). *The Classical Quarterly*, **27**(1), 187–90.

   (ed.) 1990. *Callimachus: Hecale*. Oxford.

Holmes, B. 2010. *The Symptom and the Subject: The Emergence of the Physical Body in Ancient Greece*. Princeton, NJ.

Honoré, T. 2010a. Ulpian, Natural Law and Stoic Influence. *The Legal History Review*, **78**(1/2), 199–208.

   2010b. *Justinian's Digest: Character and Compilation*. Oxford.

Hook, B. S. 2005. Oedipus and Thyestes among the Philosophers: Incest and Cannibalism in Plato, Diogenes, and Zeno. *Classical Philology*, **100**(1), 17–40.

Hopkins, K. 1980. Brother–Sister Marriage in Roman Egypt. *Comparative Studies in Society and History*, **22**(3), 303–54.

   1991. Conquest by Book. In *Literacy in the Roman World*. Ann Arbor, MI, 133–58.

Horden, P. 2005. Mediterranean Plague in the Age of Justinian. In M. Maas, ed., *The Cambridge Companion to the Age of Justinian*. Cambridge, 134–60.

Hornblower, S. 1982. *Mausolus*. Oxford.

   1995. The Fourth-Century and Hellenistic Reception of Thucydides. *The Journal of Hellenic Studies*, **115**, 47–68.

   2002. *A Commentary on Thucydides*. Oxford.

Horsfall, N. 1991. Virgil and the Poetry of Explanations. *Greece and Rome*, **38**(2), 203–11.

Horster, M., and Reitz, C. (eds.) 2010. *Condensing Texts – Condensed Texts*. Stuttgart.

Houston, G. W. 2009. Papyrological Evidence for Book Collections and Libraries in the Roman Empire. In W. A. Johnson and H. N. Parker, eds., *Ancient Literacies: The Culture of Reading in Greece and Rome*. Oxford, 233–67.

Høyrup, J. 1990. Sub-Scientific Mathematics: Observations on a Pre-Modern Phenomenon. *History of Science*, **28**(1), 63–87.

Hubbard, T. K. 1994. Elemental Psychology and the Date of Semonides of Amorgos. *The American Journal of Philology*, **115**(2), 175–97.

Huffman, C. A. 1993. *Philolaus of Croton: Pythagorean and Presocratic*. Cambridge.

   2005. *Archytas of Tarentum: Pythagorean, Philosopher and Mathematician King*. Cambridge.

Humphrey, J. H. 1986. *Roman Circuses: Arenas for Chariot Racing*. Berkeley, CA.

Hunink, V. J. C. 2005. *Tertullian: De Pallio: A Commentary*. Amsterdam.

Hunter, R. L. 1979. The Comic Chorus in the Fourth Century. *Zeitschrift für Papyrologie und Epigraphik*, **36**, 23–38.

   1989. *Apollonius of Rhodes: Argonautica Book III*. Cambridge.

   1995. Written in the Stars: Poetry and Philosophy in the *Phaenomena* of Aratus. *Arachnion*, **2**, 1–34.

2004. Epic in a Minor Key. In M. Fantuzzi and R. L. Hunter, *Tradition and Innovation in Hellenistic Poetry*. Cambridge, 191–245.

2006. *The Shadow of Callimachus: Studies in the Reception of Hellenistic Poetry at Rome*. Cambridge.

Hurtado, L. W. 2006. *The Earliest Christian Artifacts: Manuscripts and Christian Origins*. Grand Rapids, MI.

Hutchinson, G. O. 2001. *Greek Lyric Poetry: A Commentary on Selected Larger Pieces: Alcman, Stesichorus, Sappho, Alcaeus, Ibycus, Anacreon, Simonides, Bacchylides, Pindar, Sophocles, Euripides*. Oxford.

Huxley, G. 1964. Aristarchus of Samos and Graeco-Babylonian Astronomy. *Greek, Roman and Byzantine Studies*, 5(2), 123–31.

Iannaccone, L. R., Haight, C. E., and Rubin, J. 2011. Lessons from Delphi: Religious Markets and Spiritual Capitals. *Journal of Economic Behavior and Organization*, 77(3), 326–38.

Iddeng, J. W. 2006. Publica aut peri! The Releasing and Distribution of Roman Books. *Symbolae Osloenses*, 81, 58–84.

Ierodiakonou, K. 2002. Aristotle's Use of Examples in the *Prior Analytics*. *Phronesis*, 47(2), 127–52.

Inowlocki, S. 2011. Eusebius' Construction of a Christian Culture in an Apologetic Context: Reading the *Praeparatio Evangelica* as a Library. In S. Inowlocki and C. Zamagni, eds., *Reconsidering Eusebius: Collected Papers on Literary, Historical, and Theological Issues*. Leiden, 199–224.

Inwood, B. 2001. *The Poem of Empedocles: A Text and Translation with an Introduction*. Toronto.

2014. Walking and Talking: Reflections on Divisions of the Soul in Stoicism. In K. Corcilius and D. Perler, eds., *Partitioning the Soul: Debates from Plato to Leibniz*. Berlin, 63–83.

Ioppolo, A. M. 1985. Lo stoicismo di Erillo. *Phronesis*, 30(1), 58–78.

Irvine, M. 1994. *The Making of Textual Culture: Grammatica and Literary Theory 350–1100*. Cambridge.

Irwin, E. 2005. *Solon and Early Greek Poetry: The Politics of Exhortation*. Cambridge.

Jackson, H. 1920. Aristotle's Lecture-Room and Lectures. *The Journal of Philology*, 35, 191–200.

Jaeger, M. 2008. *Archimedes and the Roman Imagination*. Ann Arbor, MI.

Jaeger, W. W. 1944 [1939]. *Paideia: The Ideals of Greek Culture*, vol. III: *The Conflict of Cultural Ideals in the Age of Plato*, trans. G. Highet. Oxford.

James, A. W. 1972. The Zeus Hymns of Cleanthes and Aratus. *Antichthon*, 6, 28–38.

Janiszewski, P. 2006. *The Missing Link: Greek Pagan Historiography in the Second Half of the Third Century and in the Fourth Century AD*. Warsaw.

Janko, R. 2000. *Philodemus: On Poems: Book One*. Oxford.

Jennings, V., and Katsaros, A. (eds.) 2007. *The World of Ion of Chios*. Leiden.

Johnson, A. P. 2011. Eusebius the Educator: The Context of the *General Elementary Introduction*. In S. Inowlocki and C. Zamagni, eds.,

*Reconsidering Eusebius: Collected Papers on Literary, Historical, and Theological Issues*. Leiden, 99–118.

Johnson, R. 1959. Isocrates' Methods of Teaching. *The American Journal of Philology*, **80**(1), 25–36.

Johnson, W. A. 2000. Toward a Sociology of Reading in Classical Antiquity. *The American Journal of Philology*, **121**(4), 593–627.

2004. *Bookrolls and Scribes in Oxyrhynchus*. Toronto.

2010. *Readers and Reading Culture in the High Roman Empire: A Study of Elite Communities*. Oxford.

Johnston, A. W. 1987. IG II 2 2311 and the Number of Panathenaic Amphorae. *Annual of the British School at Athens*, **82**, 125–9.

Johnstone, S. 2014. A New History of Libraries and Books in the Hellenistic Period. *Classical Antiquity*, **33**(2), 347–93.

Joly, R. 1983. Hippocrates and the School of Cos. In M. Ruse, ed., *Nature Animated*. Dordrecht, 29–47.

Jones, A. H. M., Martindale, J. R., and Morris, J. 1971–92. *The Prosopography of the Later Roman Empire*, 3 vols. Cambridge.

Jones, A. R. 1990. Ptolemy's First Commentator. *Transactions of the American Philosophical Society*, **80**(7), i–vi, 1–61.

1991. Hipparchus's Computations of Solar Longitudes. *Journal for the History of Astronomy*, **22**(2), 101–25.

(ed.) 1999. *Astronomical Papyri from Oxyrhynchus (P. Oxy. 4133–4300a)*, 2 vols. Philadelphia.

2003. The Stoics and the Astronomical Sciences. In B. Inwood, ed., *The Cambridge Companion to the Stoics*. Cambridge, 328–44.

2005. Ptolemy's *Canobic Inscription* and Heliodorus' Observation Reports. *SCIAMVS*, **6**, 53–98.

2006. The Astronomical Inscription from Keskintos, Rhodes. *Mediterranean Archaeology and Archaeometry*, **6**(3), 215–22.

2010. Ancient Rejection and Adoption of Ptolemy's Frame of Reference for Longitudes. In A. R. Jones, ed., *Ptolemy in Perspective: Use and Criticism of His Work from Antiquity to the Nineteenth Century*. Dordrecht, 11–44.

Jones, C. P. 1986. *Culture and Society in Lucian*. Cambridge, MA.

Jory, E. J. 1981. The Literary Evidence for the Beginnings of Imperial Pantomime. *Bulletin of the Institute of Classical Studies*, **28**(1), 147–61.

Jouanna, J., and Demont, P. 1981. Le sens d'ἰχώρ chez Homère (*Iliade* V, v. 340 et 416) et Eschyle (*Agamemnon*, v. 1480) en relation avec les emplois du mot dans la collection hippocratique. *Revue des études anciennes*, **83**(3/4), 197–209.

Ju, A. E. 2013. Posidonius as Historian of Philosophy: An Interpretation of Plutarch, *de Animae Procreatione in Timaeo* 22, 1023b–c. In M. Schofield, ed., *Aristotle, Plato and Pythagoreanism in the First Century BC: New Directions for Philosophy*. Cambridge, 95–117.

Kahn, C. H. 1996. *Plato and the Socratic Dialogue: The Philosophical Use of a Literary Form*. Cambridge.

1997. Greek Religion and Philosophy in the Sisyphus Fragment. *Phronesis*, **42**(3), 247–62.

Kaldellis, A. 2007. *Hellenism in Byzantium: The Transformations of Greek Identity and the Reception of the Classical Tradition*. Cambridge.

2015. *Byzantine Readings of Ancient Historians: Texts in Translation, with Introductions and Notes*. London.

Kanavou, N. 2011. *Aristophanes' Comedy of Names: A Study of Speaking Names in Aristophanes*. Berlin.

Kaschnitz von Weinberg, G. 1926. *Spätrömische Porträts*. Leipzig.

Kassel, R., and Austin, C. 1983–2001. *Poetae comici graeci*, 8 vols. Berlin.

Kaster, R. A. 1988. *Guardians of Language: The Grammarian and Society in Late Antiquity*. Berkeley, CA.

Kaufman, R. R. 1974. The Patron–Client Concept and Macro-Politics: Prospects and Problems. *Comparative Studies in Society and History*, **16**(3), 284–308.

Kechagia, E. 2011. *Plutarch against Colotes: A Lesson in History of Philosophy*. Oxford.

Keenan, J. G. 1985. Notes on Absentee Landlordism at Aphrodito. *The Bulletin of the American Society of Papyrologists*, **22**(1/4), 137–69.

Kelly, G. 2003. The New Rome and the Old: Ammianus Marcellinus' Silences on Constantinople. *The Classical Quarterly*, **53**(2), 588–607.

Kemezis, A. M. 2010. Lucian, Fronto, and the Absence of Contemporary Historiography under the Antonines. *The American Journal of Philology*, **131**(2), 285–325.

Kennedy, G. A. 1959. The Earliest Rhetorical Handbooks. *The American Journal of Philology*, **80**(2), 169–78.

1980. Later Greek Philosophy and Rhetoric. *Philosophy and Rhetoric*, **13**(3), 181–97.

1994. *A New History of Classical Rhetoric*. Princeton, NJ.

Kennell, N. M. 2013. Who Were the Neoi? In P. Martzavou, and N. Papazarkadas, eds., *Epigraphical Approaches to the Post-Classical Polis: Fourth Century BC to Second Century AD*. Oxford, 217–32.

Kenney, E. J. 1979. The Typology of Didactic. *The Classical Review*, **29**(1), 71–3.

Kerkhof, R. 2001. *Dorische Posse, Epicharm und attische Komödie*. Munich.

Kessels, A. H., and van der Horst, P. W. 1987. The Vision of Dorotheus (Pap. Bodmer 29): Edited with Introduction, Translation and Notes. *Vigiliae Christianae*, **41**(4), 313–59.

Keyser, P. T. 2001. The Geographical Work of Dikaiarchos. In W. W. Fortenbaugh and E. Schütrumpf, eds., *Dicaearchus of Messana: Text, Translation, and Discussion*. New Brunswick, NJ, 353–72.

2006. (Un)Natural Accounts in Herodotos and Thucydides. *Mouseion: Journal of the Classical Association of Canada*, **6**(3), 323–51.

Keyser, P. T., and Irby-Massie, G. L. (eds.) 2008. *Encyclopedia of Ancient Natural Scientists: The Greek Tradition and Its Many Heirs*. London.

Kidd, D. A. 1997. *Aratus, Edited with Introduction, Translation and Commentary*. Cambridge.

Kidd, I. G. 1978. Philosophy and Science in Posidonius. *Antike und Abendland*, **24**, 7–15.

Kienast, H. 1990. The Tunnel of Eupalinos. In *Ancient Technology*. Helsinki, 38–45.

Kim, L. 2007. The Portrait of Homer in Strabo's Geography. *Classical Philology*, **102**(4), 363–88.

2010. *Homer between History and Fiction in Imperial Greek Literature*. Cambridge.

Kim, Y. R. 2010. Reading the *Panarion* as Collective Biography: The Heresiarch as Unholy Man. *Vigiliae Christianae*, **64**(4), 382–413.

Kindstrand, J. F. 1976. *Bion of Borysthenes: A Collection of the Fragments with Introduction and Commentary*. Uppsala.

1986. Diogenes Laertius and the Chreia Tradition. *Elenchos*, 7, 217–43.

Kirk, G. S., Raven, J. E., and Schofield, M. 1983. *The Presocratic Philosophers*, 2nd edn. Cambridge.

Kittler, W., Koch, H. G., and Neumann, G. 1994. *Franz Kafka: Drucke zu Lebzeiten*. Frankfurt.

Kivilo, M. 2010. *Early Greek Poets' Lives*. Leiden.

Knight, V. 1991. Apollonius, *Argonautica* 4.167–70 and Euripides' *Medea*. *The Classical Quarterly*, **41**(1), 248–50.

Knoepfler, D. 1991. *La Vie de Ménédème d'Érétrie de Diogène Laërce: Contribution à l'histoire et à la critique du texte des Vies des Philosophes*. Basel.

Knorr, W. R. 1975. *The Evolution of the Euclidean Elements: A Study of the Theory of Incommensurable Magnitudes and Its Significance for Early Greek Geometry*. Dordrecht.

1980. On the Early History of Axiomatics: The Interaction of Mathematics and Philosophy in Greek Antiquity. In J. Hintikka, D. Gruender and E. Agazzi, eds., *Theory Change, Ancient Axiomatics, and Galileo's Methodology*. Berlin, 145–86.

1982. Observations on the Early History of the Conics. *Centaurus*, **26**(1), 1–24.

1983. Construction as Existence Proof in Ancient Geometry. *Ancient Philosophy*, **3**(2), 125–48.

1986. *The Ancient Tradition of Geometric Problems*. Mineola, NY.

1989. *Textual Studies in Ancient and Medieval Geometry*. Berlin.

1993. Arithmêtikê Stoicheiôsis: On Diophantus and Hero of Alexandria. *Historia Mathematica*, **20**(2), 180–92.

Knox, B. M. 1968. Silent Reading in Antiquity. *Greek, Roman and Byzantine Studies*, **9**(4), 421–35.

Kõiv, M. 2011. A Note on the Dating of Hesiod. *The Classical Quarterly*, **61**(2), 355–77.

Kolb, A. 2004. Römische Meilensteine: Stand der Forschung und Probleme. In R. Frei-Stolba, ed., *Siedlung und Verkehr im Römischen Reich*. Bern, 135–55.

Kolde, A. 2006. Euphorion de Chalcis, poète hellénistique. In M. A. Harder, R. F. Regtuit and G. C. Wakker, eds., *Beyond the Canon*. Leuven, 141–66.

Konkola, K. 2000. "People of the Book": The Production of Theological Texts in Early Modern England. *The Papers of the Bibliographical Society of America*, **94**, 5–33.

Kontoleon, N. M. 1963. Archilochus und Paros. In *Entretiens sur l'antiquité classique*, vol. X: *Archiloque*. Geneva, 37–86.

Kortus, M. 1999. *Briefe des Apollonios-Archives aus der Sammlung Papyri Gissenses*. Giessen.

Kosak, J. C. 2004. *Heroic Measures: Hippocratic Medicine in the Making of Euripidean Tragedy*. Leiden.

Kovacs, D. 2005. Text and Transmission. In J. Gregory, ed., *A Companion to Greek Tragedy*. New York, 377–93.

Krebs, C. B. 2015. The Buried Tradition of Programmatic Titulature among Republican Historians: Polybius' Πραγματεία, Asellio's *Res Gestae*, and Sisenna's Redefinition of *Historiae*. *The American Journal of Philology*, **136**(3), 503–24.

Kremmydas, C. 2007. P. Berl. 9781 and the Early Reception of Demosthenes. *Bulletin of the Institute of Classical Studies*, **50**(1), 19–48.

   2013. Hellenistic Oratory and the Evidence of Rhetorical Exercises. In C. Kremmydas and K. Tempest, eds., *Hellenistic Oratory: Continuity and Change*. Oxford, 139–64.

Krevans, N. 2010. Bookburning and the Poetic Deathbed: The Legacy of Virgil. In P. Hardie and H. Moore, eds., *Classical Literary Careers and Their Reception*. Cambridge, 197–208.

Kroll, W. 1892. Ein neuplatonischer Parmenidescommentar in einem Turiner Palimpsest. *Rheinisches Museum für Philologie*, **47**, 599–627.

   1924. Die Kreuzung der Gattungen. In *Studien zum Verständnis der römischen Literatur*. Stuttgart, 202–24.

Krueger, D. 2011. *Writing and Holiness: The Practice of Authorship in the Early Christian East*. Philadelphia.

Kudlien, F. 1964. Herophilus und der Beginn der medizinischen Skepsis. *Gesnerus*, **21**, 1–13.

   1968. The Third Century AD: A Blank Spot in the History of Medicine. In L. G. Stevenson and R. P. Multhauf, eds., *Medicine, Science, and Culture: Historical Essays in Honor of Owsei Temkin*. Baltimore, 25–34.

   1976. Medicine as a "Liberal Art" and the Question of the Physician's Income. *Journal of the History of Medicine and Allied Sciences*, **31**(4), 448–59.

Kuhn, T. S. 1957. *The Copernican Revolution: Planetary Astronomy in the Development of Western Thought*. Cambridge, MA.

Kundera, M. 1980 [1979]. *The Book of Laughter and Forgetting*, trans. M. H. Heim. New York.

Kurke, L. 1991. *The Traffic in Praise: Pindar and the Poetics of Social Economy*. Ithaca, NY.

   2011. *Aesopic Conversations: Popular Tradition, Cultural Dialogue, and the Invention of Greek Prose*. Princeton, NJ.

Kurzová, H. 2009. What Worried the Crows in Callimachus' Epigram? *Graeco-Latina Brunensia*, **14**, 125–9.

Kyrkos, V. A. 1980. *Ho Menedemos kai he Eretrike schole (Anasystase kai Martyries): Symvole sten historia tes hellenistikes philosophias*. Athens.

Lada-Richards, I. 2007. *Silent Eloquence: Lucian and Pantomime Dancing.* London.

Lages, M. F. 1971. The Hierosolymitain Origin of the Catechetical Rites in the Armenian Liturgy. *Didaskalia*, 1, 233–50.

Laird, W. R. 1991. Archimedes among the Humanists. *Isis*, 82(4), 628–38.

Laks, A. 1983. *Diogène d'Apollonie: La dernière cosmologie présocratique.* Lille.

  2005. Die Entstehung einer (Fach) Disziplin: Der Fall der vorsokratischen Philosophie. In G. Rechenauer, ed., *Frühgriechisches Denken.* Göttingen, 19–39.

Lamari, A. A. 2017. *Reperforming Greek Tragedy: Theater, Politics, and Cultural Mobility in the Fifth and Fourth Centuries BC.* Berlin.

Lamotta, V. M., and Schiffer, M. B. 1999. Formation Processes of House Floor Assemblages. In P. M. Allison, ed., *The Archaeology of Household Activities.* London, 19–29.

Lanata, G. 1968. Linguaggio scientifico e linguaggio poetico: Note al lessico del *De morbo sacro. Quaderni urbinati di cultura classica*, 5, 22–36.

Lane Fox, R. 2000. Theognis: An Alternative to Democracy. In R. Brock and S. Hodkinson, eds., *Alternatives to Athens: Varieties of Political Organization and Community in Ancient Greece.* Oxford, 35–51.

Lang, P. 2004. Medical and Ethnic Identities in Hellenistic Egypt. *Apeiron*, 37(4), 107–32.

  2012. *Medicine and Society in Ptolemaic Egypt.* Leiden.

Lankila, T. 2008. Proclus' Art of Referring with a Scale of Epithets. *Arctos*, 42, 123–33.

Lardinois, A. 1996. Who Sang Sappho's Songs? In E. Greene, ed., *Reading Sappho: Contemporary Approaches.* Berkeley, CA, 150–72.

Lasserre, F. 1966. *Die Fragmente des Eudoxos von Knidos.* Berlin.

Lauer, J.-P. 1955. *Les statues ptolémaïques du Sarapieion de Memphis.* Paris.

Lausberg, M. 1982. *Das Einzeldistichon: Studien zum antiken Epigramm.* Paderborn.

Lauxtermann, M. D. 1997. The Palladas Sylloge. *Mnemosyne*, 50(3), 329–37.

Lavelle, B. M. 2002. The Apollodoran Date for Archilochus. *Classical Philology*, 97(4), 344–51.

Law, V., and Sluiter, I. 1995. *Dionysius Thrax and the Technē grammatikē.* Münster.

Layton, R. A. 2004. *Didymus the Blind and His Circle in Late-Antique Alexandria: Virtue and Narrative in Biblical Scholarship.* Urbana, IL.

Lear, J. 1979. Aristotelian Infinity. *Proceedings of the Aristotelian Society*, 80, 187–210.

  1982. Aristotle's Philosophy of Mathematics. *The Philosophical Review*, 91(2), 161–92.

Lee, H. D. P. 1935. Geometrical Method and Aristotle's Account of First Principles. *The Classical Quarterly*, 29(2), 113–24.

Lee, L., Frederick, S., and Ariely, D. 2006. Try It, You'll Like It: The Influence of Expectation, Consumption, and Revelation on Preferences for Beer. *Psychological Science*, 17(12), 1054–8.

Leesen, T. G. 2009. *Gaius Meets Cicero: Law and Rhetoric in the School Controversies*. Leiden.

Lefkowitz, M. R. 1980. The Quarrel between Callimachus and Apollonius. *Zeitschrift für Papyrologie und Epigraphik*, **40**, 1–19.

1981. *The Lives of the Greek Poets*. Baltimore.

Lehoux, D. 2012. *What Did the Romans Know? An Inquiry into Science and Worldmaking* Chicago.

Leith, D. 2009. The Qualitative Status of the *Onkoi* in Asclepiades' Theory of Matter. *Oxford Studies in Ancient Philosophy*, **36**, 283–320.

2012. Pores and Void in Asclepiades' Physical Theory. *Phronesis*, **57**(2), 164–91.

Lennox, J. G. 1994. The Disappearance of Aristotle's Biology: A Hellenistic Mystery. *Apeiron*, **27**(4), 7–24.

2012. The Complexity of Aristotle's Study of Animals. In C. Shields, ed., *The Oxford Handbook of Aristotle*. Oxford, 287–305.

Lenski, N. 1997. *Initium mali Romano imperio*: Contemporary Reactions to the Battle of Adrianople. *Transactions of the American Philological Association*, **127**, 129–68.

Leroi, A. M. 2014. *The Lagoon: How Aristotle Invented Science*. London.

Lesher, J. H. 1978. Xenophanes' Scepticism. *Phronesis*, **23**(1), 1–21.

Leszl, W. 2006. Democritus' Works: From Their Titles to Their Contents. In A. Brancacci and P.-M. Morel, eds., *Democritus: Science, the Arts, and the Care of the Soul*. Leiden, 11–76.

Letrouit, J. 1995. Chronologie des alchimistes grecs. In D. Kahn and S. Matton, eds., *Alchimie: Art, histoire et mythes*. Paris, 11–93.

LeVen, P. A. 2014. *The Many-Headed Muse: Tradition and Innovation in Late Classical Greek Lyric Poetry*. Cambridge.

Levin, H. 2003. *The Labor of Life: Selected Plays*, trans. B. Harshav. Stanford, CA.

Levy, C. 2012. Other Followers of Antiochus. In D. N. Sedley, ed., *The Philosophy of Antiochus*. Cambridge, 290–306.

Lewis, D. 1991. *Parts of Classes*. Oxford.

Lewis, M. E. 1999. *Writing and Authority in Early China*. Albany, NY.

Lewis, N. 1965. Exemption of Physicians from Liturgy. *The Bulletin of the American Society of Papyrologists*, **2**(3), 87–92.

1974. *Papyrus in Classical Antiquity*. Oxford.

Lieberman, M. B., and Montgomery, D. B. 1988. First-Mover Advantages. *Strategic Management Journal*, **9**(1), 41–58.

Liebeschuetz, W. 2007. Was There a Crisis of the Third Century? In O. Hekster, G. de Kleijn and D. Slootjes, eds., *Crises and the Roman Empire*. Leiden, 11–20.

Lightfoot, J. L. 1998. An Early Reference to Perfect Numbers? Some Notes on Euphorion, *SH* 417. *The Classical Quarterly*, **48**(1), 187–94.

(ed.) 1999. *Parthenius of Nicaea: The Poetical Fragments and the Erōtika Pathēmata*. Oxford.

Lindberg, D. C. 1992. *The Beginnings of Western Science: The European Scientific Tradition in Philosophical, Religious, and Institutional Context, 600 BC to AD 1450*. Chicago.

Lissarrague, F. 2000. Aesop, between Man and Beast: Ancient Portraits and Illustrations. In B. Cohen, ed., *Not the Classical Ideal: Athens and the Construction of the Other in Greek Art*. Leiden, 132–49.

Livingstone, R. 2011. Better at Life Stuff: Consumption, Identity, and Class in Apple's "Get a Mac" Campaign. *Journal of Communication Inquiry*, **35**(3), 210–34.

Livrea, E. (ed.) 1978. *Anonymi fortasse Olympiodori Thebani Blemyomachia: (P. Berol. 5003)*. Meisenheim.

Lloyd, G. E. R. 1970. *Early Greek Science: Thales to Aristotle*. New York.

    1975. A Note on Erasistratus of Ceos. *The Journal of Hellenic Studies*, **95**, 172–5.

    1979. *Magic, Reason and Experience: Studies in the Origins and Development of Greek Science*. Cambridge.

    1990. *Demystifying Mentalities*. Cambridge.

    1991. *Methods and Problems in Greek Science: Selected Papers*. Cambridge.

Lo Cascio, E. 2006. The Role of the State in the Roman Economy: Making Use of the New Institutional Economics. In P. F. Bang, M. Ikeguchi and H. G. Ziche, eds., *Ancient Economies, Modern Methodologies: Archaeology, Comparative History, Models and Institutions*. Bari, 215–34.

Løkke, H. 2008. The Stoics on Sense Perception. In S. Knuuttila and P. Kärkkäinen, eds., *Theories of Perception in Medieval and Early Modern Philosophy*. Dordrecht, 35–46.

Long, A. A. 1991. The Harmonics of Stoic Virtue. *Oxford Studies in Ancient Philosophy*, **9**(supp.), 97–116.

    1992. Stoic Readings of Homer. In R. Lamberton and J. J. Keaney, eds., *Homer's Ancient Readers: The Hermeneutics of Greek Epic's Earliest Exegetes*. Princeton, NJ, 41–66.

    1996a. The Socratic Tradition: Diogenes, Crates, and Hellenistic Ethics. In B. Branham and M. O. Goulet-Cazé, eds., *The Cynics: The Cynic Movement in Antiquity and Its Legacy*. Berkeley, CA, 28–46.

    1996b. *Stoic Studies*. Cambridge.

    1999. The Socratic Legacy. In K. Algra, J. Barnes, J. Mansfeld and M. Schofield, eds., *The Cambridge History of Hellenistic Philosophy*. Cambridge, 617–41.

Long, A. A., and Sedley, D. N. 1987. *The Hellenistic Philosophers*, 2 vols. Cambridge.

Longrigg, J. 1989. Presocratic Philosophy and Hippocratic Medicine. *History of Science*, **27**(1), 1–39.

Lord, C. 1986. On the Early History of the Aristotelian Corpus. *The American Journal of Philology*, **107**(2), 137–61.

Lowe, E. A. 1934–71. *Codices Latini Antiquiores: A Palaeographical Guide to Latin Manuscripts Prior to the Ninth Century*, 12 vols. Oxford.

Lowe, N. J. 2007. *Comedy*. Cambridge.

Luginbill, R. D. 1997. Rethinking Antiphon's Περὶ Ἀληθείας. *Apeiron*, **30**(3), 163–88.

Luhtala, A. 2005. *Grammar and Philosophy in Late Antiquity: A Study of Priscian's Sources*. Amsterdam.

Luiselli, R. 2016. The Circulation and Transmission of Greek Adespota in Roman Egypt. In G. Colesanti and L. Lulli, eds., *Submerged Literature in Ancient Greek Culture*, vol. II: *Case Studies*. Berlin, 289–310.

Luraghi, N. 2010. The Local Scripts from Nature to Culture. *Classical Antiquity*, **29**(1), 68–91.

Lutsyshyna, O. 2012. Classical Sāṁkhya on the Authorship of the Vedas. *Journal of Indian Philosophy*, **40**(4), 453–67.

Lynch, J. P. 1972. *Aristotle's School: A Study of a Greek Educational Institution*. Berkeley, CA.

Lyons, J. 1968. *Introduction to Theoretical Linguistics*. Cambridge.

Ma, J. 2003. Peer Polity Interaction in the Hellenistic Age. *Past and Present*, **180**, 9–39.

   2013. *Statues and Cities: Honorific Portraits and Civic Identity in the Hellenistic World*. Oxford.

McCabe, A. E. 2007. *A Byzantine Encyclopaedia of Horse Medicine: The Sources, Compilation, and Transmission of the Hippiatrica*. Oxford.

MacCary, W. T. 1970. Menander's Characters: Their Names, Roles and Masks. *Transactions and Proceedings of the American Philological Association*, **101**, 277–90.

McClelland, J. S. 1989. *The Crowd and the Mob: From Plato to Canetti*. London.

McClure, S. M., Li, J., Tomlin, D., Cypert, K. S., Montague, L. M., and Montague, P. R. 2004. Neural Correlates of Behavioral Preference for Culturally Familiar Drinks. *Neuron*, **44**(2), 379–87.

MacCoull, L. S. 1988. *Dioscorus of Aphrodito: His Work and His World*. Berkeley, CA.

McDermott, W. C. 1977. Plotina Augusta and Nicomachus of Gerasa. *Historia: Zeitschrift für Alte Geschichte*, **26**(2), 192–203.

MacDonald, W. L. 1982. *The Architecture of the Roman Empire: An Introductory Study*. New Haven, CT.

Mace, S. T. 1993. Amour, Encore! The Development of δηὖτε in Archaic Lyric. *Greek, Roman and Byzantine Studies*, **34**(4), 335–64.

McGill, S. 2005. *Virgil Recomposed: The Mythological and Secular Centos in Antiquity*. Oxford.

McKirahan, V. T. 1994. The Socratic Origins of the Cynics and Cyrenaics. In P. A. Vander Waerdt, ed., *The Socratic Movement*. Ithaca, NY, 367–91.

McKitterick, R. 1989. *The Carolingians and the Written Word*. Cambridge.

Macleod, C. W. 1979. The Poetry of Ethics: Horace, *Epistles*. *The Journal of Roman Studies*, **69**, 16–27.

MacMullen, R. 1982. The Epigraphic Habit in the Roman Empire. *The American Journal of Philology*, **103**(3), 233–46.

   1986. Frequency of Inscriptions in Roman Lydia. *Zeitschrift für Papyrologie und Epigraphik*, **65**, 237–8.

McNamee, K. 1995. Missing Links in the Development of Scholia. *Greek, Roman and Byzantine Studies*, **36**(4), 399–414.

1998. Another Chapter in the History of Scholia. *The Classical Quarterly*, **48**(1), 269–88.

2007. *Annotations in Greek and Latin Texts from Egypt*. Ann Arbor, MI.

McNelis, C. 2002. Greek Grammarians and Roman Society during the Early Empire: Statius' Father and His Contemporaries. *Classical Antiquity*, **21**(1), 67–94.

Maeyama, Y. 1984. Ancient Stellar Observations: Timocharis, Aristyllus, Hipparchus, Ptolemy – the Dates and Accuracies. *Centaurus*, **27**(3), 280–310.

Mallette, K. 2009. Beyond Mimesis: Aristotle's *Poetics* in the Medieval Mediterranean. *PMLA*, **124**(2), 583–91.

Manetti, D. 1986. Note di lettura dell'Anonimo Londinese: Prolegomena ad una nuova edizione. *Zeitschrift für Papyrologie und Epigraphik*, **63**, 57–74.

2012. I problemi di Cassio Iatrosofista: Difficoltà di datazione e scoperte preziose. *Journal of History of Medicine*, **24**(2), 423–40.

Mann, C. 2009. Gladiators in the Greek East: A Case Study in Romanization. *The International Journal of the History of Sport*, **26**(2), 272–97.

Mann, C., and Scholz, P. (eds.) 2012. *"Demokratie" im Hellenismus: Von der Herrschaft des Volkes zur Herrschaft der Honoratioren?* Heidelberg.

Mansfeld, J. 1983a. The Historical Hippocrates and the Origins of Scientific Medicine. In M. Ruse, ed., *Nature Animated*. Dordrecht, 49–76.

1983b. Intuitionism and Formalism: Zeno's Definition of Geometry in a Fragment of L. Calvenus Taurus. *Phronesis*, **28**(1), 59–74.

1994. *Prolegomena: Questions to Be Settled before the Study of an Author or a Text*. Leiden.

1998. *Prolegomena Mathematica: From Apollonius of Perga to Late Neoplatonism: With an Appendix on Pappus and the History of Platonism*. Leiden.

Marrone, L. 1984. Proposizione e predicato in Crisippo. *Cronache Ercolanesi*, **14**, 135–46.

Marsden, E. W. 1971. *Greek and Roman Artillery: Technical Treatises*. Oxford.

Marshall, A. 1890. *Principles of Economics*. London.

Marshall, C. W. 2006. *The Stagecraft and Performance of Roman Comedy*. Cambridge.

Martano, A., Matelli, E., and Mirhady, D. (eds.) 2012. *Praxiphanes of Mytilene and Chamaeleon of Heraclea: Text, Translation, and Discussion*. New Brunswick, NJ.

Martens, P. 2012. *Origen and Scripture: The Contours of the Exegetical Life*. Oxford.

Martin, J. 1956. *Histoire du texte des Phénomènes d'Aratos*. Paris.

1998. *Aratos: Les Phénomènes*. Paris.

Martin, R. P. 1993. The Seven Sages as Performers of Wisdom. In C. Dougherty and L. Kurke, eds., *Cultural Poetics in Archaic Greece: Cult, Performance, Politics*. Oxford, 108–28.

2005. Pulp Epic: The *Catalogue* and the *Shield*. In R. L. Hunter, ed., *The Hesiodic Catalogue of Women: Constructions and Reconstructions*. Cambridge, 153–75.

2017. Crooked Competition: The Performance and Poetics of Skolia. In E. J. Bakker, ed., *Authorship and Greek Song: Authority, Authenticity, and Performance*. Leiden, 61–79.

Massar, N. 2010. "Choose Your Master Well": Medical Training, Testimonies and Claims to Authority. In M. Horstmanshoff, ed., *Hippocrates and Medical Education*. Leiden, 169–86.

Mastronarde, D. J. (ed.) 2002. *Euripides: Medea*. Cambridge.

Matelli, E. 2004. Hieronymus in Athens and Rhodes. In W. W. Fortenbaugh and S. A. White, eds., *Lyco of Troas and Hieronymus of Rhodes: Text, Translation, and Discussion*. New Brunswick, NJ, 289–314.

Mates, B. 1953. *Stoic Logic*. Berkeley, CA.

Mathiesen, T. J. 1999. *Apollo's Lyre: Greek Music and Music Theory in Antiquity and the Middle Ages*. Lincoln, NE.

Mattern, S. P. 2008. *Galen and the Rhetoric of Healing*. Baltimore.

 2013. *The Prince of Medicine: Galen in the Roman Empire*. Oxford.

Matthaios, S. 2015. Greek Scholarship in the Imperial Era and Late Antiquity. In F. Montanari, S. Matthaios and A. Rengakos, eds., *Brill's Companion to Ancient Greek Scholarship*. Leiden, 184–296.

Mattusch, C. C., and Lie, H. 2005. *The Villa dei Papiri at Herculaneum: Life and Afterlife of a Sculpture Collection*. Los Angeles.

May, R. 2009. An Ass from Oxyrhynchus: P.Oxy. LXX.4762, Loukios of Patrae and the Milesian Tales. *Ancient Narrative*, 8, 1–26.

Mayer, R. 2008. The Early Empire: AD 14–68. In S. Harrison, ed., *A Companion to Latin Literature*. New York, 58–68.

Meijer, P. A. 2007. *Stoic Theology: Proofs for the Existence of the Cosmic God and of the Traditional Gods: Including a Commentary on Cleanthes' Hymn on Zeus*. Delft.

Meineke, A. 1849. *Stephanus Byzantius: Ethnica*. Berlin.

Meister, K. 1990. *Die griechische Geschichtsschreibung: Von den Anfängen bis zum Ende des Hellenismus*. Stuttgart.

Mejer, J. 1981. Demetrius of Magnesia: On Poets and Authors of the Same Name. *Hermes*, **109**(4), 447–72.

 1998. A Life in Fragments: The *Vita Theophrasti*. In J. M. van Ophuijsen and M. van Raalte, eds., *Theophrastus: Reappraising the Sources*. New Brunswick, NJ, 1–28.

 2004. The Life of Lyco and the Life of the Lyceum. In W. W. Fortenbaugh and S. A. White, eds., *Lyco of Traos and Hieronymus of Rhodes: Text, Translation, and Discussion*. New Brunswick, NJ, 277–87.

Mellown, E. W. 1965. The Reception of Gerard Manley Hopkins' "Poems," 1918–30. *Modern Philology*, **63**(1), 38–51.

Mendell, H. 1998. Reflections on Eudoxus, Callippus and Their Curves: Hippopedes and Callippopedes. *Centaurus*, **40**(3/4), 177–275.

 n.d. *Simplicii in Aristotelis de caelo libros commentaria* 491–510 and Related Texts. www.calstatela.edu/faculty/hmendel/Ancient%20Mathematics/Ph ilosophical%20Texts/Astronomy/Simplicius%20InDeCael.pdf, accessed May 1, 2019.

Merkelbach, R., and Stauber, J. 1998–2004. *Steinepigramme aus dem griechischen Osten*, 6 vols. Munich.

Meyer, E. A. 1990. Explaining the Epigraphic Habit in the Roman Empire: The Evidence of Epitaphs. *The Journal of Roman Studies*, **80**, 74–96.

Mickey, K. 1981. Dialect Consciousness and Literary Language: An Example from Ancient Greek. *Transactions of the Philological Society*, **79**(1), 35–66.

Miguélez-Cavero, L. 2008. *Poems in Context: Greek Poetry in the Egyptian Thebaid 200–600 AD*. Berlin.

Millar, F. 1969. P. Herennius Dexippus: The Greek World and the Third-Century Invasions. *The Journal of Roman Studies*, **59**, 12–29.

  1983. Empire and City, Augustus to Julian: Obligations, Excuses and Status. *The Journal of Roman Studies*, **73**, 76–96.

Millis, B. W., and Olson, S. D. (eds.) 2012. *Inscriptional Records for the Dramatic Festivals in Athens: IG II2 2318–2325 and Related Texts*. Leiden.

Miron, D. 2010. *From Continuity to Contiguity: Toward a New Jewish Literary Thinking*. Stanford, CA.

Mitchell, J. G. 2006. The Aural *Iliad*: Alexandrian Performances of an Archaic Text. Dissertation, Stanford University.

Mitchell, M. M. 2005. Patristic Rhetoric on Allegory: Origen and Eustathius Put 1 Samuel 28 on Trial. *The Journal of Religion*, **85**(3), 414–45.

Momigliano, A. 1971. *The Development of Greek Biography*. Cambridge, MA.

Monson, A. 2012. *From the Ptolemies to the Romans: Political and Economic Change in Egypt*. Cambridge.

Montana, F. 2011. The Making of Greek Scholiastic Corpora. In F. Montanari and L. Pagani, eds., *From Scholars to Scholia: Chapters in the History of Ancient Greek Scholarship*. Berlin, 105–61.

Montana, F., and Porro, A. (eds.) 2014. *The Birth of Scholiography: From Types to Texts*. Berlin.

Montenegro, N. V. 2004. *Die Tabulae Iliacae: Mythos und Geschichte im Spiegel einer Gruppe frühkaiserzeitlicher Miniaturreliefs*. Berlin.

Montevecchi, O. 1988. *La papirologia*. Milan.

Montiglio, S. 2005. *Wandering in Ancient Greek Culture*. Chicago.

Moretti, F. 1999. *Atlas of the European Novel, 1800–1900*. London.

  2000. The Slaughterhouse of Literature. *Modern Language Quarterly*, **61**(1), 207–27.

  2009. Style, Inc.: Reflections on Seven Thousand Titles (British Novels, 1740–1850). *Critical Inquiry*, **36**(1), 134–58.

Morgan, A. M. 2014. Family Matters in Roman Asia Minor: Elite Identity, Community Dynamics and Competition in the Honorific Inscriptions of Imperial Aphrodisias. Doctoral dissertation, University of Texas, Austin.

Morgan, K. A. 2000. *Myth and Philosophy from the Presocratics to Plato*. Cambridge.

Morgan, T. 1998. *Literate Education in the Hellenistic and Roman Worlds*. Cambridge.

  2003. Tragedy in the Papyri: An Experiment in Extracting Cultural History from the Leuven Database. *Chronique d'Egypte*, **78**, 187–201.

Morlet, S. 2011. Eusebius' Polemic against Porphyry: A Reassessment. In
S. Inowlocki and C. Zamagni, eds., *Reconsidering Eusebius: Collected Papers on Literary, Historical, and Theological Issues*. Leiden, 119–50.

Morris, I. 2004. Economic Growth in Ancient Greece. *Journal of Institutional and Theoretical Economics*, 160(4), 709–42.

    2005. Archaeology, Standards of Living, and Greek Economic History. In J. Manning and I. Morris, eds., *The Ancient Economy: Evidence and Models*. Stanford, CA, 91–126.

    2010. *Why the West Rules – for Now: The Patterns of History and What They Reveal about the Future*. London.

Morris, J. 2016. Shaping the Empire: Agrimensores, Emperors and the Creation of the Roman Provincial Identities. Doctoral dissertation, University of Leicester.

Most, G. W. 2006. *Hesiod*, vol. 1: *Theogony, Works and Days, Testimonia*. Cambridge, MA.

    2014. Quellenforschung. In R. Bod, J. Maat and T. Weststeijn, eds., *The Making of the Humanities*, vol. III: *The Modern Humanities*. Amsterdam, 207–17.

Mouritsen, H. 2005. Freedmen and Decurions: Epitaphs and Social History in Imperial Italy. *The Journal of Roman Studies*, 95, 38–63.

Mueller, I. 1981. *Philosophy of Mathematics and Deductive Structure in Euclid's Elements*. Cambridge, MA.

    1991. On the Notion of a Mathematical Starting Point in Plato, Aristotle, and Euclid. In A. C. Bowen, ed., *Science and Philosophy in Classical Greece*. Princeton, NJ, 59–97.

Mueller, K. 2006. *Settlements of the Ptolemies: City Foundations and New Settlement in the Hellenistic World*. Leuven.

Müller, C. W. 1984. *Zur Datierung des sophokleischen Ödipus*. Wiesbaden.

Münscher, K. 1920. *Xenophon in der griechisch-römischen Literatur*. Leipzig.

Murphy, T. M. 2004. *Pliny the Elder's Natural History: The Empire in the Encyclopedia*. Oxford.

Murray, O. 1972. Herodotus and Hellenistic Culture. *The Classical Quarterly*, 22(2), 200–13.

    2007. Philosophy and Monarchy in the Hellenistic World. In T. Rajak, S. Pearce, J. Aitken and J. Dines, eds., *Jewish Perspectives on Hellenistic Rulers*. Berkeley, CA, 13–28.

Nachmanson, E. 1941. *Der griechische Buchtitel*. Gothenburg.

Nagy, G. 1979. *The Best of the Achaeans: Concepts of the Hero in Archaic Greek Poetry*. Baltimore.

    1996. *Poetry as Performance: Homer and Beyond*. Cambridge.

    1997. Homeric Scholia. In I. Morris and B. B. Powell, eds., *A New Companion to Homer*. Leiden, 101–22.

    2004. Transmission of Archaic Greek Sympotic Songs: From Lesbos to Alexandria. *Critical Inquiry*, 31(1), 26–48.

    2007. Did Sappho and Alcaeus Ever Meet? In A. Bierl, R. Lämmle and K. Wesselmann, eds., *Literatur und Religion*, vol. I: *Wege zu einer mythisch-rituellen Poetik bei den Griechen*. Berlin, 211–69.

2010. The Meaning of homoios (ὁμοῖος) in *Theogeny* 27 and Elsewhere. In P. Mitsis and C. Tsagalis, eds., *Allusion, Authority, and Truth: Critical Perspectives on Greek Poetic and Rhetorical Praxis*. Berlin, 153–68.

Natali, C. 2013. *Aristotle: His Life and School*. Princeton, NJ.

Nautin, P. 1977. *Origène: Sa vie et son oeuvre*. Paris.

Nervegna, S. 2007. Staging Scenes or Plays? Theatrical Revivals of "Old" Greek Drama in Antiquity. *Zeitschrift für Papyrologie und Epigraphik*, **162**, 14–42.

Nesholm, E. J. 2010. Language and Artistry in Cicero's *Pro Archia*. *The Classical World*, **103**(4), 477–90.

Netz, R. 1997. Classical Mathematics in the Classical Mediterranean. *Mediterranean Historical Review*, **12**(2), 1–24.

1998a. The First Jewish Scientist? *Scripta Classica Israelica*, **17**, 17–33.

1998b. Deuteronomic Texts: Late Antiquity and the History of Mathematics. *Revue d'histoire des mathématiques*, **4**(2), 261–88.

1999a. *The Shaping of Deduction in Greek Mathematics: A Study in Cognitive History*. Cambridge.

1999b. Proclus' Division of the Mathematical Proposition into Parts: How and Why Was It Formulated? *The Classical Quarterly*, **49**(1), 282–303.

2000a. Why Did Greek Mathematicians Publish Their Analyses? In P. Suppes, J. Moravcsik and H. Mendell, eds., *Ancient and Medieval Traditions in the Exact Sciences: Essays in Memory of Wilbur Knorr*. Stanford, CA, 139–57.

2000b. Insight by Oversight. *Apeiron*, **33**(2), 171–9.

2001. On the Aristotelian Paragraph. *The Cambridge Classical Journal*, **47**, 211–32.

2002a. Greek Mathematicians: A Group Picture. In C. Tuplin and T. E. Rihll, eds., *Science and Mathematics in Ancient Greek Culture*. Oxford, 196–216.

2002b. Counter Culture: Towards a History of Greek Numeracy. *History of Science*, **40**(3), 321–52.

2003. Plato's Mathematical Construction. *The Classical Quarterly*, **53**(2), 500–9.

2004a. Eudemus of Rhodes, Hippocrates of Chios and the Earliest Form of a Greek Mathematical Text. *Centaurus*, **46**(4), 243–86.

2004b. *The Transformation of Mathematics in the Early Mediterranean World: From Problems to Equations*. Cambridge.

2005. The Pythagoreans. In T. Koetsier and L. Bergmans, eds., *Mathematics and the Divine: A Historical Study*. Amsterdam, 77–97.

2009. *Ludic Proof: Greek Mathematics and the Alexandrian Aesthetic*. Cambridge.

2011. The Bibliosphere of Ancient Science (outside of Alexandria). *NTM Zeitschrift für Geschichte der Wissenschaften, Technik und Medezin*, **19**(3), 239–69.

2012. Reasoning and Symbolism in Diophantus: Preliminary Observations. In K. Chemla, ed., *The History of Mathematical Proof in Ancient Traditions*. Cambridge, 327–61.

2013. Authorial Presence in the Ancient Exact Sciences. In M. Asper, ed., *Writing Science: Medical and Mathematical Authorship in Ancient Greece*. Berlin, 217–53.

2014a. The Problem of Pythagorean Mathematics. In C. A. Huffman, ed., *A History of Pythagoreanism*. Cambridge, 167–84.

2014b. A Possible Etymology for the Greek Anatomical Term kleitorís. *Studi italiani di filologia classica*, 1, 99–105.

2015. Were There Epicurean Mathematicians? *Oxford Studies in Ancient Philosophy*, 49, 283–319.

2016. Archimedes' Liquid Bodies. In T. Buchheim, D. Meissner and N. Wachsmann, eds., *Soma [ΣΩMA]: Körperkonzepte und körperliche Existenz in der antiken Philosophie und Literatur*. Hamburg, 287–322.

2017a. The Authority of Mathematical Expertise and the Question of Ancient Writing *More Geometrico*. In J. König and G. Woolf, eds., *Authority and Expertise in Ancient Scientific Culture*. Cambridge, 374–408.

2017b. Nothing to Do with Apollonius? *Philologus*, **161**(1), 47–76.

2017c. *The Works of Archimedes: Translation and Commentary*, vol. II: *On Spirals*. Cambridge.

2018. Divisions, Big and Small: Comparing Archimedes and Liu Hui. In G. E. R. Lloyd and J. J. Zhao, eds., *Ancient Greece and China Compased*. Cambridge, 259–89.

Netz, R., and Noel, W. 2007. *The Archimedes Codex: How a Medieval Prayer Book Is Revealing the True Genius of Antiquity's Greatest Scientist*. London.

Netz, R., Noel, W., Tchernetska, N., and Wilson, N. G. (eds.) 2011. *The Archimedes Palimpsest*, 2 vols. Cambridge.

Neugebauer, O. 1938. *Über eine Methode zur Distanzbestimmung Alexandria–Rom bei Heron*. Copenhagen.

Newman, J. K. 1986. *The Classical Epic Tradition*. Madison, WI.

Nichols, M. F. 2009. Social Status and the Authorial Personae of Horace and Vitruvius. In L. B. Houghton and M. Wyke, eds., *Perceptions of Horace: A Roman Poet and His Readers*. Cambridge, 109–22.

Nicolet, C. 1965. L'inspiration de Tibérius Gracchus (à propos d'un livre récent). *Revue des études anciennes*, **67**(1/2), 142–58.

Niehoff, M. R. 2007. Did the *Timaeus* Create a Textual Community? *Greek, Roman and Byzantine Studies*, **47**(2), 161–91.

Nielsen, T. H. 2007. *Olympia and the Classical Hellenic City-State Culture*. Copenhagen.

Nightingale, A. W. 1995. *Genres in Dialogue: Plato and the Construct of Philosophy*. Cambridge.

Nisbet, R. G. M., and Hubbard, M. 1970. *A Commentary on Horace: Odes*. Oxford.

Nock, A. D. 1959. Posidonius. *The Journal of Roman Studies*, **49**, 1–15.

Nolan, D. 2006. Stoic Gunk. *Phronesis*, **51**(2), 162–83.

Noreña, C. F. 2001. The Communication of the Emperor's Virtues. *The Journal of Roman Studies*, **91**, 146–68.

Noussia, M. 2006. Fragments of Cynic "Tragedy". In M. A. Harder, R. F. Regtuit and G. C. Wakker, eds., *Beyond the Canon*. Leuven, 185–203.

Nünlist, R. 2009. *The Ancient Critic at Work: Terms and Concepts of Literary Criticism in Greek Scholia*. Cambridge.

Nutton, V. 1971. L. Gellius Maximus, Physician and Procurator. *The Classical Quarterly*, **21**(1), 262–72.

1977. *Archiatri* and the Medical Profession in Antiquity. *Papers of the British School at Rome*, **45**, 191–226.

1987. Numisianus and Galen. *Sudhoffs Archiv für Geschichte der Medezin und der Naturwissenschaften*, **71**(2), 235–9.

1997. Galen on Theriac: Problems of Authenticity. In A. Debru, ed., *Galen on Pharmacology: Philosophy, History and Medicine*. Leiden, 133–51.

2004. *Ancient Medicine*. London.

2005. The Fatal Embrace: Galen and the History of Ancient Medicine. *Science in Context*, **18**(1), 111–21.

2008. Greek Medical Astrology and the Boundaries of Medicine. In A. Akasoy, C. Burnett and R. Yoeli-Tlalim, eds., *Astro-Medicine: Astrology and Medicine, East and West*. Florence, 17–31.

2009. Galen's Library. In C. Gill, T. Whitmarsh and I. Wilkins, eds., *Galen and the World of Knowledge*. Cambridge, 19–34.

Nylan, M. 2001. *The Five "Confucian" Classics*. New Haven, CT.

Obbink, D. D. 1988. Hermarchus, against Empedocles. *The Classical Quarterly*, **38**(2), 428–35.

Ober, J. 1989. *Mass and Elite in Democratic Athens: Rhetoric, Ideology, and the Power of the People*. Princeton, NJ.

2008. *Democracy and Knowledge: Innovation and Learning in Classical Athens*. Princeton, NJ.

2015. *The Rise and Fall of Classical Greece*. Princeton, NJ.

O'Brien, D. 1994. Plotinus and the Secrets of Ammonius. *Hermathena*, **157**, 117–53.

O'Day, R. 2009. Universities and the Professions in the Early Modern Period. In P. Cunningham, S. Oosthuizen and R. Taylor, eds., *Beyond the Lecture Hall: Universities and Community Engagement from the Middle Ages to the Present Day*. Cambridge, 79–102.

O'Hara, J. J. 1996. Sostratus *Suppl. Hell.* 733: A Lost, Possibly Catullan-Era Elegy on the Six Sex Changes of Tiresias. *Transactions of the American Philological Association*, **126**, 173–219.

Oldfather, C. H. 1923. *The Greek Literary Texts from Greco-Roman Egypt: A Study in the History of Civilization*. Madison, WI.

Oliver, J. H. 1936. The Sarapion Monument and the Paean of Sophocles. *Hesperia: The Journal of the American School of Classical Studies at Athens*, **5**(1), 91–122.

1970. *Marcus Aurelius: Aspects of Civic and Cultural Policy in the East*. Princeton, NJ.

Olson, S. D. (ed. and trans.) 2012. *Athenaeus: The Learned Banqueters*, vol. VIII: *Book 15; Index*. Cambridge, MA.

O'Meara, D. J. P. 2003. *Platonic Political Philosophy in Late Antiquity*. Oxford.

2006. Patterns of Perfection in Damascius' *Life of Isidore*. *Phronesis*, **51**(1), 74–90.

O'Neill, E. N. 2004. *Plutarch's Moralia: Index.* Cambridge, MA.

Osborne, C. 1987. Empedocles Recycled. *The Classical Quarterly,* 37(1), 24–50.

Osborne, R. 1993. Competitive Festivals and the Polis: A Context for Dramatic Festivals at Athens. In A. H. Sommerstein, ed., *Tragedy, Comedy, and the Polis.* Bari, 21–38.

2005. Ordering Women in Hesiod's *Catalogue.* In R. L. Hunter, ed., *The Hesiodic Catalogue of Women: Constructions and Reconstructions.* Cambridge, 5–24.

O'Sullivan, L. 2002. The Law of Sophocles and the Beginnings of Permanent Philosophical Schools in Athens. *Rheinisches Museum für Philologie,* 145(3/4), 251–62.

O'Sullivan, N. 1997. Caecilius, the "Canons" of Writers, and the Origins of Atticism. In W. J. Dominik, ed., *Roman Eloquence: Rhetoric in Society and Literature.* New York, 32–49.

Otranto, R. 2000. *Antiche liste di libri su papiro.* Rome.

Overduin, F. 2014. *Nicander of Colophon's Theriaca: A Literary Commentary.* Leiden.

Pack, R. A. 1965. *The Greek and Latin Literary Texts from Greco-Roman Egypt,* 2nd edn. Ann Arbor, MI.

Packman, Z. M. 1991. The Incredible and the Incredulous: The Vocabulary of Disbelief in Herodotus, Thucydides, and Xenophon. *Hermes,* 119(4), 399–414.

Palme, B. 2009. The Range of Documentary Texts: Types and Categories. In R. S. Bagnall, ed., *The Oxford Handbook of Papyrology.* Oxford, 358–94.

Parke, H. W. 1986. The Temple of Apollo at Didyma: The Building and Its Function. *The Journal of Hellenic Studies,* 106, 121–31.

Parker, D. C. 2012. *Textual Scholarship and the Making of the New Testament.* Oxford.

Parker, H. N. 2009. Books and Reading Latin Poetry. In W. A. Johnson and H. N. Parker, eds., *Ancient Literacies: The Culture of Reading in Greece and Rome.* Oxford, 186–229.

Parkin, T. G. 2003. *Old Age in the Roman World: A Cultural and Social History.* Baltimore.

Patterson, R. 1982. The Platonic Art of Comedy and Tragedy. *Philosophy and Literature,* 6(1/2), 76–93.

Pellegrin, P. 2006. Ancient Medicine and Its Contribution to the Philosophical Tradition. In M. L. Gill and P. Pellegrin, eds., *A Companion to Ancient Philosophy.* London, 664–85.

Pelliccia, H. 2009. Simonides, Pindar and Bacchylides. In F. Budelmann, ed., *The Cambridge Companion to Greek Lyric.* Cambridge, 240–62.

Penella, R. J. 1984. Plato's Birthday Again. *The Classical World,* 77(5), 295.

1990. *Greek Philosophers and Sophists in the Fourth Century AD: Studies in Eunapius of Sardis.* Leeds.

Penland, E. C. 2010. Martyrs as Philosophers: The School of Pamphilus and Ascetic Tradition in Eusebius's "Martyrs of Palestine". Dissertation, Yale University.

Pepper, T. W. 2010. A Patron and a Companion: Two Animal Epitaphs for Zenon of Caunos (*P.Cair.Zen.* IV 59532 = SH 977). In T. Gagos, ed., *The Proceedings of the 25th International Congress of Papyrology*. Ann Arbor, MI, 605–22.

Pernot, L. 2006. The Rhetoric of Religion. *Rhetorica: A Journal of the History of Rhetoric*, 24(3), 235–54.

Perrone, S. 2009. Lost in Tradition: Papyrus Commentaries on Comedies and Tragedies of Unknown Authorship. *Trends in Classics*, 1(2), 203–40.

Petrain, D. 2014. *Homer in Stone: The Tabulae Iliacae in Their Roman Context.* Cambridge.

Petrides, A. K. 2014. *Menander, New Comedy and the Visual.* Cambridge.

Pfeiffer, R. 1968. *History of Classical Scholarship*, vol. I. Oxford.

Piketty, T. 2013. *Capital in the Twenty-First Century.* Cambridge, MA.

Pinto, P. M. 2012. The Title of Isocrates' *Antidosis. Hermes*, 140(3), 362–8.

Plassmann, H., O'Doherty, J., Shiv, B., and Rangel, A. 2008. Marketing Actions Can Modulate Neural Representations of Experienced Pleasantness. *Proceedings of the National Academy of Sciences*, 105(3), 1050–4.

Plommer, H. 1973. *Vitruvius and Later Roman Building Manuals.* Cambridge.

Pöhlmann, E., and West, M. L. (eds.) 2001. *Documents of Ancient Greek Music: The Extant Melodies and Fragments.* Oxford.

Polinskaya, I. 2006. Lack of Boundaries, Absence of Oppositions: The City–Countryside Continuum of a Greek Pantheon. In R. M. Rosen and I. Sluiter, eds., *City, Countryside, and the Spatial Organization of Value in Classical Antiquity.* Leiden, 61–92.

Poli-Palladini, L. 2001. Some Reflections on Aeschylus' *Aetnae(ae). Rheinisches Museum für Philologie*, 144(3), 287–325.

Polito, R. 1999. On the Life of Asclepiades of Bithynia. *The Journal of Hellenic Studies*, 119, 48–66.

2007. Was Skepticism a Philosophy? Reception, Self-Definition, Internal Conflicts. *Classical Philology*, 102(4), 333–62.

Porro, A. 1994. *Vetera alcaica: L'esegesi di Alceo dagli alessandrini all'età imperiale.* Milan.

Pouilloux, J., and Salviat, F. 1983. Lichas, Lacédémonien, archonte à Thasos, et le livre VIII de Thucydide. *Comptes rendus des séances de l'Académie des Inscriptions et Belles Lettres*, 127(2), 376–403.

Pounds, N. J. G. 1994. *An Economic History of Medieval Europe.* New York.

Powell, B. B. 1991. *Homer and the Origin of the Greek Alphabet.* Cambridge.

Powell, J. G. F. 2013. The Embassy of the Three Philosophers to Rome in 155 BC. In C. Kremmydas and K. Tempest, eds., *Hellenistic Oratory: Continuity and Change.* Oxford, 219–47.

Prager, F. D. 1974. *Pneumatica: The First Treatise on Experimental Physics: Western Version and Eastern Version.* Wiesbaden.

Prandi, L. 1996. *Fortuna e realtà dell'opera di Clitarco.* Stuttgart.

Priestley, J. 2014. *Herodotus and Hellenistic Culture: Literary Studies in the Reception of the Histories*. Oxford.

Prioux, É. 2009. On The Oddities and Wonders of Italy: When Poets Look Westward. In M. A. Harder, R. F. Regtuit and G. C. Wakker, eds., *Nature and Science in Hellenistic Poetry*. Leuven, 121–48.

Pritchett, W. K. 1975. *Dionysius of Halicarnassus: On Thucydides*. Berkeley, CA.

Privitera, I. 2012. Aristotle and the Papyri: The Direct Tradition. *Quaestio*, 11, 115–40.

Puech, B. 2002. *Orateurs et sophistes grecs dans les inscriptions d'époque impériale*. Paris.

Puglia, E. 1988. *Aporie testuali ed esegetiche in Epicuro (PHerc. 1012)/Demetrio Lacone*. Naples.

Pyzyk, M. 2015. Economies of Expertise: Knowledge and Skill Transfer in Classical Greece. Doctoral dissertation, Stanford University.

Rapp, C. 2013. *Holy Bishops in Late Antiquity: The Nature of Christian Leadership in an Age of Transition*. Berkeley, CA.

Rashed, M. 2007. *Essentialisme: Alexandre d'Aphrodise entre logique, physique et cosmologie*. Berlin.

Rathbone D. W. 1990. Villages, Land and Population in Graeco-Roman Egypt. *The Cambridge Classical Journal*, 36, 103–42.

1991. *Economic Rationalism and Rural Society in Third-Century AD Egypt: The Heroninos Archive and the Appianus Estate*. Cambridge.

Raven, M. 2006. Britain, 1750–1830. In F. Moretti, ed., *The Novel*. Princeton, NJ, 429–54.

Rawson, E. 1981. Chariot-Racing in the Roman Republic. *Papers of the British School at Rome*, 49, 1–16.

1982. The Life and Death of Asclepiades of Bithynia. *The Classical Quarterly*, 32(2), 358–70.

1985. *Intellectual Life in the Late Roman Republic*. Baltimore.

Reed, A. Y. 2002. Apocrypha, "Outside Books," and Pseudepigrapha: Ancient Categories and Modern Perceptions of Parabiblical Literature. Lecture given October 10, Princeton University. Available at http://ccat.sas.upenn.edu/ps co/year40/areed1.html.

Regenauer, J. 2016. *Mesomedes: Übersetzung und Kommentar*. Bern.

Relihan, J. C. 1984. On the Origin of "Menippean Satire" as the Name of a Literary Genre. *Classical Philology*, 79(3), 226–9.

Renner, T. 2009. Papyrology and Ancient Literature. In R. S. Bagnall, ed., *The Oxford Handbook of Papyrology*. Oxford, 282–302.

Rice, E. E. 1983. *The Grand Procession of Ptolemy Philadelphus*. Oxford.

Richardson, G. 2008. Brand Names before the Industrial Revolution, Working Paper 13930. Cambridge, MA.

Richter, D. S. 2011. *Cosmopolis: Imagining Community in Late Classical Athens and the Early Roman Empire*. Oxford.

Richter, G. M. A. 1955. The Origin of Verism in Roman Portraits. *The Journal of Roman Studies*, 45, 39–46.

1965. *The Portraits of the Greeks*, 3 vols. London.

Richter, G. M. A., and Smith, R. R. R. 1984. *The Portraits of the Greeks*, rev edn. Ithaca, NY.

Richter, M. 1997. Zwei neue philosophische Papyri: P.Heid. Inv. G 1108 und 1109. *Studi e Testi per il Corpus dei Papiri Filosofici*, **8**, 85–138.

Riggsby, A. M. 2007. Guides to the Wor(l)d. In J. König and T. Whitmarsh, eds., *Ordering Knowledge in the Roman Empire*. Cambridge, 88–107.

2010. *Roman Law and the Legal World of the Romans*. Cambridge.

Riginos, A. S. 1976. *Platonica*. Leiden.

Riley, M. 1987. Theoretical and Practical Astrology: Ptolemy and His Colleagues. *Transactions of the American Philological Association*, **117**, 235–56.

Robert, L. 1930. Pantomimen im griechischen Orient. *Hermes*, **65**(1), 106–22.

1938. *Études épigraphiques et philologiques*. Paris.

1940. *Les gladiateurs dans l'Orient grec*. Paris.

Roberts, C. H., and Skeat, T. C. 1983. *The Birth of the Codex*. Oxford.

Robertson, D. G. 2004. Chrysippus on Mathematical Objects. *Ancient Philosophy*, **24**(1), 169–91.

Robinson, E. W. 2011. *Democracy beyond Athens: Popular Government in the Greek Classical Age*. Cambridge.

Robinson, J. M. (ed.) 1984. *The Nag Hammadi Library in English*. Leiden.

Roller, D. W. (ed.) 2010. *Eratosthenes' Geography*. Princeton, NJ.

Roman, L. 2014. *Poetic Autonomy in Ancient Rome*. Oxford.

Romm, J. S. 1989. Aristotle's Elephant and the Myth of Alexander's Scientific Patronage. *The American Journal of Philology*, **110**(4), 566–75.

Rondholz, A. 2012. *The Versatile Needle: Hosidius Geta's Cento "Medea" and Its Tradition*. Berlin.

Roochnik, D. 1996. *Of Art and Wisdom: Plato's Understanding of Techne*. University Park, PA.

Roselli, A. 1990. Appunti per una storia dell'uso apologetico della filologia: La nuova edizione di Demetrio Lacone. *Studi classici e orientali*, **40**, 117–38.

Rosenfeld, B. Z., and Menirav, J. 2005. *Markets and Marketing in Roman Palestine*. Leiden.

Rosenmeyer, P. A. 1992. *The Poetics of Imitation: Anacreon and the Anacreontic Tradition*. Cambridge.

Rösler, W. 1980. *Dichter und Gruppe: Eine Untersuchung zu den Bedingungen und zur historischen Funktion früher griechischer Lyrik am Beispiel Alkaios*. Munich.

Rothfus, M. A. 2010. The "Gens Togata": Changing Styles and Changing Identities. *The American Journal of Philology*, **131**(3), 425–52.

Rowland, I. D. 2016. Three Seaside Wonders. In M. M. Miles, ed., *A Companion to Greek Architecture*. New York, 440–53.

Ruffini, G. 2008. *Social Networks in Byzantine Egypt*. Cambridge.

Runia, D. T. 1988. Philosophical Heresiography: Evidence in Two Ephesian Inscriptions. *Zeitschrift für Papyrologie und Epigraphik*, **72**, 241–3.

Ruschenbusch, E. 2003. Was Hellanikos the First Chronicler of Athens? *Klio*, 85(1), 7–8.

Russo, L. 1998. The Definitions of Fundamental Geometric Entities Contained in Book I of Euclid's *Elements*. *Archive for History of Exact Sciences*, 52(3), 195–219.

2004 [1996]. *The Forgotten Revolution: How Science Was Born in 300BC and Why It Had to Be Reborn*, trans. S. Levy. Berlin.

Russo, L., and Medaglia, S. M. 1996. Sulla presunta accusa di empietà ad Aristarco di Samo. *Quaderni urbinati di cultura classica*, 53, 113–21.

Rusten, J. S. 2006. Who "Invented" Comedy? The Ancient Candidates for the Origins of Comedy and the Visual Evidence. *The American Journal of Philology*, 127(1), 37–66.

Rutherford, R. B. 1995. *The Art of Plato: Ten Essays in Platonic Interpretation*. Cambridge, MA.

Ryholt, K. 2002. Nectanebo's Dream or the Prophecy of Petesis. In A. Blasius and B. U. Schipper, eds., *Apokalyptik und Ägypten: Eine kritische Analyse der relevanten Texte aus dem griechisch-römischen Ägypten*. Leuven, 221–41.

2011. New Light on the Legendary King Nechepsos of Egypt. *The Journal of Egyptian Archaeology*, 97(1), 61–72.

Rylaarsdam, D. 2014. *John Chrysostom on Divine Pedagogy: The Coherence of His Theology and Preaching*. Oxford.

Sadurska, A. 1964. *Les tables iliaques*. Warsaw.

Saito, K., and Sidoli, N. 2010. The Function of Diorism in Ancient Greek Analysis. *Historia Mathematica*, 37(4), 579–614.

2012. Comparative Analysis in Greek Geometry. *Historia Mathematica*, 39(1), 1–33.

Saller, R. P. 1982. *Personal Patronage under the Early Empire*. Cambridge.

Sambursky, S. 1959. *Physics of the Stoics*. Princeton, NJ.

Sandbach, F. H. 1985. *Aristotle and the Stoics*. Cambridge.

Sanders, L. J. 1987. *Dionysius I of Syracuse and Greek Tyranny*. London.

Sandnes, K. O. 2011. *The Gospel "According to Homer and Virgil": Cento and Canon*. Leiden.

Sandwell, I. 2007. *Religious Identity in Late Antiquity: Greeks, Jews and Christians in Antioch*. Cambridge.

Sandy, G. 1994. New Pages of Greek Fiction. In J. R. Morgan and R. Stoneman, eds., *Greek Fiction: The Greek Novel in Context*. London, 130–45.

Sarton, G. 1952. *A History of Science*, vol. I: *Ancient Science through the Golden Age of Greece*. Cambridge, MA.

Sassi, M. M. 2011. Ionian Philosophy and Italic Philosophy: From Diogenes Laertius to Diels. In O. Primavesi and K. Luchner, eds., *The Presocratics from the Latin Middle Ages to Hermann Diels*. Stuttgart, 19–44.

Sauer, E. 2014. Milestones and Instability (Mid-Third to Early Fourth Centuries AD). *Ancient Society*, 44, 257–305.

Savage-Smith, E. 2002. Galen's Lost Ophthalmology and the *Summaria Alexandrinorum*. *Bulletin of the Institute of Classical Studies*, 45(supp.), 121–38.

Schaffer, S. 1986. Scientific Discoveries and the End of Natural Philosophy. *Social Studies of Science*, **16**(3), 387–420.

Schärlig, A. 2001. *Compter avec des cailloux: Le calcul élémentaire sur l'abaque chez les anciens Grecs*. Lausanne.

Scheidel, W. 1996. Finances, Figures and Fiction. *The Classical Quarterly*, **46**(1), 222–38.

  1997. Quantifying the Sources of Slaves in the Early Roman Empire. *The Journal of Roman Studies*, **87**, 156–69.

  1999. Emperors, Aristocrats, and the Grim Reaper: Towards a Demographic Profile of the Roman Elite. *The Classical Quarterly*, **49**(1), 254–81.

  2001. Roman Age Structure: Evidence and Models. *The Journal of Roman Studies*, **91**, 1–26.

  2002. A Model of Demographic and Economic Change in Roman Egypt after the Antonine Plague. *Journal of Roman Archaeology*, **15**, 97–114.

  2003. The Demographic Background of the Greek Expansion. *The Journal of Hellenic Studies*, **123**, 120–40.

  2004. Creating a Metropolis: A Comparative Demographic Perspective. In W. V. Harris and G. Ruffini, eds., *Ancient Alexandria between Egypt and Greece*. Leiden, 1–31.

  2007. Demography. In W. Scheidel, I. Morris and R. P. Saller, eds., *The Cambridge Economic History of the Greco-Roman World*. Cambridge, 38–86.

  2009a. Disease and Death in the Ancient City of Rome, Princeton/Stanford Working Paper in Classics 040901. Princeton, NJ.

  2009b. In Search of Roman Economic Growth. *Journal of Roman Archaeology*, **22**, 46–70.

  2010. Real Wages in Early Economies: Evidence for Living Standards from 1800 BCE to 1300 CE. *Journal of the Economic and Social History of the Orient*, **53**(3), 425–62.

  2013a. Explaining the Maritime Freight Charges in Diocletian's Prices Edict. *Journal of Roman Archaeology*, **26**, 464–8.

  2013b. The First Fall of the Roman Empire. Ronald Syme lecture, given at Wolfson College, University of Oxford, October 31.

  2017. *The Great Leveler: Violence and the History of Inequality from the Stone Age to the Twenty-First Century*. Princeton, NJ.

Scheidel, W., and Friesen, S. J. 2009. The Size of the Economy and the Distribution of Income in the Roman Empire. *The Journal of Roman Studies*, **99**, 61–91.

Schepens, G. 2005. Polybius' Criticism of Phylarchus. In G. Schepens and J. Bollansee, eds., *The Shadow of Polybius: Intertextuality as a Research Tool in Greek Historiography*. Leuven, 141–64.

Schiefsky, M. J. 2005. *Hippocrates: On Ancient Medicine*. Leiden.

  2007. Art and Nature in Ancient Mechanics. In B. Bensaude-Vincent and W. R. Newman, eds., *The Artificial and the Natural: An Evolving Polarity*. Cambridge, MA, 67–108.

2014. The Epistemology of Ptolemy's *On the Criterion*. In M. K. Lee, ed., *Strategies of Argument: Essays in Ancient Ethics, Epistemology, and Logic.* Oxford, 301–31.

Schiesaro, A., Mitsis, P., and Clay, J. S. (eds.) 1994. *Mega Nepios: Il destinatario nell'epos didascalico.* Pisa.

Schiffer, M. B. 1996. *Formation Processes of the Historical and Archaeological Records.* Albuquerque, NM.

Schmalzriedt, E. 1970. *Peri physeos: Zur Frühgeschichte der Buchtitel.* Munich.

Schmidt, M. 1997. Variae lectiones oder Parallelstellen: Was notierten Zenodot und Aristarch zu Homer? *Zeitschrift für Papyrologie und Epigraphik,* **115**, 1–12.

Schneider, I. 1979. *Archimedes: Ingenieur, Naturwissenschaftler und Mathematiker.* Darmstadt.

Schofield, M. 1983. The Syllogisms of Zeno of Citium. *Phronesis,* **28**(1), 31–58.

1984. Ariston of Chios and the Unity of Virtue. *Ancient Philosophy,* **4**(1), 83–96.

1991. *The Stoic Idea of the City.* Cambridge.

1999a. Academic Epistemology. In K. Algra, J. Barnes, J. Mansfeld and M. Schofield, eds., *The Cambridge History of Hellenistic Philosophy.* Cambridge, 323–51.

1999b. Social and Political Thought. In K. Algra, J. Barnes, J. Mansfeld and M. Schofield, eds., *The Cambridge History of Hellenistic Philosophy.* Cambridge, 739–70.

2003. Stoic Ethics. In B. Inwood, ed., *The Cambridge Companion to the Stoics.* Cambridge, 233–56.

Scholz, P. 2004. Peripatetic Philosophers as Wandering Scholars: Some Remarks on the Socio-Political Conditions of Philosophizing in the Third Century BCE. In W. W. Fortenbaugh and S. A. White, eds., *Lyco of Troas and Hieronymus of Rhodes: Text, Translation, and Discussion.* New Brunswick, NJ, 315–53.

Schöne, R. 1897. *Damianos Schrift über Optik.* Berlin.

Scott, A. 1998. The Date of the *Physiologus. Vigiliae Christianae,* **52**(4), 430–41.

Scullion, S. 2002. Tragic Dates. *The Classical Quarterly,* **52**(1), 81–101.

2003. Euripides and Macedon, or the Silence of the *Frogs. The Classical Quarterly,* **53**(2), 389–400.

Sedley, D. N. 1976. Epicurus and the Mathematicians of Cyzicus. *Cronache Ercolanesi,* **6**, 23–54.

1977. Diodorus Cronus and Hellenistic Philosophy. *The Cambridge Classical Journal,* **23**, 74–120.

1984. The Negated Conjunctions in Stoicism. *Elenchos,* **5**, 311–16.

1998. *Lucretius and the Transmission of Greek Wisdom.* Cambridge.

1999. The Stoic–Platonist Debate on Kathekonta. In K. Ierodiakonou, ed., *Topics in Stoic Philosophy.* Oxford, 128–52.

2003. Philodemus and the Decentralisation of Philosophy. *Cronache Ercolanesi,* **33**, 31–41.

2008. Atomism's Eleatic Roots. In P. Curd and D. W. Graham, eds., *The Oxford Handbook of Presocratic Philosophy*. Oxford, 305–32.

2011. P.Hibeh II 184: Platonist Logic in the Third Century BC? *Studi e Testi per il Corpus dei Papiri Filosofici*, **16**, 227–39.

(ed.) 2012. *The Philosophy of Antiochus*. Cambridge.

Sefrin-Weis, H. (ed. and trans.) 2010. *Pappus of Alexandria: Book 4 of the Collection*. Berlin.

Segal, C. 1990. *Lucretius on Death and Anxiety: Poetry and Philosophy in De Rerum Natura*. Princeton, NJ.

Sela, S. 2001. The Fuzzy Borders between Astronomy and Astrology in the Thought and Work of Three Twelfth-Century Jewish Intellectuals. *Aleph*, **1**(1), 59–100.

Selden, D. L. 1994. Genre of Genre. In J. Tatum, ed., *The Search for the Ancient Novel*. Baltimore, 39–64.

1998. Alibis. *Classical Antiquity*, **17**(2), 289–412.

Sell, R. 1984. The Comedy of Hyperbolic Horror: Seneca, Lucan and 20th Century Grotesque. *Neohelicon*, **11**(1), 277–300.

Sellars, J. 2003. Simon the Shoemaker and the Problem of Socrates. *Classical Philology*, **98**(3), 207–16.

Sens, A. (ed.) 2011. *Asclepiades of Samos: Epigrams and Fragments*. Oxford.

Serres, M. 2000 [1977]. *The Birth of Physics*, trans. J. Hawkes. Manchester.

Shanks, M. 2004. *Art and the Early Greek State: An Interpretive Archaeology*. Cambridge.

Sharples, R. W. 2011. Strato of Lampsacus: The Sources, Texts and Translations. In M. L. Desclos and W. W. Fortenbaugh, eds., *Strato of Lampsacus: Text, Translation and Discussion*. New Brunswick, NJ, 5–230.

Shaw, B. D. 1985. The Divine Economy: Stoicism as Ideology. *Latomus*, **44**(1), 16–54.

Sheppard, A. 2016. The Development of Epigram in Classical Greece. Doctoral dissertation, Stanford University.

Shipley, D. G. J. 2012. Pseudo-Skylax and the Natural Philosophers. *The Journal of Hellenic Studies*, **132**, 121–38.

Shklovsky, V. 1990 [1925]. *Theory of Prose*, trans. B. Sher. Champaign, IL.

Shotter, D. C. A. 1969. The Trial of Clutorius Priscus. *Greece and Rome*, **16**(1), 14–18.

Sider, D. 1997. *The Epigrams of Philodemos*. Oxford.

Sidoli, N. 2004. Hipparchus and the Ancient Metrical Methods on the Sphere. *Journal for the History of Astronomy*, **35**(1), 71–84.

2011. Heron of Alexandria's Date. *Centaurus*, **53**(1), 55–61.

2014. Mathematical Tables in Ptolemy's *Almagest*. *Historia Mathematica*, **41**(1), 13–37.

2015. Mathematics Education. In W. M. Bloomer, ed., *A Companion to Ancient Education*. Chichester, 387–400.

Siebenborn, E. 1976. *Die Lehre von der Sprachrichtigkeit und ihren Kriterien: Studien zur antiken normativen Grammatik*. Amsterdam.

Sijpstein, P. M. 2009. Arabic Papyri and Islamic Egypt. In R. S. Bagnall, ed., *The Oxford Handbook of Papyrology*. Oxford, 425–72.

Sinclair, R. K. 1988. *Democracy and Participation in Athens*. Cambridge.

Sivan, H. 1993. Numerian the Intellectual: A Dynastic Survivor in Fourth Century Gaul. *Rheinisches Museum für Philologie*, **136**(3/4), 360–5.

Skeat, T. C. 1982. The Length of the Standard Papyrus Roll and the Cost-Advantage of the Codex. *Zeitschrift für Papyrologie und Epigraphik*, **45**, 169–75.

1995. Was Papyrus Regarded as "Cheap" or "Expensive" in the Ancient World? *Aegyptus*, **75**(1/2), 75–93.

1999. The Codex Sinaiticus, the Codex Vaticanus and Constantine. *The Journal of Theological Studies*, **50**(2), 583–625.

Slater, N. W. 2000. *Plautus in Performance: The Theatre of the Mind*. Amsterdam.

Sluiter, I. 1995. The Embarrassment of Imperfection: Galen's Assessment of Hippocrates' Linguistic Merits. In P. J. van der Eijk, H. F. J. Horstmanshoff and P. H. Schrijvers, eds., *Ancient Medicine in Its Socio-Cultural Context*, vol. II. Amsterdam, 519–35.

Small, J. P. 2003. *The Parallel Worlds of Classical Art and Text*. Cambridge.

Smith, A. 1993. *Porphyrii Philosophi: Fragmenta*. Stuttgart.

Smith, A. M. 1987. Descartes's Theory of Light and Refraction: A Discourse on Method. *Transactions of the American Philosophical Society*, **77**(3), 1–92.

Smith, M. 1972. Pseudepigraphy in the Israelite Literary Tradition. In K. von Fritz, ed., *Pseudepigrapha*. Geneva, 191–215.

Smith, R. M. 1995. A New Look at the Canon of the Ten Attic Orators. *Mnemosyne*, **48**(1), 66–79.

Smith, R. R. R. 1998. Cultural Choice and Political Identity in Honorific Portrait Statues in the Greek East in the Second Century AD. *The Journal of Roman Studies*, **88**, 56–93.

Smolders, R. 2004. Two Archives from the Roman Arsinoites. *Chronique d'Egypte*, **79**, 233–40.

Snell, B. 1953 [1946]. *The Discovery of the Mind: The Greek Origins of European Thought*, trans. T. G. Rosenmeyer. Cambridge, MA.

1971. *Tragicorum Graecorum Fragmenta*, vol. I. Göttingen.

Snodgrass, A. 1986. Interaction by Design: The Greek City State. In C. Renfrew and J. Cherry, eds., *Peer–Polity Interaction and Social-Political Change*. Cambridge, 47–58.

Snyder, H. G. 2002. *Teachers and Texts in the Ancient World: Philosophers, Jews and Christians*. London.

Snyder, T. D. (ed.) 1993. *120 Years of American Education: A Statistical Portrait*. Collingdale, PA.

Sogno, C. 2017. The Letter Collection of Quintus Aurelius Symmachus. In C. Sogno, B. K. Storin and E. J. Watts, eds., *Late Antique Letter Collections: A Critical Introduction and Reference Guide*. Berkeley, CA, 175–89.

Solmsen, F. 1981. The Academic and the Alexandrian Editions of Plato's Works. *Illinois Classical Studies*, **6**, 102–11.

Sommerstein, A. H. 1984. Aristophanes and the Demon Poverty. *The Classical Quarterly*, **34**(2), 314–33.

2010. The History of the Text of Aristophanes. In G. W. Dobrov, ed., *Brill's Companion to the Study of Greek Comedy*. Leiden, 399–422.

Sorabji, R. 1972. Aristotle, Mathematics, and Colour. *The Classical Quarterly*, **22**(2), 293–308.

Spanoudakis, K. (ed.) 2002. *Philitas of Cos*. Leiden.

Squire, M. 2011. *The Iliad in a Nutshell: Visualizing Epic on the Tabulae Iliacae*. Oxford.

Staab, G. 2002. *Pythagoras in der Spätantike: Studien zu De Vita Pythagorica des Iamblichos von Chalkis*. Berlin.

Stadter, P. A. 1978. The *Ars Tactica* of Arrian: Tradition and Originality. *Classical Philology*, **73**(2), 117–28.

Stanley, C. D. 1990. Paul and Homer: Greco-Roman Citation Practice in the First Century CE. *Novum Testamentum*, **32**(1), 48–78.

Stanley, R. P. 1997. Hipparchus, Plutarch, Schröder, and Hough. *The American Mathematical Monthly*, **104**(4), 344–50.

Stannard, J. 1961. Book Review: *Physics of the Stoics* S. Sambursky. *Philosophy of Science*, **28**(1), 83–4.

1964. Materia Medica and Philosophic Theory in Aretaeus. *Sudhoffs Archiv für Geschichte der Medezin und der Naturwissenschaften*, **48**(1), 27–53.

Starr, R. J. 1987. The Circulation of Literary Texts in the Roman World. *The Classical Quarterly*, **37**(1), 213–23.

Stem, R. 2005. The First Eloquent Stoic: Cicero on Cato the Younger. *The Classical Journal*, **101**(1), 37–49.

Stephens, S. A. 1994. Who Read the Ancient Novels? In J. Tatum, ed., *The Search for the Ancient Novel*. Baltimore, 405–18.

Stevens, P. T. 1956. Euripides and the Athenians. *The Journal of Hellenic Studies*, **76**, 87–94.

Stiehle, R. 1856. Der Geograph Artemidorus von Ephesos. *Philologus*, **11**(1), 193–244.

Stöger, J. 2011. *Rethinking Ostia: A Spatial Enquiry into the Urban Society of Rome's Imperial Port-Town*. Leiden.

Strange, S. 2007. Porphyry and Plotinus' Metaphysics. *Bulletin of the Institute of Classical Studies*, **50**(supp.), 17–34.

Striker, G. 1991. Following Nature: A Study in Stoic Ethics. *Oxford Studies in Ancient Philosophy*, **9**, 1–73.

Strobel, C. 2009. The Lexica of the Second Sophistic: Safeguarding Atticism. In A. Georgakopoulou and M. Silk, eds., *Standard Language and Language Standards: Greek, Past and Present*. Farnham, UK, 93–108.

Strootman, R. 2011. Kings and Cities in the Hellenistic Age. In R. Alston, O. M. van Nijf and C. Williamson, eds., *Political Culture in the Greek City after the Classical Age*. Leuven, 141–53.

Stroppa, M. 2009. Some Remarks regarding Commentaries on Codex from Late Antiquity. *Trends in Classics*, **1**(2), 298–327.

Stroup, S. C. 2010. *Catullus, Cicero, and a Society of Patrons: The Generation of the Text*. Cambridge.

Stückelberger, A. 1994. *Bild und Wort: Das illustrierte Fachbuch in der antiken Naturwissenschaft, Medizin und Technik*. Mainz.

Sumner, G. V. 1973. *The Orators in Cicero's Brutus: Prosopography and Chronology*. Toronto.

Svenbro, J. 1988. *Phrasikleia: Anthropologie de la lecture en Grèce ancienne*. Paris.

Swerdlow, N. M. (ed.) 1999. *Ancient Astronomy and Celestial Divination*. Cambridge, MA.

Swiderek, A. 1954. Le mime grec en Egypte. *Eos*, 47, 63–74.

Syme, R. 1958. *Tacitus*, vol. I. Oxford.

  1960. Piso Frugi and Crassus Frugi. *The Journal of Roman Studies*, 50, 12–20.

  1982. The Career of Arrian. *Harvard Studies in Classical Philology*, 86, 181–211.

  1988. The Date of Justin and the Discovery of Trogus. *Historia: Zeitschrift für Alte Geschichte*, 37(3), 358–71.

Taisbak, C. M. 1974. Posidonius Vindicated at All Costs? Modern Scholarship versus the Stoic Earth Measurer. *Centaurus*, 18(4), 253–69.

Tanner, J. 2000. Portraits, Power, and Patronage in the Late Roman Republic. *The Journal of Roman Studies*, 90, 18–50.

Tannery, P. 1912 [1896]. Sur la religion des derniers mathématiciens de l'antiquité. In *Mémoires scientifiques*, vol. II: *Sciences exactes dans l'Antiquité*. Toulouse, 527–39.

Taplin, O. 1986. Fifth-Century Tragedy and Comedy: A Synkrisis. *The Journal of Hellenic Studies*, 106, 163–74.

  1993. *Comic Angels: And Other Approaches to Greek Drama through Vase-Painting*. Oxford.

  2007. *Pots and Plays: Interactions between Tragedy and Greek Vase-Painting of the Fourth Century BC*. Los Angeles.

Tarán, L. 1969. Asclepius of Tralles: Commentary to Nicomachus' *Introduction to Arithmetic*. *Transactions of the American Philosophical Society*, 59(4), 1–89.

  1975. *Academica: Plato, Philip of Opus, and the Pseudo-Platonic Epinomis*. Philadelphia.

  1981. *Speusippus of Athens: A Critical Study with a Collection of the Related Texts and Commentary*. Leiden.

Tarditi, G. (ed.) 1968. *Archilochus*. Rome.

Tarn, W. W. 1948. *Alexander the Great*. Cambridge.

Tarrant, H. 1983. Middle Platonism and the Seventh Epistle. *Phronesis*, 28(1), 75–103.

Taruskin, R. 2010. *The Oxford History of Western Music*. Oxford.

Taub, L. C. 1993. *Ptolemy's Universe. The Natural Philosophical and Ethical Foundations of Ptolemy's Astronomy*. Chicago.

Tchernetska, N. 2005. New Fragments of Hyperides from the Archimedes Palimpsest. *Zeitschrift für Papyrologie und Epigraphik*, 154, 1–6.

Tell, H. 2007. Sages at the Games: Intellectual Displays and Dissemination of Wisdom in Ancient Greece. *Classical Antiquity*, 26(2), 249–75.

Temin, P. 2006. The Economy of the Early Roman Empire. *The Journal of Economic Perspectives*, **20**(1), 133–51.

Tepedino Guerra, A. 1980. Il κῆπος epicureo nel *PHerc. 1780*. *Cronache Ercolanesi*, 10, 17–24.

Thalmann, W. G. 2011. *Apollonius of Rhodes and the Spaces of Hellenism*. Oxford.

Thom, J. C. 2005. *Cleanthes' Hymn to Zeus*. Tübingen.

Thomas, E. 2007. *Monumentality and the Roman Empire: Architecture in the Antonine Age*. Oxford.

Thomas, R. 1992. *Literacy and Orality in Ancient Greece*. Cambridge.

Thompson, D. J. 2000. Athenaeus in His Egyptian Context. In D. Braund and J. Wilkins, eds., *Athenaeus and His World: Reading Greek Culture in the Roman Empire*. Exeter, 77–84.

  2005. Posidippus, Poet of the Ptolemies. In K. Gutzwiller, ed., *The New Posidippus: A Hellenistic Poetry Book*. Oxford, 269–83.

Thompson, D. W. 1913. *On Aristotle as a Biologist: With a Prooemion on Herbert Spencer*. Oxford.

Thompson, H. A. 1959. Athenian Twilight: AD 267–600. *The Journal of Roman Studies*, **49**, 61–72.

Tieleman, T. 1996. *Galen and Chrysippus on the Soul: Argument and Refutation in the De Placitis, Books II–III*. Leiden.

Tigerstedt, E. N. 1968. Observations on the Reception of the Aristotelian *Poetics* in the Latin West. *Studies in the Renaissance*, **15**, 7–24.

Timpanaro, S. 2005 [1963]. *The Genesis of Lachmann's Method*, ed. and trans. G. W. Most. Chicago.

Tjäder, J.-O. 1955. *Die nichtliterarischen lateinischen Papyri Italiens aus der Zeit 445–700*, vol. I: *Papyri 1–28*. Lund.

  1982. *Die nichtliterarischen lateinischen Papyri Italiens aus der Zeit 445–700*, vol. II: *Papyri 29–59*. Lund.

Todisco, L. 2006. *Pittura e ceramica figurata tra Grecia, Magna Grecia e Sicilia*. Rome.

Todorov, T. 1981 [1968]. *Introduction to Poetics*, trans. R. Howard. Minneapolis.

Tolsa, C. 2013. Claudius Ptolemy and Self-Promotion. A Study on Ptolemy's Intellectual Milieu in Roman Alexandria. Doctoral dissertation, University of Barcelona.

Tomsin, A., Évrard, É., Denooz, J., and Bolland, P. 1973. *Traitement automatique de papyrus grecs*. Liège.

Toomer, G. J. 1970. Apollonius of Perga. In C. C. Gillespie, ed., *Dictionary of Scientific Biography*, vol. I. New York, 179–93.

Torjesen, K. J. 1985. *Hermeneutical Procedure and Theological Method in Origen's Exegesis*. Berlin.

Toye, D. L. 1999. Aristotle's Other Politeiai: Was the Athenaion Politeia Atypical? *The Classical Journal*, **94**(3), 235–53.

Trapp, M. B. 1990. Plato's *Phaedrus* in Second-Century Greek Literature. In D. A. Russell, ed., *Antonine Literature*. Oxford, 141–74.

Traversa, A. (ed.) 1951. *Hesiodi Catalogi sive eoearum fragmenta*. Naples.

Tribulato, O. 2010. Literary Dialects. In E. J. Bakker, ed., *A Companion to the Ancient Greek Language*. Chichester, 388–400.

Trimble, J. 2011. *Women and Visual Replication in Roman Imperial Art and Culture*. Cambridge.

Tropper, A. 2004. *Wisdom, Politics, and Historiography: Tractate Avot in the Context of the Graeco-Roman Near East*. Oxford.

Tselekas, P. 2012. The Coins. In N. Kaltsas, ed., *The Antikythera Shipwreck: The Ship, the Treasures, the Mechanism*. Athens, 216–19.

Tsouna, V. 1998. *The Epistemology of the Cyrenaic School*. Cambridge.

Turcan, M. 2007. *Tertullianus: Le manteau*. Paris.

Turner, E. G. 1963. Dramatic Representations in Graeco-Roman Egypt: How Long Do They Continue? *L'Antiquité classique*, **32**(1), 120–8.

1968. *Greek Papyri: An Introduction*. Princeton, NJ.

Tweddle, I. 2000. *Simson on Porisms*. Berlin.

Tybjerg, K. 2003. Wonder-Making and Philosophical Wonder in Hero of Alexandria. *Studies in History and Philosophy of Science*, **34**(3), 443–66.

Unschuld, P. U. 2003. *Huang Di Nei Jing Su Wen: Nature, Knowledge, Imagery in an Ancient Chinese Medical Text*. Berkeley, CA.

Urbano, A. P. 2013. *The Philosophical Life: Biography and the Crafting of Intellectual Identity in Late Antiquity*. Washington, DC.

Usener, H. 1884. Über die Organisation der wissenschaftlichen Arbeit im Altertum. *Preussische Jahrbücher*, **53**, 1–25.

Usher, M. D. 1998. *Homeric Stitchings: The Homeric Centos of the Empress Eudocia*. Lanham, MD.

Valantasis, R. 1991. *Spiritual Guides of the Third Century: A Semiotic Study of the Guide–Disciple Relationship in Christianity, Neoplatonism, Hermetism, and Gnosticism*. Minneapolis.

Vallance, J. T. 1990. *The Lost Theory of Asclepiades of Bithynia*. Oxford.

Van Dam, R. 1982. Hagiography and History: The Life of Gregory Thaumaturgus. *Classical Antiquity*, **1**(2), 272–308.

1985. *Leadership and Community in Late Antique Gaul*. Berkeley, CA.

Van den Hoek, A. 1997. The "Catechetical" School of Early Christian Alexandria and Its Philonic Heritage. *Harvard Theological Review*, **90**(1), 59–87.

Van den Kerchove, A. 2012. *La voie d'Hermès: Pratiques rituelles et traités hermétiques*. Leiden.

Van der Blom, H. 2011. Pompey in the Contio. *The Classical Quarterly*, **61**(2), 553–73.

Van der Eijk, P. J. 2000. *Diocles of Carystus: A Collection of the Fragments with Translation and Commentary*, 2 vols. Leiden.

2010. Principles and Practices of Compilation and Abbreviation in the Medical "Encyclopedias" of Late Antiquity. In M. Horster and C. Reitz, eds., *Condensing Texts – Condensed Texts*. Stuttgart, 519–54.

2015a. On "Hippocratic" and "Non-Hippocratic" Medical Writings. In L. Dean-Jones and R. M. Rosen, eds., *Ancient Concepts of the Hippocratic*. Leiden, 15–47.

2015b. Introduction: The Greek Medical "Encyclopaedias" of Late Antiquity. In E. Cancik-Kirschbaum and A. Traninger, eds., *Wissen in Bewegung: Institution – Iteration – Transfer*. Wiesbaden, 196–8.

Van Haelst, J. 1976. *Catalogue des papyrus littéraires juifs et chrétiens*. Paris.

Van Helden, A. 1985. *Measuring the Universe: Cosmic Dimensions from Aristarchus to Halley*. Chicago.

Van Leeuwen, J. 2016. *The Aristotelian Mechanics: Text and Diagrams*. Berlin.

Van Noorden, H. 2015. *Playing Hesiod: The "Myth of the Races" in Classical Antiquity*. Cambridge.

Van Thiel, H. 1992. Zenodot, Aristarch und Andere. *Zeitschrift für Papyrologie und Epigraphik*, **90**, 1–32.

Vanhaegendoren, K. 2010. Outils de dramatisation chez Phylarque. *Dialogues d'histoire ancienne*, **4**(2), 421–38.

Varner, E. R. 2004. *Mutilation and Transformation: Damnatio Memoriae and Roman Imperial Portraiture*. Leiden.

Vasiloudi, M. 2013. *Vita Homeri Herodotea: Textgesichte, Edition, Übersetzung*. Berlin.

Vegetti, M. 1998. Between Knowledge and Practice: Hellenistic Medicine. In M. D. Grmek, ed., *Western Medical Thought from Antiquity to the Middle Ages*. Cambridge, MA, 72–103.

Verde, F. 2013. *Elachista: La dottrina dei minimi nell'epicureismo*. Leuven.

Vergados, A. 2007. The *Homeric Hymn to Hermes* 51 and Antigonus of Carystus. *The Classical Quarterly*, **57**(2), 737–42.

Verhoogt, A. 2012. Papyri in the Archaeological Record. In C. Riggs, ed., *The Oxford Handbook of Roman Egypt*. Oxford, 507–15.

Vernant, J.-P. 1962. *Les origines de la pensée grecque*. Paris.

Vessey, M. 2014. Literary History: A Fourth-Century Roman Invention? In L. Van Hoof and P. Van Nuffelen, eds., *Literature and Society in the Fourth Century AD: Performing Paideia, Constructing the Present, Presenting the Self*. Leiden, 16–30.

Vitrac, B. 2002. Note textuelle sur un (problème de) lieu géométrique dans les *Météorologiques* d'Aristote (III. 5, 375 b 16–376 b 22). *Archive for History of Exact Sciences*, **56**(3), 239–83.

2006. Ératosthène et la théorie des médiétés. In C. Cusset and H. Frangoulis, eds., *Ératosthène: Un athlète du savoir*. Saint-Étienne, 77–103.

Vlastos, G. 1965. Minimal Parts in Epicurean Atomism. *Isis*, **56**(2), 121–47.

1966. Zeno of Sidon as a Critic of Euclid. In L. Wallach, ed., *The Classical Tradition: Literary and Historical Studies in Honor of Harry Caplan*. New York, 148–59.

Von Staden, H., 1975. Experiment and Experience in Hellenistic Medicine. *Bulletin of the Institute of Classical Studies*, **22**(1), 178–99.

1976. A New Testimonium about Polybus. *Hermes*, **104**(4), 494–6.

1989. *Herophilus: The Art of Medicine in Early Alexandria*. Cambridge.

1992. The Discovery of the Body: Human Dissection and Its Cultural Contexts in Ancient Greece. *The Yale Journal of Biology and Medicine*, **65**(3), 223–41.

1997. Galen and the "Second Sophistic". *Bulletin of the Institute of Classical Studies*, **41**(1), 33–54.

Von Wilamowitz-Moellendorff, U. 1881. *Antigonos von Karystos*. Berlin.

1900. Asianismus und Atticismus. *Hermes*, **35**(1), 1–52.

Vout, C. 2012. Unfinished Business: Re-viewing Medea in Roman Painting. *Ramus*, **41**(1/2), 119–43.

Walbank, F. 1967. *A Historical Commentary on Polybius*, vol. II: *Commentary on Books VII–XVIII*. Oxford.

Wallace-Hadrill, A. 1981. The Emperor and His Virtues. *Historia: Zeitschrift für Alte Geschichte*, **30**(3), 298–323.

1994. *Houses and Society in Pompeii and Herculaneum*. Princeton, NJ.

2008. *Rome's Cultural Revolution*. Cambridge.

Wallach, J. R. 2001. *The Platonic Political Art: A Study of Critical Reason and Democracy*. University Park, PA.

Wallis, W. 2016. Ancient Portraits of Poets: Communities, Canons, Receptions. Doctoral dissertation, Durham University.

Warren, J. 2002. *Epicurus and Democritean Ethics: An Archaeology of Ataraxia*. Cambridge.

Waschkies, H. J. 1977. *Von Eudoxos zu Aristoteles*. Amsterdam.

Wassink, A. 1991. Inflation and Financial Policy under the Roman Empire to the Price Edict of 301 AD. *Historia: Zeitschrift für Alte Geschichte*, **40**(4), 465–93.

Watts, E. J. 2005. Orality and Communal Identity in Eunapius' *Lives of the Sophists and Philosophers*. *Byzantion*, **75**, 334–61.

2006. *City and School in Late Antique Athens and Alexandria*. Berkeley, CA.

2007. Creating the Academy: Historical Discourse and the Shape of Community in the Old Academy. *The Journal of Hellenic Studies*, **127**, 106–22.

Wear, A. 1983. William Harvey and the "Way of the Anatomists". *History of Science*, **21**(3), 223–49.

Weber, G. 1993. *Dichtung und höfische Gesellschaft: Die Rezeption von Zeitgeschichte am Hof der ersten drei Ptolemäer*. Stuttgart.

Weber, M. 1978 [1921]. *Economy and Society: An Outline of Interpretive Sociology*, vol. I, trans. and ed. G. Roth and C. Wittich. Berkeley, CA.

Webster, C. 2015. Heuristic Medicine: The Methodists and Metalepsis. *Isis*, **106**(3), 657–68.

Webster, T. B. L. 1952. Chronological Notes on Middle Comedy. *The Classical Quarterly*, **2**(1/2), 13–26.

Weitzmann, K. 1947. *Illustrations in Roll and Codex: A Study of the Origin and Method of Text Illustration*. Princeton, NJ.

Welles, C. B. 1962. The Discovery of Sarapis and the Foundation of Alexandria. *Historia: Zeitschrift für Alte Geschichte*, **11**(3), 271–98.

West, M. L. 1971. Stesichorus. *The Classical Quarterly*, **21**(2), 302–14.

1986. The Singing of Hexameters: Evidence from Epidaurus. *Zeitschrift für Papyrologie und Epigraphik*, **63**, 39–46.

1989. The Early Chronology of Attic Tragedy. *The Classical Quarterly*, **39**(1), 251–4.

1992. *Ancient Greek Music*. Oxford.

(ed.) 1993. *Carmina Anacreontea*. Berlin.

1999. The Invention of Homer. *The Classical Quarterly*, **49**(2), 364–82.

2013. *The Epic Cycle: A Commentary on the Lost Troy Epics*. Oxford.

West, S. 1983. P.Hibeh 28: Alexandria or Utopia? *Zeitschrift für Papyrologie und Epigraphik*, **53**, 79–84.

White, M. J. 1986. What Worried the Crows? *The Classical Quarterly*, **36**(2), 534–7.

White, N. 1985. The Role of Physics in Stoic Ethics. *The Southern Journal of Philosophy*, **23**(supp.), 57–74.

White, P. 1978. Amicitia and the Profession of Poetry in Early Imperial Rome. *The Journal of Roman Studies*, **68**, 74–92.

1992. "Pompeius Macer" and Ovid. *The Classical Quarterly*, **42**(1), 210–18.

1993. *Promised Verse: Poets in the Society of Augustan Rome*. Cambridge, MA.

White, S. A. 2001. *Principes Sapientiae*: Dicaearchus' Biography of Philosophy. In W. W. Fortenbaugh and E. Schütrumpf, eds., *Dicaearchus of Messana: Text, Translation, and Discussion*. New Brunswick, NJ, 195–236.

2004. Hieronymus of Rhodes: The Sources, Text and Translation. In W. W. Fortenbaugh and S. A. White, eds., *Lyco of Troas and Hieronymus of Rhodes: Text, Translation, and Discussion*. New Brunswick, NJ, 79–276.

2007. Posidonius and Stoic Physics. *Bulletin of the Institute of Classical Studies*, **50**(supp.), 35–76.

2010. Philosophy after Aristotle. In J. J. Clauss and M. Cuypers, eds., *A Companion to Hellenistic Literature*. New York, 366–83.

Whitmarsh, T. 2001a. "Greece Is the World": Exile and Identity in the Second Sophistic. In S. Goldhill, ed., *Being Greek under Rome: Cultural Identity, the Second Sophistic and the Development of Empire*. Cambridge, 269–305.

2001b. *Greek Literature and the Roman Empire: The Politics of Imitation*. Oxford.

2004. The Cretan Lyre Paradox: Mesomedes, Hadrian and the Poetics of Patronage. In B. Borg, ed., *Paideia: The World of the Second Sophistic*. Berlin, 377–401.

2005. The Greek Novel: Titles and Genre. *The American Journal of Philology*, **126**(4), 587–611.

(ed.) 2010. *Local Knowledge and Microidentities in the Imperial Greek World*. Cambridge.

2016. *Battling the Gods: Atheism in the Ancient World*. New York.

Whittaker, H. 2001. The Purpose of Porphyry's Letter to Marcella. *Symbolae Osloenses*, **76**, 150–68.

Wickham, C. 2005. *Framing the Early Middle Ages: Europe and the Mediterranean, 400–800*. Oxford.

Wiedemann, E. J. 1985. The Regularity of Manumission at Rome. *The Classical Quarterly*, **35**(1), 162–75.

Wietzke, J. M. 2014. Knowledge in Person: The Socio-Literary Self-Fashioning of the Greek Expository Author. Doctoral dissertation, Stanford University.

2016. A Fashionable Curiosity: Claudius Ptolemy's "Desire for Knowledge" in Literary Context. In S. Ju, B. Löwe, T. Müller and Y. Xie, eds., *Cultures of Mathematics and Logic*. Cham, Switzerland, 81–105.

2017. Strabo's Expendables: The Function and Aesthetics of Minor Authority. In D. Dueck, ed., *The Routledge Companion to Strabo*. London, 233–47.

Forthcoming. Eratosthenes, Courtier? Royal Patronage and Authorial Ideology in Hellenistic Science.

Wilcox, A. 2012. *The Gift of Correspondence in Classical Rome: Friendship in Cicero's Ad Familiares and Seneca's Moral Epistles*. Madison, WI.

Wiles, D. 1991. *The Mask of Menander. Sign and Meaning in Greek and Roman Performance*. Cambridge.

Wilkinson, K. W. 2009. Palladas and the Age of Constantine. *The Journal of Roman Studies*, **99**, 36–60.

Williams, F. 2006. Cercidas: The Man and the Poet. In M. A. Harder, R. F. Regtuit and G. C. Wakker, eds., *Beyond the Canon*. Leuven, 345–56.

Williams, R. L. 2005. *Bishop Lists: Formation of Apostolic Succession of Bishops in Ecclesiastical Crises*. Piscataway, NJ.

Wilson, A. 2009. Indicators for Roman Economic Growth: A Response to Walter Scheidel. *Journal of Roman Archaeology*, **22**, 71–82.

2011. City Sizes and Urbanization in the Roman Empire. In A. Bowman and A. Wilson, eds., *Settlement, Urbanization, and Population*. Oxford, 161–95.

Wilson, M. 2008. Hippocrates of Chios's Theory of Comets. *Journal for the History of Astronomy*, **39**(2), 141–60.

Wilson, N. G. 1967. A Chapter in the History of Scholia. *The Classical Quarterly*, **17**(2), 244–56.

Wilson, P. 2000. *The Athenian Institution of the Khoregia. The Chorus, the City and the Stage*. Cambridge.

Winiarczyk, M. 1981. *Diagorae Melii et Theodori Cyrenaei reliquiae*. Leipzig.

2013. *The "Sacred History" of Euhemerus of Messene*. Berlin.

Wiseman, T. P. 1970. The Definition of *Eques Romanus* in the Late Republic and Early Empire. *Historia: Zeitschrift für Alte Geschichte*, **19**(1), 67–83.

1982. *Pete nobiles amicos*: Poets and Patrons in Late-Republican Rome. In B. K. Gold, ed., *Literary and Artistic Patronage in Ancient Rome*. Austin, TX, 28–31.

Wisse, J. 1995. Greeks, Romans, and the Rise of Atticism. In J. G. J. Abbenes, S. R. Slings and I. Sluiter, eds., *Greek Literary Theory after Aristotle*. Amsterdam, 65–82.

Witschel, C. 1999. *Krise – Rezession – Stagnation? Der Westen der römischen Reiches im 3. Jahrhundert n. Chr.* Frankfurt.

Witty, F. J. 1958. The *Pinakes* of Callimachus. *The Library Quarterly*, **28**(2), 132–6.

Woerther, F. 2008. Music and the Education of the Soul in Plato and Aristotle: Homoeopathy and the Formation of Character. *The Classical Quarterly*, **58**(1), 89–103.

Woodbury, L. 1974. Aristophanes' *Frogs* and Athenian Literacy: *Ran.* 52–53, 1114. *Transactions of the American Philological Association*, **106**, 349–57.

Woodward, L. H. 2009. Diogenes of Babylon: A Stoic on Music and Ethics. Doctoral dissertation, University College London.

Woolf, G. 1990. Food, Poverty and Patronage: The Significance of the Epigraphy of the Roman Alimentary Schemes in Early Imperial Italy. *Papers of the British School at Rome*, **58**, 197–228.

  1996. Monumental Writing and the Expansion of Roman Society in the Early Empire. *The Journal of Roman Studies*, **86**, 22–39.

Wooten, C. 1974. The Speeches in Polybius: An Insight into the Nature of Hellenistic Oratory. *The American Journal of Philology*, **95**(3), 235–51.

Wouters, A. 1979. *The Grammatical Papyri from Graeco-Roman Egypt: Contributions to the Study of the "Ars Grammatica" in Antiquity*. Brussels.

Wrightson, D. G. 2015. To Use or Not to Use: The Practical and Historical Reliability of Asclepiodotus's "Philosophical" Tactical Manual. In G. Lee, H. Whittaker and D. G. Wrightson, eds., *Ancient Warfare: Introducing Current Research*, vol. I. Newcastle, 65–93.

Yavetz, I. 1998. On the Homocentric Spheres of Eudoxus. *Archive for History of Exact Sciences*, **52**(3), 221–78.

  2010. *Galgalim u-Mazalot: Prakim be-Toldot ha-Astronomyia ha-Yevanit*. Jerusalem.

Yeo, R. 1993. *Defining Science: William Whewell, Natural Knowledge and Public Debate in Early Victorian Britain*. Cambridge.

Yona, S. 2015. The Psychology of Satire: Epicurean Ethics in Horace's Sermones. Doctoral dissertation, University of Illinois, Urbana–Champaign.

Young, F. M. 1997. *Biblical Exegesis and the Formation of Christian Culture*. Cambridge.

  1999. Greek Apologists of the Second Century. In M. Edwards, M. Goodman and S. Price, eds., *Apologetics in the Roman Empire: Pagans, Jews, and Christians*. Oxford, 81–104.

  2003. Alexandrian and Antiochene Exegesis. In A. J. Hauser and D. F. Watson, eds., *A History of Biblical Interpretation*, vol. I: *The Ancient Period*. Grand Rapids, MI, 334–54.

Zagagi, N. 1994. *The Comedy of Menander: Convention, Variation and Originality*. London.

Zambrini, A. 2007. The Historians of Alexander the Great. In J. Marincola, ed., *A Companion to Greek and Roman Historiography*. Oxford, 210–20.

Zanker, P. 1982. Herrscherbild und Zeitgesicht. In H. Klein, ed., *Römisches Porträt*. Berlin, 307–12.

  1995. *The Mask of Socrates: The Image of the Intellectual in Antiquity*. Berkeley, CA.

Zarmakoupi, M. (ed.) 2010. *The Villa of the Papyri at Herculaneum: Archaeology, Reception and Digital Reconstruction*. Berlin.

Zetzel, J. E. 1972. Cicero and the Scipionic Circle. *Harvard Studies in Classical Philology*, **76**, 173–9.

Zhmud, L. 1998. Plato as "Architect of Science". *Phronesis*, **43**(3), 211–44.

2002. Eudemus' History of Mathematics. In I. M. Bodnár and W. W. Fortenbaugh, eds., *Eudemus of Rhodes*. New Brunswick, NJ, 263–306.

2006. *The Origin of the History of Science in Classical Antiquity*. Berlin.

2012. *Pythagoras and the Early Pythagoreans*. Oxford.

2014. Sixth-, Fifth- and Fourth-Century Pythagoreans. In C. A. Huffman, ed., *A History of Pythagoreanism*. Cambridge, 88–111.

Ziegler, K. 1967. Plutarchstudien: XXII. Drei Gedichte bei Plutarch. *Rheinisches Museum für Philologie*, **110**(1), 53–64.

Zilliacus, H. 1938. Boktiteln i antik litteratur. *Eranos*, **36**, 1–41.

Zuiderhoek, A. 2009. *The Politics of Munificence in the Roman Empire: Citizens, Elites and Benefactors in Asia Minor*. Cambridge.

# Index

Philippus of Mende, 250
Philippus of Opus, 383
  *Epinomis*, 383
Philistion (medical author), 289
Philistus (historian), 280
Philitas (grammarian), 292, 296, 302, 363
  *Glossai*, 362
Philo
  papyri, 16
Philo of Alexandria, 53, 170, 484, 488
Philo of Byzantium, 295, 359
Philo of Larissa, 477, 520
Philo of Megara, 375
Philo the Dialectician, 385
Philocles, 204
Philoctetes, 138
Philodemus, 33, 192, 325, 329, 343, 389, 396, 442,
  486, 488–90, 492, 518, 622
  *Index Academicorum*, 475
  *On Music*, 441
  *On Poems*, 152
Philolaus, 247, 311, 633
Philon (historian), 291
Philonides (geometer), 444
Philonides (philosopher), 251, 263, 444
Philonides of Thebes, 410
philosophical chairs, 512
philosophical schools, 249–50, 285, 314, 322–30,
  380, 490, 512, 559, 576–8, 598, *see also*
    Academy, Epicureanism, Peripatos, Stoa
  routinization, 306, 329–30, 337, 347, 399
  scholarchs, 181
philosophy, 72, 74–5, 88, 113, 135, 228, 246, 296,
  *see also* Aristotle, Chrysippus,
    philosophical schools, Plato, Porphyry,
    Posidonius
  and comedy, 337, 346
  citations, 61
  fifth century BCE, 233
  fourth century BCE, 207, 208
  hiatus in third century CE, 702
  interest in science, 150, 423, 425–6
  literary style, 375, 376
  number of authors, 560–1, 574, 576, 587, 595
  papyri, 37, 39, 76
  portraits, 64, 65–6
  rate of attestation, 575, 578, 650, 655, 661, 662
  scale of writing, 318, 321
  spatial distribution, 306, 307–11, 312, 313,
    314–15, 317–19, 337–8, 378
  spatial structure, 629
  third century CE, 738
Philostephanus, 295
Philostratus of Athens, 73, 591, 680, 702–3, 710,
  714, 718–19, 721, 726, 733, 780

*Lives of the Sophists*, 665, 703, 708, 734, 745, 782
  on the Second Sophistic, 595
Philostratus the Elder, 138
Philostratus the Younger, 138
Philoxenus, 280
Phintias (Pythagorean), 315
Phlius, 313, 314, 317, 378, 478
Phocion, 212
Photius, 478, 492, 550–1, 557–8, 602, 708, 755, 765
  *Bibliotheca*, 550–1
Phrygia, 254, 734
Phrynichus, 183, 203–4
Phylarchus, 357
Pindar, 13, 49, 94, 113, 122, 138, 189, 223–4, 231,
    233, 305, 351, 413, 567
  and patronage, 280, 281, 283
  citations, 59, 61–2, 214
  in education, 42, 52
  longevity, 179
  papyri, 15, 22, 39, 75, 118
  portraits, 65, 67
*Pirke Avot*, 742, 745
Piso Frugi, 477
Pitane, 289
Pittacus, 307
Plague of Cyprian, 723
Plato, 49, 94, 113, 150, 189, 230, 235, 249, 305, 315,
    322, 350, 382, 385, 391, 416, 426, 441, 486,
    487, 567, 569, 581, 615, 632
  *Alcibiades*, 120, 484
  *Amatores*, 250
  and big libraries, 24, 122, 411, 795
  and mathematics, 250, 258, 285, 424–5, 466
  and the Academy, 322, 324–5, 326–7
  *Apology*, 613
  biographical tradition, 164, 613
  citations, 59, 61
  commentaries, 207, 482–4
  competition, 174, 319
  consistency of genre, 131
  *Cratylus*, 473
  dialogism, 171
  distribution of papyri, 118–19, 120
  *Hippias*, 250
  immediate response, 207–9, 313
  in Neoplatonism, 751, 753, 775
  *Laches*, 119
  *Laws*, 24, 119
  longevity, 179
  *Menexenus*, 11, 171, 174
  on medicine, 430
  papyri, 15, 23, 29, 75, 538
  *Parmenides*, 11, 120
  patronage, 280
  *Phaedo*, 23, 119, 162